Theory and

Practice

of the

Conve...

on Hum...

Rights

Theory and Practice of the European Convention on Human Rights

THIRD EDITION

by

P. van Dijk

G.J.H. van Hoof

in collaboration with

A.W. Heringa

J.G.C. Schokkenbroek

B.P. Vermeulen

M.L.W.M. Viering

L.F. Zwaak

SIM
KLUWER LAW
INTERNATIONAL
THE HAGUE · LONDON · BOSTON

A C.I.P. Catalogue record for this book is available from the Library of Congres

Published by Kluwer Law International
P.O. Box 85889
2508 CN The Hague, The Netherlands
Tel.:   + 31 70 308 1560
Fax: + 31 70 308 1515

Sold and distributed in the USA and Canada by
Kluwer Law International
675 Massachusetts Avenue
Cambridge, MA 02139, USA
Tel.:   + 1 617 345 0140
Fax: + 1 617 354 8595

Sold and distributed in all other countries by
Kluwer Law International
Libresso Distribution Centre
P.O. Box 23
7400 GA Deventer, The Netherlands
Tel.:   + 31 570 647324
Fax: + 31 570 633834

Printed on acid-free paper

Cover design: Robert Vulkers bNO

ISBN 90 411 0598 0   1001350713

Co-publication with Studie- en Informatiecentrum Mensenrechten (SIM), Utrecht, The Netherlands.

Kluwer Law International incorporates the publishing programmes of Graham & Trotman Ltd, Kluwer Law and Taxation Publishers and Martinus Nijhoff Publishers.

to S.K. Martens, former judge on the ECHR,
in appreciation of his important contribution
to the jurisprudence of human rights

From the Preface to the First Edition

.....

The present book is designed to serve a twofold purpose: it is meant to be a general textbook for university courses as well as a guide to practising lawyers.

As a textbook it may be used both as reading material and as a basis for discussion within the framework of courses and seminars on, *inter alia*, public international law, the law of international organizations, European law, constitutional law, national and international criminal law, and, of course, special courses and seminars on the international law of human rights. The book has been set up in such a way that it can be assigned for reading as a whole – for instance, when a teacher does not intend to cover all issues of the European Convention on Human Rights, but still wants the students to prepare for discussing any of these issues – or in part, when only one or a number of the provisions contained in the Convention are relevant to the subject matter of a particular course or seminar.

With regard to both students and practising lawyers, the book provides them first of all with a general survey of the history, the structure, and the functioning of the Convention. Its main part, however, is devoted to an elaborate description of the Convention's supervisory procedures and an extensive analysis of the rights and freedoms contained therein, based mainly upon the 'Strasbourg' case-law, *i.e.* the decisions on admissibility and the reports of the European Commission of Human Rights, the judgments of the European Court of Human Rights and – to a lesser extent – the resolutions of the Committee of Ministers of the Council of Europe. Extensive references to this case-law are included in the footnotes particularly for the benefit of practising lawyers, although they may prove useful also to students, for instance, as an aid in writing a comprehensive paper on a specific issue.

An analysis of the national case-law of the Contracting States related to the Convention has not been undertaken, because this would not only have exceeded the scope of the present book, but also the expertise of its authors.

Reference to the literature has been confined to cases where this offers additional authority or an additional explanation and therefore furthers a better understanding of the issue concerned.

.....

The theory and practice of the European Convention on Human Rights are important first and foremost to law-students and legal practitioners in Member States of the Council of Europe. Nevertheless, the Convention's relevance may go beyond this now that the International Covenant on Civil and Political Rights and, more recently, the American Convention on Human Rights have entered into force. Both these latter instruments contain a large number of provisions which are very similar to those contained in the Convention. It may therefore be expected that the theory and practice of the European Convention will gain the interest of an increasing number of students and practitioners from outside the Council of Europe countries. This book is intended to guide them in that interest.

.....

February 1984
P. van Dijk
Bilthoven, the Netherlands

G.J.H. van Hoof
IJsselstein, the Netherlands

Preface to the Third Edition

A new edition of the present book has been overdue for some time. The developments which have taken place under the Convention since the second edition have been numerous and comprehensive. Three Protocols have been added to the Convention in the meantime. The number of Parties to the Convention has grown from twenty-two to thirty-six, turning the Convention system into a pan-European human rights system. Most of all, however, the second edition of the book has become out-dated by the significant increase of the case-law concerning the Convention, both of the Commission and of the Court. Many questions of interpretation which had been addressed only by the Commission when the second edition was prepared, have now been answered by the Court, while many other issues have been raised 'in Strasbourg' for the first time since the second edition.

On the other hand, there was some doubt in the editors' mind about whether this was the appropriate time for a new edition. Protocol No. 11 to the Convention, which will enter into force on 1 November 1998, will drastically change the supervisory system under the Convention, establishing one Court, while the power of the Committee of Ministers of the Council of Europe to take a decision on applications brought under Articles 24 and 25 (then Article 33 and 34) will end. This implies that especially those parts of the book which relate to the role and functioning of the Commission and to this particular function of the Committee of Ministers, will soon no longer describe the prevailing situation. However, the Commission will continue to function for another year after Protocol No. 11 has entered into force, while the new Court will also perform the present functions of the Commission and may be expected to be guided by the Commission's procedures and working methods, and by its case-law concerning admissibility. Therefore, a full description of the present procedural practice and case-law of both the Commission and the Court represents the *acquis* of the Convention that should not and will not fail to have its impact felt, and will remain relevant for the practice and case-law of the new Court for many years to come. In Appendix VI the text of the amended Convention is included, with reference to the numbering of articles of the existing text.

In view of the extensive elaboration of the case-law of the Commission and the Court, there was even less need for complementary references to literature than was the case in the two previous editions. Such references have, therefore, almost completely been deleted, also in order not to make the footnotes any longer and more numerous than they are already. Bibliographies concerning the Convention and its case-law are to be found in several other monographs and commentaries, and may also be obtained from the Directorate of Human Rights of the Council of Europe.

For the present edition the editors had the privilege of co-operating with a team of five Dutch experts, who prepared revisions of parts of the book relating to their respective field of special expertise. Thus, the revision of Chapters I (except sections 5 and 6) and III-VI and of the sections on Articles 2 and 4 was prepared by Mr. Leo Zwaak. Professor Aalt Willem Heringa revised the sections dealing with Articles 8, 11 and 14 and the section on the legal effect of the Convention within the national legal system (Chapter 1, section 5), while Professor Ben Vermeulen covered the sections on the Articles 3 and 9 of the Convention and Article 2 of Protocol No. 1. Dr. Marc Viering prepared the new text concerning Article 6, with the exception of the part on the right of access to court, as well as the sections on Articles 5, 7, 10 and Protocol No. 7. Dr. Jeroen Schokkenbroek revised the sections on the remaining articles of Protocol No. 1 and the sections on the remaining Protocols and prepared a new Chapter II (any views expressed in these contributions are entirely personal and do not necessarily reflect the position of the Council of Europe). The remaining parts of the book were revised by the editors who, moreover, have commented on the draft texts and edited the whole text of the book. They all have benefited enormously from the research assistance of Nicola Jägers, and of the editorial assistance of both Nicola Jägers and Jacqueline Smith of the Netherlands Institute of Human Rights (SIM), while Annelies Bosch, also with admirable care and patience, transformed the manuscript into camera-ready pages.

This book takes account of the work of the Commission and the Court until 1 January 1997. Incidental, crucial information available up to June 1997 has been incorporated.

November 1997
P. van Dijk
Bilthoven, the Netherlands

G.J.H. van Hoof
IJsselstein, the Netherlands

Table of Contents

Chapter II
Interpretation and Application of the Rights and Freedoms of the Convention in the Strasbourg Case-Law: General Principles and Concepts

Chapter III
The Procedure Before the European Commission of Human Rights

Chapter IV
The Examination of a Case by the European Court of Human Rights

Chapter V
The Examination of a Case by the Committee of Ministers

Chapter VI
The Supervisory Function of the Secretary General of the Council of Europe under Article 57

Chapter VII
Analysis of the Rights and Freedoms

Chapter VIII
Provisions Concerning Enjoyment of the Rights and Freedoms and Concerning Restriction of these Rights and Freedoms

Appendices

List of Abbreviations

AJIL	American Journal of International Law
Appl(s)	Applications lodged with the Commission under Article 24 of the Convention
Bulletin EC	Bulletin of the European Communities
CML Review	Common Market Law Review
Coll.	Collection of Decisions of the European Commission of Human Rights
Cons. Ass.	Consultative Assembly of the Council of Europe
D&R	Decisions and Reports of the European Commission of Human Rights
HRLJ	Human Rights Law Journal
ICJ Reports	International Court of Justice, Reports of Judgments, Advisory Opinions and Orders
ILM	International Legal Materials
ILO	International Labour Organization
Jur.	Case-Law of the Court of Justice of the European Communities
Parl. Ass.	Parliamentary Assembly of the Council of Europe
Publ. ECHR, Series A	Publications of the European Court of Human Rights; Judgments and Decisions
Publ. ECHR, Series B	Publications of the European Court of Human Rights; Pleadings, Oral Arguments and Documents
RCADI	Recueil des Cours de l'Académie de Droit International de la Haye
RDH	Revue des Droits de l'Homme
Reports	Reports of Judgments and Decisions. Publication of the case-law of the Commission and the Court (as from 1996)
Res.	Resolution
UN Doc.	United Nations Documents
UNHCR	United Nations High Commissioner for Refugees
UNTS	United Nations Treaty Series
Yearbook	Yearbook of the European Convention on Human Rights

Chapter I

General Survey of the European Convention

1 THE GENESIS OF THE CONVENTION

The European Convention for the Protection of Human Rights and Fundamental Freedoms is a product of the period shortly after the Second World War, when the issue of international protection of human rights attracted a great deal of attention. These rights had been crushed by the atrocities of National Socialism, and the guarantee of their protection at the national level had proved completely inadequate.

As early as 1941 Churchill and Roosevelt, in the Atlantic Charter, launched their four freedoms: freedom of life, freedom of religion, freedom from want and freedom from fear. After the Second World War the promotion of respect for human rights and fundamental freedoms became one of the purposes of the United Nations. Within that framework the Universal Declaration of Human Rights, adopted on 10 December 1948 by the General Assembly of the United Nations, became a significant milestone.

Meanwhile, preliminary steps were also taken at the European level. In May 1948 the International Committee of the Movements for European Unity organised a 'Congress of Europe' in The Hague. This initiative gave the decisive impetus to the foundation of the Council of Europe in 1949. At the Congress a resolution was adopted, the introductory part of which reads as follows:

> The Congress
> *Considers* that the resultant union or federation should be open to all European nations democratically governed and which undertake to respect a Charter of Human Rights;
> *Resolves* that a Commission should be set up to undertake immediately the double task of drafting such a Charter and of laying down standards to which a State must conform if it is to deserve the name of democracy.

After the Council of Europe had been founded, the matter was discussed during the first session of the Consultative Assembly (at present called the Parliamentary Assembly) of the Council of Europe in August 1949. The Assembly charged its Committee on Legal and Administrative Questions to consider in more detail the matter of a collective guarantee of human rights.

From that moment onwards the Convention was drafted in a relatively short time. In September of the same year the Consultative Assembly adopted the Committee's report, in which ten rights were included that were to be the subjects of a collective guarantee, with a view to which the establishment of a European Commission of Human Rights and a European Court of Justice was proposed. In November of that year the Committee of Ministers of the Council of Europe decided to appoint a Committee of Government Experts, which was entrusted with the task of preparing a draft text on the basis of this report.

This Committee completed its work in the spring of 1950. It had made considerable headway, but it failed to find a solution to a number of political problems. The subsequently appointed Committee of Senior Officials also had to leave the ultimate decision on a number of matters to the Committee of Ministers, even though it reached agreement on the greater part of the text of the Committee of Experts.

On 7 August 1950 the Committee of Ministers approved a revised draft text, which was less far-reaching than the original proposals on a number of points. For example, the system of individual applications and the jurisdiction of the Court were made optional. This draft text was not substantially altered afterwards.

On 4 November 1950 the Convention, which according to its preamble was framed 'to take the first steps for collective enforcement of certain rights stated in the Universal Declaration', was signed in Rome.[1] It entered into force on 3 September 1953 and at the moment (October 1997) has been ratified by 39 Member States of the Council of Europe: Albania, Andorra, Austria, Belgium, Bulgaria, Cyprus, Czech Republic, Denmark, Estonia, Finland, the Federal Republic of Germany, France, Greece,[2] Hungary, Iceland, Ireland, Italy, Liechtenstein, Lithuania, Luxembourg, Macedonia ('FYROM'), Malta, the Netherlands, Norway, Poland, Portugal, Romania, San Marino, Slovakia, Slovenia, Spain, Sweden, Switzerland, Turkey and the United Kingdom. Croatia, Latvia, Moldova, the Russian Federation and Ukraine have become members of the Council of Europe and have also signed, but at present not yet ratified the Convention. Meanwhile Belarus has shown its desire to become a member of the Council of Europe and as a consequence thereof to become a party to the Convention. In January 1997, however, the Parliamentary Assembly has decided to suspend the Belorussian Parliament's special-guest status because the way in which the new legislature came into being deprived it of democratic legitimacy. Up to the present, 11 Protocols have been added to the Convention,[3] but not all of them have been ratified by all the Contracting States.[4]

---

[1] 213 UNTS, No. 2889, p. 221; Council of Europe, *European Treaty Series*, No. 5, 4 November 1950; Council of Europe, *Collected Texts*, Strasbourg, 1994, pp. 13-36.

[2] Greece withdrew from the Council of Europe in 1969, but in 1974 became a member again and re-ratified the Convention.

[3] The English text of the Protocols is included in Council of Europe, *Collected Texts*, Strasbourg, 1994, pp. 37-60. Protocol Nos 3, 5, 8 and 9 have been incorporated as amendments into the text of the Convention. Protocol Nos 10 and 11 have not yet entered into force. See also Appendix I.

[4] See Appendix I.

2 THE STRUCTURE OF THE CONVENTION

2.1 Everyone Within Their Jurisdiction

Under Article 1 of the Convention the Contracting States are bound to secure to everyone within their jurisdiction the rights and freedoms set forth in Section I of the Convention. To the extent that a State has ratified Protocol Nos 1, 4, 6, or 7, this obligation also applies to the rights and freedoms laid down in these Protocols, since the latter are considered as supplementary articles of the Convention, to which all the provisions of the Convention apply in a similar way.[5]

As stated above, the Contracting States must secure these rights and freedoms to 'everyone within their jurisdiction'. These words do not imply any limitation as to nationality. Even those alleged victims who are not nationals either of the State concerned or of any of the other Contracting States may claim this guarantee when they are in some respect subject to the jurisdiction of the State from which they claim that guarantee.[6] Furthermore it is irrelevant whether they have their residence inside or outside the territory of that State.[7] Moreover, in several cases the Commission and Court have held that although Article 1 sets limits on the scope of the Convention, the concept of 'jurisdiction' under this provision does not imply that the responsibility of the Contracting Parties is restricted to acts committed on their territory.

Accordingly the Court has held that the extradition or expulsion of a person by a Contracting Party to a country where there is a serious risk of torture or inhuman or degrading treatment or punishment, may give rise to an issue under

---

[5] See Art. 5 of Protocol No. 1, Art. 6(1) of Protocol No. 4, Art. 6 of Protocol No. 6 and Art. 7(1) of Protocol No. 7.

[6] See, *e.g.*, Appl. 788/60, *Austria* v. *Italy*, Yearbook IV (1961), p. 116 (138 and 140): 'Whereas, therefore, in becoming a Party to the Convention, a State undertakes, *vis-à-vis* the other High Contracting Parties, to secure the rights and freedoms defined in Section I to every person within its jurisdiction, regardless of their nationality or status; whereas, in short, it undertakes to secure these rights and freedoms not only to its own nationals and those of other High Contracting Parties, but also to nationals of States not parties to the Convention and to stateless persons.'

[7] The Consultative Assembly had proposed in the draft for the Convention the words 'all persons residing within the territories of the signatory States', but these were changed by the Committee of Experts in the sense mentioned. See report of the Committee of Experts to the Committee of Ministers, Council of Europe, *Collected Edition of the 'Travaux Préparatoires' of the European Convention on Human Rights*, Vol. IV, The Hague, 1977, p. 20: 'It was felt that there were good grounds for extending the benefits of the Convention to all persons in the territories of the signatory States, even those who could not be considered as residing there in the legal sense of the word.' See also Appl. 1611/62, *X* v. *Federal Republic of Germany*, Yearbook VIII (1965), p. 158 (168), where the Commission held: 'in certain respects the nationals of a Contracting State are within its jurisdiction even when domiciled or resident abroad.' See also *infra* pp. 7-11.

Article 3, and hence engage responsibility of that State under the Convention.[8] In cases where another provision than Article 3 is at stake, so far the extraditing State has not been held responsible for acts which take place thereafter in another country.[9] However, in the *Loizidou* Case, the Court held Turkey responsible for alleged violations of Article 8 and Article 1 of Protocol No. 1, which took place at the northern part of Cyprus, which is under control of Turkish forces in Cyprus which exercise an overall control in that area.[10]

2.2 Rights and Freedoms Laid Down in the Convention

Section I of the Convention contains the following rights and freedoms:

Article 2:	right to life;
Article 3:	freedom from torture and inhuman or degrading treatment;
Article 4:	freedom from slavery and forced or compulsory labour;
Article 5:	right to liberty and security of person;
Article 6:	right to a fair and public trial within a reasonable time;
Article 7:	freedom from retrospective effect of penal legislation;
Article 8:	right to respect for private and family life, home and correspondence;
Article 9:	freedom of thought, conscience and religion;
Article 10:	freedom of expression;
Article 11:	freedom of assembly and association;
Article 12:	right to marry and found a family.

Protocol No. 1 has added the following rights:

Article 1:	right to peaceful enjoyment of possessions;
Article 2:	right to education and free choice of education;
Article 3:	right to free elections by secret ballot.

Protocol No. 4 the following rights and freedoms have been included:

Article 1:	prohibition of deprivation of liberty on the ground of inability to fulfil a contractual obligation;
Article 2:	freedom to move within and choose residence in a country;
Article 3:	prohibition of expulsion of nationals and right of nationals to enter the territory of the State of which they are nationals;
Article 4:	prohibition of collective expulsion of aliens.

---

[8] See judgment of 7 July 1989, *Soering*, A.161, pp. 35-36; judgment of 20 March 1991, *Cruz Varas and Others*, A.201, p. 28; judgment of 30 October 1991, *Vilvarajah and Others*, A.215, p. 34; judgment of 23 March 1995, *Loizidou* (preliminary objections), A.310, p. 23. See also *infra* pp. 322-328.

[9] Appl. 10427/83, *X v. the United Kingdom*, D&R 47 (1986), p. 85 (95-96), where the applicant, a suspected deserter from the Indian army, had been extradited to India and claimed that he had been deprived of a fair trial within a reasonable time.

[10] Judgment of 23 March 1995 (preliminary objections), A.310, p. 23.

Protocol No. 6 has added the prohibition of the condemnation to and execution of the death penalty (Article 1).

Protocol No. 7 contains the following rights and freedoms:

Article 1:   procedural guarantees in case of expulsion of aliens lawfully resident in the territory of a State;

Article 2:   right of review by a higher tribunal in criminal cases;

Article 3:   right to compensation to a person convicted of a criminal offence, on the ground that a new or newly discovered fact shows that there has been a miscarriage of justice;

Article 4:   prohibition of new criminal proceedings for offences for which one has already been finally acquitted or convicted (*ne bis in idem*);

Article 5:   equality of rights and responsibilities between spouses.

2.3 General Provisions Concerning the Enjoyment, the Protection and the Limitation of the Rights and Freedoms

Article 13 stipulates that everyone whose rights and freedoms mentioned in the Convention are violated shall have an effective remedy before national authorities, notwithstanding the fact that the violation has been committed by persons acting in an official capacity. Article 14 requires the Contracting States to secure the rights and freedoms without discrimination on any ground whatsoever. Article 15 allows States to derogate from a number of provisions of the Convention in time of war or any other public emergency threatening the life of the nation. Under Article 16 States are allowed to impose limitations on political activities of aliens notwithstanding Articles 10, 11 and 14 of the Convention. Article 17 provides that nothing in the Convention may justify activities aimed at the destruction of any of the rights and freedoms set forth in the Convention or their limitation to a greater extent than is provided for in the Convention. Finally, Article 18 implies a prohibition of misuse of power (*détournement de pouvoir*) as to the right of Contracting States to impose restrictions on the rights and freedoms guaranteed by the Convention.

2.4 Provisions to Ensure the Observance by the Contracting Parties of Their Obligations

Besides these substantive provisions, the European Convention also contains a number of provisions to ensure the observance by the Contracting States of their obligations under the Convention. In this connection it should be noted that the supervision of the implementation of the Convention rests primarily with the national authorities, in particular the national courts (at least in States where the courts are allowed to directly apply the Convention).[11] This is also implied in

---

[11]   On this, see *infra* pp. 16-22 and 127-153.

5

Article 13 where reference is made to an 'effective remedy before a national authority'. With regard to those cases where a national procedure is not available or does not provide for an adequate remedy, or in the last resort has not produced a satisfactory result in the opinion of the injured party or of any of the other Contracting States, the Convention itself provides for a supervisory mechanism. At present, the system consists of two phases, *viz.* the procedure before the European Commission of Human Rights (Section III) and subsequently the procedure before the European Court of Human Rights (Section IV) or before the Committee of Ministers of the Council of Europe (Articles 30 and 31). In addition, the Secretary General of the Council of Europe also takes part in the supervision of the observance of the Convention (Article 57). When it enters into force, Protocol No. 11 will substantially change this system.[12]

2.5 Final Provisions

Section V contains, *inter alia*, the final provisions of the Convention (Articles 60 to 66). Article 63, concerning the territorial scope, and Article 65, which deals with denunciation of the Convention, will be discussed hereafter in another context.[13] Article 64, concerning reservations, will be dealt with separately in Chapter VIII.[14]

Article 60 embodies what has become a general rule of international human rights law, *viz.* that a legal obligation implying a more far-reaching protection takes priority over any less far-reaching obligation. The article provides that nothing in the Convention may be construed as limiting or derogating from any of the human rights and fundamental freedoms as they may be ensured under the national laws of any Contracting State or under any other international agreement to which the latter is a party.

Article 61 stipulates that the Convention shall not prejudice the powers conferred on the Committee of Ministers by the Statute of the Council of Europe.

Article 62 is aimed at leaving the supervision of the observance of the Convention at the international level exclusively in the hands of the organs designated by the Convention. The article provides that the Contracting States, except by special agreement, will not try to settle their disputes on the interpretation and application of the Convention by other means. Article 62 applies in those instances where the Convention is expressly invoked. With respect to disputes where this is not the case, but where nevertheless a right is at issue that is also protected by the Convention, the rationale for such an exclusive competence is much less self-evident. In our opinion the text of Article 62 does not dictate the exclusivity of the procedure provided for in the Convention as far as those latter cases are concerned. There is, however, still some difference of

---

[12] See *infra* p. 31.
[13] See *infra* pp. 7-11 and 15.
[14] See Chapter VIII, *infra* pp. 773-784.

opinion as to the exact scope of the obligation of the Contracting States under Article 62.

In a resolution of 1970 the Committee of Ministers:

> Declares that, as long as the problem of interpretation of Article 62 of the European Convention is not resolved, States Parties to the Convention which ratify or accede to the UN Covenant on Civil and Political Rights and make a declaration under Article 41 of the Covenant should normally utilize only the procedure established by the European Convention in respect of complaints against another Contracting Party of the European Convention relating to an alleged violation of a right which in substance is covered both (by) the European Convention (or its Protocols) and by the UN Covenant on Civil and Political Rights, it being understood that the UN procedure may be invoked in relation to rights not guaranteed in the European Convention (or its Protocols) or in relation to States which are not Parties to the European Convention.[15]

In practice, no problems have arisen yet in this respect. Since the entry into force of the UN Covenant on Civil and Political Rights in 1976, only two inter-State complaints have been dealt with in the context of the European Convention: *Cyprus* v. *Turkey*[16] and *France, Norway, Denmark, Sweden and the Netherlands* v. *Turkey*.[17] Since Turkey has not ratified the UN Covenant on Civil and Political Rights and Cyprus and France have not recognised the competence of the Human Rights Committee to receive inter-State complaints, there was no other possibility than to submit the case to the European Commission.

Finally, Article 66 contains a number of provisions about the ratification and the entry into force of the Convention.

3 THE TERRITORIAL SCOPE OF THE CONVENTION

3.1 Territories for Whose International Relations a State is Responsible

Article 63 contains a limitation of the principle of Article 1 according to which the Convention is applicable to everyone within the jurisdiction of the Contracting States. According to general international law a treaty is applicable to the whole territory of a Contracting State, including those territories for whose international relations the State in question is responsible.[18] This is different only when a reservation has been made for one or more of those territories in the treaty itself, or at the time of its ratification. Under Article 63(1), however, the European Convention extends to the latter territories only when the Contracting State concerned has agreed to this *via* a declaration to that effect addressed to the Secretary General of the Council of Europe. Such declarations were made in the course of time by Denmark with respect to Greenland,[19] by the Netherlands with

---

[15] Res. (70)17 of 15 May 1970, Council of Europe, *Collected Texts*, Strasbourg, 1994, pp. 331-332.
[16] Appl. 8007/77, Yearbook XX (1977), p. 98; D&R 13 (1979), p. 85.
[17] Appls 9940-9944/82, D&R 35 (1984), p. 143.
[18] See Art. 29 of the 1969 Vienna Convention on the Law of Treaties, ILM 8, 1969, p. 679.
[19] Since 1953 Greenland forms an integral part of Denmark.

respect to Suriname[20] and the Netherlands Antilles[21] and by the United Kingdom with respect to most of the non-self-governing territories belonging to the Commonwealth.[22] The question of what has to be understood by the words 'territory for whose international relations a State is responsible' was raised in a case concerning the former Belgian Congo. The applicants submitted that at the time to which their complaint related this area formed part of the national territory of Belgium, and that accordingly the Convention, including the Belgian declaration under Article 25, was applicable to the Belgian Congo even though Belgium had not made any declaration as referred to in Article 63 with reference thereto. The Commission, however, came to the conclusion that the Belgian Congo had to be regarded as a territory for whose international relations Belgium was responsible in the sense of Article 63, and that the complaint was not admissible *ratione loci*, since Belgium had not made any declaration under Article 63 with reference to this territory.[23]

According to paragraph 3, the provisions of the Convention are applied to the territories referred to in Article 63 with due regard to local requirements. In the *Tyrer* Case the British Government submitted in this context that corporal punishment on the Isle of Man was justified as a preventive measure, based on public opinion on the island. The Court, however, held that:

> for the application of Article 63(3), more would be needed: there would have to be positive and conclusive proof of a requirement, and the Court could not regard beliefs and local 'public' opinion on their own as constituting such proof.[24]

In the *Piermont* Case, a German member of the European Parliament had been expelled from French Polynesia and had been prohibited from returning, while a decision was taken prohibiting her from entering New Caledonia, because of certain statements which she had made at a demonstration in Tahiti. The applicant complained that these orders infringed, amongst others, her right to freedom of expression. The French Government submitted that the 'local requirements' of French Polynesia made the interference legitimate. According to the Government the 'local requirements' were the indisputable special features of protecting public order in the Pacific territories, namely their island status and distance from metropolitan France and also the especially tense political atmosphere. The Court noted that the arguments put forward by the Government related essentially to the tense local political atmosphere taken together with an election campaign and

---

[20] Suriname became independent in 1975.

[21] The reservation made with respect to the Netherlands Antilles with reference to Art. 6(3)(c) has meanwhile been withdrawn.

[22] See Council of Europe, *Collected Texts*, Strasbourg, 1994, p. 88.

[23] Appl. 1065/61, *X v. Belgium*, Yearbook IV (1961), p. 260 (266-268).

[24] Judgment of 25 April 1978, A.26, pp. 17-19 (18), from which it likewise appears that, even apart from the correctness of public opinion, the Court does not wish to regard the corporal punishment itself, intended as a preventive measure, as a local requirement in the sense of Art. 63(3), which would have to be taken into account in the application of Art. 3. See also Appl. 7456/76, *Wiggins v. the United Kingdom*, D&R 13 (1979), p. 40 (48).

therefore emphasised circumstances and conditions rather than requirements. A political situation, which admittedly was a sensitive one but also one which could occur in the mother country, did not suffice to interpret the phrase 'local requirements' as justifying an interference with the right secured in Article 10.[25]

When territories become independent, a declaration under Article 63 automatically ceases to apply, because the Contracting State which made it, is no longer responsible for the international relations of the new State.[26] This new State does not automatically become a Party to the Convention. In the majority of cases[27] it will not even be able to become a Party, since Article 66(1) makes signature possible only for Member States of the Council of Europe and membership of the latter organisation is open only to *European* States.[28]

3.2 State Responsibility for Acts of its Organs that have been Committed Outside its Territory

The fact that the Convention is applicable only to the territory of the Contracting States, with the qualification of Article 63, does not imply that a Contracting State cannot be responsible under the Convention for acts of its organs that have been committed outside its territory. Thus the Commission decided that in principle the acts of functionaries of the German embassy in Morocco might involve the responsibility of the Federal Republic of Germany.[29] And in the *Loizidou* Case the Court held that the responsibility of a Contracting Party may also arise when as a consequence of military action – whether lawful or unlawful – it exercises effective control of an area outside its national territory. The obligation to secure, in such area, the rights and freedoms set out in the Convention, derives from the fact of such control whether it be exercised directly, through its armed forces, or through a subordinate local administration.[30] Similarly, Switzerland was deemed responsible for acts committed under a treaty of 1923 concerning the incorporation of Liechtenstein into the Swiss customs area. The Commission held that acts of Swiss authorities having effect in Liechtenstein place all those to whom these acts are applicable, under Swiss jurisdiction in the sense of Article 1 of the Convention.[31] In addition, the responsibility of Contracting Parties can be

---

[25] Judgment of 27 April 1995, A.314, p. 23.

[26] See, *e.g.*, Appl. 7230/75, *X* v. *the Netherlands*, D&R 7 (1977), p. 109 (110-111).

[27] This was different in the cases of Cyprus and Malta only, which after their independence actually became members of the Council of Europe and Parties to the Convention.

[28] Art. 4 of the Statute of the Council of Europe.

[29] Appl. 1611/62, *X* v. *Federal Republic of Germany*, Yearbook VIII (1965), p. 158 (163).

[30] Judgment of 23 March 1995, A.310, p. 24.

[31] Appls 7289/75 and 7349/76, *X* and *Y* v. *Switzerland*, D&R 9 (1978), p. 57 (73). In this context see, however, Appl. 6231/73, *Ilse Hess* v. *the United Kingdom*, Yearbook XVIII (1975), p. 146 (174-176), in which the British Government was not held responsible, in the terms of the Convention, with respect to alleged violations in Spandau Prison, because the Commission concluded that the responsibility for the prison was exercised on a Four-Power basis and that the United Kingdom acted only as a partner in the joint responsibility. Since decisions could only be taken unanimously,

involved because of acts of their authorities, whether performed within or outside national boundaries, which produce effects outside their own territory.[32]

In the *Drozd and Janousek* Case the applicants complained that they had not had a fair trial before the *Tribunal de Corts* of the Principality of Andorra and held France and Spain responsible at international level for the conduct of the Andorran authorities. As regards the objection of lack of jurisdiction *ratione loci*, the Court agreed in substance with the Governments' arguments and the Commission's opinion that the Convention was not applicable at the territory of Andorra, notwithstanding its ratification by France and Spain. It also took into consideration various circumstances: the Principality was not a member of the Council of Europe, which prevented it being a Party to the Convention in its own right, and appeared never to have taken any steps to seek admission as an 'associate member' of the organisation. The territory of Andorra was not an area common to France and Spain or a Franco-Spanish condominium. The Principality's relations with France and Spain did not follow the normal pattern of relations between sovereign States and did not take the form of international agreements, even though the development of the Andorran institutions might according to the French Co-Prince, allow Andorra to 'join the international community'. The objection of lack of jurisdiction *ratione loci* was well-founded.[33]

On the other hand, a Contracting State is responsible for acts committed on its territory only to the extent that they have been committed by its own organs.[34] Thus, in the *Drozd and Janousek* Case the Court noted that judges from France and Spain sat as members of the Andorran courts, but did not do so in their capacity as French or Spanish judges. Those courts, in particular the *Tribunal de Corts*, exercised their functions in an autonomous manner, while their judgments were not subject to supervision by the authorities of France or Spain. There was nothing in the case-file to suggest that those authorities had attempted to interfere with the applicants' trial.[35]

---

the prison was not under the jurisdiction of the United Kingdom in the sense of Art. 1.

[32] Judgment of 26 June 1992, *Drozd and Janousek*, A.240, p. 29.

[33] *Ibidem*, pp. 28-31; report of 11 December 1990, A.240, p. 54.

[34] See Appl. 2095/63, *X v. Sweden, Federal Republic of Germany and other States*, Yearbook VIII (1965), p. 272 (282), where it was decided that the alleged violations of the Convention by the Supreme Restitution Court could not be held against the Federal Republic of Germany, even though this tribunal had its sessions on West German territory. It was to be considered as an international tribunal, in respect of which Germany had neither legislative nor supervisory powers. See also Appl. 235/56, *X v. Federal Republic of Germany*, Yearbook II (1958-1959), p. 256 (304), where the Commission reached the same conclusion with respect to the American Court of Restitution Appeals in Germany.

[35] Judgment of 26 June 1992, A.240, p. 29.

4 THE TEMPORAL EFFECT OF THE CONVENTION

4.1 General

By virtue of a generally accepted principle of international law a treaty is not applicable to acts or facts that have occurred, or to situations that have ceased to exist, before the treaty entered into force and was ratified by the State in question.[36] This applies also to the European Convention.[37] In the *Pfunders* Case the Commission inferred from the nature of the obligations under the Convention that the fact that the respondent State (in this case Italy) was a party to the Convention at the time of the alleged violation was decisive, without it being necessary that at that moment the applicant State (in this case Austria) had ratified the Convention.[38]

4.2 Continuing Violations

Noteworthy is the case-law of the Commission concerning complaints which relate to a continuing situation, *i.e.* to violations of the Convention which are caused by an act committed at a given moment, but which continue owing to the consequences of the original act. Such a case occurred with respect to a Belgian national who lodged a complaint concerning a conviction by a Belgian court for treason during the Second World War. The verdict had been pronounced before Belgium had ratified the Convention, but the situation complained about – the punishment in the form of, *inter alia*, a limitation of the right of free expression – continued after the Convention had become binding upon Belgium. According to the Commission the latter fact was decisive and the complaint accordingly was declared admissible.[39] Similarly the Court held in the *Papamichalopoulos* Case that the expropriation of land amounted to a continuing violation of Article 1 of Protocol No. 1. The alleged violations had begun in 1967. At that time Greece had already ratified the Convention and Protocol No. 1, and their denunciation by Greece from 13 June 1970 till 28 November 1974 during the military regime had not released it from its obligations under them 'in respect of any act which, being capable of constituting a violation of such obligations, [might] have been performed by it' earlier, as stated in Article 65(2) of the Convention. Admittedly,

---

[36] See Art. 28 of the Vienna Convention on the Law of Treaties, ILM 8, 1969, p. 679.

[37] Appl. 343/57, *Schouw Nielsen* v. *Denmark*, Yearbook II (1958-1959), p. 412 (454); Appl. 7742/76, *A.B. & Company A.S.* v. *Federal Republic of Germany*, D&R 14 (1979), p. 146 (167).

[38] Appl. 788/60, *Austria* v. *Italy*, Yearbook IV (1961), p. 116 (142).

[39] Appl. 214/56, *De Becker* v. *Belgium*, Yearbook II (1958-1959), p. 214 (244). See also Appl. 7031/75, *X* v. *Switzerland*, D&R 6 (1977), p. 124; Appl. 7202/75, *X* v. *the United Kingdom*, D&R 7 (1977), p. 102; and Appl. 8701/79, *X* v. *Belgium*, D&R 18 (1980), p. 250 (251) concerning disfranchise. See, however, the negative decision of the Commission in the joined Appls 8560/79 and 8613/79, *X and Y* v. *Portugal*, D&R 16 (1979), p. 209 (211-212), in which two servicemen complained that their transfer had taken place in contravention of Art. 6.

Greece had not recognised the Commission's competence to receive individual petitions until 20 November 1985 and then only in relation to acts, decisions, facts or events subsequent to that date, but the Government had not in the instant case raised any preliminary objection in that regard and the Court held that the question did not call for consideration by the Court out of its own motion. The Court noted merely that the applicants' claim related to a continuing situation.[40] In the cases of *Yağci* and *Saragin,* and *Mansur* the Court rejected the preliminary objection of the Turkish Government that the Court's jurisdiction was excluded in respect of events subsequent to the date of the acceptance by Turkey of the Court's compulsory jurisdiction but which by their nature were merely 'extensions of ones occurring before that date'. According to the Court, having regard to the wording of the declaration Turkey made under Article 46 of the Convention, it could not entertain complaints about events which occurred before the acceptance of the Court's compulsory jurisdiction. However, when examining the complaints relating to Articles 5(3) and 6(1) of the Convention, which articles were at stake in the present cases, the Court took account of the state of proceedings at the time when the declaration was deposited. It therefore could not accept the Government's argument that even facts subsequent to the date of the Turkey's declaration were excluded from its jurisdiction where they were merely extensions of an already existing situation. It added: 'From the critical date onwards all the State's acts and omissions not only must conform to the Convention but are also undoubtedly subject to review by the Convention institutions.'[41]

In the *Stamoulakatos* Case, the applicant was convicted, *in absentia*, by the Greek criminal courts on several occasions. The Government's primary submission was that the applicant's complaints did not come within the Court's jurisdiction *ratione temporis* because they related to events which had taken place before 20 November 1985, when Greece's acceptance of the right of individual petition took effect. The breach which the applicant complained of originated in three convictions dating from 1979 and 1980. The fact that he had subsequently lodged appeals could not affect the period that the Court had to consider in order to rule on the objection. The Court found that the events which gave rise to the proceedings against the applicant, together with the three judgments, were covered by the time-limit in Greece's declaration in respect of Article 25 of the Convention. As to his appeals and applications against those judgments, the applicant complained only that they were ineffective in that they did not enable him to obtain from a court which had heard him – as he was entitled to under the Convention – a fresh determination of the merits of the charges on which he had been tried *in absentia*. Thus, although those appeals and applications were lodged after the 'critical' date of 19 November 1985, according to the Court they were closely bound up with the proceedings that had led to his conviction. The Court was of the opinion that divorcing these appeals and applications from the events

---

[40] Judgment of 24 June 1993, A.260-B, pp. 75-76.
[41] Judgments of 8 June 1995, A.319-A, p. 16 and A.319-B, p. 48.

which gave rise to them would, in the instant case, be tantamount to rendering Greece's aforementioned declaration nugatory. It was reasonable to infer from that declaration that Greece could not be held to have violated its obligation for not affording any possibility of a retrial to those who had been convicted *in absentia* before 20 November 1985. The objection was well-founded and the Court found it could not deal with the merits of the case.[42]

4.3 Restrictions with Respect to the Acceptance of Jurisdiction

A declaration of a Contracting State as referred to in Article 25, in which the competence of the Commission to receive applications from individuals is recognised, in principle has retrospective effect to the moment of the ratification of the Convention.[43] As a consequence of this approach an individual may therefore draw the Commission's attention to an alleged violation of the Convention, even if this violation took place prior to the moment at which the respondent State made the declaration under Article 25, provided that at the moment in question the Convention was binding upon that State. When making the said declaration, a State may, however, indicate that it applies to the future only.[44] In the latter case, however, what has been said in section 4.2 about 'continuing violations' has to be taken into account.

When Turkey accepted the right of individual petition, it subjected its acceptance of the Commission's competence to a number of limitations. The Turkish Government stated, *inter alia*, that:

(i)   the recognition of the right of petition extends only to allegations concerning acts or omissions of public authorities in Turkey performed within the boundaries of the territory to which the Constitution of the Republic of Turkey is applicable;

(ii) the circumstances and conditions under which Turkey, by virtue of Article 15 of the Convention, derogates from her obligations under the Convention in special circumstances must be interpreted, for the purpose of the competence attributed to the Commission under this declaration, in the light of Articles 119 to 122 of the Turkish Constitution;

(iii) the competence attributed to the Commission under this declaration shall not comprise matters regarding the legal status of military personnel and in particular, the system of discipline in the armed forces;

(iv) for the purpose of the competence attributed to the Commission under this declaration, the notion of 'a democratic society' in paragraphs 2 of Articles 8, 9, 10, and 11 ECHR must be understood in conformity with the principles laid down in the Turkish Constitution and in particular its Preamble and its Article 13;

---

[42] Judgment of 26 October 1993, A.271, pp. 13-14.

[43] Appl. 9587/81, *X* v. *France*, D&R 29 (1982), pp. 238-239; Appl. 9990/82, *Bozano* v. *France*, D&R 39 (1984), p. 143; Appl. 12806/87, *Stamoulakatos* v. *Greece*, D&R 69 (1991), p. 144 (155-156).

[44] See, *e.g.*, the declaration of the United Kingdom, Yearbook IX (1966), p. 8. See also Appl. 6323/73, *X* v. *Italy*, D&R 3 (1976), p. 80 (82); Appls 15299/89, 15300/89 and 15318/89, *Chrysostomos, Papachrysostomou* and *Loizidou* v. *Turkey*, D&R 68 (1991), p. 216 (240). See also the Court in its judgment of 23 March 1995, *Loizidou* (preliminary objections), A.310, p. 33.

(v) for the purpose of the competence attributed to the Commission under the present declaration, Articles 33, 52 and 135 of the Constitution must be understood as being in conformity with Article 10 and 11 ECHR.[45]

The Commission and the Court had the opportunity to consider the validity of these limitations, when they were confronted with a complaint against Turkey. The Commission held that apart from the temporal limitations provided for in paragraph 2 of Article 25, the Convention did not authorise any other restriction in a declaration accepting the right of individual petition. Consequently, the limitations appearing in paragraphs (i) to (v) of the Turkish declaration were not valid. Referring to Article 31 of the Vienna Convention of the Law of Treaties, the Commission stated that as regards the ordinary meaning of Article 25(1), it considered that the wording 'the rights set forth in this Convention' presupposes total, not partial recognition. Otherwise, the Convention would in Article 25(1) have referred to 'any' or 'some' rights.[46]

In its judgment in the *Loizidou* Case the Court sought to ascertain the ordinary meaning given to Articles 25 and 46 in their context and in the light of their object and purpose. The Court held that if Articles 25 and 46 were to be interpreted as permitting restrictions (other than of a temporal nature) States would be enabled to qualify their consent under the optional clauses. According to the Court this would severely weaken the role of the Commission and Court and diminish the effectiveness of the Convention as a constitutional instrument of European public order. The consequences for the enforcement of the Convention would be so far-reaching that a power to that effect should have been expressly provided for. Neither Article 25 nor Article 46 contains such a provision. According to the Court, the subsequent practice of Contracting Parties of not attaching restrictions *ratione loci* or *ratione materiae* confirmed the view that these were not permitted.[47]

The conclusion that Article 25 only permits the temporal restrictions expressly authorised in its second paragraph is further supported by a comparison with Article 46, which sets forth in paragraph 2 that declarations recognising the jurisdiction of the Court 'may be made (...) for a specified period'. This provision is analogous to paragraph 2 of Article 25. Finally, the Court referred to Article 6(2) of Protocol No. 4 and Article 7(2) of Protocol No. 7 which stipulate that the right of individual recourse recognised by a declaration made under Article 25 of the Convention shall not be effective in relation to the Protocol unless the State concerned has made a statement recognising such a right. Such an express

---

[45] Annex to letter JJ1939C 29 January 1987; Council of Europe, Information Sheet No. 21 (1988), pp. 3-13.

[46] Appls 15299/89, 15300/89 and 15318/89, *Chrysostomos, Papachrysostomou* and *Loizidou* v. *Turkey*, D&R 68 (1991), p. 216 (237-240); Appl. 14524/89, *Yanasik* v. *Turkey*, D&R 74 (1993), p. 14 (24-25).

[47] Judgment of 23 March 1995, A.310, pp. 26-28.

stipulation permitting States to limit their acceptance under Article 25 would not have been necessary had Article 25 allowed for such limitations.[48]

A special situation occurred when several complaints concerning criminal proceedings in Italy were lodged. In its declaration under Article 25 this country had laid down that it accepted the rights of individual petition as from 1 August 1973. The procedure in the first instance in these cased had ended in 1969. On appeal, the verdict had been pronounced on 11 February 1976. To the extent that the complaint concerned the first-mentioned procedure it was rejected by the Commission *ratione temporis*, while with respect to the appeal procedure the application was declared admissible. The Commission used as the only criterion the question of whether the proceedings had terminated prior to or after the date indicated by Italy in its declaration under Article 25.[49]

The competence of the Commission to receive applications from States under Article 24 arises automatically from the fact that the Convention has become binding, so that the problem of the retrospective effect does not play a part in this respect, unless in the form discussed above of an application which relates to a moment at which the applicant State had not yet ratified the Convention.

4.4 Denunciation of the Convention

Finally, as to the temporal scope of the Convention, it has to be mentioned that, even after a State has denounced the Convention in accordance with Article 65(1), the latter remains fully applicable to that State for another six months (Article 65(2)). A complaint submitted between the date of denunciation of the Convention and that on which that denunciation becomes effective thus falls within the scope of the Convention *ratione temporis*. This occurred in the case of the second complaint, of April 1970, by Denmark, Norway and Sweden against Greece. On 12 December 1969 Greece had denounced the Convention. This denunciation was therefore to become effective on 13 June 1970. The Commission decided that in virtue of Article 65(2) Greece was still bound, at the time of the complaint, to comply with the obligations ensuing from the Convention, and that accordingly the Commission could consider the complaint.[50]

---

[48] Judgment of 23 March 1995, *Loizidou* (preliminary objections), A.310, p. 27. Appls 15299/89, 15300/89 and 15318/89, *Chrysostomos, Papachrysostomou* and *Loizidou* v. *Turkey*, D&R 68 (1991), p. 216 (240-241).

[49] Appl. 8261/78, *X* v. *Italy*, D&R 18 (1980), p. 150 (151). In this case the Commission took that date also as the starting-point for the six-month rule. However, the Commission has in the meantime reversed its case-law on this point and now strictly adheres to the point of departure that the six-month time-limit is to be calculated as from the final domestic decision.

[50] Appl. 4448/70, *Denmark, Norway and Sweden* v. *Greece*, Yearbook XIII (1970), p. 108 (120). After the admissibility declaration the Commission desisted from further examination. However, on 18 November 1974 Greece became a Party again to the Convention, and the Commission then resumed its examination of the complaint. Finally, on 4 October 1976, after both the applicant States and the defendant State had intimated that they were no longer interested in proceeding with the case, the Commission struck the case off the list; D&R 6 (1977), p. 6 (8).

5 THE EFFECT OF THE CONVENTION WITHIN THE NATIONAL LEGAL SYSTEMS

5.1 Dualism and Monism

It is primarily the task of the national authorities of the Contracting States to secure the rights and freedoms set forth in the Convention. To what extent the national courts can play a part in this, by reviewing the acts and omissions of those national authorities, depends mainly on the question of whether the provisions of the Convention are directly applicable in proceedings before those national courts. The answer to this question depends in turn on the effect of the Convention within the national legal system concerned. The Convention does not impose upon the Contracting States the obligation to make the Convention part of domestic law or otherwise to guarantee its national applicability and prevalence over national law.

In the context of the relationship between international law and municipal law there are two contrasting views. In the so-called *dualistic* view the international and the national legal system form two separate legal spheres, and international law has effect within the national legal system only after it has been 'transformed' into national law *via* the required procedure. The legal subjects depend on this transformation for the protection of the rights laid down in international law; their rights and duties exist only under national law. This is the case, for instance, in the United Kingdom; since the Convention has not (yet) been 'transformed' by Act of Parliament into national law, it cannot be invoked before a British court, at least not as such and independently.[51] In another dualistic system, that of the Federal Republic of Germany, the Convention has been transformed by a federal law (*Zustimmungsgesetz*) according to Article 59(2) of the Constitution, thereby becoming part of the domestic law of the Federal Republic.

In a dualistic system, after the Convention has been approved and transformed into domestic law, the question remains which status it has within the national legal system. The answer to this question is to be found in national constitutional law. Under German constitutional law, for instance, the Convention has no priority over the Federal Constitution, nor is it of equal rank. It has, however, the rank of a federal statute. The consequences of this have been mitigated by interpreting German statutes in line with the Convention; the German *Bundesverfassungsgericht* has even decided that priority should be given to the provisions of the Convention over subsequent legislation unless a contrary intention of the legislature could be clearly established. Even provisions of the Federal Constitution have to be interpreted in the light of the Convention.

---

[51] The British courts may, however, give application to Convention provisions in an indirect way by 'assuming' that the legislative authorities have had the intention that British law be in conformity with the Convention; C. Warbrick, 'Rights, the European Convention on Human Rights and English Law', *European Law Review*, 1994, pp. 34-46.

In the so-called *monistic* view, on the other hand, the various domestic legal systems are viewed as elements of the all-embracing international legal system, within which the national authorities are bound by international law in their relations with individuals as well, regardless of whether or not the rules of international law have been transformed into national law. In this view the individual derives rights and duties directly from international law, so that in national proceedings he may directly invoke rules of international law, which must be applied by the national courts and to which the latter must give priority over any national law conflicting with it.

However, even among the monistic systems many differences exist. Although as a general rule they accept the domestic legal effect of (approved) international treaties, the scope of this acceptance varies considerably. In the Netherlands, self-executing provisions of treaties and of decisions of international organisations (*i.e.* written international law) may be invoked before domestic courts and may set aside conflicting (*anterior* and *posterior*) statutory law, including provisions in the Constitution. In fact, the Dutch courts have actively made use of the Convention in setting aside or interpreting Acts of Parliament. In France, the *Court de Cassation*, relying upon Article 55 of the French Constitution, has accepted the prevalence of treaties (including EC-law) over national *lois* since 1975. The *Conseil d'Etat* has been much more hesitant, but finally, in 1989, accepted the supremacy of treaties over domestic legislation.

In the prevailing opinion the system resulting from the monistic view is not prescribed by international law at its present stage of development. International law leaves the States full discretion to decide for themselves in what way they will fulfil their international obligations and implement the pertinent international rules within their national legal system; they are internationally responsible only for the ultimate result of this implementation. This holds good for the European Convention as well,[52] although the Court indicated that the system according to which the Convention has internal effect, is a particularly faithful reflection of the intention of the drafters.[53] The consequence is that in some Contracting States no internal effect is assigned to the Convention, while in others it is so assigned.

In States in which the Convention has internal effect one must ascertain for each of its provision separately whether it is directly applicable – is self-executing –, so that individuals may directly invoke such a provision before the national courts. The self-executing character of a Convention provision may generally be

---

[52] See the judgment of 6 February 1976, *Swedish Engine Drivers' Union*, A.20, p. 18, in which the Court held that 'neither Article 13 nor the Convention in general lays down for the Contracting States any given manner for ensuring within their internal law the effective implementation of any of the provisions of the Convention.' In the same sense already the judgment of 23 July 1968, *Belgian Linguistic* Case, A.6, p. 35 and the judgment of 27 October 1975, *National Union of Belgian Police*, A.19, p. 20. See also the dissenting opinion of the Commission members Sperduti and Opsahl in the report of the Commission in *Ireland* v. *the United Kingdom*, B.23-I (1980), pp. 503-505.

[53] Judgment of 18 January 1978, *Ireland* v. *the United Kingdom*, A.25, p. 91.

presumed when the content of such a provision can be applied in a concrete case without there being a need for supplementary measures on the part of the national authorities.

5.2 Convention as Compared to EC-Law

The Court of Justice of the European Communities has taken a different position with respect to the relation between Community law and the law of the Member States.[54] According to the Court, directly applicable provisions of the Community Treaties and of the decisions of the Community institutions (regulations and even directives) do have internal effect within the legal systems of the Member States, regardless of what each particular national legal system provides in that respect. Moreover, in the view of the Court, the provisions with a self-executing character have priority over provisions of national law, even over those of the national Constitution. The Court infers this from the character of Community law and bases its position on the principle of Community fidelity, laid down in Article 5 EC-Treaty and on that of effectiveness (*l'effet utile*). Without priority, those rules, which form the core of Community law, would become devoid of effect, or at least could not be applied in a uniform and useful way. The premise on which the Court bases this view is that the Member States have renounced their sovereign rights in favour of the legal system of the Community in the areas coming under the Community Treaties.

The Court of Justice can disclose its view concerning the internal effect and the priority of Community law directly to the national courts by way of the preliminary rulings which the national courts may, and in the last resort even must, request if in national proceedings they are confronted with the question of the relation of national law to, and its compatibility with, Community law (Article 177 EC-Treaty). The relation between the European Court of Human Rights and the national courts is much less direct than that between the Court of Justice of the European Communities and the national courts. The former cannot give preliminary rulings; it might declare the ultimate result of the implementation of provisions of the Convention not to be in conformity with the obligations resulting from the Convention, *e.g.* from Article 13.

In view of its character the Convention would seem to contain the germs for a gradual development into a common legal system for the Contracting States, to which their national law must be subordinate. In practical terms the dynamic and evolving interpretation by the Court, and its reliance upon practices and rules, make it more and more necessary for the national courts to take the expanding impact of the Convention into account. The wish to avoid as much as possible incompatibilities between national law and the Convention (as interpreted by the Court) may gradually convince national courts of the desirability of taking into

---

[54] On this, see P.J.G. Kapteyn and P. VerLoren van Themaat, *Introduction to the Law of the European Communities*, 2nd ed., Deventer, 1989, p. 39, and the case-law cited there.

account the Convention's provisions. The subject-matter regulated by the Convention – the protection of civil and political rights – lends itself eminently to direct effect. In fact, it concerns precisely the protection of rights of individuals which can be exercised without further measures being taken by the national authorities; that is, rights which by their nature are directly applicable.[55] In our opinion the priority of the Convention over provisions of national law conflicting therewith may very well be defended, on the one hand, on the ground of the fundamental – one might say constitutional – character of the rights and freedoms protected in the Convention, and, on the other hand, on the basis of the aim of the Council of Europe as set forth in the Preamble of the Convention, *viz.* the achievement of greater unity between the Member States; a unity which is also striven for by the supervisory system provided for in the Convention. However, as will be shown later under the headings of Articles 6 and 13, the Court does not infer from the Convention the right to have national Acts of Parliament impugned before national courts whenever they conflict with the Convention. As the Court held in 1994:

> Article 13 does not go so far as to require a remedy whereby the laws of a Contracting State may be impugned before a national authority as being in themselves contrary to the Convention.[56]

Any initiative in the direction of establishing an obligation to incorporate the Convention into domestic law with priority status will therefore have to be taken either by the Council of Europe or by the national authorities, including the courts. The construction of renunciation of part of the sovereignty, used by the Court of Justice of the European Communities, might also be utilised by the national courts in deciding on the effect to be given to the Convention within the national legal system. Of course, national courts will not be able to take any initiative in this direction, if in their view constitutional law is expressly opposed to it. The constitutions of various Contracting States, however, contain provisions which make it possible in so many words to transfer sovereign rights to inter-governmental institutions.[57] In those cases the courts may have a possibility for assigning internal effect and priority to the Convention within their national legal system, even in the absence of express legal positions to that effect.

In the present legal climate, however, the chances that a development in the direction outlined above may materialise would not appear very great. In general, national courts are hardly inclined to allow provisions of international law to prevail over their own national law. This applies to an even greater extent to rules concerning human rights, which may indeed have a far-reaching impact upon the

---

[55] In those Contracting States where the Convention has internal effect, almost all the provisions of Section I of the Convention are considered as self-executing.

[56] Judgment of 9 December 1994, *The Holy Monasteries* v. *Greece*, A.301-A; judgment of 21 February 1986, *James and Others* v. *the United Kingdom*, A.98.

[57] See, *e.g.*, Art. 24 of the German, Arts 53 and 54 of the French and Art. 20 of the Danish Constitution.

national legal system, so that the national courts will shrink from being guided by rules which are relatively alien to that national legal system, so long as those rules are not based on a solid constitutional foundation as well.[58] Even within the European Communities, precisely in the matter of human rights, the willingness of some national tribunals to give unconditional priority to Community law has given rise to serious difficulties in the past, as may be seen from decisions of the highest constitutional courts in the Federal Republic of Germany and Italy.[59] This was based on the argument that these courts consider the Community system for the protection of fundamental rights and its (lack of a) democratic basis to constitute as yet too weak a foundation for subordinating thereto the national constitutional guarantees. It is true that the Court of Justice of the European Communities has taken the position that Community law includes also general principles of the law of human rights, and for these principles has sought to base itself on the constitutional principles of the Member States as well as on the European Convention,[60] but this was then evidently considered too weak a constitutional foundation by the tribunals referred to above.[61]

In the Preamble of the Single European Act express reference is being made to the Convention as well as to the European Social Charter. And Article F, section 2, of the Treaty on European Union states: 'The Union shall respect fundamental rights, as guaranteed by the European Convention for the Protection of Human Rights and Fundamental Freedoms signed in Rome on 4 November 1950 and as they result from the constitutional traditions common to the Member States, as general principles of Community law.' This provision reflects the approach already taken by the European Court of Justice that fundamental human rights do form part of Community law, which means that they can be invoked against the Union authorities, but also against national governments and legislatures when they act within the scope of Community law and if the issue in question is governed by Community provisions. This also means that in those areas the Convention can be

---

[58] See, however, for the Netherlands, P. van Dijk, 'Domestic Status of Human-Rights Treaties and the Attitude of the Judiciary; The Dutch Case', in: M. Nowak, Dorothea Steuer and Hannes Tretter (eds.), *Progress in the Spirit of Human Rights; Festschrift für Felix Ermacora*, Kehl *etc.*, 1988, pp. 631-650.

[59] See W.R. Edeson and F. Wooldridge, 'European Community Law and Fundamental Human Rights; some recent decisions of the European Court and National Courts', *Legal Issues of European Integration* (1976/1), pp. 1-55.

[60] See N.A. Neuwahl, 'The Treaty on European Union: A Step Forward in the Protection of Human Rights?', in: N.A. Neuwahl and A. Rosas (eds.), *The European Union and Human Rights*, The Hague *etc.*, 1995, pp. 1-22 (6-13).

[61] In the meantime, the Court of Justice has strengthened this foundation. Both the *Bundesverfassungsgericht* in the Federal Republic of Germany and the Italian *Corte Constituzionale* have reviewed their opinions, by holding that fundamental rights are sufficiently guaranteed in the Community's legal order, and that therefore their reservations with regard to the priority of Community law over national law could conditionally (*so lange*) be lifted. See the comments on these judgments by G. Gaja, *Common Market Law Review*, 1984, pp. 756-772 and J.A. Frowein, *Common Market Law Review*, 1988, pp. 201-206.

invoked as being part of Community law, and may thereby profit from the domestic status of Community law within the national legal orders.[62]

This construction does not, however, offer a full solution for those Member States of the European Union which have a dualist system, since it may give rise to conflicting case-law concerning the interpretation of provisions in the Convention by the European Court of Justice and the Strasbourg Court.[63] Thus, *e.g.*, in *Hoechst A.G.* v. *Commission*[64] the EC Court ruled that Article 8 of the Convention could not be extended to cover commercial premises. However, in 1989 the Strasbourg Court ruled in the *Chappell* Case that even where a search was directed solely against business activities, the applicability of Article 8 was not excluded.[65] In the *Niemietz* Case the Strasbourg Court explicitly decided that 'the search of the applicant's office constituted an interference with his rights under Article 8.'[66] In this judgment the Court mentioned the *Hoechst* judgment of the EC Court. It is to be expected that the latter Court in the future will defer to the Strasbourg Court's case-law, because of its explicit consideration in the *Hoechst* Case that there was at that time no case-law of the European Court of Human Rights on the subject. However, an ultimate guarantee of uniformity of interpretation would only be achieved if the European Union or the separate European Communities were to become parties to the Convention.[67]

5.3 Implementation of Court Decisions

A pertinent question is to what extent Court decisions can be relied upon before a national court. In the abstract the answer to this question is similar to the one given concerning the implementation of the Convention within the national legal order: it is dependent upon the national legal order to what extent Court decisions can be invoked and can affect the outcome of national proceedings. The Court itself does not enforce any effect; its judgments are of a declaratory character. They establish whether the Convention has been violated, and may be accompanied by a decision under Article 50 about financial compensation. However, in a subsequent case the Court may have the opportunity to judge on the

---

[62] See N. Grief, 'The Domestic Impact of the European Convention on Human Rights as Mediated through Community Law', *Public Law*, 1991, pp. 555-567.

[63] See R. Lawson, 'Confusion and Conflict? – Diverging Interpretations of the European Convention on Human Rights in Strasbourg and Luxembourg', in: R. Lawson and M. de Blois (eds.), *The Dynamics of the Protection of Human Rights in Europe, Essays in Honour of Henry G. Schermers*, Vol. III, Dordrecht *etc.*, 1994, pp. 219-252.

[64] [1989] E.C.R. 2859.

[65] Judgment of 30 March 1989, A.152-A, pp. 21-22.

[66] Judgment of 16 December 1992, A.251-B, p. 35.

[67] See, however, Opinion 2/94 of the EC Court on accession; G. Gaja, 'Comments', *CML Rev.*, 1969, pp. 973-989.

way in which its earlier judgment, and the interpretation it contains of one or more of the provisions of the Convention, has been taken into account.[68]

The various Contracting States have different systems with regard to the effect to be given to Court decisions within their respective legal orders. Some even have adopted special legislative provisions in order to ensure the execution of Court decisions within the national legal order. A study prepared by the Committee of Experts for the improvement of procedures for the protection of Human Rights (DHPR) under the authority of the Steering Committee of Human Rights (CDDH) contains a survey of to what extent the national legal systems allow for review of domestic judicial decisions subsequent to a finding of a violation of the Convention by the Strasbourg organs. One of the conclusions is that '(t)here seems to exist a rather limited amount of relevant case-law in member-States. In this connection it should be noted that for four (of the six) States that have adopted legislation enabling review subsequent to a finding of a violation of the Convention, these provisions appear, as yet, never to have been applied in practice.'[69] In our opinion, effective implementation of judgments of the Court within the national legal order is an important next step to be taken by the Contracting States, since it is an essential precondition for effectively ensuring that the rule of law is observed and enforced by giving relief to the applicants.

6 'DRITTWIRKUNG'

Drittwirkung is a complicated phenomenon about which there are widely divergent views. At this place only those general aspects which are directly connected with the Convention will be dealt with. Hereafter, in the discussion of the separate rights and freedoms, certain aspects of *Drittwirkung* will be discussed insofar as the case-law of the Commission and the Court calls for it. For a detailed treatment of *Drittwirkung*, in particular also as to its recognition and effect under national law, reference may be made to the literature.[70]

---

[68] An example concerning Belgium is to be found in the judgment of 29 November 1991, *Vermeire*, A.214-C (discrimination of illegitimate children). The Belgian court of first instance allowed Vermeire the same rights as a legitimate descendant, basing its decision upon the judgment given by the Court in the *Marckx* Case of 13 June 1979, A.31, p. 26. The Court reproached the Brussels Court of Appeal and the Court of Cassation of 'not complying with the findings of the *Marckx* judgment, as the Court of First Instance had done. There was nothing imprecise or incomplete about the rule which prohibited discrimination against Astrid Vermeire (...). An overall revision of the legislation (...) was not necessary at all as an essential preliminary to compliance with the Convention as interpreted by the Court in the Marckx case.'

[69] Published in: *Human Rights Law Journal*, 1992, Nos 1-2, pp. 71-78.

[70] See, *e.g.*, E.A. Alkema, 'The third-party applicability or "Drittwirkung" of the ECHR', in: *Protecting Human Rights; The European Dimension*, Köln, 1988, pp. 33-45; A. Drzemczewski, 'The domestic status of the European Convention on Human Rights; new dimensions', *Legal Issues of European Integration*, No. 1, 1977, pp. 1-85; M.A. Eissen, 'La convention et les devoirs des individus', in: *La protection des droits de l'homme dans le cadre européen*, Paris, 1961, pp. 167-194; H. Guradze, 'Die Schutzrichtung der Grundrechtsnormen in der Europäischen Menschenrechts-

What does the term *Drittwirkung* mean? Two views in particular must be distinguished. According to the first view it means that the provisions concerning human rights also *apply* in legal relations between private parties, and not only in legal relations between an individual and the public authorities. According to the second view, *Drittwirkung* is defined as the possibility for an individual to *enforce* his fundamental rights against another individual. Advocates of the latter view therefore consider that *Drittwirkung* of human rights is present only if an individual in his legal relations with other individuals is able to enforce the observance of the law concerning human rights *via* some procedure or other.

As to the latter view, it may at once be submitted that no *Drittwirkung* of the rights and freedoms set forth in the Convention can be directly effectuated *via* the procedure set up by the Convention. In fact, in Strasbourg it is possible to lodge complaints only about violations of the Convention by one of the Contracting States; a complaint directed against an individual is inadmissible by reason of incompatibility with the Convention *ratione personae*.[71] This follows from Articles 19, 24, 25, 31, 32 and 50 of the Convention, and has also been confirmed by the case-law of the Commission.[72] As a consequence, an individual can bring up an alleged violation of his fundamental rights and freedoms by other individuals in Strasbourg only indirectly, *viz.* when a Contracting State can be held responsible for the violation in one way or another.[73] In that case the investigation in the Strasbourg procedure concerns the responsibility of the State and not that of the private actor. It is, therefore, no surprise that the Strasbourg case-law provides little clarity as far as *Drittwirkung* is concerned. At best a kind of 'indirect *Drittwirkung*'[74] is recognised in cases where from a provision of the Convention – notably Articles 3, 10 and 11 – rights are inferred for individuals which, on the basis of a positive obligation on the part of Contracting States to take measures in order to make their exercise possible, must also be enforced *vis-à-vis* third private parties.[75]

The fact that in Strasbourg no complaints can be lodged against individuals need not, however, bar the recognition of *Drittwirkung* of the Convention, not even in the second sense referred to above. The possibility of enforcement which

---

konvention', *Festschrift Nipperdy*, Vol. II, 1965, pp. 759-769; M.M. Hahne, *Das Drittwirkungs-problem in der Europäischen Konvention zum Schutz der Menschenrechte und Grundfreiheiten*, Heidelberg, 1973; D.H.M. Meuwissen, *De Europese Conventie en het Nederlandse Recht* [The European Convention and Dutch Law], Leyden, 1968, pp. 201-211; A. Clapham, 'The "Drittwirkung" of the Convention', in: R.St.J. McDonald *et al.* (eds.), *The European System for the Protection of Human Rights*, Deventer, 1993, pp. 163-206.

[71] See *infra* p. 119.

[72] See *infra* p. 119, note 100.

[73] As a rule a State is not internationally responsible for the acts and omissions of its nationals or of individuals within its jurisdiction; on this, see *infra* pp. 120-123.

[74] See Alkema, *supra* note 70, p. 33.

[75] For an elaborate survey of such cases of 'indirect *Drittwirkung*' and other comparable cases of 'private abuse of human rights', see Clapham, *supra* note 70.

in this view is required does not necessarily have to be enforcement under international law, but may also arise from national law.[76] In that context two situations must be distinguished. In the first place there are States where those rights and freedoms included in the Convention, which are self-executing, can be directly applied by the national courts.[77] In those States the relevant provisions of the Convention can be directly invoked by individuals against other individuals insofar as their *Drittwirkung* is recognised by the national courts. Judgments of these national courts which conflict with the Convention, for which indeed the Contracting State concerned is responsible under the Convention, may then be submitted to the Strasbourg organs *via* the procedure under Article 25 or *via* the procedure under Article 24. In addition there are those States in whose national legal systems the provisions of the Convention are not directly applicable. Those States, too, are obliged under the general guarantee clause of Article 1 of the Convention to protect the rights and freedoms set forth in the Convention. If one starts from the principle of *Drittwirkung*, such States also have to secure to individuals protection against violations of their fundamental rights by other individuals in their national law. If the competent national authorities default in this respect or if the applicable provisions of national law are not enforced, responsibility arises for the State concerned, a responsibility which may be brought up *via* the procedure under Article 25, or Article 24, of the Convention.[78]

On the other hand, the existence of a supervisory system as described above does not in itself imply *Drittwirkung*. If in a given State individuals may directly invoke the Convention before the courts, this does not necessarily imply that the Convention is applicable to legal relations between private parties. And the nature, too, of the obligation arising from Article 1 of the Convention for those States in whose legal system the Convention is not directly applicable, is in itself not decisive for the question concerning that *Drittwirkung*. In fact, one cannot deduce from Article 1 whether the Contracting States are obliged to secure the rights and freedoms only in relation to the public authorities or also in relation to other individuals. For a possible *Drittwirkung*, therefore, other arguments have to be put forward.

What arguments for *Drittwirkung* can be inferred from the Convention itself? It is beyond doubt that the problem of *Drittwirkung* was not taken into account when the Convention was drafted, if it played any part at all in the discussions. One can infer from the formulation of various provisions that they were not written with a view to relations between private parties. On the other hand, the subject-matter regulated by the Convention – the fundamental rights and freedoms – lends itself eminently to *Drittwirkung*. Precisely on account of the fundamental

---

[76] See Hahne, *supra* note 70, pp. 81-94.

[77] That this so-called 'internal effect' of the Convention does not follow imperatively from international law according to its present state, has been explained *supra* pp. 17-18.

[78] For the above, see Hahne, *supra* note 70, pp. 89-90.

character of these rights it is difficult to appreciate why they should deserve protection in relation to the public authorities, but not in relation to private parties. It is submitted that it is not very relevant whether the drafters of the Convention had in mind *Drittwirkung*. Of greater importance is what conclusions may be drawn for the present situation from the principles set forth in the Convention, and specifically in its Preamble. In the Preamble the drafters of the Convention gave evidence of the great value they attached to general respect for the fundamental rights and freedoms.[79] From this emphasis on general respect an argument *pro* rather than *contra Drittwirkung* can be inferred. But, as has been said above, the drafters have not pronounced on this.

Neither do the separate provisions of the Convention constitute any clear arguments for or against *Drittwirkung*. Article 1 has already been discussed above.[80] Article 13 is also mentioned in this context. From the last words of this article, *viz.* 'notwithstanding that the violation has been committed by persons in their official capacity', it is inferred by some that the Convention evidently also intends to provide a remedy against violations by individuals,[81] whereas others assert that those words merely indicate that the State is responsible for violations committed by its officials,[82] or that Article 13 at all events does not afford an independent argument for *Drittwirkung*.[83] From Article 17, too, it is sometimes inferred that the Convention has *Drittwirkung*. It is, however, doubtful whether such a general conclusion may be drawn from Article 17.[84] That provision forbids not only the public authorities, but also individuals, to invoke the Convention for the justification of an act aimed at the destruction of fundamental rights of other persons. Such a prohibition of abuse of the Convention is quite another matter than a general obligation for individuals to respect the fundamental rights of other persons in their private legal relations.

Summarising one may conclude that *Drittwirkung* does not ensue imperatively from the Convention. On the other hand, nothing in the Convention prevents the States from conferring *Drittwirkung* upon the fundamental rights and freedoms within their national legal systems insofar as they lend themselves to it. In some States *Drittwirkung* of the rights and freedoms guaranteed by the Convention is already recognised, whilst in other States this *Drittwirkung* at least is not excluded in principle.[85] Some have adopted the view that it may be inferred from the changing social circumstances and legal opinions that the purport of the

---

[79] It is there stated, among other things, that the Universal Declaration, of which the Convention is an elaboration, 'aims at securing universal and effective recognition and observance of the rights therein declared' and the Contracting States affirm 'their profound belief in those Fundamental Freedoms which are the foundation of justice and peace in the world.'

[80] See *supra* p. 24.

[81] See Eissen, *supra* note 70, pp. 177 *et seq.*

[82] See Guradze, *supra* note 70, p. 764.

[83] See Meuwissen, *supra* note 70, p. 210.

[84] *Idem.*

[85] See Drzemczewski, *supra* note 70, p. 63 *et seq.*

Convention *is going to be* to secure a certain minimum guarantee to the individual also in his relations with other persons.[86] It would seem that in the spirit of the Convention a good deal may be said for this view, although in the case of such a subsequent interpretation one must ask oneself whether one does not thus assign to the Convention an effect which may be unacceptable to (a number of) the Contracting States, and consequently is insufficiently supported by their implied mutual consent.

Meanwhile it will also depend in particular on the nature and the formulation of each separate right embodied in the Convention whether *Drittwirkung* can be assigned to it at all. In this context Alkema warns us that the nature of the legal relations between private parties may be widely divergent, and that consequently *Drittwirkung* is a multiform phenomenon, about which general statements are hardly possible.[87]

7 THE EUROPEAN COMMISSION OF HUMAN RIGHTS

7.1 General

The European Commission of Human Rights, like the European Court of Human Rights, has been specially set up to ensure the observance of the engagements undertaken by the Contracting States under the Convention (Article 19).

Article 20 provides that the number of members of the Commission shall be equal to the number of the Parties to the European Convention. The same article also sets forth that no two members of the Commission may be nationals of the same State. On the other hand, it is not excluded that a national of a State which is not a Party to the Convention, or is not even a member of the Council of Europe, may be a member of the Commission. So far, however, one national of each of the Contracting States has always sat on the Commission. With a view to the powers which the Commission has under the Convention in the matter of the protection of human rights, in general each of the Contracting States will wish one of its nationals to be a member of the Commission. However, that this does not have to remain a general practice is shown by Liechtenstein in relation to the Court; the judge elected in the Court for that country is a non-national.[88]

7.2 Election of the Members

The procedure for the election of the members of the Commission is regulated in Article 21. Each national group of parliamentary representatives of the Contracting States in the Parliamentary Assembly[89] of the Council of Europe puts forward

---

[86] See Meuwissen, *supra* note 70, p. 211; and Clapham, *supra* note 70, in particular pp. 200-206.
[87] See Alkema, *supra* note 70, pp. 254-255.
[88] See *infra* p. 32.
[89] In 1974 the name Consultative Assembly was changed into Parliamentary Assembly.

three candidates, of whom at least two must be nationals of that particular State. The Bureau of the Parliamentary Assembly[90] draws up a list of these names, from which the members of the Commission are elected by an absolute majority of votes by the Committee of Ministers. The same procedure is followed when a vacancy arises, either because a new State becomes a Party to the Convention or when a sitting member of the Commission resigns or dies (Article 21(2)). In such a case only the group of parliamentary representatives of that State for whose nationality the post in question is predestined, is invited to put forward candidates.

The members of the Commission are elected for a period of six years. They may be re-elected (Article 22(1)). In the case of interim replacement of a member of the Commission by another person, the latter holds office for the remainder of his predecessor's term (Article 22(5)). Members of the Commission hold office until replaced. After their replacement they continue to deal with such cases as they already had under consideration (Article 22(6)).[91] The consequence of the last sentence of Article 22(1) is that not all the members of the Commission resign at the same time, but every three years half of them, as far as possible, so that continuity is ensured to some extent.

7.3 Qualifications Required for Membership of the Commission

The members of the Commission cannot be considered as government representatives. Article 23 provides expressly that they sit in their individual capacity. The independent position of the members of the Commission in relation to the national governments also appears from the declaration which they have to make before taking up their duties (Rule 3 of the Rules of the Commission; hereafter: the Rules[92]). This requirement of independence would seem to imply that government functionaries should not be elected as members of the Commission.[93]

---

[90] The Bureau consists of the President and the Vice-Presidents of the Parliamentary Assembly.

[91] The Commissioner for Cyprus M.A. Triantafyllides, whose office expired on 5 May 1969, remained member of the Commission until 18 January 1989, when he was replaced by L. Loucides.

[92] Rule 3: 'I solemnly declare that I will exercise all my powers and duties honourably and faithfully, impartially and conscientiously and that I will keep secret all Commission proceedings.' The Rules are included in *Collected Texts*, Strasbourg, 1994, pp. 171-200.

[93] When a vacancy arises, the President of the Parliamentary Assembly addresses himself to the chairman of the national delegation concerned, using the following words: 'National delegations of course have entire freedom of choice when preparing their lists of candidates. In the view of the Bureau of the Assembly, however, it is desirable when the choice comes to be made that the following qualities – essential for any member of the Commission who is to fulfil his duty – be taken into consideration: (a) high moral integrity; (b) recognised competence in matters concerned with human rights; (c) substantial legal or judicial experience. The Bureau has further asked me to call your attention to the difficulties in which a member of the Commission might find himself if he were at the same time a member of a national public service, and to the doubts which might arise in such circumstances as to the impartiality of the Commission.'

Although, until 1990, the criterion of Article 23 was the only one to be found in the Convention for the eligibility of the members of the Commission, in practice the additional requirement was made that candidates should be of high moral integrity, should be competent in matters concerning human rights, and should have substantial legal experience. The candidates were not always strictly confined to the circle of jurists. However, in Protocol No. 8, in addition to the requirements of independence and impartiality, and high moral character, the requirement has been expressly laid down that the candidates 'must either possess the qualifications required for appointment to high judicial office or be persons of recognised competence in national or international law.'[94] As a consequence of this Protocol these requirements have become part of the Convention, in the form of amendments to Article 21 and Article 23 respectively.

Article 59 confers on the members of the Commission, during the discharge of their functions, the privileges and immunities provided for in Article 40 of the Statute of the Council of Europe and in the agreements made thereunder.[95]

7.4 The Sessions of the Commission

The seat of the Commission is in Strasbourg, but, if desired, it may also perform its activities elsewhere (Rule 15 of the Rules). The Commission does not sit permanently. It decides every year, how many sessions will be held. In 1996, the Commission held eight sessions which amounted altogether to 16 session weeks.[96] The Commission meets at the order of its President or at the request of one-third of its members, so that extraordinary sessions are also possible. Because the Commission meets only a few times annually, the members usually also have other functions.[97] This in turn has the consequence that the members of the Commission do not have all their time available for the work in the Commission.

With the entry into force of Protocol No. 8 in 1990, Chambers have been set up, which exercise all the powers of the plenary Commission relating to individual complaints which can be dealt with on the basis of established case-law or which raise no serious questions affecting the interpretation or application of the Convention. Each Chamber is composed of at least seven members. The first Article of the Protocol in addition opens the possibility to set up Committees, each composed of at least three members, with the power to unanimously declare inadmissible or strike off its list of cases an application submitted under Article 25 when such a decision can be taken without further examination. A Chamber

---

[94] Arts 2 and 3 of Protocol No. 8.
[95] See Second Protocol to the General Agreement on Privileges and Immunities of the Council of Europe, *Collected Texts*, Strasbourg, 1994, pp. 204-207.
[96] Council of Europe, *European Commission of Human Rights, Survey of Activities and Statistics*, 1996.
[97] The President of the Commission, however, is expected to be available on a more regular basis in order to deal with urgent cases.

or Committee may at any time relinquish jurisdiction in favour of the plenary Commission (Article 20).

This last mentioned option may greatly reduce the effect of Protocol No. 8 if in practice the more complicated cases, which demand a lot of time, still have to be dealt with by the plenary Commission. An additional solution has been sought in increasing the amount of time available to the members of the Commission for dealing with cases. Both the Steering Committee for Human Rights, which reports to the Committee of Ministers, and the Commission itself reached the conclusion that membership of the Commission could not be combined with a full-time other function any longer. Since 1990, members of the Commission are expected to be available for 16 weeks of Commission meetings in Strasbourg, as well as to spend an additional 16 weeks on preparatory work. The system of remuneration has been adjusted accordingly. In practice, this has made the Commission a semi-permanent organ. Its membership has now become the main occupation of its members, still allowing them to engage in a part-time profession in their home country and thus to keep in touch with the domestic legal environment and legal practice.

Members of the Commission cannot take part in the examination of a case in which they have any personal interest or if they have participated in any decision on the facts on which the application is based, as an adviser to any of the parties, in public service or as a member of any tribunal or body of enquiry (Rule 20(1) of the Rules). If the President of the Commission considers that a member should not take part in the examination of a given case, because there are circumstances which might affect his impartiality, the Commission decides on the matter. The member in question, too, may submit the matter to the Commission (Rule 20(2) of the Rules). He may also decide for other reasons, after consultation with the President, not to take part in the examination of a given case. If no agreement about this is reached between them, the Commission decides (Rule 21 of the Rules). The President relinquishes his function during the examination of a case involving a State of which he is a national, or which has presented him as a candidate for membership of the Commission (Rule 10 of the Rules).

The quorum of the Commission consists of a number of members equal to the majority of the members of the Commission. For the examination of an application by an individual, however, seven members constitute the quorum when a decision according to Rule 48(2) of the Rules is to be made (Rule 23 of the Rules). According to this provision the Commission, on account of the report of the rapporteur, may decide to invite the individual applicant or the applicant State to submit relevant information or to give notice of the application to the respondent State and invite it to submit observations on its admissibility. Seven members also constitute a quorum if the Commission declares the application inadmissible or decides to strike it off its list, provided that no notice of the application has been given to the State concerned (Rule 23(2)(b) of the Rules).

The Commission decides by a majority of votes (Article 34). If the voting is equal, the President has a casting vote (Article 18(2) of the Rules). Unlike the procedure for the adoption of a report on the merits (Article 31),[98] in the case of a decision on admissibility the members of the Commission cannot add their individual opinion. They may, however, have a statement inserted in the records of the deliberations (Rule 19(1) of the Rules), but the minutes will be published only when the President considers this useful (Rule 13 of the Rules).

Protocol No. 11 to the Convention, which has been opened for signature on 11 May 1994 and which will enter into force once all the Contracting States have ratified it, will reform the present supervisory system. As a consequence, the present European Commission and the European Court of Human Rights will cease to exist. A new European Court of Human Rights, operating on a full-time basis, will be set up in Strasbourg. The system will be streamlined and, above all, individual applicants will have direct access to the new Court.[99]

7.5 The Secretariat of the Commission

Because of the non-permanent character of the Commission, its Secretariat plays an important part as a permanent factor in the system. The Secretariat of the Commission is provided by the Secretary General of the Council of Europe (Article 37). Together with the Secretary of the Commission, a number of qualified jurists from Contracting States make up this Secretariat. They are employed by the Council of Europe on a full-time basis and are assisted by a record department and an administrative staff. In 1996, the staff of the Secretariat consisted of: 49 lawyers, 35 administrative assistants and 4 translators.[100] Among the most important duties of the Secretariat are: conducting correspondence with persons filing applications and with governments; preparing cases for examination; submitting reports to the Commission on matters of national law and the law of the European Convention; and assisting the members of the Commission in drafting decisions and reports (*cf.* Rule 13 of the Rules).

7.6 The Non-Public Character of the Hearings of the Commission

The hearings and other meetings of the Commission are held *in camera* (Article 33). The deliberations of the Commission are confidential (Rule 17 of the Rules). Similarly, parties appearing before the Commission are not allowed to divulge information about the course of the proceedings. In certain cases transgression of this rule might lead to dismissal of the application on the ground of abuse of the

---

[98] See *infra* p. 174.
[99] See *infra* p. 35.
[100] See Council of Europe, *European Commission of Human Rights, Survey of Activities and Statistics*, 1996.

right of petition. The most important decisions of the Commission on admissibility as well as the great majority of its reports, however, are published.[101]

The confidential character of the examination of applications by the Commission has advantages as well as disadvantages for the effective protection of the rights and freedoms guaranteed in the Convention. As a result of its confidential character not all details of the supervisory procedure of the Convention become public, which may hamper confidence in the system and does not encourage the filing of applications. Moreover, publicity in itself would already constitute an element of sanction, because States would thus be exposed to the criticism of other States and of public opinion. Finally, public examination of a complaint against a given State might have a preventive effect on the behaviour of the other States. On the other hand, States will be more readily prepared to accept international supervision if this is kept out of publicity, particularly in the initial phase. The highly reserved attitude of States with respect to international supervision is quite evident from the fact that, even under the present confidential procedure, it took years, up to 1988, before all Contracting States were prepared to accept the individual right of complaint. For a proper discharge of the task with which the Commission has been entrusted in Article 28(1)(b), *i.e.* trying to secure a friendly settlement, secrecy would seem to be instrumental. In order to reach such a settlement certain concessions will in general have to be made by the States concerned. This will not be facilitated if they have previously committed themselves in public to a fixed position and will have to conduct the deliberations under the pressure of public opinion.

8 THE EUROPEAN COURT OF HUMAN RIGHTS

8.1 General

As the Commission the European Court of Human Rights has been specially set up to supervise the observance by the Contracting States of their engagements arising from the Convention (Article 19). Unlike the Commission, the number of

---

[101] The publication system of the Commission is rather complicated and therefore requires some elucidation. Not all decisions of the Commission are published, especially not those taken after summary proceedings. A number of the decisions concerning admissibility are to be found in the *Yearbook* of the European Convention on Human Rights and in the *Collection of Decisions*, continued after 1975 as *Decisions and Reports*. The reports of the Commission are published separately; in addition they are sometimes included in the *Yearbooks* and in the *Decisions and Reports*. Sometimes a decision is included in the *Yearbooks* but not in the *Collection of Decisions/Decisions and Reports* and *vice versa*. In the *Digest of Strasbourg case-law relating to the European Convention on Human Rights*, published by Carl Heymans Verlag, the complete case-law of the Commission and the Court has been incorporated. For those cases that have been referred to the Court, the main parts of the reports of the Commission are since 1985 also published as an Annex to the judgment of the Court (Series A), while before 1985 they were included in the materials published in Series B. As from 1996 the case-law of the Commission and the Court is published in *Reports of Judgments and Decisions* (hereafter Reports).

members of the Court is not related to the number of the Contracting States, but to the number of Member States of the Council of Europe. Just as in the case of the Commission, the Convention provides for the Court, in Article 38, that no two members may be nationals of the same State. And here again the possibility is left open that a national of a State which is not a member of the Council of Europe is a member of the Court. This occurred for the first time in 1980, when the Canadian MacDonald was elected in the Court after being nominated by Liechtenstein.

8.2 Election of the Members of the Court

For the election of the judges every member of the Council of Europe nominates three candidates, of whom two at least must be its nationals. From the list thus produced the Parliamentary Assembly elects the members of the Court by a majority of the votes cast (Article 39(1)).

Article 39(2) provides that the same procedure must be followed when new members are admitted to the Council of Europe, and in filling interim vacancies. In the former case only the new Member State puts forward candidates, in the latter case this is done by the State which had nominated the candidate to whose resignation or death the vacancy is due.

The members of the Court are elected for a period of nine years and may be re-elected. A member of the Court elected to replace a member whose term of office had not expired holds office for the remainder of his predecessor's term (Article 40(5)). The members of the Court hold office until replaced. After having been replaced, they continue to deal with such cases as they already had under consideration (Article 40(6)).

The end of the terms of office is staggered in the sense that, to the extent possible, every three years one-third of the judges resign (Articles 40(1) and 40(3)).[102]

8.3 Qualifications Required for Membership of the Court

The Convention lays down certain qualifications for members of the Court. Candidates must be of high moral character and must either possess the qualifications required for appointment to high judicial office or be jurisconsults of recognised competence (Article 39(3)). Originally, the Convention did not mention the independence of the judges. On this point Article 40 has been supplemented by Protocol No. 8.[103] According to Rule 3 of the Rules of

---

[102] With the entry into force of the Protocol No. 11 the term of all members of the Court will end.
[103] See Art. 9 of Protocol No. 8.

Court[104] before taking up their duties, the members must take an oath or make a declaration to the effect that they will exercise their function independently and impartially. Similarly, a judge may not exercise his function when he is a member of a government or holds a post or exercises a profession which is incompatible with his independence and impartiality (Rule 4 of the Rules of Court). Moreover, the Parliamentary Assembly has adopted a resolution concerning the qualifications to be satisfied by candidate-members of the Court. This resolution reads as follows:

The Assembly,
1. *Referring* to Recommendation 809(1977) on the qualification of candidates for the European Court of Human Rights;
2. *Recalling* that judges of the Court are elected for a term of nine years;
3. *Requests* its members not to vote for candidates:
    i.   who have not given a formal undertaking to retire from the office of judge during the year in which they reach the age of 75;
    ii. who, by nature of their functions, are dependent on government and who have not given a formal undertaking to resign the said functions upon their election to the European Court of Human Rights;
4. *Considers* that a list which includes more than one candidate in the situation indicated under paragraphs 3(i) or (ii) above should not be put to the vote, since in this case effective choice would be vitiated.[105]

Article 59 provides that the members of the Court are entitled to the privileges and immunities provided for in Article 40 of the Statute of the Council of Europe and in the agreements made thereunder,[106] which furthers the independent exercise of their function.

8.4 Sessions of the Court

The seat of the Court is in Strasbourg, but if it considers it expedient, the Court may also exercise its functions elsewhere in the territories of the Member States of the Council of Europe (Rule 15 of the Rules of Court). Rule 16 of the Rules of Court provides that the President convenes the Court at least once annually in

---

[104] The Rules of Procedure of the Court are included in *Collected Texts*, Strasbourg, 1994, pp. 215 *et seq*. The Rules of Court have been amended on 27 January 1994. This revised text exists as a separate publication. At present there are two sets of Rules of the Court: Rules of Court 'A' relating to cases concerning States which are not Party to Protocol No. 9 of the Convention and Rules of Court 'B', concerning those States, which are Party to the said Protocol. Where necessary, when referring to the latter set of Rules, a special reference will be made.

[105] Res. 655 (1977), 'On the qualification of candidates for the European Court of Human Rights', Council of Europe, Parl. Ass., Twenty-Ninth Ordinary Session, First Part, 25-29 April 1977, *Texts Adopted*. With the entry into force of Protocol No. 11 members of the Court will be nominated for a period of six years. In addition an age-limit of 70 has been provided for. Moreover, the Parliamentary Assembly has indicated that it will play a more active role in examining candidates: Res. 1082 (1996).

[106] See Fourth Protocol to the General Agreement on Privileges and Immunities of the Council of Europe, *Collected Texts*, Strasbourg, 1994, pp. 299-301.

a plenary session and also at the request of at least one-third of the members. Further, he convenes the Court whenever the exercise of its functions so requires. In practice the Court holds monthly sessions of six to nine days, except in July and December. The quorum for the sessions of the plenary Court is two-thirds of the judges (Rule 17 of the Rules of Court). For the consideration of a case a Chamber composed of nine judges is constituted from the Court (Article 43). This provision meets the drawbacks of the large number of members of the Court. Persons sitting as *ex officio* members of the Chambers are those judges who are nationals of the States Parties to the case. If such a judge is not available, the place is taken by a judge *ad hoc*; a person of the choice of the State in question, who must then satisfy the requirements of Article 39(3) of the Convention (Rules 21-23 of the Rules of Court). This has the advantage that at least one person who is familiar with the legal system of the State involved in the case is a member of the Chamber. The President or the Vice-President, too, sits as an *ex officio* member of the Chamber. The other members of the Chamber are chosen by lot (Rule 21 of the Rules of Court). For that purpose the judges are divided into three regional groups. The Chamber thus constituted may, or must, under certain conditions relinquish jurisdiction in favour of a Grand Chamber of 19 judges.[107] As a consequence the composition of the Court may vary considerably from case to case. This is even more so due to the fact that under Rule 24(5) of the Rules of the Court a judge who has been a member of a Chamber in one or more recent cases may, at his request, be exempted from sitting on a new case.

To prevent inconsistencies in the case-law, in its Rules the Court has assigned to the Chambers the right to relinquish jurisdiction in favour of the Grand Chamber when a case pending before a Chamber raises serious questions affecting the interpretation of the Convention. A Chamber is even obliged to do so where the resolution of such questions might have a result inconsistent with a judgment previously delivered by a Chamber or by the Grand Chamber (Rule 51(1) of the Rules of Court).[108] According to Rule 51(5) of the Rules of Court the Grand Chamber may exceptionally, when the issues raised are particularly serious or involve a significant change of existing case-law, relinquish jurisdiction in favour of the plenary court. Moreover, if the President of the Court finds that two cases concern the same party or parties and raise similar issues, he may refer the second case to the Chamber already constituted, or constitute a Chamber to consider both cases (Rule 21(6) of the Rules of Court). Finally, the fact that the President or the Vice-President sits as an *ex officio* member also ensures consistency to a certain degree.

Just as is the case with the members of the Commission, the judges of the Court may not take part in the consideration of any case in which they have a personal

---

[107] On 27 October 1993 the Court decided for the composition of a Grand Chamber to replace the plenary Court.

[108] See for an overview of judgments, in which Rule 51(1) of the Rules has been applied: Appendix IV.

interest or in which they have previously acted as the agent, advocate, or adviser of a party or of a person having an interest in the case, or as a member of a tribunal or commission of enquiry, or in any other capacity. If a judge considers that he should not take part in the consideration of a particular case, he informs the President, who shall exempt him from sitting. The initiative may also be taken by the President, when the latter considers that such a withdrawal is desirable. In case of disagreement the Court decides (Rule 24(2), (3) and (4) of the Rules of Court).

The hearings of the Court are public, unless the Court decides otherwise in exceptional circumstances (Rule 18 of the Rules of Court). This publicity is a logical implication of the judicial character of the procedure. Moreover, at this stage of the procedure there is less reason for secrecy to protect the defendant State against needlessly harmful publicity than in the procedure before the Commission. Indeed, no case can be brought before the Court unless it has been dealt with by the Commission, where an application has been examined for its admissibility by reference to a number of stringent requirements. Any deceptive or obviously ill-founded applications will therefore not reach the Court, since they have already been eliminated. Moreover, the Court is not involved in attempting to reach a friendly settlement. The deliberations of the Court, on the other hand, are in private (Rule 19 of the Rules of Court).

The Court takes its decisions by a majority of votes of the judges present. If the voting is equal, the President has a casting vote (Rule 20 of the Rules of Court).

All the judgments of the Court are published, as are also the documents relating to the proceedings, including the report of the Commission, but excluding any document which the President considers unnecessary to publish (Rule 56(1) of the Rules of Court).[109]

Protocol No. 11 to the Convention, which was opened for signature on 11 May 1994, provides for the setting up of a single permanent Court to replace the present supervisory system of the Convention. This Protocol has to be ratified by all Contracting States before it enters into force. The new Court will have jurisdiction to deal with both individual and inter-State applications. It will usually sit in Chambers of seven judges, but cases may be declared inadmissible by the unanimous decision of a panel of three judges. On the other hand the Chamber may, in certain circumstances, relinquish jurisdiction in favour of a Grand

---

[109] The judgments and decisions of the Court are published in: *Publications of the European Court of Human Rights, Series A*. The documents of the case, including the report of the Commission, are published in: *Publications of the European Court of Human Rights, Series B*. Since 1985, the main parts of reports of the Commission are also published as an annex in the Series A. In addition a summary is published in the *Yearbook* of the European Convention on Human Rights. Shortly after the judgment of the Court a provisional publication in mimeographed form is available and appears in the *Reports of Judgments and Decisions*. As from 1996 the Series A have ceased to exist.

Chamber of 17 judges.[110] Moreover, under certain conditions, from judgments of the Chamber appeal will lie to the Grand Chamber.

9 THE COMMITTEE OF MINISTERS

9.1 General

Unlike the Commission and the Court, the Committee of Ministers has not been set up by the Convention. Here a function has been entrusted to an already existing body of the Council of Europe. Accordingly, the composition, organisation, and general functions and powers of the Committee of Ministers are not regulated in the Convention, but in the Statute of the Council of Europe.[111]

The function assigned to the Committee of Ministers in the Convention is the result of a compromise. On the one hand, during the drafting of the Convention there was a body of opinion which in addition to the Commission wished to institute a Court with compulsory jurisdiction. Others, however, held that it was preferable to entrust supervision, apart from the Commission, only to the Committee of Ministers. Ultimately the two alternatives were combined by making the jurisdiction of the Court optional and granting the Committee the power, in those cases that are not, or cannot be, submitted to the Court, to decide on the question of whether there has been a violation of the Convention.

9.2 Composition of the Committee of Ministers

The Committee of Ministers consists of one representative of each Member State of the Council of Europe, as a rule the Minister for Foreign Affairs. In case of the latter's inability to be present, or if other circumstances make it desirable, an alternate may be nominated, who shall, whenever possible, be a member of government (Article 14 of the Statute). In practice the Committee has sessions only twice annually (see Article 21(c) of the Statute). In the intervening periods its duties are discharged by the so-called 'Committee of the Ministers' Deputies', consisting of high officials who generally are the permanent representatives of their governments with the Council of Europe. Every representative on the Committee of Ministers appoints a deputy (Rule 14 of the Rules of the Committee of Ministers).

Under its Rules of Procedure the Committee of the Ministers' Deputies is competent to take the decision provided for in Article 32 of the European Convention.[112] Whether in practice the matter is settled by the Committee of

---

[110] See also *infra* p. 194.

[111] See Arts 13-21 of the Statute of the Council of Europe.

[112] Art. 2 of the Rules of Procedure for meetings of the Ministers' Deputies provides that 'the Ministers' Deputies are competent to discuss all matters within the competence of the Committee of Ministers. Decisions taken by the Deputies in virtue of the authority given to them by the Ministers by whom they are appointed are considered as taken on behalf of the Committee of

Ministers itself will depend on the circumstances of the case, since the Deputies are not competent to make decisions about matters which in the opinion of one or more of them have important political consequences (Rule 2(3) of the Rules of the Committee of Ministers).[113]

9.3 Sessions of the Committee of Ministers

The sessions of the Committee of Ministers are not public, unless the Committee itself decides otherwise (Article 21(a) of the Statute). In principle the other rules of procedure, too, which apply to the Committee as executive organ of the Council of Europe, are applicable to its functions within the context of the European Convention. An exception is Article 32(1) of the Convention. It says that the Committee decides by a majority of two-thirds of the members entitled to sit on the Committee whether there has been a violation of the Convention, whereas under Article 20(a) of the Statute resolutions concerning important matters require the unanimous votes of the representatives casting a vote, and a majority of the representatives entitled to sit on the Committee. This departure from the voting procedure was necessary to give the Committee real powers of decision. Indeed, if the rule of Article 20(a) of the Statute had been declared applicable here as well, a State involved in a given case would actually have a right of veto with regard to the decision of that case, so that in practice the Committee in all probability would never be able to decide that there had been a violation of the Convention. On 25 March 1992, Protocol No. 10 to the European Convention was opened for signature. This Protocol amends the voting procedure of the Committee of Ministers of the Council of Europe laid down in Article 32, reducing the two-thirds majority provided therein to a simple majority. The Protocol shall enter into force when all Parties to the Convention have expressed their consent to be bound by it.

9.4 The Task of the Committee of Ministers Within the Supervisory System

As an addition to the provisions in the Convention the Committee has adopted a number of rules for the application of Article 32 of the European Convention,[114] which will be discussed in more detail below.[115] Here it suffices to mention the principal points dealt with in these rules. According to the original Rule 5, Article 32(2) of the Convention enables the Committee, in cases where it has decided that there has been a violation, to give opinions to the State concerned or to make

---

Ministers and have the same force and effect as decisions of the Committee.'
[113] For decisions of the Committee it is always mentioned in the *Yearbooks* whether the matter has in fact been dealt with by the Committee of the Ministers' Deputies.
[114] See *Collected Texts*, Strasbourg, 1994, pp. 192-196.
[115] See *infra* pp. 269-270.

recommendations that are related to the violation of the Convention.[116] It also stipulated that such opinions or recommendations are not binding on the States concerned, since they do not constitute decisions in the sense of Article 32(4) of the Convention. However, Rule 5 was deleted by the Ministers' Deputies on 19 December 1991. What kind of effect this has for the interpretation of Article 32(2), is unclear since the latter provision still implies that the Committee may require certain measures. Rule 6, which was maintained, states as the view of the Committee that the Commission is not entitled to make proposals as referred to in Article 31(3) of the Convention when the Commission holds that there has not been a violation of the Convention. If the Committee of Ministers has decided that there has been a violation, under Rule 9(2) it may request the Commission to make proposals concerning just satisfaction for the injured party. Rule 10 states that the voting rules of Article 20 of the Statute should in general apply.[117] This means in particular that States Parties to the dispute, too, have the right to vote. The opinions and recommendations referred to in Rule 5 require, in accordance with Rule 10, a two-thirds majority of the representatives casting a vote and a majority of the representatives entitled to sit on the Committee. Certain questions of procedure, however, may be determined by a simple majority of the representatives entitled to sit on the Committee. On the procedure, Rules 8 and 9 contain some very general provisions. The Chairman of the Committee obtains the opinion of the representative(s) of the State(s) involved in the dispute in regard to the procedure to be followed. The Committee specifies, if necessary, in what order and within what time-limits the required documents are to be deposited. During the examination of the case the Committee may request information on particular points in the report of the Commission.

With the entry into force of the above-mentioned Protocol No. 11 to the Convention[118] all applications concerning violations of individuals' rights will be submitted to the Court. The Committee of Ministers will no longer have jurisdiction to decide cases, though it will retain its important role of monitoring the enforcement of the Court's judgments.

---

[116] See, *e.g.*, the Resolution of the Committee of Ministers in the *Greek* Case, Yearbook XII (1969), pp. 511 *et seq.*

[117] See, however, the voting requirement of Art. 32 of the Convention mentioned on *infra* pp. 273-274.

[118] See *supra* p. 35.

10 THE SECRETARY GENERAL OF THE COUNCIL OF EUROPE

10.1 General

Besides the Committee of Ministers another organ of the Council of Europe plays a part in the Convention, *viz.* the Secretary General. The Secretary General is the highest official of the Council of Europe and is elected for a period of five years by the Parliamentary Assembly from a list of candidates which is drawn up by the Committee of Ministers (Article 36 of the Statute of the Council of Europe).

10.2 The Task of the Secretary General

The Secretary General is involved in the Convention system in various ways, on the one hand by reason of his administrative functions as they result from the Statute of the Council of Europe, and on the other hand in connection with a specific supervisory task created by the Convention.

In the first place, ratifications of the Convention must be deposited with the Secretary General (Article 66(1)), who has to notify the Members of the Council of Europe of the entry into force of the Convention and keep them informed of the names of the States which have become parties to the Convention (Article 66(4)).[119] A denunciation of the Convention must also be notified to the Secretary General, who informs the other Contracting States (Article 65). In addition, the various declarations which the Contracting States may make under the Convention must also be deposited with him. This applies, for instance, to the declaration in which a State recognises the individual right of complaint. The Secretary General further provides for the publication of such a declaration and transmits a copy of it to the other Contracting States (Article 25(3)). Deposition with the Secretary General is also required for the declaration in which a State recognises the jurisdiction of the Court as compulsory (Article 46(3)), and for the notification by a State in which the Convention is declared to extend to a territory for whose international relations it is responsible (Article 63(1)).

Moreover, any applications to be submitted to the Commission must be filed with the Secretary General (Articles 24 and 25(1)).

Finally, the Secretary General fulfils an important administrative function under Article 15(3) of the Convention. Any State availing itself under Article 15 of the right to derogate, in time of war or another emergency threatening the life of the nation, from one or more provisions of the Convention, must keep the Secretary General fully informed of the measures taken in that context and the reasons therefor. It must also inform him when such measures have ceased to operate.

The most important function assigned to the Secretary General in the Convention, however, is of quite a different nature. Under Article 57 he has the task to supervise the effective implementation by the Contracting States of the

---

[119] The same applies for all Protocols to the Convention.

provisions of the Convention. This supervisory task of the Secretary General will be dealt with in a separate chapter (Chapter VI).

11 THE RIGHT OF COMPLAINT

What is called here the 'right of complaint' under the Convention is the right to take the initiative for the supervisory procedure provided for in the Convention on the ground that the Convention has allegedly been violated by one of the Contracting States. The Convention differentiates between the right of complaint for States on the one hand and that for individuals (referred to in the Convention as 'petitions') on the other hand. These two forms will be discussed here successively.

11.1   Inter-State Applications (Article 24)

11.1.1 The Objective Character
When the Convention enters into force for a State, that State acquires the right to lodge, through the Secretary General, an application with the European Commission of Human Rights on the ground of an alleged violation of one or more provisions of the Convention by one of the other Contracting States. This right of complaint for States constitutes an important divergence from the traditional principles of international law concerning inter-State action.

According to these principles a State can bring an international action against another State only when a right of the former is at stake or when that State takes up the case of one of its nationals whom it considers to have been treated by the other State in a way contrary to the rules of international law; the so-called 'diplomatic protection'.

Under the Convention a State may also lodge a complaint about violations committed against persons who are not its nationals or against persons who are not nationals of any of the Contracting States, or are stateless, and even about violations against nationals of the respondent State. States may equally lodge a complaint about the incompatibility with the Convention of the national legislation or of an administrative practice of another State without having to allege a violation against any specified person: the so-called 'abstract applications'. Thus the right of complaint for States assumes the character of an *actio popularis*: any Contracting State has the right to lodge a complaint about any alleged violation of the Convention, regardless of whether there is a special relation between the rights and interests of the applicant State and the alleged violation.

In the *Pfunders* Case between Austria and Italy the Commission stressed that a State which brings an application under Article 24:

is not to be regarded as exercising a right of action for the purpose of enforcing its own rights, but rather as bringing before the Commission an alleged violation of the public order of Europe.[120]

The Court has similarly held that, unlike international treaties of the classic kind:

the Convention comprises more than mere reciprocal engagements between Contracting States. It creates, over and above a network of mutual, bilateral undertakings, objective obligations which, in the words of the Preamble, benefit from a 'collective enforcement'.[121]

The supervisory procedure provided for in the Convention, therefore, has an objective character; its aim is to protect the fundamental rights of the individual against violations by the Contracting States, rather than to implement mutual rights and obligations between those States. This objective character of the procedure is also stressed in other respects, to be mentioned later.

Clear examples of inter-State applications in the framework of the 'collective enforcement' mentioned by the Court are the applications of Denmark, Norway, Sweden and the Netherlands of September 1967 and the joint application of the three Scandinavian countries of April 1970 against Greece,[122] and the application of the Scandinavian countries, France and the Netherlands of July 1982 against Turkey.[123] The complaints against Greece were in fact lodged at the instance of the Parliamentary Assembly, which considered it the duty of the Contracting States to lodge an application under Article 24 in the case of an alleged serious violation.[124]

11.1.2 Cases in Which a Special Interest of the Contracting State is Involved
The Convention of course at the same time protects the particular interests of the Contracting States when they claim that the rights set forth in the Convention must be secured to their nationals coming under the jurisdiction of another Contracting State. And even though States have the right to initiate a procedure in which they have no special interest, in practice they will more readily be inclined to bring an

---

[120] Appl. 788/60, *Austria* v. *Italy*, Yearbook VI (1961), p. 116 (140). See also Appls 9940/82-9944/82, *France, Norway, Denmark, Sweden and the Netherlands* v. *Turkey*, D&R 35 (1984), p. 143 (169); joined Appls 15299/89, 15300/89 and 15318/89, *Chrysostomos, Papachrysostomou* and *Loizidou* v. *Turkey*, D&R 68 (1991), p. 216 (242).

[121] Judgment of 18 January 1978, *Ireland* v. *the United Kingdom*, A.25, p. 90; report of 4 October 1983, *Cyprus* v. *Turkey*, D&R 72 (1992), p. 5 (19), where the Commission further noted that a Government cannot avoid this collective enforcement by not recognising the Government of the applicant State.

[122] Appls 3321-3323 and 3344/67, *Denmark, Norway, Sweden and the Netherlands* v. *Greece*, Yearbook XI (1968), p. 690, and Appl. 4448/70, *Denmark, Norway and Sweden* v. *Greece*, Yearbook XIII (1970), p. 108.

[123] Appls 9940-9944/82, *France, Norway, Denmark, Sweden and the Netherlands* v. *Turkey*, D&R 35 (1984), p. 143.

[124] Res. 346 (1967), 'On the situation in Greece', Council of Europe, Cons. Ass., Nineteenth Ordinary Session, Second Part, 25-28 September 1967, *Texts Adopted*.

application when there has been a violation against persons who are their nationals or with whom they have some special link.

A case in which the applicant State's own nationals were involved occurred for the first time when Cyprus brought applications against Turkey concerning the treatment of nationals of Cyprus during the Turkish invasion and subsequent occupation of that island.[125] In total three applications emanated from this dispute.[126] In November 1994, Cyprus lodged another complaint against Turkey, which was declared admissible on 28 June 1996.[127]

Examples of applications concerning persons with whom the applicant State had a special relation other than the link of nationality are the applications of Greece against the United Kingdom, which concerned the treatment of Cypriots of Greek origin.[128] Further, Austria lodged a complaint in the above-mentioned *Pfunders* Case in connection with the prosecution of six young men by Italy for the murder of an Italian customs officer in the boundary region of Alto Adige (Upper Tyrol) disputed by both States.[129] The applications of Ireland against the United Kingdom, finally, concerned the treatment of and the legislation concerning the Roman Catholics of Northern Ireland, who aspire for union with the Irish Republic.[130]

11.1.3 Requirements of Admissibility

In order for State complaints to be admissible hardly any *prima facie* evidence is required. In fact the Commission has deduced from the English text ('alleged breach') and from the French wording ('*qu'elle croira pouvoir être imputé*') that the mere allegation of such a breach is, in principle, sufficient under this provision (Article 24).[131] The Commission bases this point of view on the fact that the provisions of Article 27(2) – empowering it to declare inadmissible any petition submitted under Article 25, which it considers either incompatible with the provisions of the Convention or manifestly ill-founded – apply, according to their express terms, to individual applications under Article 25 only, and that, consequently, any examination of the merits of State complaints must be entirely reserved for the post-admissibility stage.[132] On the other hand, the Commission is of the opinion that Article 27 does not exclude the application of a general rule according to which an application under Article 24 may be declared inadmissible if it is clear from the outset that it is wholly unsubstantiated, or otherwise lacking

---

[125] Appls 6780/74 and 6950/75, *Cyprus* v. *Turkey*, Yearbook XVIII (1975), p. 82.
[126] See also: Appl. 8007/77, *Cyprus* v. *Turkey*, Yearbook XX (1977), p. 98.
[127] Appl. 25781/94, *Cyprus* v. *Turkey* (not yet published).
[128] Appls 176/56 and 299/57, *Greece* v. *the United Kingdom*, Yearbook II (1958-1959), pp. 182 and 186 respectively.
[129] Appl. 788/60, *Austria* v. *Italy*, Yearbook IV (1961), p. 116.
[130] Appls 5310/71 and 5451/72, *Ireland* v. *the United Kingdom*, Yearbook XV (1972), p. 76.
[131] Appls 9940/82-9944/82, *France, Norway, Denmark, Sweden and the Netherlands* v. *Turkey*, D&R 35 (1984), p. 143 (161).
[132] *Idem.*

the requirements of a genuine allegation in the sense of Article 24 of the Convention.[133]

11.1.4 Practice of the Inter-State Complaint

Up to the present moment (April 1997), a total of 19 applications by States have been lodged. This very low number, moreover, provides a distorted picture. In fact, only six situations in different States have been put forward in Strasbourg by means of an inter-State application. In the 1950s, Greece complained twice about the conduct of the United Kingdom in Cyprus, Austria filed a complaint in 1960 about the course of events during proceedings against South Tyrolean activists in Italy, the five applications of the Scandinavian countries and the Netherlands concerned the situation in Greece during the military regime, Ireland lodged two applications against the United Kingdom about the activities of the military and the police in Ulster, all four applications of Cyprus were connected with the Turkish invasion of that island, while the five applications of 1982 all relate to the situation in Turkey under the military regime.

Given the number of violations that have occurred during the almost 45 years that the Convention is in force, it is evident that the right of complaint of States has proved not to be very effective. The idea contained in the Preamble, as it was also formulated by the Commission in the above-mentioned *Pfunders* Case and by the Court in *Ireland* v. *the United Kingdom, viz.* that the Contracting States were to guarantee the protection of the rights and freedoms collectively, has hardly materialised. Save for two instances,[134] the Contracting States have not been willing to lodge complaints about situations in other States where no special interest of their own was involved. Such a step generally even runs counter to their interest in that a charge of violation of the Convention is bound to be considered an unfriendly act by the other party, with all the political consequences that may be involved. On the other hand, an application by a State which does have a special interest of its own may equally create negative effects in that it may stir up the underlying conflict.

In comparison with inter-State applications, individual complaints have the advantage that in general political considerations will not play so important a part.[135] For this reason as well it is highly desirable that individual complaints can be lodged against all Contracting States. At the time when some Contracting States had not recognised the individual right of complaint, the inter-State procedure – apart from the remedy of Article 57, which so far has not been very satisfactory – was the only expedient for supervising the observance by all

---

[133] *Ibidem*, p. 162.

[134] The applications of the Scandinavian countries and the Netherlands against Greece in 1967 and 1970 and the applications of France, the Netherlands and the Scandinavian countries against Turkey in 1982.

[135] Here, too, political motives may sometimes constitute the real incentive for an application, while even if that is not the case the application may have some political implications.

Contracting States of their obligations under the Convention, a situation which was far from satisfactory.

11.2 Individual Applications (Article 25)

11.2.1 General

The individual right of complaint was not accepted without dispute during the drafting of the Convention. Initially there were great differences of opinion between the Consultative Assembly, as it was named then, and the Committee of Ministers. The Assembly wanted an individual right of complaint which could be exercised in all cases, whereas in the view of the Ministers such a right ought to be exercised only under the supervision and with the consent of the government concerned. Some less far-reaching constructions were also found to be unacceptable to the Committee of Ministers. It was proposed, for instance, to incorporate the individual right of petition into the Convention on the condition that a State might veto the examination by the Commission of a particular petition. This right of veto in turn would have to be subject to the collective supervision of the other States in order to prevent its abuse. The Consultative Assembly also proposed the formula according to which the individual right of petition was to be incorporated into the Convention, but the States could exclude this right with respect to petitions directed against them.[136] Finally, agreement was reached on the compromise as now laid down in Article 25 of the Convention: the Commission may receive an application[137] from an individual only if the State against which such an application has been lodged has expressly recognised the competence of the Commission to receive such applications. States which, *via* the so-called 'colonial clause', have declared the Convention to be applicable to one or more of the territories under their responsibility, may recognise also for those territories the competence of the Commission to receive applications of individuals (Article 63(4)).

The Commission became competent to receive applications of individuals on 5 July 1955. At that date the condition of Article 25(4) was satisfied that at least six Contracting States must have made a declaration as referred to in Article 25(1). Since 1987 an individual may lodge an application against all Contracting States, as at that time all of them had made the declaration under Article 25(1) while ever since new Contracting States have made the declaration at the time of ratification of the Convention.

Article 25 undoubtedly constitutes the most progressive provision of the Convention. It removes the principal limitation by which the position of the individual in international law was generally characterised. One improvement as

---

[136] For more details, see Council of Europe, *Collected Edition of the 'Travaux Préparatoires' of the European Convention of Human Rights*, Vol. IV, The Hague, 1977, pp. 114 *et seq.*

[137] The English version of Article 25 speaks of 'petition'. In the practice of the Commission this term has been replaced by 'application', a term which comes nearer to the French '*requête*'.

compared to the traditional institute of diplomatic protection, mentioned before, is the elimination of the condition of the link of nationality in the case of a complaint by a State. Even more, however, the individual right of complaint, despite its limitations, constitutes a considerable improvement over the classic system. Precisely because States are generally reluctant to submit an application against another State, the individual right of complaint constitutes a necessary expedient for achieving the aim of the Convention to secure the rights and freedoms of individuals against the States.

The importance of the individual right of complaint for the functioning of the supervisory system under the European Convention may appear from the large number of individual applications that are submitted to the Commission. On 31 December 1996 a total of 34,297 applications had been registered at the Secretariat of the Commission, and the Commission had taken a decision with respect to admissibility in 29,347 cases. However, it should be borne in mind that a great many cases were at once declared inadmissible. Of the remaining cases the majority were declared inadmissible after having been transmitted to the government concerned for its observations. In the course of the examination of the merits another number of cases were afterwards rejected in accordance with Article 29 for inadmissibility.[138] Only a total of 3,458 cases were therefore ultimately declared admissible.[139]

11.2.2 Who May Lodge a Complaint?

When a State has made the declaration under Article 25(1), anyone who is in some respect subject to the jurisdiction of that State and is allegedly a victim of a violation of the Convention by that State may lodge an application. As appears from Article 1 the nationality of the applicant is irrelevant. This means that the right of complaint is conferred not only on the nationals of the State concerned, but also on those of other Contracting States – regardless of whether the latter themselves have made the declaration of Article 25(1) –, on the nationals of States which are not Parties to the Convention, and on stateless persons, provided that they satisfy the condition referred to in Article 1, viz. that they were subject to the jurisdiction of the respondent State at the moment the violation allegedly took place. Lack of legal capacity does not affect the natural person's right of complaint. In several cases the Court held that minors have the right, of their own accord and without being represented by their guardians, to lodge a complaint with the Commission.[140] The same applies to persons who have lost their legal capacity after being committed to a psychiatric hospital.[141]

---

[138] On this, see infra pp. 166-168.
[139] See Council of Europe, European Commission of Human Rights, Survey of Activities and Statistics, 1996.
[140] See, e.g., the judgment of 28 November 1988, Nielsen, A.144, p. 8
[141] Judgment of 24 October 1979, Winterwerp, A.33, p. 6; judgment of 21 February 1990, Van der Leer, A.170, p. 8; judgment of 24 September 1992, Herczegfalvy, A.244, p. 8.

Besides individuals, non-governmental organisations and groups of persons may also file an application. With respect to the last-mentioned category the Commission decided during its first session that these must be groups which have been established in a regular way according to the law of one of the Contracting States. If that is not the case, the application must have been signed by all the persons belonging to the group.[142] As to the category of non-governmental organisations, the Commission decided that they must be *private* organisations, and that municipalities, for instance, cannot be considered as such.[143]

A wide range of organisations, such as newspapers,[144] churches,[145] associations,[146] and companies[147] have submitted applications. Although the rights and freedoms laid down in the Convention apply to individuals as well as to non-governmental organisations, some of the rights and freedoms are by their nature not susceptible of being exercised by a legal person. Insofar as Article 9 is concerned, the Commission made a distinction in this respect between the freedom of conscience and the freedom of religion. In contrast to freedom of religion,[148] freedom of conscience cannot be exercised by a legal person.[149] Also the right not to be subjected to degrading treatment and punishment cannot be exercised by a legal person[150] and the same is true with respect to the right of education.[151]

11.2.3 The Victim Requirement

(a) General

Whereas States may complain about 'any alleged breach of the provisions of the Convention by another High Contracting Party' (Article 24), and consequently also about national legislation or administrative practices *in abstracto*,[152] individuals must claim 'to be the victim of a violation by one of the High Contracting Parties of the rights set forth in this Convention' (Article 25). The special relation required is that the individual applicant himself is the victim of the alleged violation.[153] He may not bring an *actio popularis*, nor may he submit to the

---

[142] See the report of the session in question: DH(54)3, p. 8.

[143] Joined Appls 5767/72, 5922/72, 5929-5931/72, 5953-5957/72, 5984-5988/73 and 6011/73, *Austrian municipalities* v. *Austria*, Yearbook XVII (1974), p. 338 (352); Appl. 15090/89, *Ayuntamiento M.* v. *Spain*, D&R 68 (1991), p. 209 (214).

[144] Appl. 10243/83, *Times Newspapers Ltd, Giles, Knightly and Potter* v. *the United Kingdom*, D&R 41 (1985), p. 123.

[145] Appl. 8282/78, *Church of Scientology* v. *Sweden*, D&R 21 (1981), p. 109.

[146] Judgment of 21 June 1988, *Plattform 'Ärzte für das Leben'*, A.139.

[147] Judgment of 24 October 1986, *AGOSI*, A.108; judgment of 7 July 1989, *Tre Traktörer AB*, A.159.

[148] Appl. 8282/78, *Church of Scientology* v. *Sweden*, D&R 21 (1981), p. 109 (110).

[149] Appl. 11921/86, *Verein Kontakt Information Therapie and Hagen* v. *Austria*, D&R 57 (1988), p. 81 (88).

[150] *Idem.*

[151] Appl. 11533/85, *Ingrid Jordebo Foundation of Christian Schools and Ingrid Jordebo* v. *Sweden*, D&R 51 (1987), p. 125 (128).

[152] See *supra* p. 40.

[153] This question remains relevant throughout the examination of the application: Appl. 9320/81, *D* v. *Federal Republic of Germany*, D&R 36 (1984), p. 24 (30-31).

Commission abstract complaints.[154] The Commission has held that the mere fact that trade unions consider themselves as guardians of the collective interests of their members, does not suffice to make them victims, within the meaning of Article 25, of measures affecting those members.[155]

The Commission has, however, declared admissible individual applications which had a *partly* abstract character. Thus, a number of Northern Irishmen complained on the one hand about torture to which they had allegedly been subjected by the British during their detention, while in addition they claimed that this treatment formed part of 'a systematic administrative pattern which permits and encourages brutality.' They requested the Commission, *inter alia*, to conduct:

> a full investigation of the allegations made in the present application as well as of the system of interrogation currently employed by security forces under the control of the United Kingdom in Northern Ireland, for the purpose of determining whether or not such specific acts and administrative practices are incompatible with the European Convention for the Protection of Human Rights and Fundamental Freedoms.[156]

The British Government submitted that the second part of the application was not admissible and referred to the case-law of the Commission with respect to abstract complaints. The Commission held, however, that:

> neither Article 25, nor any other provisions in the Convention, *inter alia* Article 27(1)(b), prevent an individual applicant from raising before the Commission a complaint in respect of an alleged administrative practice in breach of the Convention provided that he brings *prima facie* evidence of such a practice and of his being a victim of it.[157]

An individual application may therefore be concerned not only with the personal interest of the applicant, but also with the public interest, and thus the procedure that originates from an individual complaint may in some respects also assume an objective character.[158] Thus the Commission has adopted the view that on the ground of the general function assigned to it in Article 19 'to ensure the observance of the engagements undertaken by the High Contracting Parties in the present Convention', it is competent to examine *ex officio*, also in case of an application by an individual, whether there has been a violation. It need not confine itself to an examination of the violations expressly alleged by the applicant.[159]

---

[154] Judgment of 6 September 1978, *Klass*, A.28, pp. 17-18; judgment of 13 June 1979, *Marckx*, A.31, p. 13.

[155] Appl. 15404/89, *Purcell* v. *Ireland*, D&R 70 (1991), p. 262 (273).

[156] Appls 5577-5583/72, *Donnelly* v. *the United Kingdom*, Yearbook XVI (1973), p. 212 (216).

[157] *Ibidem*, p. 260. In the second instance, *via* application of Art. 29, the said complaints were declared inadmissible, because of non-exhaustion of domestic remedies: Yearbook XIX (1976), p. 82 (252-254).

[158] See *supra* pp. 40-41.

[159] See, *e.g.*, Appl. 202/56, *X* v. *Belgium*, Yearbook I (1955-1957), p. 190 (192) and the joined Appls 7604/76, 7719/76 and 7781/77, *Foti, Lentini* and *Cenerini* v. *Italy*, D&R 14 (1979), p. 133 (143).

47

Another implication of this objective character is manifested in the Commission's view that, when an applicant withdraws his application or no longer shows any interest in the case, the procedure does not necessarily come to an end, but may be pursued in the public interest. Thus, in its decision in the case of *Gericke* v. *Federal Republic of Germany* the Commission expressly held:

> that the interests served by the protection of human rights and fundamental freedoms guaranteed by the Convention extend beyond the individual interests of the persons concerned; (...) whereas, consequently, the withdrawal of an application and the respondent Government's agreement thereto cannot deprive the Commission of the competence to pursue its examination of the case.[160]

For admissibility the applicant is not required to *prove* that he is the victim of the alleged violation. Article 25(1) only provides that the applicant must be a person 'claiming to be the victim' (*'qui se prétend victime'*).[161] However, this does not mean that the mere submission of the applicant that he is a victim, is in itself sufficient. The Commission examines whether, assuming that the alleged violation has taken place, it is to be deemed plausible that the applicant is a victim, on the basis of the facts submitted by the applicant and the facts, if any, advanced against them by the defendant State. If in the Commission's opinion this is not the case, it declares the application 'incompatible with the provisions of the present Convention' and, on the ground of Article 27(2), pronounces its inadmissibility.[162] On the other hand, even if the applicant does not expressly submit that he is the victim of the challenged act or omission, the Commission is nevertheless prepared to examine this point and to declare the application admissible if there appears to be sufficient ground for this.[163]

(b) The Applicant Must Be Personally Affected by the Alleged Violation

The requirement of 'victim' implies that the violation of the Convention must have *affected* the applicant in some way. According to the Court's well-established case-law 'the word "victim" in Article 25 refers to the person directly affected by

---

[160] Appl. 2294/64, Yearbook VIII (1965), p. 314 (320). See also Appl. 2686/65, *Heinz Kornmann* v. *Federal Republic of Germany*, Yearbook IX (1966), p. 494 (506-508).

[161] An amendment to replace these words by 'which has been the victim', tabled at the Consultative Assembly, was withdrawn after discussion, because it was recognised that this was a 'right to complain from the point of view of procedure' and not a 'substantial right of action': Council of Europe, Cons. Ass., First Session, Fourth Part, *Reports*, 1949, pp. 1272-1274.

[162] See, *e.g.*, Appl. 1983/63, *X* v. *the Netherlands*, Yearbook IX (1966), p. 286 (304). In a few cases the Commission declared the application 'manifestly ill-founded' because in its view the applicant could not be regarded as a victim: see, *e.g.*, Appl. 2291/64, *X* v. *Austria*, Coll. 24 (1967), p. 20 (33 and 35); and Appl. 4653/70, *X* v. *Federal Republic of Germany*, Yearbook XVII (1974), p. 148 (178). This also leads to a declaration of inadmissibility, but the ground was indicated wrongly here, since the question of whether the application is well-founded depends on whether there has been a violation of the Convention, not on the question of the effect of such a violation, if any, for the applicant.

[163] See, *e.g.*, Appl. 99/55, *X* v. *Federal Republic of Germany*, Yearbook I (1955-1957), p. 160 (161).

the act or omission at issue.'[164] To this, however, the Court usually adds a phrase of the sort that 'the existence of a violation being conceivable even in the absence of prejudice; prejudice is relevant only in the context of Article 50.'[165]

The requirement that the applicant be *personally* affected by the alleged violation has also been stressed by the Commission right from the beginning. Thus, an application in which it was submitted that the Norwegian legislation concerning *abortus provocatus* conflicted with Article 2(1) of the Convention, was declared inadmissible because of the fact that the applicant had not alleged that he himself was the victim of this legislation, but had lodged his application 'on behalf of parents who without their own consent or knowledge (...) have or will have their offspring taken away by abortus provocatus, and on behalf of those taken away by such operations – all unfit or unable to plead on their own behalf.'[166]

In an almost identical case an Austrian applicant submitted that the abortion legislation of his country conflicted with Articles 2 and 8 of the Convention. His application was also not admitted, because the Commission, as it stated, 'is not competent to examine *in abstracto* its [the disputed legislation's] compatibility with the Convention.' According to the Commission the applicant had meant to bring an *actio popularis*. He had submitted that the legislation in question actually concerned every Austrian citizen 'because of its effects for the future of the nation and for the moral and legal standard of the nation', and had declared himself willing 'to be nominated curator to act on behalf of the unborn in general'.[167]

A somewhat divergent view was taken in some other decisions of the Commission concerning cases in which abortion legislation was involved. A German Act of 1974, which removed penalties for abortion, had been declared by the *Bundesverfassungsgericht* to conflict with the German Constitution. A regulation concerning abortion was subsequently enacted which met the requirement laid down in this judicial decision and was then incorporated into a new Act of 1976. With respect to the judgment of the *Bundesverfassungsgericht* and its consequences an application was lodged on the ground of alleged violation of Article 8 of the Convention by an organisation, a man and two women. The application of the organisation was declared inadmissible by the Commission, fully in line with its decision in the above-mentioned Norwegian case, because it did not concern a physical person, but a legal person;[168] the abortion legislation

---

[164] Most recently the judgment of 15 June 1992, *Lüdi*, A.238, p. 18. See also the judgment of 22 May 1984, *De Jong, Baljet and Van den Brink*, A.77, p. 20; judgment of 22 May 1984, *Van der Sluys, Zuiderveld and Klappe*, A.78, p. 16; and judgment of 28 March 1990, *Groppera Radio AG*, A.173, p. 20.

[165] *Idem*.

[166] Appl. 867/60, *X* v. *Norway*, Yearbook IV (1961), p. 270 (276).

[167] Appl. 7045/75, *X* v. *Austria*, D&R 7 (1977), p. 87 (88). See also Appl. 7806/77, *Webster* v. *the United Kingdom*, D&R 12 (1978), p. 168 (174).

[168] See Annex II to the report of 12 July 1977, *Brüggemann and Scheuten*, D&R 10 (1978), p. 100 (121).

could not be applicable to the organisation, and the latter could not therefore itself be considered the victim.[169] The same also applied to the application of the man; the law had not been applied to him and according to the Commission he had not proved at all that the bare existence of the law had injured him to such an extent that he could claim to be the victim of a violation of the Convention.[170] However, the Commission here seems to leave open the possibility that the bare existence of abortion legislation does injure a man to such an extent that he must be considered its victim. This impression is corroborated by the decision of the Commission with respect to the two women. According to their submissions they themselves were not pregnant, nor had an interruption of pregnancy been refused to them, and they had not been prosecuted for illegal abortion either. However, they considered that the Convention had been violated *vis-à-vis* them because in consequence of the legislation in question they were obliged to either abstain from sexual relations or use contraceptives – of which they disapproved for several reasons, including health – or become pregnant against their will. The Commission recognised that both women were victims in the sense of Article 25 on the following ground:

> The Commission considers that pregnancy and the interruption of pregnancy are part of private life, and also in certain circumstances of family life. It further considers that respect for private life comprises also, to a certain degree, the right to establish and develop relationships with other human beings, especially in the emotional field, for the development and fulfilment of one's own personality (...) and that therefore sexual life is also part of private life; and in particular that legal regulation of abortion is an intervention in private life which may or may not be justified under Article 8(2).[171]

The Commission thus takes the position that a legal regulation of abortion constitutes an interference with private life, and under certain circumstances with family life as well, which may or may not be justified on the ground of Article

---

[169] In other cases, too, it was stressed that some of the rights and freedoms included in the Convention apply only to natural persons. See, *e.g.*, Appl. 9900/82, *X Union v. France*, D&R 32 (1983), p. 261 (264), where the Commission stated: 'In the present case, the applicant union as a legal person does not itself claim to be the victim of an infringement of the right to free choice of residence guaranteed by Article 2 of Protocol No. 4, since the legislative restrictions in question are only applicable to natural persons. (...) It might however be considered that the application really emanates from the members of the union, which is empowered (...) to initiate proceedings on behalf of its members. (...) However, it is noted in this context that the petition does not mention any specific case of one or more teachers alleged to be subjected to a measure constituting an infringement.' Obviously, other rights or freedoms are clearly applicable to legal persons as well: see Appl. 9905/82, *A Association and H v. Austria*, D&R 36 (1984), p. 187 (192-193), lodged by a political party and its chairman/legal representative alleging violation of Article 11 because of the prohibition of a meeting: 'As the right invoked (...) can be exercised by both the organiser of a meeting, even if it should be a legal person as in the present case, and by individual participants, the Commission accepts that both applicants are entitled to be victims of a violation of their rights under Article 11.' With regard to NGOs, see also *infra* pp. 552-553.

[170] Report of 12 July 1977, *Brüggemann and Scheuten*, D&R 10 (1978), p. 100 (121).

[171] Appl. 6959/75, *Brüggemann and Scheuten v. Federal Republic of Germany*, D&R 5 (1976), p. 103 (115).

8(2). Women may allege to be the victims of that regulation even if it has not actually been enforced against them. The consideration quoted above is formulated in very general terms and leaves scope for the interpretation that in certain cases men may also be considered victims of the bare existence of abortion legislation. As stated, in the case concerned the man was not admitted, because the victim-requirement was not satisfied as he had lodged his application in his capacity as chairman of the above-mentioned organisation. The decision, therefore, does not exclude that a man's application be declared admissible if he complains before the Commission about abortion legislation in his capacity as a husband or partner. In a case of 1980 the Commission confirmed this interpretation. There the applicant challenged the English legislation under which his wife had undergone *abortus provocatus*. According to the Commission the requirement of Article 25 had been satisfied on the simple consideration that 'the applicant, as potential father, was so closely affected by the termination of his wife's pregnancy that he may claim to be a victim.'[172]

In a case where a journalist and two newspapers alleged violation of their right to receive and impart information as a result of a ruling by the House of Lords that a lawyer had acted in contempt of court because she had allowed inspection of confidential documents by the journalist after these had been read out in the course of a public hearing, the Commission took a more restrictive position. It declared the application inadmissible because it did:

> not consider that the concept of 'victim' in Article 25(1) may be interpreted so broadly, in the present case, as to encompass every newspaper or journalist in the United Kingdom who might conceivably be affected by the decision of the House of Lords. The form of detriment required must be of a less indirect and remote nature.[173]

This decision would seem to deviate from the Commission's above-mentioned case-law as the ruling by the House of Lords clearly implied a restraint for the applicants. Furthermore, the reasoning upon which it is based is, in our opinion, not very convincing. The argument that the applicants remained free to publish articles on the disputed subject overlooks that not only the right to impart but also that to receive information was invoked. Similarly, the fact that the decision of the House of Lords was, according to the Commission 'one which affected every interested journalist in the United Kingdom', does not justify the conclusion that therefore the applicants cannot be considered victims within the meaning of Article 25(1). However, in a case where the applicants, an editor of a newspaper and a journalist, complained that the law of contempt of court prevented the preparation of a newspaper article on a case which was *sub judice*, the Commission considered that in view of the applicants' professional activities, the

---

[172] Appl. 8416/78, *X* v. *the United Kingdom*, D&R 19 (1980), p. 244 (248). See also Appl. 17004/90, *Hercz* v. *Norway*, D&R 73 (1992), p. 155 (166).

[173] Appl. 10039/82, *Leigh and Others* v. *the United Kingdom*, D&R 38 (1984), p. 74 (78).

applicants might be directly affected by the Contempt of Court Act 1981 and, therefore, might claim to be victims in respect of this legislation.[174]

(c) The Notion of Potential Victim

The Commission and the Court have accepted as victims in the sense of Article 25 a category of persons of whom it could not be ascertained with certainty that they had suffered an injury. The reason of this acceptance consisted in the fact that the applicants could not know whether the challenged legislation had or had not been applied to them. This matter came up in the *Klass* Case.[175] Three lawyers, a judge and a public prosecutor alleged violation of the secrecy of their mail and telecommunications by the authorities. The measures concerned were secret insofar that the persons in question were not informed of them in all cases, and if they were informed, then only afterwards. The Commission settled the matter of the victim-requirement in a brief consideration, stressing the secret character of the measures and concluding as follows: 'In view of this particularity of the case the applicants have to be considered as victims for purposes of Article 25.'[176] The Court dealt with the matter much more in detail. It stated at the outset that according to Article 25 individuals in principle may neither bring an *actio popularis* nor complain about legislation *in abstracto*.[177] The principle of effectiveness (*l'effet utile*), however, according to the Court, calls for exceptions to this rule. This principle implies that the procedural provisions of the Convention are to be applied in such a way as to contribute to the effectiveness of the system of individual applications. All this induced the Court to conclude that:

> an individual may, *under certain conditions*, claim to be the victim of a violation occasioned by the mere existence of secret measures or of legislation permitting secret measures, without having to allege that such measures were in fact applied to him.[178]

Such conditions were satisfied in the case under consideration, since:

> the contested legislation institutes a system of surveillance under which all persons in the Federal Republic of Germany can potentially have their mail, post and telecommunications monitored, without their even knowing this unless there has been either some indiscretion or subsequent notification.[179]

This may be summarised to imply that in case of the existence of secret measures (whether based on legislation or not) the victim-requirement under Article 25 may already be satisfied when the applicant is a *potential* victim. A comparable line of reasoning was followed by the Commission in the *Malone* Case, in which it found that the:

---

[174] Appl. 10243/83, *Times Newspapers Ltd, Giles, Knightly and Potter* v. *the United Kingdom*, D&R 41 (1985), p. 123 (130).
[175] For the examination of the merits, see *infra* pp. 707-709.
[176] Appl. 5029/71, *Klass* v. *Federal Republic of Germany*, Yearbook XVII (1974), p. 178 (208).
[177] Judgment of 6 September 1978, A.28, pp. 17-18.
[178] *Ibidem*, p. 18.
[179] *Ibidem*, pp. 19-20.

applicant is directly affected by the law and practice in England and Wales (...) under which the secret surveillance of postal and telephone communications on behalf of the police is permitted and takes place. His communication has at all relevant times been liable to such surveillance without his being able to obtain knowledge of it. Accordingly (...) he is entitled to claim (...) to be a victim (...) irrespective of whether or to what extent he is able to show that it has actually been applied to him.[180]

The reasoning of the Court in the *Klass* Case was relied upon by two mothers, who submitted, on behalf of their children, violation of Article 3 of the Convention on the ground of the existence of a system of corporal punishment at the schools in Scotland attended by their children. According to the Commission there was no direct analogy with the *Klass* Case, but it did refer to the criterion of effectiveness relied upon by the Court in that case, and it held subsequently:

> that in order to be accepted as victims under Article 25 of the Convention, individuals must satisfy the Commission that they run the risk of being directly affected by the particular matter which they wish to bring before it.[181]

Thus, here again, the mere fact of running a risk was deemed sufficient to be considered as 'victims'. According to the Commission it would be too restrictive an interpretation of Article 25 to require that the children had in actual fact been subjected to corporal punishment. It therefore considered the children as victims because they 'may be affected by the existence of physical violence around them and by the threat of a potential use on themselves of corporal punishment.'[182]

Shortly afterwards, in the *Marckx* Case, the Court reached the same decision by express reference to the *Klass* Case. In the *Marckx* Case it had been advanced that the Belgian legislation concerning illegitimate children conflicted with the Convention. Before the Court the Belgian Government submitted that this was in reality an abstract complaint, since the challenged legislation had not been applied to the applicant. The Court held that:

> Article 25 of the Convention entitles individuals to contend that a law violates their rights by itself, in the absence of an individual measure of implementation, if they run the risk of being directly affected by it.[183]

---

[180] Report of 17 December 1982, A.82, p. 52. See also report of 9 May 1989, *Hewitt and Harman*, D&R 67 (1991), p. 89 (98); Appl. 10799/84, *Radio X, S, W & A* v. *Switzerland*, D&R 37 (1984), p. 236 (239).

[181] Report of 16 May 1980, *Campbell and Cosans*, B.42 (1985), p. 36. However, in a case where a mother and her son complained about the existence of corporal punishment for breach of school discipline the Commission held that having failed to inquire about the disciplinary methods when she put her child in a private school, a mother cannot claim to be a victim direct or indirect, of a violation of the rights guaranteed in the Convention in respect of corporal punishment inflicted on the child for a breach of school discipline. See Appl. 13134/87, *Costello-Roberts* v. *the United Kingdom*, D&R 67 (1991), p. 216 (224).

[182] *Ibidem*, pp. 36-37. The Court in its judgment of 25 February 1982 did not deal with this question, as it had concluded that Art. 3 of the Convention had not been violated, A.48, p. 14.

[183] Judgment of 13 June 1979, A.31, pp. 12-14.

This was considered to be the case here. According to the Court the question of whether the applicant has actually been placed in an unfavourable position is not a criterion of the victim-requirement:

the question of prejudice is not a matter for Article 25 which, in its use of the word 'victim', denotes 'the person directly affected by the act or omission which is in issue'.[184]

In the *Dudgeon* Case, and later in the *Norris* Case and the *Modinos* Case, the applicants complained about the existence of laws which had the effect of making certain homosexual acts, between consenting adult males, criminal offences. The Court held that 'in the personal circumstances of the applicant, the very existence of this legislation continuously and directly affects his private life.'[185]

(d) The Notion of Future Victim

The question of whether applicants having a *future* interest may also be considered victims in the sense of Article 25 was avoided by the Commission in a case concerning Article 2 of Protocol No. 1. In this case forty mothers claimed that, in consequence of an Act on pre-school education promulgated in Sweden on 21 December 1973, they had been deprived of the right to send their children to the school of their choice. As to the admissibility of their application, the Commission divided the mothers into three groups. The mothers from the first group could not be regarded as victims, because their children had passed the pre-school age at the moment of the Act's effective date. The second group consisted of mothers whose children had not yet reached pre-school age at that moment. With respect to this group the Commission held as follows:

The Commission understands that these applicants consider themselves to be victims of a violation of the Convention in that the Act on Pre-School Activities may affect them in the future. The Commission notes that the children of these applicants in some cases might have reached pre-school age in the course of proceedings before the Commission. However, having regard to the fact that the applicants in Group 3 [the mothers of children that had pre-school age at the moment referred to] can be considered to be victims within the meaning of Article 25 of the Convention for the purpose of the present application, the Commission can abstain from examining as to whether the applicants in Group 2 also can be so considered.[186]

From an earlier decision of the Commission in a similar case, however, one may infer that the Commission is indeed prepared to recognise a future interest in certain cases. In that case two parents complained about legal and administrative measures concerning sexual instruction at primary schools. The measures were not

---

[184] *Idem.* See also the Commission in: Appl. 8307/78, *De Klerck* v. *Belgium*, D&R 21 (1981), p. 116 (124); Appl. 9697/82, *J and Others* v. *Ireland*, D&R 34 (1983), p. 131 (137); Appl. 11722/85, *B* v. *France*, D&R 51 (1987), p. 165 (176); Appl. 15070/89, *Modinos* v. *Cyprus*, D&R 67 (1991), p. 295 (299).

[185] Judgment of 22 October 1981, A.45, p. 18; judgment of 26 October 1988, A.142, p. 16; judgment of 22 April 1993, A.259, p. 11.

[186] Appl. 6853/74, *40 Mothers* v. *Sweden*, Yearbook XX (1977), p. 214 (236).

yet applicable to their school-age daughter. Nevertheless, the Commission admitted their application. Curiously enough, however, it did not mention the victim-requirement at all.[187] The admissibility may be justified on the ground that in cases like this one the alleged violation – in this case the application of the said measures to the child – will certainly take place in the near future. Especially in cases where otherwise the interests of the applicant would be irreparably prejudiced, this view ensues imperatively from the purpose of the legal protection envisaged by the Convention and the requirement of effectiveness.

In the *Kirkwood* Case such a situation was at stake. The case concerned a man complaining that his envisaged extradition from the United Kingdom to California would amount to inhuman and degrading treatment contrary to Article 3 of the Convention since, if extradited, he would be tried for two accusations of murder and one of attempt to murder, and would very probably be sentenced to death. He argued that the circumstances surrounding the implementation of such a death penalty, and in particular the 'death row' phenomenon of excessive delay during a prolonged appeal procedure lasting several years, during which he would be gripped with uncertainty as to the outcome of his appeal and therefore as to his fate, would constitute inhuman and degrading treatment. The Commission held as follows with respect to the victim-requirement:

> In these circumstances, faced with an imminent act of the executive, the consequences of which for the applicant will allegedly expose him to Article 3 treatment, the Commission finds that the applicant is able to claim to be a victim of an alleged violation of Article 3.[188]

In several cases where a decision had been taken to expel a person to a country where he claimed he risked being treated contrary Article 3, the Commission has held that a person who is about to be subjected to a violation of the Convention may claim to be a victim.[189] If, however, the order to leave the territory of the State concerned is not enforceable, the person concerned may not yet claim to be a victim. Only the notification of an expulsion order referring to the country of destination can, after the domestic remedies have been exhausted, confer on him the status of victim. If an alleged future prejudice cannot yet be foreseen, the application is inadmissible.[190] Thus, in the *Vijayanthan and Pusparajah* Case, the Court made a distinction between, on the one hand, the *Soering* Case (where the Home Secretary had signed the warrant for the applicant's extradition) and, on the other hand, that of *Vilvarajah and Pusparajah* (where the deportation of the applicants to Sri Lanka had taken place during the proceedings before the Commission). In respect of the latter case it found that, despite the direction to

---

[187] Appl. 5095/71, *V. and A. Kjeldsen* v. *Denmark*, Yearbook XV (1972), pp. 482-502.
[188] Appl. 10479/83, D&R 37 (1984), p. 158 (182).
[189] Appl. 17262/90, *A* v. *France*, D&R 68 (1991), p. 319 (334); Appls 17550/90 and 17825/91, *V* and *P* v. *France*, D&R 70 (1991), p. 298 (314); Appl. 19373/92, *Voulfovitch and Oulianova* v. *Sweden*, D&R 74 (1993), p. 199 (207).
[190] Appl. 2358/64, *X* v. *Sweden*, Coll. 23 (1967), p. 147 (151).

leave French territory, not enforceable in itself, and the rejection of Mr *Vilvarajah's* and *Pusparajah's* application for exceptional leave to remain, no expulsion order had been made with respect to the applicants. If the Commissioner of Police were to decide that they should be removed, the appeal provided for in French law would be open to the applicants, with all its attendant safeguards. The applicants could not, as matters stood, claim 'to be the victim(s) of a violation' within the meaning of Article 25(1).[191]

(e) The Notion of Indirect Victim

It is conceivable that an individual may experience a personal injury owing to a violation of the Convention against another. Under certain circumstances, therefore, an individual may lodge an application on his own account concerning a violation of the Convention against another, without the applicant himself having directly suffered a violation of one of his rights or freedoms. In such a case the applicant must have so close a link with the direct victim of the violation that he himself is also to be considered a victim. On that basis the Commission has developed in its case-law the concept of 'indirect victim', meaning that a near relative of the victim or any other third party can refer the matter to the Commission on his own initiative insofar as the violation concerned is (also) prejudicial to him or insofar as he has a personal interest in the termination of that violation.[192] Thus, a spouse was considered a victim in view of the fact that she had suffered financial and moral injury in consequence of a violation of the Convention committed against her husband.[193] That a purely non-material interest, too, is sufficient for the admissibility of the action of an applicant as the indirect victim becomes evident, for example, from the decision by the Commission that a complaint of a mother about the treatment of her detained son was admissible.[194] On the other hand, an applicant was not admitted who

---

[191] Judgment of 27 August 1992, A.241-B, pp. 86-87.

[192] Appl. 100/55, *X* v. *Federal Republic of Germany*, Yearbook I (1955-1957), p. 162 (162-163).

[193] Appl. 1478/62, *Y* v. *Belgium*, Yearbook VI (1963), p. 590 (620). See also Appl. 7467/76, *X* v. *Belgium*, D&R 8 (1978), p. 220 (221), where an applicant was regarded as an indirect victim because he had submitted that his twin brother had wrongfully been detained in a State institution, in which he had died later. And see Appls 9214/80, 9473/81 and 9474/81, *X*, *Cabales* and *Balkandali*, D&R 29 (1982), p. 176 (182): 'When the alleged violation concerns a refusal of a leave to remain or an entry clearance, the spouse of the individual concerned can claim to be a victim, even if the individual concerned is in fact staying with her, but unlawfully and under constant threat of deportation.'

[194] Appl. 898/60, *Y* v. *Austria*, Coll. 8 (1962), p. 136. See also Appl. 7011/75, *Becker* v. *Denmark*, Yearbook XIX (1976), p. 416 (450), where a German journalist challenged the repatriation of 199 Vietnamese children, proposed by the Danish Government, as contrary to Art. 3 of the Convention. And Appl. 9320/81, *D* v. *Federal Republic of Germany*, D&R 36 (1984), p. 24 (31): 'The answer to this question (whether an applicant can claim to be a victim) depends largely on the legal interest which the applicant has in a determination of his allegations of Convention breaches. In assessing this interest, any material or immaterial damage suffered (...) as a result of the alleged violation must be taken into account.' See also Appl. 9348/81, *W* v. *the United Kingdom*, D&R 32 (1983), p. 190 (198-200) and Appl. 9360/81, *W* v. *Ireland*, D&R 32 (1983), p. 211 (212-216).

submitted that his sisters had wrongfully failed to receive compensation for their sufferings during the Nazi regime, and who now claimed this as yet in his own name. This compensation related only to the sufferings of the sisters, not to those of the applicant, so that the latter could not be considered as the victim.[195]

In the case of *Open Door Counselling Ltd. and Dublin Well Women Centre Ltd.*, the Court extended the group of persons who may claim to be an indirect victim. The applications concerned restrictions imposed on the two applicant companies as a result of a court injunction prohibiting them from providing information to pregnant women as to the location or identity of, or method of communication with, abortion clinics in Great Britain. The applicant companies were engaged at the time in non-directive counselling of pregnant women. The other applicants were two of the counsellors employed by one of the companies, and two women of child-bearing age. The Government argued that the complaint submitted by the two women of child-bearing age amounted to an *actio popularis*, since they could not claim to be victims of an infringement of their Convention rights. The Court held:

> Although it has not been asserted that Mrs X and Mrs Geraghty are pregnant, it is not disputed that they belong to a class of women of child-bearing age which may be adversely affected by the restrictions imposed by the injunction. They are not seeking to challenge *in abstracto* the compatibility of Irish law with the Convention since they run a risk of being directly prejudiced by the measures complained of. They can thus claim to be 'victims' within the meaning of Article 25 § 1.[196]

Although the Court's reasoning seems to relate to the concept of 'potential victim', in fact the concept of 'indirect victim' is also at issue here, and has been considerably extended. A measure may be challenged not only by the persons to whom it is directed, but also by those who may be affected by it in another way. Since the issue was discussed at some length by the members of the Court, it must be assumed that this extension was intentional.

This extension was foreshadowed by the judgment in the *Groppera Radio AG* Case. A company which owned a radio station, its sole shareholder and two of its employees complained about an Ordinance adopted by the Federal Council prohibiting Swiss cable companies which had a community-antenna licence, from rebroadcasting programmes from transmitters which did not satisfy the requirement of the international agreements on radio and telecommunications. Groppera Radio did not satisfy these requirements. The applicants alleged a violation of Article 10. The Court dismissed the Government's preliminary objection that the applicants were not 'victims' within the meaning of Article 25 of the Convention since the Ordinance was not directed against them.[197]

---

[195] Appl. 113/55, *X v. Federal Republic of Germany*, Yearbook I (1955-1957), p. 161 (162). See also Appl. 9639/82, *B, R and J v. Federal Republic of Germany*, D&R 36 (1984), p. 139.

[196] Judgment of 29 October 1992, A.246, p. 22.

[197] Judgment of 28 March 1990, A.173, pp. 20-21.

Finally, it should be mentioned that in certain cases the Commission has qualified shareholders as victims of alleged violations of rights and freedoms of the company. It appears from its case-law that the Commission does not regard shareholders in such cases as indirect but as direct victims.[198] In these cases the individual concerned held a majority share in the company. On the other hand, in the *Yarrow* Case, the Commission held that a minority shareholder of Company A could not claim to be a victim of an interference with property rights of Company B, all the securities in which were owned by Company A, because the nationalisation measure complained of did not involve him personally. In the view of the Commission it was only open to Company A to lodge a complaint under the Convention.[199] In the *Agrotexim Hellas* Case the Commission found that the question whether a shareholder could claim to be victim of measures against a company could not be determined on the basis of the sole criterium of whether the shareholders hold the majority of the company shares. The Commission took into account, in addition to the fact that the applicants as a group held the majority of the shares in the company, that they had a direct interest in the subject matter of the application. Moreover, the company was in liquidation and was under a special regime of effective State control. Consequently, that company could not reasonably be expected to lodge an application with the Commission against the State. In these specific circumstances, the Commission found that the applicant shareholders were entitled, by lifting the veil of the company's legal personality, to claim that they were victims of the measures affecting the company's property, within the meaning of Article 25.[200] In the case of *Wasa Liv Ömsesidigt* the Commission found that a group of persons who were policyholders in an insurance company, could not be considered as victim, since the policyholders did not have any legal claim to direct ownership of the company's assets as such.[201] From the above it may be concluded that the doctrine of 'indirect victim' is not yet established in full clarity in the case-law as far as holders of financial interests in a company are concerned.

(f) The Alleged Violation Must Still Exist

Cases may occur in which the violation complained of has meanwhile been terminated, or at least no longer exists at the moment the Commission examines the case. The applicant will then not be admitted, because he can no longer allege that he is a victim.[202] If somehow the violation of the Convention complained

---

[198] Appl. 1706/62, *X* v. *Austria*, Yearbook IX (1966), p. 112 (130) and the report of 17 July 1980, *Kaplan*, D&R 21 (1981), p. 5 (23-24); Appl. 14807/89, *Agrotexim Hellas S.A.* v. *Greece*, D&R 72 (1992), p. 148 (155).

[199] Appl. 9266/81, D&R 30 (1983), p. 155 (184-185).

[200] Appl. 14807/89, D&R 72 (1992), p. 148 (156).

[201] Appl. 13013/87, D&R 58 (1988), p. 163(183-185).

[202] See, *e.g.*, Appl. 7826/77, *X* v. *the United Kingdom*, D&R 14 (1978), p. 197 (197-198). See also the report of 15 October 1980, *Foti and Others* v. *Italy*, B.48 (1986), p. 30; report of 6 July 1983, *Dores and Silveira* v. *Portugal*, D&R 41 (1985), p. 60 (19-20); Appl. 10103/82, *Faragut* v. *France*,

of has been recognised by the authorities and the applicant has got sufficient redress, he can no longer claim to be a victim of that violation.[203] In a case in which the applicants submitted that the authorities' recording of their telephone conversations with counsels was contrary to the Convention, the records had meanwhile been destroyed. In view of this the German Government advanced that the alleged violation had become moot. The Commission, however, decided that since the destruction had not taken place in response to a request of the applicants and the latter had not received reparation otherwise, 'the applicants still have to be considered as victims although the records in question no longer exist.'[204]

In the cases of *Van den Brink* and *Zuiderveld and Klappe* the respondent Government contended before the Court that the applicants could not claim to be victims of a breach of Article 5(3) as the time each one spent in custody on remand was deducted in its entirety from the sentence ultimately imposed on them. According to the Court the relevant deduction does not *per se* deprive the individual concerned of his status as an alleged victim within the meaning of Article 25 of a breach of Article 5(3). The Court added that: 'The position might be otherwise if the deduction from sentence had been based upon an acknowledgement by the national courts of a violation of the Convention.'[205]

Similarly, in the *Inze* Case the fact that a judicial settlement had been reached between the parties that might have mitigated the disadvantage suffered by the applicant, was considered insufficient reason to deprive the applicant of his status as victim. Here again the Court added that:

> The position might have been otherwise if, for instance, the national authorities had acknowledged either expressly or in substance, and then afforded redress for, the alleged breach of the Convention.[206]

Indeed, in cases where the applicant's sentence had been reduced in an express and measurable manner after a judicial finding concerning the undue length of the proceedings, the Commission took the position that he could no longer be considered to be a victim of a violation of Article 6(1).[207]

In the *East African Asians* Cases, the Commission held that where Article 3 is violated by a State's exclusion from its territory of a person on the ground of race, the violation is substantially terminated, but not redressed, by that person's

---

D&R 39 (1984), p. 186 (207).

[203] See Appl. 8865/80, *Verband Deutscher Flugleiter and Others* v. *Federal Republic of Germany*, D&R 25 (1982), p. 252 (254-255); Appl. 10092/82, *Baraona* v. *Portugal*, D&R 40 (1985), p. 118 (137); Appl. 10259/83, *Anca and Others* v. *Belgium*, D&R 40 (1985), p. 170 (177-178); Appl. 13156/87, *Byrn* v. *Denmark*, D&R 73 (1993), p. 5 (9), and as regards 'reasonable time': Appl. 8858/80, *G* v. *Federal Republic of Germany*, D&R 33 (1983), p. 5 (6-7).

[204] Appl. 8290/78, *A, B, C and D* v. *Federal Republic of Germany*, D&R 18 (1980), p. 176 (180).

[205] Judgments of 22 May 1984, A.77, p. 20 and A.78, p. 16 respectively.

[206] Judgment of 28 October 1987, A.126, p. 16.

[207] Appl. 17669/91, *Van Laak* v. *the Netherlands*, D&R 74 (1993), p. 156 (158); report of 16 February 1993, *Byrn* v. *Denmark*, D&R 74 (1993), p. 5 (9).

admission. Such a person can claim to be a victim of a violation notwithstanding admission.[208]

In the *Moustaquim* Case the applicant, a Moroccan national living in Belgium, had been deported by the Belgian authorities in 1984. The deportation order was suspended in 1989 for a trial period of two years during which the applicant was authorised to reside in Belgium. The applicant alleged that his deportation had violated, *inter alia*, Article 8. The Belgian Government submitted that the application had become devoid of purpose in that the deportation order had been suspended for a trial period of two years and the applicant was thus authorised to reside in Belgium. Since the new order had only suspended the deportation order and had not made reparation for its consequences, which the applicant had suffered for more than five years, the Court did not consider that the case had become devoid of purpose. According to the Court there had been an interference with the right to respect for family life.[209]

11.3 Representation of an Applicant

The requirement that the violation of the Convention must have caused the applicant a personal injury does not, of course, prevent an application from being lodged by his representative.[210] Furthermore, if the victim himself is not, or not very well, able to undertake an action – for example a detained person, a patient in a mental clinic, a very young person – then a close relative, a guardian, a curator, or another person may act on his behalf. In that case the name of the victim must be made known and the latter, if possible, must have given his consent for lodging the application.[211]

In case of decease of the victim his heir may lodge an application or uphold a previously lodged application only if the allegedly violated right forms part of the estate or if on other grounds he himself is to be considered the (direct or indirect) victim.[212] In the *Kofler* Case the Commission stated that 'the heirs of a deceased applicant cannot claim a general right that the examination of the application introduced by the *de cujus* be continued by the Commission.' The nature of the complaint (the application concerned the duration of the proceedings which

---

[208] Report of 14 December 1973, D&R 78-A (1994), p. 5 (63).

[209] Judgment of 18 February 1991, A.193, p. 17.

[210] Appl. 282/57, *X* v. *Federal Republic of Germany*, Yearbook I (1955-1957), p. 164 (166).

[211] See, *e.g.*, Appl. 155/56, *X* v. *Federal Republic of Germany*, Yearbook I (1955-1957), p. 163 (164); Appl. 5076/71, *X* v. *the United Kingdom*, Coll. 40 (1972), p. 64 (66).

[212] See, on the one hand, Appl. 282/57, *X* v. *Federal Republic of Germany*, Yearbook I (1955-1957), p. 164 (166), on the other hand Appl. 1706/62, *X* v. *Austria*, Yearbook IX (1966), p. 112 (124). See also Appls 7572/76, 7586/76 and 7587/76, *Ensslin, Baader and Raspe* v. *Federal Republic of Germany*, Yearbook XXI (1978), p. 418 (452). See, however, Appl. 6166/73, *Baader, Meins, Meinhof, Grundmann* v. *Federal Republic of Germany*, Yearbook XVIII (1975), p. 132 (142); Appl. 12526/86, *Björkgren and Ed* v. *Sweden*, D&R 68 (1991), p. 104 (105), where the Commission recognised the right of action of a widow and sole heir with regard to an action relating to property; Appl. 16744/90, *Dujardin* v. *France*, D&R 72 (1992), p. 236 (243).

resulted in the applicant's conviction and sentence) did not allow that complaint to be considered as transferable because the complaint was closely linked with the late applicant personally and his heirs 'cannot now claim (...) to have themselves a sufficient legal interest to justify the further examination of the application on their behalf.' The Commission considered next whether any question of general interest would justify a further examination of the application and stated: 'Such a situation can arise in particular where an application in fact concerns (...) the legislation or a legal system or practice of the defendant State.' The Commission concluded that in this case such a general interest did not exist.[213]

Accordingly, the issue is whether the widow or heir can claim that the applicant's original interest in having the alleged violation of the Convention established might be considered as an interest vested in them. Such an interest was found to exist in a case where the deceased applicant had complained about his criminal conviction. In particular he claimed that he did not have a 'fair hearing' nor did he benefit from the 'presumption of innocence'. The Commission emphasised that, by their very nature, complaints relating to Article 6 are closely linked to the person of the deceased applicant. However, the Commission continued by saying that 'this link is not exclusive and it cannot be claimed that they have no bearing at all on the person of the widow.' The widow could claim to be a victim, since she suffered the effects of the decisions concerning the seizure of property and a daily fine and civil imprisonment, both of which were enforceable against her.[214] In *X* v. *France*, the Court took an even more liberal position. In this case the applicant, who was given a number of blood transfusions, was found to have been infected with HIV. The applicant died shortly after the referral of his case to the Court, but his parents expressed the wish to continue the proceedings. The Court accepted that they were entitled to take Mr X's place in the proceedings before it.[215] Also in other cases concerning the length of proceedings the Court without restrictions showed to be willing to continue the proceedings at the wish of the heirs of the deceased applicant.[216]

If the death of the direct victim is the result of the alleged violation, *e.g.* in the case of torture, his relatives will as a rule qualify as indirect victims.

---

[213] Report of 9 October 1982, D&R 30 (1983), p. 5 (9-10). See also the report of 7 March 1984, *Altun*, D&R 36 (1984), p. 236 (259-260) and the judgment of 25 August 1987, *Nölkenbockhoff*, A.123, pp. 77-78.

[214] Appl. 10828/84, *Funke* v. *France*, D&R 57 (1988), p. 5 (25-26).

[215] Judgment of 31 March 1992, A.234-C, p. 89.

[216] Judgment of 24 May 1991, *Vocaturo*, A.206-C and judgment of 27 February 1992, *G* v. *Italy*, A.228-F. See also Appl. 14660/89, *Prisca and De Santis* v. *Italy*, D&R 72 (1992), p. 141 (147).

11.4 Contracting Parties May Not Hinder the Right of Individual Complaint

According to the last sentence of Article 25 those Contracting States which have made the declaration referred to in that article, undertake not to interfere in any way with the exercise of the individual right of complaint. In this respect the Court held in the *Cruz Varas* Case, that Article 25(1) imposes an obligation not to interfere with the right of the individual effectively to present and pursue his complaint with the Commission. Although such a right is of a procedural nature distinguishable from the substantive rights contained in the Convention, it must be open to individuals to complain of alleged infringements of the Convention. In this respect the Convention must also be interpreted as guaranteeing rights which are practical and effective as opposed to theoretical and illusory.[217]

In the *Cruz Varas* Case the question arose whether the failure on the part of the respondent State to comply with the Commission's indication of provisional measures under Rule 36 of the Rules of Procedure of the Commission[218] amounted to a violation of the obligation not to hinder the effective exercise of the right of individual petition. The Court took the position that the Convention did not contain any provision empowering the Convention organs to order interim measures. In the absence of a specific provision for such a power a Rule 36 indication cannot give rise to a binding obligation.[219] This decision by the Court is to be regretted. In our opinion the minority of the Court took the right position. In their view the protection under the Convention would be meaningless if a State had the right to extradite or expel a person without any prior possibility of clarification – as far and as soon as possible – of the consequences of the expulsion. The Court has repeatedly underlined that 'the object and purpose of the Convention as an instrument for the protection of individual human beings require that its provisions be interpreted and applied so as to make its safeguards practical and effective.' This basic principle must also be kept in mind when the procedural guarantees contained in the Convention are interpreted as to their meaning and scope.[220]

In the *Akdivar* Case concerning the alleged burning of houses by security forces in South-East Turkey, the question arose whether the Turkish authorities had hindered the effective exercise of the right of individual petition. Some of the applicants, or persons thought to be applicants in this case, had been directly interrogated by the Turkish authorities about their applications to the Commission and had been asked to sign statements declaring that no such applications had been brought. Furthermore, in the case of two of the applicants a filmed interview of

---

[217] Judgment of 20 March 1991, A.201, p. 36. See also the Commission in Appl. 14807/89, *Agrotexim Hellas v. Greece*, D&R 72 (1992), p. 148 (156).
[218] See *infra* at pp. 103-107.
[219] See judgment of 20 March 1991, A.201, p. 35.
[220] *Ibidem*, p. 39.

this procedure had taken place. The Court found a violation of Article 25(1) in this respect. It held that the applicants must be able to communicate freely with the Commission without being subjected to any form of pressure from the authorities to withdraw or modify their complaints. Given their vulnerable position and the reality that in South-East Turkey complaints against the authorities might well give rise to a legitimate fear of reprisals, the matters complained of amounted to a form of illicit and unacceptable pressure on the applicants to withdraw their applications. Moreover, it could not be excluded that the filming of the two persons, who were subsequently declared not to be applicants, could have contributed to this pressure. The Court also held that the fact that the applicants actually pursued their application to the Commission did not prevent such behaviour on the part of the authorities from amounting to a hinderance in respect of the applicants in breach of this provision.[221]

Correspondence with the Commission in which the applicants complain about the right of complaint is not considered by the Commission as a separate 'application' or '*requête*' to which the rules of admissibility are applicable. As a rule the case will be settled between the Commission and the Contracting State concerned on an administrative basis, the applicant being permitted to react to any observations which a State may make. However, if along with another complaint a complaint is also lodged on interference with the exercise of the right of complaint, the Commission appears to be prepared to examine the latter together with the first complaint.[222]

In practice difficulties arise particularly with respect to persons who have been deprived of their liberty in one way or another. The Commission does not regard every form of monitoring of the mail of detained persons addressed to it as unlawful, although it considers it more in conformity with the spirit of the Convention that the letters are forwarded unopened.[223] According to the Commission there is a conflict with Article 25 only when an applicant cannot freely submit his grievances to the Commission in a complete and detailed way.[224]

In connection with this case-law of the Commission Mikaelson has raised the question of whether an alleged violation of the last sentence of Article 25, notwithstanding its slightly different, more procedural character, would not have to be examined and dealt with by the Commission in the same way as complaints about the substantive provisions of Section I. In the present situation the Commission usually decides, even in cases where interference with the exercise of the right of complaint has been found, that no further steps are necessary ('to

---

[221] Judgment of 16 September 1996, Reports 1996-IV, Vol. 15, para. 105.
[222] See, *e.g.*, Appl. 1593/62, *X* v. *Austria*, Yearbook VII (1964), p. 162 (166-168) and Appl. 1753/63, *X* v. *Austria*, Yearbook VIII (1965), p. 174 (188); Appl. 12976/87, *G* v. *Austria*, D&R 71 (1991), p. 44 (49).
[223] Appl. 1593/62, *X* v. *Austria*, Yearbook VII (1964), p. 162 (166-168).
[224] See, *e.g.*, Appl. 892/60, *X* v. *Federal Republic of Germany*, Yearbook IV (1961), p. 240 (258) and Appl. 5265/71, *X* v. *the United Kingdom*, D&R 3 (1976), p. 5 (7).

take no further action') as long as the applicant has been able to submit his grievances in an adequate manner.[225] But precisely in view of the existence of such interference it is at least doubtful whether the Commission is really able to form an opinion as to whether the application could be submitted adequately. On the basis of a number of arguments which appear convincing to us, Mikaelson therefore concludes that it would be desirable for the Commission to change its approach in this matter.[226] In our view the most relevant argument is that Article 25 forms the corner-stone on which the whole system of the Convention depends. Indeed, if and insofar as the exercise of the individual right of complaint is restricted, the Strasbourg organs are also deprived of the principal instrument for assessing the situation as to the protection of the other rights and freedoms guaranteed in the Convention. Moreover, besides the legal protection of individuals, an element of 'European public order' is involved. Should the Commission decide to follow the course suggested by Mikaelson, the question as to the violation of the 'right' set forth in the last sentence of Article 25 will be subjected to an independent examination, although a complaint about this can, of course, be submitted only in combination with the alleged violation of one of the 'genuine' rights and freedoms. However, the former complaint would no longer depend on the admissibility or well-foundedness of the latter.

In this context the *European Agreement relating to persons participating in proceedings before the European Commission and the European Court of Human Rights* is also of interest.[227] In Article 3(2) of this Agreement States undertake to guarantee also to detained persons the right to free correspondence with the Commission and the Court.[228] This means that, if their correspondence is at all examined by the competent authorities, this may not entail undue delay or alteration of the correspondence.[229] Nor may detained persons be subjected to disciplinary measures on account of any correspondence with the Commission or the Court.[230] Finally, they have a right to speak, out of hearing of other persons, with their lawyer concerning their application to the Commission and any subsequent proceedings, provided that the lawyer is qualified to appear as a barrister before the courts of the State concerned. With respect to these provisions the authorities may impose limitations only insofar as they are in accordance with

---

[225] The case-law of the Commission, however, also discloses cases where complaints concerning interference with the exercise of the right of complaint are dealt with *via* the normal procedure, although in connection with complaints about one or more of the provisions of Section I; see Appl. 369/58, *X* v. *Belgium*, Yearbook II (1958-1959), p. 376 (380-381) and the joined Appls 5351/72 and 6579/74, *X* v. *the Netherlands*, Coll. 46 (1974), p. 85 (86-87).

[226] L. Mikaelson, *European Protection of Human Rights*, Alphen aan de Rijn, 1980, pp. 27-33.

[227] This agreement entered into force on 17 April 1971. For the text see: Council of Europe, *European Treaty Series*, 6 May 1969, No. 67. For ratifications, see Appendix I.

[228] See, *e.g.*, Appl. 4351/70, *X* v. *Federal Republic of Germany*, Yearbook XIII (1970), p. 914 (924).

[229] Appl. 530/59, *X* v. *Federal Republic of Germany*, Yearbook III (1960), p. 184 (194-196) and Appl. 2137/64, *X* v. *Federal Republic of Germany*, Yearbook VII (1964), p. 310 (312-314).

[230] Appl. 3702/68, *X* v. *Belgium*, 4 October 1968 (not published) and joined Appls 7126/75 and 7573/76, *X and Y* v. *the United Kingdom*, 9 March 1977 (not published).

the law and are necessary in a democratic society in the interests of national security, for the detection and prosecution of a crime, or for the protection of health. Despite the fact that individuals cannot rely directly on this Agreement, it is of importance for the promotion of an undisturbed exercise of the individual right of complaint, because the Commission can take its provisions into account in connection with Article 25. The scope of the State's obligation under Article 25, however, is not necessarily confined to the provisions of this Agreement.

Finally, it deserves attention that neither the Convention nor the above-mentioned *European Agreement* imposes an obligation on the Contracting States of *Rechtsmittelbelehrung*, *i.e.* an obligation to inform private parties of the possibility to file an application with the Commission after they have exhausted the domestic remedies. At any rate, according to the Commission, such an obligation cannot be inferred from the words 'not to hinder in any way the effective exercise of this right' of Article 25:

> it cannot be inferred that the Convention has conferred upon the Contracting Parties an obligation to inform persons, whose proceedings before the national courts have resulted in a final decision, of their possibility of lodging Applications with the Commission in accordance with Article 25 of the Convention.[231]

Considering the text of Article 25 this interpretation is not incomprehensible. Still, it would be in keeping with the spirit of the Convention if, in appropriate cases, after the domestic remedies have been exhausted, the attention of individuals were drawn to the possibility of lodging a complaint with the Commission. After all, a State which recognises the right of complaint according to Article 25 may be expected to assure the effective exercise of this right by giving adequate publicity to the existence of the right of complaint.

11.5 The Co-Existence of the Possibility of Lodging an Individual Complaint Under the UN Covenant on Civil and Political Rights and Under the European Convention

The co-existence of two possibilities of an individual right of complaint under the UN Covenant on Civil and Political Rights and the Convention raises in particular two questions. Is an individual, when he considers that one or more of his rights and freedoms, laid down in both treaties, has been violated, allowed to choose which action to institute? And may he also bring both actions for the same matter, either simultaneously or successively?

The first question may at once be answered in the affirmative. An individual who regards himself as the victim of a violation of one of the rights and freedoms guaranteed in the Convention as well as in the UN Covenant on Civil and Political Rights, must be considered free to use the procedure which he regards as the most

---

[231] See, *e.g.*, Appl. 1877/63, *X* v. *Austria*, 22 July 1963 (not published).

favourable for his case, since neither of the two treaties prohibits this choice.[232] This freedom of choice does not apply with respect to inter-State complaints, since Article 62 provides that the Contracting Parties agree that, except by special agreement, they will not avail themselves of treaties, conventions or declarations in force between them for the purpose of submitting, by way of petition, a dispute arising out of the interpretation of application of the Convention to a means of settlement other than those provided for in the Convention.

With respect to the second question three situations may arise: (1) identical applications are lodged at the same time with both organs; (2) the applicant tries first the procedure of the UN Covenant on Civil and Political Rights and then that of the Convention; (3) the applicant applies first to the European Commission and subsequently to the Human Rights Committee.

In the first case the applicant incurs the risk of being received by neither the Commission nor the Committee. According to Article 27(1)(b) the European Commission cannot consider an application which:

> is substantially the same as a matter which has already been submitted to another procedure of international investigation or settlement and if it contains no relevant new information.[233]

On its part, Article 5(2) of the Optional Protocol of the UN Covenant on Civil and Political Rights provides:

> The Committee shall not consider any communication from an individual unless it has ascertained that: (a) the same matter is not being examined under another procedure of international investigation or settlement.

From these provisions it appears that there is a real possibility that the application may be rejected by both organs. Such a highly unsatisfactory situation may be avoided if the Commission and the Committee pursue a flexible policy on this point. They might postpone consideration so as to enable the applicant to withdraw one of the two complaints. However, the situation where two applications are lodged at precisely the same moment is likely to occur only rarely.

It is more conceivable that applications in Geneva and Strasbourg are lodged successively. If, as in the case mentioned above sub (2), the second application is lodged in Strasbourg, this leads to its being declared inadmissible under Article 27(1)(b), unless relevant new information is put forward. In the opposite case, that of sub (3), such a conclusion does not follow imperatively from the text of Article 5(2)(a) of the Protocol. This provision provides for inadmissibility of a matter which is 'being examined under another procedure'. It is thus only the fact that the matter *is being* examined elsewhere which bars its admissibility, not the fact

---

[232] See *Secretariat Memorandum prepared by the Directorate of Human Rights on the effects of the various international human rights instruments providing a mechanism for individual communications on the machinery of protection established by the European Convention on Human Rights*, H(85)3, No. 23, p. 9.

[233] On this, see *infra* pp. 112-118.

that the matter *has been* examined elsewhere. The Human Rights Committee, therefore, has actually taken the view that no complaint submitted to it is inadmissible merely on account of the fact that this case has already been examined in another procedure.[234]

It is questionable whether it is desirable that cases considered in Strasbourg may afterwards be brought up before the Committee again. An argument against this is that such a form of 'appeal' against decisions of the Strasbourg organs is contrary to the intention of the drafters of the Convention that the outcome of the procedure provided there were to be final. This intention may be inferred from Articles 26, 27, 32 and 52 of the Convention. Moreover, reasons of procedural economy may be advanced against renewed consideration of the same case by the Human Rights Committee. In general it takes a number of years before a case has passed through the Strasbourg procedure and the preceding national procedures. One may ask oneself whether after such a long procedure the case should be re-opened again.

At all events the Committee of Ministers of the Council of Europe has answered that question in the negative. In 1970 it urged those Contracting States of the Convention, which were to ratify the Optional Protocol, to attach to their ratification a declaration denying the competence of the Human Rights Committee to receive communications from individuals concerning matters which have already been or are being examined in a procedure under the European Convention, unless rights or freedoms not set forth in the European Convention are invoked in such communications.[235] Most of the Contracting States which are also parties to the Protocol, have followed up this suggestion by making a declaration or a reservation.[236] The Netherlands, however, have refrained from making such a declaration or reservation. In the opinion of the Dutch Government there are indeed some practical objections to possible double procedures about the same matter, but they constitute an insufficient argument for preventing individuals from applying to the Human Rights Committee after having done so to the European Commission. Moreover, the Dutch Government submits that the Committee and the Commission have different powers in a number of respects. Finally, the making of declarations as suggested by the Committee of Ministers might be imitated in other regional arrangements, which might be detrimental to the world-wide system for the protection of human rights.[237] For individuals subject to the jurisdiction of the Netherlands, therefore, it is possible to initiate, after the Strasbourg procedure, the procedure provided for in the Optional Protocol to the UN Covenant on Civil and Political Rights.

---

[234] See *Report of the Human Rights Committee* of 1978, General Assembly Official Records (A/33/40), p. 100.

[235] See Yearbook XIII (1970), pp. 74-76.

[236] These States are Austria, Denmark, France, Iceland, Italy, Luxembourg, Malta, Norway, Poland, Spain and Sweden.

[237] Second Chamber, Session 1975-1976, 13 932 (R 1037), Nos 1-6, p. 42.

As regards the relevant practice of the two bodies concerned the following may be said. Up to now only a few cases have been rejected by the European Commission under Article 27(1)(b) of the European Convention. The Secretariat usually prevents this by advising an applicant, who lodges a complaint already brought before the Committee, about the content of Article 27(1)(b). In a case where two members of the *Grapo* (a antifascist revolutionary group) had brought a complaint before the Commission, the Commission noted that it appeared from their letters to the Commission, that before bringing his complaint in Strasbourg, the first applicant had brought a communication to the Human Rights Committee. The second applicant had joined this individual communication after having brought his complaint before the Commission. The Commission noted that in the relevant part of their application form the applicants omitted to mention the existence of the communication in question, then pending before the Human Rights Committee. Therefore, the Commission took the view that a situation of this type was incompatible with the spirit and letter of the Convention, which seeks to avoid a plurality of international proceedings relating to the same cases. According to the Commission the application was substantially the same as the petition submitted by the applicants to the Human Rights Committee, which was still pending before that Committee and was therefore inadmissible under Article 27(1)(b).[238] The Commission also noted that a request for suspension of the proceedings before an international body (the applicants had requested the Human Rights Committee to grant such a suspension) did not have the same effect as a complete withdrawal of the application, which was the only step allowing the Commission to examine an application also brought before it.[239]

An interesting issue came up in the case of *A.N.* v. *Denmark*. Denmark had made a reservation, with reference to Article 5(2)(a) of the Optional Protocol, in respect of the competence of the Committee to consider a communication from an individual if the matter has already been considered under other procedures of international investigation. The author of the communication had already filed an application concerning the same matter with the European Commission, which had been declared inadmissible as manifestly ill-founded. On the basis of these facts but without any further argument the Committee concluded that it was not competent to consider the communication. It thus implicitly dismissed the position taken by one of its members in his individual opinion, who argued that an application that has been declared inadmissible has not, in the meaning of the Danish reservation, been 'considered' in such a way that the Human Rights Committee is precluded from it. According to this point of view, the reservation aims at preventing a review of cases but does not seek to limit the competence of the Human Rights Committee merely on the ground that the rights of the UN Covenant on Civil and Political Rights allegedly violated may also be covered by

---

[238] Appl. 17512/90, *Calcerrada Fornielles and Cabeza Mato* v. *Spain*, D&R 73 (1992), p. 214 (223-224).

[239] *Ibidem*, p. 224.

the European Convention and its procedural requirements since it concerns a separate and independent international instrument.[240]

---

[240] *Report of the Human Rights Committee* of 1982, General Assembly Official Records (A/37/40), p. 213, and the individual opinion of the East German expert, Mr Graefrath, appended to this decision, p. 214. See also Communication No. 168/1984, *Report of the Human Rights Committee* of 1985, General Assembly Official Records (A/40/40), p. 235.

Chapter II

Interpretation and Application of the Rights and Freedoms of the Convention in the Strasbourg Case-Law: General Principles and Concepts

1 INTRODUCTION

The present chapter discusses some general principles which have a prominent place in the Commission's and the Court's interpretation and application of the Convention provisions and on which these organs rely to underpin their decision-making in concrete cases. A common feature of these principles is that their relevance is not confined to one or more specific provisions of the Convention; they emerge from, and are referred to in the case-law on a variety of provisions. Therefore, additional reference to these principles is made throughout other chapters of this book to illustrate their immediate significance for the Convention provision concerned.

With respect to the role of these general principles in the Convention case-law, a distinction may be made between two levels or aspects of the decision-making process of the Strasbourg organs. The first aspect is that of interpretation of the Convention provision invoked or deemed relevant to the case at hand. The second aspect is closely linked to the first but is of a less abstract nature. It concerns the application of the Convention provision – thus interpreted – to the facts of the case, in particular in order to answer the question of whether or not that provision has been violated.

These two aspects emerge in various forms at different stages of the Convention procedure. For example, at the admissibility stage before the Commission, the question of whether the complaint must be rejected as inadmissible for being 'manifestly ill-founded' within the meaning of Article 27(2) of the Convention requires both an interpretation, or at least an implicit understanding, of the Convention provision invoked by the applicant, and an assessment of whether there is an appearance of a violation of that provision, having regard to the facts of the case. This is true also where the Commission, after having declared a case admissible, is called upon to give an opinion as to whether the facts found disclose a breach of the State's obligations under the Convention (Article 31(1)). Finally, the two aspects appear in the decision-making by the Court where this body gives a final judgment on the merits of a case, deciding whether or not a Convention provision has been violated.

No attempt shall be made in the following to present an exhaustive overview of the general principles which play a role in the case-law. Emphasis is laid on principles particular to the Strasbourg case-law which do not, or not in the same form or with the same degree of prominence, figure in the jurisprudence of domestic courts. The purpose is merely to offer some insight into the concepts and tools which the Court and the Commission use for interpreting and applying the Convention, thus allowing for a better understanding of these organs' reasoning in concrete judgments, decisions and reports.

2 INTERPRETATION OF THE CONVENTION

2.1 Introduction

Since the Convention is an international treaty, the rules of international law for the interpretation of treaties apply. Thus, the Court stated in the *Golder* judgment that it should be guided by Articles 31-33 of the 1969 Vienna Convention on the Law of Treaties. Neither the fact that the Vienna Convention had not yet entered into force at the time of the *Golder* judgment, nor the non-retroactivity of that Convention (*cf.* Article 4) made any difference, since the Court considered that Articles 31-33 enunciate generally accepted principles of international law.[1]
    The principal rule for treaty interpretation is laid down in Article 31(1) of the Vienna Convention: a treaty shall be interpreted in good faith in accordance with the ordinary meaning to be given to the terms of the treaty in their context and in the light of its object and purpose. Article 31 further provides indications of what is the 'context' of a treaty and states that subsequent agreements and practice are also to be taken into account, as are any applicable relevant rules of international law. According to Article 31(4) a special meaning is to be given to treaty terms if it is established that the parties so intended.
    Some supplementary means of interpretation to which recourse may be had are mentioned in Article 32 (this includes recourse to the preparatory work of the treaty). As the European Convention has been authenticated in two languages (English and French), the provisions of Article 33 of the Vienna Convention are also relevant. In case of a difference of meaning between the two authentic texts, the meaning which best reconciles the texts, having regard to the object and purpose of the treaty, is to be adopted (Article 33(4)).
    The rules of the Vienna Convention do not provide clear-cut solutions to all problems of treaty interpretation. In fact, those rules themselves are not unequivocal. Depending on many factors of which the court's perception of its own role is perhaps the most important one, a court may be inclined towards an interpretation which is focused on the 'ordinary meaning' of the treaty terms or, conversely, towards an 'object and purpose'-oriented interpretation.
    There is a further reason why the rules of the Vienna Convention, while certainly relevant as a starting point, cannot be the *alpha* and *omega* of the Court's interpretation of the Convention. The Court has pointed to a number of special features of the Convention system to justify recourse to certain principles for its interpretation. As early as in 1968, the Court set held:

---

[1] Judgment of 21 February 1975, A.18, p. 14.

Given that it is a law-making treaty, it is also necessary to seek the interpretation that is most appropriate to realise the aim and achieve the object of the treaty, not that which would restrict to the greatest possible degree the obligations undertaken by the Parties.[2]

Thus, the Court distinguishes the Convention from other types of treaties which are more in the nature of contracts between the parties:

> Unlike international treaties of the classic kind, the Convention comprises more than mere reciprocal engagements between contracting States. It creates, over and above a network of mutual, bilateral undertakings, objective obligations which, in the words of the Preamble, benefit from a 'collective enforcement'. By virtue of Article 24, the Convention allows Contracting States to require the observance of those obligations without having to justify an interest deriving, for example, from the fact that a measure they complain of has prejudiced one of their own nationals.[3]

The Commission and the Court have gone even further in stressing the special character of the Convention. When assessing the validity of some of the restrictions which were attached to Turkey's declaration under Article 25 (recognising the competence of the Commission to receive individual applications), both the Commission and the Court rejected application by analogy of the State practice under Article 36(3) of the Statute of the International Court of Justice. Whereas declarations under this clause were considered mere reciprocal agreements between Contracting States, the Convention's special character as 'a constitutional instrument of European public order' was invoked as a main argument for declaring invalid the restrictions at issue.[4]

It is not surprising, then, that this special character of the Convention is reflected in the Court's approach to questions of interpretation. In the *Soering* judgment, the Court held:

> In interpreting the Convention regard must be had to its special character as a treaty for the collective enforcement of human rights and fundamental freedoms (...). Thus, the object and purpose of the Convention as an instrument for the protection of individual human beings require that its provisions be interpreted and applied so as to make its safeguards practical and effective (...). In addition, any interpretation of the rights and freedoms guaranteed must be consistent with the 'general spirit of the Convention, an instrument designed to maintain and promote the ideals and values of a democratic society' (see the *Kjeldsen, Busk Madsen and Pedersen* judgment of 7 December 1976, Series A no. 23, p. 27, § 53).[5]

The emphasis placed on object and purpose of the Convention, a treaty for the protection of human rights, has led the Court, on many occasions, to adopt a fairly

---

[2] Judgment of 27 June 1968, *Wemhoff*, A.7, p. 23.

[3] Judgment of 18 January 1978, *Ireland* v. *the United Kingdom*, A.25, p. 90.

[4] Appls 15299/89, 15300/89 and 15318/89, *Chrysostomos, Papachrysostomou and Loizidou* v. *Turkey*, D&R 68 (1991), p. 216 (242); judgment of 23 March 1995, *Loizidou (Preliminary objections)*, A.310, pp. 27 and 30. The Court not only declared invalid the territorial restrictions attached to Turkey's declaration under Art. 25, but also those attached to its declaration under Art. 46 of the Convention.

[5] Judgment of 7 July 1989, A.161, p. 34.

progressive or activist approach. This is illustrated by several principles which play a key role in constructing the Convention.

2.2 The Effectiveness Principle

The notion that the Convention is intended to guarantee not rights that are theoretical or illusory but rights that are practical and effective is, explicitly or implicitly, present in many judgments of the Court. This means, first of all, that the Court is inclined to look beyond appearances and formalities, and to focus on the realities of the position of the individual. Thus, in the *Airey* Case, the Court considered whether the applicant had had an effective right of access to the courts for obtaining a separation from her husband. The applicant claimed that she could not be represented by a lawyer before the Irish courts since she had insufficient means and no legal aid system was available in Ireland for civil cases. The Government argued that the applicant could have taken her case to court without the assistance of a lawyer, but the Court rejected this reasoning, finding it not realistic to assume that in litigations of this kind the applicant could effectively conduct her own case. Therefore, although Article 6 was not held to guarantee a right of free legal aid for every dispute relating to a 'civil right', the Court accepted that this provision may sometimes compel the State to provide for the assistance of a lawyer when such assistance is indispensable for an effective access to court, *e.g.* on account of the complexity of the procedure or of the case.[6]

This example shows that the principle of effectiveness or *effet utile* may lead the Court to adopt an extensive interpretation of the scope and content of the rights and freedoms of the Convention. In particular, the principle has been relied on for holding that a Convention provision may contain positive obligations for the Parties even where this does not appear immediately from the text of the provision.

In its judgment in the *Marckx* Case, the Court adopted an extensive interpretation of the terms 'right to respect for family life' in Article 8(1). Although the object of this provision was originally intended to be only that of protecting the individual against arbitrary interference by public authorities, the Court has accorded it a more comprehensive meaning: in addition to this negative undertaking, there may be positive obligations on the part of Contracting States inherent in an effective respect for family life. The Court explained that this means, *inter alia*, that when the State enacts in its domestic legal system a regime applicable to certain family ties (such as those between an unmarried mother and her child), it must do so in a manner calculated to allow those concerned to lead a normal family life. This implies in particular the existence of safeguards in domestic law which enable the child's integration in the family from the moment of its birth.[7]

---

[6] Judgment of 9 October 1979, A.32, p. 13 and pp. 15-16.
[7] Judgment of 13 June 1979, A.31, p. 15.

There is an obvious link between the recognition of certain positive obligations for the State and the principle that the Convention rights are intended to be practical and effective. This is particularly so where a positive obligation imposes a duty on the State to protect an individual's rights and freedoms against infringements by private parties.[8] In the Case of *X and Y* v. *the Netherlands*, which also concerned Article 8, the Court accepted the second applicant's argument that the lacuna in domestic law which made it impossible for her, as a mentally handicapped person, to initiate criminal proceedings against the person who had raped her, amounted to a violation of her right to an effective respect for her private life. The Court reiterated its view that there may be positive obligations inherent in an effective respect for private or family life and added:

> These obligations may even involve the adoption of measures designed to secure respect for private life even in the sphere of the relations of individuals between themselves.[9]

The Court, finding that civil law protection alone was insufficient in case of the wrongdoing of the kind inflicted on the applicant, held that effective deterrence is essential in this area and that it can be achieved only by criminal-law provisions. As there was no such provision in Dutch criminal law which provided the applicant with practical and effective protection, there was a failure by the State to meet its obligation to secure effective respect for her private life.[10]

Similarly, the Court accepted that genuine, effective freedom of assembly as guaranteed by Article 11, cannot be reduced to a mere duty of the State not to interfere with a demonstration. Such an approach solely based on the concept of abstention would not be compatible with the object and purpose of Article 11. Participants in an demonstration must be able to hold it without having to fear that they will be subjected to physical violence by other groups which oppose their point of view. It is the duty of the State to take reasonable and appropriate measures to enable lawful demonstrations to proceed peacefully.[11]

As a corollary to extensive interpretation of the terms of the Convention which define the scope of the rights and freedoms, the principle that exceptions to the rights guaranteed must be narrowly interpreted has been embraced in several judgments. The Court did so with respect to, for example, the restriction clauses in Articles 8 and 10[12] and the exceptions listed in Article 5(1).[13]

---

[8] *Cf.* the discussion of 'indirect *Drittwirkung*' in Chapter I, section 6 *supra*.

[9] Judgment of 26 March 1985, A.91, p. 11.

[10] *Ibidem*, pp. 13 and 14.

[11] Judgment of 21 June 1988, *Plattform 'Ärzte für das Leben'*, A.139, p. 12. For a positive obligation flowing from the effective protection of life (Art. 2(1)), see judgment of 27 September 1995 in the case of *McCann and Others*, A.324, p. 44 (obligation to investigate killings resulting from use of force by State agents).

[12] See, *e.g.*, judgment of 6 September 1978, *Klass and Others*, A.28, p. 21; judgment of 26 April 1979, *Sunday Times (I)*, A.30, p. 40; judgment of 25 March 1985, *Barthold*, A.90, p. 21; judgment of 26 November 1991, *The Observer and Guardian*, A.216, p. 29; judgment of 19 December 1994, *Vereinigung Demokratischer Soldaten Österreichs and Gubi*, A.302, p. 17.

Quite distinct from this tendency to ensure optimal effectiveness of the rights and freedoms of the Convention by their extensive interpretation, the Commission and the Court have also shown concern for the effectiveness of the protection mechanism established by the Convention. In this area, the effectiveness principle has been relied on for adopting a flexible interpretation of the 'victim' requirement of Article 25 so as to ensure access to the Commission even where, in special cases, the applicant is unable to point to a concrete measure which has affected him. The Court indicated that the efficiency of the Convention's enforcement machinery would be materially weakened if, due to the secrecy of alleged measures, no possibility of access were available.[14]

Likewise, although it is not normally for the Court to pronounce on the existence of potential violations of the Convention, the effectiveness of the Convention requires a departure from this approach in extradition or expulsion cases where the applicant faces a real risk of being subjected to treatment or punishment contrary to Article 3 in the receiving country. This entails a broad view of State responsibility under the Convention.[15]

As a final example, mention can be made of the judgment in the *Cruz Varas* Case. The Court considered that the State obligation not to hinder the effective exercise of the right of individual application (Article 25(1), last sentence) conferred upon an applicant a procedural right distinguishable from the substantive rights of Section I of the Convention. The Court, referring to the effectiveness principle, held that it flowed from the very essence of this procedural right that individuals must be able to complain of alleged infringements of it in Convention proceedings.[16]

---

[13] *Cf.* judgment of 6 November 1980, *Guzzardi*, A.39, p. 36.

[14] Judgment of 6 September 1978, *Klass and Others*, A.28, p. 18. For another example of a liberal approach to the 'victim' requirement, based on the effectiveness principle, see Appl. 14807/89 *Agrotexim* et al. v. *Greece*, D&R 72 (1992), p. 148 (156). See, however, the more restrictive view taken by the Court in this case: judgment of 24 October 1995, A.330-A, pp. 22-24.

[15] Judgment of 7 July 1989, *Soering*, A.161, p. 35 (extradition); judgment of 20 March 1991, *Cruz Varas*, A.201, p. 21 (expulsion). The same reasoning might apply, in exceptional cases, to extradition in circumstances where the individual has suffered or risks suffering a flagrant denial of a fair trial in the requesting country (*cf.* the *Soering* judgment, *ibidem*, p. 45 or where a Contracting State allows execution on its territory of a sentence handed down in third States or territories which is the result of a flagrant denial of justice: judgment of 26 June 1992, *Drozd and Janousek* v. *France and Italy*, A.240, p. 34.

[16] Judgment of 20 March 1991, A.201, p. 36. The possibility of the Court finding a violation materialised in the judgment of 16 September 1996, *Akdivar and Others* v. *Turkey*, Reports 1996-IV, Vol. 15, paras 103-106. The *Cruz Varas* Case also offers an interesting example of the limits of the application of the effectiveness principle as a tool for interpreting the Convention. See *infra* section 2.4.

2.3 The Concept of Autonomous Meaning

Another characteristic of the interpretation of the Convention is the fact that some of the terms used in this treaty are considered to have a special, autonomous meaning, which is independent from, and does not necessarily correspond to, the meaning which identical or similar terms may have in the domestic law of the Contracting States. Such an autonomous interpretation may lead to results which depart from the 'ordinary meaning to be given to the terms of the treaty' prescribed by the Vienna Convention.

A very prominent example can be found in the case-law concerning the right to a court and the fair trial guarantees embedded in Article 6(1) of the Convention. These apply to 'the determination of (...) civil rights and obligations or of any criminal charge.' In a series of judgments, the Court has held that the classification, in the national legal order, of an offence as 'disciplinary' or that of a dispute as belonging to the sphere of 'administrative law', cannot be decisive for the purposes of the Convention. In the *Engel and Others* Case, which concerned disciplinary sanctions against soldiers, the Court explained the reasons for giving an autonomous meaning to such notions:

> If the Contracting States were able at their discretion to classify an offence as disciplinary instead of criminal (...), the operation of the fundamental clauses of Articles 6 and 7 would be subordinated to their sovereign will. A latitude extending thus far might lead to results incompatible with the purpose and object of the Convention.[17]

Even where the text of the Convention refers back to national law (as, for example, in the case of the expression 'in accordance with the law' in Article 8(2) or the words 'lawful arrest or detention' in several provisions of Article 5(1)), the Court does not regard this as a complete and exclusive referral to national legal requirements. In particular, the rule of law demands that national legal standards which provide the basis for restricting rights and freedoms meet certain quality requirements, such as accessibility and foreseeability of the law, and lack of arbitrariness.[18] This allows the Commission and the Court to exercise a degree of control over the content of national legal standards.

2.4 Evolutive Interpretation

The standards of the Convention are not regarded as static, but as reflective of social changes. This evolutive approach towards interpretation of the Convention implies that the Commission and the Court take into account contemporary realities and attitudes, not the situation prevailing at the time of the drafting of the

---

[17] Judgment of 8 June 1976, A.22, p. 34. This is tantamount to saying that the result would be to render Arts 6 and 7 ineffective. The concept of autonomous notions may thus be seen as an expression of the effectiveness principle discussed in the preceding section.

[18] For a more detailed discussion of this question, see the relevant sections in Chapters VII and VIII below.

Convention in 1949-1950. This obviously reduces the relevance of the *travaux préparatoires* of the Convention as a supplementary source of interpretation.

In the *Tyrer* Case, the question arose whether judicial corporal punishment of juvenile offenders on the Isle of Man amounted to degrading punishment within the meaning of Article 3. The Court found that this was so after having implied that what was regarded as acceptable in 1950 was not necessarily acceptable in 1978 (the year of the judgment):

> the Convention is a living instrument which (...) must be interpreted in the light of present-day conditions. In the case now before it the Court cannot but be influenced by the developments and commonly accepted standards in the penal policy of the member States of the Council of Europe in this field.[19]

The principle of evolutive interpretation also played a key role in the *Marckx* judgment. The Court admitted that the distinction between the legitimate and the illegitimate family was regarded as permissible and normal in many European countries at the time the Convention was drafted but recalled that this treaty must be interpreted in the light of present-day conditions. The Court, pointing to developments in the domestic law of the great majority of Council of Europe Member States as well as to two other treaties adopted after the Convention, found that there was a clear measure of common ground amongst modern societies that there should be equality between legitimate and illegitimate children as concerns the manner of establishing, and the extent of, their family relationships, as well as their patrimonial rights.[20]

This judgment shows that evolutive interpretation is closely linked to a search for common European standards on the basis of domestic law and practice in the Member States of the Council of Europe, of other international or European instruments, and of the case-law of the Court itself.[21] Clearly, the assessment as to whether a clear European 'trend' or 'common ground' exists or not (yet), may be a very difficult one to make. Whilst the Court had no hesitation in finding that compulsory membership of a professional association constituted an interference with a right to (negative) freedom of association guaranteed by Article 11(1), having regard to 'a growing measure of common ground' in this area and to the principle of evolutive interpretation, several cases concerning the legal position of transsexuals gave rise to different views within the Court as to the existence of an emerging European standard in this field.[22]

---

[19] Judgment of 25 April 1978, A.26, p. 15.

[20] Judgment of 13 June 1979, A.31, pp. 19, 22 and 25. Similarly with respect to the distinction between married and unmarried mothers: *ibidem*, pp. 27 and 28.

[21] The possibility that the Court's own judgments may set in motion (further) European legal developments which in turn influence later rulings by the Court was recognised in the *Salesi* judgment of 26 February 1993, A.257-E, p. 59.

[22] See, with respect to Art. 11, the judgment of 30 June 1993, *Sigurjónsson*, A.264, p. 15 and, on the position of transsexuals, the judgment of 17 October 1986, *Rees*, A.106, p. 18; judgment of 27 September 1990, *Cossey*, A.184, pp. 16 and 18; judgment of 25 March 1992, *B* v. *France*, A.232-C, p. 49, as well as the various dissenting opinions in these three cases.

On a more abstract level, the principle of evolutive interpretation begs the question where treaty interpretation ends and where treaty amendment begins. On this topic, opinions are bound to differ, also within the Court itself, but there seems to be consensus that there are limits to the use of this technique of interpretation. The text of the Convention and its Protocols sets limits on any process of interpretation, even though the case-law is not consistent on where the borderline is exactly to be drawn.

In the *Soering* judgment, the Court examined the extent to which subsequent practice of the States Parties (*cf.* Article 31(3)(b) of the Vienna Convention) may warrant the adoption of a particular interpretation which departs from the text of the Convention. The question was whether, in view of a general practice of abolition of the death penalty of Contracting States, such a penalty could be regarded as inhuman or degrading punishment, prohibited by Article 3, notwithstanding the explicit wording of Article 2(1) permitting the intentional deprivation of life in the execution of a court sentence. The Court held that such a subsequent practice in the form of a generalised abolition of capital punishment could be taken as establishing the agreement of States Parties to abrogate the exception provided for under Article 2(1) and hence to remove a textual limit on its scope in favour of an evolutive interpretation of Article 3. Nevertheless, in view of the fact that Protocol No. 6 expressly provides for abolition of the death penalty in time of peace, the Court found that the Contracting Parties had intended to adopt the normal method of amendment of the text in order to introduce a new obligation. The latter had to supersede an evolutive interpretation of Article 3 as generally prohibiting the death penalty.[23]

The *Cruz Varas* judgment, however, shows a potentially different impact of subsequent practice on the interpretation of the Convention. The case raised the question of whether a failure by a State to comply with a request by the Commission under Rule 36 of its Rules of Procedure amounted to a breach of the State's obligation under Article 25(1) of the Convention not to hinder the effective exercise of the right of petition. The Commission had requested the Swedish Government not to expel the applicants. Rule 36 provides that the Commission 'may indicate to the parties any interim measure the adoption of which seems desirable in the interests of the parties or the proper conduct of the proceedings before it.' The Court noted that the Convention, unlike other international treaties, does not contain a specific provision on interim measures. In addition, the *travaux préparatoires* of the Convention are silent on this matter. Furthermore, Rule 36, which is an internal rule of procedure drawn up by the Commission, cannot in itself give rise to a binding obligation on the States Parties. Nor can, in the absence of a specific Convention provision empowering the Commission to order interim measures, an obligation to comply with Rule 36 indications be derived directly from the last sentence of Article 25(1) of the Convention. Nevertheless, the Court accepted that the practice of the Contracting States in this area showed

---

[23] Judgment of 7 July 1989, A.161, pp. 40-41.

that there had been almost total compliance with Rule 36 indications and, therefore, that it had to determine whether this amounted to subsequent practice warranting a 'new' interpretation of Article 25(1).[24]

The Court held that subsequent practice could be taken as establishing the agreement of Contracting States regarding the interpretation of a Convention provision, but not to create new rights and obligations which were not included in the Convention at the outset.[25] This reasoning is somewhat ambiguous, for a 'new' interpretation of the Convention is bound to create 'new rights and obligations'. Moreover, it is difficult to reconcile with the view expressed in the *Soering* judgment that subsequent practice may lead to the abrogation of the exception provided for under Article 2(1) of the Convention.[26]

The difficulty in drawing the line between evolutive interpretation and judicial 'revision' of the Convention is also illustrated by differences in the importance which the Court attaches, in its interpretation of the Convention, to the existence of an additional Protocol to the Convention. As was noted above, the *Soering* judgment relied on the existence of Protocol No. 6 in order to reject a wide, evolutive, interpretation of Article 3 of the Convention. In other cases, conversely, the Court has pointed to standard clauses contained in such Protocols according to which the substantive provisions of the Protocol are to be regarded as an addition to the Convention. Consequently, such additional provisions could not, in the Court's view, replace or reduce in scope the original Convention provision and their existence was not seen as an obstacle to the interpretative development of the original provision.[27]

2.5 The Proportionality Principle

The proportionality principle, which implies the need to strike a proper balance between various competing interests, permeates the whole interpretation of the Convention. In many cases, some deviation from the fundamental freedoms guaranteed will be considered acceptable under the Convention, provided, *inter alia*, that the proportionality principle is observed. The principle requires, in particular, that the extent of such deviation is not excessive in relation to the legitimate needs and interests which have occasioned it. The 'search for a fair balance between the demands of the community and the requirements of the

---

[24] Judgment of 20 March 1991, A.201, pp. 34-36.

[25] *Ibidem*, p. 36.

[26] It should be added, however, that the Court also observed that various recommendations adopted within the Council of Europe showed that the practice of compliance with Rule 36 indications cannot have been based on the belief that these indications gave rise to a binding obligation.

[27] See the judgment of 26 May 1988, *Ekbatani*, A.134, pp. 12-13 and the judgment of 22 February 1994, *Burghartz*, A.280-B, p. 28.

individual's fundamental rights' is, in the words of the Court, 'inherent' in the Convention system.[28]

The manifestations of this principle in the case-law concerning various provisions of the Convention are manifold. It is justified to say that proportionality has acquired the status of general principle in the Convention system.

Key areas in which this principle is applied are the restriction clauses in the second paragraphs of Articles 8-11 (restrictive measures must be 'necessary in a democratic society'), the non-discrimination guarantee of Article 14 and the protection of property rights under Article 1 of Protocol No. 1.

Some other areas where the Court and the Commission apply a proportionality test are Article 15 (are emergency measures 'strictly required by the exigencies of the situation'?),[29] and the so-called inherent or implied limitations.[30] Furthermore, the Court has accepted that, in determining whether or not, in a specific case, a positive obligation exists under a Convention provision, it must have regard to the fair balance to be struck between the general interest of the community and the interests of the individual.[31]

The proportionality test has not been applied in a uniform manner up until now: the Court uses different variants for different contexts. Thus, while the test is usually applied in a strict manner in the context of the 'necessary in a democratic society' requirement (is the restrictive measure proportionate to the legitimate aim pursued? is there a 'pressing social need' for the restriction and are the reasons given for it 'relevant and sufficient'?),[32] a much more flexible version is applied for examining restrictions on property rights (Article 1 of Protocol No. 1). There, the proportionality principle takes the form of the requirement that there be a 'reasonable relationship of proportionality between the means employed and the aim sought to be realised' or a 'fair balance' between the general and the individual interests at stake.[33] The first criterion is also used in the context of Article 14 for establishing whether there has been discrimination contrary to this provision.[34] As noted above, the 'fair balance' test also appears in the context of

---

[28] See, e.g., the judgment of 29 November 1988, *Brogan and Others*, A.145-B, p. 27; judgment of 7 July 1989, *Soering*, A.161, p. 35.

[29] Judgment of 18 January 1978, *Ireland* v. *the United Kingdom*, A.25, pp. 78, 80 and 83 in *fine*.

[30] On implied or inherent limitations, see Chapter VIII, section 8.2 *infra*. See, for example, as concerns limitations to the right of access to a court under Art. 6(1), the judgment of 28 May 1985, *Ashingdane*, A.93, pp. 24-26.

[31] See the judgment of 17 October 1986, *Rees*, A.106, pp. 14-15.

[32] The test is even stricter in the context of Art. 2(2) of the Convention: deprivation of life as a result of use of force 'which is no more than absolutely necessary'. See the judgment of 27 September 1995, *McCann and Others*, A.324, p. 52.

[33] See judgment of 23 September 1982, *Sporrong and Lönnroth*, A.52, p. 26 (first sentence of para. 1 of Art. 1); judgment of 21 February 1986, *James and Others*, A.98, pp. 32, 35, 36 and 37 (second sentence of para. 1 of Art. 1), and the judgment of 24 October 1986, *AGOSI*, A.108, p. 18 (para. 2 of Art. 1).

[34] See the judgment of 28 October 1987, *Inze*, A.126, p. 18.

positive obligations.[35] On the other hand, there is no reason for any proportionality test or fair balance test if an absolute right or freedom is at stake.[36]

There exists a close link between these various kinds of proportionality tests and the *margin of appreciation* which is afforded to national authorities by the Strasbourg organs. This concept is discussed in the next section.

3 THE MARGIN OF APPRECIATION[37]

3.1 Introduction

When reviewing cases under the Convention, the Commission and the Court proceed on the basis of a certain understanding of their role and responsibilities within the framework of the Convention system in relation to those of the Contracting States. The text of the Convention offers some guidelines for such an understanding, but they are no more than a starting point. According to Article 1, it is for the Contracting Parties to 'secure to everyone within their jurisdiction the rights and freedoms defined in Section I of this Convention.' The Commission and the Court have been set up 'to ensure the observance of the engagements undertaken by the High Contracting Parties' (Article 19). The respective roles, within the Convention system, of the States on the one hand and the Strasbourg organs on the other can thus be summarised as follows: the Contracting States are to observe the obligations they have undertaken, while the Commission and the Court are charged with supervising compliance with the obligations on the part of the Contracting States. Obviously, this does not yet answer the question of how exactly, given these respective roles, the Commission and the Court should exercise their supervisory powers. In order to understand the way in which these organs perceive their role in the Convention system, one must turn to their case-law.

In section 1 of this Chapter, a distinction was made between interpretation and application of the Convention. By and large, as discussed in section 2 above, the Strasbourg organs have affirmed that they have prime responsibility for interpreting the provisions of the Convention. Article 46 of the Convention expressly provides that the Court's jurisdiction extends to all cases concerning the interpretation of the Convention. The Court has affirmed that its judgments not

---

[35] See on positive obligations generally Chapter II, section 2.2 *supra*.

[36] Thus, in relation to Art. 3 of the Convention, the Court in its judgment of 15 November 1996, *Chahal*, Reports 1996-V, Vol. 22, para. 80.

[37] On this concept, see generally R.St.J. Macdonald, 'The Margin of Appreciation in the Jurisprudence of the European Court of Human Rights', in: *Collected Courses of the Academy of European Law*, Vol. I, book 2, Dordrecht, 1992, pp. 95-161; J.G.C. Schokkenbroek, *Toetsing aan de vrijheidsrechten van het EVRM* [Judicial Control of Restrictions on the Fundamental Freedoms of the ECHR, A Study of Strasbourg and Netherlands Case-Law], Zwolle, 1996, pp. 13-241 and 491-520 (English summary at pp. 521-536).

only serve to decide the cases brought before it but, more generally, 'to elucidate, safeguard and develop the rules instituted by the Convention, thereby contributing to the observance by the States of [their] engagements.'[38]

The situation is somewhat different as concerns the application of the Convention in concrete cases, that is: assessing the merits of a complaint alleging a violation of one of its provisions. Although Article 46 also refers to cases concerning the *application* of the Convention, the Court and the Commission usually adopt a more cautious attitude when it comes to determining whether, in a given case, there has been a violation of the Convention. For quite a few provisions guaranteeing rights and freedoms, the Strasbourg organs have recognised that a certain measure of discretion, a margin of appreciation, must normally be left to the States.

The rationale for allowing such a margin of appreciation was explained by the Court in its judgment in the *Handyside* Case. In this case, the Court had to examine whether the applicant's conviction – he had intended to disseminate a publication which was considered obscene by the English courts – and the confiscation of copies of the publication were restrictions on his freedom of expression which were 'necessary in a democratic society' within the meaning of Article 10(2). The case prompted the Court to formulate its views on the nature of its role in reviewing the 'necessity' of restrictions, in particular where restrictions aim at the 'protection of morals':

> The Court points out that the machinery of protection established by the Convention is subsidiary to the national systems safeguarding human rights (...). The Convention leaves to each Contracting State, in the first place, the task of securing the rights and liberties it enshrines. The institutions created by it make their own contribution to this task but they become involved only through contentious proceedings and once all domestic remedies have been exhausted (Article 26). These observations apply, notably, to Article 10 § 2. In particular, it is not possible to find in the domestic law of the various Contracting States a uniform European conception of morals. The view taken by their respective laws of the requirements of morals varies from time to time and from place to place, especially in our era which is characterised by a rapid and far-reaching evolution of opinions on the subject. By reason of their direct and continuous contact with the vital forces of their countries, State authorities are in principle in a better position than the international judge to give an opinion on the exact content of these requirements as well as on the 'necessity' of a 'restriction' or 'penalty' intended to meet them.[39]

After having interpreted the term 'necessary' as implying the existence of a 'pressing social need' and noting that it is for the national authorities to make the initial assessment of the reality of this pressing social need, the Court concluded:

> Consequently, Article 10 § 2 leaves to the Contracting States a margin of appreciation. This margin is given both to the domestic legislator ('prescribed by law') and to the bodies, judicial amongst others, that are called upon to interpret and apply the laws in force (...). Nevertheless, Article 10 § 2 does not give the Contracting States a unlimited

---

[38] Judgment of 18 January 1978, *Ireland* v. *the United Kingdom*, A.25, p. 62.
[39] Judgment of 7 December 1976, A.24, p. 22.

power of appreciation. The Court which, with the Commission, is responsible for ensuring the observance of those States' engagements (Article 19), is empowered to give the final ruling on whether a 'restriction' or 'penalty' is reconcilable with freedom of expression as protected by Article 10. The domestic margin of appreciation thus goes hand in hand with a European supervision. Such supervision concerns both the aim of the measure challenged and its 'necessity'; it covers not only the basic legislation but also the decision applying it, even one given by an independent court.[40]

3.2 Field of Application of the Doctrine

The 'margin of appreciation' doctrine is rooted in national case-law concerning judicial review of governmental action. The application of the doctrine may also make sense within the framework of the Convention. Both in the national and the European context, doctrines of judicial review may legitimately reflect the overall distribution of powers within a constitutional framework. In principle, the need to respect another authority's competence and special responsibilities may prompt a court to allow that authority a certain margin of appreciation. However, it remains to be seen in what categories of cases or types of questions such a margin of appreciation is granted by the Court (the scope of application of the doctrine).

The doctrine was first applied in the case of *Greece* v. *the United Kingdom*. The Commission showed itself prepared, in the case of derogation from the Convention under Article 15, to grant the State concerned 'a certain measure of discretion in assessing the extent strictly required by the exigencies of the situation.'[41] In the *Lawless* Case the Commission left the respondent State a rather wide discretion in connection with Article 15. Its President argued this as follows before the Court:

> The concept behind this doctrine is that Article 15 has to be read in the context of the rather special subject-matter with which it deals; namely the responsibilities of a government for maintaining law and order in times of war or public emergency threatening the life of the nation. The concept of the margin of appreciation is that a government's discharge of these responsibilities is essentially a delicate problem of appreciating complex factors and of balancing conflicting considerations of the public interest; and that, once the Commission or the Court is satisfied that the Government's appreciation is at least on the margin of the powers conferred by Article 15, then the interest which the public itself has in effective government and in the maintenance of order justifies and requires a decision in favour of the legality of the Government's appreciation.[42]

The Commission's conception of the rationale of the 'margin of appreciation', as quoted above, creates the impression that application of this doctrine was considered justified by the Commission only on the ground of the special situations to which Article 15 relates. However, both the Commission and the Court have gradually also applied the doctrine in connection with other articles of the Convention. The case-law shows examples particularly with respect to the

---

[40] *Ibidem*, pp. 22-23.
[41] Appl. 176/56, Yearbook II (1958-1959), p. 174 (176).
[42] Report of 19 December 1959, B.1 (1961), p. 408.

restrictions contained in Articles 8-11. In actual fact, however, the doctrine has been applied to most of the Convention's other rights and freedoms as well. As has been observed by Macdonald: 'In theory there is no limit to the articles of the Convention to which the margin of appreciation could be applied, for the Court has never imposed a limit.'[43] Nevertheless, it remains to be seen whether the case-law has set certain boundaries to the field of application of the margin of appreciation. Despite the rather long period of time during which the Court and the Commission have now applied the doctrine it is still very difficult to define in any precise way the conditions of its application because, although the doctrine is now well established in the Strasbourg case-law, 'its exact ambit and role are far from being fully developed.'[44] With this *caveat* in mind the following general principles may nevertheless be discerned as concerns the field of application of the doctrine.

In the first place, it may be concluded from the case-law that the margin of appreciation can come into play whenever a case raises a Convention issue that requires a balancing of interests, that is: where the Court has to determine the case by weighing up, on the one hand, the interests of the applicant and, on the other, the general interest or interests of other individuals which may be at stake. In principle, the margin of appreciation is relevant to the (numerous) elements of the Convention in respect of which a proportionality test is applied.[45] Reference can be made to the section dealing with the proportionality principle (see *supra*).

Secondly, the Court has recognised the relevance of the margin of appreciation doctrine to certain vague terms and expressions which appear in various Convention provisions. Examples are the expression 'public emergency threatening the life of the nation' in Article 15(1), the term 'persons of unsound mind' in Article 5(1)(e), the expressions 'in the public interest' and 'in accordance with the general interest' contained in Article 1 of Protocol No. 1, the notion 'respect' (for family or private life) in Article 8(1) and the terms 'for the protection of (...) morals' in Article 10(2) and other restriction clauses.[46]

In short, the margin of appreciation may come into play whenever the review of a case under the Convention requires the Court to make assessments (*appréciations*) of the weight of the various interests at stake or of the seriousness of a particular situation, especially where the national authorities, 'by reason of

[43] R.St.J. Macdonald, 'The Margin of Appreciation in the Jurisprudence of the European Court of Human Rights', in: *International Law at the time of its Codification, Essays in honour of Judge Roberto Ago*, Milan, 1987, pp. 187-208 (192).

[44] *Ibidem*, p. 207.

[45] An exception must be made for the strict proportionality test under Art. 2(2) of the Convention: see the observations *infra* on Arts 2 and 3 of the Convention.

[46] See, respectively, judgment of 26 May 1993, *Brannigan and McBride*, A.258-B, p. 49; judgment of 23 February 1984, *Luberti*, A.75, p. 12; judgment of 21 February 1986, *James and Others*, A.98, p. 32; judgment of 19 December 1989, *Mellacher and Others*, A.169, p. 25; judgment of 27 September 1990, *Cossey*, A.184, pp. 15-16; judgment of 7 December 1976, *Handyside*, A.24, p. 22 (quoted above in the introductory part of this section).

their direct and continuous contact with the vital forces of their countries', are in a better position than the European Court to make the assessment and where national opinions may legitimately vary. This suggests that the margin of appreciation will not or should not be used in relation to certain Convention guarantees or types of cases or questions.

First of all, several Convention provisions, or elements of them, lay down fairly detailed rules which leave little or no room for assessment, a balancing of interests or legitimate variations of opinion. For example, the margin of appreciation plays hardly any role in regard to the detailed requirements spelled out in Articles 5 and 6 of the Convention. As is generally borne out by the case-law, the margin is of little relevance in regard to questions of a purely procedural nature: the question of whether a national procedure is in conformity with the Convention, for example the requirements of Articles 5 and 6 or those in connection with the condition that restrictions be 'prescribed by law'/'in accordance with the law' (see paragraph 2 of Articles 8-11).

Likewise, no reference to the doctrine is to be found in the case-law under Articles 2 and 3 of the Convention. This is no surprise in view of the strictness of the wording of these provisions. Any reference to a margin of appreciation in respect of these rights would carry the unacceptable consequence that these provisions would leave room for national discretion or a balancing of interests in these areas.

Furthermore, while the margin doctrine may eventually be relevant to assessments of the facts of a given case, it will not be so as far as the establishment of the facts is concerned. In other words, the doctrine should come into play only after the facts of the case have been established on the basis of a proper inquiry by the Commission and the Court. Any difficulties in obtaining evidence of the facts should not be construed in margin of appreciation terms.[47]

Finally, there are cases which concern provisions to which a margin of appreciation may normally be applied, but the violation or non-violation of which in the concrete case is so evident to the Court that it does not consider it necessary to have recourse to this doctrine. An example of such a straightforward case is the *Darby* Case. Here, the discriminatory nature of the contested measure (a distinction between residents and non-residents in Sweden as concerns the possibility to be dispensed of the obligation to pay a 'church tax') had been virtually admitted by the respondent Government and the Court had no hesitation in finding a violation of Article 14.[48] In such cases, there is no need for the Court to adopt a cautious approach, and having recourse to the margin doctrine, as a subtle tool for affirming its subsidiary role and for expressing respect for the role of national authorities, would serve no useful purpose.

---

[47] See, for example, as concerns Art. 3, the judgment of 22 September 1993, *Klaas*, A.269, p. 17 (differing versions of the facts presented by the applicant and the Government; no reference to a margin of appreciation).

[48] Judgment of 23 October 1990, A.187, p. 13.

In other words, application of the margin of appreciation may be inappropriate in some cases because the evident nature of the violation (or the non-violation) implies that the State has clearly acted beyond (or: within) this margin.[49]

3.3 The Variable Scope of the Margin of Appreciation

While the field of application of the doctrine has, to some degree, gradually been clarified in the case-law, it is more difficult to obtain a clear view of the scope of the margin of appreciation which the Court affords to national authorities. This is because this scope may vary from case to case. It depends, amongst other things, on whether (in the words of the *Handyside* judgment) the State authorities were indeed 'in a better position than the international judge' to make the assessment of the need for measures which negatively affect the enjoyment of the Convention rights and freedoms.

No hard and fast rules governing the scope of the margin of appreciation can be identified. However, the case-law does reveal some factors or variables which are of influence. These will be outlined below.

The existence of a *European common ground* between the law and practice of the Contracting States may lead to a narrower margin of appreciation and a stricter scrutiny by the Court in judging on whether the law and practice of the respondent State are in conformity with the Convention. On the other hand, where the relevant law and practice differ widely among States, the margin of appreciation may be wider. Thus, a wide margin was accorded to national authorities in the *Handyside* (no 'uniform European conception of morals') and *Rasmussen* Cases. In the latter case, the Court held:

> The Court has pointed out in several judgments that the Contracting States enjoy a certain 'margin of appreciation' in assessing whether and to what extent differences in otherwise similar situations justify a different treatment in law (...). The scope of the margin of appreciation will vary according to the circumstances, the subject-matter and its background; in this respect, one of the relevant factors may be the existence or non-existence of common ground between the laws of the Contracting States.[50]

As concerns the alleged discriminatory nature of the Danish system of time-limits for instituting paternity proceedings, which applied to men only, the Court referred to the lack of common ground in this area and concluded that the Danish authorities 'were entitled to think that the introduction of time-limits (...) was justified by the desire to ensure legal certainty and to protect the interests of the child.'[51]

There are different ways in which the existence of common ground may be established. The Court sometimes engages in a comparative analysis of national

---

[49] This holds good even for provisions to which a wide margin is usually applied: see, for example, the judgment of 9 December 1994, *Stran Greek Refineries*, A.301-B, pp. 87-88 (unanimous finding of a violation of Art. 1 of Protocol No. 1).

[50] Judgment of 28 November 1984, A.87, p. 15.

[51] *Ibidem*, p. 15.

law and practice, but it has on many occasions equally referred to other international instruments. For example, in the *Powell and Rayner* Case, the United Kingdom was allowed a wide margin of appreciation as regards measures to minimise nuisance caused by aircraft noise. In this respect, the Court found it 'not without significance' that the relevant provisions of national law were comparable to those of the Rome Convention of 1952 on Damage Caused by Foreign Aircraft to Third Parties on the Surface.[52]

In some cases, the Court has pointed to (other provisions of) the Convention itself to demonstrate a European consensus. The *Sunday Times (I)* Case offers a clear example. In its reasoning on the margin of appreciation, the Court distinguished the case from the *Handyside* Case, in that the former concerned restrictions on freedom of expression taken with the aim of maintaining the authority of the judiciary within the meaning of Article 10(2), whereas the restrictive measures in the latter case concerned the 'protection of morals'. The Court held that its reasoning in *Handyside* on the better position of national authorities to assess the requirements of morals could not be transposed to the 'far more objective notion' of the authority of the judiciary:

> The domestic law and practice of the Contracting States reveal a fairly substantial measure of common ground in this area. This is reflected in a number of provisions of the Convention, including in Article 6, which have no equivalent as far as 'morals' are concerned. Accordingly, here a more extensive European supervision corresponds to a less discretionary power of appreciation.[53]

A second variable influencing the scope of the margin of appreciation is *the nature of the right or of the activities of the individual*.[54] For example, the States are accorded more discretion with respect to restrictions on property rights (Article 1 of Protocol No. 1) compared to restrictions on freedom of expression. In most cases concerning one of the three rules laid down in Article 1 of Protocol No. 1, the Court accepts that the margin of appreciation should be a wide one. This corresponds to a fairly loose proportionality test (see the section on proportionality above). In the area of freedom of expression, the Court frequently recalls the importance of that freedom, and especially freedom of the press, in a democratic society. In the *Barthold* Case, the Court held that the 'necessity for restricting that freedom for one of the purposes listed in Article 10(2) must be convincingly established.'[55] However, even within the area of freedom of expression, the scope of the margin of appreciation may vary, for example depending on the nature of the activities restricted. A higher level of scrutiny is generally applied where a measure restricts a free and public debate on matters of public concern, such as discussion of political issues or other matters affecting the life of the community,

---

[52] Judgment of 21 February 1990, A.172, p. 19.
[53] Judgment of 26 April 1979, A.30, pp. 36-37.
[54] See, generally, the judgment of 25 September 1996, *Buckley*, Reports 1996-IV, Vol. 16, para. 74.
[55] Judgment of 25 March 1985, A.90, p. 26.

as compared to, for example, restrictions on commercial speech. Reference is made to the discussion of the case-law in section 10 of Chapter VII below.

The importance of the right (or the activities) at issue for the well-being of the individual may also affect the scope of the margin of appreciation. Thus, with respect to Article 8, the Court recognised in margin of appreciation terms the importance of the right to a home for the personal security and well-being of the applicants in the *Gillow* Case, whereas it conceded a wide margin in respect of the restriction complained of in the *Leander* Case. According to the Court, the interference of which Mr. Leander complained 'did not constitute an obstacle to his leading a private life of his own choosing.'[56] The relevance of the nature of the right to the scope of the margin of appreciation also appears, albeit in a different guise, in the case-law concerning Articles 14 and 15 of the Convention.[57]

A third main variable is *the nature of the aim pursued by the contested measure and the circumstances or the context of that measure.* As the above comparison between the *Handyside* and *Sunday Times (I)* judgments shows, the margin of appreciation may vary according to which of the aims listed in the restriction clauses applies. This is borne out also by judgments which leave a wide discretion in cases where the protection of national security is at stake.[58] Furthermore, the margin tends to be wider in cases in which the contested measure is taken in the context of an emergency situation or at least of situations which require urgent action by the authorities.[59]

A further factor of relevance, or perhaps a variable within the last two variables mentioned above, is whether or not the case concerns *general policies (social, economic, environmental, urban and rural planning, etc.) of the State.* Here, the Court accepts that the national legislature should enjoy a wide margin of appreciation. The influence of this factor is apparent in particular in cases concerning property rights (Article 1 of Protocol No. 1, alone or in combination with Article 14) and in several cases concerning positive obligations. Especially if the case before the Court represents but one aspect of a (legitimate) broader

---

[56] Judgment of 24 November 1984, A.109, p. 22 and judgment of 26 March 1987, A.116, p. 25 respectively.

[57] In cases concerning difference of treatment solely on grounds of sex, religion, birth or nationality, the margin is much narrower (or even absent in the Court's reasoning) than in cases concerning distinctions on the ground of property. Compare, for example, the judgment of 18 July 1994, *Schmidt*, A.291-B, p. 13 with that of 21 February 1986, *James and Others*, A.98, p. 45. In the judgment of 26 May 1993, *Brannigan and McBride*, A.258-B, p. 49, the Court acknowledged that its examination, under Art. 15, of measures derogating from the rights and freedoms of the Convention has to depend also on the nature of the rights affected.

[58] See, for example, the judgment of 26 March 1987, *Leander*, A.116, p. 43.

[59] This becomes apparent from the case-law under Art. 15: see, for example, the *Brannigan and McBride* judgment cited above. In addition, the Court has held, with regard to urgent detention of 'persons of unsound mind' (Art. 5(1)(e)) that a 'wide discretion must in the nature of things be enjoyed by the national authorities empowered to order such emergency confinements'; see the judgment of 5 November 1981, *X* v. *the United Kingdom*, A.46, p. 18.

policy pursued by the national legislature, the subsidiary nature of the supervisory machinery of the Convention, in particular the fact that the Convention organs 'become involved only through contentious proceedings',[60] argues in favour of a wide margin of appreciation for national authorities. Moreover, national authorities, 'by reason of their direct and continuous contact with the vital forces of their countries', are generally better placed to take into account a multitude of local factors and to evaluate local needs and conditions.[61] The Court's cautiousness in this area is evidenced by the following passage from its judgment in the *Powell and Rayner* Case concerning policies to limit nuisance caused by aircraft:

> It is certainly not for the Commission or the Court to substitute for the assessment of the national authorities any other assessment of what might be the best policy in this difficult social and technical sphere. This is an area where the Contracting States are to be recognised as enjoying a wide margin of appreciation.[62]

The case-law shows that none of the main factors described above is in itself regarded by the Court as decisive for the scope of the margin of appreciation. Each variable has relative value. In some cases, more than one factor may be relevant; sometimes they will point in the same direction (*e.g.* a wide margin), sometimes they will not. They may reinforce or counterbalance one another.

The case-law on restrictions on the exercise of rights and freedoms which aim at the 'protection of morals' may serve to illustrate the relative weight of the various factors influencing the scope of the margin of appreciation and the interplay between them. Generally, where restrictions serve to protect morals or related matters such as the respect due to the religious feelings of other individuals, the Court has been fairly consistent in allowing a wide margin of appreciation ever since the *Handyside* judgment.[63] Here, the presumption still appears to be that, given the wide variety of opinions on moral issues between and even within the States Parties, national authorities are better placed than the Court to assess what is necessary in order to protect morality. However, the Court is prepared to adopt a stricter approach where other variables play down a lack of European common ground in moral matters. The same is true in case a common ground on more specific points does indeed exist. In cases concerning criminal law provisions prohibiting homosexual activities conducted in private between

---

[60] See the quotation from the *Handyside* judgment in the introduction of this section.

[61] *Ibidem*, p. 22 and the judgment of 25 September 1996, *Buckley*, Reports 1996-IV, Vol. 16, para. 75.

[62] Judgment of 21 February 1990, A.172, p. 19. Similar reasoning can be found in several judgments relating to property rights: see, for example, as concerns housing policies, the judgment in the case of *James and Others*, 21 February 1986, A.98, p. 32, and that in the case of *Mellacher and Others*, 19 December 1989, A.169, p. 25. See, as concerns the right to a home (Art. 8) in relation to town and country planning schemes, the judgment of 25 September 1996, *Buckley*, Reports 1996-IV, Vol. 16, para. 75.

[63] See the judgment of 25 November 1996, *Wingrove*, Reports 1996-V, Vol. 33, paras 57 and 58, with references to earlier case-law.

consenting adults, the Court attached lesser importance to the fact that these provisions purport to protect morals:

> However, not only the nature of the aim of the restriction but also the nature of the activities involved will affect the scope of the margin of appreciation. The present case concerns a most intimate aspect of private life. Accordingly, there must exist particularly serious reasons before interferences on the part of the public authorities can be legitimate for the purposes of paragraph 2 of Article 8.[64]

Even when the respondent Government pleaded special circumstances on account of the specifics of the local moral climate (in Northern Ireland), the Court did not regard these as decisive:

> As compared with the era when that legislation was enacted, there is now a better understanding, and in consequence an increased tolerance, of homosexual behaviour to the extent that in the great majority of the member States of the Council of Europe it is no longer considered to be necessary or appropriate to treat homosexual practices of the kind now in question as in themselves a matter to which the sanctions of the criminal law should be applied; the Court cannot overlook the marked changes which have occurred in this regard in the domestic law of the member States.[65]

In other words, both the importance of the activities concerned for the individual and the emergence of European common ground on the specific point at issue tipped the balance towards a narrow margin of appreciation and a strict scrutiny.

Similarly, but less explicitly, the Court attached more weight to the importance of the activities of the applicant than to the moral implications of the case in its judgment in the case of *Open Door and Dublin Well Woman* v. *Ireland*, which concerned a prohibition on providing information to pregnant women about abortion facilities abroad. The judgment places great emphasis on the importance of such information for the health and the well-being of women.[66] The Court found a violation of the right to receive and impart information (Article 10), in spite of its general assertion that 'national authorities enjoy a wide margin of appreciation in matters of morals, particularly in an area such as the present which touches on matters of belief concerning the nature of human life.'[67]

The interplay between the margin of appreciation factors makes it difficult to predict how the Court will decide the margin question in any given case, especially where the variables point in different directions. In such cases, the decision on how much latitude is to be granted to national authorities depends on the weight the Court attaches to the various factors concerned (which, incidentally, may in themselves be open to different appreciations) and this choice ultimately rests on a value judgment on the part of the Court and its individual judges.

---

[64] Judgment of 22 October 1981, *Dudgeon*, A.45, p. 21. See also the judgments of 26 October 1988, *Norris*, A.142 and of 22 April 1993, *Modinos*, A.259.

[65] Judgment of 22 October 1981, *Dudgeon*, A.45, p. 23.

[66] Judgment of 29 October 1992, A.246. See, in particular, pp. 30 and 31.

[67] *Ibidem*, p. 29.

3.4 The Margin of Appreciation and the Level of Scrutiny Exercised by the Court; Appraisal

From the case-law the margin of appreciation emerges as a review doctrine, used by the Court for determining and justifying the intensity of the supervision which is considered appropriate in concrete cases. This is clear from its rationale, as set out in the *Handyside* judgment: the doctrine rests on both the principle of subsidiarity of the Convention mechanism *vis-à-vis* domestic systems for the protection of human rights and the better position of national organs for assessing local factors and needs insofar as these are relevant to the issue before the Court.[68] This means, among other things, that the margin of appreciation is not to be understood as a reserved domain for Contracting States, a predetermined area outside the purviews of the Court's supervision.

The Court has often stated that the margin of appreciation goes hand in hand with European supervision; this means that it is for the Court and the Commission in each case to determine whether a certain margin should be left to the respondent State and, if so, how wide this margin should be.[69] Any freedom left to Contracting States under the margin of appreciation doctrine is residual and provisional, because it is the result of the Court's decision in each case on how strict its control should be, and subject to future judgments of the Court.

The Court has strongly rejected arguments to the effect that the margin of appreciation doctrine would place certain matters outside the scope of its review. Thus, while a wide margin normally applies in the field of the protection of morals, even in this field the Court does not allow States unfettered discretion. The argument advanced by the Irish Government in the *Open Door and Dublin Well Woman* Case that the proportionality test under the 'necessity' requirement of the restriction clause of Article 10(2) of the Convention was inappropriate where the life of the unborn was concerned was similarly rejected: 'To accept the Government's pleading on this point would amount to an abdication of the Court's responsibility under Article 19 "to ensure the observance of the engagements undertaken by the High Contracting Parties ..."'[70]

There is no objection of principle against the margin of appreciation doctrine as such. In fact, variations in the degree of supervision are a common phenomenon also in the case-law of domestic courts when reviewing government action and it is highly probable that, even in the absence of a margin of appreciation doctrine, there would be variations in the level of scrutiny exercised by the Strasbourg Court. From this perspective, the margin doctrine may be welcomed as an attempt,

---

[68] See the quotation from this judgment in the introductory part of this section.

[69] This becomes clear, for example, from the judgments in which the margin of appreciation is not referred to, even where they concern provisions to which the doctrine is regularly applied. *Cf.* also the judgment of 25 March 1992, *Campbell*, A.233, p. 18: 'regard *may* be had to the State's margin of appreciation' (emphasis added).

[70] Judgment of 29 October 1992, A.246, p. 29. See also the judgment of 26 October 1988, *Norris*, A.142, p. 20.

albeit an imperfect one, to make explicit considerations of judicial policy that underlie such variations. The margin of appreciation doctrine may thus contribute to transparency and consistency in the Court's reasoning.

However, the application of the doctrine can certainly be improved. In the first place, a mere reference to the margin of appreciation of national authorities without any further elucidation cannot be sufficient to justify the conclusion that there has been no violation. Nevertheless, the Court has on some occasions, after referring to the margin, been very sparse in substantiating its approach.[71] As was observed above, the margin may not serve to establish a reserved domain for Contracting States; the doctrine should be used as an expression and explanation of the Court's view of what level of scrutiny is appropriate in the case at hand.

A further problem is that the relationship between the margin of appreciation and the level of scrutiny applied in a given case is not always as clear as it should be. In some cases, the Court's use of the doctrine is difficult to explain in the light of the factors mentioned above.[72] The consistency and transparency of the Court's reasoning would be improved if more emphasis were given to the principles and factors that govern the field of application as well as the scope of the margin of appreciation and the level of scrutiny.

Nevertheless, the flexibility which the doctrine provides to the Court itself would appear to set limits on attempts to achieve a more consistent use of it. It may be doubted whether the Court will ever completely unveil the reasons for all choices of judicial policy that it makes. The doctrine allows the Court to develop the substantive standards of the Convention without running up against serious objections by Contracting States which might jeopardise its authority. Through the margin of appreciation the Court sends the message that it will not disregard national particularities. This contributes to the observance of the Court's judgments by the Contracting States, even if some of them will inevitably claim

---

[71] See, for example, the reasoning in the judgment of 28 March 1990, *Groppera radio AG and Others*, A.173, p. 28, where the arguments advanced by the Court fail to go into the necessity of the restriction in the light of its aim. Similarly the judgment of 25 August 1993, *Chorherr*, A.266-B, p. 37, where no explanation was given why the Court considered that the measures taken against the applicant were not excessive.

[72] See, for example, the judgment of 22 February 1989, *Barfod*, A.149, concerning journalistic freedom of expression. The Court's reasoning and its finding that there had been no violation of Art. 10 depart considerably from the approach adopted in the judgment of 8 July 1986, *Lingens*, A.103 (mere reference to the margin of appreciation, no application of the doctrine; strict scrutiny where restrictions on press freedom are concerned).

a wider margin of appreciation and a more elaborate use of the doctrine.[73] Therefore, the doctrine has an important rhetorical function as well.

Nevertheless, given the object and purpose of the Convention as an instrument for the protection of human rights, the Court's very use of the margin of appreciation requires close scrutiny. Great care should be taken that no undue weight is given to the doctrine to the detriment of the effective protection of the Convention's rights and freedoms. It is incumbent on the Court to give solid reasons whenever it decides to have recourse to the doctrine. Similarly, the margin of appreciation should not lead to an dilution of the proportionality requirement under various provisions of the Convention.

In this respect, some judgments are cause for concern as to the effects of the margin of appreciation on the interpretation of the 'necessary in a democratic society' requirement under Articles 8-11 of the Convention. For a long time, the Court applied a fairly strict proportionality test: were the reasons for the interference 'relevant and sufficient'? was there a 'pressing social need' for the interference? was the interference 'proportionate to the legitimate aim pursued'?. In some more recent judgments, however, a looser test is applied: was the interference 'justifiable in principle and proportionate'?; was there 'a reasonable relationship of proportionality' between the interference and the legitimate aim pursued?[74] It is suggested that the Court should maintain its established interpretation of the 'necessity' requirement. This appears all the more important in view of the accession of newly democratic Central and Eastern European States to the Convention system, which must not lead to a dilution of the standards of the Convention.

While the Court has generally been fairly progressive in developing the standards of the Convention by interpretative means, it has also recognised that the scope of its review under a number of standards may be limited especially where the latter require delicate assessments which national authorities are in a better position to make than the international judge. These two aspects of the Court's role should not be looked at in isolation. The strong affirmation of the Court's role in interpreting the Convention has enabled it to bring a broad range of issues under the protection of the Convention and hence under its supervision. The

---

[73] See, for example, the position of the Irish Government in the case of *Open Door and Dublin Well Woman*. More recently, the United Kingdom Government has made proposals for encouraging a more generous use of the margin of appreciation. According to press reports, the UK has stressed that 'democratic institutions and tribunals in Member States are best placed to determine moral and social issues in accordance with regional and moral perceptions'; that 'full regard should be had to decisions by democratic legislatures and to differing national traditions', and that 'long-standing laws and practices should be respected, except where these are manifestly contrary to the Convention.' See, *e.g.*, Paddy Smyth, 'British seek dilution of human rights court', *The Irish Times*, Tuesday 7 May 1996.

[74] See *e.g.*, as concerns the first criterion, the judgment of 25 May 1993, *Kokkinakis*, A.260-A, p. 21; judgment of 24 February 1994, *Casado Coca*, A.285-A, p. 20. As concerns the second criterion, see the judgment of 16 December 1992, *Hadjianastassiou*, A.252, p. 19; judgment of 25 August 1993, *Chorherr*, A.266-B, p. 37.

element of judicial restraint expressed in the margin of appreciation doctrine not only reflects the limited capability of courts to solve societal problems; it also bears witness to the fact that the Convention places the Court at the crossroads of international judicial supervision and national sovereignty. The margin of appreciation may be seen as a certain counterweight to the Court's interpretative activism.[75] In the final analysis, some of the general principles that feature in the Court's case-law reflect a constitutionalist approach to the Convention and the Court's supervisory role; others tend to underscore that the functioning of the Convention system and the effective protection of its rights ultimately rests upon the cooperation of the Contracting States. It may be doubted whether the former would have been possible without the latter.

---

[75] This may also emerge in individual judgments: see the judgment of 28 March 1990 in the *Groppera* Case, where the Court's innovative approach to the interpretation of the last sentence of para. 1 of Art. 10 was followed by a very limited review of the necessity of the interference (A.173, pp. 24 and 28).

Chapter III

The Procedure Before the European Commission of Human Rights

1 INTRODUCTION

The Commission has several duties. First, it considers the admissibility of the submitted applications, by reference to the admissibility conditions set forth in the Convention (Articles 26 and 27). When it accepts an application, in contact with representatives of the parties it undertakes an examination of the application in order to ascertain the facts. During this examination the Commission also places itself at the disposal of the parties with a view to securing a friendly settlement (Article 28(1)(b)). If such a settlement is secured, the Commission draws up a report with a brief statement of the facts and the solution reached, and sends the report to the States concerned, to the Committee of Ministers and, for publication, to the Secretary General of the Council of Europe (Article 28(2)). If a solution is not reached, the Commission draws up a report on the facts and states its opinion as to whether these facts disclose a violation of the Convention. This report is transmitted to the Committee of Ministers and to the parties concerned; in doing so, the Commission may make such proposals as it thinks fit (Article 31).

As stated above,[1] a year after Protocol No. 11 to the Convention has entered into force, the Commission will cease to exist. The procedure which will be described below, however, will not substantial change. As under the present system, both individual applications and inter-State applications may be lodged. As the Secretariat of the Commission does at present, the Registry of the Court will establish all necessary contacts with the applicants and, if necessary, request further information. Next, the application will be registered by a chamber of the Court and assigned to a judge-rapporteur. The judge-rapporteur may refer the application to a three-judge committee, which may include the judge-rapporteur. The committee may, by a unanimous decision, declare the application inadmissible; such a decision will be final. When the judge-rapporteur considers that the application raises a question of principle and is not inadmissible or when the committee does not unanimously reject the complaint, the application will be examined by the chamber. This procedure matches the one currently followed by the Commission.[2]

---

[1] See *supra* p. 30.
[2] See also *infra* pp. 28-29.

2 THE EXAMINATION OF ADMISSIBILITY

2.1 Registration of an Application

When the Convention was drawn up, the main task of the Commission was considered to be that of functioning as a kind of screen for the large number of applications to be expected. The examination of the admissibility was therefore regarded as the core of the procedure before the Commission. Quantitatively, it still constitutes the most important function of the Commission.

A complaint usually reaches the Secretariat of the Commission by way of a letter. As a rule such letters have the character of a first contact and not of a formal application. They do not (yet) lend themselves to official registration. The Secretariat of the Commission makes a provisional file for each case in order to obtain at the earliest possible stage as complete a picture as possible of any complaint. The applicant also receives a form for him to fill out. He may also submit documents in addition to this form. The application, which must bear his signature, must contain: the name, age, occupation and address of the applicant; the name, occupation and address of his representative, if any; the name of the Contracting State against which the application is lodged; as far as possible, the object of the application and the provision of the Convention allegedly violated; a statement of the facts and arguments on which the application is based; and finally any relevant documents, and in particular any judgment or other act relating to the object of the application.[3] Moreover, in his application the applicant must provide information showing that the conditions laid down in Article 26 concerning the exhaustion of domestic remedies and the six-month time-limit for filing the application have been complied with.[4] In general, the Commission does not treat procedural rules with the same rigidity as national courts use to do.[5] However, a communication containing only an allegation that a particular act violates one or more provisions of the Convention is considered by the Commission insufficient to constitute a full application, unless this communication sets out summarily the object of the application.[6]

If the above-mentioned requirements are satisfied and the complaint, *prima facie*, discloses a violation of the Convention, it will in general be entered in the official register of the Commission. Registration has no other meaning than that the complaint is pending before the Commission; no indications as to its admissibility may be inferred from it.

---

[3] Rule 44(1) of the Rules of Procedure of the European Commission of Human Rights, *Collected Texts*, Strasbourg, 1996 (hereafter: the Rules of Procedure). See E. Fribergh, 'The Commission Secretariat's handling of provisional files', in: F. Matscher and H. Petzold (eds.), *Protecting Human Rights: The European Dimension*, Cologne, 1988, pp. 181-191.

[4] Rule 44(2) of the Rules of Procedure.

[5] See Appl. 332/57, *Lawless* v. *Ireland*, Yearbook II (1958-1959), p. 308 (326).

[6] Appl. 18660/91, *Bengtsston* v. *Sweden*, D&R 79-A (1994), p. 11 (19).

As a rule, registration of a complaint is not refused if the party submitting it insists on registration.[7] Nevertheless, only a small part of all complaints received is actually registered.[8] The other cases are withdrawn during the phase of the first correspondence with the Secretariat of the Commission. The Secretariat has been instructed to draw the attention of potential applicants to the possibility of rejection of the complaint in cases where the case-law of the Commission points in that direction. The Secretariat does so by means of standard letters.

It is mainly because of the formulation of these letters that Mikaelson considers this practice to be contrary to the Convention. In his view, the Secretariat thus in fact makes a decision on admissibility and by doing so performs a task which the Convention has reserved exclusively to the Commission.[9] Formally, this is not correct: prior to the moment of registration there is not yet an application in the sense of the Convention, and accordingly no decision of the Commission is required. Moreover, it remains fully up to the applicant to withdraw his application or not. On the other hand, the present practice may very well create the impression 'that the Secretariat's first aim – at least in some cases – is to discourage or perhaps even frustrate the individual, in the hope that he will give up before the application is formally filed.'[10] Although one need not doubt the commonly known accuracy and caution with which the Secretariat performs its task, it may be acknowledged that for the layman it may be difficult to infer from the standard letters that these contain merely *information* supplied by the Secretariat and not a *decision* of the Commission. In our opinion, therefore, it is advisable to change this practice. The nature of the individual right of complaint – confirmed by the Commission and the Court – as the corner-stone of legal protection under the Convention entails that the whole of the Strasbourg procedure should be as 'kind to the applicant' as possible. It is the Secretariat's task to assist, not to discourage the potential applicant. In particular, the sometimes advanced efficiency grounds, derived from the limited capacity of the Commission in relation to the (large) number of applications, should not be decisive in this respect. Although efforts to eliminate patently inadmissible complaints as early as possible may be understandable and even defensible, it would seem preferable to us that any information in this respect be supplied by the Directorate of Human Rights or by a Human Rights Commissioner as proposed by the Finish Government, and not by the Secretariat, which will be identified with the Commission. Any view within the Commission on whether the (potential) application is manifestly inadmissible or ill-founded should emanate from the Commission itself.

---

[7] H. Krüger, 'The European Commission of Human Rights', HRLJ, Vol. 1, 1980, pp. 66-87.

[8] In 1996, the Secretariat of the Commission received 12,143 communications, 4,758 of which were registered; European Commission, *Survey of Activities and Statistics*, 1996.

[9] L. Mikaelson, *European Protection of Human Rights*, Alphen a/d Rijn, 1980, pp. 40-42.

[10] *Ibidem*, p. 40.

2.2 Languages

The official languages for the Commission are English and French, but the President may permit the members of the Commission and the parties to use another language.[11] In practice this means that the parties may also use any of the other languages of the Contracting States which have recognised the individual right of complaint, and that the correspondence may also be conducted in those languages.

2.3 Representation

States are represented before the Commission by their Agents, who may be assisted by (legal) advisers.[12] Individuals, non-governmental organisations, or groups of individuals may present and conduct applications before the Commission on their own behalf, but may also be represented or assisted by a lawyer or any other person residing in a Contracting State, unless the Commission at any stage decides otherwise.[13] The representative must give evidence that he/she has been authorised by the applicant to act as such.

2.4 Costs of the Proceedings

The procedure before the Commission is free of charge for the parties; the expenses are accounted for by the Council of Europe.[14] The expenses of witnesses, experts and other persons whom the Commission hears at the request of an individual applicant may in the Commission's discretion be borne by the Council of Europe.[15] The same holds true for the costs of obtaining written expert opinions and evidence.[16] Finally, in every stage of the procedure, after the written observations of the respondent government concerning the admissibility have been received or the time-limit for this has expired, or after an application has been declared admissible, the Commission may grant the applicant free legal aid if it deems this necessary for the proper discharge of its duties and the applicant does not have sufficient means.[17]

The Commission will conclude that free legal aid is necessary for the proper discharge of its duties when it is evident that the applicant has had no legal training, or when it appears from the written documents submitted by him that he is unable to defend his case adequately before the Commission. In order to

---

[11] Rule 30 of the Rules of Procedure.
[12] Rule 31 of the Rules of Procedure.
[13] Rule 32(2) of the Rules of Procedure.
[14] Art. 58 of the Convention.
[15] Rule 42(1) of the Rules of Procedure.
[16] Rule 42(3) and (4) of the Rules of Procedure.
[17] See the Addendum to the Rules of Procedure, Council of Europe, *Collected Texts*, 1996, pp. 197-203.

establish that he does not have sufficient means, the applicant must submit a declaration to that effect, certified by the appropriate domestic authorities. If the latter requirement creates difficulties for one reason or another, the Commission is satisfied when the applicant is able to prove by declaration that he would be eligible for free legal aid under the national legal system concerned. In a number of cases the Commission has refused free legal aid because it held that the income of the applicant in combination with that of his/her spouse was sufficient to defray the costs of the suit.[18]

Free legal aid may comprise not only lawyer's fees but also the travelling and subsistence expenses and any other necessary expenses of both the applicant and his lawyer.[19]

2.5 Handling of the Case after the Application has been Received

After an application has been received by the Secretary General of the Council of Europe, it is transmitted to the President of the Commission. If the application is brought by a State, the President gives notice of the application to the State against which the claim is made and invites the latter to submit written observations on the admissibility.[20]

In the case of a (registered) individual complaint this does not take place automatically. Since the amendment of the Rules of Procedure of the Commission in 1973,[21] the procedure with respect to individual complaints has been as follows: the President appoints one member of the Commission as rapporteur, who is to submit a report on admissibility. This rapporteur may request relevant further information on the complaint from the applicant and/or the State concerned, upon which he communicates any information obtained from the State to the applicant for comments.[22] At this stage the rapporteur will prepare a report for a Chamber proposing either to declare the application inadmissible, or to communicate it to the Government for observations on the admissibility and the merits. He may also propose that the case, if obviously inadmissible, should be referred to a committee of three members of the Commission, a procedure which was introduced by Protocol No. 8, which entered into force on 1 January 1990. This procedure is known as the 'summary procedure', by which the committee of three, by unanimous vote ('global formula'), may declare an application inadmissible or strike it off the list, when such a decision can be taken without further examination.[23]

---

18 See Krüger, *supra* note 7, pp. 85-86.
19 See Art. 4 of the Addendum to the Rules of Procedure, p. 198.
20 Rule 45 of the Rules of Procedure.
21 This amendment became necessary as a result of the entry into force of Protocol No. 3 to the Convention, which is incorporated in Arts 29, 30 and 34 of the Convention.
22 Rule 47(2) of the Rules of Procedure.
23 Art. 20(3) of the Convention. Art. 20(2) enables the Commission to set up Chambers of seven members to examen applications.

If the application is not declared inadmissible through the summary procedure or by unanimous vote of the committee of three, the Commission may request additional relevant information from the applicant or the State concerned and/or give notice of the application to the State and invite the State to present written observations on the admissibility of the application. The information and/or observations of the State are communicated to the applicant, so that the latter may comment on it. After receipt of the observations of the State against which the application is brought, the application is examined by the rapporteur. Before deciding upon his report on the admissibility, the Commission may invite the parties to submit further observations in writing or orally.[24] If the Commission decides to hold a hearing in this phase, the parties are invited to plead also on the merits. Such a combined procedure is intended to save time. The Commission is very strict concerning the time-limits laid down in Rule 51 of the Rules of Procedure. In an application by Turkish citizens of Kurdish origin alleging that the police had inflicted serious injuries on them and had delayed their medical treatment, the Commission found that the complaint raised important questions of fact and law. The case was communicated to the Turkish Government. After two extensions of the time-limit, the Government neither submitted observations nor requested a further extension but belatedly submitted 'preliminary observations' leaving insufficient time to obtain the applicants' observations in reply. The Government's request for adjournment of the examination of the application was therefore refused and the complaints were declared admissible.[25]

The above-mentioned difference in treatment between individual applications and applications by States as far as referring the application to the defendant State is concerned, would seem to be justified. A State may be assumed not to lodge an application lightly, on account of the political complications which such a step may involve. In the case of individual applications the chances for this to happen are greater. It would therefore not be right to communicate for comments to the governments concerned also those numerous applications which, *prima facie*, fail to satisfy the admissibility conditions. Nor does it appear to be objectionable that among individual applications a first selection is made *via* a simplified procedure, provided that the legal position of the applicant in such a procedure is not affected. It is therefore of the greatest importance that the rapporteur be obliged to transmit any information he obtains from a Government to the applicant, upon which the latter may comment. Thus, the equality of the parties is properly secured.

---

[24] Rules 48(1), (2) and 50 of the Rules of Procedure.
[25] Appl. 22493/93, *Hüseyin and Devrim Berktay* v. *Turkey*, D&R 79-A (1994), p. 97 (100-102); joined Appls 22947/93 and 22948/93, *Akkoç* v. *Turkey*, D&R 79-A (1994), p. 108 (114); Appl. 23178/94, *Aydin* v. *Turkey*, D&R 79-A (1994), p. 117 (119).

2.6 Interim Measures in Urgent Cases

A number of interrelated provisions from the Commission's Rules of Procedure on urgent cases and interim measures should be mentioned separately here. In contrast with the Rules of Court, the Commission's Rules of Procedure originally did not contain any provision for such actions, although the latter organ would appear to be in a better position than the former to take interim measures. Meanwhile, this situation has changed, a number of provisions having been included in the Rules of Procedure. Even before that time the Commission had already proved prepared to urge the Contracting States to take such interim measures as it deemed necessary. This was the case in particular where the applicants were in danger of being expelled before the Commission could consider their case.[26] This practice has now been formalised in the Rules of Procedure.

Under Rules 33 and 34 of the Rules of Procedure, in urgent cases the Commission may give precedence to a particular complaint, thus derogating from its normal procedure, according to which complaints are considered in the order in which they become ready for examination. According to Rule 46 the Secretary of the Commission then informs the respondent State of the introduction of the application and adds a summary of its contents. The purpose of this provision is of course to prevent surprise on the part of the Contracting State concerned if afterwards any interim measures prove desirable. The latter measures are regulated in Rule 36 of the Rules of Procedure:

> The Commission or, where it is not in session, the President may indicate to the parties any interim measure the adoption of which seems desirable in the interest of the parties or the proper conduct of the proceedings before it.

What is provided for here are recommendations of the Commission which involve no legal obligations for the Contracting States. This is due to the fact that the Convention does not confer on the Commission any power to impose interim measures with binding force. In the *Cruz Varas* Case, the Court had to decide on the argument that the failure to comply with the Commission's indication under Rule 36 amounted to a violation of Sweden's obligation under Article 25(1) not to hinder the effective exercise of the right of individual petition. The Court took the position that the Convention did not contain any provision empowering the Convention organs to order interim measures.[27] The Court further noted that the practice of States revealed almost total compliance with Rule 36 indications. However, subsequent practice could be taken as establishing the agreement of States regarding the interpretation of a Convention provision but not to create new rights and obligations which were not included in the Convention at the outset.

---

[26] See C.A. Nørgaard and H. Krüger, 'Interim and Conservatory Measures under the European System of Protection of Human Rights', in: Manfred Nowak, Dorothea Steurer and Hannes Tretter (eds.), *Progress in the Spirit of Human Rights*, Festschrift für Felix Ermacora, Kehl am Rhein, 1988, pp. 109-117. See also *infra* p. 215.

[27] Judgment of 20 March 1991, A.201, p. 34.

The practice was rather based on good faith cooperation with the Commission. Furthermore, no assistance could be derived from general principles of international law since no uniform legal rule existed on the matter. Accordingly, the Court found that the power to order binding interim measures could not be inferred from Article 25(1) or from other sources. According to the Court, it was within the province of the Contracting Parties to decide whether it was expedient to remedy this situation. However, the Court observed that where a State decides not to comply with a Rule 36 indication it knowingly assumes the risk of being found in breach of Article 3 by the Convention organs.[28] This rather restrictive interpretation by the Court of Article 25(1), which deviated from that of the majority of the Commission, was adopted by ten to nine votes. It may, therefore, very well be that in future cases the Court will adopt a different point of view on the issue. In our opinion, under certain circumstances the provision of Article 25 of the Convention providing that those Contracting States which have accepted the right of individual applications undertake not to hinder in any way the effective exercise of this right, may imply the obligation to take the measures as indicated by the Commission.

In the majority of cases the suggestions made by the Commission in this respect are taken very seriously by the national authorities. In fact, it is only in cases of extreme urgency that the Commission proceeds to recommend interim measures: the facts must *prima facie* point to a violation of the Convention, and the omission to take the proposed measures must result in irreparable injury to certain interests of the parties or to the progress of the examination.[29] Such would be the case if an expulsion would constitute a violation of Article 3 of the Convention, in view of a serious risk that the victim will be exposed to torture or inhuman treatment. In that case, the Commission will request a stay of expulsion until it has had the opportunity to investigate the case. Thus, an indication for an interim measure is given only where there is a high degree of probability that a violation of Article 3 is likely to occur. This is a very difficult assessment to make. It requires an applicant to state his case in a convincing manner and possibly also to present some evidence showing the danger of life or limb to which he may be exposed if expelled or extradited to a particular country. It is not sufficient for the applicant to provide information about the danger or uncertain situation in his country of origin and/or his being an opponent of the ruling Government. He must show in a credible way that he is personally at risk. It is often stated that it is practically impossible for an applicant to provide such evidence when he has fled his country in haste under threat of an immediate arrest and where documents and papers about his involvement are left behind.[30] If the expulsion only allegedly violates Article 8 of the Convention (respect for family life), an interim measure will not readily be indicated by the Commission because the damage can easily be reversed

---

[28] *Ibidem*, p. 37.
[29] See Krüger, *supra* note 7, pp. 73-75.
[30] See Nørgaard and Krüger, *supra* note 26, pp. 112-113.

by allowing the expelled person's re-entry into the State concerned.[31] In that case, therefore, it is not advisable to request for application of Rule 36 of the Rules of Procedure. It may be counterproductive to create a false impression by dramatising the effects of the alleged violation of the Convention in the hope that the Commission will be moved to action. Such an attitude is likely to diminish the willingness of the State concerned to comply with measures recommended by the Commission.[32]

As regards the manner in which requests under Rule 36 are to be presented, the following points should be mentioned. Firstly, the request should be submitted as soon as the final domestic decision has been taken, and sufficiently in advance of the execution of the expulsion order so that an intervention by the Commission is still possible. A certain time is required for the Secretary to prepare the case and, when the Commission is not in session, to communicate with the President of the Commission. The Commission should also have sufficient time to obtain information on the matter, for instance by contacting the Agent of the Government to inquire about the Government's intentions. For these reasons, making a conditional request under Rule 36 pending the decision of the domestic authorities or courts might be considered.

Secondly, the request must be in writing and should contain the required information. A telephone conversation might serve as an announcement of the request, but it cannot as such set in motion the procedure under Rule 36. On the other hand, telex or fax communication is sufficient provided it contains adequate information. In this connection it is also very important to provide the Commission with copies of relevant national judgments and decisions showing the arguments which have been put before the domestic authorities and courts and the reasons for the refusal to grant the claim.[33]

An indication under Rule 36 will not be given if it is still possible to apply for domestic remedies which have suspensive effect. The Commission has also never given an indication under Rule 36 if in the case of an expulsion or extradition the receiving State was a Member State of the Council of Europe and had recognised the right of individual complaint. Apparently, the Commission is of the opinion that in such a case there is a sufficient guarantee that the Convention will be respected, if necessary through a new application under Article 25. It may also be of relevance to the Commission whether the treatment which the applicant fears after expulsion or extradition is related to acts which are illegal in the host or in the home country. The Commission is not prepared to apply Rule 36 if the deportation is the result of a conviction for a criminal offence.

In the *Soering* Case, the applicant argued that, notwithstanding the assurance given to the United Kingdom Government, there was a serious likelihood that he would be sentenced to death if extradited to the United States of America. He

---

[31] See Krüger, *supra* note 7, pp. 73-75.
[32] See Nørgaard and Krüger, *supra* note 26, pp. 109-118.
[33] *Ibidem*, pp. 114-115.

maintained that in the circumstances and, in particular, having regard to the 'death row phenomenon' he would thereby be subjected to inhuman and degrading treatment and punishment contrary to Article 3 of the Convention.[34] He also submitted that his extradition to the United States would constitute a violation of Article 6(3)(c), because of the absence of legal aid in the State of Virginia to pursue various appeals. Finally, he claimed that, in breach of Article 13, he had no effective remedy under United Kingdom law in respect of his complaint under Article 3. The President of the Commission indicated to the United Kingdom Government, in accordance with Rule 36, that it was desirable, in the interests of the parties and the proper conduct of the proceedings, not to extradite the applicant to the United States until the Commission had had an opportunity to examine the application. This indication was subsequently prolonged by the Commission on several occasions until the reference of the case to the Court.

So far, there have been two situations in which an indication was given in circumstances other than expulsion or extradition. In the one case it was deemed necessary by the Commission in order to secure evidence. After the death of three members of the RAF, who had brought claims before the Commission concerning their treatment in prison, the President of the Commission decided that a delegation of the Commission should visit the prison concerned. This visit was intended to examine, on the spot, the conditions in which the applicants had been detained.[35] The other situation arose in the case of *Patane* v. *Italy*, where the Commission was faced with an application of a person, serving a five years' prison sentence. This person was suffering from a severe state of depression and her health was, according to medical certificates, continuously deteriorating to the point where an acute threat to her life existed. In this case the Commission gave an indication to the Italian Government that it was desirable to take at once all necessary measures to preserve the applicant's health, either by transferring her to an institution better suited for her, or by granting her provisional release. The Government informed the Commission that the applicant had been released from detention by order of an Italian court. As the applicant subsequently disappeared, the Commission decided to strike the case off its list.[36]

Finally, reference should be made to the *Altun* Case concerning a pending extradition from Germany to Turkey. The Commission gave an indication to the German Government to suspend the applicant's extradition until it had the opportunity to examine the case. The Government complied but urged the Commission to decide quickly as it was no longer possible under German law to keep the applicant in detention pending extradition. The Government maintained that, if released, the applicant would abscond. In these circumstances the Commission gave an indication to the applicant that if he was released, he should

---

[34] Judgment of 7 July 1989, A.161.
[35] Appls 7522/76, 7586/76, 7587/76, *Ensslin, Baader and Raspe* v. *Federal Republic of Germany*, Yearbook XVIII (1975), p. 132.
[36] Appl. 11488/85, *X* v. *Italy* (unpublished).

remain at the disposal of the German authorities pending the decision which the Commission was to take at its next session. During the domestic proceedings in this case, the applicant committed suicide. The Commission decided that no general interest existed for further examination of the case.[37]

2.7 Decision of the Commission

As was mentioned before, the consideration of the case by the Commission takes place *in camera* and the Commission decides by a majority of the members casting a vote.[38] The decision of the Commission on admissibility must be accompanied or followed by the reasons on which it is based. No appeal lies against this decision. A declaration of *inadmissibility* is final. A declaration of *admissibility*, however, can still be reversed in a later stage. Under Article 29 of the Convention, in the course of the examination of the merits, *i.e.* after the application has been accepted, the Commission may nevertheless decide *ex officio* and with a two-third majority of its members to reject the application if it becomes evident that after all it does not satisfy all the admissibility conditions.[39]

Thus in a case which had been initially declared admissible and in which the applicant claimed that, if he would be returned to Syria, this would be a violation of Article 3 on the ground that he would be sentenced to death or at least to fifteen years' imprisonment, the Commission considered, in the light of the parties' further observations on the merits of the case, that there were reasons to doubt the accuracy of the applicant's claim that he was a deserter. In particular, the Commission took note of the expert report concluding that the applicant was not the person or one of the persons pictured in a uniform on photographs invoked in support of his account of his purported background. This conclusion negatively affected the credibility of his submissions and the authenticity of the other documents relied on by him. Therefore, the Commission rejected the application under Article 29.[40] Moreover, as will be pointed out later,[41] the Court considers itself competent to again investigate the admissibility of an application submitted to it.

---

[37] Report of 7 March 1984, D&R 36 (1984), p. 236 (259-260).

[38] See *supra* p. 28.

[39] By the entry into force of Protocol No. 8 the original requirement of unanimity was changed into a two-third majority.

[40] Appl. 22408/93, *H* v. *Sweden*, D&R 79-A (1994), p. 85 (96).

[41] See *infra* pp. 203-213.

2.8 The Admissibility Conditions

Two of the admissibility conditions set forth in the Convention apply to applications submitted by States as well as to those submitted by individuals. These are the condition that all remedies within the legal system of the respondent State must have been exhausted before the case is submitted to the Commission, and the condition that the application must have been submitted within a period of six months from the date on which the final national decision was taken (Article 26). For the admissibility of an individual application additional requirements are that the application is not anonymous; that the application is not substantially the same as a matter which has already been examined by the Commission or has already been submitted to another procedure of international investigation or settlement and contains no relevant new information; that the application is not incompatible with the provisions of the Convention; that the application is not manifestly ill-founded; and that the application does not constitute an abuse of the right to lodge an application (Article 27(1) and (2)).

Strictly speaking, one ought to differentiate between applications which are inadmissible and applications falling outside the competence of the Commission, even though the Convention does not provide a clear basis for such a distinction. Applications by States may only be rejected on the grounds mentioned in Article 26, and not on the ground of incompatibility with the Convention mentioned in Article 27(2), a ground on which the Commission sometimes rejects individual applications with respect to which it has no competence.[42] All the same, it is evident that applications by States may also fall outside the competence of the Commission, for instance when the application relates to a period in which the Convention was not yet binding upon the respondent State. The Commission will have to reject such an application, but in this case, properly speaking, on account of incompetence, not on account of inadmissibility, the grounds for which are enumerated exhaustively in the Convention. The practice concerning individual applications, however, shows that the Commission usually rejects applications outside its competence *ratione personae, ratione materiae, ratione loci,* or *ratione temporis* on account of inadmissibility. That is why issues relating to the competence of the Commission will here be discussed under the heading of admissibility conditions.

In practice the Commission applies a particular sequence in the admissibility conditions by reference to which an application is examined. This sequence is based partly on logical, partly on practical grounds.[43] But on the very ground of practical considerations the case-law of the Commission diverges from this sequence on numerous occasions. Especially the use of the so-called 'global

---

[42] See, *e.g.*, Appl. 473/59, *X* v. *Austria*, Yearbook II (1958-1959), p. 400 (406) and Appl. 1452/62, *X* v. *Austria*, Yearbook VI (1963), p. 268 (276).

[43] See also Krüger, *supra* note 7, pp. 75-78.

formula' is striking.[44] The Commission uses this formula for rejecting an application which contains various separate complaints, as a whole on account of its manifestly ill-founded character, although the separate complaints may be inadmissible on different grounds. The Commission bases this approach on the fact that it does not consider it necessary in such a case to make a detailed examination of the separate elements of the application.

Here follows a discussion of the separate admissibility conditions in the sequence referred to above.

2.8.1   The Application must not be Anonymous (Article 27(1)(a))

This condition makes it possible to bar applications which have been lodged for purely political or propagandistic reasons, although of course cases are also conceivable in which a serious individual applicant wishes to remain anonymous for fear of repercussions. After having lodged his complaint, the applicant is asked if he objects to his identity being disclosed. If he objects, his identity will not be disclosed during the whole procedure before the Commission. The same holds true for the procedure before the Court or the Committee of Ministers. In those cases however, the application is not anonymous, since the identity of the applicant is known to the Commission.

In practice, this admissibility condition does not play an important part. The large majority of applications contains the name of the applicant and the other information which has to be supplied according to the Rules of the Commission. Moreover, the Commission takes a flexible attitude as regards the identity of the applicant. Thus, although it declared inadmissible an application that was signed 'lover of tranquillity', it did so only because the documents filed did not contain a single clue as to the identity of the applicant.[45] The Commission's flexible attitude appears, for instance, from a case in which a number of complaints had been submitted by an association. The Commission considered both the association and its individual members as applicants. With respect to the individual members the Commission held that their identity had been insufficiently established and that accordingly their application, properly speaking, was inadmissible under Article 27(1)(a). Nevertheless, the Commission pursued the examination of the case, on the presumption that this procedural defect would subsequently be redressed. Eventually, however, the application was declared inadmissible on other grounds.[46] In a case where two organisations of doctors and nurses complained of unjustified and discriminatory interference with the right of their member doctors and nurses to respect for their private lives, the Commission noted that

---

[44]   This is often formulated by the Commission as follows: 'An examination by the Commission of this complaint as it has been submitted does not disclose any appearance of a violation of the rights and freedoms set out in the Convention.'

[45]   Appl. 361/58, *X* v. *Ireland*, Case-Law Topics, No. 3, *Bringing an application before the European Commission of Human Rights*, Strasbourg, 1972, p. 10.

[46]   Appl. 3798/68, *Church of X* v. *the United Kingdom*, Yearbook XII (1969), p. 306 (318).

they did not claim to be themselves victims of a violation of the Convention. Once they had stated that they were representing various individuals, who had thus become applicants, it became essential for the associations to identify these individuals and to show that they had received specific instructions from each of them. Since this had not been done, the rest of the application had to be rejected as anonymous, within the meaning of Article 27(1)(a).[47]

2.8.2 The Application must not Constitute an Abuse of the Right of Complaint (Article 27(2))

On this ground, too, in practice very few applications are declared inadmissible. This may probably be accounted for by the fact that it is very difficult to establish such an abuse, since the applicant's motives cannot easily be ascertained, certainly not in so early a stage of the examination.

The prudence of the Commission in this respect appears from the meaning it has given to the term 'abuse'. Thus, the fact that the applicant is inspired by motives of publicity and political propaganda does not necessarily have to imply that the application constitutes an abuse of the right of complaint.[48] In such a case it is only possible to speak of an abuse if an applicant unduly stresses the political aspects of the case.[49] The Commission has also left open the question of whether an abuse is involved on the mere ground that no practical effects are envisaged with the application.[50] The Commission takes a quite lenient attitude in this respect. It held that an application alleged to be devoid of any sound juridical basis and to have been lodged for propaganda purposes may not be rejected as constituting an abuse of the right of petition unless it is clearly based on untrue statements of fact.[51]

An abuse may consist primarily in the object one wishes to attain with the application. Such an abuse of the right of complaint was found to exist in the case of *Ilse Koch*. This wife of the former commandant of the Buchenwald concentration camp had been convicted for violation of the most elementary human rights. She submitted that she was innocent and claimed her release, without invoking a specific provision of the Convention. In her application she voiced a number of accusations and complaints which were not supported in any way by the Convention. The Commission declared her application inadmissible,

---

[47] Appl. 10983/84, *Confédération des Syndicats Médicaux Français and Fédération Nationale des Infirmiers* v. *France*, D&R 47 (1986), p. 224 (229).

[48] Appl. 332/57, *Lawless* v. *Ireland*, Yearbook II (1958-1959), p. 308 (338). See also Appl. 8317/78, *McFeeley* v. *the United Kingdom*, D&R 20 (1980), p. 44 (70-71).

[49] Appl. 1468/62, *Iversen* v. *Norway*, Yearbook VI (1963), p. 278 (326).

[50] Appls 7289/75 and 7349/76, *X and Y* v. *Switzerland*, Yearbook XX (1977), p. 372 (406): 'even assuming that the concept of abuse within the meaning of Art. 27(2) in fine may be understood as including the case of an application serving no practical purpose.'

[51] Appl. 21987/93, *Aksoy* v. *Turkey*, D&R 79-A (1994), p. 60 (71).

because her sole aim evidently was to escape the consequences of her conviction, so that her application constituted a 'clear and manifest abuse'.[52]

The condition that an application must not constitute an abuse is for the Commission also an expedient tool for holding querulous applicants at bay. A German in the course of time had lodged a great many applications which had been rejected without exception, either because they were manifestly ill-founded or because of non-exhaustion of the local remedies. When – together with his wife – he once again lodged several applications, which were moreover substantially the same as previous cases submitted by him, the Commission declared them inadmissible on account of abuse, and gave the applicant to understand:

> It cannot be the task of the Commission, a body which was set up under the Convention 'to ensure the observance of the engagements undertaken by the High Contracting Parties in the present Convention', to deal with a succession of ill-founded and querulous complaints, creating unnecessary work which is incompatible with its real functions, and which hinders it in carrying them out.[53]

Not only the aim pursued in lodging an application, but also the applicant's conduct during the procedure may lead to a declaration of inadmissibility on account of abuse. Thus, applications have been rejected because the applicant had deliberately made false declarations in an attempt to mislead the Commission,[54] or because the applicant failed to furnish the necessary information even after repeated requests,[55] or because the applicant had broken bail and had fled,[56] or because he had used threatening or insulting language *vis-à-vis* the Commission or the respondent Government.[57] The fact that an applicant had omitted to inform the Commission that after the introduction of his application he had instituted before domestic courts proceedings concerning the same facts, was not considered an abuse of the right of petition.[58]

The fact that an applicant gives publicity to certain elements from the examination of his case, contrary to Article 33 of the Convention, may also induce the Commission to declare the application inadmissible on account of abuse.[59] However, the Commission has held that the appearance of an article disclosing

---

[52] Appl. 1270/61, *Ilse Koch* v. *Federal Republic of Germany*, Yearbook V (1962), p. 126 (134-136). See also Appl. 5207/71, *Raupp* v. *Federal Republic of Germany*, Coll. 42 (1973), p. 85 (90).

[53] Appls 5070, 5171, 5186/71, *X* v. *Federal Republic of Germany*, Yearbook XV (1972), p. 474 (482). See also Appls 5145/71, 5246/71, 5333/72, 5586/72, 5587/72 and 5332/72, *Michael and Margarethe Ringeisen* v. *Austria*, Coll. 43 (1973), p. 152 (153); Appl. 13284/87, *M* v. *the United Kingdom*, D&R 54 (1987), p. 214 (218).

[54] Appls 2364/64, 2584/65, 2662/65 and 2748/66, *X* v. *Federal Republic of Germany*, Coll. 22 (1967), p. 103 (109) and Appl. 6029/73, *X* v. *Austria*, Coll. 44 (1973), p. 134.

[55] Appl. 244/57, *X* v. *Federal Republic of Germany*, Yearbook I (1955-1957), p. 196 (197) and Appl. 1297/61, *X* v. *Federal Republic of Germany*, Coll. 10 (1963), p. 47 (48).

[56] Appl. 9742/82, *X* v. *Ireland*, D&R 32 (1983), p. 251 (253).

[57] Appl. 2625/65, *X* v. *Federal Republic of Germany*, Coll. 28 (1969), p. 26 (41-42) and Appl. 5267/71, *X* v. *Federal Republic of Germany*, Coll. 43 (1973), p. 154.

[58] Appl. 13524/88, *F* v. *Spain*, D&R 69 (1991), p. 185 (194).

[59] Council of Europe, *Press Release* C(78)42, 11 October 1978.

confidential information relating to the proceedings before the Commission did not constitute an abuse of the right of petition, since the applicant's representative had merely answered questions put to him by the press, who had secured their information from other sources. The Commission considered that there was no conclusive evidence that the applicant's representative was responsible for the disclosure of this information.[60]

As has been pointed out above, the present admissibility condition does not apply to applications by States. Nevertheless, the case-law of the Commission would appear not to exclude the possibility that an application by a State may likewise be rejected on account of abuse. This would not be done on the ground of the admissibility condition mentioned in Article 27(2), but on the ground of the general legal principle that the right to bring an action before an international organ must not be abused. Referring to its decision in the first *Greek* Case,[61] the Commission stated in the case of *Cyprus* v. *Turkey* that:

> even assuming that it is empowered on general principle to make such a finding, [the Commission] considers that the applicant Government have, at this stage of the proceedings, provided sufficient particularised information of alleged breaches of the Convention for the purpose of Article 24.[62]

The Commission does not exclude the possibility that applications by States are rejected on account of violation of the general prohibition of abuse of right, even though it is not to be assumed that in practice it will lightly reach such a conclusion.

2.8.3 The Application must not be Substantially the Same as a Matter which has Already been Examined by the Commission or has Already been Submitted to Another Procedure of International Investigation or Settlement Unless it Contains Relevant New Information (Article 27(1)(b))

As said above, this ground of inadmissibility does not apply with respect to inter-State complaints.[63] In practice, declarations of inadmissibility on the ground of the identical character of two or more cases submitted to the Commission do not occur frequently.[64] According to the Commission any preceding procedures

---

[60] Appl. 13524/88, *F* v. *Spain*, D&R 69 (1991), p. 185 (194).

[61] Appls 3321-3323/67 and 3344/67, *Denmark, Norway, Sweden and the Netherlands* v. *Greece*, Yearbook XI (1968), p. 690 (764).

[62] Appls 6780/74 and 6950/75, *Cyprus* v. *Turkey*, Yearbook XVIII (1975), p. 82 (124).

[63] Report of 4 October 1983, *Cyprus* v. *Turkey*, D&R 72 (1992), p. 5 (23).

[64] Some of the rare published cases in which this aspect came up for discussion are Appls 5145/71, 5246/71, 5333/72, 5586/72, 5587/72 and 5332/72, *Michael and Margarethe Ringeisen* v. *Austria*, Coll. 43 (1973), p. 152 (153); Appls 5070, 5171 and 5186/71, *X* v. *Federal Republic of Germany*, Yearbook XV (1972), p. 474 (482); and Appls 7572/76, 7586/72 and 7587/76, *Ensslin, Baader and Raspe* v. *Federal Republic of Germany*, Yearbook XXI (1978), p. 418 (452). In Appl. 3479/68, *X* v. *Austria and the Federal Republic of Germany*, Coll. 28 (1969), p. 132 (138), the Commission took into account a previously lodged complaint, 'even if it cannot strictly be said to be substantially the same'.

before the Court should also be taken into consideration.[65] In *Times Newspapers Ltd.*,[66] the applicants referred to their earlier application[67] and alleged the failure of the United Kingdom Government to implement the judgment of the Court in that case.[68] With respect to this part of the application the Commission first pointed out that the supervision of judgments of the Court under Article 54 is entrusted to the Committee of Ministers and subsequently decided that it 'cannot now examine these new developments in relation to the facts of the former case (...), as it is barred from doing so by Article 27 paragraph 1(b) of the Convention.'[69]

(a) An Application which is Substantially the Same

For an answer to the question of whether a concrete case concerns a matter which is substantially the same as a matter which has already been examined by the Commission, it is decisive whether new facts have been put forward in the application. These facts must be of such a nature that they cause a change in the legal and/or factual data on which the Commission based its earlier decision. The mere submission of one or more new legal arguments is therefore insufficient, if the facts on which the application is based are the same.[70] The Commission will not consider as new facts those which were already known to the applicant at the time of the introduction of his application and could therefore have been presented by him on that occasion.[71]

A new fact is indeed involved when an applicant whose earlier application has been declared inadmissible on account of non-exhaustion of the local remedies, has afterwards obtained a decision in the last resort in the national legal system. The Commission's flexibility in this respect is evident from the following example. An applicant had submitted in a previous application that the final decision in his case had been taken by the Court of Appeal at Liège. On that basis, his application was declared inadmissible because he was assumed not to have exhausted the local remedies. In a new application he proved that he had made a

---

[65] See Appl. 6832/74, *X* v. *Sweden* (not published): 'It is true that the Court is not mentioned in Art. 27(1)(b). The article distinguishes between a previous examination by the Commission and another procedure of international investigation or settlement. It follows, however, from a comparison with Art. 62 that the latter type of procedure is another than that provided for in the Convention. This does not therefore exclude the Commission from having regard, under Art. 27(1)(b), to proceedings before the Court.'

[66] Appl. 10243/83, D&R 41 (1985), p. 123.

[67] Appl. 6538/74.

[68] Judgment of 26 April 1979, A.30.

[69] Appl. 10243/83, *Times Newspapers Ltd. and Others* v. *the United Kingdom*, D&R 41 (1985), p. 123 (129). It is incomprehensible why the Commission without any explanation adds: 'This part of the application is therefore incompatible ratione materiae with the provisions of the Convention and must be rejected under Article 27 para. 2.'

[70] See Appl. 202/56, *X* v. *Belgium*, Yearbook I (1955-1957), p. 190 (191) and Appl. 8206/78, *X* v. *the United Kingdom*, D&R 25 (1982), p. 147 (150).

[71] Appl. 13365/86, *Ajinaja* v. *the United Kingdom*, D&R 55 (1988), p. 294 (296).

mistake, since the decision in question had in reality been taken by the Court of Cassation, from whose decisions no appeal lay. The Commission considered this as relevant new information in the sense of Article 27(1)(b).[72] Obviously, a subsequent appeal in the last resort does not avail an applicant if his earlier application has been declared inadmissible on *another* ground *as well*.

A new fact is also involved when new obligations arise from the Convention for the Contracting State in question. An example is the case where a detained person complained about the refusal of the German authorities to permit him to leave Germany and live in Poland. His application was declared inadmissible on account of incompatibility with the provisions of the Convention, because the right to leave the country was not guaranteed in the Convention. In his new application, he invoked Protocol No. 4 – which had meanwhile become binding on Germany –, Article 2(2) of which confers on everyone the right to leave a country, including that of which he is a national. As a result, the application was admissible under Article 27(1)(b). However, it was now rejected as being manifestly ill-founded, because paragraph 3 of Article 2 of Protocol No. 4 was held to permit an exception with respect to detained persons.[73]

Those cases in which the requirement of 'a fair and public hearing within a reasonable time' of Article 6 is at issue[74] may present a somewhat special feature, as is shown by the following decision of the Commission. In his first complaint the applicant alleged a violation of the Convention, because a bankruptcy procedure had been pending against him for the past three years. This application was declared manifestly ill-founded. At the moment the Commission had to give its opinion on his second – identical – complaint, the period had meanwhile increased to four years and eight months. This time the applicant was not dismissed by the Commission, on the ground that 'the time aspect constitutes in itself the relevant new information in the sense of Article 27(1)(b).'[75]

(b) The Same Applicant

From the formulation of Article 27(1)(b) it might be inferred that the words 'substantially the same matter' also cover an application that is otherwise identical but is lodged by another applicant. This provision is, however, to be interpreted in the sense that it is only directed against identical applications by *the same* applicant. It would not be in conformity with the purpose of the Convention to provide individual legal protection, if an application from X, who considers

---

[72] Appl. 3780/68, *X* v. *Belgium*, Coll. 37 (1971), p. 6 (8). See also Appl. 21962/93, *A.D.* v. *the Netherlands*, D&R 76-A (1994), p. 157 (161). See also, on the one hand, Appl. 4517/70, *Huber* v. *Austria*, Yearbook XIV (1971), p. 548, on the other hand, Appl. 6821/74, *Huber* v. *Austria*, D&R 6 (1977), p. 65.

[73] Appl. 4256/69, *X* v. *Federal Republic of Germany*, Coll. 37 (1971), p. 67 (68-69).

[74] See on this *infra* pp. 442-450.

[75] Appl. 8233/78, *X* v. *the United Kingdom*, D&R 17 (1980), p. 122 (130). *Cf.* also Appl. 9621/81, *Vallon* v. *Italy*, D&R 33 (1983), p. 217 (239), in which the continuing detention on remand constituted the relevant new information.

himself to be the victim of a violation of the Convention, would not be admitted on the ground of the fact that an identical violation in relation to Y is already being examined or has already been examined. As appears from its case-law, the Commission does not object to identical applications from *different* applicants, although it will then join such cases, if possible.[76] If an application, both in its facts and in law, is (almost) identical to the case which has already been dealt with by the Commission, it is of course not possible to join it with the previous case, but such an application may be dealt with it in a summary procedure.

Article 27(1)(b) may, however, bar applications from different applicants which concern the same violation against the same person, as in the case where in connection with one and the same violation both the direct and the indirect victim lodge an application. In its earlier case-law, the Commission opined that a new examination of the case is justified only if in each individual case a new fact is involved.[77] In a more recent case, however, the Commission was less strict. This case concerned the execution of an expulsion order from the Federal Republic of Germany to Yugoslavia. At first instance, the fiancee of the person to be expelled lodged a complaint with the Commission, several years later followed by a complaint of the person himself. With respect to the latter application, the Commission decided that it could not be rejected under Article 27(1)(b) as being substantially the same as the first application, because 'this applicant has a specific personal interest in bringing an application before the Commission.'[78] Here, the criterion was not the identity of the case, but the identity of the interests of the applicants involved. Since the second application was lodged by the direct victim, the Commission could of course hardly have decided otherwise.

The question of identical complaints may also arise in connection with the lodging of a complaint by a State as well as by an individual. Thus, in the applications of a number of Northern Irishmen, matters were denounced which had already formed the subject of the application of the Irish Government against the United Kingdom. The latter application had meanwhile been declared admissible, but the examination of the merits was still pending. The Commission did not decide on the question of whether the individual applications were now to be rejected on account of their having the same character as the application by a State, because 'The relevant part of the inter-State case has (...) not yet been

---

[76] See, *e.g.*, the successive Appls 6878/75, *Le Compte* v. *Belgium*, D&R 6 (1977), p. 79 and 7238/75, *Van Leuven and De Meyere* v. *Belgium*, D&R 8 (1977), p. 140. In its decision in the last-mentioned case the Commission held (p. 160): 'In view of all the similarities between the two applications it is desirable that they should be examined together.' The same conclusion can also be drawn from the opinion of the Commission in the Appls 5577/72-5583/72, *Donnelly* et al. v. *the United Kingdom*, Yearbook XVI (1973), p. 212 (266) that 'apart from the fact that the applicants are different in each case (...) this complaint could still not be rejected under Article 27(1)(b) of the Convention.'

[77] Appl. 499/59, *X* v. *Federal Republic of Germany*, Yearbook II (1958-1959), p. 397 (399).

[78] Appl. 9028/80, *X* v. *Federal Republic of Germany*, D&R 22 (1981), p. 236 (237).

examined within the meaning of Article 27(1)(b) of the Convention.'[79] This result in itself may be welcomed, but the reasoning on which it is based is less satisfactory. Indeed, the argument followed by the Commission leaves wide open the possibility that in similar cases, where the examination has already been completed, the Commission may decide differently. On the ground of the above-mentioned emphasis which the Convention puts on individual legal protection this is to be regretted since it might discourage individual applicants. Moreover, the complaint of a State and an individual complaint are distinctly different, both in character and as to the interests involved. The latter specially concerns the personal interests of the individual applicant, while the former is aimed much more at denouncing a general situation concerning 'European public order'. It is therefore questionable whether in the case of a succession of two applications of so different a character it is still possible to speak of 'a matter which is substantially the same'.

(c) The Application may not be the Same as a Matter which has Already been
   Submitted to Another Procedure of International Investigation or Settlement
So far very few decisions of the Commission have been published in which an application was declared inadmissible on the ground that a matter had already been submitted to another international body for investigation or settlement. In view of the small number of international organs charged with the supervision of the implementation of human rights obligations this is not surprising. This admissibility condition, however, may become more and more important in connection with the UN Covenant on Civil and Political Rights and the Optional Protocol accompanying it.[80] This Protocol confers on individuals the right to submit an application ('communication') to the Human Rights Committee,[81] so that a case like that referred to in Article 27(1)(b) is quite conceivable.[82] According to the Commission the purpose of this provision is to avoid a plurality of international proceedings relating to the same case.[83] In order not to run the risk to be declared inadmissible on this ground, the applicant has to withdraw his petition made under the other organ. It is not sufficient to request a suspension of the proceedings pending before an international body, because this does not have the same effect as a complete withdrawal of the application, which is the only step allowing the Commission to examine an application also brought before it.[84]

New events subsequent to the introduction of an application but directly related to the facts adverted to therein will be taken into account by the Commission at the time of the examination of the application. Therefore, an application

---

[79] Appls 5577-5583/72, *Donnelly* et al. v. *the United Kingdom*, Yearbook XVI (1973), p. 212 (266).
[80] The UN Covenant on Civil and Political Rights and the Optional Protocol belonging thereto entered into force on 26 March 1976.
[81] See Art. 1 of the Protocol.
[82] See *supra* pp. 65-69.
[83] Appl. 17512/90, *Calcerrada Fornielles and Cabeza Mato* v. *Spain*, D&R 73 (1992), p. 214 (223).
[84] *Ibidem*, p. 224.

introduced before the Commission by two applicants, which had the same object as the application submitted to the Human Rights Committee by one of the applicants and joined by the second after the introduction of the application before the Commission, was considered to be substantially the same as the one submitted to the Human Rights Committee.[85]

Inadmissibility might also result from the fact that the same matter has been submitted to the Court of Justice of the European Communities. Indeed, as appears from its case-law, this Court is prepared to review the acts and omissions of the Member States of the Communities and of the Community Institutions for their conformity with fundamental human rights on the ground that they form part of the general principles of Community law.[86] The chances of such a coincidence, however, are not very great. Indeed, if, in connection with the same factual situation, a case were to be brought both in Strasbourg and in Luxembourg, in the two procedures different legal issues will probably be at issue.[87] Moreover, even if the two cases are identical, the fact that a case has already been submitted to another judicial organ does not bar its admissibility under the European Convention if relevant new information is put forward to the Commission which is not or has not been examined by that other organ.

In a case where the application had been made by the Council of Civil Service Unions and six individuals, the Commission held that these applicants were not identical with the complainant before the ILO organs concerned. The complaints before the ILO were brought by the Trade Union Congress, through its General Secretary, on its own behalf. The six individual applicants before the Commission would not have been able to bring such complaints since the Committee on Freedom of Association only examines complaints from organisations of workers and employees, as opposed to individual complaints. Accordingly, the application could not be regarded as being substantially the same as the complaints before the ILO.[88] However, in a subsequent case the Commission decided the opposite. The applicants in this case were 23 former employees of a company. They had been dismissed because of the attitude they had taken as members of the works council.

---

[85] *Idem.*

[86] Standing case-law since Case 11/70, *Internationale Handelsgesellschaft*, ECR, 1970, p. 1134.

[87] An example of this is Appl. 6452/74, *Sacchi* v. *Italy*, D&R 5 (1976), p. 43, the core of which was also discussed by the Court of Justice in Luxembourg, of which the court of Biella had requested a preliminary ruling in Case 155/73, *Sacchi*, ECR, 1974, p. 409. Mr Sacchi, operator of a cable television firm (Telebiella) without a licence, refused to pay the contribution for the TV receiving sets, which was punishable under Italian law. Upon this, he was convicted. A request for a licence for transmission *via* a cable system was refused. A presidential decree of 29 March 1973 assimilated cable TV equipment to radio and TV equipment, thus making it subject to the RAI/TV monopoly. Sacchi lodged a complaint with the Commission in Strasbourg about violation of Art. 10(1) of the Convention. Questions were submitted to the Court in Luxembourg, *inter alia,* about free movement of goods and services, competition and national monopolies of a commercial nature. For the consideration of the merits, see *infra* p. 566.

[88] Appl. 11603/85, *Council of Civil Service Unions and Others* v. *the United Kingdom*, D&R 50 (1987), p. 228 (237).

The Government submitted that the World Federation of Industry Workers (WFIW) had submitted a complaint to the Freedom of Association Committee of the ILO. Therefore the complaint should be rejected as being substantially the same. The Commission noted that in the present case, although the main complainant was the WFIW, the four trade unions representing the workers at the company on the works council joined the proceedings, which precisely concerned the dismissal of the 23 applicants, the very persons who now petitioned the Commission. Although formally the 23 individual applicants before the Commission were not the complainants who appeared before the ILO organs, the Commission adopted the view that the complaint was, in substance, submitted by the same applicants. On that basis the Commission concluded that the parties were substantially the same.[89] It seems that the Commission considered it conclusive that the original applicants were also members of the trade union branches which participated in the proceedings before the ILO organs, although the Commission admitted that individual applicants could not complain before the Freedom of Association Committee of the ILO.[90]

2.8.4 The Application must not be Incompatible with the Provisions of the Convention (Article 27(2))

Incompatibility with the Convention is assumed in the case-law of the Commission: (1) if the application falls outside the scope of the Convention *ratione personae, ratione materiae, ratione loci,* or *ratione temporis*; (2) if the individual applicant does not satisfy the condition of Article 25(1); and (3) if the applicant, contrary to Article 17, aims at the destruction of one of the rights and freedoms guaranteed in the Convention. In relation to the categories referred to sub (1), it has been observed above that the Commission does not differentiate clearly between its competence and the admissibility of the application.[91] The territorial and the temporal scope of the Convention have already been discussed above.[92]

(a) Competence *Ratione Personae*

Whether an application falls within the scope of the Convention *ratione personae* is determined by the answer to the question who may submit an application to the Commission (active legitimation) and against whom such an application may be lodged (passive legitimation). This question has been answered *passim* above. An application may be lodged by the Contracting States as well as by those natural persons, non-governmental organisations and groups of individuals who come

---

[89] Appl. 16358/90, *Cereceda Martin and Others* v. *Spain*, D&R 73 (1992), p. 120 (134).

[90] Appl. 11603/85, *Council of Civil Service Unions and Others* v. *the United Kingdom*, D&R 50 (1987), p. 228 (237); Appl. 16358/90, *Cereceda Martin and Others* v. *Spain*, D&R 73 (1992), p. 120 (134).

[91] See *supra* p. 108.

[92] See *supra* pp. 7-15.

under the jurisdiction of the State against which the complaint is directed.[93] With respect to applications by States it is also to be noted that they must be lodged by a national authority competent to act on behalf of the State in international relations. In that respect regard must be had not only to the text of the Constitution but also to the practice under it.[94]

An application by a State may be directed against any other Contracting State, an individual application only against those Contracting States which have recognised the competence of the Commission to receive such applications. This means that the Commission cannot receive applications directed against a State which is not a party to the Convention[95] or, as the case may be, to the Protocols relied upon in the application,[96] or, in the case of an individual application, against a State which is a party to the Convention, but which has not made the declaration referred to in Article 25.[97]

Furthermore, an application will be declared inadmissible *ratione personae* if the alleged violation does not fall under the responsibility of the respondent State. In general, a State is internationally responsible for the acts of its legislative, executive and judicial branch of government. The question may arise as to whether a particular organ or person can be considered to belong to these government organs for the purpose of the European Convention. The case has already been mentioned of a foreign or international organ which is active in the territory of a Contracting State, but does not fall under its responsibility.[98] Furthermore, the situation may arise where a State is responsible for the international relations of a given territory, without it being possible that an application is lodged against it on account of the acts of the authorities in those territories. Indeed, the Convention is only applicable to those territories if the State in question has made a declaration as referred to in Article 63(1).[99]

Applications may be directed only against *States*, and consequently not against individuals or groups of individuals. Applications against individuals are therefore declared inadmissible *ratione personae*.[100] In practice, a comparatively large number of complaints are directed against the most widely varied categories of

---

[93] See *supra* pp. 40 and 44-46.
[94] Appls 6780/74 and 6950/75, *Cyprus* v. *Turkey*, Yearbook XVIII (1975), p. 82 (116).
[95] For some of the numerous examples, see Appl. 262/57, *X* v. *Czechoslovakia*, Yearbook I (1955-1957), p. 170; Appl. 8030/77, *Confédération Française Démocratique du Travail* v. *European Communities*, Yearbook XXI (1978), p. 530 (536-538); Appl. 21090/92, *Heinz* v. *Contracting States also Parties to the European Patent Convention*, D&R 76-A (1994), p. 125 (127).
[96] See, *e.g.*, the Appls 5351/72 and 6579/74, *X* v. *Belgium*, Coll. 46 (1974), p. 71 (80-81); Appl. 22564/93, *Grice* v. *the United Kingdom*, D&R 77-A (1994), p. 90 (97).
[97] See Appl. 62/55, *X* v. *Federal Republic of Germany*, Yearbook I (1955-1957), p. 180.
[98] See *supra* p. 9, note 31. For the special position of the British Judicial Committee of the Privy Council, see Appl. 3813/68, *X* v. *the United Kingdom*, Yearbook XIII (1970), p. 586 (598-600).
[99] On this, see *supra* pp. 7-10.
[100] See Appl. 6956/75, *X* v. *the United Kingdom*, D&R 8 (1978), p. 103 (104); Appl. 19217/91, *Durini* v. *Italy*, D&R 76-A (1994), p. 76 (79), where the complaints concerning the contents of a will were directed against the testator and did not engage the responsibility of the State.

individuals and organisations, such as judges and lawyers in their personal capacity, employers, private radio and TV stations and banks. For the rejection of such complaints the Commission generally invokes Article 19, under which it has to ensure the observance of the engagements which the *Contracting States* have undertaken, and also Article 25, which permits the Commission to consider applications if the applicant claims to be the victim of a violation of the Convention by a *Contracting State*.[101] It appears from its case-law, however, that the Commission does investigate whether a violation of the Convention by an individual may involve the responsibility of a State. Under international law a State is responsible for acts of individuals to the extent that the State has urged the individuals to commit the acts in question, or has given its consent to them, or in violation of its international obligations has neglected to prevent those acts, to punish the perpetrators, or to impose the obligation to redress the injury caused.[102] These principles also apply within the framework of the European Convention,[103] be it that Article 1 creates that responsibility with respect to the treatment of 'everyone within their jurisdiction', and not only of foreigners. The Court has also held that a State cannot absolve itself from responsibility by delegating its obligations to private bodies or individuals.[104]

The starting-point for State responsibility under the Convention is that it applies to all organs of the State, even those which under national law are independent of the Government, such as the judiciary.[105] However, it is not crystal clear in all cases whether a particular institution must be considered, with respect to the Convention, as an organ of the State concerned, so that the latter is responsible for it. It is hardly possible to provide general answers to this question; a good deal depends, in each concrete case, on the precise position of the said institution under national law[106] and the involvement of public authorities. Thus, in the *Campbell and Cosans* Case the Court held the Government of the United Kingdom responsible for acts occurring at State schools, since the State had assumed responsibility for formulating general policy.[107] In a subsequent case, where an applicant and his mother complained about corporal punishment at a private school, the Commission stated that the punishment of the applicant was administered by the headmaster of the private school for whose disciplinary regime the Government had declined responsibility under the Convention. The Commission held, however, in its decision on admissibility that the United Kingdom was responsible under the Convention, Articles 1, 3 and 8 of which having imposed a positive obligation on High Contracting Parties to ensure a legal

---

[101] See, *e.g.*, Appl. 2413/65, *X v. Federal Republic of Germany*, Coll. 23 (1967), p. 1 (7).
[102] See I. Brownlie, *Principles of Public International Law*, Oxford, 1990, pp. 444-476.
[103] See Appl. 852/60, *X v. Federal Republic of Germany*, Yearbook IV (1961), p. 346 (350-352).
[104] Judgment of 23 November 1983, *Van der Mussele*, A.70, pp. 14-15.
[105] See, *e.g.*, Appl. 7743/76, *J.Y. Cosans v. the United Kingdom*, D&R 12 (1978), p. 140 (149).
[106] See, *e.g.*, Appl. 1706/62, *X v. Austria*, Yearbook IX (1966), p. 112 (162-164).
[107] Judgment of 25 February 1982, A.48, p. 15.

system which provides adequate protection to children's physical and emotional integrity:

> The Commission considers that Contracting States do have an obligation under Article 1 of the Convention to secure that children within their jurisdiction are not subjected to torture, inhuman or degrading treatment or punishment, contrary to Article 3 of the Convention. This duty is recognised in English law which provides certain criminal and civil law safeguards against assault or unreasonable punishment. Moreover, children subjected to, or at risk of being subjected to ill-treatment by their parents, including excessive corporal punishment, may be removed from their parents' custody and placed in local authority care.[108]

The Commission also noted that the State obliges parents to educate their children, or have them educated in schools, and that the State has the function of supervising educational standards and the suitability of teaching staff even in independent schools. Furthermore, the effect of compulsory education is that parents are normally obliged to put their children in charge of teachers. If parents choose a private school, the teachers assume the parental role in matters of discipline under the national law while the children are in their care, by virtue of the *in loco parentis* doctrine. In these circumstances the Commission considered that the United Kingdom had a duty under the Convention to secure that all pupils, including pupils at private schools, were not exposed to treatment contrary to Article 3 of the Convention. The Commission considered that the United Kingdom's liability also extended to Article 8 of the Convention in order to protect the right to respect for private life of pupils in private schools to the extent that corporal punishment in such schools might involve an unjustified interference with children's physical and emotional integrity.[109] The case ended in a friendly settlement, once it had been referred to the Court. In the *Costello-Roberts* Case, however, the Court points out that the State has an obligation to secure to children their right to education under Article 2 of Protocol No. 1. Functions relating to the internal administration of a school, such as discipline, cannot be said to be ancillary to the educational process. In this respect, the Court notes that a school's disciplinary system falls within the ambit of the right to education which has also been recognised in Article 28 of the UN Convention of the Rights of the Child. Secondly, it holds that in the United Kingdom, independent schools co-exist with a system of public education. The fundamental right of everyone to education is a right guaranteed equally to pupils in State schools and independent schools, no distinction being made between the two. Finally, the Court refers to the above-mentioned *Van der Mussele* judgment where it held that a State could not absolve itself from responsibility by delegating its obligations to private bodies or individuals.[110]

---

[108] Appl. 14229/88, *Y v. the United Kingdom* (not published). See also the report of the Commission in this case of 8 October 1991, A.247-A, pp. 11-12.

[109] *Idem.*

[110] Judgment of 25 March 1993, A.247-C, p. 58.

With respect to so-called public industries and enterprises, the case-law of the Commission is still rather casuistic. In a number of cases it did not reach a decision on responsibility.[111] In one case the Commission described public transport companies as *entreprises para-étatiques*, for which the Government was not responsible.[112] Two later decisions, however, point in the other direction. In both cases the applicants had been discharged by British Rail, because they had refused to join a trade union (the so-called 'closed-shop system'). The Commission reached the conclusion that, as a public industry, British Rail came under the responsibility of the United Kingdom, and that accordingly the applications were admissible *ratione personae*.[113]

Does the responsibility of the Contracting States under the Convention extend still further, in the sense that it also covers cases where there is no question of a direct responsibility for the acts or omissions of governmental organs or of negligence with respect to the acts of individuals? One decision of the Commission seems to point in that direction. At issue was whether the Irish Government was responsible for certain acts of an institution which had been called into existence by law, but which otherwise was largely independent of the State. The Commission came to the conclusion that the acts concerned in this case (alleged violation of Article 11) did not fall under the direct responsibility of the Irish Government. However, the Commission subsequently accepted the submission that, despite this, the Irish Government would have violated the Convention if it were to be established that the national law does not protect one of the rights or freedoms guaranteed by the Convention, the violation of which is alleged before the Commission, or at least does not provide a remedy for enforcing such protection.[114] However, rather than a matter of State responsibility for acts of individuals this is a case of the possible violation by the State of a special obligation resulting from the Convention, *viz.* under Article 13.[115] In the *Nielssen* Case, the Government argued that the placement of a minor in a psychiatric hospital was the sole responsibility of the mother. The majority of the Commission found, however, that the final decision on the question of hospitalisation of the applicant was not taken by the holder of parental rights but by the Chief Physician of the Child Psychiatric Ward of the State Hospital, thus engaging the responsibility of the State under Article 5(1).[116] The Court disagreed with the Commission and held that the decision on the hospitalisation was in fact taken by the mother in her capacity as holder of

---

[111] Appl. 3059/67, *X* v. *the United Kingdom*, Coll. 28 (1969), p. 89 (93) and Appl. 4515/70, *X and the Association of Z* v. *the United Kingdom*, Yearbook XIV (1971), p. 538 (544).

[112] Appl. 3789/68, *X* v. *Belgium*, Coll. 33 (1970), p. 1 (3-4).

[113] Appl. 7601/76, *Young and James* v. *the United Kingdom*, Yearbook XX (1977), p. 520 (560-562) and Appl. 7806/77, *Webster* v. *the United Kingdom*, D&R 12 (1978), p. 168 (173-175).

[114] Appl. 4125/69, *X* v. *Ireland*, Yearbook XIV (1971), p. 198 (218-224).

[115] On this, see *infra* pp. 696-710.

[116] Report of 12 March 1987, A.144, p. 38.

parental rights.[117] All in all the exact scope under the Convention of State responsibility for private acts or omissions has not yet been clearly defined.

(b) Competence *Ratione Materiae*

In order to answer the question of whether an application falls within the scope of the Convention *ratione materiae*,[118] it is necessary to differentiate between State applications and individual applications.[119]

Article 24, which permits the Contracting States to lodge applications on 'any alleged breach of the provisions of the Convention by another High Contracting Party', leaves open the possibility for States to submit applications which relate to provisions of the Convention other than the articles of Section I. Articles that might be considered as such, for instance, are Article 1 concerning the obligation for a Contracting State to secure to everyone within its jurisdiction the rights and freedoms of Section I of the Convention,[120] and Article 25(1) in case of interference with the exercise of the individual right of complaint. The same applies to Articles 32(4) and 53 in case of refusal to give effect to a decision of the Committee of Ministers or the Court respectively, and Article 57 in case of refusal to furnish the requested information to the Secretary General of the Council of Europe concerning the implementation of the provisions of the Convention. So far the Contracting States have not availed themselves of this wider right of action, except where Article 1 is concerned.

The right of complaint of individuals has a somewhat more limited character. It appears from Article 25 that individuals may lodge complaints only about 'the rights set forth in this Convention', which implies that their complaints may relate only to the articles of Section I and the articles of the Protocols containing additional rights.[121] The question does arise whether an exception must be made for Article 25; in other words, whether the right of complaint itself, the exercise of which the Contracting States have undertaken not to hinder, may be considered a 'right'. As a rule the Commission deals with such a complaint in another way than with a complaint concerning one of the rights or freedoms of Section I, in that it consults directly with the Government concerned.[122]

It might be argued that apart from the right of individual complaint under Article 25, an individual who has been successful before the Court, if he feels that the judgment has not been complied with, properly may claim to be a victim of

---

[117] Judgment of 28 November 1988, A.144, p. 23.

[118] For the relationship between this admissibility condition and the requirement that the complaint must not be manifestly ill-founded, see *infra* pp. 163-164.

[119] Strictly speaking, inter-State applications cannot be rejected on this ground. As already indicated *supra* (p. 107), inter-State applications also may fall outside the competence of the Commission, and that point is in general dealt with by the Commission as an admissibility problem.

[120] On this, see *infra* pp. 695-696.

[121] For the question of whether individuals may bring an independent complaint concerning Art. 1, see *infra* p. 695.

[122] See *supra* pp. 62-65.

a violation of Article 53, which contains the obligation to abide by the judgment of the Court. In the case of *Olsson I*, the main issue was whether the decision of the Swedish authorities to take the children of the applicants into care had given rise to a violation of Article 8 of the Convention. The Court found a violation of that provision and awarded the applicants just satisfaction under Article 50 of the Convention.[123] In the case of *Olsson II*, the applicants complained that despite the Court's *Olsson I* judgment, the Swedish authorities had continued to hinder their reunion with their children. The applicants had still not been allowed to meet the children under circumstances which would have enabled them to re-establish parent-child relationships. In their view, Sweden had continued to act in breach of Article 8 and had thereby failed to comply with its obligations under Article 53 of the Convention. The Court referred to Resolution DH (88)18, adopted on 26 October 1988, concerning the execution of the *Olsson I* judgment, where the Committee of Ministers, 'having satisfied itself that the Government of Sweden has paid to the applicants the sums provided for in the judgment', declared that the Committee had 'exercised its functions under Article 54 of the Convention.' The Court held that in the circumstances of the case no separate issue arose under Article 53, since the present complaint raised a new issue which had not been determined by the *Olsson I* judgment.[124] The Court left thus open the possibility that there might be circumstances under which a complaint under Article 53 of the Convention could be examined by it. Judge Martens, as he then was, has questioned if the Committee of Ministers' competence under Article 54 of the Convention is an exclusive one. He gives two persuasive reasons for taking the view that complaints under Article 53 should not be decided by the Committee of Ministers but by the Court. In the first place, the interpretation of its judgments is, in the nature of things, better left to the Court than to a gathering of professional diplomats who are not necessarily trained lawyers possessing the qualifications laid down in the Convention. Secondly, the members of the Committee of Ministers are under the direct authority of their national administration and cannot be considered as a 'tribunal' in the sense of the Convention.[125]

The Commission cannot, of course, deal with complaints about rights or freedoms not set forth in the Convention. Complaints concerning such rights and freedoms are declared inadmissible by the Commission as being incompatible with the Convention. In practice a great many complaints concern the most widely varied 'rights and freedoms'. From the colourful case-law of the Commission the following examples of incompatibility *ratione materiae* may be cited: right to a university degree, right to asylum, right to start a business, right to diplomatic

---

[123] Judgment of 24 March 1988, A.130.
[124] Judgment of 27 November 1992, A.250.
[125] S.K. Martens, 'Individual Complaints under Article 53 of the European Convention on Human Rights', in: Rick Lawson and Matthijs de Blois (eds.), *The Dynamics of the Protection of Human Rights in Europe. Essays in Honour of Henry G. Schermers*, Vol. III, Dordrecht, 1994, pp. 253-286 (284-286).

protection, right to a divorce, right to a driving licence, a general right to free legal aid, right to free medical aid, right to adequate housing, right to a nationality, right to a passport, right to a pension, right to a promotion and the right to be recognised as a scholar. In this context it should, however, be borne in mind that a right which is not set forth in the Convention may find protection *indirectly* *via* one of the provisions of the Convention. Thus, it is conceivable that, although the right to admission to a country of which one is not a national has not been included in the Convention, under certain circumstances a person cannot be denied admission to a country if his right to respect for his family life (Article 8) would be violated. Similarly, although the Convention does not recognise a right to a pension, violation of an existing right to a pension may be contrary to Article 1 of Protocol No. 1, in which the right to the enjoyment of possessions is protected.[126]

Complaints to be equated with those concerning rights not protected in the Convention are complaints concerning rights which are indeed incorporated in the Convention, but with respect to which the respondent State has made a reservation.[127] Complaints relating to such rights are also declared inadmissible by the Commission on account of incompatibility with the Convention.[128]

For all this it is important that the Commission does not require the applicant to indicate accurately in his application the rights set forth in the Convention which in his opinion have been violated. The Commission has proved prepared to investigate *ex officio*, by reference to the submissions of the applicant, whether there has been a violation of one or more of the provisions of Section I. This approach of the Commission is in conformity with the above-mentioned objective character of the European Convention.[129] Nevertheless, it remains advisable for an applicant and his counsel to raise all important points of fact and law already during the examination of admissibility. The possible consequences if this is not done are apparent from the *Winterwerp* Case. When the question arose whether Article 6(1), too, was applicable in that case, the Commission submitted:

---

[126] For these examples, see *infra* pp. 618-625.

[127] See *infra* pp. 773-784.

[128] See, *e.g.*, Appl. 1452/62, *X v. Austria*, Yearbook VI (1963), p. 268 (276).

[129] See *supra* pp. 40-41. The approach was confirmed expressly by the Court in its judgment of 6 November 1980, *Guzzardi*, A.39, pp. 21-23. In that case the Commission had – wrongly, according to the Italian Government – also considered the complaint in the light of Art. 5, whereas the applicant had not expressly referred to it. On the basis of a detailed motivation the Court held as follows: 'The Commission and the Court have to examine in the light of the Convention as a whole the situation impugned by an applicant. In the performance of this task, they are, notably, free to give to the facts of the case, as found to be established by the material before them (...), a characterisation in law different from that given to them by the applicant' (p. 23).

This question, which was raised by the applicant's counsel in the course of the examination of the merits, relates to facts distinct from those originally presented to the Commission, which has not received any detailed submissions thereon. The Commission therefore considers that it ought not, in the present case, to express an opinion on this important new point.[130]

In this case, in our opinion, the issue of Article 6 was much more closely related to the subject-matter of the original complaint than the Commission suggested. In addition, one may wonder why the Commission had not invited the applicant to elaborate on the issue if the submissions received were not detailed enough. Anyhow, the Court held that there was an evident connection between the issue of Article 6 and the initial complaints. This, in combination with the fact that the Netherlands Government had not raised a preliminary objection on the point, induced the Court to take the alleged violation of Article 6 into consideration.[131]

(c) Incompatible with the Provisions of the Convention

The second of the above-mentioned categories of cases in which the application is not compatible with the provisions of the Convention – those cases where the applicant does not satisfy the condition of Article 25 – in fact concerns the condition which has already been discussed at length, *viz.* that an individual applicant must be able to furnish *prima facie* evidence that he is personally the victim of the violation of the Convention alleged by him, or at least has well-founded reasons for considering himself to be the victim. If he merely puts forward a violation *in abstracto*, or a violation which has done a wrong only to other persons, his application is incompatible with the provisions of the Convention.[132]

The most obvious case of incompatibility with the provisions of the Convention is the third of the above-mentioned categories. This concerns applications which are directed at the destruction or limitation of one of the rights or freedoms guaranteed in the Convention, and as such conflict with Article 17, which will hereafter be discussed in greater detail.[133] Even if Article 17 had not been written, such applications of course would still be inadmissible, *viz.* on account of abuse of the right of complaint in the sense of Article 27(2).

---

[130] Report of 15 December 1977, B.31 (1983), p. 45.
[131] Judgment of 24 October 1979, A.33, pp. 27-28.
[132] See *supra* pp. 48-58.
[133] See *infra* pp. 755-761.

2.9 The Domestic Remedies must have been Exhausted (Articles 26 and 27(3))

2.9.1 General

Article 26 provides:

> The Commission may only deal with the matter after all domestic remedies have been exhausted, according to the generally recognised rules of international law.

This is the so-called rule of the 'exhaustion of local remedies' (*épuisement des voies de recours internes*), which is to be regarded as a general rule of international procedural law.

Article 26 refers expressly to the general rules of international law in the matter, and in its case-law the Commission is indeed frequently guided by international judicial and arbitral decisions with respect to this rule, which will hereafter be called the 'local remedies rule'. The Commission referred expressly, for instance, to the judgment of the International Court of Justice in the *Interhandel* Case concerning the rationale of the local remedies rule.[134] In the *Nielsen* Case the Commission formulated this rationale as follows:

> The Respondent State must first have an opportunity to redress by its own means within the framework of its own domestic legal system the wrong alleged to have been done to the individual.[135]

Consequently, States are dispensed from answering before an international body for their acts before they have had an opportunity to provide a remedy through their own legal system. In this respect the Court pointed out in the *Akdivar* Case that this rule is based on the assumption, reflected in Article 13 of the Convention, that there is an effective remedy available in respect of the alleged breach in the domestic system irrespective of whether or not the provisions of the Convention are incorporated in national law. In this way, the Court continued, it is an important aspect of the principle that the machinery of protection established by the Convention is subsidiary to the national systems safeguarding human rights.[136]

The requirement of the prior exhaustion of the local remedies in principle holds for applications by States as well as for individual applications. This ensues from the wording of Article 27(1) and (2) as compared to that of Article 27(3). The first two paragraphs of Article 27 expressly declare the admissibility conditions mentioned therein to be applicable only to applications lodged under Article 25,

---

[134] *ICJ Reports*, 1959, p. 6 (27).

[135] Appl. 343/57, *Schouw Nielsen v. Denmark*, Yearbook II (1958-1959), p. 412 (438). See also Appl. 5964/72, *X v. Federal Republic of Germany*, D&R 3 (1976), p. 57 (60); Appl. 12945/87, *Hatjianastasiou v. Greece*, D&R 65 (1990), p. 173 (177); judgment of 20 September 1993, *Saïdi*, A.261-C, p. 55.

[136] Judgment of 16 September 1996, Reports 1996-IV, Vol. 15, para. 65; judgment of 18 December 1996, *Aksoy*, Reports 1996-VI, Vol. 26, para. 51.

while the third paragraph of Article 27, which refers to Article 26, where the local remedies rule is laid down, refers generally to 'any petition' and is therefore also applicable to applications by States. The same conclusion flows from the fact that the local remedies rule is a general rule of international procedural law.

While in the case of an individual application the local remedies must have been exhausted by the applicant himself, with respect to applications by States, the rule implies that the local remedies must have been exhausted by those individuals in respect to whom, according to the allegation of the applicant State, the Convention has been violated.[137]

In the *Pfunders* Case Austria submitted that, since the right of complaint of States is based on the principle of the collective guarantee and the public interest, and since an applicant State need not prove that an injury has been sustained, the local remedies rule does not hold for States.[138] The Commission, however, rejected this line of reasoning by referring to the terms of Articles 26 and 27, and held that the principle on which the local remedies rule is based should be applied *a fortiori* in an international system which affords protection not only to the applicant State's own nationals, but to everyone who is in one way or another subject to the jurisdiction of the respondent State.[139] By this statement the Commission confirmed its earlier point of view in the second *Cyprus* Case.[140]

The local remedies rule is not an admissibility condition with an *absolute* content. On the basis of the reference in Article 26 to the 'generally recognised rules of international law' this rule is applied with flexibility.[141] Point of departure is that each concrete case should be judged 'in the light of its particular facts'.[142] According to the Court this means, amongst other things, that it must take realistic account not only of the existence of formal remedies in the legal system of the Contracting Party concerned but also of the general legal and political context in which they operate as well as the personal circumstances of the applicants.[143] In this respect the Court noted in the *Akdivar* Case that:

> the situation existing in South-East Turkey at the time of the applicants' complaints was – and continued to be – characterised by significant civil strife due to the campaign of terrorist violence waged by the PKK and the counter-insurgency measures taken by the Government in response to it. In such a situation it must be recognised that there may be obstacles to the proper functioning of the system of the administration of justice. In

---

[137] The condition applies in international law only when the action of a State is concerned with the treatment of individuals. If a State puts forward its own legal position, the condition is not applied, since as a rule a State cannot be subjected against its will to the jurisdiction of another State.

[138] Appl. 788/60, *Austria v. Italy*, Yearbook IV (1961), p. 116 (146-148).

[139] *Ibidem*, pp. 148-152. See also Appls 6780/74 and 6950/75, *Cyprus v. Turkey*, Yearbook XVIII (1975), p. 82 (100).

[140] Appl. 299/57, *Greece v. the United Kingdom*, Yearbook II (1958-1959), p. 186 (190-196).

[141] The Court has frequently stated that Article 26 must be applied with some degree of flexibility and without excessive formalism. See *e.g.* judgment of 19 March 1991, *Cardot*, A.200, p. 18; judgment of 23 April 1992, *Castells*, A.232, p. 19; judgment of 16 December 1992, *Geouffre de la Pradelle*, A.253-B, p 40; judgment of 16 September 1996, *Akdivar*, Reports 1996-IV, Vol. 15, para. 69.

[142] Appl. 343/57, *Schouw Nielsen v. Denmark*, Yearbook II (1958-1959), p. 412 (442-444).

[143] Judgment of 16 September 1996, *Akdivar*, Reports 1996-IV, Vol. 15, para. 69.

particular, the difficulties in securing probative evidence for the purposes of domestic legal proceedings, inherent in such a troubled situation, may make the pursuit of judicial remedies futile and the administrative inquiries on which such remedies depend may be prevented from taking place.[144]

It should be mentioned at the outset that the local remedies rule does not apply at all to proceedings for affording satisfaction under Article 50 of the Convention.[145] In fact, such proceedings do not ensue from a new application, but constitute a continuation of the original application after a violation has been found by the Court. Questions of admissibility are not involved there at all.[146]

2.9.2 The Local Remedies Rule does not Apply to (Inter-State) Complaints Concerning Legislative Measures and/or Administrative Practices

(a) Inter-State Complaints
The rule does not apply when a State brings up the legislation or administrative practice of another State without the complaint being related to one or more concrete persons as victims of this legislation or administrative practice (the so-called 'abstract' complaints). In such a case there are no individuals who must have exhausted the local remedies, while the applicant State itself cannot be expected to institute proceedings before the national authorities of the respondent State. An example is the first *Cyprus* Case, where Greece submitted that a number of emergency acts which were in force in Cyprus at that time conflicted with the provisions of the Convention. In this case the Commission decided that:

> the provision of Article 26 concerning the exhaustion of domestic remedies (...) does not apply to the present application, the scope of which is to determine the compatibility with the Convention of legislative measures and administrative practices in Cyprus.[147]

Later case-law also shows that the local remedies rule does not apply if the application does not relate to individual decisions or acts of the authorities and to any concrete victim thereof, but is rather designed to have national legislation and/or an administrative practice received for their compatibility with the Convention.[148] According to the case-law, an administrative practice comprises two elements: repetition of acts and official tolerance. The first element is defined as:

---

[144] Judgment of 16 September 1996, *Akdivar*, Reports 1996-IV, Vol. 15, para. 70.
[145] On this, see *infra* pp. 241-242.
[146] Judgment of 10 March 1972, *De Wilde, Ooms and Versyp* (*'Vagrancy'* Cases), A.14, p. 8.
[147] Appl. 176/56, *Greece* v. *the United Kingdom*, Yearbook II (1958-1959), p. 182 (184); Appls 9940-9944/82, *France, Norway, Denmark, Sweden and the Netherlands* v. *Turkey*, D&R 35 (1984), p. 143 (162-163).
[148] See, *e.g.*, Appl. 5310/71, *Ireland* v. *the United Kingdom*, Yearbook XV (1972), p. 76 (242); Appl. 4448/70, *Second Greek* Case, Yearbook XIII (1970), p. 108 (134-136); and Appls 9940-9944/82, *France, Norway, Denmark, Sweden and the Netherlands* v. *Turkey*, D&R 35 (1984), p. 143 (162 *et seq.*). See also the judgment of 16 September 1996, *Akdivar*, Reports 1996-IV, Vol. 15, para. 67.

an accumulation of identical or analogous breaches which are sufficiently numerous and interconnected to amount not merely to isolated incidents or exceptions but to a pattern or system.[149]

By official tolerance is meant that:

> though acts of torture or ill-treatment are plainly illegal, they are tolerated in the sense that the superiors of those immediately responsible, though cognisant of such acts, take no action to punish them or to prevent their repetition; or that a higher authority, in face of numerous allegations, manifests indifference by refusing any adequate investigation of their truth or falsity, or that in judicial proceedings a fair hearing of such complaints is denied.[150]

In the case of *France, Norway, Denmark, Sweden and the Netherlands against Turkey*, the Commission added that 'any action taken by the higher authority must be on a scale which is sufficient to put an end to the repetition of acts or to interrupt the pattern or system.'[151] A condition is always that the applicant State should give 'substantial evidence' of the existence of the national legislation or administrative practice concerned. This requirement of 'substantial evidence' may take on a different meaning depending on whether the admissibility stage or the examination of the merits is concerned. According to the Commission:

> The question whether the existence of an administrative practice is established or not can only be determined after an examination of the merits. At the stage of admissibility *prima facie* evidence, while required, must also be considered as sufficient. (...) There is *prima facie* evidence of an alleged administrative practice where the allegations concerning individual cases are sufficiently substantiated, considered as a whole and in the light of the submissions of the applicant and the respondent Party. It is in this sense that the term 'substantial evidence' is to be understood.[152]

If the State does not succeed in doing so, the local remedies rule applies.

(b) Individual Complaints

In the case of individual applicants there can be no question of a completely abstract complaint about an administration practice. The applicant must submit that he is the victim of the alleged violation, which means that he is at the same time the person who must have exhausted all available local remedies.

When an applicant submitted that no local remedy had been available to him, because his complaint concerned the compatibility of the Belgian divorce legislation with the Convention, the Commission decided that nothing had prevented him from submitting this question to the Belgian Court of Cassation.[153] And in the case of an application against the Netherlands concerning the discriminatory character of fiscal legislation with respect to married

---

[149] Judgment of 18 January 1978, *Ireland* v. *the United Kingdom*, A.25, p. 64.

[150] Report of 5 November 1969, *Greek* Case, Yearbook XII (1969), p. 196.

[151] Appl. 9940-9944/82, *France, Norway, Denmark, Sweden and the Netherlands* v. *Turkey*, D&R 35 (1984), p. 143 (164).

[152] *Ibidem*, pp. 164-165.

[153] Appl. 1488/62, *X* v. *Belgium*, Coll. 13 (1964), p. 93 (96).

women, the Commission pointed out that the applicant could have submitted the question of the compatibility of the challenged provisions with the Convention, under (then) Article 66 of the Dutch Constitution, to the Dutch courts.[154] Both applications were declared inadmissible under Article 26.[155] It may be assumed that the Commission will take a similar position when in the case of an application by a State certain legislation or an administrative practice is submitted for review, but the complaint at the same time concerns concrete persons to whom an effective and adequate local remedy is available.

As has been mentioned above, however, a legislative measure or administrative practice may indeed be challenged by an individual applicant, provided that he proves satisfactorily that he himself is the victim of it. That a legislative measure or administrative practice may be of such a nature as to justify the presumption that the remedies of the State in question offer no prospects of effective redress. This is clearly the case if the situation complained of precisely consists of the absence of an effective judicial remedy required by one of the provisions of the Convention. Thus, for example, in *G* v. *Belgium*, the Commission concluded that 'as far as Article 5(4) is concerned, the question of exhaustion of domestic remedies does not arise.' The reason, according to the Commission, was 'that Belgian law does not provide for a judicial remedy which would make it possible to take a speedy decision as to the lawfulness of the detention of a person placed at the Government's disposal.' The procedures referred to by the Belgian Government did not fulfil the requirement of effectiveness.[156]

Ineffectiveness of remedies may particularly occur in the case of practices of torture and inhuman treatment. On that ground, in the *Donnelly* Case, the Commission took the view that in such a situation the local remedies rule is not applicable, provided that the applicant provides *prima facie* evidence that such a practice has occurred and that he is the victim of it.[157] Unlike in the above-mentioned inter-State applications, here the rule is not inapplicable because the application is assumed to have an abstract character, but as a result of the principle, also recognised in general international law, that remedies which in

---

[154] Appl. 2780/66, *X* v. *the Netherlands* (not published).

[155] The two applications mentioned were rejected on the ground of Art. 26, but might also have been declared inadmissible on the ground of Art. 27(2). In both cases the applicants had not submitted that they were victims of the alleged violation, so that these cases concerned in reality completely abstract complaints, which the Commission usually rejects on account of incompatibility with the provisions of the Convention.

[156] Appl. 9107/80, D&R 33 (1983), p. 76 (79).

[157] Appls 5577-5583/72, Yearbook XVI (1973), p. 212 (262). See also the report of the Commission of 5 November 1969 in the *Greek* Case, Yearbook XII (1969), p. 194. *Cf.* Appls 9911/82 and 9945/82, *R, S, A and C* v. *Portugal*, D&R 36 (1984), p. 200 (207), in which the Commission stated that the applicant must provide detailed allegations, if the remedy is to be considered ineffective.

advance are certain not to be effective or adequate need not be exhausted.[158] This became quite clear when in the next stage of the same *Donnelly* Case the Commission, quite unexpectedly, on the basis of its examination of the facts concluded that effective possibilities of redress were indeed present, and on that ground, by applying Article 29, declared the application inadmissible because the local remedies rule had not been complied with.[159] A given administrative practice may therefore give rise to the presumption that the local remedies are not effective, but whether that is indeed the case is a question subject to investigation by the Strasbourg organs.[160]

Several cases have been submitted by Kurdish citizens alleging that an administrative practice exists on the part of the Turkish authorities of tolerating abuses of human rights in relation to persons in police custody.[161] In one case the applicant had been killed following the submission of his application to the Commission and there were indications that to pursue the available remedies might have entailed serious risks for the other applicants. The Commission held in these cases that it was not necessary to resolve the question if there existed an administrative practice, because the applicants had done all that could be expected in the circumstances in relation to the local remedies. In the *Aksoy* Case the Commission noted the applicant's declaration that he had told the public prosecutor that he had been tortured. Moreover, when asked to sign a statement, he had answered that he could not sign because he could not move his hands. Although it was found not possible to establish in detail what happened during the applicant's meeting with the public prosecutor, the Commission found no reason to doubt that during their conversation there were elements which should have made the public prosecutor initiate an investigation or, at the very least, try to obtain further information from the applicant about his state of health or about the treatment to which he had been subjected. The Commission further noted that, after his detention, the applicant was in a vulnerable position, if he had, as he stated, been subjected to torture during his detention. The threats to which the applicant claimed to have been exposed after he had complained to the Commission, as well as his tragic death in circumstances which had not been fully clarified, were further elements which could at least support the view that the pursuance of remedies was not devoid of serious risks. The applicant could be said

---

[158] For this principle, see with respect to inter-State applications Appl. 299/57, *Greece* v. *the United Kingdom, Yearbook* II (1958-1959), p. 186 (192-194), and with respect to individual applications Appl. 5493/72, *Handyside* v. *the United Kingdom,* Yearbook XVII (1974), p. 228 (288-290).

[159] Appls 5577-5583/72, Yearbook XIX (1976), p. 84 (248-254).

[160] *Cf.* also Appl. 9471/81, *X and Y* v. *the United Kingdom,* D&R 36 (1984), p. 49 (61). Here the Commission simply concluded that, since there is no dispute between the parties where the compliance with Art. 26 is concerned, it is not necessary to go into the question whether Art. 26 is inapplicable in the present case because of the existence of a State practice.

[161] Appl. 21987/93, *Aksoy* v. *Turkey,* D&R 79-A (1994), p. 60 (70-71); Appl. 21893/93, *Akdivar* v. *Turkey* (not published); Appl. 21895/93, *Çagirga* v. *Turkey* (not published).

to have complied with the domestic remedies rule.[162] The Court accepted the facts as they had been established by the Commission and, on that basis, held that these constituted special circumstances which absolved Mr Aksoy from the obligation to exhaust the local remedies. Having reached that conclusion the Court did not find it necessary to pronounce on whether there existed an administrative practice obstructing applications being made.[163]

At an earlier occasion, three applicants who were placed in police custody and suspected of an offence coming within the jurisdiction of the State Security Council, alleged violations of Article 3 in that they were subjected to torture while held *incommunicado* in police custody. The Commission held that the Government had not mentioned any domestic remedy available to the applicants with regard to their detention *incommunicado* by the police, as such. Apparently this particular form of detention was an administrative practice.[164] In the *Akdivar* Case, the applicants maintained their allegations before the Court, which they had already made before the Commission, that the destruction of their homes was part of a State-inspired policy. That policy, in their submissions, was tolerated, condoned and possibly ordered by the highest authorities in the State aimed at massive population displacement in the emergency region of South-East Turkey. There was thus an administrative practice which rendered any remedies illusory, inadequate and ineffective. The Court concluded that there were special circumstances absolving the applicants from the obligation to exhaust their domestic remedies. The Court also emphasised that its ruling was confined to the particular circumstances of that case. It was not to be interpreted as a general statement that remedies were ineffective in that area of Turkey.[165]

2.9.3 What Remedies are Available?

In connection with the local remedies rule it is in the first place important to know what remedies are available. That question is to be answered on the basis of national law. It is for the respondent State to introduce any objection that a given applicant has not exhausted domestic remedies[166] and to meet the burden of proving the existence of available and sufficient domestic remedies.[167] The respondent State also has the burden of proving that the existing remedies are effective, albeit only in cases where there is 'serious doubt'.[168]

No definition of the term 'remedy' is to be found in the case-law of the Commission. In various places it does, however, give some indications as to its meaning. The concept of 'remedy' at all events does not cover those procedures in which one does not claim a right, but attempts to obtain a favour. Examples are

---

[162] Appl. 21987/93, *Aksoy* v. *Turkey*, D&R 79-A (1994), p. 60 (70-71).
[163] Judgment of 18 December 1996, Reports 1996-VI, Vol. 26, paras 55-57.
[164] Appls 16311/90 and 16313/90, *Hazar and Acik* v. *Turkey*, D&R 72 (1992), p. 200 (208).
[165] Judgment of 16 September 1996, Reports 1996-IV, Vol. 15, para. 77.
[166] Appl. 9120/80, *Unterpertinger* v. *Austria*, D&R 33 (1983), p. 80 (83).
[167] Appl. 9013/80, *Farrel* v. *the United Kingdom*, D&R 30 (1983), p. 96 (101-102).
[168] Appls 8805/79 and 8806/79, *De Jong and Baljet* v. *the Netherlands*, D&R 24 (1981), p. 144 (150).

the action for rehabilitation in Belgium,[169] the so-called 'petition to the Queen' in England,[170] and the right of petition under Article 5 of the Dutch Constitution.[171]

A question, which for a long time had been left undecided in the case-law is what an applicant should do when different remedies are open to him. Must he pursue them all or may he confine himself to bringing the action which in his view is most likely to be successful? The text of Article 26 appears to suggest the former, for it refers to 'all domestic remedies'. The Commission in a 1974 decision seemed to take a less stringent approach. It held that:

> where there is a single remedy it should be pursued up to the highest level. The position is not so certain where the domestic law provides a number of different remedies. In such cases the Commission tends to admit that Article 26 has been complied with if the applicant exhausts only the remedy or remedies which are reasonably likely to prove effective.[172]

In a later case the Commission added:

> Where (...) there is a choice of remedies open to the applicant to redress an alleged violation of the Convention, Article 26 of the Convention must be applied to reflect the practical realities of the applicant's position in order to ensure the effective protection of the rights and freedoms guaranteed by the Convention.[173]

It is up to the applicant in those cases to indicate which remedy he has chosen and for what reasons. These grounds have to be objective and reasonable.[174] The Commission has further held that when the applicant has sought in vain an apparently effective remedy, he cannot be required to try others which may be available but are probably ineffective.[175] Moreover, for a remedy to be considered effective it must be capable of remedying directly the situation complained of.[176] Finally, if it cannot be shown that a remedy presents at least some minimal prospect of success, the individual is not required to pursue it.[177]

With respect to the way in which and the time-limits within which proceedings must be instituted, national law is equally decisive. If in his appeal to a national court an applicant has failed to observe the procedural requirements or the time-limits, and his case accordingly has been rejected, the local remedies rule has not

---

[169] Appl. 214/56, *De Becker* v. *Belgium*, Yearbook II (1958-1959), p. 214 (236-238).

[170] Appl. 299/57, *Greece* v. *the United Kingdom*, Yearbook II (1958-1959), p. 186 (192).

[171] See the report of the Budget Committee for Foreign Affairs of the Dutch Parliament, Yearbook II (1958-1959), p. 566.

[172] Appl. 5874/72, *Monika Berberich* v. *Federal Republic of Germany*, Yearbook XVII (1974), p. 386 (418).

[173] Appl. 9118/80, *Allgemeine Gold- und Silberscheideanstalt A.G.* v. *the United Kingdom*, D&R 32 (1983), p. 159 (165).

[174] *Idem.*

[175] Appl. 9248/81, *Leander* v. *Sweden*, D&R 34 (1983), p. 78 (33); Appl. 14838/89, *A* v. *France*, D&R 69 (1991), p. 286 (302).

[176] Appl. 11660/85, *X* v. *Portugal*, D&R 59 (1983), p. 85 (92).

[177] Appl. 8378/78, *Kamal* v. *the United Kingdom*, D&R 20 (1980), p. 168 (170).

been complied with and his application is declared inadmissible.[178] However, non-exhaustion of domestic remedies cannot be held against the applicant if in spite of the latter's failure to observe the forms prescribed by law, the competent authority nevertheless examined the appeal.[179] It may be necessary for a correct exhaustion of the local remedies that the applicant calls in the assistance of a counsel, if national law requires this.[180]

The interpretation and application of the relevant provisions of national law in principle belong to the competence of the national authorities concerned. The Commission and the Court, on the other hand, are competent to judge whether, as a result of such an interpretation or application, the applicant would become the victim of a denial of justice.[181]

It is not only the *judicial* remedies which must be sought, but every remedy available under national law which may lead to a decision that is binding on the authorities,[182] including the possibility of appeal to administrative bodies, provided that the remedy concerned is adequate and effective. In a case concerning the nationalisation of Yarrow Shipbuilders under the British Aircraft and Shipbuilding Industries Act 1977 the Commission had to face the question of whether the reference of a dispute on compensation to an arbitration tribunal provided for in the 1977 Act constituted an effective remedy to be exhausted. According to the Commission the tribunal had jurisdiction to determine the amount of compensation under the statutory formula, but did not sit as a tribunal of appeal pronouncing on the adequacy of the offers made in the negotiations by the Secretary of State. It thus represented an alternative means of assessing the compensation due under the statutory formula, if agreement as to the appropriate amount could not be reached. As the substance of the applicant company's complaint was not that it received less than the Act entitled it to but that the very nature of the statutory compensation formula was such that it inevitably failed to reflect the company's proper value, the Commission held that resort to arbitration would not have constituted an effective and sufficient remedy.[183]

The question of whether extraordinary remedies must also have been sought cannot be answered in a general way. In the *Nielsen* Case the Commission required such exhaustion, insofar as this can be expected to produce an effective and adequate result. It must be decided for each individual case whether the remedy is effective and adequate. In the *Nielsen* Case the Commission considered an application to the Special Court of Revision as a remedy that should be exhausted.[184] In more recent case-law, however, applications for reopening of

---

[178] See, *e.g.*, Appl. 2854/66, *X and Y* v. *Austria*, Coll. 26 (1968), p. 46 (53-54).
[179] Appl. 12784/87, *Huber* v. *Switzerland*, D&R 57 (1988), p. 251 (259).
[180] Appl. 6878/75, *Le Compte* v. *Belgium*, Yearbook XX (1977), p. 254 (274).
[181] Appl. 1191/61, *X* v. *Federal Republic of Germany*, Yearbook VIII (1965), p. 106 (154-156).
[182] Appl. 332/57, *Lawless* v. *Ireland*, Yearbook II (1958-1959), p. 308 (322-324).
[183] Appl. 9266/81, *Yarrow P.L.C. and Others* v. *the United Kingdom*, D&R 30 (1983), p. 155 (188-190).
[184] Appl. 343/57, Yearbook II (1958-1959), p. 412 (438-442).

the proceedings were not regarded as 'domestic remedies' in the sense of Article 26 of the Convention,[185] unless it is established under domestic law that such a request in fact constitutes an effective remedy.[186]

2.9.4   Only Remedies which are Effective and Adequate have to be Exhausted

Another important question in connection with Article 26 is which of the available legal remedies must have been pursued. Here, too, a good deal depends on the relevant national law, and the answer to this question can only be given on a case-by-case basis.[187] From the very voluminous and rather casuistic case-law of the Commission the following trends may be inferred.

In the *Nielsen* Case the Commission stated quite generally that:

> the rules governing the exhaustion of the local remedies, as they are generally recognized today, in principle require that recourse should be had to all legal remedies available under the local law which are in principle capable of providing an effective and sufficient means of redressing the wrongs for which, on the international plane, the Respondent State is alleged to be responsible.[188]

An individual is dispensed from the obligation to exhaust certain local remedies if in the circumstances of his case these remedies are ineffective or inadequate.[189] In the same vein the answer to the question of whether non-judicial procedures belong to the local remedies that have to be exhausted depends on whether those procedures are provided with sufficient guarantees to ensure an

---

[185] See, *e.g.*, Appl. 2385/64, *X v. Norway*, Coll. 22 (1967), p. 85 (88). In a case which was practically identical with the *Nielsen* Case, for the future the Commission expressly left open the question of whether a petition to the Danish Special Court of Revision constitutes an effective remedy: Appl. 4311/69, *X v. Denmark*, Yearbook XIV (1971), p. 280 (316-320).

[186] Appl. 19117/91, *K. S. and K. S. AG v. Switzerland*, D&R 78-A (1994), p. 70 (74).

[187] See Appl. 343/57, *Schouw Nielsen v. Denmark*, Yearbook II (1958-1959), p. 412 (442-444): 'the competence which the Commission has in every case to appreciate in the light of its particular facts whether any given remedy at any given date appeared to offer the applicant the possibility of an effective and sufficient remedy.'

[188] Appl. 343/57, Yearbook II (1958-1959), p. 412 (440). See also Appl. 10092/82, *Baraona v. Portugal*, D&R 40 (1985), p. 118 (136), where the Commission held that 'the crucial point is (...) whether an appeal might have secured redress in the form of direct, rather than indirect, protection of the rights laid down in (...) the Convention.'

[189] See, *e.g.*, Appl. 7011/75, *Becker v. Denmark*, D&R 4 (1976), p. 215 (232-233); Appl. 7465/76, *X v. Denmark*, D&R 7 (1977), p. 153 (154). A special case is Appl. 7397/76, *Peyer v. Switzerland*, D&R 11 (1978), p. 58 (75-76), in which in the opinion of the Commission the applicant did not need to appeal, since he could not rely on the Convention before the national court, as it had not yet entered into force with respect to Switzerland, while in addition there was no legal ground on which such an appeal could be based. See also joint Appls 8805/79 and 8806/79, *De Jong and Baljet v. the Netherlands*, D&R 24 (1981), p. 144 (150), in which the action for damages of Art. 1401 of the Netherlands Civil Code was not considered effective to question a detention which was in conformity with domestic law. Similarly, in the case of *Z v. the Netherlands,* the appeal to the Judicial Division of the Council of State against the Deputy Minister of Justice was considered not effective because such proceedings do not suspend the execution of the decision to deport the applicant; Appl. 10400/83, D&R 38 (1984), p. 145 (150). See also Appl. 10078/82, *M v. France*, D&R 41 (1985), p. 103 (119).

effective legal protection against the authorities.[190] Recourse to an organ which supervises the administration but cannot take binding decisions, such as an Ombudsman, does not constitute an adequate and effective remedy in the sense of Article 26.[191]

For a given local remedy to be considered adequate and effective it is, of course, not required that the claim in question would actually have been recognised by the national court. In this stage of the examination by the Commission the question of whether the application is well-founded is not at issue, but only the question of whether, assuming that the complaint is well-founded, this particular remedy would have provided the applicant the possibility of redress.[192] In this context it must be noted that the applicant's personal view of the effectiveness or ineffectiveness of a given remedy in itself is not decisive.[193]

(a) What may be Regarded as an Effective and Adequate Remedy?

The Commission has built up a voluminous case-law concerning what may be regarded as an effective and adequate remedy. From this case-law, the following elements emerge as the most important.

In the first place the applicant must have used the remedies provided for up to the highest level, only if and insofar as the appeal to a higher tribunal can still substantially affect the decision on the merits,[194] and in addition any procedural means which might prevent a breach of the Convention should have been used.[195] An applicant may of course refrain from an appeal if the tribunal in question is not competent in the matter of his claim.[196] In some legal systems, a higher or the highest court has jurisdiction only with respect to legal issues and cannot pronounce on the facts. If the application submitted to the Commission precisely concerns facts, the applicant needs not previously have applied to such

---

[190] See, e.g., Appl. 155/56, X v. Federal Republic of Germany, Yearbook I (1955-1957), p. 163 (164).

[191] Appl. 11192/84, Montion v. France, D&R 52 (1987), p. 227 (235).

[192] Appl. 1474/62, Belgian Linguistic Case, Coll. 12 (1964), p. 18 (27).

[193] Appl. 289/57, X v. Federal Republic of Germany, Yearbook I (1955-1957), p. 148 (149). See also Appl. 6271/73, X v. Federal Republic of Germany, D&R 6 (1976), p. 62 (64); Appl. 7317/75, Lynas v. Switzerland, Yearbook XX (1977), p. 412 (442); and Appl. 10148/82, Garcia v. Switzerland, D&R 42 (1985), p. 98 (122).

[194] Appl. 788/60, Austria v. Italy, Yearbook IV (1961), p. 116 (172) and Appl. 2690/65, Televizier v. the Netherlands, Yearbook IX (1966), p. 512 (548). See also Appl. 6289/73, Airey v. Ireland, Yearbook XX (1977), p. 180 (200); Appl. 6870/75, Y v. the United Kingdom, D&R 10 (1978), p. 37 (67); Appls 9362/81, 9363/81 and 9387/81, Van der Sluijs, Zuiderveld and Klappe v. the Netherlands, D&R 28 (1982), p. 212 (219); Appl. 16839/90, Remli v. France, D&R 77-A (1994), p. 22 (29); judgment of 19 March 1991, Cardot, A.200, p. 19.

[195] Judgment of 6 December 1988, Barberà, Messegué and Jarbardo, A.146, pp. 28-29; judgment of 19 March 1991, Cardot, A.200, p. 18.

[196] See, e.g., Appl. 7598/76, Kaplan v. the United Kingdom, D&R 15 (1979), p. 120 (122). Thus also the Court: judgment of 6 November 1980, Guzzardi, A.39 (1981), pp. 21-22.

a court.[197] The same holds good with respect to the possibility of appeal to a constitutional court from a decision of another court, such as is provided for in Germany, Italy and Austria. Such an appeal belongs to the remedies that must have been exhausted if and insofar as the decision of the constitutional court may have any influence on the situation about which a complaint is lodged with the Commission.[198] In some legal systems, such as that of Italy, individuals have no direct access to the constitutional court; they are dependent on a decision of the ordinary court to refer the issue of constitutionality of a specific law to the constitutional court. In such a case, according to the Commission, the individual applicant is required to have raised the question of that constitutionality in the proceedings before the ordinary court. If he has not done so, he cannot claim that he had no access to the constitutional court.[199]

In Ireland the granting of leave for appeal to the Supreme Court lies at the discretion of the Attorney-General, and in Denmark it is the Minister of Justice who has a wide discretion in granting leave for appeal. In both legal systems, moreover, such a leave is granted only exceptionally. With respect to both cases the Commission has decided that the appeal to the Supreme Court does not constitute an effective remedy in the sense of Article 26.[200]

With regard to the right to have a court decide speedily on the lawfulness of detention, an action for damages against the State is not a remedy which has to be exhausted, because the purpose of an action for damages on the ground of the defective operation of the machinery of justice is to secure compensation for the prejudice caused by deprivation of liberty, not to assert the right to have the lawfulness of that deprivation of liberty decided speedily by that court.[201]

With regard to the length of detention in Turkey, in the case of a complaint about violation of Article 5 of the Convention the Commission noted that on a number of occasions the martial law court had considered whether to continue the applicants' detention on remand and refused their conditional release. It followed that the judicial authorities had the opportunity to put an end to the applicants' allegedly excessive detention. The Commission further noted that no appeal lay

---

[197] See, *e.g.*, Appl. 1437/62, *X* v. *Belgium* (not published) and Appl. 10741/84, *S* v. *the United Kingdom*, D&R 41 (1985), p. 226 (231).

[198] See, *e.g.*, Appl. 1086/61, *X* v. *Federal Republic of Germany*, Yearbook V (1962), p. 149 (154); Appls 5573 and 5670/72, *Adler* v. *Federal Republic of Germany*, Yearbook XX (1977), p. 102 (132).

[199] See Appl. 6452/74, *Sacchi* v. *Italy*, D&R 5 (1976), p. 43 (51).

[200] Appl. 9136/80, *X* v. *Ireland*, D&R 26 (1982), p. 242 (244) and Appl. 8395/78, *X* v. *Denmark*, D&R 27 (1982), p. 50 (52). *Cf.* also Appl. 8950/80, *H* v. *Belgium*, D&R 37 (1984), p. 5 (13); Appls 14116/88 and 14117/88, *Sargin and Yağci* v. *Turkey*, D&R 61 (1989), p. 250; Appl. 12604/86, *G.* v. *Belgium*, D&R 70 (1991), p. 125 (136).

[201] Appl. 10868/84, *Woukam Moudefo* v. *France*, D&R 51 (1987), p. 62 (81); Appl. 11256/84, *Egue* v. *France*, D&R 57 (1988), p. 47 (67); Appl. 13190/87, *Navarra* v. *France*, D&R 69 (1991), p. 165 (171); Appls 16419/90 and 16426/90, *Yağci and Sargin* v. *Turkey*, D&R 71 (1991), p. 253 (268); judgment of 27 August 1992, *Tomasi*, A.241-A, p. 34; judgment of 23 November 1993, *Navarra*, A.273-B, p. 27.

against decisions refusing to grant conditional release given by a martial law court after a bill of indictment had been preferred. In that connection it pointed out that in Turkish law there is a distinction between an order remanding the accused in custody and an order to continue detention on remand, the latter being issued at final instance by the court dealing with the case. With regard to the length of the criminal proceedings, for the purposes of Article 6(1) of the Convention, the Commission referred to previous decisions in which it had held that, having regard to the relatively protracted duration of proceedings, it is not bound to reject a complaint for failure to exhaust domestic remedies because appeals are still pending at the time when an application is introduced. The Commission further observed that the respondent Government had not established that the applicants had an effective remedy in Turkish law to expedite the proceedings whose length they complained of. The judgment to be given by the Military Court of Cassation to which the Government alluded was not as such a remedy capable of affording the applicants redress for the situation they complained of. Therefore, there was no effective remedy available.[202]

In the *Akdivar* Case the applicants alleged that there was no effective remedy available for obtaining compensation before the administrative courts in respect of injuries or damage to property arising out of criminal acts of members of the security forces. In order to demonstrate that the available remedies were not ineffective, the Turkish Government referred to a number of judgments by the administrative courts. Some of these decisions concerned cases in which the State Council had awarded compensation to individuals for damage inflicted by public officials or by terrorists, or suffered in the course of confrontations between the Government, the public and the *PKK*. According to the Government claims for compensation could also have been lodged in the ordinary civil courts. The Court considered it significant that the Government, despite the extent of the problem of village destruction, has not been able to point to examples of compensation being awarded in respect of allegations that property had been purposely destroyed by members of the security forces or to prosecutions having been brought against them in respect of such allegations. In this connection the Court noted the evidence referred to by the Delegate of the Commission as regards the general reluctance of the authorities to admit that this type of illicit behaviour by members of the security forces had occurred. It further noted the lack of any impartial investigation, any offer to cooperate with a view to obtaining evidence or any *ex gratia* payments made by the authorities to the applicants. Moreover, the Court did not consider that a remedy before the administrative courts could be regarded as adequate and sufficient in respect of the applicants' complaints, since it was not satisfied that a determination could be made in the course of such proceedings concerning the claim that their property was destroyed by members of the

---

[202] Appls 15530/89 and 15531/89, *Mitap and Müftüoglu* v. *Turkey*, D&R 72 (1992), p. 169 (189). See also Appls 16419/90 and 16426/90, *Yağci and Sargin* v. *Turkey*, D&R 71 (1991) p. 253 (267).

gendarmerie.[203] As regards the civil remedy invoked by the respondent Government, the Court attached particular significance to the absence of any meaningful investigation by the authorities into the applicants' allegations and of any official expression of concern or assistance notwithstanding the fact that statements by the applicants had been given to various State officials. It appeared to have taken two years before statements were taken from the applicants by the authorities about the events complained of, probably in response to the communication of the complaint by the Commission to the Government.[204]

In a case, where the applicant complained about the conditions of detention, the Government observed that she had not exhausted the domestic remedies, since she had not requested a transfer to another prison. The Commission, however, opined that even if this might have led to an improvement in the conditions of her detention, this would by no means have enabled her to assert her rights under the Convention, and in particular to raise her complaint under Article 3. Consequently, the Commission considered that these steps could not be taken into account for the purpose of deciding whether domestic remedies had been exhausted as required.[205] The Commission has held in respect of alleged ill-treatment contrary to Article 3, that raising criminal charges against the officials concerned or filing a civil action for compensation are effective remedies to be examined pursuant to Article 26.[206] However, in a case against Turkey, the Commission observed that the applicants raised in the proceedings before the State Security Court and then before the Court of Appeal their detailed complaints concerning their alleged ill-treatment during their time in police custody. The Commission observed that, under Turkish law, the applicants were entitled to complain at the trial if their statements to the police had been made under torture and that ill-treatment of prisoners by police officers is to be prosecuted *ex officio*. The Commission was therefore satisfied that the applicants had availed themselves of a proper remedy under Turkish law in that they raised their complaint of ill-treatment at their trial, first with the Public Prosecutor and subsequently before the State Security Court and the Court of Cassation. It concluded from the Government's submissions that the Public Prosecutor did not refer the complaint to the competent local Public Prosecutor, because he did not consider the allegations to be credible, and that, for the same reason, the court did not discard the evidence obtained during the applicants detention *incommunicado*. The Commission subsequently examined whether the applicants were nevertheless required to avail themselves of the further remedy indicated by the Government by addressing a complaint of criminal behaviour to the competent Public Prosecutor. The Commission here observed that the complaint concerned primarily a question of evidence and that the reason why

---

[203] Judgment of 16 September 1996, Reports 1996-IV, Vol. 15, paras 71-72.

[204] *Ibidem*, para. 73.

[205] Appl. 14986/89, *Kuijk v. Greece*, D&R 70 (1991), p. 240 (250).

[206] Appl. 10078/82, *M v. France*, D&R 41 (1985), p. 103 (119); Appl. 11208/84, *McQuiston v. the United Kingdom*, D&R 46 (1986), p. 182 (187); Appl. 17544/90, *Ribitsch v. Austria*, D&R 74 (1993), p. 129 (133).

the applicants were unsuccessful in raising it at their trial was that the State Security Court and the Public Prosecutor did not find that there was sufficient evidence to support their detailed allegations. The Commission therefore assumed that the applicants, if they had availed themselves of the remedy indicated by the Government, would have been faced with the same problem of proving that they had in fact been ill-treated. For this reason the applicants were not obliged to exhaust the said remedy in order to comply with Article 26 of the Convention.[207]

In the case of a decision ordering police custody, the lawfulness of which has been confirmed by the competent judicial authorities, lodging a criminal complaint constitutes an effective and sufficient remedy. In a case against Turkey, the Commission observed in this respect, however, that the legal authorities to which the complaint of criminal behaviour was referred, had held the decisions on detention to be in conformity with law and procedure. According to the case-law quoted by the Government, Turkish courts only grant compensation in cases where those responsible for criminal acts of the kind in question have previously been found guilty in a criminal prosecution. In these circumstances, the Commission was of the opinion that the applicants were not bound to attempt the means of redress indicated by the Government, given that the legal authorities to which the question of the lawfulness of their detention was referred had already taken a position and rejected the claim that the applicants' deprivation of freedom was illegal. In the circumstances, it would have served no purpose had the applicants undertaken proceedings for compensation.[208]

The possibility of obtaining compensation may in some circumstances constitute an adequate remedy, in particular where it is likely to be the only possible or practical means whereby redress can be given to the individual for the wrong he has suffered.[209] Applying this case-law, the Commission declared an application concerning the dismissal of police officers inadmissible under the local remedies rule since the police officers' action for compensation was pending before the Greek courts and the compensation which could be awarded, could be substantial enough to remedy the alleged violations.[210] However, the Commission has also held that the compensation machinery could only be seen as an adequate remedy in a situation where the authorities had taken reasonable steps to comply with their obligations under the Convention.[211]

---

[207] Appls 16311/90 and 16313/90, *Hazar and Acik* v. *Turkey*, D&R 72 (1992), p. 200 (207-208); Appls 14116/88 and 14117/88, *Sargin and Yağci* v. *Turkey*, D&R 61 (1989), p. 250 (280).

[208] Appls 14116/88 and 14117/88, *Sargin and Yağci* v. *Turkey*, D&R 61 (1989), p. 250 (278).

[209] Appl. 12719/87, *Frederiksen and Others* v. *Denmark*, D&R 56 (1988), p. 237 (244).

[210] Appl. 18598/91, *Sygounis, Kotsis and 'Union of Police Officers'* v. *Greece*, D&R 78-B (1994), p. 71 (80).

[211] Appl. 12719/87, *Frederiksen and Others* v. *Denmark*, D&R 56 (1988), p. 237 (244).

The personal appearance of the applicant before the court taking the decision may constitute so substantial an element of the procedure that the rejection of a request to that effect renders the procedure ineffective.[212]

In cases of expulsion, finally, the Commission has constantly held that a remedy which does not suspend execution of a decision to expel an alien to a specified country is not effective for the purposes of Article 26 and there is no obligation to have recourse to such a remedy.[213]

2.9.5 The Alleged Violations must have been Submitted at Least 'in Substance' to the Competent National Authorities

The local remedies rule is considered to be complied with only if the points on which an application is lodged in Strasbourg have also been put forward in national proceedings.[214] That the Commission takes a stringent attitude in this respect becomes clear from the case where a complaint was lodged against Norway on account of the refusal of a Norwegian judicial organ to publish the reasons for its judgment. Since this point had not been put forward before the highest court in Norway, in the opinion of the Commission the local remedies rule had not been complied with, although a number of other objections against the judgment in question had indeed been raised in those proceedings.[215] This decision of the Commission shows at the same time that the injured person cannot rely on an alleged obligation on the part of the national court to supplement the legal grounds *ex officio*.[216] This was expressly confirmed by the Court:

> The fact that the Belgian courts might have been able, or even obliged, to examine the case of their own motion under the Convention cannot be regarded as having dispensed the applicant from pleading before them the Convention or arguments to the same or like effect.[217]

In the case of *Kröcher and Möller* v. *Switzerland* the applicants alleged violation of Article 3 because of the conditions imposed on them both during the period of their detention on remand and during their preventive detention and while serving their sentences. As far as the first-mentioned period was concerned, it was not disputed that the applicants properly exhausted the domestic remedies available.

---

[212] Appl. 434/58, *X* v. *Sweden*, Yearbook II (1958-1959), p. 354 (374-376).

[213] Appl. 10400/83, *Z* v. *the Netherlands*, D&R 38 (1984), p. 145 (150); Appl. 10760/84, *X* v. *the Netherlands*, D&R 38 (1984), p. 224 (225); Appl. 10564/83, *X* v. *Federal Republic of Germany*, D&R 40 (1985), p. 262 (265); joined Appls 17550/90 and 17825/91, *V and P* v. *France*, D&R 70 (1991), p. 298 (315).

[214] See, *e.g.*, Appl. 5574/72, *X* v. *the United Kingdom*, D&R 3 (1976), p. 10 (15); Appls 5573/72 and 5670/72, *Adler* v. *Federal Republic of Germany*, Yearbook XX (1977), p. 102 (128); Appl. 7238/75, *Van Leuven and De Meyere* v. *Belgium*, D&R 8 (1977), p. 140 (158).

[215] Appl. 2002/63, *X* v. *Norway*, Yearbook VII (1964), p. 262 (266). See also Appl. 11244/84, *Pirotte* v. *Belgium*, D&R 55 (1988), p. 98 (104).

[216] See Appl. 2322/64, *X* v. *Belgium*, Coll. 24 (1967), p. 36 (42); Appl. 15123/89, *Braithwaite* v. *the United Kingdom*, D&R 70 (1991), p. 252 (256).

[217] Judgment of 6 November 1980, *Van Oosterwijck*, A.40, p. 19.

The final national decision, however, referred solely to the conditions of detention on remand. With respect to the last-mentioned period the Commission investigated whether the fact or conditions complained of constituted a mere extension of those complained of at the outset. It concluded that this was not the case and declared the applicants inadmissible for not having properly exhausted the domestic remedies, since the last-mentioned period had not been expressly at issue in the national proceedings.[218]

The formula used in the case-law requires that the point concerned must have been submitted 'in substance' to the national organs.[219] The precise implications of this requirement will depend on the concrete circumstances of the case. In general, the applicant will not be required to have explicitly referred to the relevant articles of the Convention in the national proceedings.[220] Thus, in a case where an applicant alleged a violation of Article 3, the Commission concluded that the applicant, in substance, had raised in the domestic procedure the argument of degrading treatment by alleging that compliance with a court order complained of would bring him into disgrace.[221] Express reference to provisions of the Convention may, however, be required in certain cases:

> In certain circumstances it may nonetheless happen that express reliance on the Convention before the national authorities constitutes the sole appropriate manner of raising before those authorities first, as is required by Article 26, an issue intended, if need be, to be brought subsequently before the European review bodies.[222]

In other words, express reference to the provisions of the Convention is necessary if there is no other possibility of submitting the case in the appropriate way to the national organs.[223]

The above exposé holds true for those Contracting States where the Convention has internal effect. Things are different, of course, in Contracting States where the

---

[218] Appl. 8463/78, *Kröcher and Möller* v. *Switzerland*, D&R 26 (1982), p. 24 (48-52).

[219] See, *e.g.*, Appl. 9186/80, *De Cubber* v. *Belgium*, D&R 28 (1982), p. 172 (175); Appl. 16810/90, *Reyntjes* v. *Belgium*, D&R 73 (1992), p. 136 (154); Appl. 14524/89, *Yanasik* v. *Turkey*, D&R 74 (1993), p. 14 (25); and judgment of 28 August 1986, *Glasenapp*, A.104, p. 24.

[220] Thus the Court in the *Van Oosterwijck* judgment of 6 November 1980, A.40, p. 19. Thus also the Commission in Appl. 1661/62, *X and Y* v. *Belgium*, Yearbook VI (1963), p. 360 (366): 'whereas an application against a State where the Convention is an integral part of municipal law (...) may thus prove to be inadmissible if the victim of the alleged violation has not given his judges an opportunity to remedy that violation because the Convention was not invoked or no other arguments to the same effect were raised.' See also Appl. 9228/80, *X* v. *Federal Republic of Germany*, D&R 30 (1983), pp. 132 (141-142); Appl. 17128/90, *Erdagöz* v. *Turkey*, D&R 71 (1991), p. 275 (282).

[221] Appl. 11921/86, *Verein Kontakt Information Therapie and Hagen* v. *Austria*, D&R 57 (1988), p. 81 (89).

[222] Judgment of 6 November 1980, *Van Oosterwijck*, A.40, p. 17.

[223] See the Court's judgment of the same date, *Guzzardi*, A.39, p. 27, where it was held: 'However, a more specific reference was not essential in the circumstances since it did not constitute the sole means of achieving the aim pursued (...). He [the applicant] (...) derived from the Italian legislation pleas equivalent, in the Court's view, to an allegation of a breach of the right guaranteed by Article 5 of the Convention.' See also Appl. 8130/78, *Hans and Marianne Eckle* v. *Federal Republic of Germany*, D&R 16 (1979), p. 120 (127-128).

Convention has not been incorporated. Indeed, in such a case directly invoking the Convention before the national authorities will in most cases be of no avail. Consequently, the Commission decided in a case against the United Kingdom:

> Before lodging this application the applicant lodged an appeal against her conviction and sentence. Although in the appeal proceedings she did not invoke the rights guaranteed in Articles 5, 9 and 10, she has to be considered to have exhausted domestic remedies because the Convention which guarantees the said rights is not binding law for the British courts and it is doubtful whether the rights and liberties in question constitute general principles which could successfully be invoked by the defence in criminal proceedings before the British courts.[224]

Here again, however, it may be required that the applicant has invoked legal rules or principles of domestic law which are 'in substance' the same as the relevant provisions of the Convention.[225]

(a) A Remedy does not have to be Sought when there Exists Well-Established
     Case-Law that it does not Offer any Real Chance of Success

A remedy is ineffective and does not therefore have to be sought if, considering well-established case-law, it does not offer any real chance of success.[226] In that case, however, the applicant must give some evidence of the existence of such case-law.[227] That the Commission is not inclined to accept an argument to that effect easily, if the case-law proves not to be as well-established as was alleged, appears from its decision in the *Retimag* Case. Retimag was a Swiss company, but it was actually controlled by the German Communist Party. The latter was declared unconstitutional by the German court, and consequently the property of Retimag was confiscated. The company invoked before the Commission the right to the peaceful enjoyment of possessions. Article 19 of the German Constitution declares the provisions on fundamental rights to be applicable to *internal* legal persons. As a result Retimag argued that it had not been able to appeal to the *Bundesverfassungsgericht* because it was a Swiss company, and accordingly not an internal legal person. However, after Retimag had lodged its application with the Commission, the *Bundesverfassungsgericht* decided that Article 19 was not to be interpreted *a contrario* and did not exclude an appeal by external legal persons. On this basis the Commission decided that Retimag had not exhausted the local remedies and it declared the application inadmissible under Article 26.[228]

---

[224] Appl. 7050/75, *Arrowsmith v. the United Kingdom*, Yearbook XX (1977), p. 316 (334-336). See Appl. 6871/75, *Caprino v. the United Kingdom*, Yearbook XXI (1978), p. 284 (286-288).

[225] Judgment of 16 December 1992, *Geouffre de la Pradelle*, A.253-B, p. 40.

[226] Appl. 27/55, *X v. Federal Republic of Germany*, Yearbook I (1955-1957), p. 138 (139). See also Appls 9362/81, 9363/81 and 9387/81, *Van der Sluijs, Zuiderveld and Klappe v. the Netherlands*, D&R 28 (1982), p. 212 (219); Appl. 10103/82, *Farragut v. France*, D&R 39 (1984), p. 186 (205); Appl. 13134/87, *Costello-Roberts v. the United Kingdom*, D&R 67 (1991), p. 216 (224).

[227] See, *e.g.*, Appl. 788/60, *Austria v. Italy*, Yearbook IV (1961), p. 116 (168); Appl. 15404/89, *Purcell v. Ireland*, D&R 70 (1991), p. 262 (274).

[228] Appl. 712/60, *Retimag v. Federal Republic of Germany*, Yearbook IV (1961), p. 384 (404-406).

A comparable situation presented itself in the case of *De Varga-Hirsch* v. *France*, which concerned, *inter alia*, the requirement of 'reasonable time' of Article 5(3). The applicant had been held in detention on remand for almost five years. Although he had repeatedly applied to the courts for release on bail, he had not appealed to the Court of Cassation, except in two cases. In these two cases, however, he did not rely on the Convention or on comparable provisions of domestic law. The applicant contended that, because of its limited jurisdiction, the Court of Cassation could not be considered as an effective remedy. The Commission rejected this argument by referring to case-law of the Court of Cassation with regard to detention on remand, dating from after the applicant's detention on remand had ended. It held that the appeal to the Court of Cassation was neither a new remedy nor an appeal likely to be dismissed as inadmissible. The Commission added that:

> if there is any doubt as to whether a given remedy is or is not intrinsically able to offer a real chance of success, that is a point which must be submitted to the domestic courts themselves, before any appeal can be made to the international court.[229]

Particularly in a common law system, where the courts extend and develop principles through case-law, it is generally incumbent on an aggrieved individual to allow the domestic courts the opportunity to develop existing rights by way of interpretation.[230]

It thus appears to be hazardous for an applicant to rely on a particular interpretation if the latter is not supported by clear and constant national case-law.[231] Moreover, an applicant cannot rely on case-law if the legal provisions on which that case-law is based have meanwhile been altered. Indeed, in such a case there is no certainty that the decision in his case would have been identical with previous decisions, so that the relevant remedy cannot in advance be qualified as ineffective and inadequate.[232]

For the converse situation reference may be made to the decision of the Commission in the so-called '*Vagrancy*' Cases, where three Belgians claimed that they had been unlawfully detained for vagrancy.[233] Up to the moment at which the applications were lodged it had been established case-law of the Belgian Council of State that the latter had no jurisdiction with respect to an appeal against such detention. After the applications had been declared admissible, the Council

---

[229] Appl. 9559/81, *X* v. *France*, D&R 33 (1983), p. 158 (211-212); Appl. 23548/94, *E.F.* v. *Czech Republic*, D&R 78-B (1994), p. 146 (151).

[230] Appl. 20357/92, *Whiteside* v. *the United Kingdom*, D&R 76-A (1994), p. 80 (88).

[231] See also Appl. 10789/84, *K, F and P* v. *the United Kingdom*, D&R 40 (1985), p. 298 (299).

[232] See Appl. 8408/78, *X* v. *Federal Republic of Germany* (not published), where the Commission also attached importance to the fact that the case-law had been formed before the Commission itself had shown in a decision that it took a different view. In other words, the Commission assumes that the relevant national court will take the Commission's view in a new case into consideration, and consequently will take a different decision.

[233] Appls 2832, 2835 and 2899/66, *De Wilde, Ooms and Versyp* v. *Belgium*, Yearbook X (1967), p. 420.

of State reversed its approach. According to the Commission this was no reason for declaring the applications as yet inadmissible because of non-exhaustion of an effective local remedy.[234] In the case of *X* v. *Belgium*, the question was raised whether a change in the case-law concerning the condition of access to a court of appeal, introduced only a few days before the applicant brought her own application, could be held against her. The Commission did not pursue this question as it declared the application inadmissible on other grounds.[235]

(b) The Length of Proceedings may be Taken into Account in Assessing the Effectiveness of a Remedy

Effectiveness is also considered to be lacking when the procedure is exceptionally protracted.[236] However, that is only the case if a given procedure is structurally protracted, *i.e.* in all cases;[237] the fact that a given procedure is very lengthy in a concrete case does not in itself set aside the condition of the Convention that such a procedure must be instituted. In fact, in that case the applicant will first of all have to seek redress against that long duration within the national legal system concerned. It is perhaps mainly for this reason that the Commission arrived at the rejection of an application filed by a Belgian at a moment at which the Court of Appeal had not yet pronounced a verdict, although the applicant had filed his appeal more than six years previously. Curiously enough the Commission held:

> It is true that the Commission finds that the length of the procedure before Belgian jurisdiction cannot be held against either the applicant or his lawyer. However, the Commission considers that it should put an end to a procedure pending before it for five years.[238]

More sense makes the Commission's decision with respect to a complaint concerning the length of criminal proceedings, where the question arose whether the accused should have instituted a procedure designed to accelerate proceedings but which could not have led to any other effect. In the Commission's opinion such a procedure cannot be considered an effective and sufficient remedy the use of which is required by Article 26.[239] With regard to the length of criminal proceedings, the Commission has held that, in case of a relatively protracted duration of proceedings, it is not bound to reject a complaint for failure to have

---

[234] Report of 19 July 1969, *De Wilde, Ooms and Versyp ('Vagrancy' Cases)*, B.10 (1971), p. 94. See also Appl. 8544/79, *Öztürk* v. *Federal Republic of Germany*, D&R 26 (1982), p. 55 (69).

[235] Appl. 9097/80, D&R 30 (1983), p. 119 (130).

[236] See, *e.g.*, Appl. 222/56, *X* v. *Federal Republic of Germany*, Yearbook II (1958-1959), p. 344 (350-351); Appl. 7161/75, *X* v. *the United Kingdom*, D&R 7 (1977), p. 100 (101); Appl. 13156/87, *Byrn* v. *Denmark*, D&R 73 (1992), p. 5 (12).

[237] See, *e.g.*, Appl. 14556/89, *Papamichalopoulos* v. *Greece*, D&R 68 (1991), p. 261 (270).

[238] Appl. 5024/71, *X* v. *Belgium*, D&R 7 (1977), p. 5 (7). See, however, Appl. 6699/74, *X* v. *Federal Republic of Germany*, D&R 11 (1978), p. 16 (23-24), where the Commission found differently, even despite the fact that the applicant had consented to postponement of the national procedure. In this case the Commission evidently reached an 'equity' standpoint in view of the emergency in which the applicant found herself.

[239] Appl. 8435/78, *X* v. *the United Kingdom*, D&R 26 (1982), p. 18 (20).

exhausted domestic remedies even though appeals are still pending at the moment an application is introduced.[240]

(c) A Remedy is not Effective if the Competent Court is not Fully Independent

Furthermore, the Commission considers the prior exhaustion of local remedies not to be required if the competent court is not fully independent, thus that the necessary guarantees for a fair trial are not present. In the *First Greek* Case, where Denmark, Norway, Sweden and the Netherlands complained about the torture of political prisoners in Greece, the applicant States alleged the existence of an administrative practice to which the local remedies rule was not applicable. In the Commission's opinion, however, the applicant States had not given 'substantial evidence' for the existence of such a practice. Nevertheless, the applications were not rejected under Article 26. The Greek Government had discharged several judges for political reasons. Under those circumstances the Commission found that there was insufficient independence of the judiciary. It concluded that the judicial procedures provided for under Greek law no longer constituted effective remedies which should have been exhausted.[241]

A comparable situation arose as a result of the Turkish military action in Cyprus. According to the Commission the action had 'deeply and seriously affected the life of the population in Cyprus and, in particular, that of the Greek Cypriots.'[242] The circumstances were such that the existing remedies 'available in domestic courts in Turkey or before Turkish military courts in Cyprus' could be considered as effective remedies which had to be exhausted according to Article 26 with respect to complaints of inhabitants of Cyprus only 'if it were shown that such remedies are both practicable and normally functioning in such cases.'[243] The Commission found that this had not been proved by the Turkish Government.

2.9.6 The Court may Examine Preliminary Objections Raised under Article 26

Ever since the *De Wilde, Ooms and Versyp* Case the Court has examined preliminary objections raised under Article 26 and has upheld them on occasion.[244] On various occasions individual judges have given dissenting opinions on this point. It has been argued that the Court's case-law on this point had two important consequences: it rendered more burdensome the proceedings of the Convention institutions, and created a further lack of equality between respondent governments and applicants, as the latter are not able to appeal against

---

[240] See, *inter alia*, Appl. 12850/87, *Tomasi v. France*, D&R 64 (1990), p. 128 (131); Appls 15530/89 and 15531/89, *Mitap and Müftüoglu v. Turkey*, D&R 72 (1992), p. 169 (189).

[241] Appls 3321-3323 and 3344/67, *Denmark, Norway, Sweden and the Netherlands v. Greece*, Yearbook XI (1968), p. 730 (774).

[242] Appls 6780/74 and 6950/75, *Cyprus v. Turkey*, D&R 2 (1975), p. 125 (137).

[243] *Ibidem*, pp. 137-138.

[244] Judgment of 6 November 1980, *Van Oosterwijck*, A.40, pp. 5-31.

findings of inadmissibility by the Commission.[245] In *B* v. *France* the Court expressly paid attention to this reasoning but saw no reason, as matters stood, for abandoning a line of case-law which has been followed constantly for over twenty years and which has found expression in a large number of judgments.[246]

2.9.7 The Burden of Proof

In general the Commission is well informed about the remedies available under the different national systems of law and, in dubious cases, may ascertain their existence *via* its Secretariat. If the Commission has established which remedies exist under national law, it is for the applicant to prove that these remedies have been exhausted or that they are not effective or adequate.

The Commission investigates *ex officio* whether the local remedies rule has been complied with. In many cases of individual applications which were declared inadmissible under this rule, that conclusion was reached on the basis of such an *ex officio* investigation, without the application first having been transmitted to the State against which it was directed. If the application is transmitted to the State concerned – and with inter-State applications this is always the case (Rule 45 of the Rules of Procedure) –, the burden of proof with respect to the local remedies rule is divided as follows: the respondent State which relies on the rule must prove that certain effective and adequate remedies exist under its system of law which should have been sought.[247] In the *Bozano* Case the Court held that the Government had to indicate in a sufficiently clear way the remedies that were open to the applicant: 'it is not for the Convention bodies to cure of their own motion any want of precision or shortcomings in respondent States' arguments.'[248] If the State succeeds in proving its plea, subsequently it is for the applicant to prove that those remedies have been exhausted, or that they are not effective or adequate.[249] In the *Akdivar* Case the Court elaborated this rule of the burden of proof by indicating that there may be special circumstances absolving the applicant from the requirement of exhaustion of domestic remedies. According to the Court one such reason may be constituted by the national authorities remaining totally passive in the face of serious allegations of misconduct or infliction of harm by State agents, for example where they failed to undertake investigations or offer assistance. In such circumstances it can be said

---

[245] Judgment of 18 June 1971, *De Wilde, Ooms and Versyp ('Vagrancy' Cases)*, A.12, pp. 49-58 and in cases since the judgment of 19 December 1989, *Brozicek*, A.167, pp. 23-28 and the judgment of 19 March 1991, *Cardot*, A.200, pp. 93-24.

[246] Judgment of 25 March 1992, A.232-C, p. 45.

[247] Thus the judgment of 18 June 1971, *De Wilde, Ooms and Versyp ('Vagrancy' Cases)*, A.12, p. 33; judgment of 27 February 1980, *De Weer*, A.35, p. 15; judgment of 16 September 1996, *Akdivar*, Reports 1996-IV, Vol. 15, para. 68. See also Appl. 17579/90, *Kelly* v. *the United Kingdom*, D&R 74 (1993), p. 139 (144).

[248] Judgment of 18 December 1986, A.111, p. 19. See also Appl. 14461/88, *Chave née Julien* v. *France*, D&R 71 (1991), p. 141 (153).

[249] See, *e.g.*, Appl. 788/60, *Austria* v. *Italy*, Yearbook IV (1961), p. 116 (168) and Appl. 4649/70, *X* v. *Federal Republic of Germany*, Coll. 46 (1974), p. 1 (17).

that the burden of proof shifts once again, so that it becomes incumbent on the respondent Government to justify its response in relation to the scale and seriousness of the matters complained of.[250]

2.9.8 The Moment the Preliminary Objection must be Raised

In a case where the applicant had indicated that she intended to bring domestic remedies for damages, but did not inform the Commission of the developments in her case, and the matter, inexplicably, did not come to the attention of the Government until shortly before the Commission's hearing in the case, the Commission held that the Government was not estopped from raising a preliminary objection at any time prior to the Commission's decision on the admissibility of the case.[251]

The Court takes cognisance of preliminary objections concerning the exhaustion of local remedies only insofar as the respondent State has raised them before the Commission, in principle at the stage of the initial examination of admissibility, if their character and the circumstances permitted the State to do so at that moment.[252] The latter qualification was at issue in the *Campbell and Fell* Case. Here the Government raised the plea of non-exhaustion in its observations on the merits after the Commission had declared the complaints admissible, because new developments had taken place in the relevant English case-law only a few days before the Government had submitted its observations on the admissibility. According to the Court, the Government could not reasonably have been expected to raise the plea of non-exhaustion at an earlier stage. There was, therefore, no estoppel on its part to do so at this stage of the proceedings. On the other hand, the Court held that it would be unjust now to find these complaints inadmissible for failure to exhaust domestic remedies, because after the Government had raised the issue the Commission had decided on the basis of Article 29 not to reject the application on this ground. Consequently, the applicant was justified in relying on the Commission's decision by pursuing his case under the Convention instead of applying to the domestic courts.[253]

The question may be raised as to whether the Commission should institute *ex officio* an inquiry into the compliance with the local remedies rule after the case has been transmitted to the State in case the respondent Government has not raised an exception as to the admissibility under Article 26. The Commission does not institute an inquiry into the admissibility of the complaint under Article 26 if the respondent State expressly waives or has waived its right to rely on the local

---

[250] Judgment of 16 September 1996, *Akdivar*, Reports 1996-IV, Vol. 15, para. 68.

[251] Appl. 17441/90, *O'Neill v. the United Kingdom*, D&R 73 (1992), p. 201 (207).

[252] See, *inter alia*, judgment of 18 June 1971, *De Wilde, Ooms and Versyp ('Vagrancy' Cases)*, A.12, pp. 29-31; judgment of 13 May 1980, *Artico*, A.37, pp. 12-14; judgment of 6 November 1980, *Guzzardi*, A.39, p. 24; and judgment of 10 December 1982, *Foti and Others*, A.56, p. 16.

[253] Judgment of 28 June 1984, *Campbell and Fell*, A.80, pp. 31-33.

remedies rule.[254] If the State has not waived this right, the Commission appears prepared to declare an application inadmissible on the ground of non-exhaustion without the respondent State having raised an exception to that effect.[255] Despite the general wording of Article 26, one might wonder whether the Commission ought not to take a somewhat more passive attitude in this matter. The local remedies rule is intended primarily to protect the interest of the respondent State. The fact that the latter has failed to rely on that protection may indicate that it does not consider it to be in its interest to raise the exception. After all, the rejection of an application after a thorough investigation may be more convincing, and consequently more satisfactory for the respondent State than a declaration of inadmissibility on formal grounds.[256] Usually, however, in cases which have been communicated to the respondent Government, the Commission does not declare the application inadmissible for failure to exhaust domestic remedies unless this matter has been raised by the Government in their observations. The Commission takes the same attitude if the respondent Government has not submitted any observations at all,[257] or if the Government, following extensions of the time-limit, has neither submitted observations nor requested further extension but has raised the question of non-exhaustion in 'preliminary observations' long after the expiry of the time-limits fixed by the Commission.[258]

2.9.9 Moment at Which the Local Remedies must have been Exhausted

The Commission takes a flexible attitude with respect to the moment at which the local remedies must have been exhausted. It considers it sufficient if the decision of the highest national court has been given at the moment when the Commission decides on the admissibility of the application.[259] Thus the Commission held that it is not obliged to reject a complaint for failure to exhaust domestic remedies on account that appeals were still pending at the time when the application was

---

[254] See, *e.g.*, Appl. 1727/62, *Boeckmans* v. *Belgium*, Yearbook VI (1963), p. 370 (396); Appl. 1994/63, *Fifty-seven inhabitants of Leuven and environs* v. *Belgium*, Yearbook VII (1964), p. 252 (258-260); and Appl. 8919/80, *Van der Mussele* v. *Belgium*, D&R 23 (1981), p. 244 (257). This is different with regard to the six-month rule. There the Commission holds that 'in view of the importance of this rule in the Convention system, the Contracting States cannot on their own authority waive compliance with it': Appl. 9587/81, *X* v. *France*, D&R 29 (1982), p. 228 (240) and Appl. 10416/83, *K* v. *Ireland*, D&R 38 (1984), p. 158 (160).

[255] See Appl. 2547/65, *X* v. *Austria*, Coll. 20 (1966), p. 79 (83) and Appl. 5207/71, *X* v. *Federal Republic of Germany*, Yearbook XIV (1971), p. 698 (708-710).

[256] The decision on Appl. 9120/80, *Unterpertinger* v. *Austria*, D&R 33 (1983), p. 80 (83), seems to go into this direction.

[257] Appl. 23178/94, *Aydin* v. *Turkey*, D&R 79-A (1994), p. 116 (119); Appl. 23182/94, *Dündar* v. *Turkey* (not published); Appl. 23185/94, *Asker* v. *Turkey* (not published); joined Appls 22947/93 and 22948/93, *Akkoç* v. *Turkey*, D&R 79-A (1994), p. 108 (115).

[258] Appl. 22493/93, *Berktay* v. *Turkey*, D&R 79-A (1994), p. 97 (102).

[259] Appl. 2614/65, *Ringeisen* v. *Austria*, Yearbook XI (1968), p. 268 (306); Appl. 13370/87, *Deschamps* v. *Belgium*, D&R 70 (1991), p. 177 (187). See also the judgment of 16 July 1971, *Ringeisen*, A.13, p. 38; Appl. 16278/90, *Karaduman* v. *Turkey*, D&R 74 (1993), p. 93 (106).

lodged.[260] And in a case concerning the length of proceedings, the Commission held that, for the purposes of Article 6(1), having regard to the protracted duration of proceedings, it was not bound to reject a complaint for failure to exhaust domestic remedies because appeals were still pending at the time when the application was introduced.[261]

The Commission's flexible attitude in this respect may, on the other hand, also cause problems for the applicant. The Commission has, for instance, decided that a remedy which was not open to the applicant at the time of the lodging of his application, but became available only afterwards as a result of a change in the case-law of the national court concerned, had nevertheless to be exhausted in order to satisfy the requirements flowing from the local remedies rule.[262]

2.9.10 The Effect of the Declaration of Inadmissibility

The effect of a declaration of inadmissibility on account of non-exhaustion of the local remedies is generally of a *dilatory* character. The applicant may submit his case again to the Commission after having obtained a decision by the highest national court. In fact, such a decision is considered as relevant new information by the Commission, so that the application will not be rejected as being substantially the same as a matter already examined by the Commission in the sense of Article 27(1)(b).[263] The question of whether the local remedies rule must also be applied if meanwhile the national time-limits for appeal have expired, so that in fact local remedies are no longer available, will have to be decided on a case-by-case basis. Application of the rule in such a case has *peremptory* effect, since both the national and the international procedure are then barred. Such a consequence appears justified only when the individual in question is to be blamed for having allowed the time-limit to expire. A cut-and-dried answer to this as well as several other questions concerning the application of the local remedies rule cannot be given *in abstracto*. For guidance, use may be made of the general starting-point that what can be demanded of the individual is not 'what is impossible or ineffective, but only what is required by common sense, namely "the diligence of a bonus pater familias".'[264]

---

[260] Appl. 9019/80, *Luberti* v. *Italy*, D&R 27 (1982), p. 181 (193); Appls 15530/89 and 15531/89, *Mitap and Müftüoglu* v. *Turkey*, D&R 72 (1992), p. 169 (189); Appl. 16278/90, *Karaduman* v. *Turkey*, D&R 74 (1993), p. 93 (106).

[261] Appl. 12850/87, *Tomasi* v. *France*, D&R 64 (1990), p. 128; Appls 15530/89 and 15531/89, *Mitap and Müftüoglu* v. *Turkey*, D&R 72 (1992), p. 169 (189).

[262] Appl. 7878/77, *Fell* v. *the United Kingdom*, D&R 23 (1981), p. 102 (112).

[263] See *supra* p. 113.

[264] Thus judge Tanaka in his separate opinion in the *Barcelona Traction* Case, *ICJ Reports*, 1970, p. 148.

2.9.11 Special Circumstances Absolving the Applicant of Prior Exhaustion of Domestic Remedies

The Commission has accepted the possibility that according to the generally recognised rules of international law there may be special circumstances in which even effective and adequate remedies may be left unutilised.[265] The following special circumstances have been invoked before in the Commission: doubt on the part of the applicant as to the effectiveness of the relevant remedy;[266] lack of knowledge on his part as to (the existence of) a particular remedy;[267] non-admittance of an appeal because of a procedural mistake by the applicant;[268] poor health of the applicant;[269] advanced age of the applicant;[270] poor financial position of the applicant or the high costs of the procedure;[271] lack of free legal aid;[272] fear of repercussions;[273] errors or wrong advice by a counsel or by the authorities;[274] two applicants filing the same complaint, while only one applicant has exhausted the domestic remedies.[275] So far, special circumstances justifying the non-exhaustion have been recognised only exceptionally in the case-law.

In the *Akdivar* Case, the Court took account of the fact that the events complained of took place in an area of Turkey subject to martial law and characterised by severe civil strife. In such a situation the Court was of the opinion that it must bear in mind the insecurity and vulnerability of the applicants' position following the destruction of their homes and the fact that they must have become dependent on the authorities in respect of their basic needs. Against such a background the prospects of success of civil proceedings based on allegations against the security forces must be considered to be negligible in the absence of any official inquiry into their allegations, even assuming that they would have been able to secure the services of lawyers willing to press their claims before the courts. In this context, the Court found particularly striking the Commission's observation that the statements made by villagers following the events complained of gave the impression of having been prepared by the gendarmes. Nor could the

---

[265] Appl. 2257/64, *Soltikow* v. *Federal Republic of Germany*, Yearbook XI (1968), p. 180 (224). See also Appl. 6861/75, *X* v. *the United Kingdom*, D&R 3 (1976), p. 147 (152).

[266] Appl. 3651/68, *X* v. *the United Kingdom*, Yearbook XIII (1970), p. 476 (510-514); Appl. 19819/92, *Størksen* v. *Norway*, D&R 78-A (1994), p. 88 (93).

[267] Appl. 5006/71, *X* v. *the United Kingdom*, Coll. 39 (1972), p. 91 (95).

[268] Appl. 23256/94, *Hava* v. *Czech Republic*, D&R 78-B (1994), p. 139 (144).

[269] Appl. 3788/68, *X* v. *Sweden*, Yearbook XIII (1970), p. 548 (580-582).

[270] Appl. 568/59, *X* v. *Federal Republic of Germany*, Coll. 2 (1960), p. 1 (3).

[271] Appl. 181/56, *X* v. *Federal Republic of Germany*, Yearbook I (1955-1957), p. 139 (140-141).

[272] Appl. 1295/61, *X* v. *Federal Republic of Germany* (not published).

[273] Appl. 2257/64, *Soltikow* v. *Federal Republic of Germany*, Yearbook XI (1968), p. 180 (228).

[274] Appl. 818/60, *X* v. *Belgium* (not published). See, however, the Court's judgment of 13 May 1980, *Artico*, A.37, p. 18. In Appl. 10000/82, *H* v. *the United Kingdom*, D&R 33 (1983), p. 247 (253), the Commission accepted that all domestic remedies were exhausted, since the applicant had received counsel's advice that a domestic remedy would have no prospects of success.

[275] Appl. 9905/82, *A. Association and H* v. *Austria*, D&R 36 (1984), p. 187 (192) where the Commission considered also the second applicant to be admissible.

Court exclude from its considerations the risk of reprisals against the applicants or their lawyers if they had sought to introduce legal proceedings alleging that the security forces were responsible for burning down their houses as part of a deliberate State policy of village clearance. Therefore, the Court considered that, in the absence of convincing explanations from the Government in rebuttal, the applicants have demonstrated the existence of special circumstances which dispensed them at the time of the events complained of from the obligation to exhaust the domestic remedies.[276]

2.9.12 Some Final Observations

The case-law of the Commission presents a great many instances which can hardly be fitted into the analysis provided in the foregoing.[277] Furthermore, in certain cases the issue of the exhaustion of the local remedies may coincide with the question of whether or not the Convention has been violated. In *X* v. *the United Kingdom*, for example, the Commission decided that:

> Having regard to the fact that the applicant has included in his application a complaint under Article 13 of the Convention concerning the absence of an effective remedy, (...) the Commission considers that it cannot reject all or part of the application as being inadmissible for failure to comply with the requirements as to the exhaustion of domestic remedies.[278]

Finally, it deserves mentioning that an applicant deprives himself of the possibility to exhaust the local remedies when he consents to a settlement of his claim with the national authorities. If that is the case, his application is declared inadmissible in Strasbourg on account of non-exhaustion.[279]

---

[276] Judgment of 16 September 1996, Reports 1996-IV, Vol. 15, paras 73-75.

[277] See, *e.g.*, the following cases: Appls 3435-3438/67, *W, X, Y and Z* v. *the United Kingdom*, Yearbook XI (1968), p. 562: purely internal measures within the military hierarchy do not constitute remedies in the sense of Art. 26; Appl. 6701/74, *X* v. *Austria*, D&R 5 (1976), p. 69 (78): the institution of a disciplinary action against judges is not in general an effective remedy; Appl. 1936/63, *Neumeister* v. *Austria*, Yearbook VII (1964), p. 224 (242): remedies which are available need not be used again if this has been done shortly before without success; Appl. 5613/72, *Hilton* v. *the United Kingdom*, Yearbook XIX (1976), p. 256 (274): the use of a remedy may be superfluous in certain circumstances; and Appl. 9816/82, *Poiss* v. *Austria*, D&R 36 (1984), p. 170 (178): the issue involved, the length of the proceedings and the continuous damage, could not be effectively raised before the competent domestic authorities.

[278] Appl. 7990/77, *X* v. *the United Kingdom*, D&R 24 (1981), p. 57 (60).

[279] See, *e.g.*, Appl. 7704/76, *X* v. *Federal Republic of Germany* (not published).

2.10 The Application must have been Submitted Within a Period of Six Months from the Date on Which the Final National Decision was taken (Article 26)

2.10.1 General

The six-month time-limit set forth in Article 26 serves to prevent that the compatibility of a national decision, action or omission with the Convention might still be questioned after a considerable lapse of time by the submission of an application to the European Commission. The Commission considers that the purpose of the six-month rule is to maintain reasonable legal certainty and ensure that cases raising issues under the Convention are examined within a reasonable time. It ought also to prevent the authorities and other persons concerned from being kept in a state of uncertainty for a long period of time. Lastly, the rule is designed to facilitate establishment of the facts of the case, which otherwise, with the passage of time, would become more and more difficult, and a fair examination of the issue raised under the Convention would thus become problematic.[280]

This again is an admissibility condition which applies to applications by States as well as individuals. As is the case for the condition of the prior exhaustion of the local remedies, this ensues from the text of Article 26 and Article 27(3) as compared with that of Article 27(1) and (2).[281]

2.10.2 Final Decision

There is a close relation between the admissibility condition of the six-month time-limit and the one concerning the exhaustion of local remedies. From the grammatical construction of Article 26, in which the two conditions are mentioned, the Commission inferred that:

> the term 'final decision', therefore, in Article 26 refers exclusively to the final decision concerned in the exhaustion of all local remedies according to the generally recognised rules of international law, so that the six-month period is operative only in this context.[282] From this the Commission concluded at a later instance that, if no local remedy is available, the challenged act or decision itself must be considered as the 'final decision'.[283]

In the case of *Christians against Racism and Fascism* v. *the United Kingdom* the applicant association complained about a police order prohibiting all public processions other than those of a religious, educational, festive or ceremonial character, for a period running from 24 February to 23 April 1978. No remedy was available to challenge the ensuing measures or their application to the association's planned procession on 22 April 1978. With respect to the six-month period the Commission decided:

---

[280] Appl. 15213/89, *M* v. *Belgium*, D&R 71 (1991), p. 230 (234).
[281] See *supra* p. 127.
[282] Appl. 214/56, *De Becker* v. *Belgium*, Yearbook II (1958-1959), p. 214 (242).
[283] See, *e.g.*, Appl. 7379/76, *X* v. *the United Kingdom*, D&R 8 (1977), p. 211 (212-213).

This period must normally be calculated from the final domestic decision, but where, as in the present case, no domestic decision is required for the application of a general measure to the particular case, the relevant date is the time when the applicant was actually affected by that measure. In the present case, this was the date of the procession planned by the applicant association, *i.e.* 22 April 1978.[284]

In the same vein the Commission treated an applicant who complained that he had not been entitled to have the lawfulness of his detention determined by a court contrary to Article 5(4). As the right guaranteed in Article 5(4) is applicable only to persons deprived of their liberty, the Commission decided that a person alleging a breach of that provision must, in the absence of a particular constitutional remedy or other similar remedies which could redress an alleged breach of Article 5(4), submit such a complaint to the Commission within six months from the date of his release.[285] And in the case of an application concerning the level of compensation after nationalisation of an industry, the Commission took the position that the six-month period did not run from the date of the Act on nationalisation but from the date on which the amount of compensation for shareholders was fixed. In the Commission's opinion Article 26 cannot be interpreted so as to require an applicant to seize the Commission at any time before his position in connection with the matter complained of has been finally determined or settled at the domestic level.[286]

The above-mentioned link between the two admissibility conditions laid down in Article 26 has as a further consequence that the criteria used by the Commission in answering the question of whether a given local remedy must or must not be sought are also relevant for the question of whether the time-limit has been observed;[287] the time-limit starts after the last national decision in the chain of local remedies that had to be exhausted. This means that remedies which the applicant did not have to pursue, for instance because they are not effective and adequate, are not taken into account as the starting-point of the time-limit. An applicant cannot, therefore, defer the time-limit, for instance by lodging a request for pardon, applying to an incompetent organ, or asking for reopening of his case.

---

[284] Appl. 8440/78, D&R 21 (1981), p. 138 (147).
[285] Appl. 10230/82, *X* v. *Sweden*, D&R 32 (1983), p. 303 (304-305).
[286] Appl. 9266/81, *Yarrow P.L.C. and Others* v. *the United Kingdom*, D&R 30 (1983), p. 155 (187). Similarly, in Appls 8588/79 and 8589/79, *Bramelid and Malmström* v. *Sweden*, D&R 29 (1982), p. 64 (84), the Commission decided that in proceedings concerning the right to purchase company shares leading to two subsequent decisions, one on the right to purchase and the other on the price, the six-month time-limit runs from the second decision to the extent that the individuals concerned complain in particular about the price.
[287] See, *e.g.*, Appl. 5759/72, *X* v. *Austria*, D&R 6 (1977), p. 15 (16); Appl. 7805/77, *Pastor X and Church of Scientology* v. *Sweden*, D&R 16 (1979), p. 68 (71); Appl. 15213/89, *M* v. *Belgium*, D&R 71 (1991), p. 230 (235).

Decisions on such requests are not regarded as final national decisions in the sense of Article 26.[288]

A curious decision of the Commission in this connection is the one in the *Nielsen* Case, discussed above. Although Nielsen's application had been lodged more than six months after the decision of the highest Danish court, still the Commission did not declare it inadmissible on that account. In fact, in the meantime Nielsen had addressed a request to the Special Court of Revision, and the Commission took the date of the decision of that Court as the starting-point of the time-limit for appeal.[289] As was mentioned above, later case-law indicates that the Commission's position with respect to this has changed.[290]

The close relation between the two admissibility conditions of Article 26 may place the applicant in a difficult situation if he is not sure whether a particular remedy must or must not be pursued. If he first brings a certain action and waits for the outcome, he incurs the risk of subsequently not being received by the Commission on account of exceeding the time-limit of six months, if the remedy in question did not have to be sought in the Commission's opinion. If, however, he does not seek that remedy, he incurs the risk of not being received on the ground of non-exhaustion. In such a case an applicant is well-advised to lodge an application with the Commission and at the same time to seek the remedy concerned. If later on the Commission concludes that exhaustion of the remedy concerned was not required, at any rate the time-limit has been complied with. And if the Commission decides otherwise, the final national decision as a rule will still be in time, since the local remedies have to be exhausted only at the moment at which the Commission decides on the admissibility.[291] If the national decision is not in time, the applicant may in any case again lodge an application with the Commission, the final national decision meanwhile pronounced constituting a new fact.[292] In matters like these the Commission again takes a flexible attitude. An Italian applicant contacted the Commission for the first time on 21 July 1978 setting out in his letter the substance of his complaints. Subsequently he sought reopening of proceedings in Italy, possibly as a result of the information provided by the Commission's Secretariat. The applicant did not contact the Commission again until 17 February 1981, at the end of the reopening procedure. The Commission nevertheless considered his application to have been introduced on 21 July 1978, and therefore in time.[293]

---

[288] See, for example, with regard to a request to re-open the case Appl. 10431/83, *G* v. *Federal Republic of Germany*, D&R 35 (1984), p. 241 (243) and Appl. 10308/83, *Altun* v. *Federal Republic of Germany*, D&R 36 (1984), p. 209 (231).

[289] Appl. 343/57, Yearbook II (1958-1959), p. 412 (434-444).

[290] See *supra* p. 136, note 185.

[291] See *supra* p. 151.

[292] See *supra* pp. 113-114.

[293] Appls 9024/80 and 9317/81, *Colozza and Rubinat* v. *Italy*, D&R 28 (1982), p. 138 (158).

2.10.3 Starting-Point of the Time-Limit

Although the six-month time-limit formally starts running at the moment at which the final national decision is taken, the Commission has adopted the date on which that decision has been notified to the applicant as the relevant moment, provided that the applicant was previously ignorant of the decision.[294] If a judgment is not delivered at a public hearing, the six-month period starts at the moment it was served on the applicant.[295] The Commission has also held that the period starts at the moment when the applicant's lawyer became aware of the decision completing the exhaustion of domestic remedies, notwithstanding the fact that the applicant only became aware of the decision later.[296] Depending on the nature of the case concerned, notification of the operative part of the judgment might be insufficient. For the six-month period to start running, the subsequent notification of the full text giving the reasons for the judgment may be decisive.[297] In this respect the Commission has emphasised that the period provided for in Article 26 fulfils the need of providing the person concerned with sufficient time to evaluate the desirability of submitting an application to the Commission and to decide on the content thereof. Such a need can only be satisfied from the moment when the applicant has been able to acquaint himself not only with the decision rendered by the national judicial authorities but also with the factual and legal grounds for that decision.[298] However, if the applicant knew that the decision was taken, but has made no further efforts to become acquainted with its contents, the date of the decision is considered the starting-point of the time-limit.[299]

Unlike in the case of the local remedies rule, where the moment at which the Commission decides on admissibility is decisive, for the time-limit of the six-month period the date of receipt of the application counts. In the case of the local remedies rule the Commission evidently relies on the English version of Article 26, which speaks of 'may only deal with the matter', while for its view concerning the time-limit for bringing the application it finds support in the French text, which speaks of *'ne peut être saisie que'*. In the *Iversen* Case, the Norwegian Government submitted that the date of registration of the application with the Secretariat was to be considered as the decisive date (see Rule 14 of the Rules of Procedure). The Commission, however, decided that for the question of whether an application has or has not been lodged in due time the relevant date is 'at the latest the date of its acknowledged arrival at the Secretariat-General.'[300] In practice the Commission takes as the decisive moment the date of the applicant's first letter, in which he states that he wishes to lodge an

---

[294] Appl. 899/60, *X* v. *Federal Republic of Germany*, Yearbook V (1962), p. 136 (144-146). *Cf.* Appl. 9991/82, *Bozano* v. *Italy*, D&R 39 (1984), p. 147 (155).

[295] Appl. 9908/82, *X* v. *France*, D&R 32 (1983), p. 266 (272).

[296] Appl. 14056/88, *Aarts* v. *the Netherlands*, D&R 70 (1991), p. 208 (212).

[297] Appl. 9299/81, *P* v. *Switzerland*, D&R 36 (1984), p. 20 (22).

[298] Appl. 10889/84, *C* v. *Italy*, D&R 56 (1988), p. 40 (57).

[299] Appl. 458/59, *X* v. *Belgium*, Yearbook III (1960), p. 222 (234).

[300] Appl. 1468/62, *Iversen* v. *Norway*, Yearbook VI (1963), p. 278 (322).

application and gives some indication of the nature of the complaint.[301] The mere submission of certain documents is not enough.[302] Since the scope of an application in respect of the date of introduction is circumscribed by the terms of the applicant's first communication, the Commission must also examine whether the further details of the application should be considered as legal submissions in respect of the applicant's main complaint to which the six-month rule would not be opposable[303] or whether they should be considered as separate complaints introduced at a later stage.[304] Thus, the Commission concluded in a case where the applicant initially complained under Article 6(1) of lack of access to court, that his subsequent submissions alleging the lack of an oral hearing amounted to a fresh complaint. The Commission found that the complaint of a lack of an oral hearing contained a distinct, precise fact in respect of the right to a fair hearing. In these circumstances, for the purposes of the six-month rule, the complaints had to be considered separately.[305]

In the case of *19 Chilean nationals and the S. Association* v. *Sweden*, the Commission was faced with the question how to treat the declaration of 18 Chileans that they adhered to an application already lodged with the Commission by another Chilean. The Commission took as the date of application for the 18 persons their declaration, and not the date of the filing of the original application.[306]

In a case where a period of almost seven years had elapsed between the initial letter to the Commission and the final completion of the application, the Commission first examined the question of the date of introduction of the application. The applicant wrote to the Commission for the first time on 12 December 1982 in a letter briefly setting out all her complaints. On 8 February 1983, the Secretariat sent her a letter drawing her attention to the need to exhaust domestic remedies. The letter also informed her that the application would be registered as soon as she returned the application form she had been given during a visit to the Secretariat. No more was heard from the applicant until 28 April 1989, on which date she sent the Commission a letter setting out in detail the complaints raised in December 1982 and including the relevant documents. On 30 June 1989 she sent the Commission a duly completed and signed application form. The Commission recalled that, according to its established practice, it considers the date of introduction of an application to be the date of the applicant's first letter indicating his intention to lodge an application and giving some indication

---

[301] Appl. 4429/70, *X* v. *Federal Republic of Germany*, Coll. 37 (1971), p. 109 (110). See also Appl. 8299/78, *X and Y* v. *Ireland*, D&R 22 (1981), p. 51 (72); Appl. 10293/83, *X* v. *the United Kingdom*, D&R 45 (1986), p. 41 (48).

[302] Appl. 9314/81, *N* v. *Federal Republic of Germany*, D&R 31 (1983), p. 200 (201).

[303] Appl. 12015/86, *Hilton* v. *the United Kingdom*, D&R 57 (1988), p. 108 (113).

[304] Appl. 10857/84, *Bricmont* v. *Belgium*, D&R 48 (1986), p. 106 (153).

[305] Appl. 18660/91, *Bengtsson* v. *Sweden*, D&R 79-A (1994), p. 11 (19-20).

[306] Appls 9959/82 and 10357/83, *19 Chilean nationals and the S. Association* v. *Sweden*, D&R 37 (1984), p. 87 (89).

of the nature of the complaints he wishes to raise. However, where a substantial interval follows before the applicant submits further information, the Commission examines the particular circumstances of the case in order to decide which date should be regarded as the date of introduction of the application.[307] Although the express obligation laid down in Article 26 of the Convention concerns only the introduction of an application, and the Commission has hitherto shown generosity in this respect by accepting that the date of introduction should be held to be the date on which the first letter setting out the complaint is submitted, without imposing any other restrictions, the Commission held that it would be contrary to the spirit and purpose of the six-month rule laid down in Article 26 of the Convention to accept that by means of an initial letter an applicant could set in motion the procedure provided for in Article 25 of the Convention only to remain inactive thereafter for an unlimited and unexplained period of time.[308] The Commission pointed to the fact that it has always rejected applications submitted more than six months after the date of the final decision, if the running of time has not been interrupted by any special circumstance. It considered that it would be inconsistent with the object and purpose of the six-month rule to deviate from this practice when the application has actually been introduced within six months from the final decision but has not been pursued thereafter.[309]

2.10.4 Violations Which took Place Before the Convention Became Binding upon the Respondent State

Applications concerning violations of the Convention which took place before the Convention became binding upon the respondent State are inadmissible *ratione temporis*. In such a case the six-month rule is not at issue at all. However, as was pointed out above, a declaration under Article 25 concerning the recognition of the right of complaint for individuals has retrospective effect insofar as an individual application may also concern a violation which took place between the entry into force of the Convention for the respondent State and the date of the said declaration by that State, provided that the declaration does not restrict the scope of the competence of the Commission in time.[310]

Can an individual still lodge an application if the final national decision dates back more than six months but was taken prior to the date on which the declaration under Article 25 was made? The Commission has originally decided that in such a case the time-limit does not start at the moment of the final national decision, but at the time of the declaration under Article 25, because the applicant did not have an earlier opportunity to apply to the Commission.[311] This approach

---

[307] Appl. 15213/89, *M* v. *Belgium*, D&R 71 (1991), p. 230 (234).
[308] *Idem.*
[309] Appl 10626/83, *Kelly* v. *the United Kingdom*, D&R 42 (1985), p. 205 (206).
[310] See *supra* p. 13 and Appl. 9587/81, *X* v. *France*, D&R 29 (1982), p. 228 (238).
[311] Appl. 214/56, *De Becker* v. *Belgium*, Yearbook II (1958-1959), p. 214 (243) and Appl. 846/60, *X* v. *the Netherlands*, Coll. 6 (1961), p. 63 (64-65).

has the disadvantage that, if the declaration has been made a long time after the entry into force of the Convention for the State concerned, the outcome may stand in the way of the legal certainty and stability aimed at by the time-limit. This seems to be the reason why in its more recent case-law the Commission has abandoned the above-mentioned approach and now feels obliged to calculate the six-month time-limit as from the date of the final national decision. The argument used is that the Commission considers the six-month rule 'an element of legal stability'.[312] This rule, according to the Commission:

> would not be observed, particularly in the case of States having ratified the Convention but not yet having recognized the right of individual petition, if the six-month time-limit were only to rule from the date of deposit of the declaration made in accordance with Article 25 of the Convention. The Commission considers consequently that the Contracting States cannot on their own authority put aside the rule of compliance with the six-month time-limit.[313]

The latter part of the quoted observations is remarkable: recognition of the right of individual complaint on the part of Contracting States obviously is not aimed at putting aside compliance with the six-month rule. Nevertheless, the substance of the Commission's decision would seem to make sense.

The rigidity with which the Commission adheres to its new approach becomes clear from a more recent decision in a case against Ireland. The applicant had submitted that there were special circumstances in his case which ought to be regarded as interrupting or suspending the running of the six-month period. The respondent Government replied that it had decided not to contest the facts alleged in support of the existence of special circumstances. The Commission pointed out that the six-month rule serves the interest not only of the respondent Government but also of legal certainty as a value in itself. On that basis it decided:

> that the decision of the respondent Government not to contest the facts alleged in support of the existence of special circumstances cannot operate as a form of waiver or be determinative of the issue and it falls to the Commission to make its own assessment of the matter in the light of the circumstances of the case.[314]

2.10.5 Continuing Situation

A special starting date for the time-limit applies to the cases, discussed above,[315] of a so-called continuing situation, where the violation is not (only) constituted by an act performed or a decision taken at a given moment, but (also) by its consequences, which continue and thus repeat the violation day by day. As long as that situation exists, the six-month period does not commence, since it serves to make acts and decisions *from the past* unassailable after a given period.[316]

---

[312] Appl. 9587/81, *X* v. *France*, D&R 29 (1982), p. 228 (240).
[313] *Idem.*
[314] Appl. 10416/83, *K* v. *Ireland*, D&R 38 (1984), pp. 159-160.
[315] See *supra* pp. 11-13.
[316] See in this respect Appl. 14807/89, *Agrotexim Hellas S.A.* v. *Greece*, D&R 72 (1992), p. 148 (158); Appl. 17864/91, *Çinar* v. *Turkey*, D&R 79-A (1994), p. 5 (7).

A well-known example is the *De Becker* Case. De Becker had been sentenced to death in 1946 for treason during the Second World War. Later this sentence was converted into imprisonment, and in 1961 he was released under certain conditions. Under Belgian criminal law, such a sentence resulted in the limitation of certain rights – including the right to freedom of expression – which limitation continued to apply after the release. The Commission held that this was a continuing situation and considered the complaint admissible *ratione temporis*. It considered that the six-month rule was not applicable here, because the issue was whether, by the application to De Becker of the Belgian legislation in question, the Convention was still being violated.[317]

The Commission disagreed, however, with an applicant who alleged the existence of a continuing violation of Article 13 insofar as no domestic remedy was available to him in respect of a deprivation of his possession. According to the Commission:

> Where domestic law gives no remedy against such a measure, it is inevitable that unless the law changes that situation will continue indefinitely. However the person affected suffers no additional prejudice beyond that which arose directly and immediately from the initial measure. His position is not therefore to be compared to that of a person subject to a continuing restriction on his substantive Convention rights.[318]

In another case the Commission held that the failure of the State to pay certain sums which were due to the applicant, created an ongoing situation in which the six-month rule did not apply.[319] The same was held to be the case when the administration failed to comply with the judgment of the Council of State which annulled the administrative decision refusing the applicants' application for a licence to establish a foreign language school.[320]

In the above-mentioned *De Becker* Case the continuing situation ensued from a legal provision. In those cases where the continuing situation is due to a judicial decision or a decision of the executive, the Commission applies the time-limit in the usual way.[321] The Commission adopts the view with respect to the latter that they are pronounced at a clearly defined moment and that the resulting consequences may be of a temporary nature and may be terminated. However, it is difficult to understand why a continuing situation could not thus be called into existence as well. Legislative measures, too, are of course taken at a clearly defined moment and, in the case of De Becker, the legal provision concerned became effective with respect to him at a specific moment. Moreover, the legal

---

[317] Appl. 214/56, *De Becker* v. *Belgium*, Yearbook II (1958-1959), p. 214 (230-234). See also Appl. 4859/71, *X* v. *Belgium*, Coll. 44 (1973), p. 1 (18).

[318] Appl. 8206/78, *X* v. *the United Kingdom*, D&R 25 (1982), p. 147 (151).

[319] Appl. 11698/85, *X* v. *Belgium* (not published); Appl. 11966/86, *X* v. *Belgium* (not published).

[320] Appl. 18357/91, *D and A H.* v. *Greece*, HRLJ, Vol. 16, No. 1-3, 1995, p. 50 (52). See also Appls 7572/76, 7586/76 and 7587/76, *Ensslin, Baader and Raspe* v. *Federal Republic of Germany*, D&R 14 (1979), p. 66 (113).

[321] See, *e.g.*, Appl. 1038/61, *X* v. *Belgium*, Yearbook IV (1961), p. 324 (334) and Appls 8560/79 and 8613/79, *X and Y* v. *Portugal*, D&R 16 (1979), p. 209.

consequences of legislative measures may also be of a temporary nature and may be terminated by the legislator. The distinction made by the Commission would therefore seem to require a more convincing reasoning.

2.10.6 Special Circumstances Absolving the Applicant to Fulfil the Requirement of the Six-Month Rule

With respect to the six-month rule, too, the Commission admits that special circumstances may occur in which the applicant need not satisfy this requirement. The case-law on this point is almost identical with that regarding special circumstances in connection with the local remedies rule.[322] In the *Toth* Case, the Court joined the liberal approach taken by the Commission and held that it was hardly realistic to expect a detainee without legal training to understand fully the complexity of the case concerned and in particular the difference of the two types of procedure involved. The applicant was therefore excused for, strictly speaking, not complying with the six-month rule.[323]

2.11 The Application Must not be Manifestly Ill-Founded (Article 27(2))

This admissibility condition applies only to individual applications. In general, inter-State applications, which may be assumed to be filed only after extensive deliberation and to have been prepared by expert legal advisers of the Government, in general may be expected not to be manifestly ill-founded. Nevertheless, while reiterating that the wording of Article 27(1) and (2) makes reference only to Article 25, the Commission:

> does not exclude the application of a general rule providing for the possibility of declaring an application under Article 24 inadmissible, if it is clear from the outset that it is wholly unsubstantiated or otherwise lacking the requirements of a genuine allegation in the sense of Article 24 of the Convention.[324]

Until now this has not occurred in practice. On the other hand a great many individual applications are declared inadmissible by the Commission on the ground of being manifestly ill-founded.

From a strictly formal viewpoint the competence of the Commission to declare an application inadmissible on account of manifest ill-foundedness does not fit in very well with the division of power laid down in the Convention. The Commission is competent only to pronounce on the *admissibility* of the application, while a decision on the *merits* is reserved to the Court or the Committee of Ministers, as the case may be. However, when the Commission declares an application to be manifestly ill-founded, in actual fact it pronounces on the merits, on the basis of a *prima facie* opinion on the alleged facts and the

---

[322] See *supra* pp. 152-153.
[323] Judgment of 12 December 1991, A.224, pp. 22-23.
[324] Appls 9940-9944/82, *France, Norway, Denmark, Sweden and the Netherlands* v. *Turkey*, D&R 35 (1984), p. 143 (161-162).

legal grounds put forward. On the other hand, the drafters of the Convention have intended to entrust the Commission with the task of acting as a screen for the great number of applications to be expected.[325] The competence of the Commission to exclude manifestly ill-founded applications would seem to fit the aim of procedural economy.

Precisely since, when declaring an application manifestly ill-founded, the Commission itself takes a *final* decision on the interpretation and application of one or more of the provisions of Section I of the Convention, the meaning which the Commission gives in its case-law to the term 'manifestly ill-founded' is of great importance. Indeed, it bars the possibility for the Court – or the Committee of Ministers – to deal with the case. In several decisions the Commission has indicated what it understands by 'manifestly ill-founded'. In the *De Becker* Case, for instance, the Commission held that it can declare an application manifestly ill-founded only if the examination of the complaint does not disclose any *prima facie* violation of the Convention.[326] The same view appears from the Commission's decision in the *Pataki* Case:

> whereas it follows that at the present stage of the proceedings the task of the Commission is not to determine whether an examination of the case submitted by the Applicant discloses the actual existence of a violation of one of the rights and freedoms guaranteed by the Convention but only to determine whether it includes any possibility of the existence of such a violation.[327]

In practice applications are declared manifestly ill-founded in particular if the facts about which a complaint is lodged evidently do not constitute a violation of the Convention, or if those facts have not been proven or are manifestly incorrect. As to the latter, the Commission requires the applicant to give *prima facie* evidence of the facts put forward by him.[328] As regards the former ground, it is not always possible to distinguish clearly between manifest ill-foundedness and incompatibility with the Convention. There is incompatibility *ratione materiae* if an application concerns the violation of a right not protected by the Convention.[329] In that case the application falls entirely outside the scope of the Convention and no examination of the merits is possible. An application is manifestly ill-founded if it does indeed concern a right protected by the Convention, but a *prima facie* examination discloses that the facts put forward cannot by any means justify the claim of violation, so that an examination of the merits is superfluous.

The case-law in this matter has not always been consistent. An obvious example is the case-law with respect to Article 14. According to this article the enjoyment

---

[325] See *supra* p. 98.
[326] Appl. 214/56, Yearbook II (1958-1959), p. 214 (254).
[327] Appl. 596/59, Yearbook III (1960), p. 356 (368). In the same sense, Appl. 7640/76, *Geerk* v. *Switzerland*, Yearbook XXI (1978), p. 470 (474-476).
[328] See, *e.g.*, Appl. 556/59, *X* v. *Austria*, Yearbook III (1960), p. 288. In the same sense the Court, judgment of 9 October 1979, *Airey*, A.32, p. 10.
[329] See *supra* pp. 123-126.

of the rights and freedoms set forth in the Convention must be guaranteed without discrimination on any ground. Applications containing complaints about discrimination with respect to rights or freedoms which the Convention does not protect have sometimes been declared to be manifestly ill-founded and sometimes incompatible with the Convention.[330] In general the Commission takes the position that applications leading to the interpretation of one or more articles of Section I of the Convention should not be rejected as being incompatible with the Convention *ratione materiae*. It seems, however, doubtful whether this criterion is adequate in all cases. If the right invoked is actually set forth in the Convention, but it is quite obvious from the alleged facts that there has been no violation, an interpretation of the article of the Convention invoked by the applicant will hardly be needed, if at all, while on the other hand the Commission may conclude that the application is incompatible with the Convention as not relating to a right protected therein, precisely on the ground of the interpretation of one or more of the provisions of Section I. Indeed, its very task is to examine whether the right invoked by the applicant can be brought under those provisions, and for this in most cases an interpretation will be necessary.

The degree of interpretation required before a decision can be taken also plays a part in the case of the declaration of manifest ill-foundedness as such. It has been stated above that the competence of the Commission to declare an application manifestly ill-founded fits into the framework of the screening function which the drafters of the Convention intended the Commission to perform. For a proper discharge of that function, however, no more is needed than the competence to reject those applications the ill-founded character of which is actually *manifest*. In several cases, however, the Commission has used this competence in a way which clearly went beyond this.

A clear example is the *Iversen* Case, in which the applicant complained about the possibility existing in Norway that dentists who had recently completed their studies could be obliged to work for some time in the public service. The complaint was declared 'manifestly ill-founded' by the Commission, while it raised such complicated questions concerning Article 4, which moreover divided the members of the Commission,[331] that a more detailed examination of the merits appeared decidedly justified. Equally, an application on account of violation of the freedom of expression was declared manifestly ill-founded by the Commission on the basis of the finding that the prohibition of a Buddhist prisoner to send a manuscript to the publisher of a Buddhist journal constituted a reasonable application of the prison rule concerned, and that this rule itself 'is necessary in a democratic society for the prevention of disorder or crime within

---

[330] For a declaration of manifest ill-foundedness, see, *e.g.*, Appl. 1452/62, *X* v. *Austria*, Yearbook VI (1963), p. 268 (278), and for a declaration of incompatibility, see, *e.g.*, Appl. 2333/64, *Inhabitants of Leeuw-St. Pierre* v. *Belgium*, Yearbook VIII (1965), p. 338 (360-362).

[331] Appl. 1468/62, *Iversen* v. *Norway*, Yearbook VI (1963), p. 278 (326-332).

the meaning of Article 10(2).'[332] There again, to put it mildly, it was doubtful whether this was so obvious an interpretation of the said provision of the Convention that no difference of opinion was possible among reasonable persons. Since such decisions bar the possibility that the Court – or the Committee of Ministers – may give its opinion on the interpretation and application of such important provisions, this case-law of the Commission gives rise to criticism as being contrary to the division of power such as it is laid down in the Convention. It is submitted that the Commission may declare an application to be manifestly ill-founded only if its ill-founded character is actually evident at first sight, or if the Commission bases its decision on the constant case-law of the Court. Therefore, we find it difficult to accept as a correct interpretation and application of this 'admissibility' requirement the position of the Commission, laid down in its report in the *Powell and Rayner* Case, that is implicit in the Commission's constant case-law that the term 'manifestly ill-founded' under Article 27(2) of the Convention extends further than the literal meaning of the word 'manifestly' would suggest at first reading. In certain cases, where the Commission considers at an early stage in the proceedings that a *prima facie* issue arises, it seeks the observations of the parties on admissibility and merits. The Commission may then proceed to a full examination of the facts and issues of a case, but nevertheless finally reject the applicant's substantive claims as manifestly ill-founded notwithstanding their 'arguable' character. In such cases the rejection of a claim under this head of inadmissibility amounts to the following finding: after full information has been provided by both parties, without the need of further formal investigation, it has now become manifest that the claim of a breach of the Convention is unfounded.[333]

Doubt about the practice of the Commission also arises in those cases where the Commission is obviously divided on the question of whether an application is or is not manifestly ill-founded, as occurred, for instance, in the *Iversen* Case. Of course, the Commission cannot derogate from the rules concerning the voting procedure and require unanimity for such decisions, but if only a bare majority can be obtained for a declaration of manifest ill-foundedness, this in itself makes it evident that the ill-foundedness is not very manifest.

---

[332] Appl. 5442/72, *X* v. *the United Kingdom*, D&R 1 (1975), p. 41 (42).
[333] Report of 19 January 1989, A.172, p. 27. See also Appl. 15404/89, *Purcell* v. *Ireland*, D&R 70 (1991), p. 262, where it hardly could be said that the applicant did not have an 'arguable claim'.

3 THE PROCEDURE AFTER AN APPLICATION HAS BEEN DECLARED ADMISSIBLE

3.1 General

After the Commission has declared an application admissible, it subjects the complaint contained therein to an examination of the merits (Article 28(1)(a)). The Commission also places itself at the disposal of the parties 'with a view to securing a friendly settlement of the matter on the basis of respect for human rights as defined in this Convention' (Article 28(1)(b)). Over 10 percent of the cases declared admissible have resulted in a friendly settlement, often providing for pecuniary compensation for the victim, and sometimes referring to a change in the law of the State concerned.[334] Where no settlement can be secured, the Commission prepares a report in which it establishes the facts and states its opinion as to whether these facts disclose a violation of the Convention. This opinion is not legally binding, the final decision resting with either the Committee of Ministers or, if the case is referred to it by the Commission or the State Party, the European Court of Human Rights. Protocol No. 9 to the Convention, which entered into force on 1 October 1994 for those States which have ratified it, gives the individual applicant also the right to refer the case to the Court, subject to leave being granted.[335] In the course of 1996 the Secretariat opened 12,143 provisional files and registered 4,758 individual applications within the meaning of Article 25 of the Convention. During the same year the Commission dealt with 3,400 applications. Nonetheless, on 1 July 1996 5,206 applications were pending before the Commission, 3,719 of which were still awaiting a first examination by the Commission, *i.e.* approximately 72 percent.[336] The structural reforms provided for by Protocol No. 11, which was opened for signature on 11 May 1994, are intended to overcome these problems.[337]

3.2 Rejection of the Application Under Article 29 and Striking the Application off the List of Cases Under Article 30

In the course of its examination of the merits of an individual application which it has accepted as admissible, the Commission may nevertheless decide to reject the application as inadmissible if, on the basis of these examinations, it reaches the conclusion that not all the conditions of Article 27 have been complied with (Article 29). Such a decision of the Commission requires a two-third majority of

---

[334] See *infra* pp. 183-185.
[335] See *infra* pp. 235-239.
[336] Council of Europe, *Survey of Activities and Statistics*, 1996, p. 2.
[337] See *supra* p. 30 and *infra* p. 194. Since the entry into force of Protocol No. 8, the backlog in cases has not decreased. On the contrary, since 1992 the number of pending cases has increased. This is partly caused by the new members from Central and Eastern Europe. See Council of Europe, *Survey of Activities and Statistics*, 1996.

its members and must state the reasons on which it is based. It is communicated to the parties. Article 29 thus enables the Commission to stop the procedure even at this phase on the ground of inadmissibility, thus preventing the Court or the Committee of Ministers from having to deal with the case.[338]

From the text of Article 29 it cannot be inferred that this provision may be applied only if *new* facts have become known to the Commission. The principle of legal security and that of honouring justified expectations might be said to plead for such a restriction of the rule.[339] However, the case-law shows that the Commission takes the view that Article 29 may also be applied on the basis of facts which were already known or might have been known to the Commission during the admissibility examination.[340]

From the *Schiesser* Case one might conclude that the Court is prepared to apply Article 29 even by analogy.[341] In that case the applicant had adduced a violation of Article 5(4), after his complaint concerning Article 5(3) had already been declared admissible by the Commission. In its report the Commission stated that, as regards Article 5(4), the requirement of previous exhaustion of the local remedies had not been complied with. When the Swiss Government subsequently requested the Court to declare the application incompatible with the requirements of Article 26, the latter took the position that it had no competence to deal with the issue, holding among other things:

> The Court takes the view that, on the point now being considered, the Commission's report amounts, in substance, to an implicit decision of inadmissibility, although it does not expressly refer to Article 29(1) or even to Article 27(3).[342]

However, there cannot possibly be a question of an implicit decision on the basis of Article 29, since the decision of the Commission had been taken with eleven votes in favour, one against and two abstentions. Since Article 29 (old) explicitly required unanimity, reference by the Court to Article 29(1) would seem to be out

---

[338] See Committee of Experts, *Explanatory Report on the Second to Fifth Protocols to the European Convention for the Protection of Human Rights and Fundamental Freedoms*, H(71)11, Strasbourg, 1971, p. 27.

[339] A new fact was concerned, for example, when the Commission found during the examination of the merits that the applicant had used the procedure before the Commission to evade her obligations of payments *vis-à-vis* her creditor and thus had abused her right of complaint in the sense of Art. 27(2) of the Convention; Appl. 5207/71, *Raupp v. Federal Republic of Germany*, Coll. 42 (1973), p. 85 (89-90).

[340] See Appls 5577-5583/72, *Donnelly v. the United Kingdom*, Yearbook XIX (1976), p. 85 (252-254). See also the decision of the Commission on the Appls 5100/71, 5354/72 and 5370/72, *Engel, Dona and Schul v. the Netherlands*, B.20 (1974-76), pp. 134-140; and the decision of 29 May 1973 on Appl. 4771/71, *Kamma v. the Netherlands* (not published). Application of Art. 29 in those cases did not lead to rejection of the applications, because the Commission held that all the conditions of admissibility had been satisfied. However, it may be inferred from the above-mentioned decisions that the Commission would have rejected them if the said conditions had not been satisfied, even if this could have been known during the examination of the admissibility.

[341] Judgment of 4 December 1979, A.34, pp. 16-17.

[342] *Ibidem*, p. 17.

of place. The Court reaffirmed its position in the *Artico* Case, where it held with reference to its *Schiesser* judgment, that:

> despite the apparent generality of the wording of Article 29, the respondent State is entitled by analogy to the benefit of the provisions governing the initial stage of the proceedings, in other words to obtain from the Commission, in a supplementary decision, *a ruling by majority vote (Article 34)* on the question of jurisdiction or admissibility submitted to the Commission by the State immediately it has been led to do so by the change in the legal situation.[343]

Furthermore, Article 30 provides that the Commission may at any stage – *i.e.* including during its examinations of the merits – of the proceedings decide to strike an application off its list of cases where the circumstances lead to the conclusion that the applicant does not intend to pursue his petition, or that the matter has been resolved, or that for any other reason established by the Commission, it is no longer justified to continue the examination of the petition. It will not make such a decision if it holds that any reason of a general character affecting the observance of the Convention justifies further examination of the application. In the case of an inter-State application a condition for striking the case off the list is that the applicant State has declared that it wishes to withdraw its application.

If the Commission decides to strike a petition off its list after having accepted it, it shall draw up a report which shall contain a statement of the facts and the decision striking off its list the petition together with the reasons therefore. This report shall be transmitted to the parties, as well as to the Committee of Ministers for information. The Commission may publish it. According to Article 30(3) the Commission may decide to restore a petition to its list of cases if it considers that the circumstances justify such a course. Thus in a case which had been struck off the list, because the applicant's lawyer did not reply to letters from the Secretariat, the Commission decided to restore the case on its list of cases, since the applicant could prove that the letters had been received at the office of his lawyer after the latter's death, but had not been referred to him.[344] It is evident that the same possibility of re-acceptance does not exist with respect to cases which have been declared inadmissible.[345]

3.3 The Examination of the Merits (Article 28(1)(a))

3.3.1 General

A proper understanding of all the aspects of the case helps the Commission in trying to secure a friendly settlement (Article 28(1)(b)) and further enables it to form an opinion on whether there has been a violation of the Convention (Article 31(1)). It is not sufficient for the Commission to examine the facts and

---

[343] Judgment of 13 May 1989, *Artico*, A.37, p. 13 (emphasis added).
[344] Appl. 13549/88, *M v. Italy*, D&R 69 (1991), p. 195 (197).
[345] Appl. 16542/90, *J v. France*, D&R 72 (1992), p. 226 (227).

circumstances of the case; it must also concern itself with the legal issues. The procedure concerning the merits has a contradictory[346] and quasi-judicial character. Like the procedure concerning admissibility, the examination of the merits takes place *in camera*.

Since the entry into force of Protocol No. 3 on 20 September 1970, the examination is no longer conducted in the first instance by a Sub-Commission. The application is initially examined by one or more rapporteurs whom the Commission appoints from among its members (Rule 54 of the Rules of Procedure). The powers of the rapporteur may be very wide. In accordance with Rule 34(2) of its Rules of Procedure the Commission may delegate one or more of its members, and consequently also the rapporteur, to take any action in its name which it considers expedient or necessary for the proper performance of its duties under the Convention, in particular the hearing of witnesses or experts, the examination of documents, or the visit to any locality. In every stage of the examination of an application under Article 25 the rapporteur may decide to invite the parties to submit further written evidence or observations. The rapporteur is to draft memoranda if the Commission asks him to do so in connection with its consideration of the case concerned (Rule 54(3)(a) of the Rules of Procedure). Finally, under Rule 54(3)(b), the rapporteur must prepare a draft report for the Commission in accordance with Rule 57 (in case a friendly settlement has been reached), Rule 60 (if no friendly settlement has been reached), or Rule 57 (when a case that has already been accepted is struck off the list).

The examination of the merits usually takes a good deal of time; apart from exceptional cases, about two years. In some cases this is inevitable, *viz.* if it is difficult to ascertain the facts, or if the attempts to reach a friendly settlement take a long time. On the whole, however, the desirability of shortening the procedure is evident, especially if it is borne in mind that the time which elapses between the moment at which an application is submitted and the date of the decision on admissibility is also rather long in many cases. Furthermore, there is the chance that the application must still pass through the procedure before the Court. Moreover, in most cases all this has been preceded by a lengthy national procedure.

Procedural improvements, in particular the introduction of Chambers and Committees under Protocol No. 8, have increased the Commission's efficiency. According to Article 1 of this Protocol, Chambers of at least seven members may examine individual petitions that can be dealt with on the basis of established case-law or which raise no serious questions affecting the interpretation or application of the Convention. Rule 20(3) of the Rules of Procedure of the Commission provides that the Commission may set up Committees of three members with the power, by unanimous vote, to reject or to strike a case off its list. Where there is a difference of opinion between members of the Committee,

---

[346] This does not necessarily imply direct contact between the parties; see Appl. 8007/77, *Cyprus* v. *Turkey*, D&R 13 (1979), p. 85 (147).

the case is referred in practice to the Chamber for a decision. The Committee may relinquish jurisdiction in favour of the plenary Commission. In addition, the Protocol enables the Commission to strike a petition off the list of cases if the applicant does not intend to pursue his petition, if the matter has been resolved, or if 'for any other reason established by the Commission, it is no longer justified to continue the examination of the petition.'[347]

At the end of 1990 the system of setting up Chambers and Committees became effective. Two Chambers and six Committees have been constituted pursuant to the provisions of Protocol No. 8. Moreover, commencing in 1990 the length of the sessions of the Commission has been extended to 16 weeks, while in addition the members of the Commission have 16 weeks available for preparatory work.[348] However, the length of time needed to deal with those cases which raise serious issues remains a cause of great concern.[349]

The Commission may apply an accelerated procedure for urgent cases (Rule 46).

3.3.2 Procedure before the Commission

The procedure before the Commission is generally characterised by great freedom to conduct the examination of the case as the Commission sees fit and to adapt it to the special circumstances of each case. Normally the parties are first invited to make written observations and subsequently to submit oral arguments at one or more hearings. Usually these will be supplementary observations, because the more fundamental legal arguments concerning the merits have already been put forward during the admissibility examination. In case the Commission decides that an oral hearing shall be hold at the admissibility stage, the members are asked to state their views of the admissibility and merits of the case. Thereafter a vote on the admissibility takes place. If admissible, a provisional vote is usually taken on the question of violation. At such a hearing any member of the Commission may, with the consent of the President, put questions to the parties and request them to elucidate particular points in addition to their written observations and/or oral arguments (Rule 40 of the Rules of Procedure).

Under Rule 34(1) and (2) of its Rules of Procedure the Commission may delegate one or more of its members to take any action which it considers expedient or necessary for the proper performance of its duties under the Convention. The Commission used this wide power of delegation, which already existed under Rule 51(1) of its old Rules of Procedure (but there only in connection with its duties under Article 28), for instance when it left the hearing

---

[347] Article 6(1)(a)-(c) of Protocol No. 8.
[348] See also *supra* pp. 28-29.
[349] See *supra* p. 166.

of evidence in the examination of the complaint of Ireland against the United Kingdom to three of its members.[350]

3.3.3 Inquiry on the Spot

If the Commission considers it necessary, it may, under Article 28(a) of the Convention in conjunction with Rule 15(2) of the Rules of Procedure, make an inquiry on the spot or order such an inquiry to be made. If it does so, it invites, through the intermediary of the Secretary General of the Council of Europe, the Contracting State in question to furnish all necessary facilities. Under the Convention the Contracting States are obliged to furnish these facilities (Article 28(1)(a)).

The Commission availed itself of this power for the first time in connection with the first complaint of Greece against the United Kingdom.[351] On that occasion an inquiry was made in Cyprus into the existence of certain practices of torture, and additionally into whether the threat to public order was such that the measures taken by the British authorities were justified. In September 1975 the Commission again went to Cyprus, this time, *inter alia*, for a visit to two refugee camps in connection with complaints of Cyprus against Turkey.[352] In the *Greek* Case, too, the Commission made use of the power in question. The Greek Government, however, refused to admit members of the Commission to the Averoff prison in Athens and a number of prison camps on the island of Leros.[353] In the *Northern Ireland* Case the cooperation was not refused, but the Court expressed its disapproval of the fact that, as the Commission had hinted in its report, the British Government had not always afforded the desirable assistance. In its judgment the Court emphasised the importance of the obligation of Contracting States set forth in Article 28(a), the present Article 28(1)(a).[354] In connection with the five applications which were lodged against Turkey, the Commission decided to send a delegation to this country in order to continue its efforts to reach a friendly settlement. The delegation had discussions with, *inter alia*, the Minister of Justice, members of the Grand National Assembly and members of the Military Court of Cassation. The delegation also met with journalists, academics and trade unionists, and it visited Military Detention Centres, where it was able to talk in private with prisoners.[355]

---

[350] Appl. 5310/71, *Ireland* v. *the United Kingdom*, Yearbook XV (1972), p. 76. See Council of Europe, *Stock-Taking on the European Convention on Human Rights*, Strasbourg, 1981, pp. 21-22.

[351] Appl. 176/56, *Greece* v. *the United Kingdom*, Yearbook II (1958-1959), p. 182.

[352] Appls 6780/74 and 6950/74, *Cyprus* v. *Turkey*, Yearbook XVIII (1975), p. 82. See Stock-Taking, *supra* note 350, p. 25.

[353] See Stock-Taking, *supra* note 350, p. 16.

[354] Judgment of 18 January 1978, *Ireland* v. *the United Kingdom*, A.25, p. 60.

[355] Report of 7 December 1985, *France, Norway, Denmark, Sweden and the Netherlands* v. *Turkey*, D&R 44 (1985), p. 31 (36-37).

In the case of individual complaints, too, sometimes witnesses are heard or evidence is collected in some other way on the spot, as happened in the case of the IRA prisoner Bobby Sands.[356]

The Convention does not provide for measures to enforce the duty of cooperation on the part of a Contracting State, nor do the present Rules of Procedure of the Commission contain any provision to that effect. The old Rules contained the rather ineffective provision that the Commission formally took note of the refusal of a Contracting State to cooperate in measures which the Commission had taken to perform its duties under Article 28 of the Convention (Rule 57(2) of those Rules of Procedure). In the *Greek* Case the consequences of the refusal were not very serious, because the Commission was able by other means to obtain sufficient information to form an opinion on the application. In a case in which in the Commission's opinion an inquiry on the spot is absolutely necessary, it would appear most appropriate for the Commission to appeal to the Committee of Ministers in case of a refusal. *Via* a resolution the latter organ might bring pressure to bear on the recalcitrant State to comply with its obligations and to cooperate in making an investigation on its territory possible. In addition, although in practice this is not very likely to occur, in such a case as a possible reaction to non-compliance with the resolution of the Committee of Ministers, another Contracting State might lodge an application against the recalcitrant State for alleged violation of Article 28. As was stated above, Article 24 permits the Contracting States to complain about 'any alleged breach of the provisions of the Convention by another High Contracting Party', so that they need not confine themselves to the rights and freedoms of Section I of the Convention, but may also bring up an article such as Article 28.[357]

3.3.4   Hearing of Witnesses or Experts

Under Rule 34 of its Rules of Procedure the Commission may, at the request of each of the parties or on its own initiative, take any action which it considers expedient or necessary for the proper performance of its duties under the Convention. It appears from the second paragraph of this provision that this also covers the hearing of witnesses. This provision was formulated already so widely in the old Rules of Procedure that the Commission could hear anyone it wanted. In the *Lawless* Case, for instance, it ordered the applicant himself and the police officer who had arrested him to appear as witnesses.[358] The present Rule 38 is formulated even more widely and refers to 'any individual applicant, expert or other person whom the Commission decides to hear as a witness.' Witnesses and experts, at their own choice, take the oath or make the declaration mentioned in Rule 39 of the Rules of Procedure.

---

[356] See Council of Europe, *Press Release C(81)16*, 24 April 1981.
[357] See *supra* pp. 41-42.
[358] See report of 19 December 1959, B.1 (1961), p. 53.

Apart from the expenses of witnesses, experts and other persons whom the Commission decides to hear on its own initiative, which expenses in any case have to be borne by the Council of Europe (Rule 42(2)), the Commission may decide, with regard to expenses of witnesses, experts and other persons whom the Commission hears at the request of one of the parties, that these expenses shall also be borne by the Council of Europe (Rule 42(1)).

With the permission of the President or the principle delegate of the Commission, witnesses, experts and other persons may be asked questions at the session by any member of the Commission or any of the parties (Rule 40). The same Rule 15(2) which authorises the Commission to carry out an inquiry on the spot[359] also empowers it to hear witnesses elsewhere than in Strasbourg. In the case of *Ireland* v. *the United Kingdom*,[360] for instance, three sessions for the hearing of witnesses were held, for security reasons, at an airport at Stavanger, Norway.[361]

The Commission does not have any means for compelling a witness, expert or other person to appear before it. Unlike the old Rules, the present Rules of Procedure no longer contain a provision about this. Rule 57 of the old Rules provided that, if the persons in question, after having been summoned by the Commission, failed to appear, refused to bear witness, or violated the oath or declaration which they were obliged to take, the Secretary General of the Council of Europe was to communicate this, at the request of the President of the Commission, to the Contracting State to whose jurisdiction the person in question was subject. Even without an express provision in the Rules of Procedure it would seem possible for such a communication to be addressed to the Contracting State concerned. This State will then have to take any appropriate measures to ensure that the persons in question will cooperate. In fact, the Contracting States are obliged to give the Commission the necessary assistance in the performance of its duties. This would seem to also ensue by analogy from Article 28(1)(a) of the Convention, which provides that, if the Commission decides to carry out an inquiry on the spot, 'the States concerned shall furnish all necessary facilities.'

3.3.5 The Report of the Commission

After conclusion of the examination the Commission may deliberate with a view to reaching a provisional opinion on the merits of the case (Rule 55). The rapporteur draws up a draft report on the basis of the provisional opinion reached by the Commission under Rule 55 (Rule 58). If the Commission was divided in its provisional opinion, this is stated in the draft report (Rule 58(2)). After consideration of the draft report and if no friendly settlement is reached, the Commission draws up its report referred to in Article 31 of the Convention. For this, it proceeds as follows. First those parts of the report are adopted in which the

---

[359] See *supra* pp. 171-172.
[360] Appl. 5310/71, Yearbook XV (1972), p. 76.
[361] See Stock-Taking, *supra* note 350, p. 22.

facts are established and the submissions of the parties are set out (Rule 59(1)). The Commission then deliberates and votes on whether the facts found disclose any violation by the State concerned of its obligations under the Convention (Rule 59(2)). Unless the Commission decides otherwise, only those members who have participated in the last-mentioned deliberations and vote are entitled to express their separate opinion in the report (Rule 59(3)).[362]

As said before, the report is published by the Registrar of the Court in cases where the application is brought before the Court under Article 48 of the Convention.[363] Originally, the Consultative Assembly had proposed to confer the power to do so on the Commission.[364] This power ultimately was not incorporated into the Convention, in order to enable the Committee of Ministers to play also a part with respect to the friendly settlement. However, *via* a provision in its old Rules the Commission had authorised itself to send its report for written observations to the individual applicant after the case had been referred to the Court.[365] More generally, the Commission has stated as its opinion:

> that in entrusting special responsibilities and functions to the Commission the High Contracting Parties intended the Commission to possess all the powers necessary for the effective discharge of those responsibilities and functions, including the power, if it thinks fit, to publish or communicate its Report to any person.[366]

In the *Lawless* Case, for instance, the Commission had reached the conclusion that there had been no violation of the Convention, but nevertheless decided to refer the case to the Court, since it was of the opinion that important legal problems were at issue. Out of fear that this might give rise to all sorts of speculations, it deemed it necessary for a proper application of the Convention to publish the conclusions of its report.[367] The Court did not pronounce on this point in its subsequent judgment in this case. On the basis of this silence it may be assumed that the Court does not regard such a procedure of the Commission as contrary to the Convention, because it would no doubt have pointed this out to the Commission, since the Court considers it as its duty 'to ensure that the Convention is respected and, if need be, to point to any irregularities.'[368]

The report is sent, through the Secretary General of the Council of Europe, to the Committee of Ministers and those States which are involved in the case.[369]

---

[362] That the above-mentioned finding of the facts and the opinion of the Commission on the question of whether the facts found disclose a violation of the Convention, have to be incorporated into the report follows from Art. 31(1) of the Convention. For what the report further has to contain, see Rule 60 of the Rules of Procedure.

[363] See Rule 29(3) of the Rules of Procedure of the Court.

[364] Council of Europe, Cons. Ass., Recommendation No. 38, 8 September 1949, Document 108, pp. 261-264.

[365] See Rule 61 of the old Rules of Procedure.

[366] Report of 19 December 1959, *Lawless*, B.1 (1961), p. 248.

[367] *Ibidem*, p. 252.

[368] Judgment of 14 November 1960, *Lawless*, A.1, p. 12.

[369] Art. 31(2) of the Convention in conjunction with Rule 60(2) of the Rules of Procedure.

The latter include the respondent State and the State of which the alleged victim is a national or, in case of an inter-State application, the applicant State(s). These States may not publish the contents of the report.[370] For those cases where Protocol No. 9 to the Convention is applicable the report will also be sent to the individual applicants, who also are not at liberty to publish its contents.[371]

In those cases where Protocol No. 9 is not applicable the Convention is silent on the question of whether in case of an individual application the report must or may also be sent to the individual applicant. Rule 61 of the old Rules of Procedure of the Commission provided that, if in such a case the application was submitted to the Court, the report was sent to the individual applicant, unless the Commission decided otherwise. However, in that case Rule 29(3) of the Rules of Court also applies, providing that, unless the President of the Court decides otherwise, the report shall be made available to the public through the Registrar as soon as possible after the case has been brought before the Court. If an individual application is not submitted to the Court and consequently is decided upon by the Committee of Ministers, point 3(b) of the Appendix to the 'Rules' which the Committee of Ministers has adopted with respect to its examination of cases,[372] provides that communication to an individual applicant of the complete text or extracts from the report of the Commission should take place only as an exceptional measure, and then only on a strictly confidential basis and with the consent of the State against which the application was lodged. The Committee of Ministers considers in each individual case whether there is occasion for sending the report to the individual applicant, for instance with a view to obtaining his observations on the report.

It is remarkable indeed that the very person who has taken the initiative for the procedure and may therefore be deemed to be primarily concerned, is not kept informed of the contents of one of the most important documents in that procedure as soon as it is adopted. When the Convention was drafted, this was a point of discussion. A body of opinion in the Consultative Assembly considered the publication of the report as a form of redress for an individual applicant after the lodging of an application with the Commission.[373] An argument against publication was that this might endanger any attempt of the Committee of Ministers to secure a friendly settlement.[374] Publication of the report on an unlimited scale (in the press, for instance), could entail such a disadvantage, but on the other hand it must be borne in mind that so far only a very small number of procedures before the Committee of Ministers have been ended because the parties had reached some sort of settlement.[375] The latter would seem to indicate

---

[370] See Art. 31(2) of the Convention.
[371] Art. 2 of Protocol No. 9.
[372] See Council of Europe, *Collected Texts*, Strasbourg, 1996.
[373] See also *infra* pp. 197-198.
[374] See Council of Europe, *Collected Edition of the 'Travaux Préparatoires' of the European Convention on Human Rights*, Vol. III, The Hague, 1977, p. 272.
[375] See *infra* p. 282.

that the best chances of securing a friendly settlement exist during the procedure before the Commission, not after it. However this may be, the above objection cannot be maintained with respect to sending the report to the individual applicant on the condition that the complete report or extracts from it may not be communicated to others. In our opinion any disadvantages that might result from this in a limited number of cases is outweighed by the advantages from the viewpoint of the justified interests of the original applicant.

Under Article 32(3) the report is published when the Committee of Ministers decides by a two-third majority of the members entitled to sit on the Committee that the Contracting State in question has violated the Convention (Article 32(1)) and has not taken the measures required by the Committee under Article 32(2) within the prescribed time-limit. The publication of the report thus assumes the form of a sanction for non-compliance by the Contracting State with a decision of the Committee of Ministers. Unless there is good reason to do otherwise, the report is generally published at once when the Committee has decided that there has been no violation of the Convention; in that case publication has the character of furnishing information, and in fact constitutes a form of redress for the respondent State in respect of the accusation brought against it.

The opinion of the Commission laid down in the report is not a legally binding decision.[376] The decision on the merits is made either by the Court or by the Committee of Ministers. These two organs are not bound by the views set forth in the report of the Commission, but it does constitute the most important document in the proceedings before the two other organs. As to the question whether the Commission itself is bound by the conclusions in its reports in other cases, the Commission takes the view that in principle it is free to reach different conclusions in two cases of the same character. In practice, however, the case-law of the Commission is fairly constant, both as to admissibility and with respect to the interpretation of the rights and freedoms set forth in the Convention.

Apart from the ordinary reports, with respect to which the Convention expressly contains provisions (Articles 28(2) and 31), in practice two special kinds of reports have developed, because in special cases the Commission follows a slightly different procedure. Hereafter, the so-called summary reports will be discussed, which the Commission transmits to the Committee of Ministers when at the request of the parties the case is struck off the list as a result of a non-official settlement.[377] Another special kind is the so-called provisional report, which the Commission draws up when at a given moment, for one reason or another, the examination of a case must be stopped prematurely. In the *Second Greek* Case, for example, in which the Greek Government did not put up a defence, the Commission, with a view to the 'special and unprecedented circumstances described in its subsequent report, also reached the conclusion that it could not,

---

[376] Thus also expressly the then President of the Commission in the *Lawless* Case, B.1 (1961), pp. 264-268.

[377] See *infra* p. 190.

in the present situation, continue its function adequately in the case with a view to the eventual adoption of a report under Article 30 and 31 of the Convention.'[378] After the application had been declared admissible, the Commission refrained from dealing with the case. After Greece had become a party to the Convention again on 18 November 1974, the Commission resumed its examination of the application. However, after both the applicant States and the respondent State had stated that they were no longer interested in continuance of the case, the Commission struck the case off the list on 4 October 1976.[379]

With the adoption of its report, the procedure before the Commission has come to an end, but its conciliatory task is not necessarily completed. Even during the proceedings before the Court or the Committee of Ministers the consideration of the case may be terminated on the basis of an arrangement made between the parties, and for this, too, the Commission may offer to mediate. This matter will be dealt with below in connection with the proceedings before the two other Strasbourg organs.

3.3.6 Proposals of the Commission (Article 31(3))

Under Article 31(3) of the Convention the Commission, in transmitting its report to the Committee of Ministers, may add such proposals as it thinks fit. In practice such proposals are addressed to the Committee of Ministers as well as to the respondent State. An example of the former is to be found in the *Pataki* Case and the *Durnshirn* Case.[380] During the procedure before the Commission the legal regulations complained of were abolished by means of an amendment of the law. In reaction the Commission proposed that:

> the Committee of Ministers take note of this report, express its appreciation of the legislative measures adopted in Austria with a view to giving full effect to the Convention of Human Rights, and decide that no further action should be taken in the present cases.[381]

In the *Greek* Case the Commission made a great many proposals to the Greek Government aimed at altering the situation in Greece on those points which it had found to be in violation of the Convention.[382] In the *Pfunders* Case a communication of the Commission was addressed to the respondent Government,[383] recommending that:

---

[378] Report of 4 October 1976, D&R 6 (1977), p. 5 (6).
[379] *Ibidem*, p. 8.
[380] Appl. 596/59, *Pataki v. Austria*, Yearbook III (1960), p. 357; Appl. 789/60, *Durnshirn v. Austria*, Yearbook IV (1961), p. 187.
[381] See Yearbook VI (1963), p. 734.
[382] See *Greek* Case, Yearbook XII (1969), pp. 514-515.
[383] Appl. 788/60, *Austria v. Italy*, Yearbook IV (1961), p. 117.

the Commission considered it desirable for humanitarian reasons, among which may be counted the youth of the prisoners, that measures of clemency be taken in their favour.[384]

The peculiar aspect there was that in its report the Commission had reached the conclusion that Italy had not violated the Convention.

In Rule 6 of the 'Rules' adopted by the Committee of Ministers for the application of Article 32 the latter has expressed its view that the Commission is not entitled to make proposals under Article 31(3) in cases where it considers that there has not been a violation of the Convention.[385] Such a provision is not binding upon the Commission, but it is clear that a proposal of the Commission addressed to the Committee of Ministers, when it considers that there has been no violation of the Convention, will not be effective if the Committee abides by its interpretation in this matter. Against the competence of the Commission to make proposals in such a case it may be argued that Article 19 of the Convention defines the duties of the Commission as 'to ensure the observance of the engagements undertaken by the High Contracting Parties', which could be said to imply that it can make proposals under Article 31(3) only in cases where it has actually reached the conclusion that this 'observance' is at stake. On the other hand, Article 31(3) provides that the Commission may make such proposals 'as it thinks fit', without any further qualification. This appears to imply complete freedom for the Commission. Moreover, a proposal of the Commission, even if it has not reached the conclusion that there has been a violation of the Convention, may have a preventive effect because it may induce the respondent State to take certain measures in the spirit of the Convention. As such, the competence of the Commission to make proposals fits in with its duty 'to ensure the observance of the engagements undertaken by the High Contracting Parties in the present Convention' and may have certain positive effects. Italy, for instance, actually granted a pardon to the youngest of the prisoners in the *Pfunders* Case after the above-mentioned proposal of the Commission.

3.4 The Friendly Settlement (Article 28(1)(b))

3.4.1 General

From the terms of Article 28 it is clear that the drafters of the Convention intended the attempts to reach a friendly settlement to take place simultaneously with the examination of the merits. This makes sense. In fact, on the one hand a complete examination of the merits is superfluous if a friendly settlement is reached. On the other hand the Commission cannot mediate in an effective way with a view to reaching such a settlement until it has gained some insight into the question of whether or not the application is well-founded. Moreover, the

---

[384] Appl. 788/60, Yearbook VI (1963), p. 800.
[385] See Council of Europe, *Collected Texts*, Strasbourg, 1996.

provisional views within the Commission on the latter question may put pressure on (one of) the parties to cooperate with reaching a settlement.

The friendly settlement is a form of *conciliation*, one of the traditional methods of peaceful settlement of international disputes. The term 'conciliation', which refers particularly to inter-State disputes, has been replaced in the European Convention by 'friendly settlement' because disputes between States and individuals may be – and for the most greater part are – concerned.[386] With the method of the friendly settlement a non-legal element has been introduced into the procedure. Indeed, this method is not necessarily based on exclusively legal considerations; other factors may also play a part in it.

3.4.2 The Way in Which the Commission Secures a Friendly Settlement

The Commission has great discretion with respect to the way in which it may try to secure a friendly settlement. Its Rules of Procedure contain only one general provision: Rule 53 provides that the Commission, with a view to securing a friendly settlement, shall decide on the procedure to be followed. The Convention, too, does not impose any limitations on the Commission in this matter, with the exception of the requirement to be discussed below that the settlement reached must be based on respect for human rights as defined in the Convention.

This flexible and informal character of the procedure enables the Commission to create an atmosphere which makes it easier for the parties to reach a compromise. In this context the fact that the consideration of the application by the Commission takes place *in camera* plays an important part. Furthermore, the fact that it may be attractive for the respondent State to avoid continuation of the procedure, which will involve a thorough examination of the facts and may result in a public condemnation if the Commission is of the opinion that there has been a violation of the Convention, helps to create a situation in which States may be willing to accept a compromise. The individual applicant may also benefit from the compromise by having certainty about the outcome of the dispute, and reparation, if any, of the damages incurred, at the earliest possible moment. He may, therefore, generally also wish to avoid lengthy proceedings before the Court, involving the risk of an unfavourable judgment.

On the other hand the procedure of the friendly settlement entails the drawbacks for a non-public procedure. Owing to the fact that it is a compromise, the friendly settlement, without further qualifications, would involve the risk that ultimately an agreement may be reached which does not satisfy the standards with respect to human rights set by the Convention. However, the concluding words of Article 28(1)(b) require the settlement to be reached 'on the basis of respect for Human Rights as defined in this Convention.' It is the duty of the Commission to see to this. Besides the parties concerned, the Commission must agree to the content of the settlement. In some cases, for instance, it is not unlikely that the victim of a

---

[386] See *Collected Edition of the 'Travaux Préparatoires' of the European Convention on Human Rights*, Vol. III, The Hague, 1977, pp. 271-272.

violation is ready to accept a given sum of money with which the Government concerned might as it were wish to buy off the violation, while the cause of the violation, for instance in the form of a legal provision or an administrative practice conflicting with the Convention, would continue to exist. In such a case the Commission will have to demand that the Government concerned, in addition to giving compensation to the victim, shall take measures to alter the law or administrative practice in question. In its attempts to secure a friendly settlement, too, the Commission therefore has a duty with respect to the public interest, which constitutes a further indication of the 'objective' character of the procedure provided for in the Convention.[387]

Besides the public interest in the maintenance of the legal order created by the Convention, that of the *Rechtsfrieden* (peace through justice) also plays a part here. Indeed, if the Commission did not see to it that the existing violation be ended, there would be considerable risk that repeated applications might be submitted about the same situation conflicting with the Convention in a given Contracting State.

As far as we are informed the Commission has not refused a proposed settlement for the reason that it had not been reached 'on the basis of respect for Human Rights as defined in this Convention.'[388]

About the actual course of the attempts to reach a friendly settlement and the role of the Commission only a few general remarks can be made, precisely because the procedure takes place *in camera* and data about it are therefore scanty.[389]

Article 28 states that the Commission places itself at the disposal of the parties.[390] Immediately after a complaint has been declared admissible, the Secretary of the Commission invites the parties to state whether they wish to make proposals for a possible settlement. In this early phase this will usually not be the case. In a later phase, when the Commission is informed of all the elements of the merits, it may be important for it to avail itself of the power, conferred on it in Rule 61 of its Rules of Procedure, to give a provisional opinion on the merits. Such a provisional opinion, which is notified orally and confidentially to the parties, may of course stimulate the willingness of the parties to reach a settlement. Further, it will depend on the circumstances of each individual case

---

[387] See *supra* pp. 40-41. That the Court, too, is not prepared to strike the case off the list when the parties have reached some sort of settlement, but the essence of the case has not yet been resolved, appears from its judgment of 25 April 1978, *Tyrer*, A.26, pp. 12-14.

[388] See H. Krüger and C.A. Nørgaard, 'Reflections concerning friendly settlement under the European Convention on Human Rights', in: F. Matscher and H. Petzold (eds.), *Protecting Human Rights: The European Dimension*, Cologne, 1988, pp. 329-334 (332).

[389] On this, see a somewhat more detailed discussion in the publication mentioned in the preceding note.

[390] Since the entry into force of Protocol No. 3 on 20 September 1970 the functions referred to in Art. 28 are performed by the Commission itself, and no longer by a sub-commission as provided for in the original Art. 29. However, the preparatory negotiations will as a rule be attended by the Secretary of the Commission and, where needed, its President.

whether the Commission confines itself to such a passive role, or takes steps to start the negotiations. The Commission must be deemed in the right position to do the latter, because it is well informed of the facts of the case concerned and may contact both parties in an informal way. Sometimes the Commission will first examine the possibilities for a friendly settlement in discussions with one or both of the parties separately. In other cases it will at once bring the parties into contact with each other because it considers that there are possibilities for a settlement.

The role of the Commission will also have to be more or less active depending on whether an inter-State application or an individual application is concerned. In the first case the parties are more or less on equal terms, so that the Commission may confine itself to a more passive role. In case of an individual application, on the contrary, it may be true that the parties are formally on equal terms, but the respondent State is generally better equipped to conduct the negotiations within the framework of a friendly settlement than is an individual applicant. Therefore, the latter, in taking a decision on whether or not to agree to a given settlement, may be guided largely by the attitude of the Commission. The Commission, owing to its expertise and experience, will often be better able to evaluate the content of the settlement, and by playing an active role may to some extent neutralise a factual inequality of the parties to the negotiations. However, since the notion of a settlement implies that the two parties are in agreement on the content of the settlement reached, the role of the Commission should not dominate to such an extent that it is actually the Commission which determines the terms of the settlement and imposes it more or less upon the individual applicant. Up to the present, however, there have been no indications of such a situation.

If a friendly settlement in the sense of Article 28 is reached, the Commission draws up a report in accordance with Article 28(2) containing a brief statement of the facts and the substance of the solution reached.[391] The report is transmitted to the States concerned, to the Committee of Ministers and for publication to the Secretary General of the Council of Europe. In case of an individual application the report is also transmitted to the individual applicant.

3.4.3 Friendly Settlements Reached

Up to the end of 1996, according to the available information, 324 friendly settlements had been reached.[392]

The first settlement concerned a special case. In the *Boeckmans* Case, the applicant complained about remarks made by a judge during his trial, which were alleged to be incompatible with the rights of accused persons under Article 6 of the Convention. The Belgian Government, while upholding the validity of the judgment in question, agreed to pay to Boeckmans a compensation of 65,000 Belgian francs, because the remarks were such 'as to disturb the serenity of the

---

[391] For the further points which the report has to contain, see Rule 64 of the Rules.

[392] See *European Commission of Human Rights: Survey of Activities and Statistics*, Council of Europe, Strasbourg, 1996.

atmosphere during the proceedings in a manner contrary to the Convention and may have caused the applicant a moral injury.'[393]

An Irish woman received an *ex gratia* payment after her husband was shot and killed by British soldiers in Northern Ireland. The British Government granted the compensation, considering that the death of the applicant's husband was an unfortunate mistake, and acting out of compassion without implying any admission of a violation of the Convention or any reproach against the soldiers.[394]

In a number of other cases, too, the substance of the settlement consisted merely in that the Government concerned paid compensation and/or redressed the consequences of the violation for the victim as much as possible.[395] A special case belonging to this category was the one in which, according to the Commission, a threatening deportation of a South African who had gone into exile, allegedly for political reasons, raised questions in connection with the prohibition of degrading and inhuman treatment set forth in Article 3 of the Convention. This case was eventually resolved because the Belgian authorities provided the applicant with the documents required for emigration to Senegal as desired by him, and paid his travelling expenses.[396] In another case a Jordanian citizen had been expelled to Jordania after the Commission had decided in accordance with Rule 36 of the Commission's Rules of Procedure to indicate to the Swedish Government that it was desirable in the interest of the parties and the

---

[393] Report of 17 February 1965, Yearbook VIII (1965), p. 410 (422).

[394] Report of 2 October 1984, *Farrell v. the United Kingdom*, D&R 38 (1984), p. 44 (47-48).

[395] See, *e.g.*, report of 13 December 1966, *Poerschke* v. *Federal Republic of Germany*, Yearbook IX (1966), p. 632 (640); report of 24 March 1972, *Sepp* v. *Federal Republic of Germany*, *Stock-Taking on the European Convention on Human Rights* (1954-1984), Strasbourg, 1984, p. 118; report of 12 December 1973, *Mellin* v. *Federal Republic of Germany*, ibidem, p. 121, in which the Commission accepted the view of the German Government that considerations based on the public interest could not justify continuance of the procedure, since Germany had meanwhile introduced such amendments of the law that the conflict with the Convention had been removed, and, moreover, the Commission pointed out that the same matter was concerned in two other cases pending before it; report of 19 July 1974, *Amekrane* v. *the United Kingdom*, ibidem, p. 122; report of 2 May 1978, *Nagel* v. *Federal Republic of Germany*, D&R 12 (1978), pp. 97-102, in which the applicant was granted a pardon; report of 8 March 1979, *Peyer* v. *Switzerland*, D&R 15 (1979), pp. 105-119; report of 4 May 1979, *Geerk* v. *Switzerland*, D&R 16 (1979), pp. 56-67; report of 9 July 1980, *Uppal* v. *the United Kingdom*, D&R 20 (1980), pp. 29-39, in which the deportation order issued against the applicant was withdrawn. In the report of 7 October 1986, *Widmaier* v. *the Netherlands*, D&R 48 (1986), p. 47, the applicant had been convicted for drug trafficking without being allowed to appear in person at the hearing. Under the terms of the settlement the Netherlands Government declared to be prepared not to enforce the judgment, to remove the applicant's name from the list of wanted persons and to pay him compensation. In three other cases the settlement was confined to awarding financial compensation: report of 15 May 1986, *Conroy* v. *the United Kingdom*, where the applicant was dismissed as a result of his expulsion from his trade union, D&R 48 (1986), p. 42; report of 11 May 1985, *Naldi* v. *Italy*, D&R 42 (1985), p. 63 (71-72), where the applicant had been detained in contravention of Article 5(4); report of 9 September 1988, *Van de Voorde* v. *Belgium*, D&R 57 (1988), p. 73 (80), concerning the lawfulness of a decision to place at the Government's disposal (Belgian Law of Social Protection).

[396] Report of 17 July 1980, *Giama* v. *Belgium*, D&R 21 (1981), p. 73.

proper conduct of the proceedings before the Commission not to deport the applicant to Jordan until the Commission had had an opportunity to examine the application at its forthcoming session. In the settlement reached the applicant was granted permission to return to Sweden and to reside in Sweden permanently. The Government, furthermore, revoked the prohibition to re-enter Sweden and payed the costs of his return journey and made an *ex gratia* payment to the applicant. In addition, following discussions between the Agent of the Government and the Secretary to the Commission, the Agent of the Government addressed the following letter to the Commission:

> Referring to our discussions regarding the friendly settlement in the above case, I am able to inform you that the Swedish Government, in addition to the settlement with the applicant, makes the following statement in view of the particular circumstances of this case. The Government regrets that Mr Mansi was expelled to Jordan after the indication under Rule 36 of the Rules of Procedure of the Commission had been given by the President of the Commission that he should not be expelled.[397]

Complaints concerning inhuman treatment and a breach of the right to respect for family life were raised in a similar case against Sweden by a 12-year-old Lebanese boy whose deportation was at issue. The application originally was filed also on behalf of his two elder brothers who were already deported from Sweden. Under the terms of the friendly settlement eventually arrived at, the Swedish Government agreed to grant permission to the applicant's brothers to reside and work in Sweden, their travel expenses being paid by the Government, to make an *ex gratia* payment as well as a payment for legal expenses, and to revise the relevant regulations concerning expulsion.[398]

In some cases considerations of public interest also play a part, especially in relation to the prospect that the challenged law will be amended. In the *Alam* Case, in which a complaint was lodged, *inter alia*, about Article 6(1), the Commission included in its considerations the fact that the British Government had introduced Bills in which aliens were granted the right to appeal against decisions of immigration officers.[399] Again, in a case against Austria concerning Article 6(1) the principal element of the settlement reached was the fact that the Government had proposed an amendment of the law as a result of which detained persons henceforth could also be present at hearings where an appeal lodged to their detriment was dealt with.[400] In the *Knechtl* Case, which also concerned Article 6(1), the Commission agreed to the friendly settlement after having taken note of a White Paper of the British Government in which it was suggested 'that further consideration should be given to the arrangements which are followed in

---

[397] Report of 7 December 1989, *Mansi* v. *Sweden*, D&R 64 (1990), p. 253 (258).

[398] Report of 8 December 1984, *Bulus* v. *Sweden*, D&R 39 (1984), p. 75 (78-79). See also the report of 7 October 1986, *Min, Min and Min Paik* v. *the United Kingdom*, D&R 48 (1986), p. 58, and the report of 4 July 1991, *Fadelle* v. *the United Kingdom*, D&R 70 (1991), p. 159 (162).

[399] Report of 17 December 1968, *Mohammed Alam* v. *the United Kingdom*, Yearbook X (1967), p. 478.

[400] Report of 13 October 1981, *Peschke* v. *Austria*, D&R 25 (1982), p. 182.

considering applications by prisoners to seek legal advice where negligence by officers of the Home Office is alleged' and of the assurance by the Government that this suggestion had been followed.[401]

In two other cases the friendly settlement included the readiness on the part of the United Kingdom Government to amend prison administrative practices in order to inform a prisoner's relatives in due time of his imminent transfer to another prison[402] and to better safeguard the prisoners' right to respect for their correspondence.[403]

According to the Commission a friendly settlement in the case of a complaint against Austria about inhuman and degrading treatment contrary to Article 3 satisfied the requirement of respect for human rights in the sense of Article 28, since the Austrian Minister of Justice in a directive had ordered the authorities concerned to see to it that sick or wounded prisoners were not subjected in an indirect way to 'inhuman or degrading treatment or punishment' while they were tended in public hospitals.[404] A more or less identical case concerned an application against the United Kingdom, where also a complaint was lodged about inhuman and degrading treatment contrary to Article 3, this time in connection with solitary confinement of a detained person in a clinic for mental patients. Here a settlement could be reached because the British Government showed its willingness to not only award damages to the applicant, but also supply information on the directives concerning the treatment of patients in the clinic in question, and promised to review regularly the directives for possible improvements in the future.[405] In the case of *Reed*, also against the United Kingdom, the British Government was willing to pay an *ex gratia* payment to Mr Reed as well as a payment for his lawyer's fees and disbursements, and to change the rules regarding the right of prisoners to complain about prison treatment.[406] In a case concerning the refusal to grant legal aid for appeal against a sentence, the Government of the United Kingdom issued a practice note to all appeal court chairmen and clerks opening the possibility of review in cases where legal aid had been refused and the court considered that, *prima facie*, an appellant might have substantial grounds for lodging the appeal.[407] In the case of *Schuurs* v. *the Netherlands* the Government admitted that Article 5(1)(e) had been violated and stated that it 'will, in so far as possible under national constitutional law, promote the adoption by the Upper House of Parliament of the Bill concerning particular detentions in psychiatric hospitals.'[408] In the case of *Merkier*, where the question concerned the assistance of a lawyer at the examination by a Mental Health

---

[401] Report of 24 March 1972, *Knechtl* v. *the United Kingdom*, Yearbook XIII (1970), p. 730.

[402] Report of 15 May 1986, *Seale* v. *the United Kingdom*, D&R 50 (1987), p. 70.

[403] Report of 15 May 1986, *McComb* v. *the United Kingdom*, D&R 50 (1987), p. 81.

[404] Report of 19 December 1972, *Simon-Herold* v. *Austria*, Yearbook XIV (1971), p. 352.

[405] Report of 16 July 1980, *A* v. *the United Kingdom*, D&R 20 (1980), pp. 5-18.

[406] Report of 12 December 1981, *Reed* v. *the United Kingdom*, D&R 25 (1982), p. 5 (9).

[407] Report of 13 February 1992, *Higgins* v. *the United Kingdom*, D&R 73 (1992), p. 95 (97-98).

[408] Report of 7 March 1985, *Schuurs* v. *the Netherlands*, D&R 41 (1985), p. 186 (189).

Review Board (Belgium) of the prolongation of psychiatric detention, the friendly settlement provided for re-examination of the applicant's case, in the presence of a lawyer, by a Mental Health Review Board of different composition.[409]

In the *Gussenbauer* Case against Austria, the settlement resulted in radical changes in the Austrian system of counsels assigned to prisoners.[410] In the *Zimmermann* Case, the Austrian Government was willing to propose to the Federal President to quash, by an act of grace, the conditional prison sentence of seven months imposed on Zimmermann by the Vienna Regional Court. In this case financial compensation was also offered.[411]

In the *Harman* Case, the United Kingdom Government, apart from paying all the applicant's legal costs and expenses, undertook to change the law so that it would no longer be a contempt of court to render public material that is contained in documents which are compulsorily disclosed in civil proceedings, once those documents have been read out in open court.[412] And in a case where the absence of a remedy was at stake against an order made by a judge under the English Contempt of Court Act which affected the freedom of expression, the friendly settlement was based on a law reform and payment of compensation in respect of costs.[413]

Two complaints against the Federal Republic of Germany both concerned the *presumptio innocentiae*. In the first of these cases the applicant had initially been convicted for fraud, but on appeal the action conducted against him was discontinued. The court took its decision on the ground of the insignificance of the case (*Geringfügigkeit*). The applicant, however, had to pay his own costs of the suit, because according to the court of appeal 'the outcome of the investigation and the findings of the first judge appeared to have justified the conviction.'[414] For this reason the applicant applied to the Commission, submitting violation of Article 6(1) and (2). He was willing to withdraw his complaint, after the German Government had declared, as part of the friendly settlement, that:

> pursuant to the discontinuance of proceedings by the Berlin Regional Court (...) the judgment given against the applicant on 6 May 1968 by the Tiergarten District Court in Berlin (...) is devoid of any effect. No opinion concerning the applicant's guilt may accordingly be inferred from the judgment or from the aforementioned decision of the Berlin Regional Court.[415]

In the other case the domestic procedure was discontinued on the ground of a legal provision permitting the court to abandon further prosecution if the penalty which might ensue was negligible in comparison with a penalty which had already

---

[409] Report of 13 October 1988, D&R 57 (1988), p. 38.
[410] Report of 8 October 1974, *Gussenbauer* v. *Austria*, Yearbook XV (1972), p. 558.
[411] Report of 6 July 1982, *Zimmermann* v. *Austria*, D&R 30 (1983), p. 15 (20).
[412] Report of 15 May 1986, *Harman* v. *the United Kingdom*, D&R 46 (1986), p. 57.
[413] Report of 15 July 1988, *Hodgson, Woolf Productions Ltd., National Union of Journalists and Channel Four Television Co. Ltd.* v. *the United Kingdom*, D&R 56 (1988), p. 156.
[414] Report of 9 March 1977, *Neubecker* v. *Federal Republic of Germany*, D&R 8 (1977), p. 30 (32).
[415] *Ibidem*, p. 34.

been imposed on the accused in connection with another punishable offence. Here, too, the applicant had to pay his own costs, and here, too, the complaint submitted in Strasbourg concerning violation of Article 6(2) ended with a friendly settlement, the principal part of which was formed by a declaration of the German Government to the effect that:

> the Oldenburg District Court's decision on 15 August 1973 to discontinue proceedings (...) closed the criminal proceedings opened against the applicant. This decision is final. Consequently, no appreciation of the applicant's guilt can be deduced from the decision relating to court fees taken on 22 April 1974 by the Juvenile Chamber of the Oldenburg Regional Court.[416]

A friendly settlement was also reached when the Austrian Government, as lessee, came into conflict with one of its subjects, as lessor. The latter wished to increase the rent of a garage block in a way which according to the Government was contrary to the applicable legal regulations. The lessor thereupon wished to terminate the lease, but after a procedure taking more than eight years this was ultimately refused by the highest domestic court. During the Strasbourg proceedings concerning the alleged violation of the reasonable-time requirement of Article 6, a solution was reached because the Austrian Government agreed to the termination of the contract.[417]

Two further cases concerned property rights under Article 1 of Protocol No. 1. In a complaint against the United Kingdom the applicant in addition alleged violation of his right to respect for family life and home as a result of noise and vibration nuisance affecting his property located a quarter of a mile from Heathrow Airport. The matter was settled by an *ex gratia* payment by the Government.[418] A settlement on the basis of compensation was also reached in a case against Belgium. The applicant had alleged violation of her right to peaceful enjoyment of her possessions because of the failure of the Belgian State to abide by a court judgment awarding the applicant compensation for damages suffered as a result of a refusal of a building permission. During the Strasbourg proceedings, the Government proved prepared to do so after all.[419]

In a case in which the applicant had undergone a change of sex through a medical operation, she had subsequently requested the German authorities for a change of her name and for adaptation of the register of births. However, German legislation did not provide for that possibility in the case of sex changes. A similar application was still pending before the *Bundesverfassungsgericht*. The Commission declared the complaint concerning Articles 5(1) and 6(1) admissible, but the matter was settled in a friendly way when during the proceedings the German Government declared that the following decision had been taken:

---

[416] Report of 11 May 1978, *Liebig* v. *Federal Republic of Germany*, D&R 17 (1980), p. 5 (18).
[417] Report of 4 May 1979, *Karrer* v. *Austria*, D&R 16 (1979), p. 42 (49).
[418] Report of 8 July 1987, *Baggs* v. *the United Kingdom*, D&R 52 (1987), p. 29.
[419] Report of 13 November 1987, *Leemans-Ceuremans* v. *Belgium*, D&R 54 (1987), p. 108.

By decision of the District Court in B. dated 17 January 1979, concerning entry No. ... in the birth register at the Registrar's Office in B., the relevant entry has been corrected by adding the following remark: 'By reason of a change of sex the child here designated is of female sex with effect from the date of this entry and bears the Christian name Gunde'.[420]

A number of other cases concerning alleged violations of Article 6 have been settled by way of compensation provided by the Government. In five of these cases the length of proceedings was at stake,[421] in five other cases a violation was alleged of, respectively, the requirement of an independent and impartial tribunal,[422] of access to court,[423] and of a fair and public hearing.[424]

In a number of cases matters of family law were at issue. In two of these cases, both against Sweden, the applicants complained about the taking into public care of their respective children. As in both cases the children had in the meantime returned to their mothers, they could be settled on the basis of compensation paid by the Government.[425] Two other cases dealt with proceedings concerning custody over children. In a case against Denmark the settlement was confined to an offer of compensation by the Government.[426] In a comparable case against the Federal Republic of Germany the settlement consisted in the continuation of arrangements already made, providing the applicant with access to her son as well as with the opportunity to make telephone calls every fortnight.[427] Two cases against Belgium, one against Ireland and one against Austria ended in a settlement which, apart from financial compensation for the applicants, included (proposed) legislative amendments in order to undo (formerly) existing discrimination against children born out of wedlock and out of an adulterous relationship.[428]

---

[420] Report of 11 October 1979, *X* v. *Federal Republic of Germany*, D&R 17 (1980), p. 21 (26). Moreover, the German Government afforded the prospect that legal measures in this matter were to be taken and offered the applicant compensation *(ibidem*, p. 26).

[421] Report of 11 October 1984, *Versos* v. *Portugal*, D&R 38 (1984), p. 137 (143); report of 12 July 1985, *Sacca* v. *Italy*, D&R 42 (1985), p. 5 (13); report of 12 July 1985, *Russo* v. *Italy*, D&R 42 (1985), p. 14 (22); report of 6 July 1985, *Farragut* v. *France*, D&R 42 (1985), p. 77 (83); and report of 3 March 1987, *Smidt* v. *Denmark*, D&R 51 (1987), p. 111.

[422] Report of 18 October 1985, *Stevens* v. *Belgium*, D&R 44 (1985), p. 5 (12); and report of 8 July 1987, *Nyssen* v. *Belgium*, D&R 52 (1987), p. 140.

[423] Report of 9 March 1987, *Van Hal* v. *the Netherlands*, D&R 51 (1987), p. 104.

[424] Report of 8 October 1987, *Von Sydow* v. *Sweden*, D&R 53 (1987), p. 121; report of 11 May 1988, *Vollaers*, D&R 56 (1988), p. 5.

[425] Report of 10 October 1986, *Aminoff* v. *Sweden*, D&R 48 (1986), p. 82; and report of 10 October 1986, *Widén* v. *Sweden*, ibidem, p. 93.

[426] Report of 9 March 1984, *Pedersen* v. *Denmark*, D&R 37 (1984), p. 66 (70). See also the report of 13 May 1988, *Campbell* v. *the United Kingdom*, D&R 56 (1988), p. 108; report of 5 July 1988, *Krol* v. *Sweden*, D&R 56 (1988), p. 186.

[427] Report of 14 May 1987, *D* v. *the Federal Republic of Germany*, D&R 52 (1987), p. 188.

[428] Report of 8 October 1987, *Lucile Marie de Mot and Others* v. *Belgium*, D&R 53 (1987), p. 38; report of 8 October 1987, *Jolie and Lebrun* v. *Belgium*, D&R 53 (1987), p. 65; and report of 17 December 1987, *Stoutt* v. *Ireland*, D&R 54 (1987), p. 43; and report of 16 February 1993, *Baumgartner* v. *Austria*, D&R 74 (1993), p. 40.

A number of settlements is in fact based on judgments of the Court in cases which had raised identical issues. In a case against the United Kingdom six applicants complained about their dismissal from employment after refusal to join a trade union. After the Court's judgment in the *Young, James and Webster* Case the Government settled the case by offering the applicants compensation for material loss in respect of loss of earnings, pension rights and other employment benefits.[429] Similarly, in the *Geniets* Case the admissible part of the application was similar to the *Van Droogenbroeck* Case where the Court found a breach of Article 5(4) because of the absence of an effective and accessible judicial remedy which satisfied the requirements of that provision. As a result the Belgian Government showed itself prepared to pay compensation to Geniets.[430] With respect to three complaints regarding corporal punishment of children at school, the way to a settlement was paved by the Court's judgment in the *Campbell and Cosans* Case as a result of which the United Kingdom Government changed the relevant legislation and in addition made *ex gratia* payments to the applicants concerned.[431]

Finally, mention should be made of the settlement in the case of *France, Norway, Denmark, Sweden and the Netherlands* v. *Turkey*, which was accepted by the Commission in 1985. The substantive parts of the settlement included the assurance by the Turkish Government that they would strictly observe their obligations under Article 3 of the Convention, a vague promise concerning the granting of amnesty and – as regards the derogations under Article 15 of the Convention – a reference to an even more vague declaration by the Turkish Prime Minister of 4 April 1985, stating that 'I hope that we will be able to lift martial law from the remaining provinces within 18 months.'[432] Particularly the acceptance by the applicant States of the latter part of the settlement is striking in view of the fact that when lodging their complaint the applicant States upheld that a public emergency threatening the life of the nation did not exist in Turkey in 1982. Although the application, as declared admissible, also included alleged violations of the Articles 5, 6, 9, 10, 11 and 17 of the Convention, those provisions were not explicitly mentioned in the settlement.

Because of their rather lenient attitude the applicant Governments had manoeuvred the Commission into a very difficult position. It may even be argued that the Commission was left with no choice but to accept the settlement. Indeed, in the alternative the case would have been decided by the Committee of Ministers – Turkey had not recognised the jurisdiction of the Court yet – in which organ the applicant States and Turkey would obviously have played a prominent if not

---

[429] Report of 10 December 1984, *Eaton and Others* v. *the United Kingdom*, D&R 39 (1984), p. 11 (15).
[430] Report of 15 March 1985, *Geniets* v. *Belgium*, D&R 41 (1985), p. 5 (12).
[431] Report of 23 January 1987, *Townend* v. *the United Kingdom*, D&R 50 (1987), p. 36; report of 16 July 1987, *Durairaj and Baker* v. *the United Kingdom*, D&R 52 (1987), p. 13; report of 16 July 1987, *Family A* v. *the United Kingdom*, D&R 52 (1987), p. 150.
[432] Report of 7 December 1985, D&R 44 (1985), p. 31 (39).

decisive role. Convincing as this argument may be, it does not turn the settlement into one which has been reached 'on the basis of respect for Human Rights as defined in this Convention.' It is, therefore, questionable whether the Commission has sufficiently upheld this requirement of Article 28(1)(b). In our view the Commission should at any rate have insisted on a stricter type of supervision over the observance by Turkey of its commitments under the settlement. With respect to Article 15 as well as to the granting of amnesty there was in fact no supervision at all: the Turkish Government only undertook to keep the Commission informed of further developments. As far as Article 3 is concerned, supervision was confined to a commitment by Turkey to submit three reports under Article 57 during 1986, a dialogue with the Commission on each of those reports, and a short final report on the implementation of the settlement to be prepared not later than 1 February 1987. All this, moreover, was to be conducted in a confidential manner.[433] As was to be expected, these supervisory arrangements have turned out to be inadequate. Although martial law was lifted in Turkey in the course of 1987, allegations of serious violations of human rights continued.[434]

3.5 Other Forms of Arrangements Similar to a Friendly Settlement

Apart from the friendly settlement referred to in Article 28(1)(b), the parties sometimes reach a settlement of the dispute among themselves. In those cases the applicant withdraws his complaint after having come to some kind of arrangement with the Government concerned.

A well-known example is the *Televizier* Case.[435] In that case the applicant complained about violation of its freedom of expression (Article 10) and about discriminatory treatment (Article 14) in connection with a judgment of the Dutch Supreme Court, which was based on the Copyright Act and which was unfavourable to the applicant. The case concerned information provided and comments given on radio and television programmes, for which use had been made of summaries of programmes of the Central Broadcasting Bureau in the Netherlands. Some years after the application had been submitted the parties informed the Commission that they had arrived at an arrangement and that the applicant wished to withdraw its application. Televizier had meanwhile concluded an agreement with one of the broadcasting organisations about the publication of the latter's radio and TV guide.[436]

---

[433] *Idem.*

[434] See Amnesty International, *Turkey, Brutal and Systematic Abuse of Human Rights*, London, 1989.

[435] Report of 3 October 1968, *N.V. Televizier v. the Netherlands*, Yearbook XI (1968), p. 783. See also the report of 4 October 1976, *Denmark, Norway and Sweden v. Greece*, D&R 6 (1977), p. 5; Appl. 6242/73, *Brückmann v. Federal Republic of Germany*, D&R 6 (1977), p. 57; and report of 9 October 1985, *Taspinar v. the Netherlands*, D&R 44 (1985), p. 262.

[436] For other cases belonging to the same category, see: Council of Europe, *Stock-Taking on the European Convention on Human Rights* (1954-1984), Strasbourg, 1984, pp. 143-162.

In cases like these, the Commission is willing to accept the withdrawal of the application and to strike the case off the list only if considerations of public interest do not oppose to its doing so. Thus, in the *Gericke* Case the Commission at first refused to agree to the withdrawal of the application on the ground that:

> the present application raises problems of individual freedom involved in the application of Article 5, paragraph 3, of the Convention, which may extend beyond the interests of the particular applicants.[437]

After the adoption of the report in the *Wemhoff* Case,[438] in May 1966, the Commission discontinued the procedure in the case of *Gericke*, who had been condemned as an accomplice of Wemhoff, because it held that reasons of public interest no longer made it necessary to examine the case any further.[439] A number of cases have been terminated because the issue(s) at stake had in the meantime been decided by the Court in comparable cases.[440] In some cases the main element of the informal settlement consisted of the amelioration of the legislation which was the cause of the alleged violation.[441]

With respect to these non-official settlements, before the entry into force of the new Rules of Procedure of the Commission on 13 December 1974 the question arose whether Article 30 (old), the present Article 34(2), or Article 31 of the Convention was applicable to such cases, or neither one. In the *Gericke* Case the Commission took the position that neither article could be applicable if the case were struck off the list at the request of the parties in consequence of a non-official settlement.[442] In such a case the Commission drew up a so-called summary report, which was transmitted for information and publication to the Committee of Ministers.[443] Rule 62 of the present Rules of Procedure provides for the drawing up of a report when the Commission strikes a case, which it has declared admissible, off the list.[444] The report must contain, *inter alia*, a statement of the facts, an account of the procedure, and the terms of the decision to strike the case off the list, together with the reasons.[445]

---

[437] Report of 22 July 1966, *Gericke v. Federal Republic of Germany*, Yearbook VIII (1965), p. 314 (320).

[438] Report of 1 April 1966, B.5 (1969).

[439] See Council of Europe, *Stock-Taking on the European Convention on Human Rights* (1954-1984), Strasbourg, 1984, p. 145.

[440] Report of 9 May 1987, *Bozano v. Switzerland*, D&R 52 (1987), p. 5 (11); the case was terminated after the Court's *Sanchez-Reisse* judgment, while the Case of *Scotts' of Greenock Ltd and Lithgow Ltd v. the United Kingdom*, report of 5 March 1987, D&R 51 (1987), p. 34 (37), was withdrawn on the basis of the *Lithgow* judgment.

[441] Appl. 10664/83, *Bowen v. Norway*, D&R 45 (1986), p. 158 (161); report of 7 May 1986, *Prasser v. Austria*, D&R 46 (1986), p. 81.

[442] Appl. 2294/64, *Gericke v. Federal Republic of Germany*, Yearbook IX (1966), pp. 618-620.

[443] See *Case-Law Topics, No. 3, Bringing an Application Before the European Commission of Human Rights*, Strasbourg, 1972, pp. 35-36.

[444] This competence of the Commission has meanwhile also been provided for in Art. 6 of Protocol No. 8.

[445] See *supra* pp. 169-170.

3.6 Non-Compliance with the Terms of a Friendly Settlement

Should the case occur in which the terms of a friendly settlement are not complied with by the State concerned, the Committee of Ministers, by analogy with Article 32(2) and (3) and Article 54, would seem to be the proper organ for taking suitable measures.[446] There is no express provision on this in the Convention. It would be logical if the Commission would be competent to bring cases of non-compliance before the Committee. It is self-evident that the Commission would have to investigate thoroughly whether the settlement has indeed not been complied with. The defaulting State would therefore first have to be given an opportunity to prove that it *has* complied with the obligations ensuing from the settlement. If in the Commission's opinion the State does not succeed in this, further steps would be needed. The Commission is the most suitable organ for taking such steps, because it has usually been involved intensively in the establishment of the settlement, its duty being the protection of the public interest. It would be extremely inefficient to require an application to be lodged again, even apart from the question of whether the admissibility conditions set in the Convention could then again be complied with in all cases. Moreover, a premium would be put on non-compliance with the settlement if a State could thus defer its condemnation for a considerable time, because the whole procedure would have to be gone through again from the beginning.

The construction here proposed would, however, require an amendment of the Convention, since the present Convention does not contain an express provision on the matter, while such a role of Public Prosecutor is not implied in the Commission's functions as regulated in the Convention. It would seem to be possible in the present circumstances that one of the Contracting States submits a complaint concerning non-compliance with a friendly settlement to the Committee. In fact, as members of the Council of Europe the Contracting States may take the initiative for the much more far-reaching procedure of expulsion of a Member State from the organisation under Article 8 of the Statute of the Council of Europe, when the latter Member State has seriously violated its engagements concerning human rights and fundamental freedoms. The Contracting States therefore must certainly also be considered authorised to put non-compliance with a friendly settlement before the Committee of Ministers in order to try, through that organ, to induce the State in question to comply with its obligations under the settlement. In view thereof it would be advisable if in the settlement resolution, when stating that no further steps in the respective case are necessary, the Committee of Ministers were to reserve to itself the right to take

---

[446] In this context see also Rule 49(3) of the Rules of Court, which provides that the Chamber of the Court, when it decides to strike a case off the list, informs the Committee of Ministers in order to enable it to supervise 'in accordance with Article 54 of the Convention' the execution of any undertakings which may be attached to striking a case off the list.

191

appropriate measures at a later date should one of the parties not comply with its obligations.

Often the Commission has been much less closely involved in the above-mentioned non-official arrangements. In such circumstances the case may already be struck off the list before there is a decision on admissibility, or at a time when the examination of the merits has not yet advanced very far, so that there is as yet little clarity as to whether there has been a violation of the Convention. On the other hand, a non-official settlement may also be reached when the Commission's examination of the merits is quite complete, or almost so. It must therefore be determined for each individual case what is the best solution if such a settlement is not complied with by the Contracting State in question. When a thorough examination of the merits has not yet taken place, it would seem to be most appropriate for the Commission to place the case on the list of cases again when 'the circumstances of the case as a whole justify such restoration.'[447] The consequence of this is that the original application as a whole is resuscitated, so that no additional difficulties may arise in connection with the admissibility conditions. Here again, however, the Commission will first have to ascertain whether the settlement has really not been complied with, and it will therefore have to give the State concerned an opportunity to prove the contrary.

---

[447] See *Case-Law Topics, No. 3, Bringing an Application Before the European Commission of Human Rights*, Strasbourg, 1972, pp. 31-32.

Chapter IV

The Examination of a Case by the European Court of Human Rights

1 INTRODUCTION

After an application has been declared admissible by the Commission and attempts to reach a friendly settlement have failed, within a period of three months from the date on which the Commission has transmitted its report to the Committee of Ministers, the case may be referred to the European Court of Human Rights (Articles 32(1) and 47). The following may bring a case before the Court: (1) the Commission, (2) the Contracting State of which the alleged victim is a national, (3) the Contracting State which has brought the case before the Commission and (4) the Contracting State against which the complaint is directed (Article 48).

Protocol No. 9, which entered into force on 1 October 1994, gives the individual applicant also the right to bring his case before the Court, provided that the application concerned has been brought against a State which has ratified that Protocol.[1] They may do so irrespective of whether the Commission or the State concerned has seized the Court. However, a 'filtering system' has been provided for: although the individual has an unrestricted right to seize the Court, if he is the only one who has done so, a Committee of three judges can nevertheless decide that the case in question is not one which should be examined by the Court. This Committee takes such a decision if it considers, unanimously, that the case raises no serious question concerning the interpretation or the application of the Convention or any other element that could justify its examination by the Court. In view of the entry into force of Protocol No. 9, the Court has adopted a second set of regulations, Rules of Court 'B', which apply only to cases brought against a State which has ratified the Protocol.[2] For the application of these Rules, the moment of ratification is determent, irrespective of the fact, whether the respondent State had ratified Protocol No. 9 at the moment the complaint had been lodged with the Commission.

A case can be dealt with by the Court only if the State against which the complaint is directed has previously recognised in a declaration the jurisdiction of the Court as compulsory or accepts *ad hoc* the Court's jurisdiction (Article 48 in conjunction with Article 46). The judgment of the Court is binding on the parties (Article 53) and no appeal lies against it (Article 52). Under certain conditions the Court may afford just satisfaction to the injured original applicant, to be paid by

---

[1] At the beginning of June 1997, these were the following States: Austria, Belgium, Cyprus, the Czech Republic, Denmark, Estonia, Finland, Germany, Hungary, Ireland, Italy, Liechtenstein, Luxembourg, the Netherlands, Norway, Poland, Portugal, Romania, San Marino, Slovakia, Slovenia, Sweden and Switzerland.

[2] See *Collected Texts*, Strasbourg, 1996.

the defaulting State (Article 50). The Committee of Ministers supervises the execution of the Court's judgments (Article 54).

As already said above, on 11 May 1994 Protocol No. 11, which provides a complete reform of the supervisory mechanism, was opened for ratification.[3] The main aspects of the reform are the following. (1) The present part-time monitoring institutions, namely the European Commission of Human Rights and the European Court of Human Rights, will cease to exist. A new European Court of Human Rights, operating full-time, will be set up in Strasbourg. (2) The system will be streamlined and, above all, all applicants will have direct access to the new Court. Any cases that are clearly unfounded will be sifted out of the system at an early stage by a unanimous decision of the Court, sitting as a three-judge committee. In the large majority of cases, the Court will sit as a seven-judge chamber. Only in exceptional cases will the Court, sitting as a Grand Chamber of seventeen judges, decide on the most important issues. The President of the Court and the presidents of the chambers will always be able to sit in the Grand Chamber so as to ensure consistency and uniformity of the case-law. Whichever judge is elected in respect of the State Party involved in the case will sit in the chamber dealing with the case but also in the Grand Chamber in order to ensure a proper understanding of the legal system under consideration. (3) All allegations of violations of the Convention will be referred to the Court, including all inter-State cases; the Committee of Ministers will no longer have the power to decide on such complaints, though it will retain its important role of monitoring the enforcement of the Court's judgments. (4) The right of individual application and the jurisdiction of the Court will no longer be of an optional character.[4]

2 QUESTIONS OF ADMISSIBILITY AND JURISDICTION IN THE PROCEEDINGS BEFORE THE COURT

2.1 General

As has already been observed with respect to admissibility conditions in the proceedings before the Commission, the distinction between admissibility and jurisdiction is not always strictly observed.[5] In the following discussion of questions of admissibility and jurisdiction in the proceedings before the Court it should be borne in mind that on some points there may not be agreement on the question of whether a specific issue is a matter of jurisdiction or rather of admissibility.

The following procedural requirements may come up in the proceedings before the Court: (1) the case must have been brought before the Commission and must

---

[3] See *supra* p. 350
[4] See *supra* p. 35 and *infra* p. 179.
[5] See *supra* pp. 108-109.

have been declared admissible; (2) the attempts of the Commission to reach a friendly settlement must have failed; (3) the case must have been referred to the Court within a period of three months from the date of the transmission of the Commission's report to the Committee of Ministers; (4) this must have been done by the Commission and/or by one of the States which are competent to do so under Article 48, and/or by the individual applicant if the case is covered by Protocol No. 9; and (5) the respondent State must have recognised the Court's jurisdiction as compulsory.

It is self-evident that no case could be submitted until the Court existed as such. Article 56(2) of the Convention states that no case can be brought before the Court before the first election of the members of the Court. The first paragraph of the same article provides that the first election of the members of the Court takes place after at least eight States have made the declaration concerning the recognition of the Court's jurisdiction. This condition was fulfilled on 3 September 1958, when Austria and Iceland as the seventh and the eighth State, respectively, made this declaration. In January 1959 the first election of the members took place and on 20 April 1959 the Court was inaugurated officially.

2.2 The Case must have Passed through the Whole Procedure Before the Commission and must have been Submitted to the Court within a Period of Three Months from the Date of the Transmission of the Report to the Committee of Ministers

A case cannot be submitted directly to the Court. From Articles 32(1) and 47 it is clear that an application must have passed through the whole procedure before the Commission before it can be dealt with by the Court. Article 47 provides expressly that the Court may only deal with a case after the Commission has acknowledged the failure of efforts to reach a friendly settlement, and implicitly that the Commission must first have submitted its report on the merits of the case. Applications that have been declared inadmissible by the Commission cannot be brought before the Court, as a declaration of inadmissibility by the Commission is final.[6]

The period of three months referred to in Articles 32 and 47 commences on the date of the transmission of the Commission's report to the Committee of Ministers. In the *Lawless* Case the report had been adopted by the Commission on 19 December 1959, but it had been transmitted to the Committee, and also to the Irish Government, on 1 February 1960. In view of this delay, in a preliminary objection Ireland asked the Court to declare that it had no jurisdiction, since the Commission had not proved that during this delay it had not deliberated on referring the case to the Court. In consequence of this the Irish Government felt that it had been brought into an unfavourable position in relation to the Commission, which would be contrary to the principle of equality that ensues

---

[6] See *supra* p. 97.

from the spirit of the Convention.[7] The Commission took the view that not a single provision of the Convention obliges it to transmit the report immediately after adoption, and that, since Article 31(3) permits it, in transmitting the Report, to make proposals to the Committee of Ministers, it may also deliberate for some time after adoption of the Report.[8] The Irish Government later withdrew its objection and the Court therefore did not pronounce on this point.[9] The text of the Convention appears to confirm the Commission's view.

On this point no further difficulties have arisen until in the *Instituto di Vigilanza, Figus Milone* and *Goisis* Cases, where the Italian Government made preliminary objections and submitted that the Commission had referred the three cases to the Court only on 11 December 1992, whereas its reports had been sent to the Committee of Ministers on 10 September 1992. The Court pointed out that by the terms of the French text of Article 47, it could only *être saisie d'une affaire* (be seized of a case) within the period of three months provided for in Article 32. The use of the verb '*saisir*' appeared to be incompatible with the interpretation of the word 'referred' that the Delegates of the Commission had seemed to be advocating, because in order to seize a court it was not sufficient to decide to seize it. The same applies, in the Court's opinion, to the word 'refer'. Besides, any other reading of Article 32(1) and Article 47 would be likely to produce – as regards one of the conditions to be satisfied when applying to the Commission itself – results contrary to the letter and spirit of Article 26 *in fine* and to the case-law established in the matter from the very beginning. The Court found that the Commission had exceeded – albeit by only one day – the time allowed. Furthermore, no special circumstance of a nature to suspend the running of time or justify its starting to run afresh was apparent from the file. The requests bringing the cases before the Court were consequently inadmissible as they were made out of time.[10]

In the *Morganti* Case it was the French Government, which lodged its application after the expiry of the time-limit laid down in Article 32(1). The Court noted that the French Government had referred the case to it on 13 April 1995, whereas the Commission's Report had been sent to the Committee of Ministers on 11 January 1995. It observed in the first place that the fax containing the Government's application was received by the Secretariat of the Commission at 7.33 p.m. on 12 April 1995, and was communicated to the registry on the following day. It further noted that the Government had not disputed the fact that they had exceeded the time they were allowed. It followed that the application bringing the case before the Court was inadmissible, as it was out of time.[11]

---

[7]   Report of 19 December 1959, *Lawless*, B.1 (1961), pp. 212-214.
[8]   *Ibidem*, pp. 237-241.
[9]   Judgment of 14 November 1960, *Lawless*, A.1, p. 10.
[10] Judgments of 22 September 1993, A.265-C, D and E, pp. 35, 43 and 51 respectively.
[11] Judgment of 13 July 1995, A.320-C, p. 48.

It should be mentioned here again, that once Protocol No. 11 has entered into force, Article 32 and 47 will not apply any more. The six-month period of Article 26 will then be the only applicable time-limit.

2.3 The Jurisdiction of the Court *Ratione Personae*: Active Legitimation

The jurisdiction of the Court *ratione personae* is regulated by the previously mentioned Article 48 of the Convention. Between the right to bring a case before the Court and the right to submit a complaint to the Commission there exist considerable differences. Although the former right also differs considerably from traditional international law, in this respect the Convention goes much less far than in the regulation of the right of complaint in the first stage of the procedure. From Article 48 it appears in the first place that, unlike the situation with respect to the right to submit a complaint to the Commission, not every Contracting State may bring an alleged violation of the Convention before the Court. A State bringing a case before the Court has to prove either that the alleged victim (the original applicant) is its national, or that it has submitted the case to the Commission, or that it is the State against which the complaint has been lodged.

In the *Loizidou* Case, without any substantiation the Turkish Government pointed out that they did not except the capacity of the applicant Government to represent the people of Cyprus. The Court held that the applicant Government have been recognised by the international community as the Government of the Republic of Cyprus. Its *locus standi* as the Government of a High Contracting Party was not in doubt. The Court emphasised that recognition of an applicant Government by a respondent Government was not a precondition for either the institution of proceedings under Article 24 or the referral of cases to the Court under Article 48. If it were otherwise, the system of collective enforcement which is a central element in the Convention system could be effectively neutralised by the interplay of recognition between individual Governments and States.[12]

Secondly, – and this difference is much more striking – in the original structure an individual cannot bring a case before the Court. This appears not only from Article 48, but also expressly from Article 44: 'Only the High Contracting Parties and the Commission shall have the right to bring a case before the Court'. When the Convention was drafted, the idea of also conferring *locus standi* before the European Court of Human Rights upon individuals was found not to be feasible. This situation is different with respect to those States which have ratified Protocol No. 9[13] and will change completely once Protocol No. 11 has entered into force, since this Protocol provides direct access of the individual to the Court.[14]

The disadvantages for the legal protection of the individual attached to the lack of *locus standi* if the respondent State has not ratified Protocol No. 9 should not

---

[12] Judgment of 23 March 1995, A.310, p. 18.
[13] See *supra* p. 166 and *infra* pp. 235-236.
[14] See *supra* p. 30 and p. 194.

be dramatised, since besides the States concerned the Commission also has the right to submit the case to the Court. In practice, in almost all cases referred to the Court, this is done by the Commission,[15] which will also take the interests of the individual applicant into consideration. Formally, according to Article 48, the Contracting State which has submitted the case to the Commission and the Contracting State of which the alleged victim is a national[16] are also competent to refer the case to the Court. With respect to the first-mentioned category of States it has already been observed above that States, as a rule, are inclined to file an application with the Commission only if it concerns a violation in relation to persons who are their nationals or with whom they have at least a special link.[17] Applications in which States speak up for specific persons who are not their nationals, and with whom they do not have any other special link, are therefore rare. Such a case has not yet been brought before the Court. Consequently, the first and the second category usually coincide. As to the second category of States – States of which the alleged victims are nationals –, in practice the great majority of cases is precisely formed by complaints of individuals against the State of which they are a national. In all those cases the State of which the victim is a national and the respondent State are therefore the same. Of course, the respondent State does not take into account the interests of the individual applicant when considering whether it is going to bring the case before the Court. So far only one inter-State case has been referred to the Court.[18]

When the Commission brings a case before the Court, it does so by virtue of its authority to represent the public interest.[19] Waldock, the then President of the Commission, stated in connection with the first case dealt with by the Court that the Commission brings a case before the Court 'on behalf of the governments and peoples of all the member countries of the Council of Europe.'[20] This is implied in the definition of the duty of the Commission in Article 19 of the Convention: 'To ensure the observance of the engagements undertaken by the High Contracting Parties in the present Convention.' The special position of the Commission in the proceedings before the Court will be further elaborated on below.[21]

The Commission has full discretion whether to refer a case to the Court. The Convention does not set forth any criteria for this. That the Commission itself also assumes full discretion in the matter appears from the following words of its then President:

---

[15] See *supra* p. 193.

[16] The latter situation occurred for the first time in the *Soering* Case; see the judgment of 7 July 1989, A.161, where the Federal Republic of Germany referred the case to the Court, after the respondent State had done so.

[17] See *supra* pp. 41-42.

[18] Appl. 5310/71, *Ireland* v. *the United Kingdom*, Yearbook XV (1972), p. 76.

[19] See Waldock, the then President of the Commission, *Lawless*, B.1 (1961), p. 245.

[20] *Ibidem*, p. 207.

[21] See *infra* pp. 225-228.

When we bring a case before the Court, we do so simply because we think that the appropriate tribunal for deciding the case is the Court rather than the Committee of Ministers.[22]

This shows that the criterion applied by the Commission is whether it believes that this particular case lends itself better for a decision by a judicial or rather by a political organ. The former will be the case in particular when an application raises issues, which are of importance for the interpretation and the application of the Convention in general.

This was the situation, for instance, in the *Lawless* Case. There the question was, among other things, what circumstances justify derogation by a State from its engagements under the Convention, *i.e.* a question concerning the interpretation of Article 15. The Commission had been greatly divided on this issue. Despite the fact that a majority had come to the conclusion that there had been no violation of the Convention, the Commission resolved to bring the case before the Court, the reason being that 'the present case raises issues which are of fundamental importance in the application of the Convention.'[23]

This is the most frequently adduced reason why the Commission refers a case to the Court. Another factor which sometimes plays a part is the fact that the Commission is greatly divided internally on the question of whether in the case concerned there has been a violation of the Convention.[24]

The Commission's policy has sometimes been criticised. It has been stated that the Commission makes too little use of its competence to refer cases to the Court.[25] However, as with the Commission's policy concerning admissibility, and probably for approximately the same reasons, with respect to its policy in this matter a significant change has taken place in the sense that gradually it has brought more cases before the Court. Thus, in the period from 1959 to 1976 the Court could give judgment in only 26 cases, although 142 applications had been declared admissible by the Commission in that period. From 1977 up to June 1997, 644 cases were decided by the Court. Out of the total of 670 cases, 617 were (partly) referred to the Court either by the Commission alone or by the Commission together with a State.[26] This changing policy of the Commission has had as a result that in a greater number of cases the final decision is taken in a way that is more satisfactory from the viewpoint of legal protection, *viz.* by an independent tribunal. Furthermore, it enables the Court to elaborate in greater detail the often vague provisions of the Convention, thereby promoting an effective implementation of the Convention.

---

[22] B.1 (1961), p. 266.

[23] Report of 19 December 1959, B.1 (1961), p. 206.

[24] See, *e.g.*, report of 24 June 1965, *Belgian Linguistic Case*, B.3 (1967), p. 384; report of 1 October 1968, *Delcourt*, B.9 (1970), p. 134.

[25] See, *e.g.*, F.G. Jacobs, *The European Convention on Human Rights*, Oxford, 1985, p. 262.

[26] For this, see *supra* p. 166. In these figures the judgments of the Court ex Art. 50 of the Convention are excluded.

In the *Axen* Case the Government of the Federal Republic of Germany contested the expediency of the decision to refer the case to the Court. The Court considered:

> that it is not part of its function to evaluate the expediency of the decision to bring a case before it. In this domain the Commission exercises an autonomous power conferred on it by Article 48, paragraph (a), of the Convention; the same is true, moreover, of the Contracting States listed in paragraphs (b), (c) and (d).[27]

2.4 The Jurisdiction of the Court *Ratione Personae*: Passive Legitimation

Article 48 also regulates the jurisdiction of the Court *ratione personae* with respect to the respondent State. A case can be brought before the Court only on condition that the respondent State is subject to the compulsory jurisdiction of the Court or consents *ad hoc* to the case being brought before the Court.

A State may submit to the jurisdiction of the Court by depositing with the Secretary General of the Council of Europe a so-called 'optional declaration', in which it recognises as compulsory *ipso facto* and without special agreement the jurisdiction of the Court in all matters concerning the interpretation and application of the Convention (Article 46(1)). At the present moment all Contracting States have made such a declaration.[28]

The declaration of Article 46(1) may be made unconditionally or on condition of reciprocity on the part of all or certain of the other Contracting States. It may be made for a specified period or for an indefinite time (Article 46(2)). Most of the Contracting States which have submitted to the jurisdiction of the Court have made the declaration on condition of reciprocity.[29]

In the *Loizidou* Case, the Turkish Government submitted that, in essence, the case brought against it did not concern the acts or omissions of Turkey but those of the 'Turkish Republic of Northern Cyprus' ('TRNC'), which they claimed to be an independent State established in the north of Cyprus. As the only Contracting Party to have recognised the 'TRNC', with whose authorities it has close and friendly relations, the Turkish Government saw its role before the Court as limited to that of an *amicus curiae*, since the 'TRNC' was not itself able to be a 'party' to the proceedings. The Court held that it was not within the discretion of a Contracting Party to characterise its standing in the proceedings before the Court in the manner it sees fit. It observed that the case originated in a petition made under Article 25, brought by the applicant against Turkey in her capacity as a High Contracting Party to the Convention and had been referred to the Court under Article 48(b) by another High Contracting Party. Therefore the Court considered that Turkey was the respondent Party in the case.[30]

---

[27] Judgment of 8 December 1983, A.72, p. 11.
[28] See Council of Europe, *Collected Texts*, Strasbourg, 1996, p. 86.
[29] *Idem.*
[30] Judgment of 23 March 1995, A.310, p. 20.

The condition of reciprocity, which is customary in general international law and makes good sense there because the disputes as a rule will concern legal rules which call into existence reciprocal rights for States, is not in keeping with the objective character of the European Convention and the resulting collective guarantee by the Contracting States of the rights and freedoms set forth in the Convention.[31] From that viewpoint it would be preferable that the Contracting States no longer include this condition in their declaration under Article 46(1), or that the phrase in question be cancelled from Article 46(2). This might, however, lead to a situation in which a Contracting State may bring an alleged violation of the Convention by another Contracting State before the Court, while its own acts could not be examined against its will by the Court for their conformity with the Convention because it has not submitted to the jurisdiction of the Court. Such an unequal position would not be acceptable for most States. The objective character of the supervision as provided for in the Convention will therefore not be done full justice to until ratification of the Convention by a State will at the same time imply recognition of the Court's jurisdiction.[32] This situation will be achieved with the entry into force of Protocol No. 11.[33]

The condition of reciprocity cannot, of course, be invoked against the Commission when it refers a case to the Court. The Commission cannot make a declaration as referred to in Article 46, nor can it ever get into the position of a respondent party before the Court, so that there is no question of reciprocity. When Denmark – probably erroneously – disputed *via* a preliminary objection the right of the Commission to bring the case before the Court by invoking the condition of reciprocity, this objection was hastily withdrawn again by the Danish Government at the insistence of its own parliament.[34]

Most States make the declaration referred to in Article 46(1) for a period of five years at the most. So far only Finland, Ireland, the Netherlands and Switzerland have recognised the jurisdiction of the Court for an indefinite time.[35]

The declarations under Article 46(1) which were made for a specified period, have so far always been renewed after the expiration of that period. In practice, therefore, the question has not yet arisen whether the Court has jurisdiction *ratione personae* when on the date of submission of the case the optional declaration is no longer in force, but still was on the date on which the application was filed with the Commission. A grammatical interpretation of Article 48 might lead one to conclude that in such a case the date on which the case is brought before the Court must be considered as conclusive. However, considering the nature of the supervisory procedure, where the Commission and the Court do not act in two

---

[31] See *supra* pp. 40-41.
[32] This would therefore be the same construction as is now laid down in Art. 24 with respect to the Commission in relation to inter-State complaints.
[33] *Cf. supra* p. 35.
[34] See the judgment of 7 December 1976, *Kjeldsen, Busk Madsen and Pedersen*, A.23, pp. 5-6.
[35] See *Collected Texts*, Strasbourg, 1996.

separate procedures, but in two successive stages of one and the same procedure, it would seem that a good deal may be said for regarding the date on which the application is filed with the Commission as decisive. In any way, non-renewal or withdrawal of the optional declaration for the purpose of making the submission of a given case to the Court impossible would be of little avail to a Contracting State as even then a binding decision is taken in the case. Indeed, even if it is assumed that such a non-renewal or withdrawal would bar the jurisdiction of the Court, the case will then be decided by the Committee of Ministers. Denunciation of the Convention, too, cannot release a Contracting State from the supervisory procedure of the Convention, because in that case Article 65 applies.[36]

As has already been said above,[37] a declaration as referred to in Article 46(1) has in principle retrospective effect to the moment of ratification of the Convention by the State concerned in the sense that a case which is brought before the Court after the declaration has been made may also refer to an alleged violation of the Convention that has taken place after the Convention came into force for the State in question, but before the date of its declaration under Article 46(1). This is not the case only when in the declaration the retrospective effect is expressly excluded. This may be considered as a general rule of international law, which was set forth as follows by the Permanent Court of International Justice:

> The reservation made in many arbitration treaties regarding disputes arising out of events previous to the conclusion of the treaty seem to prove the necessity for an explicit limitation of jurisdiction.[38]

In the *Stamoulakatos* Case, the Government's primary submission before the Court, as before the Commission, was that the applicant's complaint did not come within the Court's jurisdiction *ratione temporis* because it related to events which had taken place before 20 November 1985, when Greece's acceptance of the right of individual petition took effect. The breach which the applicant complained of originated in three convictions dating from 1979 and 1980. The fact that he had subsequently lodged appeals could, in the Government's opinion, not affect the period that the Court had to consider in order to rule on the objection. The Court found that the events which gave rise to the proceedings against the applicant, together with the three judgments, were covered by Greece's declaration in respect of Article 25. As to his appeals and applications against those judgments, the applicant complained only that these were ineffective in that they did not enable him to obtain from a court which had heard him – as he was entitled to under the Convention – a fresh determination of the merits of the charges on which he had been tried *in absentia*. Thus, although those appeals and applications were lodged after the 'critical' date of 19 November 1985, they were closely bound up with the proceedings that had led to his conviction. Deforcing these appeals and applications from the events which gave rise to them would, in the instant case,

---

[36] On this, see *supra* p. 15.
[37] See *supra* p. 200.
[38] *Mavrommatis Palestine Concessions* Case, *Publ. P.C.I.J.*, Series A, No. 2, p. 35.

be tantamount to rendering Greece's aforementioned declaration nugatory. It was found reasonable to infer from that declaration that Greece could not be held to have violated its obligation for not affording any possibility of a retrial to those who had been convicted *in absentia* before 20 November 1985. The objection was well-founded and the Court found it could not deal with the merits of the case.[39] In the *Yağci and Sargin*, *Mansur* and *Yağiz* Cases the Court held that having regard to the wording of the declaration Turkey made under Article 46, it could not entertain complaints about events which occurred before the date that Turkey had recognised the Court's compulsory jurisdiction.[40]

Instead of recognising the Court's jurisdiction in advance for an indefinite number of cases by means of the so-called 'optional declaration', a State may, according to Article 48, consent *ad hoc* to the consideration of a given case by the Court. This may be done explicitly by a unilateral declaration of the State in question. An example is the declaration of the British Government in the *Tyrer* Case, where the latter consented to the consideration of that case by the Court after doubt had arisen as to whether the Court had jurisdiction on the ground of the optional declaration of the United Kingdom.[41]

Since Article 48 does not contain any further requirements of form as to the giving of such a consent, it must be assumed that this can also be inferred from the behaviour of a Contracting State, such as the fact that it pleads its case on the merits without raising an objection as to the Court's jurisdiction on the ground that it had not given its consent. Such behaviour implies tacit recognition of the jurisdiction: the principle of *forum prorogatum*, which has also been recognised for the jurisdiction of the International Court of Justice.[42]

2.5 The Jurisdiction of the Court and the Examination by the Commission of the Compatibility of the Application with the Provisions of the Convention

2.5.1 Introduction
In addition to the conditions discussed above, which are listed in the Convention specifically in relation to the procedure before the Court, may preliminary objections on which the Commission has already decided explicitly or implicitly, be raised again before the Court?

The question as to the relation between the Commission's examination of admissibility and that of the procedural conditions applying to the procedure before the Court consists of two parts. In the first place the same questions of

---

[39] Judgment of 26 October 1993, A.271, p. 14; in the same sense the judgment of 8 June 1995, *Kefalas and Others*, A.318, p. 20.
[40] Judgments of 8 June 1995, *Yağci and Sargin*, A.319-A and *Mansur*, A.319-B, paras 40 and 44 respectively; judgment of 7 August 1996, *Yağiz*, Reports 1996-III, Vol. 13, para. 27.
[41] Judgment of 25 April 1978, A.26, p. 12.
[42] See S. Rosenne, *The Law and Practice of the International Court*, Leyden, 1965, pp. 344-363.

jurisdiction may arise in the two procedures, and in the second place the same questions of *admissibility* may come up.

2.5.2 *Jurisdiction of the Court* Ratione Materiae

The case-law of the Court shows that issues dealt with in a decision of the Commission concerning the compatibility of an individual application with the Convention *ratione materiae*, may also be decided by the Court in a judgment on its jurisdiction *ratione materiae*. The Commission formally does not make a distinction between questions concerning its competence and questions concerning the admissibility of the application. It puts its decision on whether a procedural condition has been fulfilled always in the form of a pronouncement on admissibility.[43] It is evident, however, that the examination by the Commission and that by the Court *ratione materiae* deal with the same question, *viz.* whether the application concerns the violation of a right that is protected by one or more provisions of the Convention or the Protocols.

Thus, in the *Belgian Linguistic* Case, Belgium asked the Court to declare that it had no jurisdiction *ratione materiae* on the ground that the right to receive education in one's own language, which had allegedly been violated according to the individual applicants, was not protected in the Convention and the Protocols.[44] The Commission requested the Court to reject the objection of Belgium concerning jurisdiction and submitted that when it has brought a case before the Court:

> the Court needs no more than a summary examination to enable it to verify that the complaints declared admissible by the Commission concern the interpretation or application of the Convention within the meaning of Article 45.[45]

With a reference to the provision of Article 49 of the Convention that 'in the event of a dispute as to whether the Court has jurisdiction, the matter shall be settled by the decision of the Court', and on the ground of the text of Article 45 'that the basis of jurisdiction *ratione materiae* of the Court is established once the case raises a question of the interpretation or application of the Convention', the Court concluded that it had jurisdiction *ratione materiae* in the case concerned.[46] What the Court actually did was no more than, in the terms of the Commission, make a 'summary examination'. However, this does not appear to have resulted from considerations inferred from the relationship between the Commission and the Court, which was the rationale behind the Commission's observations, but rather from the fact that in this case matters were fairly simple. This is evident from the conclusion of the Court 'that the jurisdiction *ratione materiae* of the

---

[43] See *supra* p. 107.
[44] Judgment of 9 February 1967, A.6, p. 13.
[45] *Ibidem*, p. 17.
[46] *Ibidem*, pp. 18-20.

Court is so evidently established in this case that it should be affirmed here and now'.[47]

Here the Commission and the Court reached the same conclusion concerning the compatibility *ratione materiae* and the jurisdiction *ratione materiae* respectively. However, if in one and the same case the two organs hold different views on the matter, an application might be rejected by the Court on a point on which the same application had been declared admissible by the Commission. In itself this is not a very felicitous situation in a procedure which must be regarded as forming a whole, and the Strasbourg organs should try to prevent such a situation.

However, it is submitted that in judging these possibilities one should distinguish between questions of *jurisdiction* and of *admissibility*. Questions of admissibility in our opinion, should be considered to belong to the exclusive competence of the Commission, and the Court ought therefore to acquiesce in the decision of the Commission on such points.[48] The matter is, however, more difficult in the case of questions of jurisdiction, specifically the question of whether the application submitted actually concerns one of the rights and freedoms guaranteed in the Convention, *i.e.* the question as to the jurisdiction *ratione materiae*.[49] The possibilities for the Commission to prevent its decision and that of the Court from differing from one another on this point are limited. In fact, it always takes its decision before the Court takes its. The Commission will of course take account as much as possible of judgments of the Court in preceding cases, but it is not obliged to do so. As regards the role of the Court, it would be conceivable for it not to consider questions concerning its jurisdiction *ratione materiae* on which the Commission has already pronounced explicitly or implicitly, thus bringing out the unity of the procedure and the connection between the organs involved. Reasons of expediency, which are very compelling in so lengthy a procedure as that of Strasbourg, would also tell in favour of this. On the other hand, it may be asking too much of a judicial organ to give up the authority over its own jurisdiction *ratione materiae*. The Court can hardly be expected to acquiesce in a decision about this by a non-judicial organ, in this case the Commission. Moreover, the final result would still be invariably that the opinion of the Court on the matter prevails over that of the Commission. Indeed, even assuming that the Court should accept a decision of the Commission in which the latter considered an application as coming within the scope of the Convention, while in fact the Court itself takes the contrary position, in the examination of the merits the application will be dismissed on account of non-violation of the Convention, precisely because it refers to an alleged violation of a right which in

---

[47] *Ibidem*, p. 19.
[48] See the next section.
[49] As has been said, the Commission's decision on compatibility *ratione materiae* with the Convention in fact is a decision on its competence, even though it is taken in the form of a decision on admissibility.

the Court's view is not protected by the Convention or the Protocols.[50] The only difference would therefore be that the application is rejected in the one case for lack of jurisdiction and in the other on the merits.

As appears from the above-mentioned case-law, the Court indeed is not prepared to take a passive attitude *vis-à-vis* the Commission, but rather decides on its jurisdiction *ratione materiae* itself.[51]

2.5.3 Delimitation of the Object of Examination

A similar all but passive attitude of the Court *vis-à-vis* the Commission becomes apparent in a question which resembles that of the jurisdiction *ratione materiae*. This concerns the delimitation of the object of examination in the proceedings before the Court. In principle that object is constituted by those elements of the original application which have been declared admissible by the Commission and have subsequently been brought before the Court.[52] In practice in a few cases doubt arose with respect to the decision of the Commission concerning the admissibility, as a result of which that decision required a further interpretation in order to establish the object of examination with accuracy. In such a case, too, the Court acts fully independently and does not in advance consider the Commission's view of the matter as decisive, even though that view plays an important part in the determination of the Court's attitude.

The *Kjeldsen, Busk Madsen and Pedersen* Case, for instance, concerned the question of how the passage from the report of the Commission was to be understood according to which the point to be examined for conflict with the Convention was 'the Danish legislation which provides for integrated sex education', not 'the manner in which the instruction is given in different schools'. A certain working document used in local schools, which the Commission had qualified as 'legislation', according to the Court could not be regarded as such and therefore could only be taken into account 'in sofar as it contributes to an elucidation of the spirit of the legislation in dispute'.[53]

Approximately the same case presented itself in *Ireland* v. *the United Kingdom*.[54] The Commission had declared admissible the complaint that 'the

---

[50] *Cf.* the finding of the Court in its judgment of 9 October 1979, *Airey*, A.32, p. 10: 'the distinction between finding an allegation manifestly ill-founded and finding no violation is devoid of interest for the Court whose task is to hold in a final judgment that the State concerned has observed, or, on the contrary, has infringed the Convention.'

[51] See also, *e.g.*, the judgment of 28 August 1986, *Glasenapp*, A.104, p. 23; judgment of 28 August 1986, *Kosiek*, A.105, p. 19; judgment of 18 December 1986, *Bozano*, A.111, p. 18.

[52] In this respect, the attitude of the Commission in the *Airey* Case was, to say the least, confusing: 'In its report, the Commission expressed the opinion that, in view of its conclusion concerning Article 6(1), there was no need for it to consider the application under Article 8. However, during the oral hearing the Principal Delegate submitted that there had also been a breach of this Article'; judgment of 9 October 1979, A.32, p. 17. See also the judgment of 2 March 1987, *Weeks*, A.114, p. 21.

[53] Judgment of 7 December 1976, A.23, pp. 22-24.

[54] Judgment of 18 January 1978, A.25.

treatment of persons in custody (...) constituted an administrative practice in breach of Article 3'. The British Government submitted in the proceedings before the Court that a number of specific complaints did not concern a 'practice', but were isolated cases and as such fell outside the object of the examination. The Court held that:

> Article 49 of the Convention provides that the Court shall settle disputes concerning its jurisdiction. It follows that, in order to rule on this preliminary plea, the Court must itself interpret the above-mentioned decision [of the Commission] of 1 October 1972, in the particular light of the Commission's explanations.

The Court concluded that:

> it has jurisdiction to take cognisance of the contested cases of violation of Article 3 if and to the extent that the applicant Government put them forward as establishing the existence of a practice.[55]

A decision going somewhat further in the same direction is the decision in the *Winterwerp* Case, where the Court held that the alleged violation of Article 6 fell under the object of the case submitted to it, in spite of the fact that at an earlier stage the Commission had decided that it should disregard the applicant's submissions about this, because they were assumed to form a separate complaint and, according to the Commission, had not been put forward until after the admissibility examination.[56]

In the *Barthold* Case the Court held that 'this complaint falls outside the ambit of the case referred to the Court', because it concerned a complaint declared inadmissible by the Commission as being incompatible *ratione materiae* and did not merely amount to a supplementary legal submission or argument adduced in support of a claim already examined by the Court.[57] In the *Bozano* Case the Court declared that it had no jurisdiction, because '[i]t is a separate complaint, and one which has been rejected in the decision setting out the limits of the dispute referred to the Court'.[58]

In the *Bönisch* Case the applicant also claimed a violation which had been declared inadmissible on the ground that it had not been put forward before the Commission at the start. The Court held that although the complaint in question was not mentioned in the applicant's written and oral arguments before the Commission, it had an evident connection with the complaints he did make; therefore the Court had jurisdiction.[59] In the *Weber* Case the Swiss Government argued that the dispute (right to a public hearing) did not come within the ambit

---

[55] *Ibidem*, pp. 61-64.
[56] See *supra* pp. 125-126. See also the judgment, there mentioned, of 6 November 1980, *Guzzardi*, A.39, pp. 21-23.
[57] Judgment of 25 March 1985, A.90, p. 27.
[58] Judgment of 18 December 1986, A.111, p. 27. See also the judgments of 23 April 1987, *Erkner and Hofauer* and *Poiss*, A.117, pp. 61 and 102 respectively.
[59] Judgment of 6 May 1985, *Bönisch*, A.92, p. 17. See also the judgment of 18 December 1986, *Johnston*, A.112, pp. 22-23.

of Article 6(1) because the proceedings taken against the applicant were not 'criminal' proceedings but disciplinary ones. The Court referred to the various criteria laid down in its case-law concerning the concept of 'criminal charge' and dismissed the Government's submissions.[60]

2.5.4 The Examination by the Court in Relation to the Commission's Examination of Admissibility

At first sight the relationship between the competence of the Commission and the jurisdiction of the Court as to admissibility issues seems to be clearer than is the case with respect to jurisdiction issues. In fact, the Convention itself seems to provide that the Commission is the organ competent to take decisions about admissibility. Nevertheless, the Court considers that it has jurisdiction in this field as well. This approach of the Court was introduced in its judgment in the *'Vagrancy'* Cases and the *Ringeisen* Case.

In the *'Vagrancy'* Cases the Belgian Government asked the Court to declare that it had jurisdiction to pronounce on the admissibility of the complaints to which the case related, and subsequently to declare these complaints inadmissible because they did not comply with the conditions contained in Article 26 of the Convention. The Commission's delegate submitted that the Court had no jurisdiction to pronounce on the decisions of the Commission concerning admissibility. However, on the ground of the wide formulation of Article 45, and with a reference to its judgment in the *Belgian Linguistic* Case mentioned above, the Court concluded that:

> once a case is duly referred to it, (...) the Court is endowed with full jurisdiction and may thus take cognisance of all questions of fact and of law which may arise in the course of the consideration of the case. It is therefore impossible to see how questions concerning the interpretation and application of Article 26 raised before the Court during the hearing of the case should fall outside its jurisdiction.[61]

It is submitted here that the Court would seem to have disregarded the fact that Article 45 cannot be viewed in isolation from the other provisions concerning the supervisory procedure provided for in the European Convention.[62] Articles 24 to 27 are especially relevant in this context. In particular from Article 27 it seems to follow that the Commission has exclusive competence with respect to questions of admissibility.[63] This results from the fact that the drafters of the European Convention did not aim at a hierarchically organised division of competence

---

[60] Judgment of 22 May 1990, A.177, p. 20.

[61] Judgment of 18 June 1971, *De Wilde, Ooms and Versyp ('Vagrancy'* Cases), A.12, pp. 29-30.

[62] Art. 31(1) of the Vienna Treaty on the Law of Treaties provides as a general rule of interpretation: 'A treaty shall be interpreted in good faith in accordance with the ordinary meaning to be given to the terms of the treaty in their context and in the light of its object and purpose'. According to para. 2, 'context' must be understood to include also the text of the treaty itself.

[63] See also the joint separate opinion of judges Ross and Sigurjonsson in the case of *De Wilde, Ooms and Versyp ('Vagrancy'* Cases), judgment of 18 June 1971, A.12, p. 50; and the separate opinions of judge Bilge (*ibidem*, p. 54) and of judge Wold (*ibidem*, pp. 55-58).

between the two organs, but juxtaposed the Commission and the Court, each of them with its own duties within the supervisory procedure, without one organ being subordinate to the other.[64] The Court, too, in its judgment held that decisions of the Commission 'to reject applications which it considers to be inadmissible are without appeal as are, moreover, also those by which applications are accepted'.[65] It is therefore all the more curious that immediately following this consideration the Court held that the decision of the Commission in which it declares an application admissible:

> is not binding on the Court any more than the Court is bound by the opinion expressed by the Commission in its final report as to whether the facts found disclose a breach by the State concerned of its obligations under the Convention (Article 31).[66]

After reading the first quotation one would expect the Court to have reached the opposite conclusion.

The parallel here drawn by the Court between the *decision* of the Commission on admissibility and its *opinion* laid down in its report on the question of whether the facts disclose a violation of the Convention by the respondent State, does not hold water in our opinion. The former has the character of a (quasi-)judicial decision, the latter serves only to inform the Court or the Committee of Ministers, as the case may be. They cannot therefore be equated as regards their legal effects.

Articles 28 to 31 inclusive would also seem to indicate that the Court has put too wide an interpretation on Article 45. In fact, it appears from the said articles that the case which, after having been declared admissible by the Commission, is brought before the Court or the Committee of Ministers, concerns only the question of whether the alleged violation of the Convention by the respondent State has taken place and whether compensation should be awarded.

Finally, the view taken by the Court leads to a dubious consequence from the viewpoint of the equality of the parties aimed at in the Convention, because the respondent State may now bring a positive decision on admissibility before the Court, but the State or the individual who has lodged the complaint may *not* do so with a negative decision on admissibility. Moreover, the answer to the question of whether the admissibility can again be considered now appears to depend on whether the case is submitted to the Court or is decided by the Committee of Ministers, because the latter organ deals exclusively with the merits and not with admissibility issues.[67] Equality would seem to require that the Convention should provide for the possibility of *appeal* to the Court from *all* decisions of the Commission or exclude reconsideration of admissibility issues altogether.

The above-mentioned viewpoint of the Court in the '*Vagrancy*' Cases did not have any great consequences for that case. The Belgian Government submitted that

---

[64] Thus also the Commission itself by the words of its then President in the case of *De Wilde, Ooms and Versyp* ('*Vagrancy*' Cases), B.10 (1971), p. 209.

[65] Judgment of 18 June 1971, *De Wilde, Ooms and Versyp* ('*Vagrancy*' Cases), A.12, p. 30.

[66] *Idem.*

[67] See *infra* pp. 268-284.

the six-month rule of Article 26 had not been observed, but the Court concluded that Belgium had lost its right to raise this objection since it did so for the first time during the hearing before the Court, *i.e.* not in the procedure before the Commission or in the written proceedings before the Court.[68] The Court also held that the submission of the Belgian Government that local remedies had not been exhausted was ill-founded.[69] Ultimately, therefore, the Court reached the same result as the Commission. The same happened in the *Ringeisen* Case. In that case, too, the Court considered that it was competent to subject an application admitted by the Commission to a renewed examination of admissibility, referring in so many words to its judgment in the '*Vagrancy*' Cases.[70] Subsequently, the submission of the Austrian Government that Ringeisen had not yet exhausted all local remedies at the moment at which he filed his application, and that consequently, under Article 26, his application ought to have been declared inadmissible by the Commission, was dismissed by the Court in this case again.[71] The viewpoint that it is competent to subject questions concerning admissibility to a renewed examination was once more confirmed by the Court in the *Klass* Case[72] and has since become constant case-law of the Court, as appears from a number of judgments which also contain decisions on matters of admissibility.[73]

Meanwhile the Commission has also contributed to this development. In the *Belgian Linguistic* Case the Commission had challenged the Court's jurisdiction in matters of admissibility. In the *Klass* Case, however, it took quite a different position. In that case the delegate of the Commission himself invited the Court to examine a particular admissibility condition by requesting the Court in his final submissions:

> to say and judge
> 1. Whether, having regard to the circumstances of the case, the applicants could claim to be 'victims' of a violation of their rights guaranteed by the Convention.[74]

The Court accordingly concluded that the Commission concurred with the Court's jurisdiction in the matter.[75] The Commission thus reversed its previously taken position and apparently was prepared to share with the Court a competence which,

---

[68] Judgment of 18 June 1971, *De Wilde, Ooms and Versyp* ('*Vagrancy*' Cases), A.12, p. 30.
[69] *Ibidem*, pp. 33-35.
[70] Judgment of 16 July 1971, A.13, pp. 35-36.
[71] *Ibidem*, pp. 36-38.
[72] Judgment of 6 September 1978, A.28, pp. 16-20.
[73] See, *inter alia*, the judgment of 9 October 1979, *Airey*, A.32, pp. 10-11; judgment of 4 December 1979, *Schiesser*, A.34, pp. 16-17; judgment of 27 February 1980, *De Weer*, A.35, pp. 14-19; judgment of 22 May 1984, *De Jong, Baljet and Van den Brink*, A.77, pp. 17-20; judgment of 22 May 1984, *Duinhof and Duijf*, A.79, p. 14: in this case the Court, referring to the *De Weer* judgment, rejected the argument of the Government of the Netherlands 'that the Commission was obliged to inquire *ex officio* into exhaustion of domestic remedies and that, consequently, the question should also be considered by the Court.' See also the judgment of 28 March 1990, *Granger*, A.174, pp. 15-16; judgment of 27 August 1992, *Tomasi*, A.241-A, pp. 33-34.
[74] Judgment of 6 September 1978, A.28, p. 15.
[75] *Ibidem*, pp. 16-17.

in our opinion, under the Convention is exclusively that of the Commission. In this case again the consequences were not far-reaching. In fact, with respect to the question of whether applicants could submit that they were victims of a violation of the Convention the Court came to the same affirmative answer as the Commission had given in an earlier stage of the procedure.

In the *Airey* Case the Commission, on the basis of a rather curious argument, tried to give a sound basis to the said change of position. In that case Ireland requested the Court to find that the Commission ought to have declared the application inadmissible on account of non-exhaustion of local remedies. The President of the Commission first of all submitted in his oral exposition during the proceedings before the Court that here no appeal against the decision of the Commission was involved, since the Convention does not provide for this, but that the Court 'has full jurisdiction to determine all issues of fact and law that arise'.[76] Subsequently he submitted that the local remedies rule has two aspects, *viz.* a procedural aspect and an aspect concerning the merits. In the procedure in which the Commission decides on admissibility, in his opinion the local remedies rule is a procedural rule. In the sequel to the procedure, and specifically in the proceedings before the Court, these facts assume a substantive character. To this he attached the following consequence:

> were the Court, when examining all the facts of the case, to consider that, even with regard to the facts presented and arising before the decision on admissibility, there was still an indication of non-exhaustion of remedies, I submit that the Court would not then be saying 'inadmissible because of non-exhaustion': it would be making a substantive decision that there were in fact remedies available at that time, and that therefore there would be no justification for proceeding further with the case. This would be a substantive decision that there was, at that stage, no breach of the Convention.[77]

According to this view the question as to what is *the matter on which* the Court makes a decision is apparently subordinate to that about *the form in which* this is done: the Court may make a decision on admissibility, provided that this decision is cast in the form of a judgment on the merits. However, in our opinion, the local remedies rule is not a question which concerns the merits, *viz.* the question of whether there has been a violation of the Convention, but a mere admissibility condition, of which the rationale is that a State should not be subjected to an international procedure so long as not all possibilities for redress within its national legal system have been put to the test. If the application has been declared admissible by the Commission and if the latter, during its examination of the merits, has not found occasion to apply Article 29, the applicant party should be secure that the Court will consider the merits of his application and not the local remedies rule or other admissibility questions. In this stage the respondent State can no longer ward off the complaint on violation of the Convention with the mere reference to a possible local remedy that has not been put to the test. That

---

[76] Council of Europe, *Cour/Misc.* (79)19, pp. 3-4.
[77] *Ibidem*, pp. 6-7.

the delegate of the Commission did not distinguish correctly here between the admissibility and the merits is also disclosed, in our opinion, in his viewpoint in this same *Airey* Case with respect to Article 29. From the fact that this provision speaks of 'reject', and not of 'declare it admissible', he inferred, *inter alia*, that:

> the approach which Article 29 is making for the Commission in respect of facts arising after the admissibility – indication of non-exhaustion, for example – is to treat this as a substantive matter for decision by the Commission when expressing its opinion, in effect, as to whether it should proceed with the application because there is no visible breach of the Convention.[78]

Considering the rationale of Article 29, the fact that this provision refers expressly to the admissibility conditions of Article 27, and the fact that in the system of the Convention the Commission does not have competence to decide on the merits, we believe this conclusion also to be wrong.

In the *Schiesser* Case the Commission seems to have acquiesced completely in the line developed by the Court. In its report the Commission had stated that Schiesser's complaint concerning Article 5(2) ought to be rejected:

> because the Convention has been incorporated into Swiss law and takes precedence over Cantonal law, Mr. Schiesser should have raised this issue before the Federal Court. Having failed to do so, he had not (...) exhausted domestic remedies in this respect.[79]

Nevertheless, the Commission requested the Court to decide 'whether the applicant could nevertheless invoke Article 5(4)', and the Commission's delegate invited the Court 'on account of the failure to comply with Article 26, to decline jurisdiction to rule on the merits of the complaint relating to Article 5(4).'[80]

The first instance in which the Court came to a different decision on admissibility from that taken by the Commission occurred in the *Van Oosterwijck* Case. This case concerned the complaint of a transsexual about the refusal of the Belgian authorities to adapt his civil status certificate to his change of sex. The admissibility issue concerned the question as to exhaustion of the local remedies. The Commission had found this requirement to be met and had declared the complaint admissible. The Court, however, decided that Van Oosterwijck had not applied for all the remedies existing in Belgium, or had not exhausted them in the proper way. Consequently, the Court decided that it could not deal with the merits.[81] Thus the Court, for the first time in the history of the Convention, passed a judgment that did not concern the merits. In the *Cardot* Case the Court also held that the applicant had not fulfilled the requirements of Article 26. The Court disagreed with the Commission as to the question whether the applicant had raised before the French courts, even in substance, the alleged violation of the Convention. It concluded that by reason of the failure to exhaust domestic

---

[78] Council of Europe, *Cour/Misc.* (79)19, pp. 7-8.
[79] Judgment of 4 December 1979, A.34, pp. 16-17.
[80] *Ibidem*, p. 17.
[81] Judgment of 6 November 1980, A.40, p. 20.

remedies, it was unable to take cognisance of the merits of the case.[82] As said above, in our opinion the approach chosen by the Court is not in line with the decision of competence laid down in the Convention.[83] Judge Martens, *inter alia*, in his dissenting opinions in the *Brozicek* Case[84] and in the *Cardot* Case[85] defended the position that the Court should leave it to the Commission to determine whether preliminary objections as to admissibility are founded or not.

3 THE PROCEEDINGS BEFORE THE COURT[86]

3.1 General

The proceedings before the Court start with a request by the Commission or an application by a State having the right under Article 48 to bring a case before the Court. If there is doubt as to whether the applicant State falls under the terms of Article 48, the question is submitted by the President to the Grand Chamber for decision (Rule 34 of the Rules of Court).[87] Moreover, the proceedings start if the case is referred to the Court by the original applicant under Protocol No. 9, unless the Screening Panel unanimously decides that the case shall not be considered by the Court.

The request or the application must contain the following data: the parties to the proceedings before the Commission; the date on which the Commission adopted its report; the date on which the report was transmitted to the Committee of Ministers; and the object of the request or application (Rule 32(1) of the Rules of Court). On the basis of these data the Court is able to ascertain whether all the conditions for the filing of an application or request laid down in the Convention have been complied with. The requirement that the Commission, too, must state the object of its request was incorporated into the Rules of Court in 1972 and was intended specifically for the case in which the Commission has not concluded that there has been a violation of the Convention, but nevertheless brings the case before the Court. In such a case the respondent State ought to know what exactly the Commission aims at with its request, in order that the State may be able to prepare itself adequately for the proceedings before the Court. If the case is referred to the Court by the original applicant under Protocol No. 9, he also has to specify why, in his opinion, the case warrants consideration by the Court (Rule 34(1)(a) of the Rules of Court 'B').

---

[82] Judgment of 19 March 1991, A.200, p. 19.
[83] See *supra* p. 128.
[84] Judgment of 19 December 1989, A.167, pp. 23-28.
[85] Judgment of 19 March 1991, A.200, p. 22.
[86] In the following text, Protocol No. 9 which confers on the individual applicant the right to refer the case to the Court, has not been taken into consideration. For Protocol No. 9, see section 6 of the present Chapter, *infra* pp. 235-239.
[87] Unless indicated otherwise the Rules of the Court refer to the Rules of the Court 'A', and not to the Rules of the Court 'B', applicable to cases concerning States bound by Protocol No. 9.

When a State has brought the case before the Court, the name and the address of the person whom the State has appointed as its Agent in the sense of Rule 28 of the Rules of Court must also be mentioned (Rule 32(1) of the Rules of Court). This Agent may be assisted by counsel and advisers. The Commission delegates one or more of its members to take part in the consideration of the case before the Court; they may be assisted by other persons (Rule 29(1) of the Rules of Court). The Delegates are appointed by the Commission in a plenary session. They represent the whole Commission and 'shall act in accordance with such directives as they may receive from the Commission' (Rule 63(1) of the Rules of the Commission). In practice, therefore, it may happen that they are not prepared to decide on a given matter unless after previous consultation with the Commission.[88] The names and addresses of these Delegates must also be communicated to the Court (Rule 32(2) of the Rules of Court). The original applicant must specify in his request the name and address of any person appointed by him (Rule 34(1)(b) of the Rules of Court 'B')

A copy of the application or request is transmitted to the members of the Court, to each of the States concerned mentioned in Article 48 insofar as they themselves have not submitted the case to the Court, and to the person, non-governmental organisation or group of individuals who lodged the complaint with the Commission under Article 25 of the Convention, hereafter referred to as 'the original applicant'. The State against which the application is directed, is invited to supply the Registrar with the name and address of its Agent. The other States here referred to are requested to inform the Registrar within two weeks whether they wish to appear as parties to the case brought before the Court. The original applicant, if he has not referred the case to the Court himself under Protocol No. 9, is also invited to notify the Registrar whether he wishes to take part in the proceedings (Rule 33(3)(d) of the Rules of Court), and if so, of the name and address of the person appointed in accordance with Rule 30. If the case has not been brought before the Court by the Commission, its members also receive a copy of the application (Rule 33(1)(c) of the Rules of Court).

After the request or the application has been filed and the constitution of a Chamber in the way described above has taken place,[89] the composition of the Chamber is communicated to the judges, the Agent of the respondent State, the Commission and the original applicant. It may be pointed out once more that, for the reasons stated above, the Chamber may or shall relinquish jurisdiction in favour of a Grand Chamber, which in its turn may exceptionally relinquish jurisdiction in favour of the plenary Court.[90]

Like the Commission, the Court applies its rules in a flexible way. The title in the Rules of Court dealing with the procedure indeed opens with the general rule

---

[88] See Verbatim Record of the public hearing by the Court, 5 October 1961, *De Becker*, B.2 (1962), p. 230.
[89] See *supra* pp. 34.
[90] See *idem*.

that for the consideration of a particular case the Court may derogate from the provisions contained in this title after having consulted the Party or Parties, the Delegates of the Commission and the applicant (Rule 26 of the Rules of Court). In the provision relating to the use of the official languages before the Court the possibility of derogation is again mentioned in so many words. It is true that French and English are to be considered as the official languages, but the Court may authorise the parties, the applicant and any person assisting the Delegates of the Commission to use another language (Rule 27 of the Rules of Court).

3.2 Interim Measures

The President of the Court or, if the Chamber has been constituted, the Chamber or its President may indicate interim measures to any Party and, where appropriate, the original applicant. This may be done at the request of a Party, the Commission, the original applicant or any other person concerned. The President, the Chamber or its President may also do so *proprio motu* (Rule 36(1) of the Rules of Court). As appears from the formulation of this provision, the Court may suggest interim measures but it cannot enforce them. That is at least the position taken by the Court so far, based upon the ground that the Convention nowhere confers the right to order interim measures.[91] As has been said, the same also applies to interim measures on the part of the Commission.[92] It would appear to be incumbent on the Commission rather than on the Court to recommend interim measures. The Commission is involved in the case at a much earlier stage. At that moment there is at least still some chance that imminent damage may be prevented or limited by the taking of interim measures. When the Court has ultimately been seized of the case, even more time has elapsed since the facts concerned have taken place. The amended Rule 36 provides that where the Commission pursuant to Rule 36 of its Rules of Procedure has indicated an interim measure, its adoption or maintenance shall remain recommended after the case has been brought before the Court, unless and until the President or Chamber decides otherwise or until paragraph 1 of Rule 36 is applied.[93]

3.3 The Examination of the Case before the Court

3.3.1 The Written Procedure
In normal cases the examination of the case starts with written proceedings. The President of the Chamber consults the Agents of the Parties, the Delegate or, if the latter has not yet been appointed, the President of the Commission, and the original applicant on whether they each consider a written procedure to be necessary. In the event of an affirmative answer by any of them, he lays down the

---

[91] See judgment of 20 March 1991, *Cruz Varaz and Others*, A.201, pp. 34-37. See *supra* pp. 103-107.
[92] See *supra* pp. 103-104.
[93] See judgment of 2 May 1997, *D* v. *the United Kingdom* (not yet published), para. 3.

time-limits within which memorials and other documents are to be filed (Rule 37(1) of the Rules of Court). Until the expiry of this time-limit the parties may file preliminary objections. The Chamber gives its decision on such objections after receipt of the replies or comments of every other party and of the Delegates of the Commission, or joins the objections to the merits (Rule 48 of the Rules of Court).

Memorials and other documents must, when they are submitted by a Party, by another State or by the Commission, be filed in forty copies. That requirement does not apply to the original applicant (Rule 39(4) of the Rules of Court 'B'). They are transmitted by the Registrar to the judges, to the Agents of the Parties, to the Delegates of the Commission and to the original applicant (Rule 37(4) of the Rules of Court). Subsequently the President of the Chamber, again after consultation with the parties concerned, fixes the date of the hearing (Rule 38 of the Rules of Court).

3.3.2 The Hearing

The President of the Chamber directs the hearings. He also prescribes the order in which the Agents, counsel or advisers of the Parties, the Delegates of the Commission, any other persons assisting the delegates and the original applicant shall be called upon to speak (Rule 39 of the Rules of Court).

A Chamber may procure information in different ways for its examination of a case. The basis of the examination is undoubtedly the report of the Commission. Whether a case is referred to the Court by a State, by the original applicant or by the Commission, the Court will in any case take into consideration the report of the Commission (Rule 29(2) of the Rules of the Court). However, the Court is bound neither by the view of the Commission on whether there has been a violation of the Convention, nor by the way the facts have been ascertained by the Commission. However, specifically as regards the latter aspect, the report constitutes an important source of information, in view also of the way in which it was drawn up.

At the request of a Party, of the Delegates of the Commission, of the original applicant or of a third party invited or granted leave to submit written comments, or *proprio motu*, the Chamber may hear witnesses, experts or any persons in another capacity whose evidence or statements seem likely to be of assistance (Rule 41(1) of the Rules of Court). The expenses of such persons are borne by the Party at whose request they have been heard, unless the Chamber decides otherwise. In other cases, the Chamber shall decide whether such costs are to be borne by the Council of Europe, or awarded against an applicant or a third party at whose request the person summoned appeared (Rule 42 of the Rules of Court). Such persons are summoned by the Registrar. If for any communication, notification or summons addressed to persons other than the Agents of the parties or the Delegates of the Commission, the Court considers it necessary to have the assistance of the Government of the Contracting State on whose territory such communication, notification or summons is to have effect, the President of the

Court shall apply directly to that Government in order to obtain the necessary facilities (Rule 31(1) of the Rules of the Court). The Convention does not contain a provision requiring the Contracting States to grant such facilities. Such an obligation may, however, be inferred from the spirit of the Convention. A Contracting State may be expected to lend its assistance if the Court tries to prepare and handle the case as well as possible through normal judicial methods. The obligation to lend assistance results from the ratification of the Convention and the consequent recognition of the existence and the function of the Court.

In case there are any objections to a particular person as a witness or an expert, the Chamber decides. Persons who cannot be heard as witnesses may, however, be heard for the purpose of information (Rule 44 of the Rules of Court). Witnesses and experts must take the oath or make the declaration mentioned in Rules 43(1) and 43(2) respectively. Like other persons appearing before the Court, they may use their own language. At the hearing they may, subject to the control of the President, be examined by the Agents, counsel or advisers of the Parties, as well as by the Delegates of the Commission and those assisting them and by the original applicant (Rule 45(2) of the Rules of Court). The same applies of course to the judges, who may also address the Agents, advocates or advisers of the Parties as well as the Delegates of the Commission and the original applicant and any other persons appearing before them (Rule 45(1) of the Rules of Court). When, without good reason, witnesses or other persons, after having been duly summoned, fail to appear or refuse to give evidence, the Contracting State to whose jurisdiction the respective person is subject may be informed. The same will apply when a witness or an expert has violated the oath taken or the declaration made by him (Rule 46 of the Rules of Court). As has been stated above with respect to the procedure before the Commission,[94] here again the effect of such a communication to the State in question may be rather limited if the national legislation does not provide for forcing such recalcitrant persons to appear before the Court and to give their evidence or make their deposition duly before the Court.

During the proceedings the Chamber may depute one or more of its members to conduct an investigation, to carry out an inquiry on the spot or to take evidence in some other manner (Rule 41(4) of the Rules of Court). For the assistance of a Contracting State in such an investigation on the spot the President shall apply to the respective Government (Rule 31(2) of the Rules of Court). Here again the obligation of the Contracting States to lend their assistance results from the mere fact that they have ratified the Convention.

Finally, the Chamber may ask any person or institution of its choice to obtain information, express an opinion or make a report upon any specific point (Rule 41(2) of the Rules of Court).

---

[94] See *supra* p. 173.

3.4 The Judgment of the Court

In most cases the proceedings before the Court conclude with a decision in the form of a judgment. Under Rule 53(1) of the Rules of Court the judgment must contain the following elements: the names of the President and the judges constituting the Chamber and the name of the Registrar or Deputy Registrar; the date on which the judgment was adopted and delivered; a description of the Party or Parties; the names of the Agents, counsel or advisers of the Party or Parties; the names of the Delegates of the Commission and of the persons assisting them; the name of the original applicant (and of his advocate or advisers if he has referred the case to the Court); an account of the procedure followed; the final submissions of the Party or Parties and, if any, of the Delegates of the Commission and of the original applicant; the facts of the case; the reasons in point of law; the operative provisions of the judgment; the decision, if any, in respect of costs; the number of judges constituting the majority; and, where appropriate, a statement as to which of the two texts, French or English, is authentic. Reasons must be given for the judgment of the Court (Article 51(1) of the Convention). Any judge who has taken part in the consideration of the case is entitled to annex to the judgment either a separate opinion, concurring with or dissenting from that judgment, or a bare statement of dissent (Article 51(2) of the Convention in conjunction with Rule 53(2) of the Rules of Court).

The judgment is signed by the President and the Registrar and is read out by the President or a delegated judge at a public hearing (Rule 55(1) and (2) of the Rules of Court). The text is submitted to the Committee of Ministers for the purpose of the supervision of its execution under Article 54 of the Convention (Rule 55(3) of the Rules of Court). Certified copies are sent to the Party or Parties, to the Commission, to the original applicant, to the Secretary General of the Council of Europe, to the Contracting States and any persons who have submitted written comments, and to any other person directly concerned (Rule 54(4) of the Rules of Court). The latter category includes, *inter alia*, any victim of the alleged violation specified in an application by a State.

Judgments of the Court are final (Article 52 of the Convention). However, a request for interpretation or revision of a judgment may be addressed to the Court.[95] Judgments and other decisions of the Court are published, as are the documents relating to the proceedings, with the exception of any document which the President considers unnecessary or inadvisable to publish. The reports of the Commission, too, are published, as well as the reports of the public hearings. Moreover, the President of the Court may order the publication of any other document which he considers useful. Documents which are not published may be inspected at the Registry, unless decided otherwise by the President of the Court either on his own initiative or at the request of a Party, the Commission, the original applicant or any person concerned. The publication of judgments,

---

[95] See *infra* pp. 259-264.

decisions, applications, petitions and the report of the Commission takes place in both official languages. The other documents are published only in the official language in which they occur in the proceedings (Rule 56(1) of the Rules of Court). In 1968 the Court decided that its judgments and decisions will be translated through the mediation of the Registrar in cases in which a State is directly concerned where English or French is not the national language or one of the national languages. In several cases this decision has been put into practice.

At the beginning of June 1997, the Court had pronounced a total of 670 decisions, including decisions concerning preliminary objections, concerning the merits, concerning the interpretation of a judgment, and concerning just satisfaction under Article 50 of the Convention.[96] At the same date, 146 cases were still pending before the Court.

The Court may also pronounce a judgment by default. Rule 52 of the Rules of Court provides that where a party fails to appear or to present its case before the Court, a decision will nevertheless be taken. The case may therefore occur in which not a single party appears in the proceedings before the Court, but the Commission alone brings in arguments.[97] In practice, however, no such case has occurred as yet.

Under Article 53 of the Convention parties have to abide by the decisions of the Court. The Committee of Ministers supervises the execution (Article 54 of the Convention). With a view to this supervisory function under Article 54 the Committee adopted a number of rules in 1976, of which the last revision took place on 19 December 1991.[98] In these rules it is laid down that, when the Court has decided that there has been a violation of the Convention and/or when it has afforded just satisfaction to the injured party, the Committee shall invite the State concerned to inform it of the measures it has taken in pursuance of the judgment of the Court (Rule 2). The Committee does not regard its function under Article 54 as having been exercised until it has taken note of the information supplied and, when just satisfaction has been afforded, until it has satisfied itself that this has actually been awarded.

If a State fails to execute a judgment of the Court, the Committee may decide on the measures to be taken by a two-third majority of the representatives casting a vote and a majority of the representatives entitled to sit on the Committee.[99] The Committee does not have the means to force a defaulting State to execute the

---

[96] See the list of judgments of the Court at the end of this book, Appendix IV.
[97] On the role of the Commission in proceedings before the Court, see *infra* pp. 225-228.
[98] See *Collected Texts*, Strasbourg, 1996.
[99] The Convention is silent on the voting procedure with respect to decisions under Art. 54. The Rules of Procedure of the Committee refer in general to Art. 20 of the Statute of the Council of Europe (Rule 10). It appears from Art. 20 that decisions concerning a number of expressly mentioned matters require unanimity or a simple majority. Decisions on all other matters, including therefore decisions under Art. 54 of the Convention, are taken with a two-third majority of the representatives casting a vote and a majority of the representatives entitled to sit on the Committee.

judgment of the Court. Given its position, however, the Committee, if it so desires, may bring considerable political pressure to bear on such a State, including suspension or even expulsion from the Council of Europe.[100]

3.5 The Striking of a Case off the List

The procedure before the Court does not always conclude with a judgment properly speaking, *i.e.* with a decision on the merits. Like the procedure before the Commission,[101] the one before the Court may be interrupted before a decision has been made. Two different situations may cause such an interruption.

Rule 49(1) of the Rules of Court deals with the possibility of striking a case off the list which has been brought before the Court by a State, when that State notifies the Registrar of its intention not to proceed with the case and the other parties agree to this. The same applies to cases referred to the Court under Protocol No. 9 (Rule 51(1) of the Rules of Court 'A'). In view of the formulation of Rule 49(1) and Rule 51(1) respectively it must be assumed that such a notification is possible at any moment during the proceedings and consequently even in the very last stage. No reasons need be given. However, in the *Van Bunkate* Case the Dutch Government notified the Court that they wished not to proceed with the case, since the Court had already found a violation in the similar *Abdoella* Case.[102] The applicant did not comment on this proposal of the Dutch Government; the Commission, however, disagreed with the Government, because in this way there would be no formal decision and the applicant would not be able to receive any just satisfaction to which, in the Commission's opinion, he was entitled. The Court agreed with the Commission that the applicant's entitlement to a formal and binding decision on the merits and to just satisfaction did override any interest the Government may have had in discontinuance of the case.[103]

Usually, however, the wish not to proceed with the case may be due to the fact that the parties have reached some sort of a settlement. And indeed Rule 49(2) of the Rules of Court provides that the Chamber may strike a case, brought before the Court by the Commission and/or a State, off the list when the Chamber is informed that a friendly settlement, arrangement or some other solution of the matter has been reached.[104] The same applies again to cases referred to the Court under Protocol No. 9 (Rule 51(2) of the Rules of Court 'A'). Finally, the Court may decide to strike a case off its list of cases when the applicant shows a lack

---

[100] See Art. 8 of the Statute of the Council of Europe.
[101] See *supra* pp. 189-190.
[102] Judgment of 25 November 1992, A.248-A.
[103] Judgment of 26 May 1993, A.248-B, pp. 29-30.
[104] Examples of cases which were struck off the list under Art. 48(2) are: judgment of 3 June 1985, *Vallon*, A.95, p. 6; judgment of 30 September 1985, *Can*, A.96, pp. 6-7, where the Court indicated that the 'case-law does already provide certain indications as to the answer to the question'; judgment of 27 November 1987, *Yaacoub*, A.127, pp. 8-9; judgment of 27 February 1992, *Birou*, A.232-B.

of interest by not responding to the request of providing further information. Thus in a number of cases concerning the length of civil proceedings, a lack of interest was manifested by the applicants in the proceedings pending before the Court, which the Court considered to be an implied withdrawal constituting a 'fact of a kind to provide a solution of the matter'. In the opinion of the Court, there were no reasons of *ordre public* for continuing the proceedings. The Court, therefore, ordered these cases to be struck off the list, subject to the possibility of their being restored thereto in the event of a new situation justifying such a course.[105]

In the *Gea Catalán* Case the Spanish Government submitted that the applicant's inactivity was tantamount to an implied withdrawal. After having indicated that he wished to take part in the proceedings before the Court, the applicant had neither lodged a memorial nor appeared at the hearing, and had submitted a claim for just satisfaction well after the expiry of the time-limit laid down in Rule 50 (1) of the Rules of Court. In the Government's opinion, such an attitude should lead the Court to strike the case off the list. The Court noted that the applicant had expressed the wish to take part in the proceedings and that he had submitted, albeit belatedly, a claim for just satisfaction. It could not therefore be inferred that he did 'not intend to pursue his complaints'. In addition, there had been neither a friendly settlement, nor an arrangement nor another fact of a kind to provide a solution of the matter, so that the first sentence of Rule 49(2) was not applicable either. The objection was accordingly dismissed.[106]

If the case has not been referred to the Court by the original applicant under Protocol No. 9, the initiative to withdraw a case before the Court cannot be taken by the individual applicant, because he is not a party to the proceedings before the Court. In the *Societé Stenuit* Case, the applicant company informed the Court of its wish to withdraw. The Government was consulted and expressed the view that the case should be struck off the list since amended legislation to a large extent remedied the problems of principle raised by the Commission in its report. The Court held that although the applicant's decision did not strictly speaking constitute a withdrawal, since it was not taken by a party to the case in view of the fact that Protocol No. 9 had not yet come into force, it was in any event a 'fact of a kind to provide a solution of the matter'. Since the Court was of the opinion that there were no reasons of *ordre public* for continuing the proceedings, it ordered this case to be struck off the list.[107]

After the notification of not proceeding with the case, or after the information about a friendly settlement the Chamber obtains the opinion of the Parties, the Commission and the original applicant on the matter and subsequently decides whether the discontinuance may be approved and the case may be struck off the list. If the Chamber agrees that the case should be struck off the list, it gives a

---

[105] Judgments of 3 December 1991, *Gilberti, Nonnis, Trotto, Cattivera, Seri, Gori, Casadio, Testa, Covitti, Zonetti, Simonetti, Dal Sasso*, A.223-C-N.
[106] Judgment of 10 February 1995, A.309, p. 10.
[107] Judgment of 27 February 1992, A.232-A, p. 8.

reasoned decision. This decision is communicated to the Committee of Ministers in order to allow the Committee to supervise the execution of any obligations which the parties may have undertaken in the settlement reached by them. This supervisory function of the Committee of Ministers runs parallel to that which is exercised under Article 54 of the Convention.

The Chamber is not obliged to strike the case off the list in the above-mentioned circumstances. Having regard to the responsibilities of the Court in pursuance of Article 19 of the Convention, the Chamber may decide that the consideration of the case should proceed (Rule 49(4) of the Rules of Court). Rule 47(3) of the old Rules, which was almost identical to the present Rule 49(4), was applied by the Court in the *De Becker* Case. During the proceedings before the Court, Belgium amended its legislation on the point to which the complaint of De Becker related. By this, the Belgian Government argued, the complaint had been satisfied. The original applicant agreed. Belgium thereupon requested the Court to strike the case off the list, to which neither the Commission nor the original applicant objected. The Court held that under Article 19 it was competent to proceed *ex officio* with the case in the interest of the maintenance of the Convention, but that in this case there was no ground for this, since the original difference of opinion underlying the case now only had historical importance.[108]

From the viewpoint of an effective maintenance of the Convention, a decision like this meets with certain objections. A declaratory judgment of the Court may have a general preventive effect even if it concerns a situation that has meanwhile been changed. Moreover, the confidence in the remedy provided for in the Convention may be impaired if proceedings can be stopped in such an advanced stage on the ground of an eleventh-hour reaction of the respondent State, which in an earlier stage refused to agree to a settlement. In this way the Court might encourage the attitude that, during the negotiations about a friendly settlement in the procedure before the Commission, States will persist longer in their positions, because they know that they can always reconsider the matter in a later stage without any harmful consequences.[109] In *K v. Austria* the Court considered it appropriate to strike the case off the list, notwithstanding the objections of the Delegate of the Commission. The Court observed that the possibility of a breach of the Convention, deriving from the manner in which the national authorities applied or might apply a provision of domestic law, could not in itself justify a refusal to strike the case off the list. It noted in addition that the Austrian Government had laid before Parliament a Bill which intended, *inter alia*, to amend some provisions of the Criminal Code and whose adoption would eliminate any public policy reason for requiring a decision on the merits of the case.[110]

---

[108] Judgment of 27 March 1962, A.4, pp. 23-27. See also the judgment of 26 October 1984, *Skoogström*, A.83, pp. 9-10.

[109] See judge Ross in his dissenting opinion, A.4, pp. 28-33; and the 7 joint dissenting opinions of judges Wiarda, Ryssdal and Ganshof van der Meersch, in the *Skoogström* Case, A.83, p. 11.

[110] Judgment of 2 June 1993, A.255-B, p. 33.

In the *Skoogström* Case a friendly settlement between the applicant and the Swedish Government was reached during the proceedings before the Court. The Swedish Commission for Revision of Certain Parts of the Code of Judicial Procedure had been asked to propose and elaborate the details for an amendment of the Code as required in order to put it beyond any doubt that it was in conformity with Article 5(3) of the Convention. In connection with this settlement the applicant was further paid a sum of SEK 5,000 for his legal costs. In the light of the settlement reached, the Swedish Government requested the Court to strike the case off its list. The Delegate of the Commission proposed that the Court should not strike the case off its list but should adjourn examination of the case 'in order to ascertain what progress has been made in the work to amend the legislation, or alternatively to ascertain the timetable for the work which will lead to those amendments'.[111] The Court, however, stated that it had no cause to believe that the settlement did not reflect the free will of the applicant. As far as the general interest was concerned, the Court did not feel able to defer judgment nor did it see any reason of public policy sufficiently compelling to warrant continuation of its proceeding on the merits of the case. The Court therefore concluded that it would be appropriate to strike the case off the list.[112]

In a number of cases the Court refused to entertain the suggestion or the request to strike the case off the list. The situation in those cases differed to some extent from that in the *De Becker* Case. In the *Kjeldsen, Busk Madsen and Pedersen* Case two of the original individual applicants (Mr and Mrs Kjeldsen) declared that they withdrew their complaint and further asked for a separate consideration of their case, but the Court refused to strike their case off the list. It held that it could not do so under Rule 47(1) (old) (the present Rule 49(1)), since that provision made it possible to strike a case off the list under certain circumstances after the intention not to proceed with the case was notified by a 'Party which has brought the case before the Court, that is to say by an Applicant Contracting State in proceedings before the Court'. In the Court's opinion the original individual applicants were not covered by this provision. Nor could a striking off the list be based on Rule 47(2) (now Rule 49(2)), which made this measure dependent upon the existence of a 'friendly settlement, arrangement or other fact of a kind to provide a solution of the matter'. The Court was of the opinion that this condition, too, had not been met in the case under consideration.[113]

On the same grounds the Court refused to strike the *Tyrer* Case off the list after a declaration of the original applicant that he wished to withdraw his complaint. The Commission had opposed such a procedure, because in its view the wishes of the applicant in this case should yield to the public interest. A proposed amendment of the law which had been mentioned by the Attorney General of the Isle of Man did not, in the Court's view, constitute a 'fact of a kind to provide a

---

[111] Judgment of 26 October 1984, A.83, p. 9.
[112] *Ibidem*, p. 10.
[113] Judgment of 7 December 1976, A.23, pp. 21-22.

solution of the matter', specifically not because the situation conflicting with the Convention was not completely redressed.[114] For the refusal to strike the case of *Koç*, in the *Luedicke, Belkacem and Koç* Case, off the list, the Court advanced almost the same arguments as in the *Kjeldsen* Case.[115]

In both the *De Weer* Case[116] and the *Guzzardi* Case[117] the respondent State submitted that the object of the complaint had ceased to exist. In the first-mentioned case the Belgian Government inferred this submission from the fact that the *Conseil d'Etat* had meanwhile nullified (a part of) the impugned legislation. In the other case the reason advanced by the Italian Government was the abolition of the measure which had given rise to the complaint (*viz.* enforced stay in the island of Asinara as part of a special supervision under which Guzzardi was placed). In both cases the Court considered, for practically the same reasons as in the cases just mentioned, that the conditions of Rule 47(2) (old) had not been satisfied, and for that reason refused to strike the case off the list. In the *Guzzardi* judgment it was expressly added that 'proceedings under the Convention frequently serve a declaratory purpose'.[118]

In the *Bagetta* Case the Italian Government contended that the applicant could no longer claim to be a victim of a violation of the Convention owing to two events that had occurred after the case was referred to the Court, namely the judgment of the Italian Court of Cassation holding that the applicant's prosecution was time-barred and the decision to recruit the applicant for a post on the railways, subject to a medical examination. The Court noted, however, that there had been neither a friendly settlement nor an arrangement. It considered that the two new facts brought to its notice were not of a kind to provide a solution of the matter and that a decision had accordingly to be taken on the merits.[119]

Although on a number of occasions the Court has accepted that the parents, spouse or children of a deceased applicant are entitled to take his place in the proceedings,[120] in the *Scherer* Case the Court held that the applicant's executor had not expressed any intention whatsoever of seeking, on the applicant's behalf, to have the proceedings reopened in Switzerland or to claim compensation for non-pecuniary damage in Strasbourg. Under these circumstances the applicant's death could be held to constitute a 'fact of a kind to provide a solution of the matter'.[121] Two other cases have been struck off the list, since the applicant's death, together with the silence of the heirs who showed no interest in the

---

[114] Judgment of 25 April 1978, A.26, pp. 12-14.
[115] Judgment of 28 November 1978, A.29, pp. 13-16.
[116] Judgment of 27 February 1980, A.35, pp. 19-20.
[117] Judgment of 6 November 1980, A.39, pp. 30-31.
[118] *Ibidem*, p. 31.
[119] Judgment of 25 June 1987, A.119, p. 31.
[120] See, *e.g.*, the judgment of 24 May 1991, *Vocaturo*, A.206-C, p. 29; judgments of 27 February 1992, *G* v. *Italy*, A.228-F, p. 65 and *Pandolfeli and Palumbo*, A.231-B, p. 16; judgment of 31 March 1992, *X* v. *France*, A.234-C, p. 89; and judgment of 22 February 1994, *Raimondo*, A.281-A, p. 8.
[121] Judgment of 25 March 1994, A.287, p. 15.

proceedings pending before the Court constituted a 'fact of a kind to provide a solution of the matter', while there was no reason of *ordre public* for continuing the proceedings.[122]

4 THE POSITION OF THE COMMISSION IN THE PROCEEDINGS BEFORE THE COURT

4.1 General

Of the various functions which the Commission exercises under the European Convention the one which it fulfils in the proceedings before the Court is the most difficult to describe. The reason for this is in the first place that the Convention does not make any reference to the fact that the Commission is involved in the proceedings before the Court.[123] The nature and the substance of the role played by the Commission during the proceedings before the Court have therefore become defined in particular in the Rules of Procedure of the Commission and the Rules of Court, and in the first cases brought before the Court. Secondly, a characterisation of the function of the Commission after the case has been brought before the Court is problematic because on certain points this function differs rather considerably from the other tasks of the Commission, to which there is express reference in the Convention.

4.2 The Role of the Commission

In the stage of the proceedings here dealt with, the Commission does not take binding decisions, as in its *quasi*-judicial function during the examination of the admissibility or when it decides on the acceptability of the substance of a friendly settlement in connection with the requirements set by the Convention. Nor is its role in the proceedings before the Court comparable with its mediatory role in the attempts to reach a friendly settlement, its role in connection with the report referred to in Article 31(1) or the initiative it may take to refer a case to the Court. The role of the Commission in the proceedings before the Court is best described as that of *amicus curiae*, an independent and impartial advisory organ with respect to questions of fact and of law concerning a case before the Court. As stated above, the position of the Commission as an organ of the Convention entails that in the proceedings before the Court, even if it has itself referred the case to the Court, it does not appear as a party, but as a representative of the public interest. The role of the Commission in the proceedings before the Court has therefore also been compared to that of an Attorney General.[124]

---

[122] Judgments of 3 December 1991, *Macaluso and Manunza*, A.223-A-B.

[123] The only provision in the Convention from which this might be inferred is that on the right conferred on the Commission in Art. 48 to submit a case to the Court.

[124] Thus Waldock, the then President of the Commission, *Lawless*, B.1 (1961), p. 360.

At all events the Commission is not a party to the proceedings before the Court on the same footing as a Contracting State may be. This is also reflected, for instance, in Rule 1 of the Rules of Court, in which the term 'Parties' is defined as 'those Contracting Parties which are the Applicant and Respondent Parties', and in the fact that a State brings a case before the Court by means of an application, while the Commission may do so by filing a request (Rule 32 of the Rules of Court).

The Commission will play its role in a more or less active way depending on whether two States confront each other in the proceedings or States are involved as respondent parties only. In the first case there are two equivalent parties in the proceedings; these proceedings are therefore completely adversary. The Delegates of the Commission may keep somewhat in the background. If, however, the case is referred to the Court by the Commission or the respondent State and no other State presents itself afterwards as a party, an element is lacking for fully adversary proceedings, *viz.* a real applicant party, and the Commission will have to play a more pronounced role in order to restore the balance to some extent.[125] In the following the last-mentioned situation will be taken as a point of departure, because it occurs most frequently in practice. If the case is referred to the Court by the original applicant under Protocol No. 9, the proceedings do have an adversary character but the fact that one of the parties is a State and the other one an individual may have some effect on the role played by the Commission.

Rule 63 of the Rules of Procedure of the Commission provides that the Commission 'shall assist the European Court of Human Rights in any case brought before the Court'. In addition, the provision that the Commission shall communicate to the Court, at its request, any memorials, evidence, documents or information concerning the case, with the exception of documents relating to the attempts to secure a friendly settlement, shows that the Commission is expected to assist the Court as much as possible (Rule 67 of the Rules of Procedure of the Commission). The Commission is eminently able to provide such assistance. It has been very closely involved in the case during the entire procedure so far, and at a given moment has been faced with the same task as that with which the Court is entrusted, *viz.* to determine whether there has been a violation of the Convention. Despite the difference in character between the task of the Commission in the proceedings before the Court and that in the earlier stage of the procedure, there is also an important element of continuity in it. The then President of the Commission declared in the *Lawless* Case:

> Our sole task remains that of ensuring the observance of the engagements of the High Contracting Parties undertaken in the Convention, which is also the task of the Court. Our function before the Court – as we see it – is therefore objectively to present to the Court the issues in the case, and all the relevant information which we, ourselves, have obtained concerning the case, and to assist the Court in its examination of the case.[126]

---

[125] On this, see further *infra* pp. 227-228.
[126] B.1 (1961), p. 267.

From this definition of function it clearly appears that in the exercise of its function the Commission wishes to be objective and impartial. In this respect, too, its functioning in the two stages of the procedure is marked by continuity. In fact, a different attitude would not be possible. If the Commission were to act as a party or as an advocate of one of the parties in the proceedings before the Court, this would seriously impair the confidence in the Commission on the part of Governments as well as individuals, in consequence of which it would not be able to idependently perform its tasks in an earlier stage of the procedure, specifically those under Article 28 of the Convention.[127]

4.3 The Manner in Which the Commission Performs its Function in Proceedings Before the Court

In practice the manner in which the Commission performs its function in proceedings before the Court depends largely on the circumstances of each individual case. The Commission has assured itself a certain latitude in this respect. In his defence of the method chosen by the Commission in the *Lawless* Case, the then President Waldock submitted:

> I do not want to be understood to be laying down any general principle which might fetter or embarrass the Commission in formulating its submission in any other type of case.[128]

In the *Lawless* Case the Commission had made its submissions to the Court in the form of the following request: 'May it please the Court (...) to decide whether or not ...'[129] The Irish Government objected to this and submitted that the Commission ought to have confined itself to asking the Court to confirm the conclusions of its report (which in this case indeed were in favour of Ireland).[130] The Commission, however, relied on Articles 44 and 48 of the Convention, which it held not to imply any limitation with regard to the manner in which it lays its submissions before the Court. In addition the Commission explained that it had reached the conclusions in favour of Ireland by a bare majority, and submitted that

> in a case where the Commission has reached conclusions by a majority of eight votes to six, and where those conclusions are in favour of the Government, the appropriate form of the submission, in our view, is the form found in our Memorial.[131]

The difference of opinion within the Commission on whether or not there had been a violation of the Convention played still another part in the proceedings before the Court. According to the Irish Government the Commission was not authorised to draw the Court's notice to the minority opinions, but ought to have

---

[127] In this sense also Waldock, the then President of the Commission, *ibidem*, p. 234.
[128] *Ibidem*, p. 266.
[129] *Ibidem*, pp. 207-208.
[130] *Ibidem*, pp. 220-221.
[131] *Ibidem*, pp. 265-266.

confined itself to the conclusion of the majority.[132] The Commission defended its action on the ground of the definition of its task under the Convention and submitted 'that we should be abdicating our responsibilities under Article 19 of the Convention if we were to ask the Court to consider only the opinions of the majority.'[133] It then added:

> As defenders of the public interest, we think it is our duty to place before you, with all objectivity and impartiality, all the elements of fact and law which appear to be relevant for you to take into consideration in reaching your decision upon the matters in this case.[134]

This objectivity and impartiality are essential to the role of the Commission before the Court, specifically also in connection with the position of the individual applicant in the proceedings before the Court, to which we now turn.

5 THE POSITION OF THE INDIVIDUAL APPLICANT IN THE PROCEEDINGS BEFORE THE COURT IF THE RESPONDENT STATE HAS NOT RATIFIED PROTOCOL NO. 9

5.1 General

If the respondent State has not ratified Protocol No. 9, an individual applicant cannot personally bring his case before the Court after his complaint has been declared admissible by the Commission and no friendly settlement has been reached.[135] For that he is entirely dependent on the Commission or the respondent State, or, in the rare cases where his complaint is not directed against the State whose national he is, on the latter State. And after his case has been brought before the Court, the original applicant holds no initiative as to the presentation of his viewpoints concerning the case to the Court.

In 1982 the Rules of the Court have been changed in order to improve this unsatisfactory position of the individual as much as possible.[136]

5.2 The Individual has no *Locus Standi*

Article 44 of the Convention provides expressly:

> Only the High Contracting Parties and the Commission shall have the right to bring a case before the Court.

---

[132] *Ibidem*, pp. 341-342.
[133] *Ibidem*, p. 360.
[134] *Idem*.
[135] On this, see *supra* pp. 197-198.
[136] See *infra* p. 229 and p. 235.

This English text of Article 44 has a somewhat less stringent formulation with regard to the role of the individual before the Court than the French version, which reads:

> Seuls les Hautes Parties Contractantes et la Commission ont qualité pour se représenter devant la Cour.

Relying on the French text, the Irish Government in the *Lawless* Case concluded that 'it was clearly intended that the individual would have no control of any kind, nor should he play any active part in the conduct of proceedings before the Court.'[137] The Commission, on the contrary, submitted that it is not possible:

> to attribute to the authors of the Convention an intention to place an impenetrable curtain between the individual and an organ specifically set up as a judicial tribunal to make a judicial determination of his case.[138]

Article 44 furnishes little clarity about the exact position of the original applicant in the proceedings before the Court. It is, however, evident, specifically from the French text, that the individual has no *locus standi*; the *travaux préparatoires*, too, do not leave any doubt about this.[139] The text of Article 44, particularly the English version, does not, however, necessitate the conclusion that the individual cannot act in any way in the proceedings before the Court. And indeed, the Rules of Court contain several provisions pointing in a different direction, especially since their 1982 revision. Rule 30 is even specifically devoted to the representation of the original applicant in the proceedings before the Court while Rule 36 also entitles the original individual applicant to request the Court to bring to the attention of the Contracting State concerned any interim measures which seem advisable. Rule 41 includes the original applicant among the persons who may request the Court to obtain evidence. Under the same provision, he may be heard by the Court as a person capable of providing clarification of the facts of the case. Finally, the original applicant belongs to the category of persons and organs to which according to Rule 55(4) a certified copy of the judgment of the Court is sent and which may request the President of the Court not to make non-published documents accessible to the public (Rule 55(2)).

Besides the arguments inferred from the text of the Convention and of the Rules of Court (in its pre-1982 edition), 'general considerations of equity and justice' induced the Commission to oppose the elimination of the individual from the proceedings before the Court, urged by the Irish Government in the *Lawless* Case.[140] According to the Commission, now that a Government may put forward new facts and arguments before the Court and is free to comment on and criticise the Commission's report, it is difficult to imagine that the original individual applicant should not have the right to inform the Court in one way or another of

---

[137] B.1 (1961), pp. 216-217 and 277.
[138] *Ibidem*, p. 254.
[139] Thus also the Commission in the *Lawless* Case, *ibidem*, p. 257.
[140] *Idem*.

its viewpoint concerning new points of fact or law, or may not give his opinion on the statements and conclusions in the Commission's report:

> The Commission doubts very much whether the authors of the Convention can be understood to have intended to create such a marked degree of inequality in the presentation of two sides of a case to a judicial tribunal.[141]

In its judgment of 14 November 1960 the Court endorsed the view of the Commission. It defined the position of the original applicant as follows:

> Whereas, in the present case, G.R. Lawless, the Applicant, although he is not entitled to bring the case before the Court, to appear before the Court or even to make submissions through a representative appointed by him, is nevertheless directly concerned in the proceedings before the Court; whereas it must be borne in mind that the Applicant instituted the proceedings before the Commission and that, if the Court found that his complaints were justified, he would be directly affected by any decision, in accordance with Article 50 of the Convention, on the substance of the case.[142]

From this description of the position of the original applicant the Court concluded that:

> the Court must bear in mind its duty to safeguard the interests of the individual, who may not be a party to any Court proceedings, and whereas the whole of the proceedings in the Court, as laid down by the Convention and the Rules of the Court, are upon issues which concern the Applicant; whereas, accordingly, it is in the interests of the proper administration of justice that the Court should have knowledge of and, if need be, take into consideration, the Applicant's point of view.[143]

5.3 The Role of the Commission to Assist the Individual in the Proceedings Before the Court

Since the individual cannot appear as a party in the proceedings before the Court and cannot therefore take the initiative to making submissions to the Court personally or through a representative, the question arose as to how the Court could then become informed of the views of the original individual applicant. The Court does know the allegations of the original applicant with regard to the factual and legal aspects of the case as contained in the Commission's report. However, in addition a fair trial of his case requires that the original individual applicant – like the respondent State – has an opportunity to advance new factual or legal arguments before the Court and/or to make his comments on or criticism of the Commission's report known to the Court. Of course, the Court may hear the original applicant as a witness or as an expert under Rule 41 (Rule 38 old) of its Rules, but as a witness or as an expert one is not of course in a position in which one can express and elucidate one's views with regard to all the aspects of the case.

---

[141] *Idem.*

[142] Judgment of 14 November 1960, *Lawless*, A.1, p. 14.

[143] *Ibidem*, p. 15.

The Commission, through its position in the proceedings before the Court, has tried to fill as effectively as possible the 'gap' which arose in consequence of the absence of the original applicant as a party to the proceedings. Because of its conception of its role as 'defender of the public interest', in view of which it considers that it must put forward all the relevant elements of the case,[144] it has made all efforts to do full justice also to the views of the original applicant before the Court. To this end the Commission included in its Rules of Procedure the following provision:

> When a case brought before the Commission in pursuance of Article 25 of the Convention is subsequently referred to the Court, the Secretary of the Commission shall immediately notify the Applicant. Unless the Commission shall otherwise decide, the Secretary shall also in due course communicate to him the Commission's Report, informing him that he may, within a time-limit fixed by the President, submit to the Commission his written observations on the said Report. The Commission shall decide what action, if any, shall be taken in respect of these observations.

This Rule 76 (old)[145] was applied by the Commission for the first time in the *Lawless* Case. The Commission had sent its report to the original applicant and the latter had submitted his observations to the Commission. Thereupon the Commission requested the Court's permission 'to submit to the Court the Applicant's comments on the Commission's report as one of the Commission's documents in the case'.[146] The Irish Government disputed the lawfulness of the Commission's action. In the first place it inferred from Article 31(2) of the Convention that the report of the Commission should in principle remain secret. According to the Irish Government it may be transmitted only to the Committee of Ministers, to the States concerned – which must not publish it – and, if the case is referred to the Court, also to the Court. Publication is possible only after a decision to that effect of the Committee or of the Court. In the opinion of the Irish Government the Commission therefore ought not to have sent the report to Lawless.[147] Furthermore the Irish Government submitted that in the proceedings before the Court the initiative for collecting new information is not to be taken by the Commission, but by the Court itself.[148] In particular it argued that an impartial organ such as the Commission cannot permit itself to receive the observations on its report from a party concerned in the case without impairing the confidence to be placed in it. The Irish Government raised the following question in that connection:

> How can that attitude of impartiality be maintained, particularly in the public mind, if there is any nexus between the Commission's own findings and the views or comments of the individual Applicant?[149]

---

[144] See *supra* p. 226.
[145] This became later Article 61, and has, for unclear reasons, been taken out of the present Rules.
[146] Judgment of 14 November 1960, A.1, p. 8.
[147] B.1 (1961), pp. 214-216.
[148] *Ibidem*, p. 284.
[149] *Ibidem*, pp. 289-290.

From the submissions of the Commission and the preliminary objections raised by the Irish Government the Court deduced three questions about which a decision had to be taken. In the first place there was the question of whether Rule 76 of the Rules of Procedure of the Commission was generally compatible with the Convention. The Court held that it could not interpret the Convention in an abstract way.[150] It referred for that position to Articles 45, 47 and 53 of the Convention. Because of this, it did not consider itself competent to decide about the validity of a provision from the Rules of Procedure of the Commission and came to the conclusion that it could not answer a question in so general a sense.

The situation was different for the second question, *viz.* whether the Commission had been permitted to send its report to Lawless or had acted contrary to the Convention in doing so. The Court first of all pointed out the public character of its proceedings in contrast with those before the Commission and the Committee of Ministers, which take place *in camera*. The Court admitted that only the reports of the sessions and the judgments are published, and the publication of other documents requires the express consent of the Court. It was, however, necessary, in the opinion of the Court, to distinguish between the publication of documents for which the consent of the Court is required, and the transmission of such documents to the individual applicant after the case has been referred to the Court, for which such consent is not required. As regards the latter aspect, in view of the importance of the proceedings before the Court for the original individual applicant, the Court concluded:

> that the Commission is enabled under the Convention to communicate to the Applicant, with the proviso that it must not be published, the whole or part of its Report or a summary thereof, whenever such communication seems appropriate; whereas, therefore, in the present case, the Commission, in communicating its Report to G.R. Lawless, the Applicant, did not exceed its powers.[151]

In addition to its own report, the Commission had also transmitted the observations of the Irish Government to the individual applicant.[152] The Irish Government had objected to this too.[153] In its judgment of 7 April 1961 the Court indicated, be it in a rather implicit way, that it also did not consider these acts to be contrary to the Convention. It referred to its judgment of 14 November 1960, in which the Commission's right had been recognised 'to take into account the Applicant's view on its own authority, as a proper way of enlightening the Court'. The Court now further explained this and held that:

> this latitude enjoyed by the Commission extends to any other views the Commission may have obtained from the Applicant in the course of the proceedings before the Court.[154]

---

[150] At that moment Protocol No. 2 was not yet in force.
[151] Judgment of 14 November 1960, *Lawless*, A.1, p. 14.
[152] B.1 (1961), pp. 348-351.
[153] *Ibidem*, pp. 353-354.
[154] Judgment of 7 April 1961, A.2, pp. 23-24.

The third question concerned the request of the Commission for permission to submit the observations of the original applicant concerning its report to the Court. The Court replied that it was unable to decide on that request, since it had not yet been able to examine the merits. It therefore reserved to itself the right to do so in a later stage.[155] It actually did so in its judgment of 7 April 1961, when it decided that:

at the present stage the written observations of the Applicant, as reproduced in paragraphs 31 to 49 of the Commission's statement of 16th December 1960, are not to be considered as part of the proceedings in the case.

It added, however:

that the Commission has all latitude in the course of debates and in so far as it believes they may be useful to enlighten the Court, to take into account the views of the Applicant concerning either the Report or any other specific point which may have arisen since the lodging of the Report.[156]

The Commission therefore acts under its own responsibility when it notifies the Court of the views of the individual applicant.

Originally, this responsibility also covered the question of whether a case could be struck off the list because some sort of settlement had been reached. In relation to that question the Court used to take note of the view of the original applicant *via* the Commission. Problems could present themselves in such a case because the Commission, on the one hand, had to defend the public interest and, on the other hand, did not want to lose sight of the interests of the original applicant and wanted to do justice to his view in the matter.[157] In the revised Rules of Court Rule 49 provides that the Court, before deciding whether to strike a case off its list, consults the original applicant directly.

Another method which the Commission has used to do justice to the views of the original applicant in the proceedings before the Court consists in inviting him to appoint a person who may be present during the proceedings before the Court. This person should then put himself at the disposal of the Delegate of the Commission in order to assist him at his request. This method is based on Rule 29(1) of the Rules of Court and was also advocated for the first time by the Commission in the *Lawless* Case.[158]

Here again the discussion between the Irish Government and the Commission focused on the question of whether, when acting in this way, the Commission could still be called impartial and objective. The Irish Government argued that:

---

[155] Judgment of 14 November 1960, A.1, p. 16.
[156] Judgment of 7 April 1961, A.2, p. 24.
[157] An illustrative example is the action of the Commission in the *De Becker* Case, B.2 (1962), pp. 212-216 and 270-280.
[158] B.1 (1961), p. 350.

If the Commission should choose counsel for the individual Applicant as one of their advisers to assist them in taking part in the deliberations of the Court, they would, in the view of the Government, cease to command the respect that an impartial body such as the Commission would be regarded as entitled to command.[159]

The Commission on the other hand took the view that it was precisely its impartiality and objectivity, and the interest of the administration of justice which demanded its action. Its then President declared that:

we feel we should be failing in our duty if, when we think there are elements which it is useful for the Court objectively to take into consideration in arriving at its judicial determination, we do not take the appropriate initiative.[160]

On this point, too, the Court followed the Commission and found that:

the Commission is entirely free to decide by what means it wishes to establish contact with the Applicant and give him an opportunity to make known his views to the Commission; whereas in particular it is free to ask the Applicant to nominate a person to be available to the Commission's delegates; whereas it does not follow that the person in question had any *locus standi in judicio*.[161]

In the '*Vagrancy*' Cases the Court further developed its viewpoint. In that case the Commission intimated its intention to be assisted by the lawyer of the original individual applicants, in the sense that it wished this lawyer to give the Court a more detailed explanation of a number of points about which the Commission itself was insufficiently informed. The Belgian Government opposed the Commission's application of Rule 29(1) of the Rules of Court in this way, arguing that Article 44 and the spirit of the Convention, which entail that individuals cannot appear before the Court, would thus be nullified. The Court, however, considered the intention of the Commission admissible:

Rule 29, paragraph 1, does not place any limit on the freedom of the Delegates in their choice of persons to assist them; and whereas, therefore, it does not preclude them, *inter alia*, from having assistance of the lawyer or former lawyer of an individual applicant.

It added, however, that:

the person assisting the Delegates must restrict himself in his statements to presenting to the Court explanation on points indicated to him by the Delegates, and this always subject to the control and responsibility of the Delegates. Whereas it is the duty of the Delegates to ensure the observance of this fundamental requirement by any person assisting them, in order to avoid any situation inconsistent with Article 44 of the Convention.[162]

In the *Golder* Case and the *National Union of Belgian Police* Case, too, the lawyer of the original individual applicants appeared as assistant of the

---

[159] *Ibidem*, p. 370.
[160] *Ibidem*, pp. 365-366.
[161] Judgment of 7 April 1961, A.2, p. 24.
[162] Judgment of 18 November 1970, A.12, pp. 6-8.

Commission before the Court in the manner described above.[163] In the meantime this method has become constant practice. In the *Schmidt and Dahlström* Case Professor Schmidt himself, one of the two original applicants, elucidated as an expert some aspects of Swedish labour law before the Court at the invitation of the Commission.[164]

As stated above, the Rules of Court as revised in 1982 contain a separate Rule 30 regulating the representation of the original applicant. Under this Rule the original applicant is in the position to present his own case or have it presented by his representative independently from the Commission. This independent position of the original applicant in the proceedings before the Court has been elaborated in Rule 37 (written procedure), Rules 38 and 39 (oral proceedings) and Rule 41 (measures for taking evidence).

From the above it appears that the main disadvantages attached to the original system of the European Convention – *i. e.* before (and until) the entry into force of Protocol No. 9 –, according to which system the individual applicant is not a party to the proceedings before the Court, have been eliminated in practice. This does not mean that the individual has fully assumed in those proceedings the place to which in our opinion he is entitled, considering the subject and the purpose of the Convention. In order for this to be achieved, the Convention itself had to be amended on this point. This was ultimately achieved by Protocol No. 9.

6 PROTOCOL NO. 9 TO THE CONVENTION: THE RIGHT OF AN INDIVIDUAL TO REFER A CASE TO THE COURT

6.1 Introduction

Although Protocol No. 9, which entered into force in 1994,[165] will cease to exist once Protocol No. 11 has entered into force, it deserves separate discussion.

As was stated above the idea of empowering individuals to seize the European Court of Human Rights is not a new one. It was put forward as early as May 1948, at the Congress of Europe, and appeared in the draft European Convention on Human Rights drawn up by the European Movement in July 1949. This idea was, however, rejected in the course of the Member States' discussions on the draft Convention, it being argued in particular that:

---

[163] *Golder*, B.16 (1975), p. 233; and *National Union of Belgian Police*, B.17 (1973-1975), pp. 157-159 and 176-184.
[164] See B.19 (1977), pp. 122 and 126-136.
[165] See *supra* p. 166.

the interests of the individual would always be defended either by the Commission, in cases where the latter decided to seek a decision of the Court, or by a State in such cases as those listed under paragraphs (b) and (c) of Article 48.[166]

The discussion was revived in the context of the examination of Assembly Recommendation 683 (1972) on a short and medium-term programme for the Council of Europe in the field of human rights. The question was also raised in the Colombo Commission's report to the Council of Europe (June 1986), recommending the 'recognition of the right of the individual to refer to the Court applications declared admissible.'[167] Finally, the third medium-term plan (1987-1991), adopted by the Committee of Ministers on 20 November 1986, listed 'the right of the individual to seize the Court of admissible cases' among those reforms which should be studied in the context of improving and adapting existing procedures under the European Convention on Human Rights. The final text of the draft Protocol was adopted by the Committee of Ministers at the 446th meeting of the Ministers' Deputies held from 22 to 23 October 1990. The text was opened for signature by Member States of the Council of Europe signatories to the European Convention on 6 November 1990, at the Committee of Ministers 87th Session held in Rome, and in conjunction with the celebration of the 40th anniversary of the signature of the Convention.

The reform brought about by Protocol No. 9 is a logical development of the Convention's system of supervision. A most significant step had already been taken, through Article 25 of the Convention, in allowing individuals who claim to be victims of human rights violations, to submit their complaints against the State concerned to an international supervisory mechanism. Secondly, through its Rules, the Court has in actual fact accorded a form of *locus standi* to the original applicant once his case has been referred to the Court. However, as has been stated above, although the new Rules of Court (adopted in 1982 and subsequently revised in 1993) have very significantly improved the procedural position of the original applicant, they have left some disparities in treatment between them and the States. To enable the individual himself to decide to take his case to the Court – rather than letting him remain dependent on the Commission or a State for this purpose – strengthens the system of legal protection.

---

[166] See report of the Committee of Experts to the Committee of Ministers, Council of Europe, *Collected Edition of the 'Travaux Préparatoires' of the European Convention on Human Rights*, Vol. IV, The Hague, 1977, p. 44.

[167] The Colombo Commission (Commission of eminent European personalities) was set up in accordance with Parliamentary Assembly Recommendation 994 (1984), with terms of reference to work out future perspectives for European cooperation beyond the present decade.

6.2 The Reform of the Supervisory System

It should be noted that once all States Parties to the Convention have consented to be bound by the Protocol, the amendments provided for in Protocol No. 9 will automatically become an integral part of the Convention.

Article 2 amends Article 31(2) of the Convention so as to provide that the Commission's report is also transmitted to the individual applicant. The latter must respect the confidentiality of the Commission's report. The term 'applicant' refers to the person, non-governmental organisation or group of individuals who has brought the complaint under Article 25. The Articles 3 and 4 of Protocol No. 9 deal with the amendments to Articles 44 and 45. Article 5 amends Article 48 of the Convention with a view to including the individual applicant among those empowered to bring a case before the Court. It is not explicitly stated that the individual only has the right to refer cases to the Court which have been declared admissible. However, this follows from the provisions of Article 47. The individual has an unrestricted right to refer his case to the Court (paragraph 1(e)), but a screening panel of the Court decides whether or not his case should be considered by the Court (paragraph 2).

According to the explanatory report to Protocol No. 9 it is clear that there is no point in bringing the panel system into play if the case is also referred to the Court by the Commission or the State concerned. Moreover, it would be inappropriate for the panel to reach a decision before it is known whether the Commission or the State wishes to refer the case to the Court. Consequently, the three-month period provided for in Article 32(1), must have expired before a panel is seized of the matter. This is expressed by the use of the word 'only' in the first sentence of paragraph 2 of Article 48 as amended. The Committee of Ministers must, of course, still be able to deal with the case in the event of the panel deciding that the case should not be considered by the Court. The difficulty here resides in the fact that under Article 32(1), the Committee of Ministers loses its potential competence *vis-à-vis* a case once it is 'referred' to the Court. The last sentence of the second subparagraph of paragraph 2 of Article 48 as amended is designed to solve this problem by expressly 're-opening' the way for the Committee of Ministers. Given the above-mentioned interplay between Article 32(1), and Article 48, the authors of the Protocol considered it preferable, in the interests of clarity, to use the expression 'referred to' rather than 'brought before' the Court throughout the text of Article 48.[168]

The panel is composed of three members of the Court, in which the 'national' judge of the respondent State is an *ex officio* member of the panel. If the case referred to the Court concerns a complaint lodged against more than one Contracting Party, the size of the panel will be increased accordingly.

---

[168] Council of Europe, *Explanatory Report to Protocol No. 9 to the Convention for the Protection of Human Rights and Fundamental Freedoms*, Treaties and Reports, p. 10.

The panel's task is to decide whether the case is to be considered by the Court. The wording of Article 48(2)(2) as amended, implies that two conditions must be fulfilled for the decision to be made that a case will not be considered by the Court: the case must not raise a serious question affecting the interpretation or application of the Convention and, in addition, must not warrant consideration by the Court for any other reason. According to the explanatory report to Protocol No. 9 cases could be regarded as not giving rise to a serious question affecting the interpretation or the application of the Convention, *inter alia,* if there is established case-law of the Court with respect to the alleged violation. A decision not to have the case considered by the Court can also be taken where the dispute relates mainly to the facts of the case. There may still be other reasons for not allowing a case to be considered by the Court. In the course of its deliberations the panel could take into account, *inter alia,* the following: the fact that the State concerned has indicated that it accepts the conclusions reached by the Commission in its report or the fact that the question of just satisfaction may be solved by a Resolution of the Committee of Ministers.[169] The latter will be the case if the Commission has adopted the opinion that the Convention has been violated. Indeed, if the panel decides that a case will not be examined by the Court, the Committee of Ministers will decide whether there has been a violation of the Convention (Article 32) and will as a rule follow the opinion of the Commission. Therefore, if the main interest of the applicant lies in pecuniary and/or non-pecuniary compensation, that interest may well be served by the Committee of Ministers deciding the case. A decision of the panel to decline consideration of a case by the Court requires a unanimous vote. This decision does not prejudge the consideration of the merits of the case by the Committee of Ministers.

During the drafting of the Protocol the question arose whether the panel is to rely exclusively on the Commission's report or instead is empowered to take into account and even seek observations from the original applicant. If the latter were the case, the State concerned would need to be given an opportunity to comment upon such observations. This issue was left to be dealt with in the Court's Rules. The present Rules of the Court 'B' do not contain any provision in that respect. Rule 26 only deals with the composition of the panel, not with its procedure. In its deliberations the panel may be expected in general to restrict itself to the report of the Commission and the arguments advanced by the applicant in his application in conformity with Rule 34(1)(a).

If the panel has not reached the unanimous conclusion that the case is not to be considered by the Court, it will be added to the list of cases. The original applicant is placed on an equal footing with the State concerned in the procedure before the Court. The Court has accordingly amended its Rules.[170] On the other hand, granting the individual the right to seize the Court should not be taken as implying that he has an absolute right to be present in person at the Court's

---

[169] *Ibidem*, p. 11.
[170] See Rule 39-44 of the Rules of Court 'B'.

hearing. Under the present procedure, applicants who, for example, are in prison cannot insist on attending the Court when their case is considered, and this may remain the position when the individual is granted the right to seize the Court. Representation of the applicant must, of course, be ensured.[171]

Granting the individual the right to seize the Court does not involve any change in the role of the Commission in the Court's proceedings as it results from the present Rules of Court. Finally, no provision has been included concerning the application of Protocol No. 9 to cases which, at the time of its entry into force, are already pending before the organs of the Convention. According to the explanatory report, the Protocol should apply to such cases on condition that the three-month period laid down in Article 32 of the Convention has not already begun.[172]

Although Protocol No. 9 brings about an important improvement of the position of the individual in relation to the Court, it still does not offer the individual full equality in comparison with the State Parties. The latter have always the possibility to have their case, if declared admissible by the Commission, considered by the Court, while the individual has to pass the screening procedure by the panel of three.

7 THE AWARD OF COMPENSATION UNDER ARTICLE 50 OF THE CONVENTION

7.1 General

When the Court finds that a violation of the Convention by a Contracting State has taken place, under Article 50 it may afford just satisfaction to the injured party, provided that the consequences of the violation cannot be fully repaired according to the internal law of the State concerned.

The initiative for having the claim for just satisfaction determined lies with the original applicant as the injured person. Originally he had to address the Commission for this (or the Government of his national State, should it decide to refer his case to the Court), which then could present a proposal concerning just satisfaction to the Court in the document instituting proceedings or at any stage of the written or oral proceedings (Rule 47*bis* of the Rules of Court before the 1982 revision). However, since the 1982 revision of the Rules of Court, which introduced for the original applicant the possibility of making written and oral statements in the proceedings before the Court, he may submit such a proposal himself. Until the 1989 revision he could do so 'at any stage of the written or oral procedure' (Rule 49 (old) of the Rules of Court). The revised first paragraph of Rule 50 (Rule 52 of the Rules of Court 'B') provides:

---

[171] See also, in this connection, the European Agreement relating to persons participating in proceedings of the European Commission and Court of Human Rights (1969).
[172] See *supra* note 168, p. 13.

> Any claims which the applicant may wish to make under Article 50 of the Convention shall, unless the President otherwise directs, be set out in his memorial or, if he does not submit a memorial, in a special document filed at least one month before the date fixed pursuant to Rule 38 for the hearing.

The revised second sentence of the first paragraph of Rule 54 provides as follows:

> If, on the other hand, this question has not been raised under Rule 50, the Chamber may lay down a time-limit for the applicant to submit any claim for just satisfaction that he may have.

Rule 56(1) of the Rules of Court 'B' contains a comparable provision.

This revision makes it clear that in cases brought before the Court after 1 April 1989 it is up to the original applicant to bring a claim for just satisfaction, and no longer to the Commission or the State which has referred the case to the Court. This seems also to imply that in inter-State applications no claim under Article 50 may be brought, since 'applicant' in the Rules of Court refers to the applicant under Article 25 only (Rule 1(k) of the Rules of Court). This does not, however, exclude the possibility that a State which acts under Article 48(b) of the Convention, requests compensation on behalf of the individual.

If a decision on the application of Article 50 is not taken in the judgment on the merits of the case, the Chamber reserves it in whole or in part and fixes the further procedure (Rule 54(1) of the Rules of Court). In that case, and also in the case that the claim by the applicant is brought after the judgment on the merits, the Chamber which rules on the application of Article 50 shall, as far as possible, be composed of those judges who sat to consider the merits of the case, even if one or more of them have ceased to be members of the Court (Rule 54(2) of the Rules of Court). This would seem appropriate from the viewpoint of procedural economy. These judges are best informed of the different aspects of the case, and for that reason most competent to determine the amount of compensation to be awarded, if any.[173]

The same idea – *viz.* that the decision on compensation should be taken in close connection with the decision on the merits – was brought up explicitly in the *Ringeisen* Case. The Austrian Government submitted that the Court could consider an application for compensation only after it had been filed in the form of a new complaint under Article 25, subsequently examined by the Commission and finally submitted to the Court in accordance with Articles 47 and 48. For this, the Austrian Government also referred to Article 52 of the Convention, which provides that 'the judgment of the Court shall be final'. The Court held that the only purpose of Article 52 is 'to make the Court's judgment not subject to any appeal to another authority'[174] and found that 'in the interests of the proper

---

[173] Not fully in conformity with this rationale Rule 54(3) of the Rules of Court provides that the plenary Court or the Grand Chamber may refer a case concerning Art. 50 to the Chamber which in the first instance had renounced jurisdiction in favour of the plenary Court or Grand Chamber.

[174] Judgment of 22 June 1972, A.15, p. 7.

administration of justice' it is preferable 'that consideration of the reparation of damage following from a violation of the Convention should be entrusted to the judicial body which has found the violation in question'.[175]

Until recently, the Court did not set any time-limit within which the Government had to pay the individual the reimbursement of costs and expenses incurred and/or the just satisfaction afforded. Nowadays the Court specifies in its judgment the period, usually three months, within which the specified sum must have been paid to the individual.[176] It is subsequently up to the Committee of Ministers under Article 54 to determine if the specified sum has been paid within the time-limit set by the Court.

7.2 An Application for Compensation is not an Independent Procedure

From the *Ringeisen* judgment referred to above, and also from the other case-law of the Court on this matter, it becomes quite clear that an application for compensation on the basis of Article 50 is not considered as an independent procedure, but is dealt with as an element of a larger whole, of which the examination of the merits forms the first part. In the '*Vagrancy*' Cases the Court stated that the application for compensation is closely linked to the proceedings concerning the merits before the Court, and cannot therefore be regarded as a new complaint, to which Articles 25, 26 and 27 of the Convention apply. For that reason the original individual applicant did not need to exhaust once more the local remedies with respect to his application for compensation.[177] In the *Barberà, Messegué and Jarbardo* Case the Court noted that there existed under Spanish law a remedy making it possible to obtain compensation in the event of the malfunctioning of the system of justice. However, referring to the aforementioned '*Vagrancy*' Cases it did not consider itself bound to stay the proceedings relating to the applicants' claims. In this respect the Court held that:

> If, after having exhausted domestic remedies without success before complaining in Strasbourg of a violation of their rights, then doing so a second time, successfully, to secure the setting aside of the convictions, and finally going through a new trial, the applicants were required to exhaust domestic remedies a third time in order to be able to obtain just satisfaction from the Court, the total duration of the proceedings would be hardly consistent with the effective protection of human rights and would lead to a situation incompatible with the aim and object of the Convention.[178]

---

[175] *Idem.*

[176] See, *e.g.*, the judgment of 28 August 1991, *Moreira De Azevedo*, A.208-C, p. 30; judgment of 21 September 1993, *Kremzow*, A.268-B, p. 49; judgment of 27 October 1993, *Dombo Beheer B.V.*, A.274, p. 21.

[177] Judgment of 10 March 1972, A.14, pp. 7-9. See also the judgment of 6 November 1980, *Guzzardi*, A.39, p. 41; judgment of 18 December 1986, *Bozano*, A.111, pp. 28-29; judgment of 13 June 1994, *Barberà, Messegué and Jabardo*, A.285-C, p. 57.

[178] Judgment of 13 June 1994, A.285-C, p. 57.

In the *Neumeister* Case the Austrian Government argued that the Commission had committed an error by transmitting Neumeister's application for compensation directly to the Court, whereas it ought to have considered and examined it as a new complaint under Article 25. This complaint was assumed to concern the alleged violation of Article 5(5) of the Convention, in which it is provided that 'Everyone who has been the victim of arrest or detention in contravention of the provisions of this Article shall have an enforceable right to compensation'. The principal argument of the Court against this line of reasoning was as follows:

> the proceedings in the present case no longer fall within Section III of the Convention but are the final phase of proceedings brought before the Court under Section IV on the conclusion of those to which the original petition of Neumeister gave rise in 1963 before the Commission.[179]

7.3 If the Court Finds that the Question of Article 50 is not Ready for Decision it may Reserve the Question and Fix the Ensuing Procedure

Article 50 appears to imply that the decision on an award of compensation must be given together with the judgment on the merits. Rule 54 of the Rules of Court, however, leaves the moment of the decision on an award of compensation entirely open. If the Chamber of the Court which deals with the case finds that there is a violation of the Convention, the Chamber gives a decision on the application of Article 50 in the same judgment only if the question, after being raised under Rule 50, is ready for decision. As an example, reference could be made to the judgment in the *Golder* Case, in which the Court, after having found that there had been a violation of Article 6(1) and Article 8, decided unanimously 'that the preceding findings amount in themselves to adequate just compensation under Article 50'.[180] Decisions concerning Article 50 which were made simultaneously with the judgment on the merits are to be found also, *e.g.*, in the *De Weer* Case,[181] the *Artico* Case,[182] the *Schönenberger and Durmaz* Case,[183] the *Berrehab* Case[184] and the *Karakaya* Case.[185]

As has been said above, if the question of compensation has been raised, but is not yet ready for decision, the Chamber reserves it in whole or in part and fixes the ensuing procedure. If the question of the compensation has not been raised, the Chamber lays down a time-limit within which this may be done by the original applicant (Rule 54(1) of the Rules of Court).[186] Owing to this very flexible arrangement the possibilities for raising the question of compensation have been

---

[179] Judgment of 7 May 1974, A.17, p. 14.
[180] Judgment of 21 February 1975, A.18, p. 23.
[181] Judgment of 27 February 1980, A.35, pp. 31-32.
[182] Judgment of 13 May 1980, A.37, pp. 19-22.
[183] Judgment of 20 June 1988, A.137, pp. 14-16.
[184] Judgment of 21 June 1988, A.138, p. 17.
[185] Judgment of 26 August 1994, A.289-B.
[186] See, for example, the judgment of 28 June 1978, *König*, A.27, pp. 40-41.

left as wide as possible. At the same time the interests of the respondent States are served in this way because, as the Court itself formulated it:

> they may be reluctant to argue the consequences of a violation the existence of which they dispute, and they may wish, in the event of a finding of a violation, to maintain the possibility of settling the issue of reparation directly with the injured party without the Court being further concerned.[187]

Even if an agreement is reached between the injured party and the State found to be liable of a violation, the Court is still involved in the matter. In fact, according to Rule 54(4) of its Rules the Court shall verify the equitable nature of such agreement and, when it finds the agreement to be equitable, strike the case off the list by means of a judgment. Such a supervision of the equitable nature of the agreement on compensation was exercised by the Court in, *e.g.*, the *Luedicke, Belkacem and Koç* Case,[188] the *Airey* Case,[189] the *Malone* Case[190] and the *Kostovski* Case.[191]

In the *Winterwerp* Case the judgment under Article 50 consisted in the unanimous decision of the Court to strike the case off the list. The reason for this was that meanwhile an arrangement had been made between the Netherlands Government and Winterwerp, which agreement was judged for its equitable nature by the Court. This arrangement in part even went beyond that originally suggested by Winterwerp's counsel. The principal elements of the arrangement were as follows:

> (1) The State shall promote that Mr. Winterwerp be placed as soon as possible in a hostel. The State Psychiatric Establishment at Eindhoven is and will remain prepared to give Mr. Winterwerp medical treatment whenever this might be necessary; (2) The State shall transfer a lump sum of ƒ 10,000 (ten thousand guilders) to Mr. Winterwerp's new guardian to be used for the resocialisation of Mr. Winterwerp.[192]

Sometimes the agreement concerns only a part of the claim of the applicant and the Court has to decide about the rest of the claim. Thus in the *Barthold* Case the settlement only concerned the claims for fees and expenses and for loss of earnings.[193] The Court took note of this agreement and considered it appropriate to strike the case off the list as far as those claims were concerned.

In a number of cases the applicants complained that as a consequence of the length of domestic proceedings they were deprived of the enjoyment of their property, thereby relying on Article 1 of Protocol No. 1. Since the Court already

---

[187] Judgment of 22 June 1972, *Ringeisen*, A.15, p. 7.
[188] Judgment of 10 March 1980, A.36, p. 7.
[189] Judgment of 6 February 1981, A.41, p. 8.
[190] Judgment of 26 April 1985, A.95, p. 4. See also the judgments of 29 September 1987, *Erkner and Hofauer* and *Poiss*, A.124, pp. 35 and 41; and the judgment of 27 June 1988, *Bouamar*, A.136, p. 48.
[191] Judgment of 29 March 1990, A.170-B, p. 30.
[192] Judgment of 27 November 1981, A.47, p. 6.
[193] Judgment of 31 January 1986, A.98, p. 7. See also the judgments of 9 June 1988, *O, H, W and R v. the United Kingdom*, A.136, pp. 7, 15, 23 and 40.

found a violation of Article 6(1), it did not find it necessary to examine the complaint based on Article 1 of Protocol No. 1. Nevertheless, in the *Brigandi* Case, where the applicant had sought compensation for loss of enjoyment, the Court found that the measures already taken by the national courts – which included compensation for loss of enjoyment – had not made full reparation for the consequences of the breach found and therefore awarded the applicant a specified sum on an equitable basis.[194] In the *Zanghì* Case, the applicant had only claimed compensation in respect of damage resulting from the alleged violation of Article 1 of Protocol No. 1. In its judgment of the same day as that in the *Brigandi* Case and concerning the same respondent State and in connection with the same type of violation, the Court observed that it was still possible that the national courts before which the applicant's action remained pending, might make reparation for the final consequences of the failure to try the case within a reasonable time. Therefore, as the matters stood, it dismissed the applicant's claim for compensation of damage.[195] After having obtained a final domestic decision, Mr Zanghì again requested compensation for the financial consequences of the failure to try the case within a reasonable time. The Court decided to re-enter the case on its list. This means that the dismissal of the claim for just satisfaction 'as the matter stood' in the Court's earlier judgment was only provisional. It also means, by implication, that the applicant was not estopped, because he relied the first time, in support of his claim, on Article 1 of Protocol No. 1 and not on Article 6 of the Convention. The Court found, however, that, as it held it unnecessary to rule on the complaint based on Article 1 of Protocol No. 1, the financial consequences of an infringement of the applicant's right to the peaceful enjoyment of his possessions could not be taken into consideration. As to the consequences of the breach of Article 6(1) of the Convention which was found by the Court on 19 February 1991, it noted at the time, even though no claim for just satisfaction had been made under that head, that it was still possible that the national courts might make reparation for them. The final domestic decision, in the opinion of the Court, was not of such a nature as to call for a reconsideration of the decision delivered on 19 February 1991.[196] Thus for the second time, and this time finally, the applicant's claim for compensation was dismissed. In its final judgment, the Court did not make clear, in which way and to what extent the final domestic decision compensated the applicant in respect of the alleged violation of Article 6, nor did it indicate how its final judgment in the *Zanghì* Case was to be reconciled with that in the *Birgandi* Case.

---

[194] Judgment of 19 February 1991, A.194-B, p. 32.
[195] Judgment of 19 February 1991, A.194-C, p. 48.
[196] Judgment of 10 February 1993, A.257-A, p. 8.

7.4 The Question of *Restitutio in Integrum*

As to the merits of the procedure for compensation under Article 50, it is especially the passage 'if the internal law of the said Party allows only partial reparation to be made for the consequences of this decision or measure' which has caused problems.

In the '*Vagrancy*' Cases the Belgian Government submitted that the application for compensation was ill-founded, because under Belgian law compensation could be obtained from the State for damage caused by an unlawful situation for which the State was responsible under national or international law. Those who claimed compensation before the Court therefore ought to have applied first to the national court.[197] The Court held that the treaties from which the text of Article 50 has been derived, undoubtedly related in particular to cases the consequences of which, considering the nature of the damage, could be eliminated altogether, but in which under the internal law of the State concerned this was impossible. However, according to the Court, this does not alter the fact that Article 50 is also applicable to cases in which such a *restitutio in integrum* is not possible precisely on account of the nature of the damage concerned. The Court added the following: 'indeed, common sense suggests that this must be so *a fortiori*'.[198] The Court distinguishes here between those cases in which *restitutio in integrum* is possible and those in which it is not, and considers it has jurisdiction in both cases; in the first case, however, only when such *restitutio in integrum* is not possible under national law. Thus, in the '*Vagrancy*' Cases, which according to the Court belonged to the second category, the Court declared that it had jurisdiction to award compensation. It held, however, that the applicants' claims for damages were not well-founded. Although in this case the decision not to grant compensation was taken unanimously, there were considerable differences of opinion within the Court on the argument described above.

In their joint separate opinion the judges Holmback, Ross and Wold put forward that the argument followed by the Court was 'unsound' and 'completely alien to the text of Article 50' for those cases in which *restitutio in integrum* was impossible.[199] In the first place they submitted with regard to the Court's argument:

> It presupposes that there is an absolute obligation on the State to restore to the applicants the liberty of which they have been deprived. But this cannot be so because of the maxim *impossibilium nulla est obligatio*.[200]

It is, however, more important in this context that they opined that in the two cases distinguished by the Court the jurisdiction of the Court should depend on the

---

[197] Judgment of 10 March 1972, A.14, p. 9.

[198] *Ibidem*, pp. 9-10.

[199] *Ibidem*, p. 14.

[200] *Idem*.

fact that 'the internal law does not allow full reparation'.[201] On the ground of Articles 5(5), 13, 53 and 54 they were of the opinion that the general rule underlying the Convention is that 'a party claiming to be injured must seek redress before national courts and not before the European Court of Human Rights'. The only exception to this is the jurisdiction conferred on the Court by Article 50 to award compensation in case the internal law in question does not make full reparation possible.[202] In their view the Court's conception led 'to the Court in fact assuming jurisdiction in respect to claims for reparation in all cases where *restitutio* is impossible, regardless of the state of internal law.'[203] The conclusion here drawn by the said judges from the Court's argument, in our opinion, goes too far, at least in the general formulation used. In its judgment in the '*Vagrancy*' Cases as well as in the subsequent *Ringeisen* Case the Court did take into account the fact that the Belgian and the Austrian Government respectively had refused compensation to the applicant.[204] But in the '*Vagrancy*' Cases it immediately added:

> The mere fact that the applicants could have brought and could still bring their claims for damages before a Belgian Court does not therefore require the Court to dismiss their claims as being ill-founded any more than it raises an obstacle to their admissibility.[205]

In the *Ringeisen* Case the Court is even more explicit. The necessity to apply Article 50 exists 'once a respondent government refuses the applicant reparation to which he considers he is entitled.'[206] Between the view of the three above-mentioned judges and that of the Court a considerable difference remains. According to the three judges the Court may award compensation only in one exceptional case, *viz.* when under internal law there is no possibility of obtaining full compensation. In the Court's view it is sufficient for the application of Article 50 that a Government has refused the compensation claimed by the applicant. The view of the three judges resembles most closely the principle of general international law that a State must previously have been enabled as much as possible to redress itself the consequences of any violation of its international obligations within the context of its own national legal system.[207] On the other hand, the Court has argued that, if for the consideration of an application under Article 50 it should be required again that the local remedies have first been exhausted, the total length of the procedure provided for in the Convention could hardly be considered compatible with the idea of effective protection of human

---

[201] *Idem.*

[202] *Ibidem*, p. 15.

[203] *Ibidem*, p. 14.

[204] Judgment of 10 March 1972, A.14, p. 10, and judgment of 22 June 1972, A.15, p. 9 respectively.

[205] Judgment of 10 March 1972, A.14, p. 10.

[206] Judgment of 22 June 1972, A.15, p. 9.

[207] Compare the corresponding principle of general international law underlying the local remedies rule, *supra* p. 127.

rights.[208] Moreover, it might be argued in support of the Court's view that the consideration of applications under Article 50 and the examination of the merits should be regarded as one and indivisible,[209] so that the decision of the Commission that the local remedies have been exhausted, in combination with the finding of the Commission that a friendly settlement has not been reached and that the State has not been found willing to pay damages, must be considered a sufficient basis for the application of Article 50. The consequence of the latter approach is that, with respect to the decision on an application for compensation under Article 50 of the Convention, the internal law of the State concerned becomes irrelevant.

In the final analysis the middle course suggested by judge Verdross in his separate opinion would appear to us the most attractive. From the text of Article 50 he infers that the Court, when dealing with an application for compensation, should first of all ascertain whether the injured individual can obtain adequate compensation under internal law. If that is the case, the respondent State should first be enabled to award compensation according to its own procedures, but with the Court remaining competent to assure itself that just satisfaction has indeed duly been given, and to fix a time within which this should take place.[210] In this construction the State concerned is given the opportunity to settle the matter within the context of its own legal system, while the Court can to judge afterwards whether the compensation is equitable and at the same time can keep the total duration of the procedure within reasonable limits.

The viewpoint of the Court set forth above appears to have become constant case-law, however, since it has been confirmed explicitly or implicitly in a series of judgments.[211] Thus, in the *De Cubber* Case the Court notes that Article 50 is applicable, because the conditions of Article 50 are fulfilled:

> the proceedings in Belgium after 26 October 1984 (...) have not redressed the violation found in its judgment of that date; they have not brought about a result as close to *restitutio in integrum* as was possible in the nature of things.[212]

In the *Barberà, Messegué and Jarbardo* Case the Spanish Government submitted that the Court's principal judgment[213] had been executed in Spain in the fullest possible manner. The Constitutional Court's judgment quashing the convictions and ordering that the proceedings in the *Audiencia Nacional* be reopened

---

[208] Judgment of 10 March 1972, *De Wilde, Ooms and Versyp ('Vagrancy'* Cases), A.14, p. 9.

[209] See *supra* pp. 241-242.

[210] Judgment of 10 March 1972, A.14, p. 16.

[211] Judgment of 10 March 1980, *König*, A.36, pp. 14-15; judgment of 13 May 1980, *Artico*, A.37, pp. 20-21; judgment of 6 November 1980, *Sunday Times*, A.38, pp. 8-9; and the judgment of 6 November 1980, *Guzzardi*, A.39, pp. 41-42.

[212] Judgment of 14 September 1987, A.124-B, pp. 17-18.

[213] Judgment of 6 December 1988, *Barberà, Messegué and Jabardo*, A.146, pp. 37-38, where the Court found a violation of Art. 6(1) based above all on 'the fact that very important pieces of evidence were not adequately adduced and discussed at the trial in the applicants' presence and under the watchful eye of the public'.

represented an innovation for the Spanish legal system, under which previously the finding of a violation by the European Court of Human Rights could not constitute grounds for reopening proceedings. In the subsequent proceedings all the guarantees laid down in Article 6 had been scrupulously complied with and they therefore afforded the most complete *restitutio in integrum* that could be obtained from the point of view of Article 50. However, the Court observed that it could not speculate as to what the outcome of the proceedings would have been had the violation of the Convention not occurred. At any rate, the applicants were kept in prison as a direct consequence of the trial found by the Court to be in violation of the Convention. There was thus, in the opinion of the Court, a clear causal connection between the damage claimed by the applicants and the violation of the Convention. In the nature of things the subsequent release and acquittal of the applicants could not in themselves afford *restitutio in integrum* or complete reparation for damage derived from their detention.[214]

7.5 The Injured Party

As to the other elements of Article 50 there are fewer differences of opinion. Thus, the term 'injured party' is fairly clear in the Court's view. 'Injured party' is a synonym for 'victim' in Article 25, and as such may be considered 'the person directly affected by the failure to observe the Convention'.[215] From this it follows, for instance, that counsel for the applicant cannot bring his fee directly under the claim for reparation pursuant to Article 50, although it may after all form part of the reparation awarded to the applicant. In the *Belkacem* Case the applicant had received free legal aid with respect to the Strasbourg proceedings and had not stated that he owed his counsel any additional amount. When the latter nevertheless claimed a supplementary fee, the Court decided that a lawyer 'cannot rely on Article 50 to seek just satisfaction on his own account'.[216]

In the *Pakelli* Case, counsel had not claimed an immediate payment of his fee because of the financial situation of his client. A reparation of costs for legal assistance was nevertheless awarded, because counsel had not waived his right to reparation of his costs (as the Government suggested). The Court noted that 'in a human rights case a lawyer will be acting in the general interest if he agrees to

---

[214] Judgment of 13 June 1994, A.285-C, pp. 56-57.

[215] See the judgment of 6 February 1981, *Airey*, A.41, p. 7 and the judgment of 6 November 1980, *Sunday Times*, A.38, p. 8. See also the judgment of 14 September 1987, *Gillow*, A.124-C, p. 29: 'Since this case relates to events and their consequences which were experienced by Mr and Mrs Gillow together, the Court considers it equitable that all sums awarded in this judgment should be paid to the survivor of them, Mrs Gillow.'

[216] Judgment of 10 March 1980, A.36, p. 8. See also the judgment of 13 May 1980, *Artico*, A.37, p. 19; judgment of 27 September 1990, *Windisch*, A.176, p. 13; judgment of 19 December 1990, *Delta*, A.191-A, p. 18.

represent or assist a litigant even if the latter is not in a position to pay him immediately'[217] and brought the payment under the reparation.

In *X* v. *France* the applicant had died during the proceedings before the Court. His parents, however, had expressed their wish to continue the proceedings. The Court decided that the parents were entitled to take his place. The applicant had claimed 150,000 francs for non-pecuniary damage. The case concerned the length of compensation proceedings brought by a haemophiliac inflicted with the AIDS virus following a blood transfusion. The applicant had claimed that the length of proceedings had prevented him from obtaining the compensation which he had hoped for, and thus from being able to live independently and in better psychological conditions for the remaining period of his life. Without further observation the Court found that the applicant had sustained non-pecuniary damage and held that France was to pay the applicant's parents the entire sum sought.[218]

7.6 Just Satisfaction

As to the term 'just satisfaction', the formulation of Article 50 makes it plain in the first place that the Court has a certain discretion in determining it 'as is borne out by the adjective "just" and the phrase "if necessary", the Court enjoys a certain discretion in the exercise of the power conferred by Article 50.[219] Taking this as a point of departure, the Court strictly upholds that the only element qualifying for satisfaction is the injury due to the previously found violation of the Convention. Injury which is connected therewith, but which in fact is due to other causes, does not qualify for satisfaction.[220] The Court therefore requires a causal link between the injury and the violation.[221] In the *Quaranta* Case the applicant had claimed compensation only in respect of the main complaint, concerning the right to liberty under Article 5, whereas the Court had only found a violation in relation to one of the subsidiary complaints. The Court rejected the compensation claim for lack of causal link.[222]

---

[217] Judgment of 25 April 1983, A.64, p. 20.
[218] Judgment of 31 March 1992, A.234-C, p. 95.
[219] Judgment of 6 November 1980, *Guzzardi*, A.39, p. 42.
[220] See the judgment of 10 March 1980, *König*, A.36, p. 16: 'The only heads of injury capable of giving rise to an award of just satisfaction are those which the applicant would not have sustained had the two actions come to a close within a reasonable time.' See also the judgment of 6 February 1981, *Airey*, A.41, pp. 8-9: 'Her decision to move appears to have been motivated not by the fact that she did not enjoy an effective right of access to the High Court for the purpose of petitioning for juridical separation but rather by her general situation underlying her wish to have such access and, in particular, by her fear of molestation by her husband.'
[221] Judgment of 23 October 1985, *Benthem*, A.97, p. 19; judgment of 2 June 1986, *Bönisch*, A.103, p. 8; judgment of 26 May 1988, *Pauwels*, A.135, p. 20; judgment of 21 June 1988, *Berrehab*, A.138, p. 17; judgment of 23 October 1990, *Huber*, A.188, p. 19.
[222] Judgment of 24 May 1991, A.205, pp. 18-19.

In the *Albert and Le Compte* Case the first claim concerned a request to the Court to direct the State to annul the disciplinary sanctions imposed on the applicants. The Court decided that, even when leaving aside the fact that the Court is not empowered to do this:[223]

> the disciplinary sanctions, which were the outcome of proceedings found by the Court not to have complied with one of the rules of Article 6 § 1 of the Convention, cannot on that account alone be regarded as the consequences of that breach. As for the criminal sentence, there is no connection whatsoever between them and the violation (...) As for the applicant's second series of claims (...), the Court considers it proper to distinguish here, as in the Case of *Le Compte, Van Leuven and De Meyere* (...), between damage caused by a violation of the Convention and the costs incurred by the applicant.[224]

As regards the last-mentioned category, a trend appears to develop in the case-law of the Court to the effect that injury pursuant to Article 50 can be made good as far as it was 'incurred by the applicants in order to try to prevent the violation found by the Court or to obtain redress therefor' and only if it fulfils specifically three criteria: costs and expenses susceptible of satisfaction must have been (1) 'actually incurred', (2) 'necessarily incurred' and (3) 'reasonable as to quantum'.[225] These criteria apply to costs described as material damage as well as to costs referable to proceedings.[226]

7.6.1 Factors Determining Whether Just Satisfaction will Be Awarded

The reparation under Article 50 is intended to place the applicant as far as possible in the position he would have been had the violation of the Convention not taken place.[227] Whether and to what extent satisfaction will be awarded by the Court depends on the circumstances of the case.

In the *Neumeister* Case there had been a violation of Article 5(3) and the Court awarded the applicant a compensation, amounting to Austrian Sch. 30,000. An important factor in the determination of the amount was the degree to which the detention under remand had exceeded reasonable limits. In this case, however, there were a number of circumstances which induced the Court to decide that compensation for material injury was not necessary. In the first place, the duration of the detention under remand counted towards the ultimately imposed imprisonment. For the remainder he had been granted a pardon. These factors also

---

[223] See *infra* pp. 258-259.

[224] Judgment of 24 October 1983, A.68, pp. 6-7. See on the said distinction also, *e.g.*, judgment of 6 November 1980, *Sunday Times*, A.38, p. 9; judgment of 18 October 1982, *Le Compte, Van Leuven and De Meyere*, A.54, p. 7; judgment of 25 April 1983, *Van Droogen-broeck*, A.63, p. 6.

[225] Judgment of 18 October 1982, *Le Compte, Van Leuven and De Meyere*, A.54, pp. 8-9; judgment of 24 February 1983, *Dudgeon*, A.59, p. 9; judgment of 30 November 1987, *H* v. *Belgium*, A.127-B, p. 38; judgment of 27 August 1991, *Philis*, A.209, p. 25; judgment of 12 May 1992, *Megyeri*, A.237-A, pp. 13-14.

[226] See, *e.g.*, judgment of 6 November 1980, *Sunday Times*, A.38, pp. 13-18; judgment of 24 February 1983, *Dudgeon*, A.59, pp. 9-11; judgment of 27 October 1987, *Bodèn*, A.125-B, p. 43.

[227] Judgment of 23 October 1984, *Piersack*, A.85, pp. 15-16.

amply counterbalanced, in the Court's opinion, the moral injury which Neumeister had sustained. Even though this did not, according to the Court, constitute a genuine *restitutio in integrum*, it approached this very closely. The sum of money was therefore awarded to him as compensation for the damage he had incurred in the form of costs in the matter of legal assistance in his attempts to prevent the violation of the Convention, subsequently to request the Commission and the Court to establish this violation, and finally to obtain compensation.[228]

In the *Engel* case, only a symbolical compensation of Dfl. 100 was awarded to Engel. Compensation was refused to De Wit, Dona and Schul, because the violation of the Convention in regard to them only consisted in the fact that the Supreme Military Court had dealt with their cases *in camera*. In its judgment on the merits the Court had already found that they did not seem to have suffered as a result. They had not since then advanced any new arguments for their claims for damages. In awarding Dfl. 100 to Engel the Court took into account the very short duration of the detention and the fact that the injury caused by the violation of Article 5(1) had been largely compensated by the circumstance that Engel had not actually had to undergo his punishment.[229]

On the other hand, in the *Guincho* Case the Court found a violation of Article 6(1), the reasonable-time requirement, which stemmed from two periods of almost total inactivity on the part of the State. The resultant lapse of time, totalling more than two years, did not only 'reduce the effectiveness of the action brought, but it also placed the applicant in a state of uncertainty which still persists and in such a position that even a final decision in his favour will not be able to provide compensation for the lost interest'. Accordingly, the Court awarded the applicant a compensation of 150,000 Escudos.[230]

Other factors can also play a part in the awarding of reparation of costs and expenses. In the *Airey* Case, for instance, it seems to have been an important factor that the British Government had already declared itself prepared before the proceedings started to award a given amount.[231] And in the *Pakelli* Case, although the applicant, because of his financial situation, did not have to pay the bill of his lawyer immediately, he could ask for the amount he needed to pay that bill.[232] On the other hand, no compensation is awarded if the fees are borne by an insurance company, since in that case 'there is no prejudice capable of being the subject of a claim for restitution'.[233] The same argument applies, if the

---

[228] Judgment of 7 May 1974, A.17, pp. 16-21.
[229] Judgment of 23 November 1976, A.22, pp. 68-70.
[230] Judgment of 10 July 1984, *Guincho*, A.81, p. 18. See also, *inter alia*, the judgment of 22 March 1983, *Campbell and Cosans*, A.60, pp. 7-13 and the judgment of 14 September 1987, *Gillow*, A.124-C, p. 26.
[231] Judgment of 6 February 1981, A.41, pp. 7-9.
[232] Judgment of 25 April 1983, *Pakelli*, A.64, p. 20.
[233] Judgment of 23 October 1984, *Öztürk*, A.85, p. 9.

applicant has received free legal aid.[234] In the *Wassink* Case the applicant also sought a specified amount for the expenses and fees of the lawyer who represented him before the Commission and the Court. The Dutch Government argued that the applicant, who had received legal aid in Strasbourg, had not shown that he had to pay his lawyer additional fees whose reimbursement he was entitled to request. In the Court's view, the mere fact that the applicant was granted legal aid did not mean that he was not under an obligation to pay the fee note drawn up by his counsel and attached to the claim submitted under Article 50. In the absence of proof to the contrary, the Court must accept that the applicant was required to pay his lawyer the amount set out in the fee note, from which the sums received from the Council of Europe are to be deducted.[235]

The fact that an applicant has accepted an out-of-court settlement is not decisive for the award of compensation. In the *Silva Pontes* Case, where the applicant had concluded an agreement with the defendant private party, in the opinion of the Court the agreement concerned the consequences of a road accident and not those, for which the State could be held responsible, flowing from the failure to comply with the reasonable time requirement. The Court, therefore, awarded the applicant with a specified sum for pecuniary and non-pecuniary damage.[236]

The Court also considers, whether the finding of a violation has effects beyond the confines of a particular case. The respondent State is then under the obligation to take the necessary measures in its domestic legal system to ensure the performance of its obligations under Article 53 of the Convention. Thus in the *Norris* Case, the Court took into account that Ireland had to take the necessary steps to ensure its obligations under Article 53. In this respect the Court referred to the change in the law, which had been effected with regard to Northern Ireland in compliance with the Court's finding of a violation in the *Dudgeon* Case. This lead the Court to the decision that its finding of a violation constituted adequate just satisfaction for the purposes of Article 50.[237] This decision of the Court seems to us somewhat premature, since the Court held in the *Dudgeon* Case that changes in the contested legislation or practice after finding of a violation cannot constitute *per se* just satisfaction in respect of facts occurred previously, although they may be taken into account for the award of non-pecuniary damage.[238] Moreover it may take several years before the respondent State has made the necessary changes. In fact, in Ireland it took almost four years before the Criminal

---

[234] Judgment of 18 December 1986, *Johnston and Others*, A.112, pp. 32-33; judgment of 25 June 1987, *Baggetta*, A.119, p. 34; judgment of 27 July 1987, *Feldbrugge*, A.124-A, pp. 9-10; judgment of 2 December 1987, *Bozano*, A.124-F, p. 48.

[235] Judgment of 27 September 1990, A.185-A, p. 15. In the same sense, see the judgment of 25 October 1990, *Koendjbiharie*, A.185-B, p. 42.

[236] Judgment of 23 March 1994, A.286-A, p. 16.

[237] Judgment of 26 October 1988, A.142, pp. 21-22.

[238] Judgment of 24 February 1983, A.59, pp. 6-8.

Law (Sexual Offences) Act 1993 modified Irish Law to decriminalise consensual homosexual acts between adult males.[239]

7.6.2 The Costs of the Proceedings

Legal costs are only recoverable insofar as they relate to the violation found.[240] In the *Eckle* Case the Court extensively went into the matter of restitution of costs of proceedings. The Court held that an applicant is entitled to an award of costs and expenses under Article 50, when these costs are incurred in order to seek, through the domestic legal order, prevention or redress of a violation, to have the same established by the Commission and later by the Court, or to obtain reparation therefor, and when they 'were actually incurred, were necessarily incurred and were also reasonable as to quantum'. Considering, however, the proceedings in which the costs were incurred in this case, the claim for restitution of costs and expenses incurred in the proceedings before the Koblenz Court of Appeal was rejected because:

> it should not be overlooked that the complaint in question was not aimed at securing a more expeditious conduct of the proceeding: the complaint was directed against the unreasonable length of the detention on remand and had as its sole object Mr. Eckle's release from custody. It could have been of relevance in relation to Article 5, para. 3 – if (...) the Commission had not declared the application inadmissible on that score – but not in relation to Article 6, para. 1.[241]

In relation to the claims for restitution of costs incurred in the 'review' procedure before the Regional Court of Trier, the Court considered that 'in view of his not having raised the issue of 'reasonable time' himself the applicant cannot recover in full Mr von Stackelberg's fees and disbursements'.[242] Concerning the recovery of costs in relation to the procedure in Strasbourg, the Government expressed the view 'that a deduction should be made in view of the applications having been unsuccessful in relation to three complaints declared inadmissible by the Commission'. The Court did not agree with this, because

> in contrast to what occurred in the case of *Le Compte, Van Leuven and De Meyere*, to which the Government referred (...), the complaints in question failed at the admissibility stage. Furthermore, the Commission did not reject them as being manifestly ill-founded, and hence after a preliminary inquiry into the merits, but for being out of time and for non-exhaustion of domestic remedies. (...) As is apparent from the decision on admissibility, the examination of these two questions of admissibility (...) was not of such complexity that its outcome could warrant the deduction called for by the Government.[243]

---

[239] D.J. Harris, M. O'Boyle and C. Warbrick, *Law of the European Convention on Human Rights*, London, 1995, p. 30.

[240] Judgment of 25 September 1992, *Pham Hoang*, A.243, p. 24; judgment of 19 April 1994, *Van der Hurk*, A.288, p. 21.

[241] Judgment of 21 June 1983, A.65, p. 13.

[242] *Ibidem*, p. 14.

[243] *Ibidem*, p. 19.

On the other hand, in the *Campbell and Fell* Case[244] the restitution of costs and expenses was made conditional on the degree in which the complaints were successful.

The costs made with respect to the Strasbourg proceedings must have been made with a view to establishing the violation of the Convention by the Commission and later by the Court. Just satisfaction may be afforded for costs incurred at all stages of the proceedings. The reimbursement may cover the costs and fees of the lawyer as well as travel and subsistence expenses. The Court will also take other costs, such as services of experts and photocopying and postal costs and translation fees, into consideration, as long as these costs are necessarily incurred. However, the applicant must seek the reimbursement of these costs himself, because according to the Court, this is not a matter which it has to examine of its own motion.[245] In the *Brogan* Case the applicants did not submit any claim for reimbursement of costs and expenses and the Court held that the question of the application of Article 50 was not ready for decision in relation to the claim for compensation for prejudice suffered.[246] When it had to deal with the question of compensation under Article 50 the applicants sought reimbursement of costs and expenses. However, the Court stated that in its principal judgment there was no call to examine the application of Article 50 in relation to reimbursement of any costs or expenses incurred. The Court referred to Article 52 according to which the earlier decision was final. Therefore the Court could not entertain the applicants' subsequent claim in this respect.[247]

7.6.3   Other Damages that might be Compensated

What other kind of damage may be compensated in addition to direct costs of proceedings? In the *König* Case, according to the Court, the extent to which the 'reasonable time' had been exceeded had left the applicant in prolonged uncertainty as to the possibilities of his career, which in the Court's opinion ought to be compensated in the form of DM 30,000 of damages.[248] In the *Goddi* Case the applicant maintained that, if he had had an opportunity of having his defence adequately presented, he would certainly have received a lighter sentence. The Court did not accept so categorical an allegation. However, it held that the outcome might possibly have been different if the applicant had had the benefit of a practical and effective defence and that, therefore, such a loss of real opportunities warranted the award of just satisfaction.[249] A similar reasoning was followed by the Court in the *Colozza* Case, where it had found a violation of

---

[244] Judgment of 28 June 1984, A.80, p. 56. See also the judgment of 18 December 1986, *Johnston and Others*, A.112, p. 33.

[245] Judgment of 24 April 1990, *Huvig*, A.176-B, p. 57; judgment of 19 February 1991, *Colacioppo*, A.197-D, p. 52.

[246] Judgment of 29 November 1988, A.145-B, p. 36.

[247] Judgment of 30 May 1989, *Brogan and Others*, A.152-B, p. 44.

[248] Judgment of 10 March 1980, A.36, p. 16.

[249] Judgment of 9 April 1984, A.76, pp. 13-14.

Article 6(1) of the Convention, since the applicant was never heard in his presence by a 'tribunal' which was competent to determine all the aspects of the matter. The Court noted that an award of just satisfaction could only be based on the fact that the applicant had not had the benefit of the guarantees of Article 6 and awarded a just satisfaction to the applicant's widow for loss of real opportunities.[250] Reparation of loss of earnings is also possible,[251] as well as the repayment of fines and costs unjustly awarded against the applicant,[252] and reimbursement of the travel and subsistence expenses met by the applicant in attending the hearings before the Commission and the Court.[253] Reparation of immaterial damage can be awarded for suffered uncertainty,[254] feeling of unequal treatment,[255] unjust imprisonment[256] and feeling of frustration.[257]

Several factors can play a part in the determination of the amount of such kinds of compensation. In the *Ringeisen* Case,[258] the Court had found that there had been a violation of Article 5(3). The Court awarded the applicant a compensation of DM 20,000, and in fixing the amount of this sum, took into account the following factors. Firstly, the fact that the detention under remand had exceeded reasonable limits by 22 months. Although the period of imprisonment to which he had ultimately been condemned was reduced by the duration of the detention under remand, he had always maintained that he was innocent, and on that account had undoubtedly felt so long a detention under remand as unjust. Secondly, the fact that his detention had been hard on him, since it had been impossible for him to undertake anything to avoid bankruptcy.

---

[250] Judgment of 12 February 1985, A.89, p. 17. See also the judgment of 2 June 1986, *Bönisch*, A.103, p. 8; judgment of 8 July 1986, *Lingens*, A.103, p. 29; judgment of 28 October 1987, *Inze*, A.126, p. 20.

[251] Judgment of 24 November 1986, *Unterpertinger*, A.110, p. 16; judgment of 21 June 1988, *Berrehab*, A.138, p. 17, where, however, no reparation of loss of earnings was awarded because of the lack of a causal link.

[252] Judgment of 27 February 1980, *De Weer*, A.35, pp. 31-32; judgment of 8 July 1986, *Lingens*, A.103, p. 29; judgment of 28 August 1992, *Schwabe*, A.242-B, p. 35.

[253] Judgment of 10 December 1982, *Corigliano*, A.57, p. 17.

[254] Judgment of 10 July 1984, *Guincho*, A.81, p. 18.

[255] Judgment of 2 June 1986, *Bönisch*, A.103, p. 8; judgment of 23 April 1987, *Lechner and Hess*, A.118, p. 22; judgments of 25 June 1987, *Capuano, Baggetta* and *Milasi*, A.119, pp. 15, 34 and 48; judgment of 8 July 1987, *Baraona*, A.122, p. 22.

[256] Judgment of 24 November 1986, *Unterpertinger*, A.110, p. 16.

[257] Judgments of 9 June 1988, *O, H, W, B and R v. the United Kingdom*, A.136-A-E, pp. 9, 17, 25, 33 and 42-43; judgment of 26 May 1994, *Keegan*, A.290, p. 23; judgment of 31 October 1995, *Papamichalopoulos and Others*, A.330-B, p. 61.

[258] Judgment of 22 June 1972, A.15, pp. 9-10. The Court did not exclude that a third factor – the deteriorated health due to the detention – could also have played a role, but Ringeisen had not advanced any evidence for that fact while from medical reports the contrary could be inferred.

In the *Artico* Case,[259] the Court took three elements into consideration, *viz.* the imprisonment actually served, the additional imprisonment which the applicant had possibly incurred in consequence of the lack of effective legal aid, and the isolated position in which he had been placed as a result of this. The Court held that

> none of the above elements of damage lends itself to a process of calculation. Taking them together on an equitable basis, as is required by Article 50, the Court considers that Mr. Artico should be afforded satisfaction assessed at three million (3,000,000) Lire.[260]

In the *Sporrong and Lönnroth* Case the Court had found a violation of Article 1 of Protocol No. 1 of the Convention. In order to decide whether or not the applicants had been prejudiced, the Court had to determine during which periods the continuation of the measures complained of had been in violation of Protocol No. 1, and then which constituent elements of damage warranted examination. The Court found it reasonable that a municipality should, after obtaining an expropriation permit, require some time to undertake and complete the planning needed to prepare the final decision on the expropriation contemplated. Whilst a comparison between the beginning and the end of the periods of damage did not show that the applicants were prejudiced in financial terms, the Court nevertheless did not conclude that there was no loss within that period. There were, in fact, other factors which also warranted attention. Firstly, there were limitations on the utilization of the properties. In addition, during the periods of damage the value of the properties in question fell. Furthermore, there were difficulties in obtaining loans, secured by way of mortgage. Above all, the applicants were left in prolonged uncertainty as they did not know what the fate of their properties would be. To these factors had to be added the non-pecuniary damage occasioned by the violation of Article 6(1) of the Convention: the applicants' case could not be heard by a tribunal competent to determine all the aspects of the matter. The applicants thus suffered damage for which reparation was not provided by the withdrawal of the expropriation permits.[261]

In the *Bozano* Case the applicant claimed just satisfaction for the violation of Article 5(1) of the Convention. The Court stated that the applicant's detention in France involved a serious breach of the Convention, which inevitably caused him substantial non-pecuniary damage. With regard to his subsequent detention in Switzerland and Italy the Court found that it had no jurisdiction to review the compatibility of that detention with the Convention, since the Commission had either declared the applicant's complaints against those two States inadmissible or struck them off its list. Nonetheless, there was a need to have regard to the

---

[259] Judgment of 13 May 1980, A.37, pp. 21-22. See further: judgment of 21 June 1983, *Eckle*, A.65, pp. 10-11; and particularly the judgment of 18 December 1984, *Sporrong and Lönnroth*, A.88, pp. 13-15.
[260] Judgment of 13 May 1980, A.37, p. 22.
[261] Judgment of 18 December 1984, A.88, pp. 12-13.

applicant's detention as it was prior to the enforcement of the deportation order. In the Court's view the real damage was that sustained as a consequence of the process of enforcing the deportation order and of the unlawful and arbitrary deprivation of liberty.[262]

If the damage or the costs do not lend themselves for a process of calculation or the calculation presented to the Court is unreasonable, the Court fixes them on an equitable basis.[263] In the *Young, James and Webster* Case there was no dispute that all three applicants had incurred pecuniary and non-pecuniary losses and also liability for legal costs and expenses referable to the Strasbourg proceedings, but certain claims exceeded as to their quantum the sums offered by the British Government during unsuccessful friendly settlement negotiations. The Court observed that:

> high costs of litigation may themselves constitute a serious impediment to the effective protection of human rights. It would be wrong for the Court to give encouragement to such a situation in its decisions awarding costs under Article 50. It is important that applicants should not encounter undue financial difficulties in bringing complaints under the Convention and the Court considers that it may expect that lawyers in Contracting States will cooperate to this end in the fixing of their fees.[264]

During the settlement negotiations, the British Government offered to have the costs in question independently assessed or 'taxed' by a Taxing Master. In the opinion of the Court, this would have been a reasonable method of assessment. However, the applicants did not take up this offer. In these circumstances the Court accepted the figure of £ 65,000 offered by the Government in respect of all legal costs and expenses.[265]

A claim for compensation will be rejected, when there is nothing to suggest with reasonable certainty that without the violation the result would have been different.[266] Other possible reasons for rejection of reparation claims are: the Court's finding that, by holding that the violation has occurred, its judgment has already furnished sufficient satisfaction for the purposes of Article 50;[267] the conclusion that the applicants did not suffer any damage;[268] the fact that the

---

[262] Judgment of 2 December 1987, A.124-F, pp. 47-48.

[263] Judgment of 13 May 1980, *Artico*, A.37, p. 22; judgment of 18 October 1982, *Young, James and Webster*, A.55, p. 7; judgment of 2 June 1986, *Bönisch*, A.103, p. 8; judgments of 9 June 1988, *O, H, W, B and R v. the United Kingdom*, A.136-A-E.

[264] Judgment of 18 October 1982, A.55, p. 8. See also the judgment of 2 June 1986, *Bönisch*, A.103, p. 9.

[265] Judgment of 18 October 1982, A.55, p. 8.

[266] Judgment of 10 March 1972, *De Wilde, Ooms and Versyp* ('*Vagrancy*' Cases), A.14, p. 11; judgment of 25 April 1983, *Van Droogenbroeck*, A.63, p. 6; judgment of 23 February 1984, *Luberti*, A.75, p. 18; judgments of 9 June 1988, *O, H, W, B and R v. the United Kingdom*, A.136-A-E.

[267] Judgment of 18 October 1982, *Le Compte, Van Leuven and De Meyere*, A.54, p. 8; judgment of 18 December 1987, *F v. Switzerland*, A.128, p. 20; judgment of 20 June 1988, *Schönenberger and Durmaz*, A.137, p. 15; judgment of 22 April 1993, *Modinos*, A.259, p. 12.

[268] Judgment of 23 November 1976, *Engel*, A.22, p. 69.

domestic court has imposed a sentence identical to that given before the judgment of the Court, but now after a trial attended by all the guarantees laid down by the Convention;[269] the circumstance that the applicant has adduced insufficient evidence or information in support of his claim;[270] or the Court's holding that the 'claims stem from matters in respect of which it has found no violation'.[271]

7.6.4 No Jurisdiction to Direct a State to Take Certain Measures

Repeatedly the Court had to declare that it lacked jurisdiction to direct the States to take certain measures, for instance to abolish the violation found by the Court, to repair the costs, *etcetera*. The Court notes regularly that it is left to the State concerned to choose the means within its domestic legal system to give effect to its obligations under Article 53.[272]

In the *Corigliano* Case the Court declared the claim inadmissible to order the State to make certain articles of the Penal Code inapplicable to 'political and social trials'. This 'falls outside the scope of the case brought before the Court', according to the Court.[273] Also the request to publish a summary of the Court's judgment in local newspapers or the removal of any reference to the applicant's conviction in the central criminal records, falls outside the scope of the jurisdiction of the Court.[274]

In the *Bozano* Case the applicant had requested the Court to recommend the French Government to approach the Italian authorities through diplomatic channels, with a view to securing either a 'presidential pardon' – leading to his 'rapid release' – or a reopening of the criminal proceedings taken against him in Italy from 1971 to 1976. The Government argued that the Court did not have the power to take such a course of action. Furthermore, they maintained that it would in any case be unconnected with the subject-matter of the dispute, since it would amount to recommending France to intervene in the enforcement of final decisions of the Italian courts. The Court did not go into these arguments. It merely pointed out that Mr Bozano's complaints against Italy were not in issue before it, as the Commission had declared them inadmissible.[275] One cannot escape the impression that the Court did not want to enter into the issue whether or not it had the power to make a recommendation as requested by the applicant. It might be

---

[269] Judgment of 23 October 1984, *Piersack*, A.85, p. 17; judgment of 28 June 1993, *Windisch*, A.255-D, p. 97.

[270] Judgment of 21 November 1983, *Foti and Others*, A.69, p. 7; judgment of 29 May 1986, *Deumeland*, A.100, p. 31; judgment of 14 September 1987, *Gillow*, A.124-C, pp. 26-27; judgment of 20 June 1988, *Schönenberger and Durmaz*, A.137, p. 15.

[271] Judgment of 18 December 1986, *Johnston and Others*, A.112, p. 32.

[272] Judgment of 25 April 1983, *Pakelli*, A.64, pp. 19-20; judgment of 24 October 1983, *Albert and Le Compte*, A.68, p. 6; judgment of 26 October 1984, *McGoff*, A.83, p. 28; judgment of 26 May 1988, *Pauwels*, A.135, p. 19; judgment of 9 June 1988, *B v. the United Kingdom*, A.136-D, p. 35.

[273] Judgment of 10 December 1982, *Corigliano*, A.57, p. 17.

[274] Judgment of 27 February 1992, *Manifattura FL*, A.230-B, p. 21; judgment of 23 April 1992, *Castells*, A.236, p. 25.

[275] Judgment of 18 December 1986, A.111, p. 28.

argued that in cases where *restitutio in integrum* is impossible, as in the present case, the Court had nothing left than to award just satisfaction. However, what Mr Bozano in addition requested from the Court was only a *recommendation* and such a recommendation should, in general, not be deemed inappropriate, comparable as it would seem to be with the recommendation of provisional measures, for which there is also no express basis in the Convention.

8 REQUEST FOR INTERPRETATION OF A JUDGMENT OF THE COURT

Rule 57 of the Rules of Court 'A' and Rule 59 of the Rules of Court 'B' deal with the possibility to request the Court for the interpretation of a judgment.

According to paragraph 1 of these Rules a Party – and in case Protocol No. 9 is in effect, the original applicant – or the Commission may request such an interpretation within three years following the delivery of the judgment. The request must state precisely the point or points in the operative provisions of the judgment on which interpretation is required (Rule 57(2) of the Rules of Court 'A' and Rule 59(2) of the Rules of Court 'B'). After receipt, the request is communicated to any other Party, to the original applicant and, where the request has been submitted by a State, to the Commission, all of which are then invited to submit written comments within a fixed time-limit (Rule 57(3) of the Rules of Court 'A'). In this procedure, too, the Court applies the principle that the request for interpretation shall be considered by the Chamber which gave the judgment and which, as far as possible, shall be composed of the same judges (Rule 57(4) of the Rules of Court 'A'). If the request is submitted by the original applicant, a Screening Panel may decide, by unanimous vote, to reject the request on the ground that there is no reason to warrant its consideration by the Court. The Panel will in principle be composed of judges who delivered also the decision to refer the case to the Court (Rule 59(3) of the Rules of Court 'B'). If the Screening Panel does not reject the request, the request for interpretation will be considered by the Chamber which gave the judgment and which, as far as possible, will be composed of the same judges (Rule 59(4) of the Rules of Court 'B').

At present (June 1997) the Court has only twice decided on a request for interpretation. On 21 December 1972, on the basis of a letter from the original individual applicant, the Commission submitted to the Court a request for interpretation of the Court's second judgment in the *Ringeisen* Case of 22 June 1972. By this judgment Ringeisen had been awarded a compensation of DM 20,000. The question whether this amount would have to be paid directly to Ringeisen or whether it might be claimed by the trustee in the bankruptcy of Ringeisen, had been left by the Court to the discretion of the Austrian Government. In this connection, however, the Court had referred to the Austrian legislation concerning compensation on account of detention under remand, which implied that no attachment or seizure may be made against such compensation. The money was, however, sent by the Austrian authorities on consignment to a judicial tribunal. The latter decided that upon request of the persons entitled to it or after a final judicial decision the money was to be paid. The Commission asked the Court what was meant by the order to pay compensation, in particular with respect to the currency and the place of the payment, and whether the term 'compensation' was to be understood as an amount that was exempt from any judicial claims under Austrian law, or on the contrary was subject to such claims. The Court replied that the compensation was to be paid in German marks and was to be made payable in the Federal Republic of Germany. Further the Court ruled that the money was to be paid to Ringeisen personally, exempt from any claim or title to it. This ruling, therefore, implied disapproval of the position taken by the Austrian authorities. Austria had called into question the competence of the Court in the matter, stating that:

> the competence of the (...) Court (...) for interpretation of its judgments (...) is based solely on the Rules of the Court. Therefore in the light of Article 52 of the (...) Convention, the well-founded question may even be raised whether this legal institution is compatible at all with the Convention.

The Court pointed out that the sole purpose of Article 52 is to exclude appeal to another authority from decisions of the Court.[276] It submitted that there is no question of appeal when the Court deals with a request for interpretation. In such a case the Court exercises inherent jurisdiction, because such a request concerns only elucidation of the purport and scope of a preceding judgment. Furthermore, the Court pointed out that Rule 56 (the present Rule 57) had been submitted to the Contracting States at the time of its adoption and that no objections had been raised against it by those States.[277]

In its judgment of 10 February 1995 in the Case of *Allenet de Ribemont* the Court awarded under Article 50 the applicant an overall sum of FRF 2,000,000 for pecuniary and non-pecuniary damage, together with FRF 100,000 for costs and expenses. In response to the applicant's request for a ruling that France should guarantee him against any application for enforcement of a judgment delivered by the Paris *tribunal de grande instance* on 14 March 1979, the Court said that 'under Article 50 it does not have jurisdiction to issue such an order to a Contracting State'.[278] In July-August 1995 the applicant was informed that an attachment of the sums awarded to him by the Court had been effected at the request of the parties in whose favour the judgment of the Paris *tribunal de grande instance* had been given. Following a request from Mr Allenet de Ribemont, the Commission submitted to the Court a request for interpretation of the judgment of 10 February 1995. The request was worded as follows:

> *Firstly*: Is it to be understood that Article 50 of the Convention, which provides for an award of just satisfaction to the injured party if the domestic law of the High Contracting Party allows only partial reparation to be made for the consequences of the

---

[276] See *supra* pp. 240-241.
[277] Judgment of 23 June 1973, A.16, pp. 4-9.
[278] Judgment of 10 February 1995, A.308, p. 23.

decision or measure held to be in conflict with the obligations arising from the Convention, means that any sum awarded under this head must be paid to the injured party personally and be exempt from attachment? *Secondly*: In respect of sums subject to legal claims under French law, should a distinction be made between the part of the sum awarded under the head of pecuniary damage and the part awarded under the head of non-pecuniary damage? and *Thirdly*: If so, what were the sums which the Court intended to grant the applicant in respect of pecuniary damage and non-pecuniary damage respectively?.

The Court observed, firstly, that when considering a request for interpretation, it is exercising inherent jurisdiction: it goes no further than to clarify the meaning and scope which it intended to give to a previous decision which issued from its own deliberations, specifying if need be what it thereby decided with binding force. The Court understood the first question put by the Commission as an invitation to interpret Article 50 in a general, abstract way. That, however, went outside not only the bounds laid down by Rule 57 of Rules of Court 'A' but also those of the Court's contentious jurisdiction under the Convention. At all events, the Court had not in the instant case ruled that any sum awarded to Mr Allenet de Ribemont was to be free from attachment. The applicant had asked the Court to hold that the State should guarantee him against any application for enforcement of the judgment delivered by the Paris *tribunal de grande instance* on 14 March 1979. In response the Court had said that 'under Article 50 it does not have jurisdiction to issue such an order to a Contracting State'. Accordingly, the question had been left to the national authorities acting under the relevant domestic law. In short, the Court had no jurisdiction to answer the first question put by the Commission. As to the Commission's second and third questions, the Court said that in its judgment of 10 February 1995 it had awarded the applicant FRF 2,000,000 'for damage' without distinguishing between pecuniary and non-pecuniary damage. In relation to the sum awarded, the Court had considered that it did not have to identify the proportions corresponding to pecuniary and non-pecuniary damage respectively. It was not bound to do so when affording 'just satisfaction' under Article 50 of the Convention. In point of fact it was often difficult, if not impossible, to make any such distinction. The Court held that the judgment it had delivered on 10 February 1995 was clear on the points in the operative provisions on which interpretation had been requested. To hold otherwise would not be to clarify 'the meaning and scope' of that judgment but rather to modify it in respect of an issue which the Court had decided with binding force. Accordingly, it was unnecessary to answer the Commission's second and third questions.[279]

---

[279] Judgment of 7 August 1996, *Allenet de Ribemont*, Reports 1996-III, Vol. 12, para. 23.

9 REQUEST FOR REVISION OF A JUDGMENT

The competence of the Court to deal with requests for revision of its judgments is likewise not regulated by the Convention. Like the competence to give an interpretation of a judgment, the competence to revise a judgment may also be considered as inherent in the jurisdiction of the Court. The procedure to be followed in connection with a request for revision is also to be found in the Rules of Court 'A', *viz.* in Rule 58 and in Rule 60 of the Rules of Court 'B'.

A request for revision of a judgment may be submitted by a Party – and if Protocol No. 9 is in effect, the original applicant in the case in which that judgment has been delivered – or by the Commission. Revision may be requested in the event of the discovery of a fact which might by its nature have a decisive influence and which, when the judgment was delivered, was unknown both to the Court, the Party and to the original applicant or the Commission now requesting revision. The request must be filed within a period of six months after the fact became known to that Party, the original applicant or the Commission, as the case may be (Rule 58(1) of the Rules of Court 'A' and Rule 60(1) of the Rules of Court 'B'). According to Rule 60(3) of the Rules of Court 'B' a request by the original applicant will be considered by a Screening Panel, (composed as described in Rule 59(4) of the Rules of Court 'B'). If the Screening Panel declares the request admissible, it shall refer the request to the Chamber which gave the judgment and which, as far as possible, shall be composed of the same judges (Rule 60(3) of the Rules of Court 'B').

A request for revision will be dealt with, according to Rule 58 of the Rules of Court 'A' and Rule 60 of the Rules of Court 'B', in proceedings largely resembling the normal proceedings before the Court. The only difference is that a request for revision is first examined for its admissibility, by reference to the conditions mentioned in Rule 58(1) of the Rules of Court 'A' and Rule 60(1) of the Rules of Court 'B', by a Chamber of the Court composed in the normal way, *i.e.* in accordance with Article 43 of the Convention. When the request is found to be admissible, the Chamber thus composed does not itself examine the merits of the request, but transmits it to the Chamber which gave the original judgment. It is only when the latter is not reasonably possible that the Chamber which has decided on the admissibility also takes a decision on the merits of the request (Rule 58(4) of the Rules of Court 'A' and Rule 60(5) of the Rules of Court 'B'). Equally, if the Screening Panel has declared a request by an original applicant admissible, it refers it to the Chamber which gave the original judgment or, if that is not reasonably possible, to a Chamber to be composed for the matter (Article 60(3) of the Rules of Court 'A'). Up to the moment of this writing (June 1997) only one request for revision had reached the Court. This is not astonishing. In general, cases in which after the final judgment an originally unknown fact of decisive importance is discovered are very rare. It is even less likely that such a situation will occur after lengthy local proceedings and the elaborate proceedings before the Commission and the Court.

In the *Prado* Case the applicant complained, *inter alia,* of a breach of his right to a fair trial. He claimed that, as a party in commercial litigation in the Aix-en-Provence Court of Appeal, he had not had the opportunity to present oral arguments on the merits, despite the fact that the President had announced that there would be a further hearing at a later date. In its judgment the Court held that there had been no violation of Article 6(1).[280] At Mr Pardo's request the Commission submitted to the Court a request for the revision of that judgment. The Commission noted that the Court, prior to its hearing on 22 March 1993, had asked the participants in the proceedings to produce certain documents. For the reasons given at the hearing, these requests were not complied with. Since then the applicant had been able to obtain certain of these documents and in particular the letter from Mr de Chessé to Mr Davin (both lawyers) of 25 March 1985 and the list of documents contained in the appeal file. The Commission took the view that, as the Court had asked for these documents to be produced, they might by their nature have had a decisive influence on its judgment. The Court took the view that the two documents submitted in support of the Commission's request (the letter from Mr de Chessé to Mr Davin of 25 March 1985 and the list of documents in the appeal file), documents to which Mr Pardo did not have access until after the delivery of the judgment of 20 September 1993, could be regarded as facts for the purposes of Rule 58(1). The Court noted that, under the terms of the second sentence of Rule 58(4), the Chamber constituted to consider the request for revision could only determine the admissibility of that request. It had, accordingly, to confine itself to examining whether, *prima facie,* the facts submitted were such as 'might by [their] nature have a decisive influence'. The task of considering whether they actually had a 'decisive influence' lay in principle with the Chamber which gave the original judgment. A decision on the admissibility of the request, therefore, in no way prejudged the merits of the request. However, in carrying out its examination the Court had to bear in mind that, by virtue of Article 52 of the Convention, its judgments were final. Inasmuch as it called into question the final character of judgments, the possibility of revision, which was not provided for in the Convention but had been introduced by the Rules of Court, was an exceptional procedure. That was why the admissibility of any request for revision of a judgment of the Court under this procedure was subject to strict scrutiny. In order to establish whether the facts on which a request for revision were based 'might by [their] nature have a decisive influence', they had to be considered in relation to the decision of the Court the revision of which was sought. The Court observed in this connection that a request to those appearing before the Court for documents to be produced was not in itself sufficient to warrant the conclusion that the documents in question 'might by [their] nature have a decisive influence'. On the other hand, the Court could not exclude the possibility that the documents in question 'might by [their] nature have a decisive influence'. It fell to the Chamber which gave the original

---

[280] Judgment of 20 September 1993, A.261-B, p. 31.

judgment to determine whether those documents actually cast doubt on the conclusions it reached in 1993. The Court accordingly declared the request for revision admissible and referred it to the Chamber which gave the original judgment.[281] In its judgment of 29 April 1997, the Court decided that the documents in question did not provide any information on the proceedings concerned whose course was in dispute before the Court. The documents would not have had a decisive influence on the original judgment and did not constitute any grounds for revision. Therefore, the request was dismissed.[282]

10 EXCURSUS: ADVISORY JURISDICTION OF THE COURT

Since the entry into force of Protocol No. 2 on 21 September 1970, the Court has jurisdiction to give advisory opinions on legal questions concerning the interpretation of the Convention and the Protocols thereto (Article 1(1) of Protocol No. 2).

Properly speaking, this jurisdiction falls outside the scope of the present chapter, which deals with the consideration of complaints or requests connected with them. The matter is, nevertheless, discussed in this chapter, since it is the chapter devoted to the Court.

The advisory jurisdiction of a court may be of great importance for a uniform interpretation and the further development of the law. With regard to international law, this is quite evident from the practice of the International Court of Justice and the Court of Justice of the European Communities. *Via* its advisory opinions the International Court of Justice has made an important contribution to the interpretation and the progressive development of particularly the law of the United Nations.[283] The advisory jurisdiction of the International Court of Justice is formulated very broadly, without any conditions being made as to the scope of such advisory opinions. According to Article 96 of the Charter of the United Nations in conjunction with Article 65 of the Court's Statute, the Court may give advisory opinions 'on any legal question', so that the most varied issues of international law may be submitted to the Court. The jurisdiction of the Court of Justice of the European Communities is very limited as to its scope, but still comprises the field of the conclusion of treaties, which is of great importance for the Communities.[284]

---

[281] Judgment of 10 July 1996, *Pardo*, Reports 1996-III, Vol. 11, paras 24-25.

[282] Judgment of 29 April 1997, *Pardo*, Reports 1997-III, Vol. 36, paras 20-22.

[283] In this context, see in particular the advisory opinions of the Court in: 'Injuries suffered in the service of the United Nations', *ICJ Reports*, 1949, p. 174; 'Certain Expenses of the United Nations', *ICJ Reports*, 1962, p. 151; and 'Legal Consequences for States of the Continued Presence of South Africa in Namibia notwithstanding Security Council Resolution 276 (1970)', *ICJ Reports*, 1971, p. 6.

[284] See Art. 228 of the EEC Treaty. See, *e.g.*, the important advisory opinion of the Court of Justice of the European Communities 1/76, *Jur.* 1977, p. 741, which partly laid the basis for the present conception of the external powers of the EEC.

The practical importance of the advisory jurisdiction of the European Court of Human Rights, on the other hand, has been reduced to a minimum from the outset because of the restrictions which are put on it in the said Protocol. In fact, Article 1(2) provides that advisory opinions of the European Court:

> shall not deal with any question relating to the content or scope of the rights or freedoms defined in Section I of the Convention and in the Protocols thereto, or with any other question which the Commission, the Court, or the Committee of Ministers might have to consider in consequence of any such proceedings as could be instituted in accordance with the Convention.

It is obvious that a high degree of inventiveness is required for the formulation of a question of any importance which could stand the test of Article 1(2) and could therefore be submitted to the Court. So far, at any rate, this has not happened, and for the future one should not expect that the Court will receive many requests for an advisory opinion. It is submitted that it is regrettable that the advisory jurisdiction of the Court does not have a wider scope. This might have the salutary effect that gaps still existing at the moment in the Court's case-law, might be filled without the necessity of the previous submission to the Commission of a complaint about an alleged violation of the Convention. This is all the more urgent since it appears in practice that, in comparison with the large number of issues that may arise in connection with the Convention and the total of the complaints submitted to the Commission, the number of cases that is submitted to the Court is still comparatively limited.[285]

Widening of the scope of the Court's advisory jurisdiction would require amendment of Protocol No. 2. In our opinion the subject-matter to which requests for an advisory opinion may relate should be extended to any legal question concerning the Convention and the Protocols, though on condition that the giving of an advisory opinion by the Court must not amount to a decision of the Court under Section IV of the Convention and that the request must not directly relate to a dispute which is pending before the Commission or the Court, while a wide discretion ought to be allowed to the Court to comply with the request or not, on the basis of character and/or the importance of the question submitted to it and in view of its case load.

Secondly, more organs should be entitled to submit a request for an advisory opinion. In the present situation only the Committee of Ministers may address a request for an advisory opinion to the Court (Article 1(1) of Protocol No. 2). However, in particular the Commission, in view of its general task of protector of the legal order created by the Convention, would seem to be eminently qualified to make such requests. In addition, the Parliamentary Assembly of the Council of Europe, and perhaps each of the individual Contracting States, might be considered for entitlement to make a request.

However, in this context too it may be said that such changes depend on the consent of the Contracting States, and that so far there has been little evidence of

---

[285] See *supra* p. 199.

willingness on their part to widen the scope of the advisory jurisdiction of the Court.

A request for an advisory opinion must indicate in precise terms the question on which the opinion of the Court is sought, and in addition the date on which the Committee of Ministers decided to request an advisory opinion, as well as the names and addresses of the person or persons appointed by the Committee to give the Court any explanations which it may require (Rule 60 of the Rules of Court). A copy of the request is transmitted to the members of the Court and to the Commission. For the remainder the Commission is involved in the proceedings only if the President of the Court takes the initiative to invite the Commission, by reason of the nature of the question, to submit written observations to the Court. Such an invitation is addressed at all events to the Contracting States (Rule 61 of the Rules of Court).

The President lays down the time-limits for the filing of written comments or other documents (Rule 62 of the Rules of Court). He also decides whether after the closure of the written procedure an oral hearing is to be held (Rule 63 of the Rules of Court).

Advisory opinions are given by majority vote of the plenary Court. They shall mention the number of judges constituting the majority, while any judge may attach to the opinion of the Court either a separate opinion, concurring with or dissenting from the advisory opinion, or a bare statement of dissent (Rule 65 of the Rules of Court).

The advisory opinion is read out by the President or his delegate at a public hearing, and certified copies are sent to the Committee of Ministers, the Contracting States, the Commission and the Secretary General of the Council of Europe (Rules 66 and 67 of the Rules of Court).

If the Court considers that the request for an advisory opinion is not within its consultative competence, it so declares in a reasoned decision (Rule 64 of the Rules of Court).

Chapter V

The Examination of a Case by the Committee of Ministers

1 INTRODUCTION

Unlike the Commission and the Court, the Committee of Ministers was not set up in connection with the adoption of the European Convention. It is the policy-making and executive organ of the Council of Europe.[1]

One of the tasks of the Committee of Ministers concerning human rights results directly from the Statute of the Council of Europe, *viz.* from Article 8. In virtue of this article the Committee supervises the observance of the obligation contained in Article 3 of the Statute, according to which every member of the Council of Europe 'must accept the principles of the rule of law and of the enjoyment by all persons within its jurisdiction of human rights and fundamental freedoms'. The more specific tasks of the Committee of Ministers with regard to human rights, however, have been laid down in the Convention.

According to Article 21 of the Convention, the Committee of Ministers elects the members of the Commission.[2] In the election of the members of the Court, too, the Committee plays a part. According to Article 39 of the Convention the judges are elected by the Consultative (read now: Parliamentary) Assembly of the Council of Europe from a list of persons nominated by the Member States of the Council of Europe.[3] Since the Committee of Ministers represents the members within the Council of Europe, it is in fact this organ which submits the lists to the Parliamentary Assembly.

2 THE SUPERVISORY TASK OF THE COMMITTEE OF MINISTERS UNDER THE CONVENTION

Apart from its function in the election procedures, the Committee of Ministers also performs a number of supervisory tasks under the European Convention. One of these, the supervision under Article 54 of the execution by the parties of the decisions of the Court, has been described above.[4]

The most important function of the Committee of Ministers, however, is that which ensues from Article 32. In those instances where, after a complaint has been declared admissible by the Commission and a report on the merits has been sent to the Committee of Ministers, the case has not been referred to the Court within a period of three months, the Committee of Ministers decides whether there has

---

[1] On the Committee, see also *supra* Chapter I, section 9.
[2] See *supra* pp. 26-27.
[3] See *supra* p. 32.
[4] See *supra* pp. 219-220.

been a violation of the Convention. With respect to those cases the Committee of Ministers has a task comparable to that of the Court, although the procedure followed by the two organs differs quite substantially. The decisions of both organs are binding: Contracting States have undertaken to regard as binding on them the decision taken by the Committee of Ministers in the case concerned (Article 32(4)). However, the State which is declared in default by the Committee of Ministers has a certain discretion in taking 'satisfactory' measures within a prescribed period (Article 32(3)), while a decision of the Court must be complied with directly (Article 53).

All in all it may be said that the Committee of Ministers performs a (quasi-) judicial function under Article 32 in the second phase of the supervisory procedure, comparable to what – alternatively – the function of the Court is. This in spite of the fact that, considering its composition,[5] procedure and functions under the Statute of the Council of Europe, the Committee of Ministers has to be regarded as a political organ.

This situation, in which a judicial function is performed by a political organ, is the result of a compromise reached during the drafting of the Convention.[6] On the one hand, it appeared impossible to find sufficient support for a Court with compulsory jurisdiction. On the other hand, it was deemed desirable that the supervisory procedure should ultimately result, in all cases, in a binding decision on whether there had been a violation of the Convention. Ultimately the solution found was to entrust that decision to the Committee of Ministers of the Council of Europe for those cases where the Court did not have jurisdiction or which were not brought before the Court.[7]

3 THE EXAMINATION OF THE CASE BY THE COMMITTEE OF MINISTERS

3.1 General

After the Commission has completed its examination of the merits of a case, it draws up a report. This report is transmitted to the Committee of Ministers. This does not yet mean that the latter organ is competent to consider the case. Such competence arises only after a period of three months from the date of transmission of the report, provided that within that period the case has not been referred to the Court (Article 32). If the respondent State is not subject to the compulsory jurisdiction of the Court, that State may give its consent to the case being brought before the Court (Article 48). The Convention does not contain any more provisions about the examination of a case by the Committee.

---

[5] See *supra* pp. 36-37.
[6] See *supra* p. 36.
[7] *Idem.*

The proceedings before the Committee of Ministers do not have a very clear-cut character. The chairman consults with the representatives of the States involved in the case to obtain their opinion about the procedure to be followed. If necessary, the Committee of Ministers subsequently specifies the order in which and the time-limits within which any written submissions and other documents are to be deposited. This equally applies to inter-State disputes and to cases which originate from individual applications. However, since Rule 8 speaks of 'State Party or States Parties to the dispute', it has to be assumed that, besides the State against which the original application was lodged, only the State by which the original application was submitted is considered as a State involved in the case, and not the State of which the individual applicant is a national.

3.2 The Procedure Followed by the Committee of Ministers

The Committee of Ministers has adopted a number of Rules in connection with the application of Article 32 of the Convention.[8] From these Rules and a number of other points discussed by the Committee of Ministers[9] the following general lines may be inferred.

Rule 1 provides that, when exercising its functions under Article 32 of the Convention, the Committee of Ministers is entitled to discuss the substance of any case on which the Commission has submitted a report, for example by considering written or oral statements of the parties and hearing of witnesses. The formulation of this rule does not appear quite accurate. Indeed, it refers to any case on which the Commission has submitted a report, while according to Article 32 of the Convention it ought to be added: 'and which has not been referred to the Court within the prescribed period'.

Rule 4 states that the Committee of Ministers must have all the necessary powers to reach a decision on the report of the Commission, but that, should the need arise, it may entrust the task of taking evidence and the like to another body. And indeed, in the second of the 'Other points discussed by the Committee of Ministers' it is stated that the Committee of Ministers 'is not well equipped to take evidence, *etc.* and ought not normally to undertake such tasks'. There the following possibilities are mentioned.

In the first place the Commission might be called in. This might be done in two ways. On the one hand a separate additional Protocol might be adopted, conferring on the Commission the power to undertake the task concerned on behalf of the Committee of Ministers. On the other hand the Committee of Ministers might invite the Commission to undertake this task on its behalf. The Commission would then have to be asked in each individual case whether it is prepared to do so.

---

[8]   Rules adopted by the Committee of Ministers for the application of Article 32 of the Convention, Council of Europe, *Collected Texts*, Strasbourg, 1996.
[9]   'Other points discussed by the Committee of Ministers', *ibidem*, pp. 319-321.

Secondly, the Committee of Ministers itself, possibly composed of so-called 'alternate members', might undertake this task. As appears from Article 14 of the Statute of the Council of Europe, the Member States are normally represented on the Committee of Ministers by the Ministers for Foreign Affairs, but they may also nominate other persons ('alternates') if this is desirable in the circumstances. For the case here referred to one might consider the Ministers of Justice, or even experts specially nominated for the purpose, or the Permanent Representatives to the Council of Europe who normally act as 'deputies'. Point 2 also provides that the Committee of Ministers may appoint a sub-committee for this purpose.

Finally, Article 17 of the Statute of the Council of Europe affords still another possibility. According to that article the Committee of Ministers may set up advisory or technical committees or commissions if it deems this desirable. The Committee of Ministers might proceed to do so for the purpose of taking evidence and other tasks within the context of its function under Article 32 of the Convention.

The Committee of Ministers has decided not to opt for an additional Protocol but to leave the choice open for a decision *ad hoc* should the need arise. In that case, in our opinion, the most appropriate solution would be to entrust the Commission with the task in question, since that organ appears to be best equipped for it and moreover has already performed the same task in an earlier phase of the procedure. If this construction is not chosen, it would seem best to leave the task to a committee specially nominated for the purpose. For the composition of such a committee it would then be possible to choose expert persons. Moreover, such a committee, although it would of course be directly subordinate to the Committee of Ministers, would perhaps be less focused on national interests than the members of the Committee of Ministers themselves or their 'alternates'.

3.3 The Composition of the Committee of Ministers

When exercising its function under Article 32 of the Convention, the Committee of Ministers is composed in the same way as for the performance of the tasks resulting from the Statute of the Council of Europe.[10] This follows in so many words from the Rules adopted by the Committee of Ministers in connection with the application of Article 32 of the Convention. In fact, Rule 2 provides that the representative of any Member State on the Committee of Ministers is fully qualified to take part in the activities of the Committee of Ministers within the context of Article 32 of the Convention, even if that State has not yet ratified the Convention. The representatives of the States which are parties to the dispute, also participate.

In its composition the Committee of Ministers therefore has some resemblance to the Court, membership of which is also coupled – but in that case with respect

---

[10] For this composition, see *supra* pp. 36-37.

to only the number of judges[11] – with membership of the Council of Europe,[12] whereas with respect to the Commission the criterion chosen for the number of the members is the number of the States which are parties to the Convention.[13]

With regard to the chairmanship of the Committee of Ministers, too, in principle the normal rules apply. This means that the chairmanship rotates among the representatives of the Member States in the alphabetical order of the States in the English language.[14] However, there is an exception to this rule in that, if the chairmanship of the Committee of Ministers is held by the representative of a Member State which is party to a dispute referred to the Committee of Ministers, under Rule 7 that representative must step down from the Chair during the discussion of the Commission's report. During that period the chairmanship is then performed by the representative of the State which in the English alphabetical order succeeds the State whose representative had to step down temporarily from the Chair.

3.4 Proposals by the Committee of Ministers

Under Article 32(2), when the Committee of Ministers has found that there has been a violation of the Convention, the Contracting State concerned is obliged to take appropriate measures within a period to be prescribed by the Committee of Ministers. In connection with that obligation, before the amendment of the Rules of the Committee of Ministers in December 1991, Rule 5 laid down the power of the Committee of Ministers to give advice or make suggestions or recommendations to the State concerned, provided that these were closely related to the violation in question. In addition, according to point 2*bis* of the appendix to the Rules of the Committee of Ministers it may consider, taking into account any proposals from the Commission, whether just satisfaction should be afforded to the injured party and, if necessary, indicate measures on this subject to the State concerned. Thus, the Committee of Ministers had stated its position that it could only recommend to the Government concerned which measures that latter should take.

The Committee of Ministers exercised this recommendary power for the first time in the *Greek* Case.[15] During the examination in the *Houart* Case concerning a violation of Article 6 on the ground of the non-public character of disciplinary proceedings, the Committee of Ministers was informed by the Belgian Government that it accepted the opinion of the Commission and that, following

---

[11] The similarity of nationality, too, exists largely in practice, although, as has been said, it is possible, and is actually the case at present, that judges may be elected in the Court who do not have the nationality of one of the Member States; see *supra* p. 26.

[12] See *supra* p. 2.

[13] See *supra* p. 26.

[14] See Rules 7 and 8 of the Rules of Procedure of the Committee of Ministers.

[15] See *Greek* Case, Yearbook XII (1969), pp. 513-514.

two judgments of the Court,[16] it had changed its legislation to the effect that certain disciplinary proceedings would henceforth be held in public. The Committee of Ministers took note of this information and recommended under Rule 5 that the Government had to pay the applicant a certain amount for the costs of the proceedings and of the defence.[17]

Since 1987 it had become standing practice that the Committee of Ministers, under Rule 5, also recommended that a certain amount of money be paid to the original applicant for expenses incurred in the proceedings before the Commission or as just satisfaction for other damages suffered.[18] According to the newly added paragraph 2 of Rule 9 the Committee of Ministers may request the Commission to make proposals concerning in particular the appropriateness, nature and extent of just satisfaction for the injured party. Such advice, suggestions, and recommendations of the Committee of Ministers were not, however, to be regarded as decisions in the sense of Article 32(4) of the Convention, and did not therefore involve any obligation on the part of the Governments to which they were addressed. In general the Contracting Parties did not object and paid the specified amount to the applicant.

The weakness of this recommendatory power under Rule 5 became evident in a number of cases against Italy concerning the violation of the length of proceedings, where the Italian Government disagreed with the proposals of the Committee of Ministers and refused to pay the applicants. In these cases the Committee of Ministers had recommended that the Government pay, within a time-limit of three months, just satisfaction to the applicants. The Committee of Ministers noted that, although the time-limit had extended, the Government still had not paid the sums it had agreed to pay following the recommendation of the Committee of Ministers. It decided to strongly urge the Government to proceed without delay to pay the specified amount to the applicants. It further decided, if need be, to resume consideration of these cases at each of its forthcoming meetings.[19]

During a special meeting of the Ministers' Deputees on 19 December 1991, the Rules of the Committee of Ministers were amended by way of deleting Rule 5. In its subsequent session, the next day, the Committee of Ministers adopted again resolutions in the Italian cases and now firmly stated that in accordance with Article 32(2) of the Convention the Government of Italy was to pay the applicants before a fixed date a certain amount in respect of just satisfaction. The Committee of Ministers invited the Government to inform it of the measures taken in consequence of the decision of the Committee of Ministers, having regard to its

---

[16] Judgment of 23 June 1981, *Le Compte, Van Leuven and De Meyere*, A.43; and judgment of 10 February 1983, *Albert and Le Compte*, A.58.

[17] Res. DH(87)10 of 25 September 1987.

[18] Res. DH(89)1 of 18 January 1989, *Sallustio*; Res. DH(89)6 of 2 March 1989, *Veit*.

[19] Res. DH(91)12 of 6 June 1991, *Azzi*; Res. DH(91)13 of 6 June 1991, *Lo Giacco*; Res. DH(91)21 of 27 September 1991, *Savoldi*; Res. DH(91)22 of 27 September 1991, *Van Eesbeeck*; Res. DH(91)23 of 27 September 1991, *Sallustio*; Res. DH 91(24) of 27 September 1991, *Minniti*.

obligations under Article 32(4) of the Convention to abide by it.[20] Finally, on 17 September 1992, the Committee of Ministers could end the consideration of these cases when it declared, after having taken note of the measures taken by the Italian Government, that it had exercised its functions under Article 32 of the Convention.[21] By deleting Rule 5, the Committee of Ministers has confirmed the binding decision-making power which it already possessed under Article 32(2) and (4). In fact Rule 5 was, according to an experienced commentator, an example of 'the Committee of Ministers' tendency not to make full use of, and even to reduce, the powers conferred upon it by the Convention. Indeed, from the very terms of Article 32, paragraphs 2 and 4, it is perfectly clear that the Committee of Ministers' decisions on remedial action or compensation have a binding character.' [22]

3.5 Voting by the Committee of Ministers

The voting procedure has been discussed above.[23] In that context it was indicated that the two-third majority required by the Convention with regard to a decision on whether or not there has been a violation diverges from the line followed in the Statute of the Council of Europe, according to which resolutions of the Committee of Ministers on important matters require the unanimous vote of the representatives casting a vote and of a majority of the representatives entitled to sit on the Committee. The two-third majority in the sense of Article 32 means 'a majority of two-thirds of the members entitled to sit on the Committee', *i.e.* a majority of two-thirds of the total number of members. Thus, the requirements of the Convention are more liberal than those set by the Statute for important matters, but more stringent if compared with the two-third majority requirement of Article 20(d) of the Statute for which a two-third majority of the representatives casting a vote and a majority of the representatives entitled to sit on the Committee is required.

On 25 March 1992, Protocol No. 10 to the European Convention was opened for signature. This Protocol amends the voting procedure of the Committee of Ministers laid down in Article 32 with a view to the reduction of the two-thirds majority provided therein to a simple majority. The Protocol shall enter into force

---

[20] Res. DH(92)3 of 20 February 1992, *Lo Giacco*; Res. DH92(4) of 20 February 1992, *Savoldi*; Res. DH(92)5 of 20 February 1992, *Van Eesbeeck*; Res. DH(92)6 of 20 February 1992, *Sallustio*; Res. DH(92)7 of 20 February 1992, *Minniti*.

[21] Res. DH(92)45 of 17 September 1992, *Azzi*; Res. DH(92)46 of 17 September 1992, *Lo Giacco*, Res. DH(92)47 of 17 September 1992, *Savoldi*; Res. DH(92)48 of 17 September 1992, *Van Eesbeeck*; Res. DH(92)49 of 17 September 1992, *Sallustio*; Res. DH(92)50 of 17 September 1992, *Minniti*.

[22] P. Leuprecht, 'The Protection of Human Rights by Political Bodies – The example of the Committee of Ministers of the Council of Europe', in: M. Nowak, D. Steurer and H. Tretter (eds.), *Progress in the Spirit of Human Rights*, Strasbourg, 1988, pp. 95-107 (105).

[23] See *supra* p. 38.

when all Parties to the Convention have expressed their consent to be bound by it.[24]

Apart from that, Rule 10 declares that the rules laid down in Article 20 of the Statute apply. This means that decisions under the second paragraph of Article 32, require a two-third majority of the representatives casting a vote and of a majority of the representatives entitled to sit on the Committee of Ministers. The same applies to the decision to discontinue the examination of the case because a friendly settlement or other arrangement has been made. Decisions concerning questions of procedure may be taken by a simple majority vote of the representatives entitled to sit on the Committee of Ministers.

As has been said, all Member States are fully entitled to take part in the activities of the Committee of Ministers within the context of Article 32 of the Convention, including those States which are parties to the dispute.[25] With respect to voting, this is expressly confirmed once more by Rule 10, where it is inferred from the general applicability of Article 20 of the Statute that parties to the dispute also have the right to vote in the Committee of Ministers.

The principle of full participation of all Member States in the procedure under Article 32 also applies in the sense that those States which were not parties to the proceedings before the Commission are also entitled, according to Rule 3, to make submissions and deposit documents in the proceedings before the Committee of Ministers *via* their representative on the Committee of Ministers. However, the Committee of Ministers has reserved its position on the possibility that they may also address to the Committee of Ministers a request which has not been made before the Commission, *e.g.* a request for damages (point 1).

3.6 Position of the Individual in the Proceedings Before the Committee of Ministers

The position of the original individual applicant in the proceedings before the Committee of Ministers is very weak if one may speak of any position at all. It is much weaker still than that in the proceedings before the Court, even as compared to the situation before the revision of the Rules of Court in 1982.[26]

In point 3 of the points discussed by the Committee of Ministers in connection with the application of Article 32 there is a reference to the decision of the Committee of Ministers not to establish a procedure permitting the communication to an individual applicant of the report of the Commission on his application, or the communication to the Committee of Ministers of the applicant's observations on the report. In comparison, in consequence of Rule 33(1) of the revised Rules of Court, the report will be transmitted to the original individual applicant. In the *Nielsen* Case the Commission gave as its opinion that the decision on communication of its report rests with the Committee of Ministers.

---

[24] For ratifications, see Appendix I.
[25] See *supra* p. 270.
[26] See *supra* p. 228.

The Committee of Ministers has adopted the view that transmission to the individual applicant of the complete text of, or extracts from the Commission's report should take place only on a strictly confidential basis, and only with the consent of the State against which the application was lodged (point 3(b)). Even under these conditions the individual applicant will not be notified of the content of the Commission's report in all cases; in the opinion of the Committee of Ministers transmission should be confined to exceptional cases where the proceedings before the Committee of Ministers render it desirable, *e.g.* when it wishes to obtain the observations of the applicant (point 3(b)). Considerations based on the interest of the individual applicant do not play a part in the decision on whether the report should be transmitted.

Even when the individual applicant addresses the Committee of Ministers in writing, such a letter is not taken into account, nor is he entitled to be heard by the Committee of Ministers. The Committee of Ministers bases this on the fact that in the system of the Convention he is not a party to the proceedings at this stage. This point of view is communicated to the individual applicant by the Secretary General when the latter informs him of the fact that the Commission's report on his case has been transmitted to the Committee of Ministers. If letters and documents addressed to the Committee of Ministers are nevertheless received from him, the Secretary General acknowledges their receipt, explaining why they will not form part of the proceedings before the Committee of Ministers and cannot be considered as documents in the case.[27]

In the past an *ad hoc* decision to transmit the report to the individual applicant was taken. More recent practice shows the tendency of transmitting the report to the individual applicant, before the publication of the report. The reason for this change is to be found in the fact that the Committee of Ministers, in case there has been a violation of the Convention, normally takes a binding decision with respect to the award of just satisfaction. In such a case the Committee of Ministers examines the proposals made by the Commission, when transmitting its report as regards just satisfaction to be awarded to the applicant. The Commission on its turn will contact the applicant and invite the latter to substantiate his claim. Therefore a practice has developed whereby the applicant now receives, in confidence, a copy of the report of the Commission which enables him to comment on the issue of just satisfaction.[28]

With the entry into force of Protocol No. 9 to the Convention, for those States which are bound by this Protocol, Article 31(2) of the Convention has been

---

[27] In 1972, the Committee of Ministers made a different decision with respect to letters of individuals in the context of the supervisory function of the Committee under Art. 54 of the Convention. When it is stated therein that no compensation has been received in accordance with a decision of the Court to that effect under Art. 50 of the Convention, or any other information is furnished in connection with the execution of such a decision of the Court, the Committee deems itself competent to take cognisance of it.

[28] See A. Drzemczewski, 'Decisions on the Merits: By the Committee of Ministers', in: R.St.J. Macdonald *et al.* (eds.), *The European System for the Protection of Human Rights*, The Hague, 1993, p. 733 (747-748).

amended in the sense that the report of the Commission shall also be transmitted to the individual applicant, if it deals with a petition submitted under Article 25. The State concerned and the applicant are not at liberty to publish it.

3.7 Position of the Commission in the Proceedings Before the Committee of Ministers

For a long time the individual applicant could also not participate as such in proceedings before the Court. The drawbacks of this system were, however, met to a large extent by the manner in which the Commission functioned in those proceedings.[29] In the proceedings before the Committee of Ministers, however, this role by the Commission is not possible. In fact, the Commission, too, in principle is not involved in the consideration of the case by the Committee of Ministers. The Committee of Ministers has even decided not to include in its Rules any provisions concerning participation of representatives of the Commission in the proceedings (point 4), and the Rules of the Commission do not contain a separate section concerning proceedings before the Committee of Ministers, such in contrast to proceedings before the Court. If the Committee of Ministers considers this desirable, it may request the Commission to supply information, but only in exceptional cases and only concerning certain specific points from its report. Consequently, even if the Commission receives such a request, its position still is not comparable to that in the proceedings before the Court, where it is able to elucidate all aspects of the case in a manner to be determined by the Commission itself.

3.8 Decision by the Committee of Ministers

Article 32(1) states that the proceedings before the Committee of Ministers result in a decision on whether there has been a violation of the Convention. However, just as is the case with proceedings before the Commission and before the Court,[30] proceedings before the Committee of Ministers have also sometimes been discontinued after the parties had reached some kind of settlement. In 1987, the Committee of Ministers added to that end to the Rules for the application of Article 32 Rule 6*bis* which reads as follows:

> Prior to taking a decision under Article 32, paragraph 1, of the Convention, the Committee of Ministers may be informed of a friendly settlement, arrangement or other fact of a kind to provide a solution of the matter. In that event, it may decide to discontinue its examination of the case, after satisfying itself that the solution envisaged is based on respect for human rights as defined in the Convention.

This added rule reflects existing practice of the Committee of Ministers.[31]

---

[29] See *supra* pp. 230-235.
[30] See *supra* pp. 189-190 and pp. 221-225 respectively.
[31] See in this respect, Res. DH(91)34 of 13 December 1991, *Garzarolli*; Res. DH(94)9 of 3 February 1994, *Gritschneder*.

In the joint cases of *Pataki* v. *Austria* and *Durnshirn* v. *Austria*[32] the applicants had alleged violation of the right to a fair trial (Article 6), because they were not represented in a particular phase of the criminal proceedings against them, whereas the Public Prosecutor was present. The Commission considered that the Austrian Penal Code conflicted with the Convention on this point. In the last phase of the proceedings before the Commission, Austria amended its legislation to eliminate this conflict. At the same time a temporary arrangement was made which enabled the applicants to have their case re-examined by the Austrian judicial authorities. At the suggestion of the Commission, the Committee of Ministers then expressed its satisfaction with the amendment of the law and decided that no further steps were necessary.[33] In the first case of *Greece* v. *the United Kingdom* the Committee of Ministers also decided that no further steps were needed after Greece and the United Kingdom had reached a settlement.[34]

The Committee of Ministers is also inclined to stop the proceedings if no settlement between the parties has been reached but certain measures have improved the situation complained of. Thus, in the *Bramelid and Malmström* Case the applicants complained that they had been compelled to surrender their shares for a price below their real value and alleged amongst others that the arbitrators to whom their dispute was referred did not constitute a 'tribunal' within the meaning of Article 6(1) of the Convention. In its report the Commission had expressed the opinion that there had been a violation of Article 6(1) of the Convention.[35] During the examination of the case, the Government of Sweden informed the Committee of Ministers that the Swedish Parliament had adopted an amendment to the legislation according to which a party not satisfied with a decision of the arbitrators could start a procedure before an ordinary court. The Committee of Ministers decided that, having regard to the information supplied by the Government of Sweden, no further action was called for.[36]

There is no objection to the Committee of Ministers accepting a settlement or other arrangement as a solution of the dispute, and thus as the end of the case, provided that it makes sure that also the original applicant consents and that the solution is in conformity with the Convention. The Committee of Ministers is a political and not a judicial organ and, in contrast with the Court, does not play a very important part in the interpretation of the Convention, so that the public interest involved in a declaratory decision as a preventive remedy plays hardly any role here. The very fact that the Commission has not referred the case to the Court and thus leaves it to the Committee of Ministers to deal with it, in general already indicates that no difficult questions of interpretation are at issue. If in such a case

---

[32] Yearbook VI (1963), p. 714 (738).
[33] *Ibidem*, p. 730. See also Res. DH(64)1 of 5 June 1964 concerning the *Glaser* Case.
[34] Res. DH(59)12 of 20 April 1959, Council of Europe, *Collection of Resolutions adopted by the Committee of Ministers in application of Article 32 of the European Convention for the Protection of Human Rights and Fundamental Freedoms 1959-1981*, Strasbourg, 1981.
[35] Report of 12 December 1983, D&R 38 (1984), p. 18 (38-41).
[36] Res. DH(84)4 of 25 October 1984, *ibidem*, p. 43.

the respondent State takes measures by which the situation conflicting with the Convention is eliminated, and moreover the original applicant has received just satisfaction, the purpose of the proceedings before the Committee of Ministers has been attained and there is no reason why the respondent State should be formally declared in default.

Strictly speaking, however, a decision of the Committee of Ministers that no further steps are required, is not in conformity with Article 32(1) of the Convention, since it ought formally to be preceded by a decision on whether there has been a violation of the Convention. In the above-mentioned cases the procedure followed by the Committee of Ministers did not involve great problems; the first case of *Greece* v. *the United Kingdom* concerned an inter-State dispute, in which the Committee of Ministers took its decision that no further steps were necessary at the instance of both States involved in the dispute. In the *Pataki* Case and the *Durnshirn* Case the decision of the Committee of Ministers was based on a suggestion of the Commission to settle the matter with the finding that no further steps were called for. The situation was somewhat different, however, in the *Fourons* Case. This case concerned the application of the Belgian linguistic legislation on education. In its report the Commission held unanimously that Belgium had violated Article 2 of Protocol No. 1 in conjunction with Article 14 of the Convention. After the transmission of the report, the Belgian legislation on this point was amended in such a way that the conflict with the Convention was abolished. In its resolution concerning this case the Committee of Ministers took cognisance of the opinion given by the Commission in its report and also of the new Belgian legislation, and subsequently decided that no further steps were called for.[37] And in a case in which the Swiss Government had ended, by means of an amendment of the law, a situation that was contrary to the Convention, the Committee of Ministers confined itself to referring to the opinion of the Commission, without itself giving any further decision.[38] In such cases, where the Commission has not been able to give its opinion on the newly arisen situation, in our view it is preferable that the Committee of Ministers adheres strictly to Article 32 of the Convention and decides that there has indeed been a violation of the Convention, but that *in its opinion* this has meanwhile been redressed by an amendment of the legislation, so that no further steps are necessary. This policy was followed, for instance, in the *Second 'Vagrancy'* Case,[39] in the *Kiss* Case[40] and in the *Hilton* Case.[41]

---

[37] Res. DH(74)1 of 30 April 1974, *Inhabitants of Les Fourons*, Yearbook XVII (1974), p. 542 (614-616).

[38] Res. DH(79)7 of 19 October 1979, *Eggs*.

[39] Res. DH(72)1 of 16 October 1972, *Second 'Vagrancy' Case*, Yearbook XV (1972), pp. 694-698.

[40] Res. DH(78)3 of 19 April 1978, *Kiss*.

[41] Res. DH(79)3 of 24 April 1979, *Hilton*. See also Res. DH(83)8 of 22 April 1983, *B* v. *the United Kingdom*; Res. DH(83)9 of 23 June 1983, *Tonwerke and Others*; Res. DH(83)14 of 27 October 1983, *Orchin*; Res. DH(84)4 of 25 October 1984, *Bramelid and Malmström*; Res. DH(85)1 of 25 January 1985, *C, Medway and Ball*; Res. DH(85)3 of 25 January 1985, *Zamir*; Res. DH(85)4 of

3.9 Situations in Which no Two-Third Majority can be Found in Order to Decide the Question Whether a Violation has Taken Place

A situation which conflicts flatly with Article 32 of the Convention, and for which at present there seems to be no solution, is the one which arises when in the Committee of Ministers the required two-third majority can be found neither for the view that there has been a violation nor for the view that no violation has occurred. In such a case no decision as required by Article 32 is taken, while there is no question of some kind of settlement between the parties, nor is there any guarantee that the situation held by the Commission to conflict with the Convention, is corrected or made good with respect to the victim by the respondent State.

An example is the *Huber* Case. In its report the Commission had given as its opinion that Austria had violated Article 6(1) of the Convention with respect to Huber.[42] The most important passage from the resolution of the Committee of Ministers in this case reads as follows:

> Voting in accordance with the provisions of Article 32(1) of the Convention, but without attaining the majority of two thirds of the members entitled to sit. Decides therefore that no further action is called for in this case.[43]

As has been said, the Committee of Ministers has been given a task under the European Convention in order to guarantee that the supervisory procedure should result at all events in a binding decision on whether or not there has been a violation. Such a guarantee does not exist under the present system, according to which a two-third majority is required, as is evident from the *Huber* Case, and also from the *East Africans* Case,[44] the *Dores and Silveira* Case,[45] the *Dobbertin* Case[46] and the *Warwick* Case.[47]

An attempt to find a solution for the problem is the adoption by the Committee of Ministers of Rule 9*bis* which provides that when a vote is taken in accordance with Article 32(1) and the majority required to decide whether there has been a violation of the Convention has not been attained, a second and final vote must be taken at one of the next three meetings of the Committee of Ministers. However, that leaves open the possibility that a two-third majority can also not be obtained at the second vote.

As has been said above, Protocol No. 10 was opened for signature on 25 March 1992, which will reduce the two-third majority requirement to a simple majority requirement. Its entry into force will reduce the problem of a deadlock substantially.

---

25 February 1985, *Marijnissen*; Res. DH(85)8 of 11 April 1985, *Neubeck*.

[42] Report of 8 February 1973, D&R 2 (1975), p. 11 (29).

[43] Res. DH(75)2 of 15 April 1975, Yearbook XVIII (1975), p. 325 (326).

[44] Res. DH(77)2 of 21 October 1977, Yearbook XX (1977), p. 642 (644).

[45] Res. DH(85)7 of 11 April 1985.

[46] Res. DH(88)12 of 28 September 1988.

[47] Res. DH(89)5 of 2 March 1989.

3.10 Measures to be Taken After the Committee of Ministers has Found a Violation

When the Committee of Ministers finds a violation of the Convention, it must prescribe, under Article 32(2), a period within which the State in question is to take the measures required in the light of the Committee's decision. So far no cases have come to our attention in which such a period has been prescribed for other measures than remunerations This may be accounted for partly by the fact that hitherto in only a few cases the Committee of Ministers has found a violation of the Convention which in its opinion called for further action other than the payment of satisfaction and costs.

The first such case was the *Greek* Case, in which the Committee of Ministers considered that a great many articles of the Convention had been violated.[48] However, before the Committee of Ministers had found in its resolution that there had been a violation of the Convention, Greece had already withdrawn from the Council of Europe and denounced the Convention.[49] Under these circumstances the Committee of Ministers observed that it was 'called upon to deal with the case in conditions which are not precisely those envisaged in the Convention' and concluded 'that in the present case there is no basis for further action under paragraph 2 of Article 32 of the Convention'.[50]

The only other case known to us is formed by the first two cases of *Cyprus* v. *Turkey*. On 21 October 1977 the Committee of Ministers decided in those cases that 'events which occurred in Cyprus constitute violations of the Convention'. In addition the Committee of Ministers requested Turkey to take measures 'in order to put an end to such violations as might continue to occur and so that such events are not repeated', and urged the parties 'to resume intercommunal talks'.[51] To our knowledge the Committee of Ministers did not prescribe a period within which these matters ought to be realised. Should this indeed be the case, the Committee of Ministers has acted contrary to the explicit provision of Article 32(2).

The foregoing means that there does not yet exist any practice concerning the length of the period referred to in Article 32(2). In general this will depend on the kind of measures which the State in question has to take in connection with the resolution of the Committee of Ministers. These measures in turn will be closely related to the nature of the violation found. Thus, a violation of the Convention consisting in a faulty application of a legal regulation by a government body can be undone with less difficulty and consequently more promptly than one where the legislation itself conflicts with the Convention.

In relation to the payment of satisfaction and costs, as mentioned before, in 1992 the Committee of Ministers for the first time expressly referred to its

---

[48] *Greek* Case, Yearbook XII (1969), p. 512.
[49] *Idem.*
[50] *Ibidem*, p. 513.
[51] Res. DH(79)1 of 20 January 1979, Yearbook XXII (1979), p. 440.

competence under Article 32(2). It did so in cases of individual applicants, where difficulties had occurred which had been caused by the refusal of a State to comply with the Committee's recommendation for payment to be made to the applicants. The Committee of Ministers decided to resume consideration of these cases at the next meeting following expiry of the time-limit set.[52]

When the Committee of Ministers prescribes a period as referred to in Article 32(2), it must also ascertain whether the State in question actually takes effective measures.[53] If this is not the case, according to the third paragraph of Article 32 the Committee of Ministers shall decide, again by a two-third majority of the members entitled to sit on the Committee of Ministers, what further steps have to be taken, and it shall publish the report of the Commission.

The sanction on the failure to act upon the decision of the Committee of Ministers under Article 32(1) is therefore twofold. It consists, on the one hand, of measures the substance and the form of which may be determined by the Committee of Ministers with a view to the circumstances of each individual case, and, on the other hand, of the publication of the Commission's report.

As has been said, in the *Greek* Case no period was prescribed, and owing to the special circumstances of that case the question as to whether or not the measures prescribed by the Committee of Ministers were acted upon has not been at issue. The Committee of Ministers did decide, however, to publish the Commission's report.[54] Also in the above-mentioned cases of *Cyprus* v. *Turkey* no period as referred to in Article 32(2) had been prescribed. By a resolution of 20 January 1979 the Committee of Ministers dealt again with the matter. It regretted to find that its request that the negotiations between the Turkish and the Greek-Cypriotic community be resumed, had not been complied with by the parties, and subsequently decided 'strongly to urge the parties to resume intercommunal talks under the auspices of the Secretary General of the United Nations in order to agree upon solutions on all aspects of the dispute', after which it stated that it considered this decision 'as completing its consideration of the case Cyprus versus Turkey'.[55]

This last part of the Committee's decision seems highly questionable to us. Even apart from the fact that a period should have been prescribed, Article 32(3), in our opinion, implies that the Committee of Ministers has to deal with a case in such a way that, and until the moment at which, this results in the States concerned having taken those measures which are required with a view to the protection of human rights envisaged by the Convention. In the case under discussion Cyprus and Turkey, contrary to Article 32(4), had not given effect to the original decision of the Committee of Ministers. Insofar as can be ascertained, at the moment when the second decision was taken there were also no indications

---

[52] See *supra* note 19.
[53] See *supra* note 15.
[54] See *Greek* Case, Yearbook XII (1969), p. 513.
[55] Res. DH(79)1 of 20 January 1979, Yearbook XXII (1979), p. 440.

that they would as yet take the measures prescribed in the original decision. In such a situation the Committee of Ministers should not have backed out of the case and shirked its responsibilities under the Convention by shifting the matter to the Secretary General of the United Nations. The Committee of Ministers did, however, also in this case decide to publish the report of the Commission.[56]

From the fact that the publication of the report referred to in Article 32(3) has the character of a sanction, one might infer that the Committee of Ministers does not proceed to such publication in cases in which it has come to the conclusion that there has not been a violation of the Convention. In practice, however, but for a few exceptions, all the reports of the Commission are published, regardless of whether or not the Committee of Ministers considers that there has been a violation. The reason for this is presumably the interest which the respondent State may have in publication when the Committee of Ministers has followed the viewpoint of the Commission in its decision and the conclusions in the Commission's report are favourable for that State. The decision to publish the report is then usually taken with the consent, or sometimes by special request, of the respondent State.

Only in a few cases has the respondent State objected against publication of the report of the Commission. This was the case in the two inter-State cases of *Greece v. the United Kingdom*, the case of *Lahaye, De Wilde, Nys and Swalens v. Belgium*, the cases of *Kiss* and *Hilton v. the United Kingdom* and in the case of *Dobbertin v. France*, while in the case of *Scheichelbauer v. Austria* the applicant objected against the publication of the report of the Commission.[57] The report of the Commission of 14 December 1973 in the case of the *East African Asians v. the United Kingdom*, has only in 1994 been made public at the request of the British Government. During the examination of the case of *Garzarolli v. Austria* a friendly settlement had been reached between the applicant and the Government, and the Committee of Ministers was informed that both the applicant and the Austrian Government did not wish the publication of the Commission's report in this case,[58] while in the case of *Sargin and Yagçi v. Turkey*, the Turkish Government objected against publication of the Commission's report.[59]

At its 307th meeting, in September 1979, the Ministers' Deputies adopted the rule that the individual applicant ought normally to be informed of the outcome of the examination of his case before the Committee of Ministers. Surprisingly enough, the decision to give this information requires a unanimous vote. This again indicates that the Committee of Ministers is more concerned with the interests of the Contracting States than with those of the individual whose rights are at issue.

---

[56] *Idem.*
[57] J. Velu, 'Report on Responsibilities for State Parties to the European Convention', *Proceedings of the Sixth International Colloquy about the European Convention on Human Rights*, Boston, 1988, p. 532 (616).
[58] Res. DH(91)34 of 13 December 1991.
[59] Res. DH(93)59 of 14 December 1993.

3.11 Other Functions Performed by the Committee of Ministers

During the Council of Europe Summit in Vienna in October 1993, one of the points discussed was the implications of the geographical enlargement of the Council of Europe as a result of the political changes which had taken place in Central and Eastern Europe as from 1989. On that occasion, the Heads of State and Government of the Member States of the Council of Europe stated that:

> the Council is the pre-eminent European political institution capable of welcoming, on an equal footing and in permanent structures, the democracies of Europe freed from communist oppression. For that reason the accession of those countries to the Council of Europe is a central factor in the process of European construction based on our Organisation's values. Such accession presupposes that the applicant country has brought its institutions and legal system into line with the basic principles of democracy, the rule of law and respect of human rights.[60]

In that context, the Committee of Ministers has repeatedly expressed the view that the opening up to the Central and Eastern European countries cannot take place at the cost of lowering the norms and standards of human rights protection established by the Council of Europe. In connection with the requests for accession of new Member States, the question arose, how to determine whether the State concerned fulfilled the requirements for membership. Apart from the procedure of Article 57 of the Convention,[61] the Council of Europe lacks a mechanism under which the Member States can be kept under constant surveillance on their compliance with the commitments accepted within the Council of Europe.

Against this background and inspired by the Vienna Summit, where the Heads of State and Government also resolved to ensure full compliance with the commitments accepted by all Member States within the Council of Europe, on 10 November 1994 the Committee of Ministers adopted a declaration on compliance with these commitments.[62] The declaration envisages a political mechanism under which the Members States of the Council of Europe, its Secretary General or its Parliamentary Assembly may refer questions of implementation of commitments concerning the situations of democracy, human rights and the rule of law to the Committee of Ministers. On 20 April 1995, the Committee of Ministers adopted the procedure for implementing the above-mentioned declaration. When considering issues referred to it, the Committee of Ministers will take account of all relevant information available from different sources such as the Parliamentary Assembly and the OSCE. The mechanism will not effect the existing procedures arising from statutory or conventional control mechanisms. At least three meetings of the Ministers' Deputies at A level, fixed in advance, will be devoted to this

---

[60] Council of Europe Summit, Vienna, 9 October 1993; see NQHR, Vol. 11, No. 4, 1993, p. 513.

[61] See *infra* pp. 287-292.

[62] Declaration of the Committee of Ministers of the Council of Europe of 10 November 1994 on the Compliance with Commitments accepted by Member States of the Council of Europe, Yearbook XXXVII (1994), pp. 461-462.

question every year. At the first meeting and subsequently every second year, unless decided otherwise, the Secretary General shall present a factual overview of the compliance with the commitments. The discussions will be confidential and held in camera 'with a view to ensuring compliance with commitments, in the framework of a constructive dialogue'. Finally, in cases requiring specific action, the Committee of Ministers may decide to request the Secretary General to make contacts, collect information or furnish advice; to issue an opinion or recommendation; to forward a communication to the Parliamentary Assembly or to take any other decision within its statutory powers.

It would be premature to give an opinion on this mechanism. It in fact does not provide the Committee of Ministers with more powers than it already had. It also may result in even less willingness on the part of the Member States to make use of the inter-State complaint mechanism under Article 24 of the European Convention. The new mechanism has, however, the advantage that it may create a platform for the Committee of Ministers and the Member States to discuss and examine on a structural basis the human rights situation in all Member States of the Council of Europe. It also provides a more convenient tool for the Member States to employ a kind of 'early warning system' when there are indications that one of the Member States does not fulfil its obligations. If the Member States are fully aware of their responsibilities concerning the collective enforcement of human rights, the new mechanism may add a new dimension to the protection of human rights in Europe. In the more than 50 years of its existence, there have been situations in which silent diplomacy might have had a better result than the existing complaint procedures.

4 COMPARISON OF THE PROCEDURE BEFORE THE COMMITTEE OF MINISTERS WITH THE ONE BEFORE THE COURT

The functioning of the Committee of Ministers under Article 32 of the Convention can hardly be described as perfect. Political elements sometimes have their advantages even in a procedure as provided for in the European Convention, as became clear in the discussion of the friendly settlement.[63] However, when a (quasi-)judicial function is concerned, the introduction of political elements normally involves considerable drawbacks. At all events the advantages would seem not to outweigh the distrust which a construction according to which a political organ has to make judicial decisions, creates among the individuals concerned.

The political character of the Committee of Ministers has its effects on the procedure under Article 32. This procedure is not public, not adversary, and takes place before a non-independent organ. Consequently, it by no means satisfies the requirements of a fair trial which Article 6 of the Convention imposes upon the Contracting States in respect of their domestic procedures.

---

[63] See *supra* pp. 178-192.

Despite the fact that the Committee of Ministers is therefore poorly equipped for its task, in practice it still takes the final decision on whether or not there has been a violation of the Convention in almost as large a number of cases as does the Court.[64] This is caused by the decisions of the Commission and the States concerned on whether or not to bring a case before the Court. As has already been observed above, the Commission's policy of referring cases to the Court, is characterised by a certain degree of reserve, even though for the past few years a striking turn of the tide has been apparent.[65] The States still do not show much inclination to leave the final decision to the Court. In general they prefer – certainly in the position of respondent States – to have their case dealt with by the Committee of Ministers. Indeed, in that organ not only can they participate in the vote on the decision to be taken, but in other respects, too, they may influence the decision *via* the discussions on the matter which precede the vote. Moreover, in the case of the Court four votes (in a Chamber of seven judges) are sufficient to arrive at a conviction, while in the Committee of Ministers in June 1997 27 votes – two-thirds of the 40 Member States – are required. The proportion of votes alone makes the chances of a conviction in the last-mentioned organ considerably smaller than in the Court.

Even though in many cases it is the Committee of Ministers which takes the final decision on whether there has been a violation of the Convention, up to the present this organ has not played an important part in the interpretation of the Convention. In practically all cases the Committee of Ministers follows in its decision the opinion of the Commission, without giving any further reasons. The contribution of the Committee of Ministers to the further development of the legal order laid down in the Convention cannot therefore be compared to that of either the Court or the Commission – apart, of course, from the competence of the Committee of Ministers, as an organ of the Council of Europe, to make recommendations to the Member States to amend the Convention.

The principal reason for this appears to be the fact that the Committee of Ministers as a political organ lacks a characteristic feature that is essential for the discharge of a judicial function, *viz.* independence. Whoever may represent the States in the Committee, Foreign Ministers, Ministers of Justice, their deputies, or even special experts, they all follow the instructions of their Government.

As stated above, Protocol No. 11 to the Convention, which will reform the supervisory mechanism under the Convention, has also consequences with respect to the supervisory task of the Committee of Ministers.[66] Once this Protocol has entered into force, all allegations of violations of individuals' rights will be

---

[64] See in this respect the regularly updated *Collection of Resolutions adopted by the Committee of Ministers in application of Articles 32 and 54 of the European Convention on Human Rights*, Council of Europe, Strasbourg.
[65] See *supra* p. 199.
[66] See *supra* p. 194.

referred to the Court. The Committee of Ministers will then no longer have the power to decide on the merits of these cases, though it will retain its role of monitoring the enforcement of the Court's judgments.

Chapter VI

The Supervisory Function of the Secretary General of the Council of Europe Under Article 57

1 INTRODUCTION

In addition to the complaint procedure, the European Convention provides for yet another procedure for supervising the observance by the Contracting States of their obligations under the Convention. This is based on Article 57 of the Convention and is entrusted to the Secretary General of the Council of Europe. Article 57 reads as follows:

> On receipt of a request from the Secretary General of the Council of Europe any High Contracting Party shall furnish an explanation of the manner in which its internal law ensures the effective implementation of any of the provisions of this Convention.

This provision originates from the work of the United Nations. In 1947, within the context of the *travaux préparatoires* of what later developed into the Universal Declaration and the two Covenants, a text was drawn up which related to civil and political rights. This text contained a provision according to which the Secretary General of the United Nations would have the right to request the States which would become Parties to the treaty then in preparation to report on the manner in which the effective implementation of the provisions of the treaty was ensured in their internal law. During the preparation of the European Convention this idea was adopted in a British proposal to the Committee of Experts and accepted by that Committee.

Under international law there are several examples of procedures in which States have to submit reports to make possible the assessment of the observance of their obligations. This system of supervision, which in general is referred to as the reporting procedure, may constitute an effective instrument of control, also in the field of the protection of human rights.

Treaties for the protection of human rights are not concerned primarily with the interests of the State, but with the interests of the individual. If such a treaty provides for an inter-State complaint procedure, the Contracting States will make their decision on whether to file an application dependent upon political considerations. And precisely because the interests of the State are affected to a less extent by a violation, States will proceed to file an application only in very exceptional cases. In this respect the practice with respect to Article 24 of the European Convention speaks for itself.[1] Owing to the lack of initiative on the side of States to start a complaint procedure, a gap in the supervision of the treaty concerned may readily arise. A reporting procedure, such as is provided for in Article 57, may fill this gap, because the initiative for this may be taken by an

---

[1] See *supra* pp. 43-44.

international organ and is not dependent on a decision of one of the Contracting States.

In the case of treaties providing for an individual right of complaint the problem of the States' lack of initiative to start the complaint procedure rises less frequently, because the initiative may also be taken by those individuals who have a personal and direct interest in it. It should, however, be borne in mind that the individual right of complaint is optional in practically all cases, which implies that it can only be employed if the State concerned has accepted that possibility. At the moment all Contracting States have accepted the right of individual complaint under Article 25 of the Convention.[2] However, situations which do conflict with the Convention but have not yet made victims in the sense of Article 25 can be complained of only by the Contracting States.[3] In such cases the supervision of the observance of the obligations under the Convention, therefore, is again dependent on the lodging of a complaint by a State, with all the disadvantages and restrictions involved. Here again a reporting procedure may be useful. Moreover there may be situations where there are victims, who, however, for one reason or another, do not take the initiative to lodge a complaint.

Even apart from the question of whether the complaint procedure provided for functions effectively or not and whether or not the initiative has been laid also in the hands of the individual concerned, the existence of a reporting procedure side by side with a complaint procedure is of great value. A reporting procedure, precisely because its character differs from that of a complaint procedure, may enhance the effectiveness of the international supervision in some respects. Thus, *via* a reporting procedure all the Contracting States can be controlled at the same time, while in a complaint procedure always the acts or omissions of only one State are examined. The first advantage of this is that the resistance to the supervision may be less if all the States are equally subjected to examination. Further, because of the possibility of comparison a more balanced picture may be obtained of the state of affairs with respect to the implementation of the treaty in question within the whole group of Contracting States, which might facilitate the taking of measures for the improvement of the situation. In addition, the reporting procedure makes it possible to complete the picture of implementation, because this form of supervision may comprise all the provisions of the treaty in question simultaneously, while in a complaint procedure only one, or at most a few, of the provisions at a time will be examined. Furthermore, it is an advantage that the international organ concerned may assure, *via* the reporting procedure, a certain continuity in the supervision, because it can itself decide which aspects are to be examined and when, while in the case of a complaint procedure one must wait until a case is submitted, in which case the supervision has a more *ad hoc* character. The continuity, owing to which a comparison with the situation in the past is also possible, naturally enhances the effectiveness of the supervision.

---

[2] See *supra* p. 44.
[3] See *supra* pp. 43-44.

Finally, the advantage may be mentioned that the reporting system will in general assume a form that is more flexible and better adapted to the particularities of States than the much more formal complaint procedure.

In view of the above-mentioned advantages it is not astonishing that many international regulations for the protection of human rights, both those concerning civil and political rights, and those concerning economic, social and cultural rights, provide for a reporting procedure.[4]

2 THE REPORTING PROCEDURE UNDER ARTICLE 57 OF THE CONVENTION

In comparison with most other treaties on human rights which include for the Contracting States the obligation to hand in reports, the provision of Article 57 of the European Convention is very brief and leaves a great number of questions unanswered. Most of this lack of clarity, however, has been removed by practice. At any rate it is clear from the text of the article that the Secretary General has the *right* to request the Contracting States to furnish an explanation of the manner in which in their internal law the effective implementation of the provisions of the Convention is ensured, and that the Contracting States have the *duty* to provide him with this information. For the rest, little can be inferred with certainty from the article.

The main question that is left unanswered is whether Article 57 confers discretionary powers upon the Secretary General or whether in the exercise of his powers he is dependent in some way on another organ of the Council of Europe. Since Article 57 is silent on this, one must assume that the Secretary General has full discretion. In a statement made before the Legal Committee of the Parliamentary Assembly the then Secretary General gave as his opinion:

> The Secretary General in making a request under Article 57 is acting under his own responsibility and at his own discretion, in virtue of powers conferred upon him by the Convention independently of any powers he may have in virtue of the Statute of the Council of Europe. His power under Article 57 is not subject to control or instruction.[5]

Until now not a single Contracting State has officially objected to this interpretation by the Secretary General of his supervisory powers. It may therefore be assumed that the above-mentioned statement constitutes an almost generally

---

[4] See, *e.g.*, Arts 22 and 23 of the Constitution of the International Labour Organisation; Art. 9 of the Convention on the Elimination of All Forms of Racial Discrimination; Arts 40 *et seq.* of the International Covenant on Civil and Political Rights; Arts 16 *et seq.* of the International Covenant on Economic, Social and Cultural Rights; Art. 19 of the Torture Convention; and Art. 21 of the European Social Charter.

[5] Statement by the Secretary General on Art. 57 of the European Convention on Human Rights made before the Legal Committee of the Consultative Assembly in Oslo on 29 August 1964, Council of Europe, *Collected Texts*, Strasbourg, 1994, pp. 235-236.

accepted interpretation of Article 57.[6] This is not to say, however, that the Secretary General's actions in this field are always welcomed by the Contracting States. Three States have refused to furnish a reply to his fourth request: the Federal Republic of Germany, Iceland and Malta, while his fifth request has met with broad opposition so far.

From these discretionary powers of the Secretary General with respect to the application of Article 57, in practice a number of more specific powers which also do not directly result from the text of that article have been inferred. Thus the Secretary General may determine the date on which, and consequently the frequency with which reports have to be submitted. Hitherto the Contracting States have been invited five times to submit reports on the application of the rights laid down in the Convention, viz. in October 1964, in July 1970, in April 1975, in March 1983 and in July 1988.

The Secretary General, when exercising his powers under Article 57, is free to refer to all or to a few of the provisions of the Convention, or to only one of them. In 1964 the Contracting States were requested to furnish information on the question of 'how their laws, their case-law and their administration practice give effect to the fundamental rights and freedoms guaranteed by the Convention and its first Protocol'.[7] In that case, therefore, they had to report on all the rights set forth in the Convention and the Protocol. In 1970, on the other hand, the request of the Secretary General concerned only Article 5(5), and in 1975 information was required on the application of Articles 8, 9, 10 and 11. Moreover, on the latter occasion, the Secretary General reserved himself the right to ask for a further explanation of certain points in connection with the reports submitted by the States.[8] In 1983, the Secretary General made an enquiry into the implementation of the Convention 'in respect of children and young persons placed in care or in institutions following a decision of the administrative or judicial authorities',[9] while in 1988 the request concerned Article 6(1).[10]

The question of whether a request to submit reports must be addressed to all the Contracting States at the same time, or whether Article 57 may also be applied with respect to one State or some of them separately, cannot yet be answered on the basis of practice. In the five cases in which the Secretary General asserted his powers under Article 57 all the States were approached indiscriminately. In our opinion, however, the above-mentioned discretionary powers of the Secretary

---

[6] See W. Pahr, 'Etude Fonctionnelle des Organes Européens de Protection Internationales des Droits de l'Homme', RDH, No. 2, 1969, pp. 199-207 (202-203). See also P. Mahoney, 'Does Article 57 of the European Convention on Human Rights Serve any Useful Purpose?', in: *Protecting Human Rights: The European Dimension; Studies in Honour of Gérard J. Wiarda*, Cologne *etc.*, 1988, pp. 373-393 (380-382) with reference to other authors. He also refers to the different opinion of the then governmental expert for the Federal Republic of Germany, Irene Maier.

[7] See Pahr, *supra* note 6, p. 203.

[8] *Idem.*

[9] See Mahoney, *supra* note 6, p. 375.

[10] Council of Europe, *Information Sheet*, No. 21, Strasbourg, 1988, p. 95.

General might permit him to request a report from one State alone, or some of them.[11] However, it is not likely to occur very often that the Secretary General examines the acts or omissions of one State or some of them only, because this is apt to be regarded as a discriminatory and unfriendly act, and may undermine the confidence in his impartiality which is necessary for an adequate discharge of his function. Moreover, in that case a number of the above-mentioned advantages of the reporting system will no longer apply. It is only in very clear cases of massive and structural violation of the Convention, which cannot be exposed in some other way, that the Secretary General might be well-advised to make use of his powers under Article 57 with respect to a particular State. Thus, one might think of a situation like that in Greece in 1967, if at that time for some reason no complaint against this State would have been submitted. It might also have been conceivable that Turkey should have been requested to submit a report on its application of Article 15, while, more generally, the situation in Turkey might have been reviewed *via* the reporting procedure as long as no complaint directed at it by a State was submitted.

Practice has produced some clarity concerning the question what is further to be done with the reports submitted by the Contracting States and what consequences, if any, may be attached to a violation of the Convention discovered in this way. The Secretary General compiles the answers of the Contracting States to his requests in a document which is subsequently brought to the notice of all the Contracting States and of the Parliamentary Assembly of the Council of Europe.[12] Before this, the States is given an opportunity to intimate that they wish certain parts of the data furnished by them not to be published.[13]

As a rule therefore the answers of the Contracting States are published. This in itself may already form an element of sanction for those cases in which, according to those answers, there has been a violation of the Convention. For that purpose some kind of (comparative) analysis with the assistance of independent experts might be desirable, as was done with the results of the third application of Article 57.[14]

In that case the defaulting State is exposed to criticism of the other States, the Parliamentary Assembly and public opinion. It is, however, doubtful whether, when serious violations have been found, this possibility will be sufficiently effective to put an end to the violation. The Secretary General has not been empowered to refer a case *via* a complaint procedure to the Commission, and, if declared admissible, to the Court. Such a possibility might enhance the effectiveness of the supervision under Article 57, although one may ask oneself whether this power would not place the Secretary General too far outside his proper function, and whether in the public interest such a right of complaint had

---

[11] In that sense also Pahr, *supra* note 6, p. 205; and Mahoney, *supra* note 6, pp. 382-383.

[12] The last report was also brought to the attention of the Commission and the Court.

[13] Pahr, *supra* note 6, p. 203.

[14] See Mahoney, *supra* note 6, p. 375.

not better be entrusted to a separate organ, which is politically less dependent on the cooperation of the States.[15]

Under the present circumstances in many cases a violation found *via* the reporting procedure can be subjected to a further examination and result in a binding decision only if one of the other States is prepared – perhaps also on the ground of the information obtained by means of Article 57 – to make use of its right under Article 24. Moreover, this can be done only if the admissibility conditions of Article 26 do not eliminate that possibility. The Secretary General himself can do little else but bring the case, if there has been a very serious violation, to the notice of the Committee of Ministers, with a view to possible measures on the ground of Article 8 of the Statute of the Council of Europe. Until now, however, the Secretary General has not given any follow-up to his initiatives.

---

[15] On this, see P. van Dijk, 'A European Ombudsman for Human Rights; Reopening a Discussion', RDH, No. 10, 1977, pp. 187-211.

Chapter VII

Analysis of the Rights and Freedoms

1 INTRODUCTION

As stated in the preamble to the Convention, the aim which the Contracting States wished to achieve was 'to take the first steps for the collective enforcement of certain of the Rights stated in the Universal Declaration'. The purpose of the Convention was therefore, within the framework of the Council of Europe, to lay down certain human rights, proclaimed in 1948 by the United Nations in the Universal Declaration of Human Rights, in a binding agreement, and at the same time to provide for supervision of the observance of those human rights provisions.

Only certain rights were included in these 'first steps'. A comparison with the Universal Declaration discloses that by no means all the rights mentioned there have been laid down in the Convention. It covers mainly those rights which were to be referred to, in the later elaboration of the Universal Declaration in the two Covenants, as 'civil and political rights', and not even all of those. The principle of equality before the law, the right to freedom of movement and residence, the right to seek and to enjoy asylum in other countries from persecution, the right to a nationality, the right to own property and the right to take part in the Government, which are included in the Universal Declaration,[1] are not to be found in the Convention.

Subsequent steps have been taken within the framework of the Council of Europe, both in the form of additional Protocols to the Convention[2] and in the form of other conventions, among them in particular the European Social Charter of 1961,[3] while Article 60 of the Convention also opens the door to further steps outside the framework of the Council of Europe.

The reason for the limited scope of the Convention was explained as follows by Teitgen, the rapporteur of the Legal Committee of the Consultative Assembly of the Council of Europe, which prepared the first draft of the Convention:

> It [*i.e.* the Committee] considered that, for the moment, it is preferable to limit the collective guarantee to those rights and essential freedoms which are practised, after long usage and experience, in all the democratic countries. While they are the first triumph of democratic regimes, they are also the necessary condition under which they operate. Certainly, professional freedoms and social rights, which have themselves an intrinsic value, must also, in the future, be defined and protected. Everyone will, however, understand that it is necessary to begin at the beginning and to guarantee political democracy in the European Union and then to co-ordinate our economies, before undertaking the generalization of social democracy.[4]

---

[1] Arts 7, 13, 14, 15, 17 and 21 respectively of the Universal Declaration.
[2] For ratifications, see Appendix I.
[3] For the text, see *European Treaty Series*, No. 35, 18 October 1961; 529 UNTS 89.
[4] Council of Europe, Cons. Ass., First Session, *Reports* (1949), p. 1144.

The drafters, therefore, concentrated on those rights which were considered essential for the integration of European democracies, which was the goal of the Council of Europe and with regard to which one might expect that an agreement could easily be reached about their formulation and about the international supervision of their implementation, since they could be deemed to have been recognised in the Member States of the Council of Europe. On the other hand, both the detailed formulation of these rights, with the possibilities of limitations and the creation of a supervisory mechanism in a binding treaty were novel and revolutionary.[5]

Precisely these two points, the formulation and the supervisory mechanism, were used as arguments for a separate regulation of, on the one hand, the civil and political rights and, on the other hand, the economic, social, and cultural rights; a solution which was ultimately also chosen within the framework of the UN. The first category of rights was considered to concern the sphere of freedom of the individual *vis-à-vis* the Government. These rights and liberties and their limitations would lend themselves to a detailed regulation, while the implementation of the resulting duty on the part of the Government to abstain from interference could be reviewed by national and/or international bodies. The second category, on the other hand, was considered to consist not of legal rights but of programmatic rights, the formulation of which necessarily is much vaguer and for the realisation of which the States must pursue a given policy, an obligation which does not lend itself to incidental review of government action for its lawfulness.[6]

It is undeniable that there are differences, roughly speaking, between the two categories of rights with respect to their legal character and their implementation. However, such differences are also present *within* those categories. Thus, the right to a fair trial and the right to periodic elections by secret ballot, unlike, for instance, the prohibition of forced labour or of torture, call not only for abstention but also for affirmative action on the part of the Governments. And in the other category the right to strike has less the character of a programmatic right than has the right to work. The classic distinction therefore, certainly for some rights, is better explained by history than by essential differences in character. In the modern welfare State – which typifies most of the Member States of the Council of Europe – the civil rights and liberties are being 'socialised' more and more and the social, economic, and cultural rights are increasingly becoming more concrete as to their content. Therefore, the question arises whether such a stringent distinction between the two categories is still justified, in particular if this entails

---

[5] In view of the emphasis placed by the drafters on democracy it may be a matter of surprise that no provision was included on the right of participation in government and on free elections. Evidently the matter was too complex and would have delayed the signing of the Convention. The issue of free elections was covered by the First Additional Protocol soon thereafter (Art. 3).

[6] See 'Annotations on the text of the draft International Covenant on Human Rights, prepared by the Secretary-General', Document A/2929, pp. 7-8. See also the statement of Henri Rolin, member of the Consultative Assembly, before the Belgian Senate, quoted in H. Golsong, 'Implementation of International Protection of Human Rights', RCADI 110, 1963-III, p. 58.

the risk that the necessary relation between the two categories of rights is misunderstood. This principle has already been stated in the Proclamation of Teheran of 1968[7] and reaffirmed in the Vienna Declaration and Programme of Action, where it has been set forth that:

> All human rights are universal, indivisible and interdependent and interrelated. The international community must treat human rights globally in a fair and equal manner, on the same footing, and with the same emphasis. While the significance of national and regional particularities and various historical, cultural and religious backgrounds must be borne in mind, it is the duty of States, regardless of their political, economic and cultural systems, to promote and protect all human rights and fundamental freedoms.[8]

This connection, and the limited value of the distinction between the two categories of rights, has also been recognised in the fact that the Council of Europe has embarked upon investigating whether certain economic and social rights should be added to the Convention, and, if so, which ones.[9]

In the present chapter the rights and freedoms laid down in the Convention and in its Protocols Nos 1, 4, 5, 6 and 7 are discussed by reference to the Decisions and Reports of the Commission and the case-law of the Court. As indicated above, a number of provisions of the International Covenant on Civil and Political Rights may entail for those Contracting States which have also ratified that Covenant[10] more far-reaching obligations than rest on them under the Convention;[11] such obligations are left intact on the basis of Article 60 of the Convention.[12]

Article 1 of the Convention does not form part of Title I which contains the substantive provisions concerning the rights and freedoms. It precedes Title I and defines in a general way the obligation of the Contracting States to secure these rights and freedoms, specifying in particular the personal scope of protection: 'to everyone within their jurisdiction'.

However, the Commission seems to have given a more specific meaning to Article 1 in connection with the extraterritorial scope of the rights and freedoms embodied in Title I.[13] In *Cyprus* v. *Turkey* the Commission held that the term

---

[7] Text of the Proclamation in Res. 2442(XLII) of the General Assembly of the United Nations, 19 December 1968.

[8] UN Doc. A/Cont.157/23, para. 5.

[9] See in this respect Protocol No. 7 to the Convention.

[10] These are all Contracting States except Andorra, Liechtenstein and Turkey.

[11] See the report of the Committee of Experts on Human Rights to the Committee of Ministers, *Problems arising from the Co-Existence of the United Nations Covenants on Human Right and the European Convention on Human Rights*, Doc. H(70)7, Strasbourg, 1970. In Protocol No. 7 the differences between the obligations resulting from the Covenant and those resulting from the Convention, have been partly taken away. This Protocol entered into force on 1 November 1988.

[12] On this, see *supra* p. 6.

[13] Appl. 10479/83, *Kirkwood* v. *the United Kingdom*, D&R 37 (1984), p. 158 (182-183); Appls 15299/89, 15300/89 and 15318/89, *Chrysostomos, Papachrysostomou and Loizidou* v. *Turkey*, D&R 68 (1991), p. 216 (244); report of 19 January 1989, *Soering*, A.161, pp. 55-56.

'within their jurisdiction' in Article 1 was not, as submitted by the respondent Government, equivalent to or limited to the national territory of the High Contracting Party concerned and stated that:

> It is clear from the language, in particular of the French text, and the object of this Article, and from the purposes of the Convention as a whole, that the High Contracting Parties are bound to secure the said rights and freedoms to all persons under their actual authority and responsibility, whether that authority is exercised within their territory or abroad.[14]

The Commission continued that it followed from this interpretation that it was competent to examine the applications, insofar as they concerned alleged violations of the Convention in the northern part of Cyprus, which is under Turkish control and is operating solely under the direction of the Turkish Government. Therefore, the Turkish armed forces were considered to be the authorised agents of Turkey and they brought any other person or property in Cyprus 'within the jurisdiction' of Turkey, in the sense of Article 1, to the extent that they exercised control over such persons or property. Consequently, insofar as these armed forces by their acts or omissions affect such persons' rights or freedoms under the Convention, the responsibility of Turkey was engaged.[15] This view was confirmed and further developed by the Commission when the Turkish Government submitted that the presence of their armed forces in that area was justified by the wish of the 'Turkish Federated State of Cyprus', proclaimed in the north of the Republic of Cyprus. The Commission concluded that Turkey's jurisdiction in the north of Cyprus, existing by reason of the presence of her armed forces there which prevented exercise of jurisdiction by the applicant Government, could not be excluded on the ground that jurisdiction in that area was allegedly exercised by the 'Turkish Federated State of Cyprus'.[16]

2 RIGHT TO LIFE (ARTICLE 2)

1.   Everyone's right to life shall be protected by law. No one shall be deprived of his life intentionally save in the execution of a sentence of a court following his conviction of a crime for which this penalty is provided by law.

2.   Deprivation of life shall not be regarded as inflicted in contravention of this Article when it results from the use of force which is no more than absolutely necessary:

(a)   in defence of any person from unlawful violence;

(b)   in order to effect a lawful arrest or to prevent the escape of a person lawfully detained;

(c)   in action lawfully taken for the purpose of quelling a riot or insurrection.

---

[14]   Appls 6780/74 and 6950/75, D&R 2 (1975), p. 125 (136).

[15]   *Ibidem*, p. 137. See also Appls 15299/89, 15300/89 and 15318/89, *Chrysostomos, Papachrysostomou and Loizidou* v. *Turkey*, D&R 68 (1991), p. 216 (244).

[16]   Appl. 8007/77, *Cyprus* v. *Turkey*, D&R 13 (1979), p. 85 (148-150); Appls 15299/89, 15300/89 and 15318/89, *Chrysostomos, Papachrysostomou and Loizidou* v. *Turkey*, D&R 68 (1991), p. 216 (246-247).

2.1 Introduction

Article 2 is formulated somewhat curiously. Unlike the corresponding Article 6 of the Covenant, it does not expressly recognise the existence of the right to life, but imposes upon the national authorities an obligation to protect everyone's right to life, followed by a prohibition of intentional deprivation of life.

As to that prohibition, it is assumed by some authors that this is addressed not only to the national authorities, but also to private persons.[17] Be that as it may, such a prohibition can be invoked in Strasbourg only when its violation is (also) due to a lack of protection on the part of the national authorities, because complaints can only be directed against acts and omissions for which the State bears responsibility.[18] For the national authorities the prohibition of intentional deprivation of life implies in addition the duty to abstain from acts which needlessly endanger life.[19]

The duty to protect the right to life seems to have been imposed by Article 2 in particular on the legislator: 'shall be protected by law'. What does this obligation imply? Is a State in default under this provision if, for instance, motorists are not subjected to speed limits, although such a measure might reduce the number of road victims? As Fawcett rightly states: 'it is not life, but the right to life, which is to be protected by law'.[20] The right to life does not afford a guarantee against all threats to life, but against intentional deprivation and careless endangering of life. The latter must be prohibited and made punishable by law except for those cases in which Article 2 permits such deprivation of life. The protection provided by the law, however, is a reality only if that law is implemented. Omission on the part of the authorities to trace and prosecute the offender in case of an unlawful deprivation of life is, therefore, in principle

---

[17] See, *e.g.*, F.G. Jacobs, *The European Convention on Human Rights*, Oxford, 1980, p. 21.

[18] The Contracting State's obligation to guarantee protection against the acts and omissions of individuals may be deemed implied in the first sentence of Art. 2 in conjunction with the provision of Art. 1; see Jacobs, *supra* note 17, p. 21. The content and the scope of this obligation, however, are difficult to indicate in abstracto. For the issue of *Drittwirkung* in general, see *supra* pp. 22-26.

[19] See, *e.g.*, Appl. 5207/71, *X* v. *Federal Republic of Germany*, Yearbook XIV (1971), p. 698 (710), where a complaint based on Art. 2 on account of an order of the national court to evict a person in poor health from her house was not considered manifestly ill-founded by the Commission; Appl. 4340/69, *Simon-Herold* v. *Austria*, Yearbook XIV (1971), p. 352 (394-398), where the complaint based on Art. 2 concerned the medical care in a prison; Appl. 7154/75, *Association X* v. *the United Kingdom*, D&R 14 (1979), p. 31 (32-33), where the Commission decided that in the case of a vaccination programme to which certain risks to life were attached it could not be said that the Government envisaged such possible consequences; and Appl. 7317/75, *X* v. *Switzerland*, Yearbook XX (1977), p. 412 (436-438), where extradition to the United States was concerned and the person in question feared reprisals on the part of the CIA, but the Commission held that this fear had been made insufficiently concrete.

[20] J.E.C. Fawcett, *The Application of the European Convention on Human Rights*, 2nd ed., Oxford, 1987, p. 37.

subjected to review by the Strasbourg organs.[21] The Commission, however, has indicated that the first sentence of the first paragraph in its opinion is not addressed exclusively to the legislator, but refers to a general obligation of the authorities to take appropriate measures for the protection of life.[22] To what extent are the authorities obliged to prevent deprivation of life by individuals? They can hardly put a bodyguard at the disposal of each citizen.[23] Their task of guarding public security does involve, however, the duty to observe a certain vigilance with respect to the lives of the individual citizens, but in this duty they cannot go so far that their obligations towards other citizens are jeopardised. Here the national authorities will have to weigh these obligations against each other, and the way they do this can be reviewed in Strasbourg for its reasonableness.[24]

Thus, in its decision on admissibility in the *Dujardin* Case, weighing the protection of the individual's right to life against the State's legitimate interests, the Commission decided that the fact that the French amnesty law adopted in the context of a settlement between various communities in New Caledonia resulted in a discontinuation of the prosecution of the suspected murderers of the applicants' close relatives, did not infringe the right protected by Article 2.[25] In the *Taylor, Crampton, Gibson and King families* Case the applicants claimed that they had been the victims of a violation of Article 2. They submitted that the State, in view of its positive obligation to protect the right to life where an unlawful killing or life-threatening attack has taken place in an environment for which it is responsible, must show that it has sought out the perpetrator and

---

[21] The Committee of Experts evidently refers to this in its report, see *supra* note 11, where it speaks of 'an obligation of States to take the necessary deterrent measures with a view to preventing by law (*i.e.* by adequate legislation and its enforcement) intentional interference with life whether by a State or by individuals'. Of course, a certain discretion will have to be allowed to the national authorities as regards the prosecution policy, but the fundamental character of the right to life stringently restricts that scope. As in the case of an individual complaint the applicant must be able to prove that he himself is the victim of the omission of the authorities, a complaint concerning deprivation of life will be possible only in the case of a so-called 'indirect' victim; see *supra* pp. 56-58.

[22] Whereas in Appl. 6839/74, *X* v. *Ireland*, D&R 7 (1977), p. 78, the Commission still left open the question of whether Art. 2 may also entail an obligation to take measures, it decided in Appl. 7154/75, *Association X* v. *the United Kingdom*, D&R 14 (1979), p. 31 (32), that the State has a duty to take appropriate steps to safeguard life. See also Appl. 9348/81, *W* v. *the United Kingdom*, D&R 32 (1983), p. 190 (199-200) and Appl. 16734/90, *Dujardin* v. *France*, D&R 72 (1992), p. 236 (243), where the Commission stated that Art. 2 'may indeed give rise to positive obligations on the part of the State'.

[23] In Appl. 9348/81, *W* v. *the United Kingdom*, D&R 32 (1983), p. 190 (200) and Appl. 9829/82, *X* v. *the United Kingdom and Ireland* (not published), the Commission added, that from Art. 2 one cannot deduce a positive obligation to exclude any possible violence.

[24] However, in Appl. 9348/81, *W* v. *the United Kingdom*, D&R 32 (1983), p. 190 (200), where the applicant complained about her husband's and her brother's dead in Northern Ireland, the Commission came to the conclusion that it is not its task, when examining a complaint under Art. 2, to consider in detail the appropriateness and efficiency of the measures taken by the United Kingdom to combat terrorism in Northern Ireland.

[25] Appl. 16734/90, D&R 72 (1992), p. 236 (243-244).

brought him/her to justice. The Commission held that the obligation to protect life includes a procedural aspect, involving the minimum requirements of a mechanism whereby the circumstances of a deprivation of life by agents of a State receive public and independent scrutiny. In this case the death and serious injuries of the children of the applicants in a public hospital had been caused by a nurse suffering from mental illness. According to the Commission, the procedural requirements of Article 2 were satisfied because there had been criminal proceedings against the nurse, which led to her conviction and imprisonment.[26] In *Cyprus* v. *Turkey*, Cyprus accused the Turkish invasion forces of having murdered citizens, including women and aged people, in cold blood. These cases were declared admissible by the Commission,[27] and the Committee of Ministers decided on the basis of the Commission's report 'that events which occurred in Cyprus constitute violations of the Convention'.[28]

In the *McCann* Case the parents of the victims who were shot dead in Gibraltar by members of the Special Air Service (SAS), which is a regiment of the British Army, alleged a violation of Article 2. The Court held that the obligation to protect the right to life required some form of effective official investigation when individuals have been killed as a result of the use of force by agents of the State. However, the Court did not deem it necessary to decide what form such an investigation should take and under what conditions it should be conducted, since public inquest proceedings in which the applicants were legally represented, and which involved the hearing of seventy-nine witnesses, had in fact taken place. Moreover, the lawyers acting on behalf of the applicants were able to examine and cross-examine key witnesses, including the military and police personnel involved in the planning and conduct of the anti-terrorist operation, and to make the submissions they wished to make in the course of the proceedings. Against this background, the Court did not consider that the alleged shortcomings in the inquest proceedings substantially hampered the carrying out of a thorough, impartial and careful examination of the circumstances surrounding the killings. In this respect there had thus been no breach of Article 2(1).[29]

In its decision in *X* v. *Austria* the Commission found that Article 2 'does (...) primarily provide protection against deprivation of life only'. It did not wish to rule out the possibility that protection of physical integrity also comes under this provision, but if so, then exclusively protection against such injuries as involve a threat to life.[30] Other injuries to the physical – and mental – integrity may in many cases be brought under Article 3.

---

[26]   Appl. 23412/94, D&R 79-A (1993), p. 127 (136).
[27]   Appls 6780/74 and 6950/75, Yearbook XVIII (1975), p. 82 (124).
[28]   Resolution of the Committee of Ministers, DH(79)1 of 20 January 1979, Yearbook XXII (1979), p. 440. See the report of 10 July 1976, *Cyprus* v. *Turkey*, in particular paras 352-354, pp. 118-119.
[29]   Judgment of 27 September 1995, A.324, p. 49.
[30]   Appl. 8278/78, D&R 18 (1980), p. 154 (156).

2.2 The Concept of the Right to Life

The most difficult interpretation problems concern the question of the beginning and the end of the physical life of the human person, which is protected in Article 2.

The word 'everyone' does not exclude the possibility that unborn life falls under the protection of Article 2, no more than this is true of 'every human being' in Article 6 of the Covenant.[31] If one takes the view that such protection is actually included, it implies that *abortus provocatus* must in principle be prohibited by the legislator and prosecuted by the authorities.

On this point, however, there is no consensus at the national and the international level.[32] The question was expressly left open by the Commission in its report in the *Brüggeman and Scheuten* Case.[33] In its later decision in *X* v. *the United Kingdom* the Commission held with respect to the word 'everyone' in Article 2 that both the use of this term in the Convention in general and the context in which the term has been used in Article 2 (for this, the Commission paid attention in particular to the restrictions in Article 2, which apply exclusively to individuals already born) indicate that the term is not meant to include the unborn child.[34] The Commission did not confine itself to this, but subsequently investigated whether the term 'life' in Article 2 refers only to the life of an individual already born or also includes the unborn life. In this connection it stated first of all that the views as to the question at what moment there is life tend to diverge widely, and that the term 'life' may also have a different meaning according to the context in which it is used.[35] Next, the Commission distinguished the following three possibilities: (1) Article 2 is not applicable to the foetus at all; (2) Article 2 recognises the right to life of the foetus with specific implied restrictions; or (3) Article 2 recognises an unqualified right to life for the foetus.[36]

---

[31] As to the latter article this point was expressly left open: UN Doc. A/3764, para. 112.

[32] See Recommendation 874 (1979) of the Parliamentary Assembly concerning a 'European Charter on the Rights of the Child', Parl. Ass., *Documents*, Doc. 4376, which contains the words 'the right of every child to life from the moment of conception'. See also Recommendation 1046 (1986) on the use of human embryos and foetuses for diagnostic, therapeutic, scientific, industrial and commercial purposes, where the Parliamentary Assembly stresses that a definition of the biological status of the embryo is necessary and expresses its awareness of the fact that scientific progress has made the legal position of the embryo and foetus particularly precarious, and that their legal status is at present not defined by law.

[33] Report of 12 July 1977, D&R 10 (1978), p. 100 (116).

[34] Appl. 8416/78, D&R 19 (1980), p. 244 (249-250). This argument would not seem very convincing, since, as the Commission itself mentions, Art. 4 of the American Convention, which uses the term 'every person', expressly protects the unborn life.

[35] *Ibidem*, pp. 250-251.

[36] *Ibidem*, p. 252.

The third possibility was excluded by the Commission, since from the mere fact that Article 2 also protects the life of the mother certain restrictions ensue with respect to the life of the unborn child, as it cannot have been intended by the drafters that priority should be given to the latter life, particularly in view of the fact that, when the Convention was drafted, nearly all the States Parties allowed abortion for the protection of the mother's life.[37] The Commission subsequently took the position that there was no need for it to take a position in a general sense on the two other possibilities, because the case under discussion concerned an interruption of pregnancy in the early stages of pregnancy and exclusively on medical opinion. Even if one were to assume that Article 2 is applicable to the first months of pregnancy, in any case an implied restriction was concerned here, *viz.* the protection of the life and the health of the mother.[38]

The ambiguous reasoning of the Commission makes it but too evident that it felt confronted here with a complicated question, which it thought could hardly be answered in a general way.[39] The rejection of the third possibility was not very problematic. However, the Commission subsequently seems to extend the exceptional case in which abortion is necessary to spare the life of the mother rather readily to the situation where it is not the life of the mother that is at stake, but the abortion is considered desirable for some other medical reason. There is, however, an essential difference between the protection of the life of the mother as a ground for restriction, which ensues directly from Article 2 itself and is narrowly defined, and the much wider ground 'medical opinion', which Article 2 is said here to imply. Even if one assumes that a woman's right to physical and mental integrity, which may be based on Article 3,[40] may be interpreted in so wide a manner that it provides protection against any conscious injury to physical and mental health, and if on the other hand one does not rule out that Article 2 protects the unborn life, it is by no means self-evident that the former right has priority, so that the protection of that right implicitly restricts the enjoyment of the latter right by the foetus. The only point that has been decided here by the Commission is, therefore, that in the Commission's opinion in the present case, even if one assumes that Article 2 protects the unborn life, the rights and interests involved had been weighed against each other in a reasonable way. As long as the question of whether Article 2 is applicable to the unborn life has not been answered in the negative, this reasonableness will have to be reviewed in each individual case. Since a generally accepted standard seems still to be lacking, such a review is likely to be marginal only.

---

[37] *Idem.*

[38] *Ibidem*, pp. 252-253.

[39] As in other difficult and highly controversial cases, here too it is astonishing that the Commission declared the complaint to be manifestly ill-founded; *ibidem*, p. 253.

[40] Art. 2 protects the physical integrity only insofar as an injury to it constitutes a threat to life. See *supra* p. 299 and Appl. 8278/78, *X* v. *Austria*, D&R 18 (1980), p. 154 (156).

In a later decision, the Commission took a somewhat different approach, but with a rather far-reaching result. Here again it started by observing that it did not exclude that in certain circumstances the foetus may enjoy a certain protection under Article 2, notwithstanding the fact that there is in the Contracting States a considerable divergence of views on whether or to what extent Article 2 protects the unborn life. The Commission continued that it did not have to decide this question because it was clear that national laws on abortion differ considerably. In these circumstances, and assuming that the Convention may be considered to have a certain bearing in this field, the Commission found that in such a delicate area the Contracting States must have a certain discretion. The Norwegian legislation in this respect was rather liberal. It allowed self-determined abortion within the first 12 weeks of pregnancy. From the 12th week until the 18th week of pregnancy a termination could be authorised by a board of doctors, if certain conditions had been fulfilled. After the 18th week termination was not allowed, unless there were serious reasons for such a step. According to the Commission, this legislation did not exceed the discretion allowed to States in this matter.[41]

Who is entitled to complain in the case of abortion? Apart from the highly unlikely case of a complaint by a State, the parents will be entitled to vindicate the rights of their unborn child. However, they will proceed to do so only if abortion has been performed without their consent or the consent of one of them. If such a case concerns parents who are married or are living together in an extramarital relationship, it would seem more appropriate for them to invoke Article 8 (the right to respect for private and family life)[42] or Article 12 (the right to found a family).[43]

The question not as to the beginning, but as to the end of the life protected in Article 2, arises in connection with euthanasia. Here again a uniform regulation in the laws of the Contracting States, and a uniform standard in general, is lacking. It would seem, however, that even in those situations where it must in reason be assumed that human life still exists, euthanasia does not *per se* conflict

---

[41] Appl. 17004/90, *H* v. *Norway*, D&R 73 (1992), p. 155 (167).

[42] See Appl. 6959/75, *Brüggemann and Scheuten* v. *Federal Republic of Germany*, D&R 10 (1978), p. 100; and Appl. 8416/78, *X* v. *the United Kingdom*, D&R 19 (1980), p. 244 (253). In its decision on Appl. 11045/84, *Knudsen* v. *Norway*, D&R 42 (1985), p. 247 (256), the Commission took the position that since the applicant was not a potential father, but a minister of religion within a State church, he was not affected differently by the abortion legislation than other citizens and therefore could not claim to be a victim. That he lost his office was, according to the Commission, not due to the Abortion Act but to the fact that he, because of his views on the Act, refused to perform functions that were duties of his office.

[43] This holds good also for cases of sterilisation and other forms of birth control against the will of the person concerned, or at least without the latter's consent. In fact, in these cases there is not yet any question of destruction of life. It is therefore curious that in connection with a man's complaint about the sterilisation of his wife without his consent the Commission held that 'an operation of this nature might in certain circumstances involve a breach of the Convention, in particular of Articles 2 and 3'; Appl. 1287/61, *X* v. *Denmark* (not published). The right to life and the right to produce life are not to be equated.

with the Convention. In fact, the value of the life to be protected can and must be weighed against other rights of the person in question, particularly his right, laid down in Article 3, to be protected from inhuman and degrading treatment. Whether the will of the person is decisive in such a case depends on whether the right to life is or is not to be regarded as inalienable. In this respect, too, a certain trend may be discerned, but not yet a *communis opinio*.[44] There is as yet hardly any standard for a strict review by the Strasbourg organs, neither as to the weighing between the various rights of the person in question, nor as to the establishment of the dividing line between human and merely vegetative life.[45]

2.3 Exceptions with Respect to the Right to Life

2.3.1 Death Penalty

Article 2 mentions a number of cases to which the prohibition of deprivation of life does not apply. In the first paragraph, in the very formulation of the prohibition, an exception is already made for the case where a person is deprived of his life in the execution of a sentence of a court following his conviction of a crime for which the death penalty is provided by law. Consequently, execution of the death penalty or extradition to a country where the death penalty is still executed does not in itself constitute a violation of Article 2.[46] In the meantime however, Protocol No. 6 concerning the abolition of the death penalty has entered into force.[47] Even for those States which have not yet ratified this Protocol, it follows from other provisions of the Convention that not every death sentence pronounced by a court is permitted under the Convention: (1) the judicial decision in question must have been preceded by a fair and public hearing in the sense of Article 6; (2) the punishment must not be so disproportionate to the crime committed, and the choice of the place and manner of execution must not be such, that these amount to an inhuman and degrading treatment in the sense of Article 3; (3) under Article 7 the crime must have been punishable by death at the moment it was committed; (4) under Article 14 no discrimination is permitted in the imposition and execution of the death penalty, and in the granting of

---

[44] See the discussion of the so-called 'euthanasia declaration' in the Hubinek/Voogd report concerning the rights of the sick and the dying, which was submitted early in 1976 in the Parliamentary Assembly of the Council of Europe; Council of Europe, Parl. Ass., Twenty-Seventh Session, *Documents*, Doc. 3699.

[45] The Hubinek/Voogd report mentioned in the preceding note, also only indicates the framework for a more uniform regulation. It holds that 'the prolongation of life should not in itself constitute the overriding aim of medical practice, which must be concerned equally with the relief of suffering'. The report contains a recommendation to the Committee of Ministers to invite the Governments of the Member States to set up committees for the drafting of ethical rules; Doc. 3699, pp. 2-3.

[46] Appl. 10227/82, *H* v. *Spain*, D&R 37 (1984), p. 93.

[47] This Protocol entered into force on 1 March 1985. See *infra* pp. 678-679.

pardon.[48] Therefore, the issue of whether the death penalty is still allowed under the Convention has to be considered in the context of several Convention provisions. As appears from the *Kirkwood* Case,[49] a difficult dilemma may present itself with regard to appeal proceedings, which will inevitably delay execution of the death sentence and during which the convicted person will be gripped with uncertainty as to the outcome of his appeal and therefore as to his fate. On the one hand a prolonged appeal system generates acute anxiety over long periods owing to the uncertain, but possibly favourable outcome of each successive appeal. This anxiety could possibly constitute an inhuman or degrading treatment and punishment contrary to Article 3. On the other hand a sound appeal system serves to ensure protection of the right to life as guaranteed by Article 2 and to prevent arbitrariness. The Commission declared the application inadmissible, because the applicant had not been tried or convicted and it could therefore not be established whether the treatment to which the applicant would be exposed, and the risk of his exposure to it, was so serious as to constitute inhuman or degrading treatment or punishment contrary to Article 3.

The British Government had taken the position that, since the second sentence of Article 2(1) of the Convention expressly provides for the imposition of the death sentence by a court, following conviction for a crime for which that penalty is provided by law, delays associated with the appeal procedure must be assumed to be compatible with both Article 2 and Article 3 of the Convention read together. The Commission rejected this argument. It acknowledged that the Convention must be read as a whole, but it stressed on the other hand that:

> its respective provisions must be given appropriate weight where there may be implicit overlap, and the Convention organs must be reluctant to draw interferences from one text which would restrict the express terms of another. As both the Court and the Commission have recognized, Article 3 is not subject to any qualification. Its terms are bald and absolute. This fundamental aspect of Article 3 reflects its key position in the structure of the rights of the Convention, and is further illustrated by the terms of Article 15(2), which permit no derogation from it even in time of war or other public emergency threatening the life of the nation. In these circumstances the Commission considers that notwithstanding the terms of Article 2(1), it cannot be excluded that the circumstances surrounding the protection of one of the other rights contained in the Convention might give rise to an issue under Article 3.[50]

The *Soering* Case concerned the imminent extradition of the applicant from the United Kingdom to the United States of America, where he feared to be sentenced to death on a charge of capital murder and would be subjected to the 'death row phenomenon'. The Court held that extradition of a person to a country where he risks the death penalty could not, in itself, raise any issue either under Article 2 or Article 3 of the Convention. The Court considered that Article 3 could not

---

[48] In the case of States which have abolished the death penalty in general, but have maintained it in respect of acts committed in time of war or imminent threat of war, the requirements under (1) and (4) apply only to the extent that derogation from them is not justified under Art. 15.

[49] Appl. 10479/83, D&R 37 (1984), p. 158 (181-190).

[50] *Ibidem*, p. 184. For further details, see the discussion of Article 3, *infra* pp. 325-328.

'have been intended by the drafters of the Convention to include a general prohibition of the death penalty since that would nullify the clear wording of Article 2(1)'. Also, the opening for signature in 1983 of Protocol No. 6 showed that:

> the intention of the Contracting Parties as recently as 1983 was to adopt the normal method of amendment of the text in order to introduce a new obligation to abolish capital punishment in time of peace and, what is more, to do so by an optional instrument allowing each state to choose the moment when to undertake such an engagement.[51]

The Court continued that the manner, however, in which the death penalty is imposed or executed, the personal circumstances of the condemned person and a disproportionality to the gravity of the crime committed, as well as the condition of the detention must not be such that an inhuman treatment in the sense of Article 3 arises.[52]

2.3.2 The Use of Force Which is no More than Absolutely Necessary

In the second paragraph three cases of deprivation of life are mentioned which also do not fall under the prohibition of the first paragraph. These are cases where deprivation of life results from the use of force for a given purpose. This is, however, subject to the condition that the force used 'is no more than absolutely necessary'. There must therefore be proportionality between the measure of force used and the purpose pursued, which moreover must be among the purposes mentioned in the second paragraph. Thus, for instance, the use of force in the case of an arrest, where the arrested person neither uses force nor attempts to flee, but only refuses to furnish certain data, will not be proportional and consequently cannot constitute a justification for a resulting deprivation of life. Moreover, the words 'absolutely necessary' have to be interpreted in such a way that there must also be some proportionality between the force used and the interest pursued. Thus, the use of force resulting in death will not be justified in the case of the escape of a prisoner, or to effect an arrest, when no serious danger is reasonably to be feared from the person concerned.

When the widow of a man killed by the police during a riot complained of a breach of Article 2 by the Belgian State, the Commission declared her complaint to be 'manifestly ill-founded', arguing that it was a case of lawful self-defence of a policeman who felt himself threatened, while there was no reason to assume that the latter had intended to kill the man.[53] By the latter argument the Commission obviously referred to the fact that the prohibition of deprivation of life in the first paragraph of Article 2 speaks of 'intentionally'. Since there was no question of this in the case under discussion, in the Commission's reasoning there was no need to examine whether the force used was absolutely necessary for one of the

---

[51] Judgment of 7 July 1989, A.161, pp. 40-41.
[52] *Idem.* See also the discussion in this respect in connection with Art. 3, *infra* pp. 326-327.
[53] Appl. 2758/66, *X* v. *Belgium*, Yearbook XII (1969), p. 174 (192).

purposes mentioned in the second paragraph. However, in this way the Commission largely deprived the second paragraph of its meaning. In fact, in the cases mentioned in the second paragraph the killing will seldom be intentional, but on the contrary will be the unintended result of the force used for a different purpose. This is also evident from the words 'when it results from the use of force'. It has therefore to be presumed that the function of the second paragraph is not merely to impose a restriction on the prohibition in the second sentence of the first paragraph. If the latter was intended, it would have been more appropriate to add the cases, mentioned in the second paragraph, to the exception of capital punishment in the first paragraph, or to refer expressly to the second sentence of the first paragraph in the second paragraph. Instead, the second paragraph contains the words 'in contravention of this Article', which imply at the same time a reference to the first sentence of the first paragraph and the general protection of the right to life contained therein. The correct interpretation, therefore, seems to be that the second paragraph prohibits any use by the authorities of force in such a measure or form that it results in death, but for the exceptions mentioned there and irrespective of the question whether the result was intended or not.

This interpretation was indeed adopted by the Commission in its decision in the *Stewart* Case. The case concerned the death of a boy as a consequence of an injury caused by a plastic baton, fired by a British soldier during a riot in Northern Ireland. The Commission had to examine whether the death of the boy was a consequence of the use of force contrary to Article 2. The British Government submitted that 'Article 2 extends only to intentional acts and has no application to negligent or accidental acts'. The Commission, however, adopted the broader view that the sphere of protection afforded by Article 2 goes beyond the intentional deprivation of life. In virtue of the object and purpose of the Convention, the Commission was of the opinion that it could not accept another interpretation. The text of Article 2, read as a whole, indicated in the Commission's opinion that paragraph 2 does not primarily define situations where it is permitted intentionally to kill an individual, but situations where the use of violence is permitted, which may then, as an unintentional consequence, result in a deprivation of life. This use of force has to be absolutely necessary for one of the purposes in subparagraphs (a), (b) or (c). With regard to this last condition the Commission stated, with reference, *inter alia*, to the *Sunday Times* Case, that (1) 'necessary' implies a 'pressing social need'; (2) the 'necessity test' includes an assessment as to whether the interference with the Convention right was proportionate to the legitimate aim pursued; and (3) the qualification of the word 'necessary' in Article 2(2), by the adverb 'absolutely' indicates that a stricter and more compelling test of necessity must be applied. This led the Commission to the conclusion that Article 2(2) permits the use of force for the purposes enumerated in (a), (b) and (c) under the condition that the employed force is strictly proportionate to the achievement of the permitted purpose. In assessing whether this condition is fulfilled, regard must be had to 'the nature of the aim pursued, the dangers to life and limb inherent in the situation and the degree of risk that the force employed might result in loss of life'.[54] The Commission followed the same line of reasoning in a case where a boy in Northern Ireland had been shot by soldiers as he attempted to drive round a vehicle checkpoint in a stolen car. In the circumstances of the case and having regard to the background of events in Northern Ireland, which was facing a situation in which killings had become a feature of life, the soldiers had reasons to believe that they were dealing with terrorists. Therefore, the use of force was justified in the terms of the second paragraph of Article 2.[55]

In the *McCann* Case the British, Spanish and Gibraltar authorities were aware that the Provisional IRA was planning a terrorist attack on Gibraltar. The intelligence assessment of the British and Gibraltar authorities was that an IRA unit (which had been identified) would carry out an attack by means of a car bomb which would probably be detonated by a remote control device. It was decided that the three suspects should be arrested. Soldiers of the SAS in plain clothes were standing by for that purpose. Allegedly thinking that the three suspects were trying to detonate remote control devices, the soldiers shot them at close range. No weapons or detonator devices were found on the bodies of the three suspects. The car which had been parked by one of the suspects was revealed on inspection not to contain any explosive device or bomb. The Court accepted that the soldiers believed that it was necessary to shoot the suspects in order to prevent them from detonating a bomb and causing serious loss of life. The actions which they took, in obedience to superior orders, were thus perceived as absolutely necessary in order to safeguard innocent lives. The Court held that the use of force by agents of the State in pursuit of one of the aims delineated in paragraph 2 of Article 2 may be justified under this provision where it is based on an honest belief which is perceived, for good reasons, to be valid at the time, but which subsequently turns out to be mistaken. Having regard to the dilemma confronting the authorities in the circumstances of the case, the reactions of the soldiers did not, in themselves, give rise to a violation of Article 2.[56]

In connection with the control and organisation of the operation the Court first observed that it had been the intention of the authorities to arrest the suspects at an appropriate stage and that evidence had been given at the inquest that arrest procedures had been practised by the soldiers and that efforts had been made to find a suitable place to detain the suspects after their arrest. The Court questioned, however, why the three suspects had not been arrested at the border immediately on their arrival in Gibraltar and why the decision was not taken to prevent them from entering Gibraltar if they were believed to be on a bombing mission. Having

---

[54] Appl. 10044/82, D&R 39 (1985), p. 162 (169-171). See also Appl. 9013/80, *Farrell* v. *the United Kingdom*, Yearbook XXV (1982), p. 124 (143); Appl. 16734/90, *Dujardin* v. *France*, D&R 72 (1992), p. 236 (243).

[55] Appl. 17579/90, *Kelly* v. *the United Kingdom*, D&R 74 (1993), p. 139 (146-147). See also the Court in its judgment of 27 September 1995, *McCann and Others*, A.324, p. 62.

[56] Judgment of 27 September 1995, A.324, p. 59.

had advance warning of the terrorists' intentions, it would certainly have been possible for the authorities to have mounted an arrest operation. The security services and the Spanish authorities had photographs of the three suspects, knew their names, as well as their aliases, and would have known what passports to look for. The Court further noted that the authorities had made a number of key assessments, in particular, that the terrorists would not use a blocking car; that the bomb would be detonated by a radio-controlled device; that the detonation could be effected by the pressing of a button; that it was likely that the suspects would detonate the bomb if challenged; that they would be armed and would be likely to use their arms if confronted. In the event, all of these crucial assumptions, apart from the terrorists' intention to carry out an attack, turned out to be erroneous. In the Court's view, insufficient allowances appeared to have been made for other assumptions. A series of working hypotheses were conveyed by the authorities to the soldiers as certainties, thereby making the use of force almost unavoidable. In the Court's view, the above failure to make provision for a margin of error had to be considered in combination with the training of the soldiers to continue shooting once they opened fire until the suspect was dead. As noted by the coroner in the inquest proceedings, all four soldiers shot to kill the suspects. Against this background, the authorities were bound by their obligation to respect the right to life of the suspects to exercise the greatest of care in evaluating the information at their disposal before transmitting it to soldiers whose use of firearms automatically involved shooting to kill. This failure by the authorities suggested a lack of appropriate care in the control and organisation of the arrest operation. In sum, the Court was not persuaded that the killing of the three terrorists constituted a use of force which was no more than absolutely necessary in defence of persons from unlawful violence within the meaning of Article 2(2)(a). There thus had been a breach of Article 2.[57]

2.4 The Right to Life is Non-Derogable

Article 2 has been included in the list of articles from which under Article 15(2) no derogation is permitted in any circumstances; it belongs to the so-called 'non-derogable' rights.[58] Consequently, as was correctly submitted by the Irish Government in the case of *Ireland* v. *the United Kingdom*, the British declarations addressed to the Secretary General, announcing that with respect to Northern Ireland measures derogating from the Convention had been taken, could not be invoked against accusations of violation of Article 2.[59]

---

[57] *Ibidem*, pp. 59-62.
[58] Art. 3 of Protocol No. 6 concerning the abolition of the death penalty also prohibits any derogation from Art. 15 of the Convention.
[59] Appl. 5310/71, Yearbook XV (1972), p. 76 (96).

3 FREEDOM FROM TORTURE AND OTHER INHUMAN OR DEGRADING TREATMENT OR PUNISHMENT (ARTICLE 3)

No one shall be subjected to torture or to inhuman or degrading treatment or punishment.

3.1 Torture; Inhuman Treatment or Punishment; Degrading Treatment or Punishment

The distinction between the notion of *torture* and that of inhuman or degrading treatment or punishment 'derives principally from a difference in the intensity of the suffering inflicted.'[60] As the Commission stated in its report in the *Greek* Case:

> It is plain that there may be treatment to which all these descriptions apply, for all torture must be inhuman and degrading treatment, and inhuman treatment also degrading.

Starting from the concept of inhuman treatment, the Commission applied the following specifications:

> The notion of inhuman treatment covers at least such treatment as deliberately causes severe suffering, mental or physical, which, in the particular situation, is unjustifiable. The word 'torture' is often used to describe inhuman treatment, which has a purpose, such as the obtaining of information or confession, or the infliction of punishment, and is generally an aggravated form of inhuman treatment.Treatment or punishment of an individual may be said to be degrading if it grossly humiliates him before others or drives him to act against his will or conscience.[61]

In the *Greek* Case the Commission came to the conclusion that it had been established that in several individual cases torture or ill-treatment had been inflicted, that there had been a practice of torture and ill-treatment by the Athens Security Police and that the conditions in the cells of the Security Police building were contrary to Article 3.[62] In its report in *Ireland* v. *the United Kingdom* the Commission based itself on the same definition. It held unanimously that the challenged English techniques of interrogation – obliging the interrogated persons to stand for a long period on their toes against the wall, covering their heads with black hoods, subjecting them to constant intense noise, depriving them of sleep and sufficient food and drink – constituted torture and inhuman treatment in the sense of Article 3.[63] However, the Court in its judgment in the same case reached

---

[60] Judgment of 18 January 1978, *Ireland* v. *the United Kingdom*, A.25, p. 66.

[61] Report of 5 November 1969, *Greek* Case, Yearbook XII (1969), p. 186. *Cf.* Art. 1 of the Declaration on the protection of all persons from being subjected to torture and other cruel, inhuman or degrading treatment or punishment, UNGA Res. 3452 (XXX) of 9 December 1975: 'Torture constitutes an aggravated and deliberate form of cruel, inhuman and degrading treatment or punishment'.

[62] *Ibidem*, pp. 504-505.

[63] Report of 25 January 1976, B.23-I (1980), p. 411.

the conclusion that these techniques of interrogation did involve inhuman treatment, but not torture. It mentioned as a distinctive element that by the term 'torture' a special stigma is attached to 'deliberate inhuman treatment causing very serious and cruel suffering' and held that the particular acts complained of 'did not occasion suffering of the particular intensity and cruelty implied by the word torture as so understood'.[64]

Recently, in the case of *Aksoy* v. *Turkey*, the Court, referring to its qualification in the *Ireland* v. *the United Kingdom* judgment, found for the first time that a treatment had to be described as torture. The case concerned an applicant who was subjected to 'Palestinian hanging': he was stripped naked, with his arms tied together behind his back, and suspended by his arms. The Court held that:

> this treatment could only have been deliberately inflicted; indeed, a certain amount of preparation and exertion would have been required to carry it out. It would appear to have been administered with the aim of obtaining admissions or information from the applicant. In addition to the severe pain which it must have caused at the time, the medical evidence shows that it led to a paralysis of both arms which lasted for some time (...). The Court considers that this treatment was of such a serious and cruel nature that it can only be described as torture.[65]

The difference between *inhuman* treatment or punishment and *degrading* treatment or punishment is likewise one of gradation in the suffering inflicted, though it should be kept in mind that in several cases the Strasbourg organs do not draw a sharp distinction and use qualifications such as 'inhuman *and* degrading treatment.'[66]

In the *Tyrer* Case the Court held 'that the suffering occasioned must attain a particular level before a punishment can be classified as "inhuman" within the meaning of Article 3'. The complaint concerned the punishment of caning for certain offences, which was provided by law and actually applied in the Isle of Man to boys between ten and seventeen. The Court concluded, in conformity with the opinion of the Commission, that this punishment did not constitute torture or inhuman punishment.[67] The Court then examined whether the punishment was to be considered degrading. Assuming that every punishment involves an element

---

[64] Judgment of 18 January 1978, *Ireland* v. *the United Kingdom*, A.25, pp. 66-67. *Cf.* also the judgment of 18 December 1996, *Aksoy* v. *Turkey*, Reports 1996-VI, Vol. 26, para. 63.

[65] Judgment of 18 December 1996, Reports 1996-VI, Vol. 26, para. 64. The Court's interpretation of the notion of 'torture' may be inspired by the definition of 'torture' in Art. 1 of the 1984 UN Convention against Torture and Other Cruel, Inhuman or Degrading Treatment or Punishment. *Cf.* also the report of 7 August 1996, *Yağiz* v. *Turkey*, Reports 1996-III, Vol. 13, paras 54-55, where the Commission, explicitly referring to this definition, found that a woman who had been hit by police officers with a truncheon on the soles of her feet was subjected to torture within the meaning of Art. 3.

[66] See the judgment of 27 August 1992, *Tomasi* v. *France*, A.241-A, p. 42; judgment of 4 December 1995, *Ribitsch* v. *Austria*, A.336, p. 26; report of 7 March 1996, *Mentes, Turhalli, Turhalli and Uvat* v. *Turkey* (not yet published), para. 190: burning of the applicants' homes by security forces amounts to 'inhuman and degrading treatment within the meaning of Article 3 of the Convention'.

[67] Judgment of 25 April 1978, A.26, p. 14.

of degradation, the Court indicated as a distinctive element of degrading punishment the degree of humiliation, which must then be judged according to the circumstances of each separate case, in particular 'the nature and context of the punishment itself and the manner and method of its execution.'[68] Decisive for this are not the views at the moment the Convention was drawn up, but the present views, since 'the Convention is a living instrument which (...) must be interpreted in the light of present-day conditions'.[69] Having regard to all the circumstances, the Court, according particular weight to the fact that physical force was used by a complete stranger in an institutionalised form, held that the punishment concerned was degrading.[70]

As may be gathered from the *Tyrer* Case a serious degree of humiliation or debasement can be an important argument to qualify a certain treatment or punishment as degrading. The Commission held in a number of cases that there is question of a degrading treatment or punishment of the person concerned 'if it grossly humiliates him before others or drives him to act against his will or conscience'.[71] As said above, the Court held in the *Tyrer* Case that humiliation or debasement of a particular level may be regarded as degrading;[72] in the *Albert and Le Compte* Case it ruled that while the withdrawal from the register of the *Ordre des médecins* had as its object the imposition of a sanction for misconduct, and not the debasement of his personality, it did not amount to a breach of Article 3;[73] and in the *Abdulaziz, Cabales and Balkandali* Case it observed that the difference of treatment as part of the United Kingdom immigration policy, since it did not denote any contempt or lack of respect for the personality of the applicants and was not designed to, and did not, humiliate or debase them, could not therefore be regarded as 'degrading'.[74]

3.2 Minimum Level of Severity

'The borderline between harsh treatment on one hand and a violation of Article 3 on the other is sometimes difficult to establish.'[75] There is no abstract, absolute standard for the kinds of treatment and punishment prohibited by Article 3. The question whether a treatment or punishment is inhuman or degrading must be judged by the circumstances of the case and the prevalent views of the time. Thus,

---

[68] *Ibidem*, p. 15.
[69] *Idem.*
[70] *Ibidem*, pp. 16-17.
[71] Report of 5 November 1969, *Greece* v. *the United Kingdom*, Yearbook XII (1969), p. 186; report of 25 January 1976, *Ireland* v. *the United Kingdom*, B.23-I (1980), p. 388; report of 14 December 1976, *Tyrer*, B.24 (1981), p. 23; and report of 7 December 1978, *Guzzardi*, B.35 (1983), p. 33.
[72] Judgment of 25 April 1978, A.26, p. 15.
[73] Judgment of 10 February 1983, A.58, p. 13.
[74] Judgment of 28 May 1985, A.94, p. 42. *Cf.* also the judgment of 25 February 1982, *Campbell and Cosans*, A.48, p. 13.
[75] Report of 4 May 1989, *McCallum*, A.183, p. 29.

in its report in the *Greek* Case the Commission considered with respect to the treatment of detainees:

> It appears from the testimony of a number of witnesses that a certain roughness of treatment of detainees by both police and military authorities is tolerated by most detainees and even taken for granted (...) This underlines the fact that the point up to which prisoners and the public may accept physical violence as being neither cruel nor excessive, varies between different societies and even between different sections of them.[76]

And in its judgment in *Ireland* v. *the United Kingdom* the Court held:

> Ill-treatment must attain a minimum level of severity if it is to fall within the scope of Article 3. The assessment of this minimum is, in the nature of things, relative; it depends on all the circumstances of the case, such as the duration of the treatment, its physical or mental effects and, in some cases, the sex, age and state of health of the victim.[77]

Thus, a certain qualification is introduced in a norm formulated in absolute terms. This is almost inevitable in the case of the application of an abstract norm which contains subjective concepts, to concrete cases. For instance, the question whether a penalty is inhuman or not may depend on the crime committed: 'an exceptionally harsh punishment for a trivial offence might raise a question under Article 3',[78] whereas the same punishment could be acceptable in case of a more serious crime. Likewise a punishment for a certain crime may be so out of proportion because of the age or the mental or physical condition of the offender that there may be an issue under Article 3, while such a punishment is entirely justified for others having committed the same type of crime. Moreover particular circumstances relating to a sentence, such as the place where or the circumstances under which it is executed, may make it inhuman, although the sentence as such is not.

In the Strasbourg case-law the national authorities are allowed a wide margin of appreciation as to the system of sanctions. Thus, the Commission has taken the position that 'the Convention does not provide as such any general right to call into question the length of a sentence imposed by a competent court.'[79] Only under exceptional circumstances may a particular sentence raise an issue under Article 3. The mere fact 'that an offence is punished more severely in one country than in another does not suffice to establish that the punishment is inhuman or degrading'.[80] Thus, for instance, although the death penalty has *de facto* been abolished in Western Europe the Court, having regard to Article 2, which expressly permits it, has not been prepared to accept that this penalty should now

---

[76] Report of 5 November 1969, *Greek* Case, Yearbook XII (1969), p. 501.
[77] Judgment of 18 January 1978, A.25, p. 65. *Cf.* also the judgment of 25 April 1978, *Tyrer*, A.26, pp. 14-15 and the judgment of 7 July 1989, *Soering* v. *the United Kingdom*, A.161, p. 39.
[78] Appl. 5471/72, *X* v. *the United Kingdom*, Coll. 43 (1973), p. 160 (160).
[79] Appl. 5871/72, *X* v. *the United Kingdom*, D&R 1 (1975), p. 54 (55); Appl. 7057/75, *X* v. *Germany*, D&R 6 (1977), p. 127 (127).
[80] Appl. 11017/84, *C* v. *Federal Republic of Germany*, D&R 46 (1986), p. 176 (181).

be considered as an inhuman and degrading punishment within the meaning of Article 3.[81] And in the *Weeks* Case the Court allowed a sentence of life imprisonment for a 17-year-old who had committed an armed hold-up, albeit with certain reservations:

> Having regard to Mr. Weeks' age at the time and to the particular facts of the offence he committed (...) if it had not been for the specific reasons advanced for the sentence imposed, one could have serious doubts as to its compatibility with Article 3 of the Convention, which prohibits, *inter alia*, inhuman punishment.[82]

In the *Bonnechaux* Case both the Commission[83] and the Committee of Ministers[84] agreed that Article 3 had not been violated in the case of a 74-year-old man suffering from diabetes and cardiovascular disease who had been detained on remand for 35 months. It may also be concluded from the case-law that the Commission, when dealing with the conditions of detention, so far has not attached much importance to developments in penitentiary views.[85]

It is clear that the answer to the question whether Article 3 has been violated, although depending on all the circumstances of the case, including such factors as the mental effects on the person concerned, is not entirely dependent on the latter's subjective appreciations and feelings. In the *East African Asians* Case the Commission did not accept the 'subjective' definition that the treatment of a person is degrading in the sense of Article 3 'if it lowers him in rank, position, reputation or character, whether in his own eyes or in the eyes of other people', and argued that – given the general purpose of this provision to prevent interferences with the dignity of man of a particularly serious nature – 'an action which lowers a person in rank, position, reputation or character can only be regarded as "degrading treatment" in the sense of Article 3 where it reaches a certain level of severity'.[86] And in *B* v. *France* the Commission found that the

---

[81] Judgment of 7 July 1989, *Soering*, A.161, p. 40.

[82] Judgment of 2 March 1987, A.114, pp. 25-26.

[83] Appl. 8224/78, D&R 15 (1979), p. 211 (241); and report of 5 december 1979, D&R 18 (1980), p. 100 (148).

[84] Res. DH(80)1, 27 June 1980, D&R 18 (1980), p. 149.

[85] In this connection, see the 'Minimum Rules for the Treatment of Prisoners', Res. (73)5 of the Committee of Ministers, European Yearbook XXI (1973), pp. 322-350; and more recently the 'European Prison Rules', laid down in Res. (87)3, adopted by the Committee of Ministers on 12 February 1987. In its decision on Appl. 7341/76, *Eggs* v. *Switzerland*, Yearbook XX (1977), p. 448 (460), the Commission took the position that 'the conditions of detention which in certain aspects did not come up to the standard of the "Minimum Rules" did not thereby alone amount to inhuman or degrading treatment'. See also Appl. 7408/76, *X* v. *Federal Republic of Germany*, D&R 10 (1978), p. 221 (222), where the Commission on the one hand found that the punishment imposed on the applicant was not in conformity with modern views of penitentiary policy, but on the other hand came to the conclusion that the treatment was not inhuman or degrading.

[86] Report of 14 December 1973, D&R 78-A (1994), p. 5 (55). *Cf.* also *ibidem*, p. 57: 'The Commission finally recalls its own statement in the First Greek Case that treatment of an individual may be said to be "degrading" in the sense of Article 3 "if it grossly humiliates him before others or drives him to act against his will or conscience". This definition is similar to the indication reached (...) above; in particular, the word "grossly" indicates that Article 3 is only concerned with

situation in which there is a discrepancy between the appearance of a transsexual and her identity papers, although creating embarrassment for her in respect of third persons to whom she is forced to reveal her particular situation, does not attain the requisite minimum degree of severity for an infringement of Article 3.[87]

The Court has followed the same approach. In the *Campbell and Cosans* Case, for instance, where it had to rule on the application of corporal punishment in British schools, the Court reached the conclusion that in that case it could not be said that a degrading treatment was involved, because the corporal punishment had not been actually applied to the children of the two applicants, and the gravity of the punishment and its degrading effect on the person concerned could not therefore be determined. They might have experienced feelings of apprehension, disquiet or alienation, but 'these effects fall into a different category from humiliation or debasement'.[88] And in the *Marckx* Case the Court held that 'while the legal rules at issue probably present aspects which the applicants may feel to be humiliating, they do not constitute degrading treatment coming within the ambit of Article 3.'[89]

Like the Commission the Court is of the opinion that ill-treatment must reach a certain (objective) level of severity in order to come within the ambit of Article 3.[90] In the *Costello-Roberts* Case the Court once again had to address the issue of corporal punishment in British schools. The applicant was a young boy punished in accordance with the disciplinary rules of the school. The Court distinguished the circumstances of this punishment from those of Tyrer's which was found to be degrading within the meaning of Article 3. Tyrer was sentenced in a juvenile court to three strokes of the birch on the bare posterior; his punishment was administered three weeks later in a police station where he was held by two policemen whilst a third administered the punishment, pieces of birch breaking at the first stroke. Costello-Roberts' punishment on the other hand amounted to being slippered three times on his buttocks through his shorts with a gym shoe by the headmaster in private. In his case the Court found that the minimum level of severity required for Article 3 to be violated was not attained.[91]

In several other cases the Court likewise ruled that the treatment, although unpleasant or even harsh, did not amount to inhuman or degrading treatment. The situation of Mr *Guzzardi*, detained on an island, was considered 'undoubtedly unpleasant or even irksome'; nevertheless his treatment did not attain the level of severity to bring it within the scope of Article 3.[92] The refusal to grant Mr

---

"degrading treatment" which reaches a certain level of severity.'
[87] Report of 6 September 1990, A.232-C, pp. 87-88.
[88] Judgment of 25 February 1982, A.48, pp. 12-14.
[89] Judgment of 13 June 1979, A.31, p. 28.
[90] Judgment of 18 January 1978, *Ireland* v. *the United Kingdom*, A.25, p. 65.
[91] Judgment of 25 March 1993, A.247-C, pp. 59-60. The United Kingdom has nevertheless responded to this judgment by passing legislation to prohibit corporal punishment in schools.
[92] Judgment of 6 November 1980, A.39, p. 40.

Berrehab a new residence permit after his divorce and his resulting deportation did not infringe Article 3, as he did not undergo suffering of a degree corresponding to the concepts of 'inhuman' or 'degrading' treatment.[93] And the conditions in which Mrs *López Ostra* and her family lived – nearby a plant for the treatment of liquid and solid waste, that despite its partial shutdown continued to emit fumes, repetitive noise and strong smells – did likewise not amount to degrading treatment within the meaning of Article 3.[94]

3.3 Other General Aspects

3.3.1 Mental Suffering

Both the Commission and the Court have left no doubt that Article 3 does not exclusively refer to the infliction of physical but also to that of mental suffering. The Commission defined the latter as covering 'the infliction of mental suffering by creating a state of anguish and stress by means other than bodily assault'.[95] Even torture does not necessarily require a 'physical act or condition'.[96]

Often there will be a combination of mental and physical suffering as may be clearly seen in the case of *X and Y* v. *the Netherlands*, in which the Commission dealt with the question of mental suffering as a result of sexual abuse of the victim.[97] There, the Commission stated that 'mental suffering leading to acute psychiatric disturbances falls into the category of treatment prohibited by Article 3 of the Convention'.[98] However, as was already stressed in section 3.2, not every measure that has emotional consequences of any kind for the individual falls within the scope of inhuman treatment, but only measures which 'inflict severe mental or physical suffering on an individual'.[99]

---

[93] Judgment of 21 June 1988, A.138, p. 16.

[94] Judgment of 9 December 1994, A.303-C, pp. 56-57.

[95] Report of 5 November 1969, *Greek* Case, Yearbook XII (1969), p. 461. For the Court, see, *inter alia*, the judgment of 18 January 1978, *Ireland* v. *the United Kingdom*, A.25, p. 65.

[96] Report of 5 November 1969, *Greek* Case, Yearbook XII (1969), p. 461; report of 14 December 1973, *East African Asians* v. *the United Kingdom*, D&R 78-A (1994), p. 5 (56). *Cf.* also the definition of 'torture' in Art. 1 of the UN Convention against Torture and Other Cruel, Inhuman or Degrading Treatment or Punishment: 'the term "torture" means any act by which severe pain or suffering, whether physical *or mental*, is intentionally inflicted on a person ...' (emphasis added).

[97] Report of 5 July 1983, A.91, pp. 22-23. In its judgment of 26 March 1985 in this case, A.91, p. 15, the Court, having found a violation of Art. 8, decided that it was not necessary to examine the case under Art. 3 as well.

[98] Report of 5 July 1983, A.91, p. 22.

[99] Appl. 9191/80, *X* v. *Federal Republic of Germany* (not published). See also Appl. 9554/81, *X* v. *Ireland* (not published). Emotional stress arising from the expropriation of one's home does not meet the requirements: Appl. 9261/81, *X* v. *the United Kingdom*, Yearbook XXV (1982), p. 200 (203).

3.3.2 Intention and Motive

Does the intention or motive of the acting person to cause physical or mental suffering, in addition to the suffering inflicted or the humiliation experienced, constitute a decisive element of the treatment prohibited in Article 3? It is obvious that a medically necessary operation or treatment, however painful it may be for the patient, is not to be considered as torture or inhuman or degrading treatment, provided that unnecessary suffering is avoided. So, in the *Herczegfalvy* Case the Court ruled that mental patients are under the protection of Article 3, but that the 'established principles of medicine are (...) decisive in such cases; as a general rule, a measure which is therapeutic cannot be regarded as inhuman or degrading.'[100] Obviously, the domestic courts and the Strasbourg organs must satisfy themselves as to the medical necessity of a particular form of treatment. A medical experiment may for lack of this necessity infringe Article 3, although the aim is not to inflict suffering, but to advance medical science.[101] Thus, in the *Herczegfalvy* Case the Commission concluded by a unanimous vote that there had been a violation of Article 3, because the treatment accorded to the applicant, who had been diagnosed as suffering from a mental illness, went beyond what was strictly necessary and extended beyond the period necessary to serve its purpose: he was forcibly administered food and neuroleptics, isolated, and attached with handcuffs to his security bed for several weeks.[102] Rather surprisingly, the Court, though expressing its worries concerning the length of time during which the hand cuffs and security bed were used, considered the necessity test to be met.[103]

Similarly a treatment of a detainee which in itself is inhuman does not lose this character through the mere fact that its only motive is the enhancement of security or the combat against crime. As the Court rightly stated in *Tomasi* v. *France*, the requirements of the investigation and the undeniable difficulties inherent in the fight against terrorism cannot result in limits being placed on the protection by Article 3 to be afforded in respect of the physical integrity of individuals.[104]

It is therefore not the intention of the acting person, but the nature of the act and its effect on the person undergoing the treatment which are decisive. Thus the Court used too general an approach when it observed, in the *Albert and Le Compte* Case, that the disciplinary measure of withdrawal of the right to practise, imposed upon a doctor, had as its object the imposition of a sanction and not the

---

[100] Judgment of 24 September 1992, A.244, p. 26.

[101] See, however, Appl. 9974/82, *X* v. *Denmark*, D&R 32 (1983), p. 282 (283-284), concerning an experiment made with a slightly different instrument, but which did not change the procedure of the operation as such. According to the Commission, the operation 'cannot be considered as such a medical experiment which, if carried out without consent, could constitute a violation of Article 3 of the Convention'.

[102] Report of 1 March 1991, A.244, p. 48.

[103] Judgment of 24 September 1992, A.244, p. 26. *Cf.* F.G. Jacobs and R.C.A. White, *The European Convention on Human Rights*, 2nd. ed., Oxford, 1996, p. 67.

[104] Judgment of 27 August 1992, A.241, p. 42. The Court repeated this view in its judgment of 4 December 1995, *Ribitsch* v. *Austria*, A.336, p. 26.

debasement of his personality; not this aspect is decisive but the issue raised next by the Court, *viz.* whether the consequences of the measure adversely affected the doctor's personality in a manner incompatible with Article 3.[105]

3.3.3 Consent

It cannot be said in general whether the absence of consent with the treatment on the part of the person in question constitutes a decisive element of the prohibition of Article 3, but it certainly is a relevant factor.[106] The consent of the person concerned may deprive an act, which would be felt by another to be inhuman or degrading, of that character. However, experiments and treatments are conceivable which are so inhuman or degrade the human person to such a degree that the person in question, in spite of his previous consent, may feel himself to be the victim of a violation of Article 3. And in any case the consent of a particular victim need not bar a complaint by an indirect victim[107] or an abstract complaint by a State concerning a general practice. On the other hand, the absence of consent does not in all cases give an inhuman character to a treatment affecting human integrity. Thus the Commission decided that the enforced administration of medicine to a mentally deranged detainee did not have that character, since that treatment had been declared medically necessary and this had been confirmed by a court decision.[108] The Court held a similar view in the *Herczegfalvy* Case.[109] However, the will of the person in question, insofar as he can be deemed capable of expressing it, must weigh heavily, since in principle he must be able himself to decide about his life and body as long as the life and the health of others are not at stake.

3.4 Imprisonment, Detention, Arrest

It is not surprising that in Strasbourg Article 3 has frequently been at issue in connection with detained persons.

As can be digested from the *Weeks* Case[110] (*supra* section 3.2), life imprisonment is not in itself a breach of Article 3. Furthermore, the Commission has held that Article 3 can not be read:

> as requiring that an individual serving a lawful sentence of life imprisonment must have that sentence reconsidered by a national authority, judicial or administrative, with a view to its remission or termination.[111]

---

[105] Judgment of 10 February 1983, A.58, p. 13.
[106] Appl. 9974/82, *X v. Denmark*, D&R 32 (1983), p. 282 (283-284).
[107] On this, see *supra* pp. 56-58.
[108] Appl. 8518/79, *X v. Federal Republic of Germany*, D&R 20 (1980), p. 193 (194).
[109] Judgment of 24 September 1992, A.244, pp. 25-26.
[110] Judgment of 2 March 1987, A.114, pp. 25-26.
[111] Appl. 7994/77, *Kotälla v. the Netherlands*, D&R 14 (1979), p. 238 (240); Appl. 15776/89, *B, H and L v. Austria*, D&R 64 (1990), p. 264 (270).

In cases where the question was raised whether solitary confinement of a detainee constituted an inhuman treatment, the Commission took the position that such confinement was in principle undesirable, particularly when the prisoner concerned was in detention on remand, and might only be justified for exceptional reasons. For the question of whether an inhuman or degrading treatment is concerned, regard must be had to the surrounding circumstances, including the particular conditions, the stringency of the measure, its duration, the objective pursued and its effects on the person concerned, and also the question of whether a given minimum of possibilities for human contact has been left to the person in question.[112] In *Kröcher and Möller* v. *Switzerland* the Commission opined: 'The question that arises is whether the balance between the requirements of security and basic individual rights was not disrupted to the detriment of the latter.'[113] In this case the prison conditions included, *inter alia*, isolation, constant artificial lighting, permanent surveillance by closed-circuit television, denial of access to newspapers and radio and the lack of physical exercise. Although the Commission expressed 'serious concern with the need for such measures, their usefulness and their compatibility with Article 3 of the Convention', it concluded that the special conditions imposed on the applicants could not be construed as inhuman or degrading treatment.[114] This conclusion was reached after it had been sufficiently shown to the Commission that these conditions were necessary to ensure security inside and outside the prison. In particular, the applicants were considered dangerous, they were alleged to be terrorists, and there was a risk of escape and collusion.[115] Other factors that have been accepted by the Commission to justify stringent measures are: extremely dangerous behaviour of the prisoner,[116] 'ability to manipulate situations and encourage other prisoners to acts of indiscipline',[117] safety of the applicant,[118] and the use of firearms at the time of arrest.[119] As regards the effects on detainees, the Commission requires applicants to submit medical evidence to show that the prison conditions have had adverse effects on their mental or physical health.[120] This medical evidence must not only show that there is a direct relationship between the prison

---

[112] Appl. 6038/73, *X* v. *Federal Republic of Germany*, Coll. 44 (1973), p. 115 (119); Appl. 6166/73, *Baader, Meins, Meinhof and Grundmann* v. *Federal Republic of Germany*, Yearbook XVIII (1975), p. 132 (144-146); Appls 7572/76, 7586/76 and 7587/76, *Ensslin, Baader and Raspe* v. *Federal Republic of Germany*, Yearbook XXI (1978), p. 418 (454-460); report of 16 December 1982, *Kröcher and Möller* v. *Switzerland*, D&R 34 (1983), p. 24 (51-55).

[113] Report of 16 December 1982, D&R 34 (1983), p. 24 (52).

[114] *Ibidem*, p. 57

[115] *Ibidem*, p. 52.

[116] Appl. 9907/82, *M* v. *the United Kingdom*, D&R 35 (1984), p. 13 (34).

[117] Appl. 8324/78, *X* v. *the United Kingdom* (not published).

[118] Appl. 8241/78, *X* v. *the United Kingdom* (not published).

[119] Appls 7572/76, 7586/76 and 7587/76, *Ensslin, Baader and Raspe* v. *Federal Republic of Germany*, Yearbook XXI (1978), p. 418 (454).

[120] See, for example, Appl. 8116/77, *X* v. *the United Kingdom* (not published) and Appl. 8601/79, *X* v. *Switzerland* (not published).

conditions complained of and the deteriorating health of the applicant,[121] but also that these conditions were such that they could 'destroy the personality and cause severe mental and physical suffering' to the applicant.[122] Finally, as the degree of isolation is concerned, it has been made clear by the Commission that absolute sensory isolation combined with complete social isolation constitutes an inhuman treatment for which no security requirements can form a justification; this in view of the absolute character of the right laid down in Article 3.[123] Moreover, the Commission has made a distinction between absolute sensory and social isolation on the one hand, and 'removal from association with other prisoners for security, disciplinary and protective reasons' on the other, and has taken the view that this form of segregation from the prison community normally does not amount to inhuman or degrading treatment or punishment.[124] In the latter case it is still possible to meet prison officers, medical officers, lawyers, relatives *etc.*, and to have contact with the outside world through newspapers, radio and television.

In a series of cases, violation of Article 3 was alleged, because of the adverse effects which the mere fact of being detained as such had on the health of the detainee. In such cases, reports by medical experts are of great importance.[125] According to the Commission, the question that has to be addressed is whether the (mental) health of the detainee is directly affected by his detention. Furthermore, the frequency of visits by the medical staff and the medical treatment are taken into account[126] as well as whether the detainee has sought medical opinion.[127] However, the latter does not take away the primary responsibility of the authorities for the medical care of the detainees.

Sometimes not the negative consequences of detention as such on the health of the detainee, but the lack of proper medical care while being detained is the main

---

[121] In the cases of *Ensslin, Baader and Raspe*, medical reports were presented, but they did not 'make it possible to establish accurately the specific effect of this isolation in relation to their physical and mental health, as compared with other factors', Yearbook XXI (1978), p. 418 (458).

[122] Appl. 8158/78, *X v. the United Kingdom*, D&R 21 (1981), p. 95 (99) and report of 16 December 1982, *Kröcher and Möller*, D&R 34 (1983), p. 24 (56).

[123] Appls 7572/76, 7586/76 and 7587/76, *Ensslin, Baader and Raspe v. Federal Republic of Germany*, Yearbook XXI (1978), p. 418 (456).

[124] Report of 25 January 1976, *Ireland v. the United Kingdom*, B.23-I (1980), p. 379; Appls 7572/76, 7586/76 and 7587/76, *Ensslin, Baader and Raspe v. Federal Republic of Germany*, Yearbook XXI (1978), p. 418 (456); Appl. 8317/78, *McFeeley v. the United Kingdom*, D&R 20 (1980), p. 44 (82); report of 16 December 1982, *Kröcher and Möller*, D&R 34 (1983), p. 24 (53); Appl. 10263/83, *R v. Denmark*, D&R 41 (1985), p. 149; Appl. 14610/89, *Treholt v. Norway*, D&R 71 (1991), p. 168 (190-191).

[125] See, for example, Appl. 9554/81, *X v. Ireland* (not published) and report of 7 October 1981, *B v. the United Kingdom*, D&R 32 (1983), p. 5 (35).

[126] See, for example, the report of 8 December 1982, *Chartier*, D&R 33 (1983), p. 41 (57-58) and Appl. 21915/93, *Lukanov v. Bulgaria*, D&R 80-A (1995), p. 108 (128-130).

[127] Appl. 9813/82, *X v. the United Kingdom* (not published).

issue.[128] In the *Hurtado* Case (eventually resolved by a friendly settlement) the Commission found that it was a breach of Article 3 not to bring the applicant to a doctor for a medical examination until eight days after his arrest in the course of which he suffered a fracture of one of his ribs.[129]

In two cases the Commission declared the applications admissible of people detained in a mental hospital who complained of violation of Article 3 on account of the treatment and living conditions in the hospitals in question. It held that at first sight these complaints were sufficiently well-founded to justify further inquiry.[130] In a case which concerned the question of whether a detainee who was not mentally deranged, could be detained in a closed ward of a mental hospital, a friendly settlement was reached with the respondent Austrian Government; the Minister of Justice issued a general order that was to prevent such a treatment in the future.[131] The placement of a mentally deranged person in a normal prison was considered allowable by the Commission after it had found that the person in question received adequate care there.[132] The segregation of accused persons from convicted persons is not prescribed by the Convention, nor does it ensue *per se* from Article 3 in the Commission's opinion.[133]

As is already clear from the discussion of the case-law concerning solitary confinement, other major elements the Commission regularly takes into account in answering the question whether a violation of Article 3 has occurred are the behaviour of the detainee, his personality and the seriousness of his crimes. Especially when the measures complained of are a result of the uncooperative attitude of the detainee, the Commission is very reticent in concluding that a violation has occurred.[134] For these reasons the Commission declared complaints

---

[128] See Appl. 7994/77, *Kotälla v. the Netherlands*, Yearbook XXI (1978), p. 522 (528), where the Commission followed the view of the Dutch court that the deterioration of the physical and mental condition of the applicant was not due to his detention. See also the report of 7 December 1978, *Guzzardi*, B.35 (1983), pp. 34-35 and the report of 5 December 1979, *Bonnechaux*, D&R 18 (1980), p. 100 (148).

[129] Report of 8 July 1993, A.280-A, p. 16.

[130] Appl. 6840/74, *X v. the United Kingdom*, Yearbook XXI (1978), p. 250 (282); Appl. 6870/75, *B v. the United Kingdom*, D&R 10 (1978), p. 37 (67). In the first-mentioned case a friendly settlement was reached, by which the authorities promised a clearer regulation concerning solitary confinement of patients: D&R 20 (1980), p. 5 (8-11). In the latter case, the Commission concluded in its Report of 7 October 1981 that, although the facilities in the hospital at that time were 'extremely unsatisfactory', they did not amount to inhuman or degrading treatment contrary to Art. 3 of the Convention; D&R 32 (1983), p. 5 (30).

[131] Appl. 4340/69, *Simon-Herold v. Austria*, Coll. 38 (1972), p. 18.

[132] Appl. 5229/71, *X v. the United Kingdom*, Coll. 42 (1973), p. 140.

[133] Appl. 6337/73, *X v. Belgium*, D&R 3 (1976), p. 83 (85). Art. 11(3) of the European Prison Rules, however, stipulates that 'in principle untried prisoners shall be detained separately from convicted persons unless they consent to being accommodated or involved together in organised activities beneficial to them'.

[134] See, *e.g.*, Appl. 8231/78, *X v. the United Kingdom*, D&R 28 (1982), p. 5 (27-28), where the detainee refused to wear prison clothes, and the report of 7 October 1981, *B v. the United Kingdom*, D&R 32 (1983), p. 5 (34-35 and 38), where the applicant had constantly refused to accept medical

of IRA prisoners about the situation in the Maze prison and the treatment they received there inadmissible;[135] however its decision does contain the important finding that the fact of the detainees carrying on a campaign against the authorities does not relieve the latter from their obligations under Article 3.[136]

Not infrequently the complaint concerns physical force used against an arrested person or a detainee by policemen or prison officers. On the one hand it is obvious that, for instance, in case of resistance to arrest, an attempt to flee or an assault on a prison officer or fellow prisoner, the use of a certain amount of force on the part of the officers may be inevitable. On the other hand the form as well as the intensity of the force must be proportionate to the nature and the seriousness of the resistance or threat. The Court has recently laid down some very useful general principles. In *Ribitsch* v. *Austria* the Court (obviously inspired by the concurring opinion of judge De Meyer in the *Tomasi* Case[137]) ruled that 'in respect of a person deprived of his liberty, any recourse to physical force which has not been made strictly necessary by his own conduct diminishes human dignity and is in principle an infringement of the right set forth in Article 3'.[138] Of course, it has to be established that the injuries actually occurred in the way alleged by the applicant, in that they resulted from physical force applied during arrest or detention.[139] However, no absolute proof is required. In the *Aksoy* Case – making explicit the principle underlying *Tomasi* and *Ribitsch* – the Court considered that 'where an individual is taken into police custody in good health but is found to be injured at the time of release, it is incumbent on the State to provide a plausible explanation as to the causing of the injury, failing which a clear issue arises under Article 3.'[140]

It is not normally for the Convention organs to substitute their own assessment of the facts for that of the domestic courts. This has been made particularly clear in the *Klaas* Case. Mrs Klaas was requested to provide a specimen of breath after allegedly committing a road offence. A struggle ensued, resulting in Mrs Klaas being handcuffed. She suffered bruising, was unconscious for a short period when she banged her head on a window-ledge and received a serious long-lasting injury to her shoulder. The Commission, basing itself on the *Tomasi* judgment, concluded

---

treatment and had refused to clean his cell himself. See also Appls 9911/82 and 9945/82, *R, S, A, and C* v. *Portugal*, D&R 36 (1984), p. 200 (208).

[135] Appl. 8317/78, *McFeeley* v. *the United Kingdom*, D&R 20 (1980), p. 44 (77-89). See also Appl. 8231/78, *X* v. *the United Kingdom*, D&R 28 (1982), p. 5 (27-33) concerning the obligation to wear prison clothes.

[136] Appl. 8317/78, *McFeeley* v. *the United Kingdom*, D&R 20 (1980), p. 44 (81). See also Appls 7572/76, 7586/76 and 7587/76, *Ensslin, Baader and Raspe* v. *Federal Republic of Germany*, Yearbook XXI (1978), p. 418 (458-460) and Appl. 9907/82, *M* v. *the United Kingdom*, D&R 35 (1984), p. 130 (133-136). In the latter case the measures taken with respect to the detainee were the result of his extremely dangerous behaviour.

[137] Judgment of 27 August 1992, A.241-A, p. 47.

[138] Judgment of 4 December 1995, A.336, p. 26.

[139] Appl. 18764/91, *Hippin* v. *Austria*, D&R 79-A (1994), p. 23 (29).

[140] Judgment of 18 December 1996, Reports 1996-VI, Vol. 26, para. 61.

that the Government had not produced any convincing explanation and the treatment of Mrs Klaas therefore had to be regarded as a disproportionate use of force that violated Article 3. The Court disagreed with the Commission. According to the Court, the injuries were consistent with either the applicant's or the arresting officers' version of events. As the national courts found against the applicant and there were no cogent reasons adduced to depart from their findings, the Court had to assume that the officers had not used excessive force, and no violation of Article 3 had occurred.[141] The relevant factor distinguishing this case from the *Tomasi* and *Ribitsch* Cases seems to be that in the latter the Governments were not able to provide a plausible explanation of how the applicant's injuries were caused.

3.5 Admission, Expulsion, Extradition

3.5.1 General Observations

The Convention does not contain a general right of admission to a certain country and also not an explicit right to asylum, while Article 4 of Protocol No. 4 prohibits only *collective* expulsion of aliens and Article 1 of Protocol No. 7 only contains certain procedural guarantees against expulsion.[142] The refusal of admission to or the expulsion from a country may, however, constitute a treatment violating Article 3.

In the case of *East African Asians* v. *the United Kingdom* the Commission concluded that legislation imposing restrictions on admission to the United Kingdom of UK citizens and Commonwealth residents in East Africa discriminated against persons of Asian origin on the ground of race, and thus constituted an interference with their human dignity which amounted to 'degrading treatment' in the sense of Article 3.[143] In a 1983 report the Commission seems to imply that 'sexual and other forms of discrimination' in immigration rules may also have such degrading aspects that Article 3 may be applicable.[144] However, because these aspects had already been dealt with in connection with Article 14, the Commission did not consider it necessary to pursue a further examination in the light of Article 3.[145] Furthermore, repeated expulsion of an individual whose

---

[141] Judgment of 22 September 1993, A.269, p. 17.

[142] Judgment of 30 October 1991, *Vilvarajah and Others* v. *the United Kingdom*, A.215, p. 34: 'the Court observes that Contracting States have the right, as a matter of well-established international law and subject to their treaty obligations including Article 3, to control the entry, residence and expulsion of aliens (...) Moreover, it must be noted that the right to political asylum is not contained in either the Convention or its Protocols.'

[143] Report of 14 December 1973, D&R 78-A (1994), p. 5 (62).

[144] Report of 12 May 1983, *Abdulaziz, Cabales and Balkandali*, A.94, pp. 56-57.

[145] *Idem*. In its judgment of 28 May 1985 in this case, A.94, p. 42, the Court did not find a violation of Article 3, because the difference of treatment did not denote any contempt or lack of respect for the personality of the applicants and the measures complained of were not designed to, and did not, humiliate or debase them.

identity it was impossible to establish, to a country where his admission is not guaranteed, may raise an issue under Article 3.[146]

Expulsion and extradition may infringe Article 3 because of their direct physical or mental effects. The Strasbourg organs apply rather strict criteria. The Commission held that extradition within a day after a second attempt to commit suicide did not violate Article 3.[147] In the *Cruz Varas* Case the Court did not consider that the applicant's expulsion to Chile exceeded the threshold set by Article 3, although he suffered from a post-traumatic stress disorder prior to his expulsion and his mental health deteriorated following his return to Chile.[148] And in *Nsona* v. *the Netherlands* the return of a nine-year-old child to Zaire that took seven days, part of which was unaccompanied, was not regarded as inhuman or degrading treatment.[149]

There may also be an issue under Article 3 in that expulsion might result in the person in question being separated from a person or group of persons with whom he has a close link, even apart from the protection of family life under Article 8.[150]

Finally the violation of Article 3 may consist in ill-treatment − torture, inhuman or degrading treatment or punishment − to which, on the basis of objective facts, the person in question may be expected to be subjected in the country to which he will be deported. According to its established case-law, the Commission has held that 'the deportation of a foreigner might, in exceptional circumstances, raise an issue under Article 3 of the Convention where there is serious reason to believe, that the deportee would be liable, in the country of destination, to treatment prohibited by this provision.'[151] In the *Soering* Case, which concerned extradition, the Court had to deal for the first time with the question whether deportation would engage the responsibility of the *deporting* State. The Court, confirming the Commission's jurisprudence, gave an affirmative answer. It held as follows:

---

[146] Report of 17 July 1980, *Giama* v. *Belgium*, D&R 21 (1981), p. 73 (89).
[147] Appl. 25342/94, *Raidl* v. *Austria*, D&R 82-A (1995), p. 134 (146-147).
[148] Judgment of 20 March 1991, A.201, p. 31.
[149] Judgment of 28 November 1996, Reports 1996-V, Vol. 23, para. 99.
[150] Judgment of 24 March 1988, *Olsson*, A.130, p. 38, where the applicants alleged a violation of Art. 3 mainly in two different respects. First, they contended that the taking away of the children from them without sufficient reasons was a deprivation of the children's right of growing up in their family. Secondly, they put forward the frequent moving of one child from one home to another and the ill-treatment in his foster-family. In the Court's view the allegations were not substantiated to give rise to a violation of Art. 3. See also Appl. 10730/84, *Berrehab and Koster* v. *the Netherlands*, D&R 41 (1985), p. 196 (209), where the Commission stated that where an expulsion raises issues under Art. 8, a complaint under Art. 3 on the same facts should not, for that reason alone, be declared inadmissible.
[151] See, *e.g.*, Appl. 11933/86, *A* v. *Switzerland*, D&R 46 (1986), p. 257 (269).

That the abhorrence of torture has such implications is recognised in Article 3 of the United Nations Convention Against Torture and Other Cruel, Inhuman or Degrading Treatment or Punishment, which provides that 'no State Party shall (...) extradite a person where there are substantial grounds for believing that he would be in danger of being subjected to torture'. The fact that a specialised treaty should spell out in detail a specific obligation attaching to the prohibition of torture does not mean that an essentially similar obligation is not already inherent in the general terms of Article 3 of the European Convention. It would hardly be compatible with the underlying values of the Convention, that 'common heritage of political traditions, ideals, freedom and the rule of law' to which the Preamble refers, were a Contracting State knowingly to surrender a fugitive to another State where there were substantial grounds for believing that he would be in danger of being subjected to torture, however heinous the crime allegedly committed. Extradition in such circumstances, while not explicitly referred to in the brief and general wording of Article 3, would plainly be contrary to the spirit and intendment of the Article, and in the Court's view this inherent obligation not to extradite also extends to cases in which the fugitive would be faced in the receiving State by a real risk of exposure to inhuman or degrading treatment or punishment prescribed by that Article.[152]

In other cases the Court has applied this principle also to expulsion.[153] The reasoning behind it is based on the idea that a returning State is itself violating Article 3 if its act of extradition or expulsion constitutes a crucial link in the chain of events leading to torture or inhuman treatment or punishment in the State to which the person is returned. Therefore in such a case the State expelling or extraditing him must be held indirectly responsible for the imminent treatment in that other State, regardless of whether that treatment is to be expected from public authorities or from non-State actors,[154] regardless of how great the – evidently not completely successful – efforts of the Government have been to prevent such

---

[152] Judgment of 7 July 1989, A.161, pp. 34-35.

[153] Judgment of 20 March 1991, *Cruz Varas* v. *Sweden*, A.201, p. 28; judgment of 30 October 1991, *Vilvarajah and Others* v. *the United Kingdom*, A.215, p. 34; judgment of 15 November 1996, *Chahal* v. *the United Kingdom*, Reports 1996-V, Vol. 22, paras 73-74; judgment of 17 December 1996, *Ahmed* v. *Austria*, Reports 1996-VI, Vol. 26, para. 39.

[154] Report of 5 July 1995, *Ahmed* v. *Austria*, Reports 1996-VI, Vol. 26, para. 68: 'the position of the Austrian Authorities that there is no substantial risk for the applicant since the State authority had ceased to exist in Somalia cannot be accepted. It is sufficient that those who hold substantial power within the State, even though they are not the Government, threaten the life and security of the applicant.' The Court adapted the same position in its judgment of 17 December 1996 in this case, para. 48. *Cf.* also the report of 7 December 1995, *H.L.R.* v. *France*, Reports 1997-III, Vol. 36, para. 45, where the Commission came to the conclusion that it would be contrary to Article 3 to deport a drug dealer to Colombia where he would risk to be killed by the mafia. In this case the Court reached a different conclusion but it followed the Commission in holding that 'owing to the absolute character of the right guaranteed, the Court does not rule out the possibility that Article 3 of the Convention may also apply where the danger emanated from persons or groups of persons who are not public officials'; judgment of 29 April 1997, Reports 1997-III, Vol. 36, para. 40. Finally, in its judgment of 2 May 1997, *X* v. *the United Kingdom*, the Court held that the expulsion of the applicant, who was suffering from AIDS, to St. Kitts, where he would be without resources or support in the final stages of his illness would constitute a violation of Art. 3.

treatment[155] and regardless of whether the latter State is or is not a party to the Convention.[156]

The case-law shows that an applicant will have to advance strong arguments to convince the Convention organs that there really is a danger of a treatment contrary to Article 3 after he will be deported[157] (see also section 3.5.3). On several occasions the Commission has held that the fact that a deportee risks criminal prosecution in the country of destination, even though the punishment may be severe,[158] is not itself enough to raise an issue under Article 3 of the Convention in connection with his deportation,[159] unless there is clear indication that the charges are 'falsely inspired'.[160]

3.5.2   Death Penalty, Loss of Life

In the *Kirkwood* Case and in the *Soering* Case the Commission has developed the view that, since Article 2 of the Convention expressly permits the imposition of the death penalty, extradition of a person to a country where he risks the death penalty cannot, in itself, raise an issue either under Article 2 or Article 3 of the Convention,[161] but that this does not exclude the possibility of an issue arising under Article 3 in respect of the manner and circumstances in which the death penalty is implemented. The Commission gave as an example protracted delay in carrying out the death penalty. In the *Kirkwood* Case, which concerned a possible extradition to California, the Commission indicated as factors to be considered in

---

[155] Appl. 10308/83, *Altun* v. *Federal Republic of Germany*, D&R 36 (1984), p. 209 (233-234); judgment of 7 July 1989, *Soering* v. *the United Kingdom*, A.161, p. 38-39.

[156] See, *e.g.*, Appl. 1802/63, *X* v. *Federal Republic of Germany*, Yearbook VI (1963), p. 462 (480). In Appl. 8088/77, *X* v. *the Netherlands* and Appl. 9822/82, *X* v. *Spain* (not published), the Commission did, however, take into account as a positive factor that the case concerned extradition to one of the State Parties to the European Convention which had accepted the right of individual petition. *Cf.* Appl. 10308/83, *Altun* v. *Federal Republic of Germany*, D&R 36 (1984), p. 209 (233-234), in which the fact that Turkey had not recognised the right of individual petition was taken into account as a negative factor.

[157] See the judgment of 29 April 1997, *H.L.R.* v. *France*, Reports 1997-III, Vol. 36, paras 39-44, where the Court assessed the situation in the third country independent of the findings by the Commission.

[158] In Appl. 11017/84, *C* v. *Federal Republic of Germany*, D&R 46 (1986), p. 176 (181) the Commission held that 'the possibility of the applicant's facing a ten-year prison sentence for refusal to perform military service does not in itself warrant the conclusion that if the applicant were sent back to Yugoslavia he would be subjected to inhuman or degrading punishment within the meaning of Article 3 (...) The mere fact that an offence is punished more severely in one country than in another does not suffice to establish that the punishment is inhuman or degrading'. *Cf.* also Appl. 22408/93, *H* v. *Sweden*, D&R 79-A (1984), p. 85 (96): 15 years imprisonment as punishment for draft evasion if returned to Syria is not contrary to Art. 3.

[159] Appl. 4162/69, *X* v. *Federal Republic of Germany*, Yearbook XIII (1970), p. 806 (822-824); Appl. 7334/76, *X* v. *Federal Republic of Germany*, D&R 5 (1976), p. 154 (155); and Appl. 10564/83, *L* v. *Federal Republic of Germany*, D&R 40 (1985), p. 262 (265).

[160] Appl. 10308/83, *Altun* v. *Federal Republic of Germany*, D&R 36 (1984), p. 209 (233).

[161] It does, of course, raise an issue under Protocol No. 6 for those Contracting States which have ratified that Protocol.

assessing whether such a delay during the appeal procedure (the 'death row phenomenon') amounts to inhuman treatment, the relevance of the appeal system for the protection precisely of the right to life, the delays caused by the backlog of cases before the appeal courts and the control over them, and the possibility of a commutation of sentence by the very reason of the duration of the detention on the 'death row'. The Commission reached the following conclusion:

> The essential purpose of the California appeal system is to ensure protection for the right to life and to prevent arbitrariness. Although the system is subject to severe delays, these delays themselves are subject to the controlling jurisdiction of the courts. In the present case the applicant has not been tried or convicted and his risk of exposure to death row is uncertain. In the light of these reasons (...) the Commission finds that it has not been established that the treatment to which the applicant will be exposed, and the risk of his exposure to it, is so serious as to constitute inhuman or degrading treatment or punishment contrary to Article 3 of the Convention.[162]

The element which the Commission adds here to its considerations, *viz.* that the applicant has not been tried or convicted and that his conviction to the death penalty is still uncertain, in our opinion is a rather strange one, since that will often be the case when the complaint concerns extradition or expulsion; what matters in those cases is that there is a real risk of the applicant's being sentenced to death.

In the *Soering* Case, which concerned a possible extradition to Virginia, the British Government had contended that the applicant did not in reality risk the death penalty, pointing to the assurance that had been given by the Commonwealth Attorney that the trial judge would be informed of the wish of the British Government that the death penalty should not be imposed or carried out. The Commission observed that the sentencing judge was not obliged under Virginia law to accept the representation made to him on behalf of the British Government and that it could not be assumed that he would have regard to the diplomatic considerations relating to the continuing effectiveness of the extradition relationship between the two countries; therefore the risk that the applicant would be sentenced to death was considered a serious one.[163] The Commission repeated the view endorsed in *Kirkwood*, that extradition of a person to a country where he risks the death penalty cannot, in itself, raise an issue either under Article 2 or Article 3 of the Convention. As to the question whether an issue arose under Article 3 in respect of the manner and circumstances in which the death penalty would be implemented the Commission reached the conclusion – be it with only six against five votes – that there was no indication that the machinery of justice

---

[162] Appl. 10479/83, D&R 37 (1984), p. 158 (190).
[163] Report of 19 January 1989, A.161, pp. 59-61 In the same sense the Court in its judgment of 7 July 1989 in this case, A.161, pp. 38-39. In Appl. 22742/93, *Aylor-Davis* v. *France*, D&R 76-B (1994), p. 164 (172), the Commission considered that there was no issue under Art. 3, while the undertaking under oath of the Dallas County prosecutor that he would not call for the death penalty excluded the risk that the applicant, after France had extradited her to the United States, would be sentenced to death and would be exposed to the 'death row phenomenon'.

to which the applicant would be subjected was an arbitrary or unreasonable one.[164]

The Court likewise held that the Convention has to be read as a whole and Article 3 should therefore be construed in harmony with the provisions of Article 2:

> On this basis Article 3 evidently cannot have been intended by the drafters of the Convention to include a general prohibition of the death penalty since that would nullify the clear wording of Article 2, paragraph 1.[165]

Furthermore, the Court emphasised that Protocol No. 6, as a subsequent written agreement, showed the intention of the Contracting States to adopt the normal method of amendment of the text in order to introduce a new obligation to abolish capital punishment and to do so by an optional instrument allowing each State to choose the moment when to undertake such an engagement. In these conditions Article 3 cannot be interpreted as generally prohibiting the death penalty.[166]

The Court added, however, that this did not mean that the circumstances relating to a death sentence could never give rise to an issue under Article 3. Whether the treatment or punishment was to be brought under Article 3 in this case depended on the particular circumstances of the case, the length of detention prior to execution, conditions on death row and the applicant's age and mental state. The Court agreed with the Commission that the machinery of justice to which the applicant would be subject in the United States was in itself neither arbitrary nor unreasonable, but, rather, respected the rule of law and afforded considerable procedural safeguards to the defendant in a capital trial. Nevertheless it concluded – unlike the Commission – that in this case the decision to extradite would amount to a violation of Article 3. It held:

> However, in the Court's view, having regard to the very long period of time spent on death row in such extreme conditions, with the ever present and mounting anguish of awaiting execution of the death penalty, and to the personal circumstances of the applicant, especially his age and mental state at the time of the offence, the applicant's extradition to the United States would expose him to a real risk of treatment going beyond the threshold set by Article 3. A further consideration of relevance is that in the particular instance the legitimate purpose of extradition could be achieved by another means which would not involve suffering of such exceptional intensity or duration. Accordingly, the Secretary of State's decision to extradite the applicant to the United States would, if implemented, give rise to a breach of Article 3.[167]

If there is a real risk that a person after deportation will lose his life not as a consequence of the execution of a death sentence within the meaning of Article 2(1) but as a result of any other treatment, the deportation may amount to a violation of Article 3. In a recent report the Commission considered that in such a case a real risk of loss of life 'would not as such necessarily suffice to make

---

[164] Report of 19 January 1989, A.161, pp. 67-68.
[165] Judgment of 7 July 1989, A.161, p. 40.
[166] *Ibidem*, p. 41.
[167] *Ibidem*, pp. 44-45.

expulsion "an intentional deprivation of life" prohibited by Article 2, although it would amount to inhuman treatment within the meaning of Article 3.'[168]

3.5.3 Asylum

In recent years Article 3 has become a very important factor in asylum cases, although the right to political asylum as such is not contained in either the Convention or its Protocols.[169] While it is not the task of the Strasbourg organs to decide whether the expulsion of an asylum seeker violates the Refugee Convention,[170] it is clear that the expulsion of an asylum seeker/refugee to his country of origin in violation of the prohibition of *refoulement* (Article 33(1) of the Refugee Convention) may also infringe Article 3 when he is thus exposed to a real risk of being subjected to a treatment going beyond the threshold set by Article 3. As the Court held in the *Vilvarajah* judgment:

> expulsion by a Contracting State of an asylum seeker may give rise to an issue under Article 3, and hence engage the responsibility of that State under the Convention, where substantial grounds have been shown for believing that the person concerned faced a real risk of being subjected to torture or to inhuman or degrading treatment or punishment in the country to which he was returned.[171]

This raises the question what the relation is between Article 3 and the Refugee Convention. It is submitted here that the two sets of norms are overlapping, in that if a person has a well-founded fear of being persecuted – in the sense of Article 1(A) of the Refugee Convention – in his country of origin, his forced return to this country would violate Article 3. It has to be admitted that for a long time the Strasbourg case-law strictly differentiated between these norms. The Commission not only held that the question whether or not a decision to deport is 'covered by the Geneva Convention of 1951 on the Status of Refugees is not at issue as such',[172] but also stated that 'the risk of political persecution, as such, cannot be equated to torture, inhuman or degrading treatment'.[173] It has often stressed that the right to asylum as such does not figure among the Convention rights, and that the expulsion or extradition of an individual could prove to be a breach of Article 3 only in exceptional cases or circumstances.[174] This case-law implied that

---

[168] Report of 13 September 1996, *Bahaddar* v. *the Netherlands* (not yet published), para. 78.

[169] Judgment of 30 October 1991, *Vilvarajah and Others* v. *the United Kingdom*, A.215, p. 34; judgment of 17 December 1996, *Ahmed* v. *Austria*, Reports 1996-VI, Vol. 26, para. 38.

[170] Appl. 4165/69, *X* v. *the Federal Republic of Germany*, Yearbook XIII (1970), p. 806 (822).

[171] Judgment of 30 October 1991, A.215, p. 34; likewise the judgment of 15 November 1996, *Chahal* v. *the United Kingdom*, Reports 1996-V, Vol. 22, paras 73-74; and the judgment of 17 December 1996, *Ahmed* v. *Austria*, Reports 1996-VI, Vol. 26, para. 39.

[172] Appl. 4165/69, *X* v. *Federal Republic of Germany*, Yearbook XIII (1970), p. 806 (822).

[173] Appl. 10760/84, *C* v. *the Netherlands*, D&R 38 (1984), p. 224 (226).

[174] Appl. 4162/69, *X* v. *Federal Republic of Germany*, Yearbook XIII (1970), p. 806 (822); Appl. 4134/69, *X* v. *Federal Republic of Germany*, Yearbook XIII (1970), p. 900 (902); Appl. 6315/73, *X* v. *Federal Republic of Germany*, D&R 1 (1973), p. 73 (75); Appl. 7465/76, *X* v. *Denmark*, D&R 7 (1977), p. 153 (154); Appl. 11017/84, *C* v. *Federal Republic of Germany*, D&R 46 (1986), p. 176 (181); Appl. 12122/86, *Lukka* v. *the United Kingdom*, D&R 50 (1987), p. 268 (273).

refoulement only raised an issue under Article 3 if the ensuing persecution would reach a high level of severity.[175] Consequently, *refoulement* of refugees leading to persecution that does not reach that level of severity has been held to be compatible with Article 3.[176]

The protection to asylum-seekers provided by Article 3 was further limited in that the Strasbourg organs, as has been said before, had adopted a restrictive approach with regard to the assessment of the risk of ill-treatment. According to their case-law the decision to expel an asylum-seeker only gives rise to an issue under Article 3 'where substantial grounds have been shown for believing that the person concerned (...) faces a real risk of being subjected to torture or to inhuman or degrading treatment or punishment' in the country to which he was returned.[177] It was not surprising that in the *Cruz Varas* Case the Court found that such substantial grounds had not been shown: the (Chilean) asylum-seeker had remained silent about his alleged clandestine activities and torture until more than 18 months after the first interrogation by the Swedish authorities; each time he was interviewed he changed his story; and in the meantime a democratic evolution was taking place in Chile which had led to improvements in the political situation.[178] Open to criticism, however, is the way in which the Court applied its (substantial grounds/real risk) standard in the *Vilvarajah* judgment, concerning the removal of five Tamil asylum-seekers to Sri Lanka, where a civil war was (and still is) going on. The Court found that their expulsion was not contrary to Article 3:

> The evidence before the Court concerning the background of the applicants, as well as the general situation, does not establish that their personal situation was any worse than the generality of other members of the Tamil community or other young male Tamils who were returning to their country. Since the situation was still unsettled there existed the possibility that they might be detained and ill-treated as appears to have occurred previously in the cases of some of the applicants (...) A mere possibility of ill-treatment, however, in such circumstances, is not in itself sufficient to give rise to a breach of Article 3.
> It is claimed that the second, third and fourth applicants were in fact subjected to ill-treatment following their return (...) Be this as it may, however, there existed no special distinguishing features in their cases that could or ought to have enabled the Secretary of State to foresee that they would be treated in this way.[179]

---

[175] Appl. 10633/83, *X* v. *the Netherlands* (not published): 'although the risk of political persecution, as such, cannot be equated to torture, inhuman or degrading treatment, the Commission does not exclude that expulsion or "refoulement" may, in a particular case, raise an issue under Article 3 if it brings about a prejudice for the individual concerned which reaches such level of severity as to bring it within the scope of this provision'. *Cf.* also Appl. 10760/84, *C* v. *the Netherlands*, D&R 38 (1984), p. 224 (226).

[176] Appl. 4162/69, *X* v. *Federal Republic of Germany*, Yearbook XIII (1970), p. 806 (822-284); Appl. 10032/82, *X* v. *Sweden* (not published).

[177] Judgment of 20 March 1991, *Cruz Varas*, A.201, p. 28; judgment of 30 October 1991, *Vilvarajah and Others* v. *the United Kingdom*, A.215, p. 34.

[178] Judgment of 20 March 1991, A.201, pp. 30-31.

[179] Judgment of 30 October 1991, A.215, p. 37.

The crux of the Court's reasoning seems to be that because of the absence of special distinguishing features in their cases there was only a general risk – 'a mere possibility' – that the asylum-seekers upon return would be treated in a manner inconsistent with Article 3. This risk, that every young male Tamil returning to his country would run, was in itself not sufficiently high to qualify as a 'real risk' to bring their removal within the scope of Article 3. From the facts of the case, however, it appears that there were enough distinguishing features to conclude that there was a real risk that the asylum-seekers would be exposed to inhuman treatment. After they were removed to Sri Lanka in February 1988 appeals were instituted on their behalf. In March 1989 the adjudicator concluded that the applicants had had a well-founded fear of persecution, that they were entitled to political asylum and should be returned to the United Kingdom.[180] In fact, ultimately they were allowed to return. The adjudicator largely believed the accounts given by the applicants of their personal situations.[181] The Government did not contest these findings, nor did the Court. It is difficult to understand why the Court thought they did not suffice as the special distinguishing features justifying the conclusion that there was indeed a real risk of a treatment contrary to Article 3 after their deportation to Sri Lanka. The Court here applied a standard of assessment that is even more restrictive than the very strict test so dominant in refugee law, that the asylum-seeker has to show that he is 'singled out for persecution'.[182] Such a restrictive approach would seem incompatible with the Court's point of departure that its examination of a risk of ill-treatment in breach of Article 3 must be a rigorous one in view of the absolute character of this provision.[183]

It seems, however, that in recent cases the Strasbourg organs have adopted a more liberal approach, which amounts to the assumption that returning a person to his country of origin who has a well-founded fear of being persecuted there *ipso facto* violates Article 3. In its earlier case-law the Commission already applied concepts which related to the refugee definition. For instance, in a case concerning extradition the Commission found it necessary 'to determine whether in this case there would be a certain risk of prosecution for political reasons which could lead to an unjustified or disproportionate sentence being passed on the applicant and as a result inhuman treatment';[184] this is a criterium that is often applied in refugee cases.[185] A more explicit reference to the concept of refugee can be found in a recent report concerning a Somalian national whose refugee

---

[180] *Ibidem*, pp. 24-25.

[181] *Ibidem*, pp. 8-21.

[182] *Cf.* on the singling out doctrine J.C. Hathaway, *The Law of Refugee Status*, Toronto/Vancouver, 1991, pp. 75-97.

[183] Judgment of 30 October 1991, *Vilvarajah and Others* v. *the United Kingdom*, A.215, p. 36.

[184] Appl. 10308/83, *Altun* v. *Federal Republic of Germany*, D&R 36 (1984), p. 209 (233). *Cf.* also Appl. 11933/86, *A* v. *Switzerland*, D&R 46 (1986), p. 257 (271).

[185] *Cf.* UNHCR, *Handbook on Procedures and Criteria for Determining Refugee Status*, Geneva, 1988, paras 57, 85 and 169.

status was forfeited by the Austrian authorities on the ground that he was convicted for particularly serious crimes within the meaning of Article 33(2) of the Refugee Convention. The Commission:

> attached particular weight to the fact that the applicant was granted asylum in May 1992. The Austrian Ministry for the Interior (...) found that he would risk persecution in Somalia. In the asylum proceedings, the Austrian authorities had to consider *basically the same elements* under Austrian law as the Commission must consider under Article 3 (emphasis added).

While the situation in Somalia had not changed fundamentally since the time when the applicant was granted asylum, the Commission concluded that he still would risk persecution, if returned to Somalia, and found that substantial grounds had been shown for believing that the applicant would then face a real risk of being subjected to treatment in breach of Article 3.[186] The Court followed the same reasoning and reached the same conclusion.[187]

Moreover, it seems that the Commission and the Court have adopted a less strict 'real risk' criterium, which resembles a more liberal 'singling out' test. In the *Chahal* judgment deportation to India of an alleged Sikh terrorist was regarded to infringe Article 3; particular weight was accorded to the general situation, especially the (non)observance of human rights.[188] However, it is not yet clear whether the Court has left the strictly individualising *Vilvarajah*-test altogether, because of Chahal's high profile as a leading figure supporting the cause of Sikh separatism which in itself set him apart from Sikhs in general, and thus made it plausible that he was 'singled out'.[189] However, that the Commission has adopted a less stringent standard of proof is evident from the *Bahaddar* Case, in which it concluded that expulsion of the applicant to Bangladesh would be in violation of Article 3, although he had not supplied much direct evidence. The Commission gave him the benefit of the doubt since it considered his account to be credible and on the whole consistent.[190]

An argument against the thesis that the deportation of an individual to a country where he has a well-founded fear of being persecuted in principle amounts to a violation of Article 3, might be that persecution in the sense of Article 1(A) of the Refugee Convention does not always attain the minimum level of severity required to fall within the scope of Article 3. Such a counter-argument misunderstands this thesis, which does not equate 'persecution' with 'treatment prohibited by Article 3', but posits that the deportation of a person to a country where he has *a well-founded fear* of being persecuted will in general amount to *a real risk* of being exposed to ill-treatment in the sense of Article 3. It may be true that not every act of persecution can be qualified as torture or inhuman or degrading treatment or

---

[186] Report of 5 July 1995, *Ahmed* v. *Austria*, Reports 1996-V, Vol. 26, paras 65, 66 and 70.
[187] Judgment of 17 December 1996, *Ahmed* v. *Austria*, Reports 1996-VI, Vol. 26, paras 42-47.
[188] Judgment of 15 November 1996, Reports 1996-V, Vol. 22, paras 98-107.
[189] *Ibidem*, para. 106.
[190] Report of 13 September 1996 (not yet published), paras 83-102.

punishment, but when a well-founded fear has been established that a person, if returned to his country, will suffer from such an act of persecution, it is plausible to assume that there is also a real risk that he will be subjected to (additional) harsher treatment, that falls within the scope of Article 3.

In conclusion, therefore, it is submitted that a person who has a well-founded fear of persecution within the meaning of Article 1(A) of the Refugee Convention and is protected by the prohibition of *refoulement* in Article 33(1) of this Convention, as a rule can also claim that he may not be returned to his country of origin because that would expose him to a real risk of being subjected to a treatment prohibited by Article 3. The reverse does not hold; Article 3 has a wider scope than Article 33(1) of the Refugee Convention. A person who fulfils the criteria of Article 1(A) of the Refugee Convention can be denied the protection of Article 33(1) when there are serious reasons for considering that he has committed crimes as mentioned in Article 1(F), as well as when he may reasonably be regarded as a danger to the security of the country of reception or, having been convicted of a particularly serious crime, constitutes a danger to the community of that country (Article 33(2)). In all these cases he is still protected by Article 3. As the Court held:

> the activities of the individual in question, however undesirable or dangerous, cannot be a material consideration. The protection afforded by Article 3 is thus wider than that provided by Article 32 and 33 of the United Nations 1951 Convention on the Status of Refugees.[191]

The protection afforded by Article 3 is also wider than the prohibition of *refoulement* in that the concept of persecution in Article 1(A) of the Refugee Convention and thus the protection against refoulement (Article 33(1)) is often believed to presuppose the existence of state authorities, and is linked with a limited number of grounds of persecution (race, religion, nationality, membership of a particular social group or political opinion), whereas the applicability of Article 3 solely depends on the character of the treatment, not on the source or the grounds of this treatment. Thus the Commission argued that the 'position of the Austrian authorities that there is no substantial risk for the applicant since the State authority had ceased to exist in Somalia cannot be accepted. It is sufficient that those who hold substantial power within the State, even though they are not the Government, threaten the life and security of the applicant.'[192] And, of

---

[191] Judgment of 15 November 1996, *Chahal* v. *the United Kingdom*, Reports 1996-V, Vol. 22, para. 80; judgment of 17 December 1996, *Ahmed* v. *Austria*, Reports 1996-VI, Vol. 26, para. 41. *Cf.* also the judgment of 7 July 1989, *Soering* v. *the United Kingdom*, A.161, p. 35: 'it would hardly be compatible with the underlying values of the Convention (...) were a Contracting State knowingly to surrender a fugitive to another State where there are substantial grounds for believing that he would be in danger of being subjected to torture, however heinous the crime allegedly committed.'

[192] Report of 5 July 1995, *Ahmed* v. *Austria*, Reports 1996-VI, Vol. 26, para. 68. *Cf.* also judgment of 17 December 1996, *Ahmed* v. *Austria*, Reports 1996-VI, Vol. 26, para. 46: the conclusion that the applicant's deportation to Somalia would amount to a violation of Art. 3 is not invalidated by 'the current lack of State authority in Somalia'.

course, *Soering* was protected by Article 3 although the inhuman treatment that he feared was not related to one of the grounds of persecution.[193]

3.6 No Derogation or Limitation

Article 3, which 'enshrines one of the fundamental values of the democratic societies making up the Council of Europe',[194] is included in the list of rights which are declared non-derogable in Article 15(2). It is therefore of an absolute character, not only in the sense that the provision itself leaves no scope for limitations by law, as a number of other provisions do, but also in the sense that no derogation can be permitted even in the event of a public emergency threatening the life of the nation.[195] The Commission accordingly stated in its report in *Ireland* v. *the United Kingdom*:

> It follows that the prohibition under Article 3 of the Convention is an absolute one and that there can never be under the Convention, or under international law, a justification for acts in breach of that provision.[196]

This implies, for instance, that 'it is never permissible to have recourse to punishments which are contrary to Article 3, whatever their deterrent effect may be.'[197] Likewise, the requirements of the investigation and the difficulties inherent in the fight against crime cannot result in limits being placed on the protection afforded by this provision.[198]

The prohibition provided by Article 3 against ill-treatment is equally absolute in expulsion and extradition cases. The States, even when protecting their communities from terrorist violence, cannot invoke national interests to override the interests of the individual where substantial grounds have been shown for believing that he would be subjected to ill-treatment when expelled.[199] Nor can they invoke the interest of the international community that suspected offenders who flee abroad should be brought to justice. That they could do so was suggested by the Court in the *Soering* judgment, where it remarked that the risk of undermining the foundations of extradition is included among the factors to be taken into account in the interpretation and application of Article 3.[200] However, in *Chahal* the Court made it clear that from these remarks it should *not* be

---

[193] Judgment of 7 July 1989, *Soering* v. *the United Kingdom*, A.161.

[194] *Ibidem*, p. 34.

[195] Judgment of 18 January 1978, *Ireland* v. *the United Kingdom*, A.25, p. 65; judgment of 15 November 1996, *Chahal* v. *the United Kingdom*, Reports 1996-V, Vol. 22, para. 79; judgment of 17 December 1996, *Ahmed* v. *Austria*, Reports 1996-VI, Vol. 26, para. 40.

[196] Report of 25 January 1976, *Ireland* v. *the United Kingdom*, B.23-I (1980), p. 390.

[197] Judgment of 25 April 1978, *Tyrer*, A.26, p. 15.

[198] Judgment of 27 August 1992, *Tomasi* v. *France*, A.241-A, p. 42.

[199] Judgment of 15 November 1996, *Chahal* v. *the United Kingdom*, Reports 1996-V, Vol. 22, paras 78-80; *Cf.* also the judgment of 17 December 1996, *Ahmed* v. *Austria*, Reports 1996-VI, Vol. 26, paras 40-41.

[200] Judgment of 7 July 1989, A.161, p. 35.

inferred 'that there is any room for balancing the risk of ill-treatment against the reasons for expulsion in determining whether a State's responsibility under Article 3 is engaged.'[201]

4 FREEDOM FROM SLAVERY, SERVITUDE AND FORCED OR COMPULSORY LABOUR (ARTICLE 4)

1. *No one shall be held in slavery or servitude.*
2. *No one shall be required to perform forced or compulsory labour.*
3. *For the purpose of this Article the term 'forced or compulsory labour' shall not include:*
   a) *any work required to be done in the ordinary course of detention imposed according to the provisions of Article 5 of this Convention or during conditional release from such detention;*
   b) *any service of a military character or, in case of conscientious objectors in countries where they are recognised, service exacted instead of compulsory military service;*
   c) *any service exacted in case of an emergency or calamity threatening the life or well-being of the community;*
   d) *any work or service which forms part of normal civic obligations.*

4.1 Introduction

In Article 4 slavery and servitude are dealt with separately from forced and compulsory labour. The first two terms refer to the entire status or situation of the person concerned. Slavery indicates that the person concerned is wholly in the legal ownership of another person, while servitude concerns less far-reaching forms of restraint and refers, for instance, to the total of the labour conditions and/or the obligations to work or to render services from which the person in question cannot escape and which he cannot change.[202] Forced labour and compulsory labour, on the other hand, do not refer to the entire situation of the person concerned, but exclusively to the involuntary character of the work and services to be performed by him, which may, and usually will, also have a temporary or incidental character.

4.2 Slavery and Servitude

The first paragraph of Article 4 has mainly been invoked in connection with complaints of detainees against the obligation to perform work in prison. In those cases the Commission took the position that the terms 'slavery' and 'servitude' are not applicable to such a situation, while from the third paragraph under (a) of

---

[201] Judgment of 15 November 1996, Reports 1996-V, Vol. 22, para. 81.

[202] See the report of 9 July 1980, *Van Droogenbroeck*, B.44 (1985), p. 30: 'in addition to the obligation to provide another with certain services, the concept of servitude includes the obligation on the part of the "serf" to live on another's property and the impossibility of changing his condition.'

Article 4 it is evident that the drafters of the Convention did not wish to prohibit the imposition of such an obligation.[203]

In the *Van Droogenbroeck* Case the applicant submitted that the fact that he had been placed at the disposal of the Government, as a recidivist, had reduced him to a condition of servitude, since in fact he was subject to arbitrary supervision by the administrative authorities. The Commission took the view that there was no question of servitude, because the measure was one of limited duration only, was subject to judicial review and did not affect the legal status of the person in question.[204]

The first paragraph was also invoked before the Commission by four young men who, at the age of 15 and 16, had joined the Navy for a period of nine years and after some time had applied for discharge. In their complaint against the refusal of the authorities to discharge them they claimed, *inter alia*, that in view of their age their service constituted a form of servitude in the sense of Article 4(1). After first having stated that military service did form an exception to the second, but not necessarily to the first paragraph, the Commission rejected the complaint as being manifestly ill-founded. The finding was based in particular on the circumstance that the relevant law prescribed for minors the consent of the parents and that in this case such consent had indeed been given.[205]

4.3 Forced or Compulsory Labour

The second paragraph of Article 4 has played a greater part in the case-law. Hitherto the Commission and the Court have refrained from giving a definition of the term 'forced or compulsory labour'. Both bodies, however, have made reference to conventions of the International Labour Organisation, which contain far more detailed norms in this respect.[206] For the meaning of the term, the Commission referred to the five categories enumerated in Convention No. 105 of the International Labour Organisation:

> political coercion or education or as a punishment for holding or expressing political views or views ideologically opposed to the established political, social, or economic system; mobilising and using labour for purposes of economic development; labour discipline; punishment for having participated in strikes; and racial, social or religious discrimination.[207]

---

[203] Appls 3134/67, 3172/67 and 3188-3206/67, *Twenty-one detainees* v. *Federal Republic of Germany*, Yearbook XI (1968), p. 528 (552). See also Appl. 7549/76, *X* v. *Ireland* (not published).

[204] Report of 9 July 1980, B.44 (1985), p. 30.

[205] Appls 3435-3438/67, *W, X, Y and Z* v. *the United Kingdom*, Yearbook XI (1968), p. 562 (596-598).

[206] See, *e.g.*, the references to ILO Convention No. 29 by the Court in its judgment of 23 November 1983, *Van der Mussele*, A.70, pp. 16-17.

[207] Appl. 7641/76, *X and Y* v. *Federal Republic of Germany*, D&R 10 (1978), p. 224 (230). ILO Convention No. 105 is to be found in: International Labour Office, *Conventions and Recommendations 1919-1966*, 1966, p. 891.

Elements of the concept 'forced or compulsory labour' mentioned by the Commission are:

> first, that the work or service is performed by the worker against his will and, secondly, that the requirement that the work or service be performed is unjust or oppressive or the work or service itself involves avoidable hardship.[208]

With respect to the first element – its involuntary nature – the Commission so far has taken the view that consent, once given, deprives the work or service of its compulsory character. If the decision mentioned above concerning the boys who had joined the Navy, which related to the first paragraph, were followed analogously in connection with the second paragraph, the consent of the parents could presumably take the place of that of their children under age.

Such an interpretation of 'forced' and 'compulsory' would appear to be too restrictive. Even if a person has voluntarily entered into a labour contract or has agreed to perform certain services, the circumstances may change in such a way or the objections to the work in question, especially in engagements of long duration, may become so far-reaching that holding the person unqualifiedly to his consent may indeed bring in issue Article 4(2). In our opinion this provision implies in such a case that alternative possibilities should be offered to the person in question, for instance different work if the objections are directed against the nature of the work, or termination of the contract coupled with the obligation to pay a reasonable compensation. And, indeed, in the *Van der Mussele* Case the Court did not hold the issue of consent to be decisive.[209]

Within the framework of the second criterion, *viz.* that the obligation to perform the work must have an unjustifiable or oppressive character, or that the work itself involves avoidable hardship for the person concerned, the Commission introduced a number of elements which allow a considerable margin of discretion to the national authorities. If this second criterion were to be applied cumulatively to the first, in fact a general ground of justification would be added to the specific grounds of the third paragraph to be discussed hereafter. Even work or a service which a person has to perform against his will and which is felt by him to be oppressive would not, in that view, constitute a violation of Article 4(2), provided that the national authorities can submit *prima facie* evidence that this oppressive character is not as bad as is alleged, or that the hardship was unavoidable. In our opinion the text of Article 4 would thus be strained and, therefore, the second criterion should rather be handled *alternatively* in the sense suggested above, *viz.* that even work or a service to which the person concerned has previously consented may assume a compulsory character for him if the obligations resulting therefrom involve such unjustified or avoidable hardship that they can no longer be deemed to be covered by his consent. In its report in the *Van der Mussele*

---

[208] Appl. 4653/70, *X* v. *Federal Republic of Germany*, Yearbook XVII (1974), p. 148 (172). Likewise Appl. 8410/78, *X* v. *Federal Republic of Germany*, D&R 18 (1980), p. 216 (219) and Appl. 9322/81, *X* v. *the Netherlands*, D&R 32 (1983), p. 180 (182-183).
[209] Judgment of 23 November 1983, A.70, p. 19.

Case, the Commission indeed speaks of 'a subsidiary argument' in connection with the second criterion.[210]

There has been considerable dissension within the Commission about the elements of the concept of 'forced' labour. This is evident from the *Iversen* Case. In that case the Norwegian legislation was brought in issue on the basis of which a dentist might be required to fill for some time a vacancy that failed to be filled after having been duly advertised. The complaint was declared by the Commission to be manifestly ill-founded. Two of the members of the Commission belonging to the majority considered the Norwegian measure justified on the basis of the ground mentioned in the third paragraph under (c), *viz.* 'emergency or calamity threatening the life or well-being of the community'.[211] Four members of the majority of six, however, held that there was no question of forced or compulsory labour, because the service to be rendered was exacted for a limited time, was properly remunerated and was in keeping with the profession chosen by Iversen, while the law in question had not been applied against him in an arbitrary or discriminatory manner.[212] A minority of four members of the Commission, finally, were of the opinion that the above-mentioned circumstances did not exclude the applicability of the second paragraph, and that the possible application of the third paragraph called for a further examination.[213] In the light of this diversity of views within the Commission it is very curious indeed that the complaint was rejected as being manifestly ill-founded, which barred a thorough examination of the facts and a decision of the Court on this evidently controversial interpretation of the second paragraph.[214]

In the case of a German lawyer who complained about having to act as unpaid or insufficiently paid defence counsel, the Commission decided that the imposed obligation was not unreasonable and did not therefore fall under the prohibition of Article 4(2). The Commission did not review this form of compulsory service for its conformity with the third paragraph. In fact, the Commission based its decision partly on the consideration that anyone who voluntarily chooses the profession of a lawyer knows that under German law lawyers are obliged to defend clients who lack the means to pay counsel's fees, in those cases where they have been nominated to do so by a judicial body. In those circumstances it could not be said that such a service had to be rendered against the will of the person

---

[210] Report of 3 March 1982, B.55 (1987), p. 33.
[211] Appl. 1468/62, Yearbook VI (1963), p. 278 (328-330).
[212] *Ibidem*, pp. 326-328.
[213] *Ibidem*, pp. 330-332.
[214] See *supra* pp. 156-157. Jacobs, *supra* note 17, p. 40, utters the supposition that in this case the Commission was guided by political motives under the influence of the stir which this case had caused in Norway and the decision of the Norwegian Government to renew the acceptance of the individual right of complaint for a period of only one year.

in question.[215] Here the Commission seems to follow the reasoning which already was hinted at by four of its members in the *Iversen* Case, *viz.* that when certain obligations are attached to a profession, the person choosing that profession accepts those obligations implicitly. A similar decision was taken in the case of a notary public who complained about the system according to which in specific cases he was allowed to charge only reduced fees for his services. The Commission stated first of all that the applicant had not advanced that he had been forced in one way or another to give his services in specific cases, so that the question might be asked whether the first element had been satisfied. With respect to the second element the Commission found that the impugned system could not be qualified as 'unjust or oppressive', since it related to a normal part of the tasks of a notary public and ensued from his almost exclusive competence as regards the services concerned.[216] And also in the case of a Dutch football player who complained that he was, after renouncing the contract with his former football club, prevented from entering another football club in view of the prohibitive transfer sum requested by the former, the Commission took the view that the applicant freely chose to become a professional football player, knowing that by doing so he would be affected by the rules governing the relationships between his future employers. Moreover, the Commission was of the opinion that the system complained of, even if it could produce certain inconveniences for the applicant, could not be considered as being oppressive or constituting avoidable hardship, especially not since it did not affect directly his contractual freedom.[217]

The above-mentioned argument applies only if the obligations form part of the normal exercise of a profession. The Commission, therefore, speaks of 'normal professional work'.[218] The obligation to lend free legal aid forms part of the normal obligations of a lawyer in the Federal Republic of Germany, as it does in most other Member States of the Council of Europe, and the obligation to take for some time, if necessary, a position in the public dental service in the northern part of the country forms part of the normal obligations of a dentist in Norway after he has completed his studies.[219] This does not, however, alter the fact that it must still be ascertained for each individual case whether the concrete content of

---

[215] Appl. 4653/70, *X* v. *Federal Republic of Germany*, Yearbook XVII (1974), p. 148 (172). Previously, two complaints of an Austrian lawyer about free legal aid had been declared admissible by the Commission, on the ground that 'these complaints raise issues of a complex nature' and could not therefore be declared manifestly ill-founded: Appls 4897/71 and 5219/71, *Gussenbauer* v. *Austria*, Coll. 42 (1973), p. 41 (48) and Yearbook XV (1972), p. 558 (562) respectively. These cases led to a friendly settlement, so that the merits have not been pronounced on; report of 8 October 1974, *Stock-Taking on the European Convention on Human Rights. A periodic Note on the Concrete Results Achieved Under the Convention. The First Thirty Years: 1954 Until 1984*, Strasbourg 1984, p. 123.

[216] Appl. 8410/78, *X* v. *Federal Republic of Germany*, D&R 18 (1980), p. 216 (219).

[217] Appl. 9322/81, *X* v. *the Netherlands*, D&R 32 (1983), p. 180 (182-183).

[218] Appl. 4653/70, *X* v. *Federal Republic of Germany*, Yearbook XVII (1974), p. 148 (172).

[219] See, however, the report of 3 March 1982, *Van der Mussele*, B.55 (1987), p. 34, where the Commission distinguishes the situation from that of the *Iversen* Case.

the obligation in question is not so oppressive for the person concerned that he can no longer be assumed to have consented to it by choosing his profession.

In another case, where a lawyer invoked Article 4(2) on account of his obligation to act as a free legal aid counsel, the Commission followed a somewhat different line of reasoning. It referred to Article 6(3)(c) and submitted that, since in the Convention the right to free legal aid has been recognised, the obligation for a lawyer to give legal aid in a concrete case cannot constitute forced or compulsory labour in the sense of Article 4(2).[220] The connection here established by the Commission between the two provisions seems to us not to be a very logical one. Indeed, the right to legal aid *per se* does not say anything about the way in which the authorities must effectuate this right and does not necessarily imply that this should be done *via* an obligation for lawyers to give such legal aid under conditions to be laid down by the authorities. In its report in the *Van der Mussele* Case the Commission impliedly indicated that this line of reasoning is rather unsatisfactory, by stating there that the obligation of the State to provide free legal aid was not decisive in that case because legal aid was organised by the Bar Association. It, therefore, again emphasised that the obligation imposed on the applicant formed part of his normal professional work and left him so much freedom that one could not speak of forced or compulsory labour, though the Commission considered it unfortunate that pupil barristers such as the applicant were not paid at all when appointed to defend indigent persons.[221]

In the same *Van der Mussele* Case the Court took a somewhat different approach. It used as a starting point for the interpretation of 'compulsory labour' the definition given in Article 2 of ILO Convention No. 29:[222]

all work or service which is exacted from any person under the menace of any penalty and for which the said person has not offered himself voluntarily.[223]

Although a refusal to act as a free legal aid counsel was not punishable by any sanction of a criminal law character, the Court concluded that there was a 'menace of any penalty', since with such a refusal the applicant would run the risk of his name being struck off the roll of pupils or a rejection of his application for entry in the register of advocates.[224] As regards the voluntary character of the service exacted, the Court held that the argument used by the Commission that the applicant consented in advance 'correctly reflects one aspect of the situation; nevertheless, the Court cannot attach decisive weight thereto'.[225] The Court subsequently observed that the applicant had to accept the requirement concerned, whether he wanted to or not, in order to become an *avocat* and that his consent

---

[220] Appl. 7641/76, *X and Y* v. *Federal Republic of Germany*, D&R 10 (1978), p. 224 (230).
[221] Report of 3 March 1982, B.55 (1987), p. 34.
[222] International Labour Office, *Conventions and Recommendations 1919-1966*, 1966, p. 155.
[223] Judgment of 23 November 1983, A.70, p. 16.
[224] *Ibidem*, p. 17.
[225] *Ibidem*, p. 18.

was determined by the normal conditions of exercise of the profession at the relevant time. Moreover, according to the Court, it should not be overlooked that the acceptance by the applicant was the acceptance of a legal regime of a general character.[226] To decide whether the service required falls within the prohibition of compulsory labour, the Court held that it should have regard to all the circumstances of the case in the light of the underlying objectives of Article 4.[227]

At first sight, the approach of the Court seems different from that of the Commission, especially since the Court distances itself from the second criterion developed by the Commission, *viz.* that of the 'unjust' or 'oppressive' character of the service to be performed.[228] It is, however, striking to see that most of the circumstances of the case taken into consideration by the Court, have also been dealt with by the Commission in its report. In fact, the main difference lies in the weight, attached to the element of 'consent in advance'. As has been stated above,[229] the view expressed by the Commission in this respect is too restrictive. The approach of the Court, therefore, is to be welcomed. However, the Court also fails to give clear guidelines with respect to the interpretation of 'forced or compulsory labour'. It restricts itself to an investigation of all the circumstances of the case, each of which, according to the Court, 'provides a standard of evaluation'.[230] These standards were in this case the following: the services did not fall outside the ambit of the normal activities of an *avocat*; a compensatory factor was to be found in the advantages attaching to the profession; the services contributed to the professional training of the applicant; the service is a means of securing the benefit, laid down in Article 6(3)(c), and can be seen as a 'normal civic obligation' as referred to in Article 4(3)(d); and, lastly, the burden imposed was not disproportionate, since it only took about 18 hours of the working time.[231]

Both the Commission and the Court concluded that, although the situation could be characterised as unsatisfactory because of the absence of any fee and the non-reimbursement of incurred expenditure, it did not constitute a violation of Article 4 of the Convention.[232]

4.4 Exceptions

With respect to the exceptions mentioned in the third paragraph, the following observations may be made. The exception formulated under (a) for the work of detainees and conditionally released persons is put in quite general terms and –

---

[226] *Ibidem*, p. 19.

[227] *Idem.*

[228] *Ibidem*, p. 20.

[229] See *supra* p. 339.

[230] Judgment of 23 November 1983, *Van der Mussele*, A.70, p. 19.

[231] *Ibidem*, pp. 19-20. *Cf.* the report of 3 March 1982, *Van der Mussele*, B.55 (1987), p. 34.

[232] *Ibidem*, pp. 21 and 35 respectively. See also Appl. 20781/92, *Ackerl, Grötzback, Glawischnig, Schwalm, Klein, Sladeck and Limberger v. Austria*, D&R 78-A (1994), p. 116 (118).

unlike Article 2(2)(c) of ILO Convention No. 29 – does not exclude work on behalf of private enterprises and foundations. Complaints with respect to work of such a character have therefore been declared inadmissible by the Commission.[233] The exception under (a) applies only to work 'in the ordinary course of detention'. In the '*Vagrancy*' Cases these words were interpreted by the Court to mean that it must be work directed at the rehabilitation of the prisoner.[234] Moreover the Court's judgment would seem to imply that Article 4 is violated if the detention itself, in the course of which the work must be performed, conflicts with the first paragraph of Article 5.[235] The view of the Commission that also in case of a conflict with the fourth paragraph of Article 5 reliance on Article 4(3)(a) by the authorities is excluded,[236] was not adopted by the Court. This is curious, since the authorities may thus refer to a situation which has been found by the Strasbourg organs to be in conformity with Article 5(1), but whose lawfulness – contrary to Article 5(4) – the applicant has not been able to have reviewed by the domestic court. Such a review could precisely have resulted in the court ordering his release, as a consequence of which the ground for the obligation to work would have ceased to exist.[237] It should finally be pointed out with respect to the exception under (a) that this exception does not relate exclusively to convicts – such as is the case in ILO Convention No. 29 – nor exclusively to persons whose detention is based on a judicial order – as Article 8 of the UN Covenant on Civil and Political Rights provides – but to all the situations of lawful deprivation of liberty mentioned in the first paragraph of Article 5.[238]

The formulation of the exception under (b), too, departs from that of Convention No. 29, where Article 2(2)(a) speaks of 'any work or service exacted in virtue of compulsory military service laws for work of a purely military character'. From the fact that in Article 4(3)(b) the confinement to 'compulsory military service' has not been adopted the Commission concluded that 'it was intended to cover also the obligation to continue a service entered into on a

---

[233] Appls 3134/67, 3172/67 and 3188-3206/67, *Twenty-one detainees* v. *Federal Republic of Germany*, Yearbook XI (1968), p. 528 (552-558) and Appl. 9449/81, *X* v. *Austria* (not published). In some of the Contracting States, however, the courts will have to apply that restriction on the ground of the direct applicability of Convention No. 29, ratified by those States.

[234] Judgment of 18 June 1971, A.12, pp. 44-45. See also Appl. 8500/79, *X* v. *Switzerland*, D&R 18 (1980), p. 238 (248-249), where in the case of the detention of a minor the Commission examined under Art. 5(1)(d) whether the required work 'was abnormally long or arduous in view of the applicant's age or was of no educational value'.

[235] Judgment of 18 June 1971, A.12, p. 44.

[236] Report of 19 July 1969, *De Wilde, Ooms and Versyp ('Vagrancy'* Cases), B.10 (1971), pp. 96-97.

[237] One might assume that the respondent State would be confronted here with the adage *nemo suam turpitudinem allegans audiendum est*. However, the Commission followed the Court in its report of 9 July 1980, *Van Droogenbroeck*, B.44 (1985), p. 31.

[238] Appl. 8500/79, *X* v. *Switzerland*, D&R 18 (1980), p. 238 (248), which was a case under Art. 5(1)(d).

voluntary basis'.[239] However, in view of the rationale of this exception, as it appears in particular from the reference to the service exacted instead of compulsory military service, such an application is justified only for those cases where this voluntary military service takes the place of compulsory military service. In fact, in other cases it cannot be appreciated why military service should be entitled to a special position as compared with other public service in the national interest, such as, for instance, service in public medical institutions or for utility companies.

The fact that Article 4(3)(b) also mentions civil service exacted instead of compulsory military service in case of conscientious objectors does not in itself mean that the Convention contains a right to such alternative service for conscientious objectors; in fact, the provision contains the limitation 'in countries where they are recognised'. If such a right for conscientious objectors is not recognised in a given country, this situation might have to be reviewed for its conformity with Article 9.[240]

The exception mentioned under (c) speaks for itself. Here the difficulty consists of course in answering the question of when an 'emergency or calamity threatening the life or well-being of the community' is involved. As has been stated above, in the opinion of some members of the Commission even a shortage of dentists could constitute such a situation.[241] It would, however, appear to be more in keeping with the terminology used not to think here of structural inconveniences like those concerned in that case, but of an acute emergency with a temporary character. Thus, services are covered by this provision like aid in extinguishing a fire, urgent repairs of transport systems and dams, supply of water and food in case of a sudden shortage, transport of wounded persons or the evacuation of persons threatened by some danger, and similar incidental services which can be required of everyone in the public interest depending on everybody's capabilities and possibilities.

The exception mentioned under (d), on the contrary, refers to 'normal' civic obligations, which means that no urgent and unforeseen calamity is required. It is still restricted, however, to work and services in the general interest. In our opinion, the difference with the provision under (c) is mainly one of gradation: the circumstances do not have to be as serious and urgent, but on the other hand the duties which are imposed may not be as burdensome for the person involved.[242] The formulation of the provision does not exclude special duties for particular professions in the public interest from being brought under it. In fact, the word

---

[239] Appls 3435-3438/67, *W, X, Y and Z* v. *the United Kingdom*, Yearbook XI (1968), p. 562 (594).

[240] Appl. 10640/83, *A* v. *Switzerland*, D&R 38 (1984), p. 219 (222-223).

[241] See *supra* p. 337.

[242] In the Strasbourg case-law a clear distinction has not yet been made, as appears from the decision on Appl. 9686/82, *S* v. *Federal Republic of Germany*, D&R 39 (1985), p. 90 (91), where the obligation of a person enjoying shooting rights in a hunting district (*Jagdpächter*) to participate in the gassing of fox holes was considered to be justified either under (c) or under (d) in view of the public interest to control epidemics.

'normal' does not necessarily refer to what may be required equally of everyone, but may also relate to what in the given circumstances may be required of the person in question according to general usage.[243] In our opinion, the rationale of this provision implies that it does not refer to the normal obligations resulting from a profession, such as the free legal aid given by lawyers, normal night duties for nurses and the like, since no compulsion in the real sense is involved there as the person concerned may quit the job. At any case the Commission would seem to have stretched the concept of 'normal civic obligations' beyond any specification in a decision in which it declared this term to be applicable to the obligation of the lessor to keep the rented premises in good repair.[244]

Finally, it is to be noted in this context that a practice based on any of the above-mentioned exceptions loses its permissible character if it involves discrimination. In virtue of Article 14 it then resumes the character of compulsory labour contrary to the Convention. This question played a part, for instance, in the *Grandrath* Case, where a member of the Jehovah's Witnesses complained that alternative civil service had been required of him as a conscientious objector to military service, although within his religious group he held a function similar to that of ministers of other religions, who were excused from service. In the discussion of Article 14 this case will be dealt with in more detail.[245]

4.5 Derogations

Under Article 15(2) no derogation from the first paragraph of Article 4 is permitted under any circumstances. Derogations from the second paragraph, apart from the cases mentioned in the third paragraph, are allowed only under the conditions and restrictions mentioned in Article 15.

5 RIGHT TO LIBERTY AND SECURITY OF PERSON (ARTICLE 5)

1. *Everyone has the right to liberty and security of person. No one shall be deprived of his liberty save in the following cases and in accordance with a procedure prescribed by law:*
    (a) *the lawful detention of a person after conviction by a competent court;*
    (b) *the lawful arrest or detention of a person for non-compliance with the lawful order of a court or in order to secure the fulfilment of any obligation prescribed by law;*
    (c) *the lawful arrest or detention of a person effected for the purpose of bringing him before the competent legal authority on reasonable suspicion of having committed an offence or when it is reasonably considered necessary to prevent his committing an offence or fleeing after having done so;*

---

[243] *Cf.* judgment of 23 November 1983, *Van der Mussele*, A.70, pp. 19-20.
[244] Appl. 5593/72, *X* v. *Austria*, Coll. 45 (1974), p. 113.
[245] See Appl. 8500/79, *X* v. *Switzerland*, D&R 18 (1980), p. 238 (249), where a detainee kept under observation complained that he was compelled to perform work, whereas this did not apply to detainees under remand.

(d) the detention of a minor by lawful order for the purpose of educational supervision or his lawful detention for the purpose of bringing him before the competent legal authority;

(e) the lawful detention of persons for the prevention of the spreading of infectious diseases, of persons of unsound mind, alcoholics or drug addicts or vagrants;

(f) the lawful arrest or detention of a person to prevent his effecting an unauthorised entry into the country or of a person against whom action is being taken with a view to deportation or extradition.

2. Everyone who is arrested shall be informed promptly, in a language which he understands, of the reasons for his arrest and of any charge against him.

3. Everyone arrested or detained in accordance with the provisions of paragraph 1(c) of this Article shall be brought promptly before a judge or other officer authorised by law to exercise judicial power and shall be entitled to trial within a reasonable time or to release pending trial. Release may be conditioned by guarantees to appear for trial.

4. Everyone who is deprived of his liberty by arrest or detention shall be entitled to take proceedings by which the lawfulness of his detention shall be decided speedily by a court and his release ordered if the detention is not lawful.

5. Everyone who has been the victim of arrest or detention in contravention of the provisions of this Article shall have an enforceable right to compensation.

5.1 Liberty of Person/Security of Person

In Article 5 the right to liberty of person and that to security of person are mentioned in the same breath, while in the following part of the article it is only the right to liberty of person that is developed. This difference in treatment has induced the Commission to state that the right to security of person, in contrast with the right to liberty of person, is formulated in absolute terms, which led the Commission to the conclusion that Article 18 of the Convention cannot have been violated in relation to the right to security of person since no restrictions to this right are permitted.[246] Otherwise, however, the Strasbourg case-law has always treated the two rights as one. Thus the Commission held in its decision on admissibility in *Adler and Bivas* v. *Federal Republic of Germany*:

---

[246] Report of 14 July 1974, *Kamma*, Yearbook XVIII (1975), p. 300 (316).

The term 'liberty' and 'security' must be read as a whole and, in view of its context, as referring only to physical liberty and security. 'Liberty of person' in Article 5(1) thus means freedom from arrest and detention and 'security of person' the protection against arbitrary interference with this liberty.[247]

And in the *Bozano* Case the Court held as follows:

> The Convention here (...) also requires that any measure depriving the individual of his liberty must be compatible with the purpose of Art. 5, namely to protect the individual from arbitrariness (...) What is at stake here is not only the 'right to liberty', but also the 'right to security of person'.[248]

The question arises, however, whether the purpose of the inclusion of the right to security of person is thus done justice. After all, the obligation to give legal protection to the right to liberty of person and the prohibition of arbitrariness in the restriction of that right result from Article 5 and the system of the Convention even without the addition of 'and security',[249] while the term 'security' according to normal usage refers to more than mere protection against limitation of liberty. The Contracting States will also have to give guarantees against other encroachments on the physical[250] security of persons and groups by the authorities as well as individuals, for instance against unnecessary threats to the physical integrity of spectators during police action or against incitement to action against a particular group of persons.[251]

5.2 Deprivation of Liberty

With respect to the right to liberty of person, in the Court's opinion Article 5 affords protection exclusively against *deprivation* of liberty, not against other restrictions of the physical liberty of a person. The Court infers this from the further elaboration of Article 5, where the terms 'deprived of his liberty', 'arrest' and 'detention' are used, and also from the fact that Article 2 of Protocol No. 4

---

[247] Appls 5573/72 and 5670/72, Yearbook XX (1977), p. 102 (146). See also Appl. 10475/83, *Dyer* v. *the United Kingdom*, D&R 39 (1984), p. 246 (256). The words 'arbitrary interference' have been elucidated by the Commission as meaning that 'any decision taken within the sphere of Article 5 must, in order to safeguard the individual's right to "security of person", conform to the procedural and substantive requirements laid down by an already existing law'; thus, *e.g.*, Appl. 7729/76, *Agee* v. *the United Kingdom*, D&R 7 (1977), p. 164 (173).

[248] Judgment of 18 December 1986, A.111, p. 23.

[249] See the judgment of 8 June 1976, *Engel*, A.22, p. 25.

[250] From its inclusion in Art. 5 it follows that, here, 'security' refers exclusively to physical security and not, *e.g.*, to mental, economic, or social security.

[251] In its decision on Appl. 6040/73, *X* v. *Ireland*, Yearbook XVI (1973), p. 388 (392-394), the Commission took the view that Art. 5(1) does not involve for the Contracting States the obligation to give a person individual protection in case of an alleged threat to his life.

contains a separate provision concerning the restriction of freedom of movement.[252]

In order to determine whether there has been *deprivation* of liberty the starting point is, in the opinion of the Court, the individual situation of the person concerned. Further, account must be taken of the special circumstances such as the type, duration, effects and manner of the implementation of the measure in question. Thus, for instance, certain restrictions of the liberty of movement of soldiers – the obligation to be present in the barracks at particular times, also during leisure – which would constitute a deprivation of liberty for civilians, may be permitted if those restrictions are not 'beyond the exigencies of normal military service'.[253] In the *Engel* Case the Court distinguished as follows: it held the so-called 'light arrest' and 'aggravated arrest' not to be in violation of Article 5, because the soldiers concerned were not confined, but were able to perform their normal service; this in contrast with 'strict arrest', which did imply confinement and therefore had to be reviewed for its justification by reference to the exceptions of Article 5.[254] The Commission, on its part, had concluded that the 'light arrest' did not, but the 'aggravated arrest' did fall under the prohibition of Article 5, because the latter sanction obliged the soldiers in question to remain within a given room during their leisure, although there was no question of confinement.[255] In the *Raimondo* Case the person concerned was placed under police supervision. He was also required to lodge a security of 2,000,000 lire as a guarantee to ensure that he complied with the constraints attaching to this measure, *e.g.* an obligation to return to his house by 9 p.m. and not to leave it before 7 a.m. unless he had valid reasons for doing so and had first informed the relevant authorities of his intention. This measure did not, according to the Commission and the Court, exceed the boundaries of the mere *restriction* of liberty.[256] A different view was expressed in the *Guzzardi* Case. In this case a measure of police supervision was combined with enforced stay on an island, where freedom of movement was limited at night to a few buildings and in the daytime to a small area of the island, while the possibilities of social contact with other persons besides the nearest relatives was very limited. The Court held that deprivation of liberty was involved.[257]

In the *Nielsen* Case the Commission and the Court differed in opinion with respect to the question of whether a deprivation of liberty was at stake. The case

---

[252] Judgment of 8 June 1976, *Engel*, A.22, p. 25; judgment of 24 October 1979, *Winterwerp*, A.33, p. 16; judgment of 6 November 1980, *Guzzardi*, A.39, p. 33; judgment of 22 February 1994, *Raimondo*, A.281-A, p. 19. In its report in the *Bozano* Case, the Commission came to the conclusion that Art. 5 amounts to a *lex specialis* in relation to the freedom of movement; report of 7 December 1984, A.111, p. 35.

[253] Report of 19 July 1974, *Engel*, B.20 (1978), p. 60.

[254] Judgment of 8 June 1976, A.22, pp. 25-26.

[255] Report of 19 July 1974, B.20 (1978), p. 60.

[256] Judgment of 22 February 1994, A.281-A, pp. 10 and 19.

[257] Judgment of 6 November 1980, A.39, p. 34.

concerned the hospitalisation for approximately six months of a 12-year-old boy in a psychiatric ward at a State hospital against his will, but with the consent of his mother as the sole holder of parental rights. The Commission, although acknowledging that the holders of parental rights are entitled to decide in matters concerning their children and that in the present case the applicant's mother gave her consent, having the best interests of the applicant in mind, found that consent not decisive for the question of whether there was a 'deprivation' at issue. The Commission based its view on the fact that the case concerned a normally developed 12-year-old child who was capable of understanding his situation and expressing his opinion clearly. As the protection under Article 5 also applies to minors, the will of the applicant was also relevant in these circumstances. And although the applicant had a room of his own in the ward and was allowed to make short visits to his mother's home, later on extended to weekend and holiday visits, and at the end went to school by taxi, the Commission reached the conclusion that the involuntary placement of the applicant under the conditions in which he stayed in the hospital must in principle be considered as being a deprivation of liberty.[258] The Court, however, although also accepting that the powers of the holder of parental authority cannot be unlimited, was of the opinion that the applicant was still of an age at which it would be normal for a decision to be made by the parent even against the wishes of the child. In the Court's opinion it must be possible for a child like the applicant to be admitted to hospital at the request of the holder of parental rights. Furthermore, the Court considered the restrictions to which the applicant was subjected in the ward to be normal requirements for the care of a child of 12 years of age receiving treatment in hospital. Therefore, the Court reached the opinion that Article 5 was not applicable in the case.[259]

Rather remarkable is the Commission's decision on admissibility in the case of three asylum seekers. The applicants were refused entry into Austria and taken to a special section of the airport transit area with a view to enable them to board a return flight. It was not possible to leave the area. According to the Commission no deprivation of liberty was involved because the applicants arrived at their own free will and they were free at any time to leave Austria.[260] The Commission took a comparable position in its report in the *Amuur* Case, but fortunately the Court did not follow this (too) formalistic approach. The Court held that the possibility to leave the transit zone of an airport is only theoretical if there is no other country that is prepared to grant entrance to the asylum-seeker and to offer him protection comparable to the protection that he expects to find in the country where he is seeking asylum.[261]

---

[258] Report of 12 March 1987, A.144, pp. 38-43.
[259] Judgment of 28 November 1988, A.144, pp. 24-26.
[260] Appl. 19066/91, *S.S., A.M. and Y.S.M.* v. *Austria* (not published).
[261] Judgment of 25 June 1996, Reports 1996-III, Vol. 11, para. 48.

From the above case-law it appears that the dividing line between deprivation of liberty and other restrictions of liberty is by no means clear-cut; the distinction is one of degree or intensity rather than one of nature or substance.[262]

If a person who has already been deprived of his liberty is subjected to additional limitations of his liberty, by way of disciplinary penalty or preventive measure, in the Commission's opinion Article 5 does not apply; such a treatment might, however, be in violation of Article 3.[263] On the other hand, the mere fact that a person has himself assented to his detention does not imply that the detention cannot be an unlawful deprivation of liberty. In the 'Vagrancy' Cases the Court held that:

> the right to liberty is too important in a 'democratic society' within the meaning of the Convention for a person to lose the benefit of the protection of the Convention for the single reason that he gives himself up to be taken into detention.[264]

5.3 Exceptions to the Prohibition of Deprivation of Liberty; General

Article 5(1) contains an enumeration of the cases in which deprivation of liberty is permitted. This is an exhaustive enumeration,[265] that must be interpreted narrowly. Only such an approach is consistent with the aim and purpose of Article 5, namely to ensure that no one is arbitrarily deprived of his liberty.[266]

As appears from the inclusion in the second sentence of the words 'in accordance with a procedure prescribed by law', it is required for all the cases mentioned that the procedure by means of which the deprivation of liberty has been imposed, be regulated in the law of the country in question. That law does not have to be written law. In the *Drodz and Janousek* Case, there was no French statutory provision, nor any international treaty which permitted the enforcement on French territory of criminal convictions pronounced in the Principality of Andorra. Nevertheless the Court held the view that the Franco-Andorron custom, dating back several centuries, had 'sufficient stability and legal force to serve as a basis' for the detention of the applicants.[267] The words 'prescribed by law' do not imply that in all cases a judicial procedure must have been followed, as is evident in particular from the cases under (c) and (f).

The question whether a detention complied with 'a procedure prescribed by law' is closely related to the question whether the detention was 'lawful'. These requirements, the latter of which is expressly mentioned in the individual

---

[262] Judgment of 6 November 1980, *Guzzardi*, A.39, p. 33 and judgment of 28 May 1985, *Ashingdane*, A.93, p. 19.

[263] Appl. 7754/77, *X v. Switzerland*, D&R 11 (1978), p. 216 (217); Appl. 19435/92, *R v. the Netherlands* (not published).

[264] Judgment of 18 June 1971, *De Wilde, Ooms and Versyp ('Vagrancy' Cases)*, A.12, p. 36.

[265] Judgment of 18 January 1978, *Ireland v. the United Kingdom*, A.25, p. 74.

[266] Judgment of 22 March 1995, *Quinn*, A.311, p. 17. See also judgment of 24 October 1979, *Winterwerp*, A.33, p. 16.

[267] Judgment of 26 June 1992, A.240, p. 33.

exceptions under (a)-(f), usually bracketed together by the Court, refer back essentially to national law. It means that the deprivation of liberty itself must be imposed in conformity with the substantive and procedural rules of the applicable national law. The Strasbourg organs are competent to satisfy themselves of this compliance, but are not called upon to give their own interpretation of national law.[268] It is also not their role to asses the facts which have led a national court to adopt one position rather than another.[269] A failure to comply with an essential procedural requirement of national law,[270] as well as the non-fulfilment of an procedural aspect even if, in the view of the Court, it is not essential, may lead to a violation of Article 5(1). The latter occurred in the *Wassink* Case, where a judge failed to comply with the national law inasmuch as he authorised the confinement of the applicant after a hearing held without a registrar.[271] The words 'prescribed by law' are not merely a reference to domestic law. They refer also to the 'quality of the law' and require that the law is 'sufficiently accessible and precise'.[272] In addition, as the Court held in the *Kemmache* Case:

> The notion underlying the term in question ['in accordance with a procedure prescribed by law'] is one of fair and proper procedure, namely that any measure depriving a person of his liberty should issue from and be executed by an appropriate authority and should not be arbitrary.[273]

The last mentioned requirement – the measure should not be taken arbitrarily – as inferred from the terms 'in accordance with a procedure prescribed by law' and 'lawful',[274] can be regarded as the guiding principle for the interpretation of Article 5. The notion 'lawful', which figures in the individual exceptions, may also imply some other requirements. These are discussed in the next section.

5.4 Exceptions to the Prohibition of Deprivation of Liberty; the Individual Exceptions

5.4.1 The Exception under (a)
The exception under (a) concerns the lawful detention of a person after conviction by a competent court. Three notions are to be discussed: 'competent court', 'lawful' and 'after conviction'.

---

[268] See, *e.g.*, judgment of 24 October 1979, *Winterwerp*, A.33, p. 20; judgment of 18 December 1986, *Bozano*, A.111, p. 25; judgment of 10 June 1996, *Benham*, Reports 1996-III, Vol. 10, paras 39-47.
[269] Judgment of 27 November 1994, *Kemmache (No. 3)*, A.296-C, p. 88.
[270] Judgment of 18 December 1986, *Bozano*, A.111, p. 23; judgment of 21 February 1990, *Van der Leer,* A.170, p. 12.
[271] Judgment of 27 September 1990, A.185-A, pp. 12-13.
[272] Judgment of 25 June 1996, *Amuur*, Reports 1996-III, Vol. 11, para. 50.
[273] Judgment of 24 November 1994, A.296-C, pp. 86-87. See also the judgment of 24 October 1979, *Winterwerp*, A.33, pp. 19-20.
[274] See, *e.g.*, the judgment of 29 February 1988, *Bouamar*, A.129, p. 20; judgment of 21 February 1990, *Wassink*, A.185-A, p. 11.

The word 'court' implies that the conviction must be imposed by a judicial organ. A decision of the police or a public prosecutor is not sufficient,[275] no more than a decision of a military commander[276] or of an administrative organ.[277] For an organ to be a judicial organ, it must be 'independent both of the executive and of the parties to the case'.[278] It is not required that the members be jurists,[279] nor that they have been nominated for an indefinite period.[280] The question whether the court is competent, is to be answered on the basis of national law.

The requirement that the deprivation of liberty must be lawful means not only that this particular penalty must find a sufficient basis in the conviction of the court concerned, but also – this in connection with Article 7 – that the facts to which the sentence relates constituted according to municipal law, at the time the offence was committed, a punishable act for which the imposition of imprisonment was possible. In addition, the sentence on which the deprivation of liberty is based must satisfy the provisions of the Convention itself. It must, for instance, have been pronounced on the basis of a fair and public hearing in the sense of Article 6. In the *Drodz and Janousek* Case the applicants were serving a term of 14 years imprisonment in France, following their conviction by a court of the Principality of Andorra. They claimed a violation of Article 5(1) because the French courts had not carried out any review of the judgment of the foreign court, whose composition and procedure was, according to the applicants, not in conformity with the requirements of Article 6. Thus, the question arose whether the above-mentioned requirement must also be made with respect to sentences that have been passed in a country which is not a party to the Convention. The Court expressed as its view that the Contracting States are obliged to refuse their cooperation if it emerges that the conviction is the result of a flagrant denial of justice. However,

---

[275] With respect to the Belgian Advocate-Fiscal, see the report of 4 March 1978, *Eggs*, D&R 15 (1979), p. 35 (62).

[276] Report of 19 July 1974, *Engel*, B.20 (1978), p. 63. A military commander can, however, order custody on remand, which is covered by para. 1 under (c): judgment of 22 May 1984, *De Jong, Baljet and Van den Brink*, A.77, pp. 21-22.

[277] For the Austrian reservation with respect to this, see Council of Europe, *Collected Texts*, Strasbourg, 1994, p. 88. If the decision of the administrative organ is based on a judicial decision, the requirement under (a) has been complied with, provided that there is a sufficiently direct link between the two: report of 1 March 1979, *Christinet*, D&R 17 (1980), p. 35 (54); report of 9 July 1980, *Van Droogenbroeck*, B.44 (1985), p. 24. See also the dissenting opinion of the Commission members Opsahl and Tenekides in the last-mentioned report.

[278] Judgment of 27 June 1968, *Neumeister*, A.8, p. 44. See also the judgment of 18 June 1971, *De Wilde, Ooms and Versyp* ('*Vagrancy*' Cases), A.12, p. 41; judgment of 16 July 1971, *Ringeisen*, A.13, p. 39; and the judgment of 8 June 1976, *Engel*, A.22, pp. 27-28.

[279] Appl. 5258/71, *X v. Sweden*, Coll. 43 (1973), p. 71 (79).

[280] The Dutch Supreme Military Court was recognised as a judicial organ in the *Engel* Case, although the four military members could be discharged from their function by the King. In the opinion of the Commission and the Court the fact that these members have taken not only the judicial, but also the military oath also did not bar their independence: judgment of 8 June 1976, A.22, pp. 27-28; report of 19 July 1974, B.20 (1978), pp. 66-67.

there is no obligation to verify whether the proceedings which resulted in the conviction were compatible with *all* the requirements of Article 6.[281] The application of this standard, which lead to the conclusion, by 12 votes to 11(!), that Article 5(1) was not violated, is justly criticised by the minority of the Court because of the fact that the French representatives in Andorra had the power to ensure that the Convention was respected: they had legislative powers and the competence to appoint judges in Andorra.[282]

The mere fact that a judicial sentence is annulled on appeal does not deprive the imprisonment imposed in execution of that sentence of its lawful character.[283] However, the matter is different if the ground for annulment is precisely a manifest error with respect to the municipal law or a violation of one of the provisions of the Convention, in particular of Articles 6 and 7.[284]

The word 'conviction' has to be understood as signifying both a finding of guilt after it has been established in accordance with the law that an offence has been committed and the imposition of a penalty or other measure involving deprivation of liberty.[285] Whenever a person is not convicted or sentenced in view of his lack of criminal responsibility his detention comes under Article 5(1) under (e) instead of (a).[286]

A person detained on remand is to be considered, from the moment of his conviction by a court of first instance, as a detainee 'after conviction', so that from that moment and during appeal proceedings the lawfulness of that detention must be reviewed by reference to the provision under (a) and no longer by reference to that under (c).[287] This holds true even if under domestic law the person is still considered as a remand prisoner.[288]

The word 'after' in Article 5(1)(a) does not, according to the Court, simply mean that 'the "detention" must follow the "conviction" in point of time', but also

---

[281] Judgment of 26 June 1992, A.240, pp. 33-35. See also the judgment of 24 October 1995, *Iribarne Pérez*, A.325-C, pp. 63-64.

[282] *Ibidem*, pp. 40-43.

[283] Appl. 3245/67, *X v. Austria*, Yearbook XII (1969), p. 206 (236); report of 9 March 1978, *Krzycki*, D&R 13 (1979), p. 57 (61).

[284] Thus the Commission in its decision on Appl. 6694/74, *Artico v. Italy*, D&R 8 (1977), p. 73 (88-89): the annulment of a judgment on the ground that the expiration of the term of limitation had not been observed by the lower court, rendered the imposed detention unlawful.

[285] Judgment of 24 June 1982, *Van Droogenbroeck*, A.50, p. 19. See also the judgment of 6 November 1980, *Guzzardi*, A.39, p. 37 and the judgment of 28 March 1990, *B v. Austria*, A.175, p. 15.

[286] Judgment of 24 September 1992, *Herczegfalvy*, A.244, pp. 21-22. See on this subject-matter *infra* p. 358.

[287] Judgment of 27 June 1968, *Wemhoff*, A.7, p. 23 and (implicitly) the judgment of 24 september 1992, *Kolompar,* A.235-C, p. 55. See, however, *infra* pp. 375-376 for the cases in which the law does not permit execution of a judgment which is not yet final.

[288] Appl. 9132/80, *N v. Federal Republic of Germany*, D&R 31 (1983), p. 154 (173). For a somewhat different system of detention after a conviction in the first instance, see the judgment of 2 March 1987, *Monnell and Morris*, A.115, pp. 19-20.

that 'the detention must result from, follow and depend or occur by virtue of the conviction'.[289]

In the *Van Droogenbroeck* Case the applicant was sentenced by a criminal court to two years of imprisonment and was ordered to be 'placed at the Government's disposal' for ten years. The Court had to decide whether there was sufficient connection, for the purpose of Article 5, between the sentence and the order, and the subsequent deprivation of liberty on two occasions as a result of the decisions by the Minister of Justice, following applicant's disappearances. According to the Court, the sentence to imprisonment and the order to be placed at the Government's disposal constitute 'an inseparable whole'. The execution of the order could take several forms, which was a matter of discretion of the Minister of Justice. In this case the way in which this discretion was exercised respected the requirements of the Convention.[290]

In the *Weeks* Case, again, the 'sufficient causal connection between conviction and deprivation of liberty' was at issue. Here the applicant was sentenced to life imprisonment, but released on licence some ten years later. However, the licence was revoked after 15 months by the Home Secretary. The reason for the sentence to life imprisonment was to make the applicant 'subject to a continuing security measure in the interests of public safety'. Since there was no medical evidence justifying an order to send him to a mental institution, this 'indeterminate sentence' would enable the Home Secretary to monitor his progress. The Court took the position that there were several similarities with an order to place someone at the disposal of the Government. However, the Court continued as follows:

> Applying the principles stated in the *Van Droogenbroeck* judgment, the formal legal connection between Mr. Weeks' conviction in 1966 and his recall to prison some ten years later is not on its own sufficient to justify the contested detention under Article 5, para. 1(a). The causal link required by subparagraph (a) (...) might eventually be broken if a position were reached in which a decision not to release or to re-detain was based on grounds that were inconsistent with the objectives of the sentencing court. In those circumstances, a detention that was lawful at the outset would be transformed into a deprivation of liberty that was arbitrary and, hence, incompatible with Article 5.[291]

Finally, the Court reached the conclusion that the sentencing judges must be taken to have known and intended that it was inherent in Mr Weeks' life sentence that his liberty was at the discretion of the executive for the rest of his life, and that it was not for the Court, within the context of Article 5, to review the appropriateness of the original sentence.[292] Thus, the Court accepted a very loose link between the original sentence and the renewed detention. However, next the Court examined whether the grounds on which the redetention was based, were

---

[289] Judgment of 5 November 1981, *X* v. *the United Kingdom*, A.46, p. 17 and judgment of 28 March 1990, *B* v. *Austria*, A.175, p. 15.

[290] Judgment of 24 June 1982, A.50, pp. 20-22.

[291] Judgment of 2 March 1987, A.114, pp. 25-26.

[292] *Ibidem*, p. 26.

sufficient. Although, here again, the Court took as a starting-point that a certain discretion has to be left to the national authorities in this matter, it conducted its own examination of the grounds in a rather detailed manner.[293]

5.4.2 The Exception under (b)

The first permissible form of deprivation of liberty mentioned under (b) – on account of non-compliance with a lawful order of a court – is clear. Here one may think, for instance, of a refusal to comply with a civil sentence[294] or to submit to a blood test,[295] or of a measure to enforce an injunction concerning a statutory declaration of assets which the applicant had refused to make.[296] In the *K v. Austria* Case the refusal to testify in a criminal case was at issue. The applicant was accused of having bought heroin from a couple, who were facing a separate prosecution. He refused to testify against the couple because of the criminal proceedings pending against himself. The court first fined him 3,000 schillings and then sentenced him to five days imprisonment. The Government contended that the measure was covered by Article 5(1) under (b), but the Commission held in its report the opposite view. The court order for the applicant to testify as a witness was made in violation of the Articles 10 and 6 of the Convention. In consequence the order to detain the applicant was also in conflict with the Convention and therefore not 'lawful' within the meaning of Article 5(1) under (b).[297]

The second form mentioned under (b) – deprivation of liberty in order to secure fulfilment of an obligation prescribed by law – is less clear. In fact, this wide formulation would seem to pave the way for a great many forms of deprivation of liberty without any judicial intervention, simply by the invocation of a legal norm, with the additional possibility of even taking preventive action before a norm has been violated. It is true that in those cases the fourth paragraph allows appeal to a court, but this does not alter the fact that such a wide interpretation of the second limb of paragraph 1(b) would erode a good many of the guarantees contained in the other provisions of Article 5. In the *Benham* Case the applicant claimed that his detention ordered by a court because he had not paid the Poll Tax owed by him, did not fall under subparagraph (b) since he did not have any means to pay the debt and therefore the detention could not have been intended 'to secure the fulfilment' of his obligation. The Court rejected this argument by merely

---

[293] *Ibidem*, pp. 26-27.
[294] In which case Art. 1 of Protocol No. 4 must be observed by those countries which have ratified that Protocol. See *infra* pp. 666-667.
[295] Appl. 8278/78, *X v. Austria*, D&R 18 (1980), p. 154 (156).
[296] Appl. 9546/81, *X v. Federal Republic of Germany* (not published).
[297] Report of 13 October 1992, A.255-B, p. 40. However, on p. 39, the Commission declares that Art. 6(1) is *not* violated on account of the applicant's obligation to give evidence. This must be a mistake.

stating that subparagraph (b) did apply because the purpose of the detention was 'to secure the fulfilment' of the applicant's legal obligations.[298]

In the *Engel* Case the Court held that 'any obligation' must relate to a 'specific and concrete obligation which the applicant has until then failed to satisfy'.[299] In this case the Supreme Military Court had invoked Article 5(1)(b) in order to justify an imposed 'strict arrest' as a provisional measure. The Court – like the Commission – rejected this viewpoint, because it considered the general obligation to comply with military discipline not sufficiently specific.[300] In the *McVeigh, O'Neill and Evans* Case the Commission held that the obligation imposed on a person, when entering the United Kingdom, to submit to examination on the requirement of an examining officer is a specific and concrete obligation and that the authorities are, therefore, in principle entitled under Article 5(1)(b) to resort to detention to secure its fulfilment. It also took the view, however, that the mere existence of an unfulfilled obligation is not of itself sufficient to justify the arrest or detention; there must be specific circumstances which warrant the use of detention as a means of securing the fulfilment of the obligation.[301] In the *Ciulla* Case in the opinion of the Commission the obligation to 'change his behaviour', mentioned in Section 3 of the Italian Act 1423/56, did not constitute a 'specific and concrete obligation'.[302] On the other hand, the obligation to go and live in the designated locality was in itself a concrete and specific one, but, according to the Court and the Commission, derived not directly from the law but from a court decision.[303]

5.4.3 The Exception under (c)

The provision under (c) in Article 5(1) permits arrest or detention if there is a reasonable suspicion that a criminal offence has been committed, or if this measure is reasonably considered necessary to prevent a criminal offence or to prevent flight after an offence has been committed. First of all, the relation between these three circumstances will be discussed. Next the terms 'competent legal authority', 'lawful'[304] and 'reasonable suspicion' will be dealt with. The third paragraph of Article 5 requires that everyone who is detained under subparagraph (c) shall be brought *promptly* before a judicial authority and is entitled to trial *within a reasonable time* or to release pending trial. This will be discussed in connection with that provision.

---

[298] Judgment of 10 June 1996, Reports 1996-III, Vol. 10, para. 39.

[299] See also the judgment of 6 November 1980, *Guzzardi*, A.39, pp. 37-38.

[300] Judgment of 8 June 1976, A.22, p. 28; report of 19 July 1974, B.20 (1978), p. 64.

[301] Report of 18 March 1981, D&R 25 (1982), p. 15 (37-43). See also the report of the Commission of 8 May 1987, *Ciulla* Case, A.148, pp. 25-26.

[302] The Court did not express its view on this point.

[303] Report of 8 May 1987, A.148, pp. 25-26; judgment of 22 February 1989, A.148, p. 16.

[304] The French version of Article 5(1) under (c) makes no express reference to '*régularité*'. This is without importance because the notion 'lawful' is a general one which applies to the whole of Art. 5(1); judgment of 6 November 1980, *Guzzardi*, A.39, p. 38.

Since the three grounds mentioned in paragraph 1 under (c) have been placed side by side and have not been made cumulative, the provision lacks clarity. In fact, in its present formulation it would appear to justify detention as a measure against persons on suspicion that they will commit crimes without their having as yet committed them. This interpretation is also corroborated by the *travaux préparatoires*, *viz.* in the report of the Senior Officials, in which it is stated as follows:

> it may (...) be necessary in certain circumstances to arrest an individual in order to prevent his committing a crime, even if the facts which show his intention to commit the crime do not of themselves constitute a criminal offence.[305]

The same line of reasoning is expressed by the Commission in the *De Jong, Baljet and Van den Brink* Case. It assigned an independent meaning to each of the three circumstances mentioned under (c): 'The wording "or" separating these three categories of persons clearly indicates that this enumeration is not cumulative and that it is sufficient if the arrested person falls under one of the above categories'.[306]

One might wonder why the fear that the accused may flee after having committed a criminal offence has been included as a separate ground, if the suspicion that such a criminal offence has been committed or will be committed is in itself already a sufficient ground for arrest? Therefore, the question arises whether another approach is not required that will do more justice to the aim and purpose of Article 5. An acceptable interpretation is reached if it is assumed that in this provision the grounds for arrest and those for continued detention have been joined. This would then produce the following picture: arrest is permitted in case of a reasonable suspicion that the accused has committed a criminal offence or if the arrest may reasonably be considered necessary to prevent his completing a criminal offence that he is about to commit or is committing. For continuation of the detention it is additionally required that it is likely that he will abscond or that there are reasonable grounds for assuming that after his release the arrested person will again commit a criminal offence.[307] In that case, however, it will also have to be assumed that these latter grounds of continuation do not constitute an exhaustive enumeration, since the Strasbourg organs have also recognised as

---

[305] Council of Europe, *Collected Edition of the 'Travaux Préparatoires' of the European Convention on Human Rights*, Vol. IV, Strasbourg, 1977, p. 260.

[306] Report of 11 October 1982, A.77, p. 34. In its judgment of 22 May 1984, A.77, pp. 21-22, the Court did not dissociate itself from this interpretation.

[307] See Recommendation R(80)11 of the Committee of Ministers of 27 June 1980 on detention on remand, where the grounds are indeed formulated cumulatively in Art. 3, while Art. 4 provides that detention on remand without one of the grounds of the second category presenting itself 'may nevertheless exceptionally be justified in certain cases of particularly serious offences'.

such grounds the risk of suppression of evidence,[308] the danger of collusion[309] and (implicitly) the danger of subordination of witnesses.[310]

If a person is arrested on reasonable suspicion that he committed an offence or in order to prevent his committing a crime or to prevent his fleeing after having done so, the conditions of the Convention are only met if the arrest or detention is really aimed at bringing the accused before a competent judicial authority. The Court took this position as early as 1961, in the *Lawless* Case. The same position was taken in the *Greek* Case,[311] and in the *Ireland* v. *the United Kingdom* Case.[312] In the *Ciulla* Case the Italian Government argued that, when drafting the provision under (c), the drafters had in mind that every legal system, in order to perform its function of maintaining social order, has to take measures to prevent criminal offences. From this the Government induced that a person constituting a danger to society may be subjected to a preventive measure imposed in the course of judicial proceedings. The Commission, however, was of the opinion that the applicant's arrest and detention were solely motivated by the fear that he might 'avoid possible security measures', but had nothing to do with pending criminal proceedings against him. In these circumstances the applicant was not detained for the purpose of bringing him before a legal authority.[313] In the *Brogan* Case the applicants alleged that their arrest and detention was not intended to bring them before the competent legal authority. In fact they were neither charged nor brought before a court. The Court held that the existence of such a purpose must be considered independently of its achievement. There was no reason to believe that the applicants' detention was not intended to further police investigation by way of confirming or dispelling concrete suspicions which grounded their arrest.[314]

In this context the very vague term 'legal authority' must, in conformity with the third paragraph of Article 5, be deemed to mean: 'judge or other officer authorised by law to exercise judicial power'.[315] The provision under (c) does

---

[308] Judgment of 27 June 1968, *Wemhoff*, A.7, p. 25.

[309] Report of 1 April 1966, *Wemhoff*, B.5 (1969), p. 89 and Appl. 9614/81, *G, S and M* v. *Austria*, D&R 34 (1983), p. 119 (121).

[310] See the judgment of 16 July 1971, *Ringeisen*, A.13, pp. 42-43, where the Court rejects the invocation by the Austrian authorities of this ground on the basis of factual data, but seems to accept the ground itself as a possibility.

[311] Report of 5 November 1969, Yearbook XII (1969), pp. 134-135.

[312] Report of 25 January 1976, B.23-I (1980), p. 110; judgment of 18 January 1978, A.25, pp. 74-75.

[313] Report of 8 May 1987, A.148, pp. 26-27. In the same sense the Court in its judgment of 22 February 1989, A.148, p. 18.

[314] Judgment of 29 November 1988, A.145-B, pp. 28-30. See also the judgment of 28 October 1994, *Murray*, A.300-A, p. 30, where the applicant was arrested for only three hours and released without being charged or being brought before the competent legal authority.

[315] Judgment of 18 January 1978, *Ireland* v. *the United Kingdom*, A.25, p. 75. In its judgment of 1 July 1961, *Lawless*, A.3, p. 51 and p. 52 respectively, the Court speaks of 'judicial authority' and of 'judge'. *Cf.* also the judgment of 4 December 1979, *Schiesser*, A.34, p. 13 and Appl. 9997/82, *X* v. *Federal Republic of Germany*, D&R 31 (1983), p. 245 (248-249). See also *infra* pp. 372-373.

not require that the warrant of arrest itself must also originate from a judicial authority.[316]

The answer to the questions of whether the court is competent and whether the arrest and detention are lawful, is determined by the law of the country concerned. The interpretation and application thereof is left to the domestic authorities, while the Strasbourg procedure provides for the marginal review of whether the national authorities have acted in good faith and reasonableness in reaching their decision.[317] That decision does not necessarily have to refer to the exact legal grounds of the arrest and/or detention, provided that these grounds are sufficiently clear by implication.[318] The mere fact that a person detained on remand is later released under a judicial decision does not render the arrest unlawful with retroactive effect.[319]

The word 'competent' constitutes a separate requirement. Rather remarkable, therefore, was the decision by the Commission on a complaint that the judge, who heard the applicant after her arrest and ordered her detention on remand, was not competent to do so. The Commission held that the procedure followed was of a judicial nature and that 'the impartiality and objectivity of the judge cannot be put in question solely by the alleged fact that he volunteered for the work'; that observation would seem to mix up the complaint concerning Article 5 with that concerning Article 6.[320]

Article 5(1)(c) requires only that there be a 'reasonable suspicion'. At the moment the arrest is made it need not yet be firmly established that an offence has actually been committed or what the precise nature of that offence is. The object of questioning during detention under subparagraph (c) is to further the investigation by way of confirming or dispelling the reason for arrest.[321] Whether the mere continuation of suspicion suffices to warrant the prolongation of the detention on remand is covered not by the first but by the third paragraph of Article 5.[322]

The term 'reasonable suspicion' presupposes the existence of facts or information which would satisfy an objective observer that the person concerned may have committed the offence. Thus, the reasonableness depends on all the circumstances of the case.[323] In the *Fox, Campbell and Hartley* Case the special circumstances in Northern Ireland were at issue. The applicants complained that their arrest under criminal legislation enacted to deal with acts of terrorism was not based on a reasonable suspicion. The Court, although acknowledging that

---

[316] Appl. 7755/77, *X* v. *Austria*, D&R 9 (1978), p. 210 (211).
[317] Appl. 2621/65, *X* v. *the Netherlands*, Yearbook IX (1966), p. 474 (478-480) and Appl. 9860/82, *X* v. *France* (not published).
[318] Appl. 9472/81, *X* v. *Austria* (not published).
[319] Appl. 8083/77, *X* v. *the United Kingdom*, D&R 19 (1980), p. 223 (225).
[320] Appl. 9997/82, *X* v. *Federal Republic of Germany*, D&R 31 (1983), p. 245 (248-249).
[321] Judgment of 28 October 1994, *Murray*, A.300-A, p. 27.
[322] Judgment of 22 May 1984, *De Jong, Baljet and Van den Brink*, A.77, p. 22.
[323] Judgment of 30 August 1990, *Fox, Campbell and Hartley*, A.182, p. 16.

terrorist crime falls under a special category, stressed that this cannot justify stretching the notion of 'reasonableness' beyond the point where the essence of the safeguard secured by subparagraph (c) is impaired. Scrutiny lead the Court to the conclusion that previous convictions for acts of terrorism cannot form the sole basis of a suspicion justifying the arrest some seven years later.[324] In the *Murray* Case the Government of the United Kingdom, without revealing its secret source that formed at least part for the reason of suspicion, succeeded in convincing the Court that there was a 'plausible and objective basis' for the suspicion that the applicant may have committed the offence of involvement in the collection of funds for the IRA.[325]

As discussed above, the detention under Article 5(1) under (c) comes to an end whenever the person on remand is convicted by a court of first instance. His further detention must then be reviewed under subparagraph (a). If no conviction or sentencing takes place because of lack of criminal responsibility on the part of the person concerned in view of his mental capacity, the eventually ordered prolonged detention comes under subparagraph (e).[326]

In the *Quinn* Case the Paris Court of Appeal set aside a judicial order extending the detention on remand of the applicant. It directed that mr Quinn should be 'released forthwith if he [was] not detained on other grounds'. This decision was not notified to the applicant nor was any step being taken to commence its execution. On the same day, eleven hours after the Court of Appeal delivered its judgment, the applicant, who was still detained in prison, was arrested with a view to extradition. The Strasbourg Court, although recognising that some delay in execution of a decision ordering release of a detainee is understandable, concluded that the continued detention (for 11 hours) was clearly not covered by subparagraph (c) and did not fall under the other subparagraphs of Article 5(1).[327]

Article 6(2) of the Convention provides that a person who is charged with an offence must be presumed innocent until proved guilty. This presumption of innocence should be respected not only during the hearing in court; out of court, too, the accused – and thus also the person detained on remand – should not be treated as if his guilt were already established. The justification of the limitations to be imposed on the person detained on remand should therefore be based on other criteria than the limitations which result from a sentence of imprisonment.[328] This might also imply that persons detained on remand must be segregated if possible from convicted persons, although, unlike in the UN

---

[324] *Ibidem*, pp. 16-18.
[325] Judgment of 28 October 1994, A.300-A, pp. 24-29.
[326] Judgment of 24 September 1992, *Herczegfalvy*, A.244, pp. 21-22. See on this subject-matter *supra* p. 351 and *infra* pp. 366-367.
[327] Judgment of 22 March 1995, A.311, pp. 17-18.
[328] See Res. (65)11 of the Committee of Ministers of the Council of Europe on detention on remand. In this Resolution it is emphasised that detention on remand should be an exceptional measure, which is applied only if 'strictly necessary'.

Covenant on Civil and Political Rights, this is not explicitly provided for in the Convention.

5.4.4   The Exception under (d)

In the first case mentioned under (d) one has to think of an order – judicial or not – to place a minor under supervision, combined with a restriction of freedom, for instance enforced stay in a reformatory institution or in a clinic.[329] Most legal systems permit such restrictions of freedom in the interest of the minor, even if the latter is not suspected of having committed any criminal offence. It is then required that it may reasonably be assumed that the development or the health of the minor is seriously endangered – for instance in the case of drug addiction and/or prostitution – or that he is being ill-treated. The text speaks only of 'lawful order', so that it does not appear to be required that the order emanates from a judicial organ. Under paragraph 4 of Article 5, however, these minors too – or if the law so provides, their legal representatives – are entitled to institute court proceedings in order that the lawfulness of the restriction of their freedom may be reviewed.[330]

The far-reaching powers emanating from Article 5(1)(d) have led the Court to require rather strict guarantees that the educational purpose is indeed served by the detention. In the *Bouamar* Case a minor was repeatedly confined in a remand prison 'for the purpose of educational supervision'. Although the confinements never exceeded the statutory limit of 15 days, the detentions (nine in total) amounted to a deprivation of liberty for 119 days in less than one year. The Court held that, in order to consider the deprivation of liberty lawful for educational supervision, the Belgian Government was under an obligation to put in place appropriate institutional facilities which meet the demands of security and educational objectives; the mere detention of a juvenile 'in conditions of virtual isolation and without the assistance of staff with educational training cannot be regarded as furthering any educational aim'.[331]

According to the *travaux préparatoires* the second case mentioned under (d) is concerned with the detention of minors for the purpose of bringing them before the court 'to secure their removal from harmful surroundings, so that they are not covered by Article 5(1)(c)'.[332] This would therefore seem to be a measure by which the minor is protected against himself in order to prevent his sliding into

---

[329] In Appl. 6753/74, *X and Y v. the Netherlands*, D&R 2 (1975), p. 118, applicant X, a minor who had run away from home, complained, *inter alia*, about the fact that she had been forced to spend a night at the police station before being taken home. The Commission declared this part of the complaint 'manifestly ill-founded' without any further argumentation, which is very unsatisfactory in view of the serious character of the measure complained of, and the justified doubt about its legality under Art. 5.

[330] See, *e.g.*, the judgment of 29 February 1988, *Bouamar*, A.129, pp. 22-25, where a breach of this provision was found to have occurred.

[331] Judgment of 29 February 1988, A.129, p. 22.

[332] Quotation in *Fawcett*, *supra* note 20, p. 82.

criminality. It is not clear, however, what specific reason there would be to bring the person concerned before a court, if no crime has been committed. The only case known to us relating to such a measure concerned an enforced stay of eight months in an observation centre, while the authorities examined whether theft and traffic offences had been committed.[333] In any case, the measure of bringing a minor before a judicial authority which decides on the prolongation of the detention, must be the purpose of the initial deprivation of liberty; consequently, there must be a sufficient ground for that measure. Which organ is competent to execute this deprivation of liberty is determined by national law ('lawful detention').

Since Article 5(1)(d) confers such far-reaching powers on the national authorities with regard to minors, the age at which a person attains majority is of the greatest importance. This age is determined by domestic law. In Resolution (72)29 the Committee of Ministers of the Council of Europe has recommended to fix this age at eighteen.[334] Domestic law also determines whether and in what cases a minor has the legal capacity to institute proceedings himself, so that a minor who has this right in the Strasbourg proceedings may be dependent on his parents or guardian for the exhaustion of the local remedies.[335]

5.4.5   The Exception under (e)

The provision under (e) deals with widely divergent categories of persons as if they were all infected by a disease from which society has to be protected, but without any further differentiation as to the character and the duration of the deprivation of liberty that is considered justified. For the latter here again the word 'lawful' forms the general criterion, while under the fourth paragraph of Article 5 the categories here referred to are also entitled to have the lawfulness of their detention reviewed by a court in accordance with the legal rules applying in the country concerned. The latter is important in particular for those cases where the detention can be ordered under municipal law by an administrative organ. If and insofar as, in performing this review, the court determines a civil right in the sense of Article 6, the rules for a fair trial set forth therein have to be observed.[336]

The scope of application of Article 5(1) under (e) is essentially determined by the terms 'infectious diseases', 'persons of unsound mind', 'alcoholics', 'drug addicts' and 'vagrants'. The Convention does not contain a definition of these concepts. In deciding whether an individual should be detained for one of the reasons stated in subparagraph (e), the national authorities do have a certain discretion. However, in reviewing these national decisions the Commission and Court are prepared to carry out an independent investigation into the question of

---

[333] Appl. 8500/79, *X* v. *Switzerland*, D&R 18 (1980), p. 238.

[334] Res. (72)29 'Lowering of the age of full legal capacity' and 'Explanatory Memorandum', Council of Europe, Strasbourg, 1972.

[335] See Stefan Trechsel, 'The Right to Liberty and Security of the Person – Article 5 of the European Convention on Human Rights in the Strasbourg Case-Law', 1 HRLJ, 1980, pp. 88-135 (119).

[336] See the judgment of 24 October 1979, *Winterwerp*, A.33, pp. 28-29.

whether the deprivation of liberty is in conformity with the Convention. In their case-law the concepts 'persons of unsound mind' and 'vagrants' have been clarified to some extent.

In the *Winterwerp* Case the Commission reviewed the definition of 'insane person' under Dutch law for its conformity with the Convention by comparing it with the ordinary meaning of this term, and investigated whether the person in question had been arbitrarily brought under that definition by the Dutch authorities.[337] This approach of giving the concept an autonomous meaning was confirmed by the Court in its judgment, in which the Court emphasised the fact that the term 'of unsound mind' implies that three minimum conditions have to be satisfied: (1) the applicant must be 'reliably shown' to be of unsound mind (which 'calls for objective medical expertise'), (2) the nature or degree of the mental disorder must be such as to justify the deprivation of liberty, and (3) continued confinement is only valid as long as the disorder persists.[338] In the *Luberti* Case the question whether the detention had continued beyond the period justified by applicant's mental disorder, was investigated by the Court in great detail.[339]

In the *De Wilde, Ooms and Versyp ('Vagrancy')* Cases the question arose whether the applicants could be considered as 'vagrants'. The Belgian Criminal Code defined vagrants as 'persons who have no fixed abode, no means of subsistence and no regular trade or profession'. According to the Court this definition did not appear to be in any way irreconcilable with the usual meaning of the term 'vagrant'. A person falling within the definition of the Belgian Criminal Code in principle comes under the exception of Article 5(1) under (e). In addition the Court held that the national courts could deduce from the information available that the persons concerned met the statual criteria.[340]

Thus, the Commission and Court, although confining themselves to a marginal review of the national law and its application, take a rather active position when it comes to a review of the conformity of that application with the wording and meaning of Article 5(1)(e). Thus a guarantee has been created against too wide a national interpretation and application of the categories mentioned under (e).[341] The necessity of a restrictive interpretation was equally emphasised by the Court

---

[337] Report of 15 December 1977, B.31 (1978-1981), pp. 36-37. See Appl. 7493/76, *X* v. *Federal Republic of Germany*, D&R 6 (1977), p. 82 (82-83), where the Commission decided that there is also question of 'unsound mind' if a person, though not mentally defective, shows such deviating traits of personality that he is constantly inclined to violate the law, but cannot be held responsible for his acts under criminal law.

[338] Judgment of 24 October 1979, A.33, pp. 16-18.

[339] Judgment of 23 February 1984, A.75, pp. 13-15. See also the report of 7 October 1981, *B* v. *the United Kingdom*, D&R 32 (1983), p. 5 (37-38).

[340] Judgment of 18 June 1971, A.12, pp. 37-38.

[341] See also the report of 16 July 1980, *X* v. *the United Kingdom*, B.41 (1985), pp. 31-32; report of 7 October 1981, *B* v. *the United Kingdom*, D&R 32 (1983), p. 5 (37-38); judgment of 23 February 1984, *Luberti*, A.75, pp. 12-13; and the judgment of 28 May 1985, *Ashingdane*, A.93, p. 18.

in the *Guzzardi* Case, where it held that it may not be inferred from the exception permitted under Article 5(1)(e) that the detention of persons who may constitute a greater danger than the categories mentioned in that article is permitted equally and *a fortiori*.[342]

The enforced placing of an accused person in an observation clinic in most cases cannot be brought under paragraph 1(e), because as a rule it is not certain in advance that he is of unsound mind. This deprivation of liberty may perhaps find its justification in paragraph 1(b), in case the measure is provided for in a judicial decision which may be enforced if it is not complied with voluntarily.

Since paragraph 1(e) does not contain any limitation as to the duration of the detention, this in contrast with the other cases of detention regulated in the same paragraph, the question is of great importance whether paragraph 4 confers on the person concerned only the right to have the lawfulness of the deprivation of his liberty as such reviewed by a court, or also the right to have recourse to a court periodically if the detention is prolonged. This question, from which the latter part has to be answered in the affirmative, will be discussed under Article 5(4).[343]

In the *Winterwerp* Case it had been argued on behalf of the applicant that Article 5(1)(e) entails for the person detained on one of the grounds mentioned there 'the right to appropriate treatment in order to ensure that he is not detained longer than absolutely necessary'. This submission, however, was rejected by the Court, which followed the Commission in this.[344] In the *Ashingdane* Case, both the Commission and the Court further elaborated on this. According to the Court, the lawfulness of a deprivation of liberty concerns not only the issuance of the order of the liberty-depriving measures, but also its execution. In other words, the measure must not only be in conformity with the domestic law, but also with the purposes of the restrictions laid down in Article 5(1). This also follows from Article 18 of the Convention. Therefore, there must be 'some relationship between the ground of permitted deprivation of liberty relied on and the place and conditions of detention'. Except for this relationship, however, Article 5(1)(e) is not concerned with suitable treatment or conditions.[345]

In relation to the provision under (e) – and to a certain extent also to the provision under (d) – it is of importance to stress again that complaints can only be brought before the Strasbourg organs against States. Therefore, the deprivation complained of must be or have been carried out under State responsibility. Thus, in the *Nielsen* Case, the issue arose if the hospitalisation of a 12-year-old boy in the psychiatric ward at a State hospital at the request of his mother, who was the sole holder of parental rights, involved State responsibility. The Commission took the view that, although the applicant was admitted into the State hospital at his

---

[342] Judgment of 6 November 1980, A.39, pp. 36-37.
[343] *Infra* pp. 385-386.
[344] Judgment of 24 October 1979, A.33, p. 21.
[345] Judgment of 28 May 1985, A.93, p. 21. *Cf.* the still somewhat stricter view of the Commission in its report of 12 May 1983, A.93, p. 37. See also the report of 7 October 1981, *B* v. *the United Kingdom*, D&R 32 (1983), p. 5 (32).

mother's request, it was the duty of the chief physician at that hospital to ensure that his admission was reasonable and justified in the circumstances. Therefore, the mother's consent did not relieve the chief physician of his responsibility in taking the final decision regarding the applicant's admission and regarding the conditions in which he was to be kept at the hospital.[346] In the Court's view, however, the decision on the question of hospitalisation was in fact taken by the mother in her capacity as holder of parental rights. Although the chief physician's decision on admission constituted indirectly a safeguard against possible abuse of parental rights, his involvement did not alter the mother's position under Danish law as the sole person with power to decide on the hospitalisation of the applicant or his removal from hospital. Consequently, the Court held Article 5 to be not applicable to the hospitalisation as such, since Article 5 is only concerned with deprivation of liberty by State authorities. The Court nevertheless investigated whether the circumstances of the case, especially the restrictions imposed upon the applicant's liberty, amounted to a violation of Article 5, thus accepting that the actual treatment in the hospital could involve State responsibility notwithstanding the original consent by the applicant's mother.[347]

5.4.6 The Exception under (f)

The great importance of the provision under (f) consists in that, although the Convention does not grant to aliens a right of admission to or residence in the Contracting States,[348] Article 5 nevertheless contains certain guarantees in case the authorities proceed to arrest or to detain an alien pending the decision on his admission, deportation or extradition. These consist first of all in the guarantee that such arrest or detention must be lawful and must therefore be in conformity with the applicable provisions of both domestic and international law[349] and may not be imposed arbitrarily.[350] This right is coupled with the right of the person in question under paragraph 4 to have this lawfulness reviewed by a court. However, Article 5 does not merely refer back to domestic law but requires also that the national law is 'sufficiently accessible and precise'. According to the Court this is especially the case with regard to asylum-seekers.[351] In the *Amuur* Case the French national law did not meet this requirement and moreover the

---

[346] Report of 12 March 1987, A.144, p. 38.
[347] Judgment of 28 November 1988, A.144, pp. 23-24.
[348] See *infra* pp. 515-521.
[349] See Appl. 6871/75, *Caprino* v. *the United Kingdom*, Yearbook XXI (1978), p. 284 (290-292), where the Commission also reviewed the detention for its conformity with an EEC directive. Review for conformity with the Convention itself for the determination of the lawfulness, according to the Commission, leads to a circular reasoning. This need not be the case if, for instance, the procedure leading to the deprivation of liberty is clearly not fair.
[350] Judgment of 18 December 1986, *Bozano*, A.111, p. 23.
[351] Judgment of 25 June 1996, *Amuur*, Reports 1996-III, Vol. 11, para. 50.

Court held, *inter alia*, that the national courts lacked jurisdiction to review the conditions of detention.[352]

The Commission distinguishes between the lawfulness of the detention and the lawfulness of the deportation or extradition itself.[353] It is obvious, however, that in reviewing the lawfulness of the detention, the lawfulness of the deportation or extradition will often also be at issue. This is especially the case when, according to national law, the lawfulness of the detention is made dependent on that of the deportation.[354]

In addition, Article 5(1)(f) implies the guarantee that the detention must have no purpose other than that of preventing the admission of the alien in question to the country or of making it possible to decide on his deportation or extradition. Article 18 of the Convention, which prohibits restrictions of the rights and freedoms for any purpose other than that for which they have been permitted, applies here as well. In the first place this means, as the Commission makes clear in the *Bozano* Case, that the deprivation of liberty is unlawful if the deportation order, and the way in which it is enforced, constitute a misuse of power.[355] In the second place it follows that the detention must not be attended with more restrictions for the person concerned and must not last longer than is required for a normal conduct of the proceedings. In the *Quinn* Case the Court stated:

> It is clear from the wording of both the French and the English versions of Article 5 § 1 (f) that deprivation of liberty under this sub-paragraph will be justified only for as long as extradition proceedings are being conducted. It follows that if such proceedings are not being prosecuted with due diligence, the detention will cease to be justified under Article 5 § 1 (f).[356]

Thus, although the duration of detention is only mentioned in paragraph 3 of Article 5 and this provision refers only to detentions under paragraph 1(c), the Court stipulates that the period of detention may not exceed a reasonable time.[357] The reasonableness of the length of detention has to be assessed in each individual case. In this respect not only the length of the extradition or deportation

---

[352] *Ibidem*, para. 53. In the report of 11 October 1983, *Zamir*, D&R 40 (1985), p. 42 (55-57), and Appl. 9403/81, *X* v. *the United Kingdom*, D&R 28 (1982), p. 235 (236-238) the Commission has found the complaints about the lack of precision of the applicable norms to be ill-founded.

[353] See Appl. 6871/75, *Caprino* v. *the United Kingdom*, where the Commission stated that 'the eventual outcome of the deportation proceedings is irrelevant for the justification of the detention provided that a lawful deportation procedure has been instituted and is being seriously pursued'; Yearbook XXI (1978), p. 284 (294). See also Appl. 9540/81, *X* v. *the United Kingdom* (not published).

[354] Report of 11 October 1983, *Zamir*, D&R 40 (1985), p. 42 (55). The fact that a domestic court has already found the deportation procedure to be illegal does not deprive the applicant of his claim to be a victim of a violation of the Convention by reason of his arrest: report of 7 December 1984, *Bozano*, A.111, p. 32.

[355] Report of 7 December 1984, A.111, pp. 32-34.

[356] Judgment of 22 March 1995, A.311, p. 19. The Court adopted the line of reasoning followed by the Commission in Appl. 7317/75, *Lynas* v. *Switzerland*, Yearbook XX (1977), p. 412 (440-442). See also Appl. 9706/82, *X* v. *Federal Republic of Germany* (not published).

[357] See also judgment of 25 June 1996, *Amuur*, Reports 1996-III, Vol. 11, para. 53.

proceedings properly is relevant, but also the length of connected procedures as, for instance, summary proceedings which may result in a stay of execution of the extradition. In the *Quinn* Case it was held that a period of almost one year and six months did not meet the requirements of the Convention.[358] If it has been decided to prolong the detention in the interest and at the request of the person concerned, *e.g.* in order to find a suitable country which is prepared to admit him, or in order to obtain certain guarantees from the extradition-requesting State with regard to his treatment,[359] he cannot claim afterwards that he is the victim of this prolonged detention. Thus, in the *Kolompar* Case the Court found the period spent in detention – it lasted for over two years – pending extradition to be unusually long. Nevertheless, it held that it did not amount to a violation of Article 5(1) under (f) because the Belgian State could not be held responsible for the delays to which the applicant's conduct gave rise.[360]

A clear example of a violation of paragraph 1(f) is offered by the *Bozano* Case. Here, the Court had to decide whether the deportation of Bozano from France to Switzerland was 'lawful' and 'in accordance with a procedure prescribed by law'. 'Lawfulness', according to the Court, also implies the absence of any arbitrariness. The circumstances of the case, *inter alia* the fact that the authorities waited about a month before serving the deportation order, prevented Bozano from making any effective use of the theoretically existing judicial remedies and the fact that they contacted only the Swiss authorities, although the Spanish border was much closer to the place where Bozano was arrested, led the Court to decide that the deprivation of liberty was neither lawful nor compatible with the right to security of person. Several French courts had reached the same conclusion. The way the deportation was executed clearly indicated what the French authorities had in mind: to get round the prohibition of extradition to Italy ordered by the Limoges Court of Appeal. That was also the reason why Bozano had been delivered to the Swiss authorities: Switzerland had an extradition treaty with Italy. The Court stated therefore that the way Bozano was deprived of his liberty amounted in fact to a disguised form of extradition.[361]

5.4.7 The Correspondence of the Individual Exceptions; Simultaneous or Consecutive Applicability of Different Exceptions

A person may be detained under different subparagraphs of Article 5(1) successively. If a person detained on remand is convicted (by a court of first instance), his detention falls no longer under subparagraph (c) but under subparagraph (a).

---

[358] Judgment of 22 March 1995, A.311, p. 19.
[359] Appl. 9706/82, *X* v. *Federal Republic of Germany* (not published).
[360] Judgment of 24 September 1992, A.235-C, pp. 56-57. See also Appl. 1983/63, Yearbook IX (1966), p. 286 (304).
[361] Judgment of 18 December 1986, A.111, pp. 25-27. See also the report of 7 December 1984, A.111, pp. 32-34.

It appears sometimes to be difficult to determine whether the exception under (a) or (e) is applicable. In the *X* v. *the United Kingdom* Case the applicant was convicted, but this conviction contained solely the establishment that he committed the criminal conduct concerned. No punishment was imposed on him. However, his admission to and detention in a mental hospital for insane offenders was ordered. In assessing under which subparagraph the detention of the applicant had to be dealt with, the Commission stated that the provisions of paragraph 1(e) and paragraph 1(a) are fundamentally different. The latter 'refers narrowly to the conviction and sentence of a person found guilty of a criminal offence, with the attendant notions of social blame and punishment'.[362] Article 5(1)(e), on the other hand, 'provides for the detention of a person by virtue of the specific state of his mental health, irrespective of criminal conduct, as a person of unsound mind, by definition, cannot be held fully responsible for his acts'.[363] The Court, however, came to the conclusion that, although it recognised the differences between the paragraphs 5(1)(a) and 5(1)(e), both paragraphs could be and were applicable to the applicant's deprivation of liberty, at least initially.[364] Even less clear are the judgments in the *Koendjbiharie* Case and the *Keus* Case on this point. The applicants were convicted to imprisonment, to be followed by two years' placement at the Government's disposal. The Court examined the applicants' complaints concerning judicial decisions for continuation of the placement at the Government's disposal in the light of paragraph 4 of Article 5, 'under which those proceedings fall in any event to be dealt with'.[365] On the other hand, in the *Herczegfalvy* Case, it did not seem difficult for the Court to choose between the applicability of subparagraphs (a) and (e). The Austrian court had not found the applicant guilty; it did not convict or sentence the applicant in view of his lack of criminal responsibility. His detention came under Article 5(1) under (e).[366] The difference between this judgment and the judgment in the *X* v. *the United Kingdom* Case is notable. Despite the fact that in the latter case the applicant was not punished either, his detention came under the paragraphs (a) and (e) together. This difference seems to originate from the difference between the applicable domestic law with respect to the criminal responsibility of persons of unsound mind. One might wonder if the Court should not change its case-law on this point and hold Article 5(1) under (e) applicable whenever, because of the unsound mind of the person concerned, criminal proceedings result in a deprivation of liberty. Such an interpretation would diminish the risk of a different application of Article 5(1) in the Contracting States.

In the *Herczegfalvy* Case the decision by which the applicant was ordered to be placed in an institution for mentally ill offenders, without convicting or sentencing

---

[362] Report of 16 July 1980, B.41 (1985), p. 30.
[363] *Idem*. See also the report of 7 October 1981, *B* v. *the United Kingdom*, D&R 32 (1983), p. 5 (36-37).
[364] Judgment of 5 November 1981, A.46, p. 17.
[365] Judgments of 25 October 1990, A.185-B, p. 40 and A.185-C, p. 65. See *infra* p. 386.
[366] Judgment of 24 September 1992, A.244, pp. 21-22.

him, was quashed on appeal. From that moment the deprivation of liberty once more came under paragraph 1(c).[367]

A person may be detained under different subparagraphs of Article 5(1) successively, but it is also possible that the detention falls under more then one subparagraph at the same time. As said before, in *the X v. the United Kingdom* Case the subparagraphs (a) en (e) were, initially at least, both applicable.[368] In the *Kolompar* Case the detention of the applicant came successively under Article 5(1)(c) only, under (c) and (f) at the same time, under (f) only, under the subparagraphs (f) and (a) at the same time and finally once more merely under subparagraph (f).[369]

5.5 The Right to be Informed of the Reasons for Arrest

5.5.1 Introduction
Article 5(2) grants to everyone who is arrested the right to be informed promptly, in a language which he understands, of the reasons for his arrest and of any charge against him. If the national authorities fail to do so, the arrest and detention are unlawful, even if they can be brought under one of the cases mentioned in paragraph 1. The rationale of this second paragraph necessarily ensues from the idea underlying Article 5: the liberty of person is the rule and is guaranteed, and an encroachment on this is allowed only in the cases expressly provided for and in conformity with the law as it stands. In order for the person arrested to be able to judge, from the moment of arrest, whether these two conditions have been met and to decide whether there are reasons for recourse to court, adequate information must be available to him.[370] Successively three notions are to be discussed: the applicability of Article 5(2), the information that should be given to the arrested person and, finally, the requirement of promptness.

A violation of paragraph 2 of Article 5 might imply also a violation of the fourth paragraph of this article. This question will be dealt with in the framework of the discussion concerning the fourth paragraph.

5.5.2 Applicability
The words 'arrest' and 'charge' used in paragraph 2 might create the impression that this provision is only relevant to cases arising under criminal law. However, the Court took a different view: the second paragraph applies not only to the detentions referred to in paragraph 1 under (c), but to any person arrested.[371] Therefore, as the Commission expressed previously, paragraph 2 applies to all

---

[367] *Ibidem*, p. 22.
[368] Judgment of 5 November 1981, A.46, p. 17.
[369] Judgment of 24 September 1992, A.235-C, pp. 54-55.
[370] On this rationale, see Appl. 8098/77, *X v. Federal Republic of Germany*, D&R 16 (1979), p. 111 (113).
[371] Judgment of 30 August 1990, *Fox, Campbell and Hartley*, A.182, p. 19; judgment of 28 October 1994, *Murray*, A.300-A, p. 31.

cases mentioned in the first paragraph of Article 5(1).[372] The Court clarified its position by invoking the autonomous meaning of the terms of the Convention and the aim and purpose of Article 5. In addition, according to the Court, the use of the words '*any* charge' ('*toute accusation*') showed that the intention of the drafters was not to lay down a condition for the applicability of Article 5(2), but to indicate an eventuality of which it takes account. Finally, the close link between the paragraphs 2 and 4 of Article 5 was considered to support this interpretation.[373]

5.5.3 *Relevant Information*

Paragraph 2 of Article 5 requires that any arrested person shall be informed of the reasons of his arrest and of any charge made against him. As the Court held in the *Fox, Campbell and Hartley* Case, he must:

> be told, in simple, non-technical language that he can understand, the essential legal and factual grounds for his arrest, so as to be able, if he sees fit, to apply to a court to challenge its lawfulness in accordance with paragraph 4.[374]

Thus, the Court, like the Commission,[375] has taken the position that the information required by Article 5(2) need not be worded in a particular form, and need not even be given in writing. Consequently, as the Court held in the *Lamy* Case, there exists at this stage of the proceedings no obligation to make the file available to the defence of the accused person for inspection.[376] Whether the content of the information conveyed is sufficient is to be assessed in each case according to its special features.[377] In the *Fox, Campbell and Hartley* Case and the *Murray* Case, the persons concerned were questioned about their alleged activities for the IRA. The Court held that the bare indication of the legal basis for the arrest, taken on its own, was insufficient for the purposes of Article 5(2).[378] However, here the obligation of paragraph 2 had been complied with because the persons concerned had been able to infer the reasons for the arrest clearly enough from the content of the interrogations that took place after the arrest. The rationale of paragraph 2 raises the question whether the Commission and Court should not be a little stricter in these respects. The interests of the arrested person which paragraph 2 is designed to protect, are sufficiently guaranteed only if the prescribed information is communicated explicitly and unambiguously to him.

---

[372] Report of 16 July 1980, *X* v. *the United Kingdom*, B.41 (1985), p. 33.

[373] Judgment of 21 February 1990, *Van der Leer*, A.170, p. 13. See further *infra* p. 382.

[374] Judgment of 30 August 1990, A.182, p. 19; reiterated in the judgment of 28 October 1994, *Murray*, A.300-A, p. 31.

[375] Appl. 1211/61, *X* v. *the Netherlands*, Yearbook V (1962), p. 224 (228). Since then this is established case-law.

[376] Judgment of 30 March 1989, A.151, p. 17.

[377] Judgment of 30 August 1990, *Fox, Campbell and Hartley*, A.182, p. 19; judgment of 28 October 1994, *Murray*, A.300-A, p. 31.

[378] *Ibidem*, p. 19 and p. 32 respectively.

If the person himself is unable to correctly understand the information, it should be transmitted to his representative.[379] And although the provision of the second paragraph refers in principle to the first arrest, in the case of continued detention it also applies if the ground for detention changes or new relevant facts present themselves.[380] According to the Strasbourg case-law, Article 5(2) does not guarantee the right to contact a lawyer.[381]

5.5.4 *Promptly*

Article 5(2) prescribes that the information about the reasons of arrest and of any charge must be given 'promptly' ('*dans le plus court délai*'). The Court indicated that it need not be related in its entirety by the arresting officer at the very moment of the arrest. In the *Fox, Campbell and Hartley* Case the applicants were informed sufficiently about the reasons for their arrest during the interrogations. These interviews took place respectively four and a half, six and a half and three hours after their arrest. These intervals could not be regarded in the context of those cases as falling outside the constraints of time imposed by the notion of promptness in Article 5(2).[382] According to the Court the arresting officer is not obliged to give the *full* information at the very moment of the arrest. This implies that at least some information should be given at once. In our opinion the aim and purpose of Article 5 requires that only very special circumstances can justify any delay in giving the full information.

5.6 Detention on Remand

5.6.1 *Introduction*

Article 5(3) relates exclusively to the category of detainees mentioned in the first paragraph under (c): those detained on remand.[383] When the accused person has been provisionally released, this provision is no longer applicable.[384] The main purpose of this paragraph, in relation to Article 5(1)(c), is to 'afford to individuals deprived of their liberty a special guarantee: a procedure of judicial nature designed to ensure that no one should be arbitrarily deprived of his liberty',[385]

---

[379] Report of 16 July 1980, *X* v. *the United Kingdom*, B.41 (1985), p. 34.

[380] *Ibidem*, pp. 33-34.

[381] Appl. 8828/79, *X* v. *Denmark*, D&R 30 (1983), p. 93 (94).

[382] Judgment of 30 August 1990, A.182, pp. 19-20. In the *Murray* Case, judgment of 28 October 1994, A.300-A, an interval of one hour and 20 minutes did not violate the provision of Art. 5(2) either (p. 33).

[383] See, *e.g.*, the judgment of 28 March 1990, *B* v. *Austria*, A.175, p. 14; judgment of 22 March 1995, *Quinn*, A.311, p. 20.

[384] Appl. 8233/78, *X* v. *the United Kingdom*, D&R 17 (1980), p. 122 (131).

[385] Judgment of 4 December 1979, *Schiesser*, A.34, p. 30. See also the reports of 13 July 1983, *McGoff*, A.83, p. 30 and of 15 July 1983, *Skoogström*, A.83, pp. 13-14.

and, furthermore, to ensure that any arrest or detention will be kept as short as possible.[386]

5.6.2   Promptly

Paragraph 3 comprises first of all, in addition to the right to prompt information conferred in the second paragraph, the right to be brought 'promptly' before a judicial authority. It is obvious that a person cannot always be heard by a judge immediately after being arrested. Unlike in the case of the obligation to inform him of the reasons for his arrest, for his first contact with a judge a third person is involved. The word 'promptly' – the French text speaks of '*aussitôt*' – therefore must not be interpreted so literally that the investigating judge must be virtually dragged out of bed to arraign the detainee or must interrupt urgent activities for this. However, adequate provisions will indeed have to be made in order that the prisoner can be heard as soon as may reasonably be required in view of his interests. Since paragraph 3 lays down an unconditional obligation upon the States to bring an arrested person automatically and promptly before a judge, it is not necessary that the arrested person first appeals against the detention order.[387]

It appears from its case-law that the Commission initially has been prepared to allow the national authorities a rather broad margin of discretion in complying with the requirement of promptness. In connection with a complaint lodged against the Netherlands it even considered a delay of four days between the arrest and the first appearance before a judge in conformity with the requirements of the Convention.[388] The Commission held that the Dutch legislation as here applied was 'consistent with the general tendency of other member States of the Council of Europe',[389] but it did not furnish any further data on the legislation and the practice of those other Member States.[390]

The Court has also given its opinion about the interpretation of the word 'promptly'. In the *De Jong, Baljet and Van den Brink* Case, the Court had to answer the question whether the referral to a judicial authority seven, eleven and six days respectively after the arrest was in conformity with the requirement of promptness of Article 5(3). Although this question was answered in the negative, the Court refrained from developing a minimum standard. It only stated that 'the issue of promptness must be assessed in each case according to its special

---

[386] See the reports mentioned in the preceding note, pp. 30-31 and p. 13 respectively.

[387] Appl. 9017/80, *McGoff* v. *Sweden*, D&R 31 (1983), p. 72 (73).

[388] Appl. 2894/66, *X* v. *the Netherlands*, Yearbook IX (1966), p. 564 (568).

[389] *Idem.*

[390] In its decision on Appl. 4960/71, *X* v. *Belgium*, Coll. 42 (1973), p. 49, the Commission added that only in exceptional circumstances a delay of five days is acceptable. In the report of 11 October 1982, *De Jong, Baljet and Van den Brink*, B.62 (1987), p. 31 and the report of 15 July 1983, *Skoogström*, A.83, p. 18, periods of seven and eleven days were not accepted. Exceptional circumstances were deemed to be present, for instance, in Appl. 4960/71, *X* v. *Belgium*, Coll. 42 (1973), p. 49 (55), where after his arrest the accused was taken at his own request to a hospital and had been nursed there for four days.

features'.[391] In other cases decided by the Court on the same day, it also refrained from indicating a minimum standard.[392]

In the *Brogan* Case the Court had to deal with the question of 'promptness' in case of arrest and detention, by virtue of powers granted under special legislation, of persons suspected of involvement in terrorism in Northern Ireland. The requirements under ordinary law in Northern Ireland as to bringing an accused before a court were expressly made inapplicable to such arrest and detention. None of the applicants was in fact brought before a judge or judicial officer during his time in custody ranging from four days and six hours to six days and sixteen and a half hours. The Commission had repeated its case-law that a period of four days in cases concerning ordinary criminal offences and of five days in exceptional cases could be considered compatible with the requirements of promptness. It had, therefore, concluded that there was a violation of Article 5(3) only in the cases where the detention had exceeded five days.[393] The Court accepted that the investigation of terrorist offences presented the authorities with special problems and that, subject to the existence of adequate safeguards, the context of terrorism in Northern Ireland had the effect of prolonging the period during which the authorities may, without violating Article 5(3), keep a person suspected of serious terrorist offences in custody before bringing him before a judge or other judicial officer. However, it also stressed that the scope for flexibility in interpreting and applying the notion of 'promptness' is very limited. In the Court's view, even the shortest of the four periods of detention, namely the four days and six hours spent in police custody, fell outside the strict constraints as to time permitted by the first part of Article 5(3). The Court held as follows:

> To attach such importance to the special features of this case as to justify so lengthy a period of detention without appearance before a judge or other judicial officer would be an unacceptably wide interpretation of the plain meaning of the word 'promptly'. An interpretation to this effect would import into Article 5, para. 3 a serious weakening of a procedural guarantee to the detriment of the individual and would entail consequences impairing the very essence of the right protected by this provision.[394]

In the *Koster* Case the applicant was not brought before the Military Court until five days after his arrest. According to the Court this period was too long. The fact that the lapse of time had occurred because of the weekend, which fell in the intervening period, and the two-yearly major manoeuvres, in which the members of the court had been participating, did not justify any delay in the proceedings. The demands of military life and justice could not alter this point of view one bit.[395]

---

[391] Judgment of 22 May 1984, A.77, pp. 24-25. See also the judgment of 28 November 1991, *Koster*, A.221, p. 10.

[392] Judgments of 22 May 1984, *Van der Sluijs, Zuiderveld and Klappe*, A.78, p. 20, and *Duinhof and Duijf*, A.79, p. 18.

[393] Report of 14 May 1987, A.145-B, p. 64.

[394] Judgment of 29 November 1988, A.145-B, pp. 33-34.

[395] Judgment of 28 November 1991, A.221, p. 10.

5.6.3 Judge or Other Officer

Paragraph 3 provides that the accused should be brought before a 'judge' or 'other officer authorised by law to exercise judicial power'. In the *Schiesser* Case the Court laid down criteria for the determination of whether a person can be regarded as such an 'officer'. It expressed that the 'officer' is not identical with the 'judge', but 'nevertheless must have some of the latter's attributes'. The first condition is independence of the executive and of the parties. This does not mean that the 'officer' may not be to some extent subordinate to other judges or officers provided that they themselves enjoy similar independence. Secondly, there is a procedural requirement: the 'officer' is obliged to himself hear the individual brought before him. Thirdly, there is a substantive requirement which places the 'officer' under the obligation to review 'the circumstances militating for or against detention', and to decide 'by reference to legal criteria, whether there are reasons to justify detention' and, if this is not the case, to order the release of the person.[396] In this case the complaint concerned the fact that the same authority who was charged in certain cases with the prosecution also had to decide on the lawfulness of the detention. The Court concluded, like the Commission, that the provision of paragraph 3 had not been violated. It held in particular that in the case under consideration there had been no blending of functions, that the functionary had been able to proceed, and had proceeded, independently, and that the procedural and substantive guarantees had been observed.[397] In the *Skoogström* Case, on the other hand, the Commission concluded that the criteria were not fulfilled. Not only was the Public Prosecutor, when deciding about the continuation of the detention, not independent because of a lack of distinction between investigating and prosecuting tasks, but she also did not hear the detainee herself. The Commission emphasised that the authorities mentioned in Article 5(3) must perform the duties, ensuing from this article, themselves; a delegation of these powers is not permitted.[398] In three cases against the Netherlands, decided by the Court on the same day, elements of the Dutch Military Code were considered to be in violation of Article 5(3). The first question raised was whether the *auditeur-militair* could be considered as an 'officer authorised by law to exercise judicial power'. Referring to its judgment in the *Schiesser* Case, the Court answered this question in the negative, since the *auditeur-militair* was only competent to make recommendations about the applicant's detention, but he had no power to order his release. The Government had submitted that, in practice, these recommendations were always followed, pending a total revision of the

---

[396] Judgment of 4 December 1979, A.34, pp. 13-14. See also the reports of 13 July 1983, *McGoff*, A.83, pp. 30-31 and of 15 July 1983, *Skoogström*, A.83, p. 13. For the procedural requirement see also the judgment of 22 May 1984, *Van der Sluijs, Zuiderveld and Klappe*, A.78, p. 19 and the judgment of 22 May 1984, *Duinhof and Duijf*, A.79, p. 16.

[397] Judgment of 4 December 1979, A.34, pp. 14-16. The presence of counsel was not included by the Court among the relevant guarantees; *ibidem*, p. 16.

[398] Report of 15 July 1983, A.83, pp. 15-17. Because of the friendly settlement between the Swedish Government and the applicant the case was struck off the list by the Court.

Military Code in order to comply with the Convention. However, in the opinion of the Court this practice was an insufficient guarantee.[399] Furthermore, as the *auditeur-militair* could also be in charge of prosecuting functions in the same case, he likewise could not be considered to be independent from the parties.[400] The Court reached the same conclusion with regard to the *officier-commissaris*, especially on the ground of the lack of power to decide on the continued detention or release.[401] In the *Pauwels* Case the investigation and prosecution functions were both performed by one and the same *auditeur-militair*. The Court held that although the *auditeur-militair* is hierarchically subordinate to the *auditeur-generaal* and the Minister of Justice, he is completely independent in the performance of his twin duties as a member of the public prosecutor's office and as chairman of the Board of Inquiry. However, the fact that the legislation entitled the *auditeur-militair* to perform investigation and prosecution functions in the same case and in respect of the same defendant, led the Court to the conclusion that the *auditeur-militair's* impartiality could give rise to doubt.[402]

In two of the three cases against the Netherlands[403] and to a lesser extent also in the *Pauwels* Case the impartiality[404] of the *auditeur-militair* was found open to doubt because he *could* also be in charge of prosecuting functions in the same case. With this reasoning, the Court implicitly deviated from its judgment in the *Schiesser* Case, where it was held that only the *effective* concurrent exercise of such functions infringed Article 5(3). This development is clearly confirmed by the *Huber* Case and the *Brincat* Case. In the latter case the Court held:

> only the objective appearances at the time of the decision are material: if it then appears that the 'officer authorised by law to exercise judicial power' may later intervene, in the subsequent proceedings, as a representative of the prosecuting authority, there is a risk that his impartiality may arouse doubts which are to be held objectively justified.[405]

5.6.4 Reasonable Time

Next, the third paragraph contains for the person detained on remand the right to be tried within a reasonable time or otherwise to be released pending trial, if necessary subject to certain guarantees for his appearance at the trial. The way this provision is formulated seems at first sight to leave a free choice to the judicial

---

[399] Judgments of 22 May 1984, *De Jong, Baljet and Van den Brink*, A.77, pp. 22-24; *Van der Sluijs, Zuiderveld and Klappe*, A.78, pp. 18-19, and *Duinhof and Duijf*, A.79, pp. 15-16.

[400] *Idem.*

[401] Judgments of 22 May 1984, *Van der Sluijs, Zuiderveld and Klappe*, A.78, pp. 19-20 and *Duinhof and Duijf*, A.79, pp. 17-18 respectively. See also the judgment of 26 May 1988, *Pauwels*, A.135, pp. 18-19.

[402] Judgment of 26 May 1988, A.135, pp. 18-19.

[403] Judgments of 22 May 1984, *De Jong, Baljet and Van den Brink*, A.77, p. 24 and *Van der Sluijs, Zuiderveld and Klappe*, A.78, p. 19.

[404] In the cases against the Netherlands the Court used the word 'independent' instead of 'impartial'.

[405] Judgment of 26 November 1992, A.249-A, p. 12. See also the judgment of 23 October 1990, *Huber*, A.188, p. 18. This case-law is closely related to the case-law on Art. 6(1). *Infra* pp. 452-457.

authorities:[406] either to prolong the detention on remand, provided that it has been imposed in accordance with paragraph 1(c), up to the moment of the judgment, which must then be given within a reasonable time, or to provisionally release the detainee pending trial, which trial would then no longer be subject to a given time-limit. Such an interpretation has been resolutely rejected by the Court. In the *Neumeister* Case the Court held with regard to Article 5(3):

> that this provision cannot be understood as giving the judicial authorities a choice between either bringing the accused person to trial within a reasonable time or granting him provisional release even subject to guarantees. The reasonableness of the time spent by an accused person in detention up to the beginning of the trial must be assessed in relation to the very fact of his detention. Until conviction he must be presumed innocent, and the purpose of the provision under consideration is essentially to require his provisional release once his continuing detention ceases to be reasonable.[407]

And in the *Wemhoff* Case the Court stated as follows:

> It is inconceivable that they [the Contracting States] should have intended to permit their judicial authorities, at the price of release of the accused, to protract proceedings beyond a reasonable time. This would, moreover, be flatly contrary to the provision in Article 6(1).[408]

The reference to Article 6(1) is indispensable for the Court's interpretation of Article 5(3); the word 'moreover' therefore might as well have been omitted by the Court. In fact, as soon as the accused has been released, Article 5(3) is no longer applicable,[409] as it also does not apply if the deprivation of liberty is a result of the execution of a prison sentence.[410] The obligation for the judicial authorities to see to it that in these cases, too, the trial takes place within a reasonable time, can be based only on Article 6(1). But precisely because Article 6(1) applies to all criminal proceedings, it is evident that Article 5(3) does not contain a choice between either release or trial within a reasonable time, but the obligation to keep a prisoner no longer in detention on remand than is reasonable and to try him within a reasonable time.

According to the quotation from the *Neumeister* Case the Court does not associate the word 'reasonable' with the processing of the prosecution and the trial, but with the length of the detention. The long delay of the trial may in itself be reasonable in view, for instance, of the complexity of the case or the number

---

[406] Literally speaking, it might even be deduced that the choice has been left to the accused himself, an interpretation which in view of the rationale of the provision, cannot have been intended.

[407] Judgment of 27 June 1968, A.8, p. 37.

[408] Judgment of 27 June 1968, A.7, p. 22.

[409] See, *e.g.*, the judgment of 13 July 1995, *Van der Tang*, A.321, p. 18.

[410] Appl. 9610/81, *X* v. *Federal Republic of Germany* (not published). In this case the applicant, during her detention on remand, also served a prison sentence. The Commission stated that the period of the prison sentence could not be taken into account in judging the reasonableness of the total period of detention under Article 5, but was of relevance for the reasonable time under Art. 6, since the investigations concerning the criminal charges could have continued during the execution of the prison sentence.

of witnesses to be summoned, but this does not mean that the continued detention is therefore also reasonable. The Court takes the view that Article 5(3) refers to the latter aspect. This implies at the same time that the criteria for 'reasonable' in Article 5(3) are different from those for the same term in Article 6(1) or, at least, have to be applied in a different way.[411] Some delays may in fact violate Article 5(3) and still be compatible with Article 6(1).[412] This is also corroborated by the view of the Court in the *Wemhoff* Case that 'an accused person in detention is entitled to have his case given priority and conducted with particular expedition'.[413]

With respect to the period that has to be taken into consideration for the determination of whether the trial has taken place within a reasonable time, the Court has taken the position in the *Wemhoff* Case that this is the period between the moment of arrest and that of the judgment at first instance.[414] If that judgment implies acquittal or discharge from further prosecution, at all events it will have to be followed by release, while in the case of conviction henceforth it is a matter of 'detention of a person after conviction' in the sense of Article 5(1)(a), to which the provisions on detention on remand no longer apply.[415] However, afterwards the Commission has pointed out that under some legal systems the execution of a sentence is not allowed as long as an appeal against it is still pending or some other ordinary remedy is sought, so that in such a case prolongation of the detention continues to have the character of a detention on remand and therefore has to be taken into consideration for the assessment of the reasonableness of the total length of this detention. In the *Ringeisen* Case it

---

[411] See also the report of 12 July 1977, *Haase*, D&R 11 (1978), p. 78 (92): 'Interpretation of "a reasonable time" in Article 5(3) must be made with regard to the fact that a person is deprived of his liberty. The time which in such cases is permissible is shorter than the time which is permissible under Article 6(1), because the aim is to limit the length of a person's detention and not to promote a speedy trial'. The relation between the two provisions is also dealt with explicitly in the judgments of 10 November 1969 in the *Stögmüller* Case and in the *Matznetter* Case, A.9, p. 40 and A.10, pp. 34-35 respectively. See also the report of 8 May 1984, *Vallon*, A.95, p. 19 and Appl. 9604/81, *X* v. *Federal Republic of Germany* (not published).

[412] Judgment of 10 November 1969, *Matznetter*, A.10, pp. 34-35; report of 8 May 1984, *Vallon*, A.95, p. 19.

[413] Judgment of 27 June 1968, A.7, p. 26.

[414] *Ibidem*, pp. 22-23. The Commission had taken the view that the commencement of the criminal proceedings should be taken as the end; B.5 (1969), p. 67. The Court bases its decision on the following two grounds: (1) it is true that the English text 'entitled to trial' leaves scope for the view of the Commission, but the French text *'le droit d'être jugée'* points clearly in the direction of the Court's view, which is not ruled out by the English text and consequently is the only interpretation which brings the two texts into conformity with one another; (2) the Court's interpretation is most in conformity with the purpose of the provision, since it cannot be appreciated why the protection of the person detained on remand against an unjustified prolongation of his detention should be less important after the commencement of the criminal proceedings. The Commission now follows the same line of reasoning as the Court. See, *e.g.*, Appl. 9132/80, *N* v. *Federal Republic of Germany*, D&R 31 (1983), p. 154 (173), and report of 8 May 1984, *Vallon*, A.95, pp. 13-14.

[415] Judgment of 27 June 1968, A.7, p. 23.

therefore requested the Court to revise its decision in the sense that in such cases the end of the period to be assessed is the moment at which the judicial decision has become final.[416] However, the Court held that the issue did not arise in the case under consideration, because the detention after conviction at first instance coincided with the detention on remand for another criminal offence.[417] Later on, in the *B* v. *Austria* Case the Court reaffirmed its decision in the *Wemhoff* Case. Thus it can be taken as established case-law that the period to be taken into consideration ends with the pronouncement of the first-instance judgment.[418] Two different periods of detention on remand for the same charge, interrupted by a release, may be taken into consideration together when determining the total period and its reasonable character,[419] but they may also be assessed separately.[420] If a detention on remand has been preceded by a detention of another character or in relation to another criminal charge, the latter detention is not taken into consideration when determining *the period* to be considered in relation to the former one.[421]

The persistence of the 'reasonable suspicion',[422] as mentioned in subparagraph 5(1) under (c), is a condition *sine qua non* for the lawfulness of the continued detention.[423] When the 'reasonable suspicion' ceases to exist, the continued detention becomes unlawful and accordingly the question as to the reasonableness does not arise at all.

When is continued detention on remand to be considered reasonable? For each individual case and at each moment the interests of the accused person will have to be weighed against the public interest, with due regard to the principle of the presumption of innocence.[424] In the first instance this weighing is in the hands of the national authorities. They must set out the relevant arguments in their decisions on the applications for release.[425] The Commission and the Court have clearly shown that they consider themselves competent, on the basis of the

---

[416] Report of 19 March 1970, B.11 (1972), pp. 44-45.

[417] Judgment of 16 July 1971, A.13, pp. 44-45.

[418] Judgment of 28 March 1990, A.175, pp. 14-16. The (majority of the) Commission had changed its view before: Appl. 9610/81, *X* v. *Federal Republic of Germany* (not published); report of 14 December 1988, *B* v. *Austria*, A.175, pp. 24-25.

[419] See, *e.g.*, the judgment of 26 June 1991, *Letellier*, A.207, p. 17; Appl. 9132/80, *N* v. *Federal Republic of Germany*, D&R 31 (1983), p. 154 (173).

[420] Judgment of 27 November 1991, *Kemmache*, A.218, p. 24.

[421] With regard to the detention of another character: judgment of 24 September 1992, *Herczegfalvy*, A.244, pp. 21 and 23.

[422] On this, *supra* pp. 357-358.

[423] See, *e.g.*, the judgment of 10 November 1969, *Stögmüller*, A.9, p. 40 and of more recent date: judgment of 28 March 1990, *B* v. *Austria*, A.175, p. 16; judgment of 27 August 1992, *Tomasi*, A.241-A, p. 35; judgment of 26 January 1993, *W* v. *Switzerland*, A.254, p. 15.

[424] See the enumeration of alternatives for (continuation of) the detention on remand in Art. 15 of Recommendation R(80)11 of the Committee of Ministers of 27 June 1980 on detention on remand.

[425] See, *e.g.*, the judgment of 26 June 1991, *Letellier*, A.207, p. 18; judgment of 27 November 1991, *Kemmache*, A.218, p. 23; judgment of 27 August 1992, *Tomasi*, A.241-A, p. 35 and judgment of 8 June 1995, *Mansur*, A.319-B, p. 49.

reasons given in these decisions and the statements of the applicant, to review for their compatibility with the Convention the grounds on which a request for release has been rejected by the national authorities.[426]

The mere fact that the 'reasonable suspicion' continues to exist is not sufficient, in the Court's opinion, to justify, after a certain lapse of time, the prolongation of the detention. According to the Court's case-law the question whether the period spent in detention on remand is reasonable, consists of two other questions. The first question to be answered is whether the (other) grounds given by the national judicial authorities are 'relevant and sufficient' to justify the continued detention. If so, the second question arises whether the national authorities displayed 'special diligence' in the conduct of the proceedings. If they did, the period spent in detention can be considered reasonable.[427] However, in case the first or second question is to be answered in the negative the period of detention on remand did exceed a 'reasonable time'.

Various grounds have been adduced by the national authorities to justify the continued detention. Thus, for example, in the *Neumeister* Case, the *Stögmüller* Case and the *Matznetter* Case the Court held that the danger of flight, even if it had initially constituted a sufficient ground for the detention on remand, afterwards had ceased to exist as a ground, specifically because of the possibility of bail.[428] It can be deduced from the *Letellier* Case and the *Tomasi* Case that the danger of the accused's absconding 'cannot be gauged solely on the basis of the severity of the sentence risked'. Such a danger must be assessed with reference to other relevant factors as well,[429] such as the character of the person involved, his morals, his assets and his contacts abroad.[430] The risk of a further offence, the other ground mentioned in paragraph 1(c), was held by the Court to

---

[426] *Ibidem.* For the Commission, see especially its report of 11 December 1980, *Schertenleib*, D&R 23 (1981), p. 137 (190), where the Commission held that even if the grounds relating to the public interest are very pertinent and sufficient to justify keeping a person in detention pending trial, that does not free the authorities from their obligations under the Convention in case of an unreasonable prolongation of detention which inflicts on the accused in the interests of public policy a greater sacrifice than would normally be demanded of a person presumed innocent. See also the report of 8 May 1984, *Vallon*, A.95, pp. 19-21, and the report of 8 July 1987, *Moudefo*, A.141-B, p. 40.

[427] See, *e.g.*, the judgment of 10 November 1969, *Matznetter*, A.10, p. 34 and, more clearly, the judgment of 28 March 1990, *B* v. *Austria*, A.175, p. 16; judgment of 26 June 1991, *Letellier*, A.207, p. 18; judgments of 12 December 1991, *Toth*, A.224, p. 18 and *Clooth*, A.225, p. 14; judgment of 26 January 1993, *W* v. *Switzerland*, A.254, p. 15 and judgment of 8 June 1995, *Mansur*, A.319-B, p. 50.

[428] Judgment of 27 June 1968, A.8, pp. 38-40 and judgments of 10 November 1969, A.9, pp. 43-44, and A.10, p. 34 respectively. In the *Wemhoff* Case the Court involved in its different finding the fact that on the part of the detainee there was no evident willingness to give bail; judgment of 27 June 1968, A.7, p. 25.

[429] Judgment of 26 June 1991, A.207, p. 19 and judgment of 27 August 1992, A.241-A, p. 37 respectively. See also the judgment of 27 June 1968, *Wemhoff*, A.7, p. 25; judgment of 8 June 1995, *Mansur*, A.319-B, p. 50.

[430] Judgment of 26 January 1993, *W* v. *Switzerland*, A.254, pp. 16-17.

have continued to exist in the *Matznetter* Case and the *Toth* Case,[431] while it rejected that ground for prolonged detention in the *Stögmuller* Case and the *Ringeisen* Case.[432] In the *Clooth* Case the danger of repetition was founded on the psychological deficiencies of the applicant. Nine months after the beginning of the detention an expert report described the applicant as dangerous and mentioned the need for him to be taken into psychiatric care. In these circumstances the national courts should not extend the period of detention on remand without ordering an accompanying therapeutic measure. They did not order such a measure, consequently the risk of repetition was not sufficient to justify the continued detention.[433] When reviewing the lawfulness of the (prolongation of the) detention, the Court does not consider itself confined to the grounds for detention on remand expressly mentioned in paragraph 1(c), but has also accepted as such grounds the risk of suppression of evidence,[434] the seriousness of the offence,[435] (implicitly) the danger of subornation of witnesses,[436] the danger of collusion[437] and the risk of pressure being brought to a witness.[438] With respect to the two last-mentioned grounds the Court pointed out that in the normal course of events these risks diminish with the passing of time.[439] In the case of *Letellier* the French Government relied among other arguments on the preservation of public order to justify the continued detention. The Court held that, at least for a time, grave offences may give rise to a 'social disturbance' capable to justify pre-trial detention. However, it added that:

---

[431] Judgment of 10 November 1969, A.10, p. 34 and judgment of 12 December 1991, A.224, p. 19, respectively. See also Appl. 9451/81, *X* v. *Federal Republic of Germany* (not published).

[432] Judgment of 10 November 1969, A.9, p. 43, and judgment of 16 July 1971, A.13, p. 43 respectively.

[433] Judgment of 12 December 1991, A.225, p. 15.

[434] Judgment of 27 June 1968, *Wemhoff*, A.7, p. 25.

[435] Judgment of 27 November 1991, *Kemmache*, A.218, p. 24; judgment of 27 August 1992, *Tomasi*, A.241-A, pp. 35-36. In both cases the Court expressed that the existence and persistence of serious indications of the guilt of the person who is under suspicion of serious offences, cannot alone justify a long period of pre-trial detention. In these cases the detention lasted five years and seven months and nearly two years and nine months respectively. See also the judgment of 8 June 1995, *Mansur*, A.319-B, pp. 50-51.

[436] See the judgment of 16 July 1971, *Ringeisen*, A.13, pp. 42-43, where the Court rejects the invocation by the Austrian authorities of this ground on the basis of factual data, but seems to accept the ground itself as a possibility.

[437] Judgment of 28 March 1990, *B* v. *Austria*, A.175, p. 16; judgment of 12 December 1991, *Clooth*, A.225, p. 16 and judgment of 26 January 1993, *W* v. *Switzerland*, A.254, p. 17.

[438] Judgment of 26 June 1991, *Letellier*, A.207, p. 19; judgment of 27 November 1991, *Kemmache*, A.218, pp. 25-26; judgment of 27 August 1992, *Tomasi*, A.241-A, p. 37.

[439] Judgment of 26 June 1991, *Letellier*, A.207, p. 19; judgment of 12 December 1991, *Clooth*, A.225, p. 16; judgment of 27 August 1992, *Tomasi*, A.241-A, p. 37; and judgment of 26 January 1993, *W* v. *Switzerland*, A.254, p. 17.

this ground can be regarded as relevant and sufficient only provided that it is based on facts capable of showing that the accused's release would actually disturb public order. In addition detention will continue to be legitimate only if public order remains actually threatened.[440]

This wording, that can be regarded as established case-law,[441] places the national courts under the obligation to state their reasons carefully when deciding to prolong the detention on remand. The mere use of stereotype criteria referring to the requirements of public order will not suffice for the purpose of Article 5(3). This conclusion *mutatis mutandis* seems to hold good for the other grounds capable of justifying the continued detention on remand.[442]

As has been observed above, if the prolonging of the detention on remand is based on well-founded reasons, the question remains whether the authorities showed 'special diligence' in the conduct of the proceedings. Article 5(3) does not imply a maximum length of pre-trial detention; the reasonableness cannot be assessed in the abstract.[443] The case-law shows that even a very long duration of the detention on remand – in the *W* v. *Switzerland* Case this was slightly more than four years – may still be deemed acceptable. On the other hand in the *Toth* Case a period of two years and one month exceeded the reasonable time limit.[444] With regard to the criteria by which the reasonableness is to be assessed, three factors seem to be of crucial importance: the complexity of the case, the conduct of the detainee and the conduct of the authorities. In case the length of a period spent in detention on remand does not appear to be essentially attributable either to the complexity of the case or to the applicant's conduct[445] and the authorities did not act with the necessary promptness, Article 5(3) will be violated.[446] If a detention on remand has been preceded by a detention of another character or in relation to another criminal charge, the latter detention is not taken into consideration when determining *the period* to be considered in relation to the former one.[447] However, that preceding detention must be taken into account in assessing the *reasonable character* of the period spent in detention

---

[440] Judgment of 26 June 1991, *Letellier*, A.207, p. 21.

[441] See the judgment of 27 November 1991, *Kemmache*, A.218, p. 25 and the judgment of 27 August 1992, *Tomasi*, A.241-A, p. 36.

[442] See, *e.g.*, the judgment of 12 December 1991, *Clooth*, A.225, p. 16 (danger of collusion); judgment of 27 August 1992, *Tomasi*, A.241-A, p. 37 (danger of absconding); judgment of 8 June 1995, *Yağci and Sargin*, A.319-A, p. 19 (danger of absconding).

[443] Judgment of 27 June 1968, *Wemhoff*, A.7, p. 24 and judgment of 26 January 1993, *W* v. *Switzerland*, A.254, p. 15.

[444] Judgment of 12 December 1991, A.224, p. 21.

[445] The right of a prisoner on remand 'to have his case examined with particular expedition must not unduly hinder the efforts of the judicial authorities'. See, *e.g.*, the judgment of 12 December 1991, *Toth*, A.224, pp. 20-21.

[446] See the judgment of 12 December 1991, *Toth*, A.224, p. 21 and the judgment of 27 August 1992, *Tomasi*, A.241-A, p. 39.

[447] Judgment of 22 March 1995, *Quinn*, A.311, p. 20.

on remand.[448] Finally, mention may be made of the Commission's decision in *X* v. *Federal Republic of Germany* to the effect that the period which the accused had spent in detention in Italy pending a decision on the request of the Federal Republic of Germany to extradite him could not be brought under the responsibility of the Federal Republic of Germany, and consequently could not be included in the assessment of the reasonableness of the detention in Germany.[449] The reasoning of the Commission is incorrect in our view. Although the Federal Republic of Germany is not responsible for what happens in Italy, the detention undergone in another country may quite well constitute one of the circumstances which have to be taken into consideration in assessing the reasonableness of the total length of the detention, even if that other detention does not fall under the category of paragraph 1(c) and accordingly has to be judged as a separate detention.

Article 5(3) expressly allows for making the release of the person detained on remand dependent on guarantees to appear for trial. The rationale of this is obvious: if and as long as prolongation of the detention would be allowed, certain guarantees may be asked for release. The express provision is important in particular because of the obligation and the limitations resulting from it for the national authorities.

Although Article 5(3) does not guarantee an absolute right to release on bail,[450] the possibility of demanding bail laid down there entails for the judicial authorities the obligation to ascertain whether by means of such a guarantee the same purpose can be achieved as is aimed at by the detention on remand. If there are sufficient indications for this, but this possibility is not offered to the detainee, the detention loses its reasonable, and as a consequence also its lawful character. This will be the case in particular if the only ground for the detention is the risk of flight.[451] If the detainee declines the offer without suggesting an acceptable alternative, he has only himself to blame for the continued detention.[452]

On the other hand, the guarantee demanded for release must not impose heavier burdens on the person in question than are required for obtaining a reasonable degree of security. If, for instance, the detainee is required to give bail the amount of which he cannot possibly raise, while it may be assumed that a lower sum would also provide adequate security for his compliance with a summons to appear for trial, the prolongation of the detention is

---

[448] Report of 8 May 1984, *Vallon*, A.95, p. 19; judgment of 8 June 1995, *Mansur*, A.319-B, p. 49; and – not very clear – judgment of 24 September 1992, *Herczegfalvy*, A.244, p. 23.

[449] Appl. 5078/71, Coll. 46 (1974), p. 35 (40).

[450] Appl. 8097/77, *X* v. *the United Kingdom* (not published).

[451] Thus also the Court in the *Wemhoff* Case, judgment of 27 June 1968, A.7, p. 25. See further the judgment of 26 June 1991, *Letellier*, A.207, p. 20 and the report of 11 December 1980, *Schertenleib*, D&R 23 (1981), p. 137 (195).

[452] In the Court's opinion that was the situation in the *Wemhoff* Case, judgment of 27 June 1968, A.7.

unreasonable.[453] This also means that the nature and the amount of the security demanded must be related to the grounds on which the detention on remand is based; thus, in the determination of the amount the damage caused by the accused may not be taken into account.[454] On the other hand, the financial situation of the person concerned and/or his relation to the person who stands bail for him must be taken into consideration.[455] The accused must provide the requisite information about this,[456] but this does not relieve the authorities from the duty of making an inquiry into it themselves, in order to be able to decide on the possibility of releasing him on bail.[457]

5.7 The Right to Judicial Review of the Lawfulness of the Detention

5.7.1 Introduction
Article 5(4) grants to everyone who is deprived of his liberty by arrest or detention the right to take proceedings by which the lawfulness of such deprivation of liberty will be reviewed speedily by a court and his release ordered if the latter decides that the detention is unlawful. This is in fact the remedy of *habeas corpus*, originating from English law. It follows from the goal of Article 5(4) that this provision ceases to be applicable once a detainee has been released from detention. If he is not detained any more, Article 5(4) can only be still invoked in relation to the complaint that the decision concerning release was not taken 'speedily'.[458]

The fourth paragraph constitutes an independent provision: even if the Commission or the Court has found that the first paragraph has not been violated and that the detention, accordingly, had a lawful character, an inquiry into the possible violation of the fourth paragraph may nevertheless be made.[459] This implies that even if the review by the Strasbourg organs leads to the conclusion that the detention was lawful, an assessment must be made if the detained person at the time had the possibility to have the lawfulness reviewed by a domestic court. The procedure of paragraph 4 must therefore also be considered as independent of the possibility of applying for release on bail.[460]

---

[453] Judgment of 27 June 1968, *Neumeister*, A.8 (1968), pp. 40-41. See the report of 12 July 1984, *Can*, A.96, p. 21.

[454] *Ibidem*, p. 40.

[455] *Idem.*

[456] Report of 5 December 1979, *Bonnechaux*, D&R 18 (1980), p. 100 (144).

[457] Report of 11 December 1980, *Schertenleib*, D&R 23 (1981), p. 137 (197).

[458] Report of 11 October 1983, *Zamir*, D&R 40 (1985), p. 42 (59). More specifically, Art. 5(4) has no application for the purpose of obtaining, after release, a declaration that a previous detention or arrest was unlawful: Appl. 10230/82, *X v. Sweden*, D&R 32 (1983), p. 303 (304-305). On the requirement of 'speed', see *infra* pp. 388-389.

[459] See, *inter alia*, the judgment of 24 October 1979, *Winterwerp*, A.33, p. 22 and the judgment of 24 September 1992, *Kolompar*, A.235-C, p. 57.

[460] Report of 11 October 1983, *Zamir*, D&R 40 (1985), p. 42 (59).

The fourth paragraph of Article 5, like the second paragraph, requires that the arrested person be informed of the reasons of his arrest in order to be in a position to take proceedings with a view to having the lawfulness of his detention determined.[461] The correspondence of these two paragraphs is still unclear. In *X* v. *the United Kingdom* the Court considered that the issue under Article 5(2) was absorbed by the fact that a violation was found of Article 5(4),[462] but on the other hand it decided in the *Van der Leer* Case that it was not necessary to examine the question of information under paragraph 4 because it dealt with it under the second paragraph.[463]

5.7.2 *Applicability*

In the *'Vagrancy'* Cases the Court held that the provision of the fourth paragraph does not apply to those cases of detention which are already based on a judicial decision, provided that such a decision is the outcome of proceedings which provide adequate guarantees.[464] This view was based on the assumption that in those cases the judicial review of the lawfulness of the detention, which is guaranteed by Article 5(4), has already taken place. Later on the Court developed a more differentiated approach. In the *X* v. *the United Kingdom* Case the applicant was convicted for causing bodily harm and was committed to a mental hospital for an indefinite period. According to the Court this deprivation of liberty fell, initially at least, within the ambit of both Article 5(1)(a) and Article 5(1)(e). The Court held that:

> By virtue of Article 5 para. 4, a person of unsound mind compulsorily confined in a psychiatric institution for an indefinite or lengthy period is thus in principle entitled, at any rate where there is no automatic periodic review of a judicial character, to take proceedings at reasonable intervals before a court to put in issue the 'lawfulness' (...) of his detention, whether that detention was ordered by a civil or criminal court or by some other authority.[465]

The *Van Droogenbroeck* Case concerned the placing of a recidivist at the Government's disposal for ten years by court order. This order was given together with a sentence to two years imprisonment. On the completion of his principal sentence, Van Droogenbroeck was placed in semi-custodial care, but he disappeared and, after his arrest, was sent to prison by a decision of the Minister

---

[461] Judgment of 5 November 1981, *X* v. *the United Kingdom*, A.46, p. 28.

[462] *Idem.*

[463] Judgment of 21 February 1990, A.170, p. 14. See further on this matter the reports of the Commission of 14 July 1988, *Van der Leer*, A.170, p. 14 and of 4 October 1989, *Keus*, A.185-C, p. 75.

[464] Judgment of 18 June 1971, A.12, pp. 40-41.

[465] Judgment of 5 November 1981, A.46, p. 23. The Court, moreover, emphasised that given the scheme of Article 5, read as a whole, the notion of 'lawfulness' implies that the same deprivation of liberty should have the same significance in paragraphs 1(e) and 4. See also the judgment of 28 May 1985, *Ashingdane*, A.93, pp. 22-23. In the *Weeks* Case the Commission added that Art. 5(4) not only requires the right to take proceedings at reasonable intervals, but also 'at the moment of any return to detention after being in liberty'; report of 7 December 1984, A.112, p. 47.

of Justice. Although the Court held that the resulting deprivation of liberty occurred 'after conviction' in accordance with Article 5(1)(a), it considered the fourth paragraph of Article 5 to be applicable, which required in the instant case:

> an appropriate procedure allowing a court to determine 'speedily' (...) whether the Minister of Justice was entitled to hold that detention was still consistent with the object and purpose of the 1964 Act.[466]

The same line of reasoning was followed in the *Weeks* case. The applicant, at the age of 17, was convicted for armed robbery and sentenced to life imprisonment. This indeterminate sanction was not imposed because of the gravity of the offence. The sentencing judge took account of the age and dangerous and unstable personality of the convict and decided that he should impose the sentence of life imprisonment to enable the Secretary of State to release him whenever he had become responsible with the passing of years. After nearly ten years the applicant was released on licence, but subsequently this license was revoked. He complained that he had not been able, either on his recall to prison or at reasonable intervals throughout his detention, to take proceedings as required by Article 5(4). The Court stated that the decisions of the executive to release or to re-detain the applicant should be consistent with the objectives of the sentencing court. If not, the detention would not longer be lawful for the purposes of subparagraph (a). Because the grounds relied on by the sentencing judges for deciding that the length of deprivation should be subject to the discretion of the executive were 'by their nature susceptible of change', the Court concluded that Mr Weeks was entitled to take proceedings as mentioned under paragraph 4.[467]

In the *Thynne, Wilson and Gunnel* Case each of the applicants had committed grave offences and had been sentenced to life imprisonment. The question of whether this sentence should be imposed was at the discretionary of the trial judge. In addition to the need of punishment the applicants were considered to be suffering from a mental disturbance and to be dangerous and in need of treatment. The discretionary life sentence was imposed to enable the administration to assess their improvements and to act accordingly. The Court decided, in line of the *Weeks* Case, that the applicants were entitled to take proceedings, but it had to establish from what point of time. Therefore it distinguished between the punitive and security element of the sentence[468] and concluded that the punitive period of the life imprisonment had expired.[469] If a mandatory life sentence is imposed the convicted prisoner is not entitled to take proceedings under paragraph 4. In

---

[466] Judgment of 24 June 1982, A.50, p. 27.
[467] Judgment of 2 March 1987, A.114, p. 29.
[468] This distinction was confirmed by English law. At least, according to the Court. The Government took the opposite view.
[469] Judgment of 25 October 1990, A.190, pp. 28-30.

such a case the guarantee of this paragraph is satisfied by the original conviction.[470]

To sum up, in fact the Court distinguishes between 'the conviction by a competent court' in the sense of Article 5(1)(a) as 'the decision depriving a person of his liberty', on the one hand, and the 'ensuing period of detention in which new issues affecting the lawfulness of the detention might subsequently arise', on the other hand. The 'conviction' does not purport to deal with the latter period. Thus, whenever the latter period starts the lawfulness of the detention is no longer incorporated in the initial conviction.

Does the fourth paragraph also apply to the detention on remand, now that the third paragraph already prescribes that an accused person, after his arrest, shall be brought promptly before a judge or other officer authorised by law to exercise judicial power? Even in the case that the person in question has thus been brought to trial it can hardly be said that he has been able to exercise the right 'to take proceedings', while moreover not in all cases there is a decision on the lawfulness of the detention by a 'court' in the strict sense. The position would therefore appear justifiable that in certain cases Article 5(4) grants to the person detained on remand a right of recourse to a court after the (judicial) decision to detain him or to prolong the detention has been taken.[471] In the *De Jong, Baljet and Van den Brink* Case, the Court reached the same conclusion by holding that the procedure, prescribed in Article 5(3):

> may admittedly have a certain incidence on compliance with paragraph 4. For example, where that procedure culminates in a decision by a 'court' ordering or confirming deprivation of the person's liberty, the judicial control of lawfulness required by paragraph 4 is incorporated in this initial decision. (...) However, the guarantee assured by paragraph 4 is of a different order from, and additional to, that provided by paragraph 3.[472]

In the *Toth* Case the Commission and the Court held that Article 5(4) did not cover proceedings instituted by an investigating judge for the extension of the pre-trial period. The national court that had to decide on the request of the judge had to confine itself to 'setting out a framework' within which the investigating judge was free to take decisions. The national court itself did not review the

---

[470] *Ibidem*, pp. 27-29 and judgment of 18 July 1994, *Wynne*, A.294-A, pp. 13-15. In the judgments of 21 February 1996, *Singh* and *Hussain*, Reports 1996-I, Vol. 4, paras 55-62 and paras 47-54 respectively, the Court held that the mandatory sentence of detention 'during her Majesty's pleasure' imposed in the United Kingdom on persons under the age of 18 who killed another, came closer to the discretionary life sentence than to the mandatory life sentence. Consequently the applicants were entitled to a review under Art. 5(4). See also the judgment of 24 October 1995, *Iribarne Pérez*, A.325-C, pp. 63-64.

[471] See Recommendation R(80)11 of the Committee of Ministers of 27 June 1980 on detention on remand, Art. 14 of which provides: 'Custody pending trial shall be reviewed at reasonably short intervals which the law or the judicial authority shall fix. In such a review, account shall be taken of all the changes in circumstances which have occurred since the person concerned was placed in custody'.

[472] Judgment of 22 May 1984, A.77, pp. 25-26.

'lawfulness' of the detention, nor gave it a decision on the question of whether the applicant should be released.[473]

5.7.3 Review of Lawfulness at Reasonable Intervals
In the *Winterwerp* Case the Court took the view that a case of detention of a person of unsound mind 'would appear to require a review of lawfulness to be available at reasonable intervals'.[474] This requirement was initially solely connected with persons of unsound mind.[475] In the *Bezicheri* Case, however, the applicant was detained on remand. Subsequent to a first judicial review of the lawfulness of the detention, according to the Court he was entitled 'after a reasonable interval, to take proceedings by which the lawfulness of his continued detention' was decided.[476]

According to established case-law the right to take proceedings exists *at any rate* where there is no 'automatic periodic review of judicial character'.[477] It is not yet clear if this right also exists in case the national legislation does provide for such a system. Anyway, the wording of paragraph 4 suggests clearly an answer in the affirmative. On the other hand, one might presume that the national authorities must be left the possibility to reject an application for judicial review if no new facts are adduced and shortly before an automatic periodic review of judicial character amounted to a negative decision for the applicant.[478] In the *Bezicheri* Case the person concerned, detained under Article 5(3), submitted his application for release one month after the first judicial review. The Italian Government argued that this period was too short to be reasonable, but the Court held that 'detention on remand calls for short intervals'. Consequently, in this case a period of one month was not unreasonable. In the *Herczegfalvy* Case, concerning the automatic periodic review of the detention of a person of unsound mind, intervals of fifteen months and two years respectively between two judicial decisions were not considered as 'reasonable intervals'. However, a period of nine months was not criticised by the Court and therefore seemed to meet the requirements of the fourth paragraph.[479]

---

[473] Judgment of 12 December 1991, A.224, pp. 24.

[474] Judgment of 24 October 1979, A.33, p. 23. See also the judgment of 23 February 1984, *Luberti*, A.75, p. 15, and the judgment of 22 May 1984, *De Jong, Baljet and Van den Brink*, A.77, pp. 25-26.

[475] See, *e.g.*, the judgment of 23 February 1984, *Luberti*, A.75, p. 31.

[476] Judgment of 25 October 1989, A.164, p. 10. The restriction to 'persons of unsound mind' was reiterated in the judgment of 12 May 1992, *Megyeri*, A.237-A, p. 11, but, on the other hand, was lacking in the judgment of 23 November 1993, *Navarra*, A.273-B, pp. 27-28 (concerning a prisoner on remand).

[477] See, *e.g.*, the judgment of 5 November 1981, *X* v. *the United Kingdom*, A.46, p. 23; judgment of 12 May 1992, *Megyeri*, A.237-A, p. 11.

[478] Compare the report of the Commission of 15 December 1977, *Winterwerp*, B.31 (1983), p. 40 and pp. 43-44 respectively.

[479] Judgment of 24 September 1992, A.244, pp. 24-25.

In the *De Jong, Baljet and Van den Brink* Case the applicants were seven, eleven and six days respectively without any remedy against their deprivation of liberty. The Court held that this amounted to a breach of Article 5(4).[480]

5.7.4 Court

Paragraph 4 entitles the accused to a decision by a 'court'. In the *Neumeister* Case the Court indicated as the decisive criterion for this that the competent authority 'must be independent both of the executive and of the parties to the case'.[481] Subsequently the Court added that the right to judicial review is not of such a scope as to empower the national courts to questions of pure expediency.[482] However, the review of the national court should comply with 'both the substantial and procedural rules of the national legislation' and be conducted in conformity with the aim of Article 5, the protection of the individual against arbitrariness.[483] What guarantees must be attached to the procedure under the fourth paragraph of Article 5 must be judged by the circumstances of each case, in which context in particular the consequences resulting for the person concerned from the decision to be taken in that procedure must be considered.[484] Consequently, the guarantees which the procedure of Article 5(4) must afford need not necessarily be the same as those prescribed in Article 6(1) for a 'fair trial'.[485]

In the *Winterwerp* Case the detention of a person of 'unsound mind' under paragraph 1(e) was at stake. The Court considered it essential for the person concerned to have access to court and to be enabled to be heard in person or, if necessary, through a representative. According to the Court it is possible that the mental condition of the person makes specific restrictions or derogations necessary as to the exercise of this right, but this cannot in any case justify an encroachment on the right in its essence, but on the contrary calls for special procedural guarantees.[486] The Court concluded that in this case the initial decision of detention was not taken by a 'court' and that later the applicant did not have access to a 'judicial procedure'.[487] In the *Megyeri* Case the national court had to assess whether the continued detention of the applicant was necessary. The applicant was heard in person but that did not meet the requirements of Article 5(4). The Court considered it doubtful whether the

---

[480] Judgment of 22 May 1984, A.77, pp. 26-27.

[481] Judgment of 27 June 1968, A.8, p. 44. In this case the procedure itself was not yet considered decisive by the Court. See also the judgment of 18 June 1971, *De Wilde, Ooms and Versyp* ('*Vagrancy*' Cases), A.12, p. 42; judgment of 25 October 1989, *Bezicheri*, A.164, p. 10.

[482] See, *e.g.*, the judgment of 24 June 1982, *Van Droogenbroeck*, A.50, p. 26; judgment of 29 August 1990, *E v. Norway*, A.181-A, pp. 21-22; judgment of 25 October 1990, *Thynne, Wilson and Gunnell*, A.190, p. 30.

[483] Judgments of 25 October 1990, *Koendjbiharie*, A.185-B, p. 40 and *Keus*, A.185-C, p. 66.

[484] Judgment of 18 June 1971, *De Wilde, Ooms and Versyp* ('*Vagrancy*' Cases), A.12, p. 42.

[485] Judgment of 24 October 1979, *Winterwerp*, A.33, p. 24.

[486] *Idem.*

[487] *Ibidem*, p. 26. See also the judgment of 21 February 1990, *Van der Leer*, A.170, p. 14.

applicant was capable of adequately presenting the relevant points. It concluded, also taking into consideration the fact that the applicant had spent more than four years in a psychiatric hospital, that a counsel should have been appointed to assist the applicant in the proceedings.[488] The same point of view was adopted by the Court in the *Bouamar* Case, taking into consideration, *inter alia*, that the proceedings concerned a juvenile.[489] In the *Toth* Case, the *Lamy* Case and the *Sanchez-Reisse* Case, the lack of truly adversarial proceedings was found to amount to a breach of the fourth paragraph.[490] In the latter case the applicant, against whom action had been taken with a view to extradition, complained also about the fact that he had not been able to apply *directly* to a court. However, the Strasbourg Court had no objections to the requirement of a previous administrative procedure, provided that this did not violate the 'speed'-requirement.[491] The Court seems to have deviated from this point of view in the *Singh* Case and the *Hussain* Case, where it held that the lack of an oral and adversarial hearing in the proceedings before the Parole Board could not be compensated by the possibility to institute proceedings for judicial review. It was crucial for the Court that the applicants risked a considerable term of imprisonment and that the decision which had to be taken by the Parole Board on the dangerousness of the applicants involved questions with regard to their 'personality and level of maturity'.[492] In the *Wassink* Case, a failure to comply with national law (according to the Court the requirement concerned was not an essential one) did not lead to the conclusion that Article 5(4) was violated.[493] Article 5(4) does not require the institution of a second level of proceedings. However, if the question whether the detained person should be released will be heard on appeal, the Contracting States in principle have to offer the persons concerned the same guarantees as at first instance.[494]

In the *Brannigan and McBride* Case the Court concluded, like the Commission did in the *De Jong, Baljet and Van den Brink* Case,[495] that the right, laid down in Article 5(4), is a *lex specialis* in relation to the right to an effective remedy, laid down in Article 13.[496]

---

[488] Judgment of 12 May 1992, A.237-A, pp. 12-13.

[489] Judgment of 29 February 1988, A.129, pp. 23-25.

[490] Judgment of 12 December 1991, A.224, p. 23; judgment of 30 March 1980, A.151, pp. 15-17 (concerning lack of access to documents that were essential for the applicant) and judgment of 21 October 1986, A.107, p. 19 respectively. Compare further the judgment of 13 July 1995, *Kampanis*, A.318-B, pp. 46-48, where the Court held that the national court should have given the applicant the opportunity to appear at the same time as the prosecutor to ensure equality of arms.

[491] Judgment of 21 October 1986, *Sanchez-Reisse*, A.107, pp. 17 and 54.

[492] Judgments of 21 February 1996, Reports 1996-I, Vol. 4, paras 68-69 and paras 60-61 respectively.

[493] Judgment of 27 September 1990, A.185-A, p. 13.

[494] Judgment of 12 December 1991, *Toth*, A.224, p. 23 and judgment of 23 November 1993, *Navarra*, A.273-B, p. 28.

[495] Report of 11 October 1982, A.77, p. 39.

[496] Judgment of 26 May 1993, A.258-B, p. 57.

5.7.5 Speedily

Paragraph 4 explicitly requires that the judicial review shall take place 'speedily'. Compliance must be assessed in the light of the specific circumstances of the case.[497] With regard to the period that has to be taken into consideration the Court has taken as starting point the day the application for release has been made.[498] The relevant period comes to an end on the day the 'court' has given judgment.[499] If the proceedings have been conducted at two levels of jurisdiction an overall assessment must be made in order to determine whether the requirement of 'speedily' has been complied with.[500]

In assessing the speedy character required by paragraph 4 comparable factors may be taken into consideration as those which play a role with respect to the requirement of trial within a reasonable time under paragraph 3 and under Article 6(1), such as, for instance, the conduct of the applicant and the way the authorities have handled the case.[501] Neither an excessive workload,[502] nor a vacation period[503] can justify a period of inactivity on the part of the judicial authorities.

The notion of 'speedily' ('*aussitôt*') indicates a lesser urgency than that of 'promptly' ('*à bref délai*') in Article 5(3).[504] In the *Sanchez-Reisse* Case the time which elapsed between the lodging of two requests and the decisions thereon, 31 days and 46 days respectively, did not satisfy the 'speed'-requirement of Article 5(4). With respect to a period of nearly one year and five months in which six judicial decisions were given[505] the Court entertained certain doubts about the overall length of the period. Nevertheless, it took into consideration the fact that the applicant had retained the right to submit further applications for release, which were all dealt with in short periods,[506] and reached the conclusion that paragraph 4 was not violated.[507] In the *Fox, Campbell and Hartley* Case two applicants instituted proceedings for *habeas corpus*. They were

---

[497] See, *e.g.*, the judgment of 21 October 1986, *Sanchez-Reisse*, A.107, p. 20 and the judgment of 29 August 1990, *E* v. *Norway*, A.181-A, pp. 27-28.

[498] See, *e.g.*, the judgment of 25 October 1989, *Bezicheri*, A.164, p. 11 and the judgment of 21 February 1990, *Van der Leer*, A.170, p. 14. This holds also good in case the request for release opens an administrative stage of the proceedings. See the judgment of 21 October 1986, *Sanchez-Reisse*, A.107, p. 20.

[499] *Idem.*

[500] See, *e.g.*, the judgment of 23 February 1984, *Luberti*, A.75, p. 16 and the judgment of 23 November 1993, *Navarra*, A.273-B, p. 28.

[501] See, *e.g.*, the judgment of 23 February 1984, *Luberti*, A.75, pp. 15-18; judgment of 21 February 1990, *Van der Leer*, A.170, p. 15.

[502] See, *e.g.*, the judgment of 25 October 1990, *Bezicheri*, A.164, p. 12.

[503] Judgment of 29 August 1990, *E* v. *Norway*, A.181-A, p. 28.

[504] *Ibidem*, p. 27.

[505] With respect to one application for release the applicant appealed three times to the Court of Cassation.

[506] Periods of from eight to twenty days.

[507] Judgment of 26 June 1991, *Letellier*, A.207, p. 22. See also the judgment of 23 November 1993, *Navarra*, A.273-B, pp. 28-29.

released 44 hours after their arrest, before judicial control on the lawfulness of their detention had taken place. The Court held that they were released speedily and did not find it necessary to examine their complaint under Article 5(4).[508]

5.8 An Enforceable Right to Compensation

Article 5(5) grants a right to compensation if an arrest or detention is found to be in contravention of the preceding provisions of Article 5. At first sight this provision appears superfluous by the side of the general provision concerning just satisfaction in Article 50 of the Convention.[509] The difference, however, is that Article 50 confers a competence on the Court, while Article 5(5) grants a right *vis-à-vis* the national authorities, the violation of which right may constitute the object of a separate complaint and may subsequently lead to the Court's application of Article 50. This difference may be illustrated by the following example. If an arrest has been declared unlawful by the national court and the prisoner has subsequently been released under Article 5(4), he can still file an application with the Commission for violation of Article 5 if his claim for compensation has not been received or has been rejected. If, on the other hand, a given treatment of a detainee has been stopped after having been found by the national court to conflict with Article 3, but no damages are awarded to the injured person, there is no ground for filing an application with the Commission, since Article 3 itself does not grant a right to compensation and Article 50 applies only after the Court has established violation of – in this case – Article 3.

In its earlier case-law the Commission took insufficient account of this distinction and held that a complaint based on Article 5(5) could only be examined after the violation of one of the other provisions of Article 5 had been established by the Court or the Committee of Ministers.[510] In its decision in the *Huber* Case, however, the Commission, after referring to this case-law, opined as follows:

> On further consideration the Commission would be inclined partially to revise or develop its earlier jurisprudence and consider that where a breach of paras (1)-(4) has been established by a national court – either directly if the said provisions form a part of the domestic law concerned, or in substance – the applicant who has been denied compensation can bring before the Commission a breach of Article 5(5) after exhaustion of domestic remedies in this respect.[511]

On the other hand, the fact that the injured person has invoked Article 5(5) neither before the national court nor before the Commission bars an award of compensation under Article 50 for damage caused by a deprivation of liberty.[512]

---

[508] Judgment of 30 August 1990, A.182, pp. 20-21.

[509] On Art. 50, see *supra* pp. 239-259.

[510] Report of 1 April 1966, *Wemhoff*, B.5 (1969), p. 90. Thus also Appl. 4149/69, *X* v. *Federal Republic of Germany*, Coll. 36 (1971), p. 66 (68).

[511] Appl. 6821/74, *Huber* v. *Austria*, D&R 6 (1977), p. 65 (69).

[512] Judgment of 7 May 1974, *Neumeister*, A.17, pp. 12-14.

In the *Brogan* Case the Government argued that the aim of paragraph 5 is to ensure that the victim of an 'unlawful' arrest or detention should have an enforceable right to compensation. In this regard they also contended that 'lawful' is to be construed as essentially referring back to domestic law and in addition as excluding any element of arbitrariness. They concluded that even in the event of a violation being found of any of the first four paragraphs, there had been no violation of paragraph 5 because the applicants' deprivation was lawful under Northern Ireland law and was not arbitrary. The Court held that such a restrictive interpretation was incompatible with the terms of paragraph 5, which refers to arrest or detention 'in contravention of the provisions of this Article'.[513]

As was pointed out by the Court in the *Ciulla* Case the effective enjoyment of the right guaranteed in paragraph 5 must be ensured in the Contracting States with 'a sufficient degree of certainty'.[514] The damage to be compensated may be material as well as non-material.[515] However, in the *Wassink* Case the Court took the view, unlike the Commission,[516] that the Contracting States are entitled to make the award of compensation dependent of the real existence of any damage resulting from the violation of Article 5.[517] In this case the detention under Article 5(1) was unlawful because there was no registrar present at the hearing, as was required by national law. For this reason it was hard for the applicant to prove any damage; it was uncertain that proceedings conducted in conformity with Article 5, would have led to the release of the applicant. The question of whether damage is involved concerns the merits and will have to be decided by the Strasbourg organs.

5.9 Derogation

Article 5 is not included in the enumeration of Article 15(2). Under the conditions mentioned in the first paragraph of that article the Contracting States may therefore derogate from the provision of Article 5 if, insofar as, and as long as this is necessary. In the *Brannigan and McBride* Case the derogation made by the United Kingdom Government was upheld by the Court. Surprisingly, the Court stated, before examining the derogation, that Article 5(3) and (5) had not been

---

[513] Judgment of 29 November 1988, A.145-B, p. 34. See also the judgment of 10 June 1996, *Benham*, Reports 1996-III, Vol. 10, para. 50.

[514] Judgment of 22 February 1989, A.148, p. 18. See further the judgment of 30 August 1990, *Fox, Campbell and Hartley*, A.182, p. 21 and the judgment of 25 October 1990, *Thynne, Wilson and Gunnel*, A.190, p. 31.

[515] Judgment of 22 June 1972, *Ringeisen*, A.15, pp. 9-10. See also the judgment of 2 December 1987, *Bozano*, A.124, p. 46.

[516] Report of 12 July 1989, A.185-A, p. 27. See also the report of 4 October 1989, *Keus*, A.185-C, pp. 79-80.

[517] Judgment of 27 September 1990, A.185-A, p. 14. See also the judgment of 10 March 1972, *'Vagrancy'* Cases, A.14, p. 11.

complied with.[518] In our opinion this consideration should not have been made if indeed the derogation met the requirements of the Convention.[519]

6 RIGHT TO A FAIR AND PUBLIC HEARING (ARTICLE 6)

1.   *In the determination of his civil rights and obligations or of any criminal charge against him, everyone is entitled to a fair and public hearing within a reasonable time by an independent and impartial tribunal established by law. Judgment shall be pronounced publicly but the press and public may be excluded from all or part of the trial in the interest of morals, public order or national security in a democratic society, where the interests of juveniles or the protection of the private life of the parties so require, or to the extent strictly necessary in the opinion of the court in special circumstances where publicity would prejudice the interests of justice.*
2.   *Everyone charged with a criminal offence shall be presumed innocent until proved guilty according to law.*
3.   *Everyone charged with a criminal offence has the following minimum rights:*
   a) *to be informed promptly, in a language which he understands and in detail, of the nature and cause of the accusation against him;*
   b) *to have adequate time and facilities for the preparation of his defence;*
   c) *to defend himself in person or through legal assistance of his own choosing or, if he has not sufficient means to pay for legal assistance, to be given it free when the interests of justice so require;*
   d) *to examine or have examined witnesses against him and to obtain the attendance and examination of witnesses on his behalf under the same conditions as witnesses against him;*
   e) *to have the free assistance of an interpreter if he cannot understand or speak the language used in court.*

6.1 Introduction

For the interpretation of the first paragraph of Article 6 the Court in its *Delcourt* judgment set forth the following guideline:

> In a democratic society within the meaning of the Convention, the right to a fair administration of justice holds such a prominent place that a restrictive interpretation of Article 6(1) would not correspond to the aim and the purpose of that provision.[520]

In thus rejecting a restrictive interpretation of that provision, the Court gives guidance not only for its own case-law and that of the Commission, but also to the national authorities which have to apply Article 6. Indeed, its case-law to be discussed hereafter shows that the Court considers itself competent to an in-depth examination of the way in which Article 6 has been interpreted and applied by the national authorities.

---

[518] Judgment of 26 May 1993, A.258-B, p. 48.
[519] See the declaration of Thór Vilhjálmsson, *ibidem*, p. 59.
[520] Judgment of 17 January 1970, A.11, p. 15. Thus also in its judgment of 26 October 1984, *De Cubber*, A.86, p. 16.

The first issue to be discussed is the scope of Article 6. Thereafter, the various express and implied requirements embodied in the three paragraphs of this provision will be mapped out.

6.2 The Scope of Article 6

6.2.1 Determination of Civil Rights and Obligations; Drafting History

Unlike the second and the third paragraph of Article 6, which apply exclusively to criminal cases, the first paragraph also applies to all those proceedings in which the determination of civil rights and obligations is (also) at issue.[521] The meaning of the words 'determination of his civil rights and obligations' ('*contestations sur ses droits et obligations de caractère civil*') is rather vague and, consequently, leaves ample scope for 'creative' interpretation and even 'judicial policy'.[522] If, as is the case here, 'the ordinary meaning to be given to the terms'[523] does not provide a sufficient guideline for this interpretation, recourse may be had to 'supplementary means of interpretation, including the preparatory work of the treaty and the circumstances of its conclusion'.[524] One may wonder why, up until now, the Court has paid so little attention to the 'preparatory work' of the Convention as a 'supplementary means of interpretation' of Article 6; at least as far as can be deduced from the text of its judgments.[525] This is the more surprising since the drafting history of the words 'civil rights and obligations' was studied in depth at an early stage by several authors, whose conclusions seem to indicate, *inter alia*, that certain elements introduced by the Court in the interpretation of these words, are not self-evident, to say the least.[526] More in

---

[521] Judgment of 8 June 1976, *Engel*, A.22, p. 36.

[522] Thus the representative of the Commission before the Court, Fawcett, in the *König* Case, B.25 (1982), p. 179: 'There is no obvious demonstration of what the purpose and scope of Article 6 really is. I submit that there are choices here of judicial policy on the part of the Court in the interpretation of Article 6'.

[523] See Art. 31(1), of the Vienna Convention on the Law of Treaties; 8 *International Legal Materials*, 1969, p. 679.

[524] See Art. 32 of the same Convention. Thus also the minority opinion of Commission members in the *Benthem* Case, A.97, p. 37.

[525] The Court itself has not yet given its opinion about the conclusions that might be drawn from the *travaux préparatoires* with regard to the interpretation of 'civil rights and obligations'. With respect to these *travaux préparatoires*, the position has been taken in Strasbourg, on the one hand, that they provide no clarity as to the meaning of 'civil rights and obligations' (separate opinion of judge Matscher attached to the judgment of 28 June 1978, *König*, A.27, p. 45), and on the other hand, that they point in the direction of a restrictive interpretation (report of the Commission of 19 March 1970, *Ringeisen*, B.11 (1972), pp. 70-71; joint dissenting opinion attached to the judgments of 29 May 1986, *Feldbrugge*, A.99, p. 21 and pp. 26-27, and *Deumeland*, A.100, pp. 33 and 38-39), while an extensive interpretation was also considered by some as being in conformity therewith (minority view of the Commission in the *Benthem* Case, A.97, p. 37).

[526] See, especially, in chronological order: Jacques Velu, 'Le problème de l'application aux juridictions administratives, des règles de la Convention européenne des droits de l'homme relatives à la publicité des audiences et des jugements', *Revue de Droit International et de Droit Comparé*, 1961,

particular, these studies show that the drafting history of Article 14 of the International Covenant on Civil and Political Rights, which was used as a model by the drafters of Article 6 of the Convention, offers a rather strong indication that it was not the intention to restrict the scope of the right of access to court, apart from determinations of a criminal-law character, to determinations of rights and obligations of a private law character. On the contrary, one is struck by the fact that proposals which might imply the risk of such a restriction, were criticised for that reason and rejected or amended.[527]

The *travaux préparatoires* of the European Convention do not contain any indication of a discussion in any of the bodies involved in the drafting concerning the formula here at issue. In the French text of Article 6 the formula of Article 14 of the Covenant was adopted without any change. In the English text 'rights and obligations in a suit at law' was altered, at the very last stage of the drafting, into 'civil rights and obligations'. The reason for this is not traceable, but apparently it was not considered to have any implications for the scope of Article 6. One may assume that the only reason for it was that, in the eyes of continental lawyers (and of the linguists involved), 'suit at law' was not the obvious equivalent for '*de caractère civil*'.[528] In conclusion, there is no indication that the more restrictive approach adopted in the Strasbourg case-law could be based upon the drafting history of either Article 14 of the Covenant or Article 6 of the Convention. The Committee of Experts on Human Rights of the Council of Europe, when making a comparison between the two provisions, also reached the conclusion with respect to the words here under discussion that 'in view of the fact that the French texts use identical terms (...) the intention was the same'.[529]

It may be true that the original intention of the drafters of a treaty may become less relevant as time lapses, especially after States have become parties whose representatives did not participate in the drafting, but this argument is less

---

pp. 129-171; Karl Josef Partsch, *Die Rechte und Freiheiten der europäischen Menschenrechts-konvention*, Berlin, 1966, pp. 143-150; Thomas Buergenthal and Wilhelm Kewenig, 'Zum Begriff der Civil Rights in Artikel 6 Absatz 1 der Europäischen Menschenrechtskonvention', *Archiv des Völkerrechts*, 1966/67, pp. 393-411; Frank C. Newman, 'Natural Justice, Due Process and the New International Covenants on Human Rights: Prospectus', *Public Law*, Winter 1967, pp. 274-313.

[527] For the same conclusion, see Velu *supra* note 526, pp. 145-154. See especially his reference, at p. 150, to a statement by the delegate of the USSR, Mr Pavlov. At p. 154 Velu says: 'Au fond, toutes les délégations étaient d'accord pour que les garanties de procédures prévues s'appliquent à toutes les juridictions'. For a more recent, detailed analysis, see P. Lemmens, *Geschillen over burgerlijke rechten en verplichtingen* [Disputes concerning Civil Rights and Obligations], Antwerp, 1989, pp. 218-220, and M.L.W.M. Viering, *Het toepassingsgebied van artikel 6 EVRM* [The Scope of Article 6 ECHR], Zwolle, 1994, pp. 33-49. Both these authors also discuss the intervention by the Danish delegate, Mr Sørensen, who proposed to exclude disputes between a private party and a public authority but did not influence the outcome of the debates on that point.

[528] See Velu, *supra* note 526, p. 159.

[529] Council of Europe, *Problems arising from the co-existence of the United Nations Covenants on Human Rights and the European Convention on Human Rights; Differences as regards the Rights Guaranteed*, Report of the Committee of Experts on Human Rights to the Committee of Ministers, Doc. H(70)7, Strasbourg, September 1970, p. 37.

convincing as long as there is no common and unambiguous legal opinion and/or uniform practice which deviates from that original intention.

6.2.2 Determination of Civil Rights and Obligations; Case-Law

In the *Benthem* Case the Court expressly declined to give an abstract definition of 'civil rights and obligations',[530] notwithstanding the Commission's invitation in its report in that case.[531] That is not to say, however, that the Court has given no guidance at all on the interpretation of these words. In its case-law the Court has drawn the following main lines.

(a) 'Rights and Obligations'

Although for the determination of whether a right or obligation is at stake the domestic legal system concerned has to be taken as a starting point, the Strasbourg case-law has made it clear that, as part of a provision of the Convention, the words 'rights and obligations' have an autonomous meaning. Thus, the Commission held in the *Kaplan* Case:

> These concepts [rights and obligations] are in themselves autonomous to some degree. Thus it is not decisive that a given privilege or interest which exists in a domestic legal system is not classified or described as a 'right' by that system. However in deciding whether it is a 'right' for the purpose of Article 6(1), account must be taken of its 'substantive content and effects', the object and purpose of the Convention and the national legal systems of other Contracting States.[532]

If, according to this line of interpretation, a certain claim is considered to be a 'right', the Court's case-law requires for the applicability of Article 6 that this right 'can be said, at least on arguable grounds, to be recognised under domestic law'.[533] The words 'on arguable grounds' leave the Commission and Court sufficient ground to make an assessment independently of the arguments advanced by the defendant State on the issue.[534] And the fact that the claim concerned was addressed as an issue in national proceedings constitutes sufficient ground for the 'arguability' of the existence of a right.[535] On the other hand, if domestic law expressly excludes the claim concerned, the Court takes the position that 'to this extent' there can be no arguable right which would make Article 6 applicable.[536]

---

[530] Judgment of 23 October 1985, A.97, p. 16.

[531] Report of 8 October 1983, A.97, p. 24. More expressly Mr Danelius and Mr Melchior, as delegates of the Commission, in the hearing before the Court; Cour/Misc (85)30, 26 February 1985, pp. 3 and 8 respectively.

[532] Report of 17 July 1980, D&R 21 (1981), p. 5 (24).

[533] See, *inter alia*, the judgment of 21 February 1986, *James and Others*, A.98, p. 46; judgment of 12 October 1992, *Salerno*, A.245-D, p. 55.

[534] See the judgment of 8 July 1987, *O v. the United Kingdom*, A.120-A, p. 24.

[535] Judgment of 26 March 1992, *Editions Périscope*, A.234-B, p. 65. Here the Court used the phrase 'sufficiently tenable' instead of 'on arguable grounds'.

[536] Judgment of 21 February 1990, *Powell and Rayner*, A.172, p. 16. See also Appl. 7729/76, *Agee v. the United Kingdom*, D&R 7 (1977), p. 164 (175), where parliamentary immunity was involved and, therefore, the right to protection of one's reputation could not be effectuated. And see the

However, the fact that the authorities enjoy discretion in their decision-making and that, therefore, the person concerned cannot claim a specific outcome, does not mean that no right is involved. He is entitled to the authorities respecting the limits of their discretion. Indeed, that discretion is not unfettered and, at least, has to be exercised in conformity with generally recognised legal and administrative principles.[537] The Court seems to have deviated from this line in the *Masson and Van Zon* Case and the *Leutscher* Case. The domestic legislation concerned provided that a former suspect may be granted compensation by the court for certain damages suffered as a result of the investigation against him, if reasons in equity exist for that. Because of the use of the word 'may' instead of 'shall', which is used in other relevant provisions of Dutch law, the Court concluded that 'the measure of discretion indicates that no actual right is recognised in law'.[538] In our opinion this point of view is unfortunate because it makes the applicability of Article 6 dependent on the measure of discretion which the domestic law provides. Thus it enables the Contracting States to evade the operation of Article 6 by granting capacious discretionary powers to the national authorities.

The determination of the existence of an 'obligation' will be less problematic; that issue has not played an important role in the case-law so far.

(b) Legal Dispute ('*Contestation*') Concerning Civil Rights and Obligations
From the use of the word '*contestations*' in the French text of Article 6(1), which has no equivalent in the English text, it has been inferred that for Article 6 to be applicable the settlement of a dispute concerning a right or obligation must be at issue.[539] This concept of 'dispute', however, should not be construed too technically and should be given a substantive rather than a formal meaning: a difference of opinion between two or more (legal) persons who have a certain relation to the right or obligation at issue is sufficient, provided that it is 'genuine and of a serious nature'.[540] One of the (legal) persons may be a public authority

---

report of the Commission of 14 January 1993, *Holy Monasteries*, A.301-A, p. 55. In the latter case the question of whether any 'arguable claim' existed, did not play a role in the judgment of the Court of 9 December 1994, A.301-A, pp. 36-38.

[537] Judgment of 7 July 1989, *Tre Taktörer AB*, A.159, pp. 17-18; judgment of 25 October 1989, *Allan Jacobsson*, A.163, p. 20.

[538] Judgment of 28 September 1995, A.327-A, pp. 19-20 and judgment of 26 March 1996, Reports 1996-II, Vol. 6, para. 24 respectively.

[539] Judgment of 23 June 1981, *Le Compte, Van Leuven and De Meyere*, A.43, p. 20. The Court said, however, 'Even if ...' See also the judgment of 23 October 1990, *Moreira da Azevedo*, A.189, p. 17: 'In so far as the French word "*contestation*" would appear to require the existence of a dispute, if indeed it does so at all ...'

[540] Judgment of 23 June 1981, *Le Compte, Van Leuven and De Meyere*, A.43, p. 20. See also the judgment of 23 October 1985, *Benthem*, A.97, p. 15; judgment of 26 June 1986, *Van Marle and Others*, A.101, p. 11; judgments of 27 October 1987, *Pudas* and *Bodén*, A.125, pp. 14 and 40 respectively.

whose act or decision affects the other (legal) person.[541] If the act or decision is a favourable one and is not contested by the addressee, but is challenged by another public authority or other (legal) person, a 'contestation' has emerged.[542]

The 'contestation' must be of a legal character: it must concern the alleged violation of a right and the alleged illegality of that violation.[543] As observed before, this does not exclude cases in which the administrative authority has discretionary powers, provided that the way in which these powers have been exercised is challenged on legal and not only on policy grounds.[544] These legal grounds may relate to the way in which the limits of the discretion set by law have been respected,[545] or to the issue of whether the challenged act is in conformity with generally recognised legal and administrative principles.[546] The legal-character requirement also does not mean that the difference of opinion may not relate to facts, provided that they have some implications for the determination of rights or obligations.[547] In this respect, in our opinion, the *Van Marle* judgment of the Court was not well reasoned.[548] In the national proceedings, which had taken place before a judicial body, the dispute concerned both facts and legal aspects, as the Court itself recognised. That the legal issue was not pursued in the Strasbourg procedure would seem to be not relevant for the applicability of Article 6. Indeed, the mere fact that a judicial authority had considered itself competent to deal with the dispute gives the latter a legal character

In the *Baraona* Case the Court rejected the Government's submission that the impugned measure had no basis in national law at that time and accordingly could not give rise to liability on the part of the State and, therefore, could not be the subject of a 'dispute'. The Court adopted the position that it was not for the Court to assess either the merits of the applicant's claim under domestic law or the influence of the revolutionary situation in Portugal on the application of domestic law; this belonged to the exclusive jurisdiction of the national courts. The applicant, however, could claim on arguable grounds to have a right that was recognised under national law as he understood it.[549] And in the *Moreira de Azevedo* Case the Court held that, although the applicant was only *assistente* in criminal proceedings and had not filed a formal claim for damages, there was a

---

[541] Judgment of 16 July 1971, *Ringeisen*, A.13, p. 39; judgment of 28 June 1978, *König*, A.27, p. 32; judgment of 23 September 1982, *Sporrong and Lönnroth*, A.52, pp. 29-30; judgment of 27 October 1987, *Bodén*, A.125-B, pp. 40-41.

[542] Judgment of 23 October 1985, *Benthem*, A.97, p. 15.

[543] Judgment of 23 June 1981, *Le Compte, Van Leuven and De Meyere*, A.43, p. 44.

[544] Judgment of 26 June 1986, *Van Marle and Others*, A.101, pp. 11-12; judgment of 27 October 1987, *Pudas*, A.125-A, p. 15.

[545] Judgment of 25 October 1989, *Allan Jacobsson*, A.163, p. 20.

[546] Judgment of 28 June 1990, *Skärby*, A.180-B, p. 37.

[547] Judgment of 26 June 1986, *Van Marle and Others*, A.101, p. 11; judgment of 27 October 1987, *Pudas*, A.125-A, pp. 14-15.

[548] Judgment of 26 June 1986, A.101, p. 12.

[549] Judgment of 8 July 1987, A.122, p. 17.

contestation concerning his civil rights.[550] It seems to be crucial for the latter case that the consequences of intervening as an *assistente* were not clear under Portuguese law, since the Court reached the conclusion in the subsequent *Hamer* Case that there had been no 'dispute' over a civil right because of the failure of the applicant to lodge a formal claim for damages.[551]

(c) 'Determination' of Civil Rights and Obligations

The (claimed[552]) judicial proceedings must lead to a 'determination' of civil rights or obligations. This requirement means that there must be a connection between the dispute to be solved and any such right or obligation. A tenuous connection or remote consequence does not suffice.[553] On the other hand, this 'determination' need not form the main point or even the purpose of the proceedings. It is sufficient that the outcome of the (claimed) judicial proceedings may be 'decisive for',[554] or may 'affect',[555] or may 'relate to'[556] the determination and/or the exercise of the right, or the determination and/or the fulfilment of the obligation, as the case may be; the effects need not be legal but may also be purely factual.[557] That right or obligation does not have to constitute the object of the procedure;[558] it may, for instance, have been the object or one of the objects of a challenged administrative decision or may be implied in the challenged sanction. It may even be a right claimed by a third party who intervenes in criminal proceedings to obtain damages.[559] And the fact that the person concerned is in an identical legal position with many others does not

---

[550] Judgment of 23 October 1990, A.189, p. 17.

[551] Judgment of 7 August 1996, Reports 1996-III, Vol. 13, paras 74-79.

[552] According to the Court, Art. 6(1) not only contains procedural guarantees in relation to judicial proceedings, but also grants a right to judicial proceedings for the cases mentioned in this article. See *infra* p. 418.

[553] Judgment of 23 June 1981, *Le Compte, Van Leuven and De Meyere*, A.43, p. 21.

[554] Judgment of 16 July 1971, *Ringeisen*, A.13, p. 39; judgment of 23 June 1981, *Le Compte, Van Leuven and De Meyere*, A.43, p. 21; judgment of 22 October 1984, *Sramek*, A.84, p. 17; judgment of 27 October 1987, *Pudas*, A.125, p. 15; judgment of 24 October 1989, *H* v. *France*, A.162-A, p. 20; judgment of 19 July 1995, *Kerojärvi*, A.322, p. 13; judgment of 21 November 1995, *Aquaviva*, A.333-A, pp. 14-15.

[555] Judgment of 24 October 1979, *Winterwerp*, A.33, p. 28; judgment of 23 September 1982, *Sporrong and Lönnroth*, A.52, p. 30; judgment of 27 October 1987, *Bodén*, A.125-B, p. 41; judgments of 23 April 1987, *Ettl and Others*; *Erkner and Hofauer*; and *Poiss*; A.117, pp. 16, 60 and 102 respectively.

[556] Judgment of 28 June 1990, *Skärby*, A.180-B, p. 36.

[557] Judgment of 23 September 1982, *Sporrong and Lönnroth*, A.52, p. 30.

[558] See the *Winterwerp* Case, where the object was the deprivation of liberty, which had, however, direct consequences for Mr Winterwerp's legal capacity to perform private law acts; judgment of 24 October 1979, A.33, p. 28.

[559] Judgment of 23 October 1990, *Moreira de Azevedo*, A.189, p. 17. In the same way, in our opinion, if an administrative decision does (also) affect civil rights of third parties, *e.g.* the neighbours of a piece of land for which a building permit has been granted, the latter also have the right of access to court; Viering, *supra* note 527, pp. 95-96.

make the connection remote or tenuous.[560] Moreover, the determination need not necessarily concern the existence of a right or obligation, but may also relate to its scope or modalities,[561] or to the prohibition of interferences with the exercise of a right.[562] Despite this big-hearted approach the Court held Article 6 to be not applicable with regard to one of the applicants in the *McMichael* Case. Mr McMichael had failed to take the requisite prior steps to obtain legal recognition of his parental rights. Therefore, the care-proceedings, insituted by Mr and Mrs McMichael, did not concern the determination of Mr McMichael's rights as a father.[563]

If a remedy is not provided for under national law, it is not possible to determine what effect the outcome of the proceedings have had or may have had. In those cases the Court investigates whether the challenged decision or refusal to decide was decisive for a civil right or obligation.[564]

(d) Autonomous Meaning of 'Civil Rights' and 'Civil Obligations'

To the words 'civil rights and obligations' an autonomous meaning must be assigned. It must first be examined what the nature of the right or obligation at issue is according to the law of the respondent State.[565] On the one hand, if the right or obligation forms part of private law, the first paragraph of Article 6 applies.[566] The same holds good if the features of private law are 'predominant'.[567] On the other hand, however, the mere fact that the right or obligation at issue is governed by public law, does not exclude the applicability of the first paragraph of Article 6; what matters are the contents and effect of that right or obligation rather than its legal classification.[568]

Moreover, the nature of the right or obligation under domestic law is not decisive: what matters is whether according to general objective principles – in which context the legal systems of the other Contracting States must also be taken into consideration[569] – the character of a 'civil right' or 'civil obligation' can be assigned to the right or obligation at issue, taking into account in particular the capacity in which a person claims a right and the conditions in which he wishes

---

[560] Judgment of 25 October 1989, *Allan Jacobsson*, A.163, p. 20.

[561] Judgment of 23 June 1981, *Le Compte, Van Leuven and De Meyere*, A.43, p. 22; judgment of 23 October 1985, *Benthem*, A.97, p. 15; judgment of 26 June 1986, *Van Marle and Others*, A.101, p. 11.

[562] Judgment of 23 September 1982, *Sporrong and Lönnroth*, A.52, pp. 29-30.

[563] Judgment of 24 February 1995, A.307-B, p. 52.

[564] Judgment of 27 October 1987, *Bodén*, A.125-B, p. 41; judgment of 28 June 1990, *Skärby*, A.180-B, pp. 36-37.

[565] Judgment of 28 June 1978, *König*, A.27, p. 30; judgment of 29 May 1986, *Feldbrugge*, A.99, pp. 12-13.

[566] Judgment of 28 November 1984, *Rasmussen*, A.87, pp. 12-13.

[567] Judgment of 29 May 1986, *Feldbrugge*, A.99, p. 16.

[568] Judgment of 28 June 1978, *König*, A.27, p. 30.

[569] *Idem* and judgment of 29 May 1986, *Feldbrugge*, A.99, pp. 12-13.

to exercise it or exercises it.[570] This point of view, too, serves to make the scope of Article 6(1) less dependent on the national legislator.

It is also not decisive for the 'civil' nature of a right or obligation whether the underlying dispute is one between individuals or one between an individual and a public authority. Even if in the latter case that public authority is involved in the proceedings in a sovereign capacity, those proceedings can relate to the determination of 'civil rights and obligations'.[571] It is equally not decisive whether the proceedings take place before a civil court or before another body vested with jurisdiction.[572] And, finally, the fact that in legal relations between individuals great public interests may also be involved does not bar the applicability of Article 6(1).[573]

Up to the present the Court has held the first paragraph of Article 6 applicable, in addition to proceedings with a private-law character, to the following proceedings as determining civil rights or obligations:
- proceedings concerning a permission, licence or other act of a public authority which forms a condition for the legality of a contract to be concluded with a private party;[574]
- proceedings which may lead to the cancellation or suspension by the public authorities of the qualification for practising a particular profession or carrying on an economic activity;[575]
- proceedings concerning the grant or revocation of a licence by the public authorities which is required for setting-up a certain business or carrying on certain economic activities on a particular site;[576]
- those stages in expropriation, consolidation and planning proceedings, and procedures concerning building permits and other real-estate permits, which have direct consequences for the right of ownership with respect to the property

---

[570] Judgment of 30 November 1987, *H v. Belgium*, A.127-B, pp. 33-34.

[571] Judgment of 28 June 1978, *König*, A.27, p. 30; judgment of 23 October 1985, *Benthem*, A.97, p. 16; judgment of 29 May 1986, *Feldbrugge*, A.99, p. 12; judgment of 8 July 1987, *Baraona*, A.122, p. 18; judgment of 24 October 1989, *H v. France*, A.162-A, p. 20.

[572] Judgment of 16 July 1971, *Ringeisen*, A.13, p. 39; judgment of 28 June 1978, *König*, A.27, pp. 29-30; judgment of 8 July 1987, *Baraona*, A.122, p. 18.

[573] Judgment of 28 November 1984, *Rasmussen*, A.87, p. 13.

[574] Judgment of 16 July 1971, *Ringeisen*, A.13; judgment of 22 October 1984, *Sramek*, A.84.

[575] Judgment of 28 June 1978, *König*, A.27; judgment of 23 June 1981, *Le Compte, Van Leuven and De Meyere*, A.43; judgment of 10 February 1983, *Albert and Le Compte*, A.58; judgment of 30 November 1987, *H v. Belgium*, A.127-B; judgment of 19 April 1993, *Kraska*, A.254-B; judgment of 26 September 1995, *Diennet*, A.325-A.

[576] See, *e.g.*, judgment of 23 October 1985, *Benthem*, A.97; judgment of 27 October 1987, *Pudas*, A.125-A; judgment of 17 July 1989, *Tre Traktörer Aktiebolag*, A.159; judgment of 18 February 1991, *Fredin*, A.192.

involved;[577] and more in general proceedings the outcome of which has an impact on the use or the enjoyment of property;[578]

- proceedings in which a decision is taken on entitlement, under a social security scheme, to health insurance benefits,[579] to industrial-accident insurance benefits,[580] to welfare (disability) allowances,[581] to State pensions,[582] and to invalidity pensions;[583]
- proceedings against public authorities in which rights and obligations concerning family law are at issue;[584]
- proceedings against the public administration concerning contracts[585] and concerning damages in administrative proceedings[586] or in criminal proceedings;[587]

---

[577] Judgment of 23 September 1982, *Sporrong and Lönnroth*, A.52; judgments of 23 April 1987, *Ettl and Others*; *Erkner and Hofauer*; and *Poiss*, A.117; judgment of 27 October 1987, *Bodén*, A.125-B; judgment of 21 February 1990, *Håkansson and Sturesson*, A.171-A; judgment of 28 June 1990, *Mats Jacobsson*, A.180-A; judgment of 28 June 1990, *Skärby*, A.180-B; judgment of 27 February 1992, *Cifola*, A.231-A; judgment of 23 June 1993, *Ruiz-Mateos*, A.262.

[578] Judgment of 18 February 1991, *Fredin*, A.192, p. 20; judgment 19 February 1991, *Zanghi*, A.194-C; judgment of 27 November 1991, *Oerlemans*, A.219; judgment of 27 February 1992, *Pandolfelli and Palumbo*, A.231-B; judgment of 16 December 1992, *De Geouffre de la Pradelle*, A.253-B; judgment of 25 November 1993, *Zander*, A.279-B.

[579] Judgment of 29 May 1986, *Feldbrugge*, A.99.

[580] Judgment of 29 May 1986, *Deumeland*, A.100.

[581] Judgment of 26 February 1993, *Salesi*, A.257-E.

[582] Judgments of 26 November 1992, *Francesco Lombardo* and *Giancarlo Lombardo*, A.249-B and A.249-C; judgment of 24 August 1993, *Massa*, A.265-B.

[583] Judgment of 24 June 1993, *Schuler-Zgraggen*, A.263. At p. 17 the judgment states in general that 'the development in the law (...) and the principle of equality of treatment warrant taking the view that today the general rule is that Article 6 § 1 does apply in the field of social insurance, including even welfare assistance'.

[584] Judgment of 28 November 1984, *Rasmussen*, A.87; judgments of 8 July 1987, *O and H v. the United Kingdom*, A.120; judgments of 8 July 1987, *W, B and R v. the United Kingdom*, A.121; judgment of 22 June 1989, *Eriksson*, A.156; judgment of 27 November 1992, *Olsson (No. 2)*, A.250; judgment of 26 May 1994, *Keegan*, A.290.

[585] Judgment of 27 August 1991, *Philis*, A.209.

[586] Judgment of 8 July 1987, *Baraona*, A.122; judgment of 27 April 1989, *Neves e Silva*, A.153; judgment of 24 October 1989, *H v. France*, A.162-A; judgment of 26 March 1992, *Editions Periscope*, A.234-B; judgment of 31 March 1992, *X v. France*, A.234-C; judgment of 23 November 1993, *Scopelliti*, A.278. See, on the one hand, the judgment of 13 July 1983, *Zimmerman and Steiner*, A.66, p. 10, where the civil character of a claim for damages concerning aircraft noise was recognised and, on the other hand, the judgment of 21 February 1990, *Powell and Rayner*, A.172, pp. 15-16, where in a comparable case the applicability of Article 6 was denied, since under English law liability in nuisance with regard to the flight of aircraft was excluded in the circumstances at issue, which meant that no substantive right could be claimed.

[587] Judgment of 23 October 1990, *Moreira de Azevedo*, A.189; judgment of 27 February 1992, *Casciaroli*, A.229-C.

– proceedings in which a decision is taken on the obligation to pay contributions under a social security scheme;[588]
– patent application proceedings.[589]

In the *Schouten and Meldrum* Case the Court held in a *obiter dictum* that the obligation to pay 'criminal' fines and obligations which are pecuniary in nature and derive 'from tax legislation or [are] otherwise part of normal civic duties' do not fall under the notion of 'civil obligations'.[590]

In a number of cases which have not reached the Court or where the Court did not go into the matter of whether a 'civil right' was at stake, the Commission expressed its opinion on the issue. Thus, already in an early stage, the Commission took the view that proceedings which concern the legal position of civil servants in their relation to the public authorities do not come under the application of the first paragraph of Article 6.[591] Even if, as a starting point, this position has found support in the *Lombardo* judgments,[592] there the Court made the important exception for cases where the State is performing a legal obligation. The Commission also found Article 6 to be not applicable to proceedings in which a public authority decides whether an employer is permitted to fire an employee.[593] It also considered proceedings concerning compensations out of public funds[594] not to affect civil rights and obligations. So far the Commission has also considered the first paragraph of Article 6, to be not applicable to

---

[588] Judgment of 9 December 1994, *Schouten and Meldrum*, A.304, pp. 20-24. Initially the Commission took a different point of view: Appl. 2248/64, *X v. the Netherlands*, Yearbook X (1967), p. 170 (174-176).

[589] Judgment of 20 November 1995, *British-American Tobacco Company Ltd*, A.331, p. 23. Thus it is questionable whether the assessment of the Commission in Appl. 8000/77, *X v. Switzerland*, D&R 13 (1979), p. 82 can be upheld.

[590] Judgment of 9 December 1994, A.304, pp. 20-21. The Commission also held Art. 6 not applicable to proceedings concerning taxation: Appl. 2145/64, *X v. Belgium*, Yearbook VIII (1965), p. 282 (310-312); Appls 1904, 2029, 2094 and 2217/64, *A, B, C and D v. the Netherlands*, Yearbook IX (1966), p. 268 (284); Appl. 9908/82, *X v. France*, D&R 32 (1983), p. 266 (272). See also on this matter *infra* p. 620.

[591] Appl. 423/58, *X v. Federal Republic of Germany*, Coll. 1 (1960) (pages not numbered through); Appl. 9248/81, *Leander v. Sweden*, D&R 34 (1983), p. 78 (83); Appl. 10878/84, *Jakobsson v. Sweden*, D&R 41 (1985), p. 247 (248-249).

[592] Judgments of 26 November 1992, *Francesco Lombardo* and *Giancarlo Lombardo*, A.249-B, p. 26 and A.249-C, p. 42: 'Even though disputes relating to the recruitment, employment and retirement of public servants [c.q. judges] are as a general rule outside the scope of Article 6 par. 1'. The meaning of the words 'Even though' is, however, not very clear; the French text uses the words '*Même si*'.

[593] Appl. 8974/80, *X v. the Netherlands*, D&R 24 (1981), p. 187 (188-189).

[594] Appl. 4523/70, *X v. Federal Republic of Germany*, Yearbook XIV (1971), p. 622 (630-634). See also the, in our opinion highly disputable, decision on Appl. 9543/81, *X v. Federal Republic of Germany* (not published), that the procedure concerning the grant of a *Vertriebenenausweis* does not concern a 'civil right'; this in spite of the great importance of such an identity card for the economic and social activities of the bearer.

401

proceedings concerning admission and expulsion of aliens.[595] In some earlier cases the Commission seemed to indicate that this would be different if the right of respect for family life as a 'civil right' was at issue[596] or if expulsion constituted a violation of the right to education,[597] but in a later decision it held that the expulsion decision did not determine the right to respect of family life.[598] In view of the Court's very extensive interpretation of 'civil rights and obligations' in disputes of an administrative character, it would seem to be doubtful that it will follow the Commission in its restrictive approach.[599] The position that Article 6 is not applicable to cases concerning military service[600] and to cases concerning the right to vote and to be elected,[601] would seem to find more support in the Court's case-law.

In case of expropriation the proceedings in which the damages are determined have been considered by the Commission as a 'determination of a civil right'.[602] In the *Kaplan* Case, in which the Commission – following the same line as in the *König* Case – recognised that the restrictions imposed by the public authorities on conducting an insurance enterprise affected 'civil rights', Article 6 nevertheless was deemed not to be applicable, because the applicant did not claim that the challenged decision was unlawful; he only differed from the Secretary of State on questions of judgment concerning the propriety of his conduct, which made that the issue of the civil rights involved was not susceptible of determination by a judicial decision.[603] In its decision in *X v. the United Kingdom* the Commission also made a distinction in comparison with the *König* Case by holding that the disciplinary proceedings against the medical practitioner did not concern the latter's possible suspension, but might only result in a reprimand, so that a purely disciplinary affair was involved, which did not result in a 'determination' of a

---

[595] Appl. 3225/67, *X, Y, Z, V and W v. the United Kingdom*, Coll. 25 (1968), p. 117 (122-123) (admission) and Appl. 9285/81, *X, Y and Z v. the United Kingdom*, D&R 29 (1982), p. 205 (211-212) (expulsion).

[596] Appl. 3225/67, *X, Y, Z, V and W v. the United Kingdom*, Coll. 25 (1968). See also Appls 2991 and 2992/66, *Alam, Kahn and Singh v. the United Kingdom*, Yearbook X (1967), p. 478 (500-504). See, however, Appl. 8244/78, *Singh Uppal and Others v. the United Kingdom*, D&R 17 (1980), p. 149 (157), where the Commission rejected the claim that the refusal of admission interfered with the right to join one's family.

[597] Appl. 7841/77, *X v. the United Kingdom* (not published).

[598] Appl. 8971/80, *X v. the United Kingdom* (not published).

[599] See Viering, *supra* note 527, pp. 136-142.

[600] Appls 3435-38/67, *W, X, Y and Z v. the United Kingdom*, Yearbook (1968), pp. 602-604. See however the judgment of 19 July 1995, *Kerojärvi*, A.322, p. 14, where the Court held that a dispute concerning the entitlement to compensation under the 1948 Military Injuries Act, came within the scope of Article 6. The Court did see no reason 'to distinguish this case from previous cases in which it has found that disputes over benefits under a social-security scheme concern "civil rights".'

[601] Appl. 11068/84, *Priorello v. Italy*, D&R 43 (1985), p. 195 (197).

[602] Report of 8 March 1982, *Andorfer Tonwerke*, D&R 32 (1982), p. 94 (107-108). See also the report of 7 March 1984, *Lithgow*, A.102, p. 117.

[603] Report of 17 July 1980, D&R 21 (1981), p. 5 (23-34).

'civil right'.[604] An individual's right to respect for his reputation by a private person was considered to be a 'civil right'.[605] The Commission held Article 6 not applicable in a case in which the person concerned tried to obtain rehabilitation through criminal proceedings in order to have a penalty imposed on the culprit.[606] However, in the *Helmers* Case the Court held that the requirements of Article 6 do apply in the case of a private prosecution instituted for the protection of one's reputation.[607] In our opinion, if judicial proceedings with a civil-law character are not provided for, an alternative must be available which satisfies the requirements of Article 6(1), since the lack of access to court for the determination of a civil right in itself already conflicts with Article 6.[608] On the other hand, if a certain procedure which affects a person's reputation does not itself determine rights or obligations but is only investigative of nature, it does not have to fulfil the requirements of Article 6.[609]

6.2.3 Is 'Civil' to be Equated with 'Private'?

The case-law as described above has as its consequence that, even if it is assumed that 'civil' should be equated with private, the first paragraph of Article 6 is applicable to a great many proceedings which in themselves have a public character according to their form and subject, but the outcome of which is of direct interest for the determination and/or content of a private right or private obligation.

Is 'civil' in Article 6 to be equated with 'private'? Although the Court has explicitly left this question open by considering that:

> [it is not] necessary in the present case to decide whether the concept of 'civil rights and obligations' within the meaning of [Article 6] extends beyond those rights which have a private nature,[610]

---

[604] Appl. 10331/83 (not published).

[605] Appl. 808/60, *ISOP v. Austria*, Yearbook V (1962), p. 108 (122); report of 7 April 1993, *Al Fayed and Others*, A.294-B, p. 6; report of 17 January 1994, *Tolstoy Miloslavsky*, A.316-B, p. 8. If statements made in Parliament are involved, an invocation of Article 6 is blocked by the principle of 'parliamentary immunity': Appl. 7729/76, *Agee v. the United Kingdom*, D&R 7 (1977), p. 164 (175). See also Appl. 9248/81, *Leander v. Sweden*, D&R 34 (1983), p. 78 (83): refusal to appoint someone to a post cannot, as such, be considered to be an attack on the person's reputation.

[606] Appl. 7116/75, *X v. Federal Republic of Germany*, D&R 7 (1977), p. 91 (92). The situation is different, however, if within the framework of criminal proceedings a civil claim can be and actually has been submitted: Appl. 8366/78, *X v. Luxembourg*, D&R 16 (1979), p. 196 (198).

[607] Judgment of 29 October 1991, A.212-A, p. 14. See also the judgment of 13 July 1995, *Tolstoy Miloslavsky*, A.316-B, p. 78.

[608] See *infra* p. 420.

[609] Judgment of 21 September 1994, *Fayed*, A.294-B, pp. 47-48.

[610] Judgment of 28 June 1978, *König*, A.27, p. 32. See also the judgment of 23 June 1981, *Le Compte, Van Leuven and De Meyere*, A.43, p. 22, and the judgment of 30 November 1987, *H v. Belgium*, A.127-B, p. 32.

for a long time it has created the impression that it started from the assumption that 'civil' meant 'private', and that it employed these terms as synonyms.[611] Article 6 does not speak, however, of 'private rights and obligations', but of 'civil rights and obligations', while the French text does not speak of *'droits et obligations civils'*, but of *'droits et obligations de caractère civil'*. Moreover, that 'civil rights' should be equated with 'private rights' appears not to be supported by the *travaux préparatoires* of Article 6 as described above.[612]

As from its *Benthem* judgment[613] the Court speaks of the 'civil' character of the right involved without relying for that on its 'private' character, and it has recognised the civil character of rights which in addition to private features had also strong public features.[614] However, the implications thereof can still not be fully estimated.

The present Strasbourg case-law concerning 'civil rights and obligations' therefore still lacks clarity and certainty. It lacks clarity because still no general definition of 'civil rights and obligations' can be inferred from it, while the construction of the effect of the outcome of the procedure for a right or obligation of a civil character is complex and not very specific. It lacks certainty because the elements actually developed in the case-law for such a definition appear still to lead within and between the Court and the Commission to different views in concrete cases, while the numbers of the adherents to the various views are almost equal.[615] In our opinion this lack of clarity and certainty, which constitutes an undesirable situation not only for the individual seeking justice, but also for the public authorities within the Contracting States, can only be eliminated if the Court departs from its present casuistic approach and develops a general and readily applicable definition of 'civil rights and obligations' in the exercise of its function to give direction to the interpretation and application of the Convention.

Some members of the Commission went quite a long way in the direction of a definition in their minority opinion in the *Benthem* report. On the basis, allegedly, of the case-law of the Court, these members proposed the following definition of 'civil rights':

---

[611] Thus, for instance, the judgment of 28 June 1978, *König*, A.27, p. 32 and the judgment of 23 June 1981, *Le Compte, Van Leuven and De Meyere*, A.43, p. 22. See also the judgments of 23 April 1987, *Ettl and Others*; *Erkner and Hofauer*; and *Poiss*, A.117, pp. 16, 60 and 102 respectively.

[612] See *supra* pp. 392-394.

[613] Judgment of 23 October 1985, A.97, p. 16.

[614] Judgment of 29 May 1986, *Feldbrugge*, A.99, pp. 13-16.

[615] Thus the Court decided in the *Benthem* Case, A.97, that Art. 6(1) was applicable, by eleven to six votes, while the Commission had taken a contrary standpoint by nine votes to eight. In the *Feldbrugge* Case, A.99, the proportion in the Court was ten to seven, and in the Commission eight to six. In the *Deumeland* Case, A.100, this was nine to eight and eight to six respectively.

all those rights which are individual rights under the national legal system and fall into the sphere of general individual freedom, be it professional or any other legally permitted activity.[616]

It is to be regretted, however, that the proponents of this broad interpretation at the same time created a new source of complexity and uncertainty by introducing as a criterion the measure of discretion on the part of the deciding authorities, adding that in cases in which on the part of the authorities there exists an absolutely discretionary competence, there is no question of a right, and consequently also not of a 'civil right'.[617] Firstly, the applicability of the first paragraph of Article 6 is thus again made dependent on what the domestic law provides for, and this *nota bene* with regard to the very complex and controversial distinction between subjective rights and reflex rights.[618] Secondly, this position implies unintentionally an invitation to the national legislator to abolish the legal restrictions to which the exercise of discretionary competence is tied down, in order thus to evade the consequences of Article 6(1). Moreover, an exception is thus created for a situation – *viz.* that of absolute discretion, if possible at all under the Rule of Law – which, also according to the Court,[619] would not be in conformity with generally recognised legal and administrative principles. But an even stronger element of uncertainty is introduced by the very vague exception for rights which the individual is not entitled to as a private person, but as a citizen:

i.e. where a special status or specific legal relations with the public institutions of the State as such are at issue (*e.g.* public service, fiscal matters, military service, immigration matters, electoral matters).[620]

From the examples given in the minority opinion it is quite clear how great an uncertainty would be built-in with this proposed distinction. Indeed, very broad categories are mentioned there, parts of which may be directly connected not only with *civil* rights and obligations, but even with *private* rights and obligations; one need only think of the family-law aspects of the immigration policy and the labour-law aspects of the position of civil servants. This uncertainty was clearly demonstrated by the *auctores intellectuales* themselves of the definition, when in the next two cases – the *Feldbrugge* Case and the *Deumeland* Case – they disagreed among each other about the application of their own definition, in consequence of which Frowein joined the majority and Melchior continued to belong to the minority. Against this background one can only hope that the

---

[616] Judgment of 23 October 1995, A.97, p. 36. In his presentation of the minority standpoint before the Court, Melchior amended the words 'any other legally permitted activity' to 'any other activity which is not absolutely prohibited by law'; Cour/Misc (85)30, p. 10.

[617] *Ibidem*, pp. 36-37.

[618] A distinction which has evoked a good deal of discussion, especially among German jurists of administrative law. See P. van Dijk, *Judicial Review of Governmental Action and the Requirement of an Interest to Sue*, Alphen a/d Rijn, 1980, pp. 178-190.

[619] Judgment of 27 October 1987, *Pudas*, A.125-A, pp. 14-15.

[620] Judgment of 23 October 1995, *Benthem*, A.97, p. 37.

Court's consideration in the *Feldbrugge* and the *Deumeland* judgments that the applicant in each of these two cases:

> was not affected in her relations with the public authorities as such, acting in the exercise of discretionary powers, but in her personal capacity as a private individual[621]

does not point to adoption by the Court of this new source of uncertainty. In the *Schouten and Meldrum* Case the Court held that:

> There may exist 'pecuniary' obligations *vis-à-vis* the State or its subordinate authorities which, for the purpose of Article 6 § 1, are to be considered as belonging exclusively to the realm of public law and are accordingly not covered by the notion of 'civil rights and obligations'. Apart from fines imposed by way of 'criminal sanction', this will be the case, in particular, where an obligation which is pecuniary in nature derives from tax legislation or is otherwise part of normal civic duties in a democratic society.[622]

As long as the meaning of the words 'normal civic duties' is not clarified, this approach does not provide clarity either. In addition, the dividing-line between 'civil' and 'non-civil' that the Court seems to draw is rather arbitrary. It is hard to understand why an obligation to pay contribution under a social security scheme is a 'civil' obligation – as the Court held in the *Schouten and Meldrum* judgment – and an obligation to pay for example wage-tax does not fall under Article 6. There exist close links between both obligations and the contract of employment of the person concerned.

In our opinion, the most satisfactory way to end legal uncertainty and maximalise effective legal protection is to recognise that the first paragraph of Article 6 is applicable to all cases in which a determination by a public authority of the legal position of a private party is at stake, regardless of whether the rights and obligations involved are of a private character.

6.2.4 Determination of a Criminal Charge

The words 'determination of (...) any criminal charge' ('*décidera (...) du bien-fondé de toute accusation en matière pénale*') also raise problems of interpretation, because on this point as well there are many differences between the legal systems of the Contracting States. Originally this induced the Commission to choose an easy way out by adopting the position that these words only apply to 'persons charged with offences under the ordinary penal code'.[623] However, this interpretation would clearly result in substantial differences in the scope of application of Article 6 in the different national legal orders, and would carry the risk of this application being eroded by the introduction of non-criminal legal norms and procedures. Therefore, here too, the adoption of an autonomous

---

[621] Judgments of 29 May 1986, A.99, p. 15, and A.100, p. 24 respectively.

[622] Judgment of 9 December 1994, A.304, p. 21.

[623] Appl. 734/60, *X v. Federal Republic of Germany*, Coll. 6 (1961), p. 29 (33). Later on, it changed its position and considered the classification under national law not decisive: report of 8 February 1973, *Huber*, Yearbook XVIII (1975), p. 326 (356).

interpretation, independent of the national legal systems, was unescapable. And indeed, in its judgment in the *Adolf* Case the Court stated with respect to 'criminal charge' in so many words:

> These expressions are to be interpreted as having an 'autonomous' meaning in the context of the Convention and not on the basis of their meaning in domestic law.[624]

6.2.5 Concept of 'Charge'

In the *Deweer* Case the Court adopted as a guideline for the autonomous interpretation of 'criminal charge', in addition to the general rule, defined in the *Delcourt* Case, 'that a restrictive interpretation of Article 6, paragraph 1 would not correspond to the aim and purpose of that provision',[625] that:

> the prominent place held in a democratic society by the right to a fair trial (...) prompts the Court to prefer a 'substantive', rather than a 'formal', conception of the 'charge' contemplated by Article 6, paragraph 1.[626]

In that same *Deweer* judgment the Court held that a 'charge' may already exist in the stage in which the prosecuting authorities make a proposal for settlement, even if that proposal is made in the framework of an inspection that is not performed within the context of the repression of crime and even if there is no notification of impending prosecution, while the settlement will prevent such prosecution.[627] On the other hand, the Commission decided on a number of occasions that the mere fact that the police are making an investigation or witnesses are being heard, or that a judicial organ makes a preliminary inquiry, does not yet mean that a 'criminal charge' exists.[628] In order to decide whether Article 6 is applicable, there is a need for clear criteria to determine if and from which moment on the person concerned is confronted with a 'charge'.

In its *Deweer* judgment the Court gave the following description of the concept of 'charge' in the sense of Article 6: 'the official notification given to an individual by the competent authority of an allegation that he has committed a criminal offence.'[629] The notification marks the beginning of the applicability of Article 6, even if it is formulated in a language which the person concerned does not understand[630] or if it did not reach him.[631]

---

[624] Judgment of 26 March 1982, A.49, p. 14. Earlier, in the same direction, judgment of 28 June 1978, *König*, A.27, pp. 29-30; judgment of 27 February 1980, *Deweer*, A.35, p. 22.

[625] Judgment of 17 January 1970, A.11, p. 15.

[626] Judgment of 27 February 1980, A.35, p. 23.

[627] *Ibidem*, pp. 22-24.

[628] Appl. 4483/70, *X v. Federal Republic of Germany*, Coll. 38 (1972), p. 77 (78-79); Appl. 4649/70, *X v. Federal Republic of Germany*, Coll. 46 (1974), p. 1 (18); Appl. 8089/77, *X v. Austria* (not published).

[629] Judgment of 27 February 1980, A.35, p. 24. See also the judgment of 15 July 1982, *Eckle*, A.51, p. 33.

[630] Judgment of 19 December 1989, *Brozicek*, A.167, pp. 18-19.

[631] Judgment of 19 February 1991, *Pugliese*, A.195-C, p. 42. For convictions *in absentia*, see the judgment of 12 February 1985, *Colozza*, A.89, p. 15.

In the *Foti* Case the Court made it clear, however, that the existence of a charge is not always dependent of an official act:

> it may in some instances take the form of other measures which carry the implication of such an allegation and which likewise substantially affect the situation of the suspect.[632]

Examples of such measures are the search of the person's home and/or the seizure of certain goods,[633] the request that a person's immunity be lifted[634] and the confirmation by the judge of the sealing of a building.[635]

The mere fact that a criminal prosecution is terminated or results in dismissal of the case does not mean that, in retrospect, Article 6 was not applicable to the procedure concerned, in particular not when the procedure has produced certain prejudicial consequences for the person who was originally accused.[636]

Article 6 is also applicable to proceedings by which a preventive detention is imposed or prolonged on the ground of an existing suspicion, although these proceedings themselves are not directed at the determination of the charge.[637]

Since the prohibition to enter a country does not amount to a criminal penalty, Article 6 cannot be applicable under the 'criminal charge' formula,[638] but may apply for other reasons, *e.g.*, when civil rights are involved. The same holds good for the removal of an illegal entrant, since the determination of a breach of the immigration regulations is not the determination of a criminal charge, and the removal not a disguised criminal penalty.[639] Finally, extradition proceedings are held, thus far, not to be covered by Article 6 on the ground that 'determination' involves the full process of the examination of an individual's guilt or innocence of an offence, and not the mere process of determining whether a person can be extradited to another country.[640]

Whether the proceedings resulting in a criminal prosecution were instituted by an individual or by a public authority is irrelevant for the applicability of Article 6.[641] However, the individual who takes the initiative to the proceedings is not himself entitled to a determination of the charge by a court; he may be entitled to the determination of his civil rights if a civil claim can be, and actually has been

---

[632] Judgment of 10 December 1982, A.56, p. 18; judgment of 21 february 1984, *Öztürk*, A.73, p. 21. See also the judgment of 19 December 1989, *Brozicek*, A.167, p. 18.

[633] Judgment of 15 July 1982, *Eckle*, A.51, pp. 33-34.

[634] Judgment of 19 February 1991, *Frau*, A.195-E, p. 73.

[635] Judgment of 18 July 1994, *Venditelli*, A.293-A, p. 10.

[636] Appl. 8269/78, *X v. Austria*, Yearbook XXII (1979), p. 324 (340-342). See also the judgment of 26 March 1982, *Adolf*, A.49, p. 16, concerning a decision that an offence was not punishable.

[637] Judgment of 28 November 1978, *Luedicke, Balkacem and Koç*, A.29, p. 20.

[638] Appl. 9593/81, *X v. Switzerland* (not published).

[639] Appl. 9174/80, *Zamir v. the United Kingdom*, D&R 29 (1982), p. 153 (163-164).

[640] Appl. 10227/82, *H v. Spain*, D&R 37 (1984), p. 94.

[641] Judgment of 25 March 1983, *Minelli*, A.62, p. 15.

submitted in the criminal proceedings.[642] On the other hand, if a third person is affected in an adverse manner in his rights by measures consequential upon the prosecution of others, no criminal charge has been brought against the former, who therefore cannot invoke the guarantees of Article 6 concerning criminal proceedings. This approach, adopted in the *Agosi* Case,[643] leads to the conclusion in the *Air Canada* Case that the seizure of an aircraft by which drugs were brought into the United Kingdom could not be considered as a 'criminal charge' brought against the airways company. The fact that the company regained the aeroplane only after it had paid an amount of £ 50,000, did not alter this conclusion.[644]

6.2.6 Concept of 'Criminal'; Disciplinary Proceedings and Administrative Sanctions

The question of whether Article 6 is also applicable to disciplinary procedures has been answered in the negative by the Commission for a long time.[645] In the *Engel* Case, however, both the Commission and the Court took the position that the character of a procedure under domestic law cannot be decisive for the question of whether Article 6 is applicable, since otherwise the national authorities would be able to evade the obligations of that provision by introducing disciplinary proceedings with respect to offences which, in view of their nature or the character of the sanction imposed, (also) form, or at any rate should form, part of criminal law.[646] As the Court stated in its judgment:

> If the Contracting States were able at their discretion to classify an offence as disciplinary instead of criminal or to prosecute an author of a mixed offence on the disciplinary rather than on the criminal plane, the operation of the fundamental clauses of Articles 6 and 7 would be subordinated to their sovereign will.[647]

For an answer to the question of whether disciplinary proceedings also imply a 'criminal charge' in the sense of Article 6 the Court in its judgment developed the following criteria.[648]

---

[642] Appl. 8366/78, *X* v. *Luxembourg*, D&R 16 (1979), p. 196 (198); Appl. 9660/82, *X* v. *France*, D&R 29 (1982), p. 241 (244).

[643] Judgment of 24 October 1986, A.108, p. 22.

[644] Judgment of 5 May 1995, A.316-A, pp. 19-20.

[645] See the case-law mentioned in the report of 19 July 1974, *Engel and Others*, B.20 (1978), pp. 68-69.

[646] *Ibidem*, p. 70 and the judgment of 8 June 1976, A.22, p. 34.

[647] Judgment of 8 June 1976, *Engel and Others*, A.22, p. 34.

[648] *Ibidem*, p. 35. The Commission, which had mentioned other criteria in its report, adopted the criteria of the Court in its later case-law: Appl. 6224/73, *Kiss* v. *the United Kingdom*, Yearbook XX (1977), p. 156 (174-176). In its report of 14 December 1981, *Albert and Le Compte*, B.50 (1986), p. 36, the Commission proposed yet a fourth criterion: the applicable rules concerning evidence. In general, in disciplinary proceedings the person concerned has no right to remain silent and no right to invoke professional secrecy. This does not, however, appear to be a correct independent criterion, since it forms a consequence of the choice made by the national legislature between criminal and disciplinary proceedings, and moreover a consequence that is detrimental to the

(a) Classification under National Law

The first criterion to be applied is the classification of the allegedly violated norm under the applicable domestic legal system. Does it belong to criminal law or to disciplinary (or administrative) law?

It has to be pointed out, however, that the autonomy of the interpretation of 'criminal charge' is a one-way autonomy[649] insofar that, whenever an offence is classified as criminal, Article 6 applies without there being room for an investigation of whether that classification is the right one according to general objective principles of criminal law. Criminalisation of certain behaviour may be reviewed for its conformity with other provisions of the Convention,[650] but its justification is not an issue under Article 6. Only if an offence is not classified as criminal, or is decriminalised, is there the danger of evasion of the guarantees of Article 6 which makes a further examination of the applicability of that provision necessary. This may require some investigation and interpretation by the Court of the relevant domestic law[651] or case-law.[652] Even if Article 6 is found to be applicable, that does not mean that the disciplinary proceedings have to be changed into criminal proceedings; the only requirement is that they meet the conditions of Article 6.

Precisely in view of this danger of evasion, if an offence has been classified as 'disciplinary' (or 'administrative') under national law, the criterion of the classification serves only as a preliminary point of departure for the ultimate assessment of the applicability of Article 6. This assessment has to be made on the basis of objective principles. For that purpose the Court has developed two other criteria.

(b) The Nature of the Offence

The second criterion relates to the scope of the violated norm and the purpose of the penalty.

The scope of the norm concerns the circle of addressees: is the norm only addressed to a specific group, or is it a norm with a generally binding character? A provision of disciplinary law only addresses persons belonging to the disciplinary system. As a starting point the circle of addressees offers a useful indication, but a certain conduct which constitutes an offence under disciplinary law may also amount to an offence under criminal law.[653] On the other hand,

---

position of the person concerned.

[649] Thus also the Court in its *Engel* judgment, A.22, p. 34.

[650] See the judgment of 22 October 1981, *Dudgeon*, A.45, pp. 23-24, where the legislation in Northern Ireland, prohibiting homosexual intercourse between consenting male persons over 21 years of age, was held to violate Article 8.

[651] Judgment of 28 June 1984, *Campbell and Fell*, A.80, p. 36; judgment of 25 March 1983, *Minelli*, A.62, p. 15.

[652] Judgment of 21 February 1984, *Öztürk*, A.73, p. 18; judgment of 27 August 1991, *Demicoli*, A.210, p. 16.

[653] Judgment of 29 April 1984, *Campbell and Fell*, A.80, p. 36.

there are several prohibitions of criminal law which can only apply to certain persons: minors or adults, parents and guardians, spouses, captains, civil servants, *etc.* Therefore, the distinguishing feature implied in this criterion is not the number of addressees, but their quality as members of a specific group, combined with the interests protected by the rule. Thus, in the *Eggs* Case the Commission took into consideration not only that the violated rule was addressed to persons belonging to the army, but also that it governed the operation of the armed forces and did not, in the particular sector of the armed forces, affect the general interests of society normally protected by criminal law.[654]

The indeterminate character of the criterion came clearly to the fore in the *Weber* Case. The applicant had filed a criminal complaint of defamation against the author of a 'reader's letter' in a newspaper. Pending the proceedings he held a press conference to inform the public about his complaint In summary proceedings he was fined for breaching the secrecy of the investigation. Since his appeal against the conviction was dismissed without public hearing, he claimed that Article 6 had been violated. The Commission had adopted the view that the violated rules were disciplinary rules and that neither the penalty imposed nor the maximum penalty could by their nature make the offence a criminal one.[655] The Court, however, made the following distinction:

> Disciplinary sanctions are generally designed to ensure that the members of particular groups comply with the specific rules governing their conduct. Furthermore, in a great majority of the Contracting States disclosure of information about an investigation still pending constitutes an act incompatible with such rules and punishable under a variety of provisions. As persons who above all others are bound by the confidentiality of an investigation, judges, lawyers and all those closely associated with the functioning of the courts are liable in such an event, independently of any criminal sanction, to disciplinary measures on account of their profession. The parties, on the other hand, only take part in the proceedings as people subject to the jurisdiction of the courts, and they therefore do not come within the disciplinary sphere of the judicial system. As Article 185 [of the relevant Swiss Code], however, potentially affects the whole population, the offence it defines, and to which it attaches a punitive sanction, is a 'criminal' one for the purposes of the second criterion.[656]

In this case, since the provision was not restricted to a group of persons in one or more specific capacities, it was not (exclusively) disciplinary in character.[657] Surprisingly, in the rather similar *Ravnsborg* Case[658] and *Putz* Case[659] the Court reached the opposite conclusion.

The purpose of the penalty as a subcriterion mainly serves to distinguish criminal sanctions from purely administrative sanctions. This subcriterion was introduced in the *Öztürk* Case to determine whether the decriminalisation of

---

[654] Appl. 7341/76, *Eggs* v. *Switzerland*, D&R 15 (1979), p. 35 (65). See also Appl. 9208/80, *Saraiva de Carvalho* v. *Portugal*, D&R 26 (1982), p. 262 (268).

[655] Report of 16 March 1989, A.177, pp. 30-32.

[656] Judgment of 22 May 1990, A.177, p. 18.

[657] See also the judgment of 27 August 1991, *Demicoli*, A.210, p. 17.

[658] Judgment of 23 March 1994, A.283-B, pp. 28-31.

[659] Judgment of 22 February 1996, Reports 1996-I, Vol. 4, paras 34-38.

certain offences under domestic law had as a consequence that Article 6 would no longer be applicable. The Court held this not to be the case as long as the sanction that could be applied had kept its 'deterrent' and 'punitive' character.[660]

Whereas the three criteria developed by the Court are not cumulative, the two subcriteria of the second criterion are; this means that for the nature of an offence which is not criminal under national law to be considered criminal in the sense of Article 6, the scope of the violated norm has to be general and the purpose of the sanction has to be deterrent and punitive.[661]

(c) The Nature and Severity of the Penalty

The third, and in many cases decisive criterion is that of the nature and the severity of the penalty with which the violator of the norm is threatened.

The element of the 'nature' of the penalty should not be confused with that of the 'purpose' of the penalty, discussed under the second criterion.[662] If the purpose of the sanction does not make the second criterion applicable, because the scope of the violated norm is not of a general character, the nature and severity of the penalty may still make Article 6 applicable.[663] On the other hand, if, on the basis of the second criterion – the nature of the offence – the proceedings must be deemed to be of a criminal character, the nature and severity of the penalty are not relevant anymore; the two criteria are alternative and not cumulative.[664]

As far as the nature of the penalty is concerned, the case-law shows that imprisonment is considered to be the criminal penalty *par excellence* and, therefore, gives an otherwise disciplinary or administrative procedure a criminal character to such an extent that Article 6 must be held applicable. It goes without saying that the same holds good *a fortiori* for capital punishment; Article 6 no doubt applies to the court proceedings to which Article 2(1) refers. And the same

---

[660] Judgment of 21 February 1984, A.73, p. 53. See also the judgment of 25 August 1987, *Lutz*, A.123, pp. 25-26; judgment of 22 May 1990, *Weber*, A.177, p. 18; judgment of 27 August 1991, *Demicoli*, A.210, p. 17.

[661] Thus Viering, *supra* note 527, p. 178.

[662] That the Court brings the element of the purpose of the sanction under the second rather than the third criterion is clear from the *Weber* judgment, A.177, p. 18: 'As article 185, however, potentially affects the whole population, the offence it defines, and to which it attaches a punitive sanction is a "criminal" one for the purposes of the second criterion.'

[663] Judgment of 8 June 1976, *Engel and Others*, A.22, p. 36; judgment of 22 May 1990, *Weber*, A.177, p. 18; judgment of 27 August 1991, *Demicoli*, A.210, p. 17.

[664] Judgment of 21 February 1984, *Öztürk*, A.73, p. 21; judgment of 25 August 1987, *Lutz*, A.123-A, p. 23. One might deduct on strict logical grounds from the *Bendenoun* judgment (judgment of 24 February 1994, A.284, p. 27) that the Court changed its case-law on this point. However, we believe that this is not the case since the judgment of the Court was given by a Chamber of the Court and not by the Grand Chamber, which indicates that the Chamber did not think its judgment to be inconsistent with previous case-law (see Rule 51 of the Rules of the Court). Moreover, in the *Ravnsborg* Case, judgment of 23 March 1994, A.283-B, p. 28, the Court took into account 'the three alternative criteria'. The Court explained its *Bendenoun* judgment in its judgment of 24 September 1997, *Garyfallou AEBE* (not yet published), para. 33. See also the judgment of 22 February 1996, *Putz*, Reports 1996-I, Vol. 4, para. 33.

would be true for any corporal punishment, if such punishment would be allowed under Article 3.[665] Thus, in the *Engel* Case, although the Court reached the conclusion that the offences at issue were against norms regulating the functioning of the Dutch armed forces, so that they could justly form the object of disciplinary procedures, it held that, since for some of these offences an imprisonment of considerable duration could be imposed, the conditions of Article 6(1) ought to have been observed in the disciplinary procedures in question.[666]

This judgment makes it clear, first of all, that in the opinion of the Court not every limitation of liberty is a deprivation of liberty. As in the case of Article 5,[667] whether a limitation of liberty meets the requirements of a deprivation depends on the factual conditions.[668] Moreover, the deprivation of liberty must be 'liable to be imposed as a punishment',[669] which excludes deprivations of liberty such as civil imprisonment, the detention of mentally ill people, or the detention of aliens with a view of deportation or expulsion. In the *Kiss* Case, which concerned disciplinary measures against a prisoner, the Commission arrived at a negative opinion as to the applicability of Article 6, because it did not consider the possible penalty, loss of the prospect of reduction of the penalty, a deprivation of liberty.[670] However, in the *Campbell and Fell* Case, where the procedure could have resulted in refusal of remission of part of the imprisonment, the Court held that the practice of remission of the penalty creates for the detainee the justifiable expectation that he will be released before the end of the detention period. The procedure might therefore, in the Court's opinion, have such serious consequences for the person concerned as to the duration of his detention that it was to be considered of a criminal character.[671] In its decision concerning *X* v. *Switzerland* the Commission came to the conclusion that isolated confinement of a person who is already detained, as a penalty for late return from leave of absence, is a purely disciplinary matter, for which the procedural guarantees prescribed in Article 6(1) need not be complied with.[672] The Commission here took into consideration that for a person already deprived of his liberty such a confinement is not of such a 'severity' as meant by the Court.

The *Engel* judgment also makes it clear that not every deprivation of liberty

---

[665] In its judgment of 25 April 1978, *Tyrer*, A.26, pp. 15-17, the Court held that the punishment of birching, as practised on the Isle of Man to boys between 10 and 17 years old for certain offences, was 'degrading' and therefore in violation of Article 3.

[666] Judgment of 8 June 1976, A.22, p. 36.

[667] See *supra* pp. 345-348.

[668] In the *Engel* Case the Commission and the Court differed of opinion as far as the penalty of 'aggravated arrest' was concerned. For its opinion that no deprivation of liberty was at issue, the Court held it to be decisive that, although under that regime the soldiers, in off-duty hours, had to serve the arrest in a specially designated place which they were not allowed to leave for recreation purposes, they were not 'kept under lock and key'; A.22, p. 26.

[669] *Ibidem*, p. 35.

[670] Appl. 6224/73, *Kiss* v. *the United Kingdom*, Yearbook XX (1977), p. 156 (176).

[671] Judgment of 28 June 1984, A.80, pp. 37-38.

[672] Appl. 7754/77, D&R 11 (1978), p. 216 (218).

renders Article 6 applicable. Its effects on the person concerned must be of a certain severity, *inter alia*, due to its duration. Thus, although the 'strict arrest' was held a deprivation,[673] in this case the maximum duration of two days was considered insufficient by the Court for it to be regarded as a criminal penalty,[674] whereas the Court took a different position with regard to the detention of some months to which the applicants De Wit, Dona and Schul could have been sentenced.[675] The relevant duration is the maximum penalty that *may* be imposed by the authority which is called upon to determine the charge; that is to say not the penalty actually imposed but the maximum that the person concerned risked when committing the offence is decisive in this respect, even if practice shows that this maximum is seldom, if ever, imposed.[676]

On the ground of the duration criterion, the Commission held in the *Eggs* Case, which also concerned a case of military discipline and in which the penalty imposed was five days of strict arrest in a civil prison:

> Although relatively harsh, this freedom-restricting penalty could not, either by its duration or by the conditions of its enforcement in Basle prison, have caused serious detriment to the applicant. It could not, therefore, in this case be classified as criminal.[677]

These elements of duration and conditions of enforcement as indications of the seriousness of the consequences of the penalty, make the third criterion a rather unpredictable one as long as fixed standards are lacking. In our opinion, it would be desirable and create the required clarity if the third criterion were applied in such a way that in any case where the penalty may consist of a deprivation of liberty in the sense assigned thereto in the case-law concerning Article 5, the guarantees of Article 6 should be observed in the procedure that may result in such a deprivation.[678]

In the *McFeeley* Case, which concerned IRA prisoners, the Commission took the position that for the determination of the severity of the penalty the cumulative effect of repeatedly imposed penalties should not be taken into account, because for the applicability of Article 6 each sentence must be considered by itself.[679]

---

[673] Judgment of 8 June 1976, *Engel and Others*, A.22, p. 26.

[674] *Ibidem*, p. 36.

[675] *Idem*.

[676] After some unclarity this is standing case-law: judgment of 22 May 1990, *Weber*, A.177, p. 18: 'that the fine could amount to ...'; judgment of 27 August 1991, *Demicoli*, A.210, p. 17.

[677] Report of 4 March 1978, D&R 15 (1979), p. 35 (65).

[678] Thus judge Cremona in his separate opinion in the *Engel* Case, A.22, pp. 52-53. In its report in the *Albert and Le Compte* Case the Commission indeed observed quite generally with regard to a certain disciplinary measure: 'it cannot be treated as being equivalent to a penal sanction, such as the deprivation of liberty'; report of 14 December 1981, B.50 (1986), p. 35. In its decision on Appl. 8209/78, *Sutter v. Switzerland*, D&R 16 (1979), p. 166 (173), the Commission also argued quite generally: 'The applicant was charged with an offence under the Military Penal Code, punishable by imprisonment, and therefore he was undoubtedly accused of a criminal offence'. Also in a general sense: report of 6 May 1981, *Minelli*, B.52 (1986), p. 21.

[679] Appl. 8317/78, D&R 20 (1980), p. 44 (94).

This position seems to have been confirmed by the Court in the *Ravnsborg* Case[680] and *Putz* Case.[681] In our opinion this position leads to unsatisfactory results. In fact, although the view of the Strasbourg organs is formally correct, it may have the consequence that without any intervention of a court a person may be subjected to restrictions which in combination amount to a much heavier burden for him than the sanction which in a separate case would be of sufficient duration to confer a criminal-law character on the procedure. The question arises whether, if the duration criterion is appropriate at all in cases of deprivation of liberty, one ought not to seek a certain analogy here with the Court's case-law concerning Article 5(3), where, for the determination of the reasonableness of the period, also successive periods of detention for various charges are taken into account together,[682] so that the total situation in which the person finds himself is taken as the frame of reference, and not the separate measures taken against him.

The fact that Article 6 also applies to legal persons raises the issue whether 'deprivation of liberty' of a legal person may also make Article 6 applicable. In its report in the *Kaplan* Case the Commission held that the restrictions imposed by administrative measures on the activities of the company did not concern a 'criminal charge', because these restrictions did not fall into the category of criminal sanctions.[683]

It has also not yet been clarified in the case-law if and to what extent other disciplinary penalties than deprivations of liberty may be considered severe enough to make Article 6 applicable. In its decision in *X* v. *Belgium*, concerning a disciplinary reprimand *vis-à-vis* a solicitor the Commission gave as its opinion that 'the sanction imposed was intrinsically not a severe one', creating the impression that it was the severity and not so much the character of the sanction which was considered decisive.[684] And in its decision in *X* v. *Austria* the Commission, in fact, took into consideration the amount of fines which the applicant risked, in addition to the length of the detention. The Commission concluded that:

> the sanctions which the applicant had to face in this case attained the level of severity which, according to the common standard of the Convention States, must be considered as being proper to 'criminal charges' in the sense of the Convention.[685]

It is, however, this 'common standard' which is not clear and has not yet sufficiently developed in the Strasbourg case-law. In the *Weber* Case, which concerned proceedings where the fine could amount to 500 Swiss francs and could be converted into a term of imprisonment in certain circumstances, the Court held,

---

[680] Judgment of 23 March 1994, A.283-B, p. 31.

[681] Judgment of 22 February 1996, Reports 1996-I, Vol. 4, para. 37.

[682] Judgment of 27 June 1968, *Neumeister*, A.8, p. 37; judgment of 16 July 1971, *Ringeisen*, A.13, pp. 41-42.

[683] Report of 17 July 1980, D&R 21 (1981), p. 5 (35).

[684] Appl. 8249/78, D&R 20 (1980), p. 40 (42).

[685] Appl. 8998/80, D&R 32 (1983), p. 150 (153).

with a general reference to its third criterion and without further reasoning, that what was at stake was 'sufficiently important to warrant classifying the offence as a criminal one under the Convention',[686] leaving it unclear to what extent the fact that the fine could be converted into imprisonment was decisive. The same unclarity was left in the *Demicoli* judgment.[687] The more recent *Ravnsborg* Case, *Schmautzer* Case and *Putz* Case seem to make it even more difficult to fathom the Court's case-law on this point. In the *Ravnsborg* Case the imposed maximum fine of 1000 Swedish crowns did not make the sanction a 'criminal' one. In addition to the amount the Court took into account that the fine was not registered in the police records and that conversion into a term of imprisonment could only take place if a special procedure, including an oral hearing, was followed.[688] This term of imprisonment amounted at least two weeks. In the subsequent *Schmautzer* Case the Court held that driving without wearing a safety-belt, an administrative offence under Austrian law, was criminal in nature. It used as an additional argument that the imposed fine (of 200 Austrian schillings) had been accompanied by an order for committal to prison in case of non-payment. The maximum term of imprisonment was 24 hours.[689] In the *Putz* Case, however, the Court held with reference to its reasoning in the *Ravensborg* Case that a possible maximum penalty of 20.000 Austrian schillings, that could have been converted into a term of imprisonment of ten days, did not come within the ambit of Article 6.[690]

Outside the sphere of disciplinary proceedings, with respect to 'fiscal penalties', the Court has adopted the position that those penalties which are not compensatory in nature, but are of a punitive character, such as fines and disqualification, give the proceedings a criminal character for the purposes of Article 6.[691] In our opinion the same approach should be followed with respect to disciplinary penalties: if they are of a clearly punitive character which makes them similar to criminal sanctions as to their nature and effect, there would seem to be no convincing reason why their imposition should not, in the final resort, be subjected to a judicial review that fulfils the requirements of Article 6.

---

[686] Judgment of 22 May 1990, A.177, p. 18.

[687] Judgment of 27 August 1991, A.210, p. 17.

[688] Judgment of 23 March 1994, A.283-B, p. 31.

[689] Judgment of 23 October 1995, A.328-A, p. 13, *juncto* pp. 8-9. See also, of the same date, five other cases against Austria: *Umlauft*, A.328-B; *Gradinger*, A.328-C; *Pramstaller*, A.329-A; *Palaoro* A.329-B, *Pfarrmeier*, A.329-C. In these cases the imposed fines varied from 5,000 Austrian schillings (in the event of defaulting of payment 200 hours of imprisonment) in the *Pfarrmeier* Case till 50,000 schillings (fifty days of imprisonment) in the *Pramstaller* Case. The maximum penalties that could have been imposed varied from 300 (24 hours of imprisonment) in the *Pfarrmeier* Case till 100,000 schilling (three months of imprisonment) in the *Pramstaller* Case.

[690] Judgment of 22 February 1996, Reports 1996-I, Vol. 4, para. 37.

[691] Judgment of 7 October 1988, *Salabiaku*, A.141-A, p. 14.

6.2.7 Decriminalisation and 'Petty Offences'

For a long time there has been a lack of clarity as to whether Article 6 applies to all criminal proceedings, even when offences of a less serious nature are concerned.[692] Since Article 6 does not distinguish between criminal charges of a serious and those of a less serious nature, and the determination of a criminal charge concerning a petty offence may be of great importance for the person in question, all proceedings in which there is question of a determination of a criminal charge should fall under the guarantees of Article 6.

This view has been adopted by the Court. In the *Adolf* Case, in which a petty offence was involved, which on that ground was declared non-punishable, the Court held:

non-punishable or unpunished criminal offences do exist and Article 6 of the Convention does not distinguish between them and other criminal offences; it applies whenever a person is 'charged' with any criminal offence.[693]

And in the *Öztürk* Case the Court held:

There is in fact nothing to suggest that the criminal offence referred to in the Convention necessarily implies a certain degree of seriousness (...). Furthermore, it would be contrary to the object and purpose of Article 6, which guarantees to 'everyone charged with a criminal offence' the right to a court and to a fair trial, if the State were allowed to remove from the scope of this Article a whole category of offences merely on the ground of regarding them as petty.[694]

The Court indicated in the *Öztürk* Case that it does not conflict with the Convention to distinguish between different categories of offences, but that such a classification is not decisive for the question whether Article 6 is applicable.[695] In this case an offence was involved which was not qualified under German law as a criminal but as a 'regulatory' offence: an *Ordnungswidrigkeit*. Quite in line with its previous case-law concerning Article 6 the Court, here again, is on its guard against erosion of the guarantees aimed at in that article:

if the Contracting States were able at their discretion, by classifying an offence as 'regulatory' instead of criminal, to exclude the operation of the fundamental clauses of Articles 6 and 7, the application of these provisions would be subordinated to their sovereign will. A latitude extending thus far might lead to results incompatible with the object and purpose of the Convention.[696]

Consequently, it remains decisive whether the nature of the offence, and that of the sanction that may be imposed, confer a criminal character on the proceedings,

---

[692] See Appl. 8537/79, *X v. Federal Republic of Germany* (not published).

[693] Judgment of 26 March 1982, A.49, p. 16.

[694] Judgment of 21 February 1984, A.73, p. 21. See also the report of 18 October 1985, *Lutz*, A.123, p. 33 and judgment of 29 April 1988, *Belilos*, A.132, p. 28.

[695] *Ibidem*, pp. 17-18.

[696] *Ibidem*, p. 18.

irrespective of whether formally they still have that character under domestic law.[697]

6.2.8 A Punitive Sanction Makes the Charge 'Criminal'

As in the case of 'civil rights and obligations' the Court should lift the uncertainty and ambiguity with respect to 'criminal charge' which its case-law has left, especially concerning the criterion of the nature and severity of the penalty. As to the nature of the penalty, in our opinion Article 6 should be held to be applicable in all those proceedings which may result in the imposition of a punitive sanction that as to its nature and/or its consequences is so similar to criminal sanctions that there is no justification of excluding judicial review, except by free and unambiguous waiver. This would include in particular deprivations of liberty and fines, but could also concern restrictions of economic or professional freedom of a punitive character (which, moreover, could affect civil rights and obligations).

As far as the severity of the penalty is concerned, it is submitted that, since the Court has adopted the position that Article 6 makes no distinction between serious and less serious offences and that it may even apply to proceedings which lead to no penalty at all, there would seem to be no convincing reason to distinguish between detentions of short and of longer duration and between fines of a small and of a large amount for the applicability of Article 6 to disciplinary and administrative proceedings; after all, if the severity of the penalty is not a decisive element for the applicability of Article 6 in case there exists a 'criminal charge', it should also not be determinant for the question whether certain proceedings have criminal features which make Article 6 applicable.

6.3 Access to Court

6.3.1 Introduction

Article 6(1) not only contains procedural guarantees in relation to judicial proceedings, but also grants a right to judicial proceedings for the cases mentioned in this article: the right of access to court. This right has not been laid down in express terms in Article 6. Its first paragraph only refers to entitlement to a fair and public hearing by a court, leaving it unclear whether this entitlement only exists in cases where judicial proceedings have been provided for under domestic law, or implies – or rather presupposes – a right to such judicial proceedings. This unclarity was lifted by the Court in its *Golder* judgment. There the Court held that Article 6 must be read in the light of the following two legal principles: (1) the principle whereby a civil claim must be capable of being submitted to a judge, as

---

[697] The criteria handled by the Court in such a case have been set forth at length in the *Öztürk* judgment, *ibidem*, pp. 17-22. In its judgment of 25 August 1987, *Lutz*, A.123, p. 23, the Court indicates that these criteria are alternative, and not cumulative.

one of the universally recognised fundamental principles of law; and (2) the principle of international law which forbids the denial of justice:[698]

> Taking all the preceding considerations together, it follows that the right of access constitutes an element which is inherent in the right stated by Article 6, paragraph 1. This is not an extensive interpretation forcing new obligations on the Contracting States: it is based on the very terms of the first sentence of Article 6, paragraph 1 read in its context and having regard to the object and purpose of the Convention, a lawmaking treaty (..), and to general principles of law.[699]

The right of access is not dependent on whether the domestic legal system in question provides for a judicial procedure for the case concerned; indeed, if the latter is not the case, it constitutes a violation of Article 6.[700] Accordingly, Article 6(1) also applies to cases where domestic law traditionally does not provide for judicial review.[701] With this extensive, teleological interpretation the Court wanted to prevent the erosion of the guarantees of Article 6, which might well occur if in the Contracting States judicial review in some fields would be restricted or even eliminated, and in other fields its introduction would be omitted.[702]

When interpreted in this way, paragraph 1 of Article 6 to a considerable extent takes over the function of Article 13, which guarantees a right to an effective remedy. Article 6 goes much further, because it implies a right of recourse to a *court* and applies to all determinations of civil rights and obligations, and not only to those which are related to one of the rights laid down in the Convention. However, at least for the time being, Article 13 remains important for cases of violation of rights which according to the Strasbourg case-law are not 'civil rights' in the sense of Article 6(1).[703]

The right of access has its full meaning only if the court concerned has full jurisdiction to determine the case brought before it. This means that the court must have competence to judge both on the facts and on the law as a basis of its 'determination'.[704] However, in the *Bryan* Case the Court has chosen a less strict approach. The Court relied on the fact that town and country planning is a specialised area of the law, on the safeguards surrounding the quasi-judicial procedure prior to the court proceedings and held that the power of the national

---

[698] Judgment of 21 February 1975, A.18, pp. 17-18.

[699] *Ibidem*, p. 18. See, however, the dissenting opinion of judge Fitzmaurice, *ibidem*, p. 54.

[700] Judgment of 21 February 1975, *Golder*, A.18, pp. 13-18; judgment of 23 June 1981, *Le Compte, Van Leuven and De Meyere*, A.43, pp. 20-23.

[701] This was the case, *e.g.*, with the Crown appeal proceedings in the Netherlands: judgment of 23 October 1985, *Benthem*, A.97, p. 18.

[702] See the judgment of 21 February 1975, *Golder*, A.18, pp. 17-18.

[703] Thus the Court in its judgment of 21 February 1975, *Golder*, A.18, p. 16.

[704] Judgment of 23 June 1981, *Le Compte, Van Leuven and De Meyere*, A.43, p. 23; judgment of 10 February 1983, *Albert and Le Compte*, A.58, p. 18; judgment of 21 September 1993, *Zumtobel*, A.268-A, pp. 13-14 and judgment of 26 April 1995, *Fisher*, A.312, p. 17. See also judgment of 23 October 1995, *Umlauft*, A.328-B, pp. 39-40.

court had been sufficient to comply with Article 6, although the court's jurisdiction over the facts had been limited.[705]

6.3.2 Access to Court; 'Civil' Cases

The right of access to court means that the person concerned not only has a right to apply to a court for the determination of his rights or obligations and to present his case properly and satisfactory,[706] but – as mentioned before – also has a right to it that there is an independent and impartial court to make this determination; otherwise his right of access is not secured.[707] In addition, that court must have the required jurisdiction to make the determination. Thus, in the cases of *W, B* and *R* v. *the United Kingdom* the Court held that, although the parents could apply for judicial review or institute wardship proceedings and thereby have certain aspects of the authority's access decisions examined by an English court, during the currency of the parental resolutions the court's powers were not of sufficient scope to fully satisfy the requirements of Article 6(1), as they did not extend to the merits of the matter.[708] And in the *Obermeier* Case the Court held that there had been a violation of the right of access to court, since the court in question could only determine whether the administrative authorities had exercised their discretionary power in a way compatible with the object and purpose of the applicable law.[709]

In the *Airey* Case it was held that the right of access to court of the first paragraph of Article 6, although it does not imply an automatic right to free legal aid in civil proceedings, *does* involve the obligation for the Contracting States to make access to court possible and effective. This may compel the State to provide for the assistance of a lawyer when this proves indispensable for an effective access to court, either because legal representation is rendered compulsory or by reason of the procedural complexity of the case. The State may also, if appropriate and possible, opt for abolition of compulsory representation and simplification of procedure to the effect that effective access to the court no longer requires a lawyer's assistance.[710]

In an unpublished decision of 1982, the Commission concluded that, although it was recognised that the intended action would require the assistance of a lawyer, the refusal of legal aid did not constitute a denial of access to court, since the

---

[705] Judgment of 22 November 1995, A.335-A, pp. 17-18.

[706] Judgment of 9 October 1979, *Airey*, A.32, p. 13.

[707] Judgment of 23 June 1981, *Le Compte, Van Leuven and De Meyere*, A.43, p. 20; judgment of 23 September 1982, *Sporrong and Lönroth*, A.52, p. 29; judgment of 28 May 1985, *Ashingdane*, A.93, p. 24.

[708] Judgments of 8 July 1987, A.121, pp. 35-36, 79-80 and 125-126 respectively.

[709] Judgment of 28 June 1990, A.179, pp. 22-23.

[710] Judgment of 9 October 1979, A.32, pp. 15-16. See also Appl. 8158/78, *X* v. *the United Kingdom*, D&R 21 (1981), p. 95 (101), and Appl. 9353/81, *Webb* v. *the United Kingdom*, D&R 33 (1983), p. 133 (138-141), where the Commission made an independent investigation in the complexity of the case, the supporting evidence, *etc.*, to assess the need of legal assistance.

argument given by the Swedish authorities for the refusal, *viz.* that the applicant did not have a justified interest to have her case treated, was not arbitrary.[711] This would put the decision on the justified interest in the hands of an authority other than the court, while the right of access to court precisely requires the opposite. In our opinion, if such a practice were accepted in cases where access to court is only possible through counsel, the very essence of the right of access to court might be impaired, to use a phrase from the *Ashingdane* and *Lithgow* judgments.[712]

In the *Golder* Case the Court attached to its view that Article 6 implies a right of access to court and that 'hindering the effective exercise of a right may amount to a breach of that right, even if the hindrance is of a temporary character', the consequence that a refusal to permit detainees to correspond with persons providing legal aid or their counsel is contrary to this provision.[713] Moreover, the detainee has a right to contact with counsel or a person giving legal aid without the presence of a prison authority.[714]

6.3.3 Access to Court; 'Criminal' Cases

For criminal cases, and for cases with certain criminal features which make Article 6 applicable, the right of access to court implies that the person who is 'charged' has a claim that his case is dealt with by a court which fulfils the requirements of Article 6. It does not imply that the person 'charged' may demand the continuation of the prosecution and an ultimate trial by a court, but only that, when a 'determination of the charge' is made, this is done by a court.[715] However, if the charge is dropped on the basis of a financial transaction between the accused and the prosecuting authority, without there being question of a free choice on the part of the accused, he is actually denied access to court contrary to Article 6.[716] And if the case is dropped under circumstances in which the odium of guilt would continue to cling to the person in question, Article 6 has nevertheless been violated; this also in the light of the presumption of innocence of the second paragraph.[717]

---

[711] Appl. 9649/82, *X v. Sweden* (not published).

[712] Judgment of 28 May 1985, A.93, pp. 24-25; judgment of 8 July 1986, A.102, p. 71.

[713] Judgment of 21 February 1975, A.18, pp. 12-20. See also the report of 11 October 1980, *Silver*, B.51 (1987), pp. 100-101; judgment of 28 June 1984, *Campbell and Fell*, A.80, pp. 46-47; the report of 3 December 1985, *Byrne, McFadden, McCluskey and McLarnon*, D&R 51 (1987), p. 5 (15).

[714] Judgment of 28 June 1984, *Campbell and Fell*, A.80, p. 49.

[715] Report of 18 October 1985, *Lutz*, A.123, p. 35.

[716] Judgment of 27 February 1980, *Deweer*, A.35, pp. 25-29. In this case the person in question was subject to the threat that his shop would be closed if he did not agree to the transaction.

[717] Judgment of 25 March 1983, *Minelli*, A.62, pp. 17-18. See, however, the judgment of 26 March 1996, *Leutscher*, Reports 1996-II, Vol. 6, paras 30-32, where the applicant had been tried at first instance *in absentia*, but the court of appeal had declared the prosecution time-barred and subsequently refused to order the reimbursement of the legal costs of the applicant and *infra* p. 463.

The right of access to court does not imply the right for the victim of a criminal offence to institute himself criminal proceedings or to claim prosecution by the public prosecutor.[718]

Against the background of the Court's judgment in the *Airey* Case concerning 'effective' access,[719] the Commission's view that the fact of excessive costs being involved for the accused in taking evidence does not imply a violation of Article 6 had to be modified.[720] It did so in an unpublished decision of 1984, where the Commission concluded that in certain circumstances the high costs could raise a problem under Article 6(1).[721] And the statement in the *Golder* judgment, referred to above,[722] that the right of access to court implies the right of free correspondence and consultations in private with a lawyer, also holds good for criminal cases, to the extent that this guarantee does not already follow from the third paragraph under (b). Moreover, the right of (effective) access to court may also play a role in assessing whether free legal aid should have been granted under paragraph 3(c)[723] and whether the State should be held responsible for a manifest failure by a legal aid counsel to provide effective representation.[724]

6.3.4 (Access to) Judicial Appeal Proceedings and the Application of Article 6

Appeal to a higher court constitutes a domestic remedy that has to be previously exhausted according to Article 26. And, indeed, an appeal court may remedy the fact that the proceedings before the lower court were not in conformity with Article 6 in all respects.[725] Nonetheless, the right of appeal to a higher court is not laid down and is also not implied in Article 6(1).[726] However, if appeal is provided for and has been lodged and the court in that instance is called to make a 'determination', the first paragraph of Article 6 applies.[727] This is deemed not to be the case, for instance, when appeal is lodged with a constitutional court and concerns exclusively the constitutionality of the previous judicial decision; that

---

[718] Judgment of 29 October 1991, *Helmers*, A.212-A, p. 14. See also Appl. 6224/73, *Kiss* v. *the United Kingdom*, Yearbook XX (1977), p. 156 (178-180); Appl. 9777/82, *T* v. *Belgium*, D&R 34 (1983), p. 158 (171-172).

[719] Judgment of 9 October 1979, A.32.

[720] Case 1982/63, *X* v. *Austria* (not published).

[721] Appl. 9379/81, *X* v. *Switzerland* (not published).

[722] *Supra* p. 421.

[723] Judgment of 28 March 1990, *Granger*, A.174, pp. 17-19.

[724] Judgment of 19 December 1989, *Kamasinski*, A.168, p. 33.

[725] Judgment of 16 December 1992, *Edwards*, A.247-B, p. 35.

[726] Judgment of 23 July 1968, *Belgian Linguistic Case*, A.6, p. 33; judgment of 17 January 1970, *Delcourt*, A.11, p. 14.

[727] Judgment of 17 January 1970, *Delcourt*, A.11, pp. 14-15; judgment of 22 February 1984, *Sutter*, A.74, p. 13; judgment of 29 May 1986, *Deumeland*, A.100, p. 26; judgment of 2 March 1987, *Monnell and Morris*, A.115, p. 21; judgment of 26 May 1988, *Ekbatani*, A.134, p. 12; judgment of 19 December 1989, *Kamasinki*, A.168, p. 44; judgment of 28 August 1991, *F.C.B.*, A.208-B, pp. 20-22; judgment of 22 April 1992, *Vidal*, A.235-B, pp. 31-33; judgment of 12 October 1992, *C.-T* v. *Italy*, A.245-C, pp. 41-42; judgment of 16 December 1992, *Hadjianastassiou*, A.252, pp. 15-17; judgment of 23 November 1993, *Poitrimol*, A.277-A, pp. 13-15.

phase then does not concern a full 'determination',[728] unless there is a 'close link between the subject-matter' of the proceedings before the constitutional court and that of the proceedings which led to the referral of the matter to the constitutional court.[729] If Article 6 is applicable, the specific characteristics of the appeal proceedings in question must be taken into account.[730] Thus, for instance, it must be examined whether the requirement of publicity of the trial in appeal proceedings[731] and in cassation proceedings[732] still has the same fundamental importance.

The Commission has concluded a few times that Article 6 was not applicable to proceedings in which a decision is taken about leave of appeal, for instance the procedure in which three judges of the *Bundesverfassungsgericht* take a decision about the admission of a *Verfassungsbeschwerde*.[733] It is disputable, however, whether this view is correct in its generality, since in these proceedings a negative decision may also be based on the manifestly ill-founded nature of the appeal, so that there may indeed be a 'determination'.[734] A more correct view was adopted by the Commission in the *Monnell and Morris* Case, in which Article 6 was deemed to be applicable on account of the close connection of the decision about admission of the appeal with the merits of the appeal proceedings themselves, and because these preliminary proceedings might already lead to an extension of the detention.[735]

In some legal systems the person who has been convicted at first instance, but for whom some remedies against this sentence are still available, is no longer regarded as one against whom a charge is pending, but as a convicted person, so that in such a case, strictly speaking, Article 6 would not be applicable. However, in the *Delcourt* Case, in which the Court stressed the desirability of an extensive interpretation of Article 6, it held that the charge has not yet been determined in the sense of Article 6(1) as long as the verdict of acquittal or conviction has not become final.[736] This means on the one hand that, although for criminal cases, too, Article 6 does not grant a right of appeal[737] – Protocol No. 7 contains a

---

[728] Judgment of 22 October 1984, *Sramek*, A.84, p. 17.

[729] Judgment of 23 June 1993, *Ruiz-Mateos*, A.262, p. 24.

[730] Judgment of 17 January 1970, *Delcourt*, A.11, p. 15; judgment of 25 April 1983, *Pakelli*, A.64, p. 14; judgment of 8 December 1983, *Pretto and Others*, A.71, p. 12; judgment of 28 March 1990, *Granger*, A.174, pp. 17-19.

[731] Judgment of 26 May 1988, *Ekbatani*, A.134, p. 13; judgments of 29 October 1991, *Helmers*; *Andersson*; and *Fejde*, A.212-A, pp. 16-17, 45-46 and 68-70 respectively.

[732] Judgment of 22 February 1984, *Sutter*, A.74, p. 13.

[733] Appl. 9508/81, *X* v. *Federal Republic of Germany* (not published). See also Appl. 6916/75, *X, Y and Z* v. *Sweden*, D&R 6 (1977), p. 107 (111-112); Appl. 10663/83, *X* v. *Denmark* (not published).

[734] *Cf.* also the report of 15 March 1985, *Adler*, D&R 46 (1986), p. 36 (44-45).

[735] Report of 11 March 1986, A.115, p. 36, followed by the Court in its judgment of 2 March 1987, *ibidem*, p. 21.

[736] Judgment of 17 January 1970, A.11, pp. 14-15.

[737] *Idem*.

provision about this in Article 2 for those States which have ratified that Protocol[738] – the proceedings in appeal and in cassation do form part of the 'determination', and therefore must equally satisfy the minimum standard laid down in Article 6.[739] The fact that the court of cassation in its investigation is confined to the legal grounds on which the lower court has based its sentence does not alter this,[740] no more than the circumstance that in some cases appeal and cassation no longer relate to the validity of the criminal prosecution as such, but exclusively to the penalty imposed.[741] On the other hand, procedures in which a decision is taken on requests for conditional release, revision, pardon or mitigation of penalty are not covered by Article 6, since in those cases there is a sentence which has acquired the force of *res judicata*.[742] However, in the case of a revocation of a conditional release there is question of 'determination of a criminal charge' in the sense of Article 6(1), because such a procedure may result in a renewed imposition of a penalty.[743] And in the above-mentioned cases Article 6(1) *is* of course applicable again if they simultaneously involve civil rights or obligations.[744]

6.3.5 In what Stage of the Proceedings is There a Right of Access to Court?

In its judgment in the *Le Compte, Van Leuven and De Meyere* Case the Court held that Article 6(1) does not prescribe the Contracting States:

> to submit '*contestations*' (disputes) over 'civil rights and obligations' to a procedure conducted at each of its stages before 'tribunals' meeting the Article's various requirements. Demands of flexibility and efficiency, which are fully compatible with the protection of human rights, may justify the prior intervention of administrative or professional bodies and, *a fortiori*, of judicial bodies which do not satisfy the said requirements in every respect.[745]

In the *Albert and Le Compte* Case the Court elucidated this as follows:

---

[738] In September 1997 this was the case for Albania, Austria, the Czech Republic, Denmark, Estonia, Finland, France, Greece, Hungary, Iceland, Italy, Latvia, Lithuania, Luxembourg, Moldova, Norway, Romania, San Marino, Slovakia, Sweden, Switzerland, Ukraine and the former Yugoslav Republic of Macedonia.

[739] Judgment of 17 January 1970, A.11, p. 14.

[740] *Ibidem*, pp. 13-14; judgment of 22 February 1984, *Sutter*, A.74, p. 13.

[741] Appl. 4623/70, *X* v. *the United Kingdom*, Yearbook XV (1972), p. 376 (394-396).

[742] Appl. 1760/63, *X* v. *Austria*, Yearbook IX (1966), p. 166 (174), and the case-law mentioned there. See also Appl. 9813/82, *X* v. *the United Kingdom* (not published), concerning a change of prison location, and Appl. 10733/84, *Asociación De Aviadores de La República, Mata* et al. v. *Spain*, D&R 41 (1985), p. 211 (224): a decision concerning an amnesty after conviction does not determine a 'criminal charge'.

[743] Appl. 4036/69, *X* v. *the United Kingdom*, Coll. 32 (1970), p. 73 (75).

[744] Thus implicitly also the Commission: Appl. 1760/63, *X* v. *Austria*, Yearbook IX (1966), p. 166 (174).

[745] Judgment of 23 June 1981, A.43, p. 23.

in such circumstances the Convention calls at least for one of the two following systems: either the jurisdictional organs themselves comply with the requirements of Article 6, paragraph 1, or they do not so comply but are subject to subsequent control by a judicial body that has full jurisdiction and does provide the guarantees of Article 6, paragraph 1.[746]

This means that, for instance, the situation in which appeal against administrative action lies with an administrative body, does not conflict with Article 6, also not if the appeal proceedings amount to a determination of civil rights and obligations or a criminal charge, provided that there is in the last resort the possibility of review by a court. It was precisely that last requirement which, in the opinion of the Court, had not been fulfilled in the Dutch procedure of Crown appeal.[747] It also means that in the case of a criminal charge the penalty may be determined by an administrative body, e.g., the Revenue[748] or the public prosecutor,[749] or by (summary) court proceedings not fulfilling all the requirements of Article 6, provided that from this decision appeal lies to a court with full jurisdiction.

However, in the *De Cubber* Case the Court has qualified the viewpoint that only the last stage of the proceedings has to fulfil all the requirements of Article 6 by holding that this applies only to those cases in which under the domestic law the proceedings are not of a civil or criminal but, e.g., of a disciplinary or administrative character, and moreover the decision is not in the hands of what within the domestic system are considered 'courts of the classic kind'. If, on the contrary, proceedings are concerned which are to be classified as 'civil' or 'criminal', both in virtue of the Convention and under domestic law, and if the body which makes the 'determination' is a 'proper court in both the formal and the substantive meaning of the term', Article 6 applies to this body irrespective of whether its decision is open to appeal. The flexible standpoint with regard to disciplinary and administrative proceedings, according to the Court:

> cannot justify reducing the requirements of Article 6, paragraph 1 in its traditional and natural sphere of application. A restrictive interpretation of this kind would not be consonant with the object and purpose of Article 6, paragraph 1.[750]

---

[746] Judgment of 10 February 1983, A.58, p. 16. See also the reports of 8 July 1986, *Van Lierde* (not officially published), para. 44 and *Houart*, D&R 53 (1987), p. 5 (24-25) and the judgment of 22 June 1989, *Langborger*, A.155, p. 15.

[747] Judgment of 23 October 1985, *Benthem*, A.97. See, however, the judgment of 27 November 1991, *Oerlemans*, A.219, pp. 21-22, where the Court accepted the argument of the Dutch Government that, since the *Benthem* judgment, the procedure of Crown appeal could still be followed by review by a civil court.

[748] Judgment of 24 February 1994, *Bendenoun*, A.284, pp. 19-20.

[749] Judgment of 16 December 1992, *Hennings*, A.251-A.

[750] Judgment of 26 October 1984, A.86, p. 18.

Moreover, it is investigated very critically in Strasbourg whether appeal is really open in all cases to the appellate body that is indicated by the respondent Government as satisfying Article 6, and whether this is a full appeal.[751]

6.3.6 Limitations of the Right of Access to Court

In the *Klass* Case a drastic restriction was imposed on the right of access to court as developed in the Strasbourg case-law. Article 6(1) was invoked by the applicants because the challenged legislation, which permitted interference with correspondence and wire-tapping for security reasons without the knowledge of the person concerned, had excluded the normal recourse to a court and had replaced it by supervision by a parliamentary committee. Leaving open the question of whether this case concerned civil rights or a criminal charge, the Court held that a distinction should be made between the stage in which the measures were still applied without the person's knowledge, and the stage in which the measures had been terminated and in which, consequently, there was no longer any ground for secrecy. In relation to the first stage the Court held as follows:

> As long as it [the security control exercised] remains validly secret, the decision placing someone under surveillance is thereby incapable of judicial control on the initiative of the person concerned, within the meaning of Article 6; as a consequence, it of necessity escapes the requirements of that Article.[752]

With respect to the second stage the Court reached the following conclusion:

> The decision can come within the ambit of the said provision [*i.e.* Article 6] only after discontinuance of the surveillance. According to the information supplied by the Government, the individual concerned, once he has been notified of such discontinuance, has at his disposal several legal remedies against the possible infringements of his rights; these remedies would satisfy the requirements of Article 6.[753]

The Court was faced here with the dilemma between, on the one hand, unlimited application of the principle of 'access to court', a principle which it had itself developed in its case-law, and, on the other hand, the necessity for the national authorities to be able to carry out an effective security control for the protection of the democratic values underlying the Convention. The Court has opted for the latter, imposing restrictions on the first-mentioned principle *via* what might be called a systematic interpretation of Article 6(1) in connection with Article 8(2). But the Court also emphasised – as the German *Bundesverfassungsgericht* had done – that the secrecy *vis-à-vis* the person concerned must not last any longer than is required for the protection of the interest envisaged by the measures, after which period access to court is fully open again for the person in question.[754]

---

[751] See in particular the report of 3 July 1985, *Ettl and Others*, A.117, pp. 23-26. In its judgment of 23 April 1987 in that case, A.117, p. 19, the Court held that there was no question of violation of Article 6, since Austria had made a reservation in this respect upon ratification of the Convention.

[752] Judgment of 6 September 1978, A.28, p. 32.

[753] *Ibidem*, p. 33.

[754] *Ibidem*, pp. 32-33 in conjunction with p. 31.

The said parliamentary committee will then have to take particular care that the person in question is indeed informed as soon as the situation permits, since otherwise the national judicial review as well as the Strasbourg review might be rendered completely illusory.

In the *Leander* Case, which also concerned secret surveillance, the Commission had declared the complaint concerning Article 6 incompatible with the Convention *ratione materiae* on the basis of its case-law that litigation concerning access to or dismissal from the civil service falls outside the scope of Article 6.[755] Consequently, the Court could not pronounce on the issue. However, it nevertheless gave a clear indication of its point of view by following, with respect to Article 13, its *Klass* judgment in holding that:

> an effective remedy under Article 13 must mean a remedy that is as effective as can be, having regard to the restricted scope for recourse inherent in any system of secret surveillance for the protection of national security.[756]

In its report in *R.V. and Others* v. *the Netherlands*, which concerned a request of access to information held by the Dutch Military Intelligence Services (MIS), although no complaint under Article 6 had been lodged but only under Article 8, the Commission based its conclusion that the interference was not 'in accordance with the law', *inter alia*, on the fact that the Royal Decree governing the activities of the MIS did not contain any safeguard mechanism, thus leaving it open whether the safeguards referred to in the Government's observations, which were provided for in a broader framework (investigation by a parliamentary committee and by the National Ombudsman), were sufficiently effective.[757]

The right of access to court laid down in Article 6 is also not an absolute right insofar as it may be waived, provided that this has been done unambiguously.[758] That waiver may concern the right of access as such[759] or certain of its elements, *e.g.*, the publicity of the proceedings,[760] or may limit the proceedings to the determination of specified questions of law.[761] Moreover, certain implicit restrictions apply in the sense that a criminal prosecution may also be terminated without intervention of the court, provided that this does not lead to a formal or factual 'determination'. The authorities may also lay down specific restrictive rules for access to a court with regard to, for instance, minors or persons of unsound minds.[762] These restrictions, however, may not impair the right of access in its

---

[755] Appl. 9248/81, *Leander* v. *Sweden*, D&R 34 (1983), p. 78 (83).

[756] Judgment of 26 March 1987, A.116, p. 32.

[757] Report of 3 December 1991 (not officially published), paras 45-46.

[758] Judgment of 7 May 1974, *Neumeister*, A.17, pp. 15-16. See also the judgments of 12 February 1985, *Colozza* and *Rubinat*, A.89, p. 14.

[759] This can be done, *e.g.* in an arbitration clause, but also then there must be no question of constraint: Appl. 1197/61, *X* v. *Federal Republic of Germany*, Yearbook V (1962), p. 88 (94-96).

[760] Judgment of 23 June 1981, *Le Compte, Van Leuven and De Meyere*, A.43, pp. 25-26; judgment of 10 February 1983, *Albert and Le Compte*, A.58, p. 19.

[761] Judgment of 5 May 1995, *Air Canada*, A.316-A, p. 21.

[762] Judgment of 21 February 1975, *Golder*, A.18, p. 19.

very essence for the (legal) person concerned[763] and must be 'sufficiently clear' or the provisions concerned must contain safeguards against misunderstanding.[764] Moreover, the limitations applied must pursue a legitimate aim, while there must be a reasonable relationship of proportionality between the means employed and the aim sought to be achieved.[765] In the special circumstances of the 'civil' *Tolstoy Miloslavsky* Case the obligation to pay an amount of 124,900 English pound as security for costs to pursue an appeal did meet this requirement.[766]

6.4 The Right to a Fair Trial

6.4.1 Introduction

Article 6 requires a 'fair hearing'. The notion of 'hearing' may be equated with that of 'trial' or 'trial proceedings'. This follows firstly from the French wording of the provision: *'toute personne a droit à ce que sa cause*(!) *soit entendue'*. Secondly, the right to be heard within a reasonable time, embodied in the first paragraph, refers to the proceedings as a whole[767] and, thirdly, the second sentence of the first paragraph allows the exclusion of the public and the press from all or part of the *trial*. Thus, the notion of 'hearing' may not be seen as equivalent to 'hearing in person' or 'oral hearing', although these two aspects may be elements of the notion of 'fair and public hearing' as contained in Article 6.[768]

When is a hearing 'fair'? In the *Kraska* Case the Court took as a starting-point that the purpose of Article 6 is, *inter alia*:

> to place the 'tribunal' under a duty to conduct a proper examination of the submissions, arguments and evidence adduced by the parties, without prejudice to its assessments of whether they are relevant to its decision.[769]

However, the Commission and the Court have avoided to give an enumeration of criteria in the abstract. In each individual case the course of the proceedings has to be assessed to decide whether the hearing concerned has been a fair one. What counts is the picture which the proceedings as a whole present,[770] although

---

[763] Judgment of 24 October 1979, *Winterwerp*, A.33, p. 29 and the judgment of 9 December 1994, *Holy Monasteries*, A.301-A, pp. 37-38.

[764] Judgment of 4 December 1995, *Bellet*, A.333-B, p. 42. See also the judgment of 16 December 1992, *Geouffre de la Pradelle*, A.253-B, p. 43.

[765] Judgment of 28 May 1985, *Ashingdane*, A.93, pp. 24-25; judgment of 8 July 1986, *Lithgow and Others*, A.102, p. 71; judgment of 21 September 1994, *Fayed*, A.294-B, pp. 50-56.

[766] Judgment of 13 July 1995, A.316-B, pp. 78-81.

[767] See *infra*.

[768] See section 6.4.3.

[769] Judgment of 19 April 1993, A.254-B, p. 49. See also, *e.g.*, the judgment of 6 December 1988, *Barberà, Messegué and Jabardo*, A.146, p. 31.

[770] Report of 15 March 1961, *Nielsen*, Yearbook IV (1961), p. 494 (568). This is standing case-law. See, *e.g.*, Appl. 9000/80, *X v. Switzerland*, D&R 28 (1982), p. 127 (133-135); judgment of 6 December 1988, *Barberà, Messegué and Jabardo*, A.146, p. 31; judgment of 20 November 1989, *Kostovski*, A.166, p. 19.

certain aspects *per se* may already conflict with the principle of a fair hearing in such a way that an opinion can be given about the fairness of the trial irrespective of the further course of the proceedings,[771] *e.g.*, the way in which the evidence is collected during a preliminary hearing. Depending on the stage of the proceedings and its special features, the manner of application of Article 6 may differ.[772] The publicity requirement for example may be less strict as far as cassation proceedings are concerned.[773]

Certain aspects of a 'fair hearing' are expressly stated for criminal cases in paragraphs 2 and 3 of Article 6. These aspects in principle also apply to civil cases. However, from the lack of such an enumeration with regard to civil cases, the Court has concluded that the requirements inherent in the notion of a 'fair hearing' in civil cases are not necessarily identical to the requirements in criminal cases and that there exists a 'greater latitude' for the national authorities when dealing with civil cases than when dealing with criminal procedures.[774]

Although the enumeration in the second and third paragraph might create a different impression, the content of the term 'fair hearing' in 'criminal' cases is not confined to the provisions of paragraphs 2 and 3 of Article 6.[775] The guarantees implied in the requirement of a 'fair hearing' in paragraph 1 fully apply to criminal proceedings as well, and this *a fortiori*.[776] Consequently, the finding that the proceedings are in conformity with the requirements of the second and third paragraph does not make a review for their conformity with the 'fair-hearing' principle superfluous in all cases. The proceedings as a whole may, for instance, create the picture that the accused has had insufficient possibilities to conduct an optimal defence, although none of the explicitly granted minimum guarantees has been violated. As the Commission observed in the *Adolf* Case: 'Art. 6(3) merely exemplifies the minimum guarantees which must be accorded to the accused in the context of the 'fair trial' referred to in Art. 6(1).'[777] This implies, on the one hand, that a negative answer to the question whether the first paragraph has been violated renders an investigation of an alleged infringement of the third paragraph superfluous,[778] while on the other hand, the investigation of a possible violation of the fair-trial principle laid down in the first paragraph must not be confined to an examination of the third paragraph. However, once a violation of one of the parts of the third paragraph has been found, the

---

[771] Appls 8603, 8722, 8723 and 8729/79, *Crociani* et al. v. *Italy*, Yearbook XXIV (1981), p. 222 (254).
[772] See, *e.g.*, the judgment of 26 May 1988, *Ekbatani*, A.134, p. 13; judgment of 29 October 1991, *Helmers*, A.212-A, p. 16.
[773] See section 6.5.
[774] Judgment of 27 October 1993, *Dombo Beheer B.V.*, A.274, p. 19.
[775] See the report of 15 March 1961, *Nielsen*, Yearbook IV (1961), p. 494 (548-550). See also Appl. 8289/78, *X* v. *Austria*, D&R 18 (1980), p. 160 (166-167).
[776] Appl. 1169/61, *X* v. *Federal Republic of Germany*, Yearbook VI (1963), p. 520 (572). See also Appl. 7413/76, *X* v. *the United Kingdom*, D&R 9 (1978), p. 100 (101).
[777] Report of 8 October 1980, B.43 (1985), p. 29.
[778] *Idem.* See also the judgment of 27 February 1980, *Deweer*, A.35, pp. 30-31.

Commission and the Court tend not to examine the alleged violation of the first paragraph any more.[779]

Article 6 demands a 'fair hearing'. Thus, it does not in itself 'guarantee any particular content for (civil) rights and obligations'.[780]

Various aspects of the right of a 'fair trial' are discussed in the next paragraphs. Sometimes it is very difficult to distinguish the various aspects, since they are often closely connected. In criminal cases the Court regularly uses the rather vague notion of 'rights of the defence'. This wording seems equal to the concept of a 'fair trial'.[781]

6.4.2 Equality of Arms

An important element of the fair hearing requirement is constituted by the principle of equality of arms. This principle implies, as the Court held in the case of *Dombo Beheer B.V.* with regard to civil proceedings:

> that each party must be afforded a reasonable opportunity to present his case – including his evidence – under conditions that do not place him at a substantial disadvantage *vis-à-vis* his opponent.[782]

For criminal cases, where the very character of the proceedings involves a fundamental inequality of the parties, this principle of 'equality of arms' is even more important, and the same applies, though to a lesser degree, to administrative procedures.[783] The principle can play a role in every stage of the proceedings and with regard to many subjects.

The principle of 'equality of arms' entails that the parties must have the same access to the records and other documents in the case, at least insofar as these play a part in the formation of the court's opinion.[784] However, the access to the file may be restricted to an accused's lawyer.[785] A particular way in which the information from the file must be given or be available does not follow from this principle, provided that no insuperable obstacles are created which in fact

---

[779] Report of 12 December 1981, *Pakelli*, B.53 (1987), p. 29. Implicitly the judgment of 13 May 1980, *Artico*, A.37, pp. 15 and 18-19.

[780] Judgment of 21 February 1986, *James and Others*, A.98, p. 46; judgment of 8 July 1986, *Lithgow and Others*, A.102, p. 70; judgment of 25 April 1996, *Gustafsson*, Reports 1996-II, Vol. 9, para. 66. See also the judgment of 24 October 1995, *Agrotemix and Others*, A.330-A, pp. 26-27.

[781] See, *e.g.*, the judgment of 24 February 1994, *Bendenoun*, A.284, pp. 21-22.

[782] Judgment of 27 October 1993, A.274, p. 19. See also the judgment of 22 September 1994, *Hentrich*, A.296-A, p. 22 and judgment of 9 December 1994, *Stran Greek Refineries and Stratis Andreadis*, A.301-B, p. 81.

[783] Judgment of 29 May 1986, *Feldbrugge*, A.99, p. 17.

[784] Appl. 7317/75, *Lynas* v. *Switzerland*, Yearbook XX (1977), p. 412 (445-446); Appl. 9433/81, *Menten* v. *the Netherlands*, D&R 28 (1982), p. 233; judgment of 24 February 1995, *McMichael*, A.307-B, pp. 53-54; judgments of 20 February 1996, *Vermeulen*, Reports 1996-I, Vol. 3, para. 33, and *Lobo Machado*, Reports 1996-I, Vol. 3, para. 31.

[785] Judgment of 19 December 1989, *Kamasinski*, A.168, pp. 39-40 and judgment of 21 September 1993, *Kremzow*, A.268-B, p. 42.

amount to withholding information.[786] In our opinion, the parties should in principle have the opportunity to make copies from the relevant documents in the case-file. The case-law on this point is not clear, although the Court in the *Schuler-Zgraggen* Case, when deciding the question whether the access of the applicant to the case-file did meet the requirements of Article 6, expressly mentioned the ability of the applicant to make copies.[787] A lack of access to the case-file may be remedied by a an appeal court.[788]

The one party must be given the opportunity to oppose the arguments advanced by the other party. In the *Feldbrugge* Case, for example, the Court came to the conclusion that Article 6(1) had been violated, since the applicant had not been given the opportunity to comment upon the report of a medical expert, which was of decisive importance for the outcome of the proceedings.[789] In the *Hentrich* Case the Revenue exercised the right of pre-emption because it held the sale price of a piece of land too low. The applicant did not get a real opportunity to challenge the decision of the Revenue, because the tribunals, on the one hand, refused her the possibility to prove that the sale price corresponded to the real market value of the land and, on the other hand, allowed the Revenue to give a meaningless motivation for its decision to exercise the right of pre-emption.[790] These facts amounted to a breach of Article 6(1).[791] In the *Stran Greek Refineries and Stratis Andreadis* Case Greece violated the applicants' rights under Article 6 by enacting a law that influenced the proceedings, already pending before the courts, between the applicants and the Greek State, in a way favourable to the State.[792] The Commission reached a comparable conclusion in the *Pressos Compania Naviera S.A.* Case, where the Belgian State had enacted legislation with retrospective effect exempting the Belgian State and private companies offering pilot services from liability for damage occasioned to shipping as a result of pilots' negligence.[793]

The principle further entails that the parties are afforded the same possibility to summon witnesses. In the *Dombo Beheer B.V.* Case the central question in the national proceedings was whether a certain agreement had been concluded between the applicant company and its bank. The person who represented the bank at the meeting where the alleged agreement was concluded, was allowed to testify before the Court. The person who represented the applicant company,

---

[786] Appl. 8289/78, *X* v. *Austria*, D&R 18 (1980), p. 160 (167-168).

[787] Judgment of 24 June 1993, A.263, p. 18.

[788] *Idem. Cf.* also the judgment of 21 September 1993, *Zumtobel*, A.268-A, pp. 14-15.

[789] Judgment of 29 May 1986, A.99, pp. 17-18. See also, *e.g.*, the judgment of 23 June 1993, *Ruiz-Mateos*, A.262, pp. 25-26; judgment of 19 April 1994, *Van de Hurk*, A.288, pp. 18-19.

[790] The Revenue confined its motivation to stating that the price was too low.

[791] Judgment of 22 September 1994, *Hentrich*, A.296-A, p. 22.

[792] Judgment of 9 December 1994, A.301-B, pp. 81-82.

[793] Report of 4 July 1994, A.332, p. 38. The Court, having found a violation of Article 1 of Protocol No. 1, held it not necessary to express an opinion on this point: judgment of 20 November 1995, A.332, p. 25.

however, could not give evidence, because the national court identified him with the company itself. Thus, there was 'a substantial disadvantage' of the company *vis-à-vis* the bank in breach of Article 6.[794]

In addition, the parties must have the same possibility to call experts and these should in turn receive the same treatment. In the *Bönisch* Case the Court found that the expert involved in the proceedings and the powers given to him insufficiently guaranteed the latter's neutrality, so that he had to be considered as a witness for the prosecution rather than as an expert. Since the accused had not been given the same opportunity to call such an 'expert', the principle of the 'equality of arms' had been violated.[795]

Phases in the examination during which neither of the parties was present fulfil the principle of 'equality of arms' and as a consequence, in that respect do not prejudice the fairness of the proceedings as a whole.[796]

In the *Delcourt* Case the Court held the fact that in Belgium the *Procureur général* participates in the deliberations of the court of cassation to be not in conflict with the principle of the 'equality of arms', because of his independent position in relation to the Minister of Justice and of the fact that the latter cannot give orders or instructions to the *Procureur général* in concrete cases.[797] However, the Court changed its view in the *Borgers* Case. It emphasised the correctness of the *Delcourt* judgment in as far as the independence and impartiality of the Court of Cassation and its *Procureur général* are concerned, but nevertheless concluded that the rights of the defence and the principle of equality of arms require that the defendant should have the possibility to reply to the submissions made by the member of the *Procureur général*'s department, which are unfavourable to him.[798] The same holds good for civil cases.[799]

---

[794] Judgment of 27 October 1993, A.274, p. 19.

[795] Judgment of 6 May 1985, A.92, pp. 14-16. The mere fact that an expert is a member of the staff of an institute which did report the initial suspicions, does not suffice to regard the expert as a 'witness for the prosecution': judgment of 28 August 1991, *Brandstetter*, A.211, p. 21.

[796] Appl. 1793/62, *X v. Austria*, Yearbook VI (1963), p. 458 (460); Appl. 7413/76, *X v. the United Kingdom*, D&R 9 (1978), p. 100 (101); Appl. 11129/84, *Brown v. the United Kingdom*, D&R 42 (1985), p. 269 (272).

[797] Judgment of 17 January 1970, A.11, pp. 16-19. The same view was adopted by the Commission with regard to the Dutch cassation procedure. Appl. 3692/68, *X v. the Netherlands*, Yearbook XIII (1970), p. 516 (522).

[798] Judgment of 30 October 1991, A.214-B, pp. 31-32. See also the judgment of 21 September 1993, *Kremzow*, A.268-B, pp. 41-42; judgment of 22 February 1996, *Bulut*, Reports 1996-II, Vol. 5, paras 48-50.

[799] Judgments of 20 February 1996, *Vermeulen*, Reports 1996-I, Vol. 3, para. 33 and *Lobo Machado*, Reports 1996-I, Vol. 3, para. 31.

6.4.3 The Right to be Present at the Trial and the Right to an Oral Hearing

The precept of a 'fair hearing' in principle entails the right of the parties to be present in person at the trial. This right is closely connected to the right to an oral hearing[800] and the right to be able to follow the proceedings.[801] In the *Colloza* Case the Court held that:

> although this is not expressly mentioned in para. 1 of Article 6, the object and the purpose of the Article as a whole show that a person 'charged with a criminal offence' is entitled to take part in the hearing.[802]

There may be exceptions to this principle as far as a trial at second or third instance is concerned. The answer to the question whether such an exception is allowed, depends on the circumstances of the case. In the first place it seems that an exception is permissible only if the accused was entitled to be present at the hearing at first instance.[803] According to the Commission the same holds good for 'civil' cases,[804] although the Court's case-law on this point does not provide sufficient clarity yet.[805] In addition the Court takes into account the nature of the national (appeal) system,[806] the scope of the powers of the national court and the 'manner in which the applicant's interests were actually presented and protected' before the national (appeal) court.[807] In the *Ekbatani* Case and the *Kremzow* Case, both concerning criminal proceedings, the Court held that the

---

[800] See the judgment of 23 February 1993, *Fredin (No.2)*, A.283-A, pp. 10-11 and the judgment of 26 April 1995, *Fischer*, A.312, pp. 20-21.

[801] Judgment of 23 February 1994, *Stanford*, A.282-A, pp. 10-11. In this case the applicant complained about the poor acoustics of the courtroom.

[802] Judgment of 12 February 1985, A.89, p. 14. See also the judgment of 2 March 1987, *Monnell and Morris*, A.115, p. 25; judgment of 6 December 1988, *Barberà, Messegué and Jabardo*, A.146, pp. 33-34; judgment of 19 December 1989, *Brozicek*, A.167, p. 19; judgment of 28 August 1991, *F.C.B.* v. *Italy*, A.208-B, pp. 20-22; judgment of 12 October 1992, *T* v. *Italy*, A.245-C, pp. 41-42.

[803] In the *Ekbatani* Case, judgment of 26 May 1988, A.134, p. 12, the Court stated that the notion of a 'fair trial' implies that persons charged with a criminal offence, *as a principle*, are entitled to be present at the first instance trial. However, there does not seem to exist any room for an exception to this principle: in nearly all the subsequent cases where the Court excepted the non-entitlement for the accused to be present at the second or third instance trial, it expressly gave attention to the fact that the person concerned had been present at the first instance trial. See, *e.g.*, judgment of 29 October 1991, *Jan-Åke Andersson*, A.212-B, pp. 44-46 and the judgment of 29 October 1991, *Fejde*, A.212-C, pp. 67-69. See, however, also judgment of 21 September 1993, *Kremzow*, A.268-B, p. 44.

[804] Report of 2 October 1990, *Muyldermans*, A.214-B, p. 18.

[805] The *Fredin (No.2)* Case, judgment of 23 February 1994, A.283-A, p. 11, leaves room for an exception to the entitlement to an oral hearing at the first instance trial. However, the judgment of 29 October 1991, *Helmers*, A.212-A, pp. 15-17, points at the opposite direction. See also the judgment of 26 April 1995, *Fischer*, A.312, p. 20.

[806] See, *e.g.*, the judgment of 2 March 1987, *Monnell and Morris*, A.115, p. 22 with regard to proceedings for leave to appeal and compare the judgment of 22 February 1996, *Bulut*, Reports 1996-II, Vol. 5, paras 41-42.

[807] Judgment of 26 May 1988, *Ekbatani*, A.134, p. 13; judgment of 29 October 1991, *Helmers*, A.212-A, p. 15.

gravity of what was at stake could not deprive the applicants of the right to be present at the trial.[808] A different conclusion was reached in the *Jan Åke Andersson* and *Fejde* Cases. The Court attached importance to the facts that the appeal raised questions which could be decided on the basis of the case-file, the minor character of the offence and the prohibition against the increase of the sentence on appeal.[809] The latter aspect, however, is not, at least not in itself, decisive. Despite the fact that the aggravation of the punishment by the appeal court was also prohibited in the *Kremzow* Case the applicant, as pointed out above, should have been enabled to be present at the appeal trial.

In the *Helmers* Case, concerning the 'civil' right to enjoy a good reputation, the Court developed with regard to the entitlement of the applicant to be present at the appeal hearing the same line of reasoning as in the 'criminal' cases.[810] The seriousness of what was at stake – the professional career of the applicant – did not justify an encroachment on the right to be present.[811]

In some 'civil' cases the Court has accepted that the right to be present at the trial may be waived. If one of the parties omits to request for an oral hearing while national law prescribes that the proceedings will be conducted without an oral hearing unless one of the parties will ask for such a hearing, the omission may be explained as an unequivocal waiver of the right to be present.[812] With regard to 'criminal' cases the case-law is less clear. A few times the Court has expressly refused to answer the question 'whether and under what conditions an accused can waive exercise of his right to appear at the hearing'.[813] On the other hand, however, the *Colozza* judgment seems to indicate that the right to be present may in principle be waived.[814] Be that as it may, it is clear that the national legislation may discourage the unjustified absence of an accused at the trial, although the measures taken may not be disproportionate.[815]

The foregoing of course does not bar judgment by default, provided that the person in question has been summoned by the prescribed procedure and sufficient

---

[808] Judgment of 26 May 1988, *Ekbatani*, A.134, p. 14; judgment of 21 September 1993, *Kremzow*, A.268-B, pp. 44-45. See also the judgment of 19 February 1996, *Botten*, Reports 1996-I, Vol. 3, paras 48-53, concerning a judgment of the Norwegian Supreme Court in which it had made its own assessment of the facts without hearing the applicant.

[809] Judgments of 29 October 1991, *Jan-Åke Andersson*, A.212-B, p. 46; *Fejde*, A.212-C, pp. 69-70. See further the judgment of 19 December 1989, *Kamasinski*, A.168, pp. 44-45.

[810] Especially its *Jan Åke Andersson* and *Fejde* judgments of 29 October 1991 respectively A.212-B and A.212-C.

[811] Judgment of 29 October 1991, A.212-A, pp. 15-17. See further the judgment of 23 February 1994, *Fredin (No. 2)*, A.283-A, pp. 10-11.

[812] Judgment of 24 June 1993, *Schuler-Zgraggen*, A.263, pp. 19-20; judgment of 21 September 1993, *Zumtobel*, A.268-A, p. 14.

[813] Judgment of 28 August 1991, *F.C.B.* v. *Italy*, A.208-B, p. 21; judgment of 12 October 1992, *T* v. *Italy*, A.245-C, p. 41.

[814] Judgment of 12 February 1985, A.89, p. 12.

[815] Judgment of 23 November 1993, *Poitrimol*, A.277-A, p. 15. In this case the absence of the accused was punished by 'ignoring the right to legal assistance' and 'the inadmissibility of the appeal on points of law'. These sanctions could not be regarded as proportional.

guarantees are attached to this procedure, also considering the provisions applying in other Contracting States in this respect.[816] If it is not certain whether the accused is really aware that proceedings against him are taking place and that he has been summoned for a hearing, the Court examines the carefulness of the procedure by means of which contact has been sought with him.[817] In any case, the fact that the accused is detained, is no reason for his not being heard,[818] at least not at a first instance trial.[819]

6.4.4 Various Requirements

The principle of 'fair hearing' also entails specific requirements with respect to evidence. From the fact that an accused person is entitled in principle to 'take part in the hearing and to have his case heard' the Court has deduced that 'all the evidence must in principle be produced in the presence of the accused (...) with a view to adversarial argument.'[820] The evidence produced must be sufficiently 'direct' if it is to admit actually refutation during the public hearing.[821] In the *Bricmont* Case the lack of confrontation between the accused persons and a member of the Belgian royal family, as the party seeking damages, amounted to a breach of paragraphs 1 and 3 of Article 6 taken together.[822] The case-law with regard to the opportunity of the accused to challenge and question a witness is further discussed in section 6.9.5. As will be seen, it may be concluded from this case-law that a court decision which is exclusively or almost exclusively based upon indirect evidence of witnesses, has not been taken in accordance with the fair-trial requirement, unless in some way or another an adequate possibility for contradiction and counter-evidence has been afforded. The same holds good with respect to other evidence, such as tape recordings; defence against its contents must be allowed and still be practicable. According to the Court, Article 6(1) does not require access to the tape itself. Its relevance for the fairness of the trial

---

[816] See Res. (75)11 of the Committee of Ministers 'on the criteria governing proceedings held in the absence of the accused'; Council of Europe, *Resolutions by the Committee of Ministers relating to crime problems*, Vol. III, 1977.

[817] Judgment of 12 February 1985, *Colozza and Rubinat*, A.89, p. 12; judgment of 28 August 1991, *F.C.B. v. Italy*, A.208-B, pp. 21-22; judgment of 12 October 1992, *T v. Italy*, A.245-C, pp. 41-42.

[818] Report of 11 March 1986, *Monnell and Morris*, A.115, p. 41; judgment of 2 March 1987, *Monnell and Morris*, A.115, pp. 22-24.

[819] The judgment of 19 December 1989, *Kamasinski*, A.168, pp. 44-45, seems to indicate a different point of view with regard to appeal proceedings.

[820] Judgment of 6 December 1988, *Barberà, Messegué and Jabardo*, A.146, p. 34. See also the judgment of 20 November 1989, *Kostovski*, A.166, p. 20; judgment of 27 September 1990, *Windisch*, A.186, p. 10.

[821] See in this context Appl. 8414/78, *X v. Federal Republic of Germany*, D&R 17 (1980), p. 231 (233-234) and Appl. 8417/78, *X v. Belgium*, D&R 16 (1979), p. 200 (207-208). In the *Kamasinski* Case the Commission held it to be in violation of Art. 6(1) that no note had been given to the applicant or his representative of the contents of the information which the judge, acting as rapporteur, had obtained by telephone from the judge of the regional court who had presided over the trial, report of 5 May 1988, A.168, pp. 62-63.

[822] Judgment of 7 July 1989, A.158, pp. 29-31.

depends, *inter alia*, on the vital character of the contents of the tape for the evidence, while it is also relevant whether the transcript of the tape has been verified by an independent person.[823] In the *Kerojärvi* Case concerning the alleged entitlement to compensation for injuries which were alleged to be the consequence of military service, the court omitted to communicate documents, which it received from several authorities, to the applicant. This omission amounted to a breach of the fair trial principle. The question whether these documents were important for the outcome of the domestic procedure seemed to be of little relevance.[824]

The prosecuting authorities are obliged 'to disclose to the defence all material evidence for or against the accused'.[825] The evidence must have been collected by legal means.[826] Evidence that has been obtained contrary to the norms laid down in the Convention itself, such as statements extracted *via* torture or other inhuman treatment, contrary to Article 3, or evidence that has been collected by means of encroachment on privacy, contrary to Article 8, conflicts on that ground alone with the Convention. As to the admissibility according to domestic law, the Strasbourg organs are guided in the first place by the opinion of the national court. However, if the latter has taken the position that it may use the evidence, though unlawfully obtained, in forming its opinion, a Strasbourg review of the way in which use is made of this evidence is very urgently needed if the principle of 'fair trial' is not to be frustrated.[827]

The 'fair hearing' requirement implies the right of the accused 'to remain silent and not to contribute to incriminating himself'.[828] However, this right is not absolute. The Court held in the *John Murray* Case that the drawing of adverse inferences from the accused's silence, regulated by law, had not been contrary to Article 6. In its motivation at length the Court took account of several safeguards designed to respect the rights of the defence. For instance, the applicant had been warned that adverse inferences might be drawn, the adverse inferences could only be drawn if a failure to express oneself might 'as a matter of common sense' lead to the conclusion that the accused had been guilty and if there existed very strong other evidence against the accused.[829]

A fair trial may imply the right to have the assistance of a lawyer, also during the phase preceding the trial. This aspect will be discussed under paragraph 3(c) of Article 6. Is it also possible to infer a right to free legal aid from the principle

---

[823] Judgment of 24 November 1986, *Gillow*, A.109, p. 28. See also the judgment of 12 July 1988, *Schenk*, A.140, pp. 29-30.

[824] Judgment of 19 July 1995, A.322, p. 16.

[825] Judgment of 16 December 1992, *Edwards*, A.247-B, p. 35.

[826] The Commission was rather too laconic in this respect in Appl. 7450/76, *X v. Belgium*, D&R 9 (1978), p. 108 (110).

[827] The Strasbourg organs consider themselves competent to do so: Appl. 8876/80, *X v. Belgium*, D&R 23 (1981), p. 233 (235).

[828] Judgment of 25 February 1993, *Funke*, A.256-A, p. 22.

[829] Judgment of 8 February 1996, Reports 1996-I, Vol. 1, paras 44-58.

of fair hearing? From paragraph 3(c) it might be concluded *a contrario* that this is not the case.[830] In fact, paragraph 3(c) only guarantees this right for criminal proceedings, and even then only 'when the interests of justice so require'. However, if one party does have the means to secure legal aid and the other does not, there is no 'equality of arms' if the latter does not obtain the assistance of a lawyer as well. Above, the view of the Commission and the Court has been mentioned that the mere right of 'access to court' which is implied in Article 6(1), entails the obligation for the Contracting States to make legal aid available, or at least financially possible, if the person in question would otherwise be faced with an insuperable barrier to defend himself adequately.[831] In that context the Commission and Court make an independent examination of the complexity of the case and other relevant factors such as the applicable rules of evidence and the emotional involvement of the applicant in the outcome of the proceedings.[832] Other expenses, too, for instance those for a translator or an interpreter, may be so onerous that the principle of 'fair trial' is at stake.[833]

The same applies to the question of whether under Article 6(1) the parties are entitled to have witnesses and experts summoned and examined. From the fact that Article 6(3)(d) contains explicit provisions about this for criminal cases it might be inferred *a contrario* that such a right does not hold good for the parties in civil proceedings. However, here again the case-law recognises the possibility that the court's refusal to have a particular witness summoned by a party to a dispute, or to hear him, constitutes an encroachment on the right to a 'fair hearing'.[834]

The failure of a member of the court concerned to thoroughly read an important document of the case-file may jeopardise the fairness of the proceedings. On this ground in the *Kraska* Case the majority of the Commission reached the conclusion that the first paragraph of Article 6 had been violated. The Court, however, taking into account the circumstances of the case, took the opposite view.[835]

Finally, an additional element of 'fair hearing' is the requirement that the judicial decision must state the reasons on which it is based. The extent of this duty depends on 'the nature of the decision' and can only, according to the Court, be assessed in the circumstances of each individual case.[836] As matters stand, only a few observations with regard to the content of this requirement can be made. A remarkable situation occurred in the *Schuler-Zgraggen* Case. The national court based its decision with regard to the alleged entitlement of the

---

[830] See, *e.g.*, Appl. 6202/73, *X and Y* v. *the Netherlands*, D&R 1 (1975), p. 66 (71).
[831] *Supra* p. 420.
[832] Appl. 9353/81, *Webb* v. *the United Kingdom*, D&R 33 (1983), p. 133 (138-141).
[833] Report of 18 May 1977, *Luedicke, Belkacem and Koç*, B.27 (1982), p. 26.
[834] See, *e.g.*, Appl. 5362/72, *X* v. *Austria*, Coll. 42 (1973), p. 145; Appl. 9000/80, *X* v. *Switzerland*, D&R 28 (1982), p. 127 (133-135).
[835] Judgment of 19 April 1993, A.254-B, pp. 49-50.
[836] Judgments of 9 December 1994, *Ruiz Torija*, A.303-A, p. 12; *Hiro Balani*, A.303-B, pp. 29-30.

female applicant to an invalidity pension on the mere assumption that 'women give up work when they give birth to a child'. This reasoning amounted to a breach of Article 6 in conjunction with Article 14.[837] The 'tribunal' is not obliged to give a detailed answer to every argument.[838] When a motivation is lacking altogether, however, the remedies provided for are likely to become illusory.[839] The detail into which the statement of the reasons must go is therefore determined by what an effective remedy against the decision requires in each particular case.[840] The practice existing in some countries to provide certain judgments in criminal cases with a motivation only if an appeal has been instituted, is at odds with this point of departure, since the decision to institute an appeal or not may precisely be determined also by the motivation of the judgment. If, on the other hand, a court of appeal agrees with the reasons of the lower court, it does not have to restate these reasons.[841]

6.5 Public Trial and the Public Pronouncement of Judgment

Article 6(1) requires that the hearing shall be public. In its report in the *Axen* Case the Commission sets forth the rationale of this requirement as follows:

> the public nature of the proceedings helps to ensure a fair trial by protecting the litigant against arbitrary decisions and enabling society to control the administration of justice (...) Combined with the public pronouncement of the judgment, the public nature of the hearings serves to ensure that the public is duly informed, notably by the press, and that the legal process is publicly observable. It should consequently contribute to ensuring confidence in the administration of justice.[842]

In addition to the interest which the parties to the dispute may have in a public hearing, it therefore serves a public interest as well: verifiability of and information about, and thus confidence in the administration of justice. Consequently, the question arises whether the parties can waive their right to a public hearing to an unlimited degree or whether the court may only comply with a request to that effect if one of the grounds explicitly mentioned for this in Article 6 presents itself. In *Le Compte, Van Leuven and De Meyere*[843] and in *H v. Belgium*[844] the Court seemed to have taken the first position. This is

---

[837] Judgment of 24 June 1993, *Schuler-Zgraggen*, A.263, pp. 21-22.

[838] Judgment of 19 April 1994, *Van de Hurk*, A.288, p. 20; judgments of 9 December 1994, *Ruiz Torija*, A.303-A, p. 12 and *Hiro Balani*, A.303-B, pp. 29-30.

[839] See the judgment of 16 December 1992, *Hadjianastassiou*, A.252, pp. 16-17 and *infra* section 6.9.3.

[840] Appl. 5460/72, *The Firestone Tire and Rubber Co. v. the United Kingdom*, Yearbook XVI (1973), p. 152 (168); Appl. 8769/79, *X v. Federal Republic of Germany*, D&R 25 (1982), p. 240 (241).

[841] Appl. 10773/84, *X v. Italy* (not published).

[842] Report of 14 December 1981, B.57 (1987), p. 24. See also the judgment of 22 February 1984 in this case, A.72, p. 12; judgment of 8 December 1983, *Pretto*, A.71, pp. 11-12; judgment of 22 February 1984, *Sutter*, A.74, pp. 12-13; judgment of 28 June 1984, *Campbell and Fell*, A.80, p. 43; report of 12 March 1985, *Adler*, D&R 46 (1986), p. 36 (55).

[843] Judgment of 23 June 1981, A.43, pp. 25-26.

[844] Judgment of 30 November 1987, A.127-B, p. 36.

confirmed by the *Håkansson and Sturesson* judgment, where the Court without any restriction held that 'neither the letter, nor the spirit' of the provision does oppose to an express or tacit waiver of the right to a public hearing.[845] In this case the Court concluded, unlike the Commission, that a tacit waiver did occur. The proceedings concerning the lawfulness of an auction sale usually took place in camera. For this reason, in the Court's view, the omission of the applicants to ask the competent authorities for a public hearing could be regarded as a waiver of their entitlement to have their case heard in public.[846] With a view to the public interest which is served by publicity, in particular in criminal cases, it will, however, have to be assumed that there is merely a possibility to waive the right to a public hearing, not a right to a hearing *in camera*, and that, if a request for a hearing *in camera* is made, the court may refuse this on the ground of the weighing of the interest of the party concerned against the public interest.[847] The court then will, of course, also have to take into account the protection of the private life of the party, as one of the explicitly mentioned grounds of restriction, and also the danger which publicity may constitute for the *praesumptio innocentiae* protected in the second paragraph.

The text of Article 6 does not contain any exceptions to the right to a public hearing as far as the phase of the proceedings is concerned. However, the Court makes a distinction between a trial before a court at first instance and a trial before an appeal court. The essence of this case-law comes to the fore in three judgments against Sweden:

> The Court fully recognises the value attaching to the publicity of the proceedings such as those indicated by the Commission (...) However, even where a court of appeal has jurisdiction to review the case both as to facts and as to law, the Court cannot find that Article 6 always requires a right to a public hearing irrespective of the nature of the issues to be decided. The publicity requirement is certainly one of the means whereby confidence in the courts is maintained. However, there are other considerations, including the right to trial within a reasonable time and the related need for expeditious handling of the court's case-load, which must be taken into account in determining the necessity of a public hearing at stages in the proceedings subsequent to the trial at first instance. Provided a public hearing has been held at first instance, the absence of such a hearing before a second or third instance may accordingly be justified by the special features of the proceedings at issue. Thus, leave to appeal proceedings and proceedings involving only questions of law, as opposed to questions of fact, may comply with the requirements of Article 6, although the appellant was not given an opportunity of being heard in person by the appeal or cassation court.[848]

As far the publicity requirement is concerned this quotation does in itself not raise any difficulty. However, the last clause, 'although the appellant was not given an opportunity of being heard in person by the appeal or cassation court', may cause

---

[845] Judgment of 21 February 1990, A.171-A, pp. 20-21.
[846] *Idem.* See also the judgment of 24 June 1993, *Schuler-Zgraggen*, A.263, pp. 19-20 and, for a different point of view, the report of 13 October 1988, *Håkansson and Sturesson*, A.171-A, p. 35.
[847] Judgment of 21 February 1990, *Håkansson and Sturesson*, A.171-A, p. 21.
[848] Judgments of 29 October 1991, *Helmers*, A.212-A, p. 16; *Jan-Åke Andersson*, A.212-B, p. 45 and *Fejde*, A.212-C, pp. 68-69.

confusion. The question whether a person should be heard in person has strictly speaking nothing to do with the publicity requirement. In fact the Court confuses the right to a public hearing – that means a public *trial* – with the right to be heard in person. Finally, in these cases the crucial question did not concern the publicity requirement but appeared to be whether the court of appeal could, 'as a matter of fair trial', properly decide to examine the case without the applicants having a right to present their arguments at a hearing.[849]

For pragmatic reasons the standpoint would seem to be justified that the requirement of a public judgment has been complied with if during a public session this is confined to the reading of the dictum,[850] and that even this may be omitted if the dictum contains no more than the determination that the appeal has been rejected or the case is referred back.[851] In that case the parties must receive a copy of the text of the judgment as soon as possible, while also the publication of at any rate those judgments in which legal questions of a more public interest are at issue, is of special importance for the verifiability.[852]

As to the grounds of restriction, it is striking that Article 6 permits restrictions exclusively with respect to the public nature of the proceedings, not with respect to the judgment. With respect to the possibilities of restriction the following observations must suffice here.

On the one hand, the Strasbourg organs appear to be willing to leave the national authorities, and specifically the national courts, a certain 'margin of appreciation' in the assessment of the question whether there is any reason for application of one of the restrictions, such as this is also the case with respect to the grounds of restriction included in other provisions of the Convention.[853] On the other hand, they appear also to make an independent examination themselves of the reasons of the restriction,[854] in which context they are not prepared to accept simply a developed practice, but require that it be stated specifically for each case which ground of restriction is invoked.[855]

When the protection of public order is at issue, one is inclined to think of the prevention of disorder. When Article 14 of the Covenant was drafted, this interpretation was indeed advocated, on the part of Great Britain, and on that

---

[849] Judgments of 29 October 1991, *Helmers*, A.212-A, p. 17; *Jan-Åke Andersson*, A.212-B, p. 46; and *Fejde*, A.212-C, pp. 69-70. The question whether a person has the right to be present at the trial is discussed *supra* pp. 433-435.

[850] Appls 8603, 8722, 8723 and 8729/79, *Crociani et al. v. Italy*, D&R 22 (1981), p. 147 (228); judgment of 8 December 1983, *Pretto*, A.71, pp. 12-13.

[851] Report of 14 December 1979, *Le Compte, Van Leuven and De Meyere*, B.38, p. 24; report of 15 March 1985, *Adler*, D&R 46 (1986), p. 36 (45).

[852] See *ibidem*, p. 24 and p. 45 respectively.

[853] See *supra*, Chapter II, section 3.

[854] See, *e.g.*, the report of the Commission and the judgment of the Court in the *Le Compte, Van Leuven and De Meyere* Case, B.38, pp. 43-44 and A.43, p. 25 respectively; and the report of the Commission and the judgment of the Court in the *Albert and Le Compte* Case, B.50, pp. 40-41 and A.58, p. 18 respectively.

[855] Judgment of 8 June 1976, *Engel*, A.22, p. 37.

ground objections were raised – in vain – to the addition of the French term *ordre public* in the English text.[856] Now that the text of Article 6 (and of Article 14) in its present form has been adopted, a comparison with Articles 10(2) and 11(2), where for the protection of public order the English text has 'the prevention of disorder' and the French text '*la défense de l'ordre*', renders it difficult to maintain this interpretation, although, on the other hand, the English and the French text of Article 9(2) show that the drafters have not been very consistent in this matter. However this may be, the prevention of disorder in the court room may in any case be brought under the ground 'the interests of justice'. What then means 'public order' in this context? In the *Le Compte, Van Leuven and De Meyere* Case the Belgian Government invoked this ground, alleging that publicity of the medical disciplinary cases might lead to violation of the medical professional secrecy. The Commission subsequently indeed examined this aspect under that denominator.[857] This seems to point in the direction of public order in the sense of *ordre public*. The medical professional secrecy has also been invoked in the *Diennet* Case, where the French Government has tried to justify the fact that disciplinary proceedings against a medical practitioner had been held in camera. However, according to the Commission and Court the proceedings in question concerned only 'the methods of consultation by correspondence' adopted by the applicant and thus, in principle, not the private life of patients of the applicant.[858]

The interest of national security so far has hardly played a part, if at all, in the Strasbourg case-law with respect to the public nature of the trial, but it is easy to conceive of situations in which in proceedings State secrets are involved, or other information that is security-sensitive. The court will then have to form an independent opinion about this. Everything that the authorities prefer to be kept secret does not for that reason alone concern national security.

Cases involving the protection of the private life of the parties, except for cases in which the interests of minors are involved, seem to require that a decision to consider the matter *in camera* can only be taken if the parties indeed appear to appreciate such protection.[859]

The last ground of restriction – the interests of justice – is explicitly left to the opinion of the domestic court concerned. Here again, however, an ultimate supervision by the Strasbourg organs is fitting, although this is likely to be

---

[856] See E/CN.4/SR.318, p. 10: 'the proper conception was that closed hearings could be held with a view to preventing disorder'.

[857] See the report of 14 December 1979, B.38 (1984), pp. 43-44. See also the report of 14 December 1981, *Albert and Le Compte*, B.50 (1986), pp. 40-41.

[858] Judgment of 26 September 1995, A.325-A, p. 15.

[859] Thus apparently also the Commission in its report in the *Albert and Le Compte* Case, B.50, pp. 40-41. In its decision on Appl. 7366/76, *X* v. *the United Kingdom* (not published), consideration *in camera* was deemed justified by the Commission on this ground against the wishes of the applicant, but this concerned divorce proceedings, so that the private life of the spouse and possibly the interests of one or more minor children were also involved.

marginal.[860] And here again the Commission and the Court will not accept a mere reference to an existing practice. In its decision in *X* v. *the United Kingdom* the Commission seems to suggest that witnesses whose testimony may constitute a danger for them may rely on Article 6(1) in complaining that the court has omitted to hear them *in camera*.[861] It may indeed be accepted that the interests of justice entail that witnesses are granted adequate protection; they, too, can claim a 'fair trial'.[862] The interests of justice may also require that the space available for the public does not become overcrowded and that agitators are excluded. But, on the other hand, the interest of publicity requires that the administration of justice takes place at locations where a reasonable accommodation for the public is available.

6.6 The Reasonable-Time Requirement

6.6.1 Introduction

Article 6 stipulates in its first paragraph that the hearing of the case by the court must take place 'within a reasonable time' (*dans un délai raisonnable*). Just as with regard to these same words in Article 5(3)[863] this raises the difficult question as to what criteria have to be applied for the assessment of what is reasonable, and also what period has to be taken into account in this respect.

In the case of Article 5(3) it is at all events clear what should be considered as the beginning of the relevant period: this is the moment of the arrest. The rationale of that provision is that the detention on remand does not last longer than is strictly necessary. The purpose of the reasonable-time requirement of Article 6(1), however, is to guarantee that within a reasonable time and by means of a judicial decision, an end is put to the insecurity into which a person finds himself as to his civil-law position or on account of a criminal charge against him; this in the interest of the person in question as well as of legal certainty. This rationale entails that the provision also applies in cases where there is no question of detention on remand.[864]

The judgments with regard to the reasonable-time requirement are quite numerous. However, since the middle of the eighties the main lines seem to have been charted.

---

[860] See the report of 14 December 1981, *Axen*, B.57 (1987), pp. 24-25, in which reference of the Government to the necessity to reduce the workload of the judiciary was not accepted without further argument by the Commission as an excuse for the elimination of the requirement of a 'public hearing' in cassation-proceedings. See on this subject however the quotation, *supra* at p. 439.

[861] Appl. 8016/77, *X* v. *the United Kingdom* (not published).

[862] See on this *infra* pp. 473-477.

[863] On this, see *supra* pp. 373-381.

[864] For the relation between the two provisions, see the judgment of 10 November 1969, *Stögmüller*, A.9 , p. 40 and the report of 12 July 1977, *Haase*, D&R 11 (1978), p. 78 (92), where it is also stated that with respect to the reasonableness of the duration more stringent requirements must be made in the case of Art. 5(3).

6.6.2 The Relevant Period

(a) Dies a Quo

In the determination of the relevant period, the *competentio ratione temporis* must be taken into account. Thus, in the case of an individual complaint concerning proceedings which were already in progress at the moment the State concerned recognised the individual's right of complaint under Article 25, only the length of the period from that moment can be taken into account. However, for the assessment of the reasonableness of that period the stage in which the proceedings were at that moment is also taken into consideration.[865]

With respect to criminal cases, the Court has held that as the beginning of the relevant period must be taken the moment at which a 'criminal charge' is brought, since it is only from that moment that the 'determination of (...) any criminal charge' can be involved.[866] However, the rationale mentioned above implies that the period may not in all cases begin at the moment at which the person in question is officially indicted. Even before that he may have realised that he is suspected of a criminal offence, so that from that moment he has an interest in that a decision about this suspicion be made by the court. This is quite evident in those cases where an arrest precedes the moment of the formal charge.[867] It is, therefore, important here as well that in the Strasbourg case-law an autonomous meaning is assigned to the concept of 'charge', the starting-point being that a substantive and not a formal concept of 'charge' must be used because of the great importance of the principle of a fair trial for a democratic society.[868] As the Court held in the *Foti* Case and in the *Corigliano* Case:

> Whilst 'charge' (...) may in general be defined as the official notification given to an individual by the competent authority of an allegation that he has committed a criminal offence, it may in some instances take the form of other measures which carry the implication of such an allegation and which likewise substantially affect the situation of the suspect.[869]

---

[865] See, *e.g.*, the judgment of 10 December 1982, *Foti*, A.56, p. 18; judgment of 26 October 1988, *Martins Moreira*, A.143, p. 16; judgment of 19 February 1991, *Brigandi*, A.194-B, p. 31; judgment of 8 June 1995, *Yaği and Sargin*, A.319-A, p. 20; judgment of 25 March 1996, *Mitap and Müftüoglo*, Reports 1996-II, Vol. 6, para. 31.

[866] Judgment of 27 June 1968, *Neumeister*, A.8, p. 41; judgment of 27 February 1980, *Deweer*, A.35, p. 22.

[867] In its judgment of 27 June 1968, *Wemhoff*, A.7, p. 26, the Court assumed that the two moments coincided. See further, *e.g.*, the judgment of 28 March 1990, *B* v. *Austria*, A.175, p. 18; judgment of 19 February 1991, *Alimena*, A.195-D, p. 53; judgment of 25 February 1993, *Dobbertin*, A.256-D, pp. 116 and 110. In the latter case there seems to exist a clear difference between the moment of arrest and the formal 'charge'. The Court took the moment of arrest as starting-point.

[868] See *supra* pp. 407-409.

[869] Judgments of 10 December 1982, *Foti and Others*, A.56, p. 18; *Corigliano*, A.57, p. 13.

Thus, the existence of a 'charge' is not always dependent of an official act.[870] Examples of such 'other measures' are the search of the person's home and/or the seizure of certain goods,[871] and the request that a person's immunity be lifted.[872] In some cases the 'charge' may not constitute the *dies a quo* of the relevant period: if the accused did not receive the official notification and was tried in absence, one has to presume that there exists a 'charge',[873] but the reasonable-time requirement is not at stake (yet), because the accused did not live under the pressure of being prosecuted.[874] The period that an accused, who is aware of the 'charge', is on the run, is excluded from the calculation of the relevant period.[875]

With respect to the determination of civil rights and obligations, as the beginning of the period may in general be taken the moment at which the proceedings concerned are instituted[876] or at which, within the framework of other proceedings, such a right or obligation is put forward in a defence. If prior to the judicial proceedings another action, for instance an administrative appeal[877] or a request for formal confirmation,[878] must have been brought, the beginning is shifted to the moment of that action.[879] A negotiation phase preceding the proceedings, however, is not counted as part of the relevant period.[880]

---

[870] Initially the Court took, unlike the Commission, a formal criterion to determine the starting-point of the relevant period: judgment of 27 June 1968, *Neumeister*, A.8, p. 41. Subsequently, it developed a substantive approach in the judgment of 15 July 1982, *Eckle*, A.51, p. 24, which culminated in the *Foti* judgment and the *Corigliano* judgment.

[871] Judgment of 15 July 1982, *Eckle*, A.51, p. 34.

[872] Judgment of 19 February 1991, *Frau*, A.195-E, p. 73.

[873] Judgment of 12 February 1985, *Colozza*, A.89, p. 15. The applicant was sentenced by default and did have, according to the Court, a right to a 'fresh determination of the merits of the charge'.

[874] This consequence does not fully correspond with the definition of 'charge' as cited from the *Foti* judgment. The contradiction can be lifted by deleting the word 'likewise'. Compare further the decision of the Commission on Appl. 9433/81, *Menten* v. *the Netherlands*, D&R 27 (1982), p. 233 (237), where the period between 1950 and 1976 was not calculated for the duration, because in that time, in consequence of the declaration of the Minister of Justice that he would not be prosecuted, Menten was not 'affected'.

[875] Judgment of 19 February 1991, *Girolami*, A.196-E, p. 55; judgment of 12 October 1995, *Boddaert*, A.235-D, p. 81; judgment of 26 May 1993, *Bunkate*, A.248-B, p. 30.

[876] See, *e.g.*, the judgment of 23 November 1993, *Scopelliti*, A.278, p. 8; judgment of 23 March 1994, *Muti*, A.281-C, p. 56; judgment of 27 October 1994, *Katte Klitsche de la Grange*, A.293-B, p. 37.

[877] Judgment of 28 June 1978, *König*, A.27, p. 33; report of 8 March 1982, *Andorfer Tonwerke*, D&R 32 (1983), p. 94 (108).

[878] Judgment of 9 December 1994, *Schouten and Meldrum*, A.304, pp. 24-25.

[879] Compare also the *Vallee* Case, judgment of 26 April 1994, A.289, p. 17, where the submission of the preliminary claim for compensation to the administrative authority, required under national law, constituted the starting-point of the relevant period.

[880] Report of 7 March 1984 and judgment of 8 July 1986, *Lithgow*, A.102, pp. 120 and 72 respectively. See, however, also the judgment of 23 April 1996, *Phocas*, Reports 1996-II, Vol. 7, para. 69, concerning, *inter alia*, negotiations, expressly recognised by law, prior to formal expropriation proceedings before a court. The Court did asses whether the duration of the preliminary proceedings

(b) Dies ad Quem

The above-mentioned rationale of this part of Article 6 entails that the end of the period to be taken into consideration is the moment at which the court has put an end to the uncertainty concerning the legal position of the person in question. That is not, therefore, in civil proceedings the moment at which the hearing in court starts, but the moment at which the decision is taken at highest instance[881] or has become final through the expiration of the time-limit for appeal.[882] Thus, as far as appeal or cassation proceedings 'are capable of affecting the outcome of the dispute', these proceedings must be taken into account in determining the relevant period.[883] The possibility of extraordinary remedies must be left out of consideration.

The same holds good for 'criminal' cases. As the Court held in its *Wemhoff* judgment:

> there is (...) no reason why the protection given to the persons concerned against the delays of the courts should end at the first hearing in a trial: unwarranted adjournments or excessive delays on the part of trial courts are also to be feared.[884]

The determination of the charge, for example by acquittal or dismissal, must be final.[885] As far as conviction is concerned, the determination of the penalty affords the certainty to the accused,[886] and then only at the moment at which he can reasonably be assumed to have been informed of the final verdict and its motivation.[887] The decision to refrain from further prosecution may also imply the final determination of the 'charge'.[888]

---

was reasonable.

[881] See, *e.g.*, the judgment of 24 May 1991, *Vocaturo*, A.206-C, p. 32; judgment of 12 October 1992, *Salerno*, A.245-D, p. 55.

[882] See, *e.g.*, the judgment of 24 May 1991, *Pugliese (II)*, A.206-A, p. 8; judgment of 27 February 1992, *Diana*, A.229-A, p. 10.

[883] See, *e.g.*, the judgment of 23 April 1987, *Poiss*, A.117-C, p. 103 and judgment of 21 November 1995, *Acquaviva*, A.333-A, p. 15.

[884] Judgment of 27 June 1968, A.7, p. 26.

[885] See, *e.g.*, the judgments of 19 February 1991, *Pugliese (I)*, A.195-C, p. 42; *Viezzer*, A.196-B, p. 21; *Angelucci*, A.196-C, p. 31.

[886] Judgment of 15 July 1982, *Eckle*, A.51, p. 35. In the same way, for civil proceedings, a judgment in which the right to compensation has been established but not its amount, does not mean the end of the proceedings; judgment of 10 July 1984, *Guincho*, A.81, p. 10. In the case of cumulative impositions of penalties the moment at which the last penalty became final constitutes the endpoint: judgment of 15 July 1982, *Eckle*, A.51, pp. 34-35.

[887] Report of 8 May 1984, *Vallon*, A.95, pp. 22-23.

[888] Report of 8 February 1973, *Huber*, Yearbook XVIII (1975), p. 324 (360).

6.6.3   Reasonable Time

When the length of the relevant period has been established, it must subsequently be determined whether this period is to be regarded as reasonable. In many cases the Court only makes an overall assessment,[889] in other cases however, it assesses the lapse of time in each stage of the proceedings.[890] The reasonableness cannot be judged in the abstract but has to be assessed in view of the circumstances of each individual case.[891] The interests of the person concerned in as prompt a decision as possible will have to be weighed against the demands of a careful examination and a proper conduct of the proceedings.[892]

When assessing the reasonableness of the relevant period the Court applies, according to established case-law, in particular three criteria: the complexity of the case, the conduct of the applicant, and the conduct of the relevant authorities. Only delays attributable to the State may cause a violation of the reasonable-time requirement.[893] The question whether a case is complex, is hard to be answered in general. The Court has attached importance to several factors as, for instance, the nature of the facts to be established,[894] the number of accused persons[895] and witnesses,[896] the need to obtain the file of the trial conducted abroad,[897] the joinder of the case to other cases,[898] and the intervention of other persons in the procedure.[899] The complexity may concern questions of fact as well legal issues.[900]

An attitude or behaviour of the party in question which has led to a delay, weakens his complaint about that delay.[901] However, an accused person is not

---

[889] See, *e.g.*, the judgment of 19 February 1991, *Colacioppo*, A.197-D, p. 51; judgment of 27 February 1992, *G* v. *Italy*, A.228-F, p. 67; judgment of 26 November 1992, *Giancarlo Lombardo*, A.249-C, p. 43; judgment of 18 July 1994, *Venditelli*, A.293-A, p. 10.

[890] See, *e.g.*, the judgment of 23 November 1993, *Scopelliti*, A.278, pp. 9-10; judgment of 23 March 1994, *Silva Pontes*, A.286-A, p. 15.

[891] See, *e.g.*, the judgments of 19 February 1991, *Santilli*, A.194-D, p. 61; *Maj*, A.196-D, p. 43.

[892] See, *e.g.*, the judgment of 8 July 1987, *H* v. *the United Kingdom*, A.120, pp. 59 and 62-63; judgment of 31 March 1992, *X* v. *France*, A.234-C, pp. 90-91; judgment of 23 March 1994, *Silva Pontes*, A.286-A, p. 15.

[893] See, *e.g.*, the judgment of 20 February 1991, *Vernillo*, A.198, p. 13; judgment of 27 February 1992, *Pierazzini*, A.231-C, p. 30.

[894] See, *e.g.*, the judgment of 19 February 1991, *Triggiani*, A.197-B, p. 24; judgment of 30 October 1991, *Wiesinger*, A.213, p. 21; judgment of 27 February 1992, *Vorrasi*, A.230-E, p. 52; judgment of 25 February 1993, *Dobbertin*, A.256-D, p. 117.

[895] Judgment of 19 February 1991, *Angelucci*, A.196-C, p. 31.

[896] Judgment of 27 February 1992, *Andreucci*, A.228-G, p. 76.

[897] Judgment of 19 February 1991, *Manzoni*, A.195-B, p. 29.

[898] Judgment of 27 February 1992, *Diana*, A.229-A, p. 10.

[899] Judgment of 27 February 1992, *Manieri*, A.229-D, p. 42.

[900] Judgment of 27 February 1992, *Lorenzi, Bernardini, and Gritti*, A.231-G, p. 75; judgment of 27 October 1994, *Katte Klitsche de la Grange*, A.293-B, p. 38.

[901] Judgment of 16 July 1971, *Ringeisen*, A.13, p. 45; judgment of 28 June 1978, *König*, A.27, pp. 35-36; judgment of 6 May 1981, *Buchholz*, A.42, p. 19; judgment of 15 July 1982, *Eckle*, A.51, p. 362; judgment of 10 July 1984, *Guincho*, A.81, pp. 21-22; judgment of 8 December 1983, *Pretto*, A.71, p. 15; judgment of 29 May 1986, *Deumeland*, A.100, p. 27; judgment of 27 February 1992,

required to cooperate actively in expediting the proceedings which may lead to his own conviction.[902] This is different for parties to civil proceedings.[903] A party to proceedings can not be blamed for making use of his right to bring an appeal.[904] It is evident that this prolongs the proceedings, but this prolongation, too, must stand the test of reasonableness.[905]

The Commission and the Court have also taken into account the conduct of the other party in its considerations concerning the reasonableness. In the Strasbourg supervision, since complaints must be directed against States, this can only play a part if that other party is a public authority, or if at least that conduct can partly be imputed to the authorities.[906] If in a criminal case with two accused persons one of them retards the case, the prosecutor must separate the cases if possible, in order that the other accused does not become the victim of the delay.[907]

With regard to the third criterion, the conduct of the authorities, the efforts the judicial authorities have made to expedite the proceedings as much as possible play an important part.[908] In this respect a special duty rests upon the court concerned to see to it that all those who play a role in the proceedings do their utmost to avoid any unnecessary delay. This holds good in criminal as well civil cases, where the initiative in the proceedings in principle may be left to the parties.[909] In the *Capuano* Case the Italian Government drew attention to the fact that the delays in the proceedings in first instance, which lasted for more than six years, were attributable to the experts, who filed their opinions too late. The Court held the court concerned responsible for the delays in preparing expert opinions.[910] In the *Idrocalce* and *Tumminelli* Cases the Court reached the same

---

Arena, A.228-H, p. 85; judgment of 12 October 1992, *Cesarini*, A.245-B, p. 26.

[902] Judgment of 15 July 1982, *Eckle*, A.51, p. 36; judgment of 25 February 1993, *Dobbertin*, A.256-D, p. 117.

[903] Appl. 1794/63, *X* v. *Federal Republic of Germany*, Yearbook IX (1966), p. 179 (212). See also the judgment of 23 March 1994, *Muti*, A.281-C, p. 57.

[904] See, *e.g.*, the judgment of 15 July 1982, *Eckle*, A.51, p. 36. Compare also the judgment of 24 October 1994, *Katte Klitsche de la Grange*, A.293-B, p. 38. The applicant had applied to the Court of Cassation for a preliminary ruling on jurisdiction of the lower court. Although he could have made a subsequent appeal, his conduct was not open to criticism.

[905] Judgment of 23 April 1987, *Lechner and Hess*, A.118, p. 19.

[906] Judgment of 6 May 1981, *Buchholz*, A.42, p. 16; judgment of 8 July 1987, *Baraona*, A.122, p. 21; judgment of 26 October 1988, *Martins Moreira*, A.143, p. 17; judgment of 9 December 1994, *Schouten and Meldrum*, A.304, pp. 25-26.

[907] Appl. 6541/74, *Bonnechaux* v. *Federal Republic of Germany*, D&R 3 (1976), p. 86 (87).

[908] Judgment of 27 June 1968, *Wemhoff*, A.7, p. 27; judgment of 27 June 1968, *Neumeister*, A.8, pp. 41-43; judgment of 16 July 1971, *Ringeisen*, A.13, p. 45; judgment of 28 June 1978, *König*, A.27, pp. 34-40; judgment of 6 May 1981, *Buchholz*, A.42, pp. 15-21; judgment of 28 March 1990, *B* v. *Austria*, A.175, p. 19; judgment of 23 March 1994, *Silva Pontes*, A.286-A, p. 15.

[909] Judgment of 20 February 1991, *Vernillo*, A.198, pp. 12-13.

[910] Judgment of 25 June 1987, A.119, p. 13. See also the judgment of 26 February 1992, *Nibbio*, A.228-A, p. 10; judgment of 23 November 1993, *Scopelliti*, A.278, p. 9.

conclusion with reference to the delays in hearing witnesses.[911] The mere fact that the national authorities fail to comply with legal time-limits is in itself not contrary to Article 6(1).[912] Legislation or a judicial practice placing obstacles in the way of a plaintiff for a prompt institution of proceedings, as well as legislation enabling him to leave the other party for a long time in uncertainty as to whether or not an action will be brought, without a reasonably short term of limitation preventing this, does not satisfy Article 6(1).

The Strasbourg organs appear to be prepared to pay attention to special interests which may be involved for the applicant. Thus in the *H* v. *the United Kingdom* Case, which concerned the length of the proceedings instituted by the applicant regarding her claimed access to her child, which had been entrusted to the care of a local authority, the Court put special emphasis on the importance of what was at stake for the applicant in the proceedings in question. Not only were these proceedings decisive for her future relations with her child, but they had a particular quality of irreversibility, involving as they did what the High Court graphically described as the 'statutory guillotine' of adoption. In these circumstances the Court expected an exceptional diligence on the part of the authorities.[913] Subsequently the Court held in general that a particular diligence is required in cases concerning civil status and capacity,[914] employment disputes, which include pension disputes,[915] decisions with regard to the determination of compensation for the victims of road accidents[916] and for persons infected with HIV as the result of blood transfusion at hospitals.[917]

Overburdening of the judiciary in general is not recognised as an excuse, since the Contracting States have the general duty to organise the administration of justice in such a way that the various courts can meet the requirements of Article 6.[918] According to constant case-law Contracting States are not-liable in the event of a temporary backlog of business in their courts, provided that they take, with the requisite promptness, remedial action to deal with an exceptional situation

---

[911] Judgments of 27 February 1992, *Idrocalce S.r.l.*, A.229-F, p. 64; *Tumminelli*, A.231-H, pp. 84-85. See also from the same date *Cooperativa Parco Cuma*, A.231-E, p. 52.

[912] Judgment of 27 February 1992, *G* v. *Italy*, A.228-F, p. 67.

[913] Judgment of 8 July 1987, A.120, pp. 62-63.

[914] Judgment of 29 March 1990, *Bock*, A.150, p. 23. See also the judgments of 27 February 1992, *Taituti*, A.229-I, p. 93; *Masciariello*, A.230-A, p. 10; *Gana*, A.230-H, p. 82.

[915] Judgments of 26 February 1992, *Nibbio*, A.228-A, p. 10; *Borgese*, A.228-B, p. 21; judgment of 27 February 1992, *Ruotolo*, A.230-D, p. 39.

[916] Judgment of 26 October 1988, *Martins Moreira*, A.143, p. 21 and judgment of 23 March 1994, *Silva Pontes*, A.286-A, p. 15.

[917] Judgment of 8 February 1996, *A. and Others* v. *Denmark*, Reports 1996-I, Vol. 2, para. 78.

[918] Judgment of 10 November 1969, *Stögmüller*, A.9, pp. 40-41; judgment of 26 October 1984, *De Cubber*, A.86, p. 20; judgment of 26 November 1992, *Francesco Lombardo*, A.249-B, p. 27; judgment of 25 February 1994, *Dobbertin*, A.256-D, p. 117; judgment of 9 December 1994, *Schouten and Meldrum*, A.304, p. 26.

of this kind.[919] The measures taken are assessed as to their effectiveness,[920] and it is also ascertained whether they have been taken in good time; measures taken afterwards cannot make up for the fact that the reasonable period has been exceeded.[921] When making this assessment the Court is prepared to take into consideration the political and social background in the country concerned.[922]

The application of the criteria, the complexity of the case, the conduct of the applicant and the conduct of the authorities, may lead to different conclusions. In the *Bunkate* Case for instance, a criminal case, the relevant period lasted two years and ten months. This lapse of time was amongst other factors caused by a period of total inactivity of fifteen and a half months between the filing of the appeal on points of law and the reception of the case-file by the registry of the Supreme Court. This period in itself infringed the reasonable-time requirement.[923] On the other hand, in the *Boddaert* Case it took slightly more than six years to determine the 'criminal charge'. This lapse of time did not violate Article 6.[924] Comparable differences may be noted as far as civil proceedings are concerned. In the *Ciricosta and Viola* Case an overall period of more than 15 years did meet the requirements of Article 6(1),[925] but a lapse of time that lasted four years and five months in the *Pugliese II* Case did not pass muster.[926]

If it is argued against the person who complains about an unreasonable delay of the proceedings that, contrary to Article 26, he has not waited for the outcome of the national proceedings, the decision about reasonableness may also be decisive for the question whether he is required still to do so, which indeed will lead to an even greater delay. If at first sight the complaint does not appear ill-founded, the Commission would be well-advised to request the national authorities to suspend the domestic proceedings pending the decision in Strasbourg, unless the possibilities for a later continuation of the proceedings would be disproportionately prejudiced as a result of such a suspension. The applicant, for his part, must be able to demonstrate that in the domestic proceedings he has used any possible remedies which might have expedited the matter.

If the proceedings concern war crimes, in the Commission's opinion the 'criteria determining the reasonableness of the length of ordinary criminal proceedings' are not automatically applicable, but the length of the proceedings

---

[919] Judgment of 13 July 1983, *Zimmermann and Steiner*, A.66, pp. 11-13; report of 12 March 1984, *Marijnissen*, D&R 40 (1985), p. 83 (90); judgment of 25 June 1987, *Baggetta*, A.119, p. 33; judgment of 26 October 1988, *Martins Moreira*, A.143, p. 20.

[920] Report of 12 December 1983, *Neubeck*, D&R 41 (1985), p. 13 (32-33).

[921] Report of 12 March 1984, *Marijnissen*, D&R 40 (1985), p. 83 (90).

[922] See, *e.g.*, the judgment of 25 June 1987, *Milasi*, A.119, p. 47, where the Court took into account the disturbances in the Region concerned and the judgment of 7 July 1989, *Unión Alimentaria S.A.*, A.157, p. 15.

[923] Judgment of 26 May 1993, A.248-B, pp. 30-31.

[924] Judgment of 12 October 1992, A.235-D, pp. 81-83.

[925] Judgment of 4 December 1995, A.337-A, pp. 10-11.

[926] Judgment of 24 May 1991, A.206-A, pp. 8-9.

has to be assessed in the light of the exceptional character of such an action.[927] For this view the Commission has not advanced any further arguments. Since Article 1 accords the protection of the Convention to 'everyone', while, if the normal criteria are applied, it is possible to take the special complexity of the case, in particular the difficulty to collect evidence, sufficiently into account, it is hard to understand why special criteria should apply. In the *Menten* Case this view was not repeated.[928]

The requirement of a trial within a reasonable time equally entails that this time may not be unreasonably short, in consequence of which it is not possible for the parties to prepare the case properly. What is expressly provided in paragraph 3(b) for criminal proceedings, in virtue of the general requirement of a fair hearing in the first paragraph applies to civil proceedings as well.

Article 6(1) does not stipulate what the consequences for the proceedings are, if the reasonable-time requirement has not been met. It would seem to ensue from this provision that, if the reasonable time has been exceeded and, consequently, the determination can no longer be made within a reasonable time, the proceedings would have to be stopped and the civil action or criminal charge to be declared inadmissible. However, the Strasbourg organs have adopted a more flexible view and indicated that:

> an excessive length of criminal proceedings can in principle be compensated for by measures of the domestic authorities, including in particular a reduction of the sentence on account of the length of procedure.[929]

This point of view, which seems difficult to be reconciled with the text of Article 6(1), offers the most appropriate solution in certain cases. In civil proceedings the applicant should not become the victim of an unreasonable delay for which the public authorities are to be blamed; both parties can be victims of the delay and be entitled to some form of just satisfaction. And in criminal procedures the public interest in the prosecution and conviction of the criminal may be so great that the prosecution should not be stopped for the sole reason that the reasonable time has been transgressed; another, more proportionate compensation should be awarded to the victim of that transgression.

---

[927] Appl. 6946/75, *X* v. *Federal Republic of Germany*, D&R 6 (1977), p. 114 (115-116). This does not imply that the requirement of a reasonable time in those cases would not apply, but only that other criteria would apply for that reasonableness.

[928] Appl. 9433/81, *Menten* v. *the Netherlands*, D&R 27 (1982), p. 233 (237).

[929] Report of 12 December 1983, *Neubeck*, D&R 41 (1985), p. 13 (34). See also Appl. 10884/84, *H* v. *Federal Republic of Germany*, D&R 41 (1985), p. 252 (254); judgment of 15 July 1982, *Eckle*, A.51, p. 31.

6.7 Independent and Impartial Tribunal

6.7.1 Introduction

Finally, the first paragraph of Article 6 provides that the determination there referred to, be in the hands of an independent and impartial tribunal, established by law. The tribunal need not be 'a court of law of the classic kind, integrated within the standard judicial machinery of the country'.[930] For the notion of 'tribunal' it is essential that there exists a power to decide matters 'on the basis of rules of law, following proceedings conducted in a prescribed manner'[931] and a power to set aside the decisions of the bodies below 'on questions of law and fact'.[932] The decision taken by the tribunal may not be deprived of its effect by a non-judicial authority to the disadvantage of the individual party.[933]

The adjectives 'independent' and 'impartial' are the expression of two different concepts. The notion of 'independence' refers to the connection between the judge and the administration, whereas the 'impartiality' must exist in relation to the parties to the suit. However, the Court has not always drawn a clear borderline between the two concepts, as will be seen in the next sections.

The principles established in the Court's case-law with regard to the notions of independence and impartiality apply as well to professional judges and lay judges as to jurors.[934]

6.7.2 Independence

In the *Ringeisen* Case the Court held that the Regional Commission could be regarded as a 'tribunal' as it was 'independent of the executive and also of the parties'. The latter element, however, refers in fact not to the independence but to the required impartiality of the court. The Court added that the members of the Regional Commission had been appointed for five years and the proceedings before it did offer the necessary guarantees.[935] A comparable line of reasoning was developed in the *Langborger* Case:

---

[930] Judgment of 28 June 1984, *Campbell and Fell*, A.80, p. 29; judgment of 22 October 1984, *Sramek*, A.84, p. 17. See also the judgment of 24 February 1995, *McMichael*, A.307-B, pp. 53-54, with regard to an adjudicatory body composed of three 'specially trained persons with substantial experience of children' and the judgment of 20 November 1995, *British-American Tabacco Company Ltd.*, A.331, p. 25, concerning patent application proceedings.

[931] Judgment of 22 October 1984, *Sramek*, A.84, p. 36 and the report of 8 December 1982 in this case, A.84, p. 31. See also the judgment of 23 October 1985, *Benthem*, A.97, p. 17; judgment of 30 November 1987, *H* v. *Belgium*, A.127-B, p. 34; judgment of 27 August 1991, *Demicoli*, A.210, p. 18.

[932] See, *inter alia*, the judgments of 23 October 1995, *Schmautzer*, A.328-A and *Pfarrmeier*, A.329-C, p. 15 and p. 66, respectively.

[933] Judgment of 19 April 1994, *Van de Hurk*, A.288, pp. 16-18.

[934] Judgment of 22 June 1989, *Langborger*, A.155, pp. 15-16; judgment of 23 April 1996, *Remli*, Reports 1996-II, Vol. 8, paras 46-48; judgment of 10 June 1996, *Pullar*, Reports 1996-III, Vol. 11, paras 31-32.

[935] Judgment of 16 July 1971, A.13, p. 39.

> In order to establish whether a body can be considered 'independent' regard must be had, *inter alia*, to the manner of appointment of its members and their term of office, to the existence of guarantees against outside pressures and to the question whether the body presents an appearance of independence.[936]

These various characteristics of the notion of independence seems to fall into three categories. Firstly, the tribunal must function independently of the executive, base its decisions on its own free opinion about facts and legal grounds. Secondly, there must be guarantees to enable the court to function independently. As far as the latter requirement is concerned, it is not necessary that the judges have been appointed for life, provided that they cannot be discharged at will or on improper grounds by the authorities.[937] Thirdly, even a semblance of dependence must be avoided. In the *Bryan* Case the Court held that the very existence of the power of the Secretary of State to revoke the power of an inspector to decide an appeal under the Town and Country Planning Act, was enough to deprive the inspector from the appearance of independence.[938] And in the *Sramek* Case, where a member of the court was hierarchically subordinate to one of the parties to the suit, the Court held:

> Litigants may entertain a legitimate doubt about his independence. Such a situation seriously affects the confidence which the courts must inspire in a democratic society.[939]

However, this aspect no longer refers to the independence, but to the impartiality of the court.

6.7.3 Impartiality

For the impartiality it is required that the court is not biassed with regard to the decision to be taken, does not allow itself to be influenced by information from outside the court room, by popular feeling, or by any pressure whatsoever, but bases its opinion on objective arguments on the ground of what has been put forward at the trial. Although a judge of course also has personal emotions, also during the proceedings, he must not allow himself to be led by them during the hearing of the case and in the formation of his opinion.[940] And although judges

---

[936] Judgment of 22 June 1989, A.155 p. 16. See also the judgment of 29 April 1988, *Belilos*, A.132, p. 29; judgment of 28 September 1995, *Procola*, A.326, p. 16; judgment of 22 November 1995, *Bryan*, A.335-A, p. 15.

[937] Implicitly the judgment of 16 July 1971, *Ringeisen*, A.13. Explicitly the report of 12 October 1978, *Zand*, D&R 15 (1979), p. 70 (81-82), and the report of 14 December 1979, *Le Compte, Van Leuven and De Meyere*, B.38 (1984), p. 40. With regard to military tribunals, see the judgment of 8 June 1976, *Engel*, A.22, pp. 27-28.

[938] Judgment of 22 November 1995, A.335-A, para. 38.

[939] Judgment of 22 October 1984, A.84, pp. 19-20.

[940] See Appl. 1727/62, *Boeckmans* v. *Belgium*, Yearbook VI (1963), p. 370 (416-420), where the complaint concerned a judge who in his indignation about a specific defence uttered a warning that its upholding might lead to an increase of the penalty. Later this case was settled: report of the subcommittee of 17 February 1965.

may also have a political preference and/or adhere to a specific philosophy of life, and although it is of course right that the various political streams and philosophies of life are also 'represented' within the judiciary, it must not make an essential difference for the person involved whether he is tried by a judge with one or another preference.[941]

Publicity surrounding a criminal case, where the difference between 'suspected of' and 'guilty of' is not always taken into account, may constitute a threat to the right to a fair and impartial trial, in particular also when this publicity proceeds from the authorities, *e.g.*, from the public prosecutor charged with the examination.[942] The judge should duly take this risk into account when forming his opinion, this also in connection with the presumption of innocence as guaranteed in the second paragraph.[943] In cases with a markedly political background the said risk and the necessity for the court to be on the alert against improper influences may even apply to a higher degree.[944] In the Strasbourg case-law it is assumed, however, that a professional judge will in general be very well aware of these external factors and will not readily allow himself to be influenced thereby, while moreover on appeal the higher court, in this respect, too, may correct the attitude of the lower court.[945] Thus, in the *Menten* Case the Commission held that the great publicity and the utterance of hostile feelings in this case could not be avoided, but that the Supreme Court had accurately ascertained on what testimony the lower courts had based their considerations.[946] In cases of trial by jury the risk of the jury being influenced by public opinion or by biassed statements of witnesses or experts is more obvious.[947]

The requirement in Article 10(2) that the freedom of expression may be restricted 'for maintaining the authority and impartiality of the judiciary'[948] is most closely connected with the point of publicity surrounding a trial. This restriction, which relates to the prohibition of 'contempt of court' embedded in Anglo-American law, was discussed at length in Strasbourg in the *Sunday Times* Case. The complaint there concerned the prohibition, imposed by the English courts up to the highest instance, to publish during a given time an article about the so-called 'thalidomide children', children who had been born with serious

---

[941] Appls 8603, 8722, 8723 and 8729/79, *Crociani* et al. v. *Italy*, D&R 22 (1981), p. 147 (222).

[942] Appl. 8403/78, *Jespers* v. *Belgium*, D&R 22 (1981), p. 100 (127).

[943] Thus the Commission in, *e.g.*, the *Pfunders* Case (*Austria* v. *Italy*), Yearbook VI (1963), p. 740 (782-784). See also Appl. 7542/76, *X* v. *the United Kingdom* (not published), where in a case which attracted much publicity the Commission attached great importance to the fact that the judge had drawn the jury's attention to the risk of prejudice.

[944] Appls 8603, 8722, 8723 and 8729/79, *Crociani* et al. v. *Italy*, D&R 22 (1981), p. 147 (222-223 and 227).

[945] Appl. 3444/67, *X* v. *Norway*, Yearbook XIII (1970), p. 302 (324); Appl. 3860/68, *X* v. *the United Kingdom*, Coll. 30 (1970), p. 70 (74-75).

[946] Appl. 9433/81, *Menten* v. *the Netherlands*, D&R 27 (1982), p. 233 (238).

[947] This risk was emphasised several times by the Commission: Appl. 1476/62, *X* v. *Austria*, Coll. 11 (1963), p. 31 (43); Appl. 3444/67, *X* v. *Norway*, Yearbook XIII (1970), p. 302 (324).

[948] See on this subject, *infra* pp. 583-585.

physical deformities in consequence of the use of the sedative thalidomide by their mothers during pregnancy. The prohibition had been imposed because at that moment various proceedings against the manufacturer of thalidomide were pending and the publication might lead to a 'contempt of court'. The Commission and the Court, though with a narrow majority, came to the conclusion that in this case the prohibition was not justified. They took into account, *inter alia*, that a court is not readily influenced by publications of this kind.[949]

In testing whether a 'tribunal' or judge has been prejudiced the Court makes a distinction between a subjective and an objective approach to impartiality. The subjective approach refers to the personal impartiality of the members of the tribunal involved; this impartiality is presumed as long as the contrary has not been proved.[950] The establishment of a personal bias is difficult. Even when the reasons are included in a judicial decision, it is extremely difficult to ascertain by what motives a court has been led. It will therefore only be possible to conclude that a judge is biassed when this becomes quite clear from his attitude during the proceedings or from the content of the judgment. It will be even more difficult to prove the prejudice of (the members of) the jury because a decision of the jury does not include a written statement of reasons.[951] In its case-law the Commission evidently assumes that if a verdict of a jury has been appealed from to a court and the latter has not found any partiality, there is no longer any reason for the Commission to review the jury's verdict in this respect,[952] and that also during the proceedings themselves in which the jury reaches its decision, the court, *via* its attitude and statements, may have a neutralising effect on undue influences.[953]

The objective approach refers to the question whether the way in which the tribunal is composed and organised, or whether a certain coincidence or succession of functions of one of its members, may give rise to doubt as to the impartiality of the tribunal or that member. If there is reason for such doubt, even if subjectively there is no concrete indication of partiality of the person in question, this already amounts to an inadmissible jeopardy of the confidence which the court must inspire in a democratic society.[954] The fear that the tribunal or a particular

---

[949] Report of 18 May 1977, B.28 (1982), pp. 71-74; judgment of 26 April 1979, A.30, pp. 28-42.

[950] Judgment of 1 October 1982, *Piersack*, A.53, pp. 14-16; judgment of 26 October 1984, *De Cubber*, A.86, pp. 15-16; judgment of 25 June 1992, *Thorgeir Thorgeirson*, A.239, p. 23; judgment of 24 February 1993, *Fey*, A.255, p. 12; judgment of 26 February 1993, *Padovani*, A.257-B, p. 20; judgment of 22 April 1994, *Saraiva de Carvalho*, A.286-B, p. 38.

[951] Compare the judgment of 10 June 1996, *Pullar*, Reports 1996-III, Vol. 11, paras 31-32.

[952] Appl. 3444/67, *X* v. *Norway*, Yearbook XIII (1970), p. 302 (324-326); Appl. 3860/68, *X* v. *the United Kingdom*, Coll. 30 (1970), p. 70 (74-75).

[953] Report in the *Nielsen* Case, Yearbook IV (1961), p. 490 (568), where the complaint concerned the fact that the jury had been influenced by a witness-expert.

[954] See the judgment of 1 October 1982, *Piersack*, A.53; judgment of 26 October 1984, *De Cubber*, A.86; judgment of 25 June 1992, *Thorgeir Thorgeirson*, A.239; judgment of 24 February 1993, *Fey*, A.255-A; judgment of 26 February 1993, *Padovani*, A.257-B; judgment of 22 April 1994, *Saraiva de Carvalho*, A.286-B.

judge lacks impartiality must 'be held to be objectively justified', so the standpoint of the accused on this matter, although important, is not decisive.[955]

This objective-approach-test has been applied in several cases. Despite the casuistic case-law some main lines can be discerned. The fact that a judge has taken decisions in the case prior to the trial and subsequently officiates as a trial judge is in itself not incompatible with the requirement of impartiality. What matters is the 'scope and nature' of the measures taken prior to the trial.[956] The fear of prejudice cannot for instance be justified solely by the fact that the judge has taken decisions on the prolongation of the detention on remand. Only special circumstances can give rise to a different conclusion.[957] Such special circumstances did occur in the *Hauschieldt* Case. In ordering the continued pre-trial detention the judge had to be convinced that there was 'a very high degree of clarity as to the question of guilt'. The difference between this assessment and the assessment that had to be made when giving judgment thus became (too) tenuous.[958] In case the prolongation of the detention on remand may be ordered if the judge is convinced that there exists *'prima facie* evidence', no problem with regard to the impartiality arises.[959] In the *Piersack* Case the president of the tribunal had been involved in an earlier phase of the case as a public prosecutor.[960] In the *De Cubber* Case and the *Yaacoub* Case a judge was involved who had previously in the same case acted as an investigating judge and as a president of a chamber respectively. In all these cases it was held that these facts created too much doubt about the impartiality of the judge concerned in an objective sense.[961] In the *Padovani* Case, however, the questioning of the accused and the taking of measures restricting his liberty in the pre-trial phase by a person who subsequently was a trial judge, did not amount to a violation of Article 6.[962] The required impartiality does not imply that a superior court which

---

[955] Judgment of 24 May 1989, *Hauschildt*, A.154, p. 21; judgment of 25 June 1992, *Thorgeir Thorgeirson*, A.239, p. 23; judgment of 24 February 1993, *Fey*, A.255, p. 12; judgment of 26 February 1993, *Padovani*, A.257-B, p. 20; judgment of 22 April 1994, *Saraiva de Carvalho*, A.286-B, p. 38.

[956] Judgment of 24 August 1993, *Nortier*, A.267, p. 15; judgment of 22 April 1994, *Saraiva de Carvalho*, A.286-B, p. 38. In the *Fey* Case, judgment of 24 February 1993, A.255-A, p. 12, the Court held 'the extent and nature' to be decisive.

[957] Judgment of 24 May 1989, *Hauschieldt*, A.154, p. 22; judgment of 16 December 1992, *Sainte-Marie*, A.253-A, p. 16.

[958] Judgment of 24 May 1989, A.154, p. 23.

[959] Judgment of 24 August 1993, *Nortier*, A.267, p. 16; judgment of 22 April 1994, *Saraiva de Carvalho*, A.286-B, p. 39.

[960] Judgment of 1 October 1982, A.53, p. 14.

[961] Judgment of 26 October 1984, *De Cubber*, A.86, pp. 15-16; report of 7 May 1985, *Yaacoub*, A.127, pp. 11-13; judgment of 29 April 1988, *Belilos*, A.132, p. 30. See also the report of 8 March 1989, *Jón Kristinsson*, A.171-B, p. 53 and the judgment of 7 August 1996, *Ferrantelli and Santangelo*, Reports 1996-III, Vol. 12, paras 53-59.

[962] Judgment of 26 February 1993, A.257-B, pp. 20-21. See also the judgment of 24 February 1993, *Fey*, A.255-A, pp. 13-14 and compare the *Thorgeir Thorgeirson* Case, judgment of 25 June 1992, A.239, pp. 23-24, where the applicant's claim that the court lacked impartiality because it had taken

quashes the decision of a lower court is obliged to send the case back to another court or to a differently composed chamber of the lower court.[963]

The successive carrying out of an advisory and a judicial function in the same case was at stake in the *Procola* Case. Procola, an association under Luxembourg law, challenged the lawfulness of four ministerial orders for the Judicial Committee of the *Conseil d'Etat*. In deciding the case the Judicial Committee also had to give its opinion on the lawfulness of a regulation that had been subjected to an advisory opinion of the *Conseil d'Etat*. In fact, the *Conseil d'Etat* had recommended the inclusion of the very provision that was challenged by Procola. The Judicial Committee was composed of five members. The fact that four of them had pronounced on the lawfulness of the regulation in their advisory capacity, was, according to the Court, sufficient reason to doubt the impartiality of the Luxembourg *Conseil d'Etat*.[964]

In the *Bulut* Case the question arose whether the applicant had waived his right under domestic law to object to the participation of a judge in a criminal trial, who had taken part previously in the questioning of two witnesses. The approach of the Court in this case seems to be ambiguous. On the one hand it held that it was irrelevant whether a waiver had been made or not, because it was anyhow incumbent on the Court to assess whether the composition of the trial court could cast doubt on its impartiality.[965] On the other hand, however, it concluded that the objective approach could offer the applicant no success, since he had refrained from his right to challenge the composition of the Court.[966]

The mere fact that lay assessors also sit on a tribunal, as is frequently the case in disciplinary tribunals, does not mean on this ground alone that they are not impartial. But if persons are concerned who are closely allied to one of the parties, which is often the case in arbitration tribunals, their impartiality may be open to doubt.[967] An issue under Article 6(1) will then rise only when not all the parties or their interests are equally represented in the tribunal in question. Thus in the *Le Compte, Van Leuven and De Meyere* Case, where three medical practitioners had been summoned before a disciplinary tribunal on account of their opposition to the obligatory membership of a professional association of medical practitioners, the Commission reached the conclusion that there was no impartial course of proceedings, since the tribunal judging at first instance, the Provincial Council, was composed largely of persons who had been elected by members of

---

over the public prosecutor's functions in the legal absence of the latter, was not upheld by the Court, and the judgment of 22 February 1996, *Bulut*, Reports 1996-II, Vol. 5, para. 34, concerning a judge who had questioned witnesses in the pre-trial phase.

[963] Judgment of 16 July 1971, A.13, p. 40; judgment of 26 September 1995, *Diennet*, A.325-A, pp. 16-17. See also the judgment of 10 June 1996, *Thomann*, Reports 1996-III, Vol. 11, paras 27-37, concerning a criminal trial *in absentia* and retrial in the presence of the accused by the same judges.

[964] Judgment of 28 September 1995, A.326, pp. 15-16.

[965] Judgment of 22 February 1996, Reports 1996-II, Vol. 5, para. 30.

[966] *Ibidem*, para. 34.

[967] Report of 12 December 1983, *Bramelid and Malmström*, D&R 38 (1984), pp. 40-41.

the professional association, while the Appeal Council consisted of medical practitioners and judges on a fifty-fifty basis. The fact that appeal to the Court of Cassation was also possible did not, in the Commission's opinion, eliminate this defect, because review was possible only on the ground of procedural errors or misapplication of the law.[968] The Court, however, did not follow the Commission. Since an appeal had been lodged with the Appeal Council, in the Court's view the impartiality of the Provincial Council did not require examination. With regard to the Appeal Council the Court held that the impartiality of such a tribunal must be presumed, unless the contrary can be proved, which had not been done in the present case in the Court's opinion.[969] However, in the *Langborger* Case the Court did apply the objective-impartiality-test and reached the conclusion that the predominance of lay assessors who had close links with two associations who had an interest – contrary to the interest of the applicant – in the outcome of the proceedings, did raise legitimate doubts as to the impartiality.[970] A comparable line of reasoning lead in the *Holm* Case to the conclusion that the impartiality (and independence) of the jury was open to doubt,[971] but in the *Pullar* Case the fact that a member of the jury was a junior employee in the firm of one of the witnesses for the prosecution, could pass the objective-impartiality-test: Article 6 had not been violated.[972] In the *Remli* Case a national court refused to check in a criminal procedure against two Algerians whether the allegation was true that one of the jurors had said, outside the court, 'What's more, I'm a racist.' The refusal constituted a breach of the impartiality-requirement.[973]

The independence and impartiality of the members of the *Procureur général*'s department of the Belgian Court of Cassation was tested in the *Borgers* Case. The Court concluded, affirming its previous case-law, that on this point no violation of Article 6 arose. However, the fact that there did not exist any possibility for the defence to react to the submissions of the *Avocat général*, who participated in an advisory capacity in the deliberations of the Court of Cassation, did amount to a violation of the rights of the defence.[974]

6.7.4 Established by Law

The prescription that the tribunal must be 'established by law' implies the guarantee that the organisation of the judiciary in a democratic society is not left to the discretion of the executive, but is regulated by law. In the Commission's

---

[968] Report of 14 December 1979, B.38 (1984), pp. 40-42.
[969] Judgment of 23 June 1981, A.43, p. 25; judgment of 10 February 1983, *Albert and Le Compte*, A.58, pp. 17-18; judgment of 28 June 1984, *Campbell and Fell*, A.80, p. 41.
[970] Judgment of 22 June 1989, A.155, p. 16.
[971] Judgment of 25 November 1993, A.279-A, p. 16.
[972] Judgment of 10 June 1996, Reports 1996-III, Vol. 11, paras 33-41.
[973] Judgment of 23 April 1996, Reports 1996-II, Vol. 8, paras 46-48.
[974] Judgment of 30 October 1991, A.214-B, pp. 30-32. See also the judgment of 17 January 1970, *Delcourt*, A.11, p. 19.

view this does not, however, rule out the possibility that parts of this organisation, e.g., the institution of specific judicial bodies, may be left by law to the executive by virtue of delegation, provided that sufficient guarantees are built in to counteract arbitrariness.[975] And in any case no right to be tried by the ordinary court can be inferred from the provision, provided that a legal basis is present for the special court as well.[976] In its report in the *Piersack* Case the Commission evidently takes the view that not only the establishment, but also the organisation and the functioning of the tribunal in question must have a legal basis, but for the question of whether this tribunal has applied these legal rules in the right way it apparently relies on the opinion of the (higher) national court.[977] In this case the Court did not deal with this point after it had held the complaint concerning the violation of the requirement of impartiality to be well-founded.[978] In the *Bulut* Case, however, the Court took the interpretation of domestic law by the national courts, like the Commission in the *Piersack* Case, more or less for granted.[979]

In the *Oberschlik* Case the applicant complained about a violation of national legislation that did offer guarantees against impartiality. He stated that the Vienna Court of Appeal lacked impartiality and was not established by law, because, contrary to national legislation, it was presided over by the same judge as in the first set. However, his submissions did not result in a separate examination of the requirement 'established by law', because the Court concluded that the applicant's two complaints coincided in substance.[980]

6.8 The Presumption of Innocence

Article 6(2) sets forth that the person who is charged with a criminal offence shall be presumed innocent until proved guilty according to law. As in the case of the third paragraph, this paragraph deals with a special aspect of the general concept of 'fair trial' in criminal cases. For that reason no further inquiry is made as to a possible violation of this provision when a violation of the first paragraph has already been found.[981] From the case-law concerning the autonomous meaning of the concept of 'criminal charge' in the first paragraph it follows that the second

---

[975] Report of 12 October 1978, *Zand*, D&R 15 (1979), p. 70 (79-81); report of 14 December 1979, *Le Compte, Van Leuven and De Meyere*, B.38 (1984), pp. 39-40; Appls 8603, 8722, 8723 and 8729/79, *Crociani* et al. v. *Italy*, D&R 22 (1981), p. 147 (219).

[976] Appl. 8299/78, *X and Y* v. *Ireland*, D&R 22 (1981), p. 51 (73).

[977] Report of 13 May 1981, B.47 (1986), p. 23.

[978] Judgment of 1 October 1982, A.53, p. 16.

[979] Judgment of 22 February 1996, Reports 1996-II, Vol. 5, para. 29.

[980] Judgment of 23 May 1991, A.204, p. 23. See also the judgment of 25 February 1992, *Pfeifer and Plankl*, A.227, pp. 16-17.

[981] Judgment of 27 February 1980, *Deweer*, A.35, pp. 30-31. Thus also the Commission in its report of 5 October 1978 in this case, B.33 (1983), pp. 29-30. In its judgment of 19 December 1990, *Delta*, A.191-A, p. 16, however, the Court suggested that in special circumstances there is room for a separate investigation under para. 2, despite the fact that a violation of the first paragraph has been established already.

and third paragraphs are also applicable to other than criminal proceedings – *e.g.*, disciplinary proceedings – which are to be equated with criminal proceedings by means of the criteria developed in the *Engel* Case.[982]

In the *Minelli* Case the second paragraph was defined by the Court in the sense that this provision has been violated if:

> without the accused's having previously been proved guilty according to law and, notably, without his having had the opportunity of exercising his rights of defence, a judicial decision concerning him reflects an opinion that he is guilty.[983]

A reasoning by which it is only suggested that the person in question is guilty is already sufficient for such a violation. The presumption may be violated not only by a court but also by other public authorities,[984] including the legislator.[985]

The most important aspect of the presumption of innocence concerns the foundation of the conviction. This aspect is very closely connected with the requirement of the court's impartiality discussed above. The court has to presume the innocence of the accused without any prejudice and may sentence him only on the basis of evidence put forward during the trial, which moreover has to constitute 'lawful' evidence recognised as such by law. The Court has formulated the essence as follows:

> Paragraph 2 embodies the principle of the presumption of innocence. It requires, *inter alia*, that when carrying out their duties, the members of a court should not start with the preconceived idea that the accused has committed the offence charged; the burden of proof is on the prosecution, and any doubt should benefit the accused. It also follows that it is for the prosecution to inform the accused of the case that will be made against him, so that he may prepare and present his defence accordingly, and to adduce evidence sufficient to convict him.[986]

The evidence put forward at the trial may refer back to statements previously made by the accused or testimony by witnesses, provided that the latter can be revoked or refuted during the trial.[987] If a witness wishes to remain anonymous or for other reasons does not wish to act as a witness during the trial and can advance a legitimate reason for it, there is no objection to a reading of previous testimony, provided that the right of the defence to question witnesses is sufficiently upheld, *e.g.* by having provided the opportunity to interrogate and contradict that witness in an earlier phase of the proceedings. If this condition has

---

[982] Judgment of 10 February 1983, *Albert and Le Compte*, A.58, pp. 19-20.

[983] Judgment of 25 March 1983, A.62, p. 18. See also the judgments of 25 August 1987, *Lutz, Englert*, and *Nölkenbockhoff*, A.123, pp. 25, 55 and 81 respectively.

[984] Judgment of 10 February 1995, *Allenet de Ribbemont*, A.308, p. 16.

[985] Judgment of 7 October 1988, *Salabiaku*, A.141-A, pp. 15-16.

[986] Judgment of 6 December 1988, *Barberà, Messegué and Jabardo*, A.146, p. 33.

[987] Appl. 8414/78, *X* v. *Federal Republic of Germany*, D&R 17 (1980), p. 231 (233-234); Appl. 8417/78, *X* v. *Belgium*, D&R 16 (1979), p. 200 (233-234).

not been met, the verdict must not be based exclusively or largely on such testimony.[988]

Every instance giving rise to the least doubt with regard to the evidence has to be construed in favour of the accused.[989] This does not necessarily mean that the evidence put forward must be absolutely conclusive – in several legal systems ultimately the conviction on the part of the court is the point that matters[990] – but it does mean that the court must base its conviction exclusively on the evidence put forward during the trial.[991] A sentence may of course also be based on a confession of guilt on the part of the accused. In that case, however, the court will have to ascertain thoroughly that this confession has been made in complete freedom,[992] while from a statement of the accused which is not intended to be a confession of guilt no such confession may be inferred.[993]

If during the trial statements are made or produced by the prosecutor, witnesses or experts from which bias on their part is evident, the court has to make a stand against those statements if it is to avoid the semblance of being biassed as well. If the court does so, the accused can no longer complain of such bias on the part of the first-mentioned persons.[994] The same holds good if a sentence which the accused alleges to have been dictated by bias has been upheld on appeal, while the court of appeal has made an inquiry into this very matter. In that case the accused will be able to complain only of bias on the part of this court of appeal or of the fact that the injury caused by the bias of the lower court has not been redressed by the higher court.[995]

If there has been publicity surrounding the proceedings in which publicity the guilt of the accused is assumed, the latter will have to prove to some extent that his ultimate conviction was also influenced by that publicity. This will not be

---

[988] Judgment of 24 November 1986, *Unterpertinger*, A.110, pp. 14-15. On the issue of anonymous witnesses, see *infra* pp. 475-476.

[989] Report of 31 March 1963, *Pfunders (Austria v. Italy)*, Yearbook VI (1963), pp. 782-784; judgment of 6 December 1988, *Barberà, Messegué and Jabardo*, A.146, p. 33.

[990] See, *e.g.*, for the Netherlands Art. 338 of the Code of Criminal Procedure.

[991] The Commission does not consider itself competent to pronounce on the value of that conviction: Appl. 7628/76, *X v. Belgium*, D&R 9 (1978), p. 169.

[992] Appl. 5076/71, *X v. the United Kingdom*, Coll. 40 (1972), p. 64 (66-67). Insofar as the confession has been extorted by illegal means, such as physical or mental torture, this follows already from the words 'according to law'; report of 31 March 1963, *Pfunders (Austria v. Italy)*, Yearbook VI (1963), p. 784.

[993] In this context, see the disputed decision of the Commission on Appl. 4483/70, *X v. Federal Republic of Germany*, Coll. 38 (1972), p. 77 (79), where the Commission appears not to have examined the complaint at all for this aspect. See also Appl. 2645/65, *Scheichelbauer v. Austria*, Yearbook XII (1969), p. 156 (170-172).

[994] Report of 31 March 1963, *Pfunders (Austria v. Italy)*, Yearbook VI (1963), p. 740 (784); report of 15 March 1961, *Nielsen*, Yearbook IV (1961), p. 490 (568). For a case in which the accused, on the contrary, complained that the court had influenced the jury to his detriment by using the word 'killing': Appl. 5881/72, *X v. the United Kingdom* (not published). The Commission's consideration that the court had not used this word with that intention seems to cut no ice.

[995] Report in the *Pfunders* Case, *idem*.

easy.[996] With respect to the practice where during the trial the criminal record, if any, of the accused is brought to the notice of the court, the Commission has given as its opinion that this practice does not constitute a conflict with Article 6(2).[997] It is obvious, however, that such information may promote a presumption of guilt on the part of the court or the jury, so that the person in question has at least to be given an opportunity to advance evidence that the criminal record has unduly influenced the court.

In addition to the establishment of guilt, Article 6(2) also has consequences for the treatment of the accused; in this respect, too, his innocence must be presumed. This applies to the treatment of the accused during the preliminary examination and the trial, as well as to the treatment of a person detained on remand: that treatment may not have a punitive character. If the conditions of Article 5(1)(c) have been fulfilled, the restrictions imposed on the detainee have to bear a relation to the purpose of the detention on remand.[998]

The principle embodied in paragraph 2 also applies in those criminal cases where the issue of guilt is not a central issue. In the *Salabiaku* Case the Court stated that the Contracting States are in principle free, subject to certain conditions, to establish an offence on the basis of an objective fact as such, irrespective of whether it results from criminal intent or from negligence. The applicant was convicted not for the mere possession of unlawfully imported prohibited goods, but for smuggling such goods, while the legal presumption of accountability was inferred from their possession which led to his conviction. The Court stressed the relative nature of the distinction between presumption of accountability and presumption of guilt. Presumptions of fact or of law operate in every legal system; this is not contrary to the Convention. The Contracting States are, however, under the obligation to remain within reasonable limits in this respect as regards their criminal law provisions, taking into account the importance of what is at stake, and to maintain the rights of the defence. Indeed, the guarantee

---

[996] See, *e.g.*, Appls 7572, 7586 and 7587/76, *Ensslin, Baader and Raspe* v. *Federal Republic of Germany*, Yearbook XXI (1978), p. 418 (462). The applicants alleged violation of Art. 6(2) on account of the press campaign against them, in which they were called criminals and murderers, and on account of the exceptional security measures around the suit, which could not but create an impression of guilt. The Commission took the position that the challenged publications and measures were a reaction to their own declarations and behaviour and were not aimed at creating an atmosphere unfavourable for the accused, and that a professional judge is sufficiently immune to any influence that might result from this. See also *supra* p. 453 and the *Menten* Case there mentioned.

[997] Appl. 2742/66, *X* v. *Austria*, Yearbook IX (1966), p. 550 (554).

[998] See Recommendation R(80)1 of the Committee of Ministers in the matter of custody on remand of 27 June 1980, Art. 1 of which states: 'Being presumed innocent until proved guilty, no person charged with an offence shall be placed in custody pending trial unless the circumstances make it strictly necessary. Custody pending trial shall therefore be regarded as an exceptional measure and it shall never be compulsory nor be used for punitive reasons'. See also Art. 10(2)(a) of the UN Covenant on Civil and Political Rights in the matter of the special treatment of detainees on remand.

of Article 6(2) must also be respected by the legislature while, according to the Court, the words 'according to law' are not to be construed exclusively with reference to domestic law but contain a reference to the fundamental principle of the rule of law.[999]

In the *Hentrich* Case the exercise of the right of pre-emption by the French tax authorities because the sale price of land was too low, appeared not to imply an accusation of tax evasion and, accordingly, could not lead to a violation of Article 6(2).[1000]

Article 6(2) may even be relevant after the formal determination of the 'charge', for instance when a decision has to be taken with regard to the costs of the suit or the compensation for pre-trial detention claimed by the former suspect. Article 6 applies to these decisions as long as the question to be answered can be regarded as 'a consequence and, to some extent, the concomitant of the criminal proceedings'.[1001] In the *Minelli* Case, where the court had concluded that the plaintiffs in an action for insult could not sue since the period of limitation had expired, but still had condemned the defendant to pay two thirds of the trial costs and to pay compensation in respect of the prosecutor's expenses, because in the court's opinion he would in all probability have been found guilty if the limitation had not barred the continuance of the proceedings, the Court held that the fact that the accused is made to pay some of the costs of the suit if he is discharged need not yet in itself conflict with Article 6(2), but that this *is* the case if the presumable guilt of the accused is used as the criterion for it, without the guarantees of Article 6 being observed.[1002] In the *Adolf* Case, in which the court had discharged the accused, but in formulating its decision had nevertheless created the impression that the accused had committed the crime with which he had been charged, although no evidence had been furnished, the Commission concluded that Article 6(2) had been violated.[1003] The Court largely followed the Commission in its argumentation, but not in its conclusion, because in the opinion of the Court the judicial decision concerned could not be viewed independently of the subsequent decision of the Austrian Supreme Court, ruling expressly that the dismissal of the case did not imply any pronouncement on

---

[999] Judgment of 7 October 1988, A.141-A, pp. 15-17. See also the judgment of 25 September 1992, *Pham Hoang*, A.243, pp. 21-22.

[1000] Judgment of 22 September 1994, A.296-A, pp. 23-24.

[1001] Judgment of 25 August 1993, *Sekanina*, A.266-A, p. 13. See also the judgments of 25 August 1987, *Lutz*, A.123, p. 23 and *Nölkenbockhoff*, A.123, p. 79.

[1002] Judgment of 25 March 1983, A.62, pp. 15-18. See also Appl. 6650/74, *Liebig* v. *Federal Republic of Germany*, Yearbook XIX (1976), p. 330 (342) and Appl. 7640/76, *Geerk* v. *Switzerland*, Yearbook XXI (1978), p. 470 (476). In both cases a friendly settlement was reached. See also Appl. 9688/82, *C. Family* v. *Switzerland*, D&R 35 (1984), p. 98 (102). The Commission declared the complaint inadmissible, since the decision that the applicants had to pay the costs of the proceedings was based on the fact that the applicants had prompted the opening of the criminal proceedings by their own negligent behaviour.

[1003] Report of 8 October 1980, B.43 (1985), pp. 25-28.

guilt.[1004] In the *Lutz, Englert* and *Nölkenbockhoff* Cases the Court held that the decision to refuse reimbursement to a person 'charged with a criminal offence' in the event of discontinuance of the proceedings against him, may raise an issue under Article 6(2) if the supporting reasons amount in substance to a determination of the accused's guilt without his having previously been proved guilty according to the law, in particular without having had an opportunity to exercise the right of defence.[1005]

6.9 Minimum Rights for the Criminal Suspect

6.9.1 Introduction

Article 6(3) contains an enumeration of the minimum rights to which everyone charged with a criminal offence is entitled. This provision, unlike the first paragraph, does not relate to proceedings concerning the determination of civil rights and obligations. On the one hand, however, if a party to civil proceedings is denied the rights mentioned in paragraph 3, under certain circumstances this may entail that there is no 'fair hearing' in the sense of the first paragraph.[1006] On the other hand, the fact that 'civil rights and obligations' are at issue does not exclude that the proceedings have a criminal character.[1007]

The specific enumeration in the third paragraph for criminal proceedings does not imply that an examination for compatibility with the third paragraph makes an examination for compatibility with the first paragraph superfluous. As the Commission held in its *Adolf* report: 'Art. 6(3) merely exemplifies the minimum guarantees which must be accorded to the accused in the context of the "fair trial" referred to in Art. 6(1).'[1008] The enumeration of the third paragraph is not limitative in that respect, and it is therefore possible that, although the guarantees mentioned there have been satisfied, the trial as a whole still does not satisfy the requirements of a fair trial. As a result of an extensive and functional interpretation of the third paragraph in the Strasbourg case-law, however, examination for compatibility with the third and with the first paragraph is in fact likely to more or less coincide. With respect to the interpretation of the guarantees of the third paragraph the Commission has taken the following position:

[1004] Judgment of 26 March 1982, A.49, pp. 18-19.
[1005] Judgments of 25 August 1987, A.123, pp. 25-26, 54-55 and 78-81 respectively. See also the *Sekanina* judgment of 25 August 1993, A.266-A, pp. 13-16, concerning the refusal to pay a contribution to the costs of the defence and a compensation for the detention on remand after an acquittal and the judgment of 26 March 1996, *Leutscher*, Reports 1996-II, Vol. 6, paras 30-32, where the applicant had been tried at first instance *in absentia*, but the court of appeal had declared the prosecution time-barred and subsequently refused to order the reimbursement of the legal costs of the applicant.
[1006] The lack of free legal aid may, for instance, bar the exercise of the right of 'access to court'; see *supra* pp. 420-421.
[1007] Judgment of 25 March 1983, *Minelli*, A.62, p. 15.
[1008] Report of 8 October 1980, B.43 (1985), p. 29. See also the judgment of 12 February 1985, *Colozza*, A.89, p. 14.

They exemplify the notion of fair trial (...) but their intrinsic aim is always to ensure, or contribute to ensuring, the fairness of the criminal proceedings as a whole. The guarantees enshrined in Art. 6(3) are therefore not an aim in themselves, and they must accordingly be interpreted in the light of the function which they have in the overall context of the proceedings.[1009]

At all events, in the case of a positive outcome of the examination for compatibility with the first paragraph an examination with regard to the third paragraph is deemed superfluous.[1010] This is to be regretted, since it restricts the development of specific case-law concerning the third paragraph.

6.9.2 Information of the Accused

Under 3(a) the accused is granted the right to be informed promptly, in a language which he understands and in detail, of the nature and cause of the accusation against him. This right is very closely related to the right granted under 3(b) that he must have adequate time and facilities for the preparation of the defence.[1011] Indeed, for the latter it is required that the accused be informed of the charge promptly and in a way which he can understand and which is sufficiently specific. In this context not only the nature of the charge must be specified, but also the factual and legal grounds on which the charge is based.[1012] However, in this phase it is not yet necessary to furnish any evidence in support of the charge.[1013]

The question whether the required information has been furnished promptly (*dans le plus court délai*) has to be assessed in each individual case on the basis of its specific circumstances. Precisely in order to enable the accused to prepare his defence, the prosecutor will have to inform him as soon as it has been decided to institute criminal proceedings and, if necessary, make provisions for a translation or for the presence of an interpreter. On that occasion he will have to provide the relevant data available at that moment, which afterwards are to be supplemented, if need be, in particular when the summons is issued. However, adequate defence may be of great importance already in the phase preceding the ultimate decision as to whether or not to institute proceedings, and it may even affect this decision, so that it results from the rationale of paragraphs 3(a) and 3(b) that even before this formal decision the accused must be kept informed as fully as possible of the suspicion against him.

[1009] Report of 12 July 1984, *Can*, A.96, p. 15.
[1010] Judgment of 27 February 1980, *Deweer*, A.35, pp. 30-31.
[1011] This has repeatedly been emphasised by the Commission. See, *inter alia*, Appl. 524/59, *Ofner* v. *Austria*, Yearbook III (1960), p. 322 (344); Appl. 8490/79, *X* v. *Austria*, D&R 22 (1981), p. 140 (142); report of 2 March 1988, *Brozicek*, A.167, p. 31.
[1012] See the cases mentioned in the preceding note, *idem* and compare the judgment of 19 December 1989, *Brozicek*, A.167, pp. 18-19. An alternative charge satisfies this requirement of specificity: Appl. 3894/68, *X* v. *the Netherlands*, Coll. 32 (1970), p. 47 (50).
[1013] Appl. 7628/76, *X* v. *Belgium*, D&R 9 (1978), p. 169 (173); report of 5 May 1983, *Collozza and Rubinat*, A.89, p. 28.

Paragraph 3(a) requires that the information must be furnished 'in detail'. In its decision in *X* v. *Federal Republic of Germany* the Commission stated rather cryptically that this does not imply that information 'in minute detail' is required.[1014]

A proposal made by the public authorities, acting as a civil party, to the registry of the Court of Appeal to reclassify the criminal acts, without informing the defendant of this proposal, does violate the third paragraph under (a).[1015]

From the words 'in a language which he understands' it follows in our opinion that if the accused is insufficiently master of the vernacular, the information must be translated for him. For this no particular form is prescribed, but the Court justly seems to require a written translation. An oral elucidation by the person who serves the writ of summons upon the accused, or by an interpreter would seem to be an insufficient basis for the preparation of his defence.[1016] It also seems dubious to us whether paragraph 3(a) has been satisfied if the information is sent to counsel who is master of the vernacular and may find ways to inform his client, since in this way the authorities shift an obligation resting upon them on to counsel, while it is important for the accused that he himself is also able to follow the defence put forward on his behalf as adequately as possible. In the *Brozicek* Case the Commission considered it contrary to the spirit and the letter of Article 6(3)(a) to presume that an accused who is resident in his own country, can understand the content of an official communication in the language of a foreign country which has instituted proceedings against him.[1017] The Court concluded that the applicant was not of Italian origin, did not reside in Italy and informed the judicial authorities that he did not understand the Italian language. In such a case, according to the Court, it is for the judicial authority to procure a translation unless it can be established that the person concerned is objectively capable of understanding the content of the notification.[1018]

6.9.3 Time and Facilities for the Defence

Under paragraph 3(b) the accused is guaranteed the right to have adequate time and facilities for the preparation of his defence. Apart from the above-mentioned relation with paragraph 3(a), there is also a close connection with paragraph 3(c), regulating legal aid. In that context the Commission has emphasised that here not only the rights of the accused are concerned, but equally the rights of counsel, so that for the assessment of the overall situation the position of both of them has to be taken into account.[1019] However, the 'facilities' do not include the possibility

---

[1014] Appl. 1169/61, Yearbook VI (1963), p. 520 (584).
[1015] Report of 16 March 1989, *Chichlian and Ekindjian*, A.162-B, p. 52. Before the Court gave judgment, a friendly settlement was reached.
[1016] Judgment of 19 December 1989, *Kamasinski*, A.168, pp. 36-37. See also the report of 5 May 1988 in that case, A.168, p. 53.
[1017] Report of 2 March 1988, A.167, pp. 33-34.
[1018] Judgment of 19 December 1989, A.167, p. 18.
[1019] Appl. 524/59, *Ofner* v. *Austria*, Yearbook III (1960), p. 322 (352).

to choose counsel or have one assigned, since the right to legal aid is provided for under paragraph 3(c).

The question of whether the accused has been allowed adequate time for the preparation of his defence will have to be decided afterwards, according to the circumstances in which both the accused and his counsel found themselves,[1020] and on the basis of the nature of the case.[1021] If the accused has great confidence in a particular lawyer, who is very occupied at the relevant time, the judicial authorities will have to take this into account as much as possible. On the other hand, in that case the accused cannot advance the resulting delay as a ground for violation of the first paragraph of Article 6. If for one reason or another the accused has to change counsel, the new lawyer will have to be given adequate time to become acquainted with the case.[1022] If there is a right to free legal aid, a lawyer has to be assigned in good time.[1023] The accused, however, cannot complain if through his own fault he has created a situation in which a lawyer has to be appointed shortly before the hearing is to be held.[1024]

If appeal is open, the time-limit has to be such that a thorough study of the judgment can be made to enable a decision as to whether an appeal is to be brought,[1025] while the moment of the hearing of the appeal in turn will have to leave adequate time for the preparation of the hearing.[1026] The words 'preparation of his defence', therefore, may not be interpreted to mean that the provision of paragraph 3(b) is not applicable to the appeal proceedings in case the accused has been convicted at first instance and consequently acts not as defendant

---

[1020] *Idem* and Appl. 4042/69, *X* v. *the United Kingdom*, Yearbook XIII (1970), p. 690 (696). See also Appl. 5523/72, *Huber* v. *Austria*, Yearbook XVII (1974), p. 314 (332), where the complaint about the very short period indeed of 14 days was declared ill-founded with a view to the nevertheless voluminous commentary which the defence had produced. This, however, is not indicative of the period granted for defence but rather of the special efforts of counsel.

[1021] Appl. 7909/77, *X and Y* v. *Austria*, D&R 15 (1979), p. 160 (162-163), where the Commission investigated whether the time of ten working days available to counsel was adequate, considering the complexity of the case and the fact that he could communicate with his client only with difficulty because of her poor psychological and physical condition.

[1022] Although it is not quite clear from the decision, the Commission accepted this perhaps implicitly in its decision on Appl. 1850/63, *Köplinger* v. *Austria*, Yearbook IX (1966), p. 240 (262). See also Appl. 4319/69, *Samer* v. *Federal Republic of Germany*, Yearbook XIV (1971), p. 322 (340).

[1023] Appl. 7909/77, *X and Y* v. *Austria*, D&R 15 (1979), p. 160 (162), where the Commission stated that here again the question what period is adequate for this cannot be answered *in abstracto*.

[1024] Appl. 8251/78, *X* v. *Austria*, D&R 17 (1980), p. 166 (169-170).

[1025] See Appl. 441/58, *X* v. *Federal Republic of Germany*, Yearbook II (1958-1959), p. 391 (395), where the Commission considered a period for appeal of two weeks sufficient, since for the institution of the appeal a summary indication of the grounds for appeal could suffice. In its decision on Appl. 5523/72, *Huber* v. *Austria*, Yearbook XVII (1974), p. 314 (332), where the period for appeal was equally short, while here it was required that the grounds were already accurately indicated in the appeal, the Commission held that such a determination 'could in some circumstances raise a problem under Article 6(3)(b)'.

[1026] In the judgment of 21 September 1993, *Kremzow*, A.268-B, pp. 41-42, a period of three weeks between the receipt of the Attorney General's position paper (the so-called *croquis*) and the hearing of the Supreme Court did suffice to formulate a reply to the *croquis*.

but as plaintiff in these proceedings. In the *Hadjianastassiou* Case the applicant had to give notice of appeal on points of law within a time-limit of five days without having the opportunity to take cognisance of the written version of the judgment. The Court took the view that it is essential for the exercise of the defendant's right of appeal that the national courts indicate unambiguously the reasons on which they base their verdicts. As the applicant was barred in the circumstances of the case to submit an additional memorial, the Court concluded that paragraph 3 under (b) in conjunction with paragraph 1 had been violated.[1027]

The reclassification of an offence in the course of proceedings does not violate subparagraph (b) as long as the defendant has been made aware that the offence may be reclassified and has the opportunity to reorganise his defence accordingly.[1028]

In the *Bricmont* Case the Commission stated that subparagraph (b) recognises the right of the accused to have at his disposal, for the purposes of exonerating himself or of obtaining a reduction of his sentence, all relevant elements that can be collected by the competent authorities.[1029] The accused cannot complain about lack of facilities if he does not cooperate in producing elements to his defence.[1030]

Finally, the possibility of inspection of the files must also be mentioned as an important element of the 'facilities'.[1031] The Commission took the position that a right of access to the files as such is not guaranteed in Article 6(3)(b), but that this provision may imply 'that under certain circumstances the person concerned or his lawyer must have reasonable access to the file'.[1032] The more recent case-law of the Court, however, seems to indicate that the right of access is incorporated in the provision under (b), although restriction of this right to the defendant's counsel is not incompatible with Article 6.[1033]

[1027] Judgment of 16 December 1992, A.252, pp. 16-17.

[1028] Report of 16 March 1989, *Chichlian and Ekindjian*, A.162-B, p. 53.

[1029] Report of 15 October 1987, A.158, p. 47. See also the report of 14 December 1981, *Jespers*, D&R 27 (1982), p. 61 (88), where the Commission held that the adjective 'adequate' implies that the facilities which must be granted to the accused are restricted to those which assist or may assist him in the preparation of his defence and the judgment of 16 December 1992, *Edwards*, A.247-B, p. 35.

[1030] Report of 15 October 1987, *Bricmont*, A.158, p. 49.

[1031] At least from the moment of the charge: Appl. 4622/70, *X* v. *Austria*, Coll. 40 (1972), p. 15 (18).

[1032] Appl. 7138/75, *X* v. *Austria*, D&R 9 (1978), p. 50 (52) and report of 14 December 1981, *Jespers*, D&R 27 (1982), p. 61 (86-92). See also the report of 5 May 1988, *Kamasinski*, A.168, p. 54.

[1033] Judgment of 19 December 1989, *Kamasinski*, A.168, pp. 39-40; judgment of 21 September 1993, *Kremzow*, A.268-B, p. 42.

6.9.4   The Right to Defend Oneself in Person or Through Legal Assistance
(a) Introduction
Paragraph 3(c) guarantees the right of the accused to defend himself in person or through legal assistance of his own choosing or (and), if he has not sufficient means to pay for legal assistance, to be given it free when the interests of justice so require. In the *Pakelli* Case the Court, referring to 'the object and purpose of this paragraph, which is designed to ensure effective protection of the rights of the defence', opted for the '*et*' in the French text, and not for the 'or' in the English text. This resulted in the following interpretation by the Court:

> a 'person charged with a criminal offence' who does not wish to defend himself in person must be able to have recourse to legal assistance of his own choosing; if he does not have sufficient means to pay for such assistance, he is entitled under the Convention to be given it free when the interests of justice so require.[1034]

There are therefore three juxtaposed rights included in this provision.

The provision under paragraph 3(c) does not contain an 'unlimited right to use any defence arguments'. It does not in principle object to a subsequent prosecution of the accused because he made 'false suspicions of punishable behaviour' concerning another person.[1035]

The manner in which the provision applies (in conjunction with the first paragraph of Article 6) in appeal and cassation proceedings or during a preliminary investigation depends on the characteristics of the proceedings in question.[1036]

If domestic law attaches consequences to the attitude of the accused at the initial stage of police interrogation, Article 6 in principle requires the assistance of a lawyer in the pre-trial phase.[1037] In the *John Murray* Case the applicant had been denied access to a lawyer for the first 48 hours of police interrogation. He had been told by the police that he had the right to remain silent but that adverse inferences could be drawn from his silence. Thus, he had been confronted at the beginning of the interrogation with a 'fundamental dilemma' concerning his defence. The Court held that in this situation the denial of access to a lawyer had constituted a breach of Article 6(1) in conjunction with paragraph 3(c).[1038] In case the assistance of a lawyer at the beginning of during the interrogation is not required by Article 6, it is considered to be highly relevant that the evidence is evaluated by the court during the trial in the presence of the accused and his counsel, who then have the opportunity to contradict the evidence, and that any confession is proved by the prosecution to have been made voluntarily.[1039] In

---

[1034]   Judgment of 25 April 1983, A.64, p. 15.
[1035]   Judgment of 28 August 1991, *Brandstetter*, A.211, pp. 23-24.
[1036]   Judgment of 2 March 1987, *Monnell and Morris*, A.115, p. 22; judgment of 22 February 1994, *Tripodi*, A.281-B, p. 45; judgment of 28 October 1994, *Boner*, A.300-B, p. 74 and with regard to the preliminary investigation judgment of 24 November 1993, *Imbrioscia*, A.275, p. 14.
[1037]   Judgment of 8 February 1996, *John Murray*, Reports 1996-I, Vol. 1, para. 63.
[1038]   *Ibidem*, paras 66-70.
[1039]   Appl. 9370/81, *X v. the United Kingdom* (not published).

as far as the rights of the defence has not been irretrievable prejudiced a failure to comply with the requirement of paragraph 3(c) may in principle be cured in appeal on the condition that the appeal court may carry out a full review.[1040]

(b) The Right to Defend Oneself in Person

The right for the accused to defend himself in person is subject to restrictions by national law and the judicial authorities concerned.[1041] The Court accepted in the *Gillow* Case the requirement of representation by a lawyer to lodge an appeal as 'a common feature of the legal systems in several Member States of the Council of Europe'.[1042] From paragraph 3(c) it then results that, if the national law stipulates or the judicial authorities decide that the accused must be assisted by a lawyer, he must be able himself to choose this lawyer and, in case of inability to pay for such legal aid, must have a lawyer assigned to him; indeed, in that case such legal aid is evidently considered necessary by the national law or the judicial authorities in the interests of justice.

Although some restrictions to the right of the accused to defend himself in person are permitted, these restrictions cannot go so far that the protection offered by the Convention becomes illusory. In the *Kremzow* Case the situation at issue was that the national legislation granted the right of a detained person to be present at the hearing of an appeal against sentence only if the person concerned made a request to this effect in his appeal. The applicant had failed to make such a request. Nevertheless, because the applicant risked a substantial increase of his sentence of imprisonment, the Court held that the national authorities had been obliged to enable the applicant to be present at the hearing and to 'defend himself in person'. The failure to fulfil this duty amounted to a breach of paragraph 6(1) in conjunction with the provision under (c).[1043] The right to be present in person in court is indeed very closely linked with that to a fair trial and has been discussed in that context above.[1044]

(c) Legal Assistance; Implied Rights

As regards the contact with counsel, the Court has attached to the right of access to court, implied in Article 6(1), the consequence that this right has been violated if a detainee is not permitted to correspond with a lawyer or another person giving legal assistance. The Court held that: 'hindering the effective exercise of a right

---

[1040] Judgment of 24 May 1991, *Quaranta*, A.205, p. 18.

[1041] Appl. 2676/65, *X* v. *Austria*, Coll. 23 (1967), p. 31 (35); Appl. 5923/72, *X* v. *Norway*, D&R 3 (1976), p. 43 (44). For the reverse case, but then in the sphere of a civil suit, for which para. 3 does not apply, see Appl. 1013/61, *X and Y* v. *Federal Republic of Germany*, Yearbook V (1962), p. 158: the court need not recognise a representative nominated by a party if the character of the case is not such that the principle of a 'fair hearing' as laid down in Art. 6(1) makes such a representation necessary.

[1042] Judgment of 24 November 1986, A.109, p. 27.

[1043] Judgment of 21 September 1993, A.268-B, p. 45.

[1044] *Supra* pp. 433-435.

may amount to a breach of that right, even if the hindrance is of a temporary character.'[1045] Consequently, as soon as a detainee wants to institute an action or wishes to prepare his defence against a criminal charge, such contact must be possible. This may hold good in the pre-trial phase[1046] and even with regard to an internal preliminary inquiry.[1047]

The provision under (c) embodies the right of an accused to communicate with his counsel out of hearing of a third person. Without this requirement the guarantee offered by the Convention would not be practical and effective.[1048] However, the risk of collusion may justify some restrictions on this right. In *S* v. *Switzerland* the fear that the lawyer of the applicant would collude with the lawyer of a co-accused was based on the fact that the lawyers proposed to coordinate their defence-strategy. This fact could not justify the restriction on the free communication of the accused and his lawyer.[1049] In the *Can* Case the Commission took the view – with regard to subparagraph 6(3)(b) – that restrictions constitute a violation only if they are of such a nature that they affect the position of the defence during the proceedings, and thus also the outcome.[1050] Such a criterion, however, would appear difficult to apply in practice, since such an impact can only be established afterwards, and even then not with certainty. If the starting-point is to be maintained that the confidential relation calls for a private conversation, an adverse influence of restrictions of this private character on the defence will have to be assumed, and the burden of proof for the necessity of the restriction should rest on the authorities.

Searching of counsel and inspection of the correspondence of counsel with his detained client by the prison authorities are in principle also incompatible with the position of counsel. Measures of this kind are justified only in very exceptional circumstances, where the authorities have sound reasons to assume that counsel himself is abusing his position or is allowing it to be abused.[1051] And even then

---

[1045] Judgment of 21 February 1975, *Golder*, A.18, pp. 12-20. Thus also the Commission in its report of 11 October 1980, *Silver*, B.51 (1987), pp. 100-101.

[1046] Judgment of 8 February 1996, *John Murray*, Reports 1996-I, Vol. 1, paras 66-70.

[1047] Appl. 7878/77, *Fell* v. *the United Kingdom*, D&R 23 (1981), p. 102 (113). See also the report of 12 May 1982, *Campbell and Fell*, A.80, pp. 76-77.

[1048] Judgment of 28 November 1991, *S* v. *Switzerland*, A.220, p. 16. The Court reached this conclusion by referring to the Standard Minimum Rules for the Treatment of Prisoners and the European Agreement Relating to Persons Participating in Proceedings of the European Commission and Court of Human Rights.

[1049] *Ibidem*, p. 16.

[1050] Report of 12 July 1984, A.96, pp. 16-17. See also the report of 8 October 1987, *Lamy*, A.151, p. 26.

[1051] In its decision on Appl. 2375/64, *X* v. *Federal Republic of Germany*, Coll. 22 (1967), p. 45 (47), the Commission deemed inspection of the correspondence inherent to the detention on remand. The Commission here wrongly applied only Art. 8 and not Art. 6, although the applicant had stated that the challenged control had also led to great delay in the correspondence. Since the restriction grounds of Art. 8(2) do not necessarily also apply in the context of Art. 6(3)(b), the conformity of the measure with the latter provision should also have been reviewed.

there will have to be complete openness, so that those concerned are aware of the surveillance.[1052]

The provision under paragraph 3(c), taken together with the first paragraph of Article 6, also implies that counsel who attends the trial must be enabled to conduct the defence in the absence of the accused, regardless of whether or not there exists an excuse for the latter's absence.[1053]

(d) Legal Assistance; The Right to Choose a Lawyer

According to the Strasbourg case-law the right of the accused to choose his own lawyer is not an absolute right; he is bound by the provisions applying in the relevant legal system with regard to the question as to who may act as counsel in court.[1054] If the court is given the power to exclude a specific lawyer or group of lawyers from the defence, for specific accused persons this might constitute an acute problem for an optimal defence, since in certain cases it may be very difficult to find a suitable lawyer. It is therefore important that in the *Goddi* Case the Commission took the view that:

> In most cases a lawyer chosen by the accused himself is better equipped to undertake the defence. It follows that as a general rule an accused must not be deprived, against his will or without his knowledge, of the assistance of the defence counsel he has appointed.[1055]

In the past the Commission has taken the view that in the case of free legal aid the accused does not have the right to make his own choice or to be consulted as to the assignment.[1056] The *Pakelli* judgment, however, in which a juxtaposition of the two rights was opted for through the word *et* in the French text,[1057] pointed already in a different direction and more recently, in the *Croissant* Case, the Court expressed as its opinion that national courts when appointing defence counsel must take into account the accused's wishes. However, those wishes may be overridden if required 'in the interests of justice'.[1058] In any case, if it should be found that there exists or arises such an unsatisfactory relationship between the accused and the lawyer assigned to him that an adequate defence is impossible,

---

[1052] See the judgment of 28 June 1984, *Campbell and Fell*, A.80, p. 49. The Dutch Supreme Court had declared the practice of wire-tapping in the *Menten* Case unlawful, even though this was done by order of the investigating judge: Supreme Court, 10 April 1979, *NJ*, 1979, No. 374. This induced the Commission to declare a complaint manifestly ill-founded which Menten nevertheless raised on this point; Appl. 9433/81, *Menten v. the Netherlands*, D&R 27 (1982), p. 133 (138).

[1053] Judgments of 22 September 1994, *Lala*, A.297-A, p. 13 and *Pelladoah*, A.297-B, pp. 34-35.

[1054] Appl. 722/60, *X v. Federal Republic of Germany*, Yearbook V (1962), p. 104 (106); Appls 7572, 7586 and 7587/76, *Ensslin, Baader and Raspe v. Federal Republic of Germany*, Yearbook XXI (1978), p. 418 (464).

[1055] Report of 14 July 1982, B.61 (1987), p. 25.

[1056] See, *e.g.*, Appl. 6946/75, *X v. Federal Republic of Germany*, D&R 6 (1977), p. 114 (116-117).

[1057] Judgment of 25 April 1983, A.64, p. 15. See *supra* p. 468.

[1058] Judgment of 25 September 1992, A.237-B, p. 33. In this case the applicant contested the necessity of the appointment of a third defence counsel.

or if the qualifications of the assigned lawyer are found to be inadequate considering the nature and/or complexity of the case, paragraph 1 and paragraph 3(b) may imply that another lawyer must be assigned to the accused at the latter's request.[1059] In the *Kamasinski* Case, however, the Court, like the Commission, held that the responsibility rests in the first place on the applicant:

> the competent national authorities are required under Article 6 § 3 (c) to intervene only if a failure by legal aid counsel to provide effective representation is manifest or sufficiently brought to their attention in some other way.[1060]

In this context the Court emphasised in the *Artico* Case that the authorities have not complied with their obligation by the mere assignment of a lawyer, since Article 6(3)(c) speaks of 'assistance' and not of 'nomination', so that it must be sufficiently ensured that real assistance is provided.[1061] Here again, however, the accused can forfeit his right by personally creating the situation in which at the very last moment before the hearing another lawyer must be nominated.[1062]

(e) Free Legal Assistance

Article 6(3)(c) stipulates that legal assistance should be given free to the accused if he has not sufficient means to pay for it and when the interests of justice so require. A system that does not contain any obligation to pay costs for the accused who is acquitted but requires the reimbursement of the costs of appointed lawyers in case the person concerned is convicted, is in itself not incompatible with the Convention. Surprisingly the Court left open the question whether it would be consistent with the provision under (c) for the national authorities to seek partial or even full reimbursement after it had been established in enforcement proceedings subsequent to the trial that the convicted person lacks sufficient means to pay the costs of his defence.[1063] We believe that on this point the text of Article 6(3)(c) leaves no room for doubt: if the accused has no sufficient means to bear the costs of legal assistance, which is required in the 'interests of justice', it should be given to him free, without restrictions.

In order to establish whether in a given case the 'interests of justice' require free legal assistance, the Court applies two criteria: the seriousness of the alleged offence in conjunction with the severity of the penalty that the accused risks and, secondly, the complexity of the case.[1064] The personal circumstances and

---

[1059] *Idem.*

[1060] Judgment of 19 December 1989, *Kamasinski*, A.168, p. 33. See also the judgment of 24 November 1993, *Ibrioscia*, A.275, p. 14. In the *Kamasinski* Case the Court expressly mentioned that the responsibility rests in the first place on the defendant 'whether counsel be appointed under a legal aid scheme or be privately financed'. This passage was lacking in the *Imbrioscia* Case. Compare further the judgment of 22 February 1994, *Tripodi*, A.281-B, p. 46.

[1061] Judgment of 13 May 1980, A.37, pp. 15-16.

[1062] Appl. 8251/78, *X v. Austria*, D&R 17 (1980), p. 166 (169-170).

[1063] Judgment of 25 September 1992, *Croissant*, A.237-B, p. 34.

[1064] Judgment of 28 March 1990, *Granger*, A.174, pp. 18-19; judgment of 24 May 1991, *Quaranta*, A.205, pp. 17-18; judgment of 10 June 1996, *Benham*, Reports 1996-III, Vol. 10, paras 60-64.

development of the accused seem to fall within the framework of the latter criterium.[1065] However, not in all cases the Court has followed exact the same line of reasoning and its rather casuistic approach has not produced further clarity yet.[1066] Be that as it may, if on the ground of the requirements of a fair hearing of the first paragraph an accused is entitled to free legal aid, that aid will also have to be considered to be required in the interests of justice, while the general interest of the case exceeding the interests of the accused may also call for legal assistance. If it has been recognised with regard to the written phase of the proceedings that the interests of justice require the assignment of legal aid, as a rule, and even *a fortiori*, this will also have to apply for the subsequent oral phase.[1067] If a lawyer has been assigned to an accused, but the behaviour of the latter has induced counsel to withdraw, the refusal of the court to assign a new lawyer may be in conformity with the 'interests of justice', provided that from that moment the accused himself is given sufficient opportunity to defend himself in person.[1068]

In the *Poitrimol* Case the Court accepted that, in principle, national legislation may discourage the unjustified absence of an accused at the trial. However, the sanction of suppression of the right to legal assistance was held disproportionate in the circumstances of the case.[1069]

The fact that the applicant has not suffered any damage from the non-fulfilment of the requirement under paragraph 3(c) does not exclude that this provision has been violated.[1070]

6.9.5 The Right to Summon and Examine Witnesses

Paragraph 3(d) grants to the accused the right to examine or have examined witnesses against him, and to obtain the attendance and examination of witnesses on his behalf under the same conditions as witnesses against him. This provision is closely related to the principle of the 'equality of arms' as an element of a 'fair hearing' in the sense of the first paragraph. Consequently, the Court often examines an alleged violation of the provision under (d) under the two provisions taken together. Although subparagraph 3(d) is included among the guarantees applying specifically to criminal proceedings, in the case-law the possibility has been recognised that the refusal by the court to permit a party to civil proceedings

---

[1065] Judgment of 24 May 1991, *Quaranta*, A.205, p. 17. See also the judgment of 25 September 1992, *Pham Hoang*, A.243, p. 23.

[1066] See, *e.g.*, the judgments of 28 October 1994, *Boner*, A.300-B, pp. 75-76 and *Maxwell*, A.300-C, pp. 97-98.

[1067] Judgment of 25 April 1983, *Pakelli*, A.64, pp. 16-18.

[1068] Appl. 8386/78, *X v. the United Kingdom*, D&R 21 (1981), p. 126 (130-132).

[1069] Judgment of 23 November 1993, A.277-A, pp. 14-15.

[1070] Judgment of 19 February 1991, *Alimena*, A.195-D, p. 56.

to have a particular witness summoned or examined constitutes a violation of the right to a fair hearing.[1071]

The notion of 'witness' is interpreted autonomously. Statements not made in court in person, but for example to the police, are to be regarded as statements of 'witnesses' as far as the national courts take account of these statements.[1072] Complaints concerning the hearing or summons of an expert do not fall under the provision of subparagraph 3(d) but under the general rule of the first paragraph of Article 6.[1073] In principle the Court does not assess whether statements of witnesses have been properly admitted as evidence.[1074] Thus, it is a matter for the domestic courts to assess whether a statement given by a witness in open court and on oath should be relied on in preference to another statement of the same witness, even when the former is contradictory to the latter.[1075]

The Court has deduced from the fact that an accused person is 'entitled to take part in the hearing and to have his case heard in his presence by a tribunal', that all the evidence should 'in principle be produced in the presence of the accused at a public hearing with a view to adversarial argument.'[1076] However it is not inconsistent with paragraph 3(d) and paragraph 1 to use as evidence statements made at the pre-trial stage as long as the accused has been given:

> an adequate and proper opportunity to challenge and question a witness against him, either at the time the witness was making his statement or at some later stage of the proceedings.[1077]

If there did not exist 'an adequate and proper opportunity' for the accused to question the witness, his conviction cannot solely or mainly be based on the testimony of the latter.[1078] The case-law does not seem to leave much room for exceptions to this rule. The use as evidence of a statement made in the pre-trial phase by a person who subsequently, in accordance with national law, refuses to give evidence in court, is in itself not incompatible with the Convention. However,

---

[1071] Judgment of 27 October 1993, *Dombo Beheer B.V.*, A.274, p. 19. See also, *e.g.*, Appl. 5362/72, *X v. Austria*, Coll. 42 (1973), p. 145.

[1072] Judgment of 19 December 1990, *Delta*, A.191-A, p. 15; judgment of 19 February 1991, *Isgrò*, A.194-A, p. 12; judgment of 26 April 1991, *Asch*, A.203, p. 10; judgment of 28 August 1992, *Artner*, A.242-A, p. 10.

[1073] Judgment of 6 May 1985, *Bönisch*, A.92, p. 15; judgment of 28 August 1991, *Brandstetter*, A.211, p. 20. See *supra* p. 432.

[1074] Judgment of 20 November 1989, *Kostovski*, A.166, p. 19.

[1075] Judgment of 26 March 1996, *Doorson*, Reports 1996-II, Vol. 6, para. 78.

[1076] Judgment of 6 December 1988, *Barberà, Messegué and Jabardo*, A.146, p. 34, with reference to the judgment of 12 February 1985, *Colozza*, A.89, pp. 14 and 16.

[1077] Judgment of 20 November 1989, *Kostovski*, A.166, p. 20. See also the judgment of 24 November 1986, *Unterpertinger*, A.110, pp. 14-15; judgment of 19 December 1990, *Delta*, A.191-A, p. 16; judgment of 26 April 1991, *Asch*, A.203, p. 10; judgment of 15 June 1992, *Lüdi*, A.238, p. 21; judgment of 20 September 1993, *Saïdi*, A.261-C, p. 56.

[1078] Judgment of 20 November 1989, *Kostovski*, A.166, p. 21; judgment of 27 September 1990, *Windisch*, A.186, p. 11; judgment of 19 February 1991, *Isgrò*, A.194-A, pp. 12-13; judgment of 28 August 1992, *Artner*, A.242-A, p. 10; judgment of 20 September 1993, *Saïdi*, A.261-C, p. 57.

it may lead to a conviction only if there exists evidence that corroborates the statement.[1079] The same hold good for a statement of a witness who has disappeared and therefore cannot be summoned to appear in court.[1080] This approach is also reflected in the case-law with regard to the admissibility of the testimony by anonymous witnesses that has been developed by the Court in the *Kostovski* Case, the *Windisch* Case and the *Doorson* Case. In the latter case the Court held that 'a conviction should not be based either solely or to a decisive extent on anonymous statements'.[1081] There seems to be no exceptions to this rule.[1082] Moreover, the use of anonymous statements seems to be permissible only if they meet strict requirements. In the *Doorson* Case the Court took as a starting-point that the interests of the defence should be balanced 'against those of witnesses or victims called upon to testify'.[1083] Subsequently it took account of the circumstances of the case, concerning the prosecution of a drug dealer, and concluded that the reasons to maintain the anonymity of some witnesses were relevant and sufficient. Finally, it held that the handicaps of the defence were 'sufficiently counterbalanced by the procedures followed by the judicial authorities' and based its conclusion on several facts: the witnesses had been questioned by an investigating judge who was aware of their identity, the national court had been able due to the report of the investigating judge to draw conclusions about the reliability of the witnesses, counsel of the defence had been offered the opportunity to question them except in so far their identity was concerned and the witnesses had identified the applicant from a photograph.[1084] In the *Kostovski* Case and the *Windisch* Case the Court held that the lack of a direct confrontation with the witnesses could not be repaired by the opportunity to put written questions. The awareness of the identity of the witnesses was of crucial importance to enable the defence to challenge their statements.[1085] In the *Lüdi* Case, however, the Court reached in respect of an undercover agent, a sworn police-officer whose function was known to the investigating judge, a different conclusion: Article 6 did not object to the examination by the defence of an undercover agent without revealing the *real* identity of the agent, because the

---

[1079] Judgment of 24 November 1986, *Unterpertinger*, A.110, pp. 14-15; judgment of 26 April 1991, *Asch*, A.203, pp. 10-11.

[1080] Judgment of 28 August 1992, *Artner*, A.242-A, pp. 10-11.

[1081] Judgment of 26 March 1996, Reports 1996-II, Vol. 6, para. 76.

[1082] In this respect the judgment of 20 November 1989, *Kostovski*, A.166, p. 21 is less clear, where the Court concluded that the handicaps of the defence that had been caused by the anonymous statements were not 'counterbalanced by the procedures followed by the judicial authorities'. Thus, the Court suggested that a conviction could have been based mainly on anonymous, but sufficiently counterbalanced, statements. This uncertainty was not, at least not clearly, lifted in the judgment of 27 September 1990, *Windisch*, A.186.

[1083] Judgment of 26 March 1996, Reports 1996-II, Vol. 6, para. 70.

[1084] *Ibidem*, paras 71-75.

[1085] Judgment of 20 November 1989, *Kostovski*, A.166, p. 20; judgment of 27 September 1990, *Windisch*, A.186, pp. 10-11.

accused knew the agent by physical appearance.[1086] In the *Baegen* Case, prior to the *Doorson* Case, the conviction of the applicant for rape had been based partly on the anonymous statements of the victim. The Commission held that, despite the lack of any opportunity for the applicant or his lawyer to examine the victim directly, the proceedings had not been unfair.[1087] The case has not been pursued before the Court,[1088] but it is uncertain whether the Court would have followed the Commission, having regard to the *Doorson* Case. Although the Court, as mentioned before, has recognised that the interests of the defence should be balanced 'against those of (...) victims called upon to testify',[1089] it remains questionable whether in the *Baegen* Case the handicaps for the defence had been sufficiently counterbalanced.

Thus far, the question whether a testimony of a so-called crown witness is permissible, has not been brought before the Court. The Commission has recognised that an issue under Article 6 may arise, but seems to have no objections of principle to this practice.[1090]

The provision under (d) does not contain any restriction with respect to the questions which the accused wants to ask the witnesses against him. However, in the case-law of the Commission this provision has been deprived of a great deal of its effect because the Commission leaves very wide discretion to the national court on this point.[1091] If in this respect the court gives evidence of bias, the right to a fair hearing has been violated,[1092] but this can hardly be proved. In our opinion, the rationale of paragraph 3(d) is satisfied only if the court affords the accused or counsel ample opportunity for the examination and only makes restrictions in case of manifest abuse or improper use of the right to examination.

In the *Unterpertinger* Case the Commission took the position that the provision of Article 6(3) under (d) had not been violated, because the prosecution, too, had not had the opportunity to examine the persons concerned.[1093] Fortunately this position was not adopted by the Court. Here the Commission transposed the equality principle, which is of decisive importance for the second limb of paragraph 3(d), *viz.* the right to summon witnesses for the defence, to the right to examine witnesses for the prosecution. That position is untenable already from a

---

[1086] Judgment of 15 June 1992, *Lüdi*, A.238, p. 21. Article 6 had nevertheless been violated because the defence did not have any opportunity to question the undercover agent.

[1087] Report of 20 October 1994, A.327-B, pp. 44-45.

[1088] The case has been struck out of the list by the Court since the applicant did not respond to writings of the Registrar. Judgment of 27 October 1995, A.327-B, pp. 39-40.

[1089] Judgment of 26 March 1996, *Doorson*, Reports 1996-II, Vol. 6, para. 70.

[1090] Appl. 7306/75, *X v. the United Kingdom*, D&R 7, p. 115 (118); Appl. 25982/94, *Sylvin Clifford Flanders* (not yet published); Appl. 18666/91, *René Salmon Menesses* (not yet published).

[1091] See Appl. 4428/70, *X v. Austria*, Yearbook XV (1972), p. 264 (282). Appl. 8417/78, *X v. Belgium*, D&R 16 (1979), p. 200 (207); report of 15 October 1987, *Bricmont*, A.158, p. 45.

[1092] This possibility was recognised by the Commission in its decision on Appl. 4428/70, *X v. Austria*, Yearbook XV (1972), p. 264 (284-286).

[1093] Report of 11 October 1984, A.110, pp. 19-20.

systematical and grammatical point of view.[1094] Moreover, an inequality occurs if the prosecution puts forward a testimony made in a previous phase, since in that previous phase the prosecution has had the opportunity to examine the person in question, albeit perhaps only *via* the police, while the accused has not.

The second limb of paragraph 3(d) clearly allows for the discretion of the national court because its only requirement is that the prosecution and the accused receive equal treatment in this respect. So it does not require the presence and examination of every witness the accused expressly requests.[1095] With regard to the summoning of witnesses for the defence and their examination, domestic law and the courts may set conditions and impose restrictions, provided that these equally apply in respect of the witnesses for the prosecution.[1096] Moreover, some initiative on the part of the accused is required as to the calling of witnesses, as well as, of course, during the examination; the court need not call witnesses of its own accord.[1097] However, here again the fact that paragraph 3(d) has not been violated does not yet mean that the requirements of the first paragraph have been satisfied. Moreover, the Commission and Court have restricted the discretion of the courts somewhat by requiring that the national courts should state the reasons for rejecting a request of the accused to summon a witness.[1098]

6.9.6 The Right to the Free Assistance of an Interpreter

Paragraph 3(e), finally, grants to the accused the right to have the free assistance of an interpreter if he cannot understand or speak the language used in court. Thus, the fact that counsel of the accused understands the language used in court does not do away with the latter's right to an interpreter. From paragraph 3(e) it follows that the accused cannot claim that the trial or the examination is conducted in a language other than the official vernacular.

The provision under (e), too, is linked so closely with the principle of a 'fair hearing' of the first paragraph that also in cases of a determination of civil rights and obligations the necessary costs for a translator or an interpreter may be so

---

[1094] See the dissenting opinion of Trechsel, *ibidem*, p. 25.

[1095] Judgment of 22 April 1992, *Vidal*, A.235-B, p. 32. See also the judgment of 26 March 1996, *Doorson*, Reports 1996-II, Vol. 6, para. 82.

[1096] Judgment of 22 April 1992, *Vidal*, A.235-B, p. 32. See further Appl. 4428/70, *X* v. *Austria*, Yearbook XV (1972), p. 264 (282). Thus also Appl. 9433/81, *Menten* v. *the Netherlands*, D&R 27 (1982), p. 233 (234-238).

[1097] Appl. 5881/72, *X* v. *the United Kingdom* (not published). In its decision the Commission stated that the calling of witnesses 'was a matter which was within the discretion of the applicant's solicitor and counsel and the fact that they apparently chose to call only one medical witness does not suggest in any way that the applicant's rights under this provision [*i.e.* Art. 6(3)(d)] were not respected'. See also Appl. 5282/71, *X* v. *the United Kingdom*, Coll. 42 (1973), p. 99 (102).

[1098] Report of 15 October 1987, *Bricmont*, A.158, p. 46; judgment of 22 April 1992, *Vidal*, A.235-B, p. 33.

burdensome for a party to the proceedings that the non-reimbursement may conflict with the first paragraph.[1099]

The right to interpretation is not limited to the trial, but also applies to the pre-trial investigations.[1100] In the *Luedicke, Belkacem and Koç* Case the Court stated that Article 6(3) under (e) relates to 'all those documents or statements in the proceedings instituted against him which it is necessary for him to understand in order to have the benefit of a fair trial.'[1101] However, according to the Court, this does not imply that all items of written evidence or official documents should be translated. The requirement of the provision under (e) is met if the accused is enabled to follow, and form an opinion of, the proceedings, so he can put before the Court his comment on the events.[1102]

In the *Kamasinski* Case the questions put to the witnesses were not interpreted separately. The interpretation at the trial was 'consecutive and summarising'. This does in itself not amount to a violation of the provision under (e).[1103] Neither does the absence of a written translation of the verdict, as long as the accused has sufficient knowledge of the judgment and its reasoning to judge whether he should give notice of appeal.[1104]

The obligation to appoint an interpreter rests on the competent authorities, although some personal initiative of the accused may be required.[1105] However, the obligation is not fulfilled by merely appointing an interpreter. If the authorities 'are put on notice in the particular circumstances, [it] may also extend to a degree of a subsequent control over the adequacy of the interpretation provided.'[1106] In German legal practice paragraph 3(e) was applied in such a way that an interpreter was indeed freely made available to begin with, but the expense involved was ultimately made to fall under the general regulation concerning the costs of the suit. This was justly considered by the Commission and the Court to be contrary to the word 'free'.[1107] Moreover, the Court indicated that paragraph 3(e) refers not only to the expenses of an interpreter, but also to translation expenses, and then not only to the expenses relating to the hearing itself, but also to those concerning the translation of the charge brought against the accused, as referred to in Article 6(3)(a), and of the reasons for the arrest and the charges

---

[1099] Report of 18 May 1977, *Luedicke, Belkacem and Koç*, B.27 (1982), p. 26, and report of 9 March 1977, *Airey*, B.30 (1983), p. 32.

[1100] Judgment of 19 December 1989, *Kamasinski*, A.168, p. 36. See also the report in this case of 5 May 1988, A.168, p. 58.

[1101] Judgment of 28 November 1978, A.29, p. 20. See also the judgment of 19 December 1989, *Kamasinski*, A.168, p. 35.

[1102] Judgment of 19 December 1989, *Kamasinski*, A.168, p. 35.

[1103] *Ibidem*, p. 38.

[1104] *Idem*.

[1105] Appl. 2689/65, *X v. Belgium*, Yearbook X (1967), p. 282 (318).

[1106] Judgment of 19 December 1989, *Kamasinski*, A.168, p. 35.

[1107] Report of 18 May 1977, *Luedicke, Belkacem and Koç*, B.27 (1982), p. 26; judgment of 28 November 1978 in the same case, A.29, p. 19.

against him, mentioned in Article 5(2).[1108] Even when the accused is discharged on account of the little importance of the case, or because the period of limitation has expired, the services of an interpreter during the trial should be paid by the authorities.[1109]

6.10 Derogation

Article 6 is not included among the non-derogable rights listed in the second paragraph of Article 15.

7 FREEDOM FROM RETROSPECTIVE EFFECT OF PENAL LEGISLATION (ARTICLE 7)

1. *No one shall be held guilty of any criminal offence on account of any act or omission which did not constitute a criminal offence under national or international law at the time when it was committed. Nor shall a heavier penalty be imposed than the one that was applicable at the time the criminal offence was committed.*
2. *This Article shall not prejudice the trial and punishment of any person for any act or omission which, at the time when it was committed, was criminal according to the general principles of law recognised by civilised nations.*

7.1 The Scope of Article 7

The scope of Article 7 is essentially determined by the concepts of 'criminal offence' and of 'heavier penalty'. It seems to be obvious that the meaning of the words 'criminal offence' is closely related to the notion of 'criminal charge' of Article 6. Thus, it is appropriate to argue that Article 7 is also applicable to those disciplinary and administrative convictions which come within the scope of Article 6.

Preventive measures, however, are not covered by it,[1110] no more than deportation orders[1111] and decisions concerning extradition[1112] as far as the applicable extradition law – apart from the criminal law elements involved – is concerned.

The notion of 'penalty' is to be interpreted autonomously to make the protection of Article 7 effective. In virtue of the wording of Article 7 the measure in question must be imposed following a conviction for a 'criminal offence'. The Court takes this as a starting-point. Other factors that may be relevant are: 'the characterisation of the measure under national law, its nature and purpose, the

---

[1108] *Idem.*
[1109] This follows from the judgment of 26 March 1982, *Adolf*, A.49, pp. 14-17, and the reports of 12 May 1982, *Öztürk*, B.58 (1987), pp. 24-32 and of 6 May 1981, *Minelli*, B.52 (1986), pp. 21-22.
[1110] Judgment of 14 November 1960, *Lawless*, A.1, p. 54.
[1111] Report of 12 October 1989, *Moustaquim*, A.193, p. 34.
[1112] Appl. 7512/76, *X v. the Netherlands*, D&R 6 (1977), p. 184 (186).

procedures involved in the making and implementation of the measure and its severity'.[1113] In the *Welch* Case the assessment of these criteria lead to the conclusion that a confiscation order imposed in addition to a sentence of imprisonment did constitute a 'penalty',[1114] while in the *Jamil* Case it was held that the prolongation of a term of imprisonment in default also amounted to the applicability of Article 7.[1115]

The word 'heavier' in the second sentence of Article 7(1) seems to refer merely to the measure of the punishment, but the rationale of this provision entails that also a punishment of a different kind than the one formerly provided for, which may be felt as more burdensome by the person in question, shall not be applied with retrospective effect.

Article 7 clearly does not oppose to a retrospective application of the criminal law in the accused's favour.[1116]

7.2 *Nullum Crimen, Nulla Poena Sine Lege*

The first paragraph of Article 7 contains the following two separate principles, shich are essential elements of the Rule of Law:[1117] (1) a criminal conviction can only be based on a norm which existed at the time of the incriminating act or omission (*nullum crimen sine lege*); (2) on account of the infringement of that norm no heavier penalty may be imposed than the one that was applicable at the time the offence was committed (*nulla poena sine lege*). Thus, Article 7 intends to offer 'essential safeguards against arbitrary prosecution, conviction and punishment'.[1118]

That these are two separate principles means, *inter alia*, that even a purely declaratory judgment in which a norm of criminal law is applied with retrospective effect and is declared to have been infringed, but in which no punishment or other measure is imposed on the offender, constitutes a violation of Article 7. This is not without importance, because such a declaratory judgment, when registered, may still have prejudicial consequences for the person in question, even apart from the social repercussions that it may also entail.

[1113] Judgment of 9 February 1995, *Welch*, A.307-A, p. 13; judgment of 8 June 1995, *Jamil*, A.317-B, pp. 27-28.

[1114] Judgment of 9 February 1995, *Welch*, A.307-A, pp. 13-15. The Court distinguished several punitive elements. The combination of these gave the confiscation order the character of a 'penalty'. The Court stressed, *inter alia*, that the severity of the order was not in itself decisive because 'many non-penal measures of a preventive nature may have a substantial impact on the person concerned'. The Commission held Art. 7, by seven votes to seven(!), to be not applicable.

[1115] Judgment of 8 June 1995, A.317-B, p. 28. It seems to be crucial that the sanction imposed was intended to be deterrent and could lead to a punitive deprivation of liberty.

[1116] Judgment of 25 May 1993, *Kokkinakis*, A.260-A, p. 22; judgment of 27 September 1995, *G* v. *France*, A.325-B, p. 38.

[1117] Judgments of 22 November 1995, *S.W.* v. *the United Kingdom*, A.335-B and *C.R.* v. *the United Kingdom*, A.335-C, p. 41 and p. 68 respectively.

[1118] *Idem.*

Beside the principles of *nullum crimen* and *nulla poena* the Court has distinguished a third principle: the authority applying criminal law shall interpret it not extensively, *i.e.* by analogy, unless such an application operates in favour of the accused. From this third principle follows, according to the Court, that the legislature shall formulate the norms of criminal law clearly.[1119] The provisions have to be sufficiently foreseeable and accessible.[1120] This requirement serves to avoid that a criminal conviction is based on a legal norm of which the person concerned could not, or at least need not, have been aware beforehand. It is satisfied where the wording of the provision, if necessary with the help of the courts' interpretation, makes clear to the individual what behaviour will make him liable.[1121] In our opinion this third principle is not a separate one, but is embodied in the rationale of the *nullum crimen* and *nulla poena sine lege* principles. The various elements of these principles also form part of the established case-law of the Commission.[1122] In this context the Commission deems itself competent to review the interpretation and application of municipal law by the national court:

> Whereas, although it is not normally for the Commission to ascertain the proper interpretation of municipal law by national courts (...), the case is otherwise in matters where the Convention expressly refers to municipal law, as it does in Article 7; whereas under Article 7 the application of a provision of municipal penal law to an act not covered by the provision in question directly results in a conflict with the Convention, so that the Commission can and must take cognisance of allegations of such false interpretation of municipal law.[1123]

The Commission added, however, that it 'exercises in this respect a purely supervisory function and must carry out its task with caution.'[1124] The case-law of the Commission shows that the national authorities hardly have to fear an autonomous interpretation of municipal law by the Commission. As an example may serve the decision in *X* v. *Austria*. In that case a person who had been convicted for homosexual practices invoked Article 7, alleging that the relevant criminal provision referred to 'unnatural indecency' and that the behaviour for which he had been convicted – reciprocal masturbation – could only be deemed to fall thereunder if those words were interpreted in a very extensive sense. There is no evidence at all of an independent opinion of the Commission on whether the behaviour referred to could be deemed to be covered by the term 'unnatural

---

[1119] Judgment of 25 May 1993, *Kokkinakis*, A.260-A, p. 22.

[1120] Judgment of 27 September 1995, *G* v. *France*, A.325-B, p. 38.

[1121] Judgment of 25 May 1993, *Kokkinakis*, A.260-A, p. 22; judgments of 22 November 1995, *S.W.* v. *the United Kingdom*, A.335-B and *C.R.* v. *the United Kingdom*, A.335-C, pp. 41-42 and pp. 68-69 respectively.

[1122] Appl. 1852/63, *X* v. *Austria*, Yearbook VII (1965), p. 190 (198); Appl. 6683/74, *X* v. *the United Kingdom*, D&R 3 (1976), p. 95 (96); Appl. 7721/76, *X* v. *the Netherlands*, D&R 11 (1978), p. 209 (211); Appl. 8141/78, *X* v. *Austria*, D&R 16 (1979), p. 141 (142); Appl. 10980/84, *G* v. *Liechtenstein*, D&R 38 (1984), p. 234 (238).

[1123] Appl. 1852/63, *X* v. *Austria*, Yearbook VIII (1965), p. 190 (198).

[1124] *Ibidem*, pp. 198-200.

indecency' in a restrictive interpretation. It confined itself to considering that the interpretation here followed by the highest Austrian court was generally accepted at the time the acts were committed and at the time of the conviction.[1125] The Commission was evidently of the opinion that for that reason the person in question knew, or could have known, that his behaviour was considered punishable – in other words that there existed a established case-law – and that it was not for the Commission to review the correctness of this case-law.[1126] But then it should have clearly pointed to the existence of a such case-law and based its decision on the latter; it should not argue, as it did on a few occasions, that it is not its duty to review, as a kind of court of appeal, the correctness of the interpretation followed by the national court.[1127]

In the *Kokkinakis* Case the Court did base its decision on the existence of a constant case-law. The Court held that the applicant, who was born in a orthodox family, could have known that the conversion to the religion of the Jehovah's witnesses made him liable under the Greek law that declared proselytism a criminal offence. It did so by referring to its conclusion in the same judgment, under Article 9 of the Convention: the legal limitation of the freedom of religion met the requirement 'prescribed by law' because there existed an established case-law concerning the relevant legal provision, that was 'published and accessible'.[1128]

Not only written statutes, but also rules of common law or customary law may provide a sufficient legal basis for a criminal conviction, provided that the law is adequately accessible and is formulated with sufficient precision to enable the citizen to regulate his conduct.[1129] Since common law is by definition law developed by the courts, Article 7(1) may cause difficulties. This problem has been tackled by the Court in the *S.W.* v. *the United Kingdom* Case and the *C.R.* v. *the United Kingdom* Case, where it held that Article 7:

> cannot be read as outlawing the gradual clarification of the rules of criminal liability through judicial interpretation from case to case, provided that the resultant development is consistent with the essence of the offence and could reasonably be foreseen.[1130]

[1125] Appl. 4161/69, Yearbook XIII (1970), p. 798 (804-806).

[1126] See also Appls 6782-6784/74, *X, Y and Z* v. *Belgium*, D&R 9 (1978), p. 13 (22 in conjunction with 20), where with regard to the applicants' allegation that the act for which they had been convicted (including distribution of the journal *Sekstant*) did not constitute a violation 'according to the principles of European morality', the Commission referred to the Court's judgment in the *Handyside* Case, to the effect that a uniform European conception of morals does not exist.

[1127] See, *e.g.*, Appl. 4080/69, *X* v. *Austria*, Coll. 38 (1972), p. 4 (7); Appl. 7721/76, *X* v. *the Netherlands*, D&R 11 (1978), p. 209 (210).

[1128] Judgment of 25 May 1993, A.260-A, p. 22 in conjunction with pp. 19-20.

[1129] Appl. 8710/79, *X Ltd. and Y* v. *the United Kingdom*, D&R 28 (1982), p. 77 (80-81). For these conditions, *cf.* the judgment of 26 April 1979, *Sunday Times*, A.30, p. 31.

[1130] Judgments of 22 November 1995, A.335-B, p. 42 and A.335-C, p. 69 respectively.

In these cases the Court finally reached the conclusion that the decision of the national courts to lift the immunity of a man from prosecution for rape upon his wife constituted a 'reasonably foreseeable development of law'. Moreover, since the 'essentially debasing character of rape' was manifest, the applicants could not claim that they had been subjected to an arbitrarily prosecution, conviction and punishment.[1131] In the case of *X Ltd. and Y* v. *the United Kingdom* the Commission held that constituent elements of an offence, such as, *e.g.*, the particular form of culpability required for its completion, may not be essentially changed, at least not to the detriment of the accused, but that it is not objectionable that the existing elements of the offence are clarified and adapted to new circumstances which can reasonably be brought under the original concept of the offence.[1132] When the national court has relied on previous case-law, the Strasbourg authorities have to be on the alert that this case-law does not imply in fact an aggravation of the norm since the time the act was committed.[1133]

In principle the national legislature is free to decide what act or omission is to be qualified as an offence and has to be penalised. Article 7 is not in issue there. The European review in that case is confined to the question of whether any of the other provisions of the Convention has been violated by that legislation.[1134]

The *nulla poena* principle in its requirement of legal certainty does not go to such lengths that the exact measure of the penalty, or an exhaustive enumeration of alternatives, must be laid down in the criminal law provision. If, as is customary in several legal systems, only the maxima are indicated, the legal subjects know what is the maximum penalty they may incur upon violation of the norm. If violation of the norm is penalised without a maximum being laid down, in the literal sense there can be no question of 'a heavier penalty (...) than the one that was applicable at the time the criminal offence was committed', unless at the latter time a different penalty was provided for. In that case, however, the second sentence of Article 7(1) will have to be interpreted to mean that the 'applicable

---

[1131] *Ibidem*, pp. 44-45 and pp. 71-72 respectively.

[1132] Appl. 8710/79, *X Ltd. and Y* v. *the United Kingdom*, D&R 28 (1982), p. 77 (80-81). See also Appl. 10038/82, *Harman* v. *the United Kingdom*, D&R 38 (1984), p. 53 (63), where the applicant complained about an unforeseeable conviction for contempt of court. She maintained that until then it was not considered to be an offence when documents were shown to a journalist after they had been read out in court. The Government submitted that the court had applied generally accepted principles of law to a factual situation which it had not previously had to consider. After the Commission had declared the application admissible a friendly settlement has been reached.

[1133] See Appl. 6683/74, *X* v. *the United Kingdom*, D&R 3 (1976), p. 95 (96), where the English court invoked a precedent which dated from the period subsequent to the moment the fact had been committed, and even subsequent to the commencement of the proceedings. For a rather thorough review by the Commission, see Appl. 8710/79, *X Ltd. and Y* v. *the United Kingdom*, D&R 28 (1982), p. 77 (81-82).

[1134] Thus the Commission in its decision on Appl. 7705/76, *X* v. *Federal Republic of Germany*, D&R 9 (1978), p. 196 (204), in connection with the applicant's allegation that refusal to perform military service does not cause anyone an injury and therefore cannot constitute a criminal offence in the sense of Art. 7.

penalty' is the penalty which is usually inflicted for that particular offence within the legal system concerned, or which at all events was reasonably to be expected for the offender.

What is the situation if after the time the offence was committed, but before the trial, the norm of criminal law or the measure of the penalty has been modified in a sense which is more favourable for the accused? Do the courts then have to apply that modified provision? With respect to the measure of the penalty, Article 15 of the UN Covenant on Civil and Political Rights expressly provides:

> If, subsequent to the commission of the offence, provision is made by law for the imposition of a lighter penalty, the offender shall benefit thereby.

Such a provision is lacking in Article 7 of the Convention. The words 'at the time the criminal offence was committed' suggest that this provision does not confer a right to application of the norm as subsequently alleviated, or of the lowered measure of the penalty.[1135] However, as stated above, Article 7 clearly does not prohibit such an application either.[1136] It may even be prescribed by domestic law, as was the case in G v. France.[1137] The lack of a provision of this import in Article 7 is to be regretted in our opinion. It can only be hoped that every court, apart from special circumstances,[1138] will exercise this clemency if its domestic law leaves any scope for doing so.

7.3 Application with Retrospective Effect

The use of the term 'retrospective effect' in the title of this subsection is misleading insofar that under Article 7(1) it is of course equally prohibited to continue to apply in the old form any norms of criminal law or sanctions which had already been repealed or modified before the time of the offence.[1139] Accordingly, it also forms part of the review by the Strasbourg organs to investigate whether and to what extent the norm of criminal law applied still had effect at the relevant time. Since this is essentially a question of national (constitutional) law, they will be guided to a high degree by the opinion of the national court on the matter.[1140] Nevertheless, it is ultimately incumbent upon them to decide whether Article 7 has been correctly applied.

If it is evident from the legal practice in the country concerned that a particular norm of criminal law has fallen completely into desuetude, so that the offender

---

[1135] Appl. 3777/68, X v. the United Kingdom, Coll. 31 (1970), p. 120 (122); Appl. 7900/77, X v. Federal Republic of Germany, D&R 13 (1979), p. 70 (71-72).

[1136] Supra p. 480.

[1137] Judgment of 27 September 1995, A.325-B.

[1138] As an example may serve the circumstance that the fact was committed in a special situation which no longer was present at the moment of the adjudication – one might think of special emergency legislation – which rendered the fact specially deserving of punishment.

[1139] Appl. 1169/61, X v. Federal Republic of Germany, Yearbook VI (1963), p. 520 (588); Appl. 7721/76, X v. the Netherlands, D&R 11 (1978), p. 209 (211).

[1140] Idem.

could not reasonably presume that acting contrary to this norm would result in prosecution, it conflicts with Article 7 if that norm is applied in his case. It is, however, obvious that in such a case a heavy burden of proof rests on the applicant.[1141]

The words 'be held guilty' and 'be imposed' at first sight point in the direction that Article 7 can only be held to have been violated if a norm of criminal law has actually been applied with retrospective effect, not merely on the basis of the fact that such a retrospective effect has been made possible by the legislature.[1142] However, one should not overlook the fact that the Convention is addressed to the Contracting States, and accordingly to all the organs of these States, including the legislature. If the legislature gives retrospective effect to a provision of criminal law, Article 7 of the Convention has been violated. It is true that such a violation in general cannot be the object of an individual complaint, because it is not yet possible to speak of a victim.[1143] It is, however, one of the characteristic features of the equally provided possibility of State complaints that legislation may be submitted *in abstracto* to review for its compatibility with the Convention without it being necessary to allege that there are (already) individual victims of the application of that law.[1144]

7.4 'National or International Law'

Article 7 refers to 'a criminal offence under national or international law'. With respect to the word 'national' the question arises whether exclusively the national law of the State concerned is meant or whether this State may also attach certain criminal law consequences to the violation, within another State, of a provision of the criminal law of the latter State which does not form part of the criminal law of the first-mentioned State. On this point the Strasbourg case-law does not provide clarity. In its decision in *X* v. *Federal Republic of Germany* the Commission did not consider it to be contrary to Article 7 when the authorities of a State include in a person's police record a foreign conviction for an offence that is not punishable in that State itself.[1145] One may, however, wonder whether such a registration, as well as, for instance, the execution of a criminal judgment

---

[1141] The possibility seems to have been recognised in principle by the Commission in its decision on Appl. 7721/76, *X* v. *the Netherlands*, D&R 11 (1978), p. 209 (211), where, however, the applicant's reference to one single example was deemed insufficient. See also Appl. 4161/69, *X* v. *Austria*, Yearbook XIII (1970), p. 798 (804-806), where the applicant alleged that the case-law had changed, but the Commission found that this change dated from prior to the moment the fact was committed.

[1142] This view seems to be implied in the report in the *Greek* Case, Yearbook XII (1969), p. 185: 'It is not disputed that the penalties provided (...) have not been imposed in any actual case'.

[1143] In specific cases, however, the mere existence of a criminal law provision, even when it has not yet been applied in a concrete case, may hinder a person so much in his freedom of action that he can already be regarded as a victim. On this, *supra* pp. 54-56.

[1144] See *supra* p. 40.

[1145] Appl. 448/59, Yearbook III (1960), p. 254 (270).

pronounced abroad, really fall under the prohibition of Article 7. The English text 'be held guilty' could have a wider scope than the French text '*être condamné*', which points to the pronouncement of the judgment itself and not to later consequences to be attached to that judgment. The words 'national (...) law' in our view must be understood to mean that a criminal judgment can be based only on the national law of the State in question, and not on the law of another State; but the wording of Article 7 would not appear to exclude the possibility that certain consequences are attached in State A to a judgment pronounced in State B on the basis of the criminal law applying in State B at that time, even if the fact concerned is not punishable according to the law of State A. This does not alter the fact, however, that this practice is hard to be reconciled with the idea of the rule of law underlying Article 7, and such a practice in our opinion is objectionable on that ground.

The reference to international law in the first paragraph of Article 7 raises the question of the internal effect of international law within the national legal order. Above, in Chapter I, we have already mentioned that, according to the prevalent opinion, international law as it stands does not oblige States to give internal effect to provisions of international law without their prior 'transformation' into domestic law. Neither does such an obligation ensue from the Convention.[1146] The effect of international law within the national legal order is regulated by national constitutional law. In those Contracting States where international law has no internal effect, this effect cannot be given in incidental cases to an international criminal law provision. Here again compliance with Article 7 depends on whether the person concerned could reasonably know that the offence committed by him was prohibited and punishable within the relevant legal system at that time, either in virtue of a national legal provision or in virtue of a directly applicable international legal provision with internal effect.

7.5 The Exception of the Second Paragraph

The second paragraph of Article 7 contains an exception to the first paragraph for the case of the trial and punishment of an act or omission which, at the time when it was committed or omitted, was a criminal offence according to general principles of law. Although this provision is formulated in a general way, it has evidently been incorporated in particular to enable the application of the national and international legislation, enacted during and after World War II, in respect of war crimes, collaboration with the enemy and treason, to facts committed during the war.[1147] In that sense it forms a codification of the principles laid down by

---

[1146] *Supra* pp. 16-22.

[1147] Thus also the Commission in its decision on, *e.g.*, Appl. 1038/61, *X* v. *Belgium*, Yearbook IV (1961), p. 324 (336).

the tribunals of Nuremberg and Tokyo.[1148] As such the provision is still important for those Contracting States where the limitation in respect of war crimes has been suspended.[1149] However, this effect of the provision does not fit in well with the system of the Convention, since Article 15(2) guarantees that the *nullum crimen-nulla poena* principle also applies to war situations.

However, the second paragraph may also have effect with respect to other cases than those mentioned above. In fact, it does not relate exclusively to war crimes, but to all acts and omissions which are criminal 'according to the general principles of law recognised by civilised nations'. The words from Article 7(2) here quoted have been taken from Article 38 of the Statute of the International Court of Justice. Even the term 'civilised nations', which is virtually meaningless, was copied; this in contrast with Article 15(2) of the UN Covenant on Civil and Political Rights, which refers to 'the community of States'. The principal source of these general principles of law is constituted by the national systems of law. In that context, the general principles of law are those which have been recognised in (practically) all States *in foro domestico*. Since Article 7(2) does not refer to 'the principles of law common to the Contracting States', but to 'the general principles of law recognised by civilised nations', the Contracting States may not be treated as an isolated group in this respect. The legal rule concerned will also have to be recognised outside this circle by a 'representative' group of States, if the principle of law is to be regarded as a general one. In addition, or frequently also in correlation therewith, general principles of law may emerge from the developing international law, usually on the basis of a pattern of treaties which have been concluded and/or of an international practice which has been or is in the process of being formed. They can then hardly be distinguished from customary international law. Be this as it may, in our opinion the concept of general principles of law as here referred to requires that the facts concerned are not only made punishable in the legal systems of nearly all countries and/or under international law, but that their punishable character ensues from a fundamental legal principle. Indeed, otherwise the guarantee of the first paragraph would be seriously jeopardised in all those cases where the legislature deliberately derogates from the criminal law as it applies in most countries in a way which is detrimental for the accused.

All this makes it difficult to establish with any accuracy what offences are meant by Article 7(2). This is particularly the case because here not the responsibility of the State but the responsibility of individuals is at issue, a matter which usually is not regulated by international law. In addition to the above-

---

[1148] See Principle II of the Nuremberg Principles as formulated in 1950 by the International Law Commission, Yearbook I.L.C., 1950, Vol. II, p. 379: 'The fact that international law does not impose a penalty for an act which constitutes a crime under international law does not relieve the person who committed the act from responsibility under international law.'

[1149] See also the Convention on the Non-Applicability of Statutory Limitations to War Crimes and Crimes against Humanity, drafted in 1968 within the framework of the UN, ILM 8, 1969, p. 68.

mentioned war crimes one will have to think in particular of the so-called crimes against peace and crimes against humanity. A definition is contained in the Charter of the International Military Tribunal,[1150] but in later documents the category of crimes against humanity has also been placed outside the war context.[1151] It seems logical to also link the general principles of law of Article 7(2) with fundamental principles in the field of human rights. One could think in this context, in particular, of the right to life and to the physical and psychological integrity of the person, the prohibition of slavery and torture, and the prohibition of racial discrimination. For the applicability of Article 7(2) it is required that the violation of these principles by individuals is punishable according to the national law of (practically) all countries, or that under international law not only the State but also the offender individually is responsible for it. Only then is it possible to speak of a 'criminal act or omission'.[1152] Violation of the above-mentioned fundamental rights will be punishable in one form or another in most national systems. However, to the extent that general principles of international law have not been incorporated in one way or another in domestic law, they can serve as a basis for the conviction of individuals only in those cases where the violation of these principles can be qualified as a 'crime against humanity'.[1153] In other cases, in our opinion, the individual responsibility is not yet established clearly enough under international law as it stands at present.

7.6 Derogation

According to Article 15(2) the guarantee implied in Article 7(1) is non-derogable. As has been said, however, the consequence of the second paragraph of Article 7 is that with respect to certain offences this guarantee is not an absolute one, neither in the situations referred to in Article 15(1) nor in other cases.[1154]

[1150] See Art. 6 of the Charter of the International Military Tribunal, AJIL 39, 1945, Supplement, p. 257.

[1151] Art. I(b) of the Convention on the Non-Applicability of Statutory Limitations to War Crimes and Crimes against Humanity (ILM 8, 1969, p. 68), speaks of 'crimes against humanity, whether committed in time of war or in time of peace', and mentions as examples 'inhuman acts resulting from the policy of apartheid and the crime of genocide'. Compare also the enumeration in the Statute of the International Tribunal for the Prosecution of Persons Responsible for Serious Violations of International Humanitarian Law Committed in the Territory of the Former Yugoslavia since 1991, UN Doc. S25704.

[1152] For war crimes and crimes against humanity this individual responsibility has been laid down in the above-mentioned documents. See also Art. I of the Convention on the Prevention and Punishment of the Crime of Genocide; Art. 1(2) of the International Convention on the Suppression and Punishment of the Crime of Apartheid; and Art. 7 of the Statute of the Yugoslavia Tribunal.

[1153] 'Crimes against humanity' used in the sense of also including war crimes, genocide and apartheid. See the preceding note.

[1154] See *supra* p. 487.

8 RIGHT TO RESPECT FOR PRIVACY (ARTICLE 8)

1. *Everyone has the right to respect for his private and family life, his home and his correspondence.*
2. *There shall be no interference by a public authority with the exercise of this right except such as is in accordance with the law and is necessary in a democratic society in the interests of national security, public safety or the economic well-being of the country, for the prevention of disorder or crime, for the protection of health or morals, or for the protection of the rights and freedoms of others.*

8.1 Introduction

Since any further definition is lacking, the rights laid down in this article cannot be clearly distinguished from each other. This is true in particular for the right to respect for private life, on the one hand, and the other three rights belonging to the private sphere, on the other hand. In fact, a clear delimitation is not necessary, since a complaint concerning violation of the private sphere can be based on the article as a whole. Thus, it was held by the Commission in the case of a stepmother:

> It is here not necessary to decide whether, in the absence of any legal relationship, the ties between the applicant and the child amounted to 'family life' (...) Bearing in mind that the applicant has cared for the child for many years and is deeply attached to him, the separation ordered by the court undoubtedly affects her 'private life'.[1155]

As a collective noun designating the rights involved in Article 8, the 'right to privacy' is often used nowadays. However, this term also comprises other rights than those expressly mentioned in Article 8. In Resolution 428(1970) of the Consultative Assembly (now: Parliamentary Assembly) of the Council of Europe, which contains the Declaration concerning the Mass Media and Human Rights, the right to privacy has been defined as follows:

> The right to privacy consists essentially in the right to live one's own life with a minimum of interference. It concerns private, family and home life, physical and moral integrity, honour and reputation, avoidance of being placed in a false light, non-revelation of irrelevant and embarrassing facts, unauthorised publication of private photographs, protection from disclosure of information given or received by the individual confidentially.[1156]

And in the final conclusions of the Nordic Conference of Jurists on the Right to Respect for Privacy of 1967 the following additional elements of the right to privacy are listed: the prohibition to use a person's name, identity or photograph without his consent; the prohibition to spy on a person; respect for

---

[1155] Appl. 8257/78, *X* v. *Switzerland*, D&R 13 (1979), p. 248 (252). See also Appls 7289/75 and 7349/76, *X and Y* v. *Switzerland*, Yearbook XX (1977), p. 372 (408-410).
[1156] Council of Europe, Cons. Ass., Twenty-First Ordinary Session (Third Part), Texts Adopted (1970).

correspondence; and the prohibition to disclose official information.[1157] The Commission has linked the right to privacy of Article 8 also to the right to freedom of expression of Article 10 by stating that 'the concept of privacy in Article 8 also includes, to a certain extent, the right to establish and maintain relations with other human beings for the fulfilment of one's personality'.[1158]

Two elements of the right to privacy as defined above which are not mentioned in Article 8 are referred to expressly in Article 10(2) as grounds for restriction of the freedom of expression: the protection of a person's reputation and the prevention of disclosure of information received in confidence. In order to rely on such grounds, however, an express legal basis is required; the restrictions must be such 'as are prescribed by law'. Moreover, it has been recognised by the Court that the right to protection of one's reputation constitutes a 'civil right' in the sense of Article 6(1).[1159] Whether these and other, comparable interests also find protection in Article 8 depends on the content given in the national and European case-law to the rights expressly mentioned therein. In this context it is noteworthy that, although the *travaux préparatoires* appear to point in a different direction, the Court and the Commission seem to have implicitly recognised the possibility that attacks on a person's reputation may constitute a breach of Article 8.[1160] In the *Niemietz* Case the Court referred to the applicant's 'professional reputation' as a relevant and important element in the context of Article 8.[1161]

In view of the present discussion concerning euthanasia a decision of the Commission of 1983 is of special interest, where the Commission took the position that the activities for which the applicant was convicted, namely aiding and abetting suicide, cannot be described as falling in the sphere of his private life in the sense of Article 8. While these activities might be thought to touch directly on the private lives of those who sought to commit suicide, in relation to the person who committed the acts of aiding and abetting, they were excluded from the concept of privacy 'by virtue of their trespass on the public interest of protecting life'.[1162]

[1157] See J. Velu, 'The European Convention on Human Rights and the Right to Respect for Private Life, the Home and Communications', in: A.H. Robertson (ed.), *Privacy and Human Rights, Third International Colloquy*, Brussels, 1970, Manchester, 1973, p. 12 (33).

[1158] Appl. 8962/80, *X and Y v. Belgium*, D&R 28 (1982), p. 112 (124).

[1159] Judgment of 21 September 1994, *Fayed*, A.294-B, in which the Court ascertained whether the contested limitation on the applicants' ability to take legal proceedings to challenge the findings and conclusions in the Inspectors' report which were damaging to their reputations satisfied the conditions stated in the Court's case-law. After an analysis of the facts the Court concluded that they did not constitute an unjustified denial of the 'right to a court'. The Commission has also accepted the applicability of Art. 6 in the context of protection of one's reputation: Appl. 808/60, *ISOP v. Austria*, Yearbook V (1962), p. 108 (122).

[1160] Judgment of 21 September 1994, *Fayed*, A.294-B, pp. 50-51; Appl. 2413/65, *X v. Federal Republic of Germany*, Coll. 23 (1967), p. 1 (7).

[1161] Judgment of 16 December 1992, A.251-B, p. 36.

[1162] Appl. 10083/82, *R v. the United Kingdom*, D&R 33 (1983), p. 270 (271-272).

8.2 Private Life

In this section on privacy the following aspects will be discussed: Registration (of persons, files and data); medical examination; homosexuality, abortion, transsexualism, grouped together under the heading 'sexual privacy'; name; and physical integrity. These aspects do not cover all issues, which may be related to the private life element of Article 8. One needs only to think of new genetic and medical techniques. However, they do cover the existing case-law of the Court and provide a sufficient framework to discuss that case-law.

8.2.1 Registration

As to the respect for private life, the question of the registration of persons attracts the greatest amount of attention at present. In the Commission's opinion registration by the police does not conflict with Article 8, not even when the registration concerns persons who do not have any criminal record.[1163] In this form, without any further qualifications, such a viewpoint would appear to be hardly tenable. It must be examined explicitly whether one of the grounds of restriction mentioned in the second paragraph is applicable. Moreover, a review of the collection and use of the data for its compatibility with the *détournement de pouvoir* provision of Article 18 might be required. Such a review actually took place in a case which concerned the transmission of personal data by the police to a criminal court. The Commission considered this justified in the interest of the prevention of crime, although this case concerned the prosecution of a crime and not its prevention. The Commission left open the question of whether the act complained of conflicted at all with the first paragraph.[1164]

In the *Leander* Case the complaint concerned the fact that information derived from the secret police register had prevented the applicant from obtaining permanent employment and had led to his dismissal from provisional employment, while the authorities had refused to disclose that information to him. In that case review for justification on the basis of the second paragraph was performed after the Court had reached the conclusion that the facts (storing and release in a secret police-register of information relating to Leander's private life, coupled with a refusal to allow Leander an opportunity to refute it) disclosed an interference with the applicant's right to respect for his private life. The Commission had agreed with the Government that the issue depended on the contents of the register concerned. A register which only contains, for instance, the name and address of an individual does, in their opinion, not normally involve any interference with

---

[1163] See Appl. 5877/72, *X v. the United Kingdom*, Yearbook XVI (1973), p. 328 (388), where the complaint concerned the taking, and storing in a file, of photographs of the applicant by the police for possible future identification purposes. The Commission evidently considered it decisive here that the photographs had not been released for publication or used for purposes other than police ends.

[1164] Appl. 8170/78, *X v. Austria*, Yearbook XXII (1979), p. 308 (320-322).

Article 8. The Court did not make this distinction. It simply stated that it was 'uncontested that the secret police-register contained information relating to Mr. Leander's private life.'[1165] The Court granted a wide margin of appreciation to the respondent State in assessing the pressing social need of the interference, and in particular in choosing the means for achieving the legitimate aim of protecting national security:

> There can be no doubt as to the necessity, for the purpose of protecting national security, for the Contracting States to have laws granting the competent domestic authorities power, firstly, to collect and store in registers not accessible to the public information on persons and, secondly, to use this information when assessing the suitability of candidates for employment in posts of importance for national security. Admittedly, the contested interference adversely affected Mr Leander's legitimate interests through the consequences it had on his possibilities of access to certain sensitive posts within the public service. On the other hand, the right of access to public services is not as such enshrined in the Convention (see, inter alia, the *Kosiek* judgment of 28 August 1986, Series A no. 106, p. 20 par. 34-35), and, apart from those consequences, the interference did not constitute an obstacle to his leading a private life of his own choosing.[1166]

After a detailed discussion of the intelligence system concerned (*inter alia*, the efficacy of control procedures) the Court stated as its conclusion that:

> Having regard to the wide margin of appreciation available to it, the respondent State was entitled to consider that in the present case the interests of national security prevailed over the individual interests of the applicant. The interference to which Mr Leander was subjected cannot therefore be said to have been disproportionate to the legitimate aim pursued.[1167]

The *Gaskin* Case concerned a complaint about refusal of access to a file. Mr Gaskin wished to have access to the whole file relating to his period in care. The applicant was taken into care at a very young age, after the death of his mother, and had remained in care until he attained his majority. The complaint was presented against the background of his severe psychological problems, which he ascribed to the way in which he was treated while in care. This case differed from the *Leander* Case as far as the character of the data is concerned but also in that in the latter case the personal information on file constituted the basis of decisions which Mr Leander complained were detrimental to him, while in the *Gaskin* Case no use at all was currently made of the file in relation to the applicant or any other person. In fact, Gaskin did not complain about the fact that information was compiled and stored about him, nor did he allege that any use was made to his detriment. He challenged rather the failure to grant him unimpeded access to that information. The Court expressly held Article 8 to be relevant. It agreed with the Commission that:

[1165] Judgment of 26 March 1987, A.116, p. 22.
[1166] *Ibidem*, p. 25.
[1167] *Ibidem*, p. 27.

[the file] no doubt contained information concerning highly personal aspects of the applicant's childhood, development and history and thus could constitute his principal source of information about his past and formative years. Consequently lack of access thereto did raise issues under Article 8.[1168]

This aspect, according to the Court, directly related to a positive obligation on the part of the Contracting State flowing from Article 8. In its judgment the Court concentrated on the question whether a fair balance had been struck between the general interests of the community and the interests of the individual:

> In the Court's opinion, persons in the situation of the applicant have a vital interest, protected by the Convention, in receiving the information necessary to know and to understand their childhood and early development. On the other hand, it must be borne in mind that confidentiality of public records is of importance for receiving objective and reliable information, and that such confidentiality can also be necessary for the protection of third persons. Under the latter aspect, a system like the British one, which makes access to records dependent on the consent of the contributor, can in principle be considered to be compatible with the obligations under Article 8, taking into account the State's margin of appreciation. The Court considers, however, that under such a system the interests of the individual seeking access to records relating to his private and family life must be secured when a contributor to the records either is not available or improperly refuses consent. Such a system is only in conformity with the principle of proportionality if it provides that an independent authority finally decides whether access has to be granted in cases where a contributor fails to answer or withholds consent. No such procedure was available to the applicant in the present case. Accordingly, the procedure followed failed to secure respect for mr. Gaskin's private and family life, as required by Article 8 of the Convention. There has therefore been a breach of that provision.[1169]

In *X* v. *the United Kingdom* the obligation to complete a census form was challenged. The Commission took the view that a compulsory public census, including questions relating to the sex, marital status, place of birth and other personal details may constitute *a prima facie* interference with the right to respect for private and family life which fails to be justified under the terms of the second paragraph of Article 8. Here again, however, as in the *Leander* Case, the Commission found that the interference was justified as being necessary in a democratic society – in this case 'in the interest of the economic well-being of the country'.[1170]

In *Filip Reyntjens* v. *Belgium* the Commission dismissed complaints about the Belgian system implying an obligation to carry an identity-card and to show it to the police on request. Since this card only contains information concerning name, sex, date of birth and place of living the Commission was of the opinion that there was no interference in the private life of the applicant.[1171]

[1168] Judgment of 7 July 1989, A.160, p. 15.

[1169] *Ibidem*, p. 20.

[1170] Appl. 9702/82, D&R 30 (1983), p. 239 (240-241).

[1171] Appl. 16810/90, D&R 73 (1992), p. 136 (152). See also recommendation No. R(87)15 of the Committee of Ministers to Member States regulating the use of personal data in the police sector, Yearbook XXX (1987), pp. 212-218.

In addition to the registration by the police[1172] and the judiciary, and to public census, all of which have a long tradition, registration of all sorts of personal data by public authorities and private institutions is taking place to an increasing degree, in particular as a result of the development of technology, which makes the automatic storage and processing of data possible. In most cases the use that is made of such data cannot be checked by the person concerned, so that, even if he has furnished the data of his own free will, that use may still imply an interference with his private life. In this respect the public authorities are bound by Article 8, and, according to the *Gaskin* judgment, the individual concerned in principle can claim a right to access.[1173]

As regards private institutions, the issue of the *Drittwirkung* of Article 8 arises.[1174] The second paragraph of Article 8 expressly mentions 'interference by a public authority'. The development by the Court of the concept of positive obligations, however, leads to an interpretation according to which the Contracting States are under an obligation to actively protect the right of privacy, also against infringements by private parties.[1175] Of course this does not mean that in Strasbourg a complaint against a private individual could be submitted,[1176] but it would imply that Article 8 could be invoked before the national courts against a private individual in those systems in which the Convention has internal effect. Moreover, Article 8 then would imply the obligation for the Contracting States to assure respect for privacy by individuals to the best of their ability *via* the legislature, the administration and the courts.[1177]

8.2.2 Medical Examination

Another example of interference with private life is the compulsory subjection to a medical or psychological examination. As the Commission has pointed out: 'A compulsory medical intervention, even if it is of minor importance, must be considered as an interference with this right.'[1178] The Court, in the *Herczegfalvy* Case, also accepted the applicability of Article 8 in the context of the compulsory the compulsory administering of food. Considering the facts of the case it

---

[1172] See recommendation No. R(87)15 of the Committee of Ministers to Member States regulating the use of personal data in the police sector, Yearbook XXX (1987), pp. 212-218.

[1173] Judgment of 7 July 1989, A.160, p. 20.

[1174] See *supra* pp. 22-26.

[1175] Art. 3 of the 1981 Council of Europe Convention for the Protection of Individuals with Regard to Automatic Processing of Personal Data (European Treaty Series No. 108) stipulates: 'The Parties undertake to apply the Convention to automated personal data files and automatic processing of personal data in the public and private sectors.' See about positive obligations in general *supra* pp. 74-75 and in the context of Art. 8 *infra* in this chapter.

[1176] See *supra* pp. 119-120.

[1177] In its report of 1 March 1979, *Van Oosterwijck*, B.36 (1983), p. 24, the Commission held that 'Article 8 does not expressly guarantee the right to be protected by the law against interferences with private life', but in the construction here defended not a legal right but a reflex effect would be in issue.

[1178] Appl. 8278/78, *X v. Austria*, D&R 18 (1980), p. 155 (156).

dismissed the applicant's allegations because, according to the psychiatric principles generally accepted at the time, medical necessity justified the treatment in issue and because of:

> the lack of specific information capable of disproving the Government's opinion that the hospital authorities were entitled to regard the applicant's psychiatric illness as rendering him entirely incapable of taking decisions for himself. Consequently, no violation of Article 8 has been shown in this respect.[1179]

Most complaints of persons who had to undergo a compulsory medical or psychological examination as suspects so far were not based upon Article 8, but upon Articles 3, 5, and 6. The Commission held in those cases that such examinations constituted a normal and frequently also desirable element of the investigations concerned.[1180] Had the Commission reviewed, *ex officio*, such examinations for their compatibility with Article 8, it should have ascertained whether they were authorised by law and whether subjection thereto could be justified on the basis of one of the grounds of limitation of the second paragraph. In a case where the applicant did invoke Article 8, it was indeed recognised by the Commission that a compulsory psychiatric examination constituted a breach of the first paragraph of this provision, and the measure was reviewed for its justification under the second paragraph.[1181] A similar review should take place – and in a number of cases was actually performed by the Commission – in connection with other encroachments on the private life of suspects, such as the search of the person, his luggage and his car,[1182] the taking and circulation of photographs, the taking of fingerprints and blood tests,[1183] and the making of tape-recordings which are later used during the trial as evidence against the suspect.[1184]

[1179] Judgment of 24 September 1992, A.244, p. 26. For similar reasons the Court also concluded that Art. 3 had not been shown to have been violated.

[1180] Appl. 986/61, *X* v. *Federal Republic Germany*, Yearbook V (1962), p. 192 (198).

[1181] Appl. 8355/78, *X* v. *Federal Republic of Germany* (not published). The Commission held that such an examination was justified in this case 'for the prevention of disorder or crime and for the protection of health'.

[1182] See, *e.g.*, Appl. 5488/72, *X* v. *Belgium*, Yearbook XVII (1974), p. 222 (226).

[1183] For the blood test aimed at the determination of the alcohol permillage of the bloodstream in connection with the traffic legislation, see: Appl. 8239/78, *X* v. *the Netherlands*, D&R 16 (1979), p. 184 (189), where the Commission considered the test justified 'for the protection of the rights of others'. For a blood test aimed at the determination of paternity, see Appl. 8278/78, *X* v. *Austria*, D&R 18 (1980), p. 155 (157), where the Commission considered the test permissible on the same ground.

[1184] The justification of the latter by the Commission without an *ex officio* review for its justification under Art. 8(2), would therefore appear to be incorrect: Appl. 2645/65, *Scheichelbauer* v. *Austria*, Yearbook XII (1969), p. 156 (172). The problem of wire-tapping and the opening of correspondence between the accused and his counsel has been discussed *supra* pp. 470-471. See also *infra* pp. 566-567.

8.2.3 'Sexual Privacy'

Another aspect of private life with regard to which far-reaching restrictions are laid down in the legislation of most of the Contracting States is that of sexuality: prohibition of sexual intercourse with minors, prohibition of homosexual practices, prohibition of the use (or the sale) of contraceptives, prohibition of abortion and non-recognition or limited recognition of (the consequences of) transsexualism. The Strasbourg case-law has expressly recognised that sexual life constitutes an important part of a person's private life.[1185]

(a) Homosexuality

A general prohibition of homosexual practices was accepted as justified by the Commission in an early decision on the basis of the protection of health and morals relied upon by the respondent State.[1186] The Commission did not provide any arguments for this. In particular it does not appear from its decision whether the Commission has undertaken an independent inquiry into the necessity and proportionality of the restriction in relation to the interests to be protected, or whether, if it has done so, it has taken into account the developments in the opinions on the subject within the country concerned and within the entire region in which the Convention applies. The importance of such an inquiry became evident when the legislation in that same country was modified some time afterwards to the effect that exclusively homosexual intercourse with persons under 18 years of age remained punishable; from this it could be deduced that opinions had indeed changed about the necessity in a democratic society of the absolute and general prohibition.[1187] The issue of the scope of the inquiry to be made by the Strasbourg organs will be discussed below.[1188] Here we confine ourselves to mentioning that on a later occasion, with a similar complaint of a person prosecuted for homosexual acts, the Commission clearly showed to be prepared to undertake an inquiry into the justification of the restriction concerned and to take into account new developments within the country in question and elsewhere.[1189] In a later stage a couple of complaints of homosexuals against the United Kingdom, in which a breach of Article 8 was alleged, was declared admissible[1190] and examined as to their merits.[1191] The first of these cases

---

[1185] For the Commission, see, e.g., its decision on Appl. 5935/72, X v. Federal Republic of Germany, Yearbook XIX (1976), p. 277 (284-286). For the Court, see the judgment of 22 October 1981, Dudgeon, A.45, pp. 18-19; judgment of 26 October 1988, Norris, A.142, p. 17.

[1186] Appl. 104/55, X v. Federal Republic of Germany, Yearbook I (1955-1957), p. 228 (229).

[1187] See Appl. 5935/72, X v. Federal Republic of Germany, Yearbook XIX (1976), p. 277 (284).

[1188] Infra pp. 771-772. With regard to the discrimination aspect in this case, see also infra p. 712.

[1189] See Appl. 5935/72, X v. Federal Republic of Germany, Yearbook XIX (1976), p. 277 (284-286), where the Commission took into consideration in particular the current opinions on the possible effect which a homosexual relationship has on juveniles, and on the question of what age limit would have to be laid down in that respect.

[1190] Appl. 7215/75, X v. the United Kingdom, Yearbook XXI (1978), p. 354 (372); and Appl. 7525/76, X v. the United Kingdom, Yearbook XXII (1979), p. 156 (184).

resulted in a resolution of the Committee of Ministers,[1192] the second in a judgment of the Court.[1193]

The first case concerned a complaint against application of the English Sexual Offences Act, by which homosexual intercourse with male persons under 21 years of age was declared punishable. Here the Commission – followed in this by the Committee of Ministers – found that the prosecution and the punishment were justified on the ground of 'the protection of the rights and freedoms of others'.[1194] The second case concerned a complaint against the legislation in Northern Ireland, prohibiting homosexual intercourse even between consenting male persons over 21 years of age. In this case both the Commission and the Court concluded that this penalisation could not be deemed necessary for the protection of morals in a democratic society, whereas the justification of the prohibition with regard to male persons under 21 years of age, here again, was deemed justifiable by both the Commission and the Court.[1195] Another complaint about the Irish legislation penalising certain homosexual acts in private between consenting adult males was dealt with in the *Norris* Case. The Commission and Court referred to the *Dudgeon* Case and held that there was no 'pressing social need' to make such acts criminal offences.[1196] In the *Modinos* Case the Court stuck to its previous case-law in the *Dudgeon* and *Norris* Cases by ruling that a prohibition of homosexual relations in private between consenting adults constitutes an interference; since the respondent Government did not argue that there existed a justification under paragraph 2 of Article 8, the Court decided that, having regard to the Court's case-law in *Dudgeon* and *Norris*, a re-examination of this question was not called for. Accordingly, it concluded that there was a breach of Article 8.[1197]

In a decision of 1983 (that is before the *Norris* and *Modinos* judgments of the Court) the Commission repeated in a general sense the case-law that 'the prohibition by criminal law of homosexual acts committed in private between consenting males amounts to an interference with the "private life" of those concerned under Article 8(1)'.[1198] Here the age of the partners, or one of them, was not at issue, but the fact that the prohibiting regulation concerned soldiers. The Commission here accepted that homosexual conduct by members of the armed

---

[1191] Report of 12 October 1978, *X* v. *the United Kingdom*, D&R 19 (1980), p. 66; and report of 13 March 1980, *Dudgeon*, B.40 (1984), pp. 32-43.
[1192] Res. DH(79)5 of 12 June 1979, D&R 19 (1980), pp. 82-83.
[1193] Judgment of 22 October 1981, *Dudgeon*, A.45.
[1194] Report of 12 October 1978, *X* v. *the United Kingdom*, D&R 19 (1980), p. 66 (75).
[1195] Report of 13 March 1980, *Dudgeon*, B.40 (1984), p. 41; judgment of 22 October 1981, A.45, pp. 23-24. See also the Voogd Report on discrimination of homosexuals, submitted to the Parliamentary Assembly of the Council of Europe; Doc. 4755, 8 July 1981.
[1196] Report of 12 March 1987 and judgment of 26 October 1988, A.142, p. 33 and pp. 20-21 respectively.
[1197] Judgment of 22 April 1993, A.259, pp. 11-12.
[1198] Appl. 9237/81, *B* v. *the United Kingdom*, D&R 34 (1983), p. 68 (71).

forces may pose a particular risk to order within the forces, which would not arise in civilian life. It referred for that to the evidence given by the Ministry of Defence to the House of Commons Select Committee, which is quoted in the Commission's decision and which the Commission accepted as justified.[1199] However, if one reads that 'evidence', one is struck by the old-fashioned and prejudiced reasoning on which it is based and which seems to neglect that the real risk to order within the forces, if any, is not created by homosexual conduct as such, but rather by the discriminatory attitude towards it in and outside military circles, against which the Convention and its organs ought to protect the individual. It remains to be seen whether this decision is still to be considered as a valid precedent, taking into account the Court's position in the *Norris* and *Modinos* Cases.

(b) Abortion

A complaint against a decision of the German *Bundesverfassungsgericht* in which provisions in the new German legislation on abortion were declared unconstitutional, and against the subsequently introduced amendments, both challenged, *inter alia*, under Article 8, was declared admissible by the Commission insofar as the two female applicants were concerned. The Commission based its decision on the following, very widely formulated ground:

> the Commission considers that pregnancy and the interruption of pregnancy are part of private life, and also in certain circumstances of family life. It further considers that respect for private life "comprises also, to a certain degree, the right to establish and to develop relationships with other human beings, especially in the emotional field, for the development and fulfilment of one's own personality" (...) and that therefore sexual life is also part of private life; and in particular that legal regulation of abortion is an intervention in private life which may or may not be justified under Article 8(2).[1200]

As has been observed above, this formulation would appear to leave sufficient scope for the admissibility also of complaints of men against a prohibition or restriction of voluntary abortion, but the male applicant in this case had insufficiently proved the injury sustained by him.[1201] In its report on the merits of the case the Commission held that the new regulation, adopted in consequence of the decision of the *Bundesverfassungsgericht*, having regard to the weighing of interests on which it was based, did not conflict with Article 8(1),[1202] and the Committee of Ministers agreed with this point of view.[1203]

In *X* v. *the United Kingdom* it was submitted that the legislation permitting abortion without the father's consent constituted an interference with the latter's

---

[1199] *Ibidem*, p. 72.

[1200] Appl. 6959/74, *Bruggemann and Scheuten* v. *Federal Republic of Germany*, Yearbook XIX (1976), p. 382 (414).

[1201] See *supra* p. 50.

[1202] Report of 12 July 1977, D&R 10 (1978), p. 100 (114-118). See, however, the dissenting opinion of Commission Member Fawcett, *ibidem*, p. 144.

[1203] Res. DH(78)1 of 17 March 1978, D&R 10 (1978), pp. 121-122.

right to respect for his family life. The Commission found that, insofar as abortion constitutes an interference with the right of the father, the interference was justified here for the protection of the rights of another person, since the decision to apply abortion had been taken at the request of the mother in order to protect her physical and mental health. The Commission adopted also the view that the father's right to respect for his family life could not be interpreted so broadly that a right to be consulted beforehand in case of an abortion could be derived from it.[1204] The Commission arrived at this latter conclusion 'having regard to the right of the pregnant woman'. It is not evident, however, that the woman's right to respect for her private life should rule out that the man might in principle derive from his right to respect for his family life a right to be consulted. After all, the second paragraph of Article 8 would seem to offer sufficient possibility to give priority to the woman's right, should the man refuse his consent.

In an application against Norway the applicant complained about the abortion that his female friend had of their child. The Commission declared his complaints, based upon the Articles 2, 3, 6, 8, 9, 13 and 14 of the Convention, inadmissible. In general the Commission noted that it was clear that national laws on abortion differ considerably: 'In these circumstances, and assuming that the Convention may be considered to have some bearing in this field, the Commission finds that in such a delicate area the Contracting States must have a certain discretion'.[1205] With regard to Article 8 the Commission adopted the following reasoning:

> It is true that Articles 8 and 9 of the Convention guarantee the right to respect for private and family life and freedom to manifest one's religion. However, the Commission finds that any interpretation of the potential father's right under these provisions in connection with an abortion which the mother intends to have performed on her, must first of all take into account her rights, she being the person primarily concerned by the pregnancy and its continuation or termination. The Commission therefore finds that any possible interference which might be assumed in the circumstances of the present case was justified as being necessary for the protection of the rights of another person. It follows that this part of the application is also manifestly ill-founded within the meaning of Article 27 para. 2 of the Convention.[1206]

In *Open Door and Dublin Well Women* v. *Ireland* two of the applicants also alleged a violation of Article 8 because they were denied access to information concerning abortion abroad, and two other applicants, counselling organisations, alleged a violation of that article because they were hindered in counselling their clients concerning their privacy rights. The Court, however, did not consider it

---

[1204] Appl. 8416/78, D&R 19 (1980), p. 244 (253-254).

[1205] Appl. 17004/90, *Hercz* v. *Norway*, D&R 73 (1992) p. 155 (168).

[1206] *Idem.* See on abortion also Appl. 8416/79, *X* v. *the United Kingdom*, D&R 19, p. 244. It is open for speculation how the Court would have decided the same issue. In the *Keegan* Case, concerning the giving up of a child for adoption by the mother, without consulting the father and without the father having a legal remedy, the Court found a violation of Article 8; judgment of 26 May 1994, A.290, p. 22.

necessary to examine this part of the claims now that it had found a violation of Article 10.[1207]

(c) Transsexualism

The right to respect for private life was also invoked in five applications by transsexuals who complained about the refusal of the national authorities to take account of the change in their status which was the result of a sexual conversion operation. In one of the cases a friendly settlement was reached, after the German authorities had proceeded to enter the change of name and the change of sex in the birth register.[1208] In the *Van Oosterwijck* Case the Commission concluded that the refusal of the Belgian authorities to take account of 'an essential element of his personality: his sexual identity resulting from his changed physical form, his physical make-up, and his social rôle', amounted to 'a veritable failure to recognise the respect due to his private life within the meaning of Article 8(1) of the Convention'.[1209] The Court did not reach a judgment on the merits because of its decision that Van Oosterwijck had not exhausted the local remedies.[1210]

In the *Rees* Case the Commission confirmed its view that Article 8 must be understood as protecting a transsexual against the non-recognition of his/her changed sex as part of his/her personality. In the opinion of the Commission, this does not mean that the legal recognition must be extended to the period prior to the specific moment of change, but 'it must be possible for the individual after the change has been effected to confirm his/her normal appearance by the necessary document'.[1211] In the case of Mr Rees this requirement was not met in the Commission's view, because it was made impossible for him to have his birth certificate altered to show his male sex, which resulted for him in being treated as an ambiguous being with all annoying consequences involved.[1212] The Court joined the Commission in the view that Article 8 not only protects the individual against arbitrary interference, but may also imply positive obligations on the part of the authorities. The Court disagreed with the Commission, however, by holding that the positive obligations do not extend so far as to require the Government to make possible annotations to the birth register as applied for by Mr Rees and to enact detailed legislation regulating the effects of such annotations. The Court indicated the intermediate character of its judgment by stating:

> That being so, it must for the time being be left to the respondent State to determine to what extent it can meet the remaining demands of transsexuals. However, the Court is conscious of the seriousness of the problems affecting these persons and the distress

---

[1207] Judgment of 29 October 1992, A.246-A, p. 32.
[1208] Appl. 6699/74, *X* v. *Federal Republic of Germany*, D&R 17 (1980), p. 21.
[1209] Report of 1 March 1979, B.36 (1983), p. 26.
[1210] Judgment of 6 November 1980, A.40, pp. 13-19.
[1211] Report of 12 December 1984, A.106, p. 25.
[1212] *Ibidem*, p. 26.

they suffer. The Convention has always to be interpreted and applied in the light of current circumstances (...). The need for appropriate legal measures should therefore be kept under review having regard particularly to scientific and societal developments.[1213]

This 'consciousness', on the part of the Court, of Mr Rees' distress will hardly have comforted him. It is difficult to understand why the problems with which the Government is confronted by the demands of transsexuals were given more weight by the Court than these demands themselves, which concerned the formal recognition of so vital an element of their personality as their sex.[1214]

In 1990 the Court was confronted with similar issues in the *Cossey* Case. It therefore had to determine whether the two cases were distinguishable on their facts or whether it should stick to or depart from the judgment in the *Rees* Case. The main distinctions between the two cases (Mr Rees had no partner whereas Ms Cossey wished to marry; Ms Cossey was a male-to-female transsexual whereas Mr Rees was a female-to-male transsexual) were not considered to have a relevancy for the case. The Court thus concluded that the *Cossey* Case was not materially distinguishable on its facts from the *Rees* Case. With regard to Article 8 the Court set out to answer whether an effective respect for Miss Cossey's private life imposed a positive obligation on the United Kingdom in this regard:

There have been certain developments since 1986 in the law of some of the member States of the Council of Europe. However, the Reports accompanying the resolution adopted by the European Parliament on 12 September 1989 (OJ No C 256, 9. 10. 1989, p. 33) and Recommendation 1117 (1989) adopted by the Parliamentary Assembly of the Council of Europe on 29 September 1989 – both of which seek to encourage the harmonisation of laws and practices in this field – reveal, as the Government pointed out, the same diversity of practice as obtained at the time of the Rees judgment. Accordingly this is still, having regard to the existence of little common ground between the Contracting States, an area in which they enjoy a wide margin of appreciation (see the Rees judgment, p. 15, par. 37). In particular, it cannot at present be said that a departure from the Court's earlier decision is warranted in order to ensure that the interpretation of Article 8 on the point at issue remains in line with present-day conditions. (...) The Court accordingly concludes that there is no violation of Article 8. The Court would, however, reiterate the observations it made in the Rees judgment (p. 19, par. 47). It is conscious of the seriousness of the problems facing transsexuals and the distress they suffer. Since the Convention always has to be interpreted and applied in the light of current circumstances, it is important that the need for appropriate legal measures in this area should be kept under review.[1215]

Only two years later the Court was again confronted with a claim with regard to Article 8 by a transsexual, this time concerning France. First of all the Court pointed out that as yet there was no sufficiently broad consensus between the Member States of the Council of Europe to persuade the Court to reach opposite

---

[1213] Judgment of 17 October 1986, A.106, pp. 15-19.

[1214] See also the dissenting opinion of judges Bindschedler-Robert, Russo and Gersing, *ibidem*, pp. 21-22.

[1215] Judgment of 27 September 1990, A.184, pp. 16-17. See also the comprehensive and critical dissenting opinion of judge Martens, *ibidem*, pp. 22-41.

conclusions to those in its *Rees* and *Cossey* judgments. However, the Court attached great value to noticeable differences between France and England with reference to their law and practice on civil status, change of forenames, use of identity documents, *etc.* In the Court's opinion it was relevant:

> that nothing would have prevented the insertion, once judgment had been given, in Miss B's birth certificate, in some form or other, of an annotation whose purpose was not, strictly speaking, to correct an actual error, but to bring the document up to date so as to reflect the applicant's present position. Furthermore, numerous courts of first instance and courts of appeal have already ordered similar insertions in the case of other transsexuals, and the *procureur's* office has hardly ever appealed against such decisions, the great majority of which have now become final and binding (...). The Court of Cassation has adopted a contrary position in its case-law, but this could change (...).[1216]

Further the Court considered as a relevant factor from the point of view of Article 8 that a change of forename was refused to the applicant and that there was an indication of the original sex on identity cards and on documents using the identification number. According to the Court this resulted in inconveniences that reached 'a sufficient degree of seriousness to be taken into account for the purposes of Article 8'.[1217] Consequently, the Court concluded that there had been a violation of Article 8. This judgment, compared with the *Rees* and *Cossey* judgments, does not create much clarity concerning the protection offered by Article 8 to transsexuals. The Court itself is divided, as appears for instance from the harnessed dissent of judge Martens in the *Cossey* Case and from the careful distinguishing by the Court between the facts in the *Cossey* Case on the one hand those in *B* v. *France* on the other. The reasons given by the Court in order to find a violation in *B* v. *France* as opposed to *Cossey* do not seem very convincing, taking into account the fundamental problems confronting transsexuals in both these cases.

8.2.4 Name

In the same case of *B* v. *France* the Court ruled that the refusal to allow the applicant to change her first name was also a relevant factor from the point of view of Article 8. The question whether *in itself* a (first) name does enjoy the protection of Article 8 was not yet settled. In 1994 the Court was directly confronted with this question. It ruled as follows:

> As a means of personal identification and of linking to a family, a person's name none the less concerns his or her private and family life. The fact that society and the State have an interest in regulating the use of names does not exclude this, since these public-law aspects are compatible with private life conceived of as including, to a certain degree, the right to establish and develop relationships with other human beings, in professional or business contexts as in others (see, mutatis mutandis, the *Niemietz* v.

[1216] Judgment of 25 March 1992, *B* v. *France*, A.232-C, p. 51.
[1217] *Ibidem*, p. 53.

Germany judgment of 16 December 1992, series A no. 251-B, p. 33, par 29). In the instant case, the applicant's retention of the surname by which, according to him, he has become known in academic circles may significantly affect his career. Article 8 therefore applies.[1218]

In the *Stjerna* Case the Court confirmed this approach by again holding that the issue of one's (family) name falls within the scope of private and family life, protected under Article 8. The Contracting States do, however, possess a broad margin of appreciation concerning the rules with regard to the change of names, since these rules still differ significantly among them:

> As to the instances of inconvenience complained of by the applicant, the Court is not satisfied on the evidence adduced before it that the alleged difficulties in the spelling and pronunciation of the name can have been very frequent or any more significant than those experienced by a large number of people in Europe today, where movement of people between countries and language-areas is becoming more and more common-place. (...) no sufficient grounds have been adduced to justify the Court coming to a conclusion different from that of the Finnish authorities.[1219]

8.2.5 Physical Integrity

The concept of 'private life' also covers a person's physical and moral integrity, as was established in *X and Y* v. *the Netherlands*.[1220] In the *Costello Roberts* Case the Court held, with respect to corporal punishment in a school:

> The Court does not exclude the possibility that there might be circumstances in which Article 8 could be regarded as affording in relation to disciplinary measures a protection which goes beyond that given by Article 3. Having regard, however, to the purpose and aim of the Convention taken as a whole, and bearing in mind that the sending of a child to school necessarily involves some degree of interference with his or her private life, the Court considers that the treatment complained of by the applicant did not entail adverse effects for his physical or moral integrity sufficient to bring it within the scope of the prohibition contained in Article 8. While not wishing to be taken to approve in any way the retention of corporal punishment as part of the disciplinary regime of a school, the Court therefore concludes that in the circumstances of this case there has also been no violation of that Article.[1221]

[1218] Judgment of 22 February 1994, *Burghartz*, A.280-B, p. 28.
[1219] Judgment of 25 November 1994, A.299-B, p. 62.
[1220] Judgment of 26 March 1985, A.91, p. 11.
[1221] Judgment of 25 March 1993, A.247-C, p. 61. See also the report of the Commission in *Y* v. *the United Kingdom*, A.247-A, p. 15, in which the Commission concluded that the corporal punishment complained of constituted a violation of Art. 3. It therefore considered that the Art. 8 issue was absorbed by that finding and that there was no need to pursue a separate examination of the applicant's claims of an unjustified interference with his right to respect for private and family life. The Court decided to strike the case off the list, because of a friendly settlement reached by the Government and the applicant; judgment of 29 October 1992, A.247-A.

8.3 Family Life

8.3.1 Scope/Autonomous Concept

The notion of 'family life' in Article 8 is an autonomous concept, which must be interpreted independently of the national law of the Contracting States.[1222] Moreover, the family life to be considered is not *de jure* family life, but *de facto* family life. As the Court held:

> In the present case, it is clear that the applicants, the first and second of whom have lived together for some fifteen years (...), constitute a 'family' for the purposes of Article 8. They are thus entitled to its protection, notwithstanding the fact that their relationship exists outside marriage ...[1223]

Thus the Commission and the Court took the view that the fact of birth, *i.e.* the biological tie between mother and child, as a rule creates family life in the sense of Article 8, also in the case of a mother and an illegitimate child.[1224] The Contracting States may, however, set up a procedure to establish the truth of the alleged family links.[1225]

The traditional European concepts of the countries of the Council of Europe is also not considered decisive; a family composed according to a different cultural pattern – *e.g.* a polygamous family – is equally entitled to protection.[1226] The same respect for different cultural patterns applies in principle to the way in which parents bring up their children. Respect for family life comprises respect for a style of education which differs from that which is common in a given society, provided that the treatment involved is not to be considered criminal and punishable under the general standards prevailing in the Contracting States.[1227]

In the *Berrehab* Case the Court held that cohabitation is not an indispensable element for the existence of family life between parents and their minor children:

> It follows from the concept of family on which Article 8 is based that a child born of such a union [*viz.* a lawful and genuine marriage] is *ipso jure* part of the relationship; hence, from the moment of the child's birth and by the very fact of it, there exists between him and his parents a bond amounting to 'family life' even if the parents are not then living together.[1228]

[1222] Thus, for the first time, the Commission in its report of 10 December 1977, *Marckx*, B.29 (1982), p. 44. Ever since this has been the standing case-law.

[1223] Judgment of 18 December 1986, *Johnston*, A.112, p. 25.

[1224] See the decision on Appl. 6833/74, *Marckx* v. *Belgium*, Yearbook XVIII (1975), p. 248 (270), and the case-law there mentioned. Thus also the judgment of 13 June 1979 in this case, A.31, p. 14, where the Court uses the argument that a different standpoint would amount to discrimination on the ground of birth, contrary to Art. 14.

[1225] Appl. 8378/78, *Kamal* v. *the United Kingdom*, D&R 20 (1980), p. 168.

[1226] Implicitly recognised by the Commission in its decision in Appls 2991/66 and 2992/66, *Alam, Kahn and Singh* v. *the United Kingdom*, Yearbook X (1967), p. 478. This leaves apart the question of whether a State must permit the practice of polygamy.

[1227] Appl. 9253/81, *X* v. *Federal Republic of Germany* (not published).

[1228] Judgment of 21 June 1988, A.138, p. 14.

Subsequent events, of course, may break that tie, but this was not so in the instant case, according to the Court, and consequently Article 8 was found to be applicable. It is a little peculiar that the Court here seems to give a special, stronger position to children born out of a lawful marriage precisely in a case where the subsequent divorce indicated that the marriage had ended in a failure. It can safely be assumed from the relevant case-law that the Court will not easily accept that this tie has been severed. Attempts to keep in touch and to arrange visits suffice to accept the continuation of family life.[1229]

In the *Keegan* Case, the Court combined the criteria used in the *Johnston* Case and in the *Berrehab* Case:

> The Court recalls that the notion of the 'family' in this provision is not confined solely to marriage-based relationships and may encompass other de facto 'family' ties where the parties are living together outside of marriage (...). A child born out of such a relationship is ipso jure part of that 'family' unit from the moment of his birth and by the very fact of it. There thus exists between the child and his parents a bond amounting to family life even if at the time of his or her birth the parents are no longer co-habiting or if their relationship has then ended (...). In the present case, the relationship between the applicant and the child's mother lasted for two years during one of which they co-habited. Moreover, the conception of their child was the result of a deliberate decision and they had also planned to get married (...). Their relationship at this time had thus the hallmark of family life for the purposes of Article 8. The fact that it subsequently broke down does not alter this conclusion any more than it would for a couple who were lawfully married and in a similar situation. It follows that from the moment of the child's birth there existed between the applicant and his daughter a bond amounting to family life.[1230]

The importance attached by the Court to the *de facto* situation was made very clear in the *Kroon* Case. The case dealt with the impossibility under Dutch law then in force for a biological father to have legally recognised family ties established with his child, if the latter is born out of a relationship with a woman who at that moment was still married to another man. The respondent Government had argued that the relationship between the father and his biological child did not amount to family life, since the child was born out of an extramarital relationship, the father did not live with the woman and the child and did not contribute to the child's upbringing. According to the Court:

> In any case, the Court recalls that the notion of 'family life' in Article 8 is not confined solely to marriage-based relationships and may encompass other de facto 'family ties' where parties are living together outside marriage (...). Although, as a rule, living together may be a requirement for such a relationship, exceptionally other factors may also serve to demonstrate that a relationship has sufficient constancy to create de facto 'family ties'; such is the case here, as since 1987 four children have been born to Mrs Kroon and Mr Zerrouk. A child born of such a relationship is ipso jure part of that 'family unit' from the moment of its birth and by the very fact of it (...). There thus exists between Samir and Mr Zerrouk a bond amounting to family life, whatever the contribution of the latter to his son's care and upbringing. Article 8 is therefore applicable.[1231]

[1229] Judgment of 19 February 1996, *Gül* v. *Switzerland*, Reports 1996-I, Vol. 3, p. 159 (174).
[1230] Judgment of 26 May 1994, A.290, pp. 17-18.
[1231] Judgment of 27 October 1994, A.297-C, pp. 55-56.

Despite the importance of the factual situation it goes without saying that a natural family relationship is not terminated by reason of the fact that the child is taken into public care.[1232]

Relations between an adoptive parent and an adoptive child are also covered by Article 8.[1233] It has not yet been decided by the Court whether foster parents and foster children also fall under 'family life'. Since for all practical purposes protection of identical interests is at stake here and the factual situation is also quite similar, in our opinion this question ought to be answered in the affirmative, no matter whether the foster parent has or has not been (temporarily) entrusted with the guardianship, be it that – especially in the latter case – these interests may have to yield to those of the natural parents.[1234] And in any case the private life of the foster parents and foster children may be involved here.[1235]

Concerning the relationship of a homosexual couple the Commission has taken the view that 'despite the modern evolution of attitudes towards homosexuality', that relationship does not fall within the scope of the right to respect for family life, but that, here again, the right to respect for private life may be involved.[1236] The Commission does not indicate on which criterion it based its decision. In our opinion the difference with an unmarried couple in relevant respects is not evident, while there seems to be a clear similarity of interests. Developments in the law of the Member States of the Council of Europe in this area may be expected to have their impact on the Strasbourg case-law.

The mere existence of a family relationship is not sufficient for the applicability of Article 8; only in the case of a sufficiently close factual tie is there a question of family life.[1237] In fact, if the relationship does not imply genuine ties, an *interference* is not possible. Whether such genuine ties exist is determined, *inter alia*, by the nature of the family relationship invoked by the applicant; for married

---

[1232] Judgment of 22 June 1989, *Eriksson*, A.156, p. 24; and judgment of 25 February 1992, *Margareta and Roger Andersson*, A.226-A, p. 25.

[1233] Appl. 9993/82, *X* v. *France*, D&R 31 (1983), p. 241. But the granting of an adoption order may constitute an interference with the natural parent's right to respect for his family life of a particularly serious nature; see judgment of 26 May 1994, *Keegan*, A.290, p. 18.

[1234] See in this connection the dissenting opinion of Commission member Schermers, attached to the report of the Commission of 14 July 1988, *Cecilia and Lisa Eriksson* v. *Sweden*, A.156, p. 56: 'Normally, there will be family life (as a fact) between foster parents and their children'.

[1235] See the judgment of 8 July 1987, *W* v. *the United Kingdom*, A.121, p. 28 and the judgment of 26 May 1994, *Keegan*, A.290, p. 20-21: 'As has been observed in a similar context, where a child is placed with alternative carers he or she may in the course of time establish with them new bonds which it might not be in his or her interests to disturb or interrupt by reversing a previous decision as to care (...). Such a state of affairs not only jeopardised the proper development of the applicant's ties with the child but also set in motion a process which was likely to prove to be irreversible, thereby putting the applicant at a significant disadvantage in his contest with the prospective adopters for the custody of the child.'

[1236] Appl. 9369/81, *X and Y* v. *the United Kingdom*, D&R 32 (1983), p. 220 (221).

[1237] See, *e.g.*, the judgment of 13 June 1979, *Marckx*, A.31, p. 15: 'with the result that a real family life existed and *still* exists between them'. See also Appl. 7626/76, *X* v. *the United Kingdom*, D&R 11 (1978), p. 160 (166).

couples and children born out of that marriage, and for other close family relationships they are assumed unless their absence is evident or proven.[1238] For other relationships the genuineness of the family ties is determined by factual circumstances, e.g. by the question whether the persons concerned belong to the same household.[1239] In the case of a relationship other than between a couple, consideration is also given to the age and dependence of the alleged victim.[1240] Thus, a parent who has been, or threatens to be, separated from her or his child under age will in general have a stronger claim to respect for family life than a person who desires to be reunited with his or her adult child or brother or sister.[1241] And for an adult the fact that he or she has to live at some distance from his or her parents abroad, in general will be less likely to constitute an interference with family life than for a minor.[1242]

A prolonged voluntary separation creates a presumption that the persons concerned do not feel the need of a close family tie. While, in some instances, the Commission seemed to take this too readily for granted,[1243] the Court in the *Moustaquim* Case was not willing to exclude the applicability of Article 8 in a case where the applicant's relations with his family were strained. He had run

---

[1238] Thus the Court held in the *Marckx* judgment, A.31, p. 21, that 'family life' in the sense of Art. 8 'includes at least the ties between near relatives, for instance those between grandparents and grandchildren, since such relatives may play a considerable part in family life'. See also the judgment of 21 June 1988, *Berrehab*, A.138, p. 14.

[1239] Thus, e.g., in the case of an uncle and a nephew: Appl. 3110/67, *X* v. *Federal Republic of Germany*, Yearbook XI (1968), p. 449 (518). See also Appls 7289/75 and 7349/76, *X and Y* v. *Switzerland*, Yearbook XX (1977), p. 372 (408-410), which concerned an extra-marital relationship.

[1240] Thus, e.g., in the case of a mother-daughter relationship the age of the latter was considered relevant in addition to the fact that she was married, lived together with her husband, and had a full-time job: Appl. 5269/71, *X and Y* v. *the United Kingdom*, Yearbook XV (1972), p. 564 (574). On the criterion of the 'financial (in)dependency', see Appl. 8157/78, *X* v. *the United Kingdom* (not published).

[1241] In Appl. 1380/62 (not published), where the complaint concerned the refusal of a visitor's visa for a brother living in Hungary, the Commission did not refer at all to Art. 8. Here the fact that this concerned a family visit, and the persons in question therefore evidently did not intend to live together in the future, was an argument against finding an interference with family life. In the parent-child relationship, however, there may actually still be question of a family tie, even if the intention to live together permanently is not (no longer) present. This very possibility of regular contacts *via* visits is advanced in many cases by the Commission as an argument that the family tie has not been affected; Appls 7289/75 and 7349/76, *X and Y* v. *Switzerland*, Yearbook XX (1977), p. 372 (410).

[1242] See Appl. 1855/63, *X* v. *Denmark*, Yearbook VIII (1965), p. 200 (204), where a refusal to grant a visitor's permit was deemed not to conflict with Art. 8, since the case concerned a 41-year-old son, who had lived abroad already for twenty years and had an opportunity to visit his parents and other relatives regularly for a reasonable time.

[1243] Thus, e.g., Appls 2991/66 and 2992/66, *Alam, Kahn and Singh* v. *the United Kingdom*, Yearbook X (1967), p. 478 (500) and Appl. 5532/72, *X* v. *the United Kingdom*, Coll. 43 (1973), p. 119 (121).

away and had been imprisoned. However, he had never broken off relations with them.[1244]

In our opinion, in cases concerning family ties one must take account, *inter alia*, of the question who took the initiative for the separation in the past, of the nature of the continued ties, and of the family traditions within the religious, ethnic, and/or cultural community to which the persons in question belong. For instance, in several cultures it is a self-evident obligation for a grandchild to adopt his grandparent into his household after his parents have died, even if he and his grandparent may have been separated for many years. Furthermore, the degree of dependence of the applicant on his parents or other relatives, in material or in immaterial respects, must be considered.[1245] And in any case the mere fact that a person has grown up does not mean that he is no longer entitled to any form of protection of the family unit of which he formed part as a child, not even when he himself has married meanwhile.[1246]

8.3.2 Guarantees Implied in the Obligation to 'Respect' Family Life

The right to respect for family life implies the right to recognition of a legal relationship between members of a family.[1247] On that ground the Belgian law was found contrary to Article 8 insofar as, in addition to the production of the birth certificate of an illegitimate child, it set other conditions for the coming into existence of a legal relationship between mother and child, such as recognition by the mother or a procedure of legitimisation of the child.[1248] And the same view was taken with respect to the denial to an illegitimate child, 'adopted by the mother', of legal relations with the parents of the mother,[1249] and the denial to an illegitimate child of rights equal to those of a legitimate child.[1250] With respect to legal relationships it has also been recognised that Article 8 does not merely require the State to abstain from interferences, but may also require certain

---

[1244] Judgment of 18 February 1991, A.193, p. 18.

[1245] See on the one hand, Appl. 5532/72, *X* v. *the United Kingdom*, Coll. 43 (1973), p. 119 (121), and, on the other hand, Appl. 5269/71, *X and Y* v. *the United Kingdom*, Yearbook XV (1972), p. 564 (574).

[1246] The possibility of violation of Art. 8 in such a case was examined by the Commission in the case of Appl. 5269/71, mentioned in the preceding note.

[1247] Judgment of 27 October 1994, *Kroon*, A.297-C, p. 57: 'The Court recalls that in the instant case it has been established that the relationship between the applicants qualifies as "family life" (...). There is thus a positive obligation on the part of the competent authorities to allow complete family ties to be formed between Mr Zerrouk and his son Samir as expeditiously as possible.'

[1248] Report of 10 December 1977, *Marckx*, B.29 (1982), pp. 44-45; judgment of 13 June 1979 in the same case, A.31, pp. 16-17. The Commission refers to Art. 2 of the Draft General Principles on Equality and Non-Discrimination in respect of Persons born out of Wedlock of the Sub-Commission for the Prevention of Discrimination and for the Protection of Minorities of the UN Commission for Human Rights, *Study of Discrimination against Persons born out of Wedlock*, United Nations, New York, 1967, pp. 225-227.

[1249] *Ibidem*, pp. 47 and 21 respectively. Here, too, the Commission refers to the Draft General Principles, *viz.* to Art. 7.

[1250] *Ibidem*, pp. 48-49.

positive measures. Thus, in the *Rasmussen* Case the Commission and the Court gave as their opinion that effective respect for family life obliges the Contracting States to make available to the alleged father of a child an effective and accessible remedy by which he can establish whether he is the biological father of the child.[1251] In its judgment the Court did not reach the conclusion that in this case there was a violation of Article 8. It focused its examination on the fact that Mr Rasmussen alleged that his right to contest his paternity of a child born during marriage was subject to time-limits, whereas his former wife was entitled to institute paternity proceedings at any time. The Court did not go into the issue of Article 8 separately, although it declared that the facts of the case fell within the ambit of that article,[1252] but directly dealt with the issue of Article 14. It concluded that the difference in treatment was not discriminatory.[1253]

The *Johnston* Case concerned the absence of the possibility under Irish law of divorce, and of recognition of the family life of persons living in a family relationship outside marriage after the breakdown of the marriage of one of those persons and a third person. The Commission and the Court took the position that, while respect for private and family life may require provision relieving parties from the obligation to live together, it must, in principle, be left to the State to decide what form the remedy should take.[1254] More or less as a logical consequence of this position the Commission and the Court took the view that, although a genuine family relationship may exist between two persons living together outside marriage and their child, one could not derive from Article 8 an obligation on the part of Ireland to establish for unmarried couples a status analogous to that of married couples.[1255] There is, however, at the very least the obligation of non-interference in the family life between them and the children born out of that new relationship.[1256] With respect to the legal status of the child born out of a relationship outside marriage the Commission, followed by the Court, concluded that here Irish law was in violation of Article 8, because it did not recognise family-law relationships between the child and her parents. As a consequence the father was not regarded, as of right, as the legal guardian of his daughter, which involved far-reaching consequences for both of them. In addition the child could never be legitimated, not even after the death of her father's wife. And further the succession rights of the child could under certain circumstances be inferior to those of legitimate children. In the Commission's view, all this constituted a failure by the State to provide a framework for the proper ordering of relations between the child and her parents, and the appropriate legal regime for the proper development of their family lives. The Commission found no

---

[1251] Report of 5 July 1983, A.87, pp. 20-21; judgment of 28 November 1984, A.87, p. 13.
[1252] *Idem.*
[1253] *Ibidem*, p. 16.
[1254] Report of 5 March 1985, A.112, p. 43; judgment of 18 December 1986, A.112, pp. 26-28.
[1255] *Ibidem*, pp. 48-49 and 28 respectively.
[1256] *Ibidem*, pp. 48-49 and 25 and 30 respectively.

justification for this failure which met the requirements of the second paragraph of Article 8.[1257]

Article 8 does not contain a specific regulation concerning the question which parent has to be awarded the custody of the children if the family unit is disrupted by divorce or judicial separation; in principle this is left to the national authorities, on the basis of the relevant national law.[1258] From Article 8, therefore, no priority for one of the two parents may be derived.[1259] In the *Hoffmann* Case, however, the Court underlined that concerning the question which parent to award parental rights Article 14 has to be taken into account. In that case the national courts heavily relied upon the religion of the mother (a Jehovah-witness) in order to grant parental rights to the father. The Court ruled that essentially a distinction had been made based on a difference in religion alone. This was considered to be a violation of Article 8 taken in conjunction with Article 14.[1260] Every decision about awarding custody of the children implies by definition an encroachment on the right to respect of family life of one or both of the parents, but in addition of course has consequences for the exercise of the right to respect of family life of the child in question and of any other children forming part of the family unit.

As has been shown in the previous section, the fact that after the divorce not all the members of the family live together under one and the same roof any more, does not put an end to their family life nor necessarily to the genuineness of their family ties.[1261] If the parents cannot reach agreement on this point or if their proposal is ignored, reliance by the national authorities on the restriction ground 'protection of health and morals' or 'protection of the rights and freedoms of others' in the second paragraph would seem to usually find favour with the Commission, apart from cases of manifest unreasonableness.[1262] However, for the parent who still has genuine ties with his child but to whom the custody of the child has not been awarded, a right of access follows from Article 8,[1263] unless the authorities can invoke one of the grounds of the second paragraph for its

---

[1257] *Ibidem*, pp. 49-51; in about the same wording the Court came to the same conclusion; *ibidem*, p. 31.

[1258] Appl. 1449/62, *X* v. *the Netherlands*, Yearbook VI (1963), p. 262 (266); Appl. 5486/72, *X* v. *Sweden*, Coll. 44 (1973), p. 128 (129).

[1259] Thus the Commission in its decision on Appl. 1449/62, *X* v. *the Netherlands*, Yearbook VI (1963) and in its decision on Appl. 7770/77, *X* v. *Federal Republic of Germany*, D&R 14 (1979), p. 175 (176).

[1260] Judgment of 23 June 1993, A.255-C, pp. 58-60.

[1261] Judgment of 21 June 1988, *Berrehab*, A.138, p. 14. See also the judgment of 26 May 1994, *Keegan*, A.290, p. 18; and the judgment of 27 October 1994, *Kroon*, A.297-C, pp. 55-56.

[1262] See, *e.g.*, the very marginal review in this respect in the case of Appl. 2699/65, *X* v. *Federal Republic of Germany*, Yearbook XI (1968), p. 366 (376); and of Appl. 5486/72, *X* v. *Sweden*, Coll. 44 (1973), p. 128 (129).

[1263] Appl. 172/56, *X* v. *Sweden*, Yearbook I (1955-1957), p. 211 (217); Appl. 7911/77, *X* v. *Sweden*, D&R 12 (1978), p. 192 (193); report of 8 March 1982, *Hendriks*, D&R 29 (1982), p. 5 (14-16).

denial.[1264] As Opsahl rightly observes, the justification for the award of the custody to one parent rather than to the other cannot be automatically relied upon as a ground for the denial of the right of access to the latter; very serious arguments have to be put forward for the justification of the complete cutting off of the ties between parent and child.[1265] All this applies in principle equally in the case of the termination of the relationship between a parent and his or her illegitimate child.[1266] And the same holds good for the deprivation of parental rights, since that also constitutes a problem directly affecting the right to protection of family life of the persons concerned, because the family ties do not end by the fact that the child is taken into public care.[1267] Such a measure will in general meet with few objections in Strasbourg if 'the protection of the rights and freedoms of others', mentioned in the second paragraph, is invoked, because of the very marginal inquiry into the reasonableness of such a justification.[1268]

In *O v. the United Kingdom* the applicant alleged a violation of Article 8 by the procedures followed to terminate the applicant's access to his children and because of the absence of a remedy against that decision. The Commission found no violation of Article 8 since it interpreted the complaint as being apparently confined to the absence of an effective remedy against the decision to deprive him of access and not as also alleging that the law was applied in a manner which lacked justification under Article 8(2). Consequently, the Commission concluded that there had been no violation of Article 8 of the Convention as a result of the alleged lack of a right to a hearing before a court and of an effective legal remedy in respect of his claim for access to his children.[1269] The Court held with respect to the first part of the complaint that the information provided about the procedures followed was insufficient to establish a violation of Article 8. With respect to the second part the Court had already found a violation of Article 6(1) and did not find it necessary to examine the complaint under Article 8.[1270]

H v. the United Kingdom concerned proceedings instituted by the applicant regarding access to her child. Here the Court held that, in view of the delays, the proceedings had failed to show respect for the applicant's family life since the proceedings related to a fundamental element of family life and the procedural delay led to a *de facto* determination of the matter at issue. The Court, therefore,

---

[1264] Appl. 5608/72, *X v. the United Kingdom*, Coll. 44 (1973), p. 66 (68-69); Appl. 7911/77, *X v. Sweden*, D&R 12 (1978), p. 192 (193); report of 8 March 1982, *Hendriks*, D&R 29 (1982), pp. 37-40.

[1265] T. Opsahl, 'The Convention and the Right to Respect for Family Life', in: A.H. Robertson (ed.), *Privacy and Human Rights*, Manchester, 1973, p. 215.

[1266] See Appl. 7658/76, *X v. Denmark*, D&R 15 (1979), p. 128.

[1267] Judgments of 8 July 1987, *W, B and R v. the United Kingdom*, A.121, pp. 27, 71 and 117 respectively; judgment of 24 March 1988, *Olsson (No. 1)*, A.130, p. 29.

[1268] See, *e.g.*, Appl. 5132/71, *X v. Denmark*, Coll. 43 (1973), p. 57 (60-61).

[1269] Report of 3 December 1985, A.120, pp. 35-36.

[1270] Judgment of 8 July 1987, A.120-A, pp. 28-29.

considered that the duration of the proceedings was a factor that could properly be taken into account in the present context.[1271]

In *W, B* and *R* v. *the United Kingdom* the complaints concerned the applicants' access to their children in the care of a local authority. According to the Commission the procedures which led to the determination of issues relating to family life had to be such as to show respect for family life. In particular, parents normally should have a right to be heard and to be fully informed in this connection.[1272] The Court took the view that Article 8 contains no explicit procedural requirements, but that this was not conclusive for the matter. The relevant considerations to be weighed by a local authority in reaching decisions on children in its care must include the views and interests of the natural parents. The decision-making process must therefore be such as to secure that their views and interests are made known to and duly taken into account by the local authority and that they are able to exercise in due time any remedies available to them. In the Court's view:

> what therefore has to be determined is whether, having regard to the particular circumstances of the case and notably the serious nature of the decisions to be taken, the parents have been involved in the decision-making process, seen as a whole, to a degree sufficient to provide them with the requisite protection of their interests. If they have not, there will have been a failure to respect their family life and the interference resulting from the decision will not be capable of being regarded as 'necessary' within the meaning of Article 8.[1273]

The Court found a violation of Article 8 after examining the procedure relating to the authority's decisions to place the children with long-term foster parents with a view to adoption, and to terminate access by the applicants. In the Court's view, it revealed insufficient involvement of the applicants.[1274]

These procedural requirements inherent in Article 8 are not identical to the guarantees laid down in Article 6. Article 6(1):

> affords a procedural safeguard, namely the 'right to a court' in the determination of one's civil rights and obligations' (...); whereas not only does the procedural requirement inherent in Article 8 cover administrative procedures as well as judicial proceedings, but is ancillary to the wider purpose of ensuring proper respect for, *inter alia*, family life.[1275]

In this particular *McMichael* Case the violation of Article 8 consisted of the fact that the applicants had been unfairly treated in care-proceedings concerning their child. The content of some relevant documents had not been disclosed to them.

In the *Olsson* Case the applicants asserted that the decision to take their children into care, the manner in which the decision had been implemented and the refusals

---

[1271] Judgment of 8 July 1987, A.120, pp. 63-64.
[1272] Report of 15 October 1985, A.121, p. 45; and reports of 4 December 1985, A.121, pp. 86 and 131.
[1273] Judgments of 8 July 1987, A.121, pp. 28, 73-74 and 119 respectively.
[1274] *Ibidem*, pp. 29-31, 74-76 and 119-121 respectively.
[1275] Judgment of 24 February 1995, *McMichael* v. *the United Kingdom*, A.307-B, p. 57.

to terminate care had given rise to violations of Article 8. As regards the question of the taking into care and the refusals to terminate care the Court held the view that the applicants had been involved in the decision-making process, seen as a whole, to a degree sufficient to provide requisite protection of their interests. As to the taking into care the Court held that it is not sufficient justification that the child will be better off if placed in care. In order to determine whether the reasons for deciding to take the children into care could be considered 'sufficient' for the purposes of Article 8, the Court held that it must have regard to the case as a whole and notably to the circumstances in which the decision was taken.[1276] The decisions were based on social reports supported by statements from persons well acquainted with the case and the decisions were confirmed by courts which were able to form their own impression of the case and whose judgments were not reversed on appeal. Therefore, the Swedish authorities, having regard to their margin of appreciation, were in the Court's view entitled to think that the taking into care was necessary. However, the implementation of the care decision was held by the Court to be in violation of Article 8. It was not the quality of the care given that was at issue, but the separation of the children and the placement of two of them at a long distance from the applicants' home and the restrictions on their visits, which impeded easy and regular access by the members of the family to each other and thus ran counter to the ultimate aim of its reunification. In these respects, and despite the applicants' uncooperative attitude, the measures of implementation of the care decision were not supported by sufficient reasons justifying them as proportionate to the legitimate aim.[1277]

In the *Eriksson* Case the Commission and the Court were confronted with the question whether the prohibition for the mother to remove her daughter from the foster home and the restrictions on her right of access constituted a violation of Article 8. The child was taken in care one month after she was born. When the child was five years old the care order was lifted, but in the same decision it was decided to prohibit the mother from removing the daughter from the foster home until further notice. Its effect was that the mother, although there were no longer any reproaches against her for inability to care for her daughter, was still deprived of the factual care. Another effect of the prohibition on removal was that the mother could not secure a formal decision on her right of access to her daughter. The Commission considered that:

> once a decision to return a child to its natural parents has been taken it must be in the interests of all parties involved that such a decision is implemented as quickly as possible. A prohibition on removal temporarily suspends the removal of the child and is therefore, although it may be justified during a transitional period, a measure which by its very nature is likely to increase the tension between those involved in the transfer of the child. If such a situation prevails for a long time there is a great risk that, as time

---

[1276] Judgment of 24 March 1988, A.130, pp. 33-34.
[1277] *Ibidem*, pp. 33-37.

goes by, the conflicts will increase and that it gradually will become more difficult to establish the close relationship between the child and his or her natural parent which is a necessary condition for the transfer.[1278]

The Commission came to the conclusion that the interference with the mother's right to respect for her family life was not necessary in the interest of the child. It put heavy weight on the fact that the Supreme Administrative Court had ordered that the child should return to the mother while the measures taken since that judgment could not be considered adequate to promote this aim. In particular, the regulations and arrangements concerning access to the child were inadequate to promote the aim of reunification of the applicants. The Court as well found a violation of Article 8, considering the factual and legal situation concerning the possibilities for the applicants to meet and develop their relationship with a view to being reunited.[1279]

In the *Margareta and Roger Andersson* Case the Court was confronted with a situation in which Roger was placed in a foster home, and, together with his mother, complained about restrictions on access, including restrictions on communication by correspondence and telephone. In this case the Court reaffirmed that Article 8 includes a parent's and child's right to the taking of measures with a view to their being reunited. The Court reached the conclusion, after having reviewed all the facts, that during a specific period the restrictions were particularly far-reaching. Therefore they had to be supported by convincing reasons and to be consistent with the ultimate aim of reuniting the Andersson family in order to be justified under Article 8(2). The Court held:

> The reasons adduced by the Government are of a general nature and do not specifically address the necessity of prohibiting contact by correspondence and telephone. The Court does not doubt that these reasons were relevant. However, they do not sufficiently show that it was necessary to deprive the applicants of almost every means of maintaining contact with each other for a period of approximately one and a half years. Indeed, it is questionable whether the measures were compatible with the aim of reuniting the applicants.[1280]

For this reason the Court concluded that the restrictions imposed on meetings, correspondence and telephone were disproportionate, and therefore not necessary in a democratic society.

In the *Olsson (No. 2)* Case the Court also had to rule upon the legality of restrictions on access and of a prohibition on removal. The Court reiterated the principle that Article 8 includes a right for the natural parents to have measures taken with a view to their being reunited with their children[1281] and an obligation on the part of the national authorities to take such measures. In this case, however, it concluded that in the light of all the facts and the margin of

---

[1278] Report of 14 July 1988, A.156, p. 44.
[1279] Judgment of 22 June 1989, A.156, p. 30.
[1280] Judgment of 25 February 1992, A.226-A, p. 31.
[1281] See also judgment of 22 April 1992, *Rieme*, A.226-B, p. 71.

appreciation 'it has not been established that the social welfare authorities failed to fulfil their obligation to take measures with a view of the applicants being reunited with Helena and Thomas'.[1282]

In the *Keegan* Case the applicant maintained that the State failed to respect his family life by facilitating the secret placement of his daughter for adoption without his knowledge or consent and by failing to create a legal nexus between himself and his (illegitimate) daughter from the moment of birth. His relationship with the mother had come to an end before the birth of the child. The Court reiterated the principle established in previous case-law, *i.e.* that legal safeguards must be created that render possible as from the moment of birth the child's integration in his family. The Court then noted, while considering whether the interference was necessary in a democratic society, that where a child is placed with alternative caretakers he or she may in the course of time establish with them new bonds which it might not be in his or her interests to disturb or interrupt by reversing a previous decision as to care. According to the Court:

> Such a state of affairs not only jeopardised the proper development of the applicant's ties with the child but also set in motion a process which was likely to prove to be irreversible, thereby putting the applicant at a significant disadvantage in his contest with the prospective adopters for the custody of the child. The Government have advanced no reasons relevant to the welfare of the applicant's daughter to justify such a departure from the principles that govern respect for family ties.[1283]

The strictness used by the Court in demanding that legally recognised family ties can be established between a father and his child was also reflected in the *Kroon* Case, referred to above. The Court in rather strong terms disapproved of the legislation in force in the Netherlands, that prevented a (biological) father to recognise his child, as long as the mother was still married to an other man. In the present case the father and the mother already had a few children together. The Court held:

> In the Court's opinion, 'respect' for 'family life' requires that biological and social reality prevail over a legal presumption which, as in the present case, flies in the face of both established fact and the wishes of those concerned without actually benefiting anyone. Accordingly, the Court concludes that, even having regard to the margin of appreciation left to the State, the Netherlands has failed to secure to the applicants the 'respect' for their family life to which they are entitled under the Convention.[1284]

8.3.3 Admission and Expulsion of Aliens

The right of a foreigner to enter or reside in a particular country has not been laid down in the Convention, but the immigration policy of the Contracting States has, of course, to be in conformity with their obligations under the Convention. Thus,

---

[1282] Judgment of 27 November 1992, A.250, p. 37.
[1283] Judgment of 26 May 1994, A.290, p. 21.
[1284] Judgment of 27 October 1994, A.297-C, p. 58.

the exclusion of a person from a country in which his close relatives reside may raise an issue under Article 8.[1285]

Refusal of admittance or the expulsion of a husband or wife has for a long time been held by the Commission not to conflict with Article 8 if the other partner has the opportunity to follow the person concerned abroad and this can reasonably be required of him or her.[1286] From this and other rather restrictive elements of its approach, it is evident that the Commission does not wish to thwart the national immigration policy too much, in particular not when that policy is apparently intended to restrict fictitious marriages or marriages which were contracted at a moment when the partners were fully aware of the risk that one of them would not be admitted or would be expelled.[1287] If persons are involved who have already resided in the country for a considerable time and have founded a family there, the Commission appears to be inclined to accept more readily that the partner and children have good reasons for not wishing to go abroad themselves.[1288] The mere opportunity to do so is not therefore decisive as to whether non-admission or expulsion violates Article 8.[1289] It is also considered to be relevant whether the person who applies for admission or appeals against expulsion has established strong ties with the country concerned,[1290] or whether he is still a minor and dependent for his care on the parent(s) with whom reunion sought.[1291]

In the *Abdulaziz, Cabales and Balkandali* Case the applications were lodged by three women who were lawfully and permanently settled in the United Kingdom, but whose husbands or prospective husbands were refused permission to remain in the United Kingdom. As to the applicability of Article 8, the Court confirmed the Commission's established case-law by holding that:

> although some aspects of the right to enter a country are governed by Protocol No. 4 as regards States bound by that instrument, it is not to be excluded that measures taken in the field of immigration may affect the right to respect for family life under Article 8.[1292]

[1285] See, *e.g.*, Appl. 9492/81, *Family X v. the United Kingdom*, D&R 30 (1983), p. 232 (234).

[1286] See the case-law mentioned in: Council of Europe, *Case Law Topics,* No. 2, 'Family Life', 1972, pp. 6-13. See also Appl. 7729/76, *Agee v. the United Kingdom*, D&R 7 (1977), p. 164 (174).

[1287] See, *e.g.*, Appl. 2535/65, *X v. Federal Republic of Germany*, Coll. 17 (1966), p. 28 (30); and Appl. 9285/81, *X, Y and Z v. the United Kingdom*, D&R 29 (1982), p. 205 (209).

[1288] Appl. 6357/73, *X v. Federal Republic of Germany*, D&R 1 (1975), p. 77 (77-78). See also Appl. 8244/78, *Singh Uppal and Others v. the United Kingdom*, D&R 17 (1980), p. 149 (156), where the grandparents and the children were allowed to stay in the country, but the parents were threatened to be expelled. In this case, which had been declared admissible by the Commission on account of its complexity, a friendly settlement was reached.

[1289] Expressly Appl. 8061/77, *X v. Switzerland* (not published).

[1290] See, *e.g.*, Appl. 24968/94, *X v. the Netherlands* (not published).

[1291] Report of 17 May 1995, *Salah and Soufiane Ahmut v. the Netherlands*, Reports 1996-VI, Vol. 24, paras 50-54. See, however, the judgments of 19 February 1996, *Gül*, Reports 1996-I, Vol. 3 and of 28 November 1996, *Ahmut*, Reports 1996-VI, Vol. 24.

[1292] Judgment of 28 May 1985, A.94, p. 31.

The Court also observed that, although by guaranteeing the right to respect for family life Article 8 presupposes the existence of a family, this does not mean that all *intended* family life falls entirely outside its ambit. Therefore, even if the family life was not yet fully established for all the applicants at the moment when permission was asked for the men to enter or remain in the United Kingdom, this did not exclude the applicability of Article 8. In this case the Court found sufficient ground for this applicability in the fact that the couples, at least in their own opinion, were married and had lived together or wished to live together.[1293] Next, confirming its case-law that there may be positive obligations inherent in an effective 'respect' for the rights protected in Article 8, but that a wide margin of appreciation has to be left to the Contracting States in determining the steps to be taken with due regard to the needs and resources of the community and of individuals, the Court held as follows:

> In particular, in the area now under consideration, the extent of a State's obligation to admit to its territory relatives of settled immigrants will vary according to the particular circumstances of the persons involved. Moreover, the Court cannot ignore that the present case is concerned not only with family life but also with immigration and that, as a matter of well-established international law and subject to its treaty obligations, a State has the right to control the entry of non-nationals into its territory.[1294]

The Court further observed that:

> The duty imposed by Article 8 cannot be considered as extending to a general obligation on the part of a Contracting State to respect the choice by married couples of the country of their matrimonial residence and to accept the non-national spouses for settlement in that country.[1295]

The Court found that the applicants had not shown that there were obstacles to establishing family life in their own or their husbands' home countries, or that there were special reasons why that could not be expected of them, and that all three applicants, at the time of their (planned) marriage, were aware of the risk that their husbands would not get a permanent residence permit for the United Kingdom. It, therefore, concluded that there was no lack of respect for family life and, hence, no breach of Article 8 taken alone.[1296] However, the Court found that the applicants were victims of discrimination on the ground of sex, in violation of Article 14 in conjunction with Article 8, because of the difference made in the 1980 Statement of Changes in Immigration Rules as to the possibility for male and female immigrants settled in the United Kingdom to obtain permission for their non-national spouses or fiancé(e)s to enter or remain in the country. The assumed difference between the respective impact of men and

---

[1293] *Ibidem*, pp. 32-33.
[1294] *Ibidem*, p. 34. See also the judgment of 19 February 1996, *Gül*, Reports 1996-I, Vol. 3, p. 159 (175).
[1295] Judgment of 28 May 1985, A.94, p. 34.
[1296] *Idem*.

women on the domestic labour market was considered by the Court to be not sufficiently important to justify this difference in treatment.[1297]

In order to determine whether it can reasonably be required that the family unit be continued or restored abroad, the disadvantages involved for the persons concerned have to be weighed against the interests of the respondent State served by its immigration policy. First of all, reunion abroad must be possible. In the *Gül* Case, the question therefore was whether Mr Gül's son's move to Switzerland would be the only way for the applicant to develop family life with his son. This evidently is a narrow criterion. Since there were no obstacles for Mr Gül preventing him from developing family life in Turkey while moreover he had only a residence permit on humanitarian grounds and his son had always lived in Turkey,[1298] the Court concluded that Switzerland has not failed to fulfil the obligations arising under Article 8(1), and there had therefore been no interference in the applicant's family life.[1299]

There are also other factors, which are deemed to be relevant for determining whether reunion abroad is possible and can reasonably be expected. If, for instance, the State where the member of the family applying for admission resides, or to which he or she has been or is threatened to be expelled, is not prepared to admit the other member or members of the family, the expulsion or the refusal of admission – if a family relationship is indeed involved – constitutes a breach of Article 8.[1300] The same holds true if an inhuman treatment in the sense of Article 3 were to await a member of the family when required to settle abroad.[1301] If reunion of the family abroad is possible but the applicant for admission is a minor, the Commission generally assumes that the child has the right to be reunited with his parents or guardians in the country of their residence, and that the latter cannot reasonably be expected to move abroad in order to join the child.[1302] However, the Court has recently adopted a more stringent view in this respect.[1303]

[1297] *Ibidem*, p. 37.

[1298] Precisely on this aspect the Court distinguished the *Gül* Case from the *Berrehab* Case (*infra*), in which the daughter was born and raised in the Netherlands and therefore could not be expected to have family life in her father's country (Morocco).

[1299] Judgment of 19 February 1996, *Gül*, Reports 1996-I, Vol. 3, p. 176.

[1300] See Appl. 8061/77, *X* v. *Switzerland* (not published), where the wife alleged that for that reason she could not follow her husband to Yugoslavia.

[1301] See *supra* pp. 323-324.

[1302] See Council of Europe, *Case Law Topics*, No. 2, 'Family Life', 1972, pp. 40-41. See also Appls 2991/66 and 2992/66, *Alam, Kahn and Singh* v. *the United Kingdom*, Yearbook X (1967), p. 478 (502); and Appl. 7816/77, *X and Y* v. *Federal Republic of Germany*, D&R 9 (1978), p. 219 (221); and report of 17 May 1995, *Salah and Souffiane Ahmut* v. *the Netherlands*, Reports 1996-VI, Vol. 24, paras 50-54.

[1303] Judgments of 19 February 1996, *Gül*, Reports 1996-I, Vol. 3 and of 28 November 1996, *Ahmut*, Reports 1996-VI, Vol. 24.

Other aspects which the Convention organs involve in their weighing of the interests are, *inter alia*: the links with the other country;[1304] the prospect of joint residence in the respondent State at the time when the family was founded;[1305] the existence of ties with other relatives outside the family;[1306] and the economic consequences of a removal to another country.[1307] If this weighing of interests results in the conclusion that the other members of the family cannot reasonably be required to follow the person in question abroad, and that therefore non-admittance or expulsion would violate the latter's family life, the respondent State may still rely on one of the restriction grounds of the second paragraph.[1308]

As has been mentioned above, in the *Abdulaziz, Cabales and Balkandali* Case the Court held that although Article 8 presupposes the existence of a family, this does not mean that all *intended* family life falls entirely outside its ambit. There, the Court declared Article 8 also applicable to a situation where admission was applied for in order to get married.[1309] The applicants could also have relied on Article 12 in that case.

In the case of a divorce, the parent who is entrusted with the custody over the children can of course not reasonably be required to follow the other parent abroad in order to maintain the family ties between the latter and the children. In the *Berrehab* Case the applicant, a Moroccan national, was divorced from his Dutch wife and was appointed as co-guardian of the child born after the divorce. Because of his divorce he was refused prolongation of his residence permit. This resulted in an expulsion order. The Court took into consideration that until his expulsion from the Netherlands, Mr Berrehab saw his daughter four times a week

---

[1304] Appl. 5301/71, *X v. the United Kingdom*, Coll. 43 (1973), p. 82 (84); judgment of 18 February 1991, *Moustaquim*, A.193, p. 19; judgment of 26 March 1992, *Beldjoudi*, A.234-A, p. 28. Especially foreign children of the 'second generation' appear to have a rather strong position in that respect.

[1305] Appls 5445-5446/72, *X and Y v. the United Kingdom*, Coll. 42 (1973), p. 146. See also Appl. 7048/75, *X v. the United Kingdom*, D&R 9 (1978), p. 42 (43), where the Commission decided that Art. 8 does not *per se* guarantee the right for a married couple to move their residence to a specific country, where one of the two has a visitor's permit. See also the judgment of 28 November 1996, *Ahmut*, Reports 1996-VI, Vol. 24, para. 71.

[1306] Appl. 5269/71, *X and Y v. the United Kingdom*, Yearbook XV (1972), p. 564 (574); judgment of 18 February 1991, *Moustaquim*, A.193, p. 19.

[1307] Appl. 5269/71, *X and Y v. the United Kingdom*, Yearbook XV (1972), p. 564 (574). See also Appl. 9492/81, *Family X v. the United Kingdom*, D&R 30 (1983), p. 232 (234-235), where the Commission found that the fact that the expulsion would prevent the son from continuing his study in the UK did not constitute an interference with the right of respect for family life.

[1308] See Appl. 312/57, *X v. Belgium*, Yearbook II (1958-1959), p. 352 (353-354); and Appl. 8061/77, *X v. Switzerland* (not published), where the Commission was of the opinion that there was a justification under the second paragraph and for that reason did not inquire the question of whether the wife could really obtain the required permission of the Yugoslav authorities to join her husband.

[1309] Judgment of 28 May 1985, A.94, p. 31. See, however, Appl. 7229/75, *X and Y v. the United Kingdom*, D&R 12 (1978), p. 32 (34).

for several hours at a time. The fact that there were frequent and regular contacts with his daughter led to the conclusion that it could not be maintained that the ties of 'family life' between them had been broken. Although the Court made allowance for the margin of appreciation that is left to the Contracting States and accepted that the Convention does not in principle prohibit Contracting States from regulating the entry and length of stay of aliens, it found a violation of Article 8, having regard to the particular circumstances, since there was in its opinion a disproportion between the means employed and the legitimate aim pursued.[1310]

In the case of *deportation* of foreigners who have committed serious crimes, the ground of prevention of disorder or crime mentioned in the second paragraph of Article 8 in general will provide sufficient justification. However, the Court has indicated that this will not easily be the case if the foreigner concerned is a person of the so-called 'second generation'.

In the *Moustaquim* Case the Belgian authorities intended to deport the applicant, a Moroccan national, living in Belgium, because of his having committed a large number of offences and the serious risk of his reoffending. The Court had to assess the necessity of this deportation order, since it interfered with his family life because his parents and other family lived in Belgium. The Court took into consideration that the applicant's offences all went back to the period when he was an adolescent; that all his close relatives had been living in Belgium for a long while; that he was less than two years old when he arrived in Belgium where he had lived for about twenty years; and that he had returned to Morocco only twice, for holidays, and had received all his schooling in French. For these reasons the Court found that his family life was thus seriously disrupted. It concluded that the deportation order was disproportionate.[1311]

In the *Beldjoudi* Case the Court also concluded that a deportation order of Mr Beldjoudi, who was born in France of parents who originated from a territory which was French at the time, namely Algeria, was not proportionate and did therefore violate Article 8. In this case Mr Beldjoudi's criminal record appeared much worse than that of Mr Moustaquim. However, the Beldjoudi's were married in France over twenty years ago. Mr Beldjoudi spent his whole life in France and was deemed to have lost his French nationality in 1963 as his parents had not made a declaration of recognition. In 1970 he manifested his wish to recover the French nationality and was consequently declared to be fit for national service. His wife was born in France of French parents, had always lived there and had French nationality. The deportation might imperil the unity or even the very existence of the marriage. Because of these reasons the Court concluded, from the point of view of respect for the applicants' family life, that the deportation order was disproportionate.[1312]

[1310]   Judgment of 21 June 1988, A.138, pp. 14-16.
[1311]   Judgment of 18 February 1991, A.193, pp. 18-20.
[1312]   Judgment of 26 March 1992, A.234-A, pp. 26-28.

In *Nasri* v. *France* the Court again showed its preparedness to independently review a deportation order as to its proportionality and its impact on the applicant's family life. The special circumstances in this case make it difficult to draw specific conclusions as to the permissibility of a deportation, other than the willingness of the Court to actively and intensely assess the balance between the reasons leading to the deportation order and the (harsh) consequences for the individual concerned.[1313]

In general it can be concluded that the relevant factors include the question of how lang a foreigner has lived in the country that wishes to deport him; the intensity of the links he (still) has with his country of origin, and the harshness of the consequences of a deportation/expulsion. These aspects determine the Court's attitude towards the proportionality of the proposed measure of deportation and its compatibility with Article 8. It even appears that these factors are conclusive, whatever the (seriousness of) the offenses committed. The nature of the offenses could, however, be important in those instances in which there is still a link with the country of origin. In the three cases mentioned, however, the applicants had been living (almost) all their lives in France/Belgium, which made any deportation to have an extremely (disproportionate) harsh effect upon them and their family life.

8.3.4 Detention

With regard to detainees the Commission starts from the point of view that the separation between a detainee and his family, and the distress resulting from it, are inherent in detention.[1314] Thus, it held that a general limitation of visiting facilities to relatives and close friends of the prisoners was reasonable and constituted no interference with the prisoners' right to respect for private life.[1315] The touchstone in the final analysis is whether the interference with the right of family life, to which the detainee is also entitled, 'goes beyond what would normally be accepted in the case of an ordinary detainee'.[1316] If the restrictions cannot stand this test, the Commission appears to be inclined nevertheless to allow the national authorities a very wide margin of appreciation in the limitation of family contacts on the basis of one of the grounds of the second paragraph.[1317]

The Commission accepted, for instance, the Austrian practice according to which those who are serving a sentence of imprisonment of more than one year, are on that ground alone denied visits from their children under age, for the

---

[1313] Judgment of 13 July 1995, A.320-B.
[1314] See, *e.g.*, Appl. 2676/65, *X v. Austria*, Coll. 23 (1967), p. 31 (37). See also the report of 18 March 1981, *McVeigh, O'Neill and Evans*, D&R 25 (1982), p. 5 (51-52).
[1315] Appl. 9054/80, *X v. the United Kingdom*, D&R 30 (1983), p. 113 (115).
[1316] Appl. 5712/72, *X v. the United Kingdom*, Coll. 46 (1974), p. 112 (116).
[1317] See, *e.g.*, Appls 1420/62, 1477/62 and 1478/62, *X and Y v. Belgium*, Yearbook VI (1963), p. 590 (628), and Appl. 5712/72, *X v. the United Kingdom*, Coll. 46 (1974).

protection of the morals of these minors.[1318] In the case of a refusal of the English authorities to permit a detainee to attend his daughter's wedding, and in another case his mother's funeral, the Commission concluded that there was no evidence that the authorities in question did not have sufficient reason to believe that this refusal was necessary on one of the grounds mentioned in the second paragraph.[1319] Performed in this way, the international review would seem to have too automatical a character. In addition to an examination as to whether the justification of the restrictions by the national authorities on one of the grounds of paragraph 2 was indeed reasonable in the particular case, the Strasbourg organs should see to it that the restriction is not imposed on the prisoner as a disguised sanction on his behaviour, which would indeed constitute a breach of Article 18. But even in those cases where the restriction is not intended as an additional punishment, it will nevertheless, as a result of the detention, in many cases actually have the same effect. As examples one may think of the detention at a place that is so far removed from where the family members live that regular visits are practically impossible,[1320] and of the refusal of (regular) conjugal intercourse for detainees, which still is the rule in most countries.[1321] In those and similar cases, both the national authorities and the reviewing organs in Strasbourg should take to heart the view set forth by Jacobs:

> Quite apart from purely legal considerations, it would be contrary to modern phenological standards to restrict unnecessarily the family life of prisoners. If they are to be able to take their place again in society, they should have the greatest contact with the outside world that is consistent with the fact of their detention. Progressing standards of penal policy may even be legally relevant, since it is sometimes legitimate to interpret the Convention in the light of the practice of the Contracting Parties. Thus, restrictions which would at one time have been justified may cease to be permitted as standards are raised.[1322]

[1318] Appl. 2306/64, *X* v. *Austria*, Coll. 21 (1967), p. 23 (33). See also Appl. 6564/74, *X* v. *the United Kingdom*, D&R 2 (1975), p. 105 (106).

[1319] Appl. 4623/70, *X* v. *the United Kingdom*, Yearbook XV (1972), p. 370 (374); and Appl. 5229/71, *X* v. *the United Kingdom*, Coll. 42 (1973), p. 140 (141).

[1320] See, *e.g.*, Appl. 9466/81, *S* v. *the United Kingdom*, D&R 36 (1984), p. 41 (44).

[1321] See Appl. 3603/68, *X* v. *Federal Republic of Germany*, Yearbook XIII (1970), p. 332 (338) and the comparative study evidently made there by the Commission. Thus also in Appl. 8166/78, *X and Y* v. *Switzerland*, D&R 13 (1979), p. 241 (243), where the Commission also refers to the Standard Minimum Rules for the Treatment of Prisoners, recommended by the Committee of Ministers in Resolution (73)5. If in a specific case it is possible for a detainee to reside together with his family in the place of detention, the Commission deems it possible that Art. 8 has been violated if the authorities make the living conditions for the family unbearable; report of 7 December 1978, *Guzzardi*, B.35 (1983), pp. 35-36.

[1322] F. Jacobs and R. White, *The European Convention on Human Rights*, 2nd ed., Oxford, 1996, p. 206.

8.4 Respect for the Home/Protection against Nuisance

8.4.1 Respect for the Home

In view of the Strasbourg approach of a predominantly restrictive review of the justification of restrictions, the right to respect for the home affords only limited guarantees in most situations, since in many cases of interference with that right the national authorities will be able to successfully invoke one of the grounds of the second paragraph. In fact, as long as the national legislation in question makes this possible, the national authorities can search the home of a suspected person in case of any concrete, but also any vague suspicion of a criminal offence, and also all those other homes where clues might possibly be found.[1323] However, in so serious a case of interference with the right to respect for the home as the case of Cypriotic citizens being expelled from their homes by the Turkish occupying forces and the latter making return to these homes impossible, the Commission concluded that none of the grounds mentioned in the second paragraph could be advanced for its justification.[1324] And the Court held in the *Akdivar* Case that the deliberate burning of the applicants' homes constituted a serious interference with their right to respect for their homes for which no justification had been offered by the Turkish Government.[1325]

The concept of 'home' was at issue in the *Gillow* Case. Mr and Mrs Gillow owned the house 'Whiteknights' in Guernsey, which they had occupied with their family until they left the country to take employment with the FAO in 1960. During their absence they rented the house to various tenants, but they continued the ownership and retained their furniture in the house. When they returned to Guernsey to live there in 1979, they were not granted the required licence, since they did not fulfil all the requirements, some of which were introduced by legislation during the period of their absence. The Commission considered that ownership of a house is not in itself sufficient to establish it as one's home, when one has never in fact lived in the house. However, where continued ownership follows occupation of a house as one's home, such ownership is evidence of a strong continuing link with the house. In the case of the Gillows this link was further illustrated by the fact that they had left their furniture in the house. The Commission opined that the question whether the house was still the applicants' 'home' at the time of their return to it in 1979, was in part dependent on their intentions and attitude towards the house prior to and on their return, of which the key element was their actual return in 1979 to live in the house. The Commission concluded that this return was a return to their 'home' within the meaning of Article 8. The fact that they were not granted the licence to live in that home and that proceedings were taken against them for unlawful occupation of the house constituted an interference with their right to respect for their home. This

---

[1323] See, *e.g.*, Appl. 530/59, *X* v. *Federal Republic of Germany*, Yearbook III (1960), p. 184 (190).
[1324] Report of 10 July 1976, *Cyprus* v. *Turkey* (not officially published), paras 209 and 210.
[1325] Judgment of 16 September 1996, Reports 1996-IV, Vol. 15, para. 88.

interference was considered by the Commission to be disproportionate in relation to the aim pursued by the authorities in making the residence requirements, and not corresponding with any pressing social need. Consequently, it was held not to have been necessary in a democratic society within the meaning of Article 8(2).[1326] The Court also found a violation of Article 8 in this case. According to the Court it was not the contested legislation which gave rise to the violation, but the manner in which the Housing Authority had exercised its discretion. The Housing Authority had given insufficient weight to the applicants' particular circumstances. They had built 'Whiteknights' as a residence for themselves and their family. At that time they possessed 'residence qualifications' and continued to do so until the entry into force of the Housing Law of 1969. By letting it over a period of 18 years to persons approved by the Housing Authority, they had contributed to the Guernsey housing stock. On their return in 1979, they had no other 'home' in the United Kingdom or elsewhere; 'Whiteknights' was vacant and there were no prospective tenants. Therefore, the refusals as well as the conviction and fining of the applicants constituted interferences which were disproportionate to the legitimate aim pursued.[1327]

In the *Langborger* Case the Court ruled that the power conferred on the Tenants' Union to negotiate on the tenant's behalf the amount of the rent for the flat in which he lived did not come within the scope of Article 8. The notion of 'home' in this article, therefore, does not apply to issues concerning rents, nor to rights and obligations deriving from the lease.[1328]

The *Chappell* Case concerned the search of a house in connection with the suspicion that video cassettes were made in breach of copyright by a company controlled by the applicant. The premises were used for both business and residential purposes. In the Commission's view, although the search was directed against the applicant's and his company's business activities, it indirectly impinged on the applicant's private life and the private sphere of items and associations which are attributes of a home. The Commission left open the question whether some private papers of the applicant constituted correspondence within the meaning of Article 8, as the interference therewith anyway fell within the private life sphere. The Commission reached the conclusion that the interference was necessary in a democratic society for the protection of the rights of others.[1329] The Court was of the same opinion.[1330]

In the *Niemietz* Case[1331] and the *Crémieux* Case[1332] the Court was also confronted with searches. It dealt with them in the context of Article 8, without

---

[1326] Report of 3 October 1984, A.109, pp. 32-41. See also Appl. 6202/73, *X and Y v. the Netherlands*, D&R 1 (1975), p. 66 (70).
[1327] Judgment of 24 November 1986, A.109, pp. 22-23.
[1328] Judgment of 22 June 1989, A.155, p. 17.
[1329] Report of 14 October 1987, A.152-A, p. 29.
[1330] Judgment of 30 March 1989, A.152-A, p. 27.
[1331] Judgment of 16 December 1992, A.251-B.
[1332] Judgment of 25 February 1993, A.256-B.

explicitly distinguishing between 'private life' and 'home'. It may be concluded from this that an infringement of the right to respect of one's 'home' always also includes an interference with one's 'private life'.

With respect to the notion of private life the Court did not consider:

> it possible or necessary to attempt an exhaustive definition of the notion of 'private life'. However, it would be too restrictive to limit the notion to an 'inner circle' in which the individual may live his own personal life as he chooses and to exclude therefrom entirely the outside world not encompassed within that circle. Respect for private life must also comprise to a certain degree the right to establish and develop relationships with other human beings.[1333]

This implies according to the Court that there is no reason to exclude activities of a professional or business nature from the concept of private life. And the same is true for the word 'home'. The interpretation of the words 'private life' and 'home' as including certain professional and business activities or premises is consonant, according to the Court, with the essential object and purpose of Article 8, namely to protect the individual against arbitrary interference by the public authorities.[1334]

In the *Velosa Barreto* Case the Court explicitly held that 'effective protection of respect for private and family life cannot require the existence in national law of legal protection enabling each family to have a home for themselves alone'. In this particular case the applicant, who lived with his family and his parents-in-law, inherited from his parents a house. This house had been let, and the applicant started proceedings to have the lease terminated on the ground that he needed the house as his own home. The Portuguese courts, however, held that there was no sufficient 'need' as required by Portuguese legislation to have the lease terminated. Since Article 8 does not contain the right to have a home, it follows that it 'does not go so far as to place the State under an obligation to give the landlord the right to recover possession of a rented house on request and in any circumstances'. Under national law the termination of the lease was possible whenever the landlord needed the property to live there. The Court held that this clause 'pursues a legitimate aim, namely the social protection of tenants, and that it thus tends to promote the economic well-being of the country and the protection of the rights of others.' In applying this national provision the Portuguese courts had not acted arbitrarily or unreasonably, neither had they failed to discharge their obligation to strike a fair balance between the respective interests.[1335]

It may be inferred from this judgment that Article 8 also applies to relations between individuals and that the Contracting States are under the obligation to effectuate this *Drittwirkung*. However, this horizontal effect implies a balancing between conflicting interests; in the *Velosa Barreto* Case, the right of the landlord to have a home and to be protected in one's home against the same rights of the

---

[1333] Judgment of 16 December 1992, *Niemietz*, A.251-B, p. 33.
[1334] *Ibidem*, p. 34.
[1335] Judgment of 21 November 1995, A.334, pp. 11-12.

tenant. The Court seems to allow that national State a large discretion in solving this horizontal conflict of interest by introducing the test of 'arbitrariness or unreasonableness'. It is likely that this rather marginal test is influenced, on the one hand, by the broad concept of 'economic well-being of the country' as a ground of restriction invoked in this particular case, and on the other hand by the 'social right' nature of the right at issue: the right to a home. Interference in this matter could easily lead the Court into the thicket of judging upon social and economic issues of housing policies. The absence of a clear emergency situation on the part of the applicant may also explain and justify this approach in this particular case.

It may also be inferred from the *Velosa Barreto* Case that the Court at present does not seem prepared to fully accept that the right to respect for the home also implies a right to a (decent) home.[1336] Recognition of such a right would amount to a considerable socialisation of Article 8, which the Court only accepts in those circumstances in which there is a finding of a serious infringement of one's personal life as well as a disproportional balancing (arbitrariness, unreasonableness) of the conflicting interests. This approach, which can also be noted in the case-law dealt with in the following section, leaves room for a gradual expansion of Article 8 by allowing for social rights elements to be included, while taking one step at a time.

8.4.2 Protection Against Nuisance

A form of indirect interference with the right to respect for the home which, if recognised, would substantially enlarge the scope of Article 8 and which, in our opinion, would not stand in the way of direct applicability, are deteriorations of living conditions by certain measures or circumstances. Thus, in *Arrondelle* v. *the United Kingdom,* which case was declared admissible by the Commission because of its complexity, the applicant complained about violation of Article 8 by the British authorities on account of the great nuisance which she experienced in her home near Gatwick Airport from the descending and ascending aircraft, and from the traffic on the motor road.[1337]

In the *Powell and Rayner* Case the Court went along with this approach. Again the case dealt with complaints about excessive noise generated by air traffic, this time in and out of Heathrow Airport. The question before the Court was not whether Article 8 had been violated, but whether both applicants had an arguable claim (within the meaning of Article 13) of violation of Article 8. The Court held as follows:

[1336] Thus already the Commission in its decision on Appl. 159/56, *X* v. *Federal Republic of Germany,* Yearbook I (1955-1957), p. 202 (203).

[1337] Appl. 7889/77, D&R 19 (1980), p. 186 (198). In this case a friendly settlement has been reached: D&R 26 (1982), p. 5.

In each case, albeit to greatly differing degrees, the quality of the applicant's private life and the scope for enjoying the amenities of his home have been adversely affected by the noise generated by aircraft using Heathrow Airport (...). Article 8 is therefore a material provision in relation to both Mr Powell and Mr Rayner.[1338]

In view of the 'fair balance that has to be struck between the competing interests of the individual and of the community as a whole' and taking into account the measures adopted by the authorities to control, abate and compensate for aircraft noise, the Court reached the following conclusion:

In view of the foregoing, there is no serious ground for maintaining that either the policy approach to the problem or the content of the particular regulatory measures adopted by the United Kingdom authorities give rise to violation of Article 8, whether under its positive or negative head. In forming a judgment as to the proper scope of the noise abatement measures for aircraft arriving at and departing from Heathrow Airport, the United Kingdom Government cannot arguably be said to have exceeded the margin of appreciation afforded to them or upset the fair balance required to be struck under Article 8.[1339]

Despite the outcome of this case, the principle was firmly established: Article 8 does also cover infringements upon private life and home by noise and disturbances.

This principle was confirmed in the *Lopez Ostra* Case. The applicant complained about smells, noise and polluting fumes caused by a plant for the treatment of liquid and solid waste sited a few metres away from her home. She held the Spanish authorities responsible, alleging that they had adopted a passive attitude. The Court, after reviewing all events, stated that it only needed to establish whether the national authorities took the measures necessary for protecting the applicant's right to respect for her home and for her private and family life under Article 8. It concluded as follows:

The Court notes, however, that the family had to bear the nuisance caused by the plant for over three years before moving house with all the attendant inconveniences. They moved only when it became apparent that the situation could continue indefinitely and when Mrs Lopez Ostra's daughter's paediatrician recommended that they do so (...). Under these circumstances, the municipality's offer could not afford complete redress for the nuisance and inconveniences to which they had been subjected.
Having regard to the foregoing, and despite the margin of appreciation left to the respondent State, the Court considers that the State did not succeed in striking a fair balance between the interests of the town's economic well being – that of having a waste-treatment plant – and the applicant's effective enjoyment of her right to respect for her home and her private and family life.[1340]

The full applicability of Article 8 in the context of environmental nuisance has now been established. It will depend on the conduct of the public authorities in comparison to the level of nuisance whether the Court is likely to hold that there has been no fair balance. The public authorities can be held responsible under

---

[1338] Judgment of 21 February 1990, A.172, p. 18.
[1339] *Ibidem*, pp. 19-20.
[1340] Judgment of 9 December 1994, A.303-C, p. 56.

Article 8 even for their failures to act, to the extent that Article 8 is held to include a positive duty to protect the right to respect for the home, health and private life.

8.5 Correspondence

With regard to the right to respect for correspondence interesting developments have taken place in the case-law of the Court in respect of public authorities' opening and censoring letters or interfering with other means of communication.

At first the Commission took the view that an invocation of the second paragraph was not necessary if the censorship or the restriction on correspondence concerned detainees, since such restrictions were to be considered inherent in detention. The Commission did not even deem a reference to paragraph 2 necessary for such serious cases as restriction or delay of the correspondence with defence counsel.[1341] However, in the 'Vagrancy' Cases, and later more clearly in the Golder Case, the Court rejected this so-called 'inherent features' theory for provisions like Article 8, where restrictions are expressly provided for, and held that every restriction has to be reviewed for its justification on one of the grounds mentioned explicitly in the second paragraph.[1342] At the same time, however, the Court recognised in the Golder Case that, in doing so, the special position of the prisoner may be taken into account.[1343]

This change in the case-law is, of course, hardly of avail to the prisoner, if a very wide discretion is still allowed to the prison authorities and the prosecuting authorities in censoring incoming and outgoing letters and in other interferences with the correspondence of prisoners.[1344] More recent case-law suggests, however, that the Convention organs are inclined to conduct a more independent inquiry into the reasonableness of interference with the correspondence of prisoners by the authorities concerned. A number of cases were joined by the Commission and led to a detailed inquiry resulting in its report in the Silver Case.[1345] There the Commission categorically rejected the doctrine of the implied restrictions, and on that ground took the view that restrictions imposed on detainees can find their justification only in one of the grounds contained in the second paragraph. At the same time it rejected the thesis of the British Government that the contents of letters destined for publication are not covered

---

[1341]   See, e.g., Appl. 2375/64, X v. Federal Republic of Germany, Coll. 22 (1967), p. 45 (47).
[1342]   Judgment of 18 June 1971, A.12, p. 45; judgment of 21 February 1975, A.18, p. 21. See also the report of 12 December 1980, Schönenberger and Durmaz, A.137, p. 18.
[1343]   Judgment of 21 February 1975, A.18, p. 21. See also the judgment of 25 March 1983, Silver, A.61, pp. 37-38.
[1344]   See Council of Europe, Case Law Topics, No. 1, 'Human Rights in Prison', 1971, pp. 24-30. See also Appl. 6166/73, Baader, Meins, Meinhof, and Grundmann v. Federal Republic of Germany, Yearbook XVIII (1975), p. 132 (146).
[1345]   Report of 11 October 1980, B.51 (1987), p. 72.

by the term 'correspondence'.[1346] With regard to the requirement, laid down in paragraph 2, that the restriction must be necessary in a democratic society, the Commission held in its report:

> In the context of present-day conditions of imprisonment, the requirements of a democratic society involve the striking of a balance between the legitimate interests of public order and security and that of the rehabilitation of prisoners.[1347]

In its judgment in this case the Court noted that since the Commission's report the practice in England and Wales on the control of prisoners' correspondence had undergone substantial modification, but it held that it was not empowered to review the control regime introduced after the events giving rise to the case.[1348] Both the Commission and the Court reached the conclusion that, with the exception of the censorship of those letters in which violence was threatened or crimes were discussed, the grounds on which letters of the detained applicants had been held back could find no justification in the second paragraph, at least not if one considered the way in which the relevant rules had been applied in these cases.[1349]

In the *Boyle and Rice* Case the Court found that the stopping by the Prison Governor of a letter to a 'media personality' was in breach of Article 8. The Government had acknowledged before both the Commission and the Court that the rules had been wrongly applied since the letter was a purely personal one and should have been allowed to pass.[1350] In the *Schönenberger and Durmaz* Case the Court had to deal with the stopping of a letter addressed by a lawyer to a person held on remand. The Government relied in the first place on the contents of the letter in issue. According to the Government, it gave Mr Durmaz advice relating to pending criminal proceedings which was of such a nature as to jeopardise their proper conduct. The Court took the view that Mr Schönenberger sought to inform the second applicant of his right 'to refuse to make any statement', advising him that to exercise it would be to his 'advantage':

> In that way, he was recommending that Mr Durmaz adopt a certain tactic, lawful in itself since, under Swiss Federal Court's case-law – whose equivalent may be found in other Contracting States – it is open to an accused person to remain silent.[1351]

The fact that the lawyer was not instructed by Mr Durmaz was of little importance, since Mr Schönenberger was acting on the instructions of Mr Durmaz'

[1346] *Idem.*

[1347] *Ibidem*, pp. 75-76.

[1348] Judgment of 25 March 1983, A.61, pp. 30-31.

[1349] Report of 11 October 1980, B.51 (1987), pp. 76-98 and judgment of 25 March 1983, A.61, pp. 34-40. See also Appl. 7630/76, *Reed* v. *the United Kingdom*, D&R 19 (1980), p. 113 (141).

[1350] Judgment of 27 April 1988, A.131, p. 22.

[1351] Judgment of 20 June 1988, A.137, p. 13.

wife. The contested interference was deemed not justifiable as necessary in a democratic society.[1352]

In the *Pfeifer and Plankl* Case the Court reiterated the applicable principles set forth in the *Silver* Case. In this case the relevant issue concerned the deletion by the investigating judge of certain passages in Mrs Plankl's letter to Mr Pfeiffer:

> The Court recognises that some measure of control over prisoners' correspondence is not of itself incompatible with the Convention, but the resulting interference must not exceed what is required by the legitimate aim pursued. According to the investigating judge, the deleted passages contained 'jokes of an insulting nature against prison officers (...). The text was not, however, reconstructed before the Austrian courts. (...) In the case of Silver and Others v. the United Kingdom, the Court held that it was not 'necessary in a democratic society' to stop private letters 'calculated to hold the authorities up to contempt' or containing 'material deliberately calculated to hold the prison authorities up to contempt' (...) The deletion of passages is admittedly a less serious interference, but in the circumstances of the case this too appears disproportionate.[1353]

In the *Campbell* Case the applicant complained that correspondence to and from his solicitor and the Commission was opened and read by the prison authorities. In this case the Court gave additional indications as to when and how the authorities are allowed to open correspondence with lawyers. Its point of departure is that correspondence with lawyers is privileged under Article 8 and, consequently, interference requires solid justification:

> This means that the prison authorities may open a letter from a lawyer to a prisoner when they have reasonable cause to believe that it contains an illicit enclosure which the normal means of detection have failed to disclose. The letter should, however, only be opened and should not be read. Suitable guarantees preventing the reading of the letter should be provided, e.g. opening the letter in the presence of the prisoner. The reading of a prisoner's mail to and from a lawyer, on the other hand, should only be permitted in exceptional circumstances when the authorities have reasonable cause to believe that the privilege is being abused in that the contents of the letter endanger prison security or the safety of others or are otherwise of a criminal nature. (...) The possibility of examining correspondence for reasonable cause (...) provides a sufficient safeguard against the possibility of abuse.[1354]

The Court did not accept the respondent Government's argument that the opening of the applicant's correspondence did not prevent him from having an effective opportunity to communicate in confidence with his solicitor during prison visits. In that respect the Court observed that:

[1352] *Ibidem*, p. 14. See on controls of correspondence of a prisoner also the judgment of 30 August 1990, *McCallum*, A.183, in which the Government, the applicant and the Court agreed with the Commission that Art. 8 had been violated.

[1353] Judgment of 25 February 1992, A.227, pp. 16-17.

[1354] Judgment of 25 March 1992, A.233, pp. 19-20.

[the] right to respect for correspondence is of special importance in a prison context where it may be difficult for a legal adviser to visit his client in person, because, as in the present case, of the distant location of the prison (...). Finally, the objective of confidential communication with a lawyer could not be achieved if this means of communication were the subject of automatic control.[1355]

The freedom of correspondence with the Secretariat of the Commission constitutes a separate issue, because the prohibition of interference ensues from Article 25 for the authorities of those Contracting States which have recognised the individual right of complaint,[1356] and the restrictions of Article 8(2) therefore, strictly speaking, should not apply. Moreover, this matter has been regulated in more detail in a special convention.[1357] However, if it is alleged by an applicant that in his contacts with the Strasbourg organs he has been hindered contrary to Article 25, the point is not dealt with by the Commission as a separate complaint, but in combination with the main complaint, if consultation between the Secretary of the Commission and the authorities concerned has not resulted in abolition of the obstacles.[1358] In the *Campbell* Case the complaint was dealt with together with complaints about other interferences with correspondence. There the Court found a violation of Article 8 because it considered the opening of letters from the Commission to the detained applicant to be not necessary in a democratic society. The Court was of the opinion that there was no compelling reason why letters from the Commission should be opened.[1359]

A case which led to an extensive investigation by the Commission as well as the Court into the scope of the possibilities of restriction under the second paragraph with respect to the freedom of correspondence and other forms of communication, is the *Klass* Case. This case concerned German legislation authorising letter-opening and wire-tapping for the protection of the free democratic system or national security, without notification of the person in question and with exclusion of the normal legal remedies. After an extensive inquiry into the substance and application of the challenged legislation, which application by its very nature calls for secrecy, the Commission as well as the Court concluded that the German legislature could in reasonableness take the view that the measures in question were necessary for the protection of the above-mentioned interests.[1360] This judgment will be discussed in detail later.[1361]

Another case directed against the Federal Republic of Germany concerned wire-tapping of a solicitors' office, a measure which the authorities had carried out on the ground of suspicion that the office played a part in the exchange of

---

[1355] *Ibidem*, p. 20.
[1356] At present, all Contracting States have made such a declaration of recognition. See *supra* p. 2.
[1357] See *supra* pp. 64-65.
[1358] See *supra* pp. 62-64.
[1359] Judgment of 25 March 1992, A.233, p. 22.
[1360] Report of 9 March 1977, B.26 (1982), pp. 37-39; judgment of 6 September 1978, A.28, pp. 20-22.
[1361] *Infra* pp. 707-709. See also *infra* p. 698.

information between prisoners who were suspected of or convicted for terrorist activities. A number of persons whose conversations with the office had been tape-recorded, complained that, contrary to the decision of the investigating judge, those conversations, which apparently were not incriminating, were not erased immediately after recording. Although the Commission considered it regrettable that the instructions of the investigating judge had not been complied with, it held that this did not constitute a violation of Article 8. For this it advanced the argument that the measure, as carried out, had been found by the German court to be in conformity with German law, and that this same court had decided that it could not be determined until the end of the proceedings which recordings were and which were not relevant.[1362] Here the Commission goes very far indeed in sheltering behind the point of view of the national court, without making an independent inquiry into the restrictions of the second paragraph relied upon. In the light of the decision in the above discussed *Campbell* Case and the Court decisions concerning telephone-tapping, to be discussed *infra (Malone, Kruslin, Huvig)*, it is unlikely that this approach taken by the Commission in 1980 does reflect present-day standards under Article 8.

More thorough was the Strasbourg review of interception of telephone calls by or at the request of the police in the *Malone* Case. Mr Malone was charged with dishonest handling of stolen goods. The police officer in charge of the investigation had ordered interception of a telephone conversation on the authority of a warrant issued by the Secretary of State for the Home Department. Moreover, Mr Malone's telephone had been 'metered' on behalf of the police by a device which automatically recorded all numbers dialled. The Court agreed with the Commission that the laws and practices existing in England and Wales which permit secret surveillance of communications, amounted to an interference with the applicant's rights under Article 8. Although this interference was lawful under the relevant law of England and Wales, both the Commission and the Court reached the conclusion that it was not 'in accordance with the law' in the sense of the second paragraph of Article 8, since the relevant law did not lay down with reasonable clarity the essential elements of the authorities' powers in this domain.[1363] As to the 'metering', the Court disagreed with the Government that, since the Post Office only recorded signals sent to itself as the provider of the telephone service and did not intercept conversations, it did not entail interference with any right guaranteed by Article 8. Release of that information without the consent of the subscriber did, in the Court's opinion, amount to such an interference. And since there appeared to be no legal rules concerning the scope and manner of exercise of the discretion enjoyed by the public authorities, this practice also was not 'in accordance with the law' within the meaning of Article 8(2).[1364]

[1362] Appl. 8290/78, *A, B, C and D* v. *Federal Republic of Germany*, D&R 18 (1980), p. 176 (180).
[1363] Judgment of 2 August 1984, A.82, pp. 31-36.
[1364] *Ibidem*, pp. 37-38.

This approach has been adapted and elaborated particularly in two cases against France: the *Kruslin* Case and the *Huvig* Case. Undisputed in both cases was that telephone-tapping by the police amounted to an interference by a public authority with the exercise of the applicant's right to respect for his correspondence and his private life. The Court therefore had to assess whether France had acted in conformity with the requirements laid down in paragraph 2. It held as follows:

> Tapping and other forms of interception of telephone conversations represent a serious interference with private life and correspondence and must accordingly be based on a 'law' that is particularly precise. It is essential to have clear, detailed rules on the subject, especially as the technology available for use is continually becoming more sophisticated.[1365]

In that respect the Court was of the opinion that French law (written and unwritten) did not:

> indicate with reasonable clarity the scope and manner of exercise of the relevant discretion conferred on the public authorities. This was truer still at the material time, so that Mr. Kruslin did not enjoy the minimum degree of protection to which citizens are entitled under the rule of law in a democratic society.[1366]

In *A v. France* the Court ruled that the recording of a telephone conversation, even if conducted on the initiative and with the consent of one of the interlocutors and even though it exclusively and deliberately dealt with matters of a criminal nature, did concern the right to respect for the applicant's correspondence. The French Government had argued that the recorded conversation fell outside the scope of private life. The Court, however, ruled that it was not necessary to consider whether the recording also affected the applicant's private life. It concluded also that the interference with the right to respect for the correspondence had no basis in domestic law. It therefore found a breach of Article 8.[1367]

In the *Lüdi* Case the applicant complained about two infringements of Article 8. His first complaint concerned the use of an undercover agent 'who had made use of the personal contact established by deceit to obtain information and influence the conduct of the applicant'. The second alleged breach of Article 8 followed from the fact that this undercover agent had used technical devices in order to gain access to the applicant's home and record conversations which had been provoked by trickery and wrongly incriminated him. The Court judged that the activities by the undercover agent, either alone or in combination with the telephone interception, did not affect private life within the meaning of Article 8. The reason was that the undercover agent's actions took place within the context of a deal relating to 5 kg cocaine:

[1365] Judgments of 24 April 1990, A.176-A, p. 23 and A.176-B, p. 55 respectively.
[1366] *Ibidem*, pp. 24-25 and 56-57 respectively.
[1367] Judgment of 23 November 1993, A.277-B, pp. 48-50.

Mr Lüdi must therefore have been aware from then on that he was engaged in a criminal act punishable under Article 19 of the Drugs Law and that consequently he was running the risk of encountering an undercover police officer whose task would in fact be to expose him.[1368]

Concerning the telephone interception the Court agreed with the applicant that it was an interference with his private life and correspondence. It ruled, however, that it was in conformity with the requirements laid down in paragraph 2.

The consequence of the Court's approach apparently is that those who engage in criminal activities take the chance of infringements upon their private lives. Therefore, their private life is not affected when the authorities, through the use of undercover agents, decide to act and to gain information. This – implied – notion of 'estoppel' is an approach which raises many questions. The first is why the Court resorted to it only in the context of the activities of the undercover agent. Is it not true in general that criminals do run the risk of having their phones tapped, and being exposed to all kinds of prosecution techniques and tactics? Still the Court accepted that telephone interception (even of supposed criminals) was an interference with Article 8 and had to meet the standards of the second paragraph. In our opinion it does not make sense to accept this approach, while at the same time accepting that a criminal is estopped from invoking Article 8 in the context of the activities of an undercover agent. This seems to be too restrictive an interpretation of the scope of the first paragraph of Article 8, while activities by an undercover agent could very well be covered by the requirements of the second paragraph.

8.6 Positive Obligations

8.6.1 General

Within the scope of Article 8 the Court has frequently made use of the concept of 'positive obligations', the assumption being that the national authorities may be under an obligation to actively respect the individual's rights protected under Article 8.

The issue of the scope of the positive obligations involved in Article 8 was discussed in *X and Y* v. *the Netherlands*. There a father complained that a person who had sexually abused his mentally handicapped daughter, was not prosecuted by the Dutch authorities, on the mere ground that the victim was incapable of lodging the required complaint and the father was not legally empowered to do so as her substitute. The Court held that the positive obligations inherent in Article 8 may involve the adoption of measures designed to secure respect for private life even in the sphere of the relations of individuals between themselves. It found that neither the protection afforded by Dutch civil law nor that offered by the current Criminal Code was sufficient, and that, therefore, taking account of the nature of

---

[1368]   Judgment of 15 June 1992, A.238, p. 19.

the wrongdoing in question, the daughter was the victim of a violation of Article 8.[1369]

The concept of positive obligations has been further developed in the *Rees* Case, the *Powell and Rayner* Case, the *Cossey* Case, *B* v. *France*, and the *Lopez Ostra* Case (all discussed above). In these cases the Court considered the term 'respect' in paragraph 1 as being not clear-cut, especially as far as the positive obligations inherent in that concept are concerned. In determining whether or not a positive obligation exists 'regard must be had to the fair balance that has to be struck between the general interests of the community and the interests of the individual ...'[1370] In the *Powell and Rayner* Case the Court explicitly ruled that the applicable principles in this balancing are broadly similar to those restrictions in paragraph 2, which are applicable in case of an interference by a public authority:

> Whether the present case be analysed in terms of a positive duty on the State to take reasonable and appropriate measures to secure the applicants' rights under paragraph 1 of Article 8 or in terms of an 'interference by a public authority' to be justified in accordance with paragraph 2, the applicable principles are broadly similar. In both contexts regard must be had to the fair balance that has to be struck between the competing interests of the individual and of the community as a whole, and in any case the State enjoys a certain margin of appreciation. (...) Furthermore, even in relation to the positive obligations flowing from the first paragraph of Article 8, 'in striking [the required] balance the aims mentioned in the second paragraph may be of a certain relevance'...[1371]

Within the context of the concept of family life the Court has also resorted to the concept of positive obligations. It is standard case-law to deduce from the wording of Article 8 active obligations for the States to promote and guarantee the effective enjoyment of family life. In the *Kroon* Case the Court summarised its approach in this respect as follows:

> The Court reiterates that the essential object of Article 8 is to protect the individual against arbitrary action by the public authorities. There may in addition be positive obligations inherent in effective 'respect' for family life. However, the boundaries between the State's positive and negative obligations under this provision do not lend themselves to precise definition. The applicable principles are nonetheless similar. In both contexts regard must be had to the fair balance that has to be struck between the competing interests of the individual and of the community as a whole; and in both contexts the State enjoys a certain margin of appreciation (...). According to the principles set out by the Court in its case-law, where the existence of a family tie with a child has been established, the State must act in a manner calculated to enable that tie to be developed and legal safeguards must be established that render possible as from the moment of birth or as soon as practicable thereafter, the child's integration in his family ...[1372]

[1369] Judgment of 26 March 1985, A.91, pp. 13-14.
[1370] Judgment of 27 September 1990, *Cossey*, A.184, p. 15.
[1371] Judgment of 21 February 1990, A.172, p. 18. See also the judgment of 9 December 1994, *Lopez Ostra*, A.303-C, pp. 54-55.
[1372] Judgment of 27 October 1994, A.297-C, p. 56.

8.6.2 Positive Obligations and the Second Paragraph

Does the second paragraph of Article 8 have the same relevance if a positive obligation has been found to exist and to have been violated as in the context of 'negative' interferences? In recent judgments the Court seems to have 'merged' the two tests more or less. The Court seems less and less inclined to explicitly distinguish between negative and positive obligations in this respect. In the *Kroon* Case the Court used the same formulation as in the *Keevan* Case.[1373] However, in a more recent decision the formula used by the Court is slightly different. First of all the Court stated that the applicable principles are '*broadly*' similar. And secondly the Court added:

> Furthermore, even in relation to the positive obligations flowing from the first paragraph of Article 8, in striking the required balance the aims mentioned in the second paragraph may be of a certain relevance.[1374]

The upshot of the Court's most recent case-law seems to be that for the weighing of the interests involved it is becoming less relevant whether the alleged violation of Article 8 is a violation of a positive obligation on the part of the State or rather an interference.

8.7 Procedural Safeguards

In various cases referred to above the Court has developed specific guarantees inherent in the protection afforded by Article 8. In the *Kruslin* Case and the *Huvig* Case (both dealing with telephone tapping) the Court indicated that certain procedures and guarantees had to be laid down in national law in order to have the national law meet the standards implied in the notion 'in accordance with the law' of paragraph 2. The essential requirements in that respect appear from the Court's finding that the French system did not:

> afford adequate safeguards against various possible abuses. For example, the categories of people liable to have their telephones tapped by judicial order and the nature of the offences which may give rise to such an order are nowhere defined. Nothing obliges a judge to set a limit on the duration of telephone tapping. Similarly unspecified are the procedure for drawing up the summary reports containing intercepted conversations; the precautions to be taken in order to communicate the recordings intact and in their entirety for possible inspection by the judge (who can hardly verify the number and length of the original tapes on the spot) and by the defence; and the circumstances in which recordings may or must be erased or the tapes be destroyed, in particular where an accused has been discharged by an investigating judge or acquitted by a court.[1375]

[1373] Judgment of 26 May 1994, A.290, p. 19. See also the judgment of 21 February 1990, *Powell and Rayner*, A.172, p. 18; judgment of 27 October 1994, *Kroon* A.297-C, p. 56; and judgment of 28 November 1996, *Ahmut*, Reports 1996-VI, Vol. 24, para. 63.

[1374] Judgment of 9 December 1994, *Lopez Ostra*, A.303-C, p. 55.

[1375] Judgments of 24 April 1990, A.176-A, p. 24, and A.176-B, p. 56 respectively. In its judgment of 6 September 1978, *Klass*, A.28, p. 23, the Court already stressed the necessity for the relevant legislation and practice to afford adequate and effective safeguards against abuse. In its judgment of 25 February 1993, *Crémieux*, A.256-B, pp. 62-63, the Court also referred to this principle and

In the *Herczegfalvy* Case the Court also dealt with the necessity of protection under national law against arbitrary interferences with the rights safeguarded by paragraph 1. According to the Court it is necessary that the national law offers a minimum degree of protection against arbitrariness. And again the basis for this fundamental guarantee, flowing from the rule of law, is to be found in the concept of 'law' in the second paragraph.[1376]

In the *Niemietz* Case the Court introduced the requirement of specific guarantees by relying upon the 'necessary in a democratic society' clause. It considered that 'the search of a lawyer's office [was] not accompanied by any special procedural safeguards, such as the presence of an independent observer'.[1377] According to the Court, special circumstances deserve special procedural guarantees.

8.8 Restrictions

Restrictions to the rights laid down in the first paragraph of Article 8 may be justified, when they meet the requirements of the second paragraph. A general description of the content and meaning of the different restriction grounds, as interpreted and applied by the Court, is to be found in Chapter VIII, section 8. Here, only certain special issues are discussed which deserve particular attention in the context of Article 8.

8.8.1 *Proportionality*

Within the concept of the 'necessary in a democratic society' test the Court relies heavily upon the principle of 'proportionality'. This enables the Court to balance all the relevant interests and factual circumstances, and also to take into account the intensity of the infringement as well as the question whether the essence of the right invoked has been infringed. The scale the Court utilises seems to imply that the more far-reaching the infringement or the more essential the aspect of the right that has been interfered with, the more substantial or compelling the legitimate aims pursued must be.

In the context of family life this has induced the Court in certain cases to impose upon the Contracting States a heavy burden to prove that an infringement was legitimate. An example of this approach is the *Margareta and Roger Andersson* Case, concerning restrictions of contact between a mother and her child. Here the Court held as follows:

---

reached the conclusion that the legislation in force was insufficient in this respect.

[1376] Judgment of 24 September 1992, A.244, pp. 27-28.

[1377] Judgment of 16 December 1992, A.251-B, p. 36. Also in its judgment of 25 February 1993, *Crémieux*, A.256-B, pp. 62-63, the Court, on the ground of the absence of sufficient safeguards against abuse, concluded that the interference was not proportionate to the legitimate aim pursued and therefore not necessary in a democratic society.

The reasons adduced by the Government are of a general nature and do not specifically address the necessity of prohibiting contact by correspondence and telephone. The Court does not doubt that these reasons were relevant. However, they do not sufficiently show that it was necessary to deprive the applicants of almost every means of maintaining contact with each other for a period of approximately one and a half years. Indeed, it is questionable whether the measures were compatible with the aim of reuniting the applicants. Having regard to all the circumstances of the case, the Court considers that the aggregate of the restrictions imposed by the social welfare authorities on meetings and communications by correspondence and telephone between the applicants was disproportionate to the legitimate aims pursued and, therefore, not 'necessary in a democratic society'. There has accordingly been a breach of Article 8.[1378]

The heavy burden of proof that is sometimes placed upon the States when family ties and reunification of the family are at issue, came also to the fore in the *Keegan* Case. The Court concluded that the state of affairs complained about:

not only jeopardised the proper development of the applicant's ties with the child but also set in motion a process which was likely to prove to be irreversible, thereby putting the applicant at a significant disadvantage in his contest with the prospective adopters for the custody of the child. The Government have advanced no reasons relevant to the welfare of the applicant's daughter to justify such a departure from the principles that govern respect for family ties.[1379]

Particularly important to note in this quotation is the Court's reference to *'such a departure from the principles'*. The intensity and effect of the infringement seem to have been conclusive. In the case of deportation the Court seems also to be applying a rather strict approach whenever an applicant's family life is to be severely interfered with.[1380]

Some encroachments deserve more justification than others. In the *Niemietz* Case, with respect to the search of a law office, the Court paid special attention to the fact that a lawyer's professional secrecy was involved. It held as follows:

More importantly, having regard to the materials that were in fact inspected, the search impinged on professional secrecy to an extent that appears disproportionate in the circumstances; it has, in this connection, to be recalled that, where a lawyer is involved, an encroachment on professional secrecy may have repercussions on the proper administration of justice and hence on the rights guaranteed by Article 6 of the Convention. In addition, the attendant publicity must have been capable of affecting adversely the applicant's professional reputation, in the eyes both of his existing clients and of the public at large.[1381]

And in the *Kruslin* Case and the *Huvig* Case the Court apparently differentiated the necessary degree of precision of the 'law' depending of the seriousness of the interference. In these cases the Court argued that:

[1378] Judgment of 25 February 1992, A.226-A, p. 31.
[1379] Judgment of 26 May 1994, A.290, p. 21.
[1380] See, *e.g.*, the judgment of 26 March 1992, *Beldjoudi*, A.234-A, pp. 26-28.
[1381] Judgment of 16 December 1992, A.251-B, p. 36.

Tapping and other forms of interception of telephone conversations represent a serious interference with private life and correspondence and must accordingly be based on a 'law' that is particularly precise. It is essential to have clear, detailed rules on the subject, especially as the technology available for use is continually becoming more sophisticated.[1382]

The relevance of the seriousness of the interference was also reflected in the *Pfeifer and Plankl* Case, concerning the control of letters of a prisoner. In this case letters had not been stopped but some (apparently abusive) passages had been deleted. Still the Court concluded that this violated Article 8, but it remarked at the same time that 'The deletion of passages is admittedly a less serious interference, but in the circumstances of the case this too appears disproportionate.'[1383]

8.8.2 *Implied Restrictions?*

As has been shown above the Court does reject in the context of Article 8 the concept of 'inherent limitations'.[1384] However, some situations do imply restrictions which the Court is likely to allow, since they are inherent in a specific situation or status like that of soldier or prisoner. This should not imply, however, that in those cases the test under the second paragraph is no longer relevant; only that the Contracting State may be confronted here with a less severe and less probing attitude on the part of the Commission and the Court. In actual fact, however, at times the testing under the second paragraph is hardly noticeable or not performed at all.

In the *Campbell* Case the Court concluded 'that some measure of control over prisoners' correspondence is called for and is not of itself incompatible with the Convention, regard being paid to the ordinary and reasonable requirements of imprisonment.[1385] A similar reasoning was adopted by the Court in the *Costello-Roberts* Case, concerning corporal punishment at school. In that respect the Court observed that measures taken in the field of education may, in certain circumstances, affect the right to respect for private life, but not every act or measure which may be said to affect adversely the physical or moral integrity of a person necessarily gives rise to such an interference. Regarding the applicability of Article 8 the Court added that the sending of a child to school necessarily involves some degree of interference with his or her private life. Therefore the Court considered 'that the treatment complained of by the applicant did not entail adverse effects for his physical or moral integrity sufficient to bring it within the scope of the prohibition contained in Article 8.'[1386] In the *Lüdi* Case the Court

---

[1382] Judgments of 24 April 1990, A.176-A, p. 23 and A.176-B, p. 55 respectively.
[1383] Judgment of 25 February 1992, A.227, p. 19.
[1384] See *infra* pp. 763-765.
[1385] Judgment of 25 March 1992, A.233, p. 18. See also the judgment of 25 March 1983, *Silver*, A.61, p. 38 and the judgment of 25 February 1992, *Pfeifer and Plankl*, A.227, p. 18.
[1386] Judgment of 25 March 1993, A.247-C, pp. 60-61.

accepted an interference with Article 8 by the use and activities of an undercover agent because the applicant must have been aware, by engaging in criminal activities, 'that consequently he was running the risk of encountering an undercover police officer whose task would in fact be to expose him'.[1387]

It may be concluded from this case-law that, although in general the Court does not accept the concept of inherent or implied restrictions, in specific cases some restrictions are nevertheless accepted by the Court, if these have their basis in a specific legal situation or status.

8.8.3 *Necessary in a Democratic Society*

Application of the 'necessary in a democratic society' concept sometimes implies a very extensive and probing scrutiny by the Court, replacing the opinions of the national authorities by its own judgment and its own criteria. Although the general concept of necessity as used by the Court is undoubtedly the same in all cases in which the Court refers to it, nevertheless the intensity of the Court's control does differ and is dependent upon many circumstances. They differ depending on factors like the seriousness of the infringement or the position of the applicant. An example of a very probing scrutiny by the Court certainly is its judgment in the *Campbell* Case. In that judgment the Court adopted a very strict approach as against the national authorities with respect to their opening letters of prisoners. But the Court even went further by giving indications to the Contracting State on how to proceed when wishing to control a prisoner's correspondence with a lawyer.[1388]

In the area of orders to place children into care, on the contrary, the Court in general adopts a more restrained attitude:

> In exercising its supervisory jurisdiction the Court must determine whether the reasons given for the prohibition on removal, its maintenance in force until the transfer of custody and the restrictions on access which were in operation throughout this period were 'relevant and sufficient' in the light of the case as a whole.[1389]

In order to give this test some more strictness, however, the Court added an extra requirement for the respondent State: to make efforts for reunification of the family. This still leaves more scope for the States than is allowed to them when control of letters to and from prisoners is concerned.

[1387] Judgment of 15 June 1992, A.238, p. 19.
[1388] See *supra* pp. 530-531.
[1389] Judgment of 27 November 1992, *Olsson (No. 2)*, A.250, p. 34. See also the judgment of 24 March 1988, *Olsson*, A.130, p. 32.

8.9 Derogation

Article 8 does not pertain to the rights that are non-derogable in virtue of Article 15(2). This means that the Contracting States can take measures in derogation of Article 8 in the circumstances referred to in Article 15 and under the conditions laid down therein.

9 FREEDOM OF THOUGHT, CONSCIENCE AND RELIGION (ARTICLE 9)[1390]

1. *Everyone has the right to freedom of thought, conscience and religion; this right includes freedom to change his religion or belief and freedom, either alone or in community with others and in public or private, to manifest his religion or belief, in worship, teaching, practice and observance.*
2. *Freedom to manifest one's religion or beliefs shall be subject only to such limitations as are prescribed by law and are necessary in a democratic society in the interests of public safety, for the protection of public order, health or morals, or for the protection of the rights and freedoms of others.*

9.1 Protection of the *Forum Internum*

The right to freedom of thought, conscience and religion, the inviolability of the *forum internum*, is guaranteed in the Convention without qualification. Restrictions are possible only with respect to the *external expressions* of thought, conscience and religion, *viz.* in pursuance of the second paragraph of Article 9 with respect to the manifestation of religious and other beliefs,[1391] and in pursuance of the second paragraph of Article 10 with respect to the expression of one's opinion in general.

This absolute freedom to entertain any thought, moral conviction or religious view is not without practical importance. It is true that thoughts and views, as long as they have not been expressed, are intangible and that convictions are really valuable for the person concerned only if he can express them. This does not render the (inner) freedom of thought, conscience and religion useless. Its guarantee also implies that one cannot be subjected to a treatment intended to change the process of thinking, that any form of compulsion to express thoughts,

---

[1390] A good survey of the case-law up to 1989 is given by N. Blum, *Die Gedanken-, Gewissens- und Religionsfreiheit nach Art. 9 der Europäischen Menschenrechtskonvention,*Berlin, 1990. *Cf.* also B.P. Vermeulen, 'The Freedom of Thought, Conscience and Religion. Reflections on Article 9(1) of the European Convention on Human Rights, in Particular with Regard to the Position of Minorities', in: J.A. Smith and L.F. Zwaak (eds.), *International Protection of Human Rights*, SIM Special No. 15, Utrecht, 1995, pp. 101-114.

[1391] Judgment of 25 May 1993, *Kokkinakis* v. *Greece*, A.260-A, p. 18: 'The fundamental nature of the rights guaranteed in Article 9 § 1 is also reflected in the wording of the paragraphs providing for limitations on them. Unlike the second paragraphs of Articles 8, 10 and 11, which cover all the rights mentioned in the first paragraphs of those Articles, that of Article 9 refers only to "freedom to manifest one's religion or belief".'

to change an opinion, or to divulge a religious conviction is prohibited,[1392] and that no sanction may be imposed either on the holding of any view whatever or on the change of a religion or conviction: it protects against indoctrination by the State.[1393] On the other hand, the obligation for children to attend moral and social education lessons that do not expose them to religious indoctrination or any other form of indoctrination does not constitute an interference with the freedom of thought and conscience.[1394] Likewise the Court has held that the obligation to take part in a school parade without military overtones is not such as to offend the parent's religious convictions, and therefore does not amount to an interference with the right to freedom of religion.[1395]

In our opinion even the obligation to reveal one's religion or conviction in a census or other registration conflicts with Article 9: the freedom to have a religion or conviction includes the right not to disclose it. It seems furthermore that the Commission deduces from Article 9 the right to have one's religion or belief correctly registered by the authorities: it considered the complaint that the municipal authorities refused to provide the applicant with a certificate indicating his religion falling under the scope of Article 9.[1396] Compulsory voting has not been considered contrary to Article 9, because this is only a duty to attend, and not a duty actually to register one's vote.[1397]

9.2 Freedom of Conscience[1398]

The freedom to *act* in accordance with one's thought, conscience and religion is only guaranteed by Article 9 in as far as from an objective point of view it may be regarded as a manifestation of religion or belief (section 9.4). This implies for instance that the freedom to act according to one's (subjective) conscience – external freedom of conscience – is as such not protected by Article 9.

In fact, it must be ruled out that such freedom may be protected by a general provision in a human rights treaty. While every type of action may have conscience as its motivational base, every legal obligation may imply a restriction of the (external) freedom of conscience. It is clear that such freedom cannot be

---

[1392] From the Teitgen-report it can be gathered that the drafters of the Convention intended the freedom of thought *etc.* to protect the individual against 'ces abominables moyens d'enquête policière ou d'instruction judiciaire qui privent le suspect ou l'inculpé du contrôle de ses facultées intellectuelles et de sa conscience' (Recueil des *Travaux Préparatoires*, Vol. I, The Hague, 1975, p. 223).

[1393] Appl. 23380/94, *C.J., J.J. and E.J.* v. *Poland*, D&R 84-A (1996), p. 46 (56).

[1394] Appl. 17187/90, *Bernard and Others* v. *Luxembourg*, D&R 75 (1993), p. 57 (73).

[1395] Judgment of 18 December 1996, *Valsamis* v. *Greece*, Reports 1996-VI, Vol. 27, paras 34-38; judgment of 18 December 1996, *Efstratiou* v. *Greece*, Reports 1996-VI, Vol. 27, paras 35-39.

[1396] Appl. 16319/90, *H* v. *Greece* (not published).

[1397] Appl. 1718/62, *X* v. *Austria*, Yearbook VIII (1965), p. 168 (172); Appl. 4982/71, *X* v. *Austria*, Yearbook XV (1972), p. 468 (472-474).

[1398] *Cf.* European Consortium for Church-State research, *Conscientious Objection in the EC-Countries*, Milan, 1992; Council of Europe, *Freedom of Conscience*, Strasbourg, 1993.

unlimited. However, the 'boundlessness' of conscience excludes that the limitations of this freedom are laid down in a general, strictly formulated restriction clause. Other human rights such as the freedom of speech, religion *etc.* are concerned with certain specifiable areas of action, are connected with social institutions, have to do with foreseeable patterns of behaviour; this makes it possible to define their restriction clauses in general terms. As the external freedom of conscience lacks such an identifiable object it is not possible to frame a satisfactory and workable provision containing the relevant restrictions. Therefore on logical grounds it must be assumed that Article 9 cannot be held to guarantee the external freedom of conscience.

A systematic argument, derived from Article 9 itself, supports such a narrow interpretation. It must be stressed that the freedom of conscience in Article 9(1) cannot be subjected to limitations: Article 9(2) only allows restrictions of the freedom to manifest one's religion or belief(s).[1399] If the freedom of conscience would comprise the right to act in accordance with the dictates of conscience this freedom would be unlimited in the sense that every legal obligation would have to yield to (an appeal to) conscientious objections. Unrestricted freedom of conscience in *foro externo* implies the abolition of the legal order as a binding system of general rules. Therefore it must be concluded that the freedom of conscience in Article 9 does not cover the 'external manifestations' but only the 'inner world' (the *forum internum*).

It seems that until the 1970s the Commission held the view that Article 9 also guarantees the right to act according to conscience. The Commission dealt with several complaints in which conscientious objections to legal obligations were raised: compulsory affiliation for dairy farmers with a service for preventing and combatting cattle disease,[1400] an obligation to pay social security premiums,[1401] and a compulsory motorcar insurance.[1402] Furthermore, a staff member of the *Sosjale Joenit*, an organisation assisting runaway children, relied on Article 9, submitting that the prohibition under Dutch law to deprive parents of their parental authority over minors by keeping those minors concealed, burdened his conscience.[1403] In none of these cases the Commission found a violation of Article 9. The argument was, however, that this provision was not violated because the challenged obligation could reasonably be justified by reference to one of the limitation grounds mentioned in the second paragraph. This implies that according to the Commission Article 9 as such was applicable.

In more recent cases – foreshadowed in the *Arrowsmith* Case[1404] – the Commission has decided otherwise, arguing that:

[1399] Judgment of 25 May 1993, *Kokkinakis* v. *Greece*, A.260-A, p. 18.
[1400] Appl. 1068/61, *X* v. *the Netherlands*, Yearbook V (1962), p. 278 (284).
[1401] Appl. 1497/62, *Reformed Church of X* v. *the Netherlands*, Yearbook V (1962), p. 286 (297).
[1402] Appl. 2988/66, *X* v. *the Netherlands*, Yearbook X (1967), p. 472 (476).
[1403] Appl. 6753/74, *X and Y* v. *the Netherlands*, D&R 2 (1975), p. 118 (120).
[1404] Report of 12 October 1978, D&R 19 (1980), p. 5 (19).

Article 9 primarily protects the sphere of personal beliefs and religious creeds, *i.e.* the area which is sometimes called the forum internum. In addition, it protects acts which are intimately linked to these attitudes, such as acts of worship or devotion which are aspects of the practice of a religion or belief in a generally recognised form.[1405]

The phrase 'acts which are intimately linked to these attitudes', *etc.* probably refers to the last part of Article 9(1), the 'freedom to manifest his religion or belief', while the phrase 'the sphere of beliefs and religious creeds, *i.e.* the area which is sometimes called the forum internum' sums up the first part of this provision, the right to 'freedom of thought, conscience and religion' and the 'freedom to change his religion or belief'. This implies that also according to the Commission the freedom of conscience in this provision only covers the *forum internum*, only guarantees the internal freedom of conscience.

9.3 Conscientious Objections to Military and Substitute Service

With respect to the exercise of the freedom of conscience, both in national and in Strasbourg case-law the issue of conscientious objections of a religious or other nature against military and substitute service takes the most important place. Several international institutions seem to subscribe to the view that at least conscientious objections against military service are covered by Article 9. In 1967 the Parliamentary Assembly of the Council of Europe inferred from Article 9, *inter alia*, that:

1. Persons liable to conscription for military service who, for reasons of conscience or profound conviction arising from religious, ethical, moral, humanitarian, philosophical or similar motives, refuse to perform armed service shall enjoy a personal right to be released from the obligation to perform such service.
2. This right shall be regarded as deriving logically from the fundamental rights of the individual in democratic Rule of Law States which are guaranteed in Article 9 of the European Convention on Human Rights.[1406]

And in 1987, the Committee of Ministers adopted a recommendation on the same subject. There, the 'basic principle' is laid down that:

[1405] Constant case-law since 1983: Appl. 10358/83, *C* v. *the United Kingdom*, D&R 37 (1984), p. 142 (147); Appl. 10678/83, *V* v. *the Netherlands*, D&R 39 (1984), p. 267 (269); Appl. 11308/84, *Vereniging Rechtswinkels Utrecht* v. *the Netherlands*, D&R 46 (1986), p. 200 (202); Appl. 22838/93, *Van den Dungen* v. *the Netherlands*, D&R 80-A (1995), p. 147 (150).

[1406] Res. 337 (1967), Council of Europe, Cons. Ass., Eighteenth Ordinary Session (Third Part), *Texts Adopted* (1967), reiterated by the Parliamentary Assembly in its Res. 816(1977), adopted on 7 October 1977; Council of Europe, *Collected Texts*, Strasbourg, 1987, pp. 222-223. The European Parliament adopted the same point of view in a resolution of 7 February 1983.

> Anyone liable to conscription for military service who, for compelling reasons of conscience, refuses to be involved in the use of arms, shall have the right to be released from the obligation to perform such service, on the conditions set out hereafter. Such persons may be liable to perform alternative service.[1407]

The Resolution and the Recommendation are not legally binding. Nevertheless they may be considered as an authoritative interpretation of Article 9, which cannot simply be ignored by the national authorities and the Strasbourg institutions. Indeed the Commission has decided that conscientious objections to military service fall 'into the realm of Article 9',[1408] presumably because such objections must in general be regarded as manifestations of a religion or belief. This does not imply that the Commission has found that the right to conscientious objection is as such guaranteed by Article 9. On the contrary, it has taken the position that the Convention contains no obligation for the Contracting States to exempt conscientious objectors from compulsory military service. For its position the Commission refers to the words in Article 4(3)(b): 'conscientious objectors *in countries where they are recognized*'[1409] (emphasis added). The argument is evidently that, since the drafters of the Convention meant to leave the States free to recognise or not to recognise conscientious objectors to military service, they cannot have intended to deprive them of this same freedom in another provision of the same Convention.

A positive aspect of the Commission's reasoning is that because conscientious objections fall within the ambit of Article 9, measures taken with regard to conscientious objectors must be in conformity with Article 14. This does not imply, however, that imposition of an alternative civilian service is not allowed. Since in Article 4(3)(b):

> it is expressly recognized that civilian service may be imposed on conscientious objectors as a substitute for military service, it must be concluded that objections of conscience do not, under the Convention, entitle a person to exemption from such service.[1410]

[1407] Recommendation No. R(87)8, Council of Europe, *Information Sheet* No. 21, H/INF(87)1, p. 160. See also Res. 1987/46 of 10 March 1987 of the United Nations Commission on Human Rights on conscientious objection to military service, where the Commission, *inter alia*, 'appeals to States to recognize that conscientious objection to military service be considered a legitimate exercise of the right to freedom of thought, conscience and religion recognized by the Universal Declaration of Human Rights and the International Covenant on Civil and Political Rights.'

[1408] Appl. 10410/83, *N v. Sweden*, D&R 40 (1985), p. 203 (207); Appl. 17086/90, *Autio v. Finland*, D&R 72 (1992), p. 245 (249); Appl. 20972/92, *Raninen v. Finland*, D&R 84-A (1996), p. 17 (30).

[1409] See the report of 29 June 1967, *Grandrath*, Yearbook X (1967), p. 626 (672-674). See also Appl. 5591/72, *X v. Austria*, Coll. 43 (1973), p. 161; Appl. 7565/76, *Conscientious objectors* v. *Denmark*, D&R 9 (1978), p. 117 (118); Appl. 7705/76, *X v. Federal Republic of Germany*, D&R 9 (1978), p. 196 (203); Appl. 10640/83, *A v. Switzerland*, D&R 38 (1984), p. 219 (223); Appl. 10410/83, *N v. Sweden*, D&R 40 (1985), p. 203 (206); Appl. 11850/85, *G v. the Netherlands*, D&R 51 (1987), p. 180 (182).

[1410] Report of 29 June 1967, *Grandrath*, Yearbook X (1967), p. 626 (672-674).

Therefore, the Convention does not prevent a State from taking measures to enforce performance of substitute civilian service or from imposing sanctions on those who refuse to perform such service.[1411] It does imply however that differential treatment between those who do their military service and those who have opted for substitute service has to be justified to the extent that the persons concerned are in a comparable position. For instance, the difference in duration of military and substitute service is often challenged in court as being unjustified. Until now without success: according to constant national and international case-law substitute service is to be regarded as less arduous than military service, so that the additional time the conscientious objector has to serve is deemed necessary to avoid refusal of military service for that reason.[1412] Even a system in which the length of the substitute service is twice as long as the length of the military service was not found to amount to a violation of Article 14 in conjunction with Article 9.[1413]

Another consequence of the applicability of Article 14 is that differential treatment between various categories of conscientious objectors must have an objective and reasonable justification. On this ground the fact that in some countries (only) Jehovah's Witnesses are exempted from military and substitute service has been and still is severely criticised. According to the Commission the certainty that membership of the Jehovah's Witnesses provides concerning the genuineness of their objections also guarantees that their privileged position does not undermine the military system itself. It is unlikely that one should join such a sect in order to avoid to do substitute service. This twofold guarantee is lacking with regard to other groups and persons, which justifies why only the Jehovah's Witnesses, and not other 'total objectors' are exempted from substitute service.[1414] This issue reveals a complex conflict between freedom and equality. On the one hand: is it justifiable that Jehovah's Witnesses are exempted from military and substitute service while other 'total objectors' are imprisoned?[1415] On the other hand: would it be justifiable that Jehovah's Witnesses also have to serve that sentence in order to be treated in the same way as (comparatively few) other 'total objectors'?

[1411]   Appl. 10600/83, *Johansen* v. *Norway*, D&R 44 (1985), p. 155 (165); Appl. 20972/92, *Raninen* v. *Finland*, D&R 84-A (1996), p. 17 (32).

[1412]   Appl. 11850/85, *G* v. *the Netherlands*, D&R 51 (1987), p. 180 (182).

[1413]   Appl. 17086/90, *Autio* v. *Finland*, D&R 72 (1992), p. 245 (250), concerning the system in Finland (military service lasts 8 months, substitute service lasts 16 months).

[1414]   Appl. 10410/83, *N* v. *Sweden*, D&R 40 (1985), p. 203 (207); Appl. 20972/92, *Raninen* v. *Finland*, D&R 84-A (1996), p. 17 (33).

[1415]   According to the Human Rights Committee such differential treatment is incompatible with Article 26 of the UN Covenant on Civil and Political Rights. In its view of 27 July 1993, Communication No. 402/1990, it concludes 'that the State Party [the Netherlands] should give equal treatment to all persons holding equally strong objections to military and substitute service, and it recommends that the State Party review its relevant regulations and practice with a view to removing any discrimination in this respect.'

9.4 The Freedom to Have and Change One's Religion or Belief

The freedom to accept a religion or belief and to change one's religion or belief is unlimited. This freedom also includes the freedom not to have a religion or belief, and not to be obliged to act in a way that entails the expression of the acceptation of a church, religion or belief that one does not share.

The Strasbourg case-law in this matter is limited. It can be deduced from the case-law about church taxes that the obligation to pay such taxes does not violate the freedom of religion or belief when the freedom to resign from the church community is safeguarded.[1416] A formal and unambiguous confirmation of such a decision may however be required.[1417] Furthermore, in the *Darby* Case the Court held that exemptions from these taxes must not be granted in a discriminative way.[1418] Unfortunately the Court examined the problem of church taxes in the *Darby* Case exclusively from the angle of Article 1 of Protocol No. 1.[1419]

That a church imposes specific restrictions on its ministers and others employed by it, in order to preserve the purity of the doctrine and to guarantee unity in religious profession, has been considered in conformity with Article 9 by the Commission. It opined as follows:

> Through the rights granted to its members under Art. 9, the church itself is protected in its right to manifest its religion, to organise and carry out worship, teaching practice and observance, and it is free to act out and enforce uniformity in these matters. Further, in a State church system its servants are employed for the purpose of applying and teaching a specific religion. Their individual freedom of thought, conscience or religion is exercised at the moment they accept or refuse employment as clergymen, and their right to leave the church guarantees their freedom of religion in case they oppose its teachings. In other words, the church is not obliged to provide religious freedom to its servants and members, as is the State as such for everyone within its jurisdiction.[1420]

This reasoning demonstrates, in our opinion, a sound balancing of rights and interests.

The obligation to join an association of, *e.g.*, architects which applies to all persons of this category has no link with the members' personal beliefs, and leaves them free to set up separate associations and express their personal ideas in other ways, and is consequently not regarded as an interference with Article 9.[1421]

It is not clear to what extent the right to have and change one's religion or belief also implies protection against the imposition of a particular conception of

---

[1416] Appl. 9781/82, *E and G.R.* v. *Austria*, D&R 37 (1984), p. 42 (45).

[1417] Appl. 10616/83, *J and B Gottesmann* v. *Switzerland*, D&R 40 (1985), p. 284 (289).

[1418] Judgment of 23 October 1990, A.187, p. 13.

[1419] The Commission found that the church tax violated Art. 9 as well as Art. 14 in conjunction with Art. 9 (report of 9 May 1989, A.187, pp. 20-22).

[1420] Appl. 7374/76, *X* v. *Denmark*, D&R 5 (1976), p. 157 (158); Appl. 11045/84, *Knudsen* v. *Norway*, D&R 42 (1985), p. 247 (257-258); Appl. 12356/86, *Karlsson* v. *Sweden*, D&R 57 (1988), p. 172 (175).

[1421] Appls 14331/88 and 14332/88, *Revert and Legallais* v. *France*, D&R 62 (1989), p. 309 (318).

morals. In this respect the judgment of the Court in the *Johnston* Case is worth mentioning. Here, the applicants complained about the prohibition of divorce in Ireland. One of the applicants invoked Article 9 of the Convention, submitting that the impossibility to live together with one of the other applicants in a marital relationship, because he had already been married with a woman with which he did not live together anymore, conflicted with his conscience. Both the Commission and the Court concluded that in this case there was no violation of Article 9. According to the Court, Article 9, 'in its ordinary meaning', was not involved.[1422]

9.5 The Freedom to Manifest his Religion or Belief

9.5.1 *Religion or Belief*

Article 9 refers to the freedom 'to manifest his religion or belief'. It does not refer to the freedom of expression in general, a right which finds regulation in Article 10. However, the Commission appears to be prepared to put a broad interpretation on the words 'religion or belief'. They do not only cover the traditional religions and (non-religious) beliefs, but also all kinds of minority views. For instance pacifism,[1423] and probably also communism is regarded as a 'belief' falling within the ambit of Article 9.[1424] Even Veganism (strict vegetarianism) may fall within the scope of this article.[1425] This does not mean that every individual opinion or preference is a 'religion or belief'. This concept is more akin to the concept of 'religious and philosophical convictions', views that attain a certain level of cogency, seriousness, cohesion and importance'.[1426] For instance, the preference for a certain language is not a belief in the sense of Article 9.[1427] The magic wishes of a *Wicca*-adept were rightly rejected because the applicant failed to specify the content of clearness of the *Wicca*-religion.[1428] The same reasoning was followed with regard to the complaint of a *Lichtanbeter*.[1429] And in the case concerning a soldier who had stated at a private party that the Holocaust was a lie of Zionists, the Commission concluded that these remarks 'did not reflect a "belief" within the meaning of Article 9 of the Convention which is essentially

---

[1422] Judgment of 18 December 1986, A.112, p. 27. See for the Commission's report of 5 March 1985, A.112, pp. 51-52.
[1423] Report of 12 October 1978, *Arrowsmith*, D&R 19 (1980), p. 5 (19); Appls 11567/85 and 11568/85, *Le Court Grandmaison and Fritz v. France*, D&R 53 (1987), p. 150 (160).
[1424] Appls 16311/90, 16312/90 and 16313/90, *N.H., G.H. and R.A. v. Turkey*, D&R 72 (1992), p. 200 (212).
[1425] Appl. 18187/91, *W v. the United Kingdom* (not published).
[1426] Judgment of 25 February 1982, *Campbell and Cosans v. the United Kingdom*, A.48, p. 16.
[1427] Judgment of 23 July 1968, *Belgian Linguistic* Cases, A.6, p. 32.
[1428] Appl. 7291/75, *X v. the United Kingdom*, D&R 11 (1978), p. 55 (56).
[1429] Appl. 4445/70, *X v. Federal Republic of Germany*, Coll. 37 (1971), p. 119 (121-122).

destined to protect religions, or theories on philosophical or ideological universal values.'[1430]

9.5.2 The Freedom to Manifest his Religion or Belief in Practice

With regard to the terms 'manifest' and 'practice' the Commission has followed a more restrictive interpretation, for the first time explicitly formulated in the *Arrowsmith* Case. Arrowsmith had claimed that she was entitled to distribute leaflets (to troops in a British army camp) in which she advocated the view that they should not serve in Northern Ireland, as Article 9 gave her the right to express her pacifist belief in this practice. The Commission, however, argued that a strictly subjective criterion would not do: 'the term "practice" as employed in Article 9(1) does not cover each act which is motivated or influenced by a religion or belief'. The Commission applied an objective standard: 'when the actions of individuals do not actually express the belief concerned they cannot be considered to be as such protected by Article 9(1), even when they are motivated by it', and concluded, that since the pamphlets 'did not express pacifist views' the applicant did not manifest her belief in the sense of Article 9 and therefore could not invoke this provision.[1431]

This line of argument has been consistently followed in later decisions. The terms 'manifestation' and 'practice' do not cover each act which is motivated by a religion or belief;[1432] actions which do not actually express a belief cannot be considered to be protected by Article 9.[1433] The Commission decided for instance that the wish to be buried in a certain place does not fall within the scope of Article 9 because it is not a 'manifestation of any belief in the sense that some coherent view on fundamental problems can be seen as being expressed thereby';[1434] and the choice of a particular doctor does not in itself express a belief.[1435] In cases of conscientious objections against financing (by means of taxes) pension schemes, military expenditure and nuclear energy, the Commission decided that only acts 'which are aspects of the practice of a religion or belief in

---

[1430] Appl. 19459/92, *F.P.* v. *Federal Republic of Germany* (unpublished). The Commission has left undecided whether fascist propaganda falls within the scope of Art. 9: Appl. 6741/74, *X* v. *Italy*, D&R 5 (1976), p. 83 (85).

[1431] Report of 12 October 1978, D&R 19 (1980) p. 5 (19-20). In a case concerning an applicant disseminating leaflets in the vicinity of an abortion clinic the Commission held that the applicant's activities were primarily aimed at persuading women not to have an abortion, although the content of the leaflets clearly expressed religious views (Appl. 22838/93, *Van den Dungen* v. *the Netherlands*, D&R 80-A (1995), p. 147 (150)).

[1432] Appl. 10358/83, *C* v. *the United Kingdom*, D&R 37 (1984), p. 142 (147); Appl. 16278/90, *Karaduman* v. *Turkey*, D&R 74 (1993), p. 93 (108); Appl. 22838/93, *Van den Dungen* v. *the Netherlands*, D&R 80-A (1995), p. 147 (150).

[1433] Appl. 19898/92, *B.C.* v. *Switzerland*, D&R 75 (1993), p. 223 (230).

[1434] Appl. 8741/79, *X* v. *Federal Republic of Germany*, D&R 24 (1981), p. 137 (138).

[1435] Appl. 19898/92, *B.C.* v. *Switzerland*, D&R 75 (1993), p. 223 (230).

a generally recognised form' are protected by Article 9.[1436] For that reason the objections concerned were not regarded as manifestations of a religion or a belief. With regard to the obligation to pay taxes the Commission argued that:

> Article 9 does not confer on the applicant the right to refuse, on the basis of his convictions, to abide by legislation, the operation of which is provided for by the Convention, and which applies neutrally and generally in the public sphere, without impinging on the freedoms guaranteed by Article 9.[1437]

In the same way it is argued that the duty to participate in a pension scheme does not restrict the freedom to manifest one's (anthroposophic) belief: 'the obligation to participate in a pension fund applies to all general practitioners on a purely neutral basis, and cannot be said to have any close link with their religion or beliefs.'[1438] In a similar vein actions which are motivated by political idealism but as such do not express a religion or belief in a recognisable form are not regarded as manifestations of a religion or belief.[1439]

This restrictive interpretation may in general be unavoidable. A legal system consisting of general binding rules cannot afford to leave to (the subjective convictions of) this person the answer to the question whether a person manifests his religion or belief and can rely on Article 9. It should answer this question itself on the basis of objective criteria, primarily related to the outward appearance of the expression.

However, for less known minorities who are not linked up with one of the world religions or ideologies this entails the danger that a behaviour will only be considered the expression of a belief, in case a sufficient resemblance can be found with the known patterns of familiar spiritual movements.[1440] To a certain extent this problem may be mitigated by giving an applicant who claims that a certain type of behaviour is an expression of his religion or belief, the benefit of the doubt.

Furthermore, it must be stressed that general regulations on a neutral basis may restrict the freedom of religion and belief in specific circumstances. For instance planning legislation, limiting the use of buildings to particular purposes, in general

---

[1436] Appl. 10358/83, *C* v. *the United Kingdom*, D&R 37 (1984), p. 142 (147); Appl. 10678/83, *V* v. *the Netherlands*, D&R 39 (1984), p. 267 (268); Appl. 11308/84, *Vereniging Rechtswinkels Utrecht* v. *the Netherlands*, D&R 46 (1986), p. 200 (202).

[1437] E.g. Appl. 10358/83, *C* v. *the United Kingdom*, D&R 37 (1984), p. 142 (147); Appl. 17522/90, *Ortega Moratilla* v. *Spain*, D&R 72 (1992), p. 256 (262).

[1438] Appl. 10678/83, *V* v. *the Netherlands*, D&R 39 (1984), p. 267 (268).

[1439] Appl. 11308/84, *Vereniging Rechtswinkels Utrecht* v. *the Netherlands*, D&R 46 (1986), p. 200 (202): 'although the aims of the applicant association are of an idealistic nature, *viz.* providing legal advice to prisoners and looking after their interests on a non-commercial basis, it cannot be said that in the present case it exercises the right contained in Article 9.' *Cf.* Appl. 15928/89, *J.K.* v. *the Netherlands* (not published): the applicant was not manifesting a belief by unfolding a banner with the words 'No Olympics' in order to protest against the candidature of Amsterdam for the 1992 Olympic Games.

[1440] K. Rimanque, 'Freedom of Conscience and Minority Groups', in: Council of Europe (ed.), *Freedom of Conscience*, Strasbourg, 1993, pp. 155-157.

does not interfere with the exercise of the right to freedom of religion, even though it may restrict the possibility to employ it for religious activities. However, when a building is already used for such activities an issue under Article 9 may arise.[1441] The Court recently decided that the applicants' conviction for using premises as a place of worship without prior authorisation in the instant case constituted an interference with the exercise of their freedom of religion.[1442]

The freedom to manifest one's religion or belief does not in general imply a right to be exempted from criticism or ridicule by others,[1443] because these actions cannot generally be regarded as an interference with this freedom. Only in extreme cases, where the effect of particular methods of opposing or denying religious or other beliefs can be such as to inhibit those who hold those beliefs from exercising their freedom to hold and express them, the State may be obliged to repress certain forms of conduct in order to guarantee the right under Article 9 to the holders of these beliefs. In *Otto-Preminger-Institut* v. *Austria* the Court held otherwise. The Court ruled that the right to respect for the religious feelings of believers as guaranteed by Article 9 could legitimately be thought to have been violated by *Das Liebeskonzil*, a film supposedly blasphemic in the eyes of the Roman Catholic majority. For this reason it decided that the seizure and forfeiture of the film was justified under Article 10(2), being necessary for the protection of the right of this majority to respect for their freedom as protected by Article 9.[1444] It is submitted that this decision is mistaken. The screening of this film in no way would have limited or inhibited Roman Catholics in manifesting their religion, and therefore did not restrict their rights under Article 9. The Court has unjustifiably extended the right (flowing from Article 9) to be protected against vicious attacks of fellow-citizens on a religion or belief that could endanger the actual enjoyment of the freedom to manifest this religion or belief – particularly relevant for minorities – to a general right – even of dominant majorities – not to be insulted in one's religious or non-religious views. However, such a right, relied upon 'to sanction improper attacks on objects of religious veneration' and 'to prevent that some people should feel the object of attacks on their religious beliefs in an unwarranted and offensive manner',[1445] is not included in Article 9, but is on the contrary inconsistent with the 'pluralism indissociable from a democratic society', embedded in Article 9.[1446]

[1441] Appl. 20490/92, *ISKCON* v. *the United Kingdom*, D&R 76-A (1994), p. 90 (106); judgment of 9 December 1994, *Holy Monasteries* v. *Greece*, A.301-A, p. 38.

[1442] Judgment of 26 September 1996, *Manoussakis* v. *Greece*, Reports 1996-IV, Vol. 17, para. 36.

[1443] Appl. 17439/90, *Choudhury* v. *the United Kingdom* (not published), concerning the refusal of the authorities to bring criminal proceedings against the author (Rushdie) and the publisher of the book 'Satanic Verses'.

[1444] Judgment of 20 September 1994, A.295-A, p. 21.

[1445] *Idem.*

[1446] Judgment of 25 May 1993, *Kokkinakis* v. *Greece*, A.260-A, p. 18.

9.5.3 The Collective Dimension of the Freedom of Religion and Belief; the Rights of Churches and Other Organisations

The freedom to manifest a religion or belief is not an exclusively individual right, but has also a collective dimension, recognised in Article 9 through the words 'in community with others'. It seems plausible then that collectivities such as churches should also be regarded as subjects of this right. However, the Commission initially held that a church, 'being a legal and not a natural person, is incapable of having or exercising the rights mentioned in Article 9, paragraph (1) of the Convention', and on that ground cannot claim to be itself the victim of the alleged violation of Article 9.[1447] This position of the Commission has rightly been criticised. Whereas the freedom of thought and conscience, as well as the freedom to choose a religion or belief are strictly personal freedoms, the right to freedom of religion has not only an individual but also a collective dimension, and the very functioning of churches depends on respect for this right. Churches appear, therefore, to be in an eminent position to stand up for that respect, the more so as Article 25 expressly provides for the possibility of complaints by non-governmental organisations and groups.[1448]

In a decision of 1979 the Commission revised its position, and labelled the distinction made between a church body and its members artificial. In this context it held:

> When a Church body lodges an application under the Convention, it does so in reality on behalf of its members. It should therefore be accepted that a church body is capable of possessing and exercising the rights contained in Art. 9(1) in its own capacity as a representative of its members.[1449]

But even that reasoning seems to us to be too narrow, as was in fact recognised by the Commission in its earlier decision, referred to above, that a church has *its own right* to manifest its religion.[1450]

The right of a collectivity to manifest its religion is not restricted to churches. Other organisations such as denominational charities may also be capable of possessing and exercising the right to freedom of religion.[1451] And even a limited liability company may enjoy this freedom.[1452]

[1447] Appl. 3798/68, *Church of X v. the United Kingdom*, Yearbook XII (1969), p. 306 (314); Appl. 4733/71, *X v. Sweden*, Yearbook XIV (1971), p. 664 (674).
[1448] See *supra* p. 46.
[1449] Appl. 7805/77, *Pastor X and Church of Scientology v. Sweden*, Yearbook XXII (1979), p. 244 (246). *Cf.* also Appl. 12587/86, *A.R.M. Chappell*, D&R 53 (1987), p. 241 (246); and Appl. 24019/94, *Finska Församlingen i Stockholm and T. Hautaniemi v. Sweden*, D&R 85-A (1996), p. 94 (96).
[1450] Appl. 7374/76, *X v. Denmark*, D&R 5 (1976), p. 157 (158).
[1451] Appl. 20490/92, *ISKCON v. the United Kingdom*, D&R 76-A (1994), p. 90 (106).
[1452] In Appl. 7865/77, *Company X v. Switzerland*, D&R 16 (1979), p. 85 (87) and Appl. 11921/86, *Verein Kontakt Information Therapie and Hagen v. Austria*, D&R 57 (1988), p. 81 (88), the Commission held that such a company, given the fact that it concerns a profit-making corporate body, can neither enjoy nor rely on the rights referred to in Art. 9. However, in Appl. 20471/92, *Kustannus et al. v. Finland*, D&R 85-A (1996), p. 29 (43) the Commission ruled otherwise: 'The

It does not suffice if a Contracting State guarantees the right to manifest one's religion only to the individual or the collectivity. The Commission rightly endorses the view that:

> the right to manifest one's religion 'in community with others' has always been regarded as an essential part of the freedom of religion and finds that the two alternatives 'either alone or in community with others' in Article 9(1) cannot be considered as mutually exclusive, or as leaving a choice to the authorities, but only as recognising that religion may be practised in either form.[1453]

9.5.4   Freely Accepted Obligations Limiting the Expression of Religion or Belief

Article 9 does not imply that one can back out of one's obligations, contracted freely and without explicit reservation. *E.g.*, a muslim teacher who regularly neglects his duties in order to participate in the common prayer on Friday afternoon in the mosque near the school has to make a choice between fulfilling this religious prescription and his position as a teacher.[1454] The same principle applies in case of conflict between an ecclesiastical hierarchy and a servant or member of the church who no longer agrees with the hierarchy. The individual must choose between submitting to ecclesiastical discipline or leaving the church.[1455] In a similar vein the Commission has argued that by choosing to pursue her higher education in a secular university a student submits to certain university rules, so that dress regulations that prohibit wearing Muslim headscarves do not constitute an interference with her freedom of religion.[1456] And likewise it has held that by enroling in a military academy an officer cadet submits of his own accord to military rules that may make his freedom to practise his religion subject to limitations as to time and place, but do not interfere with the right guaranteed in Article 9(1).[1457] On the other hand, the Commission recently decided that a disciplinary dismissal of a military judge because of his religious opinions (allegedly incompatible with the principles of the secular State) had to be regarded as an interference with Article 9.[1458]

Commission would therefore not exclude that the applicant association is in principle capable of possessing and exercising rights under Article 9 para. 1.'

[1453]   Appl. 8160/78, *X* v. *the United Kingdom*, D&R 22 (1981), p. 27 (33-37).

[1454]   *Idem.*

[1455]   Appl. 7374/76, *X* v. *Denmark*, D&R 5 (1976), p. 157 (158); Appl. 11045/84, *Knudsen* v. *Norway*, D&R 42 (1985), p. 247 (257-258); Appl. 12356/86, *Karlsson* v. *Sweden*, D&R 57 (1988), p. 172 (175). *Cf.* also Appl. 12242/86, *Rommelfanger* v. *Federal Republic of Germany*, D&R 62 (1989), p. 151 (161).

[1456]   Appl. 16278/90, *Karaduman* v. *Turkey*, D&R 74 (1993), p. 93 (108-109).

[1457]   Appl. 14524/89, *Yanasik* v. *Turkey*, D&R 74 (1993), p. 14 (26-27).

[1458]   Report of 27 February 1996, *Kalaç* v. *Turkey* (not yet published), paras 34-36.

9.5.5 Special Rights

Special rights can be derived from the profession of a particular religion or belief only if these rights are indispensable for free profession.[1459] The Commission, therefore, declared ill-founded a complaint that the non-recognition by the public authorities of a marriage concluded exclusively in accordance with a religious ritual was contrary to Article 9.[1460] The Commission relied on Article 12, which leaves the regulation of marriage to the national laws. In our opinion, however, it might have confined itself to submitting that, as long as the religious celebration of the marriage is not prohibited, the legal requirement of a supplementary non-religious procedure if the marriage is to be legally valid, does not imply an encroachment on the freedom of religion.

A matter related to that of conscientious objections discussed above is that of the exemption from military service for certain ministers of religious communities. Unlike in the case of recognised conscientious objectors, as a rule no alternative civilian service is imposed on these ministers. A right to such an exemption exists in some States only if such an exemption is necessary for the practice of the religion by the person himself and by the community for which he has been appointed. This certainly is in conformity with Article 9. If an arrangement for the exemption of ministers has been made, however, the arrangement itself and its application must not lead to discrimination.[1461] The case-law relating to this issue will be discussed below with reference to Article 14.[1462]

9.6 The Restriction Clause

The freedom to manifest one's religion or beliefs can only be restricted through such limitations as are prescribed by law and are necessary in a democratic society in the interests of public safety, for the protection of public order, health or morals, or for the protection of the rights and freedoms of others: Article 9(2). Comparing this clause with Articles 8(2), 10(2) and 11(2) it is evident that Article 9(2) comprises a relatively small list of interests as grounds for restriction. Furthermore, Article 9(2) refers to 'the protection of public order', whereas the other provisions use the term 'the prevention of disorder'. In its judgment in the *Engel* Case the Court decided that 'disorder' refers not only to 'public order' but 'also covers the order that must prevail within the confines of a special social group.'[1463] From this it seems to follow that 'public order' in Article 9(2) does only refer to the notion of 'order in places accessible to everyone'.

Nevertheless there seems to be no difference between the way the Strasbourg organs apply the restriction clause of Article 9 and the restriction clauses of

---

[1459] The existence of the religion and its profession by the applicant will then have to be proved: Appl. 7291/75, *X* v. *the United Kingdom*, D&R 11 (1978), p. 55 (56).

[1460] Appl. 6167/73, *X* v. *Federal Republic of Germany*, D&R 1 (1975), p. 64 (65).

[1461] Report of 7 March 1996, *Tsirlis and Koulompas* v. *Greece* (not yet published), paras 112-120.

[1462] See *infra* pp. 725-726.

[1463] Judgment of 8 June 1976, A.22, p. 41.

Articles 8, 10 and 11. The emphasis is always laid on whether a restriction is necessary; what interest is sought to be protected is of less importance.

In two cases the Court concluded that Article 9 was violated. In the *Kokkinakis* Case the Court decided that the conviction of a Jehovah's Witness for proselytism constituted a breach of this provision because it was not shown that the applicant's conviction was justified in the circumstances of the case by a pressing social need: the Greek courts had established his liability by merely reproducing the relevant section of the law, without specifying in what way he had attempted to convince his neighbour by improper means. Therefore the measure taken did not appear to be proportionate to the aim pursued (the protection of the rights and freedoms of others).[1464] Although the outcome of the *Kokkinakis* Case is satisfactory the Court's reasoning may be criticised. In concentrating on the *application* of the legislation the Court sidestepped the issue of whether the legislation as such constituted a breach of Article 9.[1465]

In the *Manoussakis* Case the Court had to rule on the compatibility of a conviction of Jehovah's Witnesses for having set up and operated a place of worship without the authorisation of the Minister of Education and Religious Affairs. According to the Court the right to freedom of religion excludes any discretion on the part of the State to determine whether religious beliefs or means used to express such beliefs are legitimate. The authorisation requirement was consistent with Article 9 only insofar as it was intended to allow the Minister to verify whether formal conditions laid down in the relevant enactments were satisfied. The Court observed that the State tended to use this requirement to impose rigid, or indeed prohibitive, conditions on practice of religious beliefs by certain non-orthodox movements. Moreover, to date (1996) the applicants had not received an express decision on their requests made in 1983/1984. The Court concluded that the impugned conviction could not be regarded as proportionate to the aim pursued, nor could it be regarded as necessary in a democratic society.[1466] Once again, however, the question was passed over whether this type of legislation is *per se* incompatible with Article 9, as judge Martens concluded in his concurring opinion.[1467]

In particular when considering the Commission's case-law with respect to prisoners one cannot avoid the impression that the Commission tends to assume

---

[1464] Judgment of 25 May 1993, A.260-A, pp. 21-22. The Commission ruled likewise in its report of 12 September 1996, *Larissis, Mandalaris and Sarandis* v. *Greece* (not yet published), paras 72-76. However, the Commission also found that the conviction of military persons for the proselytism of subordinates was, in view of the special character of the relationship between a superior and a subordinate in the army, not disproportionate to the aim pursued, 'the protection of the rights and freedoms of others' (*ibidem*, paras 77-82).

[1465] *Cf.* the opinions of judges Pettiti, De Meyer and Martens.

[1466] Judgment of 26 September 1996, Reports 1996-IV, Vol. 17, paras 45-53.

[1467] In its report of 27 February 1996, *Pentidis, Katharios and Stagopulos* v. *Greece* (not yet published), para. 47, the Commission doubts whether this type of regulations is as such compatible with Art. 9.

rather lightly that restrictions imposed on prisoners in the manifestation of their religion or conviction are inherent to detention and therefore are justified by one of the restriction aims of paragraph 2. It makes sense to assume that Article 9 does not imply an obligation on the authorities to provide prisoners at public expense with the books which they request for the practice of their religion and the development of their philosophy of life,[1468] or to make a minister available to prisoners who profess a religion which is not current in the country of their detention.[1469] In that situation, however, they should allow such books sent by others, and admit a minister of that religion who presents himself, although some supervision may be permitted for security reasons.[1470] But what are we to think of the Commission's acceptance of the justification of the prohibition for a Buddhist prisoner to grow a beard[1471] and of the refusal to take religious precepts into account in providing food,[1472] both on the ground of 'protection of public order'?[1473] And although it sounds reasonable that, if prisoners are required to clean their own cells, all prisoners have to do this, as soon as it is recognised that a particular prisoner's religion does not allow cleaning floors, it is too easy to conclude that this interference with Article 9 is justified 'as necessary in a democratic society for the protection of the applicant's and other prisoners' health'.[1474] It cannot be maintained that this protection requires cleaning by the prisoners themselves. In more or less the same laconic way the Commission dealt with the arguments by a Sikh prisoner that his religious principles required him to wear his own clothes rather than prison clothes.[1475]

[1468] Appl. 1753/63, *X* v. *Austria*, Yearbook VIII (1965), p. 174 (184). From the decision it is not clear whether the books desired were already present in the prison library, or would have to be purchased as yet. If the former was the case, the decision would be incorrect. In its decision on Appl. 6886/75, *X* v. *the United Kingdom*, D&R 5 (1976), p. 100 (101), the fact that a book was kept back which had indeed a philosophical character, but contained a chapter on techniques of self-defence, was considered as a restriction of the freedom of religion by the Commission, but it was deemed justified on the basis of the restriction 'protection of the rights and freedoms of others'.

[1469] Appl. 2413/65, *X* v. *Federal Republic of Germany*, Coll. 23 (1967), p. 1 (8).

[1470] It strikes us as incorrect when the Commission, without any further motivation, takes the view that writings published by Catholics do not form religious reading for a Buddhist: Appl. 1753/63, *X* v. *Austria*, Yearbook VIII (1965), p. 174 (184).

[1471] Appl. 1753/63, *X* v. *Austria*, Yearbook VIII (1965), p. 174 (184).

[1472] Mentioned in: Council of Europe, *Case-Law Topics* No. 1, 'Human Rights in Prison', 1971, p. 31. *Cf.* Appl. 5947/72, *X* v. *the United Kingdom*, D&R 5 (1976), p. 8 (8-9).

[1473] From these decisions it may be gathered that the Commission gives a broader interpretation of this phrase than 'order in places accessible to everyone'.

[1474] Appl. 8231/78, *X* v. *the United Kingdom*, D&R 28 (1982), p. 5 (38).

[1475] *Ibidem*, pp. 26-27.

9.7 Derogation

Article 9 does not lists among the provisions included in the second paragraph of Article 15 as non-derogable. On this point the Convention differs from the UN Covenant on Civil and Political Rights, where in Article 4(2) the freedom of thought, conscience, and religion laid down in Article 18 is declared non-derogable. For those Contracting States, which are also parties to the UN Covenant on Civil and Political Rights, the prohibition to derogate from the obligation that is incumbent on them under Article 18 of the Covenant also applies under the Convention. In fact, Article 15(1) of the Convention provides that the measures taken by a State must not be 'inconsistent with its other obligations under international law', while Article 60 excludes any reference to the Convention which would have the effect of limiting or derogating from any obligation incumbent on the Contracting States under other conventions in the field of human rights.

In the foregoing a distinction was made between the right to freedom of thought, conscience and religion, on the one hand, and the freedom to express one's thoughts, conscience and religion, on the other hand.[1476] With respect to the former right it would seem doubtful whether even the derogations permitted under Article 15 could have any application here. On the one hand, a provision of the Convention cannot be brought under the special protection of the second paragraph of Article 15 if it is not expressly mentioned there, however desirable the incorporation of Article 9 into that provision *de lege ferenda* may be. On the other hand, even for those States which are not parties to the UN Covenant on Civil and Political Rights it will be extremely difficult, if not impossible, to make it plausible that any interference with the freedom of thought, conscience, and religion *per se* is 'strictly required by the exigencies of the situation' in the sense of Article 15(1). Precisely on a point where the European norm is lower than the universally accepted one, a very critical examination of that necessity by the national and Strasbourg organs would seem appropriate.

10 FREEDOM OF EXPRESSION (ARTICLE 10)

1. *Everyone has the right to freedom of expression. This right shall include freedom to hold opinions and to receive and impart information and ideas without interference by public authority and regardless of frontiers. This Article shall not prevent States from requiring the licensing of broadcasting, television or cinema enterprises.*
2. *The exercise of these freedoms, since it carries with it duties and responsibilities, may be subject to such formalities, conditions, restrictions or penalties as are prescribed by law and are necessary in a democratic society, in the interests of national security, territorial integrity or public safety, for the prevention of disorder or crime, for the protection of health or morals, for the protection of the reputation or rights of others, for preventing the disclosure of information received in confidence, or for maintaining the authority and impartiality of the judiciary.*

[1476] *Supra* pp. 541-542.

10.1 The Scope of Article 10

10.1.1 Introduction
With respect to the freedom of expression, as incorporated in Article 10 of the Convention, the Court held in the *Handyside* Case that it constitutes 'one of the essential foundations of a democratic society and one of the basic conditions for its progress.[1477] From this starting-point, which can be regarded as standing case-law,[1478] the Court has developed a broad interpretation of the right embodied in the first paragraph of Article 10, which can be invoked by natural and legal persons.[1479] With regard to the former it is irrelevant to the applicability of Article 10 whether they have a special status like servicemen[1480] or civil servants.[1481] However, the special status may be relevant under the second paragraph of Article 10.[1482]

As is expressly provided for in the first paragraph of Article 10, the freedom of expression includes 'the freedom to hold opinions and to receive and impart information and ideas'. The 'freedom to hold opinions' can hardly be distinguished from the 'freedom of thought' discussed under Article 9.[1483] The freedom to impart information can still be regarded as an expression of an opinion, of the informant himself or of a third person. The seeking of information, however, precedes the formation of an opinion by the person who seeks the information, and consequently also its expression.

The fact that Article 10 protects the free expression of opinions implies that a rather strong emphasis is laid on the protection of the specific means by which the opinion is expressed. Any restriction of the means will imply a restriction of the freedom 'to receive and impart information and ideas'.[1484] However, the means by which a particular opinion is expressed are protected only insofar as they are means which have an independent significance for the expression of the opinion.[1485] Even if the person who provides the means is not the holder of the

---

[1477] Judgment of 7 December 1976, A.24, p. 23.
[1478] Judgment of 8 July 1986, A.103, *Lingens*, p. 26; judgment of 23 May 1991, *Oberschlick*, A.204, p. 25; judgment of 23 April 1992, *Castells*, A.236, p. 22; judgment of 23 September 1994, *Jersild*, A.298, p. 23; judgment of 27 March 1996, *Goodwin*, Reports 1996-II, Vol. 7, para. 39. In the *Handyside* Case, the *Lingens* Case and the *Oberschlick* Case the Court also added that the freedom of expression is a basic condition for each individual's self-fulfilment. In subsequent judgments this phrase was lacking.
[1479] Judgment of 22 May 1990, *Autronic AG*, A.178, p. 23.
[1480] Judgment of 8 June 1976, *Engel and Others*, A.22, p. 41; judgment of 16 December 1992, *Hadjianastassiou*, A.252, p. 17; judgment of 19 December 1994, *Vereinigung Demokratischer Soldaten Österreichs and Gubi*, A.302, p. 14.
[1481] Judgment of 26 September 1995, *Vogt*, A.323, p. 22.
[1482] See *infra* pp. 575-579.
[1483] See *supra* pp. 541-542. The correspondence between Art. 9 and Art. 10 will be discussed in section 10.1.6.
[1484] Judgment of 22 May 1990, *Autronic AG*, A.178, p. 23. See also the judgment of 23 September 1994, *Jersild*, A.298, p. 23; judgment of 23 May 1991, *Oberschlick*, A.204, p. 25.
[1485] See in particular section 10.1.2.

opinion, he is protected by Article 10. Thus, in the *Müller* Case, the organisers of the exhibition of Mr Müller's paintings were considered to exercise their freedom of expression.[1486]

10.1.2 Freedom to Receive and Impart Information and Ideas; General
This section contains a general survey of the case-law concerning the freedom 'to receive and impart information and ideas'. Some special subjects will be discussed in sections 10.1.3-10.1.5.

The freedom 'to receive and impart information and ideas' has been frequently at issue before the Court. The Court has expressly refused to give a definition of these terms,[1487] but it is clear that the first paragraph of Article 10 offers a broad protection. The content of the expressions seems to be irrelevant. In many cases the Court has held, with reference to the demands of 'pluralism, tolerance and broad-mindedness without which there is no democratic society', that Article 10 is not only applicable to 'information' or 'ideas' 'that are favourable received or regarded as inoffensive or as a matter of indifference, but also to those that offend, shock or disturb'.[1488] The fact that the information concerned is of a commercial nature[1489] or that the freedom of expression is not exercised in a discussion of matters of public interest[1490] is also indifferent to the applicability of Article 10. Due to this approach the Court has been able to assess a wide range of cases.

In many cases concerning civil and criminal proceedings against journalists and other authors of (newspaper) articles,[1491] the Court has stressed the importance of the freedom of the press, which is essential to the concept of a democratic society. It is incumbent on the press, with regard to the print media as well as the audio-visual media,[1492] to impart information and ideas which the public has the right to receive. Otherwise, the press would not be able 'to play its vital role of public watchdog'.[1493] This approach is not only reflected in the case-law concerning the second paragraph discussed below, but also in the interpretation of the first paragraph. In the *Goodwin* Case a journalist received information about

---

[1486] Judgment of 24 May 1988, A.133, p. 19.
[1487] Judgment of 28 March 1990, *Groppera Radio AG and Others*, A.173, p. 22.
[1488] See, *e.g.*, the judgment of 7 December 1976, *Handyside*, A.24, p. 23; judgment of 26 November 1991, *The Observer and Guardian*, A.216, p. 30; judgment of 25 June 1992, *Thorgeir Thorgeirson*, A.239, p. 27; judgment of 26 April 1995, *Prager and Oberschlick*, A.313, p. 19.
[1489] Judgment of 20 November 1989, *Markt intern Verlag GmbH and Klaus Beermann*, A.165, p. 17; judgment of 24 February 1994, *Casado Coca*, A.285-A, p. 16.
[1490] Judgment of 23 June 1994, *Jacubowski*, A.291, p. 13.
[1491] See, *e.g.*, the judgment of 8 July 1986, *Lingens*, A.103; judgment of 23 April 1992, *Castells*, A.236; judgment of 25 June 1992, *Thorgeir Thorgeirson*, A.239; judgment of 26 April 1995, *Prager and Oberschlick*, A.313; judgment of 13 July 1995, *Tolstoy Miloslavsky*, A.316-B.
[1492] Judgment of 23 September 1994, *Jersild*, A.298, p. 23.
[1493] See, *e.g.*, the judgment of 26 November 1991, *The Observer and Guardian*, A.216, p. 30; judgment of 25 June 1992, *Thorgeir Thorgeirson*, A.239, p. 27; judgment of 23 September 1994, *Jersild*, A.298, p. 23.

the financial problems of a company. When he contacted the company to verify the facts, it appeared that the information had been derived from a confidential company report. These events eventually resulted in an injunction restraining the journalist (and the publishers he worked for) from publishing the information and a court order to disclose the identity of Goodwin's source. The Court held, undisputed by the British Government, that the disclosure order had to be examined under the second paragraph of Article 10 and thus took for granted that the protection of a journalistic source – in itself not an expression of an opinion – comes within the ambit of Article 10.[1494]

The question of whether freedom of expression implies the right of reply or rectification still has not been clarified.[1495] Such an interpretation seems to have been suggested by the Commission, but in the case concerned it did not reach a decision on this point, because in the Commission's opinion the arguments advanced constituted an insufficient ground for the decision that the accused State was responsible for the impugned publication by the daily papers.[1496] A complicating issue here is that of the *Drittwirkung* of Article 10[1497] and also that of the liability of the State – which is the only party against which a complaint may be brought in Strasbourg – for violation of Article 10 by private parties.[1498] Indeed, the publications involved will usually be due to a private party, and the publication of the reply or rectification will have to be effected in most cases by a private party as well. From Article 10 might then be derived an obligation on the part of the State to create a legal obligation to publish the reply or rectification and to provide for a judicial remedy, either on the ground of a civil claim to that effect or in combination with a criminal conviction for insult. Such an obligation of publication would not constitute an unlawful interference with the freedom of expression laid down in Article 10 for the person on whom it would be imposed, since the justification might be found in the restriction ground 'protection of the reputation or rights of others'.

In the *Müller* Case, which concerned the conviction for having published obscene material and the confiscation of paintings, the Court concluded that the freedom of artistic expression of a painter, although not mentioned expressly, is also covered by Article 10.[1499] Other remarkable cases concern, *inter alia*, the complaint about the conviction of a publisher for having in his possession copies

---

[1494] Judgment of 27 March 1996, Reports 1996-II, Vol. 7, para. 28.
[1495] Within the framework of the UN a special convention was concluded on this in 1953: the Convention on the International Right of Correction, 435 UNTS, p. 191.
[1496] Appl. 1906/63, *X* v. *Belgium* (not published).
[1497] On *Drittwirkung*, see *supra* pp. 22-26.
[1498] In the case of Appl. 4515/70, *X and the Association of Z* v. *the United Kingdom*, Coll. 38 (1972), p. 86 (88), which concerned complaints about the BBC, the Commission expressly left the question of State liability open. See, however, Appl. 6586/74, *X* v. *Ireland* (not published), where the Commission took the view that the restraint upon staff expressing their views is a common feature of many working situations arising from the relationships of the people concerned and not from written regulations for which the State could be held responsible.
[1499] Judgment of 24 May 1988, A.133, p. 19.

of the 'Little Red School Book', and their destruction as pornography;[1500] the injunction of the Irish Supreme Court restraining companies from giving information to pregnant women about the possibility to obtain abortion abroad;[1501] the seizure and subsequent forfeiture of a film;[1502] the refusal of the competent authorities to add a magazine to the list of periodicals distributed by the Austrian army,[1503] and the amount of damages awarded by a court for libel.[1504] In the *Groppera AG and Others* Case the Court held with reference to the third sentence of the first paragraph that broadcasting of programmes over the air and cable retransmissions of such programmes also come within the ambit of Article 10,[1505] while the same holds good for the (im)possibility to set up a radio or television station.[1506] However, according to the Commission, the right to impart and distribute information does not include a general and unfettered right to have access to broadcasting time on radio or TV.[1507] This stands to reason, just as it does not imply a right to have one's information inserted in a daily or weekly paper. However, the Commission has rightly added that certain circumstances may occur in which the barring of a specific person or group may result in a violation of Article 10, either in combination with Article 14 or by itself.[1508]

In its report in *De Geïllustreerde Pers* v. *the Netherlands* the Commission distinguished between 'information' and 'ideas'. A publisher claimed that Article 22 of the Dutch Broadcasting Act, which prohibited publication of radio and television programmes in any other way than on behalf or by authorisation of the NOS – the Netherlands Broadcasting Foundation – was contrary to Article 10 of the Convention. In the case of information, according to the Commission, the only one who has the right of free distribution of that information is the party who is 'the author, the originator or otherwise the intellectual owner' of the information in question.[1509] The publisher, therefore, did have a protected right to publish the programmes if he himself had drawn up a survey of them by means of information which he had sought from the individual broadcasting licensees, but no right to copy the survey coordinated by the NOS. The Commission did not

---

[1500] Judgment of 7 December 1976, *Handyside*, A.24.

[1501] Judgment of 29 October 1992, *Open Door and Dublin Well Woman*, A.246-A.

[1502] Judgment of 20 September 1994, *Otto-Preminger-Institut*, A.295-A. See also the report of the Commission of 14 January 1993, *Scherer* Case, A.287, pp. 17-20.

[1503] Judgment of 19 December 1994, *Vereinigung Demokratischer Soldaten Österreichs and Gubi*, A.302.

[1504] Judgment of 13 July 1995, *Tolstoy Miloslavsky*, A.316-B.

[1505] Judgment of 28 March 1990, A.173, p. 22. See also Appl. 8962/80, *X and Y* v. *Belgium*, D&R 28 (1982), p. 112 (124), where the Commission held that a conviction for having used a transceiver for private purposes without the required authorisation constituted an interference with the right to receive and impart information and ideas.

[1506] Judgment of 24 November 1993, *Informationsverein Lentia and Others*, A.276, p. 13.

[1507] Appl. 4515/70, *X and Association of Z* v. *the United Kingdom*, Coll. 38 (1972), p. 86 (88).

[1508] *Idem.*

[1509] Report of 6 July 1976, D&R 8 (1977), p. 5 (13).

elaborate on the question what rule applies with respect to the distribution of ideas. Its reasoning seems to imply, however, freedom of such distribution irrespective of the source from which those ideas are derived, subject to such limitations as are prescribed by law in conformity with the second paragraph. This distinction would seem rather far-fetched to us and is not corroborated by the text of Article 10. In fact, the Commission seems to disregard altogether the words 'to receive (...) information'. These words indicate that the collection of information from any source whatever should in principle be free, although restrictions can be made under paragraph 2. In our view, therefore, the Commission should have found that the restriction imposed upon the publisher was contrary to the first paragraph of Article 10, and subsequently should have ascertained whether this restriction was justified on the basis of one or more of the restrictions of the second paragraph, in particular the one of 'protection of the (...) rights of others'.

When a parliamentarian complained about the fact that a motion proposed by him had not been placed on the agenda, and invoked Article 10 for this, his complaint was declared inadmissible by the Commission.[1510] The Commission gave no further motivation for its decision. In our opinion that motivation might have been that the procedural decision about which the parliamentarian complained formed part of the very means which he wished to use for the expression of his opinion: Parliament.

In *Agee v. the United Kingdom*, a former CIA agent claimed that his expulsion from England was contrary, *inter alia*, to Article 10, because his opportunity to exercise the right conferred therein was restricted by the expulsion. The Commission took the position that the right to stay in a country and the right to freedom of expression have to be distinguished.[1511] Abode in a country does not constitute an independent means or independent condition for the expression of one's opinion, unless it were to be firmly established that no other country is to be found in which that particular opinion may be put forward. In the latter case, the expelling country is responsible for that situation abroad; it may then only proceed to expel the person concerned on grounds mentioned in the second paragraph. However, as the *Piermont* Case shows, an expulsion order may also come within the ambit of Article 10 if the expulsion order is specifically aimed at the restriction of the freedom of expression. This case concerned an order directing the expulsion of the applicant from the French Polynesia territory and a ban on re-entering as well as an order prohibiting her to enter the territory of New-Caledonia. Mrs Piermont had taken part in a demonstration on the territory of French Polynesia in favour of the independence of French Polynesia and during that demonstration had made a speech in which she supported the anti-nuclear and independence positions of some of the local political parties. The orders in question had been imposed by the French authorities and had the clear intention to prevent Mrs Piermont from supporting publicly the opposition against the

---

[1510] Appl. 7758/77, *X* v. *Switzerland*, D&R 9 (1978), p. 214 (218).
[1511] Appl. 7729/76, D&R 7 (1976), p. 164 (174).

French authorities in French Polynesia and New-Caledonia. According to the Court, the expulsion order coupled with the prohibition to re-enter French Polynesia as well as the ban on entering New-Caledonia constituted an interference with the freedom of expression.[1512]

Relatively new means to provide and receive information, for instance internet, are increasingly important. Since the case-law attributes to the first paragraph of Article 10 a broad protection, one may expect that these new means, as far as they have an independent significance for the expression of opinions, will also come within the ambit of Article 10.

10.1.3 Legal Requirements for Employment

In general Article 10 does not prohibit making access to certain professions subject to regulations, not even when the exercise of those professions consists mainly in the expression of opinions. For the person in question access to such a profession as a rule does not in itself form a means which has an independent significance for expressing a specific opinion; the normal channels for doing this are not cut off or restricted if he is not admitted to that profession. Only if a person wishes to exercise a profession or start an enterprise precisely in order to be able to express his opinion in a certain way or by certain means – one might think of a publisher publishing manuscripts which may be assumed not to be accepted elsewhere or of a publisher who wishes to start a periodical of a specific character – is Article 10 at issue and can the person concerned be considered a direct or indirect victim of the violation of that article in case the possibilities to exercise the profession or start the enterprise are restricted by certain regulations. In the *De Becker* Case, in which the Commission concluded that Article 10 had been violated, the penal sanctions imposed on De Becker also comprised the prohibition to exercise the profession of publisher. However, it cannot be clearly inferred from the words which the Commission used in referring to these sanctions, *viz.* 'insofar as they affect freedom of expression',[1513] whether the Commission considered this part of the prohibition also to constitute a violation.

If the legal requirements for appointment on a certain post themselves concern the freedom of opinion or expression, Article 10 is applicable. The Commission took that position in the *Kosiek* Case and the *Glasenapp* Case, both concerning teaching jobs. Mr Kosiek was an active member of the National Democratic Party of Germany and Mrs Glasenapp was alleged to support the policies of the Communist Party of Germany. The Commission took the view that the provision of the German Civil Servants Act, prescribing that every civil servant owed an obligation of loyalty and allegiance to the Constitution as a condition for

---

[1512] Judgment of 27 April 1995, A.314, p. 22 and p. 27. With regard to the ban on entering New-Caledonia the Commission had reached a different conclusion; report of 20 January 1994, A.314, pp. 46-47.

[1513] Report of 8 January 1960, B.2 (1962), p. 11 (128). The Court struck the case off the list on account of an interim adaptation of the Belgian legislation: judgment of 27 March 1962, A.4, pp. 23-27.

appointment and for continued employment in the civil service, directly circumscribed and impinged upon the right guaranteed by Article 10(1).[1514] Both cases were referred to the Court, which first dealt with the Government's argument that the cases concerned the right – not guaranteed under the Convention – of access to a post in the civil service, and not Article 10 of the Convention. With respect to Mrs Glasenapp, the Court noted that under the Land Civil Servants Act the applicant could only become a secondary school teacher with the status of probationary civil servant, if she afforded a guarantee that she would consistently uphold the free democratic constitutional system within the meaning of the Basic Law. This requirement, according to the Court, 'applies to recruitment to the civil service, a matter that was deliberately omitted from the Convention, and it cannot in itself be considered incompatible with the Convention.'[1515] In relation to Mr Kosiek the Court adopted a comparable reasoning.[1516] In both cases the Court came to the conclusion that in the light of the facts of each case access to the civil service lay at the heart of the issue submitted to it. In refusing such access, the authority took account of the applicants' opinions and attitude merely in order to satisfy itself as to whether they possessed one of the necessary personal qualifications for the post in question. There was, therefore, in the Court's view no interference with the exercise of the right protected in paragraph 1 of Article 10.[1517] The most recent case on this matter is the *Vogt* Case, which concerned the dismissal of a teacher from the civil service because of her political activities on behalf of the German Communist Party. The Court held Article 10 to be applicable because 'civil servants do not fall outside the scope of the Convention' but, nevertheless, stuck to its point of view in the *Kosiek* Case and *Glasenapp* Case by stressing that the *Vogt* Case did not concern the right to recruitment to the civil service.[1518] In our opinion, the Court should have followed the opinion of the Commission in the *Kosiek* Case and *Glasenapp* Case. Not the intended purpose of a certain regulation and its application, but their effects on the freedom of expression of the person concerned are decisive for the question whether Article 10 is applicable. In the *Kosiek* Case and *Glasenapp* Case it was evident that the applicants could have access to the desired posts only by accepting certain restrictions on their freedom of expression. Consequently, the Court should have examined whether these resulting restrictions were justified under paragraph 2 of Article 10.[1519]

[1514] Reports of 11 May 1984, A.105 and A.104, p. 32 and p. 39 respectively.
[1515] Judgment of 28 August 1986, A.104, pp. 26-27.
[1516] Judgment of 28 August 1986, A.105, p. 21.
[1517] *Ibidem*, pp. 27 and 21 respectively. See also the judgment of 26 March 1987, *Leander*, A.116, p. 28.
[1518] Judgment of 26 September 1995, A.323, p. 23.
[1519] This criticism holds good also for the judgment of 26 March 1987, *Leander*, A.116.

10.1.4 The Right to Remain Silent

The freedom of expression entails the right not to express oneself. In the *Young, James and Webster* Case a connection was made by the Commission and the Court between compulsory membership of a trade union and Article 10: as a result of that compulsory membership the employee in question is no longer free to dissent from a view propagated by the trade union.[1520] The Commission took the same approach in *K* v. *Austria* where it held Article 10 to be applicable to a person who refused to give evidence.[1521] In this case the Commission held that forcing the applicant to testify against his will constituted an interference with the negative aspect of his right to freedom of expression; his right to remain silent.

10.1.5 Obligations on the Part of the Authorities

It is still not clear whether – and if so, to what extent – the freedom to receive information entails an obligation on the part of the authorities to impart information. At first sight the judgment in the *Leander* Case gives an answer in the negative. The competent authorities refused to appoint Mr Leander as a museum technician at the Naval Museum, adjacent to a Naval base, on the basis of secret information. With regard to the refusal to reveal the information to the applicant the Court held that:

> the right to freedom to receive information basically prohibits a Government from restricting a person from receiving information that others wish or may be willing to impart to him. Article 10 does not, in circumstances such as those of the present case, confer on the individual a right of access to a register containing information on his personal position, nor does it embody an obligation on the Government to impart such information to the individual.[1522]

In the *Gaskin* Case, which concerned the failure to grant a person unimpeded access to his case record which had been drawn up while he was in child-care, the Court reached the same conclusion.[1523] However, the considerations of the Court are expressly based on the specific circumstances of the case and moreover the Court uses the word 'basically' (*'essentiellement'* in the French text). Therefore, there still seems to be some room to argue that the freedom of expression may entail a duty on the part of the authorities to impart information of public interest. An interpretation to that effect is laid down in a resolution of the Consultative (Parliamentary) Assembly of the Council of Europe, a document which is not legally binding, but which may be taken to indicate a trend in the legal opinion within the Contracting States or some of them. This resolution sets forth with respect to the right to freedom of expression:

[1520] Report of 14 December 1979, B.39 (1984), p. 48; judgment of 13 August 1981, A.44, pp. 23-24.
[1521] Report of 13 October 1992, A.255-B, p. 38. See also *supra* p. 353.
[1522] Judgment of 26 March 1987, A.116, p. 29.
[1523] Judgment of 7 July 1989, A.160, p. 21.

> This right shall include freedom to seek, receive, impart, publish and distribute information and ideas. There shall be a corresponding duty for the public authorities to make available information on matters of public interest within reasonable limits and a duty for mass communication media to give complete and general information on public affairs.[1524]

A comparable matter concerns the question of whether the right to receive information calls for pluriformity in imparting information, which then has to be guaranteed by the authorities, for instance by making grants to persons and institutions imparting information, where this is necessary for such pluriformity.[1525] In *Vereinigung Demokratischer Soldaten Österreichs and Gubi* v. *Austria* the Austrian army had been distributing free of charge its own publications and publications of private associations of soldiers in all the country's barracks, but had refused to distribute *der Igel*, a magazine published by the first applicant. The Court held that this difference in treatment considerably reduced the chances of *der Igel* to increase its readership among service personnel and constituted a violation of Article 10.[1526] Having regard to this judgment and the fact that the Commission and the Court regard pluralism of particular importance as far as the press is concerned,[1527] it is in any case evident that the authorities, once they proceed to subsidise or in any other way support persons and institutions imparting information, have the duty to do so without discrimination.

10.1.6 Freedom of Expression and Other Convention Rights

Article 10 has often been invoked in close connection with other articles of the Convention.

In *K* v. *Austria* the applicability of Article 10 and Article 6 coincided. The applicant claimed that his obligation to testify in a criminal procedure implied an obligation to testify against himself, contrary to Article 6,[1528] and that the imposition of a fine and detention for his refusal to give evidence constituted a breach of Article 10. In deciding whether the interference of Article 10 could be regarded as 'necessary' the Commission took into account the principle of a fair trial embodied in Article 6. It concluded that there had been a violation of Article

---

[1524] Res. 428(1970), Council of Europe, Cons. Ass., Twenty-First Ordinary Session (Third Part), 22-30 January 1970, *Texts Adopted.*

[1525] In its decision on Appl. 6452/74, *Sacchi* v. *Italy*, D&R 5 (1976), p. 43 (50), the Commission held as regards its previously given opinion that Art. 10(1) does not rule out a government monopoly for TV broadcasts: 'the Commission would not now be prepared purely and simply to maintain this point of view without further consideration'. However, it did not answer the question.

[1526] Judgment of 19 December 1994, A.302, pp. 17-18.

[1527] See, *e.g.*, the report of 30 September 1975, *Handyside*, B.22 (1976), p. 45 and the judgment of 7 December 1976 in this case, A.24, p. 23; judgment of 24 November 1993, *Informationsverein Lentia and Others*, A.276, p. 16.

[1528] See also *supra* p. 436.

10 and that, therefore, it was unnecessary to consider the complaint under Article 6 separately.[1529]

Since correspondence, telephone and similar means of communication, protected in Article 8, also constitute means for the expression of an opinion, there is a close connection between that article and Article 10. This connection was put forward in the *Silver* Case, which concerned the right of detainees to respect for their correspondence. Both Commission and Court took the view that in the examination of the complaints with respect to Article 8 the freedom of expression *via* correspondence had already been dealt with at such length that a separate examination with regard to Article 10 was not necessary.[1530] However, in the subsequent *McCallum* Case, also concerning the correspondence of a detainee, the Commission took a somewhat different approach by stating that 'where interference is alleged in the communication of information by correspondence, Article 8 is the *lex specialis* and no separate issues arise under Article 10'.[1531] This appears to us too general a statement, since the aim of the two articles is not identical: in Article 8 the main point is the protection of the private character of the means of communication referred to, while in Article 10 its character as a means of expressing an opinion and of providing and receiving information is at issue.

A remarkable decision of the Commission is the one in which a complaint concerning Article 10 by a prisoner convicted for homosexual practices was declared admissible. The applicant had claimed, *inter alia*, that his right to express feelings of love for other men was interfered with by his detention. The Commission held with respect to this 'that there may be an issue under Article 10 regarding his (...) claim that the fact of imprisonment denied him his right to express feelings of love for other men'.[1532] While in the *Brüggemann and Scheuten* Case sexual intercourse had been brought under Article 8,[1533] in *X* v. *the United Kingdom* thus the possibility of a connection with Article 10 was left open. In its report on the merits of the latter case, however, the Commission took the position, on the ground of the text of paragraph 2, that:

[1529] Report of 13 October 1992, A.255-B, pp. 37-39. Strictly speaking the Commission concluded (p. 39) that Art. 6 had not been violated, but this conclusion would seem to be inaccurate since it cannot be deduced from the preceding arguments. Due to a friendly settlement the case was struck off the list by the Court, judgment of 2 June 1993, A.255-B.

[1530] Report of 11 October 1980, B.51 (1987), p. 99; judgment of 25 March 1983, A.61, p. 41. See also the judgment of 20 June 1988, *Schönenberger and Durmaz*, A.137, p. 23.

[1531] Report of 4 May 1989, A.183, p. 25. The claim under Art. 10 was not pursued before the Court. The Commission took the same position in Appl. 8383/78, *X* v. *Federal Republic of Germany*, D&R 17 (1980), p. 227 (228-229).

[1532] Appl. 7215/75, *X* v. *the United Kingdom*, Yearbook XXI (1978), p. 354 (374).

[1533] See *supra* p. 498.

the concept of 'expression' in Art. 10 concerns mainly the expression of opinion and receiving and imparting information and ideas (...). It does not encompass any notion of the physical expression of feelings in the sense submitted by the applicant.[1534]

In the *Crémieux* Case the Commission rejected the claim of the applicant that the seizure of private correspondence at his home was contrary to Article 8 and Article 10 of the Convention. With regard to Article 8, the Commission found the infringement to be justified under the second paragraph. With regard to Article 10, however, the reasoning was rather concise and poor. The Commission just stated that it failed to see how there could have been an infringement.[1535] A remarkable example of imparting information was involved in a case where two persons complained that during a 45 hour detention they had been prevented from contacting their wives. The Commission declared the total of the complaints admissible, on account of their complexity.[1536] In its report the Commission dealt with this complaint in conjunction with Article 8. After having found a breach of Article 8, it considered it unnecessary to decide the issue under Article 10.[1537]

The freedom of expression is closely related to the freedom of thought, conscience and religion in Article 9 of the Convention. This is the more so to the extent that in the case of the freedom of expression emphasis is laid upon the *content* of the opinion expressed. This does not alter the fact that Article 10 has a wider scope than Article 9. While for the applicability of Article 9 it is required that the opinion which is expressed reflects the conviction of the person who puts this opinion forward,[1538] Article 10 envisages the protection of every expression of an opinion, be it that the measure of protection may vary according to the nature of the opinion expressed.[1539]

There is also a close connection between Article 10 and the freedom of assembly protected in Article 11. In the *Ezelin* Case, concerning a disciplinary penalty imposed on a lawyer because he had participated in a demonstration in which protests were made against judicial decisions and had refused to give evidence to the investigating judge, the Court held that 'the protection of opinions, secured by Article 10, is one of the objectives of freedom of peaceful assembly and freedom of expression as enshrined in Article 11'.[1540] Articles 10 and 11 will both be applicable in those situations where several persons jointly express

---

[1534] Report of 12 October 1978, D&R 19 (1980), p. 66 (80). The conclusions of the report were adopted by the Committee of Ministers in Res. DH(79)5 of 12 June 1979.
[1535] Report of 8 October 1991, A.256-B, p. 73. In the judgment of 25 February 1993, A.256-B, pp. 59-63, the Court concluded that there had been a breach of Art. 8 and deemed it unnecessary to consider Art. 10 separately.
[1536] Appls 8022, 8025 and 8027/77, *X, Y and Z v. the United Kingdom*, D&R 18 (1980), p. 66 (76).
[1537] Report of 18 March 1981, *McVeigh, O'Neill and Evans*, D&R 25 (1982), p. 15 (53).
[1538] Report of 12 October 1978, *Arrowsmith*, D&R 19 (1980), p. 5 (19-20).
[1539] See *infra* pp. 573-575.
[1540] Judgment of 26 April 1991, A.202, p. 20. See also the judgment of 26 September 1995, *Vogt*, A.323, p. 30.

a given opinion. Thus, a demonstration always constitutes an expression of opinion, even if it has the character of a silent procession; at the same time there is an assembly. This overlap need not, however, give rise to problems in practice, since the restrictions on the two rights partly coincide, while the specific restrictions of Article 10 clearly refer to the opinion expressed, and not to the question of whether it has been expressed by one person or by several persons jointly. The approach of the Court on this point seems to differ from case to case. In the *Ezelin* Case the Court held that in the circumstances of the case Article 11 should be regarded as a *lex specialis* in relation to Article 10.[1541] In the *Sigurdur A. Sigurjónsson* Case, however, in which the compulsive membership of a organisation for taxicab operators was at stake, the Court concluded that there had been a violation of Article 11 and that there was no need to consider whether there had also been breaches of Articles 9 and 10.[1542] Finally, in the *Vogt* Case the Court took the position that the dismissal of a teacher from civil service because of her political activities on behalf of the German Communist Party amounted to a breach of Articles 10 and 11. With regard to the latter article the Court based its decision in particular on the arguments adduced with regard to Article 10.[1543]

The emphasis on the question whether the means of expression have an independent significance may delimit the applicability of Article 10 *vis-à-vis* other freedoms, which are related to the possibility to express specific opinions, but cannot be considered as means which have an independent significance apart from other means available to the person concerned. Thus, in the *Belgian Linguistic* Case the Commission rightly took the position that freedom of expression does not comprise the right to be offered the opportunity to express one's opinion in a language of one's choice, the consequence of which would be the right to being taught that language.[1544] Here Article 2 of Protocol No. 1 is at issue, not Article 10. This would only be otherwise if, for instance, an alien were denied access to being taught the vernacular or if the required facilities for this were not provided, since he would then be deprived of an independent means of expression: expression in a locally understood language. However, in such a case, too, it would seem to make more sense to invoke Article 2 of Protocol No. 1.

That the right to vote is not protected by Article 10 is established case-law of the Commission.[1545] No arguments are given for this. It can hardly be denied that taking part in elections is a form of expressing an opinion. Article 3 of Protocol No. 1 refers to 'the free expression of the opinion of the people'. Nor can

---

[1541] Judgment of 26 April 1991, A.202, p. 20.
[1542] Judgment of 30 June 1990, A.264, p. 42. See also the judgment of 13 August 1981, *Young, James and Webster*, A.44, p. 26.
[1543] Judgment of 26 September 1995, A.323, p. 31.
[1544] Appl. 1474/62, *Belgian Linguistic* Case, Yearbook VI (1963), p. 332 (342); Appl. 1769/62, *X* v. *Belgium*, Yearbook VI (1963), p. 444 (454-456).
[1545] See, *e.g.*, Appl. 6573/74, *X* v. *the Netherlands*, D&R 1 (1975), p. 87 (89) and Appl. 6850/74, *Association X, Y and Z* v. *Federal Republic of Germany*, D&R 5 (1976), p. 90 (93).

it be subject to doubt that it forms a means for the expression of that opinion which has an independent character. On the other hand, however, it seems logical to assume that the drafters of Article 10 did not intend to include the right to vote. This may be inferred from the incorporation of a specific provision concerning elections into Protocol No. 1. The duty to vote is not in violation of Article 10 – nor of Article 9 – as long as the secret character is guaranteed; in that case the person concerned is free to express any opinion or no opinion at all.

10.1.7 Regardless of Frontiers

The words 'regardless of frontiers' in the first paragraph of Article 10 indicate that the authorities must also admit information from beyond the frontiers of the country and allow the imparting of information from across those frontiers, subject, of course, to the possibilities laid down in the second paragraph.[1546] This does not, of course, offer a guarantee that such information is not held back outside the frontiers, since the State bears no responsibility for measures taken to that effect abroad.[1547]

10.2 Restriction of the Freedom of Expression

10.2.1 Introduction

Besides restrictions, the second paragraph of Article 10 also mentions formalities, conditions and penalties as measures to which the freedoms of the first paragraph may be subjected. At first sight it is remarkable that precisely with respect to the right to freedom of expression, to which the Western democracies attach such great value, the restrictions are formulated more broadly than with respect to other rights and freedoms. However, in practice this broad formulation is of little impact. The imposition of conditions or formalities in fact also amounts to restrictions, while on the other hand the failure to observe a restriction prescribed by law will also be subject to a sanction in most cases. It does not matter much, therefore, whether the complaint is directed against the application of the legal norm restricting the exercise of the freedom or against the penalty imposed because of the violation of that norm. Indeed, the restriction implied in the imposition of a penalty must also not serve the mere purpose of a retaliation, but should be intended to protect the interests enumerated in paragraph 2.

Article 10 guarantees the freedom of expression 'without interference by public authority'. In the *Casado Coca* Case the Spanish Government tried to escape from its responsibility by submitting that the disciplinary penalty imposed on a member of the Bar for contravening the ban on advertising, had been imposed by the

---

[1546] Judgment of 28 March 1990, *Groppera Radio AG and Others*, A.173 and the judgment of 22 May 1990, *Autronic AG*, A.178, concerned the imparting and receiving of information from abroad.

[1547] Appl. 7597/76, *Bertrand Russell Peace Foundation Ltd.* v. *the United Kingdom*, D&R 14 (1979), p. 117 (124).

Barcelona Bar Council and, therefore, not by a 'public authority'. This argument was rejected by the Court. It held that, according to Spanish law, the Bar Council was a public law corporation, that the Bar served the public interest and, moreover, that the penalty had been upheld by the Spanish courts, which are State institutions.[1548]

The Court has taken the position that the exceptions to the freedom of expression 'must be narrowly interpreted and the necessity for any restrictions must be convincingly established'.[1549] Preventive restraints on publications, as such not incompatible with Article 10, call for the most strict supervision of the Strasbourg organs since, even if they are temporary, they may deprive the information to be published from all its interests.[1550] The strict supervision of preventive restraints is also reflected in those cases where the Court held that the intended purpose of the ban on publication, the prevention of the disclosure of information, could no longer justify the prohibition because the information had already become public from another source.[1551]

In assessing whether an infringement of the first paragraph has been 'necessary' the Court has referred often to the 'duties and responsibilities' mentioned in the second paragraph of Article 10 of those who exercise the freedom of expression. This concept will be discussed in section 10.2.4.

The interests enumerated in the second paragraph are not identical to the interests mentioned in the Articles 8, 9 and 11 of the Convention. Therefore, three of the aims laid down in the second paragraph of Article 10 deserve special attention: 'territorial integrity', 'preventing the disclosure of information received in confidence' and 'maintaining the authority and impartiality of the judiciary'.

The 'freedom to hold opinions', mentioned separately in Article 10, can hardly be distinguished from the 'freedom of thought' provided for in Article 9.[1552] As has been stated with regard to Article 9, here again it is submitted that the restrictions mentioned in the second paragraph should not be applied to this 'freedom to hold opinions'.[1553]

Here only special elements of the restrictions of Article 10(2) and important case-law concerning this provision will be discussed. For the remainder, the second paragraph has been covered by the general section on restrictions.[1554]

[1548] Judgment of 24 February 1994, A.285-A, p. 17.
[1549] Judgment of 26 November 1991, *The Observer and Guardian*, A.216, p. 30.
[1550] Judgments of 26 November 1991, *The Observer and Guardian*, A.216, and *The Sunday Times (No. 2)*, A.217, p. 30 and pp. 29-30 respectively.
[1551] *Ibidem*, pp. 33-35 and pp. 30-31 respectively. See also the judgment of 22 May 1990, *Weber*, A.177, p. 23 *juncto* p. 9; judgment of 9 February 1990, *Bluf*, A.306-A, p. 16.
[1552] See *supra* pp. 541-542.
[1553] Thus also the Report of the Committee of Experts, *supra* note 11, p. 45, with the argument that 'any restrictions on this right would be inconsistent with the nature of a democratic society'.
[1554] *Infra* pp. 761-773.

10.2.2 Facts and Value-Judgments

The *Lingens* Case concerned criminal proceedings instigated by the former Austrian Chancellor, Mr Kreisky, in which the applicant, a journalist, was convicted for public defamation. The Government relied on the 'protection of the reputation of others' as a ground to justify the conviction. According to the Court, the penalty imposed on Mr Lingens amounted to a kind of censure, which would be likely to discourage him from making criticism of that kind again in the future. In the political field such a sanction was liable to hamper the press in performing its task as purveyor of information and as public watchdog. The Court subsequently examined the judicial decisions at issue. The passages held against Mr Lingens were value-judgments, so that his freedom of opinion and his right to impart ideas had been at issue. As regards value-judgments, the requirement to prove the truth of the statements in order to escape conviction is an impossible one, according to the Court.

> In the Court's view, a careful distinction needs to be made between facts and value-judgments. The existence of facts can be demonstrated, whereas the truth of value-judgments is not susceptible of proof. The Court notes in this connection that the facts on which Mr. Lingens founded his value-judgments were undisputed, as was also his good faith.[1555]

Finally, the Court concluded, like the Commission, that the interference on Mr Lingens' freedom of expression was not necessary for the protection of the reputation of others.[1556]

The distinction between facts and value-judgments, which is standing case-law, may be crucial to the question whether Article 10 has been violated. Thus, it is of great importance that the Commission and the Court are willing to assess whether the classification of the arguments as facts or as value-judgments by the national authorities is correct. Fortunately the Strasbourg supervision appears to be rather strict on this point.[1557] Accordingly, the question whether statements made by the person who exercises his freedom of expression have an objective and factual basis does not escape from the Strasbourg review.[1558] In the *Castells* Case the offer by the applicant to prove that his statements about the alleged involvement of the Government in murders in Basque Country were true, had been refused by the national courts. According to the Court, the impossibility to 'plead the defences of truth and good faith' amounted to a breach of Article 10.[1559]

An exception to the strict Strasbourg control seems to occur if the maintenance of the 'authority of the judiciary' has been relied on to justify a restriction. In the *Prager and Oberschlick* Case the Court took the classification as facts or as value-

---

[1555] Judgment of 8 July 1986, A.103, p. 28.
[1556] *Idem.*
[1557] See, *inter alia*, the judgment of 23 May 1991, *Oberschlick*, A.204, p. 27; judgment of 28 August 1992, *Schwabe*, A.242-B, p. 34.
[1558] Judgment of 25 June 1992, *Thorgeir Thorgeirson*, A.239, pp. 27-28.
[1559] Judgment of 23 April 1992, A.236, p. 24.

judgments made by the national authorities for granted.[1560] In our opinion, there are no good reasons for this reserved approach.

10.2.3 The Subject and Content of the Expression

The Strasbourg organs attach great importance to the freedom of the press.[1561] It is the task of the press 'to impart information and ideas on political issues just as on those in other areas of public interest.'[1562] This emphasis on the public interest is reflected in the case-law concerning the restrictions on the freedom of expression. In the *Lingens* Case the Court stressed the importance of the 'freedom of political debate', which is 'at the very core of the concept of a democratic society', and then held that:

> The limits of acceptable criticism are accordingly wider as regards a politician as such than as regards a private individual. Unlike the latter, the former inevitably and knowingly lays himself open to close scrutiny of his every word and deed by both journalists and the public at large, and he must consequently display a greater degree of tolerance.[1563]

In the *Castells* Case the Court introduced a further refinement where it held that the bounds of permissible criticism are even wider with regard to the Government than in relation to a politician.[1564] Moreover, it set forth that the freedom of expression is especially important for an elected representative of the people and that, therefore 'interferences with the freedom of expression of an opposition Member of Parliament call for the closest scrutiny on the part of the Court.'[1565] The press enjoys a considerable freedom with regard to the methods of reporting. In the *Jersild* Case the Court even concluded that the Court and the national courts are not entitled 'to substitute their own views for those of the press as to what technique of reporting should be adopted by journalists.'[1566] However, the scope of the words 'technique of reporting' should not be taken too broad. In the subsequent *Prager and Oberschlick* Case the Court criticised a journalist because he had not undertaken adequate research.[1567] In case the allegations that have been made by a journalist are very serious, the journalist may be obliged to give the person concerned the possibility to comment on the accusations.[1568]

[1560] Judgment of 26 April 1995, A.313, p. 18.

[1561] See *supra* section 10.1.2.

[1562] Judgment of 8 July 1986, *Lingens*, A.103, p. 26. See also the judgment of 23 May 1991, *Oberschlick*, A.204, p. 25; judgment of 23 April 1992, *Castells*, A.236, p. 23; judgment of 25 June 1992, *Thorgeir Thorgeirson*, A.239, p. 27; judgment of 23 September 1994, *Jersild*, A.298, p. 23. The wording in these cases is not fully identical.

[1563] Judgment of 8 July 1986, A.103, p. 26.

[1564] Judgment of 23 April 1992, A.236, p. 23.

[1565] *Idem.* See also the judgment of 27 April 1995, *Piermont*, A.314, p. 26.

[1566] Judgment of 23 September 1994, A.298, p. 23.

[1567] Judgment of 26 April 1995, A.313, pp. 18-19.

[1568] *Idem.*

The case-law mentioned in this subsection so far concerned 'information and ideas' on issues of public interest. The *Markt Intern Verlag and Klaus Beerman* Case concerned the question of freedom of the press in business matters. The applicants, a publishing company and its editor, had reported on a dissatisfied client of a mail-order firm. The mail-order firm obtained an injunction, prohibiting publication of the report. According to the Court, the contested article did not directly concern the public as a whole and contained information of a commercial nature.[1569] This conclusion appeared to be relevant with regard to the margin of appreciation of the national authorities. The Court held that:

> Such a margin (...) is essential in commercial matters and, in particular, in an area as complex and fluctuating as that of unfair competition. Otherwise, the European Court of Human Rights would have to undertake a re-examination of the facts and all the circumstances of each case. The Court must confine its review to the question whether the measures taken on the national level are justifiable in principle and proportionate.[1570]

From this point of view the Court reached the conclusion – by nine votes to nine, with the casting vote of the President – that the requirements of the protection of 'rights of others' carried more weight than the publication of the information concerned.[1571] In the *Casado Coca* Case a member of the Spanish bar complained about the disciplinary penalty that had been imposed on him for breaching the prohibition of commercial advertising. The approach of the Court in assessing whether the penalty was 'necessary' in the interests of 'the protection of the (...) rights of others' would seem to be a bit ambiguous. On the one hand the Court reiterated its wording from the *Markt Intern Verlag and Klaus Beerman* Case, just quoted, thus leaving a broad margin of appreciation to the national authorities. On the other hand it held that 'in some contexts, the publication of even objective, truthful advertisements might be restricted (...) Any such restrictions must, however, be closely scrutinised by the Court.'[1572] Finally, the Court referred to the differences that exist between the regulations in the Contracting States and concluded that the national authorities were in a better position to determine the right balance between the various interests concerned.[1573]

The *Jacubowski* Case concerned the prohibition to distribute a circular under the Unfair Competition Act. The supervision of the Court with regard to the question whether the interference of the first paragraph of Article 10 was

---

[1569] Judgment of 20 November 1989, A.165, p. 17.
[1570] *Ibidem*, p. 20.
[1571] *Ibidem*, pp. 20-21. The Commission reached a different conclusion where it held that the approach of the domestic courts failed to distinguish between the freedom of the business-oriented press to impart specialist information on the one hand and a competitor's advertising interests on the other. This failure rendered the injunction disproportionate. *Ibidem*, pp. 38-43.
[1572] Judgment of 24 February 1994, A.285-A, p. 20.
[1573] *Ibidem*, pp. 20-21. See also the report of the Commission of 19 October 1992, *Colman*, A.258-D, pp. 114-115.

necessary appeared to be rather loose. The Court left a considerable margin of appreciation to the German courts and based its conclusion that Article 10 had not been violated, amongst other arguments, on the fact that Mr Jacubowski could use other means to express his opinions.[1574] Having regard to the *Markt Intern Verlag and Klaus Beerman* Case, the *Casado Coca* Case and the *Jacubowski* Case, it may be concluded that the margin of appreciation of the national authorities increases when commercial speech is involved, which goes hand in hand with a less strict Strasbourg supervision.[1575]

The *Barthold* Case shows that the Strasbourg organs may be critical towards the question whether the information or ideas expressed are of a commercial character. The case concerned an interview given by the applicant, in which he stated that his veterinary clinic provided a night service on a voluntary basis. He had further expressed the view that a regular night service should be established with the participation of private veterinary surgeons. The interview, which subsequently appeared in the newspaper, was accompanied by the applicant's photo and mentioned his name and the name of his clinic. A court action claiming unfair competition led to an injunction against the applicant, prohibiting him, under a penalty of a fine or imprisonment, from repeating specified statements in the general press. Both the Commission and the Court held that the restricted publication was a normal press interview and not an advertisement in the sense in which this term is generally understood. It was held to be not necessary in a democratic society to restrict the freedom of expression of members of a liberal profession by forbidding them to disclose their identity and function when expressing an opinion in matters of public concern, even if they relate to their sphere of professional activity.[1576]

10.2.4 Duties and Responsibilities; Special Status

It is clear from the text of the second paragraph of Article 10 that everyone – including artists and those who promote their work[1577] – who exercises the right contained in the first paragraph undertakes 'duties and responsibilities'. Those words imply the possibility to differentiate, in assessing the necessity of restricting the freedom of expression, according to 'the particular situation of the person exercising freedom of expression and the duties and responsibilities attaching to that situation'.[1578] For the person concerned that special responsibility may then lead to a broader or a narrower interpretation of the possibilities to restrict his freedom of expression.

[1574] Judgment of 23 June 1994, A.291, pp. 14-15.
[1575] Already in the egg the Commission has taken the same view: Appl. 7805/77, *Pastor X and Church of Scientology* v. *Sweden*, Yearbook XXII (1979), p. 244 (252-254).
[1576] Report of 13 July 1983, A.90, pp. 38-40; judgment of 25 March 1985, A.90, pp. 25-26.
[1577] Judgment of 24 May 1988, *Müller and Others*, A.133, p. 22.
[1578] Report of 30 September 1975, *Handyside*, B.22 (1976), p. 44. See also the judgment of 7 December 1976 in this case, A.24, p. 23; the report of 11 May 1984, *Kosiek*, A.105, p. 44; judgment of 26 September 1995, *Vogt*, A.323, p. 26.

Although the Court has often referred to the 'duties and responsibilities', it appears that this concept plays an important part in particular in three circumstances. Firstly, if the freedom of the press is involved. Secondly, in case the person who exercises the freedom of expression possesses a special status, like a serviceman or a civil servant, and thirdly, a less clear category, if the restriction of the protection of morals is involved.

As far as the first category is concerned, as stressed before,[1579] the Court has often held that it is incumbent on the press 'to impart information and ideas on political issues just as on those in other areas of public interest'.[1580] This implies that the general rule according to which the exceptions to the freedom of expression must be interpreted narrowly[1581] is of particular importance to the press.[1582]

The second category, the 'duties and responsibilities' of a person with a special status, calls for a discussion at somewhat more length. In the *Engel and Others* Case the position of the Dutch Government that the prohibition imposed on soldiers to publish and distribute a stencilled sheet was necessary in a democratic society, found favour with the Court mainly on the basis of the special duties and responsibilities of members of the armed forces.[1583] In our opinion, the observations are formulated too widely in this case. The mere fact that a person has a special status does not yet provide a sufficient reason for a special treatment. There has to be a relation between the special status of the person in question, the content of the opinion expressed or to be expressed, and/or the medium chosen for it. This relation is quite evident in the case of the distribution of information which is available to a person by virtue of his function. The Court seems to have adopted this approach in the *Hadjianastassiou* Case, where it held that the applicant, a captain in the air force who had been in charge of an experimental missile programme, 'was bound by an obligation of discretion in relation to anything concerning the performance of his duties'.[1584] In any case, a more balanced approach is found in *Vereinigung Demokratischer Soldaten Österreichs and Gubi* v. *Austria*. The Austrian army had been distributing free of charge its own publications and publications of private associations of soldiers in all the country's barracks. However, the Minister for Defence had refused to distribute *der Igel*, a magazine published by the first applicant, to the servicemen. According to the Government the content of *der Igel* was a threat to military discipline. The Court referred to the *Engel and Others* Case but, this time, placed its own view with regard to the content of the magazine beside that of the Government. It held

---

[1579] See *supra* p. 559.
[1580] Judgment of 8 July 1986, *Lingens*, A.103, p. 26.
[1581] See *supra* p. 571.
[1582] See, *inter alia*, the judgment of 26 November 1991, *The Observer and Guardian*, A.216, p. 30; judgment of 25 June 1992, *Thorgeir Thorgeirson*, A.239, pp. 27-28; judgment of 23 September 1994, *Jersild*, A.298, pp. 23-26.
[1583] Judgment of 8 June 1976, A.22, p. 41.
[1584] Judgment of 16 December 1992, A.252, p. 19.

that the criticism in *der Igel* did not overstep 'the bounds of what is permissible (...) in the army of a democratic State'.[1585] The difference between the *Vereinigung Demokratischer Soldaten Österreichs and Gubi* Case and the *Engel and Others* Case can be explained, according to the Court, by the fact that in the former case the Austrian authorities refused to distribute the magazine in all the barracks, while in the latter the banned magazine had been distributed in only one barrack where unrest had occurred.[1586]

The special status of civil servants was at issue in the reports of the Commission in the *Glasenapp* Case and the *Kosiek* Case.[1587] The Commission pointed to the fact that the rule contained in Article 11(2) permitting certain restrictions on the exercise of freedom of assembly and association on members of the armed forces, of the police or of the administration of the State, is not expressly included in Article 10(2). However, in the opinion of the Commission, this is no sufficient ground for arguing that the drafters of the Convention have not intended to impose specific restrictions of the kind included in Article 11(2) also on the freedom of opinion, since the effect of the provision in Article 11(2) may be to limit some forms of expression of opinion, such as membership of political organisations by certain categories of public employees. According to the Commission, that connection between the two provisions is reflected in the requirement laid down in Article 10(2) that the restriction imposed must be necessary in a democratic society in the light of the actual duties and responsibilities which the exercise of freedom of expression and opinion by the person concerned carries with it; its necessity must flow from the applicant's circumstances. On this basis the Commission adopted the view that the requirement that a schoolteacher dissociated herself completely from the German Communist Party could not be considered a necessary condition and restriction on her freedom of opinion and expression,[1588] whereas the dismissal of a lecturer on the basis of his personal and public identification with the extreme policies of the National Democratic Party of Germany, in which he was a leading figure, was considered justified, because the dismissal could be deemed necessary and proportionate.[1589] The *Vogt* Case concerned the dismissal of a teacher from the civil service because of her political activities on behalf of the German Communist Party. The Court took the position that the Contracting Parties are entitled to require civil servants to be loyal to their constitutional values[1590] and held that the 'duties and responsibilities' are 'to a certain extent' also incumbent on teachers

---

[1585] Judgment of 19 December 1994, A.302, p. 17.
[1586] *Ibidem*, pp. 17-18.
[1587] The Court held Art. 10 not to be applicable because the 'access to the civil service', a right not secured in the Convention, laid at the heart of the case. Judgments of 28 August 1986, A.104 and A.105, p. 27 and p. 21 respectively. See also *supra* p. 564.
[1588] Report of 11 May 1984, *Glasenapp*, A.104, pp. 45 and 53-54.
[1589] Report of 11 May 1984, *Kosiek*, A.105, pp. 37-38 and 44-45.
[1590] Judgment of 26 September 1995, A.323, p. 28.

outside school.[1591] However, in this case, the Court found the circumstances provided by the Government not sufficient to justify the dismissal. The Court referred, *inter alia*, to the fact that Mrs Vogt in the performance of her duty had been beyond reproach, that the German Communist Party had not been banned and that there was no evidence, even outside the school, of any anti-constitutional statements. Thus, the dismissal had been disproportionate to the aim pursued.[1592]

This case-law shows that the Commission and the Court, as far as servicemen and civil servants are concerned, are not inclined to accept easily that the special 'duties and responsibilities' may lead to a restriction of the freedom of expression. In this respect the *Engel and Others* Case may be regarded as a false start.

Finally, there is the third category: the concept of 'duties and responsibilities' seems to play an important part also if 'the protection of morals' has been invoked to justify a restriction of the freedom of expression. In the *Handyside* Case, the Government of the United Kingdom relied on this aim to justify the conviction of a publisher for having in his possession copies of the 'Little Red School Book', and their destruction as pornography. The reference to the special responsibility of the publisher constituted an argument for a reserved Strasbourg review.[1593] This case may be compared with the *Otto-Preminger-Institut* Case, concerning the seizure and subsequent forfeiture of a film. According to the Austrian authorities this film had disparaged the Roman Catholic religious doctrine. The Government relied on 'the protection of (...) rights of others'. This was accepted by the Court, but it indicated that in this case that aim came very close to the concept of 'morals'. The Court referred to the 'duties and responsibilities' and held:

> Amongst them – in the context of religious opinions and beliefs – may legitimately be included an obligation to avoid as far as possible expressions that are gratuitously offensive to others and thus an infringement of their rights, and which therefore do not contribute to any form of public debate of furthering progress in human affairs.[1594]

The Court concluded that Article 10 had not been violated.[1595] The case-law mentioned under the third category seems to indicate that the reference to 'duties and responsibilities' leads to a broad margin of appreciation if at the same time on good grounds the concept of 'morals' is involved. However, with regard to this conclusion some prudence is called for, since the number of cases that support the conclusion is rather small.

With regard to Article 10, too, prisoners stand out as a special group in the case-law of the Commission, and this not in connection with the above-mentioned special duties and responsibilities which may be incumbent on a person in a given

---

[1591] *Ibidem*, p. 29.

[1592] *Ibidem*, pp. 29-30. The Court did not express clearly which aim was involved. The Government relied on the interest of national security, the prevention of disorder and the protection of rights of others; *ibidem*, p. 25.

[1593] Judgment of 7 December 1976, A.24, p. 23. See also, less clear, the judgment of 24 May 1988, *Müller and Others*, A.133, p. 22.

[1594] Judgment of 20 September 1994, A.295-A, p. 19.

[1595] *Ibidem*, pp. 19-21.

capacity, but on the basis of the special requirements assumed to be involved in detention. While here again in some cases the Commission took the view that certain restrictions on the freedom to receive and impart information and ideas are inherent in detention and consequently are not contrary to the right laid down in the first paragraph,[1596] in other cases such restrictions have been considered justified on the basis of the second paragraph, in particular on the basis of a very broad interpretation of the restriction 'prevention of disorder'. On that ground, for instance, the Commission considered justifiable the refusal by the prison authorities to make available, at the prisoner's request, a copy of the provisional regulations on the execution of penalties; this because he wanted to use the information in a discussion with the press.[1597] The prohibition for a Buddhist prisoner to send an article to a Buddhist journal was also permissible in the eyes of the Commission,[1598] as was the prison rule that in principle no journals from outside the United Kingdom were admitted.[1599] It is clear that this case-law needs some qualification on the basis of a stricter necessity test.

10.2.5 Licensing of Broadcasting, Television or Cinema Enterprises

For the most important media besides written publications, *viz.* broadcasting, television and cinema, Article 10 provides that they may be subjected to a licensing system. This provision is contained in the first, not in the second paragraph, so at first sight one would expect that when refusing a licence, the authorities are not confined to the restriction grounds mentioned in the second paragraph. However, in *Groppera Radio AG and Others* v. *Switzerland* and in *Informationsverein Lentia and Others* v. *Austria* the Court has developed a different approach. The *Groppera Radio AG and Others* Case concerned the ban on cable retransmissions in Switzerland of the programmes that had been broadcasted by a radio station from Italy. The Court held that the third sentence of the first paragraph permits the Contracting States 'to control the way in which the broadcasting is organised', especially with regard to 'technical aspects', but that otherwise the licensing measures had to comply with the requirements of the second paragraph.[1600] This point of view was further elucidated in the *Informationsverein Lentia and Others* Case. The applicants complained that the impossibility to set up a radio and television station because of the monopoly of the Austrian broadcasting company constituted a breach of the third sentence of

---

[1596] Thus, *e.g.* in Appl. 2795/66, *X* v. *Federal Republic of Germany*, Yearbook XII (1969), p. 192 (204), where the applicant alleged that he had been given insufficient opportunity to consult an annotated text of the German Criminal Code for the preparation of his request for a new hearing of his case. See also Appl. 4517/70, *Huber* v. *Austria*, Yearbook XIV (1971), p. 548 (568).
[1597] Appl. 1860/63, *X* v. *Federal Republic of Germany*, Yearbook VIII (1965), p. 204 (216).
[1598] Appl. 5442/72, *X* v. *the United Kingdom*, D&R 1 (1975), p. 41 (42).
[1599] Appl. 5270/72, *X* v. *the United Kingdom*, Coll. 46 (1974), p. 54 (59-60).
[1600] Judgment of 28 March 1990, A.173, pp. 23-24. See also the judgment of 22 May 1990, *Autronic AG*, A.178, p. 24.

the first paragraph. The Court referred to its judgment in the *Groppera Radio AG and Others* Case and held that:

> Technical aspects are undeniable important, but the grant or refusal of a licence may also be made conditional on other considerations, including such matters as the nature and objectives of a proposed station, its potential audience and the obligations deriving from international legal instruments. This may lead to interferences whose aims will be legitimate under the third sentence of paragraph 1, even though they do not correspond to any of the aims set out in paragraph 2. The compatibility of such interferences with the Convention must nevertheless be assessed in the light of other requirements of paragraph 2.[1601]

As far as the aims are concerned the Contracting States do have a considerable freedom to set up a licensing system. Thus, if the licensing system is 'prescribed by law' the guarantees offered by Article 10 in this respect seems to lie mainly in the necessity-test of the second paragraph. The *Autronic AG* Case and the *Informationsverein Lentia and Others* Case show that the supervision of the Court can be rather strict on this point. In the former case the refusal of the Swiss authorities to authorise a company to receive by means of a private dish aerial uncoded television programmes, in absence of the consent of the broadcasting State, did not meet the requirements of the necessity-test[1602] and in the latter case the Court held that the impossibility to set up a radio and television station did not either.[1603]

Under Article 14 no discrimination is permitted in the granting of licences and, in case of a State monopoly, the broadcasting time granted to a political party, trade union or other institution of a specific political, religious, philosophical or ethical character may not be disproportionate. For the assessment of whether discrimination or disproportionality has occurred, all facets of the political, religious and social climate of the community concerned will have to be taken into account. Thus, departure from the arithmetical proportionality on the ground that otherwise a small political party would not be entitled to any broadcasting time at all, or to a uselessly short time only, does not constitute discrimination.

In its decision in *X* v. *the United Kingdom* the Commission took the view that, since the first paragraph envisages legislation requiring the licensing of broadcasting organisations, a State is also allowed to take measures against those who seek to promote or encourage unlicensed 'pirate' stations by advertising them or making them known in some other way.[1604]

The *Jersild* Case concerned the criminal liability of a television journalist who had taken the initiative of making a television programme about a group of young people who were known for their racist ideas. Subsequent to the broadcasting of a summary of the interview in which the members of the group ventilated their racist statements and insulted various people, criminal proceedings had been

---

[1601] Judgment of 24 November 1993, A.276, p. 14.
[1602] Judgment of 22 May 1990, A.178, pp. 26-28.
[1603] Judgment of 24 November 1993, A.276, pp. 15-17.
[1604] Appl. 8266/78, D&R 16 (1979), p. 190 (192).

instituted and Mr Jersild had been convicted and sentenced for aiding and abetting the dissemination of racist statements. According to the national courts Mr Jersild had not clearly counterbalanced the expressed racist views. In assessing the claim of the applicant about violation of Article 10, the Court accepted that the interference pursued 'the protection of the reputation or rights of others'. Next, the Court made a distinction between print media and audio-visual media by stating that the audio-visual media 'have often a much more immediate and powerful effect'. However, according to the Court, this fact did not justify the Court or the national courts 'to substitute their own views from those of the press as to what technique of reporting should be adopted by journalists'.[1605] Moreover, the Court seemed to leave no margin of appreciation to the national authorities with regard to evaluating the attitude of the applicant. The Court expressly disagreed with the national courts and held that Mr Jersild clearly dissociated himself from the person interviewed. Accordingly, Article 10 had been breached.[1606]

10.2.6 The Protection of Journalistic Sources

In the *Goodwin* Case the applicant, a British journalist, received information about the financial problems of a company. When he contacted the company to verify the facts, it appeared that the information had been derived from a confidential company report. These events eventually resulted in an injunction restraining the journalist (and the publishers he worked for) from publishing the information and a court order to disclose the identity of Goodwin's source. With regard to the question whether the alleged interference was 'necessary in a democratic society' to protect the company's rights, the Court labelled the protection of journalistic sources as 'one of the basic conditions for press freedom' and held that 'limitations on the confidentiality of journalistic sources call for the most careful scrutiny.'[1607] The Court took the position that the purpose of the injunction, the prevention of the dissemination of the confidential information, and of the disclosure order had been basically the same and therefore the disclosure order was not 'supported by sufficient reasons' for the purpose of the second paragraph. The interest of the company to unmask a disloyal employee who had disclosed the secret plan did not constitute a sufficient reason for the disclosure order either. Consequently, the Court reached the conclusion that the disclosure order and the fine imposed upon the journalist for having refused to comply with the order had been contrary to Article 10.[1608] From this it is clear that the Convention offers a very strong, though not absolute, protection of journalistic sources.

[1605] Judgment of 23 September 1994, A.298, p. 23.
[1606] *Ibidem*, pp. 24-26.
[1607] Judgment of 27 March 1996, Reports 1996-II, Vol. 7, para. 40.
[1608] *Ibidem*, paras 37-46.

10.2.7 Territorial Integrity
In the *Piermont* Case the French Government relied on the 'territorial integrity' to justify an infringement of the first paragraph of Article 10. Mrs Piermont had taken part on the territory of French Polynesia in a demonstration in favour of the independence of French Polynesia. During that demonstration she had made a speech in which she supported the anti-nuclear and independence demands of some of the local political parties. The applicant claimed that Article 10 had been violated by the subsequent order by the French authorities, directing her expulsion from the French Polynesia territory coupled with a ban on re-entering and the order prohibiting her to enter the territory of her next destination, New-Caledonia. The Court accepted that the interference pursued two aims, the prevention of disorder and the interest of territorial integrity.[1609] With regard to the necessity-requirement the Court referred, *inter alia*, to the importance of a free political debate, the fact that the speech had been held during an authorised and non-violent demonstration and that the demonstration had not been followed by any disorder.[1610] The Court reached the conclusion that the orders had not been 'necessary in a democratic society'.[1611]

10.2.8 Preventing the Disclosure of Information Received in Confidence
The wide formulation of the restriction 'for preventing the disclosure of information received in confidence' overlaps with other grounds. Insofar as it refers to the right of the authorities to take measures against the leakage of State secrets, the ground 'in the interests of national security, territorial integrity or public safety' would appear to sufficiently serve that purpose. And insofar as it refers to the possibility of being exempted from a legal duty to impart information when information received in confidence is involved, for instance as a witness in judicial proceedings, what is involved is not a restriction, but on the contrary a confirmation of the freedom of expression, since the first paragraph entails the right to be silent.[1612] And if the protection of a person's privacy is concerned, the restriction 'protection of the reputation or rights of others' will suffice. All the same, cases may occur in which information received in confidence is revealed without one of the above-mentioned interests being involved, for instance when

---

[1609] Judgment of 27 April 1995, A.314, p. 25 and (less clear) pp. 27-28.

[1610] In the judgment of 25 August 1993, *Chorherr*, A.266-B, pp. 37-38, the Court accepted a reference by the Austrian Government to the fear of disorder during a military parade and held that Art. 10 had not been violated.

[1611] Judgment of 27 April 1995, A.314, pp. 25-27 and p. 28. The Government relied also on the Arts 63 and 16 to justify the interference. The Court rejected these arguments, pp. 22-23 and pp. 23-24 respectively.

[1612] This holds not true if the first paragraph is also taken to contain a right to seek information and accordingly a duty of the authorities to enforce the obligation to impart information. On this, see *supra* pp. 565-566.

a civil servant reveals or intends to reveal on his own initiative an official secret which does not affect either national security or the rights of others.[1613]

10.2.9 *Maintaining the Authority and Impartiality of the Judiciary*

Another specific feature of the second paragraph of Article 10 in comparison with the restrictions in other articles of the Convention is the restriction ground 'for maintaining the authority and impartiality of the judiciary'. This restriction ground would seem to have been included mainly with a view to the prohibition, familiar from Anglo-Saxon law, of 'contempt of court', which is intended to prevent that the authority and the independence of the court as well as the rights of the parties to the proceedings[1614] are impaired by publications and other acts. In the *Weber* Case the Court held that the application of a provision of the criminal code was intended 'to ensure the proper conduct of the investigation' and, therefore, also came within the ambit of this restriction.[1615]

The restriction was discussed at length in Strasbourg in the *Sunday Times* Case. In this case the publisher, the editorial staff and the general editor of the Sunday Times complained about the ban for a given period, imposed by an English court, on the publication of an article concerning the so-called 'thalidomide children', *i.e.* children born with serious malformations of limbs, because their mothers had used the sedative thalidomide during pregnancy. The reason given for the prohibition was the prevention of 'contempt of court', because at that time claims for damages were pending before the English court. In order to be able to answer the question of whether the ban on publication could be justified on this ground, the Commission undertook an independent inquiry into the circumstances under which the prohibition had been imposed. Ultimately it concluded that the nature of the prohibited publication did not tend to affect the impartiality of the court, since the article contained only information with which the court had already become familiar from another source. Nor could the authority of the court be impaired by the publication. In fact, at the moment of the prohibition, in the majority of these cases the parties were negotiating in order to reach a friendly settlement, while the role of the court consisted only in approving such a settlement if reached and in protecting the interests of the minors concerned. Moreover, the proposed publication was precisely also meant to protect the interests of those minors. In this particular situation, therefore, the court was not called upon to pronounce on the liability of the producer of the medicine, the issue which the publication dealt with. And as to the few cases in which the parents were quite averse to reaching a settlement, the proceedings, in the opinion of the majority of the Commission, were still in so early a stage that the influence of the publication on the ultimate outcome was negligible. Moreover, the Commission took into consideration the

---

[1613] See, *e.g.*, Appl. 4274/69, *X* v. *Federal Republic of Germany*, Yearbook XIII (1970), p. 888 (892).

[1614] Judgment of 26 April 1979, *Sunday Times*, A.30, p. 34; judgment of 26 November 1991, *The Observer and Guardian*, A.216, p. 28.

[1615] Judgment of 22 May 1990, A.177, p. 28.

circumstance that, although this was a civil action, a public interest was involved in the case as well. Since that public interest had not been brought out, either in a criminal prosecution or in an inquiry instituted by the authorities, only very compelling reasons could justify a prevention of information being imparted by private persons. The Commission considered that no such compelling reasons existed.[1616] The Court basically concurred – though with the bare majority of 11 votes to 9 – with the opinion of the majority of the Commission.[1617] *The Observer and Guardian* Case concerned interlocutory injunctions restraining two newspapers from publishing, pending proceedings which had been instituted by the Attorney General to obtain permanent injunctions, details of the manuscript of a book (Spycatcher) containing the memoirs of a former agent of the British Security Service. The Court held that the injunction had been permissible initially, but could no longer be justified once the book had been published in the United States, because from that very moment the confidentiality of the material had been destroyed.[1618]

In the *Barfod* Case the Danish Government relied on the 'protection of the reputation or rights of others' and indirectly on the restriction of 'maintaining the authority of the judiciary' for a quite different reason. A journalist had been convicted for writing an article of an allegedly defaming character. In his article he criticised a judgment in a case in which two lay judges had participated, who were both employed as civil servants in the local government, which was the defendant party in that case. The applicant's conviction was based on the fact that he suggested that the two lay judges cast their votes rather as employees of the local government than as independent and impartial judges. In the opinion of the Commission this statement concerned matters of public interest involving the functioning of the public administration, including the judiciary. According to the Commission, in such a case the test of necessity of the interference must be a particularly strict one:

> It follows that even if the article in question could be interpreted as an attack on the integrity or reputation of the two lay judges, the general interest in allowing a public debate about the functioning of the judiciary weighs more heavily than the interest of the two judges in being protected against criticism of the kind expressed in the applicant's article.[1619]

The Commission furthermore indicated that the aim mentioned in Article 10(2) to maintain the authority of the judiciary cannot be used as a basis for restraining criticism of the composition of a court which is improperly constituted under the applicable rules. Unlike the Commission, the Court held that the interference with

---

[1616] Report of 18 May 1977, B.28 (1982), pp. 71-74.

[1617] Judgment of 26 April 1970, A.30, pp. 28-42. The issue of 'contempt of court' also arose in Appl. 10038/82, *Harman* v. *the United Kingdom*, D&R 38 (1984), p. 53 (61-63), where a lawyer had given access to a journalist to documents which were exclusively meant for purposes of the trial.

[1618] Judgment of 26 November 1991, A.216, p. 34. See also the judgment of 26 November 1991, *The Sunday Times (No. 2)*, A.217, pp. 30-31.

[1619] Report of 16 July 1987, A.149, p. 21.

the applicant's freedom of expression did not aim at restricting his right under the Convention to criticise publicly the composition of the court in question. It was quite possible to question the composition of that court without at the same time attacking the two lay judges personally. The State's legitimate interest in protecting the reputation of the two lay judges was accordingly not in conflict with the applicant's interest in being able to participate in free public debate on the question of the structural impartiality of the High Court.[1620] The Court reached the conclusion that the conviction could not be regarded as disproportionate and that, therefore, Article 10 had not been violated. In our opinion it is difficult to make a distinction between the 'personal attack' on the two judges and the complaint about the improper constitution of the court. One may wonder whether the control of the Court in this case should not have been more strict. The same holds good for the *Prager and Oberschlick* Case concerning the complaint of a journalist and a publisher that their conviction for defamation of a judge constituted a breach of Article 10. The rejection of these claims was partly based on the Court's opinion that the classification of the insults in the published article as allegations of fact and value-judgments comes within the ambit of the margin of appreciation of the national authorities.[1621]

10.3 Derogation

Article 10 is not mentioned in the enumeration of Article 15(2), and the right to freedom of expression therefore is not a non-derogable right. In the *Greek* Case, accordingly, a violation of the Convention on account of a breach of Article 10 could only be established after the Commission had investigated whether the Greek Government had rightly invoked Article 15, and after it had reached a negative conclusion in that respect.[1622]

Just as has been submitted with regard to Article 9, here again it may be submitted that in fact the exceptions provided for in Article 15 can never be applicable to the 'freedom to hold opinions' contained in Article 10, since an exception to that right can in no circumstance be 'strictly required' in the sense of Article 15(1).[1623]

[1620] Judgment of 22 February 1989, A.149, pp. 13-14.
[1621] Judgment of 26 April 1995, A.313, p. 18.
[1622] Report of 5 November 1969, Yearbook XII (1969), p. 1 (75-76 and 100).
[1623] See *supra* p. 557.

11 FREEDOM OF ASSOCIATION AND ASSEMBLY (ARTICLE 11)

1. *Everyone has the right to freedom of peaceful assembly and to freedom of association with others, including the right to form and to join trade unions for the protection of his interests.*
2. *No restrictions shall be placed on the exercise of these rights other than such as are prescribed by law and are necessary in a democratic society in the interests of national security or public safety, for the prevention of disorder or crime, for the protection of health or morals or for the protection of the rights and freedoms of others. This Article shall not prevent the imposition of lawful restrictions on the exercise of these rights by members of the armed forces, of the police or of the administration of the State.*

11.1 Introduction

In the Convention the freedom of association and that of peaceful assembly are treated in one and the same provision. Freedom of association in fact presupposes freedom of assembly, since without regular meetings of its members an association cannot lead an effective existence. Freedom of assembly is also important, however, outside the framework of associations, for instance in connection with the right to freedom of expression laid down in the preceding article and in connection with the periodical free elections by secret ballot guaranteed in Article 3 of Protocol No. 1.[1624]

Both the freedom of association and the freedom of assembly are closely connected with the freedom of thought, conscience and religion provided for in Article 9, and with the freedom of expression of Article 10. In fact, the exercise of the right to freedom of association and of the right to freedom of assembly will generally involve the holding and propagation of specific opinions. This was expressly indicated by the Commission and the Court in the *Young, James and Webster* Case. In this case the Commission regarded Article 11 as a *lex specialis* in relation to the two other provisions, and on that account left the latter provisions out of consideration after having concluded that Article 11 had been violated.[1625] The Court in a somewhat different reasoning came to the same result. It treated the freedoms set forth in Articles 9 and 10 as elements of Article 11 and considered their violation as constituting an additional argument for the finding of a violation of Article 11.[1626] This interpretation is now established case-law since the Court invariably repeats its opinion that Article 11 must also be considered in the light of Articles 9 and 10. In the *Ezelin* Case the Court added

---

[1624] See the report of 5 November 1969, *Greek* Case, Yearbook XII (1969), p. 1 (170-171).

[1625] Report of 14 December 1979, B.39 (1984), p. 48. Thus also in Appl. 8191/78, *Rassemblement jurassien et Unité jurassienne* v. *Switzerland*, D&R 17 (1980), p. 93 (118), and Appl. 8440/78, *Christians against Racism and Fascism* v. *the United Kingdom*, D&R 21 (1981), p. 138 (147-148).

[1626] Judgment of 13 August 1981, A.44, pp. 23-24.

that '(t)he protection of personal opinions, secured by Article 10, is one of the objectives of freedom of peaceful assembly as enshrined in Article 11'.[1627]

In the *Vogt* Case the Court came to the same result *via* a somewhat different approach. The relevant issue in this case was the compatibility with Articles 10 and 11 of the dismissal of the applicant from her post as a civil servant on the ground of her having persistently refused to dissociate herself from the DKP (the German Communist Party) claiming that membership of that party was not incompatible with her duty of loyalty. The Court first concluded that Article 10 had been violated. It then held that the facts which gave rise to that conclusion, also constituted a breach of Article 11. Its main argument was that the requirements of paragraph 2 are identical to those laid down in paragraph 2 of Article 10 (with an exception for the last sentence of paragraph 2 of Article 11). The finding that there had been a disproportionality with respect to the legitimate aim pursued in the context of Article 10 therefore automatically resulted in the conclusion that there also had been a violation of Article 11.[1628]

This approach implies that the Court's method of interpretation and the margin of appreciation it accords to a State is influenced, also in the context of Article 11, by the basic principle that freedom of expression (and consequently also the freedom of association) is one of the essential foundations of a democratic society. Interferences with the freedom of association will therefore be reviewed more strictly whenever political associations or opinions are concerned, in line with the Court's approach towards 'political speech'. These different approaches, varying according to the nature of the opinion or association involved, can be equally discerned when comparing the *Vogt* Case with the *Gustafsson* Case. In the latter case the Court granted the respondent Government a wide margin of appreciation because in this case the freedom of association did not involve political associations or opinions but trade union freedom and the freedom not to participate in collective bargaining.[1629]

11.2 Peaceful Assembly

Although, as the Commission held, the right to freedom of peaceful assembly, like the right to freedom of expression, 'is a fundamental right in a democratic society and (...) is one of the foundations of such a society',[1630] freedom of assembly still has not played an important part in the Strasbourg case-law.

Until now the Court has not expressly laid down similar basic principles for the freedom of peaceful assembly as it has elaborated in the context of Article 10, underlining that the freedom of expression is one of the essential foundations of

---

[1627] Judgment of 26 April 1991, A.202, p. 20.
[1628] Judgment of 26 September 1995, A.323, p. 31.
[1629] Judgment of 25 April 1996, Reports 1996-II, Vol. 9, to be discussed in detail *infra* pp. 590-591.
[1630] Appl. 8191/78, *Rassemblement jurassien et Unité jurassienne* v. *Switzerland*, D&R 17 (1980), p. 93 (119).

a democratic society; and that Article 10 also protects those ideas that offend, shock or disturb. Nevertheless, in the *Ezelin* Case, which concerned a lawyer who had been disciplined because of having participated in a peaceful assembly, the Court referred to 'the special importance of freedom of peaceful assembly and freedom of expression, which are closely linked in this instance'. The Court proceeded to apply *de facto* a test which has the same strictness as that applied in 'pure' freedom of expression cases:

> The Court considers, however, that the freedom to take part in a peaceful assembly –
> in this instance a demonstration that had not been prohibited – is of such importance
> that it cannot be restricted in any way, even for an *avocat*, so long as the person
> concerned does not himself commit any reprehensible act on such occasion.[1631]

In the *Vogt* Case the Court applied these criteria, which it has elaborated in the context of freedom of expression, equally in order to review the compatibility with Article 11.[1632] It may therefore safely be assumed that peaceful assemblies (including demonstrations) are to be judged on the basis of the same strict standard as other means of expression. It would seem to be preferable, however, that the Court formulates these strict standards *expressis verbis* for all freedoms and activities covered by Article 11.

The adjective 'peaceful' has restricted the scope of the protection offered by the first paragraph to a very large extent. If the authorities concerned could reasonably have believed that a planned assembly would not have a peaceful character or if this has become apparent during the assembly, its prohibition or restriction, as the case may be, in the Commission's opinion does not conflict with the first paragraph of Article 11. Consequently, the second paragraph need not be relied upon in that case and it is not therefore required that the prohibition or restriction be 'prescribed by law'. However, again according to the Commission, the fact that a peacefully organised demonstration runs the risk of resulting in disorder by developments beyond the control of the organisers, for example through a violent counter-demonstration, does not for that reason fall outside the scope of Article 11(1) of the Convention.[1633]

Especially for assemblies of a public character the above observations mean that they may be subjected to a system of permits. No case-law of the Court exists establishing the standard of scrutiny in this respect. Which, for instance, are the requirements that have to be met by the national authorities when imposing a system of permits?[1634] In any case, if the adjective 'peaceful' allows for the use

---

[1631] Judgment of 26 April 1991, A.202, p. 23.

[1632] Judgment of 26 September 1995, A.323, p. 31.

[1633] Appl. 8440/78, *Christians against Racism and Fascism v. the United Kingdom*, D&R 21 (1981), p. 138 (148); Appl. 10126/82, *Plattform 'Ärzte für das Leben' v. Austria*, D&R 44 (1985), p. 65 (72).

[1634] In the context of Art. 10 prior control can also be exercised by the authorities. However, 'the dangers inherent in prior restraints are such that they call for the most careful scrutiny on the part of the Court'; judgment of 26 November 1991, *Spycatcher*, A.217. This most careful scrutiny has until now never been applied in the context of permits for assemblies.

of a standard which does not need to be covered by the restrictions of the second paragraph, such a system of permits and its application may then only relate to that peaceful character and must not affect the right of assembly as such. The latter, for instance, is the case if the prohibition has a general character or concerns a very wide category of assemblies.[1635] The prohibition may also not be of such a nature that an independent means of expression is thus in fact excluded altogether for one or more groups. The latter cases must, therefore, be reviewed on the basis of the second paragraph. Thus, in its report in the *Greek Case* the Commission reviewed the restrictions applied by Greece at that time with regard to both public and private assemblies, and assemblies of a political as well as of a non-political character, for their conformity with the second paragraph of Article 11 and, on the basis of the very wide discretion which the law left to the authorities, concluded that they could not find a sufficient justification in any of the grounds of restriction mentioned therein.[1636]

In the aforementioned *Ezelin* Case the Court was confronted with a demonstration that had not been prohibited, but during which some disturbances had occurred. The applicant had been disciplined for not having dissociated himself from offensive and insulting acts committed by other demonstrators.[1637] From the position adopted by the Court in that case it may be concluded, in the first place, that an individual participating in an assembly that has not been prohibited cannot afterwards be confronted with allegations that he took part in a non-peaceful assembly that lacks the protection of Article 11. Secondly, an individual participant enjoys the full protection of Article 11 ('his right cannot be restricted in any way') so long as he abstains from non-peaceful behaviour.

11.3   Positive Obligations/Horizontal Effect

It is established case-law of the Court that the Convention does not merely oblige the authorities of the Contracting States to respect the rights and freedoms embodied in it, but in addition requires them to secure the enjoyment of these rights and freedoms by preventing and remedying any breach thereof, and that therefore the obligation to secure the effective exercise of Convention rights may involve positive obligations on the part of the State, even involving the adoption of measures in the sphere of the relations between individuals. On that basis the Court took the view that the right to freedom of assembly includes the right to protection against counter-demonstrators, because it is only in this way that its

---

[1635] Appl. 8440/78, *Christians against Racism and Fascism* v. *the United Kingdom*, D&R 21 (1981), p. 138 and Appl. 8191/78, *Rassemblement jurassien et Unité jurassienne* v. *Switzerland*, D&R 17 (1980), p. 93.

[1636] Report of 5 November 1969, Yearbook XII (1969), p. 1 (171). In the case of Appl. 8440/78, *Christians against Racism and Fascism* v. *the United Kingdom*, D&R 21 (1981), p. 138 (150), however, a general prohibition of demonstrations for the prevention of disorder was deemed justified because there was 'a real danger' of such disorder.

[1637] Judgment of 26 April 1991, A.202.

effective exercise can be secured to groups wishing to demonstrate for certain principles in highly controversial issues. If the protection provided by the authorities proves to be insufficient to enable a free exercise of the right to freedom of assembly, this amounts to a restriction which has to be reviewed for its justification on the basis of the second paragraph. Thus, in the case of *Plattform 'Ärzte für das Leben'*, the Court reviewed the measures taken to protect the two demonstrations involved against interference by counter-demonstrators for their reasonableness and appropriateness to enable the demonstrations to proceed peacefully. The Court held that the participants of a demonstration must:

> be able to hold the demonstration without having to fear that they will be subjected to physical violence by their opponents; such a fear would be liable to deter associations or other groups supporting common ideas or interests from openly expressing their opinions on highly controversial issues affecting the community. In a democracy the right to counter-demonstrate cannot extend to inhibiting the exercise of the right to demonstrate.

The Court concluded from this that:

> Genuine, effective freedom of peaceful assembly cannot, therefore, be reduced to a mere duty on the part of the State not to interfere: a purely negative conception would not be compatible with the object and purposes of Article 11. Like Article 8, Article 11 sometimes requires positive measures to be taken, even in the sphere of relations between individuals, if need be.[1638]

With respect to the content of these measures, the Court held that the Contracting States have a wide discretion in the choice of the means to be used.[1639]

The same approach was applied by the Court in the *Young, James and Webster* Case,[1640] and has been continued in recent decisions. In the *Sibson* Case, to be discussed in greater detail *infra*, the Court reiterated that even if a case involves no direct interference on the part of the State, the responsibility of the State would nevertheless be engaged if the infringement of the rights under Article 11 resulted from a failure on its part to secure those rights in its domestic law.[1641]

In the *Gustafsson* Case the Court further elaborated upon its tendency to accept State responsibility in the case of infringements committed by private individuals. The issue in dispute was the permissibility of union action against the applicant's business in order to force him to meet the union's demand to become a party to a collective agreement. The Court laid down the following general principles in this respect:

> The matters complained of by the applicant, although they were made possible by national law, did not involve a direct intervention by the State. The responsibility of Sweden would nevertheless be engaged if those matters resulted from a failure on its part to secure to him under domestic law the rights set forth in Article 11 of the

---

[1638] Judgment of 21 June 1988, A.139, p. 12. The Court refers to its judgment of 26 March 1985, *X and Y v. the Netherlands*, A.91, p. 11.

[1639] Judgment of 21 June 1988, A.139, p. 12.

[1640] Judgment of 13 August 1981, A.44, p. 20.

[1641] Judgment of 10 April 1993, A.258-A, p. 13. See *infra* p. 595.

Convention (...). Although the essential object of Article 11 is to protect the individual against arbitrary interferences by the public authorities with his or her exercise of the rights protected, there may in addition be positive obligations to secure the effective enjoyment of these rights. (...) national authorities may, in certain circumstances, be obliged to intervene in the relationships between private individuals by taking reasonable and appropriate measures to secure the effective enjoyment of the negative right to freedom of association (...). In view of the sensitive character of the social and political issues involved in achieving a proper balance between the competing interests and, in particular, in assessing the appropriateness of State intervention to restrict union action aimed at extending a system of collective bargaining, and the wide degree of divergence between the domestic systems in the particular area under consideration, the Contracting States should enjoy a wide margin of appreciation in their choice of the means to be employed.[1642]

11.4 Association

An autonomous meaning should be assigned to the word 'association'. The legal form chosen and the legal consequences attached thereto by national law cannot be decisive here, since otherwise the guarantee of Article 11 might be rendered illusory by the national legislature, and there might exist great differences in scope of that guarantee among the legal systems of the various Contracting States.

By expressly mentioning the trade unions in Article 11, the drafters obviously wanted to put it beyond doubt that the important right to trade union freedom falls under the protection of this provision, no matter whether according to national law a trade union can be considered an association. As the Court puts it: 'the right to form and join trade unions in Article 11 is an aspect of the wider right to freedom of association'.[1643] That political parties also fall under the term 'association' was implicitly assumed by the Commission in its *KPD* decision,[1644] and more recently also by the Court in the *Vogt* Case, in which it found that the dismissal of the applicant from a post as a civil servant on the ground that she had persistently refused to dissociate herself from the DKP, constituted an interference with the right protected by paragraph 1 of Article 11.[1645]

In the *Young, James and Webster* Case, however, in respect of one of the allegations of the British Government, the Commission took the position that the term 'association' presupposes a voluntary organisation for a common purpose, and that there was no such organisation in the case of the mere relationship between employees of the same employer, since that relationship is based on the contractual connection between the employee and the employer.[1646] In its decision in *Association X* v. *Sweden* the Commission gave the following definition

---

[1642] Judgment of 25 April 1996, Reports 1996-II, Vol. 9, para. 45.
[1643] See, *e.g.*, the judgment of 30 June 1993, *Sigurdur A. Sigurjónsson* v. *Iceland*, A.264, p. 14.
[1644] Appl. 250/57, *Kommunistische Partei Deutschland* v. *Federal Republic of Germany*, Yearbook I (1955-1957), p. 222.
[1645] Judgment of 26 September 1995, A.323, p. 31. The respondent Government had not contested the applicability of Art. 11.
[1646] Report of 14 December 1979, B.39 (1984), p. 47.

of 'freedom of association': 'a general capacity for the citizens to join without interference by the State in associations in order to attain various ends'.[1647] It may therefore be assumed that this freedom includes any voluntary association by several natural and/or legal persons for a certain period of time with a an institutional structure and for common purposes.[1648]

A professional organisation established by the Government and governed by public law, which as a rule is intended not only to protect the interests of the members, but also certain public interests, is not an 'association' in the sense of Article 11. The Commission and the Court adopted this opinion in the *Le Compte, Van Leuven and De Meyere* Case with regard to the Belgian *Ordre des médecins*. On the other hand, Article 11 was considered to be involved if the existence of such a public law institution ruled out the voluntary association of the colleagues in question in private professional organisations.[1649] In the aforementioned *Sigurdur A. Sigurjónsson* Case the Court explicitly answered the question whether the 'trade union' involved ('Frami') was a public-law association outside the ambit of Article 11 or a private-law association within the meaning of this article:

> Frami performed certain functions which were to some extent provided for in the applicable legislation and which served not only its members but also the public at large (...). However, the role of supervision of the implementation of the relevant rules was entrusted primarily to another institution, namely the Committee, which in addition had the power to issue licences and to decide on their suspension and revocation (...). Frami was established under private law and enjoyed full autonomy in determining its own aims, organisation and procedure. According to its Articles, admittedly old and under revision, the purpose of Frami was to protect the professional interests of its members and promote solidarity among professional taxicab drivers; to determine, negotiate and present demands relating to the working hours, wages and rates of its members; to seek to maintain limitations on the number of taxicabs and to represent its members before the public authorities (...). Frami was therefore predominantly a private-law organisation and must thus be considered an 'association' for the purposes of Article 11.[1650]

While here the Court explicitly referred to the distinction between private and public associations, this distinction did not receive any attention from the Commission in a number of previous cases in which compulsory membership was at issue. Thus, in a case involving the compulsory membership of the *Landbouwschap*, a Dutch public agricultural organisation, the Commission confined itself to the general observation that this organisation formed part of 'an

---

[1647] Appl. 6094/73, D&R 9 (1978), p. 5 (7).

[1648] In Appl. 7729/76, *Agee v. the United Kingdom*, D&R 7 (1977), p. 164 (174), this former CIA agent invoked for his complaint against his expulsion, *inter alia*, Art. 11, referring to his regular contacts in England with foreign intelligence agents. The Commission here left open the question of whether such a loose relation could still be considered as an association. In its decision on Appl. 8317/78, *McFeeley v. the United Kingdom*, D&R 20 (1980), p. 44 (97-98), however, the Commission submitted that freedom of association 'does not concern the right of prisoners to share the company of other prisoners or to "associate" with other prisoners in this sense'.

[1649] Report of 14 December 1979, B.39 (1984), p. 23 and judgment of 23 June 1981, A.43, pp. 26-27 respectively. See also the judgment of 10 February 1983, *Albert and Le Compte*, A.58, p. 21.

[1650] Judgment of 30 June 1993, A.264, p. 14.

elaborate system for organising effectively the economic life of the country', and that the challenged system of organisation was not contrary to the Convention.[1651] And for dairy farmers the compulsory membership of a health service was accepted without any further argument.[1652]

In *Association X* v. *Sweden* the Commission considered it to be characteristic of a professional organisation that it 'upholds ethics and discipline within the profession or defends its members' interests in outside disputes', and of a trade union that it 'shall represent [its members] in a labour conflict situation against an employer'.[1653] This served to show that a students' association belongs to neither of the two categories. With respect to a complaint that membership of a particular students' association was required for admission to a certain university, the Commission adopted the view that this association was to be regarded as part of the university, a State institution, so that Article 11 was not applicable.[1654] An analogy with a political party would have been more appropriate than the comparison made by the Commission with a professional association or trade union, particularly since the Commission itself recognised that *via* the students' association participation by students in the administration of the university was regulated, and that there was the possibility that the association may adopt political positions.

The present model, adopted by the Court, serves to carefully investigate the dominant features of an association in order to determine its public or private law aspects.

11.4.1 Trade Unions

It is remarkable that only with respect to the trade unions does Article 11 mention the right to *form* an association. However, one must assume that this is implied in the freedom of association as such. Indeed, if people want to associate in a new association, the right to set up an association forms a necessary condition for the exercise of the freedom of association. That seems to be also the Commission's view,[1655] although the Commission has differentiated in that respect between membership on the one hand and participation on the board of an association on the other hand and, curiously enough, considered that the latter aspect was not protected by Article 11.[1656]

[1651] Appl. 2290/64, *X* v. *the Netherlands*, Coll. 22 (1967), p. 28 (32).

[1652] Appl. 1068/61, *X* v. *the Netherlands*, Yearbook V (1962), p. 278 (284).

[1653] Appl. 6094/73, D&R 9 (1978), p. 5 (8).

[1654] *Idem.*

[1655] See Appl. 1038/61, *X* v. *Belgium*, Yearbook IV (1961), p. 324 (336), where the Commission speaks of 'the right to set up an association or a trade union'. In its report in the *Young, James and Webster* Case it was emphasised by the Commission that trade union freedom is not a separate right, but an element of the right to freedom of association; report of 14 December 1979, B.39 (1984), p. 44. Thus also the judgment of 13 August 1981 in that case, A.44, p. 21.

[1656] Appl. 1038/61, *X* v. *Belgium*, Yearbook IV (1961), p. 324 (336-338). See, however, *infra* p. 597 and note 1673.

Since Article 11 refers to 'the right (...) to join trade unions', the question arises whether this implies at the same time protection against compulsory membership. This is important in particular with regard to the practice of compulsory trade union membership, the so-called 'closed shop'. From the *travaux préparatoires* of Article 11 one might conclude that the drafters did not intend to prohibit such a practice.[1657] The Commission, however, opined as early as in its decision on *X* v. *Belgium* that 'the very concept of freedom of association with others also implies freedom not to associate with others or not to join unions'.[1658] In that case, the Commission held the complaint on this point to be manifestly ill-founded. In later cases the Commission characterised this problem as very complex and declared admissible complaints concerning compulsory membership of a professional organisation or a trade union.[1659]

In the first two of these cases the question was not examined any further, because the Commission and the Court held that the professional association in question was not an association in the sense of Article 11.[1660] In the *Young, James and Webster* Case, however, the question of compulsory membership was discussed at length. There the complaint concerned the discharge of the applicants on account of their refusal to join a trade union. Both the Commission and the Court considered the *travaux préparatoires* not decisive for answering the question of whether the closed-shop system was contrary to Article 11.[1661] Both organs, however, avoided making a general pronouncement on the compatibility of the closed-shop system with Article 11, but restricted themselves to holding that Article 11 had been violated in this particular case. For this the Commission referred to the fact that the closed-shop agreement between the unions and the enterprise in question dit not yet exist when the applicants entered into employment with the firm, but was concluded only afterwards. In the Commission's opinion that situation in any case constituted a breach of the applicants' freedom to decide for themselves which union they wished to join or to set up their own union, while the discharge amounted to a sanction on their use of that freedom.[1662] The Court left open the question of whether compulsory membership of a trade union is always contrary to Article 11, but regarded the threat of discharge for those who did not wish to join a given union as a form of coercion which affects the essence of the freedom guaranteed in Article 11. The Court, too, took into account that the compulsory membership had been introduced after the applicants had entered into employment, while it also referred to the fact

---

[1657] See the quotation in the judgment of 13 August 1981, *Young, James and Webster*, A.44, p. 21.
[1658] Appl. 4072/69, Yearbook XIII (1970), p. 708 (718). See also Appl. 9926/82, *X* v. *the Netherlands*, D&R 32 (1983), p. 274 (280).
[1659] Appl. 6878/75, *Le Compte* v. *Belgium*, Yearbook XX (1977), p. 254 (276); Appl. 7238/75, *Van Leuven and De Meyere* v. *Belgium*, Yearbook XX (1977), p. 348 (368); and Appl. 7601/76, *Young and James* v. *the United Kingdom*, Yearbook XX (1977), p. 520 (564).
[1660] See *supra* p. 592.
[1661] Report of 14 December 1979, B.39 (1984), p. 46; judgment of 13 August 1981, A.44, pp. 21-22.
[1662] Report of 14 December 1979, B.39 (1984), p. 46.

that the number of unions from which they could choose was extremely limited.[1663] Finally, the Court expressed as its opinion that the compulsion imposed on the applicants could not deemed to be 'necessary in a democratic society' in the sense of the second paragraph.[1664] On the basis of this judgment the Commission later on achieved a friendly settlement in two applications against the United Kingdom.[1665] In the same case the Commission and the Court also assigned to Article 11 a certain *Drittwirkung* by recognising the liability of the British authorities for a violation by an enterprise of Article 11 such as was at issue here. Practices like those complained of in this case are therefore prohibited under Article 11, regardless of whether they are imposed by the authorities or not, and can be put forward in Strasbourg whenever the national legislation of the respondent State allows such practices.[1666]

In the *Sibson* Case the Court stuck to its opinion that Article 11 does not *per se* prohibit a compulsion to join a particular trade union; only a form of such compulsion which strikes at the very substance of the freedom of association guaranteed by Article 11 constitutes an interference. In the particular case the Court concluded that the applicant 'was not subjected to a form of treatment striking at the very substance of the freedom of association guaranteed by Article 11'.[1667] An important distinction with the *Young, James and Webster* Case was that the three applicants in that case were faced with a threat of dismissal involving loss of livelihood, whereas for Mr Sibson alternative employment was available with no significantly less favourable working conditions. In a strong dissent judges Morenilla and Russo argued that the Court disregarded an evolutive interpretation of Article 11 in the light of present-day conditions according to the developments that had taken place in national and international legislation, entailing a recognition of the right not to join an organisation.

Only a few months later the Court reversed its position in the *Sigurdur A. Sigurjónsson* Case. In this judgment the Court went beyond its *Young, James and Webster* judgment by concluding that 'Article 11 must be viewed as encompassing a negative right of association'.[1668] It, however, did not go so far as to accept a full-blown substantive negative right of association, because the Court added that it 'is not necessary for the Court to determine in this instance whether this right is to be considered on an equal footing with the positive right'.[1669] Why did the Court change its mind and was it willing to accept in principle the negative right of association? The most important reason was already indicated in the dissenting opinion of judge Morenilla in the *Sibson* Case: the emergence of common ground

---

[1663] Judgment of 13 August 1981, A.44, pp. 22-23.
[1664] *Ibidem*, pp. 24-26.
[1665] Appl. 9520/81, *Reed* v. *the United Kingdom*, D&R 34 (1983), p. 107; and Appls 8476/79-8481/79, *Eaton* et al. v. *the United Kingdom*, D&R 39 (1984), p. 11.
[1666] See *supra* section 11.3.
[1667] Judgment of 10 April 1993, A.258-A, p. 14.
[1668] Judgment of 30 June 1993, A.264, p. 16.
[1669] *Idem*.

at the international level and in the legal orders of the Contracting States as to the recognition and protection of the negative right of association. The Court devoted much attention to many international treaties and recommendations as well as to national legislation:

> Compulsory membership of this nature, which, it may be recalled, concerned a private-law association, does not exist under the laws of the great majority of the Contracting States. On the contrary, a large number of domestic systems contain safeguards which, in one way or another, guarantee the negative aspect of the freedom of association, that is the freedom not to join or to withdraw from an association. A growing measure of common ground has emerged in this area also at the international level. As observed by the Commission, in addition to the above mentioned Article 20 § 2 of the Universal Declaration (...), Article 11 § 2 of the Community Charter of the Fundamental Social Rights of Workers adopted by the Heads of State or Government of eleven member States of the European Communities on 9 December 1989, (...). Moreover, on 24 September 1991 the Parliamentary Assembly of the Council of Europe unanimously adopted a recommendation, amongst other things, to insert a sentence to this effect into Article 5 of the 1961 European Social Charter (...). Even in the absence of an express provision, the Committee of Independent Experts set up to supervise the implementation of the Charter considers that a negative right is covered by this instrument and it has in several instances disapproved of closed-shop practices found in certain States Parties, including Iceland. With regard to the latter, the Committee took account of, *inter alia*, the facts of the present case (...). Following this, the Governmental Committee of the European Social Charter issued a warning to Iceland (...). Furthermore, according to the practice of the Freedom of Association Committee of the Governing Body of the International Labour Office (ILO), union security measures imposed by law, notably by making union membership compulsory, would be incompatible with the Conventions Nos. 87 and 98'. [1670]

On that basis the Court concluded that Article 11 had been violated, because the applicant ran a risk of losing his taxi-licence as a result of his unwillingness to become a member of a specific private-law association. The Court also attached importance to the fact that the applicant objected to being a member of the association in question 'partly because he disagreed with its policy in favour of limiting the number of taxicabs and, thus, access to the occupation'. This aspect led the Court to consider Article 11 also 'in the light of Articles 9 and 10', and to the conclusion that the very essence of Article 11 had been infringed.[1671]

Summing up it may be observed that the Strasbourg case-law has now recognised that Article 11 in general also protects the freedom not to join an association or trade union. Recent developments in the Court's case-law have brought Article 11 in this respect in line with other international instruments. The negative right of association is not only interfered with after a dismissal, but also when other serious 'sanctions' have been imposed, or in case the individual's refusal to become a member is inspired by personal convictions or opinions. In the latter case the protection offered by Article 11 gathers strength because of the direct link it presents with Articles 9 and 10.

[1670] *Ibidem*, pp. 15-16.
[1671] *Ibidem*, p. 17.

11.4.2 Other Trade Union Rights

The case-law has gradually refined the right to freedom of association – and in particular that of trade union freedom – in the sense that this right now also includes those rights and freedoms which are important for its enjoyment.

Above the example has been given of the right to *form* an association,[1672] which was apparently deemed by the Commission to be implied in Article 11. And in its decision in *X* v. *Ireland* the Commission, referring to Convention No. 87 of the International Labour Organisation, held that the freedom of association concerned not only an unobstructed membership, but that intimidation of an employee to make him relinquish his function within the trade union might likewise constitute an encroachment on this freedom.[1673] In the aforementioned *Vogt* Case the Court held that the dismissal of the applicant from a post as a civil servant because she had refused to dissociate herself from a particular political party constituted a violation of Article 11.[1674] In its decision in *Van der Heijden* v. *the Netherlands* the Commission likewise gave as its opinion that a court decision terminating an employee's contract because of his activity in a political party constituted an interference with the exercise of the right guaranteed by this provision. In this case the Commission concluded that the interference could be held to be necessary in a democratic society for the protection of the rights of others, as the political party in question was known to have objectives opposed to those of the employer, a foundation concerned with the welfare of immigrants.[1675]

On the other hand, the State must protect the individual against abuse by associations of their dominant position. Expulsion from a trade union in breach of the union's rules or decided pursuant to arbitrary rules, or entailing exceptional hardship for the individual concerned, may constitute such an abuse.[1676]

In principle the right to form trade unions involves the right of trade unions to draw up their own rules, to administer their own affairs and to establish and join trade union federations. Such trade union rights are explicitly recognised in Articles 3 and 5 of ILO Convention No. 87, which must be taken into account in the present context. Accordingly, in principle trade union decisions in these domains must not be subject to restrictions and control by the State except on the basis of Article 11(2).[1677]

In three judgments concerning trade union freedom, on the basis of the words 'for the protection of his interests', the Court took the position that this freedom entitles the union members to a union that is able to serve their interests as workers. It is therefore incumbent on the authorities to allow the unions sufficient

---

[1672] See *supra* p. 593 and note 1655.
[1673] Appl. 4125/69, Yearbook XIV (1971), p. 198 (222).
[1674] Judgment of 26 September 1995, A.323, p. 31.
[1675] Appl. 11002/84, D&R 41 (1985), p. 264 (271).
[1676] Appl. 10550/83, *Cheall* v. *the United Kingdom*, D&R 42 (1985), p. 178 (186).
[1677] *Ibidem*, p. 185.

scope in this respect. This implies, for instance, that the trade union must be heard by the authorities in order that it may be able to stand up for those interests, although the Court held that this obligation does not necessarily take the specific form that the authorities have to consult the unions before taking certain decisions,[1678] or that the authorities as employers are obliged to conclude a collective agreement with a particular union.[1679] With regard to other employers, too, Article 11 does not entail a *right* for trade unions to conclude collective agreements, which the authorities would then be obliged to uphold, but only the *freedom* to conclude them, which the authorities must help to make possible.[1680] If one were to assume such a *right*, to be upheld by the authorities, a more far-reaching obligation would be construed than the Contracting States have undertaken under Article 6(2) of the European Social Charter, *viz.*:

> to promote, where necessary and appropriate, machinery for voluntary negotiations between employers and employers' organizations and workers' organizations, with a view to the regulation of terms and conditions of employment by means of collective agreements.[1681]

In the *Gustafsson* Case the Court referred to Article 6 of the European Social Charter in order to accept trade union activities that were aimed at forcing an employer to submit himself to a system of collective agreements. The employer concerned alleged that he had suffered considerable losses because of trade union action, consisting of a boycott. The Court argued that the union action pursued legitimate interests consistent with Article 11. With respect to the right not to enter into a collective agreement, alleged by the applicant, the Court stated that Article 11 does not as such guarantee the negative right not to participate in collective bargaining. Thus, the Court seems to draw the consequences from the fact that, in its opinion, Article 11 does not guarantee a positive right to participate in collective bargaining either. The Court also concluded that the freedom of association had not been significantly affected, to such an extent as to conclude that it had been violated.[1682] Judge Martens dissented from the Court's reasoning and against the outcome. He observed that the freedom to negotiate labour agreements is necessarily inherent in the freedom of association. In this respect he referred to Articles 5 and 6 of the European Social Charter and the findings of the Committee of Independent Experts, as well as to the conclusions of the ILO Committee on Freedom of Association.[1683]

[1678] Judgment of 27 October 1975, *National Union of Belgian Police*, A.19, p. 18.

[1679] Judgment of 6 February 1976, *Swedish Engine Drivers' Union*, A.20, pp. 15-16. The same applies to the collective bargaining as such: Appl. 7361/76, *Trade Union X* v. *Belgium*, D&R 14 (1979), p. 40 (47).

[1680] See, for example, Appl. 9792/82, *Association A* v. *Federal Republic of Germany*, D&R 34 (1983), p. 173 (174).

[1681] Thus the Court in its judgment of 6 February 1976, *Swedish Engine Drivers' Union*, A.20, p. 15.

[1682] Judgment of 25 April 1996, Reports 1996-II, Vol. 9, p. 656.

[1683] *Ibidem*, pp. 670-671.

Strikes are considered by the Strasbourg organs as a very important, but not an exclusive means for union members to protect their interests. Referring to the European Social Charter, the Court held that a right to strike, assuming that it is protected by Article 11, may in any case be subjected to restrictions by the national legislature.[1684] The authorities have to leave the trade unions sufficient scope to stand up for the interests of the affiliated employees, since trade union freedom would otherwise be illusory, but it is largely for the authorities to decide what means to this end they allow the unions.

11.4.3 Positive Obligations/Drittwirking

In Article 11(1) the words 'for the protection of his interests' are grammatically related exclusively to the trade union freedom, not to the freedom of association in general. However, associations other than trade unions are also set up precisely for the promotion and protection of common interests, and it may therefore be concluded with regard also to those associations that, if the freedom of association is not to be illusory, once they have been set up, the authorities have the obligation to leave the sufficient scope to function as associations. It is self-evident that Article 11 does not guarantee that the objectives of an association are actually realised,[1685] but efforts to that end must not be interfered with, except on the basis of the restrictions set forth in the second paragraph.[1686]

From this obligation of the authorities ensues the *Drittwirkung* also in relation to associations in general. The Court has at first expressly left undecided the question as to 'the applicability, whether direct or indirect, of Article 11 to relations between individuals *strictu sensu*'.[1687] However, the Court's position that 'the Convention requires (...) that under national law trade unions should be enabled, in conditions not at variance with Article 11, to strive for the protection of their members' interests'[1688] in fact implies that Article 11 has an indirect

---

[1684] Judgment of 6 February 1976, *Schmidt and Dahlström*, A.21, p. 16. Referred to by the Commission in Appl. 10365/83, *S v. Federal Republic of Germany*, D&R 39 (1984), p. 237 (240).

[1685] Appl. 6094/73, *Association X v. Sweden*, D&R 9 (1978), p. 5 (7). See also Appl. 7990/77, *X v. the United Kingdom*, D&R 24 (1981), p. 57 (63), where the Commission states that the authorities are not required to actively support a union or an individual union member in a particular case.

[1686] In its decision on Appl. 9234/81, *X Association v. Federal Republic of Germany*, D&R 26 (1982), p. 270 (271), the Commission states that 'private associations should be able to pursue their statutory aims by all lawful means, but this does not imply the right to have *locus standi* on all matters falling within the ambit of the statutory activities'.

[1687] Judgment of 6 February 1976, *Swedish Engine Drivers' Union*, A.20, p. 14; judgment of 6 February 1976, *Schmidt and Dahlström*, A.21, p. 15.

[1688] Judgment of 27 October 1975, *National Union of Belgian Police*, A.19, p. 18. In its report in the *Swedish Engine Divers' Union* Case the Commission speaks of 'to promote their members' economic and social interests against interference by the State and by employers', B.18 (1977), p. 49. In the *Gustafsson* Case the Court also stated that the words 'for the protection of their interests' show that Art. 11 safeguards freedom to protect the occupational interests of trade union members by trade union action.

Drittwirkung in the form of an obligation for the legislature to enable the (trade) unions, also *vis-à-vis* third parties, to enjoy the rights and freedoms set forth in that article.

This likewise implies that national law must assign legal personality to associations, or at least sufficient legal status for them to be able to stand up effectively for the interests of their members. A consequence on the international plane ought to be that associations must also be able to file on their own account an application under Article 25, not only in the case of a violation of Article 11, but in all those cases where they allegedly have been prejudiced by a violation of one of their own rights or of rights of their members which they have to protect.[1689]

11.5 Restrictions

In addition to the 'usual' restrictions, which are discussed separately,[1690] the second paragraph of Article 11 provides for the possibility that, with regard to members of the armed forces, the police and the administration of the State, lawful restrictions may be imposed on the exercise of the rights laid down in Article 11. Although most complaints of violation of Article 11 hitherto examined by the Court actually concerned police officers, civil servants or members of the armed forces, this provision was not applied in most cases.[1691] In the *Vogt* Case, the Court observed that the notion of 'administration of the State' should be interpreted narrowly, and in the light of the post held by the civil servant concerned.[1692] Consequently, the Court is likely to independently review the necessity of the restrictions imposed. In the *Vogt* Case this examination took the form of a proportionality test. In the case at hand the Court concluded that the dismissal of the applicant was disproportionate to the legitimate aim pursued (national security, prevention of disorder, rights and freedoms of others).[1693] The applicability of the last sentence of the second paragraph does not therefore stop the Court from testing whether the other conditions set forth in the second paragraph have been met. The 'lawful restrictions' that can be imposed on members of the police, the army and the administration of the State are judged on the basis of the standards of legitimate aim, pressing social need and proportionality.

The Commission did apply the second sentence of the second paragraph once, *viz.* in an unpublished decision, in which it considered the prohibition to set up a trade union, imposed on a Belgian police officer, to be justified on that

---

[1689] See *supra* p. 46.
[1690] See *infra* pp. 761-772.
[1691] The Court referred to the provision in its judgment of 8 June 1976, *Engel*, A.22, p. 23.
[1692] Judgment of 26 January 1995, A.323, p. 31.
[1693] *Idem.*

ground.[1694] This decision would appear to be questionable in the sense that the Commission did not apply the necessity test. As a result of such an approach the person concerned can be completely deprived of trade union freedom, while it is undoubtedly intended that restrictions can be imposed only with regard to particular ways of exercising this freedom, since a restriction may never affect a right in its essence.

Although it is not prescribed with regard to the restriction in question that it must be 'necessary in a democratic society', the Court nevertheless applies this test. This approach seems to be the appropriate one, since the purposes of the Convention and the legal order established by it implicate that for any restriction of the rights and freedoms laid down in the Convention such a necessity is a *condition sine qua non*.

11.6 Derogation

Article 11 is not listed in the enumeration in Article 15(2) of provisions which are non-derogable. It has to be taken into account, however, that the right to trade union freedom has developed, in particular in the International Labour Organisation, into a right which has to be respected by the States regardless of whether they have undertaken to do so in a treaty.

12 RIGHT TO MARRY AND TO FOUND A FAMILY (ARTICLE 12)

Men and women of marriageable age have the right to marry and to found a family, according to the national laws governing the exercise of this right.

12.1 The Scope of Article 12

Article 12 does not include a second paragraph laying down possibilities for restrictions. However, considering the inclusion in Article 12 of the formula 'according to the national laws governing the exercise of this right', it would not be very realistic to conclude that it guarantees an absolute right. On the contrary, the national legislature has been allowed considerable scope for subjecting the exercise of the right laid down in Article 12 to certain conditions, for regulating the legal consequences of marriage, and for laying down provisions concerning the family and the resulting family ties. Far-reaching limitations as to the exercise of

---

[1694] Mentioned by F. Castberg, *The European Convention on Human Rights*, Leyden, 1974, p. 152. See also Appl. 10365/83, *S v. Federal Republic of Germany*, D&R 39 (1984), p. 237 (240), where the Commission held that a disciplinary penalty imposed on a civil servant who was a committee member of a union, and who called on civil servants to strike, did not constitute a violation of the right to exercise freedom of association, since in this case the right to strike was prohibited by law for civil servants and that prohibition as such was not inconsistent with the right of freedom of association.

the right to marry and to found a family, consequently, may result from national law.

While Article 12 thus does not imply an absolute obligation on the part of the authorities to refrain from interference with regard to the exercise of the right to marry and to found a family, it is even more difficult to interpret the provision as entailing a duty for the authorities in concrete cases to provide the material means which must enable the persons concerned to marry and to found a family. However, if they proceed to do so, they are not allowed to discriminate. And more generally their policy has to be of such a nature that the exercise of the right to marry and to found a family is not unnecessarily interfered with.[1695]

Since the exercise of the right to marry always depends on the free consent of the partners, the right to marry cannot be invoked against a law which makes divorce at the request of the other partner possible.

The right to marry and to found a family entails for the authorities the prohibition to put a sanction on the marital and/or parental status. Thus, in general, the Government as an employer (and private employers, *via* the *Drittwirkung* of Article 12?) is not allowed to discharge an employee on the mere ground that the person has married or has become a parent. However, loss of, *e.g.*, disability benefits because of marriage is not a sanction and does not constitute an interference with the exercise of the right to marry.[1696] Discharge does not constitute a violation when a person has promised *in full freedom* not to marry, or at least has accepted the consequence that marriage will constitute a ground for discharge. That situation occurs, for instance, when a Roman Catholic priest is relieved from his priestly and directly related functions after having given up his celibate status. Toleration of this by the authorities does not then conflict with Article 12.

Article 12 does not relate to the legal consequences attached to the dissolution of marriage such as the right to visit and keep in touch with the children, unless the dissolution is imposed by the authorities. However, Article 8 may apply here.

In the *Marckx* Case, Article 12 had been put forward because under Belgian law the granting to an illegitimate child of the same status as a legitimate child was linked with his or her legitimisation, which could only take place through the marriage of the natural parents. The Court was of the opinion that there was no need for it to pronounce on the question of whether the Convention also protects the right not to marry, since in the Court's view the freedom to marry or not was not involved, and the discrimination against a child born out of wedlock fell outside the scope of Article 12.[1697]

[1695] Report of 13 December 1979, *Hamer*, D&R 24 (1981), p. 5 (14).
[1696] Appl. 10503/83, *Kleine Staarman* v. *the Netherlands*, D&R 42 (1985), p. 162 (165).
[1697] Judgment of 13 June 1979, A.31, pp. 28-29. Thus also the report of 10 December 1977, B.29 (1982), p. 55.

In the *Johnston* Case the Commission held that it is clear that the concept of 'family life' under Article 8 is not limited to the marriage-based family, but refers to people actually living together as a genuine family. However, according to the Commission, Article 8 does not oblige the State to grant a right to custody and care to a natural father of a child born out of wedlock where the parents were free to marry but had chosen not to do so.[1698]

That 'family' in the meaning of Article 8 is a broader concept than the marriage-based family has also been recognised by the Court, *e.g.* in the *Berrehab* Case, although the members of a family based on a 'lawful and genuine marriage' were still given a certain preferential treatment.[1699] This case-law has not yet resulted in the adoption of an equally broad interpretation of 'family' in Article 12.

That Article 12, according to the Commission, does not include the right to marry a deceased person posthumously, can hardly have come as a surprise.[1700]

In the *Abdulaziz, Cabales and Balkandali* Case the Court held that the expression 'family life' in the case of a married couple normally comprises cohabitation. In the Court's view this proposition is reinforced by the existence of Article 12, 'for it is scarcely conceivable that the right to found a family should not encompass the right to live together'.[1701]

12.2 The Right to Marry and National Law

Article 12 refers to national law and, consequently, accepts the possibility that the legal systems may vary among the Contracting States. In some Contracting States, for instance, the law attaches to the religious marriage ceremony the legal consequences of matrimony, whereas in other Contracting States this is not the case.[1702] And the question of when a person has reached marriageable age also needs not be answered the same way in all Contracting States. However, this does not mean that there are no common norms which the national law and those applying it have to respect and against which that law and application can be reviewed in Strasbourg. The very fact that Article 12 puts the *right* first and foremost implies that domestic regulations concerning the exercise of that right must not be of such a nature that the right itself would be affected in its essence. As the Commission stated in its report in the *Hamer* Case:

[1698] Report of 5 March 1985, A.112, p. 46.
[1699] Judgment of 21 June 1988, A.138, p. 14.
[1700] Appl. 10995/84, *M* v. *Federal Republic of Germany*, D&R 41 (1985), p. 259 (261).
[1701] Judgment of 28 May 1985, A.94, p. 32.
[1702] With regard to this, the Commission took the position that the refusal to register a marriage which has not been concluded according to the procedure legally prescribed, does not constitute a violation of Art. 12: Appl. 6167/73, *X* v. *Federal Republic of Germany*, D&R 1 (1975), p. 64 (65).

Whilst this is expressed as a 'right to marry (...) according to the national laws governing the exercise of this right', this does not mean that the scope afforded to national law is unlimited. If it were, Art. 12 would be redundant. The role of national law, as the wording of the Article indicates, is *to govern the exercise* of the right.[1703]

If the right to marry is denied to a person who is already married, this may be justified on the ground that the legislation prohibiting bigamy is so firmly anchored in the national legal order of most of the Contracting States that the Convention was not intended to change this. After all, for a person who is already married the essence of the right to marry is not affected by this prohibition. Similar reasoning applies with regard to the legislation according to which the right to marry is denied to persons below a given age. As long as there is a reasonable relation between that age limit and the concept of 'marriageable age', the essence of the right is not affected. But if the right to marry is denied to a person because of his limited mental faculties, his state of health, or his financial situation, the relevant national law cannot be justified as not affecting the essence of that right, assuming of course that such persons can be deemed capable of determining their free will to consent to the marriage.

Moreover, the conditions and restrictions set by domestic law may not amount to a violation of any of the other provisions of the Convention and its Protocols. Reference may be made, first of all, to Article 14, which prohibits the national authorities from discriminating in regulating the enjoyment of the rights and freedoms.[1704] Another instance to be thought of is the prohibition of inhuman treatment in Article 3; preventing a person from marrying or founding a family – one may think, for instance, of laws permitting compulsory sterilisation in certain cases – may assume the character of an inhuman treatment.[1705] That Article 8 would entail restrictions for regulating the right to marry is less imaginable, since both provisions will be interpreted in close correlation.[1706]

Article 12 does not provide a solution for cases in which the conclusion of a marriage involves links with various legal systems. The general reference to

---

[1703] Report of 13 December 1979, D&R 24 (1981), p. 5 (14). See also the report of 10 July 1980, *Draper*, D&R 24 (1981), p. 72 (78). In the same sense already the report of 1 March 1979, *Van Oosterwijck*, B.36 (1983), p. 27. In all three reports the Commission refers to the case-law of the Court to the effect that measures concerning the exercise of a right 'must never injure the substance of the right'.

[1704] The equality of the spouses as to marriage, during marriage and in the event of its dissolution is provided for in Art. 5 of Protocol No. 7 and will be discussed *infra*.

[1705] The prohibition imposed on a detainee to marry during his detention was not considered by the Commission as an inhuman or degrading treatment: Appl. 6564/74, *X v. the United Kingdom*, D&R 2 (1975), p. 105.

[1706] See, *e.g.*, Appl. 8041/77, *X v. Federal Republic of Germany* (not published), in which the applicant submitted that his deportation to the United States would destroy his marriage, because his wife would not be admitted to the United States. The Commission took the position that, since it had concluded that a violation of the first paragraph of Art. 8 found its justification in the second paragraph, it did not have to review the matter independently for its conformity with Art. 12.

national law implies that this is left to the rules of private international law (conflicts of law) applying in the country where the marriage is to take place.[1707] This means, for instance, that a person whose national law permits polygamy cannot rely on this law under Article 12 in a country where polygamy is prohibited by law and this norm is applied as being one of public policy. Here again, of course, application of a certain rule of private international law may not lead to discrimination. Because of the implications of nationality in this respect, changing a person's nationality may, under certain circumstances, entail restrictions for his possibility to marry. In the *Beldjoudi* Case the Commission addressed this issue but did not find, in the facts referred to by the applicants, any appearance of a violation of Article 12.[1708]

12.3 The Right to Marry of Persons of the Same Sex

A more difficult point is the question of how to regard national legislation which only permits two persons of the opposite sex to marry. Can homosexuals of marriageable age claim a right to marry a person of the same sex, submitting that marriage with a person of the opposite sex does not present a genuine marriage for them? It may safely be assumed that, when the text of Article 12 was drawn up, the term 'marriage' alluded exclusively to an institutionalised relationship between two persons of the opposite sex. And indeed, in its report in the *Van Oosterwijck* Case the Commission emphasises that 'a marriage requires the existence of a relationship between two persons of the opposite sex'.[1709] And in a case against Sweden the Commission took the same position in respect of two persons who biologically were not of the same sex, but where one of the partners had adopted the same sex as the other partner through a voluntary act recognised under domestic law.[1710] However, the question would seem justified whether a more flexible interpretation is not called for in this respect under the influence of changing views in society.

In the *Van Oosterwijck* Case the complaint concerned the fact that Belgian law prohibited Van Oosterwijck, who had been entered in the birth registry as a woman, from marrying a woman. That case was different from the question raised above insofar as Van Oosterwijck submitted that he was mentally as well as physically a man, so that according to that submission this would not be a marriage between partners of the same sex. In this case the Commission held that:

[1707] Appl. 9057/80, *X* v. *Switzerland*, D&R 26 (1982), p. 207 (208).
[1708] Report of 6 September 1990, A.234-A, p. 47.
[1709] Report of 1 March 1979, B.36 (1983), pp. 27-28. See also the opinion of the Commission members Fawcett, Tenekides, Gözübüyük, Soyer and Batliner annexed to the report of 12 December 1984, *Rees*, A.106, pp. 28-29, and the Court's judgment of 17 October 1986, *Rees*, A.106, p. 19.
[1710] Appl. 14573/89, *Eriksson and Goldschmidt* v. *Sweden*, D&R 63 (1989), p. 213 (215-216).

by raising in advance to any application to marry an indirect objection based merely on the statements in the birth certificate and the general theory of the rectification of civil status certificates without examining the matter more thoroughly, the government has in fact failed in the instant case to recognise the applicant's right to marry and found a family within the meaning of Article 12 of the Convention.[1711]

The words 'without examining the matter more thoroughly' would seem to leave the door open as regards the question raised above.[1712] The applicant's complaint was based on Articles 8 and 12. According to the Commission the Belgian State had violated both articles.

However, some years later, in the *Rees* Case, the Commission changed or clarified its position.[1713] In the Commission's unanimous opinion Article 12 had not been violated, but the Commission was divided as to the reasons for this conclusion. There were two lines of reasoning. Five members of the Commission were of the opinion that the complaint under Article 12 was a necessary consequence of the violation of Article 8: 'There is no reason to believe that once this obstacle [the applicant is not recognised as a "man"] has been removed the applicant is still not able to marry.'[1714] The other five members of the Commission wanted to separate the application of Article 8 from the application of Article 12:

> The protection of private life includes (...) the recognition (...) of a person's civil status as a man or a woman (...), but the national law can clearly require men and women protected by Article 8 (...) to satisfy specific requirements in order to marry and found a family with respect to the formalities required for contracting a marriage (...), and may also exclude certain specified categories of men and women.[1715]

These five members based their view that Article 12 was not violated on the interpretation that the 'social purpose' of Article 12 includes the physical capacity to procreate since the 'references to marriageable age and to the different sex of the spouses are obviously intended to refer to the physical capacity to procreate'. This led them to the following conclusion:

> It follows that a Contracting State must be permitted to exclude from marriage persons whose sexual category itself implies a physical incapacity to procreate either absolutely (in the case of a transsexual) or in relation to the sexual category of the other spouse (in the case of individuals of the same sex).[1716]

The question whether, even if the latters' interpretation was correct for the moment the Convention was drafted, this social purpose may have lost that exclusive orientation in the years in which the Convention has been in existence

---

[1711] Report of 1 March 1979, B.36 (1983), p. 27.
[1712] See, however, the dissenting opinion of the Commission members Sperduti and Kiernan, annexed to the report.
[1713] Report of 12 December 1984, A.106, p. 27.
[1714] Opinion of Frowein, Busuttil, Trechsel, Carrilo and Schermers, *ibidem*, p. 27.
[1715] Opinion of Fawcett, Tenekides, Gözübüyük, Soyer and Batliner, *ibidem*, pp. 28-29.
[1716] *Idem.*

as a 'living instrument', was not expressly addressed. The view expressed by the latter five Commission members was in clear contradiction with the earlier statement of the Commission in the *Van Oosterwijck* Case that 'there is nothing to support the conclusion that the capacity to procreate is an essential condition of marriage or even that procreation is an essential purpose of marriage.'[1717] However, their opinion seems to have received support from the Court. In the *Marckx* Case the Court had already indicated that all the legal effects attaching to marriage do not have to apply equally 'to situations that are in certain respects comparable to marriage'.[1718] In its *Rees* judgment the Court held without much argument that:

> the right to marry guaranteed by Article 12 refers to the traditional marriage between persons of the opposite biological sex. This appears also from the wording of the Article which makes it clear that Article 12 is mainly concerned to protect marriage as the basis of the family.[1719]

The Court was of the opinion that a legal impediment to the marriage of persons who are not of the opposite biological sex cannot be said to restrict or reduce the right in such a way or to such an extent that the very essence of the right is impaired.

It is submitted here that this statement may be correct in an abstract sense, but is subject to serious doubt in the concrete situation of homosexuals or transsexuals. Indeed, what essence of the right to marry is left for them? And what is the essential difference in this respect between partners of the same sex on the one hand, and partners of the opposite sex who cannot or do not wish to have children on the other hand? Does one speak also of an 'improper marriage' in the latter case?

In the *Cossey* Case the Commission, once again, changed its view. By a majority of ten to six it held, basing itself on the fact that the applicant was anatomically no longer of male sex and had a male partner wishing to marry her, that the situation of this transsexual fell under the protection of Article 12:

> The Commission agrees, in principle, with the Court, that Article 12 refers to the traditional marriage between persons of opposite biological sex. It cannot, however, be inferred from Article 12 that the capacity to procreate is a necessary requirement for the right in question. Men or women, who are unable to have children, enjoy the right to marry just as other persons. Therefore, biological sex cannot for the purpose of Article 12 be related to the capacity to procreate.[1720]

The Court did not follow the majority of the Commission. By fourteen votes to four it held as follows:

[1717] Report of 1 March 1979, B.36 (1983), p. 28.
[1718] Judgment of 13 June 1979, A.31, p. 29.
[1719] Judgment of 17 October 1986, A.106, p. 19.
[1720] Report of 9 May 1989, A.184, p. 51.

607

Although some Contracting States would now regard as valid a marriage between a person in Miss Cossey's situation and a man, the developments which have occurred to date (...) cannot be said to evidence any general abandonment of the traditional concept of marriage. In these circumstances, the Court does not consider that it is open to it to take a new approach to the interpretation of Article 12 on the point at issue.[1721]

The Court also repeated its view that the legal impediment on the marriage of persons who are not of the opposite biological sex cannot be said to impair the very essence of the right to marry.[1722]

Of the members belonging to the minority, judge Martens presented an extensive and quite comprehensive dissenting opinion. In his view, a true reconsideration of the issues arising under Article 12 should have led the Court to conclude that the *Rees* judgment was wrong 'or at least that present-day conditions warranted a different decision in the Cossey case'.[1723] As to the Court's view that the right to marry is not impaired in its essence by the impediments in question, judge Martens observes that the Court could take that position only because it based itself on the restrictive position that Article 12 confines the right to marry to persons who are of the opposite *biological* sex.[1724] Although he agrees with the Court that Article 12 applies to marriage as the union of two persons of the opposite sex, in his opinion that does not necessarily mean that 'sex' in this context must be interpreted as 'biological sex'.[1725] Finally, with respect to the relevance of the ability to procreate, judge Martens states in what may well be called his 'panegyric on marriage':

> Marriage is far more than a sexual union, and the capacity for sexual intercourse is therefore not '*essential*' for marriage. Persons who are not or are no longer capable of procreating or having sexual intercourse may also want to and do marry. That is because marriage is far more than a union which legitimates sexual intercourse and aims at procreating: it is a legal institution which creates a fixed legal relationship between both the partners and third parties (including the authorities); (...) it is, moreover, a species of togetherness in which intellectual, spiritual and emotional bonds are at least as essential as the physical one.[1726]

In *B* v. *France*, where the Court reached a conclusion with respect to Article 8 which differed from that in the *Rees* Case and the *Cossey* Case by distinguishing

---

[1721] Judgment of 27 September 1990, A.184, p. 18.
[1722] *Ibidem*, p. 17.
[1723] *Ibidem*, p. 22.
[1724] *Ibidem*, p. 31.
[1725] *Ibidem*, p. 32.
[1726] *Ibidem*, p. 33. See also the joint dissenting opinion of judges Palm, Foighel and Pekkanen, *ibidem*, p. 44: 'The fact that a transsexual is unable to procreate cannot, however, be decisive. There are many men and women who cannot have children but, in spite of this, they unquestionably have the right to marry'.

the facts in the former case from those in the two latter cases,[1727] Article 12 had not been relied upon by the applicant and, therefore, was not addressed by the Court. It is to be hoped that the changing attitude towards the situation which confronts transsexuals, which the Court shows in *B* v. *France*, will also lead to a change in the Court's case-law with respect to Article 12.

In *X, Y and Z* v. *the United Kingdom*, which concerns a transsexual who claims the right to be recognised as the father of the child born to his partner as a result of artificial insemination by a donor, the Commission has found a violation of Article 8. Article 12 was not relied upon by the applicants. The Commission held that this case had to be distinguished from the *Kerkhoven* Case concerning two lesbian partners, in that in the former case there has been a re-assignment of gender which means that the two partners no longer are of the same sex.[1728] The Court held that the lack of common ground amongst the European States regarding the parental rights of transsexuals affords the Contracting States a wide margin of appreciation. In this case the Court held that Article 8 had not been violated.[1729]

12.4 Does the Right to Marry Include the Right to Divorce and to Remarry?

In the *Johnston* Case, where a complaint had been lodged against Ireland where divorce is not permitted, the Court has held that Article 12 does not oblige the Contracting States to provide legal possibilities to dissolve a marriage. For an *a contrario* argument the Court refers to Article 16 of the Universal Declaration of Human Rights which, in addition to the right to marry and to found a family, provides for the entitlement to 'equal rights as to marriage, during marriage and at its dissolution', words which were deliberately left out of the Convention. The Court concludes that 'the *travaux préparatoires* disclose no intention to include in Article 12 any guarantee of a right to have the ties of marriage dissolved by divorce'.[1730] The applicants had referred to the judgment of the Court in the *Marckx* Case, where it was upheld that the Convention is a living instrument which ought to be interpreted in the light of the present-day conditions. To this the Court responds as follows:

[1727] Judgment of 25 March 1992, A.232-C, pp. 53-54. The Court took great effort to leave the impression that the fact that it reached a different conclusion here, found its reason merely in differences between the French and English systems; see *ibidem*, p. 49, where the Court states in so many words that 'there is as yet no sufficiently broad consensus between the Member States of the Council of Europe to persuade the Court to reach opposite conclusions to those in its Rees and Cossey judgments'.

[1728] Report of 27 June 1995, Reports 1997-II, Vol. 35, para. 55. See, however, the concurring opinion of Mr Schermers, who rejects the distinction made.

[1729] Judgment of 22 April 1997, Reports 1997-II, Vol. 35, para. 44.

[1730] Judgment of 18 December 1986, A.112, p. 24.

However, the Court cannot, by means of an evolutive interpretation, derive from these instruments a right that was not included therein at the outset. This is particularly so here, where the omission was deliberate.[1731]

The Court furthermore points out that the right to divorce is not included in Protocol No. 7 to the Convention. The opportunity was not taken to deal with this question in Article 5 of the Protocol, which guarantees certain additional rights to spouses, notably in the event of dissolution of marriage. Indeed, paragraph 39 of the Explanatory Report to the Protocol states that the words 'in the event of its dissolution' found in Article 5 'do not imply any obligation on a State to provide for dissolution of marriage or to provide any special forms of dissolution'.[1732] Finally, the Court holds with respect to the applicant's view that the prohibition of divorce is to be seen as a restriction on the capacity to marry that, even if this is the case, such a restriction cannot be regarded as injuring the substance of the right to marry 'in a society adhering to the principle of monogamy'.[1733] The phrase between quotation marks is difficult to understand since in many cases the possibility of divorce would precisely serve to avoid situations of factual bigamy.

In *F* v. *Switzerland* the complaint concerned Article 150 of the Swiss Civil Code, which provided for a prohibition of remarriage for a period ranging from one to three years to be imposed by the court on the party at fault in the event of divorce granted on the ground of adultery. This provision had been applied to the applicant for the maximum period. The Court rejected the Government's argument that the system of temporarily prohibiting remarriage served to protect the institution of marriage and the rights of others. The Court expressed doubt as to whether the system was an appropriate means for protecting the stability of marriage and it found that the interests of the future spouse were not protected by it and that the interests of the child born out of the relationship could be harmed. Next, the Court distinguished the present case from the *Johnston* Case by holding that:

> If national legislation allows divorce, which is not a requirement of the Convention, Article 12 secures for divorced persons the right to remarry without unreasonable restrictions.[1734]

The Court reached the conclusion that the disputed measure, which affected the very essence of the right to marry, was disproportionate to the legitimate aim pursued. Thus the Court not only addressed the question of whether the right to marry was affected in its essence but in addition introduced the criterion of proportionality. This approach seems to differ from the one adopted in the *Rees* judgment, referred to above.[1735]

[1731]   *Ibidem*, p. 25.
[1732]   *Idem.*
[1733]   *Ibidem*, p. 18.
[1734]   Judgment of 18 December 1987, A.128, p. 18.
[1735]   See *supra* p. 607.

12.5 The Right to Found a Family

With respect to the right to found a family, too, Article 12 does not guarantee a socio-economic right to, for instance, sufficient living accommodation and sufficient means of subsistence to keep a family.[1736] Article 12 primarily implies a prohibition for the authorities to interfere with the founding of a family, for instance by prescribing the compulsory use of contraceptives, ordering a non-voluntary sterilisation or abortion, or tolerating the performance thereof. Here again, it will have to be assumed that 'the national laws governing the exercise of this right' may regulate the enjoyment of this right, but may not exclude it altogether or affect it in its essence. As has been observed before, the victim of such a measure is also entitled to invoke Article 3, and in case of abortion perhaps also Article 2.[1737] Whether such an interference against the will of the person concerned is permitted in case of medical necessity depends on the question of whether the right to life has to be considered an inalienable right, for which ultimately the authorities bear responsibility.[1738]

If the person who is most directly concerned consents to the medical treatment leading to sterilisation or abortion, but the partner does not, the question arises whether the interests of the latter are also protected by Article 12, assuming that the treatment in question is permitted by law. Since Article 12 refers to both partners, in principle the answer has to be in the affirmative. However, a conflict then arises between the rights and interests of the two partners, while in the case of abortion the issue of possible rights and interests of the foetus may also play a part.[1739] The national authorities have to resolve this conflict in their law and legal practice by weighing all the interests involved. The result of this may then ultimately be submitted to the Strasbourg organs for review of its conformity with, *inter alia*, Article 12. Although no concrete solution can be worked out here, it is submitted that Article 12 entails at all events the positive obligation that the law prescribes that before the treatment in question takes place a reasonable effort should be made to obtain the consent of both partners.[1740] If no agreement is reached, in case of sterilisation the right of the most directly affected person to have control of her or his own body will have to be decisive. Indeed, just as in the case of a marriage, for the foundation of a family the agreement of both partners is required. If the consent of one of the two is lacking, it can no longer be said that the right of the other to found a family is affected in relation to the former. In the case of abortion the situation is different insofar as there the two partners have already taken a first step — whether intentional or not — to found or increase a family. If they do not agree on the question of whether the pregnancy is to

---

[1736] Appl. 11776/85, *Andersson and Kullman v. Sweden*, D&R 46 (1986), p. 251 (253).
[1737] *Supra* p. 302.
[1738] On this, see *supra* p. 303.
[1739] On this, see *supra* pp. 300-303.
[1740] For the different view of the Commission, see *supra* p. 302.

continue, here again consultation of both partners should be prescribed, but ultimately the rights and interests of the woman should have priority over those of the man. Indeed, her body is most directly concerned, and possibly her health and even her life may be at stake. In general, therefore, the consequences for the woman of the performance or non-performance of abortion will be greater than for the man. This leaves open the question of whether and, if so, how the rights and interests of the woman have to be weighed against any possible rights and interests of the foetus.[1741]

As regards adoption, the Commission has taken the position that a family may also be founded by means of adopting a child,[1742] but that Article 12 does not guarantee a *right* to adopt or otherwise integrate into the family a child who is not the natural child of the couple concerned.[1743] The two views would seem to contradict one another. In fact, if it is recognised that there are different ways of founding a family, why should only one of those ways form part of the right conferred in Article 12, even in those cases where for the person(s) in question the other way is in fact the only possible way to found a family? Of course the national authorities will have to be allowed ample scope for regulating the conditions for adoption, in which context the rights of the persons concerned will have to be weighed carefully against those of others, especially the natural parents, while the rights and interests of the child should have priority. However, this need not bar the recognition of the right as such.

In a more recent decision the Commission did not state that Article 12 does not imply a right to adopt a child, but emphasised that it was left to national law to determine whether, or subject to what conditions, the exercise of such a right should be permitted.[1744] Thus the Commission has impliedly recognised that Article 12 also applies to adoption. It should then, however, review the restrictions and conditions imposed by national law for their reasonableness, thus guaranteeing that Article 12 is not affected in its essence nor in a discriminatory way.[1745]

If any method of artificial reproduction is prohibited by the national law of a Contracting State, that would seem to affect the right to found a family in its essence for the person concerned, unless adoption is possible and may be considered to be an equivalent alternative. There is, however, no case-law on the matter.

In *X, Y and Z v. the United Kingdom* a female to male transsexual and his female partner claimed legal recognition of the former as the father of a child born to the latter as a result of artificial insemination by a donor. In that case, the

---

[1741] See *supra* pp. 300-303.
[1742] Appl. 7229/75, *X and Y v. the United Kingdom*, D&R 12 (1978), p. 32 (34). See also the report of 1 March 1979, *Van Oosterwijck*, B.36 (1983), p. 28.
[1743] Appl. 7229/75, *X and Y v. the United Kingdom*, D&R 12 (1978), p. 32 (34-35).
[1744] Appl. 8896/80, *X v. the Netherlands*, D&R 24 (1981), p. 176 (177).
[1745] A State is not obliged to recognise a foreign adoption: Appl. 7229, *X and Y v. the United Kingdom*, D&R 12 (1978), p. 32 (35).

Commission found a violation of Article 8,[1746] whereas the Court reached the opposite conclusion.[1747] Article 12, which could be relevant to the situation concerned, was not relied upon by the applicants.

The question of whether the right to found a family also implies the right to increase the family, or on the contrary has been realised with the birth or adoption of the first child, has so far been expressly left open by the Commission.[1748] It is submitted here that the question has to be answered in the former sense. After the birth of their first child some parents may take the view that they have thus founded the family they wanted, but for others this is the case only after two or more children. Since the Convention does not provide any indication in this respect and could not very well do so, it must be assumed that in national law, too, no limit may be set, since such a limitation would affect the right in its essence for some people, even apart from the possible conflict with Article 9. In our view, family planning can therefore only be stimulated on a voluntary basis.[1749]

12.6 The Relationship Between the Right to Marry and the Right to Found a Family

Must the right to found a family be deemed to be coupled with the right to marry, also mentioned in Article 12, in the sense that exclusively married couples have the former right? This was almost certainly the original intention, considering the fact that the two rights are merged into one right in Article 12 in the words 'the exercise of this right', while the words 'of marriageable age' also point in that direction.[1750] And, indeed, the Court held in the *Rees* Case that 'Article 12 is mainly concerned to protect marriage as the basis of the family'.[1751]

However, just as has been observed above with regard to the concept of 'family life' in Article 8, here again it may be submitted that since the drafting of the Convention the views with respect to the monopoly of marriage have been subject to great changes, while other forms of cohabitation, with family relations adapted thereto, are finding increasing recognition, also juridically.[1752] The text of Article 12 would seem to leave sufficient scope for an interpretation of the

---

[1746] Report of 27 June 1995, Reports 1997-II, Vol. 35.
[1747] Judgment of 22 April 1997, Reports 1997-II, Vol. 35.
[1748] Appl. 6564/74, *X* v. *the United Kingdom*, D&R 2 (1975), p. 105 (106).
[1749] *Cf.* Art. 16 of the Proclamation of Teheran of 1968; United Nations, *Human Rights; a Compilation of International Instruments*, Vol. I (First Part), New York, 1994, p. 54: 'Parents have a basic human right to determine freely and responsibly the number and the spacing of their children'.
[1750] Thus also the Commission in its decision on Appl. 6482/74, *X* v. *Belgium and the Netherlands*, D&R 7 (1977), p. 75 (77). See also the opinion of Commission members Fawcett, Tenekides, Gözübüyük, Soyer and Batliner, laid down in the report of the Commission of 12 December 1984 in the *Rees* Case, A.106, pp. 28-29.
[1751] Judgment of 17 October 1986, A.106, p. 19.
[1752] See *supra* pp. 504-508.

concept of 'founding a family' in which these developments are taken into account. In *X* v. *Belgium and the Netherlands* a bachelor invoked Article 12 in a complaint against the application of Articles 227 and 228 of the Dutch Civil Code, which made adoption possible only for married couples. In its decision the Commission left open the question of whether 'the right to found a family may be considered irrespective of marriage', although according to the formulation chosen it appears to be inclined to answer this question in the negative. It did, however, infer from the text of Article 12 that for the exercise of that right '[t]he existence of a couple is fundamental'.[1753] The issue raised here is also of direct relevance for the question whether a provision of national law which makes a differentiation between married and unmarried couples in respect of the right to found a family, will have to be reviewed for its compatibility with Article 14.

12.7 Article 12 and Deportation and Extradition

It is recognised in the case-law that from Article 12, too, restrictions may ensue for the authorities of the Contracting States as to their power of deportation or extradition and their power to refuse aliens access to their territory. As regards the right to marry, however, Article 12 can be invoked successfully only against an (imminent) measure of deportation or extradition, or against a refusal of access, if the person in question can make it sufficiently plausible that he has concrete plans to marry and that both partners cannot reasonably be expected to realise those plans outside the country concerned.[1754] And with regard to the right to found a family, just as in the case of Article 8,[1755] the Commission has usually taken the view that deportation, extradition and refusal of access to the territory of the State do not constitute a violation of Article 12, if the partner is in a position to follow the person concerned to the country of deportation or extradition, or to the country of the latter's residence or any other country, and if this may reasonably be required of the former.[1756]

In the *Abdulaziz, Cabales and Balkandali* Case the Court held that, although by guaranteeing the right to respect for family life Article 8 presupposes the existence of a family, 'this does not mean that all intended family life falls entirely outside its ambit'.[1757] This implies that couples who apply for admission of one of them in view of their intention to marry may also rely on Article 8 and that, here again, the Court will not be inclined to investigate an alleged violation of Article 12 separately after it has found a violation or non-violation of Article 8. In fact, in

---

[1753] Appl. 6482/74, D&R 7 (1977), p. 75 (77).
[1754] Appl. 7175/75, *X* v. *Federal Republic of Germany*, D&R 6 (1977), p. 138 (140).
[1755] On this *supra* pp. 520-521.
[1756] See, *e.g.*, Appl. 2535/65, *X* v. *Federal Republic of Germany*, Coll. 17 (1966), p. 28 (30), where the Commission furthermore took into account that the applicant, when she married, knew that her husband did not have a residence permit. For a case of refusal of admission, see Appl. 5301/71, *X* v. *the United Kingdom*, Coll. 43 (1973), p. 82 (84).
[1757] Judgment of 28 May 1985, A.94, p. 32.

the *Abdulaziz, Cabales and Balkandali* Case Article 12 was not invoked by the applicants.

12.8 Article 12 and Detained Persons

With regard to Article 12, too, the question has arisen whether inherent limitations ensue from detention for the exercise of the rights provided in that article.[1758]

When a person detained on remand complained about the refusal of the German authorities to give their consent to his getting married during his detention, the complaint was dismissed by the Commission as manifestly ill-founded. The Commission did not advance its own reasons for this, but mentioned in its decision the grounds on which the *Landgericht* had based its decision, *viz.* that it was expected that the person in question would be detained for a long time, so that he would not be able to cohabit with his future wife for a long time to come, which would be required to give a sound basis to a marriage; that in view of his personality and the unusually long engagement period it could not be assumed that he seriously intended to marry; and that marriages of prisoners inevitably tended to affect the maintenance of order in a prison.[1759]

The first ground would appear absolutely irrelevant since, even apart from the violation of the presumption of innocence, it is not for the authorities to prescribe to a married couple a given type of conjugal life, and this certainly must not be made a condition. Many years later, in its reports in the *Hamer* Case and the *Draper* Case, this was recognised by the Commission. In its report in the *Hamer* Case the Commission opined as follows:

> In considering whether the imposition of such a delay [in consequence of the detention] breached the applicant's right to marry, the Commission does not regard it as relevant that he could not have cohabited with his wife or consummated his marriage whilst serving his sentence. The essence of the right to marry, in the Commission's opinion, is the formation of a legally binding association between a man and a woman. It is for them to decide whether or not they wish to enter such an association in circumstances where they cannot cohabit.[1760]

For the second ground given in the decision referred to above insufficient arguments were advanced, at least judging from the decision as it was published. In cases where persons who are not detained wish to get married, their possible intention to conclude a fictitious marriage is not examined and rightly so; at most, certain legal consequences are denied to what is obviously a fictitious marriage, for instance the acquisition of a nationality. The argument of the fictitious marriage therefore can be used against a prisoner only if it is likely that the marriage ceremony is intended in reality, for example, to enable his escape, in which case there is indeed an abuse of right. It is only in the case of the third

---

[1758] For a detailed discussion of the inherent limitations, see *infra* pp. 763-765.

[1759] Appl. 892/60, *X* v. *Federal Republic of Germany*, Yearbook IV (1961), p. 240 (256).

[1760] Report of 13 December 1979, D&R 24 (1981), p. 5 (16). Similar wording is to be found in the report of 10 July 1980 in the *Draper* Case, D&R 24 (1981), p. 72 (81).

ground that we have to do with an inherent limitation, albeit a very broad and vague one, which is related to the purpose and the execution of the detention.

As has previously been observed, the doctrine of inherent limitations has been rejected by the Court, at least for those provisions of the Convention in which the restrictions are enumerated expressly, and then also exhaustively.[1761] Such an enumeration does not occur in Article 12; the only restriction mentioned there is the general one 'according to the national laws governing the exercise of this right'. Could national law contain special restrictions for prisoners? The Commission was faced with this question in the above-mentioned *Hamer* Case, where the complaint concerned the refusal of a request by a prisoner for temporary leave with a view to the conclusion of a marriage. Here the Commission departed from its earlier – almost automatic – decisions concerning inherent limitations and decided that prisoners who have the requisite age and further satisfy the legal conditions have the right to marry. If on the basis of national law restrictions may be imposed with respect to this right at all, according to the Commission – which referred to the judgments of the Court in the *Belgian Linguistic* Case[1762] and the *Golder* Case[1763] – these restrictions must not be of such a nature as to affect the *essence* of the right to marry. This means that:

> national law may not otherwise deprive a person or category of persons of full legal capacity of the right to marry. Nor may it substantially interfere with the exercise of the right.[1764]

Although admitting that some administrative arrangements must be made by the prison authorities before a prisoner can marry, the Commission was of the opinion that some positive action is required on their part to make the right effective.[1765] The Commission subsequently concluded that when a person is obliged by the authorities to defer the marriage for a considerable time (in this case, for two years), in general this affects the right to marry in its essence, regardless of whether the delay is due to legislation which is only intended to regulate the exercise of that right, to an administrative act, or to a combination of the two. In the Commission's opinion the mere fact of the detention does not provide a justification for thus affecting the said right, since 'no particular difficulties are involved in allowing the marriage of prisoners'.[1766]

When a prisoner complained that he was not allowed conjugal life and thus also could not increase his family, the Commission – leaving open the question of whether a person who already has children can still invoke Article 12[1767] – held that Article 12 indeed contains an absolute right, but does not imply for that

---

[1761] See *infra* pp. 763-765.
[1762] Judgment of 23 July 1968, A.6, p. 32.
[1763] Judgment of 21 February 1975, A.18, pp. 18-19.
[1764] Report of 13 December 1979, D&R 24 (1981), p. 5 (14).
[1765] *Ibidem*, p. 15.
[1766] *Ibidem*, pp. 15-16.
[1767] On this, *supra* p. 613.

reason that a person must at all times be given the actual possibility to beget offspring, and that the applicant had to blame himself for this temporary impossibility.[1768] Leaving aside the additional remark about the blameworthiness, which, even if tenable according to modern doctrines of criminology and forensic psychiatry, at all events may not be used as a justification of restrictions which are not justified otherwise, the Commission would appear to differentiate here between the possibility of founding a family in general and that possibility at a given moment. In the Commission's opinion measures in consequence of which a person is temporarily unable to found a family or increase his family do not constitute a violation of Article 12, since considering the preceding and the subsequent possibilities, on the whole the person in question has not been deprived of that right. It does not appear from its decision whether the Commission took into account the length of the detention, but it is obvious that this point is of relevance for the legitimacy of the reasoning followed by the Commission since, here as well, the exercise of the right may not be substantially interfered with.

In a later decision the Commission apparently followed a different line of reasoning. This decision concerned a complaint of a husband and wife, who were both detained in the same prison for pre-trial investigations and who had been refused detention in the same cell. In this case the Commission assumed a relation between the right to protection of privacy and family life in Article 8 and the right to found a family in Article 12. After first having concluded that the restrictions imposed upon the married couple with respect to their right to privacy and to respect for their family life could find their justification in the second paragraph of Article 8, the Commission subsequently held that restrictions which are not contrary to Article 8 on that ground cannot constitute a conflict with the right granted in Article 12 either.[1769] In its general formulation this argument would seem to be incorrect. Article 12 has an independent place in the Convention beside Article 8, also as regards the second element: the right to found a family. Considering the indeed notable fact that the drafters of the Convention have not included an enumeration of restrictions in Article 12, this provision must not be subjected to the regime of the second paragraph of Article 8. However, in our opinion the argumentation of the Commission *is* correct insofar as it amounts to declaring in fact Article 8, and not Article 12, applicable to a measure by which the partners to a marriage or to a comparable relationship are temporarily deprived of the opportunity for sexual intercourse. Even if the desired sexual intercourse would actually be aimed at the foundation or increase of a family, it cannot be said that their right to do so is substantially restricted by such a temporary measure. The same applies, for instance, with regard to conscript soldiers who

---

[1768] Appl. 6564/74, *X* v. *the United Kingdom*, D&R 2 (1975), p. 105 (106). The Commission quotes that passage in its report of 13 December 1979 in the *Hamer* Case, D&R 24 (1981), p. 5 (14).

[1769] Appl. 8166/78, *X and Y* v. *Switzerland*, D&R 13 (1979), p. 241 (242-244). The same reasoning was also followed in Appls 5260 and 5277/71, *X and Y* v. *Austria* (not published).

during a given period are unable to lead a normal conjugal life. The situation will, however, have to be judged separately for each individual case, because in the case of a measure applied for a longer period Article 12 may indeed come into issue. In this context it is noteworthy that the Commission has opened the door for a dynamic development by referring expressly and with approval to:

> the reformative movement in several European countries as regards an improvement of the conditions of imprisonment and the possibilities for detained persons of continuing their conjugal life to a limited extent.[1770]

12.9 Derogation

Article 12 does not belong to the category of the rights which are non-derogable in virtue of Article 15(2).

13 RIGHT TO THE PEACEFUL ENJOYMENT OF ONE'S POSSESSIONS (ARTICLE 1 OF PROTOCOL NO. 1)

Every natural or legal person is entitled to the peaceful enjoyment of his possessions. No one shall be deprived of his possessions except in the public interest and subject to the conditions provided for by law and by the general principles of international law. The preceding provisions shall not, however, in any way impair the right of a State to enforce such laws as it deems necessary to control the use of property in accordance with the general interest or to secure the payment of taxes or other contributions or penalties.

13.1 Introduction

The classification of the right to the enjoyment of one's possessions – at least in an unqualified form – among the human rights is not unchallenged. And indeed, the UN Covenant on Civil and Political Rights contains no provision equivalent to Article 17 of the Universal Declaration. That the drafters of the Convention also hesitated about the status and exact formulation of this right may appear from the fact that it was not included among the original rights and freedoms of the Convention, but was added later by Protocol No. 1.[1771] The right of property has actually lost a good deal of its inviolability, also in the Member States of the Council of Europe, under the influence of modern social policy (*Sozialstaat*). This fact is recognised in the very far-reaching limitations which Article 1 allows.

As the Court has often held, Article 1 comprises three distinct rules. The first rule, which is expressed in the first sentence and is of a general nature, lays down the principle of peaceful enjoyment of property. The second rule, in the second sentence, covers deprivation of possessions and makes it subject to certain conditions. The third rule, laid down in the second paragraph, recognises that the

---

[1770] Appl. 8166/78, *X and Y v. Switzerland*, D&R 13 (1979), p. 243. Thus also earlier in Appl. 3603/68, *X v. Federal Republic of Germany*, Coll. 31 (1970), p. 48 (50).

[1771] This Protocol entered into force on 18 May 1954. For the state of ratifications see Appendix I.

Contracting States are entitled, amongst other things, to control the use of property in accordance with the general interest, by enforcing such laws as they deem necessary for the purpose. However, these rules are not 'distinct' in the sense of being unconnected: the second and the third rule are concerned with particular instances of interference with the right to peaceful enjoyment of property. They must therefore be construed in the light of the general principle laid down in the first rule.[1772]

As with other rights and freedoms of the Convention, the Court has recognised that, in principle, the State may be responsible under Article 1 for interferences with the peaceful enjoyment of possessions resulting from transactions between private individuals. However, for the State's responsibility to be engaged, it is necessary that the facts complained of are the result of an exercise of State authority and that they do not concern exclusively contractual relations between private individuals.[1773]

Before turning to the case-law with respect to the above-mentioned three rules, we shall first examine a particular question related to the applicability of Article 1, that is: the meaning of the term 'possessions'.

13.2   The Concept of 'Possessions'

In the *Marckx* Case the Court held that 'Article 1 is in substance guaranteeing the right of property'.[1774] However, the concept of 'possessions' in the first sentence of Article 1 must not be understood in the technical-juridical meaning of the word; it is wider, as also appears from the French word '*biens*'.

In its judgment in the case of *Gasus Dosier- und Fördertechnik GmbH*, the Court confirmed that the notion of 'possessions' has an autonomous meaning which is not limited to ownership of physical goods: certain other rights and interests constituting assets can also be regarded as property rights and thus as 'possessions'. In that case, the Court considered it immaterial whether the applicant's right to a concrete-mixer (which had been seised and sold by the Dutch

---

[1772]   See, among many judgments, judgment of 23 September 1982, *Sporrong and Lönnroth*, A.52, p. 24; judgment of 21 February 1986, *James and Others*, A.98, p. 29; judgment of 8 July 1986, *Lithgow and Others*, A.102, p. 46; judgment of 24 October 1986, *AGOSI*, A.108, p. 17; judgment of 23 April 1987, *Erkner and Hofauer*, A.117, p. 65; judgment of 23 April 1987, *Poiss*, A.117, p. 107; judgment of 18 February 1991, *Fredin*, A.192, p. 14; judgment of 16 September 1996, *Matos e Silva, Lda. and Others*, Reports 1996-IV, Vol. 14, para. 81.

[1773]   See judgment of 25 April 1996, *Gustafsson*, Reports 1996-II, Vol. 9, para. 60 (applicability of Art. 1 denied). See also judgment of 21 February 1986, *James and Others*, A.98, pp. 28-29, in which the Court endorsed the view of the Commission that its examination of the applicants' complaints had to focus on the legislation which produced effects, in the form of a series of individual transactions between private persons, on their ownership rights. The applicants' view that each individual transaction had to be examined for compliance with Art. 1 was rejected.

[1774]   Judgment of 13 June 1979, A.31, p. 27.

tax authorities) was a right of ownership or a security right *in rem*.[1775] This autonomy does not mean that domestic law is completely irrelevant for determining whether there is a 'possession'. When, in the case of *Pressos Compania Naviera S.A. and Others*, the Belgian Government invoked the autonomy of the term 'possession' in order to argue that Article 1 was inapplicable to the applicants' claim under domestic tort law, the Court responded by stating that it may have regard to the domestic law where there is nothing to suggest that that law runs counter to the object and purpose of Article 1. On this basis, the Court accepted that the rules in question were rules of tort. Next, however, it held that where the domestic law of tort creates a right of compensation as soon as the damage occurs, the resulting claim constitutes an asset and therefore amounts to a 'possession' within the meaning of Article 1.[1776]

As a consequence, Article 1 may come into play in relation to a variety of claims 'constituting assets'. As the case-law on this point is still developing, it is difficult to deduce precise criteria. However, the case-law offers some general pointers.

The basic point of departure appears to be the economic value of the right or interest: where State measures do not affect this economic value, no responsibility under Article 1 is engaged. For example, the right to live in a home which one does not own is not a possession within the meaning of Article 1.[1777] Neither does Article 1 protect a particular quality of living environment, although a high level of noise nuisance may infringe the right to peaceful enjoyment of one's possessions on account of a drop in the value of real property.[1778] On the other hand, as will be seen in the remainder of this section, many rights or interests other than ownership represent an economic value and thus constitute assets for the purpose of Article 1. Recent case-law of the Commission suggests a certain link with the notion of 'civil rights and obligations' of Article 6(1) of the Convention. Where the latter provision is not applicable because there was no 'determination of civil rights and obligations', the Commission is reluctant to accept the applicability of Article 1 of Protocol No. 1.[1779]

[1775] Judgment of 23 February 1995, A.306-B, p. 46. See also judgment of 16 September 1996 in the *Matos e Silva, Lda. and Others* Case, Reports 1996-IV, Vol. 14, para. 75: although the applicants' ownership of land under domestic law was contested, the Court held that their unchallenged rights over the land for almost a century and the revenues they derived from working the land did qualify as 'possessions'.

[1776] Judgment of 20 November 1995, A.332, p. 19.

[1777] Appl. 19217/91, *Durini* v. *Italy*, D&R 76-A (1994), p. 76 (79).

[1778] Appl. 13728/88, *S* v. *France*, D&R 65 (1990), p. 250 (261).

[1779] Appl. 21775/93, *Aires* v. *Portugal*, D&R 81-B (1995), p. 48 (52); Appl. 20714/92, *Henry* v. *France*, D&R 81-B (1995), p. 24 (34). Similarly, the Court appears to have transposed the requirement under Art. 6(1) that the 'right' be of a pecuniary nature to the context of Art. 1: see the judgment of 16 September 1996, *Gaygusuz*, Reports 1996-IV, Vol. 14. This judgment will be further discussed below.

Furthermore, the object of the possessions must be adequately definable in relation to the claims based thereupon. Thus, with regard to pension schemes and social security systems, the Commission has differentiated between on the one hand systems according to which, by the payment of contributions, an individual share in a fund is created, the amount of which can be determined at each particular moment, and on the other hand systems according to which the relation between the contributions being paid and the later benefit is much looser, which makes the object of the possessions less adequately definable. The first is a property-creating system and claims to benefits constitute possessions in the sense of Article 1, while the second system 'is based on the principle of solidarity which reflects the responsibility of the community as a whole' and does not create for the participant any claim to an identifiable share, but only an expectation the amount of which depends on the conditions prevailing at the time the pension is being paid.[1780] The latter pensions are based on the principle of collective security and are not funded by contributions which can be individualised in any way.[1781] Also in the latter case there may be a right to certain benefits as long as the system is in force and the participant fulfils the prevalent conditions.[1782] However, in that case the right guaranteed by Article 1 is not a right to a particular amount, since it may be subject to fluctuations, *inter alia* due to legal regulations. Fluctuations in the amount of the benefit may only amount to a violation of Article 1 if a very substantial reduction of the benefit is concerned.[1783] And even if the right guaranteed extends, in principle, to periodic increases, it may be subjected to restrictions if the pension is to be paid abroad, since many countries apply specific restrictions to the payment of benefits to foreign countries.[1784]

In the *Feldbrugge* Case and the *Deumeland* Case the minority of the Commission put forward that even under a social security scheme the insurance of risks is financed by methods based on classical insurance techniques. In their view it is incorrect to argue that a property right is involved in old age insurance only if it is financed by a funding system and that this is not the case if the insurance is based on the pay-as-you-go system. In the minority's view the

---

[1780] See in particular Appl. 4130/69, *X* v. *the Netherlands*, Yearbook XIV (1971), p. 224 (244). See also Appl. 5763/72, *X* v. *the Netherlands*, Yearbook XVI (1973), p. 274 (290-292) concerning amounts deducted from a Dutch social security pension in respect of pension payments received under a Norwegian pension scheme.

[1781] Appl. 10094/82, *G* v. *Austria*, D&R 38 (1984), p. 84 (85-86) concerning a claim of entitlement to a survivor's pension for civil servants.

[1782] See Appl. 7624/76, *X* v. *Austria*, D&R 19 (1980), p. 100 (104-105), where the reduction of an old age pension was due to the fact that the person in question did not satisfy the conditions for a full pension due to the amount of his monthly contributions. See also Appl. 7995/77, *National Federation of Self-Employed* v. *the United Kingdom*, D&R 15 (1979), p. 198 (201), where the Commission brought an increase of contributions, without a proportional increase of pension claims in return, under the justification of the second paragraph of Art. 1 'in the general interest'.

[1783] Report of 1 October 1975, *Müller*, Yearbook XIX (1976), p. 996 (1018-1020).

[1784] Appl. 9776/82, *X* v. *the United Kingdom*, D&R 34 (1983), p. 153 (154).

important point, in fact, is that, particularly in sickness and accident insurance, the benefits are financed by contributions directly or indirectly deducted from the worker's remuneration. In their view:

> The part borne directly by the worker is of course a deduction from the income earned by his work. But the contribution borne by the employer is in fact, indirectly, a similar deduction. If there was no compulsory insurance (...) this contribution would be added to the worker's net remuneration (...) The fact that in certain cases the scheme is also funded by State contributions in addition to those of the employers does not alter the nature of the scheme involved which remains an insurance scheme.[1785]

It is not certain that the Court will follow the Commission's approach concerning the importance to be attached to the distinction between contributory and non-contributory systems. In a judgment concerning an Austrian scheme, under which emergency assistance was granted to persons who had exhausted their entitlement to unemployment benefit, the Court, while noting that the entitlement to emergency assistance was linked to the payment of contributions to the unemployment insurance fund, simply held:

> that the right to emergency assistance – insofar as provided for in the applicable legislation – is a pecuniary right for the purposes of Article 1 of Protocol No. 1. That provision is therefore applicable without it being necessary to rely solely on the link between entitlement to emergency assistance and the obligation to pay 'taxes or other contributions'.[1786]

In the third place, the right or interest must be sufficiently established. A person complaining of an interference with his property must show that such right existed. According to constant case-law, 'possessions' may be either existing possessions or valuable assets, including claims, in respect of which the applicant can argue that he has at least a 'legitimate expectation' that they will realise.[1787]

There is no question of possessions until the moment at which one can lay claim to the property concerned. As stated above, a claim as such may constitute a 'possession' in the sense of Article 1,[1788] but it should then be a concrete, adequately specified claim. Thus, the Commission decided that the claim of a notary to payment for his services does not find protection in Article 1 until it is

---

[1785] Reports of 9 May 1984, A.99, pp. 41-43, and A.100, pp. 55-57 respectively.

[1786] Judgment in the case of *Gaygusuz*, 16 September 1996, Reports 1996-IV, Vol. 14, para. 41. The Court found a violation of Art. 14 in conjunction with Art. 1 of Protocol No. 1, as the scheme distinguished between nationals and non-nationals, a distinction which lacked an objective and reasonable justification (see para. 50 of the judgment). In its report in this case, the Commission had considered that since the obligation to pay 'taxes or other contributions' (*cf.* the second paragraph of Art. 1) falls within the field of application of Art. 1, the ensuing benefits also fall within its scope; report of 11 January 1995, Reports 1996-IV, Vol. 14, para. 47). See also the judgment of 21 February 1997, *Van Raalte*, Reports 1997-I, Vol. 29, paras 34-35.

[1787] See judgment of 23 November 1983, *Van der Mussele*, A.70, p. 23; judgment of 29 November 1991, *Pine Valley Developments Ltd and Others*, A.222, p. 23; judgment of 20 November 1995, *Pressos Compania Naviera S.A. and Others*, A.332, p. 19.

[1788] See also Appl. 7742/76, *A, B and Company A.S.* v. *Federal Republic of Germany*, D&R 14 (1979), p. 146 (168).

an actual claim based on services rendered; his expectation that the applicable provisions about notarial fees were not going to be modified does not find protection in Article 1.[1789] Nor do claims which a person has as an heir during the testator's lifetime fall under the protection of Article 1, because this provision protects existing property and not the right to acquire property. It does of course protect the right of the testator to dispose of his patrimonial rights and the rights which have already been acquired by inheritance even before distribution of assets.[1790]

In the case of *Stran Greek Refineries and Stratis Andreadis*, the Greek Government argued that the applicants had no claim against the State, as neither a judgment of a domestic court of first instance nor an arbitration award was sufficient to establish the existence of such a claim. In order to determine whether the applicants had a 'possession', the Court examined whether that domestic judgment and arbitration award 'had given rise to a debt in their favour that was sufficiently established to be enforceable'.[1791] The Court then distinguished between the judgment and the award. The former was a preliminary decision which, while apparently accepting the principle that the State owed a debt to the applicants, ordered that witnesses be heard before a ruling could be made on the existence and extent of the alleged damage. According to the Court:

> The effect of such a decision was merely to furnish the applicants with the hope that they would secure recognition of the claim put forward. Whether the resulting debt was enforceable would depend on any review by two superior courts.[1792]

However:

> This is not the case with regard to the arbitration award, which clearly recognised the State's liability (...). According to its wording, the award was final and binding; it did not require any further enforcement measure and no ordinary or special appeal lay against it (...). Under Greek legislation arbitration awards have the force of final decisions and are deemed to be enforceable (...); no provision is made for an appeal on the merits.[1793]

The Court concluded that the arbitration award conferred on the applicants a right in the sums awarded. Although this right was revocable since the award could still be annulled, the ordinary courts had already twice held that there was no ground

---

[1789] Appl. 8410/78, *X* v. *Federal Republic of Germany*, D&R 18 (1980), p. 216 (219-220). See also Appl. 10426/83, *Pudas* v. *Sweden*, D&R 40 (1985), p. 234 (241); Appl. 10438/83, *Batelaan and Huiges* v. *the Netherlands*, D&R 41 (1985), p. 170 (173); and Appl. 19819/92, *Størksen* v. *Norway*, D&R 78-A (1994), p. 88 (94-95): expectations for future earnings can only be considered to constitute a 'possession', if the income had already been earned or where an enforceable claim exists.

[1790] Judgment of 13 June 1979, *Marckx*, A.31, p. 23 and pp. 27-28 respectively; judgment of 28 October 1987, *Inze*, A.126, p. 19.

[1791] Judgment of 9 December 1994, A.301-B, p. 84. See also Appl. 9676/82, *Sequaris* v. *Belgium*, D&R 29 (1982), p. 245 (249).

[1792] Judgment of 9 December 1994, A.301-B, pp. 84-85.

[1793] *Ibidem*, p. 85.

for such annulment. Therefore, the applicants' right constituted a 'possession' within the meaning of Article 1.

Two complaints of an Austrian lawyer that his obligation to render *pro-deo* services as counsel was contrary to Article 1, were declared admissible by the Commission.[1794] In these cases, however, a friendly settlement was reached.[1795] In the *Van der Mussele* Case the Court held that the absence of remuneration of expenses made by the applicant for public services was unrelated to the 'peaceful enjoyment' of applicant's existing possessions. The Court held that since the expenses were relatively small and resulted from obligations to accomplish work compatible with Article 4 of the Convention, there was no breach of Article 1.[1796]

In a number of cases, the Convention organs have considered whether a licence for carrying out certain activities constitutes a 'possession'. In its decision on the admissibility of *Pudas* v. *Sweden* the Commission had to answer the question whether a licence to conduct certain economic activities gives the licence-holder a right protected by Article 1. The Commission considered that:

> the answer will depend *inter alia* on the question whether the licence can be considered to create for the licence-holder a reasonable and legitimate expectation as to the lasting nature of the licence and as to the possibility to continue to draw benefits from the exercise of licensed activity.[1797]

And indeed in the *Tre Traktörer Aktiebolag* Case, where the complaint concerned the decision to revoke the applicant's licence to serve beer, wine and other alcoholic beverages, the Commission held that the economic interests connected with the applicant company's restaurant business were 'possessions' within the meaning of Article 1. Since that licence was an important element in the running of the restaurant and the applicant company could legitimately expect to keep the licence as long as it did not infringe the conditions thereof, the revocation of the licence was an interference with the company's rights under Article 1.[1798] The Court essentially endorsed the Commission's view, adding that the withdrawal of the licence had adverse effects on the goodwill and value of the restaurant.[1799] A licence is often granted under certain conditions. If a licence-holder no longer fulfils the conditions, he cannot be considered to have a legitimate expectation to continue his activities.[1800] Similarly, a licence-holder cannot be considered to have a reasonable and legitimate expectation to continue his activity if the licence

---

[1794] Appls 4897/71 and 5219/71, *Gussenbauer* v. *Austria*, Coll. 42 (1973), pp. 41 and 94 respectively.
[1795] Report of 8 October 1974, Yearbook XV (1972).
[1796] Judgment of 23 November 1983, A.70, p. 23. See also Appl. 8682/79, *X* v. *Federal Republic of Germany*, D&R 26 (1982), p. 97 (99-100) where the Commission held that Art. 1 is not violated when an officially appointed defence counsel is obliged to repay an advance on his fees for not having assured the accused's defence up to the end of the proceedings.
[1797] Appl. 10426/83, D&R 40 (1985), p. 234 (241).
[1798] Report of 10 November 1987, A.159, p. 29.
[1799] Judgment of 7 July 1989, A.159, p. 21.
[1800] Appl. 10438/83, *Batelaan and Huiges* v. *the Netherlands*, D&R 41 (1985), p. 170 (173).

is withdrawn in accordance with the provisions of the law which was in force when the licence was issued.[1801]

In the *Van Marle* Case the Court stated that it agreed with the Commission that the 'goodwill' relied upon by the applicants may be:

likened to the right of property embodied in Article 1: by dint of their own work, the applicants had built up a clientèle; this had in many respects the nature of a private right and constituted an asset and, hence, a possession within the meaning of Article 1.[1802]

On the other hand, the Commission rejected complaints by Greek customs officers about loss of income due to the abolition of customs barriers within the European Union. The Commission noted that, in Greece, the occupation of customs officer is a liberal profession, with no fixed income and no guaranteed turnover, but which is subjected to the hazards of economic life. The customs officers could not claim to be entitled to a guaranteed volume of business which could have qualified as a 'possession'.[1803]

Measures which are taken in order to establish who is entitled to a certain property – for instance seizure[1804] – and conditions with regard to the evidence of that entitlement in themselves do not constitute violations of Article 1, unless such conditions impose an unreasonably heavy burden of proof on the person laying claim to the property.[1805]

13.3 Peaceful Enjoyment of Possessions; The General Rule of the First Sentence

Article 1 protects 'peaceful enjoyment'. That implies that this provision may also have been violated when a person has not been affected as to his property or possessions *per se*, but is not accorded an opportunity to use that property, for instance because a necessary permit is refused to him,[1806] or because in some other way such restrictions ensue from the legislation or from government

---

[1801] Appl. 19819/92, *Størksen v. Norway*, D&R 78-A (1994), p. 88 (94).

[1802] Judgment of 26 June 1986, A.101, p. 13. See however the decision of the Commission on Appl. 10438/83, *Batelaan and Huiges v. the Netherlands*, D&R 41 (1985), p. 170 (173): the goodwill of a professional practice is an element in its valuation but does not constitute a 'possession' to the extent that it is not necessarily linked with the profession in question.

[1803] Appl. 24581/94, *Greek Federation of Customs Officers, Galouris, Christopoulos and 3,333 other customs officers v. Greece*, D&R 81-B (1995), p. 123 (128).

[1804] Appl. 7256/75, *X v. Belgium*, D&R 8 (1977), p. 161 (165-166).

[1805] See Appl. 7775/77, *Pacheco v. Belgium*, D&R 15 (1979), p. 143, which was declared inadmissible by the Commission.

[1806] See, *e.g.*, Appl. 7456/76, *Wiggins v. the United Kingdom*, D&R 13 (1979), p. 40 (46-47), concerning the refusal of a housing licence to the applicant to live in his own house.

measures to the extent that there is no longer any question of a 'peaceful enjoyment'.[1807]

In the *Loizidou* Case, which concerned denial of access to property situated in the area occupied by Turkish Cypriot forces following the civil war in Cyprus, the Commission was of the opinion that the right to the peaceful enjoyment of possessions did not include as a corollary a right of freedom of movement. However, the Court took the position that the applicant's complaint was wider: she had complained that the denial of access over a period of 16 years had gradually affected her right as a property owner and in particular her right to a peaceful enjoyment of her possessions. Against this background, the Court did not accept the characterisation of her complaint as being limited to the right of freedom of movement. Article 1 was thus held to be applicable.[1808]

That Article 1 applies to restrictions on the possibilities of using property is also clear from the second paragraph, which employs the words 'to control the use of property'. However, the distinction between 'deprivation of possessions' and 'control of the use of property' is a fluid one in certain situations. In some cases, the Court has difficulties in bringing the case under either the second sentence of Article 1 (deprivation of possessions) or the second paragraph of that article (control of use of property), although the right to peaceful enjoyment of possessions is clearly affected. In such circumstances, the case is decided on the basis of the 'general rule' laid down in the first sentence.

In the *Sporrong and Lönnroth* Case, although the expropriations left intact in law the owners' right to use and dispose of their possessions, they nevertheless in practice significantly reduced the possibility of its exercise. The expropriations also affected the very substance of ownership in that they recognised before the event that any expropriation would be lawful and authorised the City of Stockholm to expropriate whenever it found it expedient to do so. In the Court's view the applicants' right of property thus became precarious and defeasible.[1809]

In the *Erkner and Hofauer* Case and in the *Poiss* Case the applicants submitted that the provisional transfer of their land to other landowners, who were partners to a consolidation scheme, interfered with their right of property. The Court noted that the Austrian authorities did not effect either a formal expropriation or a *de facto* expropriation (Article 1, second sentence). The transfer carried out was a provisional one; only the entry into force of the consolidation plan would make

---

[1807] Report of 8 October 1980, *Sporrong and Lönnroth*, B.46 (1986), pp. 47-48, concerning, *inter alia*, restrictions on the possibility to build on land held in freehold. See also Appl. 7889/77, *Arrondelle* v. *the United Kingdom*, D&R 19 (1980), p. 186, where the complaint concerned the nuisance caused to the owner of a house by the neighbouring airfield. In this case a friendly settlement has been reached; report of 13 May 1982, D&R 26 (1982), p. 5.

[1808] Judgment of 18 December 1996, Reports 1996-VI, Vol. 26, paras 60-61.

[1809] Judgment of 23 September 1982, A.52, p. 23. See also the report of 8 October 1987, *Jacobsson* (not officially published), paras 129-130, where the Commission considered that the continued building prohibition on the applicant's property constituted an interference with his right to the peaceful enjoyment of possessions.

it irrevocable. The applicants would therefore recover their land if the final plan could not confirm the distribution made at an earlier stage of the proceedings. Nor was the provisional transfer essentially designed to restrict or control the 'use' of the land (Article 1(2)), but to achieve an early restructuring of the consolidation area with a view to improved, rational farming by the 'provisional owners'.[1810] Impliedly the Court recognised here that apart from formal expropriations the second sentence of Article 1 might also extend to *de facto* expropriations which 'can be assimilated to a deprivation of possessions'.[1811]

However, in a case where the Court concluded that there had been a *de facto* expropriation, it did not specify which sentence of Article 1 applied. In the case of *Papamichalopoulos* v. *Greece*, the applicants' land had been occupied by the Greek military authorities without any compensation. Although the Greek courts had subsequently recognised the applicants' rights to the land, it had not been returned to them. Neither had any compensatory measures been effected. Thus, the applicants, although technically still the owners of the land, were unable to dispose of it in any way. The Court had little difficulty in finding a violation:

> The loss of all ability to dispose of the land in issue, taken together with the failure of the attempts made so far to remedy the situation complained of, entailed sufficiently serious consequences for the applicants *de facto* to have been expropriated in a manner incompatible with their right to the peaceful enjoyment of their possessions.[1812]

From this formulation, it is unclear whether the Court applied the first sentence or the second sentence of Article 1, or a combination of the two rules. Conversely, in the *Hentrich* Case, the Court did specify that there had been a deprivation of possessions to which the second sentence applied, but it did not respond to the applicant's contention that there had been a *de facto* expropriation.[1813]

In other cases, in which the first sentence was identified as the applicable rule, the Court gave some criteria for its choice. In its judgment in the case of *Matos e Silva, Lda. and Others*, the Court examined a number of measures interfering with the applicants' right to the peaceful enjoyment of their possessions (parcels of land). These included so-called public interest declarations, issued as a preliminary to expropriation for the purpose of creating a nature reserve, and prohibitions on all building and on any change in the use of the land. The Court held that there was no formal or *de facto* deprivation of possessions in this case, as the effects of the measures were not irreversible as had been the case in *Papamichalopoulos*:

[1810] Judgments of 23 April 1987, A.117, pp. 65-66 and p. 108 respectively. See also judgment of 30 October 1991 in the *Wiesinger* Case, A.213, p. 26.
[1811] Judgments of 23 April 1987, *Erkner and Hofauer* and *Poiss*, A.117, pp. 65-66 and p. 108 respectively.
[1812] Judgment of 24 June 1993, A.260-B, p. 20.
[1813] Judgment of 22 September 1994, A.296-A, p. 18.

The restrictions on the right to property stemmed from the reduced ability to dispose of the property and from the damage sustained by reason of the fact that expropriation was contemplated. Although the right in question had lost some of its substance, it had not disappeared. The Court notes, for example, that all reasonable manner of exploiting the property had not disappeared seeing that the applicants continued to work the land. The second sentence of the first paragraph is therefore not applicable in this case.[1814]

In the *Phocas* Case, the Court held the first sentence to be applicable because the applicant did not complain about a deprivation of property or of specific measures restricting the use of it, but of an infringement resulting from the authorities' general conduct.[1815]

However, the importance of the classification of cases under the three rules of Article 1 should not be exaggerated. As was recalled in section 13.1 above, the Court has always held that these three rules are not unconnected: the rule concerning deprivation of possessions and that concerning the control of use of property should be construed in the light of the general principle laid down in the first sentence: the right to the peaceful enjoyment of possessions. This is made clear also by the main test applied for establishing whether or not Article 1 has been violated. Under each of the three rules, the Court applies a 'fair balance' test:

> The Court must determine whether a fair balance was struck between the demands of the general interest of the community and the requirements of the protection of the individual's fundamental rights. The search for this balance is inherent in the whole of the Convention and is also reflected in the structure of Article 1.[1816]

Here, as with other proportionality tests under the Convention, the Court accepts that a margin of appreciation must be left to the national authorities. In the context of Article 1, this margin of appreciation is usually wide.[1817]

The case-law with respect to the first sentence shows that there are two – often combined – aspects to the protection offered by the fair balance requirement: (formal) protection against lack of procedural guarantees or against protracted proceedings, and (substantive) protection against arbitrary action by the State, or action which puts an individual and excessive burden on the applicant. The absence of any compensation may also be a relevant factor under the fair balance test.

To determine whether a 'fair balance' had been achieved in the *Sporrong and Lönnroth* Case, the Court examined the possibilities for the applicants to seek a reduction of the time limits within which the expropriation of their properties

---

[1814] Judgment of 16 September 1996, Reports 1996-IV, Vol. 14, p. 114.

[1815] Judgment of 23 April 1996, Reports 1996-II, Vol. 7, p. 542 (urban development scheme which impeded the development of the applicant's property without any compensation for more than 16 years).

[1816] Judgment of 23 September 1982, *Sporrong and Lönnroth* Case, A.52, p. 26 (with respect to the first sentence of paragraph 1). See, for the second sentence of paragraph 1, judgment of 9 December 1994, *Holy Monasteries* Case, A.301-A, p. 34; for the second paragraph, see judgment of 21 November 1995, *Velosa Barreto v. Portugal*, A.334, p. 11.

[1817] See the discussion of the margin of appreciation in Chapter II, *supra* p. 82.

might be effected or to claim compensation for the damages suffered during the extremely long period during which the enjoyment of their property right had been impeded. Because remedies to that effect were not available, the Court decided that Article 1 had been violated.[1818]

Conversely, the fair balance will not be upset where the applicant has failed to make proper use of available procedures for remedying the interferences complained of, even where these interferences were *prima facie* incompatible with the fair balance requirement and even where the conduct of the authorities was not beyond reproach. Thus, in the *Phocas* Case, the Court first noted with regard to the restrictions imposed on the applicant's property on account of a development scheme for improving the crossroads where his property was situated:

> The threat of expropriation and the restrictions on building were undoubtedly an obstacle to continuing to run his business on the premises and made it doubtful that he could sell them or let them as a trader. Nor was the applicant able to convert his building as he wished, since three of his applications for planning permission were adjourned and one refused. (...) Such a situation is in principle incompatible with the fair balance required by Article 1 of Protocol No. 1.[1819]

However, the Court then observed that a remedy had been available to the applicant: he could have taken steps to have his land purchased by the local authority for whose benefit the land had been reserved under the development plan within three years of the application. Failing agreement, an application could be made to the expropriations judge to fix the price. Having regard to the applicant's conduct – he twice renewed his application to the local authority instead of turning to the expropriations judge with the result that, when he finally did apply to the judge, his application was out of time so that the judge had to decline jurisdiction – the Court found that the failure of these proceedings was attributable to him, 'even if the authorities delayed in replying to Mr Phocas's applications'. The Court concluded that Article 1 had not been violated.[1820]

The Court reached the opposite conclusion with respect to the interferences with the applicants' property rights in the above-mentioned case of *Matos e Silva, Lda. and Others.* Although it recognised that the various measures complained of did not lack a reasonable basis, the Court observed that:

[1818] Judgment of 23 September 1982, A.52, pp. 26-28. See also the Court's focus on procedural issues, including the length of the land consolidation proceedings, in the cases of *Erkner and Hofauer* and *Poiss*, judgments of 23 April 1987, A.117, p. 66 and pp. 62-63 respectively; likewise the judgment in the *Wiesinger* Case of 30 October 1991, A.213, p. 27.

[1819] Judgment of 23 April 1996, Reports 1996-II, Vol. 7, p. 544.

[1820] *Ibidem*, p. 545. Failure to make use of available remedies was also held against the applicant in the case of *Katte Klitsche de la Grange* v. *Italy*, judgment of 27 October 1994, A.293-B, p. 36. In the *Phocas* Case, judges Foighel and Palm dissented, agreeing with the Commission that the acts of the French authorities and courts had made the applicant's right of property unstable and uncertain over a very long period. Pointing to a lack of diligence on the part of the authorities and indications given by them which could reasonably lead to applicant to believe that negotiations were continuing and that a solution was imminent, these judges disagreed with the majority that the failure of the domestic proceedings was attributable to the applicant alone.

in the circumstances of the case the measures had serious and harmful effects that have hindered the applicants' ordinary enjoyment of their rights for more than thirteen years during which virtually no progress has been made in the proceedings. The long period of uncertainty both as to what would become of the possessions and as to the question of compensation further aggravated the detrimental effects of the disputed measures. As a result, the applicants have had to bear an individual and excessive burden which has upset the fair balance which should be struck between the requirements of the general interest and the protection of the right to the peaceful enjoyment of one's possessions.[1821]

In the case of *Stran Greek Refineries and Stratis Andreadis* v. *Greece*, the applicants complained of the Greek legislature's intervention which annulled an arbitration award in their favour that had become final and binding. In this case, domestic courts of first instance and of appeal had already held that there were no grounds for annulment of the arbitration award when, at the State's request, the date for the hearing by the Court of Cassation was postponed on the ground that a draft law on the case was before Parliament. Just before the hearing took place, a law was enacted which, *inter alia*, annulled the award. Subsequently, this part of the law was not held unconstitutional by the Court of Cassation. The Court, referring to the case-law of international courts and arbitration tribunals did not question the right of the State to terminate contracts with private individuals, provided it pays compensation and with the exception of arbitration clauses. The domestic courts of first instance and of appeal had recognised in this case that arbitration clauses are autonomous; moreover, they had found that the unilateral termination of the contract by the Greek State had not invalidated the applicants' existing claims. The Court concluded that Greece was:

> under a duty to pay the applicants the sums awarded against it at the conclusion of the arbitration procedure, a procedure for which it had itself opted and the validity of which had been accepted until the day of the hearing in the Court of Cassation. (...) By choosing to intervene at that stage of the proceedings in the Court of Cassation (...) the legislature upset, to the detriment of the applicants, the balance that must be struck between the protection of the right of property and the requirements of public interest.[1822]

The straightforward reasoning of the unanimous Court in this case may be explained by the dubious, *ad hoc* character of the legislation in question: as the Court stated, 'the real objective of the legislature' was to close the domestic proceedings in the present case once and for all.[1823]

[1821] Judgment of 16 September 1996, Reports 1996-IV, Vol. 14, p. 1115. The 'individual and excessive burden' criterion was applied by the Court for the first time under the first sentence of paragraph 1 in the *Sporrong and Lönnroth* judgment of 23 September 1982, A.52, p. 28. See, as regards the second sentence of paragraph 1, the judgment of 22 September 1994, *Hentrich*, A.296-A, p. 21.

[1822] Judgment of 9 December 1994, A.301-B, p. 88.

[1823] *Ibidem*, p. 34.

13.4 Deprivation of Possessions: The Second Sentence

The most important restriction to be imposed by the authorities on the peaceful enjoyment of one's possessions is regulated explicitly in the second sentence: deprivation of property in the public interest.[1824] Under this head, the Court will examine 1) whether the deprivation had a 'public interest' aim; 2) whether the measure was proportionate in relation to the aim pursued; and 3) whether the measure was lawful (*cf.* 'provided for by law' and the reference to 'the general principles of international law').[1825]

13.4.1 'In the Public Interest'

Whether a particular expropriation has been performed in the public interest will be subjected by the Strasbourg organs to a very limited review only, the main objective being to detect cases of *détournement de pouvoir*[1826] or of manifest arbitrariness.[1827] As the Commission stated in its report in the *Handyside* Case in connection with the fact that the first paragraph speaks of 'in the public interest' and not of 'necessary in a democratic society': 'Clearly the public or general interest encompasses measures which would be preferable or advisable, and not only essential, in a democratic society.'[1828] In the *James* Case the Court held, with respect to the State's margin of appreciation:

> Furthermore, the notion of 'public interest' is necessarily extensive. In particular, as the Commission noted, the decision to enact laws expropriating property will commonly involve considerations of political, economic and social issues on which opinion within a democratic society may reasonably differ widely. The Court, finding it natural that the margin of appreciation available to the legislature in implementing social and economic policies should be a wide one, will respect the legislature's judgment as to what is 'in the public interest' unless that judgment be manifestly without reasonable foundation.[1829]

Regarding the meaning of 'the public interest' the Court also stated:

[1824] On the question of whether this sentence applies also to *de facto* expropriation, see section 13.3 *supra*.

[1825] See judgment of 22 September 1994, *Hentrich*, A.296-A, where the Court examined all three requirements. In most judgments, however, the 'lawfulness' of the deprivation measure is not at issue; in fact, such measures normally take the form of legislation.

[1826] See Appl. 3039/67, *A, B, C and D v. the United Kingdom*, Yearbook X (1967), p. 506 (516-518), where the Commission uses the doctrine of the margin of appreciation also on this point. See also the Court's judgment of 9 December 1994, *Holy Monasteries*, A.301-A, p. 34 (doubts as to real reasons of a legislative measure; see *infra*).

[1827] Report of 30 September 1975, B.22 (1976), p. 50; judgment of 21 February 1986, *James*, A.98, p. 32.

[1828] *Idem.*

[1829] Judgment of 21 February 1986, A.98, p. 32. See also judgment of 8 July 1986, *Lithgow and Others*, A.102, p. 51 and judgment of 20 November 1995, *Pressos Compania Naviera S.A. and Others*, A.332, p. 20.

a deprivation of property effected for no reason other than to confer a private benefit on a private party cannot be 'in the public interest'. Nonetheless, the compulsory transfer of property from one individual to another may, depending upon the circumstances, constitute a legitimate aim for promoting the public interest.[1830]

The Court added that:

a taking of property effected in pursuance of legitimate, social, economic or other policies may be 'in the public interest', even if the community at large has no direct use or enjoyment of the property taken.[1831]

It is therefore not surprising that the Court has, so far, never ruled that a deprivation of possessions was not 'in the public interest'. For example, it accepted that the prevention of tax evasion is a legitimate objective which is in the public interest.[1832] Likewise, the purpose of constructing housing for a category of disadvantaged persons constitutes a public interest aim.[1833] In the case of *Pressos Compania Naviera S.A. and Others*, the Court accepted that a law depriving the applicants of their property pursued such an aim, without commenting in any specific way on the reasons put forward by the Belgian Government.[1834]

The Court's deference to the national legislature's assessment of what is in the public interest appears very clearly from the judgment in the *Holy Monasteries* Case. This case concerned a Greek law effectively transferring to the State full ownership of land held by the monasteries. The reasons given for this measure were to end illegal sales of the land, encroachments on it and its abandonment or uncontrolled development. The Court expressed some doubts on this point on account of the fact that the law gave the State optional power whether or not to transfer the land for use by farmers and that it mentioned also public bodies in the list of possible beneficiaries. Nonetheless, it accepted that the overall objective of the law was legitimate.[1835]

13.4.2 Proportionality of the Measure

The review by the Court is more extensive as concerns the proportionality requirement, although a wide margin of appreciation for national legislatures is normally also accepted on this score. As was already pointed out in section 13.3 above, the Court assesses the proportionality of the contested measure by

---

[1830] Judgment of 21 February 1986, A.98, p. 30.
[1831] *Ibidem*, pp. 31-32.
[1832] Judgment of 22 September 1994, *Hentrich*, A.296-A, p. 19.
[1833] Judgment of 7 August 1996, *Zubani*, Reports 1996-IV, Vol. 14, p. 1077.
[1834] Judgment of 20 November 1995, A.332, p. 22. The Belgian Government had sought to justify the interference (a law which retroactively deprived the applicants of civil law claims against the State) by referring to the need to protect the State's financial interests, the need to re-establish legal certainty and the need to bring Belgian legislation in line with that of neighbouring countries.
[1835] Judgment of 9 December 1994, A.301-A, p. 34.

determining whether a 'fair balance' has been struck between the interest of the community and the requirements of the protection of the individual's fundamental rights. This means, in particular, that:

> there must be a reasonable relationship of proportionality between the means employed and the aim sought to be realised by any measure depriving a person of his possessions.[1836]

Under this head, the Court may examine whether 'an individual and excessive burden' has been imposed on the individual.[1837] Where this is the case, there appears to be a strong presumption of a lack of proportionality, which can be refuted only if adequate remedies and procedural safeguards have been available.[1838] In the *Hentrich* Case, the applicant complained of measures taken by the French tax authorities under which she was deprived of the real property which she had purchased. French law recognised a right of pre-emption by the Revenue, where the latter considered the sale price to be too low. This right, a deterrent against tax evasion, was to be exercised by offering to pay the purchaser the sale price plus a ten percent premium. The Court first stated that, in order to assess the proportionality of this interference, it had to look at the degree of protection from arbitrariness that is afforded by the proceedings in this case. In this instance, domestic law did not require that reasons be given for the decision to exercise the right of pre-emption. The right of pre-emption allowed the tax authorities to substitute themselves for any purchaser, even one acting in perfectly good faith, for the sole purpose of general deterrence against tax evasion. In addition, this right of pre-emption, which does not exist in other States Parties, did not apply systematically every time the sale price was too low, but only rarely and scarcely foreseeably. The Court, after having pointed to other suitable methods for discouraging tax evasion, and having regard to the risk run by any purchaser that he will lose his property and the 'definite level of severity' of the consequences of a pre-emption measure, considered that 'merely reimbursing the price paid – increased by 10 percent – and the costs and expenses of the contract cannot suffice to compensate for the loss of a property acquired without any fraudulent intent'.[1839]

The Court concluded that Article 1 had been violated:

[1836] See judgment of 21 February 1986, *James and Others*, A.98, p. 34; judgment of 8 July 1986, *Lithgow and Others*, A.102, p. 50; judgment of 9 December 1994, *Holy Monasteries*, A.301-A, p. 34; judgment of 20 November 1995, *Pressos Compania Naviera S.A. and Others*, A.332, p. 21.

[1837] See the judgment of 21 February 1986, *James and Others*, A.98, p. 34 and the judgment of 22 September 1994, *Hentrich*, A.296-A, p. 21.

[1838] Similarly, in the context of the first sentence of Art. 1(1), first sentence, the judgment of 23 September 1982, *Sporrong and Lönnroth*, A.52, p. 28.

[1839] Judgment of 22 September 1994, A.296-A, pp. 20-21

Having regard to all these factors, the Court considers that, as a selected victim of the exercise of the right of pre-emption, Mrs Hentrich bore an individual and excessive burden which could have been rendered legitimate only if she had had the possibility – which was refused her – of effectively challenging the measure taken against her.[1840]

The *Hentrich* Case is perhaps a-typical in that most judgments concerning the second sentence of Article 1 focus on the question of compensation for deprivation of property. A particular feature of this case was the fact that, although compensation had been given to the applicant, the Court found that the French system offered insufficient protection from arbitrary deprivation of property.[1841]

The question of compensation is an important factor for the determination of the proportionality of the deprivation of property. A claim that the compensation paid is unfair should, therefore, not be related to the 'public interest' requirement nor to the phrase 'subject to the conditions provided for by law', which requires in the first place the existence of and compliance with adequately accessible and sufficiently precise domestic legal provisions.[1842] In the *James* Case and in the *Lithgow* Case both the Commission and Court adopted the view that the taking of property without payment of an amount reasonably related to its value would normally constitute a disproportionate interference. Legitimate objectives of 'public interest', such as pursued in measures of economic reform or measures designed to achieve a greater social justice, may however call for less than reimbursement of the full market value.[1843] And also here the Court emphasised that its power is limited to ascertaining whether the choice of compensation terms falls outside the State's margin of appreciation in this domain.[1844]

However, the Court views situations in which there has been a complete lack of compensation with a far more critical eye than those where the complaint is directed against the level of compensation. In the *Holy Monasteries* Case, the Court confirmed a principle developed in the *James* and *Lithgow* Cases that 'A total lack of compensation can be considered justifiable under Article 1 only in exceptional circumstances.'[1845] In this case, the Court disagreed with the Commission that such exceptional circumstances existed. The special relationship

---

[1840] *Ibidem*, p. 21.

[1841] In this connection, it should be noted that the Court also reached a negative conclusion as concerns the lawfulness of the interference (see *infra*). See also the judgment of 7 August 1996, *Zubani*, Reports 1996-IV, Vol. 14, p. 1078, where the Court found a violation on account of the way the national authorities had handled the applicants' situation, in spite of the fact that a considerable compensation had been awarded to them.

[1842] Judgment of 8 July 1986, *Lithgow and Others*, A.102, p. 47.

[1843] Judgment of 21 February 1986, A.98, p. 36; judgment of 8 July 1986, A.102, p. 51.

[1844] See also the report of 13 October 1988, *Håkansson and Sturesson*, A.171-A, p. 27.

[1845] Judgment of 9 December 1994, A.301-A, p. 35. See also judgment of 20 November 1995, *Pressos Compania Naviera S.A. and Others*, A.332, p. 21. In the *James* and *Lithgow* Cases, the Court had already referred to this in terms of a principle applying under the legal systems of the Member States, adding that the protection afforded by Art. 1 would be largely illusory in the absence of any equivalent principle: A.98, p. 36 and A.102, p. 50 respectively.

between the Greek Church and the State was not sufficient to justify the measures taken, which imposed a considerable burden on the applicant monasteries: when resorting to similar expropriation measures in 1952, the State had provided for compensation to monasteries of one-third of the real value of the land; no compensation measures had been taken in the case at hand.[1846]

The judgment in the case of *Pressos Compania Naviera S.A. and Others* confirms the Court's critical attitude towards legislative interference with the judicial process and the importance it attaches to rule of law considerations (*cf.* the judgment in *Stran Greek Refineries*, discussed in section 13.3 *supra*). The Court considered that the Belgian law at issue:

> quite simply extinguished, with retrospective effect going back thirty years and without compensation, claims for very high damages that the victims of the pilot accidents could have pursued against the Belgian State or against the private companies concerned, and in some cases even in proceedings that were already pending.[1847]

The serious financial considerations cited by the Government could warrant prospective legislation to derogate from the general law of tort but not:

> legislating with retrospective effect with the aim and consequence of depriving the applicants of their claims for compensation. Such a fundamental interference with the applicants' rights is inconsistent with preserving a fair balance between the interests at stake.[1848]

13.4.3 'Provided for by Law and by the General Principles of International Law'
Expropriations are permissible only if the conditions provided for by law and by the general principles of international law have been observed. As regards compliance with national legal conditions, here again the Commission and the Court do not examine whether national law has been applied correctly. They take the position that in this matter they have to refer to the judgment of the national court in the case concerned and that they must not function as a 'fourth instance'. Nonetheless, the Court has recalled, also in the context of Article 1, that the notion of 'law' within the meaning of the Convention (see, for example, paragraph 2 of Articles 8-11) requires the existence of and compliance with adequately accessible and sufficiently precise domestic legal provisions.[1849] Furthermore, there must be protection, in the form of procedural safeguards, from arbitrariness.[1850]

With respect to the reference to international legal principles, one is inclined to think first of all of the obligation to pay damages, as this obligation exists under

---

[1846] Judgment of 9 December 1994, *Holy Monasteries*, A.301-A, p. 35.
[1847] Judgment of 20 November 1995, A.332, p. 21.
[1848] *Ibidem*, p. 22.
[1849] See judgment of 8 July 1986, *Lithgow and Others*, A.102, p. 47; judgment of 22 September 1994, *Hentrich*, A.296-A, p. 19.
[1850] See judgment of 22 September 1994, *Hentrich*, A.296-A, p. 19. Here, the Court criticised the discretionary nature of the exercise of the State's right of pre-emption and the unfairness of the procedure (no adversarial proceedings respecting the principle of equality of arms).

international law or at all events existed according to the prevalent view at the moment when Protocol No. 1 was drafted.[1851] In fact, the Commission has taken that general principle of international law into consideration. It came, however, with reference to the genesis of Article 1 to the conclusion that this principle relates exclusively to the nationalisation of foreign property and cannot be invoked against the national State of the owner.[1852] In the past, this has led the Commission to conclude that in the case of expropriation in the public interest of property owned by the State's own subjects, the State is under no obligation to pay damages if this is not provided for in national law.[1853]

According to this interpretation, Article 1 of Protocol No. 1 permits a difference in treatment between the State's own nationals and aliens, this contrary to the purpose of the Convention to secure to everyone the same enjoyment of the rights and freedoms, as laid down in Articles 1 and 14. This result is all the more curious as the derogation from that purpose is an implied one and this even to the detriment of the State's own nationals, while other derogations are laid down expressly, *viz.* in Article 16 of the Convention and Article 3 of Protocol No. 4, and are to the detriment of aliens. However, in the case of Article 1 of Protocol No. 1 this does not create a fundamental difference between nationals and aliens, but one which exists only insofar and as long as general principles of international law actually prescribe a specific treatment of foreign property and these principles are different from those applying under the law of the State in question with regard to the treatment of the property of its own nationals. If any differences on this point still exist at present, developments within international law go into the direction of their minimisation.[1854] It should be added that also developments in the case-law of the Court as regards compensation for deprivation of property of nationals tend to result in a relativisation of these differences.[1855]

[1851] This conclusion was also reached at that time within the Committee of Ministers: K.J. Partsch, *Die Rechte und Freiheiten der Europäischen Menschenrechtskonvention*, Berlin, 1966, p. 224.

[1852] An interpretation in that sense has been included in the minutes of a discussion devoted to it by the Committee of Ministers at that time: Partsch, *ibidem*, p. 225.

[1853] See, *e.g.*, Appl. 511/59, *Gudmundsson v. Iceland*, Yearbook III (1960), p. 394 (422-424).

[1854] See the Charter of Economic Rights and Duties of States adopted by Res. 3281(XXIX) of the General Assembly of the UN on 12 December 1974, *International Legal Materials*, 1975, p. 251.

[1855] See the remarks made above as concerns the Court's critical attitude in cases where there has been a total lack of compensation. A further way of minimising the differences in protection between nationals and aliens appears from the Commission's report in the case of *Gasus Dosier- und Fördertechnik*, report of 21 October 1993, A.306-B, p. 56. This was a (rare) case of interference with property rights of an alien (a foreign company). The Commission considered that the seizure of the applicant company's machine – in actual possession of a Dutch company which went bankrupt – by the Dutch tax authorities for the purpose of securing payment of the taxes owed by the bankrupt company, constituted a deprivation of possessions. Nevertheless, the Commission said that this particular form of deprivation of possessions could not be compared to measures of confiscation, nationalisation or expropriation in regard to which international law provides special protection to foreign citizens and companies. The Court did not pronounce on this aspect of the case, as it examined it under the second paragraph of Art. 1.

In the *James* Case and in the *Lithgow* Case the Court, too, held that the reference to the general principles of international law in Article 1 means that those principles are incorporated into that article, but only as regards those acts to which they are normally applicable, that is to say acts of a State in relation to non-nationals. For this interpretation the Court referred to Article 31 of the Vienna Convention on the Law of Treaties: the words of a treaty should be understood to have their ordinary meaning.[1856] On that ground it rejected the grammatical argument of the applicants, based upon Article 1, that all elements of that article applied to everyone. The Court also rejected the argument of the applicants that the interpretation according to which the principle in question only applied to non-nationals, would make the reference in Article 1 to the general principles redundant since non-nationals already enjoyed the protection thereof. In the Court's view the inclusion of the reference could be seen to serve at least two purposes:

> Firstly, it enables non-nationals to resort directly to the machinery of the Convention to enforce their rights on the basis of the relevant principles of international law, whereas otherwise they would have to seek recourse to diplomatic channels or to other available means of dispute settlement to do so. Secondly, the reference ensures that the position of non-nationals is safeguarded, in that it excludes any possible argument that the entry into force of Protocol No. I has led to a diminution of their rights.[1857]

The Court also indicated that the difference in treatment did not constitute discrimination, since the differences in treatment had an 'objective and reasonable justification':

> Especially as regards a taking of property effected in the context of a social reform, there may well be good grounds for drawing a distinction between nationals and non-nationals as far as compensation is concerned.[1858]

In the Court's view non-nationals are more vulnerable to domestic legislation since, unlike nationals, they will generally have played no part in the elections. Secondly, although the taking of property must always be effected in the public interest, different considerations may apply to nationals and non-nationals and there may well be a legitimate reason for requiring nationals to bear a greater burden in the public interest than non-nationals. Finally, the Court pointed to the fact that also the *travaux préparatoires* and Resolution (52)1 of 19 March 1952 approving the text of the Protocol revealed that the reference to the general principles of international law was not intended to extend to nationals.[1859] In both cases the Court found that no violation of Article 1 had been established, since in the exercise of its margin of appreciation the United Kingdom was

---

[1856] Judgment of 21 February 1986, A.98, p. 38; judgment of 8 July 1986, A.102, p. 48.
[1857] *Ibidem*, p. 39 and p. 49 respectively.
[1858] *Idem.*
[1859] *Ibidem*, pp. 39-40 and pp. 48-49 respectively.

entitled to adopt the compensation provisions as applied to the applicants and these provisions and their application were deemed by the Court not to be unreasonable.

13.5 Control of the Use of Property: The First Part of Paragraph 2

The second paragraph of Article 1 allows the national authorities an almost unlimited power to impose restrictions on the use of property in accordance with the general interest. Here it is not the deprivation of property itself that is concerned, but restriction of its use. In this context it is remarkable that with regard to this restriction it is provided that it must be necessary, while with respect to the expropriation itself it is not.[1860]

However, the judgment as to what is necessary in the general interest is expressly left to the State: 'as it deems necessary'. Taken literally, this phrase appears to suggest that the relevant national legislation and its application can be reviewed only for their conformity with the prohibition of discrimination of Article 14, with the prohibition of *détournement de pouvoir* laid down in Article 18, and possibly with Article 17.[1861] In 1976, this was indeed the view taken by the Court in the *Handyside* Case:

> this paragraph sets the Contracting States up as sole judges of the 'necessity' for an interference. Consequently, the Court must restrict itself to supervising the lawfulness and the purposes of the restriction in question.[1862]

However, a more extensive supervision has gradually been developed in the case-law. In its report in the *Sporrong and Lönnroth* Case, the Commission concluded from the slightly modified wording used by the Court in the *Marckx* judgment[1863] that the Court only recognises the States as the 'sole judges' with respect to the law on which the restrictions are based, but not in relation to the necessity of the measures themselves. As regards the latter, in the Commission's opinion, the possibility of review by the Strasbourg organs goes further and includes, for instance, the proportionality between those measures and the purpose of the law on which they are based.[1864] In its judgment in the *AGOSI* Case, the Court adopted a similar approach, but later judgments show that the Court applies a fair balance test to assess the proportionality of the interference, both as

---

[1860] The submission by an applicant that in his case the deprivation of property could not be deemed to have been necessary was not, therefore, examined by the Commission: Appl. 3039/67, *A, B, C and D* v. *the United Kingdom*, Yearbook X (1967), p. 506 (516).

[1861] In Appl. 4984/71, *X* v. *Federal Republic of Germany*, Coll. 43 (1973), p. 28 (35-36), the Commission nevertheless seems to have reviewed the measure by which a prisoner was prohibited from spending his money, be it in a very marginal way, for its necessity in the public interest.

[1862] Judgment of 7 December 1976, A.24, p. 29.

[1863] Judgment of 13 June 1979, A.31, p. 28.

[1864] Report of 8 October 1980, B.46 (1986), pp. 48-49.

concerns enforcement measures and the underlying legislation.[1865] As the Court stated in the *Allan Jacobsson* Case:

> Under the second paragraph of Article 1 of Protocol No. 1, the Contracting States are entitled, amongst other things, to control the use of property in accordance with the general interest, by enforcing such laws as they deem necessary for the purpose. However, as this provision is to be construed in the light of the general principle enunciated in the first sentence of the first paragraph, there must exist a reasonable relationship of proportionality between the means employed and the aim sought to be realised. In striking the fair balance thereby required between the general interest of the community and the requirements of the protection of the individual's fundamental rights, the authorities enjoy a wide margin of appreciation.[1866]

Given the flexibility of the 'reasonable relationship of proportionality' criterion and the wide margin of appreciation, the Court will not easily conclude that a fair balance has not been achieved, not even when it entertains doubts on this score.[1867] Although the Court has recognised that the fair balance will be lacking where the applicant had to bear an individual and excessive burden,[1868] a complaint has better chances of success where the applicant can show that the control of the use of his property suffered from procedural irregularities such as non-implementation of domestic court judgments, or (otherwise) from a lack of application of domestic law.[1869]

In the pursuance of modern social policies, the States are entitled even to take measures which affect existing contracts:

> The Court observes that, in remedial social legislation and in particular in the field of rent control, it must be open to the legislature to take measures affecting the further execution of previously concluded contracts in order to attain the aim of the policy adopted.[1870]

Various factors may play a role in the proportionality test: the Court has, for example, on occasion referred to the fact that avenues of judicial review of the contested measures had been available to the applicant.[1871] Similarly, the fact that the applicant was engaged in a commercial venture which by its very nature involved an element of risk, the circumstance that the applicant could have sought to reduce this risk, as well as the fact that the applicant must have been aware of

---

[1865] Judgment of 24 October 1986, A.108, p. 18 (distinction between the importation prohibition as such and the enforcement of this prohibition).

[1866] Judgment of 25 October 1989, A.163, p. 17. See also the judgment of 18 February 1991, *Fredin*, A.192, p. 17. This fair balance test applies also to legislative measures: see the judgment of 19 December 1989, *Mellacher and Others*, A.169, p. 27; judgment of 28 September 1994, *Spadea and Scalabrino*, A.315-B, p. 27.

[1867] Judgment of 25 October 1989, *Allan Jacobsson*, A.163, p. 19.

[1868] Judgment of 23 February 1995, *Gasus Dosier- und Fördertechnik*, A.306-B, p. 51.

[1869] See judgment of 22 February 1994, *Raimondo*, A.281-A, p. 18; judgment of 18 July 1994, *Venditelli*, A.293-A, p. 13; and judgment of 29 September 1994, *Scollo*, A.315-C, p. 54.

[1870] Judgment of 19 December 1989, *Mellacher and Others*, A.169, p. 27.

[1871] See the judgment of 23 February 1995, *Gasus Dosier- und Fördertechnik GmbH*, A.306-B, p. 53 and the judgment of 5 May 1995, *Air Canada*, A.316-A, p. 14.

the possibility of restrictions on the use of his property, have been held against the applicant.[1872]

Although the second paragraph of Article 1 does not require explicitly that the control of use of property be in accordance with law (as does the second sentence of the first paragraph), the Court has accepted that it may review the 'lawfulness' of the measures interfering with the use of property. Therefore, even if the Court's review of compatibility with domestic law as such is limited, the usual requirements of foreseeability and accessibility of the law, as well as that of legal protection against interference by public authorities, apply also in the context of the second paragraph.[1873]

As concerns the 'general interest' aim of the interference, the Court, accepting a wide margin of appreciation, has stated that 'it will respect the legislature's judgment as to what is in the general interest unless that judgment be manifestly without reasonable foundation.'[1874] Thus, a wide variety of aims have been considered to be in the general interest, such as social and economic policy aims in the fields of housing, town planning, alcohol consumption, but also the protection of nature and of the environment, the need to combat international drugs trafficking and the need to preserve evidence of offences and to prevent aggravation of offences.[1875]

13.6 Secure the Payment of Taxes or Other Contributions or Penalties: The Second Part of Paragraph 2

A broad margin of discretion also applies in the case of the second element of the second paragraph: securing the payment of taxes or other contributions and penalties. In its older case-law, the Commission seemed to read this element as not

---

[1872] See respectively, the *Pine Valley and Others* judgment of 29 November 1991, A.222, p. 26; *Gasus* judgment of 23 February 1995, A.306-B, p. 53; and *Fredin* judgment of 18 February 1991, A.192, p. 17.

[1873] See the judgment of 7 July 1989, *Tre Traktörer*, A.159, p. 22; judgment of 18 February 1991, *Fredin*, A.192, p. 16; judgment of 5 May 1995, *Air Canada*, A.316-A, p. 14. Only in its judgment of 22 February 1994, *Raimondo*, A.281-A, p. 18, did the Court find a violation under this head (unexplained delay in execution of domestic court judgment). However, the Court has treated lack of compliance with domestic law also as being relevant under the proportionality test (see *supra*).

[1874] Judgment of 19 December 1989, *Mellacher and Others*, A.169, p. 25; judgments of 28 September 1994 in the *Spadea and Scalabrino* and *Scollo* Cases, A.315-B and A.315-C, p. 25 and p. 52 respectively.

[1875] See respectively, the judgment of 19 December 1989, *Mellacher and Others*, A.169, p. 25 (housing); judgment of 25 October 1989, *Allan Jacobsson*, A.163, p. 17 (town planning); judgment of 7 July 1989, *Tre Traktörer*, A.159, p. 22 (alcohol consumption); judgment of 18 February 1991, *Fredin*, A.192, p. 16 (protection of nature); judgment of 29 November 1991, *Pine Valley and Others*, A.222, p. 25 (protection of the environment); judgment of 5 May 1995, *Air Canada*, A.316-A, p. 14 (combatting international drugs trafficking); and judgment of 18 July 1994, *Venditelli*, A.293-A, p. 12 (preservation of evidence of offences and prevention of aggravation of offences).

placing any particular limit on national measures in this area.[1876] Under this approach, the power of the national authorities to levy taxes, to impose penalties (duly respecting Article 7), to make social security contributions compulsory and to impose other levies[1877] was left intact as long as there existed a legal basis for them, no discrimination was involved, and the power was not used for a purpose other than that for which it had been conferred.[1878]

However, the Commission has gradually moved to an interpretation which affords a wider protection. It accepts that a taxation scheme does not escape its powers of review under the second paragraph of Article 1, notably as concerns the requirements of a 'fair balance' and a 'reasonable relationship of proportionality'. In the area of taxes and other contributions, the Commission has taken the position that:

> the financial liability arising out of the raising of tax or contributions may adversely affect the guarantee secured under this provision if it places an excessive burden on the person or the entity concerned or fundamentally interferes with his or its financial position.[1879]

Nevertheless, the States Parties have a wide margin of appreciation in deciding on the type of tax or contributions they wish to levy, given the assessment of political economic and social considerations that is involved. Thus, in a case where the Commission recognised that a particular system of deducting tax advances created a substantial burden for taxpayers, it nevertheless considered that 'the applicants have not proved that such a burden seriously undermined their financial situation'.[1880]

A considerable margin of appreciation is also accepted in relation to measures taken by tax authorities to enforce tax obligations. In the case of *Gasus Dosier-*

[1876]   In its report in the *Greek* Case, therefore, the Commission held with regard to this latter provision that it does not prescribe any limitation, either of form or of size; *Greek* Case, Yearbook XII (1969), p. 185.

[1877]   *E.g.* a levy for the construction of a road: Appl. 7489/76, *X* v. *Federal Republic of Germany*, D&R 9 (1978), p. 114. See also Appl. 7669/76, *Company X* v. *the Netherlands*, D&R 15 (1979), p. 133 (134): contribution to a professional organisation, required in virtue of a collective agreement declared generally binding by the Government.

[1878]   A complaint of discrimination in relation to tax legislation was upheld by the Court in its judgment of 23 October 1990, *Darby*, A.187, p. 13.

[1879]   Appl. 13013/87, *Wasa Liv Omsesidigt* v. *Sweden*, D&R 58 (1988), p. 163 (188); Appl. 15117/98, *Travers and 27 Others* v. *Italy*, D&R 80 (1995), p. 5 (11).

[1880]   See Appl. 15117/89, *Travers and 27 Others* v. *Italy*, D&R 80 (1995), p. 5 (12). One may assume that this wide margin of appreciation will apply *a fortiori* in relation to the level of taxation. See, however, the Court's judgment of 23 February 1995 in the case of *Gasus Dosier- und Fördertechnik*, A.306-B, pp. 48-49, which leaves open the question of whether the State's right to 'enact (...) laws (...) to secure the payment of taxes' is limited to procedural tax laws or whether it also covers substantive tax laws (laws that define the circumstances under which tax is due and the amounts payable). This rather mysterious statement could be taken to mean that the Court reserved the question of whether it is competent to review taxation levels under Art. 1.

und Fördertechnik GmbH, the Court held, with respect to Dutch legislation which enabled the authorities to recover tax debts against a third party's assets, that:

> in passing such laws, the legislature must be allowed a wide margin of appreciation, especially with regard to the question whether – and if so, to what extent – the tax authorities should be put in a better position to enforce tax debts than ordinary creditors are in to enforce commercial debts. The Court will respect the legislature's assessment unless it is devoid of reasonable foundation.[1881]

Nevertheless, the Court went on to examine the case on the basis of the requirements of a 'fair balance' and of a 'reasonable relationship of proportionality'. The applicant company in this case had complained that, by seizing and selling its possessions which were held by a third party which went bankrupt, the Dutch authorities had deprived it of its property in order to secure payment of a tax debt owed by that third party, for which debt it was in no way responsible. The Court held that such a system of recovery of debts was not uncommon and not incompatible *per se* with the requirements of Article 1. The Court pointed, amongst other things, to the fact that the applicant company was engaged in a commercial venture which naturally entailed risks (in this case: bankruptcy of a debtor), which it could have sought to reduce or eliminate in various ways. The Court, considering also that the tax authorities have fewer possibilities than commercial creditors to protect themselves against insolvency of debtors and that legal remedy against the seizure had been available to the applicant, concluded that the proportionality requirement had been satisfied in this case.[1882]

Also outside the area of taxation, enforcement measures such as forfeiture or even preventive measures such as seizure have been examined by the Convention organs for their compatibility with the second paragraph of Article 1.[1883] The *AGOSI* Case concerned a forfeiture, by court order, of smuggled gold coins belonging to a third party and the subsequent refusal by the customs authorities to restore the goods. The Commission observed that AGOSI complained not of the seizure of the coins, but of their forfeiture and the denial of their return. It was not for the Commission to decide upon AGOSI's innocence or complicity in smuggling, but to examine whether the decision not to restore the coins to the applicant and the procedure which had led to that decision satisfied the procedural requirement inherent in Article 1. The Commission first recalled its case-law that forfeiture constitutes a control of the use of property, not a deprivation. In this

---

[1881] Judgment of 23 February 1995, A.306-B, p. 49.

[1882] *Ibidem*, pp. 51-53.

[1883] As concerns preventive measures, see the judgment of 22 February 1994, *Raimondo*, A.281-A, pp. 16-17 (seizure and confiscation not held disproportionate, having regard to the importance of the fight against the mafia); a violation was found because the confiscation continued even after a domestic court had ordered that the possessions be returned: see p. 18. See also judgment of 18 July 1994, *Venditelli*, A.293-A, pp. 12-13 (sequestration of a flat – to preserve evidence of offence and prevent any aggravation of the offence – which lasted well beyond the judgment ending the criminal proceedings placed a disproportionate burden on the applicant).

case, since the smuggling of the coins was intended to circumvent customs legislation, the forfeiture found its justification in the security which the authorities sought to obtain for the payment of customs duties and penalties. The forfeiture presupposes that the smuggler owns the property. If he does not and if the lawful owner is unaware of the smuggling and suffers loss, the specific justification for forfeiture may be absent and it may amount to confiscation without any specific justification *vis-à-vis* the owner. In the opinion of the Commission the rule of proportionality requires that the innocent owner be given an opportunity to assert his property right and show that he is an innocent owner, this being a necessary balancing factor to the State's forfeiture powers. The Commission concluded that this proportionality requirement was not fulfilled by the legislation and the procedures concerned.[1884] Contrary to the Commission, the Court concluded that it was not established that the British system failed either to ensure that reasonable account be taken of the behaviour of the applicant company or to afford it a reasonable opportunity to put its case.[1885]

13.7 Derogation

Since Article 5 of Protocol No. 1 provides on the one hand that 'all the provisions of the Convention shall apply accordingly', while on the other hand no separate mention is made of Article 15(2), it follows from this that none of the rights mentioned in Protocol No. 1 is non-derogable.

14 RIGHT TO EDUCATION (ARTICLE 2 OF PROTOCOL NO. 1)

No person shall be denied the right to education. In the exercise of any functions which it assumes in relation to education and to teaching, the State shall respect the right of parents to ensure such education and teaching in conformity with their own religious and philosophical convictions.

14.1 The Right to Education

Article 2 of Protocol No. 1 comprises two different, though interconnected rights. While its first sentence guarantees a right to education, its second sentence obliges the State to respect the right of parents to ensure education for their children in conformity with their fundamental convictions. The right to education is the primary right:[1886] the article 'constitutes a whole that is dominated by its first sentence (...) The right set out in the second sentence is an adjunct of this fundamental right to education.'[1887]

[1884] Report of 11 October 1984, A.108, pp. 35-37.
[1885] Judgment of 24 October 1986, A.108, pp. 20-21.
[1886] Report of 21 March 1975, *Kjeldsen, Busk Madsen and Pedersen*, B.21 (1979), p. 2.
[1887] Judgment of 7 December 1976, *Kjeldsen, Busk Madsen and Pedersen*, A.23, p. 26; judgment of 25 February 1982, *Campbell and Cosans*, A.48, p. 16.

The negative formulation of the first sentence seems to emphasise that the right to *freedom of* education is involved here, rather than the social and cultural *right to* education entailing a positive obligation on the part of the State. And, indeed, in the *Belgian Linguistic* Cases the Court held that Article 2 does not require that the Contracting States ensure at their own expense, or subsidise, education of a particular type, but merely implies for those who are under the jurisdiction of one of the Contracting States the right 'to avail themselves of the means of instruction existing at a given time'.[1888] Therefore, its primary objective is to guarantee a right of equal access to the existing educational facilities.

In addition, according to the Court, the article obliges the State to give official recognition in one form or another to those who have completed a given type of education with good results, since otherwise the exercise of this right would not be effective.[1889] Whether this also applies to education pursued abroad, has been left open so far; in any case the person in question may be required to undergo an examination in the country where recognition is requested.[1890]

As the Court observed in its judgment in the *Belgian Linguistic* Cases, the right to education in Article 2 comprises the right to avail oneself of the 'means of instruction existing at a given time'. This implies that the scope of the right to education may vary from one country to another, and is subject to developments. If in a given country a new branch or a new type of education is introduced, persons in that country have a right of access to it, provided that they satisfy the conditions of entry. This right of access refers to all levels of education. As the Commission held in the *Belgian Linguistic* Cases, it 'includes entry to nursery, primary, secondary and higher education'.[1891] The position the Commission has taken in more recent cases, *viz.* that the 'right to education envisaged in Article 2 is concerned primarily with elementary education',[1892] is corroborated neither by the text of Article 2 nor by the Court's case-law. According to the Court's interpretation Article 2 does not require the States to provide a particular level of education – in the Member States of the Council of Europe elementary education must be assumed to be the absolute minimum – but it does oblige them to give access to everyone to all existing educational facilities in accordance with the relevant rules.

Although Article 2 in principle confers a right to access to any type and any level of education existing in the country concerned, this does not mean that everyone should have access to any type of education for which he applies and be

---

[1888] Judgment of 23 July 1968, A.6, p. 31.
[1889] *Idem.*
[1890] Appl. 7864/77, *X v. Belgium*, D&R 16 (1979), p. 82 (83-84); Appl. 11655/85, *Glazewska v. Sweden*, D&R 45 (1986), p. 300 (302).
[1891] See the judgment of 23 July 1968, A.6, p. 22. *Cf.* also Appl. 5492/72, *X v. Austria*, Coll. 44 (1973), p. 63 (64).
[1892] Appl. 5962/72, *X v. the United Kingdom*, D&R 2 (1975), p. 50; Appl. 7010/75, *X v. Belgium*, D&R 3 (1976), p. 162 (164); Appl. 14524/89, *Yanasik v. Turkey*, D&R 74 (1993), p. 14 (27); Appl. 24515/94, *Sulak v. Turkey*, D&R 84-A (1996), p. 98 (99).

permitted to pursue the education concerned as long as he likes.[1893] It is an inherent feature of education that one can complete a particular kind of studies or training successfully only when one has reached the required level. Conditions of entry referring to an objective assessment of this level therefore are not contrary to the freedom of education.[1894] The same holds good for restrictions resulting from admission decisions, fixed numbers of entries, maxima as regards the length of the period one is allowed to spend on one's studies and the like, caused by the limited availability of facilities at a given moment in relation to the demand. Since from Article 2 there does not ensue the obligation to increase this availability, once again there is no question of violation of the Convention as long as no discrimination takes place in the admission.

The right to education by its nature calls for a certain regulation on the part of the Government. However, this regulation may never be of such a nature and scope that the essence of the right[1895] is affected or one of the other rights and freedoms guaranteed by the Convention is violated as a result. This was confirmed by the Court in its judgment in the *Campbell and Cosans* Case. In this case the parents complained, *inter alia*, that their children were actually denied the right to education because they did not receive the guarantee that at the school in question no corporal punishment would be applied, while there was no alternative for them. Since the refusal of Jeffrey Cosans to accept that he should receive corporal punishment in a concrete case had resulted in his suspension, and the requirement itself to submit to that kind of punishment conflicted with the parents' right laid down in the second sentence of Article 2, in the Court's opinion there was no longer any question of a reasonable regulation of access to education, and it consequently concluded that the right to education had been violated.[1896]

On the other hand, reasonable disciplinary measures are compatible with Article 2. For instance, it is not incompatible with this provision for pupils who have committed disciplinary offenses or who have been caught cheating, to be suspended or expelled from the institution concerned.[1897]

[1893] Appl. 5492/72, *X* v. *Austria*, Coll. 44 (1973), p. 63 (64).

[1894] Appl. 6598/74, *X* v. *Federal Republic of Germany* (not published). See also Appl. 8844/80, *X* v. *the United Kingdom*, D&R 23 (1981), p. 228 (229), in which it was found compatible with Art. 2 of Protocol No. 1 that a person was not readmitted to the university because of the fact that he failed the first-year examination and had a poor attendance record.

[1895] For the question as to what this 'essence' is, in our opinion the difference between elementary and other education has to be taken into consideration.

[1896] Judgment of 25 February 1982, A.48, p. 19.

[1897] Appl. 14524/89, *Yanasik* v. *Turkey*, D&R 74 (1993), p. 14 (27); Appl. 24515/94, *Sulak* v. *Turkey*, D&R 84-A (1996), p. 98 (100).

14.2   Compulsory Education

Does the freedom of education also imply the freedom not to receive education? In other words: is a system of compulsory education contrary to Article 2? Article 2 protects free access to and a certain degree of free choice of education, but does not seem to prohibit compulsory education in which sufficient scope is left for such a free choice. Accordingly, the Commission has adopted the view that:

> it is clear that Article 2 of Protocol No. 1 implies a right for the State to establish compulsory schooling, be it in State schools or private tuition of a satisfactory standard, and that verification and enforcement of educational standards is an integral part of that right.

In that particular case the Commission concluded:

> that to require the applicant parents to cooperate in the assessment of their children's educational standards by an education authority in order to ensure a certain level of literacy and numeracy, whilst, nevertheless, allowing them to educate their children at home, cannot be said to constitute a lack of respect for the applicant's rights under Article 2 of Protocol No. 1.[1898]

It is interesting to note that the Commission does not attach so much weight to the form of the (primary) education, but rather to the responsibility of the State for its quality; a certain level of literacy and numeracy, leaving the rights of the parents unimpaired as much as possible. After all, even though compulsory education is not contrary to Article 2, it is limited by certain rights of the children and their parents, in particular the right to respect for their private lives.

14.3   The Obligation to Set Up and Support a System of Education

The primary objective of Article 2 of Protocol No. 1 is to guarantee a right of non-discriminatory access to the existing educational facilities. This provision does not in general require that the Contracting States establish and subsidise education of a particular type or at a particular level.[1899] They are, for instance, not obliged to provide for particular types of adult education.[1900] They are also not required to establish or subsidise schools in which education is provided in a given language,[1901] nor is it their duty to guarantee the availability of schools which are in accordance with a certain religious conviction of the parents,[1902] or to

---

[1898]   Appl. 10233/83, *Family H v. the United Kingdom*, D&R 37 (1984), p. 105 (106).

[1899]   Judgment of 23 July 1968, *Belgian Linguistic* Cases, A.6, p. 31; followed by the Commission: Appl. 6853/74, *40 Mothers* v. *Sweden*, Yearbook XX (1977), p. 214 (238); Appl. 7527/76, *X and Y* v. *the United Kingdom*, D&R 11 (1978), p. 147 (150); Appl. 9461/81, *X and Y* v. *the United Kingdom*, D&R 31 (1983), p. 210 (211); Appl. 23419/94, *Verein Gemeinsam Lernen* v. *Austria*, D&R 82-A (1995), p. 41 (45).

[1900]   Appl. 7010/75, *X* v. *Belgium*, D&R 3 (1976), p. 162 (164).

[1901]   Judgment of 23 July 1968, *Belgian Linguistic* Cases, A.6, p. 42.

[1902]   Appl. 7527/76, *X and Y* v. *the United Kingdom*, D&R 11 (1978), p. 147 (150).

recognise and subsidise private denominational schools.[1903] They are equally not required to place a dyslexic child in a private specialised school, with fees paid by the State, when a place is available in an ordinary State school which has special teaching facilities for disabled children.[1904]

However, the exercise of the right to education, understood as a right of equal access, requires by implication the existence and the maintenance of a minimum of education provided by the State, since otherwise that right would be illusory, in particular for those who have insufficient means to maintain their own institutions. Denying a person the possibility to receive primary education has such far-reaching consequences for the development of the person and for his possibilities to enjoy the rights and freedoms of the Convention to the full that such a treatment is contrary, if not to the letter of Article 2, at all events to the whole system of the Convention, in the light of which Article 2 has to be interpreted.

14.4 The Right to Establish Private Schools

The question has been raised whether the right to education only comprises the right to receive education, or also implies the right to provide for education. Does it, for instance, include the right to provide for private education outside the system of public schools?

Since the first sentence of Article 2 only refers to education, while the second sentence distinguishes between education and teaching, the interpretation that the former includes the right to provide for (private) education does not seem to have originally been intended. In its report in the *Kjeldsen, Busk Madsen and Pedersen* Case, however, the Commission took the view that also the right to 'the establishment of and access to private schools or other means of education outside the public school system' falls under the provision of Article 2.[1905] In its judgment in this case the Court restricted itself to holding that the *travaux préparatoires*:

> indisputably demonstrate (...) the importance attached by many members of the Consultative Assembly and a number of governments to freedom of teaching, that is to say, freedom to establish private schools.[1906]

[1903] Appl. 7782/77, *X v. the United Kingdom*, D&R 14 (1979), p. 179 (181); Appl. 11533/88, *Ingrid Jordebo Foundation of Christian Schools and Ingrid Jordebo v. Sweden*, D&R 51 (1987), p. 125 (128).

[1904] Appl. 14688/89, *Simpson v. the United Kingdom*, D&R 64 (1990), p. 188 (195).

[1905] Report of 21 March 1975, B.21 (1979), p. 44. This position would seem to imply that the Commission then also ought to revise its standpoint that legal persons cannot complain on their own account about violation of Art. 2 (Appl. 3798/68, *Church of X v. the United Kingdom*, Yearbook XII (1969), p. 306 (314)).

[1906] Judgment of 7 December 1976, A.23, pp. 24-25.

In the Commission's view, the first sentence of Article 2 guarantees the right to establish and run a private school, but does not contain a positive obligation for the State to fund it.[1907]

14.5 Parental Rights

14.5.1 The Scope of Parental Rights

The second sentence of Article 2 does not concern the freedom of education of those receiving education, but the right of parents to ensure education for their children in conformity with their own religious and philosophical convictions.[1908] This right has to be *respected*; it is not sufficient that it is taken into account. The Court rejected the defence of the British Government, that it fulfilled the obligation of Article 2 with regard to parents who objected to corporal punishment at school, since it pursued a policy of gradual abolition of this punishment. Referring to the *travaux préparatoires*, the Court held:

> As is confirmed by the fact that, in the course of the drafting of Article 2, the words 'have regard to' were replaced by the word 'respect' (...), the latter word means more than 'acknowledge' or 'take into account'; in addition to a primarily negative undertaking, it implies some positive obligation on the part of the State.[1909]

What kind of obligation does this right entail for the Government? Has the Government fulfilled its obligation to respect the religious and philosophical convictions of the parents if it leaves sufficient scope for instruction in conformity with these convictions in private schools? In other words: is it not obliged to insure respect for these convictions also in public schools? In essence this was contended by the Danish Government in the *Kjeldsen, Busk Madsen and Pedersen* Case. In that case the Danish legislation was challenged which made sex education obligatory at public schools, as integrated with the teaching of other subjects, so that the parents could avoid such education for their children only by sending them to a private school. The argument of the Danish Government as such was rejected by the Court. The second sentence of Article 2 refers to *all* activities of the Government and consequently also implies an obligation concerning the organisation of public education.[1910] At the same time, however, the Court observed that the fact that the State makes an essential contribution to the defrayment of the costs of private education must be taken into consideration

---

[1907] Appl. 11533/85, *Ingrid Jordebo Foundation of Christian Schools and Ingrid Jordebo* v. *Sweden*, D&R 51 (1987), p. 125 (128); Appl. 23419/94, *Verein Gemeinsam Lernen* v. *Austria*, D&R 82-A (1995), p. 41 (45).

[1908] The question as to who are to be considered in a concrete case as the parents of a minor is determined by national law; in this context awards of guardianship, adoptions and the like also have to be taken into account, see Appl. 7626/76, *X* v. *the United Kingdom*, D&R 11 (1978), p. 160 (167-168).

[1909] Judgment of 25 February 1982, *Campbell and Cosans*, A.48, p. 17.

[1910] Judgment of 7 December 1976, A.23, p. 25. This point of view was followed by the Commission in its decision on Appl. 6853/74, *40 Mothers* v. *Sweden*, Yearbook XX (1977), p. 214 (238).

when deciding whether the obligation ensuing from Article 2 has been fulfilled.[1911] How much weight the Court is prepared to attach to this aspect in a concrete case was not revealed, since it reached the conclusion that the obligatory sex education was of such a nature as not to conflict with the interests of the parents protected in Article 2.

In its report in the *Campbell and Cosans* Case, in regard to the argument advanced by the British Government that there existed private schools where the challenged corporal punishment was not applied, the Commission took the position that this did not absolve the Government from the obligation to respect at public schools the religious and philosophical conviction of the parents, while the fact that private schools required a high financial contribution from the parents or that these schools were situated at a great distance could render the alternative unrealistic.[1912] In a later decision, however, the Commission did away without any argument with the factor that the parents could not afford private education as an alternative.[1913]

The above-mentioned judgment in the *Kjeldsen, Busk Madsen and Pedersen* Case has produced two more clarifications as to the second sentence of Article 2. In the first place, the Court rejected the submission of the Danish Government that this provision referred exclusively to specific religious instruction. According to the Court, in *all* education activities with which the Government is concerned the rights of parents ensured in Article 2 have to be respected.[1914]

Secondly, the Court clearly stated that the subjective views of the parents are not decisive for the question whether the content of the instruction is in conformity with their religious and philosophical convictions: this question should be examined by reference to objective criteria.[1915] The Court held that the second sentence of Article 2 'aims in short at safeguarding the possibility of pluralism in education, which possibility is essential for the preservation of the "democratic society" as conceived by the Convention'. And 'in view of the power of the modern State, it is above all through State teaching that this aim must be realized'.[1916] As the Government is responsible for the curriculum it is entitled to include in the teaching also the transmission of information of a directly or indirectly religious or philosophical kind, integrated with other subjects, since they

---

[1911] *Idem*. See also Appl. 7782/77, *X v. the United Kingdom*, D&R 14 (1979), p. 179 (181).

[1912] Report of 16 May 1980, B.42 (1985), pp. 38-39.

[1913] Appls 10228/82 and 10229/82, *W & D.M. and M & H.I. v. the United Kingdom*, D&R 37 (1984), p. 96 (100). See also its decision on Appl. 7527/76, *X and Y v. the United Kingdom*, D&R 11 (1978), p. 147 (151), where the Commission took into consideration that the parents had been offered a place for their son at a Roman Catholic school in a neighbouring municipality.

[1914] Judgment of 7 December 1976, A.23, p. 25.

[1915] *Cf.* judgment of 18 December 1996, *Valsamis v. Greece*, Reports 1996-VI, Vol. 27, pp. 2324-2325, and judgment of 18 December 1996, *Efstratiou v. Greece*, Reports 1996-VI, Vol. 27, pp. 2359-2360: the Court could not discern any military overtones in the school parade, in which the child of Jehovah's Witnesses had to take part, that could possibly offend their pacifist convictions to an extent prohibited by the second sentence of Art. 2.

[1916] Judgment of 7 December 1976, A.23, p. 25.

will inevitably be implied in the subject-matter to be taught. Article 2 has been violated only if the transmission of ideas does not take place in an objective, critical and pluralistic way, but on the contrary assumes the character of indoctrination. The question of whether the latter was the case here, was examined independently by the Court; it took into account particularly the purpose of sex education, the content of the instruction to be given in that respect, the fact that the instruction given did not affect the rights of the parents to advise and guide their children in line with their convictions, and the possibility of taking action against abuse at a particular school or by a particular teacher.[1917]

If the State prescribes a certain instruction, such instruction must not be indoctrinating but objective and pluralistic. In the case of integrated instruction, this requirement of pluralism always applies. On the other hand, religious instruction based on a particular State religion provided at a public school is not necessarily contrary to Article 2, provided that parental beliefs are respected by granting exemptions.[1918] From the prohibition of discrimination in Article 14 follows that the State, when granting exemptions on the ground of religious belief, should also allow exemptions on the ground of non-religious philosophical convictions.[1919]

Although parents have the right to keep their children away from religious instruction at a public school, they cannot lay claim to separate instruction as an alternative. The State is not required to provide for special facilities to accommodate particular convictions;[1920] nor is the State obliged to set up and support schools serving such beliefs.[1921]

The Commission has not yet decided whether opinions of parents about the appropriate school for their disabled child can be said to be based on philosophical convictions. Even assuming that this is the case, the wide margin of discretion left to the authorities implies that the second sentence of Article 2 does not require the

---

[1917] *Ibidem*, pp. 26-28. See also the Commission, Appl. 6853/74, *40 Mothers* v. *Sweden*, Yearbook XX (1977), p. 214 (238-240), and Appl. 7527/76, *X and Y* v. *the United Kingdom*, D&R 11 (1978), p. 147 (151). Furthermore, see Appl. 8811/79, *Seven Individuals* v. *Sweden*, D&R 29 (1982), p. 104 (116): reference to policy statements of a general character in official publications cannot be held to be indoctrination.

[1918] Appl. 10491/83, *Angeleni* v. *Sweden*, D&R 51 (1987), p. 41 (46).

[1919] However, the Commission seems to accept that exemptions of moral and social education lessons are exclusively conditional on adherence to a religious belief: Appl. 17187/90, *Bernard and Others* v. *Luxembourg*, D&R 75 (1993), p. 57 (74-75).

[1920] Appl. 7782/77, *X* v. *the United Kingdom*, D&R 14 (1979), p. 179 (180); Appl. 13887/88, *Graeme* v. *the United Kingdom*, D&R 64 (1990), p. 158 (165); Appl. 25212/94, *Klerks* v. *the Netherlands*, D&R 82-A (1995), p. 129 (132).

[1921] Appl. 7527/76, *X and Y* v. *the United Kingdom*, D&R 11 (1978), p. 147 (151); Appl. 9461/81, *X and Y* v. *the United Kingdom*, D&R 31 (1983), p. 210 (211).

placing of such a child in a regular school with additional facilities rather than in an available place in a special school,[1922] nor *vice versa*.[1923]

Since Article 2 in principle also refers to secondary and higher education to the extent available, it must be assumed that the obligation of the State to ensure pluriformity in religious and philosophical respects in providing for education applies also to education for adults. For this they may rely on the first sentence of Article 2, interpreted in the light of the whole of Article 2.

14.5.2 Philosophical Convictions

In the *Campbell and Cosans* Case the Court clarified the concept of 'philosophical convictions'. It did not equate these convictions with 'mere' opinions or ideas:

> the word 'conviction', taken on its own, is not synonymous with the words 'opinions' and 'ideas', such as are utilised in Article 10 of the Convention, which guarantees freedom of expression; it is more akin to the term 'beliefs' (...) appearing in Article 9 – which guarantees freedom of thought, conscience and religion – and denotes views that attain a certain level of cogency, seriousness, cohesion and importance.

Nevertheless, it gave a wide interpretation:

> Having regard to the Convention as a whole, including Article 17, the expression 'philosophical convictions' in the present context denotes, in the Court's opinion, such convictions as are worthy of respect in a 'democratic society' (...) and are not incompatible with human dignity; in addition, they must not conflict with the fundamental right of a child to education, the whole of Article 2 being dominated by its first sentence.[1924]

In that context and with respect to objections submitted to corporal punishment, the Court held:

> The applicant's views relate to a weighty and substantial aspect of human life and behaviour, namely the integrity of the person, the propriety or otherwise of the infliction of corporal punishment and the exclusion of the distress which risk of such punishment entails. They are views which satisfy each of the various criteria listed above; it is this that distinguishes them from opinions that might be held on other methods of discipline or on discipline in general.[1925]

[1922] Appl. 14135/88, *P.D. and L.D.* v. *the United Kingdom*, D&R 62 (1989), p. 292 (297); Appl. 13887/88, *Graeme* v. *the United Kingdom*, D&R 64 (1990), p. 158 (166); Appl. 25212/94, *Klerks* v. *the Netherlands*, D&R 82-A (1995), p. 129 (133).

[1923] Appl. 14688/89, *Simpson* v. *the United Kingdom*, D&R 64 (1990), p. 188 (195).

[1924] Judgment of 25 February 1982, A.48, p. 16. See also Appl. 8566/79, *X, Y and Z* v. *the United Kingdom*, D&R 31 (1983), p. 50 (53). *Cf.* the definition of the Commission in its report of 16 May 1980, B.42 (1985), p. 37: 'those ideas based on human knowledge and reasoning concerning the world, life, society, etc., which a person adopts and professes according to the dictates of his or her conscience. These ideas can more briefly be characterised as a person's outlook on life including, in particular, a concept of human behaviour in society'. See also p. 36, where the Commission abandoned its much narrower interpretation in the *Belgian Linguistic* Cases that 'philosophical opinions were added in order to cover agnostic opinions'.

[1925] *Ibidem*, pp. 16-17. In order to be respected, those philosophical convictions must of course have been brought to the attention of the authorities: see Appl. 8566/79, *X, Y and Z* v. *the United Kingdom*, D&R 31 (1983), p. 50 (53).

The respect for 'philosophical convictions' does not extend to the domain of language. In the *Belgian Linguistic* Cases the Court concluded that Article 2:

> does not require of States that they should, in the sphere of education or teaching, respect parents' linguistic preferences, but only their religious and philosophical convictions. To interpret the terms 'religious' or 'philosophical' as covering linguistic preferences would amount to a distortion of their ordinary and usual meaning and to read into the Convention something which is not there.[1926]

14.5.3 Education and Teaching

In its *Campbell and Cosans* judgment the Court has also given a definition of the words 'education' and 'teaching':

> the education of children is the whole process whereby, in any society, adults endeavour to transmit their beliefs, culture and other values to the young, whereas teaching or instruction refers in particular to the transmission of knowledge and to intellectual development.[1927]

On the basis of these definitions the submission of the British Government that discipline at school does not form a part of these concepts was rejected:

> it is (...) an integral part of the process whereby a school seeks to achieve the object for which it was established, including the development and moulding of the character and mental powers of its pupils.[1928]

Furthermore, it was clearly established that, once the Government has assumed responsibility for education, no distinction can be made between aspects of education falling under that responsibility and aspects not falling under it; certainly not where education at public schools is concerned. That responsibility, therefore, extends beyond the curriculum and also embraces the way in which discipline is maintained at the school, even though the Government does not concern itself with such maintenance day by day.[1929]

14.5.4 Parental Authority

The broad definition of 'education' in the *Campbell and Cosans* Case implies that the second sentence also applies to situations outside the framework of teaching institutions. In the *Olsson* Case parents complained of a violation of that provision because their son had been placed in a foster family that belonged to a religious denomination and attended church with him, whereas they did not wish their children to receive a religious upbringing. The Commission first referred to its earlier case-law that in case of adoption or when the courts have removed a parent's right to custody, that parent no longer has the right to determine the child's education, since this is an integral part of the right to custody (and *a fortiori* of the rights of the adoptive parents). Whether Article 2 of Protocol No.

[1926] Judgment of 23 July 1968, A.6, p. 32.
[1927] Judgment of 25 February 1982, A.48, p. 14.
[1928] *Idem.*
[1929] *Ibidem*, p. 15.

1 imposes on the public authorities an obligation not to transfer parental authority over a child to persons who do not share the convictions of the natural parents in matters of education, was expressly left open by the Commission.[1930] Subsequently, it held that a decision to take a child into care was of a different character and did not mean that the right to custody was removed from the parents. However, since a care order temporarily transfers certain parental rights to the public authorities, it is inevitable, according to the Commission, that the contents of the parent's rights in Article 2 of Protocol No. 1 must be reduced accordingly. On the other hand, the responsible authorities must, in the exercise of their rights under a care order, have due regard to these rights. In the case under consideration the Commission, followed by the Court, concluded that there were no serious indications that the applicants had, prior to the care order, been particularly concerned with giving their children a non-religious upbringing and that, moreover, there was no reason to believe that the religious education of their son in the foster home would be in conflict with the education previously given by the applicants.[1931]

14.6 Foreigners and Detainees

A *foreigner* cannot, by referring to Article 2, claim admittance to a Contracting State in order to receive education there, since only those who are already under the jurisdiction of the Contracting State may derive rights from Article 2. If, however, Article 2 is interpreted to include the right to give instruction, this may imply that, for instance, a religious group established in the country may, in principle, claim admittance for its members to attend a congress, a course of study, and the like, or may claim the admittance of a person who is specifically qualified to teach.[1932]

Can a foreigner challenge the refusal of an extension of his stay permit by referring to Article 2? This was done by 15 foreign students in a complaint against the United Kingdom. The Commission, however, declared this complaint manifestly ill-founded, holding that the power of the States to decide for themselves who may reside in their territory is not limited by Article 2, unless perhaps in cases where expulsion might result in the person concerned being deprived of any elementary education.[1933] It seems that with respect to the right to primary education the line has been followed that the situation in the country of origin must also be included in the assessment of a possible violation of the

---

[1930] Appl. 7626/76, *X* v. *the United Kingdom*, D&R 11 (1978), p. 160 (167); Appl. 7911/77, *X* v. *Sweden*, D&R 12 (1978), p. 192 (194).

[1931] Report of 2 December 1986, A.130, pp. 63-64; judgment of 24 March 1988, A.130, p. 40.

[1932] The Commission, however, rejected such a construction in its decision on Appl. 3798/68, *Church of X* v. *the United Kingdom*, Yearbook XII (1969), p. 306 (320-322), after it had first taken the disputable view that an organisation cannot derive an independent right from Art. 2.

[1933] Appl. 7671/76 and 14 other complaints, *15 Foreign Students* v. *the United Kingdom*, D&R 9 (1978), p. 185 (186-187).

Convention (as is usual in expulsion cases where Articles 3, 8 and 12 are invoked).

As long as a foreigner resides lawfully in a Contracting State, he of course also has the right to education. However, this does not imply the right to receive education in his own vernacular if that is not already offered by the State concerned; there is only a right of access to the existing educational facilities (*cf.* section 14.1). In the Court's opinion the interest in receiving education in one's own language or in the language of one's choice is also not protected by the second sentence of Article 2, because an interpretation of the terms religious and philosophical in that sense 'would amount to a distortion of their ordinary and usual meaning', while it is evident from the *travaux préparatoires* that this provision was not intended 'to secure respect by the State of a right for parents to have education conducted in a language other than that of the country in question.'[1934] The question remains, however, whether in virtue of the first sentence of Article 2 it is not at least incumbent on the Government to create additional facilities within the existing educational institutions for the benefit of those aliens having taken up residence in the territory for a considerable time who do not yet have sufficient command of the language in which education is conducted; otherwise the right to education will remain illusory for them for a long time. At least as regards elementary education, in our opinion this question should be answered in the affirmative on the same grounds as have been given above for minimum provisions for elementary education in general (section 14.3).

Article 2 does not contain a restriction clause, which raises the difficult question to what extent foreigners without a residence permit can derive from this provision a right to education. As we observed in section 14.1, this article primarily guarantees a right of *equal access* to the existing educational institutions. Is the fact that these persons do not have such a permit a sufficient reason for differential treatment and to deny them the right of access to educational institutions of nationals and legally residing foreigners? It seems to us that at least with regard to primary education this is not the case[1935] as far as it concerns foreigners who, although not legally residing here, are likely to stay here for an indefinite period of time (for instance because they cannot be expelled for humanitarian reasons). Denying these persons the possibility to receive primary education has such far-reaching consequences, that the fact that they do not legally reside here is not a reasonable justification for this differential treatment, which therefore is contrary to Article 2 (independently or in conjunction with Article 14).

With regard to *detainees* the question of inherent limitations arises, since Article 2 does not contain an enumeration of restrictions. Prisoners, too, are in principle

---

[1934] Judgment of 23 July 1968, *Belgian Linguistic* Cases, A.6, p. 32.
[1935] Appl. 7671/76 and 14 other complaints, *15 Foreign Students* v. *the United Kingdom*, D&R 9 (1978), p. 185 (186-187), points in this direction: expulsion is not limited by Art. 2, unless perhaps in cases where it might result in the person concerned being deprived of any elementary education.

entitled to make use of the existing educational facilities if this is compatible with the rationale of the detention on remand or the penalty of imprisonment, taking also into consideration changing views of penitentiary policy. Thus, correspondence courses or courses *via* radio and television, subject to the necessary security measures, must as a rule be permitted, as must also the purchase of books for purposes of study. The argument advanced by the Commission that no facilities for the desired education were available within prison[1936] is in itself insufficient. If a type of education is available which prisoners can follow without unacceptable consequences for the execution of the penalty – for instance a correspondence course – it is difficult to understand why they should not have the right 'to avail themselves of the means of instruction existing at a given time'.[1937] But it follows from the negative formulation of Article 2 that the Government is not obliged to defray the costs.

14.7   Derogation

Article 2 of Protocol No. 1 is not exempted from Article 15(1) of the Convention. This means that derogating measures may be taken under the conditions laid down in Article 15.

15   FREE ELECTIONS BY SECRET BALLOT (ARTICLE 3 OF PROTOCOL NO. 1)

The High Contracting Parties undertake to hold free elections at reasonable intervals by secret ballot, under conditions which will ensure the free expression of the opinion of the people in the choice of the legislature.

15.1   Introduction

The importance of Article 3 does not consist in the first place in the obligation of the States to hold free elections at reasonable intervals by secret ballot, but in the connection between those elections and the composition of the legislature. In fact, this means, as was observed by the Commission in its report in the *Greek* Case, that Article 3 presupposes the existence of a representative legislature, elected at reasonable intervals, as the basis of a democratic society.[1938]

Since such an important role has been assigned to the national legislature in ensuring the enjoyment of the rights and freedoms set forth in the Convention as well as in subjecting certain of these rights and freedoms to rules which may restrict their enjoyment, it is of eminent importance that this legislature should consist of democratically elected representatives of the holders of those rights and freedoms. Therefore, properly speaking, this Article 3 should have preceded the

---

[1936]   Appl. 5962/72, *X* v. *the United Kingdom*, D&R 2 (1975), p. 50.
[1937]   Judgment of 23 July 1968, *Belgian Linguistic* Cases, A.6, p. 31.
[1938]   Report of 5 November 1969, Yearbook XII (1969), p. 179.

provisions of Section I of the Convention as a further elaboration of the concept of 'effective political democracy' referred to in the Preamble and of 'democratic society' mentioned in various provisions of the Convention. In its first judgment with regard to Article 3 of Protocol No. 1 the Court emphasised that 'since it enshrines a characteristic principle of democracy, Article 3 of Protocol no. 1 is accordingly of prime importance in the Convention system'.[1939]

15.2   Scope of the Obligation to Hold Free Elections at Reasonable Intervals

With respect to both its formulation and its content, Article 3 constitutes an exception among the rights and freedoms laid down in the Convention and its Protocols. It is formulated neither as a right or freedom nor as an obligation for the national authorities to refrain from interfering with the exercise of a right or freedom, but as an undertaking on the part of the Contracting States to *do* something; an express and not only an implied positive obligation.

What does that obligation imply for the States? From the text of Article 3 it follows that elections must be held at regular intervals, that those elections must be free, *i.e.* without any pressure as regards the choice, and that the secrecy of the votes cast must be safeguarded. Moreover, it follows from the word 'choice' in Article 3 that there must be a real choice, which implies that the States must make possible the creation and functioning of political parties and must enable the latter – apart from the possible applicability of Article 17[1940] – to present candidates for the elections.[1941] A one-party system imposed by the State, therefore, must be considered contrary to Article 3.[1942] And although Article 3 does not prescribe any particular form of government, it follows from the tenor of Article 3 that the legislative power must rest with the body constituted as a result of those free elections, and the possibility for the Head of State or Government to rule by decree without a parliamentary mandate would be contrary to that tenor.

Conditions for the admission of a group of persons as a political party to the elections have been considered permissible by the Commission if these conditions serve the purpose of guaranteeing the public character of the political process and of avoiding confusion of the electorate by groups which cannot assume political responsibility, provided that they do not essentially interfere with free choice.[1943] Thus, the requirement of the production of a given number of signatures was considered justified, since groups standing any chance at all in the

---

[1939]   Judgment of 2 March 1987, *Mathieu-Mohin and Clerfayt*, A.113, p. 22.
[1940]   On Art. 17, see *infra* pp. 750-755.
[1941]   Report of 5 November 1969, *Greek* Case, Yearbook XII (1969), p. 180. See also Appl. 7140/75, *X v. the United Kingdom*, D&R 7 (1977), p. 95 (96).
[1942]   However, a guarantee of the right to free political opposition, which appeared in the European Movement's draft, was not included in the final text; see Partsch, *supra* note 526, pp. 241-243.
[1943]   Appl. 6850/74, *Association X, Y and Z v. Federal Republic of Germany*, D&R 5 (1976), p. 90 (93-94). For conditions in regard to the objectives of political parties, see the discussion of Art. 17, *infra* pp. 750-755.

elections will easily be able to satisfy such a requirement, while groups evidently unable to bear political responsibility will thereby be excluded.[1944] In a later decision the Commission pursued this line further with respect to the requirement that an appeal against the way in which the elections have been conducted must be supported by a given number of signatures. The Commission reached this view:

> having regard to the principles of a democratic society that the procedural rights related to the exercise of the right to stand as a candidate or to propose candidates, reflect the character of the elections as a public political process, and that these rights are accordingly circumscribed in such a way that they cannot be exercised by an individual acting alone, but only with the support of a certain minimum number of persons holding the same views.[1945]

Likewise, the Commission accepted as legitimate a French rule according to which lists standing in general elections must pay a deposit, which will only be reimbursed to lists having obtained at least five percent of the votes cast. This system was 'designed to promote the emergence of sufficiently representative currents of thought', a legitimate aim for the purposes of Article 3.[1946]

The system according to which political parties are subsidised by the Government on the basis of the results of the elections, too, was deemed permissible as one which protects the parties from undue outside pressure and at the same time reflects the real importance of each of them.[1947]

Both the constituency voting system of elections within a certain district,[1948] and the system of proportional representation[1949] are compatible with Article 3. The same must be assumed to apply to a system of indirect elections, since the word 'direct' does not appear in Article 3 and the people are able freely to express their opinion on the ultimate constitution of the legislature *via* such a system as well.[1950] In the same line it was held by the Court that Article 3 of Protocol No. 1 'does not create any obligation to introduce a specific system, (...) such as proportional representation or majority voting with one or two ballots'.[1951]

Once the people can participate in the composition of the legislature at regular intervals, the requirements set by Article 3 regarding participation in government

---

[1944] *Idem.*

[1945] Appl. 8227/78, *X* v. *Federal Republic of Germany*, D&R 16 (1979), p. 179 (180-181).

[1946] Appl. 12897/87, *Desmeules* v. *France*, D&R 67 (1991), p. 166 (173). The Commission added that it did not consider arbitrary or disproportionate the way this rule was applied in the instant case.

[1947] Appl. 6850/74, *Association A, Y and Z* v. *Federal Republic of Germany*, D&R 5 (1976), p. 90 (93-94).

[1948] In this sense concerning a complaint of a member of the British Liberal Party: Appl. 7140/75, *X* v. *the United Kingdom*, D&R 7 (1977), p. 95 (96-97).

[1949] Appl. 8364/78, *Lindsay* v. *the United Kingdom*, D&R 15 (1979), p. 247 (251), with regard to a complaint about the electoral system of Northern Ireland in connection with the elections for the European Parliament. See also Appl. 8765/79, *The Liberal Party, Mrs R and Mr P* v. *the United Kingdom*, D&R 21 (1981), p. 211 (223).

[1950] That it was indeed intended not to exclude the system of indirect elections, appears also from the *travaux préparatoires*: Partsch, *supra* note 526, p. 243.

[1951] Judgment of 2 March 1987, *Mathieu-Mohin and Clerfayt*, A.113, p. 24.

have been satisfied. In particular this provision does not require that the people shall be consulted *via* referendum about certain legislative acts.[1952]

In a case concerning the electoral system of Niedersachsen (Germany), the Commission examined whether a five-year period still constituted a 'reasonable interval' within the meaning of Article 3. It found that this question should be determined by reference to the purpose of parliamentary elections: ensuring that fundamental changes in the prevailing public opinion are reflected in the opinions of the representatives of the people. Too short an interval might impede longer-term planning for the implementation of the will of the people, while too long a period may lead to a composition of Parliament which no longer bears any resemblance to the prevailing will of the electorate. The Commission considered that a five-year interval gave appropriate weight to these various considerations and duly reflected the will of the people.[1953]

15.3 Scope of the Right to Vote and to be Elected

On the basis of the formulation of Article 3 as a government undertaking to do something, and not as an individual right, some authors have taken the position that this provision can only be the object of a complaint by a State and not of an individual complaint.[1954] The Commission never went so far, although its observation quoted above that the right of appeal against the way elections have been conducted is a right which 'cannot be exercised by an individual acting alone'[1955] seems to go somewhat in the direction of also excluding a complaint by an individual.

At first the Commission drew from the text of Article 3 the general conclusion that this provision does not imply a right of the individual citizens to vote and to be elected. Exclusion from the franchise, not only of particular persons,[1956] but also of groups of persons,[1957] was therefore considered admissible by the Commission on that ground, be it under the condition that 'such exclusion does not prevent the free expression of the opinion of the people in the choice of the legislature'.[1958] This view of the Commission was corroborated to some extent

---

[1952] Appl. 6742/74, *X* v. *Federal Republic of Germany*, D&R 3 (1976), p. 98 (103), concerning the conclusion of a treaty.

[1953] Appl. 27311/95, *Timke* v. *Federal Republic of Germany*, D&R 82 (1995), p. 158 (160).

[1954] See, *e.g.*, Partsch, *supra* note 526, pp. 243-244.

[1955] See *supra* p. 657. In that context it is rather surprising that on the other hand the Commission still left open the question of whether a political party may be the victim of a violation of Art. 3: Appl. 8765/79, *The Liberal Party, Mrs R and Mr P* v. *the United Kingdom*, D&R 21 (1981), p. 211 (223).

[1956] Thus, *e.g.*, of a detainee: Appl. 530/59, *X* v. *Federal Republic of Germany*, Yearbook III (1960), p. 184 (190), and of a collaborator: Appl. 787/60, *X* v. *the Netherlands*, Coll. 7 (1962), p. 75 (79), and Appl. 6573/74, *X* v. *the Netherlands*, D&R 1 (1975), p. 87 (89-90).

[1957] *E.g.* the exclusion of Belgian residents in Belgian Congo from the elections in Belgium: Appl. 1065/61, *X* v. *Belgium*, Yearbook IV (1961), p. 260 (268).

[1958] *Idem.*

by the *travaux préparatoires*: in fact, from the original draft the word 'universal' was cancelled,[1959] from which it might be inferred that the drafters did not wish to include a guarantee for universal suffrage. In later decisions, however, the Commission took the position that the obligation imposed on the Contracting States does imply 'the recognition of universal suffrage'.[1960] It added, however, that this did not mean that the right to take part in the elections was ensured to everyone without any restriction. In a decision of May 1975 the Commission clearly expressed its view in the following words:

> it follows both from the preamble and from Article 5 of the Protocol no. 1 that the rights set out in the Protocol are protected by the same guarantees as are contained in the Convention itself. It must, therefore, be admitted that, whatever the wording of Article 3, the right it confers is in the nature of an individual right, since this quality constitutes the very foundation of the whole Convention.[1961]

Repeating thereupon its position that Article 3 recognises universal suffrage, the Commission concluded 'that Article 3 guarantees, in principle, the right to vote and the right to stand for election to the legislature'.[1962] Here again, however, the Commission emphasised that this does not mean that it is an absolute or unlimited right. From the words 'under conditions which will ensure the free expression of the opinion of the people in the choice of the legislature' it inferred that the Contracting States are allowed to impose certain restrictions on the right to vote and to be elected, provided that this is not done arbitrarily and does not constitute interference with the free expression of the people's opinion as such. It is for the Strasbourg organs to judge ultimately whether this condition has been fulfilled.[1963]

The Commission's view was endorsed by the Court in 1987. The Court held that:

> the inter-State colouring of the wording of Article 3 does not reflect any difference of substance from the other substantive clauses of the Convention and Protocols. The reason for it would seem to lie rather in the desire to give greater solemnity to the commitment undertaken and in the fact that the primary obligation in the field concerned is not one of abstention or non-interference, as with the majority of the civil and political rights, but one of adoption by the State of positive measures to 'hold' democratic elections.[1964]

The Court approved the Commission's interpretation of the right embodied in Article 3 as a subjective right of participation, but also recognised that there are implied limitations which leave the States a wide margin of appreciation in making the rights to vote and to stand for election subject to certain conditions. The Strasbourg organs have to satisfy themselves that these conditions do not

---

[1959] See Partsch, *supra* note 526, p. 243.
[1960] Appl. 2728/66, *X* v. *Federal Republic of Germany*, Yearbook X (1967), p. 336 (338).
[1961] Appls 6745 and 6746/74, *W, X, Y and Z* v. *Belgium*, Yearbook XVIII (1975), p. 236 (244).
[1962] *Idem*.
[1963] *Idem*.
[1964] Judgment of 2 March 1987, *Mathieu-Mohin and Clerfayt*, A.113, pp. 22-23.

curtail the rights in question to such an extent as to impair their very essence and deprive them of their effectiveness; that they are imposed in pursuit of a legitimate aim; and that the means employed are not disproportionate. In particular, such conditions must not thwart 'the free expression of the opinion of the people in the choice of the legislature'.[1965] Moreover, the Court emphasises that the phrase 'conditions which will ensure the free expression of the opinion of the people in the choice of the legislature':

> implies essentially – apart from freedom of expression (already protected under Article 10 of the Convention) – the principle of equality of treatment of all citizens in the exercise of their right to vote and their right to stand for election.[1966]

A touchstone for the admissibility of limitations of the right to vote will therefore have to be, besides the prohibition of arbitrariness, the question whether the right to vote and to be elected has been conferred in a sufficiently wide and representative way to make it possible to speak of a free expression of the people's opinion as such. In addition, the restrictions have to be reviewed, in virtue of Article 5 of Protocol No. 1, for their conformity with the whole of the Convention, in particular with the prohibition of discrimination of Article 14. It is likely that the Commission's earlier view that the exclusion of citizens not residing in the country was justified,[1967] can also stand this new test; for the requirement of residence it advanced a number of grounds which it found not to be unreasonable, while it considered justified the resulting difference in treatment between categories of citizens on the ground of the different situations in which they found themselves.[1968] The establishment of a minimum age for the exercise of the right to vote and to be elected in principle also fulfils the criteria indicated in the case-law.[1969] However, when this limit is appreciably higher than is the case in most other Member States of the Council of Europe, the question of its reasonableness and the impact on the representative character of the elections will have to receive special attention.

In the *Mathieu-Mohin and Clerfayt* Case the Belgian 1980 Special Act was at issue, which required that candidates elected for the Flemish Council should take their parliamentary oath in Dutch. The applicants complained that this requirement prevented French-speaking electors from voting for a candidate who was likewise French-speaking. The Commission agreed that the Act had as an effect that a substantial minority in the district concerned could not have its own representatives on the Flemish Council and, therefore, constituted restrictions which were not compatible with Article 3 of Protocol No. 1, taken on its own. Having reached that conclusion, the Commission found it unnecessary to give its

---

[1965] *Ibidem*, p. 23.
[1966] *Idem*.
[1967] See *supra* note 1957.
[1968] See also Appl. 7566/76, *X v. the United Kingdom*, D&R 9 (1978), p. 121 (122-123), and Appl. 8987/80, *X and Association Y v. Italy*, D&R 24 (1981), p. 192 (196).
[1969] Appls 6745 and 6746/74, *W, X, Y and Z v. Belgium*, Yearbook XVIII (1975), p. 236 (244-246).

opinion on Article 14 of the Convention.[1970] The Court, by thirteen votes to five, reached a different conclusion. It attached great importance to the fact that the Act fitted into a general institutional system of the Belgian State, based on the territoriality principle, and was designed to achieve an equilibrium between the Kingdom's various regions and cultural communities by means of a complex pattern of checks and balances, and to defuse the language disputes in the country by establishing more stable and decentralised organisational structures. Against that background and given the State's margin of appreciation, the system – which was still incomplete and provisional – was not considered unreasonable by the Court. The fact that the French-speaking electors must vote either for candidates who will take the parliamentary oath in French and will accordingly join the French-language group in the (central) House of Representatives or the Senate and sit on the (regional) French Community Council, or else for candidates who will take the oath in Dutch and so belong to the Dutch-language group in the House of Representatives or the Senate and sit on the Flemish Council, was considered by the Court not to be a disproportionate limitation such as would thwart 'the free expression of the opinion of the people in the choice of the legislature'. For the same reason the Court held that there was no discrimination prejudicial to the applicants in violation of Article 14.[1971]

Denying the right to vote to women is contrary to the tenor of Article 3 as well as to the prohibition of discrimination.[1972] As to the restriction of the right to vote to the State's own nationals, this question is more difficult to answer. Article 16, which allows restriction of the political activities of aliens in certain cases, has not been linked to Article 3 of Protocol No. 1 but may operate *via* Article 14 of the Convention. It is true that the above-mentioned important role which has been assigned by the Convention to the legislature in ensuring and further regulating the enjoyment of the rights and freedoms points to an equal interest of aliens in the composition of the legislature in their host country, since Article 1 of the Convention confers the enjoyment of those rights and freedoms on them as well. Nevertheless, the Court has held in its *Mathieu-Mohin and Clerfayt* judgment that Article 3 'implies essentially equality of treatment of all *citizens* in the exercise of their right to vote and to stand for election'.[1973] Restriction of the franchise to the State's own nationals is still fairly common, and was even more so at the time Article 3 was drafted, so that it is not very likely that the drafters wished to exclude such a system for the future.[1974] However, if they have intended to express this by the word 'people', this is inadequate; it can hardly be argued that those aliens who have been residents of a given country for a long time and as

---

[1970]   Report of 15 March 1985, A.113, pp. 36-37.
[1971]   Judgment of 2 March 1987, A.113, pp. 24-26.
[1972]   See, with a reference to the situation in Switzerland, Partsch, *supra* note 526, p. 245. Switzerland, however, has not yet ratified Protocol No. 1.
[1973]   Judgment of 2 March 1987, A.113, p. 23 (emphasis added).
[1974]   Thus impliedly also the Commission: Appl. 7566/76, *X v. the United Kingdom*, D&R 9 (1978), p. 121 (122), and Appl. 7730/76, *X v. the United Kingdom*, D&R 15 (1979), p. 137 (138).

such contribute to the economic, social and cultural life of that country, without, for whatever reason, having been naturalised, do not belong to the 'people' of that country. It is therefore not a matter of course to deny the franchise to them when one takes the principle of representative democracy, as laid down in Article 3, seriously. Although the idea of granting the right to vote to aliens, in particular in local elections, is gaining more ground,[1975] it may hardly be expected that the Strasbourg case-law will force a break-through on this point.[1976]

Many legislations contain the provision that nationals can take part in elections in the country in question only if they also have residence in that country. The Commission considered this restriction as being in conformity with Article 3, and advanced the following justifications for such a restriction: (1) non-residents are less directly and continuously concerned with and less well informed on the day-by-day problems in the country; (2) candidates for the elections have less easy access to non-residents to present the different electoral issues so as to secure a free expression of opinion; (3) non-residents have less influence on the selection of candidates and the formulation of their electoral programmes; and (4) the correlation between the right to vote and the involvement in acts of the bodies elected is less.[1977] The fact that, on the other hand, in some countries nationals residing abroad who are working there in the service of their country do have the right to vote, does not in the Commission's opinion constitute discrimination in the sense of Article 14, because in view of their function they still keep a closer link with their country.[1978] Precisely in the light of the justifications for the residence requirement indicated by the Commission in the same decision, this argument does not appear quite convincing to us, because most of the reasons mentioned also apply to non-residents in public service. In the case of *X* v. *the United Kingdom* the applicant, a resident of Jersey, complained about the fact that he could not participate in elections for the United Kingdom Parliament. Although this Parliament does have legislative competence with regard to Jersey (which it exercises occasionally) and residents of Jersey are therefore British subjects, they are not considered residents of the United Kingdom. Accordingly, they cannot participate in elections for Parliament. The Commission, after considering the specific constitutional relationship between Jersey and the United Kingdom and

---

[1975] See, for example, the 1992 Council of Europe Convention on the Participation of Foreigners in Public Life at Local Level, *ETS* 144, Art. 6 of which contains an undertaking, as concerns local elections, to grant the right to vote and to stand for election to every foreign resident provided he has been a lawful and habitual resident for the five years preceding the elections. This Convention has so far been ratified by Italy, Norway, Sweden and the Netherlands.

[1976] However, the Commission has already referred to developments in this field: Appl. 7730/76, *X* v. *the United Kingdom*, D&R 15 (1979), p. 137 (138).

[1977] Appl. 7730/76, *X* v. *the United Kingdom*, D&R 15 (1979), p. 137 (139). See also Appl. 7566/76, *X* v. *the United Kingdom*, D&R 9 (1978), p. 121 (122), and with regard to the elections for the European Parliament, Appl. 8612/79, *Alliance des Belges de la Communauté européenne* v. *Belgium*, D&R 15 (1979), p. 259 (264).

[1978] Appl. 7730/76, *X* v. *the United Kingdom*, D&R 15 (1979), p. 137 (139).

after considering that Jersey has its own elected legislature, concluded that there was no breach of Article 3.[1979]

With regard to the right to vote of prisoners, whose invocation of Article 3 found no hearing under the old case-law of the Commission,[1980] it would seem to us that, if the law imposes as a penalty on a particular offence the (temporary) loss of the franchise, this is a restriction which fulfils the criteria indicated in the case-law, but that this is not the case with a general prohibition for prisoners to participate in elections, not as a punitive measure, but as a measure for maintaining order, and even less so when this is left to the discretion of the prison authorities. Since special regulations for the voting of prisoners can be made without difficulty, a general exclusion would amount to an exclusion of a group of the population which is insufficiently justified by their special status.

In the case of a Dutch conscientious objector, who complained about a rule in the Netherlands according to which every prison sentence of more than one year automatically resulted in a suspension of the exercise of the right to vote for three years, the Commission concluded that, taking into account the legislator's margin of appreciation, such a measure does not go beyond the restrictions justifiable in the context of Article 3 of Protocol No. 1.[1981] In our opinion, in this case the way in which the Netherlands authorities have used the margin of appreciation leads to a disproportionate limitation such as thwarts the free expression of the opinion of the people in the sense of Article 3.

The right to stand for election to the legislature is also not unlimited. Here the same conditions apply as with regard to restrictions of the right to vote. In its decision in *M* v. *the United Kingdom*, the Commission concluded that the condition that to be eligible one must not be a member of another legislature was not a restriction which was inconsistent with Article 3 of the Protocol.[1982]

The Commission seems to accept that Article 3 also gives protection to candidates who have suffered from irregularities in the way the elections have been conducted, to the extent that there has been an interference with the free expression of the opinion of the people in the choice of the legislature. However, where a competent national authority has ruled that the irregularities could not have prejudiced the outcome of the election, the Commission's review will be limited to whether or not that finding was arbitrary.[1983]

In the *Mathieu-Mohin and Clerfayt* Case it was emphasised by the Court that any electoral system must be assessed in the light of the political evolution of the country concerned, so long as the free expression of the opinion of the people in

---

[1979] Appl. 8873/80, D&R 28 (1982), p. 99 (104).
[1980] Appl. 530/59, *X* v. *Federal Republic of Germany*, Yearbook III (1960), p. 184 (188); Appl. 2728/66, *X* v. *Federal Republic of Germany*, Yearbook X (1967), p. 336 (338).
[1981] Appl. 9914/82, *H* v. *the Netherlands*, D&R 33 (1983), p. 242 (245-246).
[1982] Appl. 10316/83, D&R 37 (1984), p. 129 (133-134). See, as concerns the condition to present a certain number of signatures, Appl. 23151/94, *Asensio Serqueda* v. *Spain*, D&R 77 (1994), p. 122.
[1983] Appl. 18997/91, *I.Z.* v. *Greece*, D&R 76 (1994), p. 65 (68).

the choice of the legislature is ensured. In the Court's opinion it does not follow from Article 3 that:

> all votes must necessarily have equal weight as regards the outcome of the election or that all candidates must have equal chances of victory. Thus no electoral system can eliminate 'wasted votes'.[1984]

15.4 Choice of the Legislature

What is meant in Article 3 by 'legislature' (French: *'corps législatif'*)? Does Article 3 relate to the election of the highest legislative bodies in the Contracting States only,[1985] or of all bodies having legislative powers?

The Commission has taken the position that what is involved is in any case the election of a body vested with legislative power and that the constitutional law of the Contracting State in question is decisive in this respect. A body which can only propose bills, but cannot itself enact them, does not belong to the 'legislature'.[1986] The Commission has added the criterion that the legislative power has to be an autonomous power. With regard to bodies which have indeed legislative powers, but only by virtue of delegation by a superior legislator, and with regard to bodies whose legislative powers only concern a limited circle of persons, the obligation to hold free elections does not apply.[1987] The body concerned must, in that opinion, be the legislative body which derives its legislative powers directly from the written or unwritten constitution. Moreover, it will have to be the body that can really be identified as the 'legislature', and not, for instance, also the Head of State, even though the passing of a bill depends on the latter's assent. It can hardly be assumed that the drafters wished to exclude the existence of a monarchy with hereditary succession to the throne for the Member States of the Council of Europe! However, as said above, this Head of State must then not have the power to take legislative measures by decree without a parliamentary mandate.

For those States which are a federation, such as the Federal Republic of Germany, Austria and Switzerland, the highest legislative bodies of the constituent states, too, will have to be considered as belonging to the 'legislature', since they do not exercise their legislative powers by virtue of delegation by the federal

---

[1984] Judgment of 2 March 1987, A.113, pp. 23-24. See also Appl. 8765/79, *The Liberal Party, Mrs R and Mr P* v. *the United Kingdom*, D&R 21 (1981), p. 211 (224), and Appl. 8941/80, *X* v. *Iceland*, D&R 27 (1982), p. 145 (150).

[1985] In its decision on Appl. 8364/78, *Lindsay* v. *the United Kingdom*, D&R 15 (1979), p. 247 (251), the Commission expressly left open the possibility that Art. 3 also relates to international legislative bodies. See also Appl. 8612/79, *Alliance des Belges de la Communauté européenne* v. *Belgium*, D&R 15 (1979), p. 259. In both cases the European Parliament was concerned.

[1986] Appls 6745 and 6746/74, *W, X, Y and Z* v. *Belgium*, Yearbook XVIII (1975), p. 236 (240-244).

[1987] Appl. 5155/71, *X* v. *the United Kingdom*, D&R 6 (1977), p. 13, and Appl. 9926/82, *X* v. *the Netherlands*, D&R 32 (1983), p. 274 (281).

legislator, but derive these powers directly from the federal constitution.[1988] In the *Mathieu-Mohin and Clerfayt* Case the Court indeed took the position that the word 'legislature' does not necessarily mean the national parliament only. According to the Court, its meaning has to be interpreted in the light of the constitutional structure of the State in question. On that basis the Court held that the Flemish Council in Belgium was vested with competences and powers wide enough to make it a constituent part of the Belgian 'legislature' in addition to the House of Representatives and the Senate.[1989] The criterion of the autonomous power is not mentioned by the Court and might in some cases be rather inflexible. In our opinion the reasoning used by the Court leaves enough scope for the thesis that the same applies, as concerns unitary states, with regard to the legislative bodies of the provinces and municipalities, which indeed also may be said to have been vested with competences and powers wide enough to make them also constituent parts of the legislature.[1990] If one assumes – which in our opinion one should – that there is a connection between Article 3 and the guarantee incorporated in several articles of the Convention, that restrictions to be imposed on the enjoyment of rights and freedoms have to be 'prescribed by law', this broad interpretation of the word 'legislature' would also seem to follow from the broad interpretation in the case-law of the word 'law' in the latter articles.[1991]

15.5 Derogation

From the fact that Protocol No. 1 does not contain a reference to Article 15(2) of the Convention it follows also for Article 3 that it does not belong to the provisions which are non-derogable.[1992] On the other hand it has been stated above that the principle of democratic representation in the legislative bodies forms one of the basic conditions for the effectiveness of the Convention. In the supervision of the application of Article 15, and particularly in the assessment of the necessity of the temporary derogation from this principle, this fundamental character should weigh very heavily. If the derogation is of a rather long duration, the question even arises whether the country in question does not lose by this very fact the basis for its membership in the Council of Europe.

[1988] See, as regards the Diets of the German *Länder*, Appl. 27311/95, *Timke* v. *Germany*, D&R 82 (1995), p. 158.

[1989] Judgment of 2 March 1987, A.113, p. 23.

[1990] The question as to whether the Municipal Councils in the Netherlands are legislative bodies in the sense of Art. 3 was at issue in Appls 8348 and 8406/78, *Glimmerveen and Hagenbeek* v. *the Netherlands*, D&R 18 (1980), p. 187 (197), but could be passed over in silence by the Commission, because in its opinion Art. 17 of the Convention was applicable to the applicants. See also the report of 15 March 1985, *Mathieu-Mohin and Clerfayt*, A.113, p. 34.

[1991] On this *infra* pp. 765-771.

[1992] See *supra* p. 643.

16 PROHIBITION OF DEPRIVATION OF LIBERTY ON THE GROUND OF INABILITY TO FULFIL A CONTRACTUAL OBLIGATION (ARTICLE 1 OF PROTOCOL NO. 4)

No one shall be deprived of his liberty merely on the ground of inability to fulfil a contractual obligation.

16.1   Scope

This provision contains a further restriction of the powers of the authorities to deprive a person of his liberty. As such it is closely related to Article 5 of the Convention and it specifically limits the possibility of deprivation of liberty mentioned in that article *sub* (1)(b) 'for non-compliance with the lawful order of a court in order to secure the fulfilment of any obligation prescribed by law'. In those States which have ratified Protocol No. 4,[1993] the courts will not be allowed to give such an order merely on the ground that the person in question is unable to pay a debt or to meet some other contractual obligation.

Article 1 speaks of 'inability'. If a debtor is able to pay, but refuses to do so, Article 1 does not exclude deprivation of liberty. Moreover, there is the word 'merely'. If a debtor acts in a fraudulent or malicious way, Article 1 does not bar his detention on that ground, even if it is established or it appears afterwards that he was unable to pay his debt.[1994] A person whose detention had been ordered by the court because, contrary to the law, he had refused at the request of the creditor to make an affidavit in respect of his property, was deemed not to be entitled to the protection of Article 1.[1995] In its report to the Committee of Ministers, the Committee of Experts gives the following examples of cases to which Article 1 does not apply: a person orders a meal at a restaurant, knowing that he is unable to pay; through negligence a person fails to supply goods when he is under a contract to do so; a debtor is preparing to leave the country to avoid meeting his commitments.[1996] If this interpretation of the word 'merely' will be followed in the case-law the prohibition of Article 1 has only a very limited scope.

16.2   Derogation

As to the question of whether the rights and freedoms are non-derogable, for Protocol No. 4 the same reasoning applies as that set out above with regard to Protocol No. 1: since Article 6(1) of Protocol No. 4 declares that all the provisions of the Convention are applicable and does not make any provision concerning an

---

[1993] Protocol No. 4 entered into force on 2 May 1968. For a state of ratifications see Appendix I.

[1994] See the *Explanatory Reports on the Second to Fifth Protocols to the European Convention for the Protection of Human Rights and Fundamental Freedoms*, submitted by the Committee of Experts to the Committee of Ministers, H(71)11 (1971), pp. 39-40.

[1995] Appl. 5025/71, *X* v. *Federal Republic of Germany*, Yearbook XIV (1971), p. 692 (696-698).

[1996] See the Explanatory Reports mentioned *supra* in note 1994, p. 40.

addition to the enumeration of Article 15(2), it must be assumed that under the circumstances and conditions referred to in Article 15(1) derogations from the provisions of Protocol No. 4 are possible.

17 THE RIGHT TO LIBERTY OF MOVEMENT WITHIN THE TERRITORY OF A CONTRACTING STATE, TO CHOOSE ONE'S RESIDENCE THERE, AND TO LEAVE IT (ARTICLE 2 OF PROTOCOL NO. 4)

1. *Everyone lawfully within the territory of a State shall, within that territory, have the right to liberty of movement and freedom to choose his residence.*
2. *Everyone shall be free to leave any country, including his own.*
3. *No restrictions shall be placed on the exercise of these rights other than such as are in accordance with law and are necessary in a democratic society in the interests of national security or public safety, for the maintenance of ordre public, for the prevention of crime, for the protection of health or morals, or for the protection of the rights and freedoms of others.*
4. *The rights set forth in paragraph 1 may also be subject, in particular areas, to restrictions imposed in accordance with law and justified by the public interest in a democratic society.*

17.1 Introduction

In the discussion of some of the other rights and freedoms, it has been pointed out above that the Convention does not provide for a general right to be admitted to the territory of the Contracting States.[1997] Protocol No. 4 ensures such a right only to the nationals of the Contracting State in question, *viz.* in Article 3, to be discussed below. Admission of aliens has so far been left by the Convention to the national legislation and national policy, provided that the rights and freedoms which *are* ensured in the Convention are respected.

17.2 Liberty of Movement and Freedom to Choose Residence

This non-interference with the admission policy of the national authorities with regard to aliens is expressed in Article 2 in the words 'lawfully within the territory of a State' in the first paragraph. Indeed, without these words the national authorities would be prohibited from expelling, on grounds other than those mentioned in the third and the fourth paragraph, an alien who has managed to enter the country illegally. It is precisely with a view to keeping the discretion of the national authorities in this respect as wide as possible that the word 'legally' ('*légalement*') from the original draft was replaced by 'lawfully' ('*régulièrement*').[1998]

[1997] See *supra* pp. 322-325, 515, 653-655.
[1998] Explanatory Reports, *supra* note 1994, p. 40.

From the fact that Article 3 of this same Protocol contains the obligation to admit the State's own nationals and prohibits their expulsion, it follows that a national is always lawfully within the territory of his own State. It is rather curious that this consequence of Article 3 has not been explicitly stated in Article 2.

He who has been admitted to a given country is there lawfully only as long as he complies with the conditions under which he has been admitted.[1999] His presence becomes unlawful after the expiration of the period for which the stay permit applies, but also, for instance, when the person admitted no longer has sufficient means of livelihood, in violation of the conditions of admission made in that respect. The same applies from the moment an expulsion order on public order grounds is served upon a person.[2000] These conditions, however, apart from the cases mentioned in the third and the fourth paragraph, must not restrict his freedom of movement itself in the country and his freedom to choose his residence there, since the first paragraph of Article 2 would then not contain any guarantee; indeed, a right the enjoyment of which completely depends on the discretion of the authorities is not a right, but only a favour.[2001]

The restrictions of the third paragraph also apply to those persons who have always had residence in the country and not only to those who have been admitted under certain conditions. Thus, with respect to a woman who was convicted of running a 'disorderly house or brothel', the ban imposed upon her to close down her business, which according to her complaint had as a consequence that she could no longer reside with her husband, was considered justified as a measure necessary for the prevention of crime and for the protection of health and morals.[2002]

It may not always be easy to determine whether the first paragraph of Article 2 of Protocol No. 4 or some other provision of the Convention applies. This may be the case, for example, with the right to a home (Article 8),[2003] the right to respect for private life (Article 8),[2004] the right to the peaceful enjoyment of one's possessions (Article 1 of Protocol No. 1),[2005] or the right protected by

---

[1999] See Appl. 14102/88, *Aygün* v. *Sweden*, D&R 63 (1989), p. 195.

[2000] Judgment of 27 April 1995, *Piermont*, A.314, p. 21.

[2001] In a different sense, the Committee of Experts, Explanatory Reports *supra* note 1994, p. 41, where these conditions are mentioned as examples of possible conditions.

[2002] Appl. 8901/80, *X* v. *Belgium*, D&R 23 (1981), p. 237 (243).

[2003] Judgment of 24 November 1986, *Gillow*, A.109, p. 18 (case dealt with under Art. 8; the respondent State (the United Kingdom) had not ratified Protocol No. 4).

[2004] Appl. 16810/90, *Reijntjens* v. *Belgium*, D&R 73 (1992), p. 136 (152-153): in the absence of special circumstances the obligation to carry an identity card and to show it to the police whenever requested constitutes neither an interference with private life nor a restriction of liberty of movement.

[2005] See, as concerns denial of access to property in the area of Cyprus occupied by the Turkish Cypriot forces, the *Loizidou* judgment of 18 December 1996, Reports 1996-VI, Vol. 26, para. 60: denial of access over period of 16 years gradually affected the applicant's right as a property owner. The complaint therefore did not concern to the right of freedom of movement.

Article 5. On the last point, the Court has held that placing a person under special police supervision may be considered to fall under Article 2 of Protocol No. 4, as this measure does not amount to a deprivation of liberty within the meaning of Article 5. In this case (*Raimondo* v. *Italy*), the special supervision of the applicant consisted of a prohibition to leave his home without informing the police, an obligation to report to the police on specified dates and an obligation to stay at home at night unless there were valid reasons to the contrary which he had first announced to the authorities. The Court considered that, in view of the mafia threat to democratic society, the measures were in principle necessary in a democratic society for the maintenance of *ordre public* and for the prevention of crime. However, insofar as there had been a delay in notifying the applicant of a court order lifting the police supervision, the Court found a violation of Article 2 as this interference was neither provided for by law nor necessary.[2006]

In a case where the applicant, opposed to abortion on religious grounds, had been prohibited by a court order from entering the immediate vicinity of an abortion clinic where he had previously distributed anti-abortion material, the Commission noted that the injunction was of limited duration (six months) and applied to a specified, limited area. This restriction of his liberty of movement was considered proportionate to the legitimate aim of the protection of the rights of others and therefore 'necessary in a democratic society'.[2007]

17.3 Right to Leave the Country

The right to leave the country, conferred in the second paragraph, has not a very broad effective scope, because practically all conceivable motives for the authorities to refuse a person this right can be brought under the restrictions of the third paragraph.

Thus, the ground of 'the maintenance of *ordre public*' or of 'the prevention of crime' may be invoked against a person who is serving a term of imprisonment, who is detained on remand, or whose extradition has been decided on, if he should claim the right to leave the country.[2008] Indeed, one cannot seriously argue, on the ground that it is better to be rid of the person than to keep him in the country, that the refusal to let him go is not 'necessary in a democratic society'. The same grounds of the third paragraph may also justify measures which are aimed at preventing a person to leave the country, such as the requirement imposed upon

---

[2006] Judgment of 22 February 1994, A.281-A, p. 19.

[2007] Appl. 22838/93, *Van den Dungen* v. *the Netherlands*, D&R 80 (1995), p. 147 (151-152).

[2008] See Appls 3962/69, 4256/69, 4436/70 and 7680/76, all of them directed against the Federal Republic of Germany, Yearbook XIII (1970), p. 688 (690); Coll. 37 (1971), p. 67 (68-69); Yearbook XIII (1970), p. 1028 (1032-1034); D&R 9 (1978), p. 190 (193). See also Appl. 8988/80, *X* v. *Belgium*, D&R 24 (1981), p. 198 (204): forbidding a bankrupt from absenting himself was considered necessary for the maintenance of *ordre public* and for the protection of the rights and freedoms of others.

an accused or convicted person to surrender his passport as a condition for provisional or conditional release.[2009]

The Committee of Experts, referring to the words 'any country' ('*n'importe quel pays*'), has assigned a certain external effect to the second paragraph. Although of course only the Contracting States are bound by this provision, it may have as a consequence that a court, when it has to pronounce on the question of whether a person has lawfully left the territory of a non-Contracting State, should decide that reference to the law of that State is accepted only insofar as that law does not prejudice the principle of freedom to leave a country.[2010]

The Commission has accepted a fairly wide interpretation of the expression 'any country'. In a case concerning a passport refusal by Finnish authorities to a person (who had failed to report for military service) who was resident in Sweden and who could travel freely without a passport between the Nordic countries, the Commission nevertheless considered that the refusal interfered with his right: the freedom to leave 'any country' implies a right to leave for such a country of the person's choice to which he may be admitted. However, the Commission did not consider that the measure went beyond the limits of paragraph 3, in view of the wide margin of appreciation to which the Contracting States are entitled in the organisation of their national defence.[2011]

17.4 Restrictions in Particular Areas

Besides the grounds of restrictions in the third paragraph, which do not differ from the 'usual' list and for which reference is made here to their general discussion,[2012] in the fourth paragraph a special ground for restricting the rights conferred in the first paragraph has been included: the public interest in a democratic society. Restrictions which are justified on this ground may be imposed in particular areas.

This restriction has been the subject of a good deal of discussion within the Committee of Experts, as is evident from its report.[2013] It was intended to make possible restrictions which serve the public interest of the country in situations where it cannot be clearly established that the *ordre public* is also involved. Although the majority of the Committee was opposed to the express inclusion of 'economic welfare' as a ground of restriction, the chosen formulation 'in the public interest' is so wide that the economic welfare of society as a motive for the imposition of restrictions does not appear to be excluded by it. The grant of a housing licence only to those who have an economic link with the municipality

---

[2009] Appl. 10307/83, *M* v. *Federal Republic of Germany*, D&R 37 (1984), p. 113 (118-119).

[2010] Explanatory Reports, *supra* note 1994, p. 42.

[2011] Appl. 19583/92, *Peltonen* v. *Finland*, D&R 80 (1995), p. 38 (43). See also Appl. 21228/93, *K.S.* v. *Finland*, D&R 81 (1995), p. 42 (46).

[2012] *Infra* pp. 755-761. See also the cases cited in the previous footnote as well as the judgment of 22 February 1994, *Raimondo*, A.281-A.

[2013] Explanatory Reports, *supra* note 1994, pp. 43-46.

in question might be justified on that ground, and so might, for instance, the transfer of government departments, with the obligation for those employed by those departments to move, on penalty of loss of their function. The scope of application or the ground of application of the restrictive measures, however, will have to be localised, according to the text of the fourth paragraph, within particular areas – *e.g.* areas with an extraordinary dense population or with a high unemployment rate –, and consequently must not apply to the country as a whole. Furthermore, of course, here again no discrimination is permitted in the application of the restrictions.

The restriction under the fourth paragraph does not apply to the freedom to leave the country, regulated in the second paragraph. A Contracting State may not therefore prohibit emigration, in the public interest, on purely economic grounds, *e.g.* in order to prevent brain drain.

17.5 Territorial Application

Article 5(4) of Protocol No. 4 provides that, if a Contracting State has also declared the Protocol to be applicable to any territory for whose foreign relations it is responsible, this territory and the territory of the Contracting State to which the Protocol already applies by virtue of the ratification itself shall be treated as separate territories for the application of Article 2. Thus, the Court treated French Polynesia as being a separate territory, where different rules applied concerning the entry and residence of aliens as compared with metropolitan France, which is relevant to the question whether someone is 'lawfully' within the territory concerned.[2014]

17.6 Derogation

As has been said, none of the rights mentioned in Protocol No. 4 are non-derogable.[2015]

18 PROHIBITION OF EXPULSION OF NATIONALS; THE RIGHT OF NATIONALS TO BE ADMITTED TO THEIR OWN COUNTRY (ARTICLE 3 OF PROTOCOL NO. 4)

1. *No one shall be expelled, by means either of an individual or of a collective measure, from the territory of the State of which he is a national.*
2. *No one shall be deprived of the right to enter the territory of the State of which he is a national.*

[2014] Judgment of 27 April 1995, *Piermont*, A.314, p. 20.
[2015] See *supra* pp. 666-667.

18.1 Prohibition of Expulsion of Nationals

Although the term expulsion is generally used in connection with aliens and *not* with the State's own nationals, the drafters of Article 3 preferred the word 'expelled' to 'exiled', because exile is a word pregnant with meaning, which might raise many interpretation problems. It is not only exile as a penalty or as a political measure which is prohibited by Article 3, but any expulsion of a national from the territory.

According to a definition given by the Commission, expulsion is involved when 'a person is obliged permanently to leave the territory of the State (...) without being left the possibility of returning later'.[2016] The words 'permanently' and 'without being left the possibility of returning later' in this definition may create the wrong impression that temporal expulsion of nationals would be permitted. In the context in which the definition was given, these words seem to be included to support the decision of the Commission that extradition does not fall under the concept of expulsion, and consequently not under the prohibition of Article 3 either.[2017] For its point of view the Commission could rely on the *travaux préparatoires*. In fact, in its report to the Committee of Ministers, the Committee of Experts had held: 'It was understood that extradition was outside the scope of this paragraph'.[2018] This does raise the question why the drafters did not bring out this intention somewhat more clearly in the formulation of Article 3. As this provision is now worded, from a wide interpretation of the word 'expelled' one might conclude that a national enjoys protection against any measure according to which he has to leave his country under compulsion; in fact, in its report the Committee of Experts itself puts on the word 'expel' the very wide interpretation of 'to drive away from a place'.[2019]

At all events, it should be recalled that the case-law has recognised that extradition – of aliens as well as of nationals – may constitute a violation of one of the other rights and freedoms, specifically of the prohibition of inhuman treatment and of the right to respect of family life.[2020]

[2016] Appl. 6189/73, *X* v. *Federal Republic of Germany*, Coll. 46 (1974), p. 214.

[2017] *Idem.* Two weeks later, in its decision on Appl. 6242/73, *Brückmann* v. *Federal Republic of Germany*, Yearbook XVII (1974), p. 458 (478), the Commission took the same position with the following definition of the two concepts: 'Expulsion is the execution of an order to leave the country, while extradition means the transfer of a person from one jurisdiction to another for the purpose of his standing trial or for the execution of a sentence imposed upon him'.

[2018] Explanatory Reports, *supra* note 1994, p. 47.

[2019] *Idem.*

[2020] *Supra* pp. 322-325 and 515-521.

18.2 Prohibition of Deprivation of the Right to Enter One's Own Country

The second paragraph of Article 3, which contains without any restriction the right to be admitted to the State of which one is a national, would confront in particular the United Kingdom with serious problems, since numerous people outside the United Kingdom, particularly in the Commonwealth countries, have acquired British nationality by birth. However, the United Kingdom has not ratified Protocol No. 4. This does not alter the fact that, if that country, in admitting people having its nationality, should discriminate with respect to a particular racial group, it could still come into conflict with its obligations under the Convention; not under Article 14, which in that case indeed could only have been violated in conjunction with Article 3 of Protocol No. 4, but because such discrimination may constitute a degrading treatment in the sense of Article 3 of the Convention.[2021]

The same could apply in relation to a discriminatory denial of the right of entry to a national where the State Party has limited its obligations through a valid reservation to Article 3 of Protocol No. 4.[2022]

In its Explanatory Report the Committee of Experts states that the proposal to include the word 'arbitrarily' in the second paragraph, in accordance with Article 12(4) of the UN Covenant on Civil and Political Rights, was expressly rejected, but that the members of the Committee agreed that the right of the national to be admitted to his State does not confer on him an absolute right to stay within that State. The Report gives the example of a national who, after first having been extradited to another country, takes refuge again in his own State, and of a national who, after having served in the army of another State, wishes to return to his own country.[2023]

These examples, however, seem to indicate that the Committee is raising a fictitious problem here. Indeed, in those cases the absolute character of the prohibition under the second paragraph of Article 3 is not affected, but in the first example the State has the right to decide to extradite the person again, and in the second example it has the right to impose on service in the army of another State the sanction of forfeiture of nationality and of the rights associated with it.

[2021] *Supra* p. 322.
[2022] See Appl. 15344/89, *Habsburg-Lotharingen* v. *Austria*, D&R 64 (1989), p. 210 (219-220): even though it accepted the validity of the Austrian reservation with respect to Art. 3 of Protocol No. 4, the Commission went on to examine the complaint about discrimination according to the applicant's family origin under Arts 3 and 14 of the Convention; it found that the situation complained of had not been shown to constitute a distinction the effects of which were contrary to Art. 3 of the Convention, either alone or taken together with Art. 14.
[2023] Explanatory Reports, *supra* note 1994, pp. 48-49.

18.3   Territorial Application

With respect to the inhabitants of colonies and other territories for whose international relations a Contracting State is responsible, the Protocol itself already provides for a possibility of avoiding certain consequences in case of ratification. And this in connection with the first as well as the second paragraph of Article 3. First of all, at the moment of ratification States may indicate under Article 5 to what extent they also wish this Protocol to apply to these territories; this, therefore, irrespective of the extent to which they have declared the Convention itself applicable. Thus, they are able to declare that some articles of the Protocol are applicable to these territories and others are not. Moreover the fourth paragraph of Article 5 provides in relation to Article 3 that, where there is a reference to 'the territory of a State', the territory of the Contracting State itself and these territories are treated as separate territories.

18.4   Article 3 and the Acquisition and Loss of Nationality

Can a State evade its obligations under Article 3 by depriving a person of his nationality? In principle the Convention leaves it to the States to regulate the acquisition and the loss of nationality; a right to a nationality, such as it is incorporated in Article 15 of the Universal Declaration of Human Rights, does not form part of the rights and freedoms laid down in the Convention. However, if a person can be deprived of his nationality for the sole purpose of his expulsion or refusal to admit him, the protection of Article 3 may be rendered illusory.

It appears from the Explanatory Report that the Committee of Experts was aware of this problem, but that it rejected a proposal to include in Article 3 a provision according to which 'a State would be forbidden to deprive a national of his nationality for the purpose of expelling him'. Although the Committee stated that it approved of the underlying principle, the majority thought that 'it was inadvisable in Article 3 to touch on the delicate question of the legitimacy of measures depriving individuals of nationality'.[2024]

This does not answer the above question, for even though in its generality Article 3 leaves intact the right of the State to decide to whom it will grant its nationality and whom it will deprive of it, still such a decision by the national authorities in a given case may involve a violation of that article. Thus, with regard to a refusal of nationality combined with an order of expulsion it was expressly recognised by the Commission that the link between the two decisions could create the presumption that the refusal of nationality had the mere purpose of making the expulsion possible.[2025] Indeed, a measure of the national authorities which has as its sole object evasion of an obligation under the Convention is equivalent to a violation of that provision. A rule to that effect is

---

[2024]   *Ibidem*, pp. 47-48.
[2025]   Appl. 3745/68, *X* v. *Federal Republic of Germany*, Coll. 31 (1970), p. 107 (110).

implicit in the Convention as an essential requirement for the maintenance of the effective enjoyment of its rights and freedoms and is also in conformity with the rationale underlying Article 17. However, it can be assumed only in very evident cases that the national authorities actually intended *exclusively* to evade the operation of the Convention by their measure. In the above-mentioned decision the Commission in fact adopted the view that in this case nothing justified such a conclusion.[2026]

18.5 Derogation

To Article 3 again the above statement applies that none of the rights incorporated in Protocol No. 4 are non-derogable.[2027]

19 PROHIBITION OF COLLECTIVE EXPULSION OF ALIENS (ARTICLE 4 OF PROTOCOL NO. 4)

Collective expulsion of aliens is prohibited.

19.1 Introduction

This provision prohibits only the *collective* expulsion of aliens, but this without any possibility of restriction other than under Article 15. Besides the general prohibition of expulsion of a State's own nationals as laid down in the above-mentioned Article 3, the Consultative Assembly wished to make the expulsion of aliens in this article subject to stringent conditions. According to its draft, expulsion of an alien lawfully residing in a Contracting State would be permitted only on the ground of danger to national security or violation of the *ordre public* or morality. However, the Committee of Experts did not adopt this part of the draft and proposed an entirely new provision, referring exclusively to collective expulsion.[2028]

The first argument advanced by the Committee was that the subject-matter brought up in the draft of the Consultative Assembly had already been regulated in the European Convention on Establishment of 1955.[2029] Against this, however, it may at once be argued that this renders regulation in Protocol No. 4 by no means superfluous, since the Establishment Convention confers protection only on the nationals of the other States Parties to that Convention and not, as would be the case in the proposal of the Consultative Assembly, on *all* aliens residing in one of the Contracting States. Moreover, the Establishment Convention lacks an international supervisory procedure as provided for in the Convention. And since the text of the draft of the Consultative Assembly was almost identical

---

[2026] *Ibidem*, p. 111.
[2027] See *supra* pp. 666-667.
[2028] Explanatory Reports, *supra* note 1994, p. 50.
[2029] *Idem*. The Convention has been published in *European Treaty Series*, No. 19.

with that of the Establishment Convention, there was no reason to fear that those Contracting States, which have also ratified the Establishment Convention, would have to confer, *via* the operation of Articles 14 and 60 of the Human Rights Convention, on these 'other' aliens (*i.e.* those aliens who are not nationals of one of the other States Parties to the Establishment Convention) a more far-reaching protection than that which Article 4 of Protocol No. 4 itself would oblige them to confer.

The second argument put forward in favour of the cancellation – and the one which was no doubt decisive – is that the majority of the Committee did not wish to restrict the grounds for expulsion and did not wish the motives which induce a State in each individual case to expel an alien, to be subjected to international supervision.[2030]

Meanwhile Protocol No. 7 has entered into force on 1 November 1988. Article 1 provides for certain procedural guarantees in the case of expulsion of individual aliens who are lawfully resident in the territory of a Contracting State. The provision will be discussed separately hereafter.

19.2   Scope of the Prohibition

Even in its ultimate formulation Article 4 is not entirely devoid of importance, considering such practices, also existing within countries of the Council of Europe, as the expulsion of groups of gypsies seeking a camp or groups of migrant workers seeking employment.

The effect of Article 4 depends largely on the interpretation that is put on the word 'collective'. Is this to refer to expulsion of *all* aliens residing in a given State or at least of all aliens *of one particular nationality*? Or is there also question of collective expulsion if a number of people within one of those groups or any number of aliens is concerned? The first-mentioned interpretation would render Article 4 almost completely devoid of any importance. Collective expulsion of all aliens, also of those who are lawfully in a country, would, if any country should ever be able or wish to do so, only take place in very urgent and exceptional circumstances; and in those very circumstances Article 15 of the Convention would most likely deprive Article 4 of its protective effect. The same will usually apply if there are reasons for expelling all aliens of a particular nationality indiscriminately. It has therefore to be assumed that the Contracting States did not mean to restrict Article 4 to these very exceptional cases of collective expulsion, but wanted to prohibit any expulsion of aliens *as a group*.

Even then, however, the question of what exactly distinguishes the expulsion of a group of aliens from the expulsion of a number of individual aliens has not yet been answered. How large must such a group be? Is the expulsion of an entire family to be considered a collective expulsion? And is this true, for instance, for the expulsion of an orchestra or sport team consisting of foreigners? If so, why

---

[2030]   Explanatory Reports, *supra* note 1994, pp. 50-51.

then do such 'groups' deserve more protection than a foreigner who lives on his own or an individual foreign musician or sportsman? This problem can be solved only if one uses neither the number of which the group consists nor the link knitting together the members of that group as the decisive criterion for the application of Article 4, but the *procedure* followed in the expulsion. If a person is expelled along with others without his case having received an individual treatment, his expulsion is a case of collective expulsion.

This seems also to be the view of the Commission. In its opinion there is no question of collective expulsion if the decision of expulsion is based on 'particular circumstances relating to each of the applicants as individuals'.[2031] In a later decision, moreover, the Commission made that individual treatment dependent on certain minimum conditions by giving the following definition of 'collective expulsion of aliens':

> any measure of the competent authorities compelling aliens as a group to leave the country, except where such a measure is taken after and on the basis of a reasonable and objective examination of the particular cases of each individual alien of the group.[2032]

At first sight it would appear as if here the Commission has introduced a restriction to the absolutely formulated prohibition of Article 4, since Article 4 does not make any exception for cases where an examination such as that mentioned in the definition by the Commission has taken place with regard to each member of the group. However, this is not really the case. In fact, the national authorities can always evade the absolute prohibition of Article 4 by following a procedure in which there is no question of a *collective* expulsion in the proper sense. In its decision the Commission precisely indicates that a pure formality is not enough for evading Article 4, but that an objective examination must be involved, in which a reasonable weighing takes place between the interests of each individual separately and the interest envisaged by the authorities with the expulsion. The Commission therefore in fact introduces certain minimum procedural guarantees, although a proposal to that effect had been expressly rejected by the Committee of Experts.[2033]

The definition of the Commission, however much it has to be welcomed *per se*, raises the problem that for the expulsion of an alien who forms part of a particular

---

[2031]   Appls 3803 and 3804/68, *X and Y* v. *Sweden* (not published). The Commission is not very clear in its decision on Appl. 7704/76, *X* v. *Federal Republic of Germany* (not published): 'although the applicants act as a group, or rather as two groups, the official processing of the matter also shows several individual variations within these groups'.

[2032]   Appl. 7011/75, *Becker* v. *Denmark*, Yearbook XIX (1976), p. 416 (454), concerning the refusal of entry visas and stay permits to a group of Vietnamese children. See also Appl. 14209/88, *A and Others* v. *the Netherlands*, D&R 59 (1989), p. 274 (277), where the Commission furthermore emphasised the opportunities which the applicants have had and used individually to present their arguments against expulsion, both before the Minister of Justice and the courts; it concluded that there had been no appearance of a collective expulsion.

[2033]   See *supra* pp. 674-675.

group certain procedural requirements are developed, which were not prescribed for the expulsion of other aliens. Therefore, the issue remains as to when there is question of a group and why a group deserves more protection than an individual. In our opinion, a satisfactory solution is reached only if it is assumed that any expulsion of an alien as an alien, without an objective examination having been made of his individual situation and interests, in fact is part of a prohibited collective expulsion, irrespective of whether his expulsion in actual fact is or is not accompanied by the expulsion of other aliens in a comparable situation. It must be admitted, however, that thus the word 'collective' is interpreted in a rather far-fetched sense which seems to be contrary to the genesis of Article 4. As was observed above, the Convention has been complemented with Protocol No. 7, stipulating in Article 1 minimum procedural rights for aliens lawfully within a Contracting State, who are confronted with expulsion. However, not all States Parties to Protocol No. 4 have ratified Protocol No. 7, so that the issues raised above still remain valid for the situation in a number of States and have to wait for an answer by the Commission and, ultimately the Court.

Here again it has to be pointed out that the expulsion of aliens may also constitute a violation of the Convention on other grounds. One may think in particular of those cases in which the consequences of the expulsion are such that it entails an inhuman treatment contrary to Article 3 or a severance of family ties contrary to Article 8.[2034]

19.3   Derogation

As has been stated above, none of the provisions of Protocol No. 4, including Article 4, are non-derogable.[2035]

20   ABOLITION OF THE DEATH PENALTY (ARTICLE 1 OF PROTOCOL NO. 6)

The death penalty shall be abolished. No one shall be condemned to such penalty or executed.

20.1   Introduction

The abolition of the death penalty has since long been a matter of concern in- and outside the Council of Europe. As early as 1957, the European Committee on Crime Problems studied the problem of capital punishment in the States of Europe. The Parliamentary Assembly also regularly dealt with this question. In 1980 it adopted two resolutions, in which on the one hand it appealed to national parliaments to abolish capital punishment from their penal systems, if they had not

---

[2034]   See *supra* pp. 328-333 and 515-521 respectively.
[2035]   See *supra* pp. 666-667.

already done so,[2036] and on the other hand called upon the Committee of Ministers to 'amend Article 2 of the European Convention on Human Rights to bring it into line with Resolution 727'.[2037] In December 1982, the Committee of Ministers adopted the text of draft Protocol No. 6, prepared by the Steering Committee for Human Rights, and opened it for signature and ratification by the Member States of the Council of Europe on 28 April 1983. The Protocol entered into force on 1 March 1985, after it had received five ratifications.[2038]

Until recently, no death sentences had been executed in the Member States of the Council of Europe for many years. However, the enlargement of this organisation over the last few years has made this a matter of topical concern. The Parliamentary Assembly has made the willingness to sign Protocol No. 6 within one year and ratify it within three years from the time of accession and to introduce a moratorium upon accession, a prerequisite for membership of the Council of Europe on the part of the Assembly. In spite of this, a recent Report of the Assembly indicates that some of the new Member States have continued to carry out executions after their accession to the Council of Europe.[2039]

20.2 Scope of the Prohibition

Article 1 of the Protocol must be read in conjunction with Article 2 of the Convention. It follows from this that a State which wants to become a party to the Protocol first has to delete the death penalty from its criminal law. The second sentence of Article 1 underlines that it contains not only an obligation, but also a right: every individual has the right not to be condemned to the death penalty or to be executed.

However, the scope of the obligation to abolish the death penalty is limited to acts committed in peace time. Protocol No. 6 does not apply to acts committed in times of war or of imminent threat of war, provided that the law lays down the instances in which the death penalty may be applied and that the relevant provisions of the law are communicated to the Secretary General of the Council of Europe. It follows from the wording of Article 2 of Protocol No. 6 that even after a State has ratified the Protocol, it may introduce the death penalty for those situations.[2040] It may, of course, withdraw or modify this legislation later on and

---

[2036] Res. 727 of the Parliamentary Assembly, adopted on 22 April 1980 during its 32nd Session, Yearbook XXIII (1980), p. 66.

[2037] Res. 891 of the Parliamentary Assembly, adopted on 22 April 1980 during its 32nd Session, Yearbook XXIII (1980), p. 66.

[2038] For an overview of the Contracting States which have ratified Protocol No. 6, see Appendix I.

[2039] See *Report on the Abolition of the Death Penalty in Europe* (Committee on Legal Affairs and Human Rights, rapporteur: Mrs Wohlwend) of 25 June 1996, Parliamentary Assembly Document 7589.

[2040] Art. 2 of the Protocol reads as follows: 'A State may make provisions in its law for the death penalty in respect of acts committed in time of war or of imminent threat of war; such penalty shall be applied only in the instances laid down in the law and in accordance with its provisions.

notify the Secretary General of this. The requirement that in those situations the death penalty shall be applied only in the instances laid down in the law in fact is superfluous since this also stems from Article 7 of the Convention.[2041] However, Article 2 of Protocol No. 6 adds to this that this penalty shall only be applied 'in accordance with' the law, which also concerns the way the death penalty is executed. The Parliamentary Assembly of the Council of Europe has proposed that a new additional protocol be drawn up abolishing the death penalty also in war time.[2042]

There is so far little case-law under this provision, which may be explained by the fact that the Contracting States which maintain the death penalty on the statute book have not ratified this Protocol. However, Article 1 of Protocol No. 6 may also be relevant in expulsion and extradition cases, on the basis of the reasoning followed by the Court in the *Soering* Case.[2043] In this case, the Court accepted that Article 3 of the Convention cannot be interpreted as generally prohibiting the death penalty, because the existence of Protocol No. 6 showed that the intention of the drafters was to use the normal method of amendment of the text to introduce an obligation to abolish capital punishment. However, the circumstances relating to a death sentence might be such as to give rise to an issue under Article 3 and Article 3 prohibits expulsion or extradition where a person would face, in the receiving State, a real risk of exposure to inhuman or degrading treatment or punishment. The *Soering* Case concerned extradition by a State not bound by Protocol No. 6, but where the State is so bound, Article 1 of the Protocol may be violated if the State extradites or expels a person to another State where he is at serious risk that he will be sentenced to death and that sentence will be executed.[2044] In such cases, there would be no need for the organs of the Convention to proceed in an indirect manner by examining, under Article 3, the circumstances relating to the death sentence. The key question would be whether

---

The State shall communicate to the Secretary General of the Council of Europe the relevant provisions of the law.' What is meant by the phrase 'imminent threat of war' is not made clear in the Protocol or the Explanatory Memorandum thereto.

[2041] See *supra* pp. 284-285.

[2042] See Recommendation 1246 (1994) on the abolition of capital punishment. In an interim reply, the Committee of Ministers informed the Assembly that it is currently examining this and other proposals made in Recommendation 1246 (see Parliamentary Assembly Document 7466 of 22 January 1996). The same reply also states that the Committee of Ministers has encouraged Member States which have not abolished the death penalty to operate *de facto* or *de jure* a moratorium on the execution of death sentences.

[2043] This case is discussed in this Chapter, at pp. 323-324.

[2044] Appl. 22742/93, *Aylor-Davis* v. *France*, D&R 76-B (1994), p. 164 (170); the Commission does not exclude State responsibility under Protocol No. 6; assurances obtained from US authorities by France such as to exclude the risk of the applicant being sentenced to death; extradition thus not liable to expose applicant to serious risk of treatment or punishment prohibited by Art. 3 of the Convention or Art. 1 of Protocol No. 6. See, as concerns expulsion, Appl. 16531/90, *Y* v. *the Netherlands*, D&R 68 (1991), p. 299 (304): the Commission left open whether Art. 1 of Protocol No. 6 was applicable, but it went on to consider that no real risk had been shown that the death penalty would be imposed.

extradition or expulsion would expose the applicant to a real risk of being subjected to capital punishment.

20.3 Derogation

The prohibition of the death penalty is non-derogable.[2045] Moreover, according to Article 4 of the Protocol it is not possible to make any reservation in respect of the provisions of the Protocol.

21 GENERAL INTRODUCTION TO PROTOCOL NO. 7

The original aim of Protocol No. 7, as recommended by the Parliamentary Assembly in 1972, was 'to insert as many as possible of the substantive provisions of the Covenant on Civil and Political Rights in the Convention'.[2046] However, the Committee of Experts which prepared the draft of the Protocol, followed a more restrictive approach, keeping in mind 'the need to include in the Convention only such rights as could be stated in sufficiently specific terms to be guaranteed within the framework of the system of control instituted by the Convention'.[2047] Although the idea of such an extension was already born in the early seventies, it was not until 22 November 1984 that the Protocol was opened for signature. And only in 1988 sufficient States had ratified the Protocol for it to enter into force.[2048]

The enthusiasm about Protocol No. 7 appears to be not very great. This has to do with the fact that the original aim of the Protocol can hardly be said to have been achieved. In a comparative report[2049] a series of rights had been enumerated, which were included in the UN Covenant on Civil and Political Rights but not in the Convention. Only some of these rights are now included in this Protocol. A clarification of the reasons for it, other than the above-mentioned general viewpoint of the Committee of Experts, is not to be found in the Explanatory Report. Although it is true that some of the other rights do not fulfil the requirement of 'sufficiently specific terms to be guaranteed', it is by no means clear why, for example, the right of the accused to be informed of his right to have legal assistance or the right of equality before the law, have not been included in the Protocol. Furthermore, the rights that have been incorporated, are on the whole formulated rather narrowly. Most of the rights are framed in more restricted terms than their counterparts in the UN Covenant on Civil and Political

---

[2045] Art. 3 of the Protocol.

[2046] Explanatory Report on Protocol No. 7 to the Convention for the Protection of Human Rights and Fundamental Freedoms, Council of Europe, Strasbourg, 1985, p. 5.

[2047] *Ibidem*, p. 6.

[2048] Protocol No. 7 entered into force on 1 November 1988. For the state of ratifications, see Appendix I.

[2049] *Supra* note 11, pp. 4-5.

Rights. It may be concluded, therefore, that the outcome of this lengthy exercise is rather disappointing.

States which ratify or have ratified the Protocol have to make a separate declaration under Article 25 of the Convention in order to give individuals the right to submit individual applications, and have to accept separately the jurisdiction of the Court, pursuant to Article 46 of the Convention, with respect to the rights guaranteed in the Protocol.[2050]

22 EXPULSION OF ALIENS (ARTICLE 1 OF PROTOCOL NO. 7)

> *1. An alien lawfully resident in the territory of a State shall not be expelled therefrom except in pursuance of a decision reached in accordance with law and shall be allowed:*
> *a) to submit reasons against his expulsion,*
> *b) to have his case reviewed, and*
> *c) to be represented for these purposes before the competent authority or a person or persons designated by that authority.*
> *2. An alien may be expelled before the exercise of his rights under paragraph 1(a), (b) and (c) of this Article, when such expulsion is necessary in the interests of public order or is grounded on reasons of national security.*

As is clear from the text of the article, and as is emphasised in the Explanatory Report,[2051] the guarantees laid down therein only apply to certain categories of aliens, and even then not in all circumstances. Indeed, Article 1 only concerns aliens lawfully resident in the territory of the State in question. The word 'resident' is intended to exclude any alien who has arrived at the border or (air)port, but has not yet passed through the immigration control. Aliens who have been admitted for the purpose of transit or for other non-residential purposes, or who are waiting for a decision on a request for a residence permit, are also excluded from the scope of this article. The term 'lawfully' refers to domestic law. It is up to domestic law to determine the conditions for a person's presence in the territory to be considered 'lawful'. As soon as an alien does not comply any more with one or more of these conditions, his presence can no longer be considered 'lawful'.

According to the Explanatory Report the phrase 'expulsion' must be considered as an autonomous concept, independent of any domestic definition. It refers to any measure compelling the departure of an alien from the territory except extradition.[2052]

[2050] See Art. 7(2) of the Protocol.
[2051] Explanatory Report, *supra* note 2046, p. 7.
[2052] *Ibidem*, p. 8.

22.1 The Various Requirements of the First Paragraph

The Convention contains in several articles implied guarantees for aliens against whom a measure of expulsion is taken. First of all, Article 4 of Protocol No. 4 contains the prohibition of collective expulsion of aliens. In addition, in individual cases Articles 3, 5(1)(f), and 8, in conjunction with Article 13, do provide some guarantees against measures of expulsion.[2053] Article 1 of Protocol No. 7 has been added 'in order to afford minimum guarantees to such persons (aliens) in the event of expulsion from the territory of a Contracting Party'.[2054] And minimal they are indeed.

Expulsion may take place only 'in pursuance of a decision reached in accordance with law'. The word 'law' refers to domestic law. It is therefore up to domestic law to determine which authority is competent to decide about expulsion and which procedure has to be followed, provided that the requirement of an effective remedy of Article 13 of the Convention is met. A judicial authority is not required, unless in cases where Article 6 of the Convention applies. However, during the procedure, the alien concerned has some minimum rights, as set forth in paragraph 1(a)-(c).[2055] As regards the first right: to submit reasons against his expulsion, here again it is up to domestic law to determine the conditions governing the exercise of this right. This right may, however, be exercised also in the first phase of the procedure and not only at the review stage, as is clear from its formulation separately from (b).[2056]

As regards the second right: to have his case reviewed, it is emphasised in the Explanatory Report that this does not necessarily imply:

a two-stage procedure before different authorities, but only that the competent authority should review the case in the light of the reasons against expulsion submitted by the person concerned.[2057]

This 'competent authority' may be the same authority who took the original decision or a higher authority. The form of the review, again, is determined by domestic law. The minimal approach, which overshadowed the preparation of the Protocol, can be clearly inferred from the Explanatory Report where it is expressly stated that Article 1 does not relate to the stage of proceedings, existing in some States, in which aliens have the possibility of lodging an appeal against the decision taken following the review of their case:

[2053] See *supra* pp. 328-333, 364-365 and 515-521. For Art. 13 and its implications for procedural guarantees, see *infra* p. 697.

[2054] Explanatory Report, *supra* note 2046, p. 7.

[2055] See also Art. 5 of the Convention.

[2056] Explanatory Report, *supra* note 2046, p. 8.

[2057] *Idem.*

The present Article (...) does not therefore require that the person concerned should be permitted to remain in the territory of the State pending the outcome of the appeal introduced against the decision taken following the review of his case.[2058]

Also for the third right: to be represented before the competent authority or a person or persons designated by that authority, it is up to domestic law to determine the form of representation and the competent authority. It is not required that the representative is a lawyer or that the competent authority is a judicial organ. It is not even required that the authority be the authority who finally decides about the expulsion. In order to comply with this article, it is sufficient that the competent judicial or administrative authority makes a recommendation to an (other) administrative authority, who then decides about the measure of expulsion.[2059] The provision does not give the alien or his representative the right to be physically present when the case is considered, nor does the procedure – unless in cases where Article 6 of the Convention applies[2060] – have to include an oral hearing; the whole procedure may be a written one.[2061]

22.2 The Exception of the Second Paragraph

As a rule, the alien concerned has the right to make use of the minimum guarantees laid down in the first paragraph of Article 1 before being expelled. The second paragraph, however, allows for exceptions to this rule 'when such expulsion is necessary in the interests of public order or is grounded on reasons of national security'. The words 'in a democratic society', which are coupled to the necessity requirement in the several provisions of the Convention which allow for restrictions of the rights embodied therein, are lacking here for unclear reasons. However, the Strasbourg case-law has not (yet) made these words play a distinctive role. With reference to that case-law the Explanatory Report states that the exceptions have to be applied 'taking into account the principle of proportionality as defined in the case law of the European Court of Human Rights'.[2062]

When a State relies on this exception in the interest of public order, it is up to that State to show why in the particular case or cases that exception was necessary. If, however, a State grounds the exception on reasons of national security, according to the Explanatory Report 'this in itself should be accepted as sufficient justification'.[2063] Since this view would imply that review by the Strasbourg organs is not possible at all, it cannot be accepted as being in

---

[2058] *Idem.*
[2059] *Ibidem*, p. 9.
[2060] See *supra* pp. 433-435.
[2061] Explanatory Report, *supra* note 2046, p. 9.
[2062] *Idem.*
[2063] *Idem.*

accordance with the purpose of the Protocol to place the rights embodied therein under the supervisory system of the Convention; especially the necessity requirement must be subject to the review of the Strasbourg organs, be it that the latter may leave a margin of discretion to the national authorities in that respect.

In the above-mentioned cases it is only scant comfort for the alien concerned to know that he may still exercise his rights under paragraph 1 of this article after his expulsion.

22.3   Derogation

Article 1 is not a non-derogable right under Article 15 of the Convention.

23   THE RIGHT TO A REVIEW BY A HIGHER TRIBUNAL (ARTICLE 2 OF PROTOCOL NO. 7)

1. *Everyone convicted of a criminal offence by a tribunal shall have the right to have his conviction or sentence reviewed by a higher tribunal. The exercise of this right, including the grounds on which it may be exercised, shall be governed by law.*

2. *This right may be subject to exceptions in regard to offences of a minor character, as prescribed by law, or in cases in which the person concerned was tried in the first instance by the highest tribunal or was convicted following an appeal against acquittal.*

23.1   The Scope of Article 2 of Protocol No. 7

The scope of this article is essentially determined by the concepts of 'criminal offence', 'tribunal' and 'conviction or sentence'. It seems to be obvious that the meaning of the words 'criminal offence' is closely related to the notion of 'criminal charge' of Article 6 of the Convention. Thus, it is appropriate to argue that Article 2 of Protocol No. 7 also applies to those disciplinary and administrative sanctions that fall within the scope of Article 6. It seems to be not applicable, however, to preventive measures, deportation orders and decisions concerning extradition as far as no criminal law elements are involved.[2064]

Article 2 presupposes the existence of a 'conviction or sentence', which notions are to be interpreted autonomously. Article 2, consequently, would seem to be not applicable if a person is not convicted and also not sentenced in view of lack of evidence or guilt.

In the first sentence of paragraph 1 it is emphasised that the conviction must have been imposed 'by a tribunal'. According to the Explanatory Report this phrase was added to make it clear that the right laid down in this provision is not applicable to 'offences which have been tried by bodies which are not tribunals within the meaning of Article 6 of the Convention'.[2065] At first sight this is a

---

[2064]   See *supra* pp. 411-412.
[2065]   Explanatory Report, *supra* note 2046, p. 10.

somewhat strange restriction, since Article 6 of the Convention requires that the determination of criminal charges be made by an independent tribunal. Therefore, trial of a criminal offence by a non-judicial organ would in itself be a violation of the Convention. However, since the Strasbourg case-law has accepted the possibility that the determination of a criminal charge is made, in the first instance, by a non-judicial body, provided that from that determination appeal lies to a tribunal, the drafters must be assumed to have intended to make it clear that this first appeal to a tribunal is not a review in the sense of Article 2; its decision on appeal must be open to review by a higher tribunal.

23.2 The Right to a Review

The first sentence of paragraph 1 provides that everyone has the right to have the 'conviction or sentence' reviewed. The reason for using the word 'or' instead of 'and'[2066] is, again according to the Explanatory Report, that it is not required that in every case both the conviction and the sentence should be reviewed. For example, if a person has pleaded guilty and has been convicted, the right of review may be restricted to the review of the sentence. Here, too, the line of reasoning is not very convincing. Although in most cases in which a suspect has pleaded guilty the review will in fact mainly focus on the sentence, it may be necessary also to review the way the confession was obtained, and therefore the basis of the conviction. On the other hand, a review of the conviction alone, without the sentence being also reviewed, is only possible in those cases in which the suspect has been found guilty, but no sentence has been imposed. Just as in the corresponding Article 14(5) of the Covenant on Civil and Political Rights, it would therefore have been better if the word 'and' instead of 'or' had been used.

As is made clear in the second sentence of the first paragraph, the exercise of this right of appeal shall be governed by law. In other words, the modalities of the review are left for determination by domestic law. The Explanatory Report adds to this that the review may either concern a review of findings of facts and questions of law or be limited to questions of law.[2067] In the latter case the review is a rather restricted one and one may wonder why the drafters, if they considered such a restricted review sufficient, have not expressed that more clearly in the text. In any case one may expect that the Strasbourg organs will not accept as sufficient a restricted form of review of questions of law which cannot result in an annulment or alteration of the conviction and sentence.

Some countries have a system according to which persons who wish to appeal to a higher tribunal must in certain cases first apply for leave of appeal. According to the Explanatory Report such a procedure is in itself to be regarded as a form of review within the meaning of this article.[2068] It may be doubted if this

---

[2066] Art. 14(5) of the Covenant on Civil and Political Rights uses the word 'and'.
[2067] Explanatory Report, *supra* note 2046, p. 10.
[2068] *Idem.*

interpretation is in conformity with the text of the article. The decision to grant or to refuse leave of appeal may be based upon reasons of expediency and does not necessarily imply a review of the conviction or sentence as Article 2 would seem to guarantee, but rather block such a review. Moreover, one may wonder whether such a decision can be said always to amount to a review 'by a higher tribunal'. In our opinion, the Strasbourg organs should be guided by the text and purpose of Article 2 rather than by the restrictive interpretation given in the Explanatory Report on this point.

23.3 Exceptions to the Right to a Review

The second paragraph of Article 2 contains three exceptions to the right laid down in the first paragraph. The first exception concerns offences of a minor character. In practice it will not always be clear where the dividing line between serious and minor offences lies. The Explanatory Report proposes as a guiding criterion the question of whether the offence is punishable by imprisonment or not.[2069]

Although this criterion is a clear one, it is unlikely to lead to a common scope or autonomous meaning of the concept of 'offences of a minor character'. Since the question of imprisonment is entirely regulated by domestic law, major differences may occur in the Contracting States. More importantly, in several States a great many minor offences, such as infringements of traffic rules, are made punishable by imprisonment, though such sentences are never imposed in practice. It is unlikely that the drafters of the Protocol wished to make the right of review by a higher tribunal also obligatory in such cases.

The second exception concerns cases in which a person has been tried in the first instance by the highest tribunal. It refers to cases in which the domestic law has assigned the highest tribunal as a court of first instance because of the status of the accused as a minister, judge or other high official, or because of the nature of the offence. It is obvious that in those cases review by a higher tribunal is not possible.

The third exception is more controversial. It concerns cases where the conviction has been pronounced following an appeal against acquittal. For the person concerned this exception can be very unsatisfactory, especially when he thinks that the court of second instance has made an error of facts or of law. In most countries of the Council of Europe, however, the convicted person will normally have the right of appeal in cassation to a third instance. In that case, at least any error of law can be restored. One has to presume that the third exception does not apply in case the acquittal has been pronounced by a non-judicial body. Since Article 6 of the Convention requires that the determination of criminal charges be made by an independent tribunal, in this respect no consequences should ensue from a decision of a non-judicial body.

[2069] *Idem.*

23.4   Derogation

Article 2 does not belong to the non-derogable rights in the sense of Article 15(2) of the Convention.

24   COMPENSATION FOR MISCARRIAGE OF JUSTICE (ARTICLE 3 OF PROTOCOL NO. 7)

> *When a person has by a final decision been convicted of a criminal offence and when subsequently his conviction has been reversed, or he has been pardoned, on the ground that a new or newly discovered fact shows conclusively that there has been a miscarriage of justice, the person who has suffered punishment as a result of such conviction shall be compensated according to the law or the practice of the State concerned, unless it is proved that the non-disclosure of the unknown fact in time is wholly or partly attributable to him.*

24.1   The Scope of Article 3 of Protocol No. 7

Article 3 of Protocol No. 7 applies only if seven preconditions have been fulfilled. Firstly, Article 3 presupposes the existence of a 'criminal offence'. It seems to be obvious that the notion of 'criminal offence' is closely related to the notion of 'criminal charge' of Article 6 of the Convention. Thus, it is appropriate to argue that Article 3 also applies to those disciplinary and administrative sanctions that fall within the scope of Article 6.

Secondly, the person concerned must have been 'convicted'. Consequently, the article does not apply in cases where the charge is dismissed or the accused is acquitted.[2070]

Thirdly, the person concerned must have been convicted by a 'final decision'. A decision is final:

> if, according to the traditional expression, it has acquired the force of *res judicata*. This is the case when it is irrevocable, that is to say when no further ordinary remedies are available or when the parties have exhausted such remedies or have permitted the time-limit to expire without availing themselves of them.[2071]

Fourthly, the person concerned must, as a result of this final decision, have suffered punishment. Thus, if the suspect has been found guilty, but no sentence has been imposed or the sentence has not (yet) been executed, Article 3 does not apply.

Fifthly, the right laid down in this article can only be exercised, if the conviction has been reversed or pardoned.

[2070]   Explanatory Report, *supra* note 2046, p. 11. Under circumstances the fifth paragraph of Art. 5 of the Convention may offer compensation.

[2071]   Explanatory Report, *supra* note 2046, p. 11, with reference to the *Explanatory Report of the European Convention on the International Validity of Criminal Judgments, Commentary on Article 1(a)*, Council of Europe, Strasbourg, 1970, p. 22.

Sixthly, the reversal or pardon must have taken place because of new or newly discovered facts. In the latter case, it must moreover be assessed whether the circumstance that these facts were not disclosed in time is wholly or partly attributable to the person concerned. It is obvious that if a person is willingly withholding relevant information, he loses his right to compensation because the prejudice suffered is (partly) due to his own conduct. If, besides the convicted person, also others are responsible for the fact that certain relevant facts were not disclosed, it may not always be fair to put the blame solely on the former by fully denying him a right to compensation. In that case a partial compensation may be more appropriate.

Seventhly, the new or newly discovered facts on the basis of which the person's conviction has been reversed or he has been pardoned must conclusively show that there has been a miscarriage of justice. By this phrase is meant a 'serious failure in the judicial process involving grave prejudice to the convicted person'.[2072] Reversal or pardon on other grounds – especially pardon may often be granted on other grounds – does not create a right to compensation. According to the Explanatory Report, the intention is that compensation should be paid only in 'clear cases of miscarriage of justice, in the sense that there would be acknowledgement that the person concerned was clearly innocent'.[2073] In what follows the Explanatory Report seems to imply that reversal on the ground that new facts have been discovered which introduce a reasonable doubt as to the guilt of the accused is not enough.[2074] In our opinion this interpretation would be too strict, especially in view of the right to be presumed innocent, laid down in Article 6(2) of the Convention, which implies that reasonable doubt and clear innocence should lead to the same result.

24.2 The Right to Compensation

If all conditions have been fulfilled, Article 3 requires that the person who has suffered punishment as a result of such conviction shall be compensated according to the law or the practice of the State concerned.

What is meant by the phrase 'the practice of the State concerned' is not very clear. The Explanatory Report does not clarify it any further than by providing that 'the State should provide for the payment of compensation in all cases to which the Article applies'.[2075] In our opinion, this phrase, which does not appear anywhere else in the Convention, is rather unfortunate. It does not add anything to the reference that has already been made to national law and it may lead to confusion as to its meaning. Article 5(5) of the Convention, which establishes a right to compensation for victims of arrest or detention in

---

[2072] *Idem.*
[2073] *Ibidem*, p. 12.
[2074] *Idem.*
[2075] Explanatory Report, *supra* note 2046, p. 12.

contravention of the provisions of Article 5, uses the words 'an enforceable right to compensation'. This phrase should also have been adopted here.

24.3 Derogation

Article 3 does not belong to the non-derogable rights in the sense of Article 15(2) of the Convention.

25 *NE BIS IN IDEM* (ARTICLE 4 OF PROTOCOL NO. 7)

> 1. *No one shall be liable to be tried or punished again in criminal proceedings under the jurisdiction of the same State for an offence for which he has already been finally acquitted or convicted in accordance with the law and penal procedure of that State.*
> 2. *The provisions of the preceding paragraph shall not prevent the re-opening of the case in accordance with the law and penal procedure of the State concerned, if there is evidence of new or newly discovered facts, or if there has been a fundamental defect in the previous proceedings, which could affect the outcome of the case.*
> 3. *No derogation from this Article shall be made under Article 15 of the Convention.*

25.1 Criminal Proceedings

The principle that nobody may be tried or punished again is limited to 'criminal proceedings'. In the *Gradinger* Case the applicant had been convicted and punished by a criminal court. Subsequently the administrative authorities imposed a fine on him. The latter punishment was based on the same facts as the former. The applicant complained that the decision of the administrative authorities amounted to a violation of Article 6 of the Convention[2076] and Article 4 of Protocol No. 7. Thus, the Court had to asses whether Article 6 did apply to the administrative proceedings. It answered this question in the affirmative with reference to the criteria developed in its case-law. With regard to Article 4 of Protocol No. 7 the same question could have arisen. However, with regard to Article 4 the Court took the existence of the 'criminal proceedings' for granted.[2077] Thus, it may be concluded that the notion of 'criminal' in Article 4 of Protocol No. 7 is identical to the term 'criminal' in Article 6 of the Convention.

Article 4 only applies to criminal proceedings under the jurisdiction of one and the same State, thus limiting its scope to the national level. It, therefore, still allows that a person is punished more than once for the same act in two or more countries, depending on the rules on jurisdiction of the States involved. Although

---

[2076] The applicant contended that he did not have access to a 'tribunal'.
[2077] Judgment of 23 October 1995, A.328-C, pp. 61 and 65-66.

the Council of Europe had already, by adopting three Conventions,[2078] given a certain international scope to the *ne bis in idem* principle, this in itself was considered an insufficient ground for laying down an unconditional, internationally applied *ne bis in idem* principle.

25.2 An Offence for Which he has Already been Finally Acquitted or Convicted

In the *Gradinger* Case the question arose whether the 'offence' the applicant had been tried and punished for by the criminal court – causing death by negligence, while driving his car – concerned the same 'offence' as his subsequent conviction for driving under the influence of alcohol by the administrative authorities. The former offence constituted a violation of the Criminal Code and the latter came under the Road Traffic Act. The relevant provisions differed with regard to their nature and purpose. Nevertheless, the Court reached the conclusion that Article 4 of Protocol No. 7 did apply and had been violated. It appeared to be crucial in the Court's view that the decision of the criminal court under the Criminal Code and the decision of the administrative authorities under the Road Traffic Act 'were based on the same conduct'.[2079]

Paragraph 1 of Article 4 further provides that the *ne bis in idem* principle is only applicable if the conviction or acquittal has become final. Here again, just as in the preceding Article 3, a decision is to be considered final 'if, according to the traditional expression, it has acquired the force of *res judicata*'. This is the case when it is irrevocable, that is to say when 'no further ordinary remedies are available or when the parties have exhausted such remedies or have permitted the time-limit to expire without availing themselves of them'.[2080]

25.3 Re-Opening of the Case

The second paragraph of Article 4 provides that the *ne bis in idem* principle does not prevent that a case may be re-opened if there is evidence of new or newly discovered facts, irrespective of the question whether this is in favour or to the detriment of the person concerned. According to the Explanatory Report the term 'new or newly discovered facts' also 'includes new means of proof relating to previously existing facts'.[2081] What is exactly meant by these words is not clear, but it seems to be apt to lead to misuse. Is the meaning of this phrase that new technologies or previously forbidden forms of collecting evidence may lead to a

---

[2078] These Conventions are: the European Convention on Extradition (1957), the European Convention on the International Validity of Criminal Judgments (1970) and the European Convention on the Transfer of Proceedings in Criminal Matters (1972).
[2079] Judgment of 23 October 1995, A.328-C, p. 66.
[2080] Explanatory Report, *supra* note 2046, pp. 11-12.
[2081] *Ibidem*, p. 13.

re-opening of a case, if that technology or form has become available after the closing of a case? Especially when these 'facts' may also lead to a situation detrimental to the person concerned, this might create legal uncertainty for that person. In fact, a person may, even after an acquittal, be found guilty after the re-opening of a case as a result of new technologies or a change in the case-law concerning proof. This would practically mean that an accused may only feel safe after the prosecution for a criminal offence has become barred by limitation.

Re-opening of the proceedings and any other changing of the judgment, again according to the Explanatory Report, may also take place on other grounds, if this is in favour of the convicted person.[2082]

25.4 Derogation

According to the third paragraph of Article 4, the principle of *ne bis in idem* is non-derogable in the sense of Article 15(2) of the Convention.

26 EQUALITY OF RIGHTS AND RESPONSIBILITIES BETWEEN SPOUSES DURING AND AFTER MARRIAGE (ARTICLE 5 OF PROTOCOL NO. 7)

Spouses shall enjoy equality of rights and responsibilities of a private law character between them, and in their relations with their children, as to marriage, during marriage and in the event of its dissolution. This Article shall not prevent States from taking such measures as are necessary in the interests of the children.

26.1 Relations of a Private-Law Character

The rights and obligations to which this equality principle refers are of a private-law character; the equality concerns only the relations between the spouses themselves, with respect to their personal status or their property, and their relations with their children. As the Explanatory Report puts it, 'the Article does not apply to other fields of law, such as administrative, fiscal, criminal, social, ecclesiastical or labour laws'.[2083] Since under the system of the Convention complaints can be lodged against States only, the scope of the Strasbourg review is rather restricted and mainly concern the obligation of the State to enact and enforce the appropriate legislation. At the national level, however, in those legal systems where the Convention and its Protocols have internal effect, the scope may be much broader, as Article 5 clearly implies *Drittwirkung*.[2084]

To a large extent the equality of spouses is already secured by Article 8, in conjunction with Article 14 of the Convention. In the *Hokkanen* Case the applicant complained that, in breach of Article 8 of the Convention and Article 5 of

---

[2082] *Idem.*
[2083] *Idem.*
[2084] On this, see *supra* pp. 22-26.

Protocol No. 7, the public authorities had not taken the necessary steps to facilitate the speedy reunion of the applicant and his daughter. The Commission declared the complaint under both these articles admissible. However, finally it reached the conclusion, as did the Court, that Article 8 of the Convention had been violated and that no separate issue arose under Article 5 of Protocol No. 7.[2085]

26.2 During and After Marriage

The rights and obligations 'as to marriage' relate to the legal effects connected with the conclusion of marriage. Article 5 is not applicable to the period preceding marriage. It also is not concerned with the conditions of capacity to enter into marriage.[2086] It is, therefore, left to the States to determine these conditions. It is, for instance, allowed for States to make a difference between men and women with regard to the minimum age required for marriage, since this concerns the pre-marital period, provided of course that this regulation is in conformity with Article 12 in conjunction with Article 14 of the Convention.

The words 'in the event of its dissolution' in Article 5 do not imply a right to divorce. States are not obliged to provide for dissolution of marriage. In this context, it is noteworthy that the phrase referring to the dissolution of marriage in the corresponding Article 23(4) of the UN Covenant on Civil and Political Rights and Article 5 of this Protocol is identical in the French version, but not in the English version. In the French version both articles speak of '*lors de sa dissolution*'. In the English version, Article 23(4) of the UN Covenant on Civil and Political Rights uses the words 'at its dissolution', while Article 5 of Protocol No. 7 states 'in the event of its dissolution'. Apparently this change has been introduced to take into consideration the situation in some States where the dissolution of a marriage is still prohibited.

26.3 Exception to the Equality of Rights and Responsibilities

The second sentence of Article 5 contains an exception to the equal enjoyment of the rights and responsibilities. The Contracting States may take such measures as are necessary in the interests of the children, even if this results in inequality between the spouses. The Explanatory Report states in too broad a phrase that Article 5:

> should not be understood as preventing the national authorities from taking due account of all relevant factors when reaching decisions with regard to the division of property in the event of dissolution of marriage.[2087]

[2085] Report of 22 October 1993, A.299-A, pp. 37-38; judgment of 23 September 1994, A.299-A, pp. 24-25, para. 66.

[2086] Explanatory Report, *supra* note 2046.

[2087] *Idem.*

To the extent that these 'relevant factors' are related to the interests of the children, it follows from the express provision in Article 5 itself. However, since Article 5 contains no other exceptions – at least not expressly – any other limitations of the right to equal enjoyment seem to be inadmissible. If otherwise, it is to be assumed that such limitations will have to meet the requirement of an objective and reasonable justification and that of reasonable proportionality, which have been developed in the Strasbourg case-law with respect to Article 14.[2088]

26.4 Derogation

Article 5 does not belong to the non-derogable rights in the sense of Article 15(2) of the Convention.

[2088] See *infra* pp. 722-729.

Chapter VIII

Provisions Concerning Enjoyment of the Rights and Freedoms and Concerning Restriction of these Rights and Freedoms

1 INTRODUCTION

Articles 13 to 18 of the Convention form part of Section I but, unlike the preceding provisions of this Section, do not contain independent rights and freedoms. They cannot, therefore, constitute the object of a separate complaint, but can be put forward only in conjunction with one of the preceding provisions of Section I or one of the rights and freedoms set forth in Protocols Nos 1, 4, 6 and 7.

According to the prevailing opinion the same is true for Article 1, which, preceding Section I, is important for ensuring the rights and freedoms laid down therein, but cannot be put forward in Strasbourg independently of one of these rights and freedoms. In the case of an individual complaint this means that Commission and Court will not undertake a separate inquiry into the violation of Article 1; the individual applicant can allege that he is a 'victim' only if he is able to advance the violation of one of the rights and freedoms.[1] In the case of a complaint by a State the matter is more complicated, since according to the broad formulation of Article 24 – 'any alleged breach of the provisions of the Convention' – such a complaint need not be confined to the violation of a right. In fact, a State may have violated an obligation under Article 1 even if there has been no concrete violation of one of the rights and freedoms, for instance when a State has failed to take the necessary legislative and other measures so as to ensure that those rights and freedoms are respected. Since a State does not have to prove that such negligence has produced concrete victims, Article 24 would seem to leave scope for a separate examination of the alleged violation of Article 1.

In fact, a State may lodge a complaint even when it is not yet possible to identify concrete violations of any of the rights set forth in the Convention, for instance because a legal rule has not yet been applied in a concrete way. Thus, the Court held in *Ireland* v. *the United Kingdom*:

---

[1] The Commission, therefore, has so far refrained from instituting a separate inquiry into the alleged violation of Art. 1 in the case of an individual complaint. See its decisions on Appl. 5493/72, *Handyside* v. *the United Kingdom*, Yearbook XVII (1974), p. 228 (300) and Appl. 5613/72, *Hilton* v. *the United Kingdom*, Yearbook XIX (1976), p. 256 (272).

Article 24 enables each Contracting State to refer to the Commission 'any alleged breach of any of the provisions of the Convention by another State'. Such a 'breach' results from the mere existence of a law which introduces, directs or authorises measures incompatible with the rights and freedoms safeguarded.[2]

The Court stressed, however, that such an 'abstract complaint' concerning legislation must be sufficiently clear and exact to make the violation immediately manifest, since otherwise a decision on the complaint can be taken only by reference to the specific application of that legislation.[3]

It is obvious, however, that in the case of a specific complaint that a State has not fulfilled its obligations under Article 1, one or more of the other provisions will always be involved as well, in addition to Article 1. In actual fact, therefore, the question as to a violation of Article 1 has little significance independently of the question of whether the State has violated one or more of those other provisions.

The main importance, however, of Article 1 concerns the scope of application *ratione personae* of the Convention and has already been discussed above within that context.[4]

Articles 13, 14, 15(2) and 18 provide an additional guarantee for the enjoyment of the rights and freedoms laid down in the Convention. These provisions, accordingly, can also only be invoked before the Strasbourg organs in connection with a complaint concerning the violation of one or more of these rights or freedoms. Articles 15(1) and 16, on the other hand, authorise the Contracting States to limit the enjoyment of certain rights and freedoms for particular situations or with regard to a particular group of persons. They may therefore be invoked as a defence by the State against which a complaint is addressed. Article 17 contains elements of both categories.

A discussion of each of the above-mentioned articles will be followed in this chapter by some general observations on the specific restrictions mentioned in Articles 8 to 11 of the Convention, Article 2 of Protocol No. 4 and Article 1 of Protocol No. 7. The chapter concludes with a section concerning the possibility of making reservations with respect to one or more provisions of the Convention.

2 RIGHT TO AN EFFECTIVE REMEDY BEFORE A NATIONAL AUTHORITY (ARTICLE 13)

Everyone whose rights and freedoms as set forth in this Convention are violated shall have an effective remedy before a national authority notwithstanding that the violation has been committed by persons acting in an official capacity.

---

[2] Judgment of 18 January 1978, A.25, p. 91. See also the separate opinion of judge O'Donogue, *ibidem*, p. 109.
[3] *Ibidem*, p. 91.
[4] *Supra* pp. 118-123.

2.1 Introduction: Ancillary Character of Article 13 and Casuistry in the Case-Law

The status of Article 13 within the framework of the Convention is an odd one. In our opinion a general guarantee of an effective remedy for anyone who alleges that one of his or her rights or freedoms has been violated by the authorities or by an individual should be provided for. This would be warranted not only in view of the concept of the rule of law, which along with the idea of democracy constitutes one of the pillars of the Council of Europe,[5] it would also be in line with the prominent place the Court in its case-law concerning Article 6 has accorded to the principle of access to court.[6]

However, the present situation is different. It is evident from the words 'whose rights and freedoms as set forth in this Convention are violated' that Article 13 does not contain such a general guarantee. It refers exclusively to cases in which the alleged violation concerns one of the rights and freedoms of the Convention.[7] It cannot therefore be invoked independently from, but only in conjunction with one or more of these rights and freedoms.

The underrated status of the right to an effective remedy resulting from the ancillary character of Article 13 is aggravated by the way this provision is being dealt with in the case-law. In 1984 it was opined:

> that Article 13 constitutes one of the most obscure clauses in the Convention and its application raises extremely complicated problems of interpretation. This is probably the reason why, for approximately two decades, the Convention institutions avoided analysing this provision, for the most part advancing barely convincing reasons.[8]

Since then the situation has not substantially improved. In fact every single element of Article 13 still gives rise to difficulties of interpretation.

---

[5] See in particular the Preamble and Art. 3 of the Statute of the Council of Europe. See also Res. (78)8 of the Committee of Ministers, where 'the right of access to justice' is called an 'essential feature of any democratic society'; Council of Europe, *Information Bulletin on Legal Activities*, 1 June 1978, p. 48.

[6] In the *Golder* Case, judgment of 21 February 1975, A.18, p. 17, it was held that 'The principle whereby a civil claim must be capable of being submitted to a judge ranks as one of the universally "recognised" fundamental principles of law; ...'

[7] Thus also the case-law of the Commission. See, *inter alia*, Appl. 6753/74, *X and Y v. the Netherlands*, D&R 2 (1975), p. 118 (119), and the report of 17 July 1980 in the *Kaplan* Case, D&R 21 (1981), p. 5 (35).

[8] Partly dissenting opinion of judges Matscher and Pinheiro Farinha in the *Malone* Case, judgment of 2 August 1984, A.82, p. 41; in the same vain the concurring opinion of judges Bindschedler-Robert, Gölcuklu, Matscher and Spielman in the *James* Case, judgment of 21 February 1986, A.98, p. 51.

2.2 The Meaning of the Words 'are Violated' and 'has been Committed'

The words 'are violated' and 'has been committed' should, of course, not be interpreted to imply that Article 13 may be invoked in Strasbourg only if the violation of one or more of the said rights and freedoms *has been established* in advance by a national authority. In fact, such an interpretation would be in very poor keeping with the aim of the Convention, which precisely provides for the possibility of international supervision if the Convention has allegedly been applied incorrectly or not at all by the national authorities. Moreover, such an interpretation would largely deprive Article 13 of its meaning, because the very establishment of the alleged violation would indicate that the applicant has had an effective remedy before a national authority. It is also, and pre-eminently, in those cases where the national authority concerned declares that the Convention has not been violated, or where no decision about this can be obtained, that Article 13 can be put forward in Strasbourg. Indeed, even if ultimately, as a result of the Strasbourg procedure, there proves to have been no violation, the Contracting State was nevertheless obliged to provide an effective remedy for the examination of the alleged violation. In this sense Article 13 ensures an independent right even though it can only be invoked in conjunction with one of the other rights or freedoms of the Convention.

The Court in its *Klass* judgment clearly decided in the above sense. It held with respect to Article 13:

> This provision, read literally, seems to say that a person is entitled to a national remedy only if a 'violation' has occurred. However, a person cannot establish a 'violation' before a national authority unless he is first able to lodge with such an authority a complaint to that effect. Consequently, as the minority of the Commission stated, it cannot be a prerequisite for the application of Article 13 that the Convention be in fact violated. In the Court's view, Article 13 requires that where an individual considers himself to have been prejudiced by a measure allegedly in breach of the Convention, he should have a remedy before a national authority in order both to have his claim decided and, if appropriate, to obtain redress. Thus, Article 13 must be interpreted as guaranteeing an 'effective remedy before a national authority' to everyone who *claims* that his rights and freedoms under the Convention have been violated.[9]

At present the case-law of the Court and the Commission on this point may be summed up as follows:

> where an individual has an arguable claim to be the victim of a violation of the rights set forth in the Convention, he should have a remedy before a national authority in order both to have his claim decided and, if appropriate, to obtain redress.[10]

---

[9] Judgment of 6 September 1978, A.28, pp. 29-30.

[10] Judgment of 25 March 1983, *Silver and Others*, A.61, p. 42; judgment of 26 March 1987, *Leander*, A.116, pp. 29-30.

2.3 The Arguability-Test

The arguability-test, introduced in the *Silver* Case, has not been elaborated much further in the case-law until now. In fact, the Court has refrained from giving – in its own words – 'an abstract definition of the notion of arguability'.[11] Rather the test is applied on a case-by-case basis.

Nevertheless, some general indications, albeit negative ones, have been provided by the Court. On the one hand, the Court does not interpret Article 13 so as to require a remedy in domestic law in respect of any supposed grievance under the Convention that an individual may have, no matter how unmeritorious his complaint may be.[12] On the other hand, non-arguability, according to the Court, is not the same thing as manifest ill-foundedness; a complaint may be manifestly ill-founded and yet arguable. At first sight, this point of view might seem remarkable. Indeed, the Court itself has conceded that according to the ordinary meaning of the words, it is difficult to conceive how a claim that is manifestly ill-founded can nevertheless be arguable, and *vice versa*.[13] This discrepancy may be explained by the fact that the Commission, when conducting its admissibility investigation as to manifest ill-foundedness, does not confine itself to asking whether or not the applicant has a *prima facie* case, but comes close to a full-fledged examination as to the merits.[14] Conceived in this way, manifest ill-foundedness cannot be put on the same line as arguability, meaning that a claim 'only needs to raise a Convention issue which merits further examination'.[15] Indeed, this would run counter to the above-mentioned point of departure that a violation of Article 13 does not presuppose violation of one of the substantive rights or freedoms.

The link between the arguability-requirement and the concept of manifestly ill-foundedness is complicated by the fact that the former belongs to the merits of a case, while the latter is dealt with during the admissibility stage, but in a way which amounts to a full-fledged examination. The Court's position on the matter was most recently summed up in the *Powell and Rayner* judgment. There the Court elaborates its above-mentioned statement in the *Boyle and Rice* judgment according to which it is difficult to conceive how a claim that is manifestly ill-founded can nevertheless be arguable and *vice versa*. It is now added that, because both arguability and manifestly ill-foundedness are concerned with the availability of remedies:

---

[11] Judgments of 27 April 1988, *Boyle and Rice*, A.131, p. 24, and of 21 June 1988, *Plattform 'Ärzte für das Leben'*, A.139, p. 11.
[12] Judgment of 27 April 1988, *Boyle and Rice*, A.131, p. 23.
[13] *Ibidem*, pp. 23-24.
[14] See *supra* pp. 162-165.
[15] See the Commission's position before the Court in the judgment of 27 April 1988, *Boyle and Rice* A.131, p. 23.

The coherence of this dual system of enforcement is at risk of being undermined if Article 13 is interpreted as requiring national law to make available an "effective remedy" for a grievance classified under Article 27 paragraph 2 as being so weak as not to warrant examination on its merits at the international level. Whatever threshold the Commission has set in its case-law for declaring claims "manifestly ill-founded" under Article 27 paragraph 2, in principle it should set the same threshold in regard to the parallel notion of "arguability" under Article 13.[16]

However, according to the Court, the need for the Commission to take into account the coherence of the dual system in the admissibility stage does not mean that the Court in dealing with the merits is bound:

> to hold Article 13 inapplicable solely as a result of the Commission's decisions (...) declaring the applicants' substantive claims (...) to be manifestly ill-founded. Whilst those decisions are as such unreviewable, the Court is competent to take cognisance of all questions of fact and law arising in the context of Article 13 complaints duly referred to it, including the "arguability" or not of each of the substantive claims (...). In order to determine the latter question, the particular facts and the nature of the legal issues raised must be examined, notably in the light of the Commission's admissibility decisions and the reasoning contained therein. In that connection, as the case of Boyle and Rice and the case of Plattform "Ärzte fur das Leben" show, a claim is not necessarily rendered arguable because, before rejecting it as inadmissible, the Commission has devoted careful consideration to it and to its underlying facts.[17]

2.4 The Relation Between Article 13 and Other Rights and Freedoms

The troublesome character of Article 13 is also exposed by the case-law concerning the relation between this provision and other rights or freedoms contained in the Convention. Particularly Article 6 is a case in point here. When discussing Article 6(1) it was pointed out that the Court has inferred from that provision a right of access to an independent and impartial tribunal in the cases there referred to, *i.e.,* among other instances, when a 'civil right' is involved.[18] When interpreted in this way, Article 6(1) strengthens and extends on a number of points the guarantee which Article 13 is intended to provide.

First, the right to an effective national remedy consists not only in the case of an alleged violation of one of the rights and freedoms guaranteed in the Convention, but also in the case of violation of any 'civil right' in the sense of Article 6(1).[19] In the latter case, that right to a national remedy may actually constitute the object of an independent complaint, because it is guaranteed in Article 6 as one of the rights and freedoms. There, too, the violation of, or interference with, a 'civil right' has to be proven by only *prima facie* evidence and need not have been established. The Strasbourg organs would not even be competent to establish such a violation if a 'civil right' not laid down in the Convention is concerned. To what extent Article 6(1) also confers a right of

---

[16] Judgment of 21 February 1990, A.172, p. 15.
[17] *Idem.*
[18] *Supra* pp. 420-421.
[19] On the meaning of 'civil rights', see *supra* pp. 392-406.

access to a court against acts and omissions of the authorities depends on the question of whether in such a case a 'civil right' (or a 'civil obligation') may be involved.[20] Article 13 remains relevant for those cases where the complaint concerns a violation of one of the rights or freedoms of the Convention without a 'civil right' in the sense of Article 6(1) being at issue; it is of a subsidiary character.[21]

Secondly, Article 6(1) guarantees access to a court, while the term 'effective remedy before a national authority' is so wide that it also refers to procedures other than judicial ones.[22] These too will then have to be endowed with sufficient guarantees; otherwise it is not possible to speak of an 'effective remedy'.[23]

Thirdly, while Article 13 in all probability does not lend itself to direct application by the national courts, this direct applicability *has* been recognised by domestic courts for Article 6, so that this can be invoked before the national courts in those countries where the Convention has internal effect within the domestic legal order.

From the above it is evident that, if the Commission or the Court has concluded that Article 6 has not been violated, because there is no question of a 'civil right', a separate inquiry into a possible violation of Article 13 may be required. If a violation of Article 6 *has* been found, a further inquiry concerning Article 13 may be superfluous, *viz.* to the extent that the guarantees of the two provisions overlap or that of Article 13 is subordinate to that of Article 6. In a number of cases the Court has indeed used what would seem to have become a standard formula, holding that examination of the complaint under Article 13 is not necessary, because the requirements of the latter are less strict or absorbed by those ensuing from Article 6.[24] However, when a violation of Article 6 has been found, this may precisely raise the question of whether against such a violation – *e.g.* excessively long proceedings – an effective remedy was available.[25] Not surprisingly, therefore, this case-law of the Court has given rise to doubts:

---

[20] *Idem.*

[21] This also holds true with regard to other provisions of the Convention where the right to judicial proceedings forms part of the substantive right guaranteed. See Appl. 7341/76, *Eggs v. Switzerland,* Yearbook XX (1977), p. 448 (458), where this was held concerning the relation between Art. 13 and Art. 5(4).

[22] Thus also the Court in its judgment of 21 February 1975, *Golder,* A.18, p. 16, and in its judgment of 6 September 1978, *Klass,* A.28, p. 30.

[23] On this, see *infra* pp. 706-710.

[24] See, for instance, the judgment of 28 June 1984, *Campbell and Fell,* A.80, p. 51; judgment of 8 July 1987, *O v. the United Kingdom,* A.120-A, p. 29; and the judgment of 27 October 1987, *Pudas,* A.125-A, p. 17 and most recently the judgment of 23 September 1994, *Hokkanen v. Finland,* A.299-A, p. 21.

[25] Appl. 7987/77, *Company X v. Austria,* D&R 18 (1980), p. 31 (46). In such a case it will have to be a judicial remedy, since appeal to a non-judicial authority against an act or omission of a judicial organ indeed would impair the independence of the court which is also guaranteed by Art. 6. In this respect, see the individual opinion of Commission member Trechsel in the *Kaplan* report of 17 July 1980, D&R 21 (1981), p. 37.

It was only with some hesitation that we concurred in the decision that it was not necessary to examine the case under Article 13 of the Convention. We are not quite sure that such examination was made superfluous by the finding of a violation (...) of the entitlement to a hearing by a tribunal within the meaning of Article 6, para. 1. Are the 'less strict' requirements of Article 13 truly 'absorbed' by those of Article 6, para. 1? Do these provisions really 'overlap'? It appears to us that the relationship between the right to be heard by a tribunal, within the meaning of Article 6, para. 1, and the right to an effective remedy before a national authority, within the meaning of Article 13, should be considered more thoroughly.[26]

The Court and the Commission follow a comparable line of reasoning with respect to the relation between Article 13 and Article 5(4). In the case of *De Jong, Baljet and Van der Brink* both the Commission and the Court, after having found a violation of Article 5(4), decided not to examine the alleged violation of Article 13 on the basis of the argument that since Article 5(4) guarantees a right to proceedings before a 'court' and not merely before an authority of unspecified status, Article 5(4) must be considered as a *lex specialis* with respect to the general obligation to provide an effective remedy for any victim of a violation of the Convention.[27] The Court repeated this formula in its judgment in the *Brannigan and McBride* Case, where it recalled:

that it was open to the applicants to challenge the lawfulness of their detention by way of proceedings for habeas corpus and that the Court in its Brogan and Others judgment of 29 November 1988 found that this remedy satisfied Article 5 par. 4 of the Convention.[28]

However, judge Walsh was of the opinion that there had been a breach of Article 13. In his dissenting opinion he pointed out that the Court's judgment overlooked:

that the so-called safeguards are, in practice, illusory as their availability within the first forty-eight hours of detention is solely dependent upon police willingness. In the result the arrested person is secretly detained for that period and is held incommunicado and without legal assistance, or if he receives it, he may expect to have it overheard by the police (...). Even the great historic remedy of habeas corpus, theoretically available almost instantly, can be put out of reach of the arrested person by reason of non-access to the world outside the detention centre.

According to judge Walsh:

Article 13 of the Convention requires that an effective remedy shall be available before a national authority for everyone whose rights and freedoms as set forth in the Convention are violated. The application of Article 13 does not depend upon a violation being proved. No such authority is or was available in the United Kingdom and the Convention has not been incorporated in the national law. It is not correct to suggest

---

[26] Joint separate opinion of judges Pinheiro Farinha and De Meyer, judgment of 8 July 1987, *W v. the United Kingdom*, A.121, pp. 40-41. See also the partly dissenting opinion of Mr Schermers, joined by Mr Jörundsson, annexed to the report of the Commission in this case, A.121, pp. 55-56.

[27] Report of 11 October 1982, A.77, p. 39 and judgment of 22 May 1984, A.77, p. 27. See also the judgment of 29 February 1988, *Bouamar*, A.129, p. 25.

[28] Judgment of 26 May 1993, A.258-B, p. 57.

that the remedy of habeas corpus satisfies the requirements of Article 13. That remedy depends upon showing a breach of national laws. It is not available for a claim that the detention is illegal by reason of a breach of the Convention.[29]

Finally, the relationship between Article 13 and other rights and freedoms of the Convention has come up with respect to Article 8. The picture emerging from the case-law on this point is far from clear. In a case decided in 1984 the applicant raised complaints concerning, *inter alia*, the refusal to allow confidential consultation by a prisoner with his lawyer and restrictions on a prisoner's personal correspondence. Whereas with respect to the latter complaint the Court found a violation of Article 8, with respect to the former it did not.[30] These different findings did not prevent the Court from subsequently examining the alleged violation of Article 13 with respect to both complaints.[31] In our view this would seem to be the correct approach doing justice to the independent – albeit ancillary – character of Article 13 outlined above.[32]

However, in a number of other cases the Court strengthens the impression that, once a violation of a substantive provision of the Convention has been found, it is not much inclined to consider Article 13 as well. In the *Malone* Case, where the interception of postal and telephone communications as well as the release of information obtained from the 'metering' of telephones were found to be in violation of Article 8, with respect to the alleged violation of Article 13, it was held without any further argument that: 'Having regard to its decision on Article 8 (...) the Court does not consider it necessary to rule on this issue'.[33] Similarly, in *X and Y* v. *the Netherlands* the Court held that it:

> has already considered in the context of Article 8, whether an adequate means of obtaining a remedy was available to Miss Y. Its finding that there was no such means was one of the factors which led it to conclude that Article 8 had been violated. This being so, the Court does not have to examine the same issue under Article 13.[34]

Similarly, in the *Hokkanen* Case the Court first found that:

> the non-enforcement of the applicant's right to access [to his daughter] from 10 May 1990 until 21 October 1993 constituted a breach of his right to respect for his family life under Article 8. However, there has been no such violation in respect of the period thereafter.[35]

Subsequently, it was decided with respect to the alleged violation of Article 13 that 'The Court, having regard to its findings above, shares the Commission's view that it is not necessary to examine this grievance.' In these cases the Court

---

[29] *Ibidem*, p. 69.
[30] Judgment of 28 June 1984, *Campbell and Fell* v. *the United Kingdom*, A.80, p. 50.
[31] *Ibidem*, p. 52, where the Court concluded that there had been a violation of Art. 13 on both scores.
[32] See *supra* p. 697.
[33] Judgment of 2 August 1984, A.82, p. 39.
[34] Judgment of 26 March 1985, A.91, p. 15.
[35] Judgment of 23 September 1994, A.299-A, p. 18.

would seem to go far beyond what is required by the ancillary character of Article 13 and in fact reduces the independent character of that provision to the vanishing point.[36]

In a more recent case the Court went again the other way. After it had concluded that the applicant concerned had been a victim of a violation of Article 10, it held with respect to Article 13: 'In the light of the conclusion (...) above, the requirement that the complaint be "arguable" is satisfied ', and subsequently decided that there had been a violation of Article 13, because the Government had failed to show that the remedies it had adduced would have been effective in the case.[37]

2.5 'Notwithstanding that the Violation has been Committed by Persons in an Official Capacity'

From the words 'notwithstanding that the violation has been committed by persons acting in an official capacity' it might be inferred that an effective legal remedy must also, and *a fortiori*, be provided for when the violation has been committed by an individual; in this interpretation an argument for *Drittwirkung* of the rights and freedoms guaranteed in the Convention might be derived from Article 13.[38]

If this *Drittwirkung* is indeed recognised for those articles of the Convention which lend themselves to it, from the general obligation of Article 1 to guarantee the rights and freedoms ensues the obligation for the Contracting States to effectuate this *Drittwirkung* in their national system of law. Consequently, violations by an individual in cases where the State has failed to fulfil that obligation may then become the object of a complaint against that State. In that context Article 13 may also be invoked.

As to the words 'persons acting in an official capacity', the Commission has held so far that this term does not include the legislator. In its report in the *Young, James and Webster* Case it opined as follows:

> It cannot be deduced from Art. 13 that there must be a remedy against legislation as such which is considered not to be in conformity with the Convention. Such a remedy would in effect amount to some sort of judicial review of legislation because any other review – generally sufficient for Art. 13 which requires only a 'remedy before a national authority' – could hardly be effective concerning legislation. Without a clear indication in the text Art. 13 cannot be extended that far. This provision rather contains a textual element which supports the reading adopted here. As Art. 13 adds to the main guarantee the words 'notwithstanding that the violation has been committed by persons acting in an official capacity' it indicates that the Article is concerned with individuals

---

[36] With respect to Arts 8 and 10, see also the judgment of 24 September 1992, *Herczfalvy* v. *Austria*, A.244, p. 25.

[37] Judgment of 19 December 1994, *Vereinigung Demokratscher Soldaten Österreichs and Gubi* v. *Austria*, A.302, p. 14.

[38] On *Drittwirkung* and Art. 13, see *supra* p. 25.

acting for the State. Even if these words are mainly directed to exclude any doctrine of immunity of State organs, they can be used as an element to show the scope of the Article. Art. 13 does not relate to legislation and does not guarantee a remedy by which legislation could be controlled as to its conformity with the Convention.[39]

The case-law of the Court on this issue was summed up in the Court's judgment in the *Leander* Case, in which as one of the principles for the interpretation of Article 13 it was set forth that:

> Article 13 does not guarantee a remedy allowing a Contracting State's laws as such to be challenged before a national authority on the ground of being contrary to the Convention or equivalent domestic norms.[40]

As it has been recognised in the Strasbourg case-law that a legal regulation as such may impair a person's rights guaranteed in the Convention, even if this regulation has not yet been applied to him,[41] a gap exists here in the national remedies against violation of those rights, and thus in the system of Article 13.

This gap would seem to be even more serious in the case of those Contracting States where the Convention is not part of domestic law and where no constitutional procedure exists permitting the validity of laws to be challenged for non-observance of fundamental rights. In such situations the Court adheres to its above-mentioned point of departure. Thus in the *The Observer and Guardian* Case it was reiterated that there is no obligation to incorporate the Convention into domestic law and that Article 13 does not go so far as to guarantee a remedy allowing a Contracting State's laws as such to be challenged before a national authority on the ground of being contrary to the Convention.[42]

As far as the application of the laws in question to the alleged victim is concerned, the Court's judgment on the effectiveness of the available remedies seems again to depend to a large extent on the question of whether or not it finds

---

[39] Report of 14 December 1979, B.39 (1984), p. 49. Thus also the report of 17 July 1980, *Kaplan*, D&R 21 (1981), p. 5 (36).

[40] Judgment of 26 March 1987, A.116, pp. 29-30. See also the judgment of 9 December 1994, *Holy Monasteries v. Greece*, A.301-A, p. 35.

[41] See *supra* pp. 50-51.

[42] Judgment of 26 November 1991, A.216, p. 33. Judge Valticos in his separate opinion, *ibidem*, p. 45, supplemented the Court's conclusion by adding that States are of course under a duty to give effect to the Convention and that the obligation to give effect is often best fulfilled where the terms of the Convention are transposed into the domestic legal system. Judges De Meyer and Petiti in their separate opinion, *ibidem*, p. 44, took a more far-reaching position. They upheld that 'The question whether a certain treaty is, or is not, "incorporated into domestic law" may be of some interest as regards other kind of treaties. It has no relevance when fundamental rights are concerned; these are of such a nature that it cannot be necessary to have them formally "incorporated into domestic law". (...) the object and purpose of the European Convention on Human Rights was not to create, but to recognise rights which must be respected and protected even in the absence of any instrument of positive law. It has to be accepted that, everywhere in Europe, these rights "bind the legislature, the executive and the judiciary, as directly applicable law" and as "supreme law of the land, (...) anything in the constitution or laws of any State to the contrary notwithstanding".'

the law concerned to be in conformity with the substantive provisions of the Convention, such as Articles 6 and 8. If this is the case, the Court seems to be inclined to conclude that no violation of Article 13 had occurred.[43] If not, the requirements which the Court derives from Article 13 seem to turn out more strict.[44]

2.6 When is a Remedy 'Effective'?

If it comes to the examination of an alleged violation of Article 13, when can a given remedy be said to be 'effective'? In the *Vilvajarah and Others* Case[45] the Court has outlined the rationale of Article 13 as follows. When the applicant has an arguable claim, Article 13 guarantees the availability of a remedy at national level to enforce the substance of the Convention rights and freedoms in whatever form they may happen to be secured in the domestic legal order. The effect of Article 13, according to the Court, is thus to allow the competent national authority both to deal with the substance of the complaint concerned and to grant appropriate relief. From this point of departure it follows that the effectiveness of a remedy for the purposes of Article 13 does not depend on the certainty of a favourable outcome for the applicant.[46] Furthermore, Article 13 does not go so far as to require any particular form of remedy; Contracting States are afforded a margin of discretion in conforming to their obligation under this provision.

As far as particular remedies are concerned, in its *Soering* judgment[47] the Court considered judicial review proceedings to be an effective remedy in relation to the complaint concerned. Similarly, in the *Vilvajarah and Others* Case the Court concluded that:

> While it is true that there are limitations to the powers of courts in judicial review proceedings (...), these powers, exercisable as they are by the highest tribunals in the land, do provide an effective degree of control over the decisions of the administrative authorities in asylum cases and are sufficient to satisfy the requirements of Article 13.[48]

However, judges Walsh and Russo dissented on this point. They argued, *inter alia*, that the Government's claim that judicial review 'controls' the decision of immigration authorities must be qualified since in English law judicial review controls only the procedure and not the merits of the imp gned decision. According to these judges:

---

[43] See the judgment of 21 February 1986, *James and Others*, A.98, pp. 47-48, and the judgment of 8 July 1986, *Lithgow and Others*, A.102, pp. 74-75.

[44] See the judgment of 28 May 1985, *Abdulaziz, Cabales and Balkandali*, A.94, pp. 42-43.

[45] Judgment of 30 October 1991, A.215, pp. 37-38.

[46] See also the judgment of 25 March 1993, *Costello-Roberts v. the United Kingdom*, A.247-C, p. 13.

[47] Judgment of 7 July 1989, A.161, pp. 27-28.

[48] Judgment of 30 October 1991, A.215, p. 38.

a national system which it is claimed provides an effective remedy for a breach of the Convention and which excludes the competence to make a decision on the merits cannot meet the requirements of Article 13.[49]

In addition a number of general principles elaborated by the Court for the interpretation of Article 13, and summed up in its judgment in the *Leander* Case, are relevant. According to the Court, the authority referred to in Article 13 need not be a judicial authority but, if it is not, the powers and the guarantees which it affords are relevant in determining whether the remedy before it is effective.[50] In addition the Court takes the position that, in cases where no single remedy in itself entirely satisfies the requirement of Article 13, the aggregate of remedies provided for under domestic law may do so.[51]

Not listed among these principles, but in fact underlying them, is the systematic approach towards Article 13 as employed by the Court. In the *Leander* judgment this approach was explained as follows 'the Convention is to be read as a whole and therefore (...) any interpretation of Article 13 must be in harmony with the logic of the Convention.'[52]

The *Klass* Case had already indicated that this in fact means that the Court is not prepared to interpret or apply Article 13 in a way which amounts to nullifying its conclusions derived from the (preceding) interpretation of one or more of the (other) rights and freedoms set forth in the Convention.[53]

In the *Klass* Case a judge, a public prosecutor and three lawyers complained about the German legislation which allows interception of correspondence and wire-tapping in certain cases without the person concerned having to be informed of it. In addition to violation of Article 8, they alleged violation of Articles 6(1)[54] and 13.

As to Article 13, it was argued that the challenged legislation did not provide for an 'effective remedy', because the normal judicial remedies had been replaced by supervision by a committee of parliamentarians which was regularly informed by the authorities about the cases in which the legal provision here challenged had been applied. Moreover, those affected by that application were not in a position to challenge this personally, since it was not certain whether and when they would be informed of that application. The Court formulated in the first place the principle mentioned above, *viz.* that:

---

[49] *Ibidem*, pp. 42-43.
[50] Judgment of 26 March 1987, A.116, pp. 29-30.
[51] *Idem.*
[52] *Ibidem*, p. 30.
[53] Judgment of 6 September 1978, A.28, pp. 30-31.
[54] On this, see *supra* pp. 531 and 427-428 respectively.

the authority referred to in Article 13 may not necessarily in all circumstances be a judicial authority in the strict sense (...). Nevertheless, the powers and procedural guarantees an authority possesses are relevant in determining whether the remedy before it is effective.[55]

Next the Court examined the existing remedies *in concreto*. It noted that a person having an interest in the matter may request the *Bundesverfassungsgericht* to review the legislation in question for its conformity with the German Constitution. It is true that it is not the conformity of the legislation with the Convention that is reviewed, but conformity with provisions in the German Constitution. However, the relevant provisions in this case greatly resemble the relevant Article 8 of the Convention.[56] Furthermore, a person who suspects that the legal provision has been applied to him may approach the above-mentioned parliamentary committee, and thereafter may again appeal to the *Bundesverfassungsgericht*, which may then request the authorities to supply all the information desired. With respect to this, the Court held:

> Admittedly, the effectiveness of these remedies is limited and they will in principle apply only in exceptional cases. However, in the circumstances of the present proceedings, it is hard to conceive of more effective remedies being possible.[57]

And as to the complaint that the potential victim cannot defend himself because he does not know whether the provision has been applied to him, the Court, following the Commission, adopted the position – 'albeit to its regret' – that secret control may after all be necessary, and that:

> the Court cannot interpret or apply Article 13 so as to arrive at a result tantamount in fact to nullifying its conclusion that the absence of notification to the persons concerned is compatible with Article 8 in order to ensure the efficacy of surveillance measures.[58]

Thus the Court to a high degree stripped Article 13 of its autonomous character recognised in this same judgment. The issue whether it is still possible to speak of a 'remedy' and whether the latter is 'effective' was turned by the Court into a relative one, which has to be judged in accordance with the circumstances of each case. If those circumstances are such that they do not constitute a violation of one of the rights or freedoms of the Convention, no further requirements for legal protection than those circumstances allow can ensue from Article 13.

The Court thus actually created the same vicious circle which it wished to break in the first place. It is precisely the question whether these circumstances are in conformity with the Convention which the person concerned wants to have established in a national procedure. This right is conferred on him by Article 13, but then the national procedure must provide an actual and effective possibility for it. As has been observed above with respect to the application of Article 6(1) in

---

[55] Judgment of 6 September 1978, A.28, p. 30.
[56] *Ibidem*, pp. 30 and 31 in conjunction with p. 13.
[57] *Ibidem*, p. 31.
[58] *Ibidem*, pp. 30-31.

this case,[59] the Court was confronted with the choice between, on the one hand, the interest of the person in question in an effective remedy and, on the other hand, the general interest of an effective surveillance for the protection of the democratic values underlying the Convention. The Court in fact gives priority to the latter interest *via* a systematic interpretation of Article 13 in conjunction with Article 8(2). However, an argument evidently weighing heavily with the Court is the fact that, in accordance with a decision of the German *Bundesverfassungs- gericht*, the authorities are obliged to inform the person involved of the measures 'as soon as the surveillance measures are discontinued and notification can be made without jeopardising the purpose of the restriction'.[60] From that moment the normal remedy is open again to the person involved. Previously, the remedy against unlawful acts of the authorities is in the hands of the above-mentioned parliamentary committee and, if appealed to, the *Bundesverfassungsgericht*. In this phase, too, there is a certain amount of supervision of the way in which interests of national security and the rights and freedoms of individuals are being weighed against each other by the authorities, although this supervision cannot be called very effective, because the person concerned must rely on presumptions as to the application of the security measures against him.

The impact of the systematic approach as employed by the Court with respect to Article 13 can also be noticed in its judgment in the *Silver* Case concerning the effectiveness of the various remedies that were available in the case of a breach of the right of a detainee to respect for his correspondence. With respect to the relevant British legislation the Court made the following distinction:

> in those instances where the norms in question were incompatible with the Convention and where the Court has found a violation of Article 8 to have occurred there was no effective remedy and Article 13 has therefore also been violated. In the remaining case, there is no reason to assume that the applicants' complaints could not have been duly examined by the Home Secretary and/or the English courts and Article 13 has therefore not been violated.[61]

Here, too, the Court seems to be inclined to apply stricter standards if it first has found a violation of one of the rights laid down in the Convention.

That the systematic approach may entail very far-reaching consequences became clear in the *Leander* Case. This case concerned the use of information kept in a secret police-register when assessing a person's suitability for employment on a post of importance for national security. As far as Article 13 was concerned Mr Leander complained that neither he nor his lawyer had been given the right to receive and comment upon the complete material upon which the appointing authority had based its decision not to employ him and that he had not had any right to appeal to an independent authority with power to render a binding decision as to the correctness and release of information kept on him.

---

[59] See *supra* pp. 427-428.
[60] Judgment of 6 September 1978, A.28, p. 31.
[61] Judgment of 25 March 1983, A.61, p. 44.

Consequently, the Court had to review the effectiveness of the remedies which the Swedish legal system provides in cases like this. According to the Court the Chancellor of Justice and the Parliamentary Ombudsman, to both of whom complaints may be addressed, are independent of the Government, but lack the power to render a legally binding decision.[62] The other remedy, to which Mr Leander actually had recourse, consisted in fact of a complaint to the Government. The Court observes that there can be no question about the power of the Government to deliver a binding decision in this respect. On that basis it concludes that 'the aggregate of the remedies set out above (...) satisfies the conditions of Article 13 in the particular circumstances of the instant case.'[63] What the Court omits to refer to, however, is the obvious fact that Government officials are not independent of the Government.

The odd result in the *Leander* Case is premised on the systematic approach set forth by the Court:

> the requirements of Article 13 will be satisfied if there exists domestic machinery whereby, *subject to the inherent limitations of the context*, the individual can secure compliance with the relevant laws.[64]

In the instant case this context dictated that:

> an effective remedy under Article 13 must mean a remedy that is as effective as it can be, having regard to the restricted scope for recourse inherent in any system for the protection of national security.[65]

In sum, the systematic approach may permeate the Court's interpretation to the point where the meaning of Article 13 is virtually nullified. This approach is based upon the assumption that the Convention is to be interpreted in harmony with its logic. However, this assumption should not be a one way street. The question may well be raised whether a meaningful interpretation of Article 13 should not – in certain instances – have a bearing upon the interpretation of other Convention provisions instead of the other way round. This question has not yet been expressly addressed in the Strasbourg case-law despite the pivotal role of the guarantee of an effective remedy within the framework of the concept of the Rule of Law.[66]

3 PROHIBITION OF DISCRIMINATION (ARTICLE 14)

> *The enjoyment of the rights and freedoms set forth in this Convention shall be secured without discrimination on any ground such as sex, race, colour, language, religion, political or other opinion, national or social origin, association with a national minority, property, birth or other status.*

---

[62] Judgment of 26 March 1987, A.116, p. 31.
[63] *Ibidem*, p. 32.
[64] *Ibidem*, p. 30 (emphasis added).
[65] *Ibidem*, p. 32.
[66] See *supra* p. 697.

3.1 Article 14: An Accessory Right

Like Article 13, Article 14 according to its formulation does not grant an independent right, in this case the right to freedom from discrimination. Here again it may be said that such a right ought not to be lacking in the Convention. At the drafting stage of Protocol No. 4 the Consultative Assembly had advocated the inclusion of a general provision to the effect that 'all persons are equal before the law'. However, this proposal was deleted from the draft by the Committee of Experts on the ground of arguments which, weighed against the importance of the elimination of discrimination, cannot be considered very convincing,[67] and which are contradicted more or less by later case-law.

The Convention thus lags behind the developments at the global level, where the elimination of discrimination has received and still receives a good deal of attention, as has been expressed in a number of treaties: the 1952 UN Convention on the Political Rights of Women, the 1951 and 1958 Conventions of the International Labour Organisation on Equal Remuneration and on Discrimination in Employment and Occupation respectively, the 1960 UNESCO Convention against Discrimination in Education, the 1965 UN Convention on the Elimination of All Forms of Racial Discrimination, the 1979 UN Convention on the Elimination of All Forms of Discrimination against Women, and last but not least Article 26 of the UN Covenant on Civil and Political Rights. These as well as other treaties drafted within the framework of the United Nations system constitute an important addition to the, on this point defective, guarantees in the Convention insofar as the Contracting States are parties to those treaties as well.[68]

Since an addition to the Convention in this respect has not been realised thus far,[69] the developments that have taken place in the case-law with respect to Article 14 are of all the greater importance. The case-law of the Commission and the Court presents a rather complex picture because of the necessary relationship between Article 14 and the other substantive Convention provisions and because of the inherent complex nature of questions related to non-discrimination and equality.

Two closely connected questions concerning the relationship between Article 14 and the rights and freedoms of Section I are more or less interwoven in the case-law. On the one hand, there is the question whether Article 14 has its own significance independently of the rights and freedoms protected in the Convention. On the other hand, there is the question whether in relation to those rights and freedoms Article 14 grants an autonomous or only an accessory protection, that

---

[67] See Council of Europe, *Explanatory Reports on the Second to Fifth Protocols to the European Convention for the Protection of Human Rights and Fundamental Freedoms*, H(71)11, pp. 52-53.

[68] For a survey of the status of ratification of the main human rights treaties, see *Netherlands Quarterly of Human Rights*, Vol. 15, No. 3, 1997, pp. 403-416.

[69] A draft additional Protocol to that effect is at the moment being prepared by a group of governmental experts.

is whether or not it can be applied only when any of those rights or freedoms has been violated. Both questions have been summarily answered as follows by the Commission, with a reference to the Court's judgment in the *Belgian Linguistic Case*, to be discussed below:

> the guarantee of Article 14 of the Convention 'has no independent existence in the sense that, under the terms of Article 14, it relates solely to rights and freedoms set forth in the Convention'; nevertheless 'a measure which in itself is in conformity with the requirements of the Article enshrining the right or freedom in question, may however infringe this Article when read in conjunction with Article 14 for the reason that it is of a discriminatory nature'.[70]

The answer to the first-mentioned question is, therefore, that Article 14 has no significance, independently of the rights and freedoms ensured in Section I. In a later case the Commission once again expressed this as follows: 'Article 14 is not directed against discrimination in general but only against discrimination in relation to the rights and freedoms guaranteed by the Convention'.[71]

As will become apparent below, this answer is qualified to a certain extent in connection with the second above-mentioned question concerning the relationship between the protection to be afforded by Article 14 and the requirement that any of the rights and freedoms protected by the Convention has actually been violated.

As regards this second question, the earlier case-law of the Commission seems to point in the direction that the dependent character of Article 14 entails that this provision can be brought up only if there is *prima facie* evidence that one of the rights or freedoms of the Convention has been violated.[72] This accessory character then implies at the same time that the restriction grounds which are provided for in the 'main' article may be advanced for the justification of what in itself constitutes discrimination.[73]

---

[70] Appl. 4045/69, *X* v. *Federal Republic of Germany*, Yearbook XIII (1970), p. 698 (704-706). See also report of 3 March 1982, *Van der Mussele*, B.55 (1987), p. 37.

[71] Appl. 8410/78, *X* v. *Federal Republic of Germany*, D&R 18 (1980), p. 216 (220).

[72] See, *e.g.*, Appl. 808/60, *ISOP* v. *Austria*, Yearbook V (1962), p. 108 (124): since the right to a fair hearing of Art. 6(1) has not been violated, Art. 14 cannot be applicable. See also Appl. 6782/74, *X, Y, and Z* v. *Belgium*, D&R 9 (1978), p. 13 (21); Appl. 7729/76, *Agee* v. *the United Kingdom*, D&R 7 (1977), p. 164 (176); and Appl. 7742/76, *A, B, and Company A.S.* v. *Federal Republic of Germany*, Yearbook XXI (1978), p. 492 (514). For other examples, see M.A. Eissen, 'L' autonomie de l'article 14 de la Convention européenne des Droits de l'Homme dans la jurisprudence de la Commission', in: A. Pedone (ed.), *Mélanges offerts à Polys Modinos. Problèmes Des Droits De l'Homme et De l'Unification Européene*, Paris, 1968, pp. 122-145 (127-132).

[73] In this context, see the decisions in which the Commission held that the German legislation by which homosexuality between men was penalised but that between women was not, might find its justification in the protection of health and morals in the sense of Art. 8(2), and on this ground concluded that the complaint about discrimination was inadmissible as manifestly ill-founded: *inter alia*, Appl. 104/55, *X* v. *Federal Republic of Germany*, Yearbook I (1955-1957), p. 228 (229). See also the somewhat different reasoning in Appl. 5935/72, *X* v. *Federal Republic of Germany*, Yearbook XIX (1976), p. 276 (282-288), where a complaint about the said German legislation was considered manifestly ill-founded, because the criterion of 'necessity of social protection', used by the Federal Republic of Germany, was objective and reasonable in the Commission's view. Two

However, unlike Article 13, Article 14 does not refer solely to cases involving alleged *violations*, but to *every* discriminatory restriction on the enjoyment of the rights and freedoms. Even if a restriction in itself finds support in the relevant provision of the Convention, the restriction must not be applied in a discriminatory way. This interpretation has also found increasing support in the case-law of the Commission, contrary to its above-mentioned position. An example is its decision on *X* v. *the Netherlands*, where an elder of the Reformed Church, in his complaint concerning the General Old Age Insurance Act, alleged among other things that this Act implied a discrimination between two categories of conscientious objectors. After having rejected the invocation of Article 1 of Protocol No. 1 as manifestly ill-founded on the basis of the justification 'in the public interest' mentioned there, the Commission nevertheless instituted a separate inquiry into the complaint concerning Article 14.[74] The Commission clearly set forth its argument for this approach in its report in the *Belgian Linguistic* Case:

> the applicability of Article 14 is not limited to cases in which there is an accompanying violation of another Article. Such a restricted application would deprive Article 14 of any practical value. The sole effect of the discrimination would be to aggravate the violation of another provision of the Convention. Such an interpretation would hardly be compatible with the wording of Article 14: this states that the enjoyment of the rights and liberties set forth in the Convention shall be *secured (doit être assure)* without any discrimination. It thus places on States an obligation which is not simply negative.(...)
> Article 14 is of particular importance in relation to those clauses of the Convention which, while establishing a right or freedom, give States discretionary power with regard to the steps to be taken to ensure the enjoyment of that right or freedom. It is not a normative provision of the same kind as Article 8 of the Convention or Article 2 of the Protocol: it concerns the means or the extent of the enjoyment of rights and freedoms already stated elsewhere. It may happen that different measures taken by a State in respect of different parts of its territory or population entail no breach of the Article in the Convention defining the right in question, but that the differentiation entails a violation if the State's conduct is judged from the point of view of Article 14. The question would then arise of a violation not only of Article 14 but of the right in question as mentioned in the relevant Article in conjunction with Article 14: in fact, an individual who suffers prejudice as a result of a State's infringement of Article 14 does not enjoy the right or freedom in question on the conditions or to the degree laid down in the Convention viewed as a whole.[75]

In this reasoning the Commission still relates Article 14 very closely to one of the other provisions, which in itself has not, but in conjunction with Article 14 has been violated. In a number of later decisions it seems to be going further in

---

complaints against the United Kingdom concerning discrimination between homosexuality of men, on the one hand, and of women, on the other, were, however, declared admissible by the Commission: see Appl. 7215/75, *X* v. *the United Kingdom*, Yearbook XXI (1978), p. 354 (370-374) and Appl. 7525/76, *X* v. *the United Kingdom*, Yearbook XXII (1979), p. 156 (184-186). For the report on Appl. 7215/75, see D&R 19 (1980), p. 66, and for the judgment in the *Dudgeon* Case, see *infra* p. 717.

[74] Appl. 2065/63, Yearbook VIII (1965), p. 266 (272). For other examples, see Eissen, *supra* note 72, pp. 132-145.

[75] Report of 24 June 1965, B.3 (1967), pp. 305-306.

attributing an autonomous character to Article 14. Thus, in its decision in 1973, in *X* v. *the Netherlands*, the Commission first held that Article 1 of Protocol No. 1 was not applicable because social security benefits do not constitute 'possessions' in the sense of that article, but nevertheless examined whether the challenged legislation was discriminatory in its application. The argument it advanced was that 'the allegations which the applicant has made under Article 14 of the Convention *are related to* the right to peaceful enjoyment of possessions and therefore raise an issue under Article 1 of Protocol No. 1'.[76]

In a case against the Federal Republic of Germany the Commission held that for the application of Article 14 it is sufficient 'that the "subject matter" *falls within the scope* of the Article in question'.[77] In between the formulations used by the Commission in these two decisions we find that of its decision in 1975 in another case against the Netherlands: 'Article 14 may be taken in conjunction with another article which need not itself be violated. It is enough for the matter at issue *to be covered by* that other article'.[78]

This case-law shows that the Commission has qualified its above-mentioned view that Article 14 refers only to discrimination in relation to the rights and freedoms protected in the Convention. Nevertheless, it still appears from that case-law that the discrimination complained of must have some connection with one of the rights and freedoms guaranteed.[79]

The development in the case-law as just described would seem to have culminated, – at least for the time being – in a standard formula, used by the Court, according to which:

> Article 14 complements the other substantive provisions of the Convention and the Protocols. It has no independent existence, since it has effect solely in relation to 'the enjoyment of the rights and freedoms' safeguarded by those provisions. Although the application of Article 14 does not necessarily presuppose a breach of those provisions – and to this extent it is autonomous –, there can be no room for its application unless the facts at issue fall within the ambit of one or more of the latter.[80]

---

[76] Appl. 5763/72, Yearbook XVI (1973), p. 274 (296) (emphasis added).

[77] Appl. 5935/72, *X* v. *Federal Republic of Germany*, Yearbook XIX (1976), p. 276 (288) (emphasis added). See also the report of 10 December 1977, *Marckx*, B.29 (1982), p. 49.

[78] Appl. 6573/74, *X* v. *the Netherlands*, D&R 1 (1975), p. 87 (89) (emphasis added).

[79] In Appl. 6573/74, *X* v. *the Netherlands*, D&R 1 (1975), p. 87, the applicant had been disenfranchised and on that basis alleged violation of Art. 14 in conjunction with Art. 10. The Commission held that the right to vote could not be brought under Art. 10, so that Art. 10 could not be invoked nor, therefore, Art. 14. Compare Appl. 8701/79, *X* v. *Belgium*, D&R 18 (1980), p. 250 (254), where the Commission decided 'that, in the present case, the matter at issue (the right to vote) is covered by Article 3 of the First Protocol and that Article 14 may be taken in conjunction with Article 3 of this Protocol'.

[80] Judgment of 28 May 1985, *Abdulaziz, Cabales and Balkandali*, A.94, p. 35. See also the judgment of 28 November 1984, *Rasmussen*, A.87, p. 12; judgment of 23 November 1983, *Van der Mussele*, A.70, p. 22; judgment of 28 October 1987, *Inze*, A.126, p. 17; judgment of 23 October 1990, *Darby*, A.187, p. 12 (the duty to pay taxes falls within the field of application of Art. 1 of Protocol No. 1); judgment of 18 July 1994, *Karlheinz Schmidt*, A.291-B, p. 31; judgment of 16 September 1996, *Gaygusuz*, Reports 1996-IV, Vol. 14, para. 36; and judgment of 21 February 1997, *Van*

This formula makes clear that Article 14 is not independent in the sense that there has to be at least some kind of relation with the rights and freedoms of the Convention; differential treatment in a field which falls outside the scope of the Convention cannot amount to a violation of Article 14.[81] At the same time the judgment referred to bears out that Article 14 is autonomous in the sense that its application does not require the simultaneous violation of one of the Convention's rights or freedoms.

This autonomous character of Article 14 had been recognised earlier by the Court in the *Belgian Linguistic* Case, where it held as follows:

> While it is true that this guarantee [*viz.* the one laid down in Article 14] has no independent existence in the sense that under the terms of Article 14 it relates solely to 'rights and freedoms set forth in the Convention', a measure which in itself is in conformity with the requirements of the Article enshrining the right or freedom in question may however infringe this Article when read in conjunction with Article 14 for the reason that it is of a discriminatory nature.[82]

In the *Karlheinz Schmidt* Case, the Court investigated the claim based upon Article 14 and Article 4(3)(d) after having established that the obligation to pay a financial contribution in lieu of service in the fire brigade fell within the scope of the latter provision. The Court held as follows:

> Like the participants in the proceedings, the Court considers that compulsory fire service such as exists in Baden-Wurttemberg is one of the 'normal civic obligations' envisaged in Article 4 par. 3 (d). It observes further that the financial contribution which is payable – in lieu of service – is, according to the Federal Constitutional Court (...), a 'compensatory charge'. The Court therefore concludes that, on account of its close links with the obligation to serve, the obligation to pay also falls within the scope of Article 4 par. 3 (d). It follows that Article 14 read in conjunction with Article 4 par. 3 (d) applies.[83]

According to the Court, Article 14 constitutes as it were 'an integral part of each of the Articles laying down rights and freedoms'.[84]

Raalte, Reports 1997-I, Vol. 29, para. 33.

[81] See, for instance, Appl. 8493/79, *De Meester* v. *Belgium*, D&R 25 (1982), p. 210 (217): 'In the instant case, the discrimination complained of by the applicant relates to the freedom to apply for a position in the judiciary, a freedom which (...) the Convention does not protect. Consequently, Article 14 of the Convention is not relevant to the instant Case.'

[82] Judgment of 23 July 1968, A.6, p. 33. In later case-law the Court took a similar view. In its judgment in its judgment of 27 October 1975, *National Union of Belgian Police* Case, A.19, p. 19, it held: 'Although the Court has found no violation of Article 11(1), it has to be ascertained whether the difference in treatment complained of by the applicant union contravenes Articles 11 and 14 taken together (...) A measure which in itself is in conformity with the requirements of the Article enshrining the right or freedom in question may therefore infringe this Article when read in conjunction with Article 14 for the reason that it is of a discriminatory nature'. For the Court's view see also the judgment of 6 February 1976, *Swedish Engine Drivers' Union*, A.20, pp. 16-17, and the judgment of 13 June 1979, *Marckx*, A.31, p. 24.

[83] Judgment of 18 July 1994, A.291-B, p. 32.

[84] *Ibidem*, p. 34. Thus also the Commission in its report of 15 July 1983, *Rasmussen*, A.87, p. 22.

Sometimes the Court refrains from looking into Article 14 because it is of the opinion that the same guarantees are to be found in the 'main' provision of the Convention. This has been the case in respect of Article 6:

> The Court judges it superfluous to examine the contested facts also under Article 14 since in the present context the rule of non-discrimination laid down in that provision is already embodied in Article 6 par. 3 (e) (see the Luedicke, Belkacem and Koc judgment, A.29, p. 21).[85]

In summary, the case-law discussed above induces us to conclude that Article 14 contains an autonomous, though complementary guarantee in relation to the rights and freedoms protected in Section I. Even though the 'main' provision on itself has not been violated, the facts may show a violation of that provision in conjunction with Article 14 and a broad interpretation of the scope of the 'main' provision will lead to an expansion of the applicability of Article 14. In the *Gaysusuz* Case, for instance, the Court held that Article 1 of Protocol No. 1 includes pecuniary rights, such as social security benefits.[86] This means that Article 14 also covers distinctions made in a social security system.

3.2 The Subsidiary Guarantee of Article 14

Curiously enough, the Commission and the Court adopt a different attitude when a violation of one of the articles from Section I is actually found. In that case they take the position that in general it is not necessary anymore to make an inquiry into the possible violation of that article in conjunction with Article 14. In other words: in such cases Article 14 is not treated as an autonomous and complementary, but only as a subsidiary guarantee.

In its judgment in the *Airey* Case the Court formulated this view, which was repeated in later judgments, as follows:

> Article 14 has no independent existence; it constitutes one particular element (non-discrimination) of the rights safeguarded by the Convention (...). The Articles enshrining those rights may be violated alone and/or in conjunction with Article 14. If the Court does not find a separate breach of one of those Articles that has been invoked both on its own and together with Article 14, it must also examine the case under the latter Article. On the other hand, such an examination is not generally required when the Court finds a violation of the former Article taken alone. The position is otherwise if a clear inequality of treatment in the enjoyments of the right in question is a fundamental aspect of the case.[87]

Even apart from the fact that the meaning of the formulation 'clear inequality of treatment' is left vague and therefore allows different interpretations in a concrete

---

[85] Judgment of 19 December 1989, *Kamasinski*, A.168, p. 35.

[86] Judgment of 16 September 1996, Reports 1996-IV, Vol. 14, para. 41. See also the judgment of 21 February 1997, *Van Raalte*, Reports 1997-I, Vol. 29.

[87] Judgment of 9 October 1979, A.32, p. 16. See also the judgment of 22 October 1981, *Dudgeon*, A.45, p. 26.

case,[88] the line followed by the Court would appear not to be very consistent. It cannot be appreciated why Article 14 should have another character in cases where a violation of another article of the Convention has been found than in cases where there is no question of a violation of any of these articles as such. As judge Evrigenis rightly observed in his dissenting opinion in the *Airey* Case:

> Discrimination in the enjoyment of a right protected by the Convention contravenes Article 14 irrespective of whether such discrimination lies within or outside the area of violation of that right. The word 'enjoyment', within the meaning of Article 14, must cover all situations that may arise between, at the one extreme, plain refusal of a right protected by the Convention and, at the other, full embodiment of that right in the domestic system.[89]

In the *Dudgeon* Case the Court gave the following argument for the distinction it made with regard to Article 14:

> Once it has been held that the restriction on the applicant's right to respect for his private sexual life gives rise to a breach of Article 8 by reason of its breadth and absolute character (...) there is no useful legal purpose to be served in determining whether he has in addition suffered discrimination as compared with other persons who are subject to lesser limitations on the same right.[90]

From the argumentation of the Court it appears that it has in mind in particular a 'useful legal purpose' from the viewpoint of the individual applicant concerned. Even leaving aside whether in the case at issue the applicant took the same view, and whether the Court's approach not to investigate all the elements of the complaint is correct from a procedural point of view,[91] in our opinion this argument would seem to ignore the fact that decisions of the Court, as the highest organ competent to interpret the Convention, have an effect far exceeding the concrete aspects of the case submitted to it, and that these decisions may therefore also have implications of a more general character.[92]

Nevertheless, the Court's position has become standing case-law. In recent cases the Court does not even adduce arguments anymore for its position. Thus, after having found a violation of Article 8 with respect to one of the applicants – an

---

[88] See the dissenting opinions of judge Evrigenis in the *Airey* Case (A.32, p. 29) and of the judges Evrigenis and Garcia De Entecre in the *Dudgeon* Case (A.45, p. 25), who, unlike the majority of the Court, concluded that in these cases there was decidedly a question of a 'clear inequality of treatment'.

[89] Judgment of 9 October 1979, A.32, p. 29.

[90] Judgment of 22 October 1981, A.45, p. 26.

[91] See the position of judge Matscher in his dissenting opinion in the *Dudgeon* Case: 'In my view, when the Court is called on to rule on a breach of the Convention which has been alleged by the applicant and contested by the respondent Government, it is the Court's duty, provided that the application is admissible, to decide the point by giving an answer on the merits of the issue that has been raised. The Court cannot escape this responsibility by employing formulas that are liable to limit excessively the scope of Article 14 to the point of depriving it of all practical value'; A.45, p. 36.

[92] *Cf.* in this context also what has been observed *supra* p. 223, with regard to the position of the Court in the *De Becker* Case.

illegitimate child whose legal situation under Irish law differed considerably from that of a legitimate child – the Court held with respect to the allegation that Article 14 had been violated:

> Since succession rights were included among the aspects of Irish law which were taken into consideration in the examination of the general complaint concerning the third applicant's legal situation (...) the Court (...) does not consider it necessary to give a separate ruling on this allegation.[93]

In the *Philis* Case the Court held that it would serve 'no useful purpose (...) in determining whether [the applicant] has suffered discrimination' since the Court had established that the right of access to a court had been violated.[94] And in the *Castells* Case the Court refused to deal with a claim based upon Article 14, since it considered this question not to be 'a fundamental aspect of the case'.[95]

3.3 The Scope of Article 14

3.3.1 Distinctions

The concept of equality and the ensuing prohibition of discrimination constitute one of the most complex legal principles. This is not the place to extensively deal with the concept of equality.[96] The following general observations, however, would seem to be at place.

---

[93] Judgment of 18 December 1986, *Johnston*, A.112, p. 31. See also the judgment of 21 September 1993, *Kremzow*, A.268-B, p. 47; judgment of 26 March 1992, *Beldjoudi*, A.234-A, p. 29; and judgment of 22 September 1994, *Hentrich*, A.296-A. In the *Johnston* Case there was one separate opinion in this respect, partly dissenting and partly concurring, of judge De Meyer, who stated (A.112, pp. 39-40): 'I consider that in the present case the Court should, as in the *Marckx* Case, have found not only a violation of the right to respect for private and family life but also a violation, as regards that right, of the principle of non-discrimination. In my view, the latter violation arises from the very fact that, on the one hand, the legal situation of the third applicant, as a child born out of wedlock, is different from that of a child of a married couple and that, on the other hand, the legal situation of the first and second applicants [the unmarried parents of the third applicant] in their relations with or concerning the third applicant is different from that of parents of a child of a married couple in their relations with or concerning that child'. In later cases the Court unanimously considered it unnecessary to examine the complaint under Art. 14 when a violation of a substantive Convention provision had been established.

[94] Judgment of 27 August 1991, A.209, p. 24.

[95] Judgment of 23 April 1992, A.236, p. 25.

[96] For a very intense discussion on the concept of equality, see: P. Westen, 'The Empty Idea of Equality', 95 *Harvard Law Review*, 1982-1983, pp. 537-595; E. Chemerinsky, 'In Defense of Equality: A Reply to Professor Westen', 81 *Michigan Law Review*, 1983, pp. 575-595; A. D'Amato, 'Is Equality a Totally Empty Idea?', 81 *Michigan Law Review*, 1983, pp. 600-603; P. Westen, 'The Meaning of Equality in Law, Science, Math and Morals: A Reply', 81 *Michigan Law Review*, 1983, pp. 604-663; S. Burton, 'Comment on "Empty Ideas": Logical Positivist Analysis of Equality and Rules', 91 *The Yale Law Journal*, 1982, pp. 1136-1152; P. Westen, 'On "Confusing Ideas": Reply', 91 *The Yale Law Journal*, 1982, pp. 1153-1165; A. Greenawolt, 'How Empty is the Idea of Equality?', 83 *Columbia Law Journal*, 1983, pp. 1167-1185; and P. Westen, 'To Lure the Tarantula from Its Hole: a Response', 83 *Columbia Law Journal*, 1983, pp. 1186-1208.

Fundamental principles, like the principle of equality, can play a prominent role in any legal order. Because of their general character and their ensuing wide scope, principles can enhance coherence of and structure within the set of rules of which a legal order is made up. Principles, in other words, can constitute an integrating factor, if they function adequately. This implies that, conversely, the malfunctioning of principles can have very negative consequences for the legal order concerned. To the extent that, for instance, the concept of equality is insufficiently developed, this may lead to unclarity and uncertainty. It is therefore of the utmost importance that the concept of equality is well elaborated at the various levels at which it is to play its integrating role, *i.e.* at that of the legislature, that of the executive branch of government, and that of the judiciary.

For our purposes the latter level is particularly relevant and it therefore suffices to briefly outline the elements which should be taken into account if a given treatment or situation is reviewed for its conformity with the principle of equality and the prohibition of discrimination. These elements are the following. A violation of the principle of equality and non-discrimination arises if there is (a) differential treatment of (b) equal cases, (c) without there being an objective and reasonable justification, or if (d) proportionality between the aim sought and the means employed is lacking.

As far as the first element is concerned, it should be observed from the outset that Article 14 – despite the French text '*sans distinction aucune*' – does not prohibit every difference in treatment. On the contrary, the obligation contained therein may even entail unequal treatment. Indeed, Article 14 is not only concerned with *formal* equality – equal treatment of equal cases – but also with *substantive* equality: unequal treatment of unequal cases in proportion to their inequality. In other words, a difference in treatment which is aimed at eliminating an existing inequality creates substantive equality and is consequently in conformity with Article 14.

Thus, a progressive income tax is not discriminatory provided the progressive measure is proportional and consequently results in a fairer distribution of income than would be the case without it. Obviously, what may be called 'fair' and 'proportional' in such cases is to a large extent still dependent upon the national situation, so that the reasonableness of the national authorities' views on this matter can be reviewed only marginally in Strasbourg. This may explain why a complaint concerning a difference in treatment under the fiscal legislation was declared 'manifestly ill-founded' by the Commission on the basis of the very general argument indeed 'that it is a common incident of taxation laws that they apply in different ways or in different degrees to different persons or entities in the community'.[97]

This marginal approach of the review does not seem to be followed when the Commission or the Court have to investigate an unequal treatment of unequal cases. In the *Moustaquim* Case the Court was asked to pronounce upon the

---

[97] Appl. 511/59, *Gudmundsson v. Iceland*, Yearbook III (1960), p. 394 (424).

unequal treatment of foreigners from third States as compared to foreigners from European Community Member States. According to the Court:

> As for the preferential treatment given to nationals of the other member States of the Communities, there is objective and reasonable justification for it as Belgium belongs, together with those States, to a special legal order. There has accordingly been no breach of Article 14 taken together with Article 8.[98]

In the *Hoffmann* Case, which dealt with the legality of taking into account the religion of one of the parents when deciding about awarding parental rights over the children after divorce, the Court first established whether the applicant could claim to have undergone different treatment. It was only after having accepted that there had been a difference in treatment, based on the ground of religion, that the Court set out to investigate whether this difference amounted to discrimination within the meaning of Article 14.[99]

The second comparative element of the concept of equality consists of the question as to whether the cases at hand are equal or unequal in the relevant respects. In order to be able to answer that question, a yardstick has to be developed, which has to be applied to both cases, and on that basis the ensuing results have to be compared. The crux of the matter is the yardstick or the criteria used for the comparison. Since two cases can always be said to be equal in some respects and unequal in others, for the comparability test to be meaningful, the criteria used have to be adequately related to the object of the provision which prescribes equal treatment. To the extent that such is the case, the comparison which is inherent in the equality test puts in focus the goals underlying the provisions concerned. Consequently, if the comparability test is skipped or merged into the third element – the justification test – the danger arises that the interests protected and/or the goals envisaged in the provisions embodying equality become underexposed. As will be argued below, this danger materialises not infrequently in the Strasbourg case-law.

The comparability test was clearly performed by the Court in its *Van der Mussele* judgment and its judgment in the *Johnston* Case. In both cases the Court refers not to equal, but to 'analogous' situations. In the first-mentioned case it was alleged, *inter alia*, that Belgian *avocats*, unlike medical practitioners, veterinary surgeons, pharmacists, and dentists, were required to provide their services free of charge to indigent persons and that such a difference in treatment constituted arbitrary inequality. The Court pointed out that between the Bar and the other professions cited there existed fundamental differences as to legal status, conditions for entry to the profession, nature of the functions involved, manner of exercise of those functions, *etc.* The Court, consequently, did not find any similarity between the disparate situations in question, because each one was

---

[98] Judgment of 18 February 1991, A.193, p. 20.
[99] Judgment of 23 June 1993, A.255-C, pp. 58-59. *Infra*, we will deal with the Court's reasoning concerning the justification for the difference in treatment.

characterised by a corpus of rights and obligations of which it would be artificial to isolate one specific aspect.[100]

In the *Johnston* Case the two applicants alleged violation of Article 14 on the basis of the fact that the first applicant was unable to obtain a divorce in order subsequently to marry the second applicant, whereas other persons resident in Ireland and having the necessary means could obtain a divorce abroad which could be recognised *de jure* or *de facto* in Ireland. The Court, however, noted that under general Irish rules of private international law foreign divorces are recognised in Ireland only if they have been obtained by persons domiciled abroad and that, therefore, the situations of such persons and of the first and the second applicants could not be regarded as analogous.[101]

In the *Fredin* Case the Court extensively investigated the question whether the closure of applicants' pit amounted to a violation of Article 14. The applicants had not forwarded any arguments (other than their dissimilar treatment) supporting their claim that they had been discriminated against. From this, under the heading of the comparability test, the Court inferred a rule of evidence:

> In their submissions to the Court the applicants did not try to refute the Commission's assessment, nor did they adduce other evidence. Their main argument was, since theirs was the only ongoing business to have been stopped (...), it was for the Government to explain in what respect their case was dissimilar to those of the other enterprises which had been allowed to continue their activities or to give a plausible reason for their exceptional treatment.
> The Court cannot subscribe to this argument. It is true that, in the absence of further information from the Government with regard to the implementation of the 1964 Act and, in particular, the 1973 amendment thereto (...), the Court has to presume that the applicants' pit is the only one to have been closed by virtue of that amendment. However, this is not sufficient to support a finding that the applicants' situation can be considered similar to that of other ongoing business which have not been closed.[102]

In the *Sunday Times* and *The Observer and Guardian* Cases the Court held with respect to the comparability test:

> Article 14 affords protection against different treatment, without an objective and reasonable justification, of persons in similar situations (...). If and so far as foreign newspapers were subject to the same restrictions as [the Sunday Times, the Observer and the Guardian], there was no difference in treatment. If and so far as they were not, this was because they were not subject to the jurisdiction of the English courts and hence were not in a situation similar to that of [the Sunday Times, the Observer and the Guardian].[103]

And in the *Spadeo and Scalabrino* Case the Court held:

---

[100] Judgment of 23 November 1983, A.70, pp. 22-23.
[101] Judgment of 18 December 1986, A.112, pp. 26-27.
[102] Judgment of 18 February 1991, A.192, p. 19.
[103] Judgments of 26 November 1991, A.217, p. 31 and A.216, p. 35 respectively.

Article 14 will be breached where, without objective and reasonable justification, persons in 'relevantly' similar situations are treated differently. For a claim of violation of this Article to succeed, it has therefore to be established, *inter alia*, that the situation of the alleged victim can be considered similar to that of persons who have been better treated.[104]

The category of cases just referred to in fact presents relatively few difficulties, because the comparability test is clearly performed instead of being merged into the justification test, or even skipped completely. Obviously, this is not to say that the comparability test may not be very complex. It is not always easy to decide whether the situations concerned are different or equal, or rather to select the relevant criteria on which that decision has to be based. It requires an intensive investigation into the relevance of the criteria used. In this respect the Court does not go at length in analysing the (dis)similarity of the cases at hand. In most of the cases mentioned *supra* the Court readily accepts the relevance of dissimilarity which can be traced to national jurisdiction, national (or EU) citizenship and the like. In the *Fredin* Case it stated as a rule of evidence that it is up to the applicant to come forward with relevant information leading to the conclusion that his case is a similar case.[105]

3.3.2 Justifications

In the above-mentioned kind of cases the discussion goes to the heart of the matter, *i.e.* whether the situations at hand are equal or unequal. In most instances of the Strasbourg case-law, however, the comparability test is glossed over, and the emphasis is (almost) completely on the justification test.[106] This result ensues from the approach which the Court takes with respect to Article 14. According to the Court, for the purposes of Article 14 a difference of treatment is discriminatory if it has no objective and reasonable justification, that is if it does not pursue a legitimate aim or if there is no reasonable relationship of proportionality between the means employed and the aim sought to be realised.[107] This approach was developed by the Court in its judgment in the *Belgian Linguistic* Case[108] and also used by the Commission. According to this scheme, discrimination contrary to Article 14 occurs when in a given case the existence of the following three elements can be established:

---

[104] Judgment of 28 September 1995, A.315-B, p. 28.

[105] Judgment of 18 February 1991, A.192, p. 19.

[106] *E.g.* judgment of 28 September 1995, *Spadeo and Scalabrino* v. *Italy*, A.315-B. In this case the Court first notes that the similarity of the legal situation of the persons involved has to be established. Subsequently it does not do so, but immediately answers the question whether the distinction drawn was objective and reasonable given the aim of the legislation.

[107] See, for instance, the judgment of 21 February 1986, *James*, A.98, p. 44; judgment of 8 July 1986, *Lithgow*, A.102, p. 66; judgment of 28 October 1987, *Inze*, A.126, p. 18; judgment of 23 October 1990, *Darby*, A.187, p. 12; judgment of 23 June 1993, *Hoffmann*, A.255-C, p. 59; and judgment of 24 February 1995, *McMichael*, A.307-B.

[108] Judgment of 23 July 1968, A.6, p. 34.

(a) the facts found disclose a differential treatment; (b) the distinction does not have a legitimate aim, i.e. it has no objective and reasonable justification having regard to the aim and effects of the measure under consideration; and (c) there is no reasonable proportionality between the means employed and the aim sought to be realized.[109]

Review of an allegedly discriminatory act on the part of a Contracting State by reference to the above criteria has become established case-law of the Strasbourg organs.[110] Since the criteria are cumulative and not alternative, the finding that one of them has not been met may make the investigation of the other ones superfluous.[111]

As was already observed, this approach entails the danger that the interests or goals embodied in the comparability test are implicitly subordinated to those which are enhanced by an objective and reasonable justification, which is often derived from the general interest. An example of this is to be found in the Court's judgment in the *Belgian Linguistic* Case. In that case the Belgian linguistic legislation, which differentiated on a number of points between the different linguistic entities, was found by the Court not to conflict with Article 14, except on a few points; not because that legislation served to abolish existing differences, but because in the Court's opinion the differences in treatment in this case 'strike a fair balance between the protection of the interests of the community and respect for the rights and freedoms safeguarded by the Convention'.[112]

In the Court's view this was not the case only for those provisions in the challenged linguistic legislation where access to the French-language schools in some predominantly Dutch-speaking suburbs of Brussels was refused to those children who did not live in these suburbs. Since, conversely, the Dutch-language schools in those same suburbs were open to anyone irrespective of his place of residence, the majority of the Court held that there was unlawful discrimination with regard to the French-speaking parents as concerned the restriction on the right

---

[109] See the report of 6 July 1976, *Geïllustreerde Pers N.V.* v. *the Netherlands*, D&R 8 (1977), p. 5 (14-15).

[110] See for the case-law of the Court, *supra* note 107. As far as the Commission is concerned, see, *inter alia*, Appl. 5935/72 *X* v. *Federal Republic of Germany*, Yearbook XIX (1976); Appl. 6741/74, *X* v. *Italy*, D&R 5 (1976), p. 83 (85), where a complaint that an Italian law prohibiting the re-establishment of the fascist party was contrary to Art. 14 in conjunction with Arts 9, 10, and 11, was rejected by the Commission on the basis of the argument that 'the difference in treatment (...) is justified by the fact that it pursues a legitimate aim, that of protecting democratic institutions'; Appl. 7729/76, *Agee* v. *the United Kingdom*, D&R 7 (1977), p. 164 (176), where the Commission seems to imply that the status of alien in itself already constitutes an objective and reasonable justification for difference in treatment between nationals and aliens in the field of immigration legislation; and Appl. 7721/76, *X* v. *the Netherlands*, D&R 11 (1978), p. 209 (211), where the Commission seems to imply that the very fact that decisions are taken by an independent court already constitutes an objective and reasonable justification for different results in more or less equal criminal cases: 'it is a general principle that decisions in criminal matters are taken on the particular circumstances of each case.'

[111] Judgment of 21 February 1997, *Van Raalte*, Reports 1997-I, Vol. 29, para. 44.

[112] Judgment of 23 July 1968, A.6, p. 44.

of parents to choose the education of their children in accordance with their own views.[113] It is true that in this case the Court instituted an independent inquiry – five members of the Court precisely blamed the majority for having gone too far in this[114] – but it is obvious that the question of whether an inequality in treatment results in a factual equality or inequality leaves much more scope for an independent inquiry by the organs of the Convention than does the question of whether a given measure does or does not serve the general interest of the State, especially in a politically so delicate matter as the one concerned in this case.

A second clear example is the judgment in the *Dudgeon* Case.[115] In this case Northern-Irish legal provisions were at stake, which contained a general prohibition of certain homosexual acts irrespective of the circumstances in which these took place and of the age of the persons involved. A 35-year old man alleged, *inter alia*, violation of Article 14 because the legislation concerned prevented him from having sexual relations with young men under 21 – even in private and with their consent – whereas the minimum age for admissible heterosexual and lesbian acts was fixed under Northern-Irish law at 17. The Court, dealing with the complaint of inequality of treatment under Article 8 rather than under Article 14, settled the issue summarily as follows. It took as a starting-point:

> the legitimate necessity in a democratic society for some degree of control over homosexual conduct, notably to provide safeguards against the exploitation and corruption of those who are specially vulnerable by reason, for example, of their youth.[116]

Next, it adopted the view that the fixing of ages with a view to affording such safeguards falls within the competence of the national authorities.[117]

That the protection of young persons constitutes a legitimate aim is self-evident. In fact, this point had remained undisputed. The complaint, however, concerned the fact that the legislation of Northern Ireland wanted to realise this aim in very unequal ways with respect to cases which, according to Dudgeon, were comparable in all relevant respects. The Court did not go into this argument of the applicant; it skipped the comparability test and directly applied the justification test in the form of a reference to the protection of the young. This is all the more remarkable as the Court had shortly before held that 'there can be no denial that some degree of regulation of male homosexual conduct, *as* indeed *of other forms of sexual conduct* by means of criminal law can be justified' and in that context had pointed in particular to 'those who are especially vulnerable because they are young, weak in body or mind, inexperienced, or in a state of special, physical, official or economic dependence'.[118]

---

[113] *Ibidem*, pp. 69-70.
[114] See the collective dissenting opinion of the judges Holmback, Rodenbourg, Ross, Wiarda and Mast, A.6, p. 89 (95).
[115] Judgment of 22 October 1981, A.45.
[116] *Ibidem*, p. 25.
[117] *Idem*.
[118] *Ibidem*, p. 20 (emphasis added).

From these considerations it is difficult to draw any other conclusion than that as far as the protection of vulnerable groups – in particular the young – is concerned, homosexual, lesbian, as well as heterosexual acts have to be put on the same line and, therefore, be treated equally.

Something similar holds good for one of the elements of the complaint with which the Court had to deal in the *Abdulaziz, Cabales, and Balkandali* Case.[119] In this case Mrs Balkandali, among other things, alleged discrimination on the ground of birth, because the British immigration rules distinguished between female residents who themselves, or whose parents, were born in the United Kingdom and those with whom this was not the case. It was only for the foreign spouses of women belonging to the first-mentioned group that the British legislation opened the possibility to settle in the United Kingdom. The applicant was a British resident, but she as well as her parents were born in Egypt. Consequently, her Turkish husband was not permitted to take up permanent residence in the United Kingdom.

According to the Government the distinction was designed to avoid the hardship which women having close ties with the United Kingdom would encounter if, on marriage, they were obliged to move abroad in order to stay with their husbands. The Court accepted this justification without a blow. It simply stated that 'there are in general persuasive social reasons for giving special treatment to those whose link with a country stems from birth within it'.[120] It is submitted here that this may be true in general, but in special cases the criterion of birth does not appear to be the most suitable one. For the existence of close ties it is not only decisive whether or not one is born in the country, but particularly also whether or not and, if so, how long one has lived there. It is likely, for instance, that Mrs Balkandali, having lived in the United Kingdom for more than ten years, had closer ties with that country than persons whose parents are born there, but who themselves have taken up residence only recently. In fact, the Court itself conceded that 'it is true that a person who, like Mrs Balkandali, has been settled in a country for several years may also have close ties with it, even if he or she was not born there'.[121]

In other words, as far as the existence of close ties with the United Kingdom is concerned, Mrs Balkandali, although not born there, could in all relevant respects be put on the same line with female residents born in that country. Nevertheless, the Court subordinated the comparability aspect without further argument to the justification aspect.

A more recent example is to be found in the *Holy Monasteries* Case. One of the elements in this case was the complaint that only monasteries belonging to the Greek Church had been affected by a law, enabling expropriation. The Court dismissed this complaint by combining the comparability issue with that of a

---

[119] Judgment of 28 May 1985, A.94.
[120] *Ibidem*, p. 41.
[121] *Idem.*

justification. In essence it reasoned that since the legal status of the monasteries was different, the law, treating them differently, was justified:

> Given the close links between the Greek Church and the applicant monasteries, the distinction made between the latter and the monasteries coming under the Ecumenical Patriarchate of Constantinople or the patriarchates of Alexandria, Antioch and Jerusalem or under the Holy Sepulchre and the Holy Monastery of Sinai or under other denominations and religions does not lack an objective and reasonable justification. Consequently, there is no breach of Article 14 together with the aforementioned Articles of the Convention and of Protocol No. 1.[122]

From the above-mentioned examples it becomes evident that an objective and reasonable justification for differences in treatment is in some cases based on considerations derived from the public interest. It is at least questionable, however, whether such a more or less automatic subordination of individual interests to the public interest – without there being an adequate relationship in all cases between the unequal treatment and the existing inequality which the authorities wish to redress – can find support in the text and the spirit of Article 14. After all, the individual interest of enjoyment of the rights and freedoms without discrimination is given a prominent place there, while no restrictions based on the public interest are provided for, as *is* the case in various other provisions of the Convention.[123] The upshot is in our view that Article 14 in those cases has been deprived of much of its meaning, since only those inequalities for which no objective and reasonable justification can be found are considered to conflict with it, while in determining that justification only a rather loose proportionality test is applied.

This emphasis on the public interest has the additional consequence that the Strasbourg organs leave a wide margin of discretion to the national authorities in appreciating the weight of the public interest concerned as compared with the individual interests at stake.[124] In fact, as a result of the above-mentioned definition of the concept of equality in the case-law it is sometimes added that 'the Contracting States enjoy a certain margin of appreciation in assessing whether and to what extent differences in otherwise similar situations justify a different treatment in law'.[125]

Clearly, this approach would seem to further detract from the importance of Article 14 in the case-law.

An example of this approach is the *Rasmussen* judgment.[126] In this case Mr Rasmussen alleged violation of Article 14, because under a Danish Act of 1960 his right to contest his paternity of a child born during marriage was subject to

---

[122] Judgment of 9 December 1994, A.301-A, p. 39.

[123] See Arts 4(3), 5(1), 6(1), 8(2), 9(2), 10(2), and 11(2) of the Convention; Art. 1 of Protocol No. 1; Art. 2(2) of Protocol No. 4; and Art. 1(2) of Protocol No. 7.

[124] For more details on this so-called 'margin of appreciation', see *supra* pp. 82-96.

[125] See, *e.g.*, the judgment of 8 July 1986, *Lithgow*, A.102, p. 67, where the Court further observed that 'the scope of this margin will vary according to the circumstances, the subject-matter and its background'. See also the judgment of 28 May 1985, *Abdulaziz, Cabales and Balkandali*, A.94, pp. 35-36 and the judgment of 18 July 1994, *Karlheinz Schmidt*, A.291-B, p. 32.

[126] Judgment of 28 November 1984, A.87.

time-limits, whereas his former wife was entitled to institute paternity proceedings at any time. The Court started by skipping the comparability test. It felt that it did not have to deal with the question of whether or not husband and wife were placed in analogous situations, because 'the positions and interests referred to are also of relevance in determining whether the difference of treatment was justified'.[127] With respect to this latter question the Court subsequently relied on the margin of appreciation to be granted to the Contracting States, and pointed out that one of the relevant factors in this respect might be the existence or non-existence of common ground between the laws of the Contracting States on the issue concerned. The Court found no such common ground, as the position of the mother and that of the husband were regulated in different ways in the various legal systems and, therefore, concluded that the Danish authorities were entitled to think that the difference made was justified.[128]

In the same vein the Court finally decided that the proportionality requirement was fulfilled:

> the competent authorities were entitled to think that as regards the husband the aim sought to be realized would be most satisfactorily achieved by the enactment of a statutory rule, whereas as regards the mother it was sufficient to leave the matter to be decided on a case-by-case basis.[129]

Our main concern here is not whether one should agree or disagree with the Court on the outcome of this case. Whatever the outcome, the point is that this approach taken by the Court would seem to water down the significance of Article 14 to the bare minimum. However, in recent years the Court seems in some cases to have strengthened its hold upon Article 14.

Firstly, it should be noted that the Court in the context of Article 14, apart from the examples referred to *supra*, does not frequently refer to the margin of appreciation doctrine.

Secondly, the Court is not very much inclined to assist the Contracting States in looking for 'justifications'. Thus, in the *Pine Valley Developments LTD* Case the Court ruled that there had been a violation of Article 14 since, *inter alia*, the Government did not 'advance any other justification for the difference of treatment between the applicants and the other holders of permissions in the same category as theirs'.[130]

Thirdly, the Court is gradually developing a course whereby some distinctions need to be scrutinised more strictly. So far the following 'suspect' classifications can be detected in the Court's case-law:

---

[127] *Ibidem*, pp. 13-14.
[128] *Ibidem*, p. 15.
[129] *Ibidem*, pp. 15-16.
[130] Judgment of 29 November 1991, A.222, p. 27. See also the judgment of 23 October 1990, *Darby*, A.187, p. 13: 'In fact, the Government stated at the hearing before the Court that they did not argue that the distinction in treatment had a legitimate aim. In view of the above, the measure complained of cannot be seen as having had any legitimate aim under the Convention.'

1) distinctions between legitimate and illegitimate children;[131]
2) distinctions on the basis of sex;[132]
3) distinctions based upon religion;[133]
4) distinctions based upon nationality.[134]

In the area of the first two distinctions a decisive aspect in the Court's case-law is the common ground to be detected in the Member States of the Council of Europe. In, for instance, the above-mentioned *Abdulaziz, Cabales, and Balkandali* Case the Court concluded that there was a violation of Article 14 because of discrimination on the ground of sex, since the British immigration rules made it more difficult for women than for men to obtain a permit to stay with their foreign spouses. As a justification the British Government had adduced the aim of protecting the domestic labour market. In the view of the Court this was not enough reason to justify the difference in treatment, the main argument being that 'the advancement of the equality of the sexes is today a major goal in the Member States of the Council of Europe'.[135] In the *Marckx* Case the Court held that the distinction, made on different points in the Belgian legislation, between legitimate and illegitimate children, was contrary to the Convention.[136] The qualification of distinctions between legitimate and illegitimate children as 'suspect' does, however, not mean that all distinctions between natural and married fathers have to be judged with the same strict standard. In *McMichael*[137] the Court applied the objective and reasonable justification standard without the same strictness as in *Marckx*. The Court did not offer an explanation for this different approach. The conclusion that has to be drawn, however, is that the Court is careful in expanding the scope of the classifications we have identified as 'suspect'.

With regard to the second category the Court added in the *Abdulaziz, Cabales and Balkandali* Case, the *Schuler-Zgraggen* Case, the *Burghartz* Case, the *Karlheinz Schmidt* Case and the *Van Raalte* Case, that since the advancement of the equality of the sexes is a major goal, very weighty reasons would have to be advanced before a difference of treatment on the ground of sex could be regarded as compatible with the Convention.[138]

---

[131] Judgment of 13 June 1979, *Marckx*, A.31; judgment of 29 November 1991, *Vermeire*, A.214-C.
[132] Judgment of 28 May 1985, *Abdulaziz, Cabales and Balkandali*, A.94, p. 38; judgment of 24 June 1993, *Schuler-Zgraggen*, A.263, pp. 21-22; judgment of 22 February 1994, *Burghartz*, A.280-B, p. 29; judgment of 18 July 1994, *Karlheinz Schmidt*, A.291-B, pp. 32-33; judgment of 21 February 1997, *Van Raalte*, Reports 1997-I, Vol. 29, paras 39-44.
[133] Judgment of 23 June 1993, *Hoffmann*, A.255-C, p. 60.
[134] Judgment of 16 September 1996, *Gaysusuz v. Austria,* Reports 1996-IV, Vol. 14, para. 42.
[135] Judgment of 28 May 1985, A.94, p. 37.
[136] Judgment of 13 June 1979, A.31, pp. 17-27.
[137] Judgment of 24 February 1995, *McMichael*, A.307-B.
[138] Respectively the judgment of 28 May 1985, A.94, p. 38; judgment of 24 June 1993, A.263, p. 22; judgment of 22 February 1994, A.280-B, p. 22; judgment of 18 July 1994, A.291-B, pp. 32-33; judgment of 21 February 1997, Reports 1997-I, Vol. 29, para. 39.

With respect to distinctions on the basis of religion no such reasoning, based upon common ground between the Member States, has been given by the Court. In the *Hoffmann* Case the Court simply held:

> Notwithstanding any possible arguments to the contrary, a distinction based essentially on a difference in religion is not acceptable. The Court therefore cannot find that a reasonable relationship of proportionality existed between the means employed and the aim pursued; there has accordingly been a violation of Article 8 taken in conjunction with Article 14.[139]

With regard to distinctions on the basis of nationality the Court held in the *Gaysusuz* Case that:

> very weighty reasons would have to be put forward before the Court could regard a difference of treatment based exclusively on the ground of nationality as compatible with the Convention.[140]

In other areas, the approach taken by the Court implies a more restrictive interpretation of Article 14 as is also witnessed by the judgments of the Court in the *National Union of Belgian Police* Case and in the *Swedish Engine Drivers' Union* Case. In these cases the Court examined whether, with the difference in treatment complained of, the national authorities had a justified aim or whether they pursued 'other and ill-intentioned designs'.[141] The latter conclusion is likely to be reached only in cases of evident arbitrariness. In more recent cases, however, this phrase does not return. And in our opinion the stricter approach adopted by the Court does more justice to the question of discrimination. For instance, a government may decide on grounds derived from the public interest that only children of parents having sufficient means shall be admitted to universities, in order thus to restrict the government expense in the matter of scholarships. For this, objective and perhaps even reasonable criteria may be advanced. Would this not constitute prohibited discrimination? The aim of the Convention is to provide protection not only against unreasonable, but also against reasonable public authorities.

3.4 The Socialising Effect of Article 14

Article 14 may have a socialising effect on the rights and freedoms laid down in the Convention. The Convention is concerned mainly with what might broadly be called freedom rights, which by their nature do not in general require a specific performance on the part of the authorities, but oblige them to refrain from restrictive interference. If, however, the authorities proceed in one way or another to specific performance in a field connected with one or more of the rights in question, they are obliged to do so without discrimination. If, for instance, they

---

[139] Judgment of 23 June 1993, A.255-C, p. 60.
[140] Judgment of 16 September 1996, Reports 1996-IV, Vol. 14, para. 42.
[141] Judgment of 27 October 1975, A.19, p. 21, and the judgment of 6 February 1976, A.20, p. 17 respectively.

proceed to subsidise a particular religious community or to promote education in a particular language, other religious communities or other linguistic communities are in principle entitled to the same treatment. Such a right in itself is not laid down in the Convention, but derives its protection from the operation of Article 14. Here again, however, such a right does not arise when the preferential treatment by the authorities is intended precisely to remove an existing inequality or – according to the case-law developed by the Commission and the Court – may be justified on other objective and reasonable grounds.

3.5 No Exhaustive Enumeration of Discrimination Grounds

As appears from the words 'on any ground such as' (*'ou toute autre situation'*), the enumeration of grounds for a difference in treatment which constitute discrimination is not exhaustive.[142] No distinctive feature or distinctive situation whatsoever may constitute a ground for an unequal treatment, unless that inequality is precisely intended to remove for the person concerned the disadvantages resulting from the distinctive feature or the distinctive situation.

It is important to note, however, that the scope or the intensity of the review of the Court may and probably will vary according to the grounds of the distinction made. *Supra* it was concluded from the case-law of the Court that some distinctions have to be treated with a more strict scrutiny than others. Another factor, however, that could play a role is the *area* in which a specific distinction has been made. When it concerns purely economic regulations the Court probably will be more reluctant to interfere than when it has to cope with a distinction that touches upon essential elements of freedom rights.

4 DEROGATION FROM THE RIGHTS AND FREEDOMS IN CASE OF A PUBLIC EMERGENCY (ARTICLE 15)

1. *In time of war or other public emergency threatening the life of the nation any High Contracting Party may take measures derogating from its obligations under this Convention to the extent strictly required by the exigencies of the situation, provided that such measures are not inconsistent with its other obligations under international law.*
2. *No derogation from Article 2, except in respect of deaths resulting from lawful acts of war, or from Articles 3, 4 (paragraph 1) and 7 shall be made under this provision.*
3. *Any High Contracting Party availing itself of this right of derogation shall keep the Secretary General of the Council of Europe fully informed of the measures which it has taken and the reasons therefor. It shall also inform the Secretary General of the Council of Europe when such measures have ceased to operate and the provisions of the Convention are again being fully executed.*

---

[142] See, for instance, the judgment of 21 February 1986, *James*, A.98, p. 44.

4.1 Introduction: Article 15; A Special Case

Article 15 contains a general authorisation for temporary derogation from the rights and freedoms laid down in the Convention – insofar as they are not exempted in the second paragraph – in case of a public emergency threatening the life of the nation. As the Secretariat of the Commission observes in a publication, here 'the overriding rights of the State to protect its democratic institutions' are concerned.[143] This general authorisation is additional to the special restriction clauses, which are incorporated into some articles of the Convention and in which 'national security' and 'public safety' are also mentioned as grounds for such restrictions.[144]

When a Contracting State avails itself of the possibility of derogation provided for in Article 15 the consequences may be so far-reaching and the number of people affected may be so large that effective supervision on the part of the Strasbourg organs is of the utmost importance. Indeed, particularly in times of emergency threatening the life of the nation protection of human rights at the national level is likely to be defective. On the other hand, victims of violations in cases of emergency may, in general, be expected to be hesitant to lodge complaints while national courts may be under considerable pressure, assuming that possibilities for lodging complaints and for judicial review are not suspended at all precisely as a result of the derogation on the part of the State concerned.

It may be observed at the outset that effective Strasbourg supervision with respect to Article 15 has not yet materialised. This is mainly due to the approach taken by the Court and the Commission on the basis of the well-known doctrine of the margin of appreciation.

4.2 Article 15 and the Application of the Doctrine of the Margin of Appreciation

In connection with the application of Article 15, just as with respect to the special restriction clauses, two questions arise: (1) are the values which are to be protected by means of this derogation from or restriction of rights and freedoms threatened, and (2) are the legislation enacted, the measures taken, or the penalties imposed 'necessary' or, as Article 15 formulates it even more restrictively, 'strictly required' to safeguard these values?

The demarcation between, on the one hand, the discretion of the national authorities and, on the other hand, the review of its use by the Strasbourg organs, has been defined by the Commission in its report in the first case in which Article 15 was at issue: *Greece* v. *the United Kingdom*. In this case the Commission took the position that, on the one hand, the Strasbourg organs are competent to institute

---

[143] *Case-Law Topics*, No. 4, 'Human Rights and their limitations', Strasbourg, 1973, p. 3.
[144] See Arts 8(2), 9(2), 10(2) and 11(2) of the Convention; Art. 2(3) of Protocol No. 4; and Art. 1(2) of Protocol No. 7.

an inquiry into both the above-mentioned questions, but that, on the other hand 'the Government should be able to exercise a certain measure of discretion in assessing the extent strictly required by the exigencies of the situation'.[145]

Although the Commission in its report referred to the 'margin of appreciation' of the Greek Government,[146] it subsequently gave a negative answer to the first question on the basis of a detailed examination of testimony, publications in the press and other information besides the views of the Governments involved.[147] There is hardly any evidence in that report of a restriction to a marginal review of the reasonableness of the position of the Greek Government.

In the *Lawless* Case the Court set forth as a starting point for the Strasbourg supervision 'whereas it is for the Court to determine whether the conditions laid down in Article 15 for the exercise of the exceptional right of derogation have been fulfilled in the present case'.[148] Subsequently, with regard to the first of the above-mentioned questions the Court held that 'the existence at the time of a 'public emergency threatening the life of the nation' was *reasonably* deduced by the Irish Government from a combination of several factors'.[149] However, with regard to the second question, the Court appeared to institute an independent inquiry, which then resulted in the conclusion that the condition that the measures taken must be 'strictly required' had been satisfied.[150]

If on the basis of the above-mentioned case-law a lack of clarity concerning the attitude of the Strasbourg organs has arisen, this seems to have been removed by the Court in *Ireland* v. *the United Kingdom*. There the Court adopted the line of the 'margin of appreciation' with respect to Article 15, which, like the Commission, it had followed with respect to the imposition of special restrictions in the *Belgian Linguistic* Case and in the *Handyside* Case.[151] The judgment of the Court granting the State quite a wide margin of appreciation contains the following observations:

> It falls in the first place to each Contracting State, with its responsibility for 'the life of [its] nation', to determine whether that life is threatened by a 'public emergency' and, if so, how far it is necessary to go in attempting to overcome the emergency. By reason of their direct and continuous contact with the pressing needs of the moment, the national authorities are in principle in a better position than the international judge to decide both on the presence of such an emergency and on the nature and scope of derogations necessary to avert it. In this matter Article 15 § 1 leaves those authorities a wide margin of appreciation. Nevertheless, the States do not enjoy an unlimited power in this respect. The Court, which, with the Commission, is responsible for ensuring the

---

[145] Appl. 176/56, Yearbook II (1958-1959), p. 174 (176).
[146] Report of 5 November 1969, *Greek* Case, Yearbook XII (1969), p. 72.
[147] *Ibidem*, pp. 73-76.
[148] Judgment of 1 July 1961, A.3, p. 55.
[149] *Ibidem*, p. 56 (emphasis added).
[150] *Ibidem*, pp. 57-59.
[151] See *infra* pp. 772-773.

observance of the States' engagements (Article 19), is empowered to rule on whether the States have gone beyond the 'extent strictly required by the exigencies' of the crisis (...). The domestic margin of appreciation is thus accompanied by a European supervision.[152]

In exercising in this case the European supervision, mentioned at the end of the quotation, the Court indeed gave evidence of instituting an independent inquiry into the necessity of the derogations, but with respect to those points where differences of opinion were possible as to the interpretation of facts and the effectiveness of measures, it confined itself to an assessment of the reasonableness of the position taken in the matter by the respondent Government.[153] The Court has persisted in this approach up to the present. In its most recent case dealing with Article 15 it was argued by the applicants as well as a number of authoritative non-governmental organisations that strict scrutiny was required by the Court when examining derogation from fundamental guarantees for the protection of detainees. Nevertheless, the Court explicitly held that also in matters like these a wide margin of appreciation had to be left to the national authorities.[154]

Several concurring and dissenting opinions quite severely criticised this approach favoured by the Court's majority. Judge Pettiti opined that 'Even if it is accepted that States have a margin of appreciation (...), the situation relied on must be examined by the European Court.'[155] He concluded that in the *Brannigan and Mcbride* Case 'the Government's action fell outside the margin of appreciation which the Court is able to recognise'.[156]

Judge Martens concurred with the majority, but 'only after considerable hesitation'.[157] He criticises the majority's margin of appreciation approach for being solely based on a 15 years old precedent, *i.e.* the above-mentioned 1978 *Ireland* v. *the United Kingdom* judgment. His line of reasoning is noteworthy:

> Since 1978 'present day conditions' have considerably changed. (...) the situation within the Council of Europe has changed dramatically. It is therefore by no means evident that standards which may have been acceptable in 1978 are still so. The 1978 view of the Court as to the margin of appreciation under Article 15 was, presumably, influenced by the view that the majority of the then member states of the Council of Europe might be assumed to be societies which (...) had been democratic for a long time and, as such, were fully aware both of the importance of the individual right to liberty and of the inherent danger of giving too wide a power of detention to the executive. Since the accession of eastern and central European States that assumption has lost much of its pertinence.[158]

---

[152] Judgment of 18 January 1978, A.25, pp. 78-79.
[153] *Ibidem*, pp. 81-82 and 92-93.
[154] Judgment of 26 May 1993, *Brannigan and McBride* v. *the United Kingdom*, A.252-B, p. 17.
[155] *Ibidem*, p. 29.
[156] *Ibidem*, p. 33.
[157] *Ibidem*, p. 40.
[158] *Idem.*

It is interesting to compare this view with judge Makarczyk's observations on the same topic:

> The principle that a judgment of the Court deals with a specific case and solves a particular problem does not, in my opinion apply to cases concerning the validity of a derogation made by a State under Article 15 of the Convention. A derogation made by any State affects not only the position of that State, but also the integrity of the Convention system of protection as a whole. It is relevant for other member States – old and new – and even for States aspiring to become Parties which are in the process of adapting their legal systems to the standards of the Convention. For the new Contracting Parties, the fact of being admitted, often after long periods of preparation and negotiation, means not only the acceptance of the Convention obligations, but also recognition by the community of European States of their equal standing as regards the democratic system and the rule of law. In other words, what is considered by the old democracies as a natural state of affairs, is seen as a privilege by the newcomers which is not to be disposed of lightly. A derogation made by a new Contracting Party from Eastern and Central Europe would call into question this new legitimacy and is, in my opinion, quite improbable. Any decision of the Court concerning Article 15 should encourage and confirm this philosophy. In any event it should not reinforce the views of those in the new member states for whom European standards clash with the interests which they have inherited from the past. I am not convinced that the reasoning adopted by the majority fulfils these requirements.[159]

Judge Martens rejects the majority's formula by which the national authorities are granted a wide margin of appreciation not only because he is of the opinion that it is outdated, but also for reasons of principle. As to the question whether there is an objective ground for derogating which meets the requirements laid down in the opening words of Article 15, judge Martens holds:

> inevitably, in this context, a certain margin of appreciation should be left to the national authorities. There is, however, no justification for leaving them a *wide* margin of appreciation because the Court, being the 'last-resort' protector of the fundamental rights and freedoms guaranteed under the Convention, is called upon to strictly scrutinise every derogation by a High Contracting Party from its obligations.[160]

Furthermore, the question as to whether the derogation is to the extent strictly required by the exigencies of the situation, according to judge Martens:

> calls for a closer scrutiny than the words 'necessary in a democratic society' which appear in the second paragraphs of Articles 8-11. Consequently, with respect to this (...) question there is, if at all, certainly no room for a *wide* margin of appreciation.[161]

Judge Makarczyk also questioned the position taken by the majority on the margin of appreciation as far as its consequences with respect to the issue of the duration of a derogation were concerned by observing that the approach of the majority:

> does not contribute to reassure the international community that the Court is doing all that is legally possible for the full applicability of the Convention to be restored as soon as possible. On the contrary, the present wording of the judgment tends rather to perpetuate the status quo and opens, for the derogating State, an unlimited possibility

---

[159] *Ibidem* p. 42.
[160] *Ibidem*, p. 41.
[161] *Idem.*

of applying extended administrative detention for an uncertain period, to the detriment of the integrity of the Convention system and, I firmly believe, of the derogating State itself.[162]

The latter observation implies, it might be added, that in judge Makarczyk's opinion the Court's *Brannigan and McBride* judgment has also been to its own detriment; the judgment has not fostered confidence that the Court is able to provide an effective type of supervision with respect to Article 15. This raises the question whether the Court is the most appropriate body to conduct the examination on the basis of which it has to be judged whether the situation in a State meets the requirements laid down in Article 15(1) and, if so, whether the measures taken by the national authorities are strictly required in the light of that situation. At any rate it is clear that the Court is prepared to grant the Contracting States a very wide margin of appreciation and this attitude does not fail to make its impact felt on the interpretation and application of the various elements of Article 15.

4.3 'Time of War'

The interpretation of the term 'time of war' in the first paragraph of Article 15 does not raise great problems. This situation is present at any rate in case of an official declaration of war on the part of, or directed against, the State in question, or when that State is actually involved in an international armed conflict. Whether a 'time of war' can also be considered to exist in case of a civil war, a question that is of great importance for the applicability of humanitarian law of war, is not very relevant here on account of the addition 'or other public emergency threatening the life of the nation'.

4.4 'Public Emergency Threatening the Life of the Nation'

In its report in the *Lawless* Case the Commission gave the following definition of 'public emergency threatening the life of the nation':

> an exceptional situation or crisis of emergency which affects the whole population and constitutes a threat to the organised life of the community of which the State is composed.[163]

This definition was adopted by the Court in its judgment in this case.[164] In that judgment the Court held that the Irish Government could have reasonably deduced that there was a 'public emergency' at a given moment, on the basis of a combination of the following factors: (1) the existence in the territory of the Republic of a secret army which was engaged in unconstitutional activities and

---

[162] *Ibidem*, p. 42.
[163] Report of 19 December 1959, B.1 (1961), p. 82.
[164] Judgment of 1 July 1961, A.3, p. 56.

was using violence to attain its ends; (2) the fact that this army was also operating outside the territory of the State, thus seriously jeopardising the relation of the Republic with its neighbour; and (3) the steady and alarming increase in terrorist activities in the period preceding the decisive moment.[165]

In the *Greek* Case the above-mentioned definition was elaborated by the Commission. It pointed out beforehand that the French – authentic – text of the *Lawless* judgment, in which the Court adopted its definition, mentioned not only the word '*exceptionnel*', but also the word '*imminent*'. In the opinion of the Commission an emergency must have the following characteristics if it is to be qualified as a 'public emergency' in the sense of Article 15:

1) It must be actual or imminent.
2) Its effects must involve the whole nation.
3) The continuance of the organised life of the community must be threatened.
4) The crisis or danger must be exceptional, in that the normal measures or restrictions, permitted by the Convention for the maintenance of public safety, health and order, are plainly inadequate.[166]

The arguments of the Greek Government for its submission that there was a 'public emergency' were summarised as follows by the Commission: (1) communist danger, (2) crisis of constitutional government, and (3) crisis of public order.[167] In support of its submission the Greek Government had put forward in particular that the communists were preparing an armed revolt within the State and from outside and were planning to seise power, that the other political parties were collaborating with the communists and were corrupt, that the numerous changes of government had rendered the administration of the country impossible and the constant strikes had brought the State on the verge of bankruptcy, and that the violent demonstrations had led to anarchy.[168] In the Commission's opinion, however, the Government had not thus sufficiently demonstrated that the situation in Greece showed the above-mentioned characteristics at the decisive moment.[169]

In *Ireland* v. *the United Kingdom* both the Commission and the Court, on the basis of a very brief finding, concluded that the 'public emergency' invoked by the British Government indeed appeared to exist in Northern Ireland, and observed that this fact had not been contested by Ireland.[170] Since large-scale violent actions by a paramilitary organisation were concerned, which were largely directed against the British security forces, the conclusion of the Commission and the Court can indeed hardly be disputed. The brief finding might, however, create the impression that, if the existence of a 'public emergency' in the sense of Article

---

[165] *Idem.*
[166] Report of 5 November 1969, Yearbook XII (1969), p. 72.
[167] *Ibidem*, p. 45.
[168] *Ibidem*, pp. 46-71.
[169] *Ibidem*, pp. 76 and 100.
[170] Report of 25 January 1976, B.23-I (1980), p. 94; judgment of 18 January 1978, A.25, p. 78.

15 has not been disputed by the applicant, the Commission and the Court need not institute an independent inquiry into it anymore.

In its most recent judgment concerning Article 15 the Court has avoided creating that impression. In the *Brannigan and Mcbride* Case the applicants did not dispute the existence of an emergence situation. In this case too the Court confined itself to finding that 'there can be no doubt that such a public emergency existed at the relevant time' in the light of 'the extent and impact of terrorist violence in Northern Ireland and elsewhere in the United Kingdom'. The Court was explicitly 'Recalling its case-law in Lawless v. Ireland (...) and Ireland v. the United Kingdom', but meaningfully added 'and making its own assessment'.[171]

4.5 'Strictly Required by the Exigencies of the Situation'

In the determination of the 'strictly required' character of the derogating measures various elements may play a role, notably the necessity of the derogations to cope with the threat and the proportionality of the measures in view of the threat. In its *Brannigan and McBride* judgment the Court found, more specifically, that it had to give appropriate weight to such relevant factors as 'the nature of the rights affected by the derogation, the circumstances leading to, and the duration of, the emergency situation.'[172]

In the *Lawless* Case the Court held that the requirement of necessity had been satisfied, because the Irish Government had proved that the existing legislation and the normal procedures for the maintenance of the legal order were not sufficient. The requirement of proportionality had been satisfied in the Court's opinion, because, on the one hand, the Irish Government had not proceeded to take more far-reaching measures, such as the complete closure of the frontiers, while, on the other hand, in the internment system a number of guarantees against abuse of power by the authorities had been incorporated.[173]

4.6 Duration of the Emergency

The issue of the duration of the measures taken by the Irish Government was not examined by the Court in the *Lawless* Case, evidently because the Court held that the situation called for the same stringent measures during the entire relevant period. It is, however, conceivable that, even if it can be established that the 'public emergency' continues, the effect of the measures adopted or of certain developments has been such that from a given moment continuation of the derogations to the same extent can no longer be deemed 'strictly required'.

In *Ireland v. the United Kingdom* it had been argued by the Irish Government that the English internment measures had proved ineffective and after a given

---

[171] Judgment of 26 May 1993, A.258-B, p. 50.
[172] *Ibidem*, pp. 49-50.
[173] Judgment of 1 July 1961, A.3, pp. 57-59.

point in time had not therefore been applied any longer. With respect to this the following position was taken by the Court:

> It is certainly not the Court's function to substitute for the British Government's assessment any other assessment of what might be the most prudent or most expedient policy to combat terrorism. The Court must do no more than review the lawfulness, under the Convention, of the measures adopted by that Government from 9 August 1971 onward. For this purpose the Court must arrive at its decision in the light, not of a purely retrospective examination of the efficacy of those measures, but of the conditions and circumstances reigning when they were originally taken and subsequently applied.[174]

A curious reaction to a curious argument! From the side of the applicant State one would have expected the argument that the respondent State has gone to unnecessary lengths with its measures, and in doing so has exceeded the limit of proportionality, while the argument of Ireland seems to have the opposite purport, *viz.* that England has not gone far enough in fighting the IRA. But in itself the argument is valid: if certain measures are not adequate for checking or restricting the dangers against which they are aimed, those measures cannot be considered necessary and must be modified or abolished as soon as that inefficacy is established. It is certainly for the Court to judge whether this has been done and, if so, whether it has been done in good time, although the Court must allow the national authorities sufficient discretion to assess that efficacy themselves. In evident cases of inefficacy, however, the conditions of Article 15 have not been satisfied. By establishing this, the Strasbourg organs indeed do 'no more than review the lawfulness, under the Convention, of the measures', since this is a matter of review for conformity with the condition that they must be 'strictly required'.

In fact, in one of the subsequent paragraphs of the same judgment the Court did go into the obligation of the State to always ascertain, when applying derogations under Article 15, whether and to what extent the scope of these derogations can be restricted. Thus the Court found with respect to the right to judicial review, which Article 5(4) grants to everyone who has been deprived of his liberty, that it would have been preferable if this had been provided for immediately upon the introduction of the internment measures, but that the British Government *might* have been of the opinion that this was not yet possible in the initial period: 'The interpretation of Article 15 must leave a place for progressive adaptations'.[175]

In the *Brannigan and Mcbride* Case the same issue came up in the form of the question of whether the derogation had been declared prematurely by the British authorities. According to the applicants this was indeed the case because at the time of declaring the emergency the Government had not reached a firm and final view on the need to derogate and had announced that it required a further period of reflection and consultation. The Court rejected this line of reasoning:

---

[174] Judgment of 18 January 1978, A.25, p. 82.

[175] *Ibidem*, p. 83.

The validity of the derogation cannot be called into question for the sole reason that the Government had decided to examine whether in the future a way could be found of ensuring greater conformity with Convention obligations. Indeed, such a process of continued reflection is not only in keeping with Article 15 para. 3 which requires permanent review of the need for emergency measures but is also implicit in the very notion of proportionality.[176]

4.7 The Nature of the Rights Affected

This element in the evaluation of whether a derogation is strictly required also came up in the *Brannigan and McBride* Case. That case concerned Article 5(3) and (5). The Court started out its examination by stressing that:

> judicial control of interference by the executive with the individual's right to liberty provided for by Article 5 is implied by one of the fundamental principles of a democratic society, namely the rule of law.[177]

Against the background of that point of departure the way in which the Court subsequently deals with the Government's assertion that control of extended detention by a judge or other officer authorised by law to exercise judicial control was not possible, comes somewhat as a surprise. In the final analysis the Court concluded that the Government had not overstepped its margin of appreciation in deciding against judicial control because:

> in the context of Northern Ireland, where the judiciary is small and vulnerable to terrorist attacks, public confidence in the independence of the judiciary is understandably a matter to which the Government attach great importance.[178]

This is quite a remarkable line of reasoning and it is, therefore, no surprise that various dissenters reacted in quite strong terms against this position of the majority. According to judge Pettiti 'it is difficult to believe that the independence of a judge would be undermined because he took part in proceedings making it possible to grant or approve an extension of detention'.[179]

In the same vein judge Walsh observed that:

> The Government's plea that it is motivated by a wish to preserve public confidence in the independence of the judiciary is, in effect, to say that such confidence is to be maintained or achieved by not permitting them to have a role in the protection of the personal liberty of the arrested person. One would think that such a role was one which the public would expect the judges to have. It is also to be noted that neither Parliament nor the Government appears to have made any serious effort to rearrange the judicial procedure or jurisdiction, in spite of being advised to do so by the persons appointed to review the system, to cater for the requirement of Article 5 para. 3 in cases of the

---

[176] Judgment of 26 May 1993, A.258-B, p. 52.

[177] *Ibidem*, pp. 50-51.

[178] *Ibidem*, p. 54.

[179] *Ibidem*, p. 61.

type now under review. It is the function of the national authorities so to arrange their affairs as not to clash with the requirements of the Convention. The Convention is not to be remoulded to assume the shape of the national procedures.[180]

On the one hand in the *Brannigan and McBride* Case the Court *expressis verbis* sets forth the nature of the right affected as a specific element in the evaluation of whether a derogation is strictly required by the exigencies of the situation. On the other hand, however, the judgment makes it difficult to escape the impression that the Court in fact attaches hardly any weight to the nature of the right concerned as a separate element within the framework of the said evaluation. As far as the Convention is concerned it is difficult to come up with a more essential provision than the requirement of judicial control of interference by the executive with the individual's right to liberty which, as the Court itself reiterated, is implied by one of the fundamental principles of a democratic society, namely the Rule of Law.

Despite the fact that this fundamental requirement was at stake in the *Brannigan and McBride* Case and despite convincing arguments to the contrary, as for instance set forth in the dissenting opinions, the Court approved the Government's derogation. As to future cases one wonders what circumstances have to prevail for the Court to consider a derogation not justified on the basis of the nature of the rights affected, particularly when 'less fundamental' rights are concerned.

4.8 'Provided that such Measures are not Inconsistent with its Other Obligations Under International Law'

The provision in Article 15 that the measures adopted must not be inconsistent with the other obligations resting on the State under international law has played little part in the case-law thus far. In the *Lawless* Case – *ex officio*[181] –, in *Ireland* v. *the United Kingdom*[182] and in the *Brannigan and McBride* Case[183] the Court held that no evidence was found of any infringement of this condition. To the extent that obligations under other international conventions concerning human rights are concerned, the same condition also follows from Article 60 of the Convention.[184]

In this context it is of interest that the UN Covenant on Civil and Political Rights in Article 4 provides for the possibility of derogations also in case of a 'public emergency', but that more rights are 'non-derogable' there. The enumeration of Article 4(2) of the UN Covenant on Civil and Political Rights also includes Article 11 (the prohibition of imprisonment merely on the ground of inability to fulfil a contractual obligation) and Article 18 (freedom of thought,

---

[180] *Ibidem*, p. 66.
[181] Judgment of 1 July 1961, A.3, p. 60.
[182] Judgment of 18 January 1978, A.25, p. 84.
[183] Judgment of 26 May 1993, A.258-B, p. 57.
[184] On this, *supra* p. 6.

conscience and religion). A Contracting State which has also ratified the UN Covenant on Civil and political Rights therefore cannot take derogatory measures with respect to those rights either, unless, where the freedom to manifest one's religion or beliefs is concerned, the restriction is one which is supported by the third paragraph of Article 18 of the UN Covenant on Civil and Political Rights. The Court is unlikely to easily reach the conclusion that a Contracting State is in violation of Article 15 because the measures adopted are inconsistent with Article 4 of the UN Covenant on Civila and Political Rights. In the *Brannigan and McBride* Case the applicants alleged a violation of the requirement contained in the Covenant's Article 4 that an emergency has to be officially proclaimed. The Court did go into the plausibility of this argument (and rejected it), but only after having observed that it is not the Court's 'role to seek to define authoritatively the meaning of the terms "officially proclaimed" in Article 4 of the Covenant.'[185] Apart from the UN Covenant on Civil and Political Rights, other provisions that may be thought of are those of the Geneva Conventions concerning humanitarian law, which are intended to be applied in situations such as those mentioned in Article 15. The wide formulation 'other obligations under international law' also covers obligations under other than human rights and humanitarian conventions, under customary international law and under generally recognised legal principles. It is evident, however, that on this point the Strasbourg organs will not lightly go beyond the scope of conventional law, unless they can rely on clear international case-law or an express consensus within the community of States.

Besides the conditions mentioned in Article 15 itself, the exercise of the power of derogation granted in that article is also subject to conditions ensuing from a number of other articles of the Convention, *viz.* Articles 14, 17, 18 and, as stated above, Article 60.

4.9 Paragraph 2: Non-Derogable Rights

The second paragraph of Article 15 contains an enumeration of the provisions of the Convention from which no derogation may be made under any circumstances, not even under those mentioned in the first paragraph: these provisions are non-derogable. In Chapter VII, in the discussion of each individual right and freedom, the issue has been addressed whether a particular right or freedom is non-derogable.

4.10 Paragraph 3: Information to be Provided to the Council of Europe

As to the information to be given to the Secretary General of the Council of Europe, as prescribed in the third paragraph, the Court held in the *Lawless* Case that this must take place 'without delay' after the entry into force of the measures concerned. A delay of twelve days was still considered to be in conformity with

---

[185] Judgment of 26 May 1993, A.258-B, p. 57.

this obligation.[186] The Commission, in its report, had used the words 'without any avoidable delay',[187] thus evidently indicating that allowance must be made for the special difficulties with which a government may be confronted in case of a 'public emergency'. A delay of four months in the *Greek* Case, however, was considered too long by the Commission.[188] No special form is prescribed for the information, nor need it be stated expressly that it is intended as information in the sense of Article 15(3).[189] However, in the words of the Commission, the Government must:

> furnish sufficient information concerning them [the measures in question] to enable the other High Contracting Parties and the European Commission to appreciate the nature and extent of the derogation from the provisions of the Convention which these measures involve,[190]

while the information must also be sufficient to enable them to infer therefrom the reasons for the measures.[191] It is solely for the Strasbourg organs to judge whether the condition of the third paragraph has been fulfilled. However, as appears from the above-mentioned words 'reasonable' and 'avoidable', here again these organs leave some discretion to the Government concerned.

What are the consequences if a Contracting State makes use of the possibilities of derogation provided for in the Convention, but omits to inform the Secretary General thereof in the way prescribed in Article 15(3)? Since the Convention does not explicitly lay down such consequences, a number of variants are conceivable. Failure to inform the Secretary General might rule out reliance on Article 15 for the justification of derogation measures taken. On the other hand, there is the possibility that non-observance of Article 15(3) has no (legal) consequences at all. The question here referred to arose in the joined Applications of *Cypres* v. *Turkey*, where Cyprus complained about the action of the Turkish invasion forces.[192] In the first case of *Greece* v. *the United Kingdom* and in the *Lawless* Case this question had also already arisen, but then in a more indirect way. In these cases the Commission had 'reserved its view as to whether failure to comply with the requirements of Art. 15(3) may "attract the sanction of nullity or some other sanction"'.[193] The question was raised expressly, however, in the joined applications just mentioned. The Turkish Government had not furnished any information as referred to in Article 15(3), because, as it submitted, it had no

---

[186] Judgment of 1 July 1961, A.3, p. 62.
[187] Report of 19 December 1959, B.1 (1961), p. 73.
[188] Report of 5 November 1969, Yearbook XII (1969), p. 43. See also the dissenting opinion of Commission member Delahaye, Yearbook XII (1969), pp. 43-44.
[189] Report of 19 December 1959, *Lawless*, B.1 (1961), p. 73. See also the judgment of 1 July 1961 in this case, A.3, p. 62.
[190] *Idem*.
[191] Judgment of 1 July 1961, *Lawless*, A.3, p. 62.
[192] Appls 6780/74 and 6950/75, Yearbook XVIII (1975), p. 82.
[193] Report of 10 July 1976, *Cyprus* v. *Turkey* (not officially published), para. 526.

jurisdiction over the Northern part of Cyprus occupied by the Turkish forces.[194] The Commission, on the contrary, had held in its decision on the admissibility that:

> the Turkish armed forces in Cyprus brought any person or property there 'within the jurisdiction' of Turkey, in the sense of Art. 1 of the Convention, 'to the extent that they exercise control over such persons or property'.[195]

During its examination of the merits the Commission was therefore confronted with the question of the consequences of the Turkish Government's failure to provide the relevant information. Despite the fact that this question thus became prominent, the Commission, curiously enough, began its answer with the following finding: In the present case the Commission still does not consider itself called upon generally to determine the above question'.[196] It continued with the following words:

> It finds, however, that, in any case, Art. 15 requires some formal and public act of derogation, such as a declaration of martial law or state of emergency, and that, where no such act has been proclaimed by the High Contracting Party concerned, although it was not in the circumstances prevented from doing so, Art. 15 cannot apply.[197]

Thus, in a case of a failure on the part of the authorities to publicly declare the state of war or other public emergency, they are deprived of the right to invoke Article 15(1). This still leaves open the question of what are the consequences if a State has publicly declared such a state, but has failed to inform the Secretary General about it. It is to be regretted that the Commission has not taken the opportunity to also clarify the consequences of non-fulfilment of the information obligation laid down in Article 15.

4.11 The Adequacy of the Supervision over Article 15

As was already observed, given the far-reaching consequences of the application of Article 15 it is of the utmost importance that that application in practice is supervised as effectively as possible. Nothing at all is left of the supervision by the Strasbourg organs – which is already very marginal – of the application of Article 15 by the Contracting States if a reservation, as made by France with respect to Article 15, is accepted.[198] In fact, this reservation implies, *inter alia*, that the words 'to the extent strictly required by the exigencies of the situation' must not be interpreted as restrictions on the power of the President of the French

---

[194] *Idem.*

[195] *Ibidem*, para. 525.

[196] *Ibidem*, para. 527.

[197] *Idem.* The proclamation of martial law in Turkey itself, which had been notified, according to the Commission could not be deemed 'to cover the treatment of persons brought into Turkey from the northern area of Cyprus'; *ibidem*, para. 530.

[198] On the question of whether this French reservation is legitimate or not, see *infra* p. 780.

Republic to take 'measures required by the circumstances'.[199] The consequence of this is that derogation from the rights and freedoms protected in the Convention, with the exception of those mentioned in Article 15(2), remains at the free discretion of the Contracting State in question, without any real review of the use of that discretion by means of 'European supervision' being possible.

In some situations it may turn out to be difficult to judge the exact scope of the Strasbourg supervision over the observance of Article 15. In a case which has remained unique until now, France, Norway, Denmark, Sweden and the Netherlands alleged a violation of Article 15 on the part of Turkey, but subsequently reached a friendly settlement with the latter.[200] As far as Article 15 was concerned, the States concerned noted that Turkey had in the meantime progressively reduced the geographical scope of martial law and had declared that it would be lifted from the remaining provinces within 18 months, and that a number of decrees or other legal enactments, mentioned by the applicant Governments in their applications, had been changed or amended.[201] The Commission accepted the settlement by concluding that it had been secured on the basis of respect for human rights in the sense of Article 28(8).[202] In accordance with Article 30 the Commission's report is confined to a brief statement of the facts and of the solution reached. Consequently, no arguments can be found to support the Commission's conclusion that respect for human rights had indeed been secured.[203] During the second half of the 1980s the human rights situation in Turkey would seem to have been slightly improving, as might be deduced from its acceptance of the right of individual petition and the Court's compulsory jurisdiction. In addition, Turkey has limited its derogation under Article 15 to Article 5 only and to a number of specified districts in 1992 and 1993 respectively. From that time on, however, the situation seems to have been deteriorating again, as may be deduced from the numerous applications lodged against Turkey in Strasbourg. As far as Article 15 is concerned, the point here is that during the whole period Turkey in fact has been switching on and off its obligations under the Convention without any form of supervision being exercised on the part of the Strasbourg organs.

Even if Strasbourg supervision is exercised, there is no guarantee in the present situation that it is effective. This has become clear from the Court's reaction in its *Brannigan and McBride* judgment to the aftermath of its earlier *Brogan* judgment. The latter judgment held that the United Kingdom had violated, *inter alia*, Article 5(3) because the applicants, after being detained, were neither brought promptly

---

[199] For the full text of the French reservation, see Council of Europe, *Collected Texts*, Yearbook 33A (1994), p. 72.
[200] Appls 9940-9944/82, report of 7 December 1985, D&R 44 (1985), p. 31.
[201] *Ibidem*, p. 39.
[202] *Ibidem*, p. 41.
[203] On 25 May 1987, the Turkish Government informed the Secretary General of the Council of Europe that martial law would be lifted in the remaining provinces from 19 July 1987; Council of Europe, *Information Sheet*, No. 21, 1987, p. 14.

before a judicial authority nor released promptly following their arrest. As far as Article 15 is concerned, the judgment contained the following considerations:

> The Government have adverted extensively to the existence of particularly difficult circumstances in Northern Ireland, notably the threat posed by organized terrorism. (...) The Government informed the Secretary General of the Council of Europe on 22 August 1984 that they were withdrawing a notice of derogation under Article 15 which had relied on an emergency situation in Northern Ireland (...). The Government indicated accordingly that in their opinion 'the provisions of the Convention are being fully executed'. In any event, as they pointed out, the derogation did not apply to the area of law in issue in the present case. Consequently, there is no call in the present proceedings to consider whether any derogation from the United Kingdom's obligations under the Convention might be permissible under Article 15 by reason of a terrorist campaign in Northern Ireland.[204]

However, on 23 December 1988 – less than a month after the *Brogan* judgment – the British Government provided the Secretary General with a set of information in order to ensure compliance with its obligations under Article 15(3). The contents of this information was at least confusing and from the perspective of the United Kingdom's obligations under the Convention even dubious. Formally the *Note Verbale* in which the information was contained, could be taken as a notice on the part of the British Government that from 23 December 1988 it was going to make use of the possibility provided for by Article 15 to derogate from certain of the obligations ensuing from the Convention. In a technical sense there is nothing wrong with such a step. It is even fully justified, provided that the Government can convincingly argue that the circumstances prevailing in the country call for the application of Article 15. In the present case, however, that was hard to imagine. Given the above-mentioned position taken by the British Government during the *Brogan* Case, the circumstances requiring application of Article 15 could only have arisen between the date of the Court's judgment and 23 December 1988. The *Note Verbale* did not make this clear at all. On the contrary, reference was made to 'recent years' of campaigns of organised terrorism and to the year 1974, in which the Government found it necessary to introduce special measures to combat this terrorism. Since the Government did not rely on Article 15 in the *Brogan* Case, the position taken in the Note Verbale, in our view, bore witness to at least bad faith on the part of the British Government as far as the period starting from 23 December 1988 was concerned.[205]

---

[204] Judgment of 29 November 1988, A.145-B, pp. 28-29.

[205] As far as the period between the date of the judgment up to 23 December 1988 was concerned, there was an outright violation of the Convention and the *Note Verbale* did not even bother to conceal it. After recalling that, the Court held that 'even the shortest of the four periods of detention concerned (...) fell outside the constraints as to time permitted by the first part of Article 5(3)', the *Note Verbale* bluntly added that 'Following this judgment (...) the Government did not believe that the maximum period of detention should be reduced.' Finally it was concluded that 'Since the judgment of 29 November 1988 as well as previously, the Government have found it necessary to continue to exercise, in relation to terrorism connected with the affairs of Northern Ireland, the powers described above enabling further detention without charge, for periods of up to five days.' (DH(89)1, pp. 10-11)

In the *Brannigan and McBride* Case the applicants took a somewhat similar position alleging that the 1988 derogation on the part of the United Kingdom was the Government's reaction to the *Brogan* judgment and was declared in order to circumvent the consequences of that judgment. The Court first observed that the power of arrest and extended detention had been considered necessary by the British Government in dealing with the threat of terrorism since 1974. Following the *Brogan* judgment, according to the Court, the Government was then faced with the option of either introducing judicial control or lodging a derogation from their Convention obligations in this respect. The Court then simply added:

> The adoption of the view by the Government that judicial control compatible with Article 5 para. 3 was not feasible because of the special difficulties associated with the investigation and prosecution of terrorist crime rendered derogation inevitable. Accordingly, the power of extended detention without such judicial control and the derogation of 23 December 1988 being clearly linked to the persistence of the emergency situation, there is no indication that the derogation was other than a genuine response.[206]

In view of the history of the case the Court's reaction is, first of all, rather concise. Moreover, the attitude of the majority reflects a very loose type of supervision, which in our view squares uneasily with the far-reaching impact of derogation under Article 15. The approach set forth by judge De Meyer in his dissenting opinion would seem to be much more convincing. According to judge De Meyer, given the prevailing situation in Northern Ireland:

> One can (...) understand that (...) the Government of the United Kingdom have since 1957, repeatedly felt it appropriate to avail themselves of their right of derogation under Article 15 of the Convention.
> In 1984 they had come to the conclusion that this was no longer necessary.
> We have been told that one of their reasons for doing so was their belief that detaining for up to seven days a person suspected of terrorism without bringing that person before a judge or other judicial officer was not inconsistent with their obligations under the Convention.
> In our Brogan and Others v. the United Kingdom judgment of 29 November 1988 we held that this assumption was wrong, and we strongly emphasised the importance of the fundamental human right to liberty and the need for judicial control of interferences therewith.
> The Government of the United Kingdom have tried to escape the consequences of that judgment by lodging again a notice of derogation under Article 15 in order to continue the practice concerned.
> In my view, this was not permissible: they failed to convince me that such a far-reaching departure from the rule of respect for individual liberty could, either after or before the end of 1988, be "strictly required by the exigencies of the situation".
> Even in the circumstances as difficult as those which have existed in respect of Northern Ireland for many years it is not acceptable that a person suspected of terrorism can be detained for up to seven days without any form of judicial control.
> This was, in fact, what we had already decided in the Brogan and Others Case and there was no valid reason for deciding otherwise in the present one.[207]

---

[206] Judgment of 26 May 1993, A.258-B, p. 51.
[207] *Ibidem*, p. 71.

Similarly, on the basis of a comparable line of reasoning judge Pettiti concluded in his dissenting opinion that 'The State was under a duty to implement mechanisms complying with the Brogan and Other judgment and making it possible to conform thereto without resorting to derogation'.[208]

The possibility of derogation under Article 15 has been made use of several times and by different countries. This has also resulted in a number of complaints about violation of Article 15. It goes without saying that an effective maintenance of the rights and freedoms guaranteed in the Convention requires that derogations from the provisions of the Convention be minimised. This calls for a continuous and strict supervision of the observance of the conditions laid down in Article 15. One may wonder whether the supervision mechanism provided for in the Convention, which comes into operation only after submission of a complaint and consequently has an incidental character, is sufficient in this respect.

5 RESTRICTIONS ON THE POLITICAL ACTIVITY OF ALIENS (ARTICLE 16)

Nothing in Articles 10, 11 and 14 shall be regarded as preventing the High Contracting Parties from imposing restrictions on the political activity of aliens.

5.1 The Scope of Article 16

The provision now laid down in Article 16 did not occur in the draft of the Consultative Assembly; it was added thereto by the Committee of Experts.[209] It constitutes an important encroachment on the system of the Convention, which, as ensues in particular from Articles 1 and 14, guarantees the enjoyment of the rights and freedoms to everyone under the jurisdiction of one of the Contracting States, irrespective of nationality. That guarantee is restricted to a considerable degree by Article 16 for those persons who are under the jurisdiction of the Contracting State in question, but do not possess the nationality of that State.

With respect to Articles 10 and 11, Article 16 implies that the freedom of expression and freedom of association and assembly guaranteed in those articles may be restricted for aliens also in cases not provided for in the second paragraph thereof, when political activities are concerned. With regard to Article 14 it means that the national authorities may discriminate to the detriment of aliens in relation to the rights guaranteed in the Convention. The latter then applies not only to the rights provided for in Articles 10 and 11, but to all rights, insofar as this discrimination aims at the limitation of the political activities of aliens. In this context one may think especially of the right to vote and to be elected, at least if one assumes that Article 3 of Protocol No. 1 in principle confers this right on

---

[208] *Ibidem*, p. 61.
[209] Council of Europe, *Collected Editions of the 'Travaux Préparatoires' of the European Convention on Human Rights*, Vol. III, The Hague, 1976, p. 238.

aliens as well. But one may also think of restrictions on the freedom of education in connection with political activities.

5.2 'Aliens'

The term 'aliens' ('*étrangers*') refers both to persons having the nationality of one of the other Contracting States (while not also having the nationality of the State in question) and of other foreigners, including stateless persons. The Convention does not therefore grant, as does the law of the European Communities with respect to nationals of Member States of the Communities, a privileged position to those aliens who are nationals of one of the Member States of the Council of Europe. However, the Court has in fact granted a privileged status to at least some nationals of Member States of the European Union in the case of *Piermont*, which is the only case before the Court up until now raising issues concerning Article 16. Mrs Piermont, a German citizen and at the material time a member of the European Parliament, was expelled from French Polynesia for what the authorities considered interference in French internal matters during a demonstration. The Court agreed with the French Government that Piermont could not rely on European citizenship, because the Community did not at the time recognise any such citizenship. Nevertheless, the Court subsequently decided:

> that Mrs. Piermont's possession of the nationality of a member State of the European Union and, in addition to that, her status as a member of the European Parliament do not allow article 16 of the Convention to be raised against her. Especially as the people of the OT's [Overseas Territories] take part in the European Parliament elections.[210]

This is a somewhat distorted line of reasoning in view of the unambiguous text of Article 16 referring to 'aliens' without express exception.[211] It shows the Court bending backwards to avoid the consequences of the odd character of Article 16.

5.3 'Political Activity'

The rights of Articles 10 and 11 and the protection of Article 14 are not set aside with respect to aliens. Insofar as these rights relate to other than political activities, aliens are entitled to the same guarantees in relation to these articles as the nationals of the State in question. The scope of the restrictions that can be applied to them is therefore determined by the interpretation put upon the term 'political activity' ('*activité politique*').

Since Articles 10 and 11 themselves already mention as a general restriction 'the interests of national security and public safety' and Article 10 adds to that 'the prevention of disorder', while Article 11 speaks of 'peaceful assembly', the drafters evidently wished to protect other interests of the State by Article 16. In

---

[210] Judgment of 27 April 1995, A.314, p. 24.
[211] In the same vein the joint dissenting opinion by four judges; *ibidem,* pp. 31-32.

this context one should think in particular of the interest of good relations with other States. Thus, for instance, demonstrations of South Moluccans in the Netherlands directed against Indonesia, or demonstrations or publications of Moroccan migrant workers residing in the Netherlands criticising the regime in Morocco may be prohibited on that ground to the extent that the persons involved do not possess Dutch nationality. The fact that such activities of aliens often serve to promote and protect the very values on which the Convention is based, unfortunately does not stand in the way of the application of Article 16, since the latter does not contain any reservation in that respect. Even a plea for respect of the Convention itself, addressed to another Contracting State, might fall under censorship under certain circumstances, when such a plea is not advanced by a national of the State on whose territory it is aired.

But Article 16 goes further still. It also permits restriction of the freedom of expression, association and assembly, and of the prohibition of discrimination, if the political implications thereof concern exclusively the host country itself. Thus, a State would have the right to impose on migrant workers a prohibition from advocating improvement of that State's social security measures, the granting of stay permits or other measures directly concerning them. They might even be prohibited from advocating better application by that State of the Convention with regard to them, an application to which they are entitled. And all this may be done without certain interests of the State concerned, such as national security or public order, being at stake. These examples clearly demonstrate that in its present, unqualified form Article 16 hardly fits into the system of the Convention, which is based on the idea of democracy. Or is this also a value the implications of which are confined to the State's own nationals?

The question of whether in a particular case a 'political activity' is involved must ultimately be judged by the Strasbourg organs, since this concerns the interpretation of a provision of the Convention. To the best of our knowledge the question has not yet been raised before them thus far. In the light of the case-law concerning other possibilities to restrict the enjoyment of certain rights it is to be expected that for the answer to that question, too, they will leave a 'margin of appreciation' to the national authorities. However, the latter will have to advance reasonable arguments for their qualification of an activity as 'political'. Thus it is self-evident that a regulation prescribing that the responsible publishers of all journals must possess the nationality of the country in which they are published, without any differentiation between journals which do and those which do not deal with political issues,[212] may find no favour with the Commission and the Court. Precisely because of the above-mentioned far-reaching consequences of Article 16, which hardly fit into the system of the Convention, it is of great importance that the term 'political activity' shall be interpreted restrictively.

---

[212] The example has been taken from Karl Josef Partsch, *Die Rechte und Freiheiten der europäischen Menschenrechtskonvention*,Berlin, 1966, p. 261. It should be observed that such a regulation would (also) violate Art. 6 of the Treaty establishing the European Community.

5.4 Article 16: A Dead Letter to be Abolished

As was already pointed out in the foregoing, up until now there has been only one case before the Court raising an issue concerning Article 16. Fortunately, therefore, the provision has for all practical purposes remained a dead letter. This together with Article 16's odd character provides more than sufficient reason to finally follow up the 1977 recommendation of the Parliamentary Assembly in which the Committee of Ministers was urged:

> to instruct the competent committee of experts to make proposals for the amendment of the European Convention for the Protection of Human Rights and Fundamental Freedoms in such a way as to exclude restrictions at present authorised by Article 16 with respect to political activity on the exercise by aliens of the freedoms guaranteed by Article 10 (freedom of expression) and Article 11 (freedom of association).[213]

6 PROHIBITION OF ABUSE OF THE RIGHTS AND FREEDOMS SET FORTH IN THE CONVENTION AND OF THEIR LIMITATION TO A GREATER EXTENT THAN IS PROVIDED FOR IN THE CONVENTION (ARTICLE 17)

Nothing in this Convention may be interpreted as implying for any State, group or person any right to engage in any activity or perform any act aimed at the destruction of any of the rights and freedoms set forth herein or at their limitation to a greater extent than is provided for in the Convention.

6.1 Introduction

From the formulation of Article 17 it is quite clear that this provision does not have an independent character; its violation is necessarily connected with one or more of the rights and freedoms enumerated in Section I of the Convention and of Protocols Nos 1, 4, 6 and 7.[214] This connection varies somewhat depending on whether Article 17 is invoked against an individual or against a State.

6.2 The Scope of Article 17 *vis-à-vis* Private Parties

With regard to individuals and groups the aim of Article 17 is to prevent them from invoking the rights and freedoms to which they are entitled, when they use them for the purpose of destroying or limiting those rights and freedoms of others.[215] In this case Article 17 must therefore be connected both with the rights of the person against whom this article is invoked and with one or more of the rights of others. As to the first-mentioned rights, the Commission held in the *Glimmerveen and Hagenbeek* Case:

---

[213] Recommendation 799(1977) on the political rights and position of aliens, 25 January 1977; Council of Europe, Parliamentary Assembly, 28th Ordinary Session, Third Part, *Texts Adopted* (1977).

[214] See the judgment of 8 June 1976, *Engel*, A.22, p. 43.

[215] Thus also the Court in its judgment of 1 July 1961, *Lawless*, A.3, p. 45.

Article 17 covers essentially those rights which, if invoked, will facilitate the attempt to derive therefrom a right to engage personally in activities aimed at the destruction of any of the rights and freedoms set forth in the Convention.[216]

In proceedings before a national court Article 17 has the function, in a dispute between two individuals, of one of the criteria for weighing the rights of one party against those of the other party. In a dispute between an individual and a governmental body and in proceedings before the Strasbourg organs Article 17 constitutes a possible ground of justification for the respondent State to rely on against a claim of violation of the Convention.

6.3 The Scope of Article 17 *vis-à-vis* States

Article 17 not only implies a prohibition for persons and groups, but also for 'any State'. Thus it is also intended to prevent the national authorities from making use of their powers under the Convention to limit the enjoyment of the rights and freedoms in order to destroy the essence of those rights and freedoms or to limit them to a greater extent than is provided for in the Convention. In this case, therefore, Article 17 is of a dependent character in that it must be connected both with the possibilities which other provisions of the Convention allow the national authorities to limit certain rights and freedoms and with those rights and freedoms themselves. Article 17 may here be invoked by an individual against the authorities in conjunction with the complaint about violation of one of his rights protected in the Convention.

The latter characteristic of Article 17 has been very tersely summarised by the Commission in the following manner:

Where a Government seeks to achieve the ultimate protection of the rule of law and the democratic system, the Convention itself recognises in Article 17 the precedence which such objectives take, even over the protection of the specific rights which the Convention otherwise guarantees. Nevertheless, precisely because of the cardinal importance to be attached to the preservation of the rule of law and the democratic system, the Convention requires a clearly established need for any interference with the rights it guarantees, before such interference can be justified on that basis.[217]

In cases where Article 17 has the function of a justification on the part of the authorities, the decision that the invocation of Article 17 by the respondent State is well-founded, in fact is at the same time a decision on the merits, since it is thus established that the Convention has not been violated by this State. On this account, and also in view of the very important and complex questions to which such an invocation of Article 17 may give rise, it is highly desirable that the Commission, if it does not consider reliance on Article 17 by the State concerned

---

[216] Appls 8348 and 8406/78, D&R 18 (1980), p. 187 (195).

[217] Reports of 11 May 1984, *Glasenapp*, A.104, p. 49, and *Kosiek*, A.105, pp. 42-43. In both cases the Court did not deal with Art. 17, since it held that the question complained of was not covered by the Convention.

to be manifestly ill-founded, joins its examination to the merits, in order that the final decision may rest not with the Commission, but with the Court or the Committee of Ministers, as the case may be.

This policy, however, has not always been followed by the Commission. When the *Kommunistische Partei Deutschland* (KPD) submitted a complaint against the Federal Republic of Germany with respect to the decision of the *Bundesverfassungsgericht* in which it had been dissolved and had been declared a prohibited party, the Commission, apparently *ex officio*, instituted an inquiry into the applicability of Article 17. On the basis of depositions made by the KPD during the proceedings before the *Bundesverfassungsgericht* the Commission concluded that the aim of the KPD was to establish a socialist-communist system by means of a proletarian revolution and the dictatorship of the proletariat, and that it had intimated that it still adhered to these principles. Even if it should be found that the KPD was trying to seise power only *via* constitutional methods, in the Commission's opinion this did not yet mean that it had renounced these principles. On that ground the Commission deemed Article 17 to be applicable and came to the decision that the application could not be based on any of the provisions of the Convention and was therefore inadmissible as being incompatible with the Convention.[218]

In its later decision in the *Lawless* Case the Commission did join the question about the applicability of Article 17 to the merits.[219] In our view there would also have been every reason for this in the *KPD* Case. In fact, the decision taken in that case by the Commission, on the basis of exclusively written proceedings, not only was very far-reaching, but also did not as a matter of course ensue from the facts described and from the formulation of Article 17, in particular considering the words 'activity' and 'act'; indeed, the Commission's decision was based exclusively on the aims and not on the actual activities of the KPD.

In the *Glimmerveen and Hagenbeek* Case the Commission again declared the application inadmissible by invocation of Article 17. In this case Glimmerveen complained about his criminal conviction for having possessed, with the aim of distribution, leaflets of the 'Nederlandse Volks Unie', which were found to incite to racial discrimination. In addition, both applicants complained of the invalidation by the Central Voting Boards of Amsterdam and The Hague of the list of candidates of the 'Nederlandse Volks Unie'. The Commission recognised that the challenged acts constituted a breach of the freedom of expression of Article 10, and possibly a violation of the right to be elected, laid down in Article 3 of Protocol No. 1. It also called to mind the finding of the Court in the *Handyside* Case, that the freedom of expression constitutes one of the essential foundations of a democratic society. It concluded, however, that, pursuant to Article 17, the

---

[218] Appl. 250/57, Yearbook I (1955-1957), p. 222 (224-226).
[219] Appl. 332/57, Yearbook II (1958-1959), p. 308 (340). In the *De Becker* Case the invocation of Art. 17 by the Belgian Government took place only after the declaration of admissibility, during the examination of the merits. See the report of 8 January 1960 in this case, B.2 (1962), p. 133.

two applicants could not invoke this provision, or these provisions, and declared the applications 'incompatible with the provisions of the Convention'.[220] In this case, like in a number of cases to be discussed in the next subsection, in our opinion it would have been more appropriate to join the question of the applicability of Article 17 to the merits. This would also have been desirable in view of the important implications of the Commission's decision and the not indisputable foundation thereof. Indeed, it is difficult to ignore that the Commission relied on the 'softer' right of freedom from discrimination (Article 14 in conjunction with Article 3), which the Convention guarantees to a limited extent only (at least in the view thus far taken by the Commission itself), and some of the rights from Protocol No. 4, not yet ratified by the Netherlands at that moment, whereas the applicants invoked the 'hard' right of freedom of expression as laid down in Article 10 of the Convention.

The Commission – followed in this by the Court – has introduced a very important restriction on the respondent State's possibility of invoking Article 17 as a justification. Both in the *Lawless* Case and in the *De Becker* Case it was held that, even if it is firmly established that the applicant himself aims at the destruction or restriction of the fundamental rights of others, or belongs to a group with such an objective, this does not yet entail that he may therefore remain deprived of all the rights laid down in the Convention; Article 17 applies exclusively to those rights which he abuses directly for the said aim. In the *Lawless* Case this connection between that aim and the rights invoked was altogether absent in the opinion of the Commission and the Court; even if Lawless had been involved in IRA activities, his invocation, as a detained person, of the guarantees of Articles 5 and 6 in any case was not aimed at engaging in such activities.[221] And in the *De Becker* Case, where the complaint concerned the freedom of expression, the connection was absent, because De Becker's totalitarian views and activities dated from the past and it had not been shown that he would abuse his freedom of expression again for that purpose.[222] This case-law is important, for instance, for war criminals and terrorists detained in prison or meanwhile released; the mere fact of their past does not constitute a sufficient ground for denying them certain rights and freedoms.

The question of how close the link between the right claimed and the activity prohibited under Article 17 must be is of course open to discussion. When a Swiss company claimed that the confiscation of its property in the Federal Republic of germany was contrary to Article 1 of Protocol No. 1, the German Government invoked Article 17, submitting that the aim of the company was to manage and protect real property of the *Kommunistische Partei Deutschland*. However, the

---

[220] Appls 8348 and 8406/78, D&R 18 (1980), p. 187 (194-197).
[221] See the report of 19 December 1959 and the judgment of 1 July 1961 in this case, B.1 (1961), p. 180 and A.3, pp. 45-46 respectively.
[222] Report of 8 January 1960, B.2 (1962), pp. 137-138. The Court did not take a decision on this point, because the case was struck off the list after the Belgian legislation had been amended.

applicants submitted that they only claimed compensation and were able to guarantee that this would not be used for anti-constitutional activities. The request, however, was declared inadmissible on account of non-exhaustion of the local remedies, so that the Commission did not reach a decision on this point.[223] Here again a highly factual examination would have been concerned, which in our opinion the Commission should not use as a basis for a declaration of inadmissibility but should join to the merits.

6.4 Subsidiary and Complementary Character of Article 17

In the *Engel and Others* Case, the applicants alleged that the penalty imposed on them for having written an article in a journal could not be justified in this particular case by the second paragraph of Article 10 and consequently constituted a violation of Article 17. The Commission declared this part of the complaint to be admissible,[224] but it was later declared ill-founded by the Court, following the Commission in that respect, after it had been found that the challenged prohibition was justified under Article 10(2).[225] From this decision the subsidiary character of this element of Article 17 becomes particularly clear: if the restriction imposed is justified under the Convention, Article 17 has not been violated, while, if it is not justified, besides Article 17 one of the rights or freedoms will also have been violated. This is different only in those cases where the disputed measure does not directly constitute a violation of one of the rights and freedoms, but its effect amounts to a circumvention of the guarantees contained in the Convention and thus in fact leads to a restriction not provided for.[226]

This means that in the case of those articles which themselves already contain fairly wide possibilities for restrictions, Article 17 can only rarely be invoked successfully against a State; this also in view of the wide margin of appreciation which the Strasbourg organs are willing to allow the national authorities in the application of those restrictions.[227] In such cases, therefore, the Commission and the Court usually confine themselves to the statement that the restrictions imposed have been found to be in conformity with the provision in question, so that the applicability of Article 17 need not be discussed any further.[228] But in the case

---

[223] Appl. 712/60, *Retimag S.A.* v. *Federal Republic of Germany*, Yearbook IV (1961), p. 384 (392-394).

[224] Appls 5354/72 and 5370/72, Yearbook XV (1972), p. 508 (556-558).

[225] Judgment of 8 June 1976, A.22, pp. 42-43.

[226] See the report of 19 July 1974, *Engel*, B.20 (1978), p. 70, where the Commission suggested as a possibility of such a case a situation in which a State introduces or maintains a disciplinary procedure in order to evade the guarantees of Art. 6. Thus also Appl. 5916/72, *X* v. *the United Kingdom*, Coll. 46 (1974), p. 165 (166-167).

[227] On this, see *supra* pp. 84-87.

[228] Besides the report of 19 July 1974, B.20 (1978), pp. 84-85 and the judgment of 8 June 1976, *Engel*, A.22, p. 43, reference may also be made to Appl. 1747/62, *X* v. *Austria*, Yearbook VI (1963), p. 424 (442-444). If, on the other hand, the restriction imposed is already contrary to that other provision, review against Art. 17 is also considered superfluous: report of 5 November 1969, *Greek*

of a provision of the Convention which does not provide for any restrictions or in which they are defined less expressly or somewhat less broadly, Article 17 may be very important as an autonomous or a complementary criterion for the lawfulness of the restriction. Thus, in the *Sporrong and Lönnroth* Case, after having found that the restrictions imposed on the part of the authorities with regard to the peaceful enjoyment of the property by the applicants had a lawful character in virtue of Article 1 of Protocol No. 1, the Commission subsequently instituted an inquiry into the question of whether these restrictions did not after all go beyond what is provided for in the Convention.[229] Eventually the Commission concluded unanimously that there had been no violation of Article 17. After having noted the Commission's conclusion, the Court without any additional argument held that 'having found that there was a breach of Article 1 of Protocol No. 1, the Court does not consider it necessary also to examine the case under Article 17 (...) of the Convention'.[230]

The Commission seems to have pursued the approach taken in the *Sporrong and Lönnroth* Case. In the *Lithgow* Case it first found that the nationalisation measures at stake were compatible with Article 1 of Protocol No. 1 and that the taking of the applicants' property on that basis could be considered justifiable in view of the purposes of that provision. Subsequently, it dealt with the alleged violation of Article 17, but concluded that the measures concerned were not shown to have been aimed at the destruction or excessive limitation of the applicants' rights.[231]

7 PROHIBITION OF MISUSE OF POWER IN RESTRICTING THE RIGHTS AND FREEDOMS (ARTICLE 18)

The restrictions permitted under this Convention to the said rights and freedoms shall not be applied for any purpose other than those for which they have been prescribed.

7.1 Non-Autonomous Supplementary Character of Article 18

Article 18 contains for the Contracting States a general prohibition to use the restrictions permitted under the Convention for any purpose other than those for which they are intended.

This prohibition cannot constitute the object of a separate complaint, but can be advanced only in conjunction with one of the rights and freedoms; it forms one of the autonomous provisions of Section I.[232] As is the case with respect to

---

Case, Yearbook XII (1969), p. 113.

[229] Report of 8 October 1980, B.46 (1986), p. 53.

[230] Judgment of 23 September 1982, A.52, p. 28.

[231] Report of 7 March 1984, A.102, p. 115. The Court did not have to deal with this question, since the particular issue of violation of Art. 17 had not been referred to it.

[232] Report of 14 July 1974, *Kamma*, Yearbook XVIII (1975), p. 300 (316); report of 19 July 1974, *Engel*, B.20 (1978), p. 86; report of 8 October 1980, *Sporrong and Lönnroth*, B.46 (1986), p. 53; Appl. 9990/82, *Bozano* v. *France*, D&R 39 (1984), p. 119 (141).

Article 14,[233] Article 18 too has nevertheless been given a fairly autonomous character in the case-law of the Commission, in the sense that this provision may be violated in conjunction with another article, even though this latter article has not itself been violated.[234] The Court, on the other hand, has so far considered a separate examination concerning Article 18 superfluous after it has concluded that the right invoked has not been violated,[235] or if in considering the restrictions it has already gone into the aims envisaged by the limitations imposed.[236] In the latter case the Court in fact incorporates Article 18 into the provision on limitations contained in the article in question. And also when the Court has already concluded that one of the rights has been violated, it considers consideration of Article 18 superfluous.[237]

7.2 'The Restrictions Permitted under this Convention'; General Applicability of Article 18

It appears from its formulation that Article 18 refers to all restrictions permitted under the Convention. These include not only the special restrictions provided for in Articles 8 to 11 of the Convention, Article 2 of Protocol No. 4 and Article 1 of Protocol No. 7. Article 18 also applies to the general restrictions ensuing from Articles 15, 16 and 17. Thus the Commission relied in part on Article 18 in the *De Becker* Case to conclude that measures which were taken in accordance with Article 15 in connection with an emergency situation are no longer justified when they remain in force after the emergency has ceased to exist.[238] Indeed, in that situation the objective which constituted the justification for such measures have equally ceased to exist.

Moreover, Article 18 is applicable to restrictions which may ensue from the regulation of a specific right itself. This implies, conversely, that a right which is formulated in absolute terms and with respect to which consequently no restrictions are possible cannot lead to a violation of Article 18.[239] However, if and to the extent that the regulation of a right or freedom does leave scope for restrictions, their application has to be reviewed for its conformity with Article 18. Thus, in the *Sporrong and Lönnroth* Case, the Commission took Article 18 into consideration in connection with the question whether the restrictions in that case

---

[233] For this, see *supra* pp. 716-718.
[234] Report of 14 July 1974, *Kamma*, Yearbook XVIII (1975), p. 300 (316); report of 19 July 1974, *Engel*, B.20 (1978), p. 86; report of 8 October 1980, *Sporrong and Lönnroth*, B.46 (1986) p. 53.
[235] Judgment of 8 June 1976, *Engel*, A.22, p. 43.
[236] Judgment of 7 December 1976, *Handyside*, A.24, p. 30.
[237] Judgment of 8 June 1976, *Engel*, A.22, pp. 39-40.
[238] Report of 8 January 1960, B.2 (1962), p. 133. In its report in the *Greek* Case the Commission did not get as far as discussing Art. 18 in conjunction with Art. 15, because it held that even the conditions of Art. 15 itself had not been fulfilled: report of 5 November 1969, Yearbook XII (1969), p. 113.
[239] See the reports of 14 July 1974, *Kamma*, Yearbook XVIII (1975), p. 300 (316) and of 19 July 1974, *Engel*, B.20 (1978), p. 86.

were lawful measures imposed in the general interest in the sense of Article 1 of Protocol No. 1.[240] The question whether Article 18 is also applicable to 'inherent limitations' must be preceded by the question whether 'inherent limitations' are at all permitted under the Convention, and if so, to what extent.[241] Insofar as they are considered lawful, in our opinion, their application has to be reviewed for its conformity with Article 18, because they are then to be considered as 'permitted under this Convention' in the sense of that article. In that case such a review is extremely important precisely because Article 18, in conjunction with Articles 14 and 17, then constitutes the sole yardstick of the Convention.

7.3 Burden of Proof

Article 18 is a provision that is hard to apply in practice, as is the case for the prohibition of misuse of power (*détournement de pouvoir*) in general. Indeed, it requires an exact determination of the motives on the part of the authorities taking a given measure, while it must also be established that these were not in conformity with the aims envisaged when the restriction in question was incorporated into the Convention. Although bad faith does not as such constitute an element of *détournement de pouvoir*, still in most cases determination of the former is implied in that of the latter. It is thus not surprising that the Commission and the Court are not readily inclined to take Article 18 into consideration on their own motion, although on the basis of the task entrusted to them in Article 19 they are undoubtedly competent, and arguably even obliged, to do so. A particularly difficult burden of proof comes to rest on the applicant party when the latter makes Article 18 a part of his complaint, unless the intention of the national authority concerned clearly ensues from the nature of the measure or finds expression in the motivation given for it.

7.4 Application of Article 18 in the Case-Law

The most illustrative case so far in which Article 18 played a preponderant role was that of *Kamma* v. *the Netherlands*. Kamma, while in detention on remand on the suspicion of swindle and attempted robbery, had been removed for one month to the police station for interrogation in relation to another case concerning murder. He alleged that the possibility which the Convention offers the authorities to deprive a person of his liberty, *viz.* detention on remand under Article 5(1)(c), had temporarily been used for another purpose, *viz.* for a police interrogation which did not respect certain rules provided for under Dutch law and under the Convention. He submitted that as a result he had suffered an injury in that his detention on remand had thus been prolonged by one month and that he had been

---

[240] Report of 8 October 1980, B.46 (1986), p. 53.
[241] On this, *infra* pp. 763-765.

subjected to a more rigorous regime during that month as a result of his detention at the police station.

As a matter of fact, under Dutch law the suspicion of murder in itself would have been a sufficient ground for a separate decision to detain him on remand. If such a decision had been taken, Article 18 would not have come into play. The complication, however, was that the court, when it decided on detention for the period in question, was not informed of Kamma's detention at the police station and the inquiry into the murder, so that in fact that decision related only to the suspicion of swindling. The investigating judge, on the contrary, *was* informed of the second suspicion, but apparently had not considered it necessary to take a separate decision.

In its report the Commission found, *inter alia*, that (1) good reasons had been advanced for the temporary removal to a police station, in particular since not a single provision in the Convention prohibited a police station as a place of detention; (2) the interrogation of a person detained on remand with respect to a case other than that for which the decision to detain him on remand had been taken was, as such, neither contrary to Dutch law nor contrary to the Convention; (3) the actual interrogation at the police station took eighteen days in all, *i.e.* only two days more than would have been possible without a decision of the court, if Kamma had not already been detained on remand; (4) his detention at the police station was subject to a certain judicial supervision, though not of the court, but of the investigating judge; and (5) if the interrogation in the murder case had caused a prolongation of the detention on remand, Kamma himself was to blame for this, since he himself had spread the rumour about his involvement in that case and on the second day of the interrogation had made a confession without being compelled, while the continued examination had resulted in the charge being dropped in that case. This induced the Commission to find that Article 18 had not been violated.[242] Curiously enough, the Commission concluded its report with the following observation:

> The Commission has, however, duly noted that the respondent Government concluded their observations on the merits with an indication that they intend to examine the question as to whether a reform of the relevant legislation is necessary in order to avoid ambiguous situations which may, as in the present case, arise under the existing provisions concerning interrogation by the police of persons already in detention on remand.[243]

From this it may be deduced that, although the Commission concluded that the challenged acts of the authorities in question were not contrary to the Convention, it considered them undesirable.

The Commission's opinion that in this case there was no violation of Article 18 seems to be based on the following train of thought: the deprivation of liberty, which as such was lawful, has been used for another purpose: interrogation in

---

[242] Report of 14 July 1974, *Kamma*, Yearbook XVIII (1975), pp. 316-322.
[243] *Ibidem*, p. 322.

another case; however, that interrogation and the circumstances under which it took place, particularly considering the fact that Kamma was already detained, were not in themselves contrary to Dutch law or the Convention; consequently, it could not be said that the authorities pursued a (continuation of an) unlawful deprivation of liberty. Although the latter may be true, in our opinion it does not get down to the essence of Article 18. In connection with Article 18 the question is not whether the restriction of the right to liberty is or is not legitimate as such, but precisely whether that restriction, assuming that it is justified on the ground advanced for it, was really imposed on that ground and not for another purpose, for which the restriction is not permitted. The way in which the Commission has applied Article 18 in this case deprives that provision of any independent meaning in addition to the provisions in which the rights and freedoms, and any restrictions thereof, are laid down. Unfortunately, the *Kamma* Case was not referred to the Court, but was decided by the Committee of Ministers in conformity with the opinion of the Commission.[244]

In the *Engel* Case, Dona and Schul – two of the five conscripts who acted as applicants – had submitted, *inter alia*, that the disciplinary punishment imposed on them for writing articles in a barracks journal was based by the Court Martial on the restrictions of Article 10(2), but in fact was intended to restrict their trade-union freedom.[245] The Commission dismissed this complaint by submitting that with respect to Article 10 it had concluded that 'prevention of disorder' justified the restriction of the right of Article 10 under the given circumstances, and that also no violation of Article 11 had taken place: 'It is therefore clear that there has been no breach of Article 18 in this respect'.[246] The Court, too, did not go into Article 18.[247]

Against the reasoning here followed, the same objection may be raised as against the way in which Article 18 was applied by the Commission in the *Kamma* Case: it seems to ignore altogether the rationale of Article 18 and deprives that provision of all independent meaning. Article 18 does not refer to 'any purpose in violation of the said rights and freedoms', but to 'any purpose other than those for which they have been prescribed'. Even if the inquiry in connection with Article 10, on account of the invocation of the second paragraph of this provision, leads to the conclusion that this article in itself has not been violated, it must still be possible that the inquiry concerning Article 18 subsequently alters this conclusion. If the applicants Dona and Schul could furnish *prima facie* evidence that the disciplinary measure had indeed been imposed on them to restrain their trade union activities in general, and not so much out of concern for order in the barracks, Article 10 would have been violated in conjunction with Article 18, regardless of whether the result of that measure also conflicted with Article 11.

---

[244] Res. DH(75)1 of 13 March 1975, Yearbook XVIII (1975), p. 300.
[245] See the report of 19 July 1974, *Engel*, B.20 (1978), pp. 85-86.
[246] *Ibidem*, p. 86.
[247] See *supra* p. 756 and note 237.

Indeed, review on the basis of the second paragraph of Article 10 provides an answer only to the question of whether the authorities *could* hold that the measure was necessary for the protection of one of the values mentioned in it. The *real* motives of the authorities taking the measure concerned are not at issue at that stage; those are dealt with afterwards in connection with the review under Article 18. If one starts from the position that, if the first review has a positive result, the second need not be performed at all, Article 18 has no meaning at all, since if the first review has a negative result, the second is no longer necessary anyway.

In its report in the *Handyside* Case the Commission appears to have corrected its position. The applicant, a publisher who had been prohibited from publishing the so-called 'Little Red Schoolbook', submitted that in fact the authorities had not taken action against him for the protection of morals, but for other motives, such as the desire to resist the development of modern teaching techniques at schools. The Commission in its report observed first of all that the infringement of the applicant's freedom of expression ensuing from the prohibition imposed was justified on the ground of the second paragraph of Article 10. However, it continued as follows:

> Furthermore, an examination of the case as it has been submitted does not disclose any evidence which might suggest that the authorities and courts in the United Kingdom in taking the action complained of against the publication and distribution of the *Schoolbook*, have in any way been guided by motives other than those described in Article 10(2).[248]

In our opinion the Commission thus intimates that it has carried out an independent inquiry into the violation of Article 18. In the judgment of the Court in this case, in the considerations concerning Article 10 an opinion was given on what in the view of the Court was the real aim of the measures adopted, so that the Court could indeed refer back to this in dealing with Article 18.[249]

This line taken in the *Handyside* Case has been continued in later case-law.[250] In the *Bozano* Case the applicant alleged that his deportation by the French authorities to Switzerland and the ensuing deprivation of his liberty were, *inter alia*, contrary to Article 5. The Commission agreed and went on to examine the question of whether the unlawfulness of the deportation affected the applicant's detention in respect of Article 18 of the Convention as well. The Commission pointed to the fact that a French administrative court had found the deportation – and hence the applicant's detention – unlawful on the ground that the executive, by proceeding in this way, had sought to circumvent the competent judicial authority's veto on extraditing the applicant, which was binding on the French Government. Consequently, it was concluded that the applicant's detention had a

---

[248] Report of 30 September 1975, B.22 (1976), p. 52.

[249] Judgment of 7 December 1976, A.24, pp. 25 and 30.

[250] See the decisions concerning the admissibility on Appl. 6794/74, *X* v. *Federal Republic of Germany*, D&R 3 (1976), p. 104 (107), and on Appl. 7317/75, *Lynas* v. *Switzerland*, Yearbook XX (1977), p. 412 (446). See also the report of 18 May 1977, *Sunday Times*, B.28 (1982), p. 77, and the report of 8 October 1980, *Sporrong and Lönnroth*, B.46 (1986), p. 53.

purpose different from detention with a view to deportation, as provided for in Article 5(1)(f).[251] The Court, in an approach similar to the one followed in the *Handyside* Case, did not deem it necessary to examine the issue under Article 18, as it had already noted, in connection with Article 5(1) taken alone, that the deportation procedure was abused for objects and purposes other than its normal ones.[252] Thus, like Article 14, Article 18 has actually been made an integral part of all those provisions of the Convention in which the rights and freedoms are regulated, at least insofar as those provisions permit any restriction of the rights and freedoms laid down therein. In our view, only in this way is the meaning of Article 18 done justice to.

8 THE GROUNDS OF RESTRICTION, IN PARTICULAR THOSE REFERRED TO IN ARTICLES 8-11 OF THE CONVENTION, ARTICLE 2 OF PROTOCOL NO. 4 AND ARTICLE 1 OF PROTOCOL NO. 7

8.1 Introduction: The System of the Restrictions

From the discussion of the individual rights and freedoms in Chapter VII the fundamental importance of the issue of restrictions has become quite clear. Indeed, in a great many cases the very question as to the possibility of restricting the enjoyment of a particular right and as to the nature and scope of that possibility was found to be decisive for the question of whether or not a violation had taken place. The possibilities of their restriction are a determinant factor of the scope of the rights and freedoms guaranteed in the Convention.

The rights and freedoms of the Convention can be distinguished into absolute and non-absolute rights and freedoms. In this context it must be pointed out first of all that the 'restriction' of Article 17 applies to all the rights and freedoms without exception.[253] For every notion of rights, however, the prohibition of abuse is so self-evident that the provision that the enjoyment and the exercise of the rights and freedoms laid down in the Convention may not be directed at the destruction of those rights and freedoms themselves or at their limitation to a greater extent than is provided for in the Convention, cannot be considered to affect the absolute character of a right. It is precisely because of this self-evidence that the prohibition of abuse of right is to be considered a general principle of law.

Some rights and freedoms are non-derogable in the sense that no derogation from them is permitted even in times of war or other general emergency.[254] This applies under Article 15(2) for the right to life, except in respect of deaths resulting from lawful acts of war (Article 2), for the prohibition of torture and inhuman or degrading treatment (Article 3), for the prohibition of slavery or

---

[251] Report of 7 December 1984, A.111, p. 54.
[252] Judgment of 18 December 1986, A.111, p. 27.
[253] On this article, see *supra* pp. 750-755.
[254] On this, see *supra* p. 741.

servitude (Article 4(1)) and for the prohibition of retrospective effect of criminal law (Article 7). It also applies for Protocol No. 6 concerning the abolition of the death penalty and for Article 4 of Protocol No. 7 concerning the prohibition to be tried in criminal proceedings for an offence for which one has already been finally acquitted or convicted. With the exception of the right to life of Article 2 the said rights and freedoms moreover are formulated in absolute terms, so that no restriction is permitted in any case, neither in times of an emergency nor in a normal situation.

Outside the situation referred to in Article 15, and in addition to the above-mentioned articles, the Convention does also not permit restrictions with respect to Article 6(2) of the Convention and with respect to Articles 1, 3 and 4 of Protocol No. 4. These articles, too, are formulated in absolute terms.

With respect to the other rights and freedoms guaranteed in the Convention certain restrictions are possible. These restrictions may take different forms. A case apart in this respect is the possibility to restrict certain rights under Article 16. In fact, this refers to a specific category of activities: political activities; for a specific category of persons: aliens; and with reference to particular rights and freedoms: the freedom of expression and the freedom of association and assembly; while in addition it allows restrictions of the prohibition of discrimination of Article 14 with reference to the said categories.[255]

For the rest the restrictions may ensue, in the first place, from the way a right has been formulated, because certain limitations are inherent in the formulation of the right itself, or because it is expressly stated that particular cases are not covered by the right in question. The following articles belong to this category: Articles 2, 4 (with the exception of paragraph 1), 5, 6 (with the exception of paragraph 2) and 12 (in view of the words 'according to the national law governing the exercise of this right'), as well as Articles 1, 2 and 3 of Protocol No. 1, Article 1(1) of Protocol No. 7 (except in pursuance of a decision in accordance with law), and Articles 2, 3 and 5 of Protocol No. 7. The restrictions of this nature have been mentioned and discussed above in connection with the respective rights and freedoms.

Secondly, a number of articles, after having defined the guaranteed right in their first paragraph, contain in a second or third paragraph an enumeration of a number of possible restrictions. This applies to Articles 8-11 of the Convention, Article 2 of Protocol No. 4 and Article 1 of Protocol No. 7. These restrictions have been treated briefly in the discussion of the articles in question. For a more detailed discussion, however, reference has been made there to this separate section, because the enumerations in the various articles are broadly similar and the same observations need not be made about each individual article. The fact must, however, be taken into account that the separate paragraphs of one and the same article must be interpreted in connection with each other, so that a given ground for restriction in one article may have a somewhat different meaning than in

---

[255] On Art. 16, see *supra* pp. 747-750.

another article. This does not alter the fact, however, that the case-law with respect to these restrictions is broadly the same for the different articles, determined as this case-law is by the 'margin of appreciation' which the Commission and the Court allow to the national authorities in applying these restrictions.

8.2 'Inherent Limitations'

Before the special restrictions are discussed, a short reference must be made to the doctrine of 'inherent limitations'.

For a long time the Commission took the position that, in addition to the expressly mentioned restrictions or in the absence of such an express reference, the scope of the rights and freedoms laid down in the Convention may be subject to implied limitations. Unlike the express restrictions, these implied ones do not have the character of a justification of a breach of these rights and freedoms; they are inherent in those rights and freedoms themselves, so that, as long as these rights and freedoms with their inherent limitations are respected, there is no breach and the question as to possible limitations does not arise. The Commission developed this doctrine specifically with respect to persons of a special legal status, such as detained persons, psychiatric patients, soldiers and civil servants. This special status was assumed to entail for persons of these categories a more limited scope of certain rights and freedoms than for those outside these categories. Thus, according to that doctrine the right to respect for family life[256] and correspondence[257] was assumed to have a more limited character for a detained person in view of the inherent limitations which the execution of imprisonment involves for the exercise of these rights.

The Court, however, rejected this doctrine of the Commission, at any rate with respect to those articles of the Convention where express restrictions are incorporated in a separate paragraph. The Court adopted the view that the enumerations given there are exhaustive, so that there is no room for 'inherent limitations'.[258] Admittedly, the exhaustively enumerated restrictions are worded so broadly and the national authorities are allowed so wide a discretion by the Commission and the Court that the above-mentioned examples of 'inherent limitations' could in all likelihood still be brought under them in most cases. This applies all the more as the Court has also adopted the view that in the application of those restrictions by the national authorities still the fact may be taken into

---

[256] Appl. 2676/65, *X* v. *Austria*, Coll. 23 (1967), p. 31.

[257] Appl. 2375/64, *X* v. *Federal Republic of Germany*, Coll. 22 (1967), p. 45; Appl. 2749/66, *Kenneth Hugh de Courcy* v. *the United Kingdom*, Yearbook X (1967), p. 388.

[258] Judgment of 18 June 1971, *De Wilde, Ooms and Versyp ('Vagrancy' Cases)*, A.12, p. 45; judgment of 21 February 1975, *Golder*, A.18, pp. 21-22.

account that the person in question belongs to a particular category.[259] Nevertheless, the position of the Court presents the great advantage that the limitations in question are not examined only impliedly within the context of the interpretation of the right in question, but are, as restrictions, expressly subjected to the opinion of the Strasbourg organs, which then also have to review their application for its conformity with the specific justification requirements and with provisions such as Article 18.[260]

With respect to those rights which have not been provided in the Convention with express possibilities of restriction, the Court too has adopted the doctrine of 'inherent limitations'.[261] This view of the Court – and the Commission – appears to us to be wrong. It results from Article 1 that the Convention applies equally to everyone within the jurisdiction of one of the Contracting States. If the drafters should have wanted to permit special restrictions in relation to particular categories of persons, they could have stated this in each individual article, as has indeed been done, for instance, in the second paragraph of Article 11.[262] Just as from an exhaustive enumeration of the express restrictions, in our opinion it also follows from the absence of any provision to that effect that the drafters did not want to include any (other) limitations.[263] The whole system of the Convention would therefore appear to be opposed to the notion that the rights and freedoms laid down in it can be subjected to so-called 'inherent limitations'. Moreover, an argument against that notion can be derived from Article 18 of the Convention. That article provides that the restrictions permitted under the Convention may not be applied for any purpose other than those for which they have been prescribed. From the formulation of that article it follows that only those restrictions are allowed which have been permitted for a given purpose. Since no implicit purposes for restrictions are permissible, inherent limitations too must be deemed not to be allowed.

Even in the view defended here that the doctrine of 'inherent limitations' should be rejected, not all questions as to the scope of the rights and freedoms with respect to persons of a special legal status have been settled yet. So much is clear

---

[259] Judgment of 21 February 1975, *Golder*, A.18. In the *Schönenberger and Durmaz* Case the Court referred to its earlier case-law, where it held that in the case of a prisoner the pursuit of the objective of the prevention of disorder or crime may justify wider measures of interference than in the case of a person at liberty. The Court held that the same reasoning may be applied to a person being held on remand and against whom inquiries with a view to bringing criminal charges are being made, since in such a case there is often a risk of collusion; judgment of 20 June 1988, A.137, p. 13.

[260] This becomes evident, for instance, from the observations in the report of 11 October 1980, *Silver*, B.51 (1987), p. 72.

[261] Judgment of 21 February 1975, *Golder*, A.18, pp. 18-19.

[262] See also Art. 4(3)(a) and (b).

[263] *Cf.* also the report of 19 July 1974, *Engel*, B.20 (1978), p. 58: 'From this analysis of the Convention, and the method adopted therein, it is clear that the Convention is not conceived in terms of whose rights shall be protected but in terms of what rights shall be guaranteed and to what extent'.

that as to those rights and freedoms which are formulated in an absolute way no derogations or restrictions are permitted in a normal situation under any circumstances, also not on the ground of any special legal status. With respect to the other rights and freedoms, however, certain questions as to their scope still tend to arise, which may then have a special dimension for particular categories of persons. Do, for instance, the position of a prisoner and the requirements inherent in the prison regime permit him to marry, to have regular sexual intercourse with his spouse, to keep regular contacts with the family, or to take up a study?

In our opinion, in answering these questions one should not start from the conception of 'inherent limitations', but from the view that everyone, detained persons included, is entitled to these rights. Next, it has to be investigated what restrictions may be imposed on the right in question by reason of its formulation or on the basis of express grounds of restriction. To this end, all the relevant circumstances of the case must be taken into account, which may include the special legal status of the persons involved. When the imposed restrictions are tested for their conformity with the relevant provision of the Convention, account may therefore also be taken of the 'ordinary and reasonable requirements'[264] which are inherent in that special legal status. This approach differs, however, from the acceptance in advance of special 'inherent limitations' for persons in a special legal position. The question of whether the 'requirements' advanced by the national authorities are indeed 'ordinary and reasonable' may be assessed in each individual case by the Strasbourg organs with a view to the specific circumstances of that case. When confronted with the questions raised above with respect to detained persons, for instance, modern penitentiary conceptions with respect to the scope which the execution of a detention permits as to the provisions and measures required for the enjoyment of the rights in question must also be involved in the evaluation. In this matter a European standard may be gradually developed.[265]

8.3 'Prescribed by Law'; 'in Accordance with the Law'

In the enumerations of the specific limitations it is stated expressly that the latter must be 'prescribed by law' (Articles 9(2), 10(2) and 11(2) of the Convention) or 'in accordance with the law' (Article 8(2) of the Convention, Article 2(3) and (4) of Protocol No. 4 and Article 1(1) of Protocol No. 7). Thus the Convention refers

---

[264] Judgment of 21 February 1975, *Golder*, A.18, p. 21. See also the judgment of 8 June 1976, *Engel*, A.22, p. 25, where the Court speaks of 'specific demands' and 'normal restrictions'; judgment of 20 June 1988, *Schönenberger and Durmaz*, A.137, p. 13.

[265] See, *e.g.*, the report of 13 December 1979, *Hamer*, D&R 24 (1981), p. 5, where the Commission considered a two years' delay of the possibility of marrying, imposed on a detained person, in its generality an encroachment on his right to marry.

to the legal system of the State involved, which must provide an adequate basis for the restrictive measure.[266]

The interpretation of municipal law is a matter for the national authorities[267] and forms in principle an established fact for the Strasbourg organs, unless a manifest error of law is concerned. Equally, the question of whether a certain law has been enacted in the prescribed manner and is also in other respects in conformity with national (constitutional) law is not for the organs of the Convention to judge. However, this does not mean that the Strasbourg organs should simply accept the position of the respondent State – not even if that position is based upon a judgment of the highest national court – to the effect that a given restrictive measure was based on domestic law. These 'facts' may and must be tested for their conformity with the Convention. At that instance it is not the interpretation and application of domestic law that is at issue, but the interpretation and application of the words 'prescribed by law' and 'in accordance with the law' in the Convention itself. Nevertheless, also in this case the Court appears to leave quite a broad margin of appreciation to the national authorities:

> the logic of the system of safeguard established by the Convention sets limits upon the scope of the power of review exercisable by the Court in this respect. It is in the first place for the national authorities, notably the courts, to interpret and apply the domestic law: the national authorities are, in the nature of things, particularly qualified to settle the issues arising in this connection.[268]

The Court has dealt with the phrases 'prescribed by law' and 'in accordance with the law' in a number of cases. It has pointed out, first of all, that no importance is to be attached to the existence in the English text of the different formulations of the requirement of a sufficient legal basis.[269] Indeed the French text uses the words '*prévue par la loi*' for 'prescribed by law' as well as for 'in accordance with the law'. Furthermore, the Court has elaborated four principles in its case-law. It has taken as its point of departure:

> that the phrase 'in accordance with the law' does not merely refer back to domestic law but also relates to the quality of law, requiring it to be compatible with the rule of law, which is expressly mentioned in the preamble to the Convention.[270]

---

[266] This need not necessarily be the national law of that State; it may also be a provision of international law which, in virtue of the monistic system applying for that State, forms part of the national legal order, *e.g.*, a prohibition of war propaganda or the incitement to racism, as restrictions on the freedom of expression.

[267] On the other hand, the Commission has rejected the contention that justiciability is an inherent requirement of the concept of 'prescribed by law' or 'in accordance with the law'; Appl. 8231/78, *X v. the United Kingdom*, D&R 28 (1982), p. 5 (30).

[268] Judgment of 25 March 1985, *Barthold*, A.90, p. 22.

[269] Judgment of 25 March 1983, *Silver and Others*, A.61, pp. 32-33; judgment of 2 August 1984, *Malone*, A.82, p. 31.

[270] Judgment of 2 August 1984, *Malone*, A.82, p. 32. See also the Commission in its report of 11 October 1980, *Silver*, B.51 (1987), p. 74.

On that basis the Court has set forth as a first principle that the word 'law/*loi*' is to be interpreted as covering not only written law but also unwritten law.[271] According to the Court:

> it would clearly be contrary to the intention of the drafters of the Convention to hold that a restriction imposed by virtue of the common law is not 'prescribed by law' on the sole ground that it is not enunciated in legislation: this would deprive a common-law State which is a Party to the Convention of the protection of Article 10 para. 2 and strike at the very roots of that State's legal system.[272]

For the remainder the Strasbourg case-law has hardly defined the term 'law/*loi*'. The Commission and the Court have in fact accepted as a sufficient legal basis what has been qualified as such by the national authorities, including royal decrees, emergency decrees, and even internal regulations based on the law.[273] In a case against the Federal Republic of Germany the Rules of Professional Conduct for Veterinary Surgeons were at stake. These rules emanated from the Veterinary Surgeons' Council and not directly from Parliament. The Court nevertheless considered these rules as 'law' within the meaning of Article 10(2):

> The competence of the Veterinary Surgeons' Council in the sphere of professional conduct derives from the independent rule-making power that the veterinary profession (...) traditionally enjoys, by parliamentary delegation.[274]

Whether and, if so, to what extent the Court considers this 'parliamentary delegation' to be a condition, is not clear from this judgment.

It is dubious whether the legislation of the European Communities satisfies the democratic criterion. Its internal legal effect, indeed, may be said to originate from acts of parliament ratifying the EC Treaties for the separate Member States, but, as being of a higher order, its content and effect cannot be modified by the national parliaments, while the democratic character of rule-making is still highly imperfect in the Communities, even now that the European Parliament is composed of directly elected members and its legislative powers have widened.

As a second principle it has been recognised that 'the interference in question must have some basis in domestic law'.[275] In itself this principle is rather trivial and it has, consequently, been qualified in the case-law so as to include the third

---

[271] Judgment of 2 August 1984, *Malone*, A.82, p. 31.

[272] Judgment of 26 April 1979, *Sunday Times*, A.30, p. 31.

[273] See the judgment of 18 June 1971, *De Wilde, Ooms and Versyp ('Vagrancy'* Cases), A.12, p. 45. See also the decisions of the Commission on Appl. 1017/61, *X* v. *the Netherlands*, Coll. 8 (1962), p. 1 (4), and on Appl. 1983/63, *X* v. *the Netherlands*, Yearbook VIII (1965), p. 228 (264 in conjunction with 246). For legislation based on delegation, see Appl. 7736/76, *X* v. *Switzerland*, D&R 9 (1970), p. 206 (207) and Appl. 7308/75, *X* v. *the United Kingdom*, D&R 16 (1979), p. 32 (34-35).

[274] Judgment of 25 March 1985, *Barthold*, A.90, pp. 21-22. The Court took also into account, however, that 'it is a competence exercised by the Council under control of the State, which in particular satisfies itself as to observance of national legislation' and that 'the Council is obliged to submit its rules of professional conduct to the Land Government for approval.'

[275] Judgment of 2 August 1984, *Malone*, A.82, p. 31.

and the fourth principle, encompassing respectively the accessibility requirement and the foreseeability requirement.[276]

In the *Silver* Case the Court has explained the accessibility requirement as meaning that 'the law must be adequately accessible: the citizen must be able to have an indication that is adequate, in the circumstances, of the legal rules applicable to a given case.'[277]

Subsequently, the Court held that the Orders and Instructions at issue in that case did not meet this criterion because they 'were not published'.[278] The point of view that unpublished rules do not meet the accessibility requirement at first sight would seem to square uneasily with the above-mentioned first principle according to which 'law' does not only cover written but also unwritten law. However, what was at issue in the *Sunday Times* judgment was common law in general, which as such is unwritten law but which in most cases is easily accessible, often through published sources like court decisions, text books and other publications.[279] In the *Silver* Case, on the contrary, the Court was faced with internal orders and instructions which, generally speaking, could only be made accessible by their publication (or by their communication in some other way, which was not shown to be the case). In fact, however, in the *Silver* Case the Court did not have to rely solely on the unpublished Orders and Instructions. The main prescriptions in the form of the British Prison Act and the Rules were published and, therefore, satisfied the accessibility requirement. It was with respect to the interpretation and application of these published provisions – *i.e.* in the context of the foreseeability requirement – that the Court took the unpublished rules nevertheless into account. According to the Court the (unpublished) Orders and Instructions established a practice:

> which had to be followed save in exceptional circumstances (...) In these conditions, the Court considers that although those directives did not themselves have the force of law, they may – to the admittedly limited extent to which those concerned were made sufficiently aware of their contents – be taken into account in assessing whether the criterion of foreseeability was satisfied.[280]

Since the *Silver* judgment the foreseeability requirement has been developed into what now seems to be established case-law. The requirement entails as a point of departure that:

> the relevant national 'law', which includes both statute and common law (...), must be formulated with sufficient precision to enable those concerned – if need be, with appropriate legal advice – to foresee, to a degree that it is reasonable in the circumstances, the consequences which a given action may entail.[281]

---

[276] *Ibidem*, pp. 31-32.
[277] Judgment of 25 March 1983, A.61, p. 33.
[278] *Idem.*
[279] Judgment of 26 April 1979, A.30.
[280] Judgment of 25 March 1983, A.61, pp. 33-34. See also judgment of 26 March 1987, *Leander*, A.116, p. 23.
[281] Recently the judgment of 25 November 1996, *Wingrove*, Reports 1996-V, Vol. 33, para. 40.

Within this framework the Court has recognised on various occasions that:

> it may be difficult to frame laws with absolute precision and that a certain degree of flexibility may even be desirable to enable the national courts to develop the law in the light of their assessment of what measures are necessary in the interests of justice.[282]

According to the Court the level of precision required of the domestic legislation depends to a considerable degree on the content of the instrument concerned, the field it is designed to cover and the number and the status of those to whom it is addressed.[283] In other words, many laws inevitably entail a certain degree of discretion. However, according to the Court 'a law which confers a discretion must indicate the scope of that discretion'.[284] In this context, the Court has held that although safeguards must particularly exist in the case where a text bestows wide discretionary powers these have not to be enshrined in that very text.[285] The Court took the latter position in connection with its point of view, referred to above,[286] that rules governing the interpretation and application of a law do not have to be embodied in the same text but may even be contained in unpublished rules. In its *Vogt* judgment the Court seems to take this line of reasoning one step further. There it was held that the national German courts concerned had clearly defined the duty of political loyalty imposed on all civil servants by the relevant legislative provisions. As the applicant must had been aware of that case-law, she was in a position to foresee the risks she was running – *in casu* dismissal – as a result of her political activities. The applicant had alleged that there was divergence of opinion on the relevant points of law between the Federal Administrative Court and the Federal Labour Court. The Court rejected this contention in concluding that the disciplinary courts concerned had to follow the Federal Administrative Court. The Court added that:

> the mere fact that a legal provision is capable of more than one construction does not mean that it does not meet the requirement implied in the notion 'prescribed by law'.[287]

Quite illustrative for the Court's subtle approach to the foreseeability requirement is the *Olsson* judgment concerning Swedish legislation allowing the taking of children into public care. The Court held as follows:

> The Swedish legislation applied in the present case is admittedly rather general in terms and confers a wide measure of discretion, especially as regards the implementation of care decisions. (...) On the other hand, the circumstances in which it may be necessary

---

[282] For instance, the judgment of 27 March 1996, *Goodwin*, Reports 1996-II, Vol. 7, para. 33.

[283] Judgment of 25 August 1993, *Corherr*, A.266-B, pp. 35-36; and the judgment of 19 December 1994, *Vereinigung Demokratischer Soldaten Östereichs and Gubi*, A.302, pp. 15-16, where it was added: 'As far as military discipline is concerned, it would scarcely be possible to draw up rules describing different types of conduct in detail'.

[284] Judgment of 25 March 1983, *Silver and Others*, A.61, p. 22.

[285] *Ibidem*, p. 34.

[286] See *supra* p. 768.

[287] Judgment of 26 September 1995, A.323, para. 48.

to take a child into public care and in which a care decision may fall to be implemented are so variable that it would scarcely be possible to formulate a law to cover every eventuality. To confine the authorities' entitlement to act to cases where actual harm to the child has already occurred might well unduly reduce the effectiveness of the protection which he requires. Moreover, in interpreting and applying the legislation, the relevant preparatory work (...) provides guidance as to the exercise of the discretion it confers. Again, safeguards against arbitrary interference are provided by the fact that the exercise of nearly all the statutory powers is either entrusted to or is subject to review by the administrative courts at several levels (...). The Court thus concludes that the interferences were 'in accordance with the law'.[288]

The Court has accepted that the requirement of foreseeability cannot be exactly the same in the case of implementation of the law through secret measures – such as the interception of communications for the purposes of police investigations and secret controls of staff in sectors affecting national security – and implementation in other comparable fields. However:

> where the implementation of the law consists of secret measures, not open to the scrutiny by the individuals concerned or by the public at large, the law itself, *as opposed to the accompanying administrative practice*, must indicate the scope of any discretion conferred on the competent authority with sufficient clarity, having regard to the legitimate aim of the measure in question, to give the individual adequate protection against arbitrary interference.[289]

On this basis the Court concluded in the *Leander* Case:

> that Swedish law gives citizens an adequate indication as to the scope and the manner or exercise of the discretion conferred on the responsible authorities to collect, record and release information under the personnel control system.[290]

A main reason underlying this conclusion was that, although the first paragraph of section 2 of the Swedish Personnel Control Ordinance conferred a wide discretion on the National Policy Board, 'the scope of this discretion is however limited by law in important respects through the second paragraph'.[291] In its earlier *Malone* judgment the Court had reached a different conclusion:

> In the opinion of the Court, the law of England and Wales does not indicate with reasonable clarity the scope and manner of exercise of the relevant discretion conferred upon the public authorities,

because:

> it cannot be said with any reasonable certainty what elements of the powers to intercept [telephone communications] are incorporated in legal rules and what elements remain within the discretion of the executive.[292]

---

[288] Judgment of 24 March 1988, A.130, pp. 30-31. See also judgment of 22 June 1989, *Eriksson*, A.156, pp. 24-25.

[289] Judgment of 26 March 1987, *Leander*, A.116, p. 23 (emphasis added).

[290] *Ibidem*, p. 24.

[291] *Idem*.

[292] Judgment of 2 August 1984, A.82, p. 36.

Similarly, with respect to the process of so-called 'metering' – involving the use of a device which registers the numbers dialled on a particular telephone and the time and duration of each call – the Court concluded that:

> apart from the simple absence of prohibition, there would appear to be no legal rules concerning the scope and exercise of the discretion enjoyed by the public authorities. Consequently, (...) the interference resulting from the existence of the practice in question was not 'in accordance with the law' within the meaning of paragraph 2 of Article 8.[293]

The Court's approach with respect to secret measures was continued and in fact elaborated in the *Kruslin* Case and the *Huvig* Case where it was held that:

> Tapping and other forms of interception of telephone conversations represent a serious interference with private life and correspondence and must accordingly be based on a 'law' that is particularly precise. It is essential to have clear, detailed rules on the subject, especially as the technology available for use is continually becoming more sophisticated.[294]

8.4 Legitimate Aims to be Protected/'Necessary in a Democratic Society'

The Articles 8-11 of the Convention, Article 2 of Protocol No. 4 and Article 1 of Protocol No. 7 list a number of interests for the promotion or protection of which the imposed restriction must be necessary in a democratic society.

It is obvious that very wide concepts are involved here, which, if interpreted broadly, might make the guarantee aimed at by the Convention illusory. It is therefore of great importance that these concepts should be clearly defined in the Strasbourg case-law.

The review by the Strasbourg organs usually proceeds as follows. After it has been established that the right laid down in the first paragraph of the relevant article has been interfered with, it is examined whether that interference may be justified by the next paragraph of the same article. This last examination in fact consists of three parts. The first concerns the question – dealt with in the preceding section – whether the interference was 'prescribed by law' or 'in accordance with the law'. Subsequently it is examined whether the legislation on which the interference is based aims at the protection of one of the interests listed as grounds for restrictions in the relevant provision of the Convention. Finally, it must be decided whether, with a view to the interest to be protected, the interference may be considered necessary in a democratic society.

Emphasis is laid by the Strasbourg organs on the issue of the necessity of the interference.[295] In fact, the examination of the question of whether the protection of a justifiable interest is at issue generally coincides with the examination as to the necessity. As a result, the interests listed as grounds for restrictions have

---

[293] *Ibidem*, p. 38.

[294] Judgments of 24 April 1990, A.176-A, p. 23 and A.176-B, p. 55.

[295] An illustrative example of the approach followed in Strasbourg is the judgment of 22 October 1981, *Dudgeon*, A.45, pp. 18-25.

received only scant independent attention in the case-law. They are defined in relation to the evaluation of what may be considered necessary in a democratic society.

An autonomous interpretation has been given with respect to the difference between, on the one hand, 'the protection of public order' in Article 9(2) of the Convention and, on the other hand, 'the prevention of disorder' in Articles 8(2), 10(2) and 11(2). In its judgment in the *Engel* Case the Court, following the Commission,[296] decided that 'disorder' refers not only to 'public order' but 'also covers the order that must prevail within the confines of a special social group'.[297] From this it seems to follow likewise that 'public order' in the sense of Article 9(2) of the Convention – and Article 1(2) of Protocol No. 7 –, contrary to the French term *ordre public* in Article 2(3) of Protocol No. 4, does not refer to the notion of 'public policy', but to order in places accessible to everyone.

The enumerations of the interests vary somewhat from one article to another, but they are largely similar. The interests mentioned are: national security[298] and public safety,[299] public order,[300] the prevention of crimes,[301] morals,[302] health,[303] the reputation and the rights and freedoms of others,[304] the economic welfare of the country,[305] the prevention of disclosure of information received in confidence[306] and the guaranteeing of the impartiality of the judiciary.[307]

As was observed before, in general the grounds of restrictions are defined and reviewed mainly *via* demarcation of the requirement that the restriction must be

---

[296] Report of 19 July 1974, B.20 (1978), p. 210.

[297] Judgment of 8 June 1976, A.22, p. 41.

[298] See, *e.g.*, the *Klass* Case discussed *supra* pp. 707-709.

[299] See, *e.g.*, Appl. 8166/78, *X and Y* v. *Switzerland*, D&R 13 (1979), p. 241 (243), in which the refusal to married prisoners to continue their married life in prison was considered justified. See also the judgment of 25 March 1983, *Silver*, A.61.

[300] See, *e.g.*, Appl. 8191/78, *Rassemblement jurassien et Unité jurassienne* v. *Switzerland*, D&R 17 (1980), p. 93 (120), concerning a prohibition to hold demonstrations.

[301] See, *e.g.*, Appl. 8170/78, *X* v. *Austria*, D&R 16 (1979), p. 145 (152-153), in which the collection of personal data by the police for use in criminal proceedings was considered a justifiable violation of Art. 8.

[302] On this, see the judgment of 7 December 1976, *Handyside*, A.24; judgment of 22 October 1981, *Dudgeon*, A.45; judgment of 24 May 1988, *Müller*, A.133.

[303] See, *e.g.*, Appl. 8209/78, *Peter Sutter* v. *Switzerland*, D&R 16 (1979), p. 166 (173), in which with respect to the obligation for soldiers to wear their hair cut so as not to touch the collar, the Commission considered without any further argument that 'it can indeed be reasonably regarded as a measure necessary for the protection of health'.

[304] See, *e.g.*, Appl. 8239/78, *X* v. *the Netherlands*, D&R 16 (1979), p. 184 (189), in which it was held: 'while compulsory blood-testing may be seen as constituting a violation of private life within the meaning of Article 8, paragraph 1, it may also be seen as necessary for the protection of the rights of others'.

[305] See, *e.g.*, Appl. 7456/76, *Wiggins* v. *the United Kingdom*, D&R 13 (1979), p. 40 (45-46), in which this restriction formed a justification for a system of housing licences which violated the right to privacy.

[306] Appl. 4274/69, *X* v. *Federal Republic of Germany*, Yearbook XIII (1970), p. 888 (890-892).

[307] On this, see the judgment of 26 April 1979, *Sunday Times*, A.30.

'necessary in a democratic society'. This demarcation, in its turn, is determined to a large extent by application of the proportionality principle and that of the 'margin of appreciation'. These two principles, and their application in the case-law, have been discussed *supra* in sections 2.5 and 3.2, respectively, of Chapter II, to which reference is made here.

9 RESERVATIONS (ARTICLE 64)

1. *Any State may, when signing this Convention or when depositing its instrument of ratification, make a reservation in respect of any particular provision of the Convention to the extent that any law then in force in its territory is not in conformity with the provision. Reservations of a general character shall not be permitted under this Article.*
2. *Any reservation made under this Article shall contain a brief statement of the law concerned.*

9.1 Introduction

The inclusion into the Convention of the possibility of making reservations was a controversial matter at the time the Convention was drafted. The Committee on Legal and Administrative Questions of the Consultative Assembly was opposed to giving the States unlimited power to do so: 'Such a power would threaten to deprive the latter [the Convention] of its practical effect and in any case of its moral authority'. The Committee therefore proposed that the validity of a reservation would at the least have to be subjected to the approval of a qualified majority of the other Contracting States, and that the State in question would have to give reasons for every reservation. Moreover, it was suggested that a State which made a reservation should submit periodically a report in which the reasons for the maintenance of that reservation would have to be given.[308] These suggestions were not adopted by the Committee of Ministers.

Indeed, the possibility for Contracting States to make reservations would seem to be at odds with the presumption of universality of human rights. By making reservations when ratifying a human rights treaty, the State concerned excludes or modifies its obligations under that particular treaty with as a consequence that the acceptance of the human rights standards is not of a common level or intensity. Moreover, the possibility of making reservations is hard to be reconciled with the character and contents of human rights obligations as a minimum standard. As the Human Rights Committee, established under the UN Covenant on Civil and Political Rights, states in its General Comment on Issues Relating to Reservations:

it is desirable in principle that States accept the full range of obligations, because the human rights norms are the legal expression of the essential rights that every person is entitled to as a human being.[309]

---

[308] Council of Europe, Cons. Ass., Ordinary Session 1950, Documents, Part II, Doc. 6, p. 534.
[309] General Comment No. 24(52), 11 November 1994, para. 4.

What holds good for global human rights systems applies *a fortiori* for the common legal order established by the Convention.

Nevertheless, under international law as it stands at present, reservations to human rights treaties are not excluded, as is well illustrated by Article 64 of the Convention. And, in fact, several Contracting States have made reservations in respect of the Convention.[310] Most of these reservations have a limited scope and concern substantive provisions, *i.e.* the rights and freedoms protected by the Convention and the Protocols.

9.2 Supervision of the Validity of Reservations

The first general question to be discussed as to the Convention's system of reservations concerns the competence to decide on the legal validity of reservations. As was observed above, the Convention does not stipulate that a reservation requires acceptance by other Contracting States. On the other hand, the Convention embodies a specific mechanism of supervision of its observance. It seems obvious, therefore, that the said competence lies with the Convention organs.

In the *Temeltasch* Case, the Commission expressly established its competence to review and interpret reservations. Leaving aside the question of whether declarations may be the subject of express acceptance or objections by other Contracting States, it continued as follows:

> However, it emphasises that, even assuming that some legal effect were to be attributed to an acceptance or an objection made in respect of a reservation to the Convention, this could not rule out the Commission's competence to express an opinion on the compliance of a given reservation or an interpretative declaration with the Convention. In this respect, the specific nature of the Convention should be recalled, and particularly the fact that in Section III it establishes organs responsible for supervising the enforcement of its provisions by the Contracting Parties. (...) The latter, in drawing up the Convention, did not intend – as the Commission has already noted – to concede to each other reciprocal rights and obligations in pursuance of their individual national interests, but (...) to establish a common public order of the free democracies of Europe with the object of safeguarding their common heritage of political traditions, ideals, freedoms and the rule of law (...) The obligations undertaken by States are of an essentially objective character, which is particularly clear from the supervisory machinery established by the Convention. The latter 'is founded upon the concept of a collective guarantee by the High Contracting Parties of the rights and freedoms set forth in the Convention'. In view of the above considerations, the Commission considers that the very system of the Convention confers on it the competence to consider whether, in a specific case, a reservation or an interpretative declaration has or has not been made in accordance with the Convention.[311]

---

[310] The reservations made by the different Contracting States are included in *Collected Texts*, Strasbourg, 1994, pp. 68-125.

[311] Report of 5 May 1982, D&R 31 (1983), p. 120 (144-145).

In the *Belilos* Case the Court expressly adopted the same point of view[312] after having recognised its competence impliedly at two earlier occasions.[313] Indeed, the task entrusted to the Commission and the Court in Article 19 'To ensure the observance of the engagements undertaken by the High Contracting Parties' can only be fulfilled if in the last instance the Strasbourg organs, and not the States, determine the contents of the obligations as well as the validity and scope of reservations pertaining thereto.[314]

In its *Belilos* judgment the Court also decided on the important issue whether, if a reservation is held to be invalid, the State concerned must, as a consequence, be deemed not to be bound by the treaty at all. According to the Court that was not the case in the present instance, since an overall willingness on the part of the State concerned to be bound by the Convention might be presumed.[315]

The Court's straightforward assertion of jurisdiction should not obscure the fact that in many cases the question as to the validity of reservations remains open as long as it is not raised in proceedings in connection with an alleged violation of one of the rights and freedoms. This may lead to protracted uncertainty. It would therefore appear to be desirable to set up a special procedure by which the admissibility of reservations can be judged by the Court at the moment at which they are made.

9.3 Conditions for the Validity of Reservations

According to Article 19 of the Vienna Convention of the Law of Treaties, which in this respect codifies customary law,[316] the formulation of reservations is not allowed if:
a) the reservation is prohibited by the treaty;
b) the treaty provides that only specified reservations, which do not include the reservation in question, may be made; or
c) in cases not falling under subparagraphs (a) and (b), the reservation is incompatible with the object and purpose of the treaty.

As far as the category under (c) is concerned, the International Court of Justice has indicated that the following are relevant factors:
a) whether the principles underlying the treaty concerned are principles which are recognised by civilised nations as binding on States, even without any conventional obligation;
b) whether the obligation concerned is of a universal character; and

---

[312] Judgment of 29 April 1988, A.132, p. 24.

[313] Judgment of 16 July 1971, *Ringeisen*, A.13, pp. 40-41; judgment of 9 October 1979, *Airey*, A.32, p. 16.

[314] In its report of 5 May 1983, *Temeltasch*, D&R 31 (1983), p. 120 (145), the Commission has taken the same position.

[315] *Ibidem*, p. 145.

[316] Thus also the Commission in its report in the *Temeltasch* Case, D&R 31 (1983), p. 120 (146).

775

c) whether the treaty was adopted for a purely humanitarian purpose in which the States do not have any interest of their own but merely a common interest, *viz.* the accomplishment of that purpose.[317]

As was observed before, in the case of the Convention Article 64 contains an express provision concerning reservations, which makes it clear that it was the intention of the drafters to make reservations possible. It is to be regretted that Article 64 has not been modelled after Article 15 in the sense that it list the provisions of the Convention with respect to which reservations are not allowed. Now that this has not been done, Article 19 of the Vienna Convention of the Law of Treaties applies, which means that reservations are allowed under Article 64 only if and insofar as they are not incompatible with the object and purpose of the Convention. Therefore, in addition to reviewing reservations for their conformity with Article 64 itself,[318] the Commission and the Court also have to include in their review the principle laid down in Article 19 of the Vienna Convention.[319]

Article 64 provides that:

a) reservations must be made at the moment the Convention is signed or ratified;
b) the domestic law to which the reservation relates must then be in force;
c) reservations of a general character are not permitted; and
d) the reservation must contain a brief statement of the law concerned.

The requirement that the reservation must be specific may be inferred from the first sentence of the first paragraph, which provides that a reservation may only concern 'any particular provision'. From this it ensues that, when a reservation is made, the provision of the Convention to which it refers must be expressly mentioned, and the effect of the reservation remains confined exclusively to that provision.

In view of the exceptional character and far-reaching consequences of reservations the conditions laid down in Article 64 should be interpreted and applied restrictively. That is not, however, the picture the Strasbourg case-law has consistently presented. Thus, as far as this specificity requirement is concerned, in its decision on *X* v. *Austria* the Commission found that:

---

[317] Advisory opinion of 28 May 1951 on Reservations to the Convention on Genocide, *ICJ Reports*, 1951, p. 23.

[318] See, *e.g.*, the judgment of 29 April 1988, *Belilos*, A.132, p. 24, and the judgment of 22 May 1990, *Weber*, A.177, p. 19.

[319] Although the Court did not refer to Art. 19 of the Vienna Convention, that must have been the basis of its judgment of 23 March 1995, *Loizidou* (Preliminary Objections), A.310, pp. 26-30, where it held that the Turkish declaration recognising the competence of the Commission to deal with individual applications under Art. 25 and the declaration accepting the Court's jurisdiction, were valid but without any other restriction than the one *ratione temporis* 'Taking into consideration the character of the Convention, the ordinary meaning of Articles 25 and 46 in their context and *in the light of their object and purpose* and the practice of the Contracting Parties' (p. 30, emphasis added).

whereas it is true that this reservation does not make any express reference to Article 6 of the Convention; (...) whereas the Commission, in interpreting the terms of the reservation, has to take into consideration the clear intention of the Government (...); whereas, accordingly, the reservation must be extended to cover not only 'the measures for the deprivation of liberty' but also the proceedings leading up to a decision by which an accused person is deprived of his liberty in accordance with the Acts mentioned in the reservation.[320]

The condition of specificity of the reservation also implies that the reservation must be restricted to a specific law or specified legal measures, which must be indicated explicitly in the reservation. This also appears from the second paragraph: 'Any reservation made under this Article shall contain a brief statement of the law concerned'. Austria had made a reservation in respect of Article 1 of Protocol No. 1 in connection with Part IV and Part V of the State Treaty which Austria has concluded with the Western Allies and the Soviet Union in 1955. A complaint directed against Austria was concerned with a law of 1958, which had been enacted in execution of Part IV of the State Treaty, but which had not been mentioned in the reservation. The Commission nevertheless brought the law within the scope of the Austrian reservation, holding that:

in making a reservation with respect to Parts IV and V of the State Treaty, Austria must necessarily have had the intention of excluding from the scope of the First Protocol everything forming the subject matter of Parts IV and V of the said Treaty; whereas it follows that the Austrian reservation relating to Parts IV and V of the said Treaty must be interpreted as intended to cover all legislative and administrative measures directly related to the subject matter of Parts IV and V of the State Treaty.[321]

With respect to the condition of the second paragraph of Article 64 that the reservation 'shall contain a brief statement of the law concerned', the Commission concluded in the *Temeltasch* Case that the Swiss interpretative declaration did not comply with that provision. It nevertheless reached the conclusion that:

the failure by Switzerland – an omission which it would have been desirable to avoid – (...) did not prove to be decisive in the circumstances of the present case. Indeed, the very terms of the interpretative declaration were sufficient to make the applicant or his lawyer aware that the principle of the free assistance of an interpreter could not as such be invoked against Switzerland.[322]

---

[320] Appl. 1452/62, Yearbook VI (1963), p. 268 (276). See also Appl. 473/59, *X* v. *Austria*, Yearbook II (1958-1959), p. 400 (406); Appl. 2432/65, *X* v. *Austria*, Coll. 22 (1967), p. 124 (127); Appl. 4002/69, *X* v. *Austria*, Yearbook XIV (1971), p. 178 (186). In a later decision the Commission indicated that it wanted to reconsider the position here taken by it. In Appl. 8180/78, *X* v. *Austria*, D&R 20 (1980), p. 23 (27-28), it held, after an express reference to the case-law just mentioned: 'The Commission has now come to the opinion that in view of the various questions which may be raised by the scope of a reservation and its compatibility with Article 64 of the Convention, its previous decisions on this matter could usefully be reconsidered'. The reconsideration announced did not take place in this case because the complaint concerned was declared manifestly ill-founded.
[321] Appl. 2765/66, *X* v. *Austria*, Yearbook X (1967), p. 412 (418). See also Appls 1821-1822/63, *Hudetz, Haiek and Von Beringe* v. *Austria*, Yearbook IX (1966), p. 214 (236).
[322] Report of 5 May 1982, D&R 31 (1983), p. 120 (151).

More recent case-law, however, shows a somewhat stricter approach. Thus, as to the condition of specificity, the Court held in the *Belilos* Case with respect to an interpretative declaration on the part of the Swiss Government[323] that:

> By 'reservation of a general character' in Article 64 is meant in particular a reservation couched in terms that are too vague or broad for it to be possible to determine their exact meaning and scope. While the preparatory work and the Government's explanations clearly show what the respondent State's concern was at the time of ratification, they cannot obscure the objective reality of the actual wording of the declaration. The words 'ultimate control by the judiciary over the acts or decisions of the public authorities relating to [civil] rights or obligations or the determination of [a criminal] charge' do not make it possible for the scope of the undertaking by Switzerland to be ascertained exactly, in particular as to which categories of dispute are included and as to whether or not the 'ultimate control by the judiciary' takes in the facts of the case. They can therefore be interpreted in different ways, whereas Article 64 § 1 requires precision and clarity. In short, they fall foul of the rule that reservations must not be of a general character.[324]

From this it may be concluded that, according to the Court, the exact scope of the reservation must be deducible from the terms of the reservation.

With respect to the requirement contained in the second paragraph that any reservation must contain a brief statement of the law concerned, the Swiss Government attempted to justify its failure to comply with that condition by referring to the very flexible state-practice in this respect and by advancing the argument that Article 64 does not take account of the specific and allegedly almost insuperable problems faced by federal States. As to this latter argument, according to the Government:

> Switzerland would have had to mention most of the provisions in the twenty-six cantonal codes of criminal procedure and in the twenty-six cantonal codes of criminal procedure, and even hundreds of municipal laws and regulations.[325]

Neither of these arguments were honoured. The Commission, referring to its report in the *Temeltasch* Case, held that the undeniable practical difficulties put forward by the Government could not justify the failure to comply with paragraph 2 of Article 64.[326] The Court agreed with this position, adding that:

> the 'brief statement of the law concerned' both constitutes an evidential factor and contributes to legal certainty. The purpose of Article 64 § 2 is to provide a guarantee (...) that a reservation does not go beyond the provisions expressly excluded by the State concerned.[327]

---

[323] This declaration was worded as follows: 'The Swiss Federal Council considers that the guarantee of fair trial in Article 6, paragraph 1 of the Convention, in the determination of civil rights and obligations or any criminal charge against the person in question is intended solely to ensure ultimate control by the judiciary over the acts or decisions of the public authorities relating to such rights or obligations or the determination of such a charge'.

[324] Judgment of 29 April 1988, A.132, p. 26.

[325] *Ibidem*, p. 27.

[326] *Ibidem*, p. 43.

[327] *Ibidem*, pp. 27-28.

After this more strict test in the *Belilos* Case, the Austrian reservation which had also been at issue in the above-mentioned Commission decisions, came under review again in the *Chorherr* Case. The Court held that the reservation concerned did not contain the degree of generality prohibited by Article 64, because it 'encompasses a limited number of laws which, taken together, constitute a well-defined and coherent body of substantive and procedural administrative provisions'.[328] Also with respect to the condition that the reservation contains a brief statement of the law concerned, the Court took a rather lenient attitude. It accepted the mere reference to the Federal Official Gazette, as that reference made it possible for everyone to identify the precise laws concerned and to obtain any information regarding them, while it also provided safeguards against any interpretation which would unduly extend the field of application of the reservation.[329] As judge Valticos, not without good reason, observes in his partly dissenting opinion, by merely indicating where the laws in question can be found, the reservation:

clearly does not contain a 'brief statement' of the substance of this law which would make it possible to understand the law's contents and its scope, or to determine whether the text amounts to a general reservation which is not permitted under the Convention.[330]

The condition under (b) implies that the law or legal provisions concerned must have been effective at the time the reservation is made, *i.e.* at the moment of signature or ratification of the Convention by the State in question. This unambiguous provision seems to leave room for no other conclusion than that no later law may be brought within the scope of the reservation once it has been made. However, thus far the Strasbourg organs have not held on to the letter of this provision.

Thus, the Commission declared a complaint inadmissible concerning an Austrian Act of 1960 on road traffic. This Act replaced an Act of 1947 and had been enacted after the date of the Austrian reservation in question. The Commission considered that the Act of 1960 was covered by the reservation in view of the fact:

that the subject matter covered by the Road Traffic Act of 1947 and the Road Traffic Act of 1960 is substantially the same; whereas, therefore, the latter Act does not have the effect of enlarging, a posteriori, the subject matter which is excluded from the competence of the Commission by the above reservation.[331]

---

[328] Judgment of 25 August 1993, A.266-B, p. 34.
[329] *Ibidem*, pp. 34-35.
[330] *Ibidem*, p. 40.
[331] Appl. 2432/65, *X* v. *Austria*, Coll. 22 (1967), p. 124 (127). See also Appl. 3923/69, *X* v. *Austria*, Coll. 37 (1971), p. 10 (15).

A similar reasoning was applied by the Commission and the Court in the *Campbell and Cosans* Case.[332]

9.4 Are all Provisions of the Convention Subject to Reservations?

The preceding observations concerned reservations with respect to the substantive provisions of the Convention. In addition thereto, and leaving aside the Convention's final clauses, the Convention comprises two categories of provisions: provisions concerning the enjoyment and the restriction of the rights and freedoms (Articles 1 and 13-18), and provisions concerning the supervisory mechanism (Articles 19-57).

With respect to the former category of provisions reservations would seem to be impermissible. It is true that the text of Article 64 speaks of 'any particular provision', but this cannot be considered conclusive. The obligations ensuing from Articles 1 and 13-18 are of such a fundamental importance for the enjoyment of the rights and freedoms laid down in the Convention that restricting them by means of a reservation would be incompatible with the 'object and purpose' of the Convention, and consequently must be considered inadmissible.

It is submitted, therefore, that the reservation which France has made with respect to Article 15 conflicts with the Convention. This reservation is to the effect that the circumstances specified in Article 16 of the French Constitution and other relevant national legislation regarding proclamation of a state of siege or emergency:

> must be understood as complying with the purpose of Article 15 of the Convention, and (...) secondly, for the interpretation and application of Article 16 of the Constitution of the Republic, the terms 'to the extent strictly required by the exigencies of the situation' shall not restrict the power of the President of the Republic to take 'the measures required by the circumstances'.[333]

Article 15 in itself is already a highly exceptive clause. It confers on the Contracting States the power to derogate from a number of provisions of the Convention in exceptional cases. As such, Article 15 draws the line beyond which the Contracting States may not go under the Convention. It must therefore be considered inacceptable that this limit could be shifted even further in favour of the States by means of a reservation. This holds true in particular also for the French reservation since its formulation is so wide that in fact the Strasbourg supervision of the implementation of Article 15 is eliminated altogether.

---

[332] Judgment of 25 February 1982, A.48, pp. 17-18, in which it was held that the new legislation was no more than an echo of the identical provision from the old legislation and 'therefore goes no further than a law in force at a time when the reservation was made'. In the Commission's report of 16 May 1980, B.42 (1985), p. 39, it was held that the new law 'has not the effect of enlarging a posteriori the field which the United Kingdom Government wanted to exclude from the competence of the Commission'.

[333] See *Collected Texts*, *supra* note 199, p. 72.

The category of provisions pertaining to the supervisory machinery (Articles 19-57) includes two clauses – Articles 25 and 46 – which have an optional character. The Contracting States therefore can remain exempt from the procedures laid down in these provisions without having to make a reservation at the time of ratification. However, from the optional character of these provisions – the competence of the Commission to receive individual applications, and the jurisdiction of the Court – it may also be inferred that the drafters of the Convention intended that, apart from the option to make or not to make the declarations provided for in these provisions, the supervisory mechanism would operate unabridged with regard to each of the Contracting States. It is submitted that reservations with respect to these provisions are incompatible with the 'object and purpose' of the Convention. The same would seem to hold good in respect of the right of States to lodge complaints (Article 24), the binding effect of decisions of the Committee of Ministers (Article 32) and the reporting procedure at the request of the Secretary General (Article 57). It appears from the Preamble that the purpose of the Convention was 'to take the first steps for the collective enforcement of certain of the Rights stated in the Universal Declaration'. Any backing out of the mechanism set up for this 'collective enforcement', that goes beyond that expressly permitted by the Convention would, with respect to the State concerned, hamper this 'collective enforcement', and accordingly the purpose of the Convention.

A reservation with respect to Articles 25 and 46 was at issue in the *Loizidou* Case.[334] In its declaration pursuant to Article 25, by which it accepted the competence of the Commission to receive individual applications, Turkey had stated, *inter alia*:

> the recognition of the right of petition extends only to allegations concerning acts or omissions of public authorities in Turkey performed within the boundaries of the territory to which the Constitution of the Republic of Turkey is applicable.[335]

Turkey's subsequent Article 25 declarations contained a similar reservation,[336] which was also included in its declaration under Article 46 concerning the jurisdiction of the European Court.[337] The Court took as a starting point that:

> the object and purpose of the Convention as an instrument for the protection of individual human beings requires that its provisions be interpreted and applied so as to make its safeguards practical and effective.[338]

Building thereupon, the Court held as follows:

> If, as contended by the respondent Government, substantive or territorial restrictions were permissible under these provisions, Contracting Parties would be free to subscribe to separate regimes of enforcement of Convention obligations depending on the scope

---

[334] Judgment of 23 March 1995, concerning the Preliminary Objections, A.310.
[335] *Ibidem*, p. 11.
[336] *Ibidem*, pp. 13-14.
[337] *Ibidem*, pp. 14-15.
[338] *Ibidem*, p. 27.

of their acceptances. Such a system, which would enable States to qualify their consent under the optional clauses, would not only seriously weaken the role of the Commission and Court in the discharge of their functions but would also diminish the effectiveness of the Convention as a constitutional instrument of European public order (ordre public). (...) In the Court's view, having regard to the object and purpose of the Convention system as set out above, the consequences for the enforcement of the Convention and the achievement of its aims would be so far-reaching that the power to this effect should have been expressly provided for. However, no such provision exists in either Article 25 or Article 46.[339]

This led the Court to the conclusion that the restrictions *ratione loci* attached to Turkey's Article 25 and Article 46 declarations were invalid.[340] And as it did in its *Belilos* judgment, the Court took the position that the impugned restrictions could be separated from the remainder of the text of the Article 25 and Article 46 declarations, leaving intact the acceptance of the optional clauses.[341]

9.5 Interpretative Declarations

The relation between interpretative declarations and reservations was one of the issues in the *Belilos* Case.[342] In addition to two reservations Switzerland had made two interpretative declarations, one of which was relied upon by the Swiss Government. Consequently the Court was faced with 'The question whether a declaration described as "interpretative" must be regarded as a "reservation"'.[343] The Court took as a starting point that 'it is necessary to ascertain the original intention of those who drafted the declaration'[344] and that 'in order to establish the legal character of such a declaration, one must look behind the title given to it and seek to determine the substantive content.'[345]

This led the Court to examining the validity of the interpretative declaration in question, as in the case of a reservation, in the context of Article 64.[346] This flexible approach carries with it the disadvantage of legal uncertainty as to the exact scope of a State's obligations under the Convention, while a State should be aware of the difference between reservations and interpretative declarations and

---

[339] *Idem.* In the same vain the Human Rights Committee in its General Comment concerning its competence to consider individual communications under the Optional Protocol to the International Covenant on Civil and Political Rights: 'And because the object and purpose of the first Optional Protocol is to allow the rights obligatory for a State under the Covenant to be tested before the Committee, a reservation that seeks to preclude this would be contrary to the object and purpose of the first Optional Protocol, even if not of the Covenant'; UN Doc. CCPR/C/21/Rev.1/Add.6, 11 November 1994, para. 13.

[340] *Ibidem*, p. 30.

[341] *Ibidem*, p. 32.

[342] The Commission had pronounced on the issue in its report in the *Temeltasch* Case, D&R 31 (1983), p. 120 (146-148).

[343] Judgment of 29 April 1988, A.132, p. 24.

[344] *Ibidem*, pp. 23-24.

[345] *Ibidem*, p. 24.

[346] *Idem.*

its possible legal implications. On the other hand, it has to be admitted that Article 2 of the Vienna Convention, in its paragraph 1(d), defines a reservation as 'a unilateral statement, however phrased or named'.

9.6 Concluding Observations

Are the object and purpose of the Convention static concepts? The Convention as a whole is considered by the Court to be a 'living instrument' that must be interpreted and applied according to the circumstances which prevail at that particular moment.[347] This implies that the will of the States at the moment of drafting the provisions of the Convention is considered by the Court not to be decisive for their scope. If, in doing so, the Court has created a certain latitude within the Convention for taking into account the evolution of legal and social concepts, there is no reason why the same doctrine should not equally apply to the interpretation and application of its Article 64. This was expressly recognised by the Court in its *Loizidou* judgment.[348]

Following that line, if one of the purposes of the Convention, according to its Preamble, is to pursue the achievement of greater unity between the Member States of the Council of Europe through the maintenance and further realisation of human rights, than the unity aimed at may have reached a certain stage at a certain moment where there is no longer room for differences on important issues between these Member States in the obligations which they have accepted concerning the protection of human rights. Therefore, Frowein is quite right when he submits that the goal of European integration is equally valid for the Convention system and that 'under those circumstances the possibility of unilateral derogations through reservations does not seem to fit easily into the picture'.[349]

Observations like the foregoing may lead the Commission and the Court to even greater reticence in accepting and interpreting reservations made under Article 64; a reticence which has also been displayed by the Human Rights Committee in its General Comment, to which reference was made *supra*.[350] This attitude would not exclude, of course, that the Commission and the Court continue to leave the States a certain 'margin of appreciation' in implementing some of these common obligations, allowing for certain variations in interpretation and application as discussed in the introduction. Such variations leave the core of the commitment in tact and do not necessarily lower their level of protection, whereas reservations disrespect the integrity and interdependence of these commitments and negatively affect the level of protection.

---

[347] See, *e.g.*, the judgment of 25 April 1978, *Tyrer*, A.26, pp. 15-16 and the judgment of 22 October 1981, *Dudgeon*, A.45, pp. 23-24.
[348] Judgment of 23 March 1995, A.310, p. 26.
[349] J.A. Frowein, 'The European Convention on Human Rights as the Public Order of Europe', in: *Collected Courses of the Academy of European Law 1990*, Vol. I, Book 2, Dordrecht *etc.*, 1992, pp. 267-358 (288-289).
[350] General Comment No. 24(52), 11 November 1994.

Ultimately, developments in Europe may have reached such a level of integration that this allows for the conclusion that the common legal order established by the Convention, in view of the generally recognised character of its provisions, the unity aimed at between the Member States of the Council of Europe, and the principle of equality before the law and equal protection of the law which should not only apply within, but also between the States, no longer leaves any room for unilateral reservations. If such a conclusion would be shared by the political decision-makers, it should then be translated into an amendment of Article 64 of the Convention. To gradually bring the Contracting States to accepting such a change, the proposal by Alkema would be very instrumental that the Secretary General of the Council of Europe should use his power under Article 57 to ask those States which have made reservations, to explain, at regular intervals, the reasons and the necessity of maintaining them.[351] A comparison comes to mind here with Article 22 of the European Social Charter, which provides as follows:

> The Contracting Parties shall send to the Secretary-General, at appropriate intervals as requested by the Committee of Ministers, reports relating to the provisions of Part II of the Charter which they did not accept at the time of their ratification or approval or in a subsequent notification. The Committee of Ministers shall determine from time to time in respect of which provisions such reports shall be requested and the form of the reports to be provided.[352]

And the Human Rights Committee, in its General Comment, states:

> It is desirable for a State entering a reservation to indicate in precise terms the domestic legislation or practices which it believes to be incompatible with the Covenant obligations reserved; and to explain the time period it requires to render its own laws and practices compatible with the Covenant, or why it is unable to render its own laws and practices compatible with the Covenant. States should also ensure that the necessity for maintaining reservations is periodically reviewed, taking into account any observations and recommendations made by the Committee during examination of their reports. Reservations should be withdrawn at the earliest possible moment. Reports to the Committee should contain information on what action has been taken to review, reconsider or withdraw reservations.[353]

A common European legal order in the field of human rights presupposes that all Contracting States are under the same obligations in that field and subjected to the same supervisory mechanisms. At the moment that clearly still is not the case.

---

[351] E. Alkema, 'Written Communication on "Responsibilities deriving from the implementation of the European Convention on Human Rights: Responsibilities for States Parties to the Convention"', in: *Proceedings of the Sixth International Colloquy about the European Convention on Human Rights*, Dordrecht, Boston and London, 1981, pp. 706-730 (726).

[352] *European Treaty Series*, No.35, 18 October 1961; 529 UNTS 89.

[353] General Comment No. 24(52), November 1994, para. 20.

Appendix I

State of Ratifications

States	ECHR	Art. 25 ECHR	Art. 46 ECHR	P. 1 ECHR	P. 4 ECHR	P. 6 ECHR	P. 7 ECHR	P. 9 ECHR	P.10 ECHR	P. 11 ECHR
Albania	X	X	X	X	X					X
Andorra	X	X	X			X	X			X
Austria	X	X	X	X	X	X	X	X	X	X
Belgium	X	X	X	X	X	S		X	X	X
Bulgaria	X	X	X	X	S		S			X
Croatia	X	X	X	X	X	X	X	X		X
Cyprus	X	X	X	X	X	X		X	X	X
Czech Republic	X	X	X	X	X	X	X	X	X	X
Denmark	X	X	X	X	X	X	X	X	X	X
Estonia	X	X	X	X	X	S	X	X	X	X
Finland	X	X	X	X	X	X	X	X	X	X
France	X	X	X	X	X	X	X	S	S	X
Germany	X	X	X	X	X	X	S	S	S	X
Greece	X	X	X	X		S	X	S	S	X
Hungary	X	X	X	X	X	X	X	X	S	X
Iceland	X	X	X	X	X	X	X			X
Ireland	X	X	X	X	X	X	S	X	X	X
Italy	X	X	X	X	X	X	X	X	X	X
Latvia	X	X	X	X	X		X	X	X	X
Liechtenstein	X	X	X	X		X		X	X	X
Lithuania	X	X	X	X	X		X	S	X	X
Luxembourg	X	X	X	X	X	X	X	X	X	X

States	ECHR	Art. 25 ECHR	Art. 46 ECHR	P. 1 ECHR	P. 4 ECHR	P. 6 ECHR	P. 7 ECHR	P. 9 ECHR	P.10 ECHR	P. 11 ECHR
Macedonia (Former Yugoslav Republic of)	X	X	X	X	X	X	X			X
Malta	X	X	X	X		X		S	X	X
Moldova	X	X	X	X	X	X	X		X	X
Netherlands	X	X	X	X	X	X	S	X	X	X
Norway	X	X	X	X	X	X	X	X	X	X
Poland	X	X	X	X	X		S	X	X	X
Portugal	X	X	X	X	X	X	S	X	X	X
Romania	X	X	X	X	X	X	X	X	X	X
Russian Federation	S			S	S	S	S	S	S	S
San Marino	X	X	X	X	X	X	X	X	X	X
Slovakia	X	X	X	X	X	X	X	X	X	X
Slovenia	X	X	X	X	X	X	X	X	X	X
Spain	X	X	X	X	S	X	S			X
Sweden	X	X	X	X	X	X	X	X	X	X
Switzerland	X	X	X	S		X	X	X	X	X
Turkey	X	X	X	X	S		S	S		X
Ukraine	X	X	X	X	X	S	X			X
United Kingdom	X	X	X	X	S				X	X
Total number of ratifications	39	39	39	37	29	27	25	23	24	39

X = ratified   S = signed

Appendix II

Cited Decisions of the Commission on Admissibility (Applications)

Appendix III

Cited Reports of the Commission on the Merits

Appendix IV

Cited Judgments of the Court

823

Appendix V

Cited Resolutions of the Committee of Ministers

Appendix VI

Reform of the Supervisory Mechanism According to Protocol No. 11

With the entry into force of Protocol No. 11 on 1 November 1997, the text of most of the Articles of the Convention, with exception of the substantive Articles contained in Section I and the Protocols Nos 1, 4, 6 and 7, have been changed. Also the numbering of the Articles have been changed. For your convenience, you will find, where appropriate, a reference between brackets to the existing provisions. Section I of the Convention is entitled 'Rights and Freedoms' and the articles of this Section as well as the Articles of the Protocols are provided with headings. The amended Convention will enter into force on 1 November 1998.

Protocol No. 11 to the Convention for the Protection of Human Rights and Fundamental Freedoms Restructuring the Control Machinery Established Thereby

The existing text of Sections II to IV of the Convention (Articles 19 to 56) and Protocol No. 2 conferring upon the European Court of Human Rights competence to give advisory opinions shall be replaced by Section II of the Convention (Articles 19 to 51). A new Section III, entitled 'Miscellaneous Provisions' concerns Articles 52 to 59. With respect to the Protocols Nos 1, 4, 6 and 7 and these articles are reproduced in which changes have been made.

Section II – European Court of Human Rights

Article 19 – Establishment of the Court (Article 19(b))
To ensure the observance of the engagements undertaken by the High Contracting Parties in the Convention and the protocols thereto, there shall be set up a European Court of Human Rights, hereinafter referred to as "the Court". It shall function on a permanent basis.

Article 20 – Number of judges (Article 38)
The Court shall consist of a number of judges equal to that of the High Contracting Parties.

Article 21 – Criteria for office (Article 39(3) and Article 40(7))
1. The judges shall be of high moral character and must either possess the qualifications required for appointment to high judicial office or be jurisconsults of recognised competence.
2. The judges shall sit on the Court in their individual capacity.

3. During their term of office the judges shall not engage in any activity which is incompatible with their independence, impartiality or with the demands of a full-time office; all questions arising from the application of this paragraph shall be decided by the Court.

Article 22 – Election of judges (Article 39(1) and 39(2))

1. The judges shall be elected by the Parliamentary Assembly with respect to each High Contracting Party by a majority of votes cast from a list of three candidates nominated by the High Contracting Party.
2. The same procedure shall be followed to complete the Court in the event of the accession of new High Contracting Parties and in filling casual vacancies.

Article 23 – Terms of office (Article 40(1)-(6))

1. The judges shall be elected for a period of six years. They may be re-elected. However, the terms of office of one-half of the judges elected at the first election shall expire at the end of three years.
2. The judges whose terms of office are to expire at the end of the initial period of three years shall be chosen by lot by the Secretary General of the Council of Europe immediately after their election.
3. In order to ensure that, as far as possible, the terms of office of one-half of the judges are renewed every three years, the Parliamentary Assembly may decide, before proceeding to any subsequent election, that the term or terms of office of one or more judges to be elected shall be for a period other than six years but not more than nine and not less than three years.
4. In cases where more than one term of office is involved and where the Parliamentary Assembly applies the preceding paragraph, the allocation of the terms of office shall be effected by a drawing of lots by the Secretary General of the Council of Europe immediately after the election.
5. A judge elected to replace a judge whose term of office has not expired shall hold office for the remainder of his predecessor's term.
6. The terms of office of judges shall expire when they reach the age of 70.
7. The judges shall hold office until replaced. They shall, however, continue to deal with such cases as they already have under consideration.

Article 24 – Dismissal

No judge may be dismissed from his office unless the other judges decide by a majority of two-thirds that he has ceased to fulfil the required conditions.

Article 25 – Registry and legal secretaries

The Court shall have a registry, the functions and organisation of which shall be laid down in the rules of the Court. The Court shall be assisted by legal secretaries.

Article 26 – Plenary Court (Articles 41 and 43)

The plenary Court shall

a) select its President and one or two Vice-Presidents for a period of three years; they may be re-elected;
b) set up Chambers, constituted for a fixed period of time;
c) elect the Presidents of the Chambers of the Court; they may be re-elected;
d) adopt the rules of the Court; and
e) elect the Registrar and one or more Deputy Registrars.

Article 27 – Committees, Chambers and Grand Chamber

1. To consider cases brought before it, the Court shall sit in committees of three judges, in Chambers of seven judges and in a Grand Chamber of seventeen judges. The Court's Chambers shall set up committees for a fixed period of time.
2. There shall sit as an ex officio member of the Chamber and the Grand Chamber the judge elected in respect of the State Party concerned or, if there is none or if he is unable to sit, a person of its choice who shall sit in the capacity of judge.
3. The Grand Chamber shall also include the President of the Court, the Vice-Presidents, the Presidents of the Chambers and other judges chosen in accordance with the rules of the Court. When a case is referred to the Grand Chamber under Article 43, no judge from the Chamber which rendered the judgment shall sit in the Grand Chamber, with the exception of the President of the Chamber and the judge who sat in respect of the State Party concerned.

Article 28 – Declarations of inadmissibility by committees

A committee may, by a unanimous vote, declare inadmissible or strike out of its list of cases an individual application submitted under Article 34 where such a decision can be taken without further examination. The decision shall be final.

Article 29 – Decisions by Chambers on admissibility and merits

1. If no decision is taken under Article 28, a Chamber shall decide on the admissibility and merits of individual applications submitted under Article 34.
2. A Chamber shall decide on the admissibility and merits of inter-State applications submitted under Article 33.
3. The decision on admissibility shall be taken separately unless the Court, in exceptional cases, decides otherwise.

Article 30 – Relinquishment of jurisdiction to the Grand Chamber

Where a case pending before a Chamber raises a serious question affecting the interpretation of the Convention or the protocols thereto, or where the resolution of a question before the Chamber might have a result inconsistent with a judgment previously delivered by the Court, the Chamber may, at any time before it has rendered its judgment, relinquish jurisdiction in favour of the Grand Chamber, unless one of the parties to the case objects.

Article 31 – Powers of the Grand Chamber
The Grand Chamber shall
a) determine applications submitted either under Article 33 or Article 34 when a Chamber has relinquished jurisdiction under Article 30 or when the case has been referred to it under Article 43; and
b) consider requests for advisory opinions submitted under Article 47.

Article 32 – Jurisdiction of the Court (Article 45)
1. The jurisdiction of the Court shall extend to all matters concerning the interpretation and application of the Convention and the protocols thereto which are referred to it as provided in Articles 33, 34 and 47.
2. In the event of dispute as to whether the Court has jurisdiction, the Court shall decide.

Article 33 – Inter-State cases (Articles 44 and 48)
Any High Contracting Party may refer to the Court any alleged breach of the provisions of the Convention and the protocols thereto by another High Contracting Party.

Article 34 – Individual applications (Article 44)
The Court may receive applications from any person, non-governmental organisation or group of individuals claiming to be the victim of a violation by one of the High Contracting Parties of the rights set forth in the Convention or the protocols thereto. The High Contracting Parties undertake not to hinder in any way the effective exercise of this right.

Article 35 – Admissibility criteria (Articles 26 and 27)
1. The Court may only deal with the matter after all domestic remedies have been exhausted, according to the generally recognised rules of international law, and within a period of six months from the date on which the final decision was taken.
2. The Court shall not deal with any individual application submitted under Article 34 that
a) is anonymous; or
b) is substantially the same as a matter that has already been examined by the Court or has already been submitted to another procedure of international investigation or settlement and contains no relevant new information.
3. The Court shall declare inadmissible any individual application submitted under Article 34 which it considers incompatible with the provisions of the Convention or the protocols thereto, manifestly ill-founded, or an abuse of the right of application.

4. The Court shall reject any application which it considers inadmissible under this Article. It may do so at any stage of the proceedings.

Article 36 – Third-party intervention

1. In all cases before a Chamber or the Grand Chamber, a High Contracting Party one of whose nationals is an applicant shall have the right to submit written comments and to take part in hearings.
2. The President of the Court may, in the interest of the proper administration of justice, invite any High Contracting Party which is not a party to the proceedings or any person concerned who is not the applicant to submit written comments or take part in hearings.

Article 37 – Striking out applications (Article 30)

1. The Court may at any stage of the proceedings decide to strike an application out of its list of cases where the circumstances lead to the conclusion that
a) the applicant does not intend to pursue his application; or
b) the matter has been resolved; or
c) for any other reason established by the Court, it is no longer justified to continue the examination of the application.
   However, the Court shall continue the examination of the application if respect for human rights as defined in the Convention and the protocols thereto so requires.
2. The Court may decide to restore an application to its list of cases if it considers that the circumstances justify such a course.

Article 38 – Examination of the case and friendly settlement proceedings

1. If the Court declares the application admissible, it shall a pursue the examination of the case, together with the representatives of the parties, and if need be, undertake an investigation, for the effective conduct of which the States concerned shall furnish all necessary facilities;
b) place itself at the disposal of the parties concerned with a view to securing a friendly settlement of the matter on the basis of respect for human rights as defined in the Convention and the protocols thereto.
2. Proceedings conducted under paragraph 1.b shall be confidential.

Article 39 – Finding of a friendly settlement (Article 28(2))

If a friendly settlement is effected, the Court shall strike the case out of its list by means of a decision which shall be confined to a brief statement of the facts and of the solution reached.

Article 40 – Public hearings and access to documents

1. Hearings shall be public unless the Court in exceptional circumstances decides otherwise.

2. Documents deposited with the Registrar shall be accessible to the public unless the President of the Court decides otherwise.

Article 41 – Just satisfaction (Article 50)
If the Court finds that there has been a violation of the Convention or the protocols thereto, and if the internal law of the High Contracting Party concerned allows only partial reparation to be made, the Court shall, if necessary, afford just satisfaction to the injured party.

Article 42 – Judgments of Chambers (Article 52)
Judgments of Chambers shall become final in accordance with the provisions of Article 44, paragraph 2.

Article 43 – Referral to the Grand Chamber
1. Within a period of three months from the date of the judgment of the Chamber, any party to the case may, in exceptional cases, request that the case be referred to the Grand Chamber.
2. A panel of five judges of the Grand Chamber shall accept the request if the case raises a serious question affecting the interpretation or application of the Convention or the protocols thereto, or a serious issue of general importance.
3. If the panel accepts the request, the Grand Chamber shall decide the case by means of a judgment.

Article 44 – Final judgments
1. The judgment of the Grand Chamber shall be final.
2. The judgment of a Chamber shall become final
a) when the parties declare that they will not request that the case be referred to the Grand Chamber; or
b) three months after the date of the judgment, if reference of the case to the Grand Chamber has not been requested; or
c) when the panel of the Grand Chamber rejects the request to refer under Article 43.
3. The final judgment shall be published.

Article 45 – Reasons for judgments and decisions (Article 51)
1. Reasons shall be given for judgments as well as for decisions declaring applications admissible or inadmissible.
2. If a judgment does not represent, in whole or in part, the unanimous opinion of the judges, any judge shall be entitled to deliver a separate opinion.

Article 46 – Binding force and execution of judgments (Articles 53 and 54)
1. The High Contracting Parties undertake to abide by the final judgment of the Court in any case to which they are parties.

2. The final judgment of the Court shall be transmitted to the Committee of Ministers, which shall supervise its execution.

Article 47 – Advisory opinions

1. The Court may, at the request of the Committee of Ministers, give advisory opinions on legal questions concerning the interpretation of the Convention and the protocols thereto.
2. Such opinions shall not deal with any question relating to the content or scope of the rights or freedoms defined in Section I of the Convention and the protocols thereto, or with any other question which the Court or the Committee of Ministers might have to consider in consequence of any such proceedings as could be instituted in accordance with the Convention.
3. Decisions of the Committee of Ministers to request an advisory opinion of the Court shall require a majority vote of the representatives entitled to sit on the Committee.

Article 48 – Advisory jurisdiction of the Court

The Court shall decide whether a request for an advisory opinion submitted by the Committee of Ministers is within its competence as defined in Article 47.

Article 49 – Reasons for advisory opinions

1. Reasons shall be given for advisory opinions of the Court.
2. If the advisory opinion does not represent, in whole or in part, the unanimous opinion of the judges, any judge shall be entitled to deliver a separate opinion.
3. Advisory opinions of the Court shall be communicated to the Committee of Ministers.

Article 50 – Expenditure on the Court (Article 58)

The expenditure on the Court shall be borne by the Council of Europe.

Article 51 – Privileges and immunities of judges (Article 59)

The judges shall be entitled, during the exercise of their functions, to the privileges and immunities provided for in Article 40 of the Statute of the Council of Europe and in the agreements made thereunder.

Section III Miscellaneous provisions

Article 52 – Inquiries by the Secretary General (Article 57)

On receipt of a request from the Secretary General of the Council of Europe any High Contracting Party shall furnish an explanation of the manner in which its internal law ensures the effective implementation of any of the provisions of the Convention.

Article 53 – Safeguard for existing human rights (Article 60)

Nothing in this Convention shall be construed as limiting or derogating from any of the human rights and fundamental freedoms which may be ensured under the laws of any High Contracting Party or under any other agreement to which it is a Party.

Article 54 – Powers of the Committee of Ministers (Article 61)

Nothing in this Convention shall prejudice the powers conferred on the Committee of Ministers by the Statute of the Council of Europe.

Article 55 – Exclusion of other means of dispute settlement (Article 62)

The High Contracting Parties agree that, except by special agreement, they will not avail themselves of treaties, conventions or declarations in force between them for the purpose of submitting, by way of petition, a dispute arising out of the interpretation or application of this Convention to a means of settlement other than those provided for in this Convention

Article 56 Territorial application (Article 63)

1. Any State may at the time of its ratification or at any time thereafter declare by notification addressed to the Secretary General of the Council of Europe that the present Convention shall, subject to paragraph 4 of this Article, extend to all or any of the territories for whose international relations it is responsible.
2. The Convention shall extend to the territory or territories named in the notification as from the thirtieth day after the receipt of this notification by the Secretary General of the Council of Europe.
3. The provisions of this Convention shall be applied in such territories with due regard, however, to local requirements.
4. Any State which has made a declaration in accordance with paragraph 1 of this article may at any time thereafter declare on behalf of one or more of the territories to which the declaration relates that it accepts the competence of the Court to receive applications from individuals, nongovernmental organisations or groups of individuals as provided by Article 34 of the Convention.

Article 57 – Reservations (Article 64)

1. Any State may, when signing this Convention or when depositing its instrument of ratification, make a reservati in respect of any particular provision of the Convention the extent that any law then in force in its territory is not in conformity with the provision. Reservations of a gene character shall not be permitted under this article.
2. Any reservation made under this article shall contain brief statement of the law concerned.

Article 58 – Denunciation (Article 65)

1. A High Contracting Party may denounce the present Convention only after the expiry of five years from the date on which it became a party to it and after six months' notice contained in a notification addressed to the Secretary General of the Council of Europe, who shall inform the other High Contracting Parties.
2. Such a denunciation shall not have the effect of releasing the High Contracting Party concerned from its obligations under this Convention in respect of any act which, being capable of constituting a violation of such obligations, may have been performed by it before the date at which the denunciation became effective
3. Any High Contracting Party which shall cease to be a member of the Council of Europe shall cease to be a Party to this Convention under the same conditions.
4. The Convention may be denounced in accordance with the provisions of the preceding paragraphs in respect of any territory to which it has been declared to extend under the terms of Article 56.

Article 59 – Signature and ratification (Article 66)

1. This Convention shall be open to the signature of the members of the Council of Europe. It shall be ratified. Ratifications shall be deposited with the Secretary General of the Council of Europe.
2. The present Convention shall come into force after the deposit of ten instruments of ratification.
3. As regards any signatory ratifying subsequently, the Convention shall come into force at the date of the deposit of its instrument of ratification.
4. The Secretary General of the Council of Europe shall notify all the members of the Council of Europe of the entry into force of the Convention, the names of the High Contracting Parties who have ratified it, and the deposit of all instruments of ratification which may be effected subsequently.

Protocol to the Convention for the Protection of Human Rights and Fundamental Freedoms

Article 4 – Territorial application

Any High Contracting Party may at the time of signature or ratification or at any time thereafter communicate to the Secretary General of the Council of Europe a declaration stating the extent to which it undertakes that the provisions of the present Protocol shall apply to such of the territories for the international relations of which it is responsible as are named therein.

Any High Contracting Party which has communicated a declaration in virtue of the preceding paragraph may from time to time communicate a further declaration modifying the terms of any former declaration or terminating the application of the provisions of this Protocol in respect of any territory.

835

A declaration made in accordance with this article shall be deemed to have been made in accordance with paragraph 1 of Article 56 of the Convention.

Protocol No. 4 to the Convention for the Protection of Human Rights and Fundamental Freedoms securing certain rights and freedoms other than those already included in the Convention and in the First Protocol thereto

Article 5 – Territorial application

1. Any High Contracting Party may, at the time of signature or ratification of this Protocol, or at any time thereafter, communicate to the Secretary General of the Council of Europe a declaration stating the extent to which it undertakes that the provisions of this Protocol shall apply to such of the territories for the international relations of which it is responsible as are named therein.
2. Any High Contracting Party which has communicated a declaration in virtue of the preceding paragraph may, from time to time, communicate a further declaration modifying the terms of any former declaration or terminating the application of the provisions of this Protocol in respect of any territory.
3. A declaration made in accordance with this article shall be deemed to have been made in accordance with paragraph 1 of Article 56 of the Convention.
4. The territory of any State to which this Protocol applies by virtue of ratification or acceptance by that State, and each territory to which this Protocol is applied by virtue of a declaration by that State under this article, shall be treated as separate territories for the purpose of the references in Articles 2 and 3 to the territory of a State
5. Any State which has made a declaration in accordance with paragraph 1 or 2 of this Article may at any time thereafter declare on behalf of one or more of the territories to which the declaration relates that it accepts the competence of the Court to receive applications from individuals, nongovernmental organisations or groups of individuals as provided in Article 34 of the Convention in respect of all or any of Articles 1 to 4 of this Protocol.

Protocol No. 6 to the Convention for the Protection of Human Rights and Fundamental Freedoms concerning the Abolition of the Death Penalty

Article 4 – Prohibition of reservations

No reservation may be made under Article 57 of the Convention in respect of the provisions of this Protocol.

Protocol No. 7 to the Convention for the Protection of Human Rights and Fundamental Freedoms

Article 6 – Territorial application

1. Any State may at the time of signature or when depositing its instrument of ratification, acceptance or approval, specify the territory or territories to which the Protocol shall apply and state the extent to which it undertakes that the provisions of this Protocol shall apply to such territory or territories.

2. Any State may at any later date, by a declaration addressed to the Secretary General of the Council of Europe, extend the application of this Protocol to any other territory specified in the declaration. In respect of such territory the Protocol shall enter into force on the first day of the month following the expiration of a period of two months after the date of receipt by the Secretary General of such declaration

3. Any declaration made under the two preceding paragraphs may, in respect of any territory specified in such declaration, be withdrawn or modified by a notification addressed to the Secretary General. The withdrawal or modification shall become effective on the first day of the month following the expiration of a period of two months after the date of receipt of such notification by the Secretary General.

4. A declaration made in accordance with this Article shall be deemed to have been made in accordance with paragraph 1 of Article 56 of the Convention.

5. The territory of any State to which this Protocol applies by virtue of ratification, acceptance or approval by that State, and each territory to which this Protocol is applied by virtue of a declaration by that State under this Article, may be treated as separate territories for the purpose of the reference in Article 1 to the territory of a State

6. Any State which has made a declaration in accordance with paragraph 1 or 2 of this Article may at any time thereafter declare on behalf of one or more of the territories to which the declaration relates that it accepts the competence of the Court to receive applications from individuals, nongovernmental organisations or groups of individuals as provided in Article 34 of the Convention in respect of Articles 1 to 5 of this Protocol.

Article 7 – Relationship to the Convention

As between the States Parties, the provisions of Article 1 to 6 of this Protocol shall be regarded as additional Articles to the Convention, and all the provisions of the Convention shall apply accordingly.

Appendix VII

Index of Subjects